AMA
MANAGEMENT
HANDBOOK

THIRD EDITION

AMA
MANAGEMENT
HANDBOOK

THIRD EDITION

JOHN J. HAMPTON, EDITOR

amacom
American Management Association
New York • Atlanta • Boston • Chicago • Kansas City • San Francisco • Washington, D.C.
Brussels • Mexico City • Tokyo • Toronto

This book is available at a special
discount when ordered in bulk quantities.
For information, contact Special Sales Department,
AMACOM, a division of American Management Association,
135 West 50th Street, New York, N.Y. 10020.

This publication is designed to provide accurate and authoritative
information in regard to the subject matter covered. It is sold with
the understanding that the publisher is not engaged in rendering
legal, accounting, or other professional service. If legal advice or
other expert assistance is required, the services of a competent
professional person should be sought.

Library of Congress Cataloging-in-Publication Data

AMA management handbook / John J. Hampton, editor.—3rd ed.
        p. cm.
    Includes bibliographical references and index.
    ISBN 0-8144-0105-8
    1. Management. I. Hampton, John J., 1942–   . II. American
Management Association
HD31.A418 1994
658—dc20   94-6802
                                                  CIP

Printing number

10   9   8   7   6   5   4   3   2   1

BOARD OF EDITORS

CONTENTS

Foreword   *xv*
Editor's Preface   *xvii*
List of Contributors   *xxi*

Section 1
General Management
Don E. Marsh, Section Editor   1-1

Introduction   1-3
Management: From Old Designs to New Realities   1-5
Management Theories and Practices   1-11
Management Theory and Application   1-18
Quality Processes in Management   1-23
Mission Statement and Policies   1-27
Corporate Climate and Culture   1-30
Managing Ethics in the Corporation   1-32
Strategic and Tactical Planning: From Corporate Level to Department
   Level   1-36
Establishing Controls   1-43
Organizational Models and Structures   1-47
Integrating Functions and Departments   1-52
Techniques for Project Management   1-54
The Organization of the Future   1-58

Section 2
Marketing
Noel Capon, Section Editor   2-1

Introduction   2-3
The Marketing-Oriented Firm   2-5
The Tasks of Marketing Management   2-12
The Product Life Cycle   2-18

Strategic Marketing Planning Processes   2-25
Strategic Marketing Planning Tools   2-34
The Annual Marketing Plan   2-42
Marketing Research   2-48
Customer Decision Making   2-55
Corporate Marketing   2-61
Marketing and Quality   2-65
Developing New Products   2-69
Competitive New Product Strategies   2-77
Profitable Pricing   2-80
Auditing the Marketing Function   2-86
Legal Imperatives for Marketing Decisions   2-94
Industrial Marketing   2-101
Advertising and Mass Communications   2-108
Direct Marketing   2-116

Section 3
Sales and Distribution
Noel Capon, Section Editor   3-1

Introduction   3-3
The Tasks of Sales Management   3-5
Designing the Sales Organization   3-11
Managing the Distribution System   3-19
Major Account Management   3-26
Designing Sales Force Compensation   3-35
Sales Promotion   3-41

Section 4
Human Resources
Michael Z. Sincoff, Section Editor   4-1

Introduction   4-3
Effective Supervision   4-6
Human Resources Planning in the 1990s   4-12
Personnel Selection and Psychological Assessment   4-16
Managing the Diverse Work Force   4-20
New Dimensions in Work Scheduling   4-24
Training and Development to Improve Employee Performance   4-28
Employee Compensation   4-35
Employee Benefits: Options and Alternatives   4-40

Retirement and Pension Planning   4-46
Managing Pension Plans   4-51
Compliance with Government Regulations   4-55
The Performance Appraisal Process   4-60
Evaluating Human Resources Information Systems   4-64
Human Resources Management in International Operations   4-66
Dealing with Corporate Restructuring   4-69
Effective Communication   4-72
Relations with Organized Labor   4-76
Employee Health Promotion   4-86
Employee Substance Abuse   4-89
Privacy and Personnel Security Issues   4-92

Section 5
Accounting
Athar Murtuza, Section Editor   5-1

Introduction   5-3
General-Purpose Financial Reporting on Financial Statements   5-5
Managing Accounts Receivable   5-12
Inventory Valuation and Control   5-16
Analyzing Operating Results   5-23
Managerial Uses of Accounting   5-27
Federal Taxation: Management Responsibilities and Opportunities   5-31
Managing State and Local Taxes   5-37
Internal Auditing   5-40
The Independent Audit   5-43
Investor Relations   5-49
Accounting in the International Environment   5-52

Section 6
Finance
Gordon Cummings, Section Editor   6-1

Introduction   6-3
Finance's Increased Role in Management   6-5
The Role of the Chief Financial Officer   6-7
Planning, Budgeting, and Forecasting   6-9
Corporate Restructuring   6-14
Capital Expenditures: Analysis and Decision Making   6-21
Sources of Financing: Traditional and New   6-25
Cash Management   6-33
The Effects of Financial Deregulation   6-36

Global Financial Thinking   6-40
Managing Foreign Exchange   6-42

Section 7
Research and Technology
Mark D. Dibner, Section Editor   7-1

Introduction   7-3
Coping with Technological Change   7-5
Management Functions in R&D   7-11
Managing and Prioritizing Projects: Project Assessment   7-16
Project Management Methods   7-21
Setting Up the R&D Team   7-25
Managing R&D for Strategic Position   7-29
Encouraging Innovation in R&D   7-33
Taking Ideas from the Laboratory to the Market   7-36
Licensing, Protecting Intellectual Property Rights, and Other Legal
   Aspects of Technology Management   7-39
Technology Management in Consortia and Strategic Alliances   7-42
Using U.S. Federal Government Resources in R&D   7-45
Managing Technology in a Global Economy   7-47

Section 8
Manufacturing
Patricia Turnbaugh, Section Editor   8-1

Introduction   8-3
Developing Strategy in a Manufacturing Business   8-5
Planning Manufacturing Organizations   8-18
Human Resources Planning   8-22
Wage Incentives   8-26
Quality Management   8-36
Manufacturing Processes and Materials   8-51
Managing Technology in Manufacturing   8-64
Environmental Management   8-75

Section 9
Information Systems and Technology
Norbert J. Kubilus, Section Editor   9-1

Introduction   9-3
The MIS Function   9-5
Information Strategy Planning   9-10

Hardware and Equipment 9-16
Software and Applications Development 9-22
Telecommunications 9-28
Electronic Data Interchange 9-33
Intelligent Network Management 9-36
Database Management Systems 9-42
The Data Processing Center 9-48
Outsourcing 9-52
Disaster Recovery for Information Systems 9-56
Training for Users and MIS Staff 9-60
Security and Legal Issues in MIS 9-64
Managing Transitions in MIS 9-68

Section 10
Purchasing
Don Bohl and Bobby Zachariah, Section Editors 10-1

Introduction 10-3
Functions of the Purchasing Department 10-4
Purchasing Techniques and Procedures That Maximize Value 10-11
Legal Aspects of Purchasing 10-18
Controls in the Purchasing Process 10-22
Physical Distribution and Warehousing 10-27
Logistics Management 10-31
Leasing 10-33
Capital Purchasing 10-35
Electronic Data Interchange 10-38

Section 11
Corporate Relations
John D. Bergen, Section Editor 11-1

Introduction 11-3
Managing the Corporate Relations Staff 11-4
Government Relations 11-6
Media Relations in the 1990s 11-8
Shareholder and Investor Relations 11-11
Employee Relations and Communications 11-14
Corporate Philanthropy 11-17
Business-to-Business Communications 11-20
Trade Relations 11-23
Risk Management Communications 11-25
Intracorporate International Relations 11-30
Evaluating Corporate Relations Results 11-32

Section 12
Risk Management and Insurance
Sandra Gustavson, Section Editor   12-1

Introduction   12-3
The Risk Management Function   12-5
The Risk Management Process   12-8
Property and Income Loss Exposures   12-11
Liability Loss Exposures   12-16
Human Resources Loss Exposures   12-21
Loss Control   12-24
Risk Retention   12-29
Noninsurance Risk Transfer   12-33
Insurance   12-35
Risk Management Department Organization and Policy   12-41
The Role of Insurance Agents and Brokers   12-48
Global Insurance and Risk Management   12-50

Section 13
Entrepreneurship and Small Businesses
Donald A. Straits, Section Editor   13-1

Introduction   13-3
The Role of the Entrepreneur in the Economy   13-5
Preparing a Business Plan   13-6
Sources of Financing for the New Business   13-12
Human Resources Management in the Small Business   13-16
Marketing in the Small Business   13-19
Cash Management for Growing Firms   13-22
Customer Service in Small Businesses   13-26
International Opportunities for the Growing Business   13-28
Taxation and Accounting Considerations   13-30
Hiring, Firing, and Avoiding Lawyers   13-34
Family-Owned Businesses   13-37
The Franchising Route   13-39

Section 14
International Business
Jean Kelly, Section Editor   14-1

Introduction   14-3
Formulating and Implementing a Global Strategy   14-7
Looking at the Global Marketplace   14-26
Overseas Distribution, Licensing, and Technology Transfer   14-29

International Sourcing and Strategic Alliances 14-36
Managing Risks in International Joint Ventures 14-41
Problems and Opportunities in Countertrade 14-45
Management in Japan 14-48

Section 15
Service Industries
Rachel I. Vecchiotti, Section Editor 15-1

Introduction 15-3
Success in the Service Industries 15-5
Organizing for Efficient Service 15-16
Relationship Selling in the Service Industries 15-22
The Challenge of New Service Introduction 15-27
Establishing the Selling Prices for Services 15-33
The Impact of Telecommunications on the Service Industries 15-38
The Changing Nature of Professional Services 15-41

Section 16
Public-Sector and Nonprofit Management
Herrington J. Bryce, Section Editor 16-1

Introduction 16-3
Competencies of Effective Public-Sector Management 16-5
The Leadership Function in the Public Sector 16-9
The Power of Government Agencies 16-14
Evaluating Public Programs 16-18
Decision Making in the Public Sector 16-22
Ten Priniciples to Guide the Nonprofit 16-25
The Management of Nonprofit Organizations 16-27
Information Technology and the Nonprofit Manager 16-31
Public and Nonprofit Marketing 16-36
Auditing Nonprofits 16-42

Index *I-1*
About the Editor *E-1*
About American Management Association *A-1*

FOREWORD

When the last edition of the *AMA Management Handbook* was published in 1983, American quality was a joke, there was still a Soviet Union, China was screwed down tightly, downsizing wasn't institutionalized, business survived without PCs and faxes, Sears was the largest retailer in the United States, and the idea of IBM faltering was as unthinkable as the United States becoming the world's largest debtor nation.

It is now so commonplace to talk about the rapid pace of change that the concept has lost meaning . . . until you actually begin to list just those changes that come readily to mind. I was amazed at how quickly I could fill an entire page with major, far-reaching societal, political, and business events that have reshaped our lives forever.

In the context of major shifts in business practices, it was very apparent that a revision of the previous *AMA Management Handbook* would not produce a useful tool for managers in the 1990s and beyond. That's why this third edition of the *Handbook* is a completely new work. We asked leading practitioners in each discipline of management to provide a fresh perspective on their fields; to examine the new techniques of management without losing sight of those proven methods that have stood the test of time; and to present best practices, those things that really get results for successful companies from around the world.

In the following pages you'll find a full dis-cussion of new techniques such as activity-based cost accounting, process reengineering, and core competencies. In addition, you'll see how these new ideas evolved and how they can be evaluated for your particular situation. Finally, you'll see how other organizations have used them successfully. While increasing your understanding of these new concepts, you'll also get a thorough grounding in the traditional body of knowledge known as management. No other work provides such a comprehensive discussion of the proven and the innovative and then weaves the two into a coherent whole.

I want to take this opportunity to thank the many AMA members who contributed to this volume. Your expertise and support made its publication possible. My special thanks to John J. Hampton, professor of risk management and insurance at the College of Insurance and president of Princeton Consulting Group. As editor, John had the seemingly impossible task of pulling this huge work together.

After you've had a chance to use the *AMA Management Handbook, Third Edition*, I think you'll agree that the efforts of all involved have created an indispensable road map for managing your way through this ever-changing business landscape.

David Fagiano
President and Chief Executive Officer
American Management Association

EDITOR'S PREFACE

As we approach the turn of a new century, we are witnesses to a revolution in management thought. The past century was characterized by large organizations and the techniques for managing them. A bureaucracy was the model. Within a structure of rules and policies, managers planned, directed, staffed, motivated, and performed the other functions that achieved organizational goals. With rare exceptions, the process sought consistency and permanence of operation.

By the 1980s, many organizations were facing serious challenges from all sides. The world had changed in fundamental ways. Fierce competitors came from all over the world and crossed international borders with speed and ease. Governments and the courts proposed and interpreted legislation that affected all areas of operation and imposed new requirements and costs on private and nonprofit entities alike. Consumer groups allied with trial lawyers to make fundamental changes in the responsibilities of employers and producers and distributors of goods or services.

These forces were accompanied by changing technologies that opened some doors and closed others. The distinction between hardware, software, and communications channels blurred as information systems offered totally new tools and resources to manage organizations. Total quality management, reengineering, restructuring, the virtual office, the knowledge organization, and networking characterized the cutting edge of management activities.

Now, in the mid-1990s, we are beginning to see the outline of the organization of the future. In this new edition of the *AMA Management Handbook*, we build on the past hundred years of management thought and practice even as we prepare for the next century's changing work force and global marketplace. Many of the lessons of the past will carry forward into the future. Traditional management concepts are retained in this new edition; the authors may be different, but the ideas remain the same. At the same time, new ideas and methodologies are introduced to reflect technologies and emerging trends that will influence managers of the present and future.

The third edition of the *Handbook* brings together the ideas of more than two hundred experts in a wide range of disciplines, all of which can be covered under the broad umbrella of management. The final effort is the world's most comprehensive body of information dealing with the subjects that define and shape management thought. It is also a major resource identifying and explaining the fundamental issues that will affect organizations as they prepare for an increasingly uncertain future.

The lessons of this *Handbook* should be received by the reader in the context of changing cultural, social, and financial climates throughout the world. Organizations pursue their markets or other goals in an environment that changes daily. Manufacturing is shifting from the developed to the developing nations. Technology is allowing different kinds of manufacturing to grow in industrialized nations. Consumers are seeking to improve their standards of living in the face of the long-term trends of declining global resources. Hierarchies are yielding to alternative organizational structures that value partnerships, interdependency of units, and new ways to divide up the task of work.

Sure, the world is changing. Yet, some things will remain the same. Goods and services must still be priced correctly. Customers and clients will always demand improvements in service and support. New products and services must continue to be developed to allow profit and not-for-profit organizations to survive and flourish as needs change. And organizations will need to be managed, which means that managers will still have to perform a variety of appraisal, leadership, planning, implementation, and other functions.

So what does this mean for the managers of tomorrow? First, they must have a breadth of knowledge of the kinds of topics that are covered in this book. The task is nothing less than the full integration of planning, marketing, finance, and technology. The world of management ideas, as reflected in this *Handbook*, is not just "nice to have." It is essential if managers are to be familiar with ideas outside of their own specific functional area. The need for breadth has always existed for chief executive officers. In the organization of the future (or is it the organization of today?), all managers must have a broad range of knowledge and skills.

Second, managers must view learning as a lifelong process. The lessons brought from college must be augmented and updated on a regular basis if correct decisions and accurate judgments are to be part of the management process. This *Handbook* has been carefully organized and structured to allow managers to quickly find the best and brightest of new ideas and to gain a quick understanding of how those ideas might be useful in their own operations.

Peter Drucker wrote that it is not enough to ask, "What is our business? Who is our customer?" Managers, he says, must also ask, "What should our business be? Who should our customer be? How is value defined by our customer?" Drucker was ahead of his time when he asked these questions in the

1970s. Now, his time has arrived. Organizations that do not learn about the changing arena of management are or will be in trouble.

This third edition of *The AMA Management Handbook*, belongs near the manager's computer or on a nearby shelf. Its lessons will be of interest to senior executives, line and staff managers, students of management, and individuals who want a clearer understanding of the current state and range of management thought. It can be skimmed periodically as a source of new ideas. It can be used as a specific reference work in the search for technical information. It can be an adviser on thorny issues. But whatever its use, it should not remain unopened for long periods of time.

The *Handbook* has been prepared with the cooperation and efforts of many people. The front line has been manned by outstanding section editors, all experts in their respective fields and aware of new developments and current trends. These men and women have invited other experts—the individual authors—to share their knowledge, beliefs, and perspectives on specific topics. All of the material is new, even as it builds on the ideas and traditions of successful managers of the past. The writing style is practical and instructive. Underlying principles and lessons are expressed in clear language, although some "jargon" is always needed when expressing cutting-edge ideas in technical areas.

Some thanks are in order. The section editors dealt with the complexities and contradictions that often emerge when a variety of experts describe a complex and pluralistic world. Their dedication and patience exceeded normal bounds. The individual authors also deserve thanks for taking time from always busy schedules to synthesize and condense complicated thoughts. A special note of thanks goes to Don Bohl for his help in many areas. Thanks also to the reviewers of the various sections and the members of the AMA councils who helped formulate and conceive the structure of the book. And, finally, thanks to Adrienne Hickey of AMACOM Books, who stayed with the process as different viewpoints were incorporated and problems were solved.

Being a manager in the mid-1990s is a complex business. The breadth of topics in the *Handbook* gives some idea of the level of this complexity. At the same time, few things are more exciting than being a *successful* manager. All of us affiliated with the American Management Association hope this book will be helpful as managers prepare themselves and their organizations for the challenging opportunities of management in the twenty-first century.

John J. Hampton
Gillette, New Jersey

LIST OF CONTRIBUTORS

Pier A. Abetti, Rensselaer Polytechnic Institute

Frank L. Acuff, Director, Human Resources International, and Adjunct Professor, Northwestern University

Mark J. Allen, Senior Manager, KPMG Peat Marwick

Robin D. Anderson, Director, Nebraska Center for Entrepreneurship, University of Nebraska, Lincoln

Caleb S. Atwood, President, E.R.I.Q., Inc.

Marc Bassin, Vice-President, Human Resources Development, Montefiore Medical Center

Alden S. Bean, Lehigh University

Sara L. Beckman, Haas School of Business, University of California, Berkeley

James A. Belasco, Professor of Management, San Diego State University

A. Douglas Bender, School of Management, Widener University

Shelby D. Bennett, The University of North Carolina at Asheville

Keki R. Bhote, President, Keki R. Bhote Associates, and Senior Corporate Consultant (retired), Quality and Productivity Improvement, Motorola

Barry Bingham, Director, Compensation, Monsanto Company

Dan Bishop, Founder/President, National Family Business Association

Mary Jo Bitner, Associate Professor of Marketing, Arizona State University

Barry Blitstein, Vice-President of Human Resources, Monsanto Company

Jack Bologna, Associate Professor of Management, Siena Heights College

Richard E. Boyatzis, Professor, Weatherhead School of Management, Case Western Reserve University

Stephen W. Brown, Professor of Marketing and Director, The First Interstate Center for Services Marketing, Arizona State University

William Brunsen, Eastern New Mexico University

Herrington J. Bryce, School of Business, The College of William and Mary

Alethea O. Caldwell, Executive Vice-President, Corporate Services, Blue Cross of California

Noel Capon, Professor of Business, Graduate School of Business, Columbia University

Gregory S. Carpenter, Associate Professor of Marketing, J. L. Kellogg Graduate School of Management, Northwestern University

Harold Carr, Vice-President of Public Relations and Advertising, The Boeing Company

Joan H. Coll, Associate Professor of Management, School of Business, Seton Hall University

William S. Comfort, Maher, Rosenheim & Comfort

Gregory E. Conlon, Champion International Corporation

John I. Coppett, University of Houston at Clear Lake

George S. Day, Geoffrey T. Boisi Professor, The Wharton School, University of Pennsylvania

Daniel J. Dean, Vice-President, Frank Crystal & Company, Inc.

Milton F. Droege, Jr., President, Droege & Associates

Christopher A. Duncan, Director, Risk Management, Kentucky Fried Chicken Corporation

John F. Early, Vice-President Research and Development, Juran Institute, Inc.

Robert B. Edgar, Assistant Vice-President, Chubb and Son, Inc.

Phyllis Elnes, President, STI International/Sales Training Institute

Karen Epermanis, Director, Risk Management, Intermedics Inc.

Anne Farley, Former Partner, KPMG Peat Marwick

Thomas C. Farnam, Attorney-at-Law, T. C. Farnam & Associates

Linda J. Ferri, President, L. J. Ferri & Associates

Elisha W. Finney, Manager, Risk Management and Corporate Credit, Varian Associates, Inc.

Peter B. Fitzpatrick, Executive Vice-President, Center for Innovative Technology

Peter T. FitzRoy, Monash University

Michele Forzley, Managing Director, Forzley and Company

Richard N. Foster, McKinsey and Company

Donald E. Frischman, Operations Director, IBM Marketing and Services Communications

Sharon Gamsin, Vice-President, Communications, New York Stock Exchange

Jack P. Gibson, President, International Risk Management Institute, Inc.

Ronald M. Gimpel, Productivity Solutions Management, Ltd.

Bela Gold, Claremont Graduate School

Michael Goldberg, Director, Managed Care Development and Education, Blue Cross/Blue Shield of Missouri

Michael F. Grace, Insurance Consultant

James Granger, President, The Wirthlin Group

Barbara L. Gray, CEO, Barron Group Ltd.

E. Malcolm Greenlees, Linfield College

Donald Grunewald, Professor of Strategic Management, Iona College

Denis Guerette, Executive Vice-President of Operations, Meloche Monnex, Inc.

James M. Guinan, retired senior executive, major retailing corporations

T. Carter Hagaman, Kean College of New Jersey

William F. Hamilton, The Wharton School of Business, University of Pennsylvania

John J. Hampton, Principal, Princeton Consulting Group, Inc.; Professor of Insurance and Risk Management, The College of Insurance

William John Hanna, The University of Maryland, College Park

Jeffrey L. Harkins, Department of Accounting, University of Idaho

A. Douglas Hartt, Treasurer, Maritime Telegraph and Telephone

Daniel Haskin, Eastern New Mexico University

Elizabeth J. Hawk, Senior Consultant of Compensation, Monsanto Company

L. Hall Healy, Jr., Patrick Engineering, Inc.

Floyd D. Hedrick, Chief, Contracts and Logistics, Library of Congress

Jan B. Heide, Assistant Professor of Marketing, University of Wisconsin–Madison

Christopher E. Held, Director, Asian Research Center, Concordia College (Japan)

Robert W. Hiller, Vice-President and Treasurer, General Foods Corporation (retired)

William J. Hindman, Jr., Hindman and Associates

Kathleen Conlon Hinge

W. Edward Hodgson, Manchester Equipment Company, Inc.

Donna L. Hoffman, Associate Professor of Marketing, Owen Graduate School of Management, Vanderbilt University

Reed K. Holden, Professor, Boston University, and Managing Director, Strategic Pricing Group, Inc.

John Huguet, President, Commonwealth Construction Company

James M. Hulbert, R. C. Kopf Professor of International Marketing, Columbia Business School, Columbia University

Gerard Huybregts, Eastern New Mexico University

Richard C. Hyde, Hill and Knowlton, Inc.

Tom Inglesby, President, American Society for Competitiveness; formerly Editor, *Manufacturing Systems Magazine*

Thomas N. Ingram, Sales and Marketing Executives of Memphis Chair in Sales Excellence, Memphis State University

V. Bruce Irvine, Professor of Accounting, College of Commerce, University of Saskatchewan

Bruce Isaacson, Doctoral Student, Harvard Business School, Harvard University

Joseph Jackson, Crowley Maritime Corporation

Sara Joannides

Steven P. Kahn, Principal, Advanced Risk Management Techniques, Inc.

Marjorie Kalter, Executive Vice-President, Wunderman Cato Johnson

George L. Knox III, Vice-President, Public Affairs, Philip Morris Companies Inc.

Charles H. Koch, Jr., Woodbridge Professor of Law, School of Law, The College of William and Mary

Philip Kotler, Northwestern University

Margery Kraus, President and CEO, APCO Associates

Norbert J. Kubilus, Vice-President and Chief Information Officer, BCM Engineers, Inc.

Thomas D. Kuczmarski, President, Kuczmarski & Associates

Arthur Kurek, President, ALICOMP, Inc.

Raymond W. LaForge, Brown-Forman Professor of Marketing, University of Louisville

Dick Laird, Executive Director, Center for Business and Economic Education, Lubbock Christian University

Donald R. Lehmann, George E. Warner Professor of Business, Graduate School of Business, Columbia University

Wendell Leimbach, AME Group, Inc.

Herbert J. Lerner, Ernst & Young

E. J. Leverett, Jr., Professor of Risk Management and Insurance, University of Georgia

Laura A. Lies, Corning-Asahi Video Products Company

Andres Llana, Jr., Vermont Studies Group, Inc.

Christopher H. Lovelock, Lovelock Associates

Bruce Lunergan, Partner, Ash, Craig, and Thornton

J. Mike McElhone, Interamerican Transport Systems, Inc.

David S. Machlowitz, Counsel, Siemens Medical Corporation

William R. Maher, Maher, Rosenheim & Comfort

Gail H. Marcus, U.S. Nuclear Regulatory Commission

E. Nancy Markle, Information Technology Consultants

Don E. Marsh, President and CEO, Marsh Supermarkets

John F. Martin, President, John Martin & Associates, Inc.

Vance A. Mehrens, Director, International Center for Franchise Studies, University of Nebraska, Lincoln

Michael Merbaum, Professor of Psychology, Washington University-St. Louis; and Hazelwood Farms Bakeries, Inc.

D. Bruce Merrifield, Walter Bladstrom Executive Professor of Management, The Wharton School of Business, University of Pennsylvania

David J. Metz, Senior Vice-President and Director, Communications and Public Affairs, Eastman Kodak Company

W. Sanford Miller, Jr., Chief Marketing Officer/Corporate Strategist, CIGNA Corporation

Paul W. Miniard, Professor of Marketing, University of South Carolina

Graham R. Mitchell, Assistant Secretary Designate for Technology Policy, Department of Commerce

Kent B. Monroe, University of Illinois–Champaign-Urbana

Jeffrey A. Moore, Director, Corporate Planning and Development, Indiana Gas Company, Inc.

Dennis J. Morikawa, Attorney-at-Law, Morgan, Lewis & Bockius

Athar Murtuza, Associate Professor of Accounting, Seton Hall University

Thomas T. Nagle, Professor, Boston University; and Managing Director, Strategic Pricing Group, Inc.

Kent Nakamoto, Assistant Professor of Marketing, Graduate School of Business, University of Colorado

Scott A. Neslin, Professor of Business Administration, The Amos Tuck School, Dartmouth College

Tom Niland, Small Business International Trade Program, Portland Community College

Warren E. Norquist, Vice-President, Purchasing and Materials Division, Polaroid Corporation

Gerard A. Osborne, Hamilton Consultants

Stanley J. Ostaszewski, Principal, Unisys Corporation

John A. Passante, Senior Vice-President, Human Resources, Moog Automotive, Inc.

Susan L. Pedigo, Managing Editor, *The Wyatt Communicator,* The Wyatt Company

Michael Perril, President, ESI & Associates, Inc.

Robert Plaut, Digital Equipment Corporation

Charmaine Ponkratz, Vice-President, Marketing, Valley Bancorporation

George R. Quittner, Coors Brewing Company

Jack S. Rader, Executive Director, Financial Management Association

Clifford A. Rand, Partner, Cowen and Company, and Senior Vice-President and Registered Investment Advisor, Cowen Asset Management

V. Kasturi Rangan, Professor, Harvard Business School, Harvard University

Fred M. Reichman, Attorney-at-Law, Reichman & Associates

S. Theodore Reiner, Ernst & Young

David N. Richardson, Senior Vice-President, The Wirthlin Group

William H. Rodgers, Hamilton Consultants

Alvin Rohrs, President and CEO, Students in Free Enterprise, Inc.

Robert L. Rosenheim, Maher, Rosenheim & Comfort

Michael Rourke, Vice-President, Communications/Corporate Affairs, The Great Atlantic and Pacific Tea Company

Michael T. Rousseau, Vice-President, Human Resources, Intermedics Pacemaker Division, A Company of Sulzermedica

Evan E. Rudolph, Vice-President, Southern School Media

Tony W. Salinger, Quality Director, AT&T Global Video Phone Systems

Charles S. Saunders, Director, Government Relations, ICI Explosives (Division of ICI Americas, Inc.)

Victor Schachter, Partner, Schachter, Kristoff, Orenstein and Berkowitz

W. Keith Schilit, University of South Florida

Bernd H. Schmitt, Associate Professor of Business, Graduate School of Business, Columbia University

Benjamin Schneider, Department of Psychology, University of Maryland at College Park

John L. Schwab, Jr., President, John L. Schwab & Associates

Herschel V. Sellers, Director of Corporate Benefits, Monsanto Company

Donald E. Sexton, Professor of Business and Co-Director, Center for International Business Education, Graduate School of Business, Columbia University

Steve Shoaf, FHP, Inc.

Kenneth D. Sibley, Bell, Seltzer, Park & Gibson

Francoise L. Simon, Graduate School of Business, Columbia University

Jack L. Simonetti, Professor of Management, The University of Toledo

Ronald R. Sims, Associate Professor, School of Business Administration, The College of William and Mary

Ashley James Sinclair, President, Krell Capital Corporation

Kathleen D. Sincoff, Director of Human Resources, Spectrum Emergency Care

Michael Z. Sincoff, Senior Vice-President, Human Resources and Administration, DIMAC DIRECT Inc.

Andrew W. Singer, Editor and Publisher of *Ethikos: Examining Ethical Issues in Business*

Raymond W. Smilor, IC^2 Institute and Graduate School of Business, The University of Texas at Austin

Robert A. Smith, Jr., Esq., Managing Partner, Smith and Hiatt

Bert Spilker, Burroughs Wellcome Company

William A. Staples, University of Houston at Clear Lake

Ralph E. Stayer, CEO, Johnsonville Foods

Elizabeth Stearns, The Stearns Group

Jan-Benedict E. M. Steenkamp, AGB Professor of Marketing Research, Catholic University of Leuven, Belgium

Paul J. Stitzel, President, Brentwood Hospital

Diana Stork, University of Hartford

David H. Swanson, Chairman, President and CEO, Central Soya Company

Craig A. Terrill, Partner, Kuczmarski & Associates

Donald R. Tieken, Riverwood International Corporation

Jerry D. Todd, The Charles E. Cheever Chair in Risk Management, St. Mary's University

Richard Torrenzano, Director and Senior Vice-President, Corporate Affairs, SmithKline Beecham

Alan R. Tubbs, President, American Bankers Association; and President, Maquoketa State Bank

Joseph L. Tufano, Managing Partner, Management Consulting Services

Gary S. Tubridy, Senior Vice-President, The Alexander Group, Inc.

Patricia Turnbaugh, Consultant and Committee Chairperson, Foundation for Manufacturing Excellence

Rachel I. Vecchiotti, Consultant, Kuczmarski & Associates

Randall Vick, Senior Procurement Specialist, The World Bank

Julie A. Vincent, Director, Corporate Communications, Indiana Gas Company, Inc.

Cecilia L. Wagner, Associate Professor, School of Business, Seton Hall University

Larry A. Warner, Risk Management Analyst, Mars, Inc.

Charles B. Weinberg, Alumni Professor of Marketing, University of British Columbia

Leo C. B. Welt, President, Welt International

Ray O. Werner, Professor of Economics, Emeritus, The Colorado College

Bruce L. Whitaker, Eastern New Mexico University

Joseph S. Wholey, School of Public Administration, University of Southern California

Deborah Wiethop, Editor, Communications Projects, Blue Cross/Blue Shield of Missouri

Michael Williams, Abbott Laboratories

John J. Willingham, Partner, KPMG Peat Marwick

George Willis, Controller, Industry, Science, and Technology Canada

Russell S. Winer, Professor of Marketing, Haas School of Business, University of California, Berkeley

Donald T. Winski, President, DTW Associates

Ann M. Wolf, Vice-President, Robert E. La Blanc Associates, Inc.

John F. Wymer III, Partner, Jones, Day, Reavis & Pogue

Dennis R. Young, Mandel Center for Non-Profit Organizations, Case Western Reserve University

Ahmed Zaki, School of Business Administration, The College of William and Mary

Dale E. Zand, Professor of Management, Stern School of Business, New York University

Ronald E. Zier, Vice-President, Public Affairs, Warner-Lambert Company

Alan Zimmerman, President, Radley Resources, Inc.

SECTION 1

General Management

Don E. Marsh, Section Editor

Introduction   *Don E. Marsh*   1-3

Management: From Old Designs to New Realities   *Ralph E. Stayer*
    and James A. Belasco   1-5

Management Theories and Practices   *Don E. Marsh*   1-11

Management Theory and Application   *Dale E. Zand*   1-18

Quality Processes in Management   *John F. Early*   1-23

Mission Statement and Policies   *Paul J. Stitzel*   1-27

Corporate Climate and Culture   *Benjamin Schneider*   1-30

Managing Ethics in the Corporation   *Andrew W. Singer*   1-32

Strategic and Tactical Planning: From Corporate
    Level to Department Level   *Jeffrey A. Moore and*
    Julie A. Vincent   1-36

Establishing Controls   *Alethea O. Caldwell*   1-43

Organizational Models and Structures   *Joan H. Coll*   1-47

Integrating Functions and Departments   *David H. Swanson*   1-52

Techniques for Project Management   *Ronald M. Gimpel and*
    Barbara L. Gray   1-54

The Organization of the Future   *John J. Hampton*   1-58

INTRODUCTION

Don E. Marsh

Management may be defined as the process of getting things done through people. It involves elements of organization, leadership, communications skills, and the ability to set goals and figure out ways to achieve them.

Management has never been a simple task. Even when organizations were relatively simple in terms of their size, technology, and environment, good managers stood out from those who were unable to organize resources to achieve a goal. History provides many examples of effective and incompetent organizations, with some examples showing the same organization as effective in one period of time and ineffective at a later point in time.

The task of management has never been more difficult than it is in the 1990s. The processes of getting things done through people must recognize environmental, competitive, social, and economic pressures that did not exist in simpler times. The challenge and opportunities for managers are great.

This section sets the foundation for the entire *AMA Management Handbook*. Yes, management skills may be applied generically in various environments and organizations. A good manager can be effective in public or private sector situations, recognizing that time may be needed to learn what is important in any new environment. A section on "General Management" is the right place to start.

What is accomplished in this section? Essentially, the distinguished authors are sharing their insights on how to get the job done when working with others. In many ways, management is like a journey to a distant destination. This section examines the components of a successful voyage.

Management begins with the goals to be achieved. Words like *mission, objectives,* and *goals* are common in the text. Once the manager has a clear definition and understanding of the goal, a road map must be developed to reach it. Thus, the term *planning* appears prominently and often. *Implementation* is next, as managers need a vehicle to carry the passengers to the goal. Chapters examine the structure of organizations, productivity, controls, and activities. Finally, the likelihood of a successful journey is enhanced by an understanding that we are moving through a world that is not under our control. Innovation and ethical behavior are examples of the need to

---

Don E. Marsh *is chairman, president, and chief executive officer of Marsh Supermarkets, Inc., a food retailing company that owns and operates 257 supermarkets and convenience stores in the Midwest. He is a governor of the World Economic Forum and has been chairman of the International Centre for Food Trade and Industry and the Association of Publicly Traded Companies. He also spearheaded the 1991 Marsh Super Study, the first major, in-depth analysis of American supermarkets since the mid-1960s.*

take a broad and flexible view of the process of management.

The chapter authors bring different viewpoints to provide food for thought. In many cases, their lessons are entirely logical, if not always obvious. In other cases, they may stir controversy. This is all right. Management is an art—that is, it must be practiced in the real world—as opposed to a science that takes place in a laboratory. The reader is free to accept or reject the various arguments contained herein. We hope only that we have stimulated thought on the subject of general management.

MANAGEMENT: FROM OLD DESIGNS TO NEW REALITIES

Ralph E. Stayer, CEO, Johnsonville Foods
James A. Belasco, Professor of Management,
San Diego State University

America's largest export is not airplanes. Nor is it cola or blue jeans, as ubiquitous as those symbols of American culture have become worldwide. It's not even Disney's Mickey Mouse, the most widely recognized figure in the world. When the history of the twentieth century is written, America's most valuable contribution and most widely used export will be its management thought and practice. America has developed the art and science of managing large organizations and has exported its expertise to the four corners of the earth. American management is the model for the world.

The history of American management has been written largely by practitioners. The works of a Frenchman, Henri Fayol, formed the basis of American management thought and practice. He ran the French coal mines in the later nineteenth century and based his book, *Principles of Administration*, on his experience. Frederick Winslow Taylor, an industrial engineer in the steel industry, added fur-

ther insight and practices. Chester Barnard, president of New Jersey Bell in the late 1920s, wrote about his developments in management thought and practice in his book, *Functions of the Executive*. And, of course, Alfred Sloan blazed new trails in his pioneering work at General Motors as did Henry Ford at the Ford Motor Company.

But today the "old" management paradigms are under attack. They are increasingly unable to handle the "new" realities: globalization, electronic highways that transfer information instantly around the world, an educated work force, and rapid shifts in technology, markets, and customer needs.

Again, American practitioners are blazing new trails in management practice. The hierarchy is being replaced with the network. Authority is being replaced with empowerment. Conglomerates are being replaced with small customer/product-focused units. Standardized "every-one-gets-the-same" compensation systems are being replaced with customized pay-for-performance incentives. The emphasis on individual achievement is being replaced by a focus on effective teamwork. Even the venerable assembly line can now be stopped by any worker.

What follows is the distillation of what we have learned from years of running our own business and coaching the leaders of some of the largest companies and countries in the world. These insights reflect the latest learning in the field of management practice and thought. Some of these lessons were expensive in terms of money, time, and energy. The biggest lesson we learned? In most situations, "we" (management) were the biggest problem. Our attitudes, mentalities, and behaviors often were the biggest obstacles to our individual and organizational success. We had to learn to look at ourselves as the problem first, before we could really start learning how to be successful. We learned to ask ourselves, "What are we doing or not doing that is causing the problem?"

In this process, we also learned how to be the solution. We learned that our old management paradigms were our biggest obstacle. We had to learn an entirely new way of thinking about our role as leaders. In 1892, Henri Fayol stated that the five functions of management are planning, organizing, commanding, coordinating, and controlling. The expectations are far different today.

Working with many different organizations, we have found that the new task of leaders is to focus on creating an organization marked by clear definitions, value-added strategies, and continual learning on how to execute visions, values, and strategies. To implement the new approach we had to learn a new set of principles. The principles are:

1. Thinking strategically—thinking and acting with the end result in mind.
2. Getting the right people to want to own the right responsibilities—developing an organization in which people know what great performance is individually and are totally committed to achieving it.
3. Continual learning—change is the only constant. The definition of great perfor-

mance continually changes. Our pace of learning must increase to keep up.

Learning these principles will provide a foundation for using the rest of the information in this handbook.

THINKING STRATEGICALLY

Details overwhelm you. Employees, bosses, suppliers, customers, and bureaucrats attack from all sides. As one executive said, "I spend my day running down an endless, narrow, dimly lit hallway, being beat upon by shrouded figures who appear and disappear in a seemingly random fashion." Although not an easy concept to master, thinking strategically (think and act with the end result in mind) invariably leads to positive results, for example:

> PRC is a highly successful specialty chemical producer, but that was not always the case. The company came back from the brink of bankruptcy by clearly defining its end state, and then motivating each employee to think strategically in terms of what he or she could do to advance the organization toward that end state. PRC sold ink for ballpoint pens—a fiercely price-competitive business. Yet, the company commanded a premium in that commodity market. How? Its end state was not to sell ink; it was to seek a solution to the customer's problem.

While ink is only a fraction of a pen's total cost, unavailability of the right ink color at the right time can shut down an entire line, resulting in great cost to the manufacturer. So, PRC guaranteed delivery and posted a performance bond to back up its guarantee. It focused all employees on thinking strategically in order to produce the end state: production continuity through guaranteed on-time delivery. The net result was that manufacturers could rely on their performance and PRC earned 50 percent margins in a 10 percent margin business!

Learning from PRC, management should

seek to accomplish two objectives in every situation: the short-term objective of solving the immediate problem and the long-term objective of moving toward the end state.

Strategic Leadership

As the leaders of our organizations our task is to teach everyone to think strategically. Questions are a great way to teach. Begin by asking such strategic questions as, "How does this action contribute to our end state of helping people to be responsible for making this the best company in the industry? Who owns the responsibility for fixing that quality problem? Do they recognize that they own the responsibility? What are we doing to get them to want to own the responsibility? Can they measure their performance?" Inevitably, questions help people learn priorities.

Leaders execute. Leadership is a participative sport, not a spectator sport. For too long, industry practiced the conventional wisdom that managers planned, organized, commanded, coordinated, and controlled. Once our business changed and focused on execution, our jobs became easier and our organizations became much more productive.

Leaders should focus on preventing problems, not solving them. When the going gets tough, quite often it is too late. Leaders must continually look ahead and implement long-term programs to prevent problems. Leaders should ask, "What does it take to deliver world-class products and services?" And, effective leaders are more interested in doing good than looking good.

The Magic of Vision

Vision focuses. Vision inspires. Vision is our alarm clock in the morning, our caffeine in the evening. The branch manager who leads the most successful IBM branch office said, "I know the vision's working when the lights are never off in the people's eyes. Vision is the energy that keeps everyone going."

Vision paints a picture of great performance. It becomes the criterion against which all behavior is measured. Vision enables all employees to answer the question, "How does this action/decision support the vi-

sion?" Having a vision is essential to thinking strategically.

Focusing on Strategic Activities

Identify and focus on the 20 percent of activities that yield 80 percent of the results. Most managers have long "to do" lists, most of which will make no difference in terms of attaining the end state. Instead, focusing on the few "criticals" will have the greatest impact on the end state.

One of our company's clients was facing economic hardship. He learned that he had to fire customers in order to improve his performance. After analyzing his customers, he discovered that 23 percent of them provided 87 percent of his business. It cost him more to market to many of his smaller accounts than the revenue they generated. Furthermore, 11 percent of the small accounts and 14 percent of the larger ones required extra services that destroyed his operating margins. When he dropped the smallest accounts, after selecting the few potential growth situations, and charged for the special extra services, his bottom line improved. He had learned to focus on major activities.

The story is told about Henry Kissinger that further illustrates maintaining focus. Several days after an aide delivered a report, Kissinger called him into his office and asked, "Is this your best work?" "Well no," the aide replied, "I had a deadline and all this other work. It's good but not the best." "Then take it back and redo it," Kissinger said. This was repeated several times. Finally, the aide answered, "Yes, this is my best work," to which Kissinger replied, "Good, now I'll read it."

When you accept less than the best work, that is all you will ever get. A president of a large communications firm learned this lesson. He consistently complained about getting shoddy work from his vice-presidents.

We asked him the "thinking strategically" questions: "What is great performance for your people? What are you doing or not doing that is causing the current performance?" He learned how to insist on and accept only the best. He would send incomplete material back with the notation, "I don't think this is indicative of your best work." The first few times that happened it absolutely shocked the recipient. He also reassigned incomplete work to other people, and made the low number of recycles and reassigns one of the criteria for year-end bonuses. Not only did the quality of the work he received improve dramatically, but the company's decision cycle dramatically shortened.

It is easy to be immobilized by the fear of failure. It is hard to think strategically about capitalizing on the future when an employee is concerned with the consequence of the past. Concern about potential disapproval chills action. Unfortunately, most people overestimate the potential for disapproval. Most executives tell us that they want their people to be risk takers, but the people seem not to want to be. Most employees say they want to take more risks, but perceive that their executives discourage risk taking. Everyone wants to do it, but no one dares. Successful people take calculated risks. They do not wait for permission to move ahead. To assure strategic thinking, management must set the example and reward the risk takers.

GETTING THE RIGHT PEOPLE TO WANT TO OWN THE RIGHT RESPONSIBILITIES

Focusing on Your Contribution

Our company's management worked hard and we still did not accomplish as much as we wanted to. We were great "fixers." Give us a problem—a production problem, a people problem, or a quality problem—and we would fix it. But was that our job? We learned that fixing other people's problems had three negative consequences: We worked too many hours doing other people's jobs, we prevented other people from learning and growing (thus assuring ourselves of permanently working long hours), and, being further away from the point of action and information, we often made bad decisions. We *taught* our people to bring us their problems to solve, because when they chose to do it themselves we criticized them for not doing it "our way."

Finally, we announced to the staff that henceforth they were responsible for making

their own decisions. Then management sat back and waited . . . and waited . . . and waited. In due course, staff was *asked* what it would take to help them become great performers, without us making decisions in their area. That is when the business really took off. Employees told us, "Tell us the parameters—what decisions we can and can't make. Give us the criteria for a good decision so we don't have to keep checking with you. Help us make the first several decisions, but don't make them for us. But, mostly, trust us to want to do the 'right' thing and don't second-guess us." We listened and implemented their ideas.

Obstacles to Change

"One cannot confer a benefit on an unwilling recipient." Cicero made this observation more than two thousand years ago, and it remains equally true today. As long as change is something done *to* someone, it will not happen. This is why most reactive programs do not seem to work and why most training does not seem to cause change. Individuals must be willing to change, must want to learn, and must want to be different. The leader's job is to create the conditions in which that desire occurs.

People are reluctant to change even though it may well be in their own best interest. For example, everyone is in favor of quality, but it is too easy to point to all the things that prevent someone from doing quality work. Johnsonville Foods (Kohler, Wisconsin) was a family owned manufacturer of sausage when I became president in the 1960s. The company employed several hundred people. Leadership talked a great deal about quality at Johnsonville and how essential it was to our collective job security. But it was not until those who actually produced our products became responsible for quality that we significantly improved quality levels.

Our marketing department received and responded to all customer complaint letters. Because marketing handled the feedback in a vacuum, the people who made the sausage were insulated from learning what customers really thought of the products they made. When we began routing the letters directly to the people producing the sausage, customers became real people with real desires. Production personnel responded positively to the complaint letters and made changes to satisfy "their" customers. Further, to prevent continuing complaint letters, the line workers asked for and received responsibility for measuring product quality and using those measurements to improve production processes. Management created an environment where individuals demand responsibility.

People feel powerless when they experience no control over their work. Their circles of control and influence are very small and, consequently, they feel disconnected from the organization's success or failure. Obviously, this is not a condition that produces positive results.

The pattern of obeying authority continues through childhood and into adult life. We learn the concept early and it is reinforced often. Parents are responsible for their children's behavior, teachers are responsible for their students' learning and, eventually, the boss is responsible for employees' performance. In the face of all this past learning, we now ask people to change their perspective to be responsible for their own behavior, learning, and performance.

CONTINUAL LEARNING

Effective managers are good learners and learning is the key to success in management. But now, with the more rapid pace of change, we need to learn at a much faster rate. The Managing Board of Royal Dutch Shell, the most successful oil company in the world, stated, "Our principle competitive advantage is the ability of our people to learn faster than our competition."

Learning begins with a mindset of openness to learn. Unfortunately, we are not always good learners. For example, when our organization started a replacement auto parts business, we were convinced that we knew that what customers really wanted was rapid service. Thus, lots of trucks were put on the road carrying huge inventories, ready to answer any telephone order within forty-five

minutes. The company even guaranteed, "Forty-five minutes or it's free."

We soon discovered that it was not possible to carry enough inventory on each truck to supply all the parts that could be ordered by customers. Further, traffic, weather, and breakdowns translated into lots of free parts. Finally, customers really did not need the parts instantly. There were advance warning signs for these factors, but the company had a closed mind—and it cost a bundle.

Success can be a great enemy of learning, leading to an overconfident smugness. For example, in the early 1980s, IBM owned the computer business. Everyone, including Tom Peters (coauthor of *In Search of Excellence,* Harper and Row, 1982), praised its management style. IBM was the "Most Admired Company in America." But IBM lost touch with its customers. It became more concerned with selling than solving. It focused more on telling customers what to buy than listening to what customers really needed. The result? Since the 1980s, IBM's market share has declined in virtually every market. IBM recognizes that it was a victim of its own arrogance. The company is working to relearn how to treat customers in that special IBM way.

Unwillingness to leave the comfort zone behind shows up perhaps most dramatically in the military. Most armies are perfectly designed to fight the previous war. The French had the best cavalry in the world in 1939. They invested a significant portion of their defense budget in it. However, it did not do much good against German tanks.

Managers are limited by their expectations. Many people lose because they expect to lose. Vince Lombardi, legendary coach of the Green Bay Packers, expected to win, and his team did win!

Expectations become reality. The president of a media group asked my organization to help him *empower* his people to be more responsible to rapidly changing situations. We met with the group during an unusual Saturday session. After initial doubt, the group enthusiastically agreed on a number of specific actions they would take to empower themselves and others. It was late on Saturday when the president closed the session by saying, "Thanks for coming. I know there's a lot of food for thought here, but just remember, 'Rome wasn't built in a day.' It will take time to make all these changes and there will be disappointments. Have patience." The knowing looks around the table told it all.

Several weeks later the president called and complained, "Very few of the commitments made at the meeting have been met. What's wrong with these people? Why is it so difficult to get them to be responsible?" In truth, his own expectations had negatively conditioned his organization. He told the people that progress would be slow, and it was.

That great management philosopher Yogi Berra said, "You can observe a lot by just watching." Yogi is right. Our business learned a lot about customers—what they wanted and liked—by watching them buy and use our products. We learned that customers did not care if the sausage was cooked or smoked. They cared about how it tasted and how they used it (e.g., snacking, barbecuing).

CONCLUSION

Discipline comes from two Latin roots: *discipulus,* meaning "pupil," and *discer,* meaning "learning." Thus, discipline means the devotion of the pupil to learning. In a chaotic business world filled with distractions, it requires discipline to be a learner. *Beware:* The smoke from the fire of yesterday's crises can easily obscure the vision of learning for tomorrow's opportunity.

A manager is caught up in the eternal circle of doing, learning, and changing. Management is a metaphor for life. It is a classroom filled with different teachers and it is a world that runs best with flexible guidelines geared to modern realities. Think strategically. Lead the right people to want to own the right responsibilities and continually learn.

MANAGEMENT THEORIES AND PRACTICES

Don E. Marsh, President and CEO, Marsh Supermarkets

Professionally trained managers are found in large corporations, small businesses, health-care organizations, educational institutions, churches, the arts, and government. The need for skilled managers, as well as the ability to teach certain aspects of management, are reflected in large numbers of students enrolled in graduate and undergraduate schools of business. The improvement of managerial skills throughout a career is supported by thousands of managers and prospective managers who participate in management seminars and other training programs offered in-house or by outside organizations.

Management is not a new phenomenon. China had a highly developed bureaucratic system thousands of years ago. The Roman Empire possessed a fairly sophisticated approach to controlling the activities of a far-flung empire. Religious organizations, such as the Catholic Church, have long managed missionary and other efforts throughout the world.

Management theory and formal instruction in the principles of management are more recent developments. The Wharton School began formal studies in the 1880s. Other schools followed early in the twentieth century. The study of management coincided with three important developments:

1. *Growth of large corporations*—The enormous industrial organizations that began in the late nineteenth century demanded new models for managing their operations.
2. *Separation of management and ownership*—Public ownership of common stock divorced investors from those who managed enterprises on a day-to-day basis. Skills were needed by professional managers who held only a small ownership interest in a business.
3. *Development of new theories*—As business and management became formal areas of study, practitioners and academics created a body of knowledge that could be transferred through books and classroom instruction.

SCHOOLS OF MANAGEMENT THEORY

The first half of the twentieth century saw a massive growth in the ideas and theories to help managers deal with the changing realities. Classifying the various theories is a problematic task at best. Harold Koontz attempted it in his classic article "The Management Theory Jungle" (*Journal of the Academy of Management*, 1961). He identified six schools:

1. *Management process school*—These theories see management as a means of organizing practical management experience. Practice can be improved through research and an empirical testing of principles. It can further be advanced by formally teaching the process of management.
2. *Empirical school*—These theories advocate the case study approach to management. By examining the experience of managers in real-world circumstances, future managers can extricate concepts and techniques that work in actual situations.
3. *Human behavior school*—These theories focus on the psychological and sociological aspects of managing people in organizations. The school seeks lessons from a variety of disciplines, including anthropology and economics, as it pursues the human factors that affect professional management and work performance.
4. *Social systems school*—These theories focus on groups and their behavioral processes. The school seeks group factors that affect organizational performance.
5. *Decision theory school*—These theories deal with decision making and the approaches that can be used by managers. Decision-making processes are treated both quantitatively and qualitatively. The goal is for managers to gather the relevant information and process it effectively to reach rational decisions.
6. *Mathematical school*—These theories seek to reduce management, organization, planning, and decision-making processes down to their basic principles, which can be expressed by mathematical formulas. Similarities and differences among various systems can often be identified only on an abstract, mathematical level.

EARLY THEORIES

Many individuals contributed to the management literature in the early 1900s. Three important categories of thought can be identified as part of the management process school:

1. *Scientific management*—In 1911, Frederick Taylor, an American engineer, published *Scientific Management*, a book that introduced the industrialized world to new ideas of management. Taylor introduced the concept of using scientific methods to measure and control the processes of work. Taylor and his contemporaries (including Henry Gantt and Frank and Lillian Gilbreth) were dedicated to the achievement of the one best way to perform a specific function.

Scientific management sought to separate planning from doing. It made use of time and motion studies to find more efficient approaches to work. It encouraged the use of incentive payments to increase productivity. It emphasized specialization so skilled workers could perform the tasks for which they had been trained. It sought the full interchangeability of parts to reduce unnecessary complexity.

Scientific management had a major impact on the level of productivity of an industrializing world. Efficiency was achieved as companies reduced the physical effort required to produce goods. Wasteful practices, in terms of materials or energy, were reduced. The same level of goods could be produced by fewer workers using less materials and other resources.

Scientific management had a downside. As processes became more routine and workers became more interchangeable, morale suffered. Employees were seen as cogs in a machine. Workers, particularly those involved with the production of goods at the shop level, were increasingly alienated from their organizations.

2. *Bureaucratic theories*—Changes in production processes led to the need for new organizations. Max Weber, a German sociologist, and his disciples recognized that the creation of large organizations required structural changes. The traditional model, in which owners also managed the enterprise, would not work in the new world. An owner-managed business tends to reflect the personalities of the owner. Entrepreneurial personali-

ties may make decisions on the basis of whim, fail to communicate their instructions effectively, and delegate tasks unevenly or not to the right persons. Positions in the hierarchy may be assigned to friends or family members who lack the skills to successfully perform.

Max Weber contributed significantly to the concept of the ideal bureaucracy. This was an organization governed by laws rather than personalities. It was impersonal and formal, where interchangeability of parts was accompanied by interchangeability of people. The ideal bureaucracy had a clear-cut division of labor; a well-defined hierarchical structure; activities determined by a consistent system of impersonal rules; employment and advancement based on technical qualifications and protected against arbitrary dismissal; and businesslike management that transcended emotion and feelings.

Weber, building on the foundation of scientific management, made major contributions to the understanding of organization structure and management that developed during the first half of the twentieth century and beyond.

3. *Principles of management*—This school is identified with Henri Fayol, a French businessman, who published his theory in 1916 in *Administration Industrielle et Generale*. He argued that the principles of management were universal, applying to all types of organizations. He identified fourteen such principles, including:

- *Authority*—This was derived from two sources. A manager had official authority that derived from a position in a hierarchy. Such authority extends to a variety of decisions, including hiring and firing employees. A manager also had personal authority, derived from intelligence, experience, and interpersonal skills. Such authority extends to the influence possessed by a manager outside of formal channels.
- *Chain of command*—Individuals in a hierarchy have superiors and subordinates. An employee should receive orders and be responsible to a single superior. Every employee should understand his or her position in the organization.

- *Primacy of the organization*—The interests of the organization supersede the interests of employees. Decisions should be made to achieve organizational, not individual, goals.
- *Organizational goals*—Once objectives are selected, implementation should be assigned to clearly defined groups who can achieve the organizational goals.

FUNCTIONAL MANAGEMENT

Following Taylor, Weber, and Fayol, the management process school focused heavily on the functions performed by managers. Some of the major ideas that dominated the period 1920–1970 are:

- *Planning*—This is the process of formulating objectives and developing strategies for achieving them. It involves establishing a strategy and identifying policies, procedures, and programs for implementing it. Planning is required at all levels of the organization. Lower-level plans must be compatible with the organization's overall plan.

- *Unity of command*—No subordinate should report to more than one superior.

- *Division of labor*—Work must be divided into manageable tasks. Clear areas of specialization are needed to improve the technical performance of the organization. Such division of labor is not restricted to production but extends to all functions from the lowest to the highest levels.

- *Hierarchical structure*—Each activity should have a fixed place in a structure of superior-subordinate relationships.

- *Span of control*—An optimal number of subordinates should report to a single superior. Originally, the span of control was defined as five to eight subordinates. More recently, it should reflect a number of variables including the nature of the process, the complexity of the task, the skills of subordinates, and the physical proximity of subordinates and the superior.

- *Line and staff*—Line executives are responsible for carrying out primary functions, such as production, marketing, and finance, and have the authority to manage their areas. Staff specialists are essentially advisers, who assist line executives in achieving their goals.

■ *Departmentalization*—The personnel, processes, and functions of an enterprise should be separated into subunits and grouping that will contribute to achieving organizational goals. An organization can be divided many ways, including by product, by process, by function, by geographic territory, and by customer class.

■ *Decentralization*—Authority should be widely dispersed throughout the organization. A decentralized organization has far greater autonomy and effectiveness in controlling its operations. Decisions are made at appropriate levels, where information is available and managers are responsible for the results. Thus, some decisions are centralized, such as those dealing with raising capital or relations with regulatory bodies. Operational decisions, conversely, are normally decentralized.

■ *Staffing*—This is the selection, training, and promoting of personnel. It involves studying the characteristics and desired behavior for a job, developing a list of skills and behavioral characteristics for personnel who will fill these jobs, choosing instruments to measure these characteristics in applicants, and hiring applicants who best meet selection criteria. Staffing also generally includes posthiring activities. The most important is evaluation of performance to ensure that the selection process is valid.

■ *Directing*—This involves guiding employees to achieve organizational objectives. This function has evolved over the years. It does not imply authoritarian or other nonparticipative approaches to moving the members of a work group to achieve objectives. Dynamic person-to-person relationships between managers and subordinates are frequently part of direction.

HUMAN BEHAVIOR THEORIES

The functional theories of the management process school were supplemented by a human behavior school that emphasized the psychological and sociological aspects of management. Management thinkers noted that people are motivated to behave in a particular way in order to satisfy their needs. Two theories of motivation may be identified:

1. *Content theories of motivation*—These examine the factors that motivate individuals to perform. Scientific management argued that people are motivated by money. Although this is true, money alone does not achieve the best results. Elton Mayo and others studied motivation at the Hawthorn Works of Western Electric in the late 1920s and early 1930s. They showed that workers were also motivated by peer group approval and ego needs.

2. *Process theories of motivation*—These are concerned with the mechanics of motivation. The content theories focus on *what* motivates people. Process theories focus on *how* needs are met, thus causing people to exhibit desired behavior.

HUMAN RELATIONS CONTRIBUTIONS

A number of important management ideas can be attributed to the human relations school, including:

■ *Hierarchy of needs*—Abraham Maslow postulated that needs follow a hierarchical progression. Lower-order needs must be satisfied before higher-order needs will motivate people. The progression from lowest to highest is (a) physiological needs, such as food, water, and shelter; (b) security needs, including personal safety; (c) social needs, that is, a sense of belonging; (d) ego needs, including self-esteem and recognition from others; and (e) self-actualization or self-fulfillment needs. Maslow's hierarchy explains why people have different needs and why a person may be motivated by different needs at different times.

■ *Satisfiers and motivators*—Frederick Herzberg contended that factors that cause dissatisfaction are not the same as those that cause satisfaction. Hygiene factors are defined as those that can satisfy only. These include company policies, supervisory practices, work conditions, interpersonal relationships on the job, and salary. They are different from factors that motivate people to do a good job. Motivating factors are recognition, achievement, responsibility, advancement, and the nature of the work itself.

- *The X and Y theories*—Douglas McGregor identified two categories of managers, based on their view of subordinates. Theory X managers assume that the average person is lazy, lacks ambition, dislikes responsibility, and prefers to be led. Therefore, subordinates must be rewarded or punished as the situation demands and their activities must be closely supervised. Theory Y managers assume that the potential for development, the capacity for assuming responsibility, and the readiness to strive to achieve organizational goals are present in all workers. The role of management is to assist people to recognize and develop these characteristics for themselves.

- *Theory Z*—William Ouchi described a new manager in the late 1970s. The theory Z manager produces a strong commitment to the organization by paying careful attention to employees. The workplace provides job security, opportunities for advancement, and group problem solving, as managers work together with employees to achieve organizational goals.

- *Behavior modification*—B. F. Skinner proposed positive reinforcement as a means of encouraging good behavior. According to Skinner, all behavior is the result of a conditioning process that starts in infancy. Some theorists proposed that managers should continue this process by reinforcing desired behavior with psychological and material rewards. Essentially, the behavior of an individual would be manipulated into desired channels through the mechanism of operant conditioning.

- *Team problem solving*—Kurt Lewin and others advocated participative management and group problem solving as elements of a better workplace and also a more productive environment for accomplishing organizational tasks.

LEADERSHIP THEORIES

Closely related to, but distinct from, management are theories of leadership. Managing is the formal process in which organizational objectives are achieved through the efforts of superiors and subordinates. Stated differently, management is the art of getting things done through others. Leading is the process in which a person with power is able to influence the behavior of others in some desired way.

Managers have power by virtue of the positions they hold. Other forms of power in organizations do not derive from a position. Thus, organizations seek managers who are leaders by virtue of their personalities and expertise.

Two important theories of leadership are:

1. *Trait theory*—Adherents to this theory seek to identify the characteristics of leaders. This list includes intelligence, supervisory ability, self-assurance, initiative, and individuality. The assumption is that individuals who possessed these traits will be successful leaders.

2. *Behavioral theory*—Followers of this theory characterize leaders by behavioral patterns, such as:

- *Autocratic*—This leader commands, and performance or the lack of it has consequences. Enforcement depends on the autocratic leader's power to reward or punish.
- *Supportive*—This leader creates a social climate in which each person will want to do his or her best without compulsion. The supportive leader does this by showing consideration for subordinates, by consulting them in making decisions, and by general rather than close supervision.
- *Task oriented*—This leader organizes available resources and divides and assigns work. The leader makes the plans, schedules activities, and establishes standards of job performance.
- *Situational*—This theory argues that leadership can be explained in terms of the interaction between a leader and the variables in a work situation. Effective

leadership is the matching of a goal and a group of employees so as to achieve an optimal performance by the group in achieving the goal.

MANAGEMENT THEORIES TODAY

After 1960, schools of management were not so easy to identify. Contributions were made on a variety of fronts, including:

■ *Principles of management*—Peter Drucker synthesized and extended many of the best management ideas. His *Management: Tasks, Responsibilities, and Practices* (1973) is a classic interpretation of the full range of effective management practices. He describes the ''knowledge worker'' as a skilled individual who works most effectively when allowed to use independent judgment. He started the process of integrating strategic planning, marketing, and finance and broke down traditional lines between management and these areas.

■ *Management competencies*—In the 1970s, David McClelland worked to identify the competency of effective managers. His list of competencies includes:

Entrepreneurial orientation—This refers to a proactive approach toward action as opposed to inaction when pursuing efficiency and the achievement of organizational goals.
Intelligence—This refers to an ability to solve problems by reasoning. The manager must recognize patterns and conceptualize approaches to decision making.
Versatility—This refers to a group of socioemotional attributes. Effective managers are under control when dealing with subordinates, crises, and day-to-day problems. They deal with conflict in a careful and objective manner, accurately assessing their own strengths and weaknesses as well as the strengths and weaknesses of others.
Interpersonal skills—This refers to skills in dealing with subordinates and superiors.

With subordinates, it involves coaching, mentoring, and the proper use of authority and power. With superiors, it involves communications and persuasion skills.

■ *Management roles*—Henry Mintzberg's *The Nature of Managerial Work* (1973) identifies the daily roles played by managers, including:

Interpersonal roles—This refers to behavior with regard to subordinates (leading, motivating, staffing, training, rewarding), peers (other managers, customers, vendors), and position as a member of the management structure (ceremonial, social, legal).
Informational roles—This refers to the seeking of information needed to solve problems and disseminating information to people who need it to do their own jobs.
Decision-making roles—This refers to planning; budgeting; allocating resources; negotiating with subordinates, customers, and suppliers; and conflict resolution.
Management roles—This refers to organizing individuals into work groups, supervising the work itself, enforcing rules and regulations, and helping subordinates solve problems.

Changing Workplace

The principles and lessons of management form a rich pattern of theory and application. They must be applied in a changing workplace. Some of the major characteristics of the modern world that affect management practices are:

■ *Global orientation*—The world continues to shrink as organizations manufacture in one country and sell in others.
■ *Telecommunications*—Major organizations and individuals are linked in a worldwide network of computers, data transmission, and information using satellites and fiber optics.
■ *Computer processing power*—Personal computers, linked in increasingly creative networks, are changing the way information is gathered and processed.
■ *Technology*—Changing capabilities can

result in new approaches to producing goods and delivering services.

CHANGING EXPECTATIONS

The principles and lessons of management must also be applied in a context of changing employee desires, including:

- *Stakeholders*—Employees are demanding a minimum standard of treatment, whereby their needs are given as much consideration as the needs of shareholders.
- *Nontraditional work patterns*—Men and women seek new approaches to membership in the work force. Women are demanding new patterns to allow full career participation without sacrificing family values and responsibilities. Men are demanding more personal freedom and less subjugation to corporate demands and values.
- *New office and time realities*—As a result of technology, the office can be at home, and commuting to a central workplace is often a waste of time. Management must learn to deal with these new realities as the traditional nine-to-five workday becomes obsolete.
- *Changing demographics*—The work force is increasingly made of minorities who have different values but still seek full participation in the American dream of social and career opportunity.
- *Changing rate of skill obsolescence*—The skills of workers are no longer learned at the start of a career and then applied for forty or fifty years. New technologies will require periodic update of worker capabilities in order for organizations to be able to compete effectively.
- *Environmental concerns*—Businesses will increasingly have to conduct their operations with a concern for compliance with regulations designed to protect the environment.

CONCLUSION

Much has been written in the twentieth century to create the theories and practices of management. As the world changes, we can expect a continuing demand for professionally trained managers. At the same time, we can expect new skills and knowledge to be required as managers cope with new realities in the workplace and competitive markets. Management is a dynamic area of activity, both in theory and practice, which will continue into the distant future.

Note: This article includes references to a number of the classic books and writers in management theory. Many of the books are no longer in print. More detail can be obtained on the ideas of the theorists in any principles of management textbook.

MANAGEMENT THEORY AND APPLICATION

Dale E. Zand, Professor of Management, Stern School of Business, New York University

Jim Nolan, age thirty-two, is a geophysicist who was appointed manager of the exploration department of a medium-size oil company. He gave several of the geophysicists specific assignments. Following up two weeks later, he found that one senior geophysicist had not started yet because he was working on a project for Nolan's boss. The second had put the assignment aside. He said he was working on other projects. A third subordinate said he had not started his assignment because he was waiting for maps, seismic data, and logs from neighboring wells.

Nolan was astounded by these responses. He thought they were very unprofessional. Like most managers, Nolan was applying his version of the classic, directive, task-oriented management style (Hellriegel and Slocum 1978). Tell your subordinates what you want done. Follow up to see that they do it. Demand performance. Tell your subordinates when you are dissatisfied. Do not accept excuses. Do not make excuses.

NATURE AND USE OF THEORIES

Most theories are limited or partial. They work well in a narrow range of circumstances. They explain a part of reality. Once you go outside those circumstances, the theory does not work and may be completely wrong.

Several theories can exist side by side because each covers a different set of conditions. In management we have coexisting theories of directive and participative leadership, centralized and decentralized structures, differentiation and integration of units, and formal and informal networks. Applying a theory outside of its domain often makes little sense and gets poor results.

A theory tells us three things: what to look for, how to interpret what we find, and what to do. It is like a lens. It focuses our attention and screens out irrelevant data. Otherwise, we would be overwhelmed by the large number of possibilities. We would be like the novice chess player who is immobilized by the large number of possible moves and can only attend to one or two pieces at a time. Master players, however, think in terms of patterns. They look for a match between the array of pieces on the board and their theory of patterns. Their focus is selective, comprehensive, and informed.

A theory tells us what meaning to give to events. For example, using classic directive theory, Jim Nolan would interpret his subordinates' failure to complete their assignments as a threat to his authority and a sign of insufficient control.

A theory tells us what to do. Classic, directive theory would tell Nolan to reject his subordinates' lack of results and demand performance without excuses. It would tell him to insist on greater effort to install progress checkpoints and hold follow-up reviews. These actions would reassert Nolan's authority and control.

UNCERTAINTY

Uncertainty affects our approach to management theory at almost every level of analysis. Starting with theories of individual behavior, through theories of leadership and competence, to the formulation of strategy and the design of organization structures, uncertainty is a key factor. Uncertainty refers to what is unknown, or a lack of information. Sometimes it is called "imperfect" information, in contrast to certainty, which is called "perfect" information. In management, uncertainty is the difference between what we know and what we need to know when we must make a decision.

Uncertainty limits our foresight, our ability to plan, the quality of our decisions, our ability to learn and practice necessary skills, and the effectiveness of our actions. As an ideal, we would like to eliminate or reduce uncertainty. Then we could improve our decisions and program our actions. When we cannot reduce uncertainty, we must install adaptive systems that cope with it.

Situation Structure

Rather than talk about uncertainty as a general, inclusive term it is helpful to recognize that it is the structure of a situation that contributes to certainty or uncertainty (Zand 1981). A situation with high certainty or little uncertainty is well structured. It has the characteristics of repetitive, physical work or routine, simple mental tasks. We know reliably what needs to be known and we can respond repetitively with simplified, specialized behavior. We create a system to control behavior within predetermined limits, like a thermostat system that controls a furnace, circulating pumps and fans to maintain room temperature.

A situation with high uncertainty, how-

ever, is unstructured. Much is unknown, for example, exploring for oil. The situation has unique features we have not seen before, may occur infrequently, and may emerge over a long period of time. Poorly structured situations are high in uncertainty and have the characteristics of complex, creative, nonroutinized mental work. Well-structured situations are the reverse. Exhibit 1-1 matches uncertainty with the degree of structure.

Environmental and Task Uncertainty

There are two major types of uncertainty:

1. *Environmental uncertainty*—This refers to conditions outside of our organization or our subunit in an organization. Generally it consists of unpredictable demand, supply of materials, competitor behavior, and technology and changes in these items. Industries in an early stage of development with little government regulation tend to have higher environmental uncertainty than industries in a mature stage or with heavy governmental regulation. In an early stage of development, new products come to market, features are not standardized, technology and manufacturing processes are changing rapidly, product usage is evolving, and demand is diverse and volatile. In a mature, high-volume, standardized-product industry, new products are rare, features are standardized, technology and manufacturing processes change slowly, product usage is established, and demand changes slowly.

2. *Task uncertainty*—This refers to conditions in our work, that is, what is to be done, when, and how. Simple tasks that are machine determined and machine paced are highly structured, highly certain tasks. High-volume, assembly-line tasks in the auto industry and its supply companies are highly structured. In contrast, designing marketing plans for new food products is a poorly structured, uncertain task.

Tolerance of Uncertainty

Individuals differ in their tolerance of uncertainty. Some people have a need for well-

Exhibit 1-1. Matching Uncertainty and Degree of Structure

	Characteristics of Uncertainty	
Element	Well-Structured Situation	Poorly Structured Situation
Future events	Known, predictable	Unknown, unpredictable
Other's actions	Known, predictable	Unknown, unpredictable
Goals	Few, consistent	Many, contradictory
Key factors	Few, independent	Many, interdependent
Cause and effect	Known	Unknown
Change	Low	High
Repetition	High	Low
Superior decisions	Identifiable	Indeterminate
Feedback	Close, direct	Distant, indirect
Expertise	High	Low

Source: After D.E. Zand, *Information, Organization, and Power* (New York: McGraw-Hill, 1981), 62; original exhibit © by D.E. Zand.

structured, highly certain situations. They prefer stable, uncomplicated tasks and clear, well-defined directions. As they move to higher levels of management, this quality can be a strength because they make decisions and arrange activities to reduce uncertainty for the levels below.

However, the problem for managers with a low tolerance of uncertainty is that the organization's environment does not march to their need for certainty. The danger for management is that a high personal need for certainty may lead a manager to ignore, deny, misinterpret, and not cope with critical environmental uncertainty. The manager may introduce structure that is premature or inappropriate for the situation, thus diminishing the organization's ability to adapt. Therefore, in organizations facing high environmental uncertainty, and at higher levels of management, managers need a high tolerance of certainty.

CLASSICAL THEORY

Classical theory attempted to increase the level of certainty within an organization. It tried to structure tasks and relationships for both the workers and their managers. Classical theory offers the following set of principles that essentially fashion organization structure and management behavior into a control system:

1. *Division of labor*—Work should be divided into small, standardized tasks that people can learn quickly and easily. People can become specialists and develop great skill and expertise in a few tasks. Standardization of tasks makes people interchangeable. If some are absent or leave, they are more readily replaceable.

2. *Clearly defined tasks and procedures*—Each person's job should consist of well-defined tasks and responsibilities. Clear procedures and rules for performing a job should be specified. The best way to do an operating-level job should be determined by expert specialists who standardize and specify the best procedures to the worker.

3. *Unity of command*—Each person should receive orders from only one boss. There should be no overlapping authority and responsibility that might result in a person getting orders from two people. The chain of command should be clear from the top to the bottom of the organization.

4. *Limited span of supervision*—Each manager should supervise only a small number of subordinates to assure effective direction, coordination, and control. The span of super-

vision can increase as the competence of subordinates increases, as the interdependence among subordinates' jobs decreases, and as subordinates' tasks increase in simplicity and repetition.

5. *Functional organization*—An organization should group functionally similar activities into major departments such as manufacturing, marketing, and engineering. The organization then benefits from the specialized knowledge and expertise brought together within each function.

6. *Authority to match responsibility*—Managers should have sufficient authority over personnel, materials, and equipment to carry out their responsibilities.

7. *Centralization of authority*—The important organizational decisions should be made by top management, which is better able to see the organization's overall needs. This assures unity of direction and uniformity of action. Top management can use specialized staff experts to assure that the best decisions are made. Lower-level managers have limited perspective and judgment and should have little discretion to act on their own initiative.

8. *Formalization*—Unity of direction, standardized performance, and high productivity are obtained by using written procedures and formal rules for all tasks. Planning, budget, and review systems should be standardized and written. Communications between managers and across functions should be written.

HUMANISTIC THEORY

By the 1950s, U.S. society and business organizations had changed significantly from the early period when classical theory had been formulated. There was great growth in literacy, education, public information, and standard of living. Labor unions had received legislative support and had gained strength. There were great strides in science and technology. The number of middle managers and specialized knowledge workers—engineers, researchers, accountants—had greatly increased.

By its single-minded application of classical theory, management had unwittingly dehumanized work (Argyris 1964). Jobs had become so narrow and repetitive that people were bored and fatigued. The skills required were so simple that work had little challenge. Workers and managers were told so little that they did not understand how their work contributed to the final product. Employees and managers could not see how their poor performance affected others later in the flow of work and they did not care. The insensitive monolithic use of classical bureaucratic theory had increasingly alienated people from their work.

A theory of individual needs was formulated by Maslow (1954). His theory proposed that the vast array of possible human needs could be classified into five categories: (1) physiological—food, shelter, etc.; (2) safety—protection from harm and stability of income; (3) social—companionship, affection, and nurturance; (4) esteem—appreciation, respect, and status; (5) achievement—competence, self-sufficiency, and personal growth.

The needs fall into a sequence of potency with physiological needs first and achievement needs last. If the lower-order needs such as physiological needs and safety are substantially satisfied, then the higher-order needs become more significant. The relative importance of a need decreases as it is satisfied, and a person's behavior can be affected by several needs at the same time.

McGregor (1960) brought the theory of individual needs to the attention of the management community. He argued persuasively that work was as natural as play if it was designed on the right assumptions about human nature. The classical premises—which he called theory X—assumed that people were lazy, irresponsible, needed close supervision, and were motivated only by money. This was not a suitable theory of human nature in an educated, prosperous society where lower-order needs were substantially satisfied.

Instead, McGregor argued that people are responsible, ambitious, creative, growth seeking, and motivated by other needs besides money. This view he called theory Y. He was asserting that in our developed society a person's higher needs are increasingly relevant.

GROUP THEORY

Management became interested in learning how to effectively lead groups after it recognized that most of the planning, mutual adjustment, and corrective action taken in an organization require that people meet frequently face-to-face.

All groups develop norms that shape the behavior of their members. How people behave in groups and how we can improve a group's effectiveness was systematically studied after the 1950s. Two broad categories of behavior were identified:

1. *Task behavior consists of several skills.* These include initiating proposals and ideas, giving and seeking information or opinions, elaborating, evaluating, and summarizing. Task behavior moves the group ahead in selecting goals, defining priorities, and designing and implementing action plans to reach its goals.

2. *Maintenance behavior consists of different skills.* It includes encouraging others; gatekeeping, which assures that each person has a fair opportunity to speak; relieving tension; expressing the feelings of the group; developing norms; testing for consensus; and checking member commitment to different proposals. Maintenance behavior can improve interpersonal relationships, manages conflict constructively, and increases group cohesiveness.

Effective Teams

Both task and maintenance behavior are necessary to make a group effective. The leader and the members need skills in group process. Often they require special training in decision-making procedures. Membership should include people with different characteristics such as authority to make a decision, relevant information, and technical competence. It should also include those who will actually implement the solution, and people with interpersonal and process facilitation skills.

Members understand and accept their primary goal in an effective group. There is open communication, mutual trust, and mutual support.

Participation

Participation is the opportunity to influence decisions. It consists of joining with another person in the process of finding and solving problems. Participation can vary from no influence to complete influence. The amount of influence depends on the manager's decision behavior. The manager can invite participation at one or several of the stages in the decision process. These stages include preliminary definition of the problem, clarification of goals, gathering of information, redefinition of the problem, generating alternatives, defining evaluation criteria, projecting the effects of each alternative, evaluating alternatives, choosing, and action planning.

Managers are interested in participation for several reasons:

1. When subordinates influence a decision they are more likely to understand it, accept it, and be committed to implementing it.
2. Subordinates usually know the specific, practical difficulties of their jobs better than managers.
3. Participation familiarizes subordinates with the goals to be achieved and the context of a problem.
4. If subordinates feel that their participation has influenced results and they have received recognition for their contribution, they will feel more satisfied with their work and their organization.

Subordinates want to participate for several reasons:

1. They can shape their tasks and their working conditions to better meet their individual needs.
2. They want to feel a sense of competence, independence, and power by being influential rather than always being told what to do.
3. As responsible people they wish to show that they can accept and fulfill re-

sponsibility and they can contribute to their organization's effectiveness.

4. Participation offers subordinates an opportunity to grow, to learn new skills, and to find meaning and purpose by seeing how their job fits into the organization's strategy.

Participation, if well designed and managed, can now benefit all levels of an organization. It is a theory that fits the modern organizational world. We can expect it to be applied increasingly in the future.

REFERENCES

Argyris, C. 1964. *Integrating the Individual and the Organization*. New York: Wiley.

Hellriegel, D., and J. W. Slocum, Jr. 1978. *Management: Contingency Approaches.* Reading, Mass.: Addison-Wesley.

McGregor, D. 1960. *The Human Side of Enterprise*. New York: McGraw-Hill.

Maslow, A. H. 1954. *Motivation and Personality*. New York: Harper.

Zand, D. E. 1981. *Information, Organization, and Power: Effective Management in the Knowledge Society*. New York: McGraw-Hill.

QUALITY PROCESSES IN MANAGEMENT

John F. Early, Vice-President Research and Development, Juran Institute, Inc.

One of the myths of modern postindustrial society is: "Workers do not care about the quality of their work. If we could motivate workers more strongly, there would be marked improvement in quality and productivity." This myth is a major hinderance to improvement. Responsibility for quality and productivity lies squarely with the managers of an organization. In particular, that responsibility lies with the upper managers.

THE QUALITY STRATEGY

Quality is most useful when it has been adopted as a strategy. The quality strategy focuses the entire organization on one goal: delighted customers.

There are multiple strategies within a quality framework. In addition, quality provides two important complements to other strategies:

1. It provides the context for other strategic decisions. Quality keeps all other strategies consistent with delighting customers.

2. It provides the means for carrying out other strategies successfully. Application of the quality processes will make any strategy much more effective.

Dimensions of Quality

The word *quality* has been given many definitions. Most rely on either of two dimensions:

1. The quality of a good or a service is the set of features possessed by the good or service.
2. Quality is the absence of deficiencies in the good or service.

The distinction between these two dimensions has important consequences for how one manages quality.

One common definition of quality is "fitness for use"—that is, the good or service has the needed features and those features are without defect. Another is "meeting or exceeding customer expectations"—that is, providing the features the customer expects and doing so without defect. A third short definition is "doing the right thing right the first time."

Quality as Features

The features of a good or a service are those characteristics that respond to customer needs. For example, the basic family automobile has features such as acceleration, stopping distance, cargo space, and passenger room. A luxury automobile also will have other features such as an advanced stereo system, genuine wood on the dashboard, or leather seats.

Air travel has features that relate to allowances for checked baggage, convenience of departure times, and safety of equipment. First-class travel also may add express check-in, wide seats, china dishes, and premium wines.

In health care, a community hospital will offer basic diagnostic X-rays, a wide range of laboratory tests, and skilled nursing care. Regional care centers also may offer magnetic resonance imaging (MRI), neonatal intensive care, and a burn unit.

In these examples, we may speak of higher quality in the sense of having more features, or having more of a specific feature.

Quality as Freedom From Deficiencies

Even the most luxurious first-class accommodations will not eliminate customer dissatis-faction if the plane is delayed. Deficiencies in our goods and services create dissatisfaction for our customers. A deficiency is any failure to meet the features designed into a good or a service—for example, late arrival, a car engine that dies easily, or an unplanned return to surgery.

Fewer deficiencies will reduce customer dissatisfaction. They also will lower cost, because deficiencies cost more than if the deed had been done correctly the first time. Even defects that the customer never sees are costly. The work must be repaired, replaced, or redone.

TOTAL QUALITY MANAGEMENT AND PRODUCTIVITY

For many years, quality was viewed very narrowly as the absence of defects. Recent experience makes it clear that quality is more universal. Total quality management is the structured management process ensuring that all types of customers are delighted by all the goods and services produced by a company.

Productivity and quality have an important relationship. Reducing deficiencies means that fewer resources are employed inspecting, repairing, replacing, or doing work over again. If one improves quality by reducing deficiencies, fewer resources are consumed for each unit of output—that is, productivity rises!

If one provides higher-quality goods or services by doing a better job of meeting customer needs, then one has increased output as well. Effective quality planning for new products generates increased income that is disproportionate to the added resources required. Because outputs are increased by more than the inputs, productivity rises.

Quality is managed through three fundamental processes, namely:

1. *Quality planning* designs the quality of a good or service. It includes a structured process for developing features that will meet customer needs. It also pro-

vides a means for developing processes that will deliver the planned features without deficiencies.

2. *Quality control* keeps the process or product deficiency at the originally designed or improved levels.

3. *Quality improvement* removes chronic poor quality and establishes a new process with improved quality.

Quality Planning

In a structured quality planning process top management can make customer orientation a permanent and effective part of the organization. Quality planning activities rely on interdisciplinary teams. Traditional planning has been sequential—market research to product design to engineering design to production engineering to manufacturing, or some variation on that theme. Modern quality planning includes all critical functions on the team from the beginning. The team then follows a structured approach together, as follows:

1. *Identify the customers.* Customers are all those affected. They include not only the immediate paying clients but others such as each stage in the distribution chain, regulators, or the community at large. In addition to all the external customers, there is a whole cast of internal customers.

2. *Determine the customers' needs.* This should be done in their own language. Look not only for the stated needs but also for the unstated needs. Needs are revealed by actual usage, including misuse. Needs are often social or implicit in nature and considerable ingenuity is required to uncover them. Needs must be analyzed and translated into the producer's terms so that they can be measured and satisfied.

3. *Develop the features of the service or good that will satisfy those needs.* Every significant customer need will have at least one product feature that will meet or exceed that need. Each feature will also have a goal: how much, how many, how often, how fast. These goals must not only meet current customer needs but must be gauged against the competitors' performance and against anticipated *changes*

in customer needs or competitor performance.

4. *Develop a process that will deliver the service or good exactly as the quality goals were designed.* All processes have an inherent capability. In designing a process that will deliver a good or service, one must know what the inherent capability of that process is to deliver the planned features. If an existing process cannot meet the required capability, then a new process must be designed.

5. *Establish process controls.* Every customer need has at least one product feature to satisfy it and a corresponding process feature that will produce the product feature. Now each process feature requires a control to ensure that it operates as designed. Every customer need has appropriate controls and every control relates ultimately to an important customer need. There are no unnecessary controls.

6. *Transfer to operations.* Those who will operate the process must be confident that the process performs as advertised. Part of the confidence will come from their participation in the planning process. The remainder comes from formal testing.

Quality Control

Quality control is a management process with two key ideas:

1. *The feedback loop*—Exhibit 1-2 illustrates a feedback loop. A process has an output that is measured by a sensor. There is a goal for that process measurement. The actual measurement and the goal are compared. If the

Exhibit 1-2. The Feedback Loop

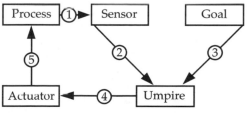

Source: From J.M. Juran, *Making Quality Happen: Upper Management's Role* (Wilton, CT, Juran Institute, 1988), F-3; © 1988 by the Juran Institute.

comparison is unfavorable, then action is taken to adjust the process to bring the actual performance and the goal into agreement. No process can be controlled without all of these elements.

2. *Planning for quality control*—These feedback loops do not happen naturally. They must be planned. If modern quality planning methods have been followed in the original product design, planning for the controls will have been included. Still, we also need to plan controls for activities that have not been through that structured design.

First, the proper control subject must be selected. It must relate to process and product features that are important to the customer, not just things that are easy to measure.

Second, a unit of measure and a method for measuring must be established. Especially in services, measurement can be quite difficult, but without measurement, quality control is impossible.

Third, a goal must be established. That goal is not usually a single value like 22 cm. It often takes the form of a range like 22 ± .01 cm. Or it may be a limit like "less than five minutes" or "more than 95-percent response rate." Goals in quality control cannot be wishes. They must be demonstrably attainable.

Variability and Process Capability. All processes vary—the radius of a wheel, the temperature of an oven, the resistance of a circuit, the time it takes to cash a check, vital signs after surgery. They are never exactly the same time after time. Some processes vary less than others, and a structured quality improvement process can reduce variability, but all processes and their results vary.

Goals for quality control are based on the *actual* variation of the process, not what we wish it would be. Quality control goals differ from the goals we set because they will satisfy customer needs. Control goals are based on actual performance. Planning goals are based on customer needs. The relationship between the goals that are desired based on customer needs and the control goals that are derived from the actual process has been called the *process capability*. If airline passengers need their luggage within fifteen minutes of arrival

95 percent of the time, and if luggage delivery operates that fast only 80 percent of the time, then the luggage delivery process is *not* a capable one.

Self-Control. One can enhance performance of a process by placing those who operate it in a state of self-control that requires the operator of a process to (1) know what is expected, (2) know how the process is performing, and (3) have the ability to regulate the process. Ability to regulate a process requires that the process is capable of meeting the goal and that the operator has the tools, knowledge, skills, and authority to make the needed adjustments. In short, self-control means that the operators of the process must have the full feedback loop at their command.

Quality Improvement

Continuous quality improvement comes through a structured process that can be summarized in seven basic steps:

1. *Identify projects.* Projects must attack the major, persistent quality problems if any meaningful progress is to be made.
2. *Organize project teams.* The most serious quality problems usually cut across different organizational units. Therefore, normal hierarchical management structures cannot deal with them. A team composed of individuals from those parts of the organization that are most affected by the problem should be organized.
3. *Discover causes.* One of the important skills is measurement of quality problems. Problems that are not measured cannot be improved.
4. *Develop remedies.* Once the cause is discovered, another set of skills is required to develop appropriate remedies.
5. *Prove effectiveness of remedy.* This simple but often overlooked step ensures that the team has fixed the problem.
6. *Deal with cultural resistance.* Every change has a technical side. It also has

a social or cultural side. People will be asked to behave in different ways or to adopt new roles. Resistance should be recognized and addressed.

7. *Establish controls to hold the gains.* Without these controls, a process may drift back into its old ways.

CONCLUSION

Application of the quality planning process has proved to be an integral part of successful efforts in the most advanced forms of employee empowerment. The pursuit of total quality management provides numerous benefits to an organization.

MISSION STATEMENT AND POLICIES

Paul J. Stitzel, President, Brentwood Hospital

Every company has a mission whether it is stated or unstated. Nature abhors a vacuum—there must be a reason for existence of everything in this world. In the case of any enterprise, there was an original purpose that brought it into existence. Although subject to change through the vagaries of the environment, a mission still exists. The reduction to writing of that mission is the *mission statement.*

As basic to business as a mission statement may be, there are many companies that have not articulated it to their employees or constituents. Unfortunately, the demise of many businesses might well be summed up in the popular phrase that, "If you don't know where you are going, any road will get you there." Frequently, that road leads to disaster rather than to success.

WHY IS A PUBLISHED STATEMENT NECESSARY?

From the customer point of view, it provides a framework of expectation. In the case of the

Goodyear Tire and Rubber Company, their simple mission statement, "Protect Our Good Name," literally assures customer satisfaction both in service and in product. Such a statement means that regardless of the technical complexity of the product involved, the buyer can be confident. By virtue of the statement alone, a customer can evaluate the priorities that drive a given organization and evaluate the organization's values and direction.

To employees, mission statements provide a sense of direction and an appreciation for the decisions that are made by management. In those enterprises where empowerment is actualized, mission statements, and the policies that necessarily follow, provide the broad parameters within which workers can make appropriate judgments. Employees are provided a framework within which individual decisions can be made.

Finally, from the perspective of management, the mission statement provides a challenge. It becomes a mandate requiring certain actions, goals, and consequences. Since the statement iterates the fundamental purpose for the existence of the organization, every management decision must be in sync.

MISSION STATEMENT AT WORK: TYLENOL

One of the most dramatic examples of the requiring nature of the mission statement occurred in 1982 with the actions of Johnson & Johnson's management in the Tylenol crisis. On September 28, 1982, Mary Kellerman died after having ingested a capsule of Extra-Strength Tylenol that had been contaminated with cyanide. Within a week, six others from the Chicago area died from the same cause. Without knowing the cause of the problem (manufacturing malfunction, a malevolent employee, or a psychotic killer), management was faced with a tough decision.

The mandate was clear. The credo of Johnson & Johnson begins with the compelling statement: "We believe our first responsibility is to the doctors, nurses and patients, to mothers and to all others who use our products and services." Empowered and controlled by that statement, the management of Johnson & Johnson issued an immediate recall of Extra-Strength Tylenol capsules. Through the media, mail, and electronic means, the company did everything possible to warn the public and the medical profession. Although the financial loss was to be in the millions, the potential loss of faith by customers would be even greater.

The results bore out the wisdom of following the credo. Johnson & Johnson regained 98 percent of its original market share. In commenting on the entire event, James Burke, chairman of Johnson & Johnson, remarked: "We had no historic precedent to rely on . . . the guidance of the credo played the single most important role in our decision making."

DEVELOPMENTAL STEPS

Accepting the reality that a formalized statement of corporate vision is necessary, how is it developed—what are the steps necessary to bring it into existence? The first step is to recognize that the statement is not necessarily static. In dynamic times, the statement itself must remain dynamic and be relevant to society at the time. To produce the finest buggy whip at the lowest possible price hardly qualifies for success in a society that is no longer dependent on horses for transportation.

Primary to the development of the mission statement is the necessity to think—alone or in group brainstorming—to identify the underlying cause for the existence of the enterprise. Why was the company started in the first place? Does that reason still prevail? Has the environment changed to the point where new directions must be defined? Is what we are doing still relevant? Those and many more questions of a similar nature must be asked to get to the core of the enterprise. The present, relevant concept justifying the existence of the organization must be identified. Although not necessarily articulated in the statement, the core value drives the statement through its recognition of the elements that will ultimately be addressed in the statement: customers, employees, community, shareholders, suppliers, and profitability.

Once the purpose for existence has been defined, the balance of the process deals with "fleshing out" a statement considering the elements mentioned in the previous paragraph. As ideas are assembled for inclusion, limits are established regarding propriety. At all times it must be remembered that the statement becomes the window through which customers, employees, and management can view the enterprise; consequently, care must be taken not to include information that might disclose the specific strategy (the "how") the organization has embraced in its competitive marketplace.

Conversely, the statement cannot be full of bland and meaningless fluff. Motherhood and apple pie have no place in dynamic, directional statements. It does become a challenge to be specific and yet not disclose the strategy. The statement might include comparative statements such as: "profits equal to that of the industry," or, "a 15-percent return on equity."

POLICIES

Policies are more focused than mission statements. As defined by *Webster's*, policies are "a definite course of action or method of action selected from among alternatives and in the light of given conditions to guide and determine present and future decisions." In respect to the foregoing, the mission statement is the vision that focuses policies in a certain direction.

Policies should be more specific than the mission statement, but not so specific that initiative and creativity are stifled. Policies are the broad guidelines against which objectives and goals are measured.

If the mission statement is a requiring statement, then policies should be considered enabling statements. Policies guide not only the objective- and goal-setting functions of the organization but provide the code of conduct employed within the organization and in relationships with entities outside the organization. For example, the mission of an organization may be in part to return to the community a certain percentage of its profits. To actualize the mission, policies would be adopted defining the types of organizations that would qualify for the beneficence as well as the formulas involved for quantifying the grants and gifts.

Unlike the mission statement, policies do not evolve from a think tank but rather from anticipating and/or reacting to events occurring in the daily operation of the business. They are frequently caused by a doubt concerning the proper response to a question, problem, or situation. Once established, once the situation has been addressed and a policy adopted to answer the need, the policy then becomes enabling, allowing decisions to be made throughout the organization that are in congruence with the policy itself—and, of course, consistent with the mission statement.

Policies are generally of two types: those that are operational and those that broaden the philosophical concepts presented in the mission statement. Operational policies focus on the rules and regulations of conduct in rather definitive ways. Personnel policies are an example. The policy may spell out the qualifications and specifications for vacations. Such a policy would address the amount of service necessary before an employee is eligible, and then indicate the amount of vacation based on length of service. Likewise, it would spell out how holidays are treated that fall within a vacation period, whether vacations could be carried over to subsequent years, the amount of accumulated vacation allowed, and so on.

Other operational policies might deal with employees' conduct, safety and security measures, credit and collection issues, and so forth. In reality this type of policy is the norm of operation—the rules and regulations of the enterprise.

At the other end of the policy spectrum are those pronouncements that are more philosophical in nature. In a hospital such a policy might be that no one would be refused care because of a lack of financial resources. In a retail establishment this type of policy might proclaim that the customer is always right. In differentiating policies between operational and philosophical, one could say that operational policies are the rules and regulations employed for the orderly conduct of business and that the philosophical policies are general guidelines to be used with discretion and interpretation by the individual involved.

There are some characteristics of policies that are unique, including the propensity for proliferation. Care should be taken regarding the authorship, or at least the qualification for authorship, of policies. So often it occurs that a response to a repeated situation takes on a life of its own and becomes "company policy." The converse of that is also true. It is not uncommon to hear the refrain, "That's not our policy," as a response to a call for action.

It is essential to define those who have the authority to write and approve policies. Within that group, a mechanism should be established to periodically review policies for their continued applicability. To aid in this periodic audit, it is essential that some numbering system be employed to identify policies and that the dates be recorded showing when the policy was written and its subsequent review times.

GOAL AND OBJECTIVES

Goals and objectives are the natural outcomes resulting from articulating the reason for the existence of the enterprise and its operational norms. Without such outcomes, the enterprise would be analogous to a finely tuned race car, ready to go, motor purring to perfection, driver behind the wheel, but with no place to go. Goals and objectives flow naturally from the knowledge of why an enterprise exists and what its operational capabilities are.

Goals and objectives fulfill another important purpose. They are an integral part of the feedback loop that is necessary in any viable organization. Feedback is necessary to determine if the organization's mission is still in tune with its environment—if the organization's policies are relevant to the real world. Going back to our original example where the manufacture of the finest buggy whips available was the mission of the organization, it is the feedback from the lack of goal attainment—the sale of buggy whips—that would cause management to reevaluate the relevance of the mission of the organization.

CONCLUSION

The successful business not only knows where it is going and how it is going to get there but it realizes that it operates in a dynamic environment and it too must remain fluid. Flexibility, and revision as it relates to external and internal dynamics, ensures that an organization remains on course and en route to potential success.

CORPORATE CLIMATE AND CULTURE

Benjamin Schneider, Department of Psychology, University of Maryland at College Park

WHAT IS CORPORATE CLIMATE?

Corporate climate refers to the perceptions employees have of the imperatives of their organizations. Two broad classes of imperatives have been identified in the research on corporate climate. The first concerns employees' perceptions of the extent to which their company promotes employee well-being. This perception answers the question: To what extent is employee well-being an imperative for the management of the organization?

Employees answer this question by sensing many facets of the workplace including the way jobs are structured and organized, how compensation and other forms of rewards (promotions, praise) are dispensed, and the nature and quality of formal and informal interpersonal relationships they encounter at work. More will be said about these later. The important point to make here is that it is the message employees get from all of these facets of the workplace that informs them about the organization's sense of imperative regarding employee well-being.

The second class of imperatives involves the strategic goals of the organization. Perceptions of goals or imperatives can have innumerable frames of reference: customer service, product innovation, manufacturing quality, profit-at-all-cost, or safety. People thus speak about a climate for service, or a climate for innovation, quality, profits, or safety. The climate perceived by employees is a function of innumerable experiences they have. The greater the consistency in what employees experience as corporate imperatives, the more likely it is that they will direct their energies to facilitating those corporate goals.

THE CLIMATE FOR WELL-BEING

The experiences that send the messages to employees about a climate for employee well-being are:

- The way work is structured. Is it challenging and of great variety, or is it boring and repetitive? Are there clear and informal work goals and guidelines?
- The nature of formal and informal interpersonal relations.
- The procedures by which rewards, including compensation, are allocated.

No one experience or perception sends a total message. Rather, it is the accumulation of multiple and consistent experiences that constitute the perception of a climate for well-being. It is a serious error to believe that, for example, employees separate issues like pay from issues like supervision or the nature of their work. The various facets of human resources practices combine to send the employee well-being message.

Organizations differ in the way they design jobs, reward people, and structure interpersonal relationships. When jobs are rewarding and challenging, when compensation is competitive and rewards are equitably dispensed,

and when interpersonal relationships are characterized by warmth and consideration, the climate of the organization will be experienced as one that promotes a sense of well-being.

STRATEGIC CLIMATE AND CORPORATE CULTURE

A climate for individual well-being, however, may not give direction to people's energies and competencies. Such direction is found in the strategic imperatives of the organization.

Strategic climates are also based on employee experiences with the marketing, financial, operations, systems, and production activities of the organization. What is the market niche? On what issues are finances targeted? What kinds of data and information are monitored? Are systems up and running? What are the standards against which production and service effectiveness are judged?

Corporate culture is what employees believe management believes and values. Corporate culture is more subtle than corporate climate because it deals with broad concepts like the beliefs in people, the nature of the world, and people's relationships to each other and the world. Culture is the way employees explain to themselves and others why their organization functions as it does with respect to employee well-being and its strategic imperatives.

Corporate culture resides in the psychology of the experience. Corporate culture is what the experience means to employees. In an organization characterized by a climate for well-being, employees might make the attribution that management really believes in people and feels that the key to success is the way people are treated. In an organization characterized by a climate for service, employees might make the attribution that management believes in promoting and maintaining harmony with the external world; customers, as people in the external world, deserve the best treatment.

In a very real sense, corporate culture concerns the gods employees believe management worships. This relates directly to the kinds of experiences management creates for them and to the strategic imperatives pursued by the different functions of the organization. Thus, whereas corporate climate is a *direct* interpretation by employees of how they experience an organization, corporate culture is one step removed from direct experience.

CHANGING CLIMATE AND CULTURE

It is easier to change corporate climate than it is to change corporate culture—but even climate is difficult to change. Climate perceptions have direct roots in the everyday experiences of employees. Culture, on the other hand, emerges out of employees' attempts to understand why things are the way they are.

Climate is difficult to change because it is a summary of many consistent experiences over time. Employees need to have a basis in experience to form new perceptions and new perceptions require consistent new experiences over a long period of time. Because culture is an attempt by employees to explain why climate is the way it is, culture will be even more difficult than climate to change. The first step in changing culture is to change climate.

As employees encounter new experiences associated with change, it will be a while before their perceptions of the climate change. This is because new information is incorporated into old perceptions for some time prior to when new information begins to overwhelm old impressions.

Because top management knows what kind of climate(s) it is trying to create, it is always ahead of employees in grasping what the new climate is. Top management must facilitate ways for employees to experience the new climate, be consistent in the messages it sends employees, and be patient for the change to occur.

MANAGING ETHICS
IN THE CORPORATION

Andrew W. Singer, Editor and Publisher, *Ethikos: Examining Ethical Issues in Business*

Organizations have moral and legal reasons to deter misconduct by their employees. Stated more broadly, they have the responsibility of encouraging high standards of conduct and moral judgment. Managing such ethics is an important part of the job of every manager.

Ethics awareness training seminars, corporate ombudsmen, hotlines, ethics committees—these are some of the programs that companies have initiated in recent years in an effort to strengthen their ethical commitment. Many have also undertaken revisions to their codes of conduct.

But do such programs really deter misconduct within an organization? Critics point to surveys showing that companies with corporate ethics codes are just as likely to run afoul of the law as those without such codes. A prime example is the numerous companies linked to Pentagon procurement scandals in the late 1980s.

Others ask how much a CEO (chief executive officer) can really do to affect the actions of the thousands of employees who comprise the modern corporation. Many contend that ethics and values cannot be taught by corporations. Does this mean so-called ethics programs are predisposed to fail? Not necessarily. But some awareness of their limitations must be realized lest the value of these programs be oversold.

Consider this analogy: Automobiles, like large corporations, are a phenomenon that arguably has improved the overall quality of life in our society. But automobiles also kill people—and the likelihood of eliminating all deaths by automobile is not realistic. By the same token, we are unlikely to halt entirely ethical and criminal trespasses by employees within corporations.

However, just as air bags reduce auto fatalities, there are concrete steps that a company can take to slash—or at least to manage—its ethical "accident" rate. As in many things, the process begins with education.

ETHICS TRAINING

Consumer advocates have been prodding Detroit for years to build stronger cars—for example, cars with sturdier bumpers that will not collapse upon impact. An organization should be looking to build stronger moral agents. Many companies have arranged for ethics awareness seminars, designed to "sensitize" employees to ethical dilemmas—to make them more resistant to the moral hazards that they may encounter on the job.

Sessions vary in breadth and intensity. They can range from several hours of classes on site, to several full-day sessions off the premises. Most of these programs usually seek to provide employees with the ethical "tools" to enable them to resolve dilemmas themselves. An ethical tool can be quite simple. It can consist of little more than asking these questions: Who is likely to be affected by my decision? Who is likely to be hurt? Who will benefit? What message is my action sending to others in the organization?

A former director of training and development offered some suggestions about ethics training programs:

1. Do not expect to change people's values in such seminars. It is often enough to raise the participant's awareness of what constitutes an ethical dilemma.
2. A program is more attractive if the boss has already been in it. If the CEO or top managers take the classes first, it often gives the program credibility.
3. Do not accept significantly different levels of managers in the same group. Those of a lesser status will be reluctant to express opinions until a consensus begins to appear. Optimum class size is twelve to eighteen. Fewer than that does not provide diversity; more tends to make discussions unwieldy.

It is a nice idea to mix disciplines, which invites different perspectives. As an example, finance people may be most concerned with fiscal integrity. The manufacturing group may focus on product quality. The differing perspectives will add breadth and depth to class discussions.

The firm should use a brief lecture and extensive class discussion. Everyone should be actively involved in the give and take of weighing typical dilemmas.

THE CEO'S ROLE

Many automobile deaths occur when one or more parties are intoxicated. Perhaps nothing would reduce automobile fatalities quite as much as cutting down on drinking and driving. This aim requires some moral authority—from parents, community leaders, manufacturers of alcoholic beverages, tavern owners, and others.

Within a corporation, the CEO must provide the moral authority. When it comes to standards and values, his or her example will determine if policies are to be taken seriously. If the CEO is willing to fire a morally reckless employee, such an action will send a potent message throughout the organization. In other words, it is the CEO's task to help keep the corporation morally sober.

THE OMBUDSMAN

Sober driving can reduce traffic fatalities significantly. But can we go even further? Experts tell us that if all drivers and car passengers wore seat belts, automobile fatalities would fall dramatically, perhaps by as much as 50 percent.

Is a moral seatbelt available to the corporation? A comparable function might be served by an organization's ombudsman or ethics committee.

What is an ombudsman? The concept goes back to nineteenth-century Sweden. *Ombudsman* is a Swedish term meaning "agent" or "representative," and the ombudsman there was a government official who recommended prosecution, where appropriate, of public officials for malfeasance in office.

It is only recently that this notion has been extended to corporations and other organizations. The idea is to create an office—a safe haven—where employees can go with problems about waste, fraud, or abuse—outside of the usual chain of command. Confidentiality is usually promised, at least as far as is legally allowed.

From the organization's perspective, an ombudsman is one way of ensuring that problems are identified early and that they do not fester. The thinking is that it is better for the organization to identify a problem itself than for it to hear of the problem through a newspaper article, a regulatory agency, or from a congressional investigating committee. The ombudsman serves as the company's safety valve, or, if you like, the organization's seat belt, mitigating the effects of a crash.

Related to the ombudsman is the corporate ethics committee. Composed of top managers—and often outside corporate directors as well—this group meets regularly to review ethics policy. The committee might also serve an "ombuds" function, dealing with difficult ethical cases. One common task of the ethics committee is to review and, when necessary, revise the company's code of conduct.

THE IMPORTANCE OF ENFORCEMENT

One shudders to think what would result if traffic laws were not enforced. By the same token, an organization's ethical rules have to be enforced to avoid moral anarchy.

In his autobiography, *Father, Son, and Company*, former IBM chief Thomas Watson, Jr., recalls an incident in which he failed to dismiss managers for breaking "rules of integrity" and came to regret it:

> After that I simply fired managers when they broke rules of integrity. I did it in perhaps a dozen cases, including a couple involving senior executives. I had to overrule a lot of people each time, who would argue that we should merely demote the man, or transfer him, or that business would fall apart without him. But the company was invariably better off for the decision and the example.

It goes without saying that employees who are to be disciplined must first be apprised of the rules. A question asked repeatedly by Texas Instruments' ethics director Carl Skooglund is: "To what extent are we convinced that the employees knew what they did was wrong?" In fact, about two thirds of the calls to Texas Instruments' ethics office are questions about ethics—not reports of violations.

CORPORATE CODES OF CONDUCT

The code of conduct is usually the place where company policies and standards are spelled out. A code of conduct can supply a measure of discipline for people who want to do the right thing. It is better not to have a code of conduct, however, "than to have one and let it collect dust," says Harvey Pitt, an expert on corporate codes. The message that sends to employees is: We have standards, but we're not serious.

A code of conduct should begin with a broad statement of corporate policy and principles. The idea is to create an atmosphere that goes beyond strict legal compliance. A bad way to begin, for instance, is: "It is a violation to . . . " Better: "We're going to exceed legal standards . . . "

LEGAL CONSIDERATIONS

Codes of conduct, ethics training programs, ombudsman offices, prompt enforcement of company rules—many companies have initiated these programs recently, for among other reasons, attracting "better" people to their organizations and maintaining the morale of the good people that they have. But if corporations are looking for a financial incentive to implement such programs, they can find it in the recent sentencing guidelines for organizational defendants developed by the U.S. Sentencing Commission.

For the first time, organizations that implement, in good faith, some of the programs described above can have penalties or fines reduced significantly in the event that they are convicted of corporate crimes. Earlier, little distinction was made at sentencing time between a company with comprehensive ethics/compliance programs and those without.

The message now, according to Jeffrey Kaplan, partner in the New York law firm of Chadbourne & Parke, is that, "You have to do things before there is a problem. Given the magnitude of the fines, it could be the difference between bankruptcy and salvation for a company that gets into trouble."

According to Kaplan, new legal guidelines are "perhaps the most important development in corporate compliance in years. Any company that is not examining these questions now is making a big mistake."

STRATEGIC AND TACTICAL PLANNING: FROM CORPORATE LEVEL TO DEPARTMENT LEVEL

Jeffrey A. Moore, Director, Corporate Planning and Development, Indiana Gas Company, Inc.

Julie A. Vincent, Director, Corporate Communications, Indiana Gas Company, Inc.

STRATEGIC PLANNING

Strategic planning is the process whereby managers establish an organization's long-term direction, set specific performance objectives, develop strategies to achieve these objectives in light of all the relevant internal and external circumstances, and execute the chosen action plans.

To develop successful strategic plans, it is necessary to have a clear understanding of the various organizational objectives articulated effectively by management. Just as importantly, a manager must have a clear understanding of and a respect for the corporate culture and recognize its limits. The best strategic ideas can be basically useless if they are not accepted internally.

After analyzing the culture and environment of the corporation, management formulates broad judgments about the firm's strengths and weaknesses, with attention given to both corporate opportunities and threats. Then, strategic choices can be made that match the company's strengths with potential opportunities and protect against threats. Organizational policies that reinforce these strategic decisions are then developed in areas such as human resources, customer service, and operations. Finally, the total plan is communicated to managers and employees in such a manner so as to motivate toward successful implementation.

It is essential that the planning process be fully linked, so department plans fully represent the goals of the corporation. Continual and periodic updating is required. Managers and other employees must be properly educated on execution. Simplicity and ease of use is important. A plan must envelop only a manageable number of objectives. Accountability must be clear. And the planning process should be fully integrated with the budgeting process. Exhibit 1-3 depicts the

Exhibit 1-3. Goals and Objective Flow Chart

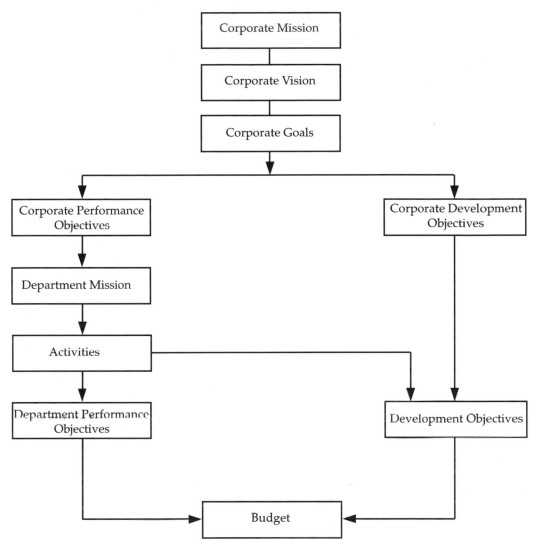

department planning process and how it links with the goals and objectives of the corporation.

Mission Statement

Strategic planning starts with the development of a mission statement, a concise statement of overall strategic direction of the unit. It explains the organization's business purpose and provides a broad framework within which corporate, division, department, and specific project strategies are developed. For example, a mission statement for a corporate communications department might be: "To influence, inform, and respond to the company's various stakeholders in order to position the company, its products and services as market driven and institutionally responsible."

Corporate Goals and Objectives

Corporate goals and objectives are the link between strategic and operational planning. With the corporate mission as a guide, management identifies specific goals and objectives that will result in the accomplishment of the company's mission. Objectives should be based on key measures of the interests of the major stakeholders of the organization.

The corporate objectives should be divided into two categories:

1. Performance objectives are quantifiable, measurable indicators of success. They are often called critical success factors or key performance indicators.
2. Development objectives are typically project oriented, usually requiring one or more years for completion.

Following are three examples of corporate stakeholders:

1. Investors are interested in return on investment, safety of the investment, and the overall integrity of the company. Quantifiable measurements for this group include earnings per share, return on equity, total return, dividends per share, yield, dividends-to-book ratio, debt-to-equity ratio, and cash flow coverage.
2. Customers look for reliable service, cost, safety, quality, and responsive service. Measurements of this performance might include the number of safety incidents, market share by segment, results versus competitor results, and customer complaints.
3. Employees want stability, fair compensation, fair treatment, job satisfaction, and two-way communication. They measure performance by employee turnover, the number and severity of grievances, wage and salary survey results, and equal employment opportunity.

DEPARTMENT PLANNING

Once the corporate directives are determined, the individual departments are responsible for developing plans that show how they will contribute to the achievement of the corporate goals and objectives.

A preferred planning process builds on the best features of top-down and bottom-up planning. It is important to realize that each group, executive management and line management, have important roles to play in the planning process. The top-down component consists of defining the goals and objectives relating to the key performance factors of the business. This top-down approach must be supported by a good communications process directed toward the middle managers. Executive management and middle management's perspective will often be different, and the gap should be closed through discussion, negotiation, and resolution.

Department Mission Statement

The starting point for department planning is the development of a mission statement. This requires managers to think about the aim or thrust of their department. It also requires a manager to look at the department's customers, and determine the best way to serve them.

Defining Functions

Once the mission is defined, the major functions performed within the department should be identified. Information should be gathered for each activity, such as purpose, user or customer, time, and financial requirements. With this information identified, it is possible to focus on ways to improve efficiency, decrease costs, and eliminate nonessential activities. During this process, input from customers should be obtained to ensure that essential functions are not eliminated or compromised. Exhibit 1-4 is a sample worksheet to aid a department head in outlining department activities.

Developing Department Objectives

Developing department objectives should be an iterative process, in which ideas flow both up and down. Subordinate input can be valu-

Exhibit 1-4. Sample Activities Worksheet

Activities	Customer Served	Estimated Annual O&M	Estimated Annual Capital	Total Annual Cost	Estimated Annual Hours	% Time	Impact Rating (A,B,C)
1.							
2.							
3.							
4.							
5.							
6.							
7.							
8.							
9.							
10.							
11.							
12.							
13.							
14.							
15.							
16. Nonproductive items							
17. Other O&M expenses							
18. Other capital							
TOTALS							

able and should be included in the planning process.

Many department objectives are interdependent and a need for coordination exists. Dealing with horizontally linked objectives requires (1) identifying objectives that potentially impact other areas and (2) coordinating efforts with respective department heads. Exhibit 1-5 is a sample department objectives worksheet.

Department objectives should be:

- *Verifiable*—Objective attainment must be verifiable at some time in the future. Specifying measurements in terms of results to be achieved gives a clear-cut basis for the objective.
- *Time oriented*—Objectives should be time oriented. Set deadlines so that results occur when the company needs them.
- *Attainable*—Targets should be achievable and realistic, yet focused on the "stretch" dimension.
- *Specific*—Each objective should specify results to be achieved in a single area. Avoid broad, sweeping statements.

Further, they should address the following concerns:

- *Financial impact*—Objectives should be of economic and financial value to the company. Specify the dollar value in terms of lower costs, improved efficiencies, and so forth. The emphasis should be placed on those strategies that offer the greatest opportunities.
- *Resource allocation*—Personnel requirements should be estimated and incorporated in objectives. Personnel estimates should include not only required hours from within the department but also any required hours from other departments.
- *Linkage*—Objectives should reflect the linkage that exists between departments within the company. Often objectives are linked to and need to be coordinated with objectives of other departments.

- *Objectives versus routine*—Each department has two dimensions, one being the day-to-day activities, the other the "stretch" dimension. The stretch dimension is that effort that is above and beyond the scope of day-to-day activities.

PROJECT PLANNING

A good plan will ensure that projects are appropriately executed and that three objectives can be accomplished: (1) to finish the project on time, (2) to complete the project within budget, and (3) to finish the project so that its technical performance objectives are achieved.

It is critical that an evaluation be made of the sources of data and that all managers in the organization understand the methods of analysis used. Project evaluation has a greater chance of success when it is a team effort of both staff and line managers.

All relevant aspects of the project should be studied in depth and converted to figures that will be used in the detailed financial analysis. The length of time for which projections are compiled will vary with the needs of the company. The five-year period used in many long-range plans will be too short for many purposes. The lead time for a major project will rarely be less than twelve months and will often exceed three years.

Not all projects will require the same length of analysis. Each project, however, should be analyzed with consideration given to the following items:

1. Marketing research should form part of most major capital expenditure studies. Market forecasts should be made a part of the overall marketing plan. The marketing plan is essential to produce realistic sales forecasts and to assess marketing and selling costs.

2. Production information includes specifications of the plant and machinery and buildings. Raw material costs, packaging material costs, and direct and indirect production costs can be estimated. This requires knowledge of the processes recommended, the capital costs of plants and buildings, the worker supply

Exhibit 1-5. Departmental Objectives Worksheet

Department Objectives	Department Performance Target	Additional O&M Cost	Additional Capital Cost	Total Additional Cost	Corporate Objective Linkage	Impact Rating (A,B,C)
Performance Objectives 1.						
2.						
3.						
4.						
5.						
Development Objectives 6.						
7.						
8.						
9.						
10.						
TOTALS						

levels required, and the types of labor required.

3. The project report should show clearly how the new proposal is to be staffed. Particular attention should be paid to key positions. Effects on existing personnel must be planned in detail. Additionally, any organizational changes should be evaluated.

4. An important aspect of the project plan is the amount of capital required. Estimates must be made of two types of capital: (a) Fixed capital needs can be assessed from the analysis just discussed, mostly derived from the production aspects. The more difficult part of analysis is determining the time when this capital is needed. In a large project, capital expenditures may be spread over a period of several years. The project analysts need to know when the capital will be needed. (b) Working capital needs will tend to increase as the business expands, and can be estimated from the sales and production figures, as these are related to raw material and finished good inventory levels, accounts receivables, and payables.

Project Analysis

There are many ways of analyzing the figures produced during the investigation. One of the most effective tools is the discounted cash flow method, enabling weight to be given to the time value of money. Cash inflows and outflows are discounted on a time basis at a rate that represents the return the company should be earning.

Using a discounted cash flow method, an acceptable project will return enough cash to do three things:

1. Pay off all interest payments to creditors who have lent money to finance the project.
2. Pay dividends and capital gains to shareholders who have put up equity for the project.
3. Pay off the original principal that was invested in the project.

Budgeting

Budgets are the primary technique used in translating strategic plans into current actions. They set standards for coordinated action and provide a basis for controlling performance to see that it is in conformance with plans. Budgeting systems must reflect the unique attributes of the company and therefore each system is different.

Budgeting has three objectives in the overall planning process:

1. To provide a means to evaluate and to quantify the upcoming year's activities and processes.
2. To assist in allocating resources.
3. To assist in monitoring and controlling expenditures.

A budgeting process must take into consideration the following:

1. Ongoing activities or functions, as defined by the departmental plan.
2. New products or services and the impact they have on the current organization, including additional staffing, new programs, and new plant and equipment.
3. Provisions made for contingencies.

The budgeting process should immediately follow the planning process, thereby providing the financial support or justification of the department's objectives.

SALES PLANNING

The first step in the budgeting process is to develop the sales forecast, as sales levels typically drive all other activities. The sales forecast should be based on economic, demographic, and specific market information. It should provide detailed information about the product mix, sales volumes, pricing strategies, new product releases, and other pertinent data.

Production Budget

Once sales volumes have been projected, the production budget can be determined. Raw materials, labor, supervision, machinery and equipment, and other production-related items need to be planned well ahead of actual production schedules so that specifications can be written and these items can be purchased at the lowest cost possible. Other considerations include warehouse capacity, transportation costs, and packaging costs.

Administrative Budgets

Other areas of the organization need to also project their expenses based on their specific departmental plans. Projects that require additional resources, as well as general company growth, should be considered. Areas such as information services, accounting, public relations, human resources, and other general and administrative areas are included in this group.

Analyzing Results

The real test of a well-prepared plan is, of course, the comparison of actual results. On a monthly basis, the results need to be reported against the budget and an analysis should be completed to determine why variances exist. If variances are justified, adjustments should be made so that the overall company objectives can be met.

ESTABLISHING CONTROLS

Alethea O. Caldwell, Executive Vice-President, Corporate Services, Blue Cross of California

Only by implementing systems of control can organizations ensure the successful achievement of their goals. Controls are an integral part of every organization's structure, forming the basis for measuring its effectiveness and ultimate success. In general, controls are tailored to an industry's or organization's particular results. Controls are, therefore, a feedback mechanism that enables management and staff to monitor how effectively they are delivering their product or service. Controls contribute to consistency, focus attention on a particular process or outcome, reduce variation, and add to the probability of success.

The controlling process begins during strategic planning when leadership establishes the organization's vision and goals. As management translates the strategic plan into action, the controls impact beyond objective measurement and become part of the corporate culture.

TRADITIONAL VS. DYNAMIC CONTROLS

Traditionally, controls have relied heavily on historical performance measurement, such as operating budgets, production rates, profit and loss statements, annual employee appraisals, sales volume, and adherence to specifications. These basic controls establish accountability for results. Although these remain valuable measures, today's rapidly changing business environment requires more dynamic controls that measure performance in multiple dimensions. In order to compete successfully, organizations must not only measure performance to today's production or service requirements but must also:

- Project what impact a product or service will have and focus resources on those that show the highest probability of success.
- Measure and track consumer response to current products or services.
- React quickly to consumer needs or acceptance.
- Measure customer perception of quality.
- Refine measures and definitions of quality.
- React quickly to economic or environmental conditions.
- Measure the timeliness of creating a new product or service, or design an old product or service to meet customer requirements.
- Measure employee responsiveness to correcting variations.
- Continuously monitor employee performance.
- Train or cross-train employees in new procedures or technologies.
- Continuously improve the service and product.

The "new generation" controls will use highly automated decision support models that are analytical and predictive in nature. The information generated will give organizations the capability to correct variations almost immediately. Organizations that use these controls will be "flatter" to allow centralized participation in design and use of controls. Emphasis will be on keeping the work force quickly and effectively prepared for anticipated and unanticipated industry changes.

CHARACTERISTICS AND CONDITIONS OF CONTROLS

Controls are based on standards established during the planning process. Once established, controls are driven by outcome, and measures of outcome become a type of control. Controls focus attention on tasks, thereby assuring that the tasks are completed. Controls identify deviations or variations from established goals, thereby facilitating correction so that future outcome is consistent. And controls give organizations the ability to measure what is important in accomplishing their goals. In short, "what gets measured gets done."

So that controls provide information upon which to take action, they should be based on objective measures. Yet the simple act of singling out a particular function for "controlling" signals that it is important, thus changing the way people view it. Therefore, to maintain as much objectivity as possible, controls must be:

- Based on predetermined standards.
- Appropriate for the function being measured.
- Timely and easily understood to immediately identify deviations.
- Practical and capable of immediate corrective action.
- Consistent.
- Based on realistic goals and fact-driven objectives.

Controls can be distinguished from each other by investigating the focus of corrective action. These foci fall into three main areas: past performance, ongoing or concurrent events, and future outcomes.

Measures of the Past

Controls are often based on historical economic and organizational performance as reflected in such traditional measures as standard cost analyses, financial statements, and profit and loss statements. With this information, management can make corrections if actual expenses, revenue, and productivity are below projections made in the strategic and financial plans. Historic controls also include annual evaluations of past employee performance, assessments of how satisfied customers were with the product or service, and measures of how well quality control standards were met. These measures gauge an organization's previous performance and provide an important initial "snapshot" pulse reading for future actions.

Ongoing Controls

Ongoing (or concurrent) measures provide timely feedback that is based on information directly related to the product or service. They monitor current operations and any deviations so that staff can take immediate corrective action. Among ongoing controls important to an organization are the monitoring of behavioral changes in employees, users, and consumers and external conditions such as changes in political, social, or economic environments that influence the behavior or choices of users of the product or service.

Other areas where ongoing controls are appropriate include monitoring product or service consistency and quality, controlling lead time between when an order is placed and the product or service is produced, tracking inventory, and managing resources. This information, when gathered and shared on a continuous basis, provides the vital feedback that management and workers need to correct any deviations from acceptable standards. That means information must be directed to the staff who impact the product or service being measured. To this end, many organizations have moved to decentralized management and decision making. They find that this "flattening out" of the organization improves communication, allows more people to participate in and contribute to the planning and operations process, and results in staff "buying in" to the organization's goals and actions because they have direct input.

Outcome Measurement and Controls

The definition of future outcomes begins with a strategic plan. Predictive models utilize both historical and current performance measures to build strategic assumptions to antici-

pate the future. Thus, a strategic plan is the ultimate control, with the milestones along the way being recorded and measured by the "new" predictive models.

The strategic plan is the broad compass that sets an organization's direction. It is based on the organization's resources, knowledge, and skills, its external market conditions, and its competitive environment. The strategic plan is driven by the desired "place in the sun" that the organization wishes to achieve. It is through the strategic plan that leaders establish the vision for the organization and set strategies for producing the changes that will allow them to make their vision a reality. Management and staff support the strategic planning process by developing models and processes that help all players determine the best path toward achieving their strategies and goals. Management also develops the supporting financial plan, procedures, timetables, and resource allocation necessary for achieving the projected outcomes.

Controlling human resources selection and development is essential for any organization committed to achieving its strategic plan. Recruiting employees who have skills, attitudes, and commitment that closely match the organization's operational needs and culture is a fundamental step in directing future outcomes.

Measure What Is Important to the Task at Hand. It is easy to fall prey to the temptation of evaluating what is convenient or what has already been measured. The challenge is to go beyond the norm and discover an indicator that is more critical to assuring the desired outcome. Measures appropriate to the task and desired outcome will be effective whereas those selected because of tradition or convenience will not be. For example, modern organizations are expert at developing and distributing mountains of information—overhead, overall sales volume, revenue, expenditures, employee turnover, and so on. This information, however, is usually not germane to the activities of supervisors and workers directly involved in production or distribution of the product or service. These individuals need to know if quality standards, production quotas, and cost estimates related to their areas of responsibility are being met. Another example is employee turnover. Whereas turnover may be insignificant when looked at on a company-wide basis, it could be critical if 90 percent of the turnover were occurring in one department.

Keep Measures Simple, Visible, and Understandable. As companies become more complex, the need for simple, understandable controls increases. Managers need to become adept at identifying two or three key controls that allow them to monitor the pulse of their area of operation at all times.

The measures must be very clearly communicated to all the workers involved in production. They must be detailed enough to communicate whether or not the result is being achieved. Front-of-mind awareness is essential to keeping energies focused on results. Therefore, measurements should be visible throughout the work area, serving as an invitation to problem solving.

Decentralizing and Sharing

The free dissemination of operational information throughout the organization is essential for establishing effective controls. Information empowers. When employees understand the vision and goals that have shaped their jobs and the results they are expected to achieve, they are more likely to give of themselves and contribute suggestions for more effectively achieving the results. Sharing basic, vital information communicates to the employees that they are valued members of the organization. Knowing that production is 10 percent behind schedule or customer satisfaction is down 25 percent is more motivational than just being told to increase production or to be more service oriented.

Many organizations are decentralizing information flow and decision making in an effort to eliminate bureaucracy, streamline operations, and speed up communications. Flattening out management levels offers more opportunities for senior management and line workers to interact with each other, enhancing the possibility of a partnership rather than the "we–them" relationships present in many companies. Decentralization also moves the planning and decision-making process further down the line, allowing companies to react quickly to external pressures. Sharing information across division, department, or unit lines can stimulate employees' competitive and creative juices and increase productivity throughout the organization. Knowing about another area's successes and failures also results in employees modifying their own behavior—either replicating or avoiding, as appropriate, the actions taken elsewhere.

THE MOST IMPORTANT ORGANIZATIONAL CONTROL FACTOR

The ultimate success for any organization's control system lies with its people. With today's increased sophistication of management information systems, workplace mechanization, and ability to monitor complex operations, some managers might develop a false sense of security in the ability of technology to substitute for the human factor. But each individual in an organization has his or her own set of personal aspirations, motivations, needs, and ideas. Balancing the needs of the organization and the needs of its employees provides management with several challenges.

The first challenge is to provide institutional incentives and deterrents that will satisfy the needs of employees. However, the incentives or deterrents chosen must be applied consistently and fairly throughout the organization.

Many organizations are using structured quality improvement processes to control outcomes. Quality improvement motivates development of work force skills and abilities, promotes communication and teamwork, builds consensus around improvement actions, and allows constructive and appropriate participation in controlling the production of high-quality products and services. The quality improvement process promotes objective management, instills values for customer satisfaction and respect for people, sets valid requirements, encourages active analysis of variance, and fosters accountability for and rapid correction of the variance.

CONCLUSION

Organizations will spend much of the next decade learning to better define and refine the measures and controls of success. They will perfect the dynamic systems now being implemented to control product and service quality. As they progress through this process, organizations will concentrate on measuring and evaluating the effectiveness of control systems and will eventually base measures of their overall organizational effectiveness on contributed value to societal and economic performance.

ORGANIZATIONAL MODELS AND STRUCTURES

Joan H. Coll, Seton Hall University

Organizational development is an ongoing effort to create and maintain a model, structure, and environment that produce the highest possible effectiveness. To be successful, such effort must be ongoing, organization-wide, and fully supported by top management. This requires an understanding of different organizational models.

MODELS

The Bureaucratic Model

The most venerable of the organizational models is the classical bureaucratic model first described by Weber in the early 1900s. The term *bureaucracy* is singularly appropriate for this model, except that the popular understanding of the term is one of unresponsiveness, red tape, and bungling inefficiency. In a well-run bureaucracy, such as the U.S. Marine Corps, nothing is further from the truth. Indeed, if people's needs are ignored, it is the most efficient model in terms of overhead cost, speed, predictability, and operational consistency. It is characterized by a strict chain of command, centralized authority, and a set of impersonal but consistent rules for all aspects of the workplace, including employee rights, duties, censure, and operating procedures.

In a bureaucracy, the organizational hierarchy is inviolable. Each position is under the direct control of the one immediately above, all the way to the CEO (chief executive officer). At every level, compliance is to the position and not to the person. Each employee has a narrow strictly defined sphere of rights, duties, powers, and expertise. Job openings are filled by appointment on the basis of certificates/degrees and technical qualifications. Employees enjoy a career ladder distinguished by promotion according to seniority and/or achievement as evaluated by their boss. Ownership is separate and distinct from management.

In recent times the bureaucratic model has experienced job alienation among employees bored by the dull repetitive nature of their work. Since these are the workers on whom the organization depends for productivity and for building quality into its products, desired levels may not be reached.

The bureaucratic model experiences deficiencies with increases in environmental uncertainty and task complexity. Because of its inflexibility, the bureaucratic model is incapable of a fast response. Nonetheless, the bureaucratic model can be effectively used in situations in which technology is minimal and the environment is stable.

The Behavioral Model

The behavioral model is a modification of the bureaucratic model that places increased emphasis on the social and psychological side of the organization. The majority of industrialized companies operate within the confines of this model. Concern for the psychological and emotional well-being of the individual is a major aspect of management activity. This interest is demonstrated by a variety of employee-oriented assistance programs, such as tuition remission, health education workshops, in-house training, flextime, quality circles, and company-sponsored outings.

Behavioral models recognize that two systems operate within an organization:

1. A technical system that produces a product/service.
2. A social system composed of the workers who operate the technical system.

If insufficient attention is paid to nurturing the social and psychological needs of the individual and groups, the technical side will presumably falter.

A second intent of the behavioral model is to empower the organization to be responsive to its external environment, as well as internal environments. As a result, behavioral model managers are provided more freedom and latitude in decision making than their bureaucratic model counterparts.

A strong behavioral model emphasizes decentralization, openness in communication up and down the hierarchy, and a weak chain of command with respect to work organization and accountability. Employees are expected to involve themselves in decision making, which is decentralized and often a group process. Authority is earned through accomplishment and successful relationships rather than from any hierarchical positioning. All members can influence departmental procedures and goals. Emphasis is placed on the individual's ability to fit in and solve problems. One of every manager's key tasks is to foster the development of his or her people by means of training.

The Organic Model

For organizations involved in areas of high uncertainty, the behavioral model might not provide sufficient flexibility. The organic model is characterized by low use of rules (except, perhaps, safety rules), total decentralization and shared decision making, broad responsibilities, few levels of hierarchy, and little division of labor. Self-starting employees possessing competence and ingenuity are the cornerstones of this model. Rules are seen as impediments that dull employee motivation and creativity. Decision making is by consensus, even when it comes to personnel evaluation, in which the judgments of co-workers and other area managers are invited.

The organic model is marked by fluidity and its capacity for rapid response to changes in environmental circumstances, such response encompassing even the potential of reorganization. An example of this model is the Swedish computing consultant company, Enator, which employs five hundred people. The company is divided into subsidiaries with a maximum of fifty people and one manager each. This facilitates a pleasant atmosphere, group loyalty, common interests, and management without hierarchical emphasis. Should a subsidiary grow to more than fifty people, it is divided in two. Flexibility and acceptance of responsibility are emphasized. An example is the borrowing of staff among subsidiaries, particularly for larger projects. The structure of subsidiaries changes as operations develop and opportunities emerge.

A second example is W. L. Gore and Associates, the makers of Goretex, an enterprise with twenty-eight plants. As with Enator, there is a limit to the number of employees per plant, in this case, two hundred. Gore has minimal hierarchy, few titles, and an almost total absence of policy manuals. New hires are told to look around and find something to do that they would enjoy and that will help the company. Every employee is encouraged to work with every other employee. It could be described as a three-ring circus. But the company is consistently profitable.

The Nebula Model

A nebula is a swirling vibrant mass in interstellar space. This conveys the intent of the nebula, or self-designing, model. It is continuously changing, continuously looking for original ways to respond to its environment and to invent its own future. A self-designing organization cherishes impermanence, conflict, the unorthodox, and inventiveness. Such an organization is unpredictable in method and orientation, often a chaotic and bizarre place to work. Many people would be unable to survive in such conditions. With respect to the business arena, this form of organization is still experimental and so established examples are not prevalent.

STRUCTURES

The models just discussed are vehicles around which structures are built. Certain models are more compatible with certain structures.

Functional Structure

In this traditional structure, the chain of command flows downward from the CEO. Marketing, finance, data processing, and other functions that are pertinent to a specific enterprise are headed by vice-presidents. Managers report to these vice-presidents. Further down the ladder, tasks are also divided functionally by process.

The functional organization is easily applicable to all sizes and types of businesses. It groups people of like orientation together, promoting skill specialization and reducing duplication of resources. It enhances quality and creativity, and encourages economies of scale.

On the other hand, maintaining cooperation among functions is complex and often problematic. Different functions have different time frames, goals, and protocols, making coordination and scheduling difficult. Additionally, a functional orientation emphasizes routine tasks, encourages parochial perspectives, and obscures accountability for outcomes.

Divisional Structure

Divisional structure divides an organization according to product/service lines, geographic regions, or customers. This structure is especially appropriate for large multiple product companies such as PepsiCo or General Foods. It reduces the technical complexity facing upper-level managers who otherwise would have to deal with totally different demands of various product lines.

Since managers must coordinate all phases of their product, the divisional structure enables them to develop meaningful breadth, flexibility, and well-rounded resourcefulness. These opportunities are not available within the functional structure. Divisional structure engenders an orientation toward outcomes and clients, ensures accountability, promotes delegation of authority, and encourages team spirit and involvement.

On the negative side, this structure may not use skills and resources to the fullest (because they reside in a specific division), may limit advancement of specialists (because specialist pools are not as large as with a functional structure), puts stressful multiple demands on managers, and promotes suboptimization (because the goals of a decision may be at odds with the goals of an organization). Opportunities for economies of scale are often lost because interdepartmental unity is not so likely.

Product structure is especially attractive when products have different and keenly competitive markets. Geographic structure is attractive when market areas require different strategies, as selling to the common market and selling to India.

Hybrid Structure

It is predictable that an organization will opt for an amalgamation of the functional and the divisional rather than for either pure form. This is the hybrid structure. In the typical hybrid organization, the products are organized as divisions in the standard divisional structure, while certain functions such as research and development, data processing, logistics, and personnel are organized as functional groups. Thus, typically, certain vice-presidents will be product leaders while other vice-presidents will be function leaders. Obviously, the purpose of the functional units is to serve the product units. Levi Strauss employs such a hybrid structure. The advantages to the product lines are the same as those given in the previous section, while the functional groups provide cost efficiency by obviating the need for duplication of various expensive resources (lawyers, mainframes, payroll systems, etc.).

Matrix Structure

Matrix structure, developed by the aerospace industry, is the most complex structure. Organization is along two dimensions simultaneously. Examples are function and geographical or customer type and product.

Picture a series of product lines (radios, TVs, cameras) listed one below the other, each with a line running horizontally across the page. Also picture a series of function names (finance, marketing, operations, etc.) spread across the top of the page, each with a line running down the page. The finance line intersects with each product, as does marketing, operations, and so on. Each of these constituencies (radios, TVs, cameras, finance, marketing, operations, etc.) is headed by a vice-president, known as a matrix boss. The point where each of the horizontal and vertical lines intersect designates a department manager. Examples are the manager of finance for radios, manager of finance for TVs, manager of marketing for radios, and so on.

These two-boss managers have the stressful distinction of owing allegiance to two supervisors. Each manager controls a department dedicated to both a function and a product. The advantage of this structure is that product functional expertise is spread to all corners of the company. Every department has a direct line to its product and to a function.

The matrix structure violates what is generally regarded as an inviolable rule of business: a single-boss chain of command. It opens up authority conflicts, loyalty conflicts, ambiguity, and responsibility lapses ("He told me to do A, which is different from the B you told me to do"). A great deal of overhead may be expended to resolve conflicts. This complex structure can lead to turmoil and confusion. A large number of companies are sold on matrix structure. It is particularly appropriate when a company must deal with pressure for quality and innovative products. The matrix structure facilitates the sharing of resources, which is important when products require scarce or expensive resources.

Network Structure

An organization with a network structure contracts out all aspects of the business. A core of idea people put together complete packages by contracting with manufacturers, transporters, marketing companies, and retail stores/chains. Any needed function is obtained with a phone call. Products never come near the company's doors. Even accounts receivable, accounts payable, and payroll functions are contracted.

At any one time all of the functions of a traditional company are in place through contractual arrangement. Rather than a chain of command, the hierarchy is a chain of purchase orders and relationships to other firms. The people in the company have no underlings. Instead, they have contacts.

Because all functions are contracted, providers can be changed easily and the network company is relieved of tensions and sunken costs. There are no employees to stimulate and no unions to mollify. If a supplier experiences a setback, such as a strike, it is a disaster for the supplier but only a problem for the network company.

If a line becomes unprofitable it can be terminated easily. There are no factories to retool and no employees to retrain. The project possibilities are limited only by the imagination of the network personnel rather than by constraints of plant capacity and technical resources. On the negative side, a network organization may find that a supplier is selling in the same market or to a competitor. Or the supplier may stop providing capacity. Quality, and other product aspects, cannot be directly controlled. Since network organizations do not have research facilities, they are not able to create state-of-the-art products.

EFFECTING MODEL/ STRUCTURAL CHANGE

The organizational development specialists recommend adjustments the organization can make in its model/structure/environment. The process includes:

- Systematically reviewing the organization and its environment for problem areas. This may involve making comparisons to competitors and similar organizations in other fields of business.
- Creating an OD (organizational development) master plan.
- Avoiding any frontal assaults on the prevailing corporate culture or the values of the employees, for such assaults will surely fail. Proposed interventions must be examined for compatibility with existing cultural values.
- Ensuring that the plan contains the simplest, most concrete intervention possible.
- Planning changes so that they can be implemented incrementally. A series of small changes has a much better chance of success than one large change.
- Promulgating the organizational development cause. The OD specialist must promote informed employee involvement. In this way, employees come to regard themselves as implementors and thus commit themselves to the changes.
- Maintaining top management's unreserved support. If top management does not enthusiastically back planned change, the changes will most likely fail.
- Expecting opposition and preparing plans to defuse it. To be successful, the OD specialist must have clear objectives, respond quickly to resistance, and quickly block off game players.
- Remaining independent. An OD specialist who takes sides or who appears to be some power group's shill loses credibility and effectiveness.

CONCLUSION

The model/structure of an organization must be tailored to its goals, its values, and the external environment. Change should be carefully planned to maintain an effective model/ structure in the face of this continuously changing environment.

INTEGRATING FUNCTIONS AND DEPARTMENTS

David H. Swanson, Chairman, President, and CEO, Central Soya Company

Organizations must make a number of decisions when designing a structure that can meet the needs of its customers and activities. Every company benefits from a periodic review of its organizational structure to assure that the existing structure is still best suited to meet changing needs and conditions. Such an analysis must examine how tasks are assigned and divided, how resources are deployed, and how departments are coordinated.

One component of any review must be an examination of each function and department to see if strategic objectives can be better achieved with a greater or lesser degree of integration of functions. Are there similar departments within like responsibilities? If so, what are the trade-offs to be made in a realignment? Each scenario will have its own answer. Often the solution will be a composite structure that features a combination of integrated and decentralized functions. No overlay can be said to work universally and be appropriate for every organization in every environment.

STAFF VS. LINE

In most cases, there will be greater potential for effective integration of a staff function than a line function. Often, the nature of staff work better lends itself to integration. Line department responsibilities involve a customer who must be pleased at all costs. Line departments may, for this reason, resist a shift toward integration.

In a large company with several operating groups, an integrated human resources department can effectively service all groups with specialized skills that are equally applicable to all. If an attempt is made to unionize a plant, the department's experienced experts can deal with the challenge more effectively than a plant human resources administrator who may never have experienced such a challenge.

The sales organization of two line divisions may not be easily integrated. If the products are different and customers demand different types and levels of service and expertise, different cultures may be needed to provide service. This is not to say that the sales department can never be integrated. At one consumer products company, an umbrella sales organization was established over its previously autonomous product divisions after major retailers demanded an end to visits from multiple sales representatives. Again, the point is not that sales can never be integrated but that the level of integration is necessarily defined by the needs of the customer.

BENEFITS FROM INTEGRATION

Apart from the cost benefits of integrating a function, there are considerable benefits in the form of greater control of critical activity. Functions that involve the gathering and dissemination of important data, for instance, become more effective when channeled through a central point. Compliance with government regulation would likely be a chaotic endeavor without a central control point.

Without belaboring an obvious point, are there significant cost savings to be gained by integrating? The purchasing function is perhaps the best example of potential economies of scale. Can you buy fasteners for thirty plants at a cheaper rate than for just the five in your own division? Probably. The divisions of a large international corporation may go to great lengths to maintain separate identities to the outside world. But by combining their purchasing, they make significant gains. They reduce expenses in the form of smaller payroll. They can negotiate significantly lower prices as a result of their combined bargaining power.

One company, a highly decentralized manufacturer whose products ranged from aerospace to automotive parts, utilized an integrated corporate purchasing database despite the fact that its business units were in different markets and used different technologies. By sharing an integrated database that encompasses thousands of vendors, each business unit could negotiate prices and terms based on the strength of the entire corporate relationship.

ISSUE OF CONTROL

In addressing the degree of integration, the level of control is an important component of the decision. How much decision-making latitude is necessary to operate effectively? What level of authority is needed to properly respond to operating challenges that may be presented?

The potential for integrating a function increases as the latitude for decision making decreases. Relatively rigid disciplines, such as finance and accounting, will generally be integrated quite effectively. Each plant can normally be measured in an "apples to apples" manner and the centralization of the function can be an effective means of measuring and comparing performance in many locations. A customer service function, in contrast, will often need to be decentralized and decisions pushed close to the marketplace in which each business unit operates. Decisions must be made quickly, and without the encumbrance that centralization can bring. Such decentralization, however, requires highly competent people, clearly defined responsibilities and levels of authority, and effective communications.

THE HUMAN ELEMENT

The decision on the level of integration of any function should be based on input from many sources. It must be recognized that a certain bias can exist in even the most well-meaning managers. Many managers are inclined to think their own needs are unique, and prefer to control their own support staffs. With the technology available today, for example, the ability may exist for the accounts payable department to be electronically linked to headquarters and to be capable of handling the same function that was formerly replicated thirty times at thirty plants. In many of those plants, however, there will be resistance to the idea from plant managers more comfortable with a staff dedicated totally to the individual plant's needs. A dedicated staff is less risky for plant managers and a change in the status quo might also be viewed as an infringement on their "kingdom."

All but the smallest organizations can benefit from the judicious integration of certain functions and departments. It is never a question of whether to integrate, but which functions can be made more effective and how much integration should be introduced? Obviously, if customers wait too long for a telephone to be answered, an order to be processed, or a billing dispute to be resolved, a consolidated function will fail. Clearly, sacrifices in customer service or product quality can never be made in the name of functional integration. Frequently, however, such a change can save time, introduce order and control, and bring harmony to a team effort. It can counter poor communication, higher inventories, and lower productivity.

Many large companies have set up truly separate strategic business units in which each unit operates as a separate business and "buys" its integrated corporate services from a central management. Others tailor an integrated approach to the needs of the business,

perhaps integrating human resources in two of three divisions, while maintaining a specialized human resources staff for an offshore division. Or, the regulatory compliance department may perform all functions for some divisions, but only selected functions for others.

CONCLUSION

Most organizations will find an effective composite that combines integrated functions and decentralized functions, and the resulting structure is efficient for that dynamic of customers, products, processes, and geography. With that proper balance, management will be efficient and productive. Without that balance, it will never operate at its most effective level.

TECHNIQUES FOR PROJECT MANAGEMENT

Ronald M. Gimpel, Productivity Solutions Management, Ltd.

Barbara L. Gray, CEO, Barron Group Ltd.

Most organizations, given competent operations management, face common issues when planning and conducting business projects. In all cases, the first task is to identify a project as differentiated from other routine business

activities. Some criteria used to distinguish the differences are:

- It usually has a highly specific justification and expected benefit.

- Its conduct is "one-time only," with a specific scope, budget, start, and end.
- It has specific completion criteria. These occur with the demonstrated achievement of a set of predetermined results.
- It frequently requires the participation and resources of multiple departments and/or vendors.
- It yields little, if any, interim benefits prior to its completion.

Actually managing a project differs, too, from managing in a routine environment. For example, a project manager (PM) will be:

- Coordinating the activities of parties not under the manager's direct supervision.
- Facilitating commitment from people at various levels of the organization to what may be broadly viewed as a short-term effort.
- Having personal job performance evaluated by nonreporting line senior managers.
- Managing in an environment where he or she may be unfamiliar with the technology or the subject matter.

Obviously there are critical factors that have the potential to lead to disaster. Our discussion of project management techniques focuses on preventing, or detecting and resolving, the causes of disaster in project management.

The project sponsor, normally a senior line executive, is required to objectively view the project in light of the company's well-being, while assuring that the intent, intergroup cooperation, and progress of the project team stay aligned with the project objectives. The position must carry the influence to resolve interorganizational conflicts, expedite administrative processes, and authorize changes in project scope, cost, or schedule.

FOLLOWING A PROJECT PROPOSAL STANDARD

We recommend the use of a project proposal standard that requires a thorough analysis of a project's business justification and underlying assumptions, its priority, dependencies, and conflicts with other projects or business operations, as well as the trade-offs of alternative approaches, where applicable. In addition to the standard project description, benefit analysis, and positional advantage profile, this standard should require an analysis of:

- Critical business measures (economic, political, legal, competitive, and market demand) that justify and/or permit the project undertaking. Where applicable, range-of-comfort estimates should be included.
- Other internal projects whose efforts and goals either complement or conflict with the proposed project.
- Initial projection of the required participation of both internal and external organizations.

PROJECT PLANNING AND ESTIMATING

The subject of project planning and estimating has been addressed by the creation of countless models and software programs. The PM should select a tool that is sufficiently robust and produces various levels of readily understandable progress and resource status reports. Embedded model plans and tutorials can both save time and guide new project managers.

Project planning and estimating go hand in hand. Estimates of time and cost are based on the detail work activities identified and the resources allocated in the project plan. If the time, resources, and cost of performing a project cannot be closely estimated, it may indicate that there is not sufficient information to define the project.

Frequently, the first planning step to be performed is commonly called milestone O or phase O. Using the project proposal as a starting point, the project manager develops a plan for the time and resources required to complete the definition of the project and the detailed project plan. He or she must verify that the project is defined well enough for the development of a project plan, and that the assumptions on which the project is initially based are validated.

In order to develop a meaningful plan, a project's scope, major work components, and generic resource requirements must be known. The PM must identify every internal and external organization having a stake or role in the project's success.

Use a Work Breakdown Structure

A project plan is normally structured into a four-level hierarchy with the total project being the first, or top, level. This planning hierarchy is referred to as the work breakdown structure. The names used in this discussion for the three levels of the hierarchy below project are milestone, submilestone, and activity. In practice, the names, but not the nature, of these levels may vary.

Milestones, also called major deliverables, major events, or phases, represent the achievement of a major component of the overall project. The project's viability and estimates are normally assessed as each milestone is completed. Milestones may also correspond to the completion of a project product that can be utilized by the organization.

Submilestones, also known as events or tasks, represent the achievement of a related set of work items (activities). These normally correspond to critical path diagram events.

Activities are the lowest level of the work breakdown structure and represent the performance of actual work. It is at this level that time estimates, resource requirements, and work step (activity) sequence are assigned.

Customize Generic Estimates

As previously discussed, project time, cost, and resource estimates are made at the level at which work is performed (activity). Cost and time estimates are based on the duration of each activity and the quantity and quality of the resources applied to it. Allocation of both human and other resources required for the activity must be included in the plan as well as the direct management responsibility for its progress. Obtaining the necessary resources may, in and of itself, require planned activities.

Estimating is neither a hard science nor an arcane art. There are frequently rules of thumb, both generic and industry/discipline specific, to guide the allocation of time and resources. The activity duration must be specific to the project and must produce a measurable unit of output. For example, if the activity is the design of a report, measure is a completed report design, delivered in a specified format to a specific party. Acceptance of the format is another activity.

The complexity level of an activity, relative to the quality of the resources assigned to the task, should be used to determine both time and resource quantity estimates. Those estimates based on a generic resource needed to perform an activity must be adjusted to reflect the actual quality of the resources available.

Monitor and Report Progress

Progress reporting has several essential elements. Reports must be timely (in order to facilitate remedial action) and meaningful. This may require the generation of reports with differing levels of detail and technical complexity. The basis of progress reporting is to provide others with the ability to determine where the project is in relation to the plan. Reports should highlight those events (submilestones and milestones) on the critical path and how well the activities leading to them are progressing. They should include all accomplishments against plan, any potential problems or issues to be resolved, and what is expected to be accomplished during the next progress reporting period.

Structure Project Testing and Acceptance

The project manager's role in testing and acceptance, aside from monitoring the progress of the testing, is to assure that the necessary resources and facilities are available when required by the project test team.

Many project managers establish a test assurance group to be responsible for coordinating the documentation of both business function and technical test criteria, developing test cases, running and monitoring the actual tests, and reporting/tracking test problems and their resolution.

Manage Change

More often than not, some changes to scope occur during the course of a project. In large-scale projects, project managers frequently have established separate change control teams. It is the responsibility of this team to ensure that any changes to the project deliverables or objectives be evaluated, estimated for impact, documented, adjudicated, and communicated to project participants and stakeholders.

Avoid Last-Minute Delays

Regardless of how well the project has been planned and estimated, Murphy's Law reminds us that whatever can go wrong, will. Some suggestions for the prevention, diagnosis, and correction of project variances include:

- Factor in slack time for those activities least controllable, for example, client review, equipment installation, and legal processes. Manage the project, however, as if no slack time was budgeted.
- Create frequent submilestones in the plan and insist on timely and objective proof of completion.
- If variances from the plan occur:

    Identify and initiate remedial actions.
    Identify the activities, submilestones, and milestones that are, or will be, impacted.
    Modify time and resource schedule where necessary.
    Immediately communicate to the project

sponsor and other impacted project participants.

Monitor the Business Environment

Business assumptions and forecasts are, to varying degrees, dynamic. Unexpected real-world variance in such areas as interest rates, consumer demand, and competitive strategies may occur at any time during the course of a project. To determine if project redirection or termination is indicated, a process for monitoring these items, that is, measuring their movement against a preestablished acceptable range, is recommended. It is far more economical to terminate a project midstream than to find it obsolete at its completion.

CONCLUSION

Although a project manager's actual use of the techniques discussed will vary with a project's size, duration, and number of participant groups, each technique discussed is potentially applicable to every project. Early consideration of the issues these techniques address will often highlight the need for additional research to clarify a project's goals, benefits, exposures, participants, acceptance criteria, and management approach. This discipline can also identify and terminate requests for projects with insufficient justification or unavailable resources.

In closing, we wish to emphasize that successful project management requires a generous blend of tools, techniques, and, perhaps most importantly, participant commitment. A project manager's leadership skills training, enthusiasm, personal character, and attention to detail can inspire the achievement of extraordinary project successes.

THE ORGANIZATION OF THE FUTURE

John J. Hampton, Principal, Princeton Consulting Group, Inc.

TRENDS OF CHANGE

Management is changing in fundamental ways that will markedly influence businesses, nonprofit corporations, and government agencies. The changes are quite fundamental and even remarkable, fueled as they are by knowledge, technology, and a world of declining resources.

Organizations of the future will be influenced by demographic, economic, and technological trends affecting the society overall. These include:

- *An information society*—Power once came from labor, capital, and natural resources. Increasingly, power will come from information.
- *Decline of middle management*—A corollary to the technological and information revolution is a decrease in the numbers of people and importance of middle management. Many of the tasks will be replaced by computers and technology.
- *Diversity in the work force*—A mobile and global economy and the laws of comparative advantage will produce a labor pool with a variety of native languages, cultures, and value systems.
- *Intuitive decision making*—The complexity of the world and information explosion will overcome the processing capa-

bility of a person's mind. The sequential reasoning that dominated business schools in the 1960s through 1980s will be joined by increasing reliance on intuition in the decision-making process.

Change in Organizational Resources

As a result of these social and other changes, we can expect some shifts in the use of resources in the organizations of the future, including:

- *Capital*—Still important, but shortages will have to be made up with better use of capital.
- *Skilled wage earners*—Still important, but the work force will be augmented by skilled contractors.
- *Skilled contractors*—Organizations will increasingly rely on independent contractors, suppliers of components and services, part-time workers, and other nontraditional sources of labor. These individuals will work for fees, not wages. In effect, people will be paid for the accomplishment of tasks, not the spending of time in an organizational setting.
- *Natural resources*—Raw materials will still be valuable but increasingly expen-

sive. The creative use of raw materials will lower their cost and stretch their availability. Waste will not be so easy on a planet with finite resources.

- *Customers*—Control over customers will be an increasingly recognized valuable resource. Sales to strangers will be less important than sales in networked structures of suppliers and customers who are reliable in meeting each other's needs. The importance of networking can already be seen as Western companies build relationships with entities in East Asia. The need for supplier–customer friendships and long-term business linkages is also evident in activities with overseas communities, such as with Poles and Chinese, where expatriates work with family and friends in their home country.
- *Time*—Increasingly, organizations will recognize that time is a limited resource for their most talented people. Time will have to be managed with the same care as money and information.

Decline of Middle Management

The career field for most corporate professional employees fifty years ago was middle management. Two factors will eliminate much of this area:

1. *Computers will manage tasks.* Many of the middle management reporting, investigating, coordinating, and controlling tasks are now automated.
2. *Self-management will replace organizational control.* We can expect managers to spend less time managing people's time and activities. Skilled and knowledgeable people, it may be argued, can manage themselves. The organization will still need to judge performance. The evaluation process will continue to shift toward results and away from activities.

Decline of the Bureaucracy

Even large organizations will no longer attempt to organize themselves on the model of the bureaucracy. They will increasingly be characterized by:

- *Small teams*—Research shows that a group of individuals working together produces both the highest level of motivation and also the highest level of productivity. These findings support a view that results are best obtained when peers also provide friendship, recognition, social interaction, support, and cooperation.
- *Cross-disciplinary skills*—Bureaucracies tend to encourage compartmentalization and specialization. Organizations of the future will increasingly need teams of individuals whose skills cross structural and disciplinary lines.
- *Autonomous units*—The bureaucracy works with functional responsibility for problem solving. Personnel problems are viewed as the domain of the human resources division. Inadequate sales are the fault of the marketing division. We now know that such divisions do not achieve the best results. Low sales may result from inadequate planning, poor product design, poor marketing, or failure to provide follow-up service after a sale. In the organization of the future, autonomous units will accept responsibility for a wide variety of problems and handle them. Outside help, as needed, will be sought on a contract basis.
- *Informal structure*—People in large organizations already know that the informal structure of alliances, cooperative agreements, and partnerships make the place run. The organization of the future is likely to recognize this situation openly. This means a flattening of the hierarchical structure or eliminating it completely.

ANTIBUREAUCRACY BEHAVIORS

Managers can influence the speed of moving toward the organization of the future by undertaking a number of on-the-job behaviors, such as:

- *Encouraging departments to become friends before coordinating their efforts.* Managers can encourage personal relations across unit boundaries. This encourages people to work together because they care about each other. It is much easier to achieve organizational goals when the different units in the organization facilitate each other's efforts to be successful.
- *Decentralizing decision making totally.* Decisions need to be made at the level where information is available to properly trained and motivated employees. The trend in management has been to move decisions to lower levels where this situation exists. New technology will accelerate this trend further, particularly since we know that decentralization also encourages people to empower themselves.
- *Requiring self-management.* Governance is the process of determining the goals and values of an organization. Management is the task of achieving the goals and fulfilling the values. Top managers increasingly are performing more governance than management functions. Teams can set their own objectives, make their own plans, set their own priorities, and manage their own workloads. Technology allows higher management levels to monitor their results and step in only as needed. Such largely self-managed activity encourages people to be responsible for their own actions and allows them to see their own results.
- *Performing two-way evaluations.* Set up a system so superiors evaluate subordinates and vice versa. This encourages people to recognize that everybody is accountable to everybody else and all roles must be performed both to achieve goals and build teams.

RECRUITING AND RETAINING HIGH-QUALITY WORKERS

In the organization of the future, managers must deal with a different work environment. Some lessons will be particularly important to recruit and retain the best people:

1. *Manager as a coach*—The hierarchical manager cannot exist in a five-star organization. The best people want to work for and with other individuals who have the skills of the effective coach, teacher, or mentor. They neither want nor need a "boss."
2. *Entrepreneurship*—Individuals seek the freedom to fail. An entrepreneurial spirit must exist.
3. *Ownership*—Individuals need to feel that they "own" a piece of the business. Ownership can be actual, as with stock, or psychic.
4. *Networking*—Individuals need the emotional rewards of working with other talented people. Department lines are unimportant. Working in a large web of caring co-workers is important.
5. *Personal growth*—Individuals grow both professionally and personally over their working careers. Organizations must have programs to support both kinds of development.

POWER SHIFT

Power is the ability to make things happen, even though other parties may not agree with the actions being taken. It is a particularly important concept because the nature of power is changing. Essentially, there are three sources of power in all kinds of organizations.

1. *Punishment*—The ability to punish is one source of power. Violence has been seen in strikes by workers, firing whistle-blowers by management, and filing lawsuits against competitors. Milder punishments consist of denying people pay increases and promotions. Such behavior is the least useful form

of power as it lacks flexibility. It can only be negatively used.

2. *Capital*—This is the second source of power in organizations. Capital was the primary source of power for industrial organizations for several centuries. It allowed companies to enter businesses and to keep others out of them. Capital is more useful than violence as it can be used positively as well as negatively.

3. *Knowledge*—Knowledge is the most useful source of power as it can be used to reward, punish, or change the organization. It also is the key to the optimal use of capital.

Bureaucracies have used punishment and capital as their primary sources of power. The organization of the future will use knowledge. *Powershift* (from *Powershift*, Alvin Toffler, Bantam Books, 1990) is a term that describes knowledge replacing violence and capital as the primary source of power in organizations. In this context, we should note that knowledge does not have the same meaning as data or information:

- *Data*—unconnected facts. Data are created by both internal systems and external databases. Modern organizations are virtually buried in data.
- *Information*—data that have been categorized or classified. Creating information has traditionally been the task of middle management. It is also the task of consultants, information services, trade associations, and other external organizations. As with data, modern organizations are virtually buried in information.
- *Knowledge*—information that has been further refined into a tool that can be used to create power. Some organizations make extensive use of knowledge. Some do not.

PROBLEM SOLVING IN BUREAUCRACIES

Bureaucracies solve problems and respond to opportunities in their own way. A convenient, if somewhat tongue-in-cheek, approach to understanding bureaucracies uses the following terms:

- *Cubbyhole*—an administrative unit of a bureaucracy.
- *Specialist*—the person who works in a cubbyhole.
- *Channel*—the place through which information flows in a bureaucracy.
- *Manager*—the person who controls the bureaucratic channel.
- *Problem or opportunity*—any situation that must be dealt with by specialists or managers in a bureaucracy. Problems or opportunities are assigned to cubbyholes for specialized knowledge and given to managers for movement in channels. Information moves back and forth from one cubbyhole to another using information channels.

KNOWLEDGE POWER STRUCTURE IN BUREAUCRACIES

The knowledge power structure in bureaucracies is under attack on all fronts:

1. The cubbyholes and channels of bureaucracies are overwhelmed by data.

2. Specialists cannot handle the fragmented data in their cubbyholes.

3. Managers cannot move the volume of information in their channels.

4. Networks of knowledge are transcending the bureaucratic system. These networks are computerized systems for rapidly and accurately gathering data, creating knowledge, and moving knowledge to wherever it is needed. An example is the chief executive officer who communicates directly with a subordinate many miles and levels away, using electronic linkages. Another example is the manager whose direct access electronically to corporate databases eliminates the need for information from the accounting department. Still another example is the specialist who can access external or internal computerized marketing research data without contacting the party who collected it.

KNOWLEDGE IN ORGANIZATIONS OF THE FUTURE

The bureaucratic model for managing data will not be carried forward into the organization of the future. Bureaucracies are notoriously slow in gathering and using knowledge, the most powerful source of power. Also, competition requires rapid and accurate responses to knowledge.

The way we organize knowledge will affect the way bureaucracies must be organized in the future. Otherwise, they will not compete effectively. Networks of knowledge will replace cubbyholes and channels as the primary organizational mode for bureaucracies in the future. This has an implication for the specialist in the cubbyhole. The specialist must be integrated into the network of knowledge. This also has an implication for the manager who gathers information and passes it through channels. The implication is unemployment.

CONCLUSION

Managers of the future must prepare to live in the organization of the future. If knowledge is to be the primary power source for organizations of the future, five-star organizations will emphasize the acquisition and use of knowledge. If cubbyholes and channels are obsolete, the successful organization will not be organized around them. If managers prepare for the changing managerial world, they are likely to survive and even prosper in the successful organizations of the future.

Marketing

Noel Capon, Section Editor

Introduction   *Noel Capon*   2-3

The Marketing-Oriented Firm   *James M. Hulbert*   2-5

The Tasks of Marketing Management   *Noel Capon*   2-12

The Product Life Cycle   *Noel Capon*   2-18

Strategic Marketing Planning Processes   *George S. Day*   2-25

Strategic Marketing Planning Tools   *Peter T. FitzRoy*   2-34

The Annual Marketing Plan   *Russell S. Winer*   2-42

Marketing Research   *Donald R. Lehmann*   2-48

Customer Decision Making   *Paul W. Miniard*   2-55

Corporate Marketing   *W. Sanford Miller, Jr.*   2-61

Marketing and Quality   *Donna L. Hoffmann and Jan-Benedict
    E. M. Steenkamp*   2-65

Developing New Products   *Thomas D. Kuczmarski*   2-69

Competitive New Product Strategies   *Gregory S. Carpenter and
    Kent Nakamoto*   2-77

Profitable Pricing   *Thomas T. Nagle and Reed K. Holden*   2-80

Auditing the Marketing Function   *William H. Rodgers,*
   Gerard A. Osborne, and Philip Kotler   2-86

Legal Imperatives for Marketing Decisions   *Ray O. Werner*   2-94

Industrial Marketing   *V. Kasturi Rangan and Bruce Isaacson*   2-101

Advertising and Mass Communications   *Bernd H. Schmitt*   2-108

Direct Marketing   *Marjorie Kalter and Elizabeth Stearns*   2-116

INTRODUCTION

Noel Capon

Regardless of whether their underlying purpose is to make profits (business firms) or to fulfill some social goal (public and not-for-profit organizations), the major task of all organizations is to create and re-create customers. Customers are truly organization assets and should be treated as such. Quite simply, organizations that fail to generate customers should not, do not, and will not survive.

Regardless of an organization member's specific function or position, serving customers is everyone's job. Such a customer, outward, or marketing orientation, however, exists only in those organizations where true customer-focused leadership is driven from the top of the organization chart and desire for serving customers with quality offers becomes a passion.

In most organizations, the major responsibility for ensuring that the organization identifies and serves its customers belongs to a marketing group or department associated with a particular line of business. If a marketing group does not exist, or is in a fledgling state of development, a corporate marketing organization can play an important role in developing line marketing skills, ensuring that the core tasks of marketing management are rigorously addressed, and imbuing the organization with a customer-driven orientation. Regardless of the specific organizational location of marketing, an independently conducted marketing audit is a useful device for assessing the degree to which marketing efforts are on target.

As the twentieth century draws to a close, the environment faced by most organizations is increasingly complex, fast changing, and global in scope. Whether we consider economic, legal, technological, social, political, or other environmental imperatives, the organization's ability to understand and predict environmental shocks and changes is ever more important. All organizations should develop a market-driven strategic planning process that is well grounded in a comprehensive set of strategic planning tools and concepts. Strategic marketing decisions, based in part on the organization's history, mission, strengths, and weaknesses, should be informed by a comprehensive understanding of marketplace realities and available opportunities and threats. In particular, the organization should acquire a thorough understanding of the developing competitive structure, key competitor strategies, and the decision-making practices of its customers; insightful marketing research is critical in this regard.

These strategic decisions, which together form a resource allocation plan for the organization as a whole, must be translated into a set of objectives and competitive marketing strategies. The annual marketing plan is the mechanism through which strategic decisions are translated into organization actions in the operating period.

The departure point for developing marketing strategy is the identification of market opportunities that seem attractive to the organization and the creative segmentation of those markets. The organization selects those segments it wishes to address, targets customers and competitors, and develops a core strategy or competitive differential advantage designed to deliver value to, and secure appropriate behavior (typically purchase or recommendation to purchase) from, customers in the face of competitive market offers. Marketing strategy is implemented through a series of action programs, frequently termed the marketing mix—product, service, price, promotion, and distribution. (We defer discussion of promotion and distribution issues to Section 3.)

An especially important implication of the fast-changing business environment is the shortening of product life cycles. Never before has the ability to produce well-designed new products at appropriate quality and cost levels been so important. In order to satisfy targeted customers' needs, the organization must develop and manage a system for developing and/or acquiring new products and services, and disposing of obsolete items in the product line. Products must thus be managed throughout their life cycles, but marketing managers must pay particular attention to developing solid competitive strategies at the critical juncture when new products are introduced.

In this section we pay special attention to pricing issues because of the huge leverage on profits from relatively small price changes. Marketers must make decisions on pricing their products and services in the context of an overall market strategy. However, rather than focus pricing strategy on costs, market-driven organizations focus on value received by customers from buying and using their products and services.

Whereas marketing concepts generalize well across many domains of marketing practice, there are, nonetheless, many domain-specific issues. Thus, the fields of industrial marketing, services marketing, and public and nonprofit marketing deserve special attention because of their unique circumstances. Finally, as the result of the postwar economic wealth of the United States, many marketers think in terms of U.S. markets. Operating abroad and especially globally requires a new frame of reference with which to deal with a new set of marketing problems.

These issues and many more are addressed in this section and related sections. The authors are an international group of leaders in their respective areas of marketing. Some are practicing businesspeople; more are business school faculty, leaders in teaching and research who daily work with marketing professionals in dealing with the tough challenges of the 1990s. The chapters comprise some of the best in practical marketing thinking. For those executives whose job responsibilities involve the tasks of creating and re-creating customers, the insight provided in this section cannot be ignored.

Cross-references: *Global Marketing,* F. L. Simon and D. E. Sexton, Section 14; *Public and Nonprofit Marketing,* C. H. Lovelock and C. B. Weinberg, Section 16; *Services Marketing,* S. W. Brown and M. J. Bitner, Section 15.

Noel Capon, Ph.D., *is Professor of Business at Columbia Business School. His teaching and research interests are in the areas of strategy and planning, and sales force management. Recipient of teaching excellence awards, Professor Capon directs several of Columbia's marketing and sales management executive programs. He is coauthor of* Corporate Strategic Planning, *a study of planning practices in major U.S. manufacturing corporations.*

THE MARKETING-ORIENTED FIRM

James M. Hulbert, R. C. Kopf Professor of International Marketing, Columbia Business School, Columbia University

THE MARKETING CONCEPT

Origins of the marketing orientation are rooted in the evolution of developed economies. When the industrial revolution began, living standards were low and markets were characterized by scarcity. The output of preindustrial artisans was severely limited in quantity and priced too high for most of the population. However, many entrepreneurs easily found markets for their mass-produced wares among those who previously could not afford such goods. Raw materials, capital, technology, and labor were viewed as scarce resources, critical to business success. Customers were not.

The turning point in business thinking is variously viewed as the 1930s depression or the post-World War II period, but certainly by the late fifties many companies were awakening to the central importance of customers. Then, large companies first established marketing departments. What led to this change and the increasingly elaborate explanations of the marketing concept or marketing orientation? Simply put, as living standards improved with economic growth, an increasing proportion of consumers' budgets became discretionary. As basic needs for food, shelter, clothing, and health care were better met, a growing portion of purchasing power was subject to consumer whim and volition. Firms grew only if they could tempt customers to spend money.

This recognition led to attempts to articulate a coherent philosophy of company goals and objectives. For example, Robert Keith, president of Pillsbury, stated that his company's purpose was to satisfy the needs and desires, actual and potential, of its customers. Perhaps Peter Drucker put it most succinctly: "There is only one valid definition of business purpose: to create a customer."

To managers experienced with the marketing concept, these insights seem unremarkable. To others, they often seem dramatic if not threatening in their implications. Most people working in smaller firms—owners, managers, or employees—are well aware that business ceases if customers stop buying. Yet, as firms grow, activities become more differentiated; specialization increases and over time a higher proportion of jobs become remote from any customer interface. A major challenge for marketing and general management in larger organizations is to communicate and gain acceptance of the marketing concept among all employees.

One of marketing's paradoxes is that an idea seen as central to business success in the 1960s seemed to disappear from senior management agendas in the 1970s and for much of the 1980s. In many instances, CEOs (chief executive officers) delegated development of marketing to others. Early on, many charged with this responsibility came from sales, in other cases from advertising. Marketing changed from a concept to a department via the addition of activities under the marketing umbrella. These activities might be restricted to advertising and promotion, or might include packaging, product design, new venture development (product and market), pricing, logistics, public relations, and, in some cases, even sales. Thus, marketing, *the concept*, grew via the addition of activities to marketing, *the department or function.* Yet something was lost in the process; marketing issues, ultimately, cannot be resolved by delegation. The same phenomenon that spawned technical expertise and sophistication in marketing the function also sowed the seeds of great difficulty. The very centrality of functional marketing spells its ultimate doom.

What must a company do to create and retain customers? Simply, it must satisfy their needs better than competitors and continue to do so on a sustained basis. Satisfying needs involves innovation as well as operations, communications as well as delivery, service as well as billing and collection. When a firm sets out to create a customer, it promises certain things. To turn a prospective customer into an actual customer, it must deliver on its promises. To keep customers, it must continue to do so. Over the long term, it must do all of the above better than competitors, at least in the eyes of targeted customers. If keeping customers is the central task in ensuring firm survival, it is also a necessary (if not sufficient) task for earning profits.

Moreover, the marketing function does not manage and control the performance of all tasks necessary to keep customer promises, nor should it. But failure in just one task breaks a promise to a customer that jeopar-

dizes the firm's ability to retain that customer. Thus, embracing the marketing concept must take place throughout the firm, not just in the marketing department. This is, and always was, the central message of the marketing concept. Why was it forgotten for so long? Largely because other problems preoccupied management. The 1970s brought floating exchange rates, energy price increases, high inflation, stagnating real incomes, and major labor force shifts. The 1980s began with recession, saw very high real interest rates, significant deregulation, and unprecedented restructuring of companies and of whole industries. Marketing departments added to the difficulty. As they grew in size, power, and influence, they often generated resentment not just in production, operations, and finance but even in sales. Further, marketers sometimes contributed by maintaining the myth that a firm's marketing problems could be solved by marketing alone!

In the mid-1980s came the realization in a few firms that marketing was not for the few but must be for the many. This now fast emerging awareness (e.g., customer driven, customer oriented) owes less to marketing professionals than to economic necessity. The heightened competitive intensity of the 1980s is continuing in the 1990s. Deregulation, technology development, economic development, and globalization of markets all combine to create greater choices for customers.

One consequence of increased competition is that the perception that customers are a scarce resource is penetrating the consciousness of even slow-learning firms. Putting customers first is not a new idea, but some firms are acting on these precepts for the first time. That customer orientation is a task in which all must be engaged is a new idea for many firms. Its acceptance has been facilitated by widespread acceptance of the total quality concept.

Increased competitiveness has also been responsible for the shift to total quality. Embracing the views of such pioneers as W. Edwards Deming and Joseph Juran, senior managers have sensitized whole organizations to the tasks involved in satisfying customers. The relative success of this movement in advancing the organization-wide concept of marketing is evidence that dominance of a functional view impeded acceptance of marketing as a concept. In adopting an organization-wide perspective, Deming and his ilk formulated more complete and effective strategies for engineering the necessary organizational changes than marketing ever did.

Paradoxically, marketing's preoccupation with customers may have been an obstacle to broader acceptance of the marketing concept. Not until competitive pressures were almost overwhelming did firms take a comprehensive view of the effectiveness of the total business system in meeting customer requirements. Even today, only a few are actively remaking themselves. We believe that firms that do not make a full-fledged commitment to the marketing orientation will increasingly find survival at risk. The bold fact that between 1980 and 1990, 46 percent of the Fortune 500 lost their independent existence should cause all senior executives more than a moment's sober contemplation.

MARKETING DECISIONS

The marketing orientation is a concept or philosophy, but to have impact it must affect management decisions, management style and, ultimately, employee behavior.

Pricing

Pricing approaches in marketing-oriented firms are very different from otherwise-oriented competitors. In marketing-oriented firms, cost plays only a supporting role in pricing; in all other cases it plays a dominant, if not exclusive, role.

In marketing-oriented firms, perceived value to customers determines the upper bound on willingness to pay. Cost plays no role in such perceptions, but marketing communications, for example, may play the major role. Pricing is an exercise in sharing the value inherent in the offer, as seen by the customer. The customer's perception of value sets the upper bound, but prices are rarely established at this level. Decisions on value sharing with customers are critically important strategic decisions; they must consider firm objectives,

competitors' objectives, customer requirements, and relevant cost structures. This approach to pricing should be reflected in resource allocation, including staffing. In marketing-oriented firms, we expect to find significant monies and persons devoted to measuring customer value—perceived and economic—delivered by the firm and competitors. Compare the scale of the company's efforts in measuring and managing costs with the efforts to measure and manage value delivered to customers—the results are usually very striking!

Customer Service

In marketing-oriented firms, customer service is a key means of customer retention and competitive advantage. Catalogue merchandisers such as Lands' End and L. L. Bean are firms for which customer service is central; for others (e.g., American Express, Marriott, Federal Express, Nordstroms') it is a key strategic element. In these firms, significant effort is directed to specialized human resource management systems (e.g., selection, training, motivation, recognition, and reward of customer service personnel). Likewise, significant infrastructure investment supports personal service effort, particularly in information systems. In other firms, customer service is a low-status, poorly staffed activity, reporting at low level with no recognition of its potentially crucial role.

Marked Differences

Marked differences in practice also occur in new product development. Marketing-oriented firms demonstrate that innovation is vital to long-term profitable relationships by their sense of urgency, organization structures, and management practices (including budgets!). Innovation is a broader issue than new product development, but the latter is the most crucial aspect. There is substantial evidence that firms that innovate early, and well, earn and retain marketing leadership. In most industries certain companies have preempted this role and use it to advantage. Compaq owes its existence to such strategies, and such firms as Kellogg (cereals) and Dupont (chemicals) have pursued such strategies successfully for decades.

Product Quality and Liability

Quality and liability may seem curious areas to group together, but when quality problems occur, firm values are demonstrated most clearly. Not long ago, companies knowingly produced and shipped defective products to customers, taking a legalistic view of obligations, caveat emptor. Today, both good management and the law demand more thoughtful approaches. Johnson and Johnson's exemplary handling of the Tylenol poisoning incidents (1986) is a textbook example of a marketing-oriented firm in action. Firestone's actions with the "500" radial tire problems (1976), and Audi's more recent (1990) faux pas regarding automatic transmissions are striking counterexamples. Johnson and Johnson treated their customers as assets in the fullest sense of the word.

Marketing Expenditures

The money spent for marketing illustrates whether the firm operates with a marketing orientation. Contrast your firm's R&D and market research spending. We do not need equality, but order of magnitude differences—which are not uncommon—should be questioned, especially when new product failures are more commonly customer- or competitor-related than technical in origin.

In recession, attitudes to customers are typically revealed in swathing cuts in advertising, selling, and even customer service. The resulting reductions in perceived customer value usually accentuate downward price pressures experienced in recession, as well as inhibiting the firm's ability to generate customers and orders when most needed. Unsurprisingly, marketing-oriented firms often gain share in recession.

Publications and Information Services

This is another important area. Try it yourself! Call a company and ask for product or service information. Note how you are treated on the phone and the time it takes to receive the information. Examine what you receive. Is it written for customers or for engineers or lawyers? Judge the brochure's quality; what is subtly communicated about the company's feeling toward you, the customer. Some companies understand that providing information is a key prepurchase service activity; others do not seem to understand this relationship to sales revenue. Since information requests typically come from prospects, because existing customers often have information, anything less than a first-class response is doubly unfortunate.

Also examine advertising. Good advertising has continuity of theme, builds ongoing customer relationships, communicates key benefits clearly, and permits easy identification of brand or company. Some advertising copy is so poor that it seems a thoughtful review could not possibly have occurred.

Planning Systems

Many large companies do not have planning systems; they have overly elaborate, glorified budgeting systems, often based heavily on projections. Budgets are not strategies: exclusive focus on budgets is detrimental to profits—it can lead to premature death!

The basic premise of planning is that if managers spend time thinking about future market conditions they should make better decisions on how to deal with them. In strategic planning, this kind of external analysis must be reemphasized. From situation analyses, firms should be able to devise better strategies and, in turn, be better able to forecast and budget. By neglecting the situation analysis and strategy formulation elements of the planning process, budget-oriented planners not only operate in strategic vacua but they probably have greater deviations in performance versus plan.

Information Systems

In some firms, the information system is primarily a control mechanism. In marketing-oriented companies, information about markets, customers, and competitors is more readily and widely available. Market research is collected more frequently, with relatively higher proportions of primary compared to secondary research.

However, information differences go far beyond market information. Accounting systems permit better identification of true direct costs, and should provide information on segment and customer profitability. Because of systemic limitations, many companies cannot even aggregate revenues by customer across product lines, let alone calculate gross margins. Ideally, firms should be able to measure net margin for all direct customers, by customer or segment. For large direct customers (or customer segments), capital productivity measures can compare and monitor customer relationships. More sophisticated marketing companies use data-based marketing to identify and track secondary (indirect) customers (including final consumers) and in some cases communicate and market to them via direct marketing techniques.

Beyond market and financial information support for decision making, sophisticated information systems are a key means to secure competitive advantage for some firms. For example, American Airlines clearly views information systems as a value-adding activity. The Sabre reservations system was followed by mileage programs, sophisticated yield management models, and other developments that reinforced its leadership position. Electronic data interchange (EDI) has developed to the point where some suppliers and customers are embedded in sophisticated electronic relationships with enormous benefits to both parties.

Customer Orientation

To develop a business system or company focused around customers, charity must begin at home. Exhorting employees to treat customers well is unlikely to succeed if employees themselves are treated poorly. A focus on meeting external customers' needs and wants fails if internal customers' needs and wants are ignored. This level of marketing orientation demands significant change in management priorities with an emphasis on teamwork and participation; a task-focused organization; a positive attitude toward learning and change; a reward structure rec-

ognizing good performance, yet perceived as equitable; an open interface with customers; in short, an organization that operates along nontraditional lines. The 1980s successful turnaround of British Airways was largely attributable to this kind of cultural engineering, accompanied by significant changes in marketing. The task is difficult, not least because of changes required in middle managers. Jack Welch, CEO of General Electric, said: "Middle Managers can be the stronghold of the organization. But their jobs have to be redefined. They have to see their roles as combination teacher, cheerleader, and liberator—not controller."

IMPLICATIONS FOR OTHER FUNCTIONS

To focus the entire organization on creating and re-creating customers—the original marketing concept—significant changes must occur in several functional areas.

Human Resources

To create a whole organization operating according to the marketing concept affects every traditional area of human resource management. In recruitment and selection, training and development, appraisal and reward, emphasis on the values and beliefs discussed here is required. In addition, specialist human resources skills are needed, since engineering major customer-focused cultural change in large firms is a difficult and complex task.

Sales

In the sales function, a customer-focused principle is unlikely to be questioned, but practice may be different. Senior sales executives in marketing-oriented firms increasingly view customers as assets to be developed, not exploited. They appreciate the difference between transactions and relationships, and are keenly aware that properly nurtured sales relationships improve both volume and bottom line for suppliers and customers alike. Short-term-oriented selling is the antithesis of the marketing concept; managers must be vigilant to ensure that sales compensation systems, sales objectives, and sales budgets do not operate against the firm's longer-term interests. Increasingly, the longer-term view is fostered by mutual dependency evident in increased seller and buyer concentration.

Manufacturing and/or Operations

Operations has seen enormous change in the 1980s, much distinctly helpful for implementing the marketing concept. Total quality management (TQM) has had substantial impact: it is a useful counterweight to traditional cost-minimization concepts that often lead to product quality problems, missed or late deliveries, and so forth. Comprehensive commitment to TQM has probably been the most successful culture change example in large firms. In several large companies the executive and team responsible for evolving the TQM shift has responsibility for focusing on customer orientation as well.

However, the revolution in manufacturing and operations is ongoing. Time-based competition is driving major changes in product design and manufacturing processes, and also facilities design. Faster product innovation and recognition of competitive advantage offered by rapid delivery and product variety are leading to broader acceptance of a market-driven need for flexible manufacturing and commensurate changes in manufacturing strategy. The previously existing vast gap between manufacturing and marketing is easing in some firms as operations managers put these new concepts to work.

Research and Development

People in this area often complain that marketing thinks too short term to provide good market-based guidance. Marketing typically counters that R&D moves too slowly, or that the firm's R&D efforts are cost ineffective. In marketing-oriented firms we still expect differences in perspective between marketing and R&D. However, the firm's policies and procedures should reflect the central need for mutual cooperation for effective innovation. Top management support and leadership are key for improving marketing and R&D cooperation, but are not enough. Successful innovators are systematically different from competitors in many ways: notably, the most innovative companies harness the power of teamwork in new product development. Adopting team-based, parallel development approaches is not simple, but pays great dividends for firms mastering them. Specific techniques, such as quality function development (QFD) and programs of customer visits, can help bridge the customer/technology gap, but careful attention to management processes and power and status relationships among team members is also vital.

Finance and Accounting

With appropriate measurement systems in place, finance and marketing can have more productive dialogues about customers as assets in which the true economics of decisions can be addressed. As companies segment markets more finely, develop more varied and individualized products and services, and actively manage individual customer relationships, the need for precise yet flexible financial analysis increases. For sophisticated practitioners of the marketing orientation, financial analysts are now part of the business team, sometimes attached to the marketing area. Much better-integrated decisions about the business result.

Few companies have yet realized the full benefits of analysis and model building for improved marketing decision making. It is an economic paradox that in some companies expenses of a few thousand dollars must be documented and justified because they are "capital expenditures," whereas advertising expenditures of several million dollars are routinely approved with little effort devoted to preassessing or postmeasuring economic effectiveness. Since true economics are based on cash flow analysis rather than arbitrary classification, this should not continue. Some companies, such as Colgate-Palmolive, have established a marketing effectiveness audit group to deal with these issues.

Among accountants there is currently considerable turmoil based on belated recognition of weaknesses in traditional standard costing systems, the need to better estimate direct costs and avoid arbitrary allocation of overhead. In too many companies, accounting systems violate many accepted principles of good management accounting. Marketing-oriented firms need the "right" information. Responsibility reporting procedures, variable budget income statements, and ready availability of key financial data are hallmarks of the right approach. In light of our earlier discussion on internal customers, if company accountants treated managers in a "management" accounting system as customers, the results might be particularly beneficial.

THE FUTURE FOR MARKETING

Why are so many major companies so far from truly implementing a marketing orientation? The answer lies in the extreme difficulty of changing corporate cultures in large firms. Major change takes time, requires great dedication, threatens existing assumptions and power bases, and perhaps requires a new type of leadership. Few senior managements have invested the time and effort to master the skills required, and none has all the answers to making change on the nature and scale we have discussed.

How many of today's large companies will successfully manage the transitions and transformations that lie ahead? To survive in the 1990s without mastery of marketing will prove increasingly difficult. Just as many large companies disappeared in the 1980s, more will go in the 1990s. In those firms that survive, however, the longer-term future of marketing raises one particularly intriguing question.

To implement fully the marketing concept requires the marketing orientation to spread through the entire organization, so that marketing is not viewed as solely a functional responsibility. Yet, if the whole firm is geared to creation and retention of customers, what need is there for a separate marketing department? Since marketing is typically a staff department, might it not be both more effective and efficient to imbue all line managers with marketing concepts and skills?

There is tentative evidence for a withering away of the functional view of marketing. Many firms now require business unit managers to have marketing experience; others require direct and more frequent exposure to customers for all functions and levels. Although we probably will not see the demise of functional marketing, continued evolution of the marketing function is likely in the future.

THE TASKS OF MARKETING MANAGEMENT

Noel Capon, Professor of Business, Graduate School of Business, Columbia University

If we were to survey marketing departments, we would find the personnel engaged in an enormous range of activities including gathering customer and competitive information, designing new products, developing advertising and direct mail brochures, and preparing advice for the sales force.

Of these and many more activities we must ask: Which are critical? What are the tasks that marketing management *must* perform for marketing to fulfill its proper role in the organization? Certainly, if a new marketing department were created where previously there was none, its members would find things to do. The pressures of organizational life deriving from role expectations of those in other parts of the organization are typically sufficient to keep people busy. But being busy with activities is no substitute for spending effort on those things that truly make a difference in the long run.

The purpose of this chapter is to identify those tasks that are essential for the ongoing health of the organization—the tasks that *must* be performed. They are:

- *Core Task 1*—Advise senior management which markets to address, where (geographically), and which products to offer.
- *Core Task 2*—In the chosen markets, identify and target market segments.

- *Core Task 3*—In the chosen market segments, identify and select customer targets.
- *Core Task 4*—Design the marketing offer: the product/package/service benefit, price mix, and communications mix for chosen customer targets in the target market segments.
- *Core Task 5*—Secure support from other functions in the organization.
- *Core Task 6*—Monitor and control appropriate execution and performance.

These core tasks must be performed in a coordinated manner. Typically, responsibility rests with a department titled marketing, but on occasion certain tasks or task elements may be performed elsewhere in the organization.

CORE TASK 1: ADVISE SENIOR MANAGEMENT WHICH MARKETS TO ADDRESS, WHERE (GEOGRAPHICALLY), AND WHICH PRODUCTS TO OFFER

A key task of the organization's senior management is to define the firm's mission, determine its geographic scope, and construct its portfolio of businesses—those product/markets in which it will compete. Three key questions comprise the firm's portfolio decisions:

1. Which of the current businesses should continue to receive investment?
2. From which businesses should the firm withdraw?
3. Which new businesses should be added?

There are important subsidiary questions. *For continuing businesses:* How much should be invested? What type of investments should be made? When should the investments occur? *For withdraw businesses:* When should withdrawal occur? How should withdrawal be accomplished? *For new businesses:* When should entry take place? Should the entry be de novo, by acquisition, or through a strategic alliance? Who should be acquired or who should be a partner?

The environment faced by organizations is increasingly turbulent. It is therefore likely that historically profitable businesses will no longer continue to be so. By the same token, environmental turbulence will create a host of new opportunities; some may be profitable for the firm to exploit, others may not! Reduced profitability from existing businesses and newly available opportunities will lead to substantial churning of firms' business portfolios in the years ahead.

Of course, the issues involved in portfolio realignment go far beyond marketing concerns; they include critical matters of strategic direction for the enterprise, financial management, human resources, operations, organizational culture, and the like. Nevertheless, marketing issues are involved and marketing has a responsibility to inject itself in this strategic decision-making process.

Of critical concern are decisions involving new businesses; here there are explicit issues concerning markets and products new to the firm. Marketing must play two key roles:

1. *Identification of opportunities*—Marketing is the one function of the organization with explicit responsibility to identify new areas of opportunity and, following appropriate in-

formation gathering and analysis, to bring these opportunities to the attention of top management. Typically, opportunities fall within the scope of the firm's mission but, since mission redefinition should take place periodically, opportunities outside the formal mission should not be automatically discarded.

Example: Banc One was for many years a consumer-oriented bank in Ohio. It was an early licensee of Bank Americard (later VISA) from Bank of America and developed a processing capability for credit slips. Banc One realized that as other banks also became licensees there was a market opportunity to become a third-party processor for these banks. As a result, processing for banks nationwide has for several years been an important profit center for Banc One.

2. *Advice on proposed strategic actions*—Marketing has an advisory role to play regarding decisions on proposed strategic actions generated by groups other than marketing. Decisions on acquisitions, strategic alliances, divestitures, and market withdrawal all have marketing implications. Few acquisitions achieve the promise anticipated at their consummation. The lack of hard marketing input in these decisions is one important factor in their failures.

Example: The acquisition of Bache Securities by the Prudential Insurance Company anticipated several marketing synergies, notably in sales effort. Insurance agents were expected to sell securities products to their clients; securities brokers to sell insurance products to their clients. Reports suggest that neither of these synergies has been realized.

CORE TASK 2: IDENTIFY AND TARGET MARKET SEGMENTS IN CHOSEN MARKETS

Market segmentation embraces three interrelated notions:

1. *Process of market segmentation* — the process of grouping actual and potential customers in a market for the purpose of selecting targets for effort and de-

signing marketing programs for them.

2. *Nature of market segments* — an identifiable group of current or potential customers who seek similar sets of benefits with similar levels of priority.
3. *Target market segments*—market segments for which the firm has decided to allocate effort.

Whereas many firms understand that market segmentation has a role to play in the marketing effort, often market segments are developed without a clear conviction of their crucial strategic importance in selecting the firm's battleground. For example, segmentation may just be a continuation of past practice based on the availability of data, may be driven by the firm's current organization, or may be based on the way competitors segment the market.

Market segmentation should proceed from a recognition that in any product category the needs and wants of current and potential customers are heterogeneous; they seek a variety of different benefits with different orders of priority. The segmentation task is to develop subgroups (segments) of customers with relatively homogeneous needs and wants. This task requires a high degree of conceptual skill, based on both creative insight and analysis of market research data.

To be useful for developing marketing strategy, each segment must be identified. Typical distinguishing characteristics are *demographic* (e.g., consumers: age, sex, income, language, wealth; organizations: industry, firm size, growth, ownership type); *behavior patterns* (e.g., usage, decision-making practices, decision-making unit); *social/psychological* (e.g., personality, lifestyle).

The number of market segments to form is a trade-off. More segments imply greater homogeneity of needs and wants per segment, more precise tailoring of market offers, and better customer need satisfaction; however, more segments also typically imply greater costs. The choice of market segments to target depends on segment sizes and anticipated growth; the level of resources available

to the firm; its current position in various segments; and anticipated actions by competitors. Key questions for the firm to ask of potentially attractive segments are: Can we develop offers that deliver important customer benefits better than competitors? Do we have the appropriate skills and resources to implement these offers? Segments with two "yes" answers warrant serious consideration; otherwise the firm should search further.

Marketing managers must understand that the complexion of customers' needs and wants changes over time. In new product categories, functional benefits typically satisfy previously unmet customer needs. When competitors later provide similar functional benefits, competitive advantage is only achieved by satisfying customers' finer-grained sets of needs. These benefits may be little related to those functional benefits that caused original adoption of the product category.

Example: Ask colleagues the basis on which they will choose an airline the next time they fly from New York to Los Angeles. Typical responses are, the one with the best on-time record; most convenient scheduling; best frequent flyer program; best meals; most leg room. Rarely, for this route, does anyone mention safety. Yet safety is clearly the most important benefit provided by the various competitors.

Why is safety not mentioned? Because it has been taken out of the decision since target consumers believe that all competitors are equivalent in delivering this benefit, regardless of whether this happens to be objectively true.

CORE TASK 3: IDENTIFY AND SELECT CUSTOMER TARGETS IN CHOSEN MARKET SEGMENTS

For any market segment the firm decides to address, three interrelated customer targeting decisions must be made: intermediary levels; organizational roles, and potential customers' current relationships to the firm.

Intermediary Levels

Many product/market situations can be viewed as vertical channel systems. The firm is often at the head of the channel; product flows through the channel via various market participants until end-use customers are reached. Mostly, these market participants fulfill a distributional function (e.g., distributors, retailers); sometimes they fulfill a manufacturing function or an influence function. The firm must decide which types of intermediary to select as customer targets. For example, if a firm introduces a new small consumer-durable product, should it attempt to sell through upscale department stores (e.g., Saks, Marshall Field), moderate-priced department stores (e.g., Sears, J. C. Penney), lower-priced stores (e.g., K-Mart), discount stores, or specialty stores?

The choice of intermediary is crucially dependent on the segment target at the end-use customer; these must be appropriately matched. Thus, Honda successfully built a distribution system of automobile retailers for its low-priced cars. However, when it introduced Acura, it built a totally different distribution system for the very different target segment of consumers. In each case, the distribution system matched the segment of end-user consumers being targeted.

Organizational Roles

The customer targeting decision at intermediary levels identifies several organization types that might be addressed. However, within each of these organization types the key targeting decision involves a choice of organizational role. For a firm targeting manufacturing organizations, should the target role be the chief engineer, manufacturing manager, purchasing agent, or general manager? Should the target within the household be the mother, father, child, or grandparents? Clearly, marketing efforts to appropriately selected intermediaries and end-user customers can fail if customer role targets are badly chosen.

Potential Customers' Current Relationships to the Firm

In a broad sense, there are three sources of increased sales volume. The firm can sell more to existing customers, make sales to competitors' customers, or sell to nonusers in the targeted market segment. In each case, the marketing job is very different. For nonusers, the firm has to convince potential customers of the value of the product form. To steal competitors' customers requires precisely chosen strategies to emphasize firm superiority. To sell more to current customers requires building on the existing reservoir of good feeling for the firm's products.

Typically, the focus early in the product life cycle is on nonusers. As the life cycle matures, the focus on retaining current customers versus stealing competitors' customers depends largely on the strength of the firm's market position. For example, AT&T largely seeks to retain current customers; Sprint and MCI focus on stealing AT&T's customers.

CORE TASK 4: DESIGN THE MARKETING OFFER

Core marketing tasks 2 and 3 deal with the selection of targets for the firm's efforts; core task 4 is focused on the design of marketing offers so that selected targets behave in the desired manner. The ultimate goal of designing marketing offers is for customers to make purchase decisions for the firm's products and services. In addition, the firm may wish to elicit other behaviors from target customer groups. For example, a firm might want brokers actively to sell products, or influencers to make strong recommendations that the product be purchased.

Marketers attempt to secure desired behavior through the design of marketing offers:

1. *Benefits* are delivered by the firm to satisfy customer needs. The manner in which benefits are delivered is designed into the product, the package, its availability, the set of accompanying services, and so forth. The greater the set of benefits, the greater the probability that target customers will behave as required.
2. *Price* represents the cost charged to the customer for behaving in the required manner.

3. *Communication* is the means by which the firm informs and persuades customers that benefits outweigh the price so that required behavior should be forthcoming.

Note the interrelationships between design elements. All things being equal, the greater the level of delivered benefits, the greater price the firm can charge. Furthermore, communication may provide benefits through reassurance and status; price may carry information about benefits. A second type of interrelationship occurs in interaction between customer targets. For example, the key benefit offered to important influencers may be the belief that the firm's product will truly deliver benefits that satisfy targeted customer needs. Influencers may also be a key element of communication by which the firm persuades targeted customers to purchase products.

The important point to bear in mind is that the focus of this marketing task is on design, not execution. A well-developed marketing offer requires many other functions of the organization to play a role for effective implementation.

In addressing a given market, firms may need to design marketing offers for multiple customer targets in multiple market segments. However, the firm typically has limited resources. Three important allocation decisions must be made:

1. What level of resources should be allocated to each market segment?
2. For each market segment, what level of resources should be allocated to each potential customer target?
3. What is the appropriate balance of resources between providing product / package / availability / service benefits, communications, and securing low costs?

Complex trade-offs must be made in allocating resources among benefits, communications, and low costs. At the first level, firms must decide between allocating resources to developing and delivering benefits; communicating benefits; and developing a low-cost operation that provides downward price flexibility.

At the second level, companies must decide on allocations within the three areas. For example: What should be the allocation between benefits related to product design, packaging, services, product and service availability, and so forth? How should resources be allocated for the communication function: sales force, mass advertising, direct marketing, and public relations?

The three types of allocation decisions (i.e., market segments, customer targets, offer design) are closely intertwined. For example, for a given market segment of consumers, how should a personal lines life insurance company balance effort between influencers (e.g., lawyers and accountants) and final consumers? Resolving this question is clearly related to the benefit/communication/low-cost resource trade-off for final consumers and to the trade-offs among different forms of communication.

To successfully complete this design task, the marketing manager must weigh both strategic considerations and the multiple response functions of returns for different allocation methods.

CORE TASK 5: SECURE SUPPORT FROM OTHER FUNCTIONS

Core task 4 focuses on the design of marketing offers for targeted customers in target market segments. However, rarely does the marketing group have line authority over the various organizational functions with responsibility for implementing elements of the offer. Core task 5 focuses on ensuring that these other functions support the offer designed by marketing and that their plans are developed so the designed marketing offers can be delivered.

"The chain is as strong as its weakest link!" If a key function is unable to play its part in implementing the marketing offer, the effort expended by all other functions may be in vain.

Example: A New York money center bank

developed several extensively advertised new consumer loan products. Response in the form of applications was as forecasted, but the bank's credit approval system was antiquated. It took so long to process applications that by the time many applicants were advised of their approval they were no longer interested.

Depending on the particular circumstances, several different functional areas may be key to implementing an offer. They may be functions that deal with the marketplace (sales force, advertising, customer service, credit control, underwriting, market research) or functions that are more internal to the organization (operations, product development, information systems, human resources).

Whereas the first four core tasks of marketing are externally focused and deal with understanding and making decisions regarding the environment, core task 5 is internally focused. Marketing must use a combination of formal authority and informal persuasion to ensure that its marketing offer design is executed appropriately.

CORE TASK 6: MONITOR AND CONTROL APPROPRIATE EXECUTION AND PERFORMANCE

The first five core tasks focus on planning; successful completion of these tasks produces a set of customer targets in targeted market segments, a series of marketing offers, and an agreement from various organizational functions to execute the marketing offers. Core task 6 focuses on execution of the offers; it is concerned with monitoring both marketing performance and execution of the agreed-upon actions.

Performance goals comprise three broad types: *profit oriented* (e.g., bottom-line profit, contribution, ROI [return on investment], ROE [return on equity], cash flow, gross spreads); *volume oriented* (e.g., unit volume, sales revenue, market share, market occupancy ratio, cross-sell ratio); and *intermediate* (e.g., awareness, intention to buy, satisfaction).

In monitoring execution and performance, two key questions must be answered: Were the set performance goals achieved? Were the agreed-upon actions executed? For marketing management to be satisfied, the answer to both questions must be yes! If so, the firm can move forward. Assuming that performance goals are set appropriately, and that no major customer, competitor, or other environmental changes are forecasted, the firm continues to execute based on the targeted segments, targeted customers, and designed marketing offers.

The other three answer combinations each have different implications:

1. *Performance goals achieved/imperfect execution*—This result implies that success was achieved without executing the agreed-upon plan. Although achievement of goals is positive, the firm must understand the reasons so as to approach the future with confidence.

Perhaps an imperfectly designed strategy was deliberately not implemented by personnel who saw its faults and acted in the firm's best interest. Or, unforeseen but significant environmental change occurred and relevant personnel made necessary adjustments. In each case, the marketing strategy should be reevaluated. In the former, better strategy making is required; in the latter, new strategy must be developed to account for environmental change.

2. *Performance goals not achieved/execution appropriate*—The major reasons for this result are twofold: first, an imperfectly designed strategy that cannot achieve desired goals even though executed as planned; second, an appropriately designed strategy based on best information at the time, but where significant environmental change occurs to which the firm does not react. The appropriate action in both cases is strategy reevaluation.

3. *Performance goals not achieved/imperfect execution*—The major reasons for this result are also twofold: First, the strategy is fine, but the goals are not reached because of imperfect execution by relevant functional areas. Second, neither the strategy design nor the execution was appropriate.

This combination is difficult to sort out

since in either case the strategy was improperly implemented. The firm should undertake a strategy review, but should place extra effort on ensuring that in the future implementation proceeds as planned.

In its performance monitoring function the firm should embrace four key principles. It should be *proactive*—heading off problems before they occur; *ongoing*—exercising the proactive role continuously; *objective*—based on objective measures rather than subjective feelings; and *flexible*—recognizing that assumptions may not hold and that modification of performance targets may be in order.

THE PRODUCT LIFE CYCLE

Noel Capon, Professor of Business, Graduate School of Business, Columbia University

The product life cycle describes the product's sales trajectory over time, from introduction to decline (see Exhibit 2-1). For these curves, *product* has four quite distinct meanings:

1. *Product class*—At the highest level of aggregation, *product* refers to all products from all competing producers which, despite differences in appearance and performance, essentially serve a set of functional needs in a roughly similar manner. Typically, different product classes (categories) offer quite distinct customer benefits in satisfying common needs. For example, the product classes of passenger automobiles, bicycles, airplanes, railroads, ships, and motorcycles all provide the common benefit of consumer transportation.
2. *Product form*—At a finer level of aggregation, *product* refers to a homogeneous grouping of products from all competing producers that are more similar in perception and use by customers than items in a product class. For example, product forms in the automobile product class include sports cars, luxury cars, compacts, and subcompacts; the computer product class comprises mainframes, minis, workstations, and personal computers as product forms.
3. *Brand*—*Product* also refers to several items in a product form produced by a single organization; thus, Jaguar, Cadillac, and Lexus are brands.
4. *Model*—Finally, *product* refers to an individual item or model produced by a single organization: a four-door Pontiac station wagon is a product in this most specific sense.

The sales trajectory for models or brands may follow a similar curve to Exhibit 2-1.

Exhibit 2-1. The Product Life Cycle

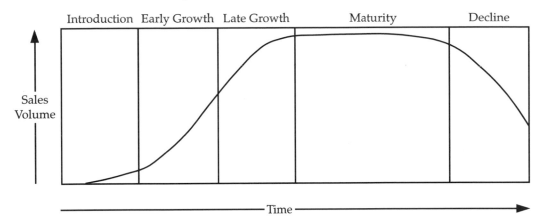

However, because individual producers make resource decisions for specific models or brands, in practice, sales curves of many different shapes are found. For example, a firm whose model has declining sales may increase advertising and reverse the decline. In addition, analysis at the model or brand level provides little insight into market factors such as competitor entry and exit. For these reasons, product life cycle analysis at the model or brand level is not very useful.

However, for both product class and product form, consistent patterns resembling Exhibit 2-1 are found for many products. Analysis at the product class level can provide important insights, but product form analysis is typically most valuable because marketing strategy is generally developed at that level. For a firm contemplating an entry in personal computers, life cycle analysis of the computer product class is of little value. Analysis of both personal computers and other computer product forms would be more worthwhile.

FACTORS AFFECTING SALES TRAJECTORIES

Sales trajectories are a function of two separate but interacting sets of variables: market potential factors and marketing strategy efforts of all competitors. Market potential re-

fers to the capacity of the population to absorb some number of units of the product form per annum. This capacity is a function of population, income levels, underlying product form need, population knowledge of the product's availability, desire to consume product items, and usage or replacement rates.

Competitors commit varying levels and types of resources to market development and sustenance via product development and design, distribution and advertising, sales and promotion expenditures. These resources determine the match with customer needs, and the population's knowledge and demand for the product form. Also, competitors can, of course, vary prices. Current and prior resource commitments to enhance population knowledge of and desire to purchase product form items interact with variables determining market potential to produce a given level of sales in any time period.

Market potential and marketing strategy variables are each based on the independent actions of many actors. Individual customers—firms or consumers—pursuing purchasing goals underlie market potential; competitor companies determine marketing strategy. The interaction of these two groups of behaviors, each with its own objective sets, results in the relatively consistent shapes of product life cycle curves found for many different product forms.

PRODUCT LIFE CYCLE STAGES

Introduction

Introduction may follow many years of research and product development by one or more organizations. Frequently, there is a single pioneer; however, competitors may enter during introduction and jointly share the market development task. Whether or not a monopoly exists depends on how difficult the product and/or production process is to imitate and whether the product or process is patented. Competitors may be attracted if they perceive the product form as profitable and/or if it threatens existing business.

Introduction is a period of much uncertainty: customers may be fearful the new product will not perform adequately; producers may be unsure of the technology and of the optimal marketing strategy. Resource requirements to develop the market and ensure product survival can be very high; they may outstrip spending for research and product development. For example, RCA's market development spending for color TV was reputedly three times its R&D spending.

Typically, there are few product designs in introduction as one or more entrants struggle to build profitable volume. Advertising educates customers about the product form to stimulate primary demand; there is less emphasis on differentiating individual brands. Personal selling informs customers and distributors about the use and value of the product and reduces uncertainties. Price may not fully cover total production costs in anticipation that volume will build and all costs, both direct and indirect, will be covered later.

The length of the introduction phase can range from a few months to many years. A major determining factor is the quantity and quality of marketing effort expended by entrants in the new and developing market. The stage is likely to be longer to the extent that innovation is radical and requires significant changes in customers' behavior; the product is complex; the demonstration of benefits is difficult; and the financial and technological risks of using the new product are high. Also, regardless of substantial product benefits, if the price is high relative to alternatives, introduction may be long. If the decision to adopt involves several people, rather than a single individual, as for an industrial product, introduction may also take longer. Other factors slowing introduction are delays in securing distribution and economic changes affecting customer purchasing power. From the producers' perspective, technical problems with production processes, early product failure, or inability to expand capacity sufficient to meet growing demand can also retard market development.

Early Growth

Increasing sales and increasing rate of growth of sales mark the close of introduction and usher in the early growth phase. Attracted by growth, competitors enter the market and by their marketing efforts help further increase sales growth. Frequently, the pioneer's inability to fully satisfy market demand eases newcomer entry.

Typically, early growth products introduced by new entrants differ little from the original: competitive entries imitate rather than involve radical design changes. As new competitors struggle for market position, new distribution channels open and promotional activity remains high. However, promotional expenditure-to-sales ratios tend to drop as the denominator, sales, increases. Advertising emphasis shifts to brand differentiation and selective demand creation. Prices fall as economies of scale associated with increasing sales permit price to be used as a competitive weapon.

Overall, though, competition is not intense in early growth as many competitors can share sales growth. Firms increase sales not at competitors' expense but from market growth. The corollary is that a firm's sales can increase while its market share decreases.

Late Growth

Sales continue to rise in late growth, but the rate of growth decreases. Strong competitors initiate tough actions to retain sales growth, forcing weaker entrants to withdraw.

Market segments are increasingly identifiable, and in contrast to imitative product strategies often found in early growth, extensive product modification occurs as competitors seek differential advantage through product design. Product variations tend to proliferate as competitors adapt products to specific customer requirements. Distribution is broad, but sales growth slowdown makes distribution outlets more selective about brands and individual items carried. Price becomes a major competitive weapon, and pressure is put on distribution margins. Purchase terms and the amount/length of credit available are more favorable to customers; warranties and service policies also become more advantageous. As weaker competitors fade, price cutting and promotional actions attempt to stave off business withdrawal.

Maturity

In maturity, sales remain relatively constant and are affected primarily by changes in basic macroeconomic and demographic factors. Most sales are to repeat users.

Pricing tends to be competitive, and attempts to segment the market rely more on packaging and promotional strategies than on basic product differentiation. Often, industry structures formed in early growth are stabilized in this period, frequently as oligopolies, and market positions achieved by early maturity often survive for many years (e.g., IBM's domination of mainframe computers; General Electric's domination of steam turbine generators).

Distribution is critical. Because differential advantage is difficult to secure in the product, producers concentrate on retaining distribution outlets. Companies with broad product lines sold through common outlets have considerable advantages over more specialized producers (e.g., Procter & Gamble's great distribution strength in supermarkets).

Cost economies and market positions achieved by entrenched competitors make entry in mature markets difficult. New entrants need significant resources to mount major promotional efforts to gain sufficient market share for competitive cost positions. Successful entrants may have advanced production technology and/or may target particular market segments.

Decline

Although the maturity phase may last many years, eventually sales turn downward and the product enters decline; decreased annual sales may range from very gradual to steep. Sales decline may be caused by growth of a new substitute product (e.g., CDs replacing LPs in recorded music) or by customer need changes that render the product obsolete. As sales decline, industry overcapacity grows, often resulting in fierce price competition. Temporary respite may be gained by more stable firms as competitors drop out and increased volume is available for those remaining. Price decreases may be difficult to sustain as excess capacity leads to increased costs, resulting in higher prices, lower volumes, and greater excess capacity, in a vicious cycle. In general, marketing expenditures drop; advertising may shift from mass media toward more specialized media to reduce advertising costs and target remaining customers more directly. Cost reductions are sought by pruning product lines to achieve greater scale economies. Late in decline, profitable opportunities may be available by selling to a core of loyal, relatively price-insensitive buyers.

Trends in the Time to Maturity

Market positions achieved by the onset of maturity are often sustained throughout the phase. Thus, it is crucial to identify long run trends in the time it takes products to reach maturity. Most evidence suggests that product life cycles are shortening dramatically. In addition, the product development cycle time in R&D is also shortening. These trends have resulted from improved technology, greater information dissemination, increased global competition, and greater consumer purchasing power.

The key implication is that whereas thirty years ago firms with new product failures could undertake more development effort and still reenter the market in the growth phase, shortening product life cycles place a heavy premium on market entry with the right strategy the first time.

BUYERS OF PRODUCTS

Firms attempting to determine product strategy through the life cycle should determine the types of consumers or firms likely to adopt the product at different stages. Consumer research has identified five general categories: innovators (2% of the population), early adopters (15%), early majority buyers (34%), late majority buyers (34%), and laggards (5%).

Innovators

These are the first purchasers of a new product. They tend to be cosmopolitan, well traveled, socially mobile, and financially privileged. They read journals and magazines extensively, are more frequently exposed to communications concerning innovation, and decide more easily than others to try something new. They may influence others to the extent that they have contact with early adopters, but their purchases do not lead to widespread imitative behavior.

Early Adopters

These are the true opinion leaders. In contrast to innovators, they are well entrenched in their communities' social structures and are among the leaders. They tend to be aware of new products through contacts with local businesspeople; other members of the social system ask them for advice. They set examples by their adoption decisions. Innovators are characterized as venturesome; in contrast, the most striking characteristic of early adopters is the respect they command.

Early Majority Buyers

Members of the early majority are slower to try new products, entering the market only after their peers have adopted the product. Their first purchases tend to be in the later parts of early growth and the early parts of late growth. They are less privileged than early adopters, but their income and social position are still above average. They have a great deal of contact with early adopters whose purchase behavior they monitor before entering the market themselves, but are less socially mobile and tend to be older.

Late Majority Buyers

These buyers make their first purchases in the late growth and maturity phases; by this time,

innovators and early adopters may have repurchased the product or moved on to new product forms. Late majority buyers are slow to adopt innovations, in part because their income is below average. They wait until prices fall to affordable levels. In contrast to previous groups, these buyers rely on mass media rather than interpersonal sources for purchase information.

Laggards

These are excessively traditionalist. They tend to be isolated from social processes in their communities; their purchases are governed by long-established habits that are slow to change. They tend to have little social mobility, are older, and have fewer financial resources than other groups. Products are well into maturity before laggards make their first purchases. The traditionalism of this group accounts for the slow death of many products. Whereas members of the other groups have moved on to new product forms, laggards are still purchasing an earlier product. Because their purchase behavior is habitual, they do not need advertising to persuade them to buy.

Industrial Consumers

Adoption of product innovations by industrial firms is less studied, but some observations can be made. Often within an industry one or two firms function as opinion leaders. They have greater resources for testing new products and efficient decision-making systems for adoption. Firms with more cumbersome decision-making systems take longer to adopt, as do firms with few resources for testing; they may let larger competitors test and adopt new products before they decide to purchase.

On the other hand, established companies may be more committed to existing products and processes by past investments than newer, smaller firms. In such cases, smaller firms may be quicker to adopt. Sometimes organizational culture mitigates against new product adoption. Management may feel secure with present purchases and may be unwilling to risk new products. Or, a not-invented-here (NIH) syndrome may cause executives to look askance at innovations developed by other firms.

Characteristics of individual industrial buyers may also be important in the adoption decision. For instance, one study found that the more well educated and experienced the buyer, as measured by the number of jobs he or she held, the earlier adoption took place.

STRATEGIC OBJECTIVES

For management contemplating market entry early in the product life cycle, a critical issue is financial results. Profit performance typically varies through the life cycle, but general statements about individual firm performance over time cannot be made because it depends both on the firm's own strategic objectives and resource commitments, and on the strategic objectives and resource commitments of competitors. Some patterns emerge, although for any given firm and product life cycle, they are impossible to predict.

One pattern often found commences with an innovator's product launch and willingness to accept losses early in the introduction phase. High costs surround start-up, and although low price sensitivity often permits high prices and high margins on direct cost, revenues frequently do not cover full production and marketing costs. Thus, profitability may be subordinated to market development as a strategic objective. As the market starts to take off, however, plant capacity fills and opportunities increase for near-term profit. The innovator seeks short-term profit to compensate for losses suffered during introduction and initial R&D. In the late growth phase, prices are cut in an attempt to maintain historic growth rates. Although reduced price levels are somewhat offset by cost efficiencies, profits may be reduced for all competitors.

When maturity commences, the industry has stabilized and competitor profitability is typically related to market share. (The innovator may have lost its dominant position by this time.) A firm entering maturity with dominant market share can, if it makes appropriate resource commitments compared to competitors, retain that position and profita-

bility throughout maturity. By contrast, a firm entering maturity with low market share may find it difficult to achieve profitability. Desire to enter maturity with a dominant market share may cause early market entrants to forgo high profits in the growth phases. Instead, market share is the key strategic objective and profitability is subordinated until maturity commences and a dominant market share is obtained.

To finance R&D for new products, and losses in the introduction and growth phases, cash must come from other parts of the organization, often from mature products with dominant market share. This cash funds products in early life cycle stages, so that they in turn become dominant in maturity and fund other new products.

The ability of firms to forgo profits early in the product life cycle depends on their ability and determination to finance the drive for market share from more mature products. Small companies may find this impossible, and even large companies may balk at postponing profits until maturity; profits in growth may be relatively more certain than in maturity, and stockholders may require short-term profits.

If at least one competitor aggressively seeks market share in early and late growth, the time from introduction to onset of maturity may be shortened considerably. Fewer companies enter the market, and they may exit more quickly as the competitive turbulence of late growth is reached sooner. Further, if a firm gains a reputation for aggressively pursuing market share in growth phases, other companies may be inhibited from competing in new product markets the firm has entered or is believed about to enter.

ENTRY STRATEGIES

Management must decide at what product life cycle stage to enter the market. Broadly speaking, there are four possible entry periods.

Pioneers

A critical requirement for a pioneer company, one that aims to launch new product classes and forms, is strong R&D. This firm must be willing to fund research to develop new products, but it must also accept inevitable R&D failures. Pioneers need large numbers of high-quality people and sufficient organizational slack to shift people when swift responses to competitive action are required. They need strong competitive intelligence to keep abreast of competitive research efforts and patent lawyers to provide them (if possible) with legal monopolies on their discoveries.

In successful pioneering firms, production, engineering, and marketing work closely together; the firm is prepared to launch products that are not completely perfect to gain a jump on competition. However, it must also fund ongoing product development necessary to upgrade early products launched in the market.

Follow-the-Leader Companies

In contrast to pioneers, follow-the-leader firms focus resources on development. Typically they wait until a pioneer has launched a product and monitor progress. If they believe the success potential is high they invest heavily in development. They afford this expense by not funding extensive research. To monitor market activity they need strong market intelligence groups; they also have staffs of patent lawyers not only to write good patents but to find ways to invent around competitors' patents. Follow-the-leader companies need extensive resources for market development. Since pioneering firms secure a head start as the product moves from introduction to early growth, follow-the-leader firms must conceive and execute development programs quickly.

Segmenters

Segmenters enter the late growth phase with modified products designed to fit specific needs of particular market segments. Segmenter companies tend to exert little effort in R&D but commit substantial resources to product design and engineering. Most important, they have strong market research departments, often skilled in advanced quantitative technologies, to identify market segments incompletely served by current competitors. Because they are late entrants, segmenters must be extremely cost conscious in deciding which applications to develop; they also need efficient manufacturing organizations. Successful segmenters have a flair for minimizing engineering and production costs by using the same parts in different products.

Me-Too Companies

Since me-too firms enter the market in maturity, they have little need for R&D departments. Product design is dominated by manufacturing cost considerations; they tend to be slim organizations with minimum overhead. They are, however, strong marketers, able to promote and price products aggressively against entrenched competitors.

Firms that attempt to span the range of entry possibilities from pioneer to me-too have severe strategy implementation problems. Firms launching me-too products require efficient manufacturing operations carrying little overhead. Such firms are also unlikely to be able to support the R&D demanded of pioneers.

PRODUCT LIFE CYCLE EXTENSION

The individual firm competing for sales and market share in a product form has basically two modes of behavior. First, it may attempt to win sales from competition by better product design, promotion, advertising, and distribution aimed at currently identified customer needs. Second, it may attempt to extend the product life cycle. Extensions can take place in several ways: increasing product use among current buyers; obtaining more varied use among current buyers; identifying new users.

More frequent product usage can be obtained through promotional activities explaining the benefits of increased use. For instance, a campaign to encourage brushing teeth after every meal might increase toothpaste sales; planned obsolescence in the auto industry leads to more frequent auto purchases.

More varied product usage can be achieved by identifying product applications not previously exploited. Church and Dwight (Arm & Hammer) expanded uses for baking soda to such areas as controlling odors in refrigerators and drains and using the product as a toothpaste, vastly increasing sales of a decline product.

New product users can be obtained by re- defining the target market. Depending on current product distribution, sales might be expanded by targeting different geographic areas, types of environment (urban, suburban, rural), age groups, or income levels.

All these ways extend product life cycles and can be enhanced by product design, price reductions, and appropriate distribution and promotion decisions.

STRATEGIC MARKETING PLANNING PROCESSES

George S. Day, Geoffrey T. Boisi Professor, The Wharton School, University of Pennsylvania

DEVELOPING STRATEGIES

How are strategies developed? They may follow the strategic planning model and be the deliberate outcome of analytic top-down processes that match opportunities with capabilities. Alternatively, strategies may emerge from piecemeal responses to events over which management has little control (e.g., new competitors, unexpected material shortages, production problems, technological improvements). The pattern of bottom-up actions and reactions of those closest to the situation coalesces to reveal overall strategic change.

For a business to be successful, both approaches are needed. A top-down, deliberate strategy imposed unilaterally on lower organization levels seriously limits learning possibilities; also, if assumptions and objectives are not understood or accepted, poor implementation is likely. But neither are incremental bottom-up strategies assured success— especially in rapidly changing environments. Strategic change is too slow, strategy elements may not form a coherent whole, and the business may be poorly positioned against aggressive competitors.

Effective planning combines the benefits of deliberation with need for flexibility and organizational learning. The framework follows the steps taken to deal with any ill-structured problem: apply intelligence (situation assessment); design possible responses (develop alternatives); choose best alternative; implement decision. Flexibility is added by shifting the focus from planning steps to issues and projects; broadening management participation in planning; treating objectives as negotiated outcomes rather than the starting point; and continuously tracking performance against objectives and assumptions.

The *situation assessment* stage begins with a comparison of past performance versus objectives. Substantial deviations (positive or negative) by product type, market segment, or channel member raise problem and opportunity flags. Causes of deviations are surfaced by specifying the realized strategy, representing actions actually taken, rather than a planned strategy that may not have unfolded as hoped. Set in an explicit business definition that bounds the planning process, the situation assessment identifies external (threats and opportunities) and internal (strengths and weaknesses) factors influencing future performance. Linkage to the next step is through a set of assumptions, about environmental and business prospects, tested for validity.

In the *strategic thinking* stage, information from the situation assessment is put to work. The business team concentrates on the few pivotal issues that must be dealt with because of their key impact on future performance. Issue resolution begins with generating creative options for dealing with each issue, followed by analysis and choice.

Decision making follows from the ongoing negotiation of objectives and resource requirements with corporate management, based on strategic options for dealing with each issue. These negotiations drive the main strategic decisions: strategic thrust shifts, option choices, and resource allocation in light of mutually acceptable objectives. Because performance objectives are negotiated for feasibility (versus imposed top-down), the business team understands and accepts them. The payoff is broad-based commitment to decisions and performance expectations that can quickly lead to action.

Implementation comprises ongoing activities that translate strategic decisions into programs, projects, and near-term functional plans. Sweating action plan details is impor-

tant for good execution: responsibilities, time frames, resource needs and their utilization (human and financial), and performance levels must be specified while organizational obstacles are overcome. Such detailed planning both fleshes out strategies and further tests feasibility. Finally, budgeting—figures attached to each revenue and expense-related activity—is essential to fit plans in the available resource envelope. Budgets also set standards and provide benchmarks for comparing actual versus expected performance. Tracking deviations completes the process and begins the next round of planning activities.

SITUATION ASSESSMENT

A key competitive strategy principle is focusing firm strength against rivals' weaknesses; a firm must know its capabilities relative to competition and the fit with present and prospective environments. The scope of situational inquiry embraces all trends, forces, and conditions that may influence business performance. The outcome is a set of assumptions (hopefully valid) about the environment, competition, and internal skills and resources.

The key distinctions in situation assessment (Exhibit 2-2) are between external factors (beyond direct control) that present opportunities or threats and internal factors reflecting skills and resources. Whether strengths can be exploited or weaknesses overcome depends primarily on comparisons with competition. Direct competitors are placed at center stage to provide reference points for strengths and weaknesses.

Environmental Dimensions

Each business unit confronts a unique multidimensional blend of environmental forces, differing in intensity. The most pressing environmental realities derive from customers, channels, and competitors in the served market. But the broader macroenvironment critically influences these realities: political, economic, social, and technological (PEST).

The political domain comprises regulatory

Exhibit 2-2. Overview of the Situation Assessment

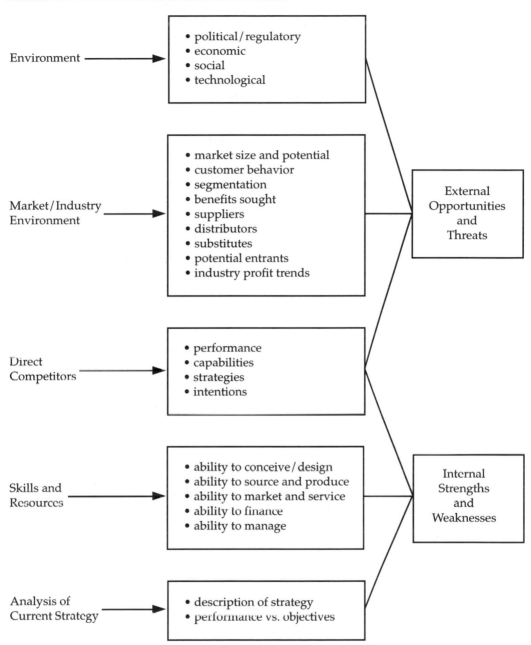

Source: From G. S. Day, *Market-Driven Strategy* (New York: Free Press, 1990).

oversight, legislative decisions, and administrative judgments (e.g., tax code interpretations, legal opinions). Addition/removal of regulatory and legislative constraints creates new markets (e.g., deregulation of trucking, communications, financial services), or eliminates market opportunities (e.g., shifts in defense spending or trade policy).

Economic forces range from general economic health (e.g., GNP [gross national product] growth, unemployment) to inflation levels. Since economies are interconnected, examining only the regional or national economy is insufficient; balance of payments and other influences on currency values must be understood.

The social dimension comprises cultural trends, the values and beliefs of society that determine lifestyles, concerns and habits of customers and employees, and demographic shifts. Demography includes age, income, education, work force participation, and geographic location. Demography influences cultural values and vice versa.

A business uses technologies in all value-creating stages: *core* technologies driving manufacturing processes or product performance; *pacing* technologies that may displace core technologies or promise new features; *supporting* technologies that facilitate information flows. Technologies have limitations—continually overcome by research—and life cycles as new technologies displace them. For example, in computer printing, the ion-deposition pacing technology threatens still-growing fiber optic and ink jet technologies, and may entirely displace the traditional impact methods.

No formulae guide the choice of environmental factors to consider; business specifics determine relevancy. Consumer-packaged food firms pay close attention to consumer trends; capital goods producers are more sensitive to economic factors. Identifying influential trends in advance is difficult. The main influences on consumer goods in the 1980s were demographic shifts, including record numbers of more affluent and active aging adults; rapid changes in the nuclear family, resulting from delays in first marriages, a significant increase in the divorce rate within ten years of marriage, and growing numbers of working women; value shifts as consumers became preoccupied with maintaining economic and emotional stability and finding personal, not social, fulfillment.

Opportunities and Threats

Opportunities are anticipated external events or trends that raise the possibility of improved performance. The opportunity may suggest a new basis for competitive advantage: new features, new production processes, new delivery systems. Other changes may disable competitors. For example, newly highly leveraged firms, following LBOs (leveraged buyouts) or expensive defenses against takeover, are vulnerable to price competition as they struggle to pay debt interest. New market segments create opportunities. For example, Avon exploited a trend to purchasing beauty products at the workplace; by 1988, 25 percent of sales were made in business locations.

Threats are the dark side of the external world. Threats may impede strategy implementation, increasing risk and required resources, or erode sustainability of present advantages and sooner or later reduce performance. In 1984, Avon saw many potential threats: a decline in home direct selling; maturing domestic markets for cosmetics, fragrances, and toiletries; fewer representatives willing to sell door-to-door; emergence of direct mail competition.

Management teams often do a good job enumerating threats and opportunities. However, the laundry list of environmental topics, trends, and possible events is marked by considerable uncertainty about timing and magnitude. Often management dwells too long on possible threats; creative efforts are focused on the myriad things that could go wrong, rather than on business-building opportunities.

Focusing the Environmental Assessment

Business teams need a procedure to identify the few environmental factors with real strategic significance to channel their scarce planning time.

Step One: For each significant environmental trend make specific assumptions with action implications. Examples:

- Energy prices will range from $16 to $21 per barrel, for the next three years.
- Excess auto production capacity in North America will be 30 percent by 1992.
- Videoconferencing will not noticeably reduce business air travel.
- The shakeout of facsimile machine manufacturing continues; only the top seven will survive.

If an assumption does not pose an obvious threat or opportunity, it probably lacks pertinence and can be put aside.

Step Two: Test the validity of each key assumption. What evidence supports the judgment about timing direction of change and magnitude? Speculation and surmise are inappropriate; corroborating evidence is crucial. What is the competitor really doing? Is the new segment big enough? Disagreements about event or trend probabilities are surfaced.

Step Three: Assess potential short- and long-run impacts of each opportunity or threat; isolate those especially critical. Watch carefully for two-edged sword trends; for example, a new technology that threatens base products but creates opportunities for lower costs and market expansion.

Assessing Strengths and Weaknesses

Strengths derive from superior skills and resources; taken together the business has the ability to do more, or better, than competitors. These distinctive capabilities can exploit opportunities and parry threats. Avon's new management team identified several significant strengths: an unmatched ability to manage direct selling systems; a strong and identifiable consumer franchise; a strong balance sheet; R&D that routinely produced six hundred new or reformulated products each year.

Weaknesses are deficiencies or constraints that inhibit the firm's ability to match or outperform competitors. Avon management identified as weaknesses heavy dependency on home direct selling; an eroding beauty image; inability to meet needs of emerging segments.

A comprehensive strengths-weaknesses analysis embraces all business areas including the functional abilities to:

- *Conceive and design*, including marketing and technological research capabilities, patents, design, and funding available for innovation.
- *Source*, comprising access to raw materials, ability to manage supply networks, achieving low input costs.
- *Produce* with respect to costs; quality, productivity, capacity and readiness to serve, and manufacturing flexibility.
- *Market*, including served market coverage, customer knowledge, product line breadth, customer response, ability to promote and advertise effectively, provide service, finance customers.
- *Finance*, considering both sources and amounts of funding, ability to generate income, parent willingness to finance growth.
- *Manage*, including leadership, depth of experience, planning capability, loyalty and turnover, ability to work as a team, effectiveness of systems and controls.

STRATEGIC THINKING: REAL-TIME ISSUES MANAGEMENT

Issues are the main currency of the strategy dialogue, and a major impetus to deep strategic thinking. Issues help to concentrate the plethora of forces, problems, and uncertainties into manageable chunks. These become focal points for decision making and specify needs for information collection and interpretation. Once all issues are properly framed, they are compared for immediacy and impact. Priorities are set so those few central problems and challenges impacting future performance are addressed. Focusing scarce management time and energy on high payoff issues is the most compelling reason for an issues orientation.

Planning Cycles vs. Budget Cycles

Real-time issues management disconnects strategic thinking from budget cycle rigidities. Issues arrive and are resolved on an event-based schedule, not the annual calendar. Triggers for scanning and sorting issues for potential impact are various: arrival of a new general manager or CEO; serious downturn in performance; industry restructuring under deregulation pressure; technological change; new customer demands. In stable environments, when strategy is on course, identification and sorting of issues every three years may be sufficient.

When issue resolution activities are distinct from budgeting formalities, the quality of strategic thinking improves. Conversely, when planning is an obvious precursor to annual budget preparation, management attention often narrows to short-run implementation concerns, rather than strategic moves with longer time frames. Myopia should not be encouraged by designing systems that promote bad habits.

Identifying and Framing Issues

A strategic issue is a condition or pressure on the business created by internal or external developments that involves possible outcomes having a high impact on future performance; controversy (reasonable people defend different possible actions); strategic consequences, since resolution may mean a strategy shift.

Useful issues are posed as questions. "Inflation" is not an issue! "The effect of inflation on relative cost position" is an issue demanding analysis and action. Correctly formulated issue questions facilitate solution discovery.

Suppose the firm is persistently unable to satisfy delivery promises. A question framed as "What should be done to reduce late deliveries?" may produce the solutions work overtime, promise realistic schedules, build buffer stocks. None tackle the underlying strategic issue. Digging deeper might reveal: "Should the business expand production capacity?" Different questions are suggested by probing other reasons for late delivery. Ideally, questions with a yes or no answer should emerge. If analysis suggests no, capacity is insufficient, several solution options can be explored. Big issues such as "How can we become more market oriented?" should be broken down to more manageable issues.

Resolving Issues

A thorough situation assessment and past performance review versus objectives in complex, fast-moving markets may uncover as many as fifty issues. Typical is a major building materials manufacturer that sold to warehouse suppliers; installers used the product in both new construction and renovation. A sampling of some of the forty-three issues surfaced in a strategy review demonstrates the richness of an issues array:

- Should we do more component manufacturing in firm-owned warehouses?
- Should we seek offshore sources of low-cost products? If so, should we make or buy?
- Will the recent LBOs of competitors X and Y affect their strategies by forcing an emphasis on short-run earnings? What share gaining opportunities does this present for us?
- What is the right number and mix of firm-owned versus independent warehouses?

Typically, no more than five to seven issues will require full management team attention. Too many more dilute time and energy, so priorities are essential. Consensus must be achieved on the immediacy and impact of each issue, using a grid such as Exhibit 2-3.

Generating and Evaluating Strategic Options

Each priority issue can be handled in many possible ways. However, the effectiveness of the action taken depends on having a wide array of options to consider. Seldom will

Exhibit 2-3. Grid for Classifying Strategic Issues

Potential Impact on Performance
(Positive or Negative)

	Major	Minor
Immediate	*Priority Issues* • Identify action alternatives	*Minor Issues* • Delegate decision authority • Resolve in context of higher-priority issues
Distant	*Emerging Issues* • Monitor closely • Hedge bets	*Nonissues*

Immediacy of Issue (Likelihood and Timing)

Source: From G. S. Day, *Market-Driven Strategy* (New York: Free Press, 1990).

"more of the same" be an acceptable option, but, without adventurous thinking about new possibilities, such a pedestrian outcome is likely.

A defining feature of effective planning is the separation of the creative act of generating options from their detailed evaluation. If critical questions and comments are not deferred until all the possibilities have been identified, the atmosphere of the meeting soon resembles a "day in court." This will quickly suppress adventurous thinking and novel solutions. What is needed is a supportive and open setting for stretch thinking that encourages half-baked ideas with potential for elaboration. The flow of ideas may lead down blind alleys, but may also trigger new options that combine the best features of several different options.

When all members of a planning team participate in the full discussion of all the options

for dealing with an issue, and understand the reasons why one was selected (or their proposal was rejected), they are much more committed to implementing the options. But besides these process advantages, it is essential to have meaningful strategic options to enter into the dialogue with corporate management on the feasible resources and objectives for the business.

DECISION MAKING: NEGOTIATING OBJECTIVES AND RESOURCES

Sound objectives mobilize and stretch an organization, and establish benchmarks for judging actual performance. Unfortunately, objective setting is too often a charade yielding flawed or meaningless objectives. One new CEO found objectives were usually written then ignored; over twenty objectives were formulated by some businesses, but not challenged; other businesses had no objectives; still others delayed presenting annual objectives until the end of the year.

Sound objectives satisfy several criteria: they are few in number, clear in direction, and measurable. Otherwise, they cannot be communicated through the organization or tested for consistency. They should also offer challenging yet realistic performance targets.

Performance variables chosen for objective setting are typically the quantitative variables guiding resource allocation decisions: return on investment, profitability, and market share growth. These numbers mean much to senior management, but little to lower organization levels where only fragments of the big picture can be seen. Consequently, these variables are not broadly shared; opportunity is lost to focus the organization's energy. These variables should be complemented with more

broadly visible and meaningful objectives such as quality and order responsiveness. They should relate to enduring key success factors and avoid episodic objectives ("Last year it was quality; this year it's productivity") that send contradictory signals and diffuse commitment.

The Negotiation Process

The outcome of negotiations reconciles stakeholders' needs and business feasibility given available resources (Exhibit 2-4). Preliminary objectives and guidelines from corporate management start the planning process. These performance expectations are influenced by (1) stakeholders' requirements, notably profits for investors (other stakeholders—such as unions, governments, and employees—also play a role); (2) the business unit's role in the corporate portfolio (i.e., build, harvest, hold); (3) support for other firm businesses through shared programs; (4)

Exhibit 2-4. Negotiating Objectives

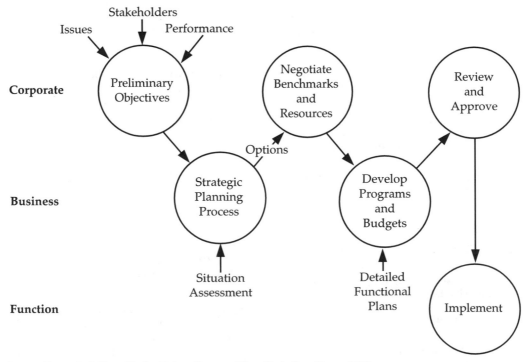

Source: From G. S. Day, *Market-Driven Strategy* (New York: Free Press, 1990).

available resources, given financial growth and competing capital demands from other businesses; (5) past growth and profit performance, and reasonable continuation prospects.

Corporate managers may also raise specific concerns. Business-specific issues may stem from customer requirement shifts, raw materials availability, or competitive moves revealed by corporate's environmental scan: Company-wide concerns and priorities may include quality enhancement, working capital conservation, and productivity, each requiring a focused program response.

Gap Analysis

Gap analysis focuses on discussions with top management. Preliminary objectives and issues trigger strategy development, but discussions must resume with corporate managers at the strategic thinking stage. The business team has identified major issues and strategic options; options are combined into discrete strategy alternatives representing internally consistent packages of strategies, ob-

jectives, and resource requirements. The building materials business noted earlier developed one strategic alternative based on incremental growth with modest capital expenditures; this "momentum" strategy required no shift in resource priorities or direction. The management team was more excited about options to expand the business rapidly by doubling investment in company-owned warehouses and moving aggressively into component manufacturing.

Preliminary objectives proposed by corporate management were compared with likely performance if "momentum" strategy was followed. A growing gap emerged, along all performance dimensions (Exhibit 2-5).

Parties to negotiating the gap are corporate management who know the resource needs of all businesses but not the details of opportunities for each business and the business unit management team with intimate knowledge of the business. Gaps are closed in two ways: changing objectives in light of what is achievable; selecting a strategy with different objectives. Generally gaps are sizable; negotiated solutions are needed to close them.

Exhibit 2-5. Gap Analysis for Building Materials Manufacturer

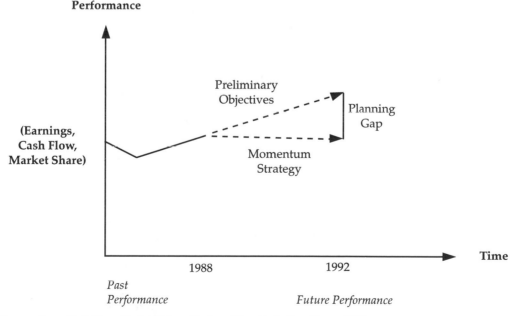

Source: From G. S. Day, *Market-Driven Strategy* (New York: Free Press, 1990).

The negotiation dialogue covers different resource requirements and objectives. Management typically explores and challenges assumptions and perhaps demands more ambitious alternatives. A favorite CEO question is, "Suppose we double your cash for two years; what can this business do?" As the dialogue proceeds, management learns more and clarifies implementation requirements. The process is messy, but it does lead to the two-way commitment that is needed to implement an option that is internally consistent, realistic, and supported at appropriate resource levels.

COMPLETING THE PLANNING PROCESS

Planning is a living, adapting, continuous process. The end of one cycle—situation assessment, strategic thinking about issues, choice of performance objectives, and courses of action culminating in implementation activities—signals the start of another cycle.

The bridge to the next cycle is a monitoring and control system that tracks whether the strategy is on course to achieve promised objectives, and whether the underlying assumptions remain valid. Key elements are performance criteria and related measures derived from objectives and key success requirements. For a strategy requiring new distribution methods, an inventory control system would be a high priority; it would ensure that inventory levels did not grow so much that they backed up the system or that corrective action was triggered. Of course, too many serious departures from the expected should initiate a complete strategy review, or spur setting up a project team to deal with the specific problem at hand.

STRATEGIC MARKETING PLANNING TOOLS

Peter T. FitzRoy, Monash University

Increased environmental complexity and change have caused managers in many industries to take a more strategic marketing approach. All industries are affected by one or more of the following factors:

- Increasing competition, often from new and global competitors.

- Product/market maturity forcing firms to seek new market opportunities.
- Rapid rates of technological change, shortening product life cycles, and hastening obsolescence.
- Increasingly complex competitive patterns with indistinct market boundaries and interindustry competition.

- Emergence of "me-too" strategies and difficulties in achieving competitive advantage.

STRATEGIC MARKETING APPROACH

To address these issues, firms have become more strategic in marketing planning and decision making. Characteristics of a strategic marketing approach are:

- Strategies are market driven, based on solid understanding of customers, markets, and competitors.
- The objective of strategy is to develop a significant and sustainable competitive advantage.
- Strategies are creative, bringing change and innovation to the market.
- Strategies are focused on the need to create and maintain customers.
- Strategic marketing skills are embedded throughout the firm, reflecting moves toward decentralization and greater autonomy.

Strategic marketing decisions can be grouped into two categories:

1. *What business(es) to be in*—This includes such issues as firm mission, investment decisions, product/market scope, growth strategy, and resource allocation. To support these decisions, we review methods to analyze industry attractiveness: why one industry is more attractive and profitable than another. We also discuss approaches to portfolio analysis: methods providing guidelines for establishing the business mission and assisting resource allocation decisions in diversified firms.

2. *How to compete in a given industry*—This includes how to develop a sustainable competitive advantage. The basis of advantage must be well grounded in industry structure; securing advantage requires a thorough understanding of customer requirements and competitive offerings. Two important ways to generate competitive advantage are discussed: achieving lowest industry cost (hence lowest price) and providing highly differentiated products (hence price premiums). Firms must be aware of costs, their determining factors, as well as methods to measure value created for customers.

A number of strategic marketing planning tools are available to help answer these questions. A few selected tools are covered here.

COMPETITIVE ANALYSIS

The financial performance of a business depends in large part on industry characteristics. An industry can be described in terms of a set of forces affecting all competitors, albeit to varying degrees. For example, in the pulp and paper industry, high exit barriers have allowed too many competitors to remain; hence, excess capacity and low prices. Long playing records (LPs) are being replaced by compact discs (CDs). These various forces determine industry profit potential and relative attractiveness. Forces affecting industries can be grouped into five major categories, as shown in Exhibit 2-6:

1. *Competition between existing firms*—If intense competition leads to lower prices or higher costs, firms find it difficult to establish an advantage that cannot be easily emulated by competitors. Rivalry is likely to be intense when a small number of equal-size competitors all strive for dominance; high fixed costs (i.e., high break-even volumes) lead to severe price-cutting tendencies when demand falls; there is limited product differentiation and consequent price competition; there are high exit barriers and industry is over capacity.

2. *Threat of entrants*—This causes concern regarding competitive methods: new entrants bring change, innovation, and capacity to the industry. The magnitude of threat depends on the nature and size of industry entry barriers, switching costs incurred by customers switching to new suppliers, economies of scale, product differentiation, and access to

Exhibit 2-6. Forces Determining Industry Competition

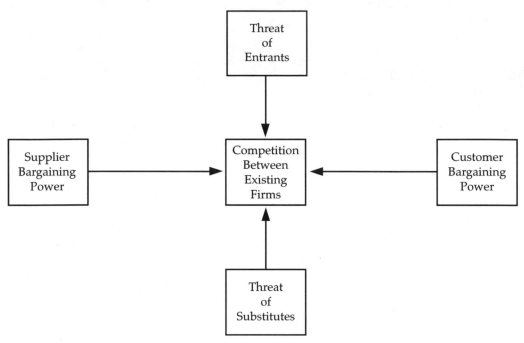

Source: After M. E. Porter, *Competitive Strategy* (New York, Free Press, 1980), 4.

distribution channels. High entry barriers generally raise industry profitability.

3. *Customer bargaining power*—This is high if customers are large and powerful and the product is important to the firm, but not to them. Customers are likely successful in bargaining down prices, and bargaining up quality and service, at the expense of industry profit. (For example, in retailing, powerful retailers can call the shots to manufacturers.) Alternatively, if customers' profits are low, they likely exert pressure to reduce input costs. Customers may also exert depressing effects on prices if backward integration is a serious possibility.

4. *Supplier bargaining power*—This is high if suppliers are few and large relative to industry participants; they may be able to pass large price increases on to customers. Power is increased if suppliers can forward integrate to compete directly with industry firms or if their products have no substitutes.

5. *Threat of substitutes*—This provides the most serious form of competition in many industries (e.g., plastics for steel in automobiles; aluminum for steel in packaging; optical fibers for copper wire in communications). Industry prices are constrained by the price/performance characteristics of substitutes, plus customer switching costs. All too often industry participants underestimate performance rate improvements and price reductions for substitutes, and fail to recognize the threats they pose. Yet substitutes can decimate an industry—witness the decline in LP records (Exhibit 2-7).

GROWTH-SHARE MATRIX

The majority of modern corporations comprise a set of divisions or strategic business units (SBUs). (An SBU is a relatively independent company unit with its own customers, technologies, products, and competitors.) In

Exhibit 2-7. Effect of Substitutes on Sales

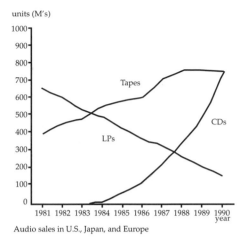

Audio sales in U.S., Japan, and Europe

Source: From *The Economist*, June 1, 1991, p. 62.

	Competitor A	Competitor B	Competitor C
Market share	20	15	5
Relative market share	1.33	.75	.25

This criterion is assumed to measure the ability of the business to generate cash. Businesses with large relative market share should be able to generate substantial levels of cash. Relative market share greater than 1.0 demonstrates industry dominance.

Four-Cell Matrix

Under the growth-share matrix, long-run market growth rate and relative market share are used to construct a four-cell matrix, as shown in Exhibit 2-8. Five businesses comprising the firm are plotted in terms of market growth and relative market share; each circle's size is proportional to business size (typically annual sales). The cut point for market growth separates high-growth from low-growth markets (commonly GNP + 3% in real terms). The cut point for relative market share is generally 1.0.

these firms, a key corporate task is deciding which businesses should comprise the firm's portfolio and how resources should be allocated across the portfolio. Each SBU faces different market conditions and represents different opportunities for the firm. Some businesses may generate more cash than needed for reinvestment; others may generate insufficient cash to support required capacity levels, R&D, and market development expenses.

The growth-share matrix, developed by the Boston Consulting Group, was the earliest developed approach to portfolio management; each business in the firm's portfolio is assessed on two criteria:

1. *Long-term market growth rate* in which the business competes. This criterion is assumed to measure business cash needs; participation in high-growth markets requires substantial cash for reinvestment.

2. *Relative market share* of the business. Relative market share measures competitive strength/weakness. It is defined as the firm's market share divided by the largest competitor's market share, as follows:

Exhibit 2-8. Four-cell Matrix

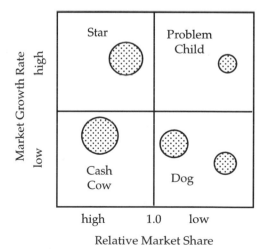

The four business categories are commonly named:

1. *Cash cow*—This segment has the dominant market share in a low-growth market. Generally these businesses have low costs relative to competitors and high profits. They require limited investment due to low market growth rates. They should generate substantial cash surpluses.
2. *Dog*—This business has a small relative market share in a low-growth market. These businesses require few funds for reinvestment but have high relative costs and thus low profits. On average, these businesses are cash neutral.
3. *Problem child*—This business has a small relative market share in a high-growth market. Because of low market shares, these businesses generate small profits yet require substantial funds to maintain position in high-growth markets. These businesses are generally cash negative.
4. *Star*—This business has a high relative market share in a high-growth market. These businesses are usually profitable and generate substantial cash; however, they also absorb large amounts of cash because of high market growth. On average, these businesses are cash neutral.

Strategies

The growth-share matrix holds that the firm should manage its collection of businesses as an entity—a portfolio; each business should not be permitted to establish its own objectives and strategy. The corporate task is to ensure that cash flows from one business category (e.g., cash cows), to another (e.g., problem children). Businesses with few cash use opportunities support businesses with significant development opportunities but insufficient internal cash generation.

Vertical movement within the matrix is largely outside management's control; businesses typically move downward as market growth slows. The key strategic issue is managing horizontal movement or relative market share: build; hold; or harvest, liquidate, or divest. Strategic considerations are:

1. *Cash cow*—These businesses should be managed to generate cash for investment in other businesses; however, they must not lose dominance. They require continued investment, but investment needs should be modest and they should be managed for substantial cash surpluses.
2. *Dog*—These low-share businesses have difficulty improving market position against well-entrenched leaders. Options are to divest or close down (depending on profitability and future outlook); acquire other similar businesses to form a "kennel" of dogs to improve competitive position; niche-operate in a small portion of the market where dominance can be established.
3. *Problem child*—These businesses may attempt share gains while the market is growing rapidly. However, share-gaining strategies require large cash infusions. Consequently, firms with several problem children must be selective and fund limited numbers for high growth. Strategies for others are divestment or niche competition.
4. *Star*—These businesses should be managed to maintain leadership; they should not lose their dominant position in any market segment. They must actively continue to search for product and process innovations and new market segments. As growth slows and the market matures, these businesses become cash cows to support the next generation of problem children and stars.

DIRECTIONAL POLICY MATRIX

A second portfolio management tool is the directional policy matrix developed by Shell Chemicals Ltd. It is based on two composite attributes:

1. *Competitive position* relative to competitors. Strong position may be indicated by high market share, low costs, high quality, and so on.
2. *Market attractiveness* in which the business competes. An attractive market may have high growth, large market size, and limited cyclicality.

The approach, and typical influencing factors for each attribute, is illustrated in Exhibit 2-9. (Assigning a business to a specific matrix position makes use of quantitative factors that are not covered in this section.)

The appropriate strategy for a business is determined by its matrix position. For example, "leader" businesses are given priority; they receive resources necessary to maintain position. "Double or quit" businesses may be future successes for the firm; only a few are adequately financed; the remainder are deleted from the portfolio or operate in market

Exhibit 2-9. Directional Policy Matrix

	strong		
strong	Leader	Try Harder	Double or Quit
Market Attractiveness size, growth differentiation cyclicality customer power entry/exit barriers substitutes	Growth	Selective	Phased Withdraw
weak	Cash Generator	Phased Withdraw	Withdraw
	strong		weak

Competitive Position
market share
perceived quality
business image
relative costs
technology
management

Source: After S. J. Q. Robinson, R. E. Hichens, and D. P. Wade, The directional policy matrix, *Long Range Planning*, 11:8–15, 1978; copyright © 1978 by Pergamon Press Ltd.

niches. This approach is not a substitute for strategic thinking; strategy is not determined solely by matrix location. However, the method provides insight into strategies for individual businesses and is a framework for assessing the overall portfolio. Caution must be exercised when interdependencies (e.g., shared distribution channels, joint R&D) occur between businesses.

COMPETITIVE ADVANTAGE

We typically find significant profit variability among companies in an industry. Some firms earn high profits; others may make losses. Our fundamental principle is that superior financial returns accrue to businesses that possess significant advantage over competitors; they provide extra customer benefits and incur low relative costs in delivering that value.

Competitive advantage may be secured in two ways:

1. *Cost leadership*—This strategy is based on achieving the lowest delivered cost to the customer. The business is the low-price competitor yet achieves above average margins. Such strategies are observed when products are relatively standardized and product differentiation is difficult, (e.g., commodity chemicals). This strategy requires firm commitment to pursue cost reductions vigorously in all business aspects, and R&D focuses on process improvements. Other competitive dimensions must be adequate (e.g., quality, delivery, service), but business success is based on low prices stemming from low costs.

2. *Differentiation*—This strategy is based on offering highly valued products or services to customers. These benefits may appeal to a broad market (e.g., Sony in electronics) or to smaller segments (e.g., Rolls Royce automobiles). Differentiation may be based on quality, delivery, reliability, technical ser-

Exhibit 2-10. Nature of Competitive Advantage

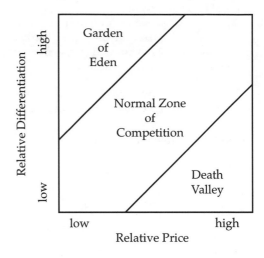

vice, sales service, and so forth; for success, customers must seek benefits other than low purchase price.

A model of competitive advantage is shown in Exhibit 2-10.

Experience Curve Sources and Graphs

In many industries (e.g., electronics, chemicals, automobile, insurance), research shows that total real costs decline in a predictable fashion by a constant percentage each time cumulative output (total product units ever produced) doubles. Magnitudes of cost decline vary by industry, but average 20 percent. On log-log graph paper, constant percent unit cost declines for each output doubling result in straight lines.

In Exhibit 2-11, cost data for electronic components in the United States and industrial products in the United Kingdom are plotted on log paper. Graphically, we can see the declines approximate a straight line in each market.

Experience curves raise two key questions: Why do they occur? What implications follow for strategic marketing decisions? Experience

Exhibit 2-11. Two Examples of Experience Curves

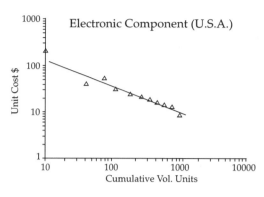

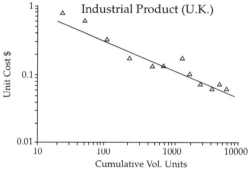

Source: After B. Hedley, A fundamental approach to strategy development, *Long Range Planning*, Dec. 1976, pp. 2–11; copyright © 1976 by Pergamon Press Ltd.

curves are not preordained; they do not happen automatically. In some industries costs may rise with experience; in competitive markets we expect them to fall. Sources of the experience curve are:

- *Learning*—productivity improvements resulting from learning by doing, including better ways to organize the firm's activities and to accomplish tasks.
- *Technology and technical improvements*—more appropriate tools, processes, raw material substitution, product redesign, and automation.
- *Economies of scale*—in production through larger plants; also, in areas such as advertising, service, and R&D.
- *Suppliers*—learning and cost reductions passed to customers.

Experience curves have major implications for marketing strategy. When costs decline rapidly with volume, the firm with the largest accumulated volume has substantial competitive cost advantage. Firms failing to reduce costs along the characteristic industry slope have uncompetitive costs; also, firms growing less rapidly build experience slowly. This can be seen in Exhibit 2-12, where competitor A has lower costs and higher margins than B and C.

Experience Curve Strategies

A successful strategy in a market with a declining experience curve involves identifying a growth market and adopting aggressive marketing and investment strategy to gain dominant market share. High profits should accrue to the largest share producer because of superior costs. This powerful strategic message has received significant empirical support; high market–share businesses are more profitable than low market–share competitors. However, some caveats are warranted:

- *Competition*—If several competitors aggressively pursue market share, industry profits may be very low until one firm establishes dominance.
- *Technological change*—Substitutes may

Exhibit 2-12. Implications of the Experience Curve

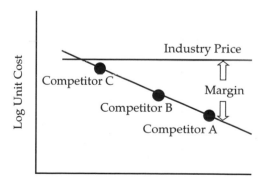

Log Accumulated Volume

decimate an industry, regardless of cost position (e.g., LPs versus CDs).
- *Differentiation*—Competitors may gain superior financial results from high-cost/high-value strategies.

- *Shared experience*—Accumulated volume is not a good measure of experience if knowledge can be readily transferred (e.g., hiring staff or licensing technology).

THE ANNUAL MARKETING PLAN

Russell S. Winer, Professor of Marketing, Haas School of Business, University of California, Berkeley

A marketing plan is a written document containing the guidelines for the business center's marketing programs and allocations over the planning period. The written plan produces multiple benefits. It encourages and requires disciplined thinking; it ensures that prior experiences are not lost; it provides a communications vehicle between the firm's functional areas (e.g., manufacturing, finance, sales) that is vital to successful plan implementation; it facilitates the pinpointing of responsibility for achieving results; it provides for continuity when management turns over and when new employees must quickly be indoctrinated to the business situation.

Marketing plans are usually written at the business center level, and the precise level for planning varies across organizations. For example, in typical brand management-organized firms, marketing plans are written for each brand, since each is a profit center (e.g., Procter & Gamble develops separate marketing plans for each toothpaste brand such as

Crest and Gleem). Alternatively, some companies write plans for groups of brands, particularly when fixed costs are difficult to allocate by product (e.g., commercial banks typically do not develop separate marketing plans for each checking account variant but instead develop overall marketing plans for larger account classes such as interest-bearing checking accounts).

The planning period for marketing plans varies from product to product. Retailing traditionally has short planning cycles to match seasonality and vagaries of fashion trends. Automobiles have long planning cycles since lead times for product development and/or modifications are longer. Other factors contributing to variation in planning horizons are technological change rates, competitive intensity, and frequency of taste shifts in relevant customer groups.

Although important for a business, marketing planning is not a panacea; some common mistakes in planning are:

- Using a process that is too time consuming on the marketing manager.
- Collecting either too little or too much data.
- Approaching planning responsibility incorrectly: line managers must be active, not professional, planners.
- Letting planning structure degenerate to a form-completion exercise.
- Writing encyclopedia-size plans.
- Not circulating plans to the functional areas most impacted by them (e.g., sales, finance, production).

Although many firms have individualized planning formats, most annual marketing plans have a common set of elements divided into five sections.

EXECUTIVE SUMMARY

Senior managers often review many marketing plans. Thus, the first section is a brief summary of the marketing plan focusing on objectives, strategies, and expected financial performance is mandatory. The overview is useful for quickly refreshing major plan elements and for easy comparison between product plans. The summary is usually one to two pages.

BACKGROUND ASSESSMENT

The second section of the marketing plan includes the data and analysis so vital for sound marketing strategies and is comprised of three parts.

Historical Appraisal

The historical appraisal identifies long-term trends and short-term market changes. This section focuses on past data; 1993 plans, developed in 1992, use 1991 and earlier information. Major interest areas include general market data such as sales and market shares; market activity information such as advertising and pricing histories; historic cost and profit data; facts concerning technology, regulatory and other environmental changes.

Since marketing planning is an ongoing activity, this plan section is not redone each year; rather it is a summary of facts accumulated over time. Sometimes these facts are stored in a separate product fact book. The fact book is the major historical repository for important product-related data and is an ideal vehicle for new manager familiarization.

Situation Analysis

The situation analysis, comprising several subsections, analyzes the current situation:

1. *Sales analysis*—attempts to better understand brand sales by decomposing total sales and market share into several subareas. Much product activity lies beneath the surface and is masked by aggregate numbers. Sales may be decomposed in several ways. First, by geographic area: an aggregate sales increase may be the net effect of increasing sales in several regions and shrinking sales in others. Second, by stock keeping unit (SKU) (e.g., individual product varieties such as color and size): increasing total sales may be the net effect of a popular size (e.g., 19-inch color television) and an unpopular size (e.g., 15-inch model). This analysis is particularly important for products with many SKUs such as apparel, and for mail order firms that must determine which products to keep and which to drop from catalogues.

2. *Defining competition*—is not a formal section of the marketing plan, but two areas of the situation analysis—industry attractiveness and competitor analysis—rely on assessing the competitive set. This may seem to be an obvious task, yet many product managers define competitors much too narrowly. The obvious competitors usually include only the most direct product subcategory (form) competition. For example, the Diet Coke product manager might say the most serious competitors are Tab (Coca Cola product) and Diet Pepsi, both other diet colas, with similar characteristics. But Diet Coke also competes with other colas and soft drinks; on some con-

sumption occasions, consumers view the choice set as all soft drinks. Thus, regular Coke and Pepsi, root beers, and so forth form a broader competitive set—product category competition. But competition is even broader; other beverages such as orange juice, beer, and milk also satisfy thirst. From the consumer's perspective, products satisfying a generic thirst-quenching need might be viewed as substitutes and, therefore, competitors. Remember, product managers do not define competition—customers do! In some cases, a broader competitor set goes beyond satisfying the generic need, but competes for disposable customer dollars.

Industry Attractiveness Analysis. This important background element provides several benefits. First, it indicates whether sustained investment is worthwhile for the firm, current competitors, or potential new entrants. Second, the analysis provides information on critical success factors highlighting product disadvantages/advantages. The industry analysis is typically updated annually, rather than totally redone.

The three main areas of inquiry in industry attractiveness include aggregate market factors, industry factors relating to major participants, and environmental factors. Aggregate market factors include:

- *Market size*—Information concerning total market sales (units and dollars) provides information on the likelihood of securing sufficient revenues to support product investment.
- *Market growth*—Fast-growing markets can sustain profits into future years, but they attract competitors and need high investment.
- *Product life cycle*—Combining market size and growth data creates the product life cycle. Market attractiveness in each phase is somewhat unclear, as firms succeed and fail with products in each stage.
- *Sales cyclicity*—Products whose sales follow business cycles may be less attractive than those less sensitive to macroeconomic factors.

- *Seasonality*—Significant intrayear sales cycles are generally not viewed positively. Because annual sales are secured in a few months, competition, which is characterized by price wars, is often intense.
- *Profits*—There is large interindustry profit variability (and profit variability by firm within industry).

Industry factors include:

- *Threat of new entrants*—Bargaining power of buyers, bargaining power of suppliers, current industry rivalry, and pressure from substitutes are in this category.
- *Industry capacity*—Chronic overcapacity is a negative sign for long-term profitability; costs are high and downward price pressure is intense.

Environmental factors include:

- *Technological factors*—In attractive industries, competitors are successful in integrating or developing new technologies into products.
- *Political factors*—Sensitivity to political factors affects attractiveness. For example, products developed for military services are very sensitive to government action.
- *Economic factors*—Sensitivity to currency exchange rates, interest rates, and GNP fluctuations are unattractive features.
- *Regulatory factors*—Sensitivity to regulatory changes generally makes for less attractive industries. Sometimes, however, regulations reduce competition by raising entry barriers.
- *Social factors*—Trends in demographics, lifestyles, attitudes, and personal values are important for both consumer and industrial goods. Some products are well positioned for such changes (e.g., VCRs, travel, products, plastics) and some are not (e.g., steel, tobacco).

Competitor Analysis. This area has received more attention in recent years for several reasons. First, many product categories have matured; competitive pressures are intense as unit sales volume gains derive only from competitors. Second, shortening product life cycles increase pressure to deliver sales and profits quickly. Finally, increased foreign competition and general market turbulence driven by technology and other industry factor changes have raised consciousness about the external environment in general.

Competitor analysis requires a structure for collecting, organizing, and analyzing competitor data in four key competitor areas:

1. *Competitors' objectives*—This analysis provides valuable data on intended competitor aggressiveness. Growth objectives usually imply growing brand units or market share. Profits are secondary. Hold objectives imply consolidation; harvest objectives are characterized by sacrificing market share for profits. If a competitor seeks increased market share at the expense of short-term profits, likely actions are price cuts, increased advertising, increased promotion (consumer and trade), and increased distribution expenses. The reverse is likely for brands being harvested. Observing such actions provides data on competitor objectives.

2. *Competitors' strategies*—Assessing competitors' current marketing strategies is critical to developing the product marketing strategy. A marketing strategy contains three key elements: product/market selection, core strategy (differential advantage or product positioning), and strategy implementation through the marketing mix. Product/market selection involves choosing which product features to offer which target customers; its focus is market segment selection. The core strategy focuses on how the product is differentiated from competitor offerings. The marketing mix is the set of tools available to product managers (e.g., advertising, promotion, distribution channel selection, price).

Competitor analysis should uncover competitor activities in these areas. A convenient way to secure much of this information is by collecting advertising, sales brochures, and other communications from rivals. Such communications provide data about target market segments pursued and the claimed positioning/differential advantage. Target market segments can be inferred from descriptors of media users where communications are observed. Positioning can be determined directly from market advertising or brochure copy. Marketing mix elements can be inferred from direct observation.

3. *Competitors' capabilities*—This assessment provides insight on the ultimate ability to execute a strategy. There are five distinct categories of necessary resources: ability to conceive and design new products; ability to market; ability to finance; ability to manage; and ability to produce. Increasingly, much competitor information can be accessed via dial-up computer databases and information on floppy disks. However, because these change rapidly, the firm should keep up-to-date on the latest resources.

4. *Competitors' future strategies*—Predicting future strategies should be possible with the information base on competitor objectives, strategies, and capabilities. Knowing what competitors are likely to do provides a sound basis for developing the firm's marketing strategy. Several forecasting methods are available. First, competitors sometimes state their intentions to the business press. Second, an examination and future extrapolation of past strategies into the future (like forecasters constructing trend lines from historical sales data) may be appropriate. Third, competitor simulation by managers role-playing major competitors and developing strategies provides valuable data for designing the firm's own marketing strategy to counter simulated strategies.

Customer Analysis. This procedure is central to marketing practice since businesses cannot survive without customers. This seems so obvious, but many marketing managers have regretted obtaining insufficient customer information in developing products or strategies. Several key questions provide a structure for analyzing customers of a product category:

1. *Who buys and uses the product?* For most industrial goods and many consumer goods,

significant differences exist between buyer and user; this distinction must always be considered.

For consumer products, the most obvious and popular basis for describing customers is a set of general demographic, socioeconomic, personality, and psychological descriptors. Other useful customer variables are behavioral characteristics—purchase quantity, brand loyalty, sensitivity to marketing mix variables (e.g., price).

For industrial products, firm characteristics (e.g., company size, location, sales levels) are key. The most widely used industrial segmentation basis in the United States is the Standard Industrial Classification (SIC) system. Two-digit codes indicate major industry groups (e.g., 34—fabricated metal products); three digits indicate broadly defined industries (e.g., 344—fabricated structural metal products); four digits indicate fairly specific industries (e.g., 3442—metal doors, sash frames, moldings, and trim).

2. *Where do customers buy?* Purchase location is very important. Where customers actually purchase (e.g., home, office, by mail) often changes over time. As a result, preferred distribution channels also change.

3. *When do customers buy?* This embraces time of year, time of month, and even time of day. For example, fast-food operators segment by "daypart": breakfast, lunch, dinner, and even "snacking" times. *When* may also embrace sales, price breaks, and rebates if customers buying on deal are different from those paying full price.

4. *How do customers choose?* Five different buying roles can be specified (for consumer and industrial buyers): initiator (identifies product need); influencer (has informational or preference input); decider (makes final decision); purchaser (makes actual purchase); user. In complex buying decisions (e.g., industrial), different individuals may occupy each role.

A threefold complexity-based category scheme describes the purchase decision process. In extensive problem solving, products are technically complex and/or new; in limited problem solving the product is known but the decision is still complex; in routinized decision making (typically for frequently purchased products) a predetermined rule is followed.

5. *Why do customers buy?* Understanding what customers value depends both on benefits offered and costs incurred. Customer value for a brand comprises three basic elements: importance of usage situation, product form effectiveness in the situation; and relative brand effectiveness. Knowing customers' value for a product makes key decisions—notably price—much easier.

Significant data for customer analysis are available from secondary sources (e.g., government documents) or syndicated services. However, much primary data are also required from methods such as surveys or focus groups (i.e., small groups of customers, led by a moderator, who discuss the product). Substantial firm commitment to marketing research is critical to performing adequate customer analysis for the annual marketing plan.

Planning Assumptions

Industry, competitor, and customer analyses provide basic background information for developing marketing objectives and strategies. However, marketing managers must develop marketplace assumptions for the plan implementation period. Two major planning assumptions are estimates of market potential and market size.

Of course, it is difficult to know maximum sales for a product. Yet, market potential is very useful for allocating resources among competing products. Also, equal potential is a useful criterion for designing sales territories. Market potential is calculated in a three-step process. First, potential customers are identified by marketing research. Second, numbers of potential customers are estimated—census data can be useful here. Third, numbers of potential customers are multiplied by the potential purchasing rate. Note that potential purchasing rates may be higher than actual rates; sometimes buying rates of heavy purchasers are good indicators of potential rates.

Many methods are available for predicting market size and they can be categorized as qualitative, quantitative/time series, and quantitative/causal. Methods include judgmental forecasts, qualitative consensus forecasts, and the Delphi method (group forecasting using iterative independent judgments by experts). Quantitative/time series methods rely on historic market size values along with a statistical model: simple approaches such as moving averages, exponential smoothing, and time trends, and more sophisticated methods such as Box–Jenkins time-series modeling. Quantitative/causal methods develop statistical models by predicting market size as a function of independent variables (e.g., advertising, sales promotion).

STRATEGY FORMULATION

The third section of the marketing plan deals with a formulation of the organization's strategy.

Marketing Objectives

These items are a subset of firm objectives ranging from corporate to product to human resources. In the annual marketing plan, focus is on the specific product or service. The most commonly set objectives are for growth in sales revenues or market share, and profitability. This dichotomy is easy to conceptualize as it is typically not possible simultaneously to optimize both in the annual planning period: activities required for ambitious market share objectives work against securing ambitious profit objectives.

"Good" brand objectives must comprise quantified performance standards (e.g., "increase market share by two points"); sufficiently ambitious goals; a time frame for achieving the objective (e.g., "increase market share by two points by the end of 1993"). Objectives should be based on the background analysis.

Marketing Strategy

The two key elements, product/market selection and core strategy (differential advantage), must be established prior to marketing decisions such as price and communications. Critical to target market selection is customer analysis. Target market selection is perhaps the most important strategy decision since target customers and their buying behavior affect both product differentiation from competitors and many marketing decisions. Current thinking on product differentiation offers two options: high quality/high price and low cost/low price. "Stuck in the middle" with neither high quality nor low price is frequently a problem. For example, in retailing, Sears, J. C. Penney, and others have found their markets drained by high-end retailers such as Nordstrom's and low-end stores such as Walmart and K-mart.

Marketing Programs

These programs comprise the marketing manager's tool kit, typically called the "four P's": price, promotion, product, and place (channels of distribution). Within each there are many options and strategies. Marketing programs must be tightly integrated with the strategy; their role is to implement the strategic elements of market segment selection and product differentiation. Also, decisions on marketing programs should be made prior to determining the plan's financial implications. Ideally, the product manager analyzes the market, develops objectives and strategies necessary for success, then figures out the cost. Of course, negotiations must take place with senior marketing and other corporate officers, but marketing planning should be proactive, rather than a means to spend limited budget on the product. A preset budget results in consideration of a set of constrained alternatives, some of which would likely be unsuccessful against aggressive competitors.

CONTROL

The fourth section of the plan deals with monitoring results once the plan is implemented.

Financial Document

This reports the plan's financial implications. It is closely tied to marketing objectives and marketing programs, themselves based on the situation analysis. The financial section also brings in data from other areas (e.g., manufacturing costs, capital costs).

Monitors and Controls

The firm should not wait until the planning period's end to examine plan results. Most companies design monitors and controls to follow progress through the year. Measures should be closely tied to marketing objectives; thus, market shares and sales should be monitored closely using syndicated services or primary data such as distributor surveys. Other measures related to marketing programs are advertising (e.g., awareness, attitudes), distri-

bution (e.g., coverage), and price (e.g., transaction price versus suggested price).

CONTINGENCY PLANS

Because assumptions may go awry—for example, new competitors enter a market or interest rates increase—contingency plans, the fifth section of the plan, are necessary. It is extremely valuable to highlight the major contingencies and to develop strategy alternatives that the firm may consider implementing if the contingency occurs. Often these strategies are developed from the alternative set created in the planning process.

MARKETING RESEARCH

Donald R. Lehmann, George E. Warner Professor of Business, Graduate School of Business, Columbia University

WHAT IS MARKETING RESEARCH?

The American Marketing Association defines marketing research as "the function which links the consumer, customer, and public to the marketer through information—information used to identify and define marketing opportunities and problems; generate, refine, and evaluate marketing actions; monitor marketing performance; and improve understanding of marketing as a process. Marketing research specifies the information required to address these issues; designs the method for collecting information; manages and implements the data collection process; analyzes

the results; and communicates the findings and their implications."

The term *research* encompasses widely disparate approaches to gaining and analyzing information:

1. *Orientation*—This can range from tightly focused research (e.g., what would be the effect on sales of a 10-percent price cut?) to very general, scholarly styled investigations (e.g., finding out what customers think about when they use a product).
2. *Formality*—While most people associate research with studies that are structured with budgets, time schedules, and

computerized analysis, both introspection and informal contacts with customers or salespersons are excellent ways to gain information.

3. *Amount of data collection*—Again, a common stereotype of marketing research is that it involves extensive data collection, usually in the form of either an experiment or a survey. Not only are there many other kinds of data collection but much marketing research involves analysis of data that are already available.

4. *Complexity of analysis*—Research can include nothing more complicated than counts of the responses to a single question (i.e., how many people bought blue shirts?) or "fancy" multivariate statistical procedures that simultaneously examine several variables in a variety of ways.

Thus, marketing research and analysis is something of a hodgepodge of different approaches and heritages. It comprises a large variety of activities, including:

- Monitoring performance (sales, margin, share, turnover, returns, satisfaction).
- Idea generation and testing (advertising copy, new product concepts).
- Industry evaluation (growth rate, technological change, regulatory environment, likely entrants and exits).
- Customer analysis (who they are; why, where, and how they buy; what they buy and intend to buy; segmentation).
- Competitor analysis (who they are, what they are doing, strengths and weaknesses, what they are likely to do).
- Potential estimation and sales forecasting.
- Marketing mix evaluation: product (concept tests, test markets); distribution (sales by channel, level of support); price (elasticity estimation, impact of promotions, determining appropriate price); advertising (what to say—copy, who to say it to—targeting, when to say

it—timing, where to say it—media selection); service (level of satisfaction, voicing of complaints, adequacy of response to complaints).

WHO DOES MARKETING RESEARCH?

Research is traditionally a staff function, often aligned with planning. Those who do marketing research are a widely disparate group. There are no marketing research schools, no certification exams, and very few schools where a marketing research major exists. Hence, the academic backgrounds of those in research tend to be varied, with psychology and statistics the two most common courses of study. Many enter research on rotational assignments from line marketing positions, so it may be somewhat surprising that there is considerable colleagueality among members of the research business. Job movement between suppliers (companies that provide research services to other companies for a fee), advertising agencies, and marketing companies is common.

More specifically, research is usually performed by an outside firm (supplier). Some are fairly large such as A. C. Nielsen (known for television audience ratings and audit and scanner-based data), IMS (specializing in medical and pharmaceutical studies), and IRI (a major source of scanner data). Many others are small operations of few people. As a consequence, dealing with research suppliers (hiring, monitoring) is a major task for most research departments.

THE ROLE OF THE MARKETING RESEARCHER VIS-À-VIS THE MANAGER

The role of the company marketing researcher is that of an internal consultant. In a research project, the role is essentially threefold. First, the researcher serves as a technical consultant providing expertise in such areas as sampling and implementation (generally by knowing available suppliers, selecting an appropriate one, and working with the supplier during execution of data collection). Second, he or she is generally responsible for performing data analysis and providing an initial interpretation of results. Third, the researcher acts as consultant to the manager in both the problem definition and action recommendation stages of the project.

By contrast, the manager is primarily responsible for defining the problem and making final recommendations. To be comfortable with the results, a manager must have at least a logical, nontechnical understanding of the research project, especially in terms of its basic design.

The manager must also maintain a reasonable perspective on what research can and cannot do. Research cannot make a bad product sell, nor can it exactly forecast sales in the year 2010. A manager who asks for a single estimate of, for example, sales, ignores the associated uncertainty. Knowing whether forecast sales of 1.2 million are reliable within 10,000 or 200,000 is critical to proper contingency planning. Also, the manager who sets unrealistic time schedules (e.g., two weeks for a study in which data collection should take three) or budgets receives relatively unreliable research. Finally, managers should recognize that some apparently simple questions (e.g., What is the effect of advertising on sales?) are actually very complex. In addition to a variety of measurement issues (Do we measure sales in terms of units, dollars, or market share; advertising in terms of dollars, exposures, media used?), the basic nature of the cause and effect relationship among variables is often unclear (e.g., Does advertising cause sales, or is the advertising budget set as percent of sales?). In short, a manager must accept research projects as a useful but imperfect aid to decision making rather than a panacea.

Conflicts occur between managers and researchers. Managers often think of research as an expensive optional expense whose benefits are difficult to measure. They view it as slow to arrive, dull, overly qualified, and overly technical. By contrast, researchers criticize managers for poor and changing problem definitions, and as technically semiliterate,

unsupportive, and superficial with a predetermined right answer. Firms that minimize such conflicts, generally through direct contact leading to mutual understanding and respect, are likely to find their research function more beneficial.

Managers do not generally like to be bothered with technical details. Basically the manager needs to do three things:

1. Manage/interpret available information.
2. Recognize when additional information is needed and contract for it.
3. Communicate clearly with both researcher and others in the organization (e.g., bosses). In particular, listen to and distill information regarding strategies and problems (e.g., from bosses) and specific research issues (for researchers).

Listening is essential to good communication. These tasks suggest a basic distinction in competencies and responsibilities between researcher and manager. The manager should have an in-depth knowledge of the business and be primarily responsible for problem detection and definition. The researcher, by contrast, should be technically knowledgeable (about sampling, data collection, and methods of analysis) and focus on project specification and analysis. Interpretation of results is a joint task that blends researcher technical skills and fresh and broader perspective with the manager's knowledge of the subtleties of the particular situation.

STAGES OF A RESEARCH PROJECT

Phase 1: Problem Definition

The first phase of a research project involves defining the problem. The manager specifies what the problem is, preferably in terms of decisions to be made, and the researcher indicates what can and cannot be reasonably expected. A joint agreement as to the problem and the research question to be answered helps prevent later disagreements and re-criminations.

Phase 2: Selection of an Approach/Design

The next phase requires selection among (or selection of a combination of) types of studies. These include:

- *Qualitative studies*—Either direct one-on-one discussions (e.g., depth interviews), group discussions (e.g., focus groups), or participant or observer narrations (in the tradition of anthropology) are used. Generally useful both early on to help define problems and later to develop a more detailed understanding of reactions and behavior, these studies have grown in popularity, fueled in part by their relatively low cost.
- *Laboratory experiments*—These involve testing of factors (e.g., different product compositions) in a controlled setting. Excellent at focusing attention on a small number of factors and removing the impact of extraneous factors, these experiments often suffer from a lack of realism and overstate the impact of the variable being studied. Hence, projection to the "real world" (also known as external validity) is suspect.
- *Field experiments*—Factors that varied in real settings and their impacts are monitored (e.g., different advertising copy may be run in two regions). Unfortunately, in real settings a number of other factors are not controlled for, which may affect the results (e.g., different preferences among the regions). As a consequence, it is often difficult to disentangle the effect of the variable of interest from the effects of many other (confounding) variables.
- *Sales and customer records*—An often overlooked source of information is customer records (except for direct marketing, which has developed extensive methods for targeting specific customers). Billing records (e.g., for phone companies and other utilities) can be used to track purchase trends. Before the advent of scanner panels, and in areas where scanner panels are not available, audits based on sales records and inventory data (i.e., keeping track of sales plus beginning and ending inventory) serve as a major source of marketing research information.

  Probably the most popular sources of customer records data are scanner panels, especially for products sold through supermarkets. These panels require a household to use a special card, shop at participating stores, and as a consequence they may capture only 80 percent of purchases of a household.

  More laborious for participants but still useful are diary panels where a sample of customers agrees to record their activities (e.g., radio listening or food purchases) for a period of time (e.g., one week). Subject to various recording (or underreporting) errors, this type of panel is generally used when more mechanistic means are not available.
- *Surveys*—These are in many ways synonymous with marketing research. Ask people their image of research and a large number answer being asked to participate in a survey either in a shopping mall or by telephone or mail. Surveys allow the collection of data or attitudes and opinions (as well as objective data) and can be made to "branch" depending on answers to previous questions. Computer-controlled interviews (often made from central locations WATS [Wide-Area Telecommunications Service] lines) are very popular for both consumer and business-to-business studies, and seem to have outpaced both personal and mail interviews as the method of choice. Of course, surveys also allow for various sources of error including misinterpretation, incorrect recording of answers, various biases involving the interaction between interviewer and respondent, and interviewer cheating.

In terms of content, areas for consideration as part of a survey include:

- Background data such as demographics or firm descriptions (for business-to-business studies).
- Product category and brand use data including awareness, brands used, occasions used for.
- Brand attitudes, preferences, and attribute importances including so-called conjoint data where various combinations of product attributes are rated.
- Intentions and plans for future behavior.
- Satisfaction and quality ratings—currently the hottest topic in research.

Phase 3: Sampling

Sampling actually has two subphases: design and execution. Design involves selecting on whom (people, companies, regions) you wish to gather data. For example, in studying the reaction to a new product formulation, one might be interested in the reactions of current users of your product (who you probably do not want to antagonize), current users of other competing products (who you want to attract), and nonusers of the product category (who you also would like to attract). Thus, you must have a reasonable number of each type in your sample. Similarly you may want diversity in terms of basic descriptive variables (i.e., age, income, sex for consumer products; industry, firm size for industrial goods). A sample must therefore be designed to get a reasonable number of each type.

Design also includes the issue of sample size. To get adequate estimates, you may need a target sample of several thousand. Moreover, if you wish the same level of precision for each subgroup (i.e., the current users between ages forty and forty-nine), the sample requirement is multiplied by the number of subgroups, which means that available budget, and not statistical precision, typically determines sample size.

A third design issue involves the selection of sample points. The key to a good sample is that it be representative of the population in which you are interested in terms of what you are measuring (i.e., as long as blue-eyed people have similar mustard preferences to the population, then a sample of all blue-eyed people may be adequate for studying mustard use). Basically designs are either random (everyone has an equal chance), modified random (such as nth name), quota (where the most available people are used to get the desired number in each subgroup), or convenience (any warm body will do). In general, modified random samples are the most useful.

The execution part of sampling involves getting the desired sample points to cooperate. This can involve prior notification, support from authorities (e.g., government agencies, bosses), and monetary and other incentives. It also involves efforts. Repeated efforts to reach sample members (callbacks) increase sample response rate, though at a decreasing rate, as does precontact. While the optimum number of callbacks is not easily determined, it is generally better to have a somewhat smaller sample size and higher response rate rather than vice versa. Otherwise, questions of response bias (i.e., why did the nonrespondents refuse to participate: lack of interest in product?) make interpretation of results open to serious question.

Execution also involves checking on the accuracy of data (verifying responses with respondents and checking coding and editing of the data). Mundane issues such as how to deal with nonresponses and inconsistent responses can have substantial impact on subsequent analysis and must be dealt with systematically and reported along with the results.

Phase 4: Analysis

The most basic form of analysis involves item by item reporting frequencies, means, and standard deviations. By careful presentation of these data, much of the information in a study can be discerned (i.e., which attributes are most important, usage rates of different products).

The next most basic form is pairwise analysis of items, which is often done as cross-tabulations (tables of frequencies with one variable as the rows, the other as columns, and the frequency of each combination of "responses" occurring appearing in each cell). This analysis is appropriate for categorical data (i.e., favorite color, region of the country) as well as metric/numerical data (i.e., number of cars owned, sales last year, ratings on 100-point scales).

Whether a statistically significant relationship exists can be tested using different techniques. Metric data can be used to generate correlations, an index that ranges in magnitude from zero (no relation) to one (perfectly linearly related) with the sign indicating the direction of the relation. Examination of cross-tabulations and correlations provides additional insight but can also be misleading. For example, the correlation between sales in units and price may be positive because of the omitted variable quality: high-priced goods are (or are perceived to be) higher in quality and it is quality and not price that is driving the relation. For this reason, more complicated/sophisticated means are needed to tease out complex or subtle relations.

One class of more complex procedures are basically data simplification methods. Factor analysis examines the consistency/redundancy among variables and is useful for simplifying the number of variables to consider by either throwing out redundant ones or combining highly correlated ones in an index. Cluster analysis focuses more on the similarity among sample points and groups them into clusters/segments with similar response profiles. Multidimensional scaling (MDS) uses similarity between sample points as a basis for a graphical presentation of the sample where similar sample members are plotted close to each other, and is often used to plot brands in a (competitive) market space.

The other main class of multivariate procedures is predictive in nature. In these, a series of predictor (independent) variables is related to a criterion (dependent) variable (i.e., intention to buy a product). A variety of such procedures exists including discriminant analysis (which focuses on exploration of the differences between groups) and logistic and logit analyses (which focus on predicting the probability that an event will occur). By far the most widely used of these procedures is regression analysis. Basically regression assumes there is a linear relation between predictive and criterion variables and estimates the impacts of the predictor variables or the criterion variable.

A new generation of procedures combines, in effect, factor analysis and regression. These procedures, known as structural equation modeling, are available in computer packages such as LISREL, PLS, and EQS. For now, however, their use is fairly limited among practitioners.

Phase 5: Interpretation

Interpreting computer outputs, typically aided by statistical tests, is fairly straightforward. Translating this analysis into meaningful prose is considerably more difficult.

One major problem with interpretation is the subtle nature of causality. In regression terms, a perfect correlation does not "prove" causality nor does a low correlation rule it out. While managers want causal results, it is rare that the conditions for demonstrating causality are all met: (1) Two items vary together. (2) Precedence exists: one clearly came first. (3) No alternative explanations exist. Unfortunately, even if numbers 1 and 2 are true, it is impossible to rule out all alternative explanations. Hence, causal interpretation requires a level of belief/faith on the part of the interpreter that can be based only partially on statistics.

Another point in interpretation concerns Bayesian methods in general and past studies in particular. Classical statistics (the type appearing in most computer outputs and taught in most courses) focus on hypothesis testing, generally against the null hypothesis, that nothing is going on (i.e., the impact of price on sales is zero). Yet somehow we know there is an effect based both on intuition/theory and past studies. Hence, the real question is what is the magnitude of the effect. Obviously the best guess is what past studies found, not zero. In the future, accumulation of past results (often via a technique known as meta analysis) will provide "prior"/base value that will be adjusted by current data. Although some companies are actively pursuing this route, this approach is not yet widely used.

Phase 6: Communication

Much of the value of research is lost in its translation, which is partly the fault of the receiver, the manager. Especially in the United States, managers are so accustomed to one-page memos, simple answers, and slick presentations that they refuse to deal with subtle relations or even uncertainty. Yet sometimes the best available evidence is fairly inconclusive and the forecast for sales five years from now does and should (for planning purposes) have a big range associated with it.

The researcher often is a major contributor to misused (and hence unused) communication as well. Selling research results is a marketing task and serious attempts need to be made to translate the results into a form (ben-

efits) useful to the manager. The reporting of reams of test statistics is counterproductive except in a nonessential appendix, and what impresses peers often alienates managers. Try talking in normal terms—you may find out it helps clarify your own thinking.

CONCLUSION

The phases described in this chapter focus on the execution of a single research project. Yet the success of research depends on the relations of past and present studies, researchers and managers, firms and suppliers. Managing on a project-by-project basis leads to loss of information from previous studies as well as almost an adversarial relation between the parties involved. A more long-term relation seems likely to be productive, as the current literature on quality suggests.

Finally, remember that customers are more than statistics. Direct contact can be very enlightening and companies that avoid such contact do so at their own peril.

CUSTOMER DECISION MAKING

Paul W. Miniard, Professor of Marketing, University of South Carolina

TRACKING CUSTOMER BEHAVIOR

Tracking customer purchase behavior over time provides valuable information to help firms assess their abilities to retain and recruit customers. Success at retaining customers is measured by the number of last period's (e.g., year, season, month, purchase occasion) customers that purchased this period. The number of this period's customers that were not customers last period is a measure of recruitment success. Whether sales are down, flat, or improved, the firm must understand performance in both areas. For instance, even if sales are improved, outstanding recruitment may mask declining retention.

Of course, aggregate measures of customers gained or lost do not identify where new customers have come from or former customers have gone. Such insights can be gleaned, however, from a switching matrix that tracks customer buying behavior from one purchase period to the next. Consider a three-competitor (A, B, C) market. We collect purchase data from 1,000 buyers concerning which firm's product was purchased in period 1 and period 2. We can then construct a switching matrix such as presented in Exhibit 2-13.

The row and column totals tell us that in period 1, firm A had a 50-percent market share (500/1,000), followed by firms B (30%)

and C (20%). In period 2, some things changed; A lost share (40%), B gained share (40%), and C held ground (20%).

Factors driving market share changes are in the heart of the exhibit. The first row represents purchases made in period 2 by the 500 customers that bought from firm A in period 1. Firm A retained 400 of 500; 20 switched to B; 80 switched to C. For B (second row), 270 of 300 period 1 buyers repurchased in period 2; 30 went to C. Finally, C retained only 90 of its original 200 customers; the rest defected to B.

These data tells us there are substantial differences in the firms' abilities to retain customers. We calculate retention rates by dividing numbers in the top/left-to-bottom/right diagonal (retained customers) by row totals (numbers of customers in period 1). Retention rates are: firm A, 80 percent (400/500); firm B, 90 percent (270/300); firm C, 45 percent (90/200). In terms of retaining customers, C needs a wake-up call!

The matrix also tells us where "lost" customers are going. Firm A lost business to both B and C, but C poses the more serious threat; it stole four times more customers (80) than B (20). Firms B and C should only worry about each other (C should be very concerned about B, which stole 55% of C's customers); firm A did not attract business from either firm.

Finally, the switching matrix provides information about each company's success at

Exhibit 2-13. Switching Matrix Example

		Firm Purchased at Period 2:			
		A	**B**	**C**	**Total**
Firm Purchased at Period 1:	**A**	400	20	80	500
	B	0	270	30	300
	C	0	110	90	200
	Total	400	400	200	1000

stealing competitors' customers. While C is less skilled at keeping customers, it is a very successful customer recruiter (110). Firm B (130) is also good at recruiting; its ability to attract new business while retaining most current customers accounts for its market share rise. Firm A, by contrast, did not attract any business from competitors.

This example assumes that all customers purchased in both periods. The analysis can be extended to incorporate period 1 buyers not purchasing in period 2, and first-time buyers in period 2. These extensions provide valuable data on new buyer recruiting and more complete data on where former customers are going.

The particular matrix design depends both on the product category and the information required. In some cases "firm" is appropriate; in other cases, "brand" (e.g., Pepsi, 7 Up, Coke, Sprite, Dr. Pepper) is appropriate. The analysis may focus on consecutive purchase occasions or purchase periods (e.g., year, month, season). For example, in some categories (e.g., restaurants) customers continually rotate purchases among an offering set. A switching matrix based on consecutive purchase occasions would suggest very low customer retention levels; a longer time span for purchase should provide better customer retention information.

In sum, tracking purchase behavior provides valuable insights into a firm's customer recruitment and retention abilities. It identifies sources of new customers, where former customers are going, and the relative competitive threat. However, it only tells what has

occurred, not why. We must dig deeper to appreciate the factors responsible for purchase behavior. One way is to focus on the process by which customers make buying decisions.

From a decision-making perspective, purchase is one element in a process that customers engage in to acquire and consume goods and services. Sometimes the process is complex and requires much time and effort; at other times customers minimize decision-making time and effort, leading to a relatively simple decision process. These differences in decision making have important marketing implications.

STAGES IN THE DECISION-MAKING PROCESS

Marketing researchers traditionally separate the purchase decision process into several stages (Exhibit 2-14). Because products are purchased to fulfill needs, customers must be aware of some unmet need(s) before they are motivated to action. This *need recognition* is the initial process stage.

Need recognition occurs when customers perceive a difference between their current state and a desired state sufficient to activate the decision process. Thus, when customers' needs are satisfied, harmony exists between current and desired states, and need recognition does not occur. However, this harmony is only temporary; the passage of time alone can lead to current state erosion, such as when products wear out.

Exhibit 2-14. Stages in the Decision-Making Process

Need Recognition

↓

Information Search

↓

Prepurchase Evaluation

↓

Purchase

↓

Postpurchase Evaluation

Although need recognition is highly dependent on the passage of time, marketers may influence need recognition by altering desired states. For example, product innovations can cause customers to redefine desired states. Reebok's "pump it up" athletic shoe led many young consumers to become disenchanted with their current footwear. Information can also change desired states. A consumer may believe her current (15.9% APR) credit card is a good deal compared to her former card (18.5%). But then she encounters a mailer promoting a 12-percent APR (annual percentage rate) card; her desired state will change.

Once need recognition occurs, the customer engages in search for potential need satisfiers. *Information search* represents the motivated activation of knowledge stored in memory (internal search) and/or acquisition of environmental information (external search). Customers start with internal search since this may be sufficient; in particular, experienced customers may have a wealth of data available in memory, particularly for relatively unchanging product categories. However, for inexperienced customers as well as experienced customers whose knowledge is "outdated" via new brands, product innovations, or price changes, internal search alone may be inadequate. External search will then be needed.

The amount and nature of search is shaped by several decisions: which brands to consider, which attributes to evaluate, which information sources to consult, which stores/suppliers to shop. Customers may select a single store/supplier and choose the lowest-priced item; alternatively, search may encompass many sources and involve comparisons across multiple brands, attributes, and stores/suppliers.

What could we learn by asking recent purchasers about their search activities? We might partition them into segments based on how much they searched (e.g., extensive, moderate, minimal) and see if purchase behavior differed. Suppose the high-search segment purchased the firm's product more often than other segments; in this regard, it represents an attractive target. Moreover, because greater search apparently enhanced the odds of customers buying the firm's product, it might try to enhance customers' search efforts (e.g., Dannon yogurt ads asking consumers to read package labels; Texas Instrument's "dare to compare" personal computer campaign).

The firm might also gain a better appreciation of its immediate competition from the customer's perspective by identifying which competitors are examined during search. Competitors considered by the firm's customers obviously pose a stronger competitive threat than those that are ignored. From this understanding of competitors, the firm can better assess the need to respond to competitor actions. A price cut to meet competitor action may be unnecessary if this competitor is not examined during search.

Search behavior among customers buying from competitors provides information relevant to customer recruitment. Since products cannot be purchased unless considered, the firm must determine if its product is being considered during decision making; if not, why not? Customers may be unaware of the firm (product), or may be aware but do not consider the offer. Firm actions are guided by reasons for nonconsideration.

Understanding the specific information sources (e.g., pharmacist, salespeople, other customers, magazine articles) consulted by customers during search helps identify which sources to monitor for data/opinion about the firm's product. Also, it provides guidance as to which sources might be used productively when trying to influence customers' purchase decisions (e.g., infrequently used sources rarely hold much promise for persuading customers).

At *prepurchase evaluation,* customers evaluate the various products under consideration and decide which to purchase. Customers form the attitudes and preferences that determine purchase behavior. Attitudes are based on customers' perceptions/beliefs regarding how well each product offering satisfies needs, given budget constraints. Examining beliefs and attitudes helps build an understanding of the reasons underlying customer purchases.

Consider a customer survey that rates three suppliers (A, B, C) along several attributes. From supplier A's perspective, we first consider the findings based on A's customers (Exhibit 2-15A). We can see that A's customers perceive it as having a very convenient location, a fairly wide product assortment, and

fairly low prices; A's shopping atmosphere is perceived poorly. For A to make changes based solely on this information is risky. For example, although performance on atmosphere is poor and changes could be made, customers may place little importance on this attribute; greater payoff may be realized by focusing efforts elsewhere. Thus, information about the attributes' relative importance would be necessary.

Exhibit 2-15B presents performance relative to competitors B and C. Supplier B poses a more serious threat to A's customer base than C. A's customers view B as offering equally convenient location and width of assortment, a more attractive atmosphere, and only slightly higher prices. Consequently, A must be particularly attentive to the actions of B. A may wish to enhance perceived differentiation between itself and B, perhaps along price and/or assortment dimensions. Whether this would require price cuts or expanded product lines depends on the accuracy of customers'

Exhibit 2-15. Ratings by Customers of Supplier A

A

convenient location	____ : _A_ : ____ : ____ : ____ : ____ : ____ : ____ : ____ : ____ : ____	inconvenient location
low prices	____ : ____ : ____ : _A_ : ____ : ____ : ____ : ____ : ____ : ____ : ____	high prices
wide assortment	____ : ____ : ____ : _A_ : ____ : ____ : ____ : ____ : ____ : ____ : ____	narrow assortment
pleasant atmosphere	____ : ____ : ____ : ____ : ____ : ____ : ____ : ____ : _A_ : ____ : ____	unpleasant atmosphere

B

convenient location	____ : _AB_ : ____ : ____ : ____ : ____ : ____ : ____ : _C_ : ____ : ____	inconvenient location
low prices	____ : ____ : ____ : _A_ : _B_ : ____ : ____ : ____ : ____ : _C_ : ____	high prices
wide assortment	____ : _C_ : ____ : _AB_ : ____ : ____ : ____ : ____ : ____ : ____ : ____	narrow assortment
pleasant atmosphere	____ : _C_ : ____ : ____ : ____ : _B_ : ____ : ____ : _A_ : ____ : ____	unpleasant atmosphere

Exhibit 2-16. Ratings by Customers of Supplier B

convenient location	___ : AB : ___ : ___ : ___ : ___ : ___ : C : ___ : ___ : ___	inconvenient location
low prices	___ : ___ : B : ___ : A : ___ : ___ : ___ : C : ___ : ___	high prices
wide assortment	___ : ___ : C : B : ___ : ___ : A : ___ : ___ : ___ : ___	narrow assortment
pleasant atmosphere	___ : ___ : C : ___ : B : ___ : ___ : ___ : A : ___ : ___	unpleasant atmosphere

perceptions. Discrepancies between customer perceptions and marketplace realities are not uncommon. If, for instance, A actually carries a substantially wider assortment than B, then A should correct the current misperception that A and B are equal on this dimension.

In developing customer recruitment strategies, examining the ratings of a competitor's customers can be very useful (Exhibit 2-16). For A, location is not a barrier to attracting B's customers, but perceptions involving the remaining attributes undermine A's attractiveness. Before taking action, A must consider each attribute's relative importance and explore perceptual accuracy. For example, contrary to B's customers' beliefs, prices at B may be higher, not lower, than at A; A should correct the misperception. However, if B's prices are in fact lower, A may have to consider price changes to attract these customers.

When customers have collected sufficient information to evaluate choice alternatives, a selection is made and *purchase* occurs. This is followed by the final decision stage: *postpurchase evaluation*. How satisfied was the customer? Customer repurchase strongly depends on whether the experience was satisfying or unsatisfying. Satisfied customers return and often recommend to other customers; dissatisfied customers take their business elsewhere and are often more active than satisfied customers in spreading the word about their consumption experiences.

Customer satisfaction depends on whether product performance meets expectations. If expectations are met or surpassed, the consumer is satisfied; if performance falls short,

dissatisfaction occurs. The dilemma for marketers is that the greater the promise (i.e., higher expectations), the more likely customers are to try. But if high expectations cannot be met, initial purchases may be gained at the loss of repeat buyers.

Monitoring customer satisfaction is a worthwhile investment. It serves as an early warning system of potential customer retention problems, and may provide ammunition for advertising copy. Each year the winner of the latest J. D. Power survey of new car buyer satisfaction spends a considerable amount of money to advertise the victory.

TYPES OF DECISION MAKING

The purchase decision process just discussed well captures complex purchase decisions. However, customer behavior is clearly different for a person buying a car versus breakfast cereal, or a firm buying capital equipment versus routine supplies. Many product categories are simply not that important or involving for customers.

Thus, while some purchase decisions involve elaborate processes, many do not. Once customers have made one or a few purchases in a product category, they may follow a habitual process. Customers simply buy the product previously purchased; other brands are not even considered. Once need recognition occurs, customers simply remember the previous purchase and buy it again.

Habitual decision making occurs because

buying the same product greatly simplifies decision making. Customers may not have strong product loyalty, but it performs well enough to satisfy their needs and mitigates investing effort to investigate purchase alternatives. Habitual decision making also occurs when customers are satisfied with the product and develop loyalty. Repurchasing is motivated more by satisfaction rather than by desire to minimize effort.

In general, it is more difficult to recruit customers following habitual decision processes, particularly when based on strong product loyalty. A product must first receive consideration before it can be purchased. Habitual decision makers only consider one product—the one previously bought. To attract habituated buyers the firm must reactivate the decision making process to gain consideration. Such efforts are not needed when customers use nonhabitual processes.

From a customer retention perspective, it is most desirable to have customers that follow habitual processes. The firm should avoid actions that push customers back into an active decision process. Noticeable declines in product quality, out-of-stocks, or significant price increases can cause customers to consider competitors. In nonhabitual processes, competitors already receive this consideration. Consequently, it is important to determine which competitors are being considered, and how they are perceived relative to the firm by its customers.

THE DECISION-MAKING UNIT

So far, the discussion of customer decision making has assumed that the customer is a single individual. Frequently, however, more than one person is involved in the purchase decision process. These members of the decision-making unit (DMU) may be family members in consumer purchases or different organization members in industrial purchasing.

The DMU normally is viewed as comprising five major roles:

1. *Initiator*—person who activates the decision process.
2. *Influencer*—person whose opinions affect what is purchased.
3. *Decider*—person responsible for the final decision.
4. *Buyer*—person who actually purchases the product.
5. *User*—the actual product or service user.

For example, a teenager tells his parents that a personal computer would be very helpful for schoolwork. The parents visit a computer store and, after a lengthy discussion with a salesperson, purchase his product recommendation. The child was the initiator and user; the parents were the decider and buyer; the salesperson was an influencer. In industrial purchasing, where the buyer is frequently a professional purchasing agent, the other roles are played by organization members in different departments and at different levels in the management hierarchy.

In general, marketing effort is more demanding as the number of persons comprising a DMU increases, in part because customer needs may vary across the DMU. If the DMU is a single person, only one person need be targeted. As the DMU increases in size, the number of potential targets increases. In complex purchasing decisions, many potential influencers may be targeted. However, not all DMU members should necessarily be targeted; effort is only justifiable when a DMU member has influence on the purchase decision. For example, in men's underwear, women account for roughly 80 percent of sales; men have relatively little purchase influence. Although they are users, they rarely initiate the buying process, nor do they commonly request a particular brand. Accordingly, marketing efforts are directed primarily toward product purchasers rather than actual product users.

CORPORATE MARKETING

W. Sanford Miller, Jr., Chief Marketing Officer/Corporate Strategist, CIGNA Corporation

The business environment is increasingly complex and fast changing; competitive challenges are growing in depth and scope. As a result, the importance to business firms of developing an external orientation is greater than ever. However, the gap between businesses that are truly marketing and customer oriented and those that are not has widened dramatically. For corporations desiring change, rather than relying solely on the operating businesses to establish a marketing orientation, a clear role exists for a corporate marketing function. However, if marketing is working well in a firm, a centralized corporate marketing organization should have a minimal or nonexistent role.

We define corporate marketing as a centralized organization designed to make a firm more marketing oriented, in contrast to the traditional line role of "doing" marketing in the operating units. Corporate marketing typically has two functions. First, it may be designed to make the operating businesses more marketing oriented. Second, it may carry out certain tasks that for cost or other reasons are better controlled centrally; advertising is a notable example.

Efforts to change marketing practices in companies are often driven by competitors. These competitors, focusing on customers and thereby improving sales and earnings, force others to react to their successes. Other firms, recognizing that embracing marketing may give them substantial competitive advantage, have initiated these changes on their own. Beyond traditional consumer packaged goods companies, some industrial and service businesses exemplify a marketing orientation (e.g., American Express, Citibank, 3M). However, these firms are the exception, not the rule.

In contrast to a strong marketing orientation, many firms are driven by a focus on such functions as finance, engineering, research, operations, or underwriting. In some firms, the ability to acquire and shed businesses is the driving force. These functions or activities set the tone for management and often focus attention internally.

To make the change to a marketing orientation, firms must become more flexible and align themselves more directly to their customers, which is easier said than done. Professor John P. Kotter searched for examples of large companies effecting such change and found only ten, including General Electric, British Air, and Xerox. "For the cynics who say it's impossible, yes, it's possible." But Kotter says, "only barely."

Of course, many firms have marketing-like departments controlled at the CEO level. However, these typically have public relations and advertising functions, operating largely at the whim of senior management. That these managers cannot initiate major cultural and strategic change is sometimes not immediately evident to management, but it is a first and necessary step in the change process. Their inability to act in a real marketing capacity is often overlooked because of their "loyal" service to management.

EVOLVING A MARKETING ORIENTATION

Structure for Change

When the decision is made to evolve to a marketing orientation, firms have several options from which to choose. First, each operating business or strategic business unit (SBU) can do the job individually with its own resources. The major drawback to this option mirrors the original problem of lack of marketing orientation: the experience of current senior management and staff is limited. In addition, costs may be prohibitive as smaller businesses may not warrant full marketing staffs.

Second, a mixture of executional aspects can take place in the operating units with assistance, coaching, and guidance from a central marketing organization operating under the CEO. This option sounds simple, but may create major organizational problems. Arguably, the biggest issue is assigning responsibility for managing the overall business: Does the responsibility go to staff or line management?

Third, guidance and coaching is offered from a corporate unit only to those who ask for it. This can be particularly effective when real progress is made and obvious disparity is created among operating businesses.

In most cases, a combination of these approaches is most likely preferable to any single approach. If a corporate marketing approach is chosen, its structure should be conceived of in horizontal, rather than vertical, terms. The traditional pyramid reinforces hierarchical behavior and limits the perception of staff value. Small groups with no apparent leader allow for equal contributions to be made by a greater number of skilled people. Businesses do not find it necessary to deal with the person in charge of research, but can deal with an equal number of qualified peo-

ple. "Higher-level" work can be completed simultaneously. This structure fosters teamwork and collaboration while breaking down inflexibility. Flexibility is important, particularly because the marketing change is sought throughout the entire organization.

Measuring Progress

Regardless which approach or approach combination is selected, the creation and use of a measurement system is an important part of the corporate role. It should be created specifically by the firm and reflect its current structure and problems. It is critical to develop common measures that allow for comparison of each SBU's progress against the others, and the continued drive toward each business developing and operating its own marketing culture.

The easiest way to construct such measures is to develop a time and activities matrix (Exhibit 2-17). Time represents phases in the evolution of marketing; activities refer to specific marketing tasks, such as marketing planning, use of research, and product development, that are important to marketing's success. Each activity is charted in various phases as its role and importance change. For example, in the strategic phase, marketing research has a more influential role than in the earlier tactical phase. While neither a new nor novel approach, this measurement system allows everyone to see how each business is progressing. As businesses move from left to right (the ultimate goal) they progress from one phase to another. Not only is each business tracked individually but the entire company's progress is tracked as well.

Change Processes and Difficulties

Marketing is a line function; few would argue it can or should be centrally managed. Big organizations broken into small organizations seem capable of functioning better. Therefore, a corporate marketing organization should always be viewed as transitional; it should change as the corporation changes. However, real change in large organizations is far more difficult and painful than most people realize. A centralized marketing structure can serve important roles in orchestrat-

Exhibit 2-17. Marketing Measurement Matrix

Phases (Time)

	Tactical	Strategic

Marketing Planning
Use of Research
Product Development
(Activities)

ing change, but such structures are fraught with problems and their mission and effectiveness should constantly be evaluated.

If the CEO has a clear view and desire to change, and operating management's ability to execute marketing is limited, a corporate marketing organization can play a primary role as catalyst and bridge between the CEO and operating divisions. In addition, change may be forced on SBUs by forces beyond their control: markets appear and disappear; competitors are smarter; new product development is faster; product life cycles are shrinking. A friendly corporate group can help cope with change.

More and more it is argued that marketing is everyone's job; marketing is too important to be left to marketing people! But in addition to fostering a shift toward the customer, CEOs often press for improved cost controls, productivity and earnings growth. These goals may be in conflict with a marketing orientation. A corporate marketing organization can bridge these differences and act as a successful intermediary between the CEO and the operating businesses in bringing clarity to how these factors work together.

There is, of course, a danger that corporate staffs often seek justification for their existence and importance, and add little or no real value. Large corporate staffs can often be properly labeled as "meddlers"; traditionally they are not good change agents. Hence, those selected for the corporate marketing organization should understand their role is not perennial, but should ultimately disappear.

Compensation can be structured with this in mind.

MARKETING STAFFING

Successful marketing is difficult without experienced marketing personnel. Simply "knighting" individuals from other functions (e.g., finance, sales, production, engineering, underwriting, actuary) to the corporate marketing position often fails. Rather, a careful balance of existing personnel and outside marketing professionals offers the best chance for success. In general, a corporate marketing organization should be staffed with fewer but better qualified and experienced people. This may require altering levels and compensation.

The corporate marketing group can play an important role in helping marketing staffing in the SBUs. The firm should search for as many internal candidates for marketing jobs as possible. Candidates should have demonstrated an affinity for customers, a penchant for externally focused strategic thinking, personal traits such as an insatiable curiosity about business, and an ability to foster cooperation and teamwork. Of course, candidates for marketing positions should not be selected merely because they have proven themselves in their own disciplines.

An internal-external people balance is necessary for rather obvious reasons. Internal people know the business, the politics, and perhaps most importantly, how to get things done. A blend with experienced marketing people from the outside creates the powerful combination needed to initiate the marketing orientation.

The corporate marketing organization can assist in ensuring the assimilation and success of these outside marketing people. In some cases, drastic steps such as altering people's compensation around the success of newly hired outsiders may be necessary. Because they represent change, new hires may be viewed as a threat. A subtle issue of concern is that marketing professionals from highly marketing-oriented firms may find it difficult to operate in information-poor environments.

ROLES FOR CORPORATE MARKETING

An important corporate marketing role is help in blending business strategies and marketing plans. Broad and nonspecific sales and financial plans must be replaced or augmented with hard market analysis that may force the elimination of markets and/or current customers from the firm's portfolio. A small corporate marketing group working with the operating businesses to review and assist in plans development can be extremely effective. Of course, these plans must be "owned" by the businesses. A particularly important role is reinforcing the efficacy of limiting and specifying strategic objectives.

As noted earlier, certain marketing functions (e.g., research, communications, advertising), more properly termed marketing services, can be greatly improved by use of a corporate marketing organization. A central marketing structure can combine communications organizations, slim down staff, upgrade personnel, and use functional responsibilities to challenge not merely the tactics but the basic tenets of strategy. In many cases, it may discover there is no strategy. Strategic improvements can be made by using these functions to challenge and push for a marketing orientation.

Corporate marketing can spot trends occurring as the marketing process unfolds and can prevent businesses from going in the wrong direction. For example, many firms discover marketing research and embark on focus group mania; anyone wanting to learn about customers advocates focus groups. However, simple conversations and informal customer interviews can be less expensive, quicker, and more valuable because they give people direct customer contact and feedback.

Also, in the area of product development, corporate marketing professionals can objectively evaluate new product concepts and ensure they reflect both the desires of the market and competitive offerings. In addition, they can teach people to develop more "complete" products designed around customer needs.

As the firm evolves so that a marketing orientation is broadly adhered to by the various functional areas, the role of the corporate marketing organization must reflect that evolution. However, corporate marketing's most significant effort should be toward a broad planning role in which it analyzes environmental changes and fosters contention within the corporation as to how best to respond.

MARKETING AND QUALITY

Donna L. Hoffman, Associate Professor of Marketing, Owen Graduate School of Management, Vanderbilt University

Jan-Benedict E. M. Steenkamp, AGB Professor of Marketing Research, Catholic University of Leuven, Belgium

Four approaches may be identified when examining the issue of perceived quality and consumer behavior. The simultaneous existence of four different methodologies often causes confusion with respect to product quality. This article examines the issue and attempts to resolve the confusion.

THE METAPHYSICAL APPROACH

The metaphysical approach to quality, which has profoundly influenced thinking on the quality concept, focuses on the "being" of quality; quality represents a mark of uncompromising standards and high achievement. This approach regards quality as an unanalyzable property that individuals can only learn to recognize through experience. People disagree about quality not because quality varies but because their experience about quality varies.

THE PRODUCTION MANAGEMENT APPROACH

By contrast, in the production management approach, quality is an objectively measurable concept, customarily defined as conformance to technical specifications. Product quality is achieved and maintained by four interrelated quality-determining parameters: (1) quality of design, (2) quality of production, (3) continuity of service, and (4) customer after-sale service.

Quality of design, which refers to the quality level the product must possess, involves three functions: (1) identifying consumers' quality needs, (2) developing a product concept that meets these needs, and (3) translating this concept into a detailed set of specifications.

Quality of production (or quality of conformance) refers to all activities undertaken to meet the design specifications during the manufacturing process. Typically, specifications include acceptable deviations (tolerances), since different factors (e.g., operator fatigue, input material variation) imply that some samples will not conform precisely to all specifications.

For durable goods two additional parameters are important. Continuity of service, involving product reliability and ease of maintenance, means that the product is in a usable state; customer service comprises speed, competence, and integrity of after-sale service.

Costs must be incurred to secure high quality. *Appraisal costs* include inspection and testing costs to measure firm output against quality specifications. *Internal failure costs* include scrap, rework, and spoilage. *External failure costs* (e.g., warranty charges) are caused when customers receive defective products. *Prevention costs* minimize failure and appraisal costs and include employee training, quality reporting, and improvement projects.

Total quality costs typically comprise 60–70 percent of internal and external failures; 25–35 percent of appraisal costs; and only 5 percent of prevention costs. Increasing prevention costs to 10–15 percent of total quality costs may both reduce total quality costs and increase product quality.

THE ECONOMIC APPROACH

Economists have historically ignored the concept of quality, since in perfect markets they assume that products are homogeneous and that consumers are fully informed. Although theories of oligopoly and monopolistic competition can incorporate *differentiated* products and imperfectly informed consumers, their major weakness regarding quality is the focus on objective product characteristics. Unfortunately, economic theory has little to say regarding consumer perception of objective reality, and those behavioral factors that must be considered in studying how consumers evaluate and assimilate quality in their purchase decisions.

THE PERCEIVED QUALITY APPROACH

The essence of the perceived quality approach deriving from marketing is that quality lies in the eye of the beholder, and is neither absolute nor objective. Quality must be subjective since it depends on the needs, goals, and perceptions of individual consumers. The perceived quality approach concentrates on the way consumers form judgments about the quality of a product on the basis of incomplete information.

Consumer Perceptions of Quality

How do consumers form impressions regarding the quality of refrigerators, cars, cereals, and other products? A managerially useful model distinguishes three core concepts: quality attributes, overall perceived quality, and quality cues. *Quality attributes* are the functional and psychosocial benefits provided by the product; they are revealed only upon consumption (e.g., taste of a cut of meat, automobile fuel consumption; a detergent's cleaning power). *Perceived quality* is a higher-level abstraction than a specific product attribute; however, overall perceived quality judgments are based on product perceptions of the quality attributes. *Quality cues* are informational stimuli received by consumers through the senses prior to consumption. Cues encompass a multiplicity of product-related characteristics including price, brand name, country of origin, advertising, store image, color, and other physical aspects. Quality cues are important, since prior to consumption the brand's benefits are unknown. Thus, consumers typically use quality cues in choosing between brands; highly involved consumers may use more quality cues.

Quality cues are observed by consumers through the senses; quality attributes are what consumers desire in the product. Cues are valued because of their perceived relationship(s) with quality attributes: the extent to which they are perceived to be a means of achieving ends that the consumers value, namely, benefits or quality attributes. For example, consumers cannot secure direct insight into the cleaning effectiveness (quality attribute) of a detergent prior to use; they must rely on quality cues such as brand name, price, and physical product attributes to gain an impression of cleaning effectiveness.

This model has been used to develop quality-based marketing strategies. It can also be used to investigate the relationship between quality cues and quality attributes. For example, advertising should concentrate on cues that consumers rate as favorable to the brand *and* that predict important quality attributes. Message content should be developed in terms of favorable cues and attributes they predict; the danger of incorporating minor cues (clutter) in the message is thus reduced. The model can also be used in consumer-based quality improvement and cost reduction programs by identifying important cues that should be modified to enhance the quality image and quality cues unused by consumers that can be modified to reduce costs.

Place of purchase may be an important cue in the formation of quality perceptions; the firm may use such data as input in evaluating selective versus mass distribution. The model may also be used to develop pricing strategy, particularly when information is available about consumers' price versus perceived quality trade-offs.

Quality and Perceived Risk

Only in rare circumstances can consumers evaluate a brand's quality with absolute certainty. Typically, relevant cues are missing, and available cues may be misunderstood. Thus, perceived quality risk must be considered as a component of the quality perception process.

Perceived quality risk is the state of tension consumers experience in the decision-making process resulting from the fact that a contemplated purchase might lead to an undesirable outcome. Quality risk has two dimensions: (1) uncertainty about the *outcome* of the decision and (2) the extent of possible *negative consequences* after purchase.

Studies show that perceived risk varies across consumers and products. Consumers perceiving higher risk are less willing to try new products; also, products with higher perceived risk are less favorably evaluated. Overall product ranking according to perceived risk tends to correspond to overall ranking based on price.

Since perceiving risk is typically a negative state, consumers develop risk-reduction strategies aimed at minimizing the likelihood of making the wrong choice when perceived risk exceeds tolerable risk. Brand loyalty is one such strategy; consumers who find a particular brand satisfactory continue purchasing so as to avoid the risk associated with buying a new (to them) brand. Other strategies are price-dominance quality evaluation (i.e., buy the more expensive brand) and reliance

on store image, warranties, or the firm's reputation. Consumers use a wide variety of quality cues to alleviate perceived quality risk. Information search via informal discussions with friends or relatives, or reading published test reports, may also reduce risk, but the empirical results are equivocal.

Marketers can reduce consumer risk and improve brand attractiveness by developing strategies along each dimension of perceived quality risk. Building brand image and providing product information are strategies aimed primarily at reducing uncertainty about decision outcomes; extended warranties, postsale service, and complaint management may reduce anxiety about possible negative consequences.

RELATIONSHIPS AMONG THE FOUR APPROACHES TO PRODUCT QUALITY

All four approaches to product quality have merit since they focus on different aspects of quality; the connections are depicted in Exhibit 2-18. The perceived quality approach is input to the production management approach. This link explicitly recognizes that product specifications should be based on

Exhibit 2–18. Relationships among the Four Approaches to Product Quality

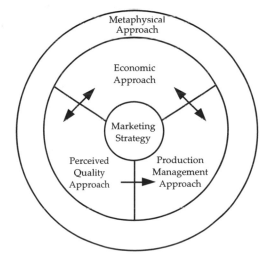

consumer needs. The firm should first identify the quality needs and perceptions of the target market (perceived quality approach), then translate these perceptions into physical product characteristics. The firm should then develop procedures to ensure that the product possesses these physical characteristics (production management approach).

This quality guidance link between the perceived quality and production management approaches expresses the alliance that must exist between marketing and marketing research, and production and research and development. Quality guidance implies that physical characteristics are linked psychophysically to quality attribute perceptions; these perceptions are combined into overall perceived quality. The firm must understand the connection between physical product characteristics and quality perceptions. Then it should identify those physical product characteristics for which consumers' tolerance for deviations from optimum are lowest; these should be modified to enhance consumers' quality perceptions.

The relationship between the perceived quality and the production management approaches is mediated by the economic approach. Firms do not select quality levels based solely on consumer perceptions. Economic considerations play an important role since firms select quality levels to achieve economic objectives (e.g., profitability, market share).

The economic approach may also benefit from the production management approach. Thus, research on production costs reveals that higher quality does not necessarily lead to higher costs; the economic approach assumes that higher quality implies higher costs. Also, the production management approach indicates that quality is useful as a competitive factor when it can be specified objectively. Finally, the economic approach may provide production managers with guidelines concerning maximum allowable level of defects for optimal profitability.

Since the metaphysical approach deals only with the *concept* of quality, not with specific aspects of quality, it provides a foundation for the other approaches. It contributes to the perceived quality approach by highlighting the idea that such intangibles as esthetics may enter into consumers' quality perceptions. Its focus on quality as a mark of uncompromising standards gives philosophical support to what many observers call the "Japanese approach to production management."

Marketing strategy is influenced by the different approaches to quality. Consumers' needs and perceptions; profits, market share, and other economic considerations; production costs, levels of defects, and other production considerations, are all input to developing marketing strategy. Firms should develop marketing strategy by first investigating quality perceptions (perceived quality approach); translating these perceptions into technical specifications (quality guidance); selecting the quality level yielding the highest profit or market share (economic approach); and finally, developing a production management and quality control system that enables the firm to maintain the selected quality level (production management approach). Firms that embrace this process are truly market oriented in their quality strategy.

DEVELOPING NEW PRODUCTS

Thomas D. Kuczmarski, President, Kuczmarski & Associates

AIMING FOR SUCCESS

In a recent survey on winning new product and service practices for the 1990s, managers cited several internal obstacles that affect their new product success. The top three barriers cited by twenty-seven new product directors who have launched over 1,100 new products during a five-year period include:

- Top management risk-aversion and short-term orientation
- Insufficient people and funding resources
- Poor understanding of the market and lack of market research

For the most part, senior management continues to pay lip service to new product development because it is risky and often requires a longer-term investment to achieve the big bang for the bucks. However, the key answer to overcoming these barriers and surmounting the top management short-term commitment obstacle is to create a systematic process for developing new products—for innovation can be managed, marshaled, and harnessed into a repeatable and routinized process that yields creative and innovative new products and services on a continuous basis.

The top five challenges of the 1990s facing firms that develop new products and services are:

1. The majority of companies are preoccupied with reducing the development time of new products—getting them to market faster as well as reducing the cycle time from idea generation to commercialization. The challenge is to reduce the time while trying to increase the success rate of new products launched.

2. Managers recognize the power and value in more innovative new products. They see the need to develop more "new-to-the-world" and "new-to-the-company" types. In fact, the most successful new product companies achieve roughly 40 percent of their new product portfolio from these higher-risk types of new products. The challenge is to convince top management that innovation pays for itself and is worth the risk.

3. Being able to kill off a new product or service enroute to commercialization is difficult for many companies. A certain momentum is established for a new product and management is reluctant to stop the process. The challenge is to set up a system that enables some of the emotional momentum to be taken out of the process and allows better resource allocation.

Exhibit 2-19. New Product Success Ladder

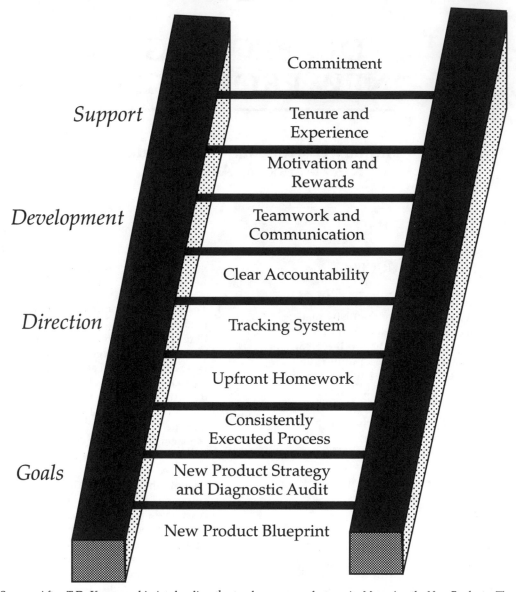

Source: After T.D. Kuczmarski, Applauding the ten key success factors, in *Managing the New Products: The Power of Innovation* (Englewood Cliffs, NJ: Prentice-Hall, 1992).

4. Most companies still need to develop tailored compensation programs that reward risk taking and provide financial recognition for achieving success. The challenge is to convince management that an innovative incentive system is valuable.

5. Most companies are still neglecting to globalize their new product development process. While they recognize the need to pursue foreign markets, they tend to make product adaptations on a regional basis more than developing global new products. The challenge is

to design a process that offers more sensitivity to global new products.

Unfortunately, there is no neatly packaged software program that provides sure success for managing new products. However, patterns continue to emerge that are similar among companies who seem to be good at developing a steady stream of profitable new products. Thus, success factors are relatively common across truly innovative companies.

The following ten success factors, depicted in Exhibit 2-19, tend to be found in winning new product companies:

1. *New product blueprint*—defines the overall direction and role of new products relative to a company's growth objectives and strategy.
2. *New product strategy*—identifies the game plan, that is, how a company plans to achieve the blueprint. Defines new product financial goals, strategic roles, new product types, product/market categories, performance benchmarks, and new product screening criteria.
3. *Consistently executed process*—Pinpoints the development stages that a new product concept passes through to reach commercialization. Offers a commonly understood and consistently applied approach for all participants in the new product process.
4. *Adequate upfront homework*—provides market, competitive, and customer information on target categories, customer needs, and business analysis of new product concepts.
5. *Tracking system*—measures progress and performance of new products relative to the amount invested in them. Identifies development costs and new product performance relative to original objectives and competitive responses after launch.
6. *Clear accountability*—designates one person responsible for managing and executing the new product strategy and process, and ensures that the roles of all new product participants are clear.

7. *Teamwork and communication*—defines how the organization will be structured, what formal and informal communication mechanisms will be utilized, and what approaches will be taken to facilitate teamwork across functions.
8. *Motivation and rewards*—encourages the use of appropriate financial compensation and incentive programs as well as nonfinancial rewards to build a risk-taking and innovative environment.
9. *Tenure and experience*—motivates the right people to stay involved in the new product development process for at least three to five years.
10. *Commitment*—enables top management to execute the new product program on a consistent basis through a supportive environment, risk-taking culture, and appropriate human and financial resources.

DEVELOPING A NEW PRODUCT PROCESS

Planning the Direction-Setting Approach

Before development begins, planning plays an integral part in establishing the right mindset for key managers. These direction-setting efforts may require three or more months to complete. The time spent is a wise investment for a winning effort.

The new product blueprint is the first step in direction setting, as shown in Exhibit 2-20. First, the new product blueprint should be viewed as a contract between functional managers and senior management. It should provide a common basis of understanding, a jointly-agreed-upon language that depicts the overall expectations and broad goals for new products, along with a broad definition of the resources required. The blueprint also should encompass the risk posture and commitment level of senior management. Thus, the essential purpose of a new product blueprint is to articulate, in writing, and place quantifiable dimensions around the role a new product is

Exhibit 2-20. Direction Setting for a New Product

---

1. Design a New Product Blueprint

- Determine revenues and profits desired from new products over a given time period.
- Identify number of people needed to commit to a new product development process.
- Define management expectations from new products and their role in the process.

↓

2. Conduct a Diagnostic Audit

- Evaluate previous new product performance.
- Assess internal strengths and weaknesses.
- Identify internal barriers to success.

↓

3. Establish New Product Roles

- Determine the growth role that new products will play during the next three to five years.
- Describe new product role as either "serving" or "defending" the existing business or a more diversifying role.
- Develop financial targets for new products to satisfy.

↓

4. Define New Product Screening Criteria

- Determine how to define a successful new product.
- Design strategic criteria for evaluating a new product concept.
- Develop financial screening hurdles that represent minimum thresholds that a new product concept needs to pass.

↓

BEGIN THE DEVELOPMENT PROCESS

anticipated to play in fulfilling the company's growth objectives.

Now that a company has determined where it wants to go with its new product program, it is best to take a historical look at new product performance from which to build a foundation. A new product diagnostic audit is the tool for providing this historical platform. The three key elements of a diagnostic audit include (1) an evaluation of previous new product performance, (2) an assessment of internal strengths and weaknesses, and (3) an identification of internal barriers to success.

Foremost in determining how a company's previous new products performed is to analyze the revenue and profits of commercialized new products. A company needs to determine how much money was spent on, as well as generated from, internally developed new products. This will help a company gauge its bang for a buck. A company must also determine its new product survival rate in the market. By taking a look at how long a product stays on the market and determining the reasons for it being on or off the market, a company can measure market acceptance rates. It is also important to compare the success of a new product to its original objectives. This provides the opportunity to evaluate success criteria and assess a company's ability to better forecast future objectives. Finally, it is important to determine the underlying reasons for success and failure of a new product. This provides important lessons learned from previous products to apply to the next project.

Beyond individual product performance, a snapshot of the company's strengths and weaknesses is necessary to assess overall new product performance. The major areas to include for the strengths and weaknesses assessment are cost-related and manufacturing factors, technology-driven factors, demand-related and marketing factors, and sales and distribution factors. Through a strengths and weaknesses assessment, a company is able to isolate what it can leverage for future new product development and what enhancements are needed to become more successful relative to the competition. Through internal

management interviews, the audit also determines a company's barriers to new product development success. Identifying the barriers is the first step to overcoming them.

The diagnostic audit has now equipped management with the necessary information for establishing new product roles because a more realistic picture can be painted of what a company can expect to achieve from new products. Next, the company must establish growth for new products. Given today's existing business, management projects where it wants to be in five years and what roles new products will play in achieving that future goal. Depending on the company's existing new product program and risk orientation, it may set either aggressive or conservative growth roles for new products. With either approach, these growth roles set up a tangible target for new product people to shoot for and commit management to provide the necessary support and resources required for fulfilling them.

A company must also establish strategic roles for new products. Management must determine whether new products will either serve or defend the existing business, or provide diversification for the existing business. If a company is positioned with a strong core business and does not want to threaten this position, its management will most likely opt for the supportive role for new products. However, if a company is facing decreasing revenues, erosion of the core business, or encroaching competitive pressure, it will most likely choose a diversification role for new products to spread the risk of doing business.

It is important to determine strategic roles for new products because each posture mentioned above results in significantly different approaches to new products. A "serve" or "defend" role is less risky and will involve less emphasis on achieving substantial financial gain from new products, but may involve significant gain in competitive positioning from new products. A diversification role, however, may involve heavier emphasis on achieving financial gain as well as competitive positioning from new products.

Finally, it is important for management to also develop financial targets for new products to satisfy. These targets can be three years out, five years out, or ten years out, but they should coincide with the established growth and strategic roles. These three factors combined will solidify an overall picture for the role of new products to fulfill in terms of the future of the company's business.

The final step in the direction-setting planning approach to new product development is to define the new product screening criteria. This process entails determining how to define a "successful" new product. There are many ways to define success. It may be that a new product meets original objectives. Or that it matches financial and strategic criteria. Or that a product is first to market. Regardless of the criteria chosen, it is important to at least pinpoint those factors that determine success and then measure a product's performance against them once a product is launched. Defining success criteria early in the process will aid in determining screening criteria to weed out less attractive product concepts. By setting screening criteria to measure the attractiveness of new product concepts, a company increases its chances for new product success. Most importantly, a company needs to design strategic screening criteria for evaluating a new product concept—not just financial screens.

It is also important, though, to develop financial screening hurdles that represent minimum thresholds that new product concepts need to pass. The purpose of screening criteria, therefore, is to provide a consistent way, with limited management emotion and bias, to compare new product opportunities against one another. Companies have also found it useful to establish primary, secondary, and tertiary screens to provide united flexibility through which different new product types can pass.

In summary, the direction-setting planning approach is the key for companies to translate corporate goals into new product realities. This approach enables a company to work from the inside out—first to focus on internal strengths, strategic roles, and screens, and then to move outside to understand potential consumer needs and wants, and finally to generate new product concepts.

The Development Process

There are ten basic steps in a new product development process (see Exhibit 2-21). It is difficult to select, develop, and launch one new product from a multitude of ideas. Therefore, screening criteria are usually applied in three stages of the development process: (1) needs and wants exploration, (2) concept development, and (3) following business analysis.

Exhibit 2-21 shows the relationship of screening criteria to the ten-step approach for guiding success in new product development. To begin focusing idea generation, the first step involves an exploration of potential customer needs and wants. This step requires upfront research. Many times a successful product is one that solves a particular customer problem.

The Canon plain-paper fax machine is an example of a product solving a customer problem. The plain paper avoids smudging, wet ink, curling edges, and fading associated with the original thermal paper fax machines. Another key benefit is that there is no need to transfer the fax onto plain paper through a copier—which also saves paper.

This upfront exploration sets up a framework for focusing the creative, brainstorming, and association-making process of idea generation. New product ideas are rarely lacking in an organization. There is, however, a need for a focused framework to solicit new ideas that fit a company's internal strengths and future goals. New product ideas can be found internally from management and all functional areas. New product ideas also originate externally from competitive analysis, technology analysis, university research, consumer behavior trends and problems analysis, foreign products analysis, focus groups, patent searches, and trade shows, to name a few.

After capitalizing on the many diverse sources for new product ideas, a company can be virtually guaranteed to have a steady stream of new product concepts in the pipeline. Turning an idea into a concept means giving the idea form, substance, and shape. The concept must describe the real, functional, or perceived benefit of the potential

Exhibit 2-21. Screening Process in Product Development

Direction-Setting Product Management

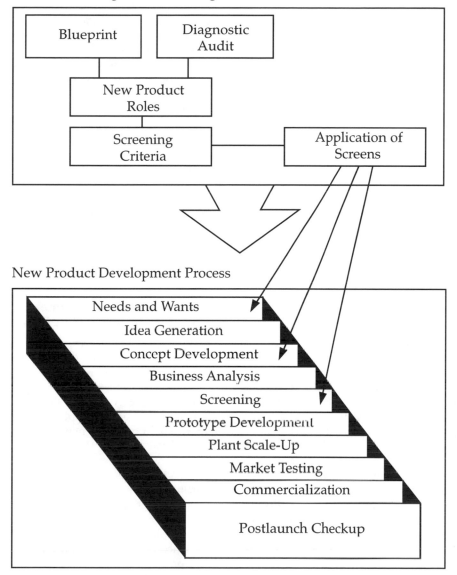

After T.D. Kuczmarski, Managing the new product process, in *Managing the New Products: The Power of Innovation* (Englewood Cliffs, NJ: Prentice-Hall, 1992).

new product. Even just a rough sketch at this point is valuable. It is important to apply the screening criteria loosely to evaluate the attractiveness of the concept. This requires some homework, including an examination of competition, relative market shares,

growth of the potential market, key success factors, and degree of capital intensity. However, this analysis is still preliminary; all in-depth business analysis will be completed for the concepts that pass the screens.

With the number of new product ideas

scaled down to a manageable quantity of product concepts, a company must perform in-depth business analysis for the most attractive product concepts. Business analysis entails examining the dynamics of the potential market and competition, cost positions, consumer buying patterns, and fit with internal strengths in order to develop financial projections of the new product concept.

The next step involves applying screening criteria to concepts to determine prototype candidates. At this stage, screens are strongly applied and the financial screens set up in the initial direction-setting activities come into play. This screening step is a "go/no-go" decision point for management approval of new product concepts to move to prototype development.

Prototype development involves designing or redesigning a product until cost of materials and manufacturing can be accurately figured. It is important for the manufacturers to become more involved during prototype development. Valuable input from them can save money and time. The end output for this stage is one or more prototypes that can be tested with potential customers.

Market testing, therefore, involves taking the prototypes to the market for the ultimate "go/no-go" decision. Many times companies forgo this stage because they are swept into the excitement of having a product so close to launch. However, this is a vital stage for determining whether a new product will succeed and for identifying what changes are needed prior to launch. The advantage is to provide a realistic direction on how to improve the positioning, packaging, pricing, advertising, shelf placement, and so on. It is an effective way for companies to reduce the risk of commercializing a product.

After market tests are completed, a company decides whether to launch a product or not. If the go ahead is given, a company initiates plant scale-up and heavy investment is incurred. Additional equipment may need to be purchased, factory lines shifted, new tooling added. The product needs to be tested in the plant on a large enough scale to ensure product quality prior to launch.

Finally, a company is ready to develop launch plans and commercialize the new product. Timing, coordination and carefully planned execution, and effective communications to the potential purchasers of the product are the cornerstones of a successful launch. The sales force must be brought up to speed and properly motivated to gain its commitment behind the product. The launch must also be closely monitored to make adjustments to the initial commercialization program.

Therefore, a company needs to monitor a new product's performance regularly against the original plan. It is important not only to measure performance against original financial forecasts but also against original strategic objectives. Sometime between six and twelve months postlaunch, the product team should meet again to discuss what has been learned from the project. These "lessons learned" can be valuable when applied to future projects.

New Product Development Processes with Staying Power

Companies that are successful at new product management tend to use the same process for a long period of time, for example, five years or more. The key benefit of this consistency is the learning economies that result from having new product people understand the approach for turning a new idea into a commercialized product.

The key to any new product development process is making it understandable and actionable for everyone in the organization involved in new products. Consistency in the way the process is interpreted and followed is vital. The process should be structured, with a sequence of steps that defines the stages a new product concept will pass through on its way to market launch. But it also has to be simple, straightforward, and systematic. The difficult part is making sure that people adhere to the steps in the process while recognizing that a certain degree of flexibility is critical for getting new products to the marketplace.

Any successful new product development process has to encourage "disciplined freedom." This term suggests the need to provide a framework for managers while enabling their creativity and analytics to flourish. Moreover, participants in the process will have a solid understanding of what their roles are in getting a new product to market. Importantly, the process must be applied uniformly by senior managers and new product development people. This commonly applied discipline offers a direction and suggests the highways to take for reaching the final destination—a commercialized new product.

COMPETITIVE NEW PRODUCT STRATEGIES

Gregory S. Carpenter, Associate Professor of Marketing, J. L. Kellogg Graduate School of Management, Northwestern University

Kent Nakamoto, Assistant Professor of Marketing, Graduate School of Business, University of Colorado

Many markets are dominated by a small number of brands, in some cases by just one. For example, Wrigley's chewing gum, Federal Express, Coca-Cola, and DuPont Stainmaster carpet have dominated their markets for some time. Launching a new product into a market dominated by such a brand is a daunting proposition. The odds of survival are small, and those that survive often secure only a small market share. Coca-Cola, for instance, has been challenged by low-calorie competitors (Diet Rite), caffeine-free alternatives (RC100), and brands differentiated by flavor (Dr. Pepper). All survived, but are dwarfed by Coke. Even time does not appear to increase the odds much; market share advantages of dominant brands can last for decades.

Traditional strategies for introducing new products into markets with dominant brands are based on the marketing concept, "give people what they want." However, as competitors increasingly focus on understanding and meeting customer needs, giving people what they want has meant giving people what competitors are also offering. As a result, new product success rates are falling at a time when, ironically, interest and resources devoted to new products are rising. Falling success rates can be traced, in large measure, to meeting consumer needs but not anticipating the role of a dominant brand in customer reactions to new products. New Coke's failure is perhaps the most vivid recent example.

DOMINANT BRAND ADVANTAGE

Dominant brands derive competitive advantage from three factors: perceptual distinctiveness in customers' minds, customers' extensive experience, and low price sensitivity.

Perceptual Distinctiveness

The dominant brand is often known by many customers and may even be representative or synonymous with the category. Indeed, it may even have defined the category as in the case of Kleenex or Jeep: for example, "It's like a Jeep except . . ." In addition, a dominant brand occupies a unique, distinctive position in customers' minds; Coca-Cola seems somehow different from all other colas. Consumers know it better, recall more favorable aspects, and may even have difficulty recalling the brand and category separately.

Being representative of all brands in the category, yet different from all brands, provides a powerful competitive advantage. The dominant brand is thought of more often and by more customers. More important, it is often simply the best—the standard of comparison. Brands that are different are perceived as less attractive: brands perceived as similar are dwarfed by it. A new product positioned far from the dominant brand appears inferior; a new product positioned near the dominant brand appears to offer nothing unique. The new brand can even reinforce the superiority of the dominant brand in customers' minds. Thus, Eveready, seeking a larger share of the battery market, positioned itself as very similar to Duracell and increased advertising spending. Eveready's comparisons highlighted Duracell's superiority and actually reduced Eveready's share. Similarly, the Pepsi-initiated cola wars increased Coca-Cola's market share.

Extensive Penetration

To establish dominance, a brand must achieve substantial trial, penetration, and repeat purchase. Trial and repeat purchase early in a market's life enable a brand to influence the evolution of customer tastes, become the standard of comparison, and achieve perceptual distinctiveness. Vaseline petroleum jelly illustrates this process well. Vaseline was introduced in 1880, advertised as a healing agent of unsurpassed purity. Sampling Vaseline, a translucent, highly pure gel, buyers learned

that its attributes produced an effective wound preparation. Generalizing from this observation they inferred that petroleum jelly's effectiveness lay in its translucence and purity (in contrast to competing black coal tar derivatives). Subsequent trials confirmed this conjecture; translucence became favored over opacity and gained more importance in brand evaluation. Moreover, all later entering brands were compared to Vaseline, and found wanting even if identical, simply because they were not Vaseline.

Building a dominant position is very expensive in the short run. Distribution and awareness must be established, trial induced, and repeat purchase generated. It also requires a willingness to take substantial risks. However, if successful, customers and distributors are less likely to switch brands. Moreover, as new customers enter the market, they encounter the dominant brand more often simply by chance, plus it is more widely distributed, has more shelf space, and is recommended by others. For example, many children have grown up in a "Crest household," using Crest for many years before another brand is sampled; this produced an enormous impact on consumer tastes and, ultimately, a sustained market share advantage.

Price Insensitivity

Brand dominance also provides some insulation from competitive price reductions. The dominant brand is distinctive among all competitors, widely available, and widely known, thus limiting the impact of competitive price reductions on the dominant brand's market share. For example, many have challenged Federal Express based on price. Purolator Courier mounted the most direct challenge, advertising its package delivery service as "overnight, not overpriced." Many aspirin-free pain relievers have also challenged Tylenol on price. These challenges were ineffective at generating large market share because the dominant brand's advantage was so strong.

NEW PRODUCT STRATEGY OPTIONS

How can firms compete against dominant brands with such formidable competitive advantages? Entry options must recognize the dominant brand's advantages, then devise strategies to exploit its *relative* weaknesses.

Challenger

One widely used option is to position near the dominant brand with high price and high advertising expenditures. By challenging the dominant brand for its position, the new entry threatens its dominance—its association with the category. This strategy requires vast advertising, and pricing at comparable levels to signal comparable value. The strategy is high risk, but has high potential payoff. If successful, the market's standard can be redefined. Pepsi's repositioning head-to-head with Coca-Cola, precipitating the so-called cola wars, exemplifies the challenger strategy—its potential cost and high rewards. Thus, Pepsi in some consumers' minds has replaced Coca-Cola as the standard. However, doing so was enormously expensive.

Differentiation

Differentiation requires adopting a highly differentiated position (i.e., emphasizing differences with the dominant brand), spending large amounts on advertising, and pricing as high as the dominant brand to convey a high value image. Differentiating and creating an attractive position far from the dominant brand can be very effective, but very expensive. DHL in overnight package delivery illustrates the potential success of this strategy. DHL faced a powerful competitor in Federal Express in the United States but not in Europe. DHL used this opportunity to distinguish itself from Federal Express and to become a differentiated player; in so doing it dominated the European market.

Me-Too

An option requiring more limited resources involves positioning near the dominant brand, emphasizing similarities, but stressing low price. Advertising is more limited and largely devoted to highlighting the price difference. Although rarely effective at generating large market share, it can be successful. Purex Bleach has built a valuable brand by

positioning as a lower-cost, unadvertised alternative to Clorox. Purex distributes its bleach in outlets where price sensitivity is high; its reputation and name implies a similarity to Clorox, but at a lower price.

Fringe

A second option requiring limited resources involves positioning the new entry far from the dominant brand, strongly emphasizing differences but spending little on advertising, and pricing below major competitors. This option works well if a small, isolated market niche can be identified. In the car rental market, Rent-a-Wreck has successfully pursued this strategy. Dominated by Hertz and Avis, Rent-a-Wreck has carved out a seemingly odd but profitable niche in the low-priced segment. The contrast with Hertz is dramatic on all important dimensions: quality and condition of the cars, service and locations and, of course, price. By drawing such a stark contrast, Rent-a-Wreck has slowly built a profitable business where others have failed competing head-to-head with the dominant players.

CHOOSING AMONG OPTIONS

The new entrant's best option depends on the resources available and the strength of the dominant brand.

Strong Dominant Brand

The best options when the dominant brand is strongly associated with the category are differentiation and me-too. Developing a differentiated position offers the opportunity to develop distinctiveness, at comparable price. 7 Up was overshadowed in comparison to Coca-Cola even though buyers preferred 7 Up in blind taste tests. The successful solution distinguished 7 Up as the "uncola," suggesting it was meaningfully different from Coke.

A me-too strategy generates lower profits than differentiation, but requires smaller investment. Over time, as buyers become more price sensitive, its success can increase (e.g., Purex Bleach). The danger is becoming the perennial also-ran or, worse, failing to generate sufficient market share to survive.

Weaker Dominant Brand

Here, challenger and fringe may be viable strategies. By challenging the dominant brand, a late entrant can gain many of the dominant brand's advantages of strong association with the category, broad trial, and even low price sensitivity. Avis's "We try harder" is a classic challenger strategy. Although dominant, Hertz was not inseparable from the category in customers' minds. Avis was positioned as similar to Hertz, but better, via high advertising and comparable price.

A fringe brand can be effective if fewer resources are available. By positioning far from the dominant brand a new product has difficulty generating short-term sales. Although compounded by limited advertising spending and low price in a market where price sensitivity is low, over time a fringe strategy can return adequate results for minimal investment. As with me-too a potential danger is becoming an also-ran.

PROFITABLE PRICING

Thomas T. Nagle, Professor, Boston University, and Managing Director, Strategic Pricing Group, Inc.

Reed K. Holden, Professor, Boston University, and Managing Director, Strategic Pricing Group, Inc.

PITFALLS OF COMMON PRICING PROCEDURES

What price is needed to cover costs? What price is needed to close the sale? What price is needed to meet competitive (e.g., market share, growth) objectives? While these questions recognize the three main forces pricing strategy must consider—costs, customers, and competition—they offer no guidelines for making trade-offs among these forces. Consequently, they lead to decisions that undermine profitability.

Cost-Driven Pricing

Cost-driven pricing is the most common pricing procedure because of its aura of financial prudence. Financial prudence is achieved by pricing each product or service to yield a "fair" return over all costs, fully and fairly allocated. In theory, it is a simple guide to profitability; in practice, it is a blueprint for mediocre financial performance.

The problem is fundamental. In most industries it is impossible, without arbitrary and unrealistic assumptions, to determine unit product cost *before* determining price. Why? Because unit costs change with volume; fixed costs must be allocated to determine full unit cost. Since fixed cost allocations depend on volume, unit cost is a moving target.

To determine unit cost, cost-based pricers must make the absurd assumption that prices do not affect volume. Failure to account for price effects on volume, and volume effects on costs, leads directly to pricing decisions that undermine profits. One tragic example was Wang Laboratory's pricing of the world's first word processor. Introduced in 1976, the product was an instant success; Wang grew rapidly and dominated the market. However, by the mid-1980s personal computers with word-processing software were credible competitors. As competition increased and growth slowed, unit costs were repeatedly recalculated, prices were increased to reflect rising overhead allocations, and sales declined even further. Before long, even Wang's most loyal customers switched to cheaper alternatives.

Cost-driven pricing is more insidious when applied to strong products since no signals (e.g., declining market share) warn of potential damage. A technological leader in international telecommunications uses cost-based pricing as a pricing starting point. Product and sales managers review cost-based target prices for consistency with market conditions, then argue for adjustments to reflect market conditions. Organization members find the system fair and reasonable. But does it foster profitability? Marketing frequently requests and receives permission to charge prices below cost-based targets. But marketing has never argued for raising target prices, despite a long order backlog on some popular products. Cost-based targets have become cost-based caps on profitability.

Cost-driven pricing leads to underpricing in strong markets and overpricing in weak markets—the reverse of prudent market-oriented strategy. But how should managers price to cover costs and achieve profit objectives? The question reflects an erroneous perception that the firm can, in order, (1) determine sales levels; (2) calculate unit cost and profit objectives; (3) set prices. In fact, sales volume (beginning assumption) depends on price (final stage); cost-based pricing puts the cart before the horse.

Managers should not price reactively to cover costs, but proactively to increase profits. The financial questions driving proactive pricing are: "What sales volume increase leads to additional profit at a lower price?" or "What sales volume decrease can we afford yet still earn more profit at a higher price?"

Answers depend on how cost changes with volume, not on whether the current product price, at current volume, covers cost and profit objectives.

Customer-Driven Pricing

Some companies recognize the fallacy and adverse profit effects of cost-based pricing and realize that pricing must reflect market conditions. Consequently, pricing authority is placed with sales or product managers. Although marketing and sales are best positioned to understand customers and likely price responses, in practice bottom-line results often disappoint.

The basic problem is that concern with short-term objectives may lead sales or marketing to price at buyers' willingness to pay, rather than on product worth. Sales objectives are met, but long-term profitability is undermined. The problem: sophisticated buyers are rarely honest about willingness to pay. Purchasing agents have financial incentive to conceal information from, and even mislead, sellers about the product's true value to their firms.

Second, profitable pricing reflects product value. Sales and marketing's job is not to process orders at the price customers are *currently* willing to pay. Rather, they should raise customers' willingness to better reflect true product value.

This problem is most dramatic with new, innovative products where product value is unproven. For example, most customers initially perceived that photocopiers, mainframe computers, food processors, and cake mixes lacked adequate value to justify their prices. Only extensive efforts to communicate and guarantee value led to market acceptance. Many companies underprice truly innovative products because they ask potential customers (ignorant of product value) what they would pay. When innovations are introduced, price has little impact on trial; only after trial does price play an important role in customer purchase decisions. *Forget what customers are initially willing to pay.* Rather, determine true product worth to customers and develop a marketing plan that communicates and guarantees that value.

Competition-Driven Pricing

Competitive conditions often dictate pricing strategy; pricing becomes a tool to achieve competitive objectives such as market share or sales growth. Such pricing is "letting the tail wag the dog." Typically firms seek market share because they believe that higher market share produces greater profits. But priorities are confused when managers reduce price simply to achieve market share goals. Pricing's goal is to find the margin and market share combination that maximizes long-term profitability. The most profitable price might substantially restrict market share relative to competition. Godiva chocolates, Mercedes cars, and Premier Industrial fasteners could probably gain substantial share if priced closer to competition. However, added share would probably not be worth forgoing their profitable and successful positioning as skim-priced brands.

The fallacy of competition-driven pricing goes beyond skim-priced products. Many companies recapitalized in the 1980s learned they could substantially increase cash flow by scaling back market share objectives. One industrial firm increased prices by 9 percent, suffered a 20-percent market share loss, and still increased profit contribution by 70 percent. An excessive market share goal had prevented the firm from capturing the value that four of five customers had for the product.

Finally, many firms use price to defend market share, but price is not the most appropriate competitive weapon. First, price is easily matched; second, using price as a competitive weapon is often too costly unless a firm has substantial cost advantage or small market share. Alternatively, product differentiation, advertising, and improved distribution do not increase market share as quickly as price, but are usually more cost effective and sustainable.

GUIDELINES FOR STRATEGIC PRICING

Managers cannot sustain superior long-run profitability by using short-term pricing tactics to solve problems with costs, customers, or competition. Long-run profitability and competitive positioning require a pricing strategy that considers (1) the firm's internal cost structure for each product, group of products, and customers; (2) customer price sensitivity and how customers value the firm's unique product attributes; (3) competitor positioning including capabilities and strategies. Profitable pricing strategy requires understanding the interactions among these three forces—costs, customers, and competition—and making optimal trade-offs among them.

Understanding Cost Structure

The key information about costs for pricing is not their per-unit level but how they change with sales changes. Understanding cost structure—are costs incremental or fixed for additional sales?—is essential for making profitable margin and market share trade-offs. The first step in changing price is determining true, incremental product costs: costs incurred if the sale is made, costs not incurred if the sale is not made. Costs that do not change have *no* impact on the profitability of pricing decisions. Fixed costs are, of course, important in determining bottom-line profitability, but they do not affect changes in profitability associated with price increases or decreases.

Having identified the true cost of a sale, managers can determine the contribution margin for the product: price minus incremental variable cost. The contribution margin enables them to calculate the break-even sales change: the additional sales necessary to profit from a price cut, or the maximum sales loss sustainable to profit from a price increase.

% Break-Even Sales Change

$$= \frac{-\text{Price Change}}{\text{Contribution} - \text{Price Change Margin}}$$

Using this formula is key to resolving the common conflicts between financial and sales management. If a sales manager seeks a lower price to stimulate sales, the formula shows how much the sales goal must increase to achieve the same financial results. If the sales manager can effectively increase prices, the formula shows how much the sales goal could be relaxed. Thus, the choice of a price can be made by those who most understand customers, properly constrained by relevant financial considerations.

Understanding Customer Price Sensitivity

Most customer behavior discussions regarding price begin with the question "How price sensitive are customers?" That's a reasonable start, but only a start. Price sensitivity is a simple indicator of a complex process. To understand and influence the process, we must go deeper.

Two useful tools can help market managers better understand customer willingness to pay. *Economic value analysis* helps identify the product's potential value to the customer, but economic value is not the only consideration driving purchase decisions. *Determinants of price sensitivity* are a set of factors that, in part, determine the importance customers place on economic value when making purchase decisions.

Economic value analysis (EVA) is the process of quantifying the value customers actually realize from buying the firm's product. EVA is a mechanism for quantifying the product's good and bad points to help establish a final price. The five steps are summarized in Exhibit 2-22.

Consider a manufacturer pricing a new technology for electronic circuit board assembly. Management knows the equipment operates 30 percent faster and with improved

quality. The firm must also determine all other benefits associated with customers using the new technology. In addition to saving machine time, increased speed reduces downtime, labor costs, and maintenance costs; increased quality reduces reworking costs. Considering all functions, a 30-percent efficiency increase may represent a greater than 30-percent value increase.

The new product also brings associated costs: worker retraining, maintenance parts inventories, and costs of removing old equipment. Subtracting from the reference and positive differentiation values produces the economic value (EVA). If a product were priced at EVA, a "rational" customer would be indifferent between the old and new equipment. Thus, a price below economic value is required to induce customers to buy. The amount of inducement varies across customers based on factors determining price sensitivity.

EVA forces a focus on customer value in pricing decisions. Product attributes adding little or no value should be excluded in establishing product value. In some markets it is difficult to measure some attribute values, whereas in others, values may be objectively quantified by studying customer costs. In markets where values are intangible, conjoint analysis and other research techniques can quantify these values. EVA is also the basis by which sales and advertising departments justify prices to customers. Customers may not be aware of the product's real value unless it is quantified for them.

Exhibit 2-22. Economic Value Analysis

Step 1.	Identify the price per unit of the product or process currently being used—reference value.
Step 2.	Identify the cost saving or value-enhancing aspects of your product or service relative to the current product or methods—positive differentiating values.
Step 3.	Identify all potential problems and costs associated with changing to your product—negative differentiating values.
Step 4.	Calculate the total economic value of the product by adding the reference and positive differentiation values and subtracting the negative differentiation value.
Step 5.	Determine the final selling price. Except for well-established products, the price must be set below the economic value. The difference is called the inducement to purchase.

Exhibit 2-23. Determinants of Price Sensitivity

1. *Reference value effect*—Buyers are more price sensitive when the price appears high relative to perceived alternatives.
2. *Unique value effect*—Buyers are more price sensitive when they are convinced that differentiating attributes offer unique benefits.
3. *Price quality effect*—Buyers are less price sensitive to the extent that higher price signals higher product quality.
4. *Difficult comparison effect*—Buyers are less price sensitive the more difficult it is to evaluate competing offers.
5. *Total expenditure effect*—Buyers are more price sensitive when the expenditure is larger.
6. *End benefit effect*—Buyers are more price sensitive when they are more sensitive to the cost of the end benefit to which the product contributes and the product's price accounts for a large share of the total cost of the end benefit.
7. *Shared cost effect*—Buyers are less price sensitive the smaller the portion of the price they actually pay.
8. *Fairness effect*—Buyers are more price sensitive when price is outside the range they perceive as "fair" or customary given the purchase context.
9. *Sunk investment effect*—Buyers are less price sensitive the greater the sunk investment they have made in anticipation of continued use of a product.
10. *Inventory effect*—Buyers are more price sensitive in the short run when they are able to hold product inventories.

In some markets (particularly business markets) customers act as "economic men": sophisticated buyers who carefully evaluate all alternatives and seek to maximize value achieved from purchases. More often, EVA is only a starting point for understanding how customers weigh price and other attributes when making purchase decisions. Customers also differ across segments and purchase situations in their awareness of alternatives, their ability to compare, the importance of the expenditures, and their prior price expectations. The ten factors in Exhibit 2-23 are a checklist for evaluating the importance of economic value in purchasing situations and for influencing customer willingness to pay. For example, a personal computer's perceived value may be strongly influenced by framing the purchase relative to a son or daughter's success in college. The attractiveness of discount long-distance telephone service is influenced by the seller's ability to convince customers that all services are essentially alike (discounter strategy) or that substitutes are inferior and pose hidden risks (AT&T strategy). Better understanding of these effects and their interrelationships leads to strategies that better capture true product value.

EVA and the ten pricing effects form the basis for segmented pricing strategies. Managers are better able to predict prices that different customer groups are willing to pay. By developing and justifying unique offers to those segments, marketers can capture the different values with different prices.

MANAGING THE COMPETITIVE PROCESS

EVA and the ten pricing effects provide useful inputs into setting prices, but in many competitive situations attribute values vanish and negotiations quickly focus on price. Rather than continually reacting to such price pressures, prudent managers carefully evaluate competition and follow strategies to eliminate the damaging effects of excessively low prices.

The first strategy insulates economic value from competitive effects by developing a unique and sustainable competitive advantage. Price is the quickest way to gain competitive advantage, but the easiest for competitors to duplicate. Price advantages are short lived, but losses from too low prices last indefinitely. Sustainable differentiation relies on preempting competition with unique advantages.

A second way of preempting damage from excessive price competition is to manage the competitive process. Even firms with significant cost or product advantage benefit from this control. Three issues are key: setting appropriate goals, managing competitive information, and allocating resources strategically.

Competitive Goals

Most marketing strategies contain goals, but they are often unrealistic with regard to competitive market conditions. Setting market share and growth goals must realistically anticipate competitor strategies. If not, intense price competition results as competitors individually try to meet collectively inconsistent goals. By anticipating such inconsistencies, managers can either avoid competitive conflicts or respond in less costly, more effective ways.

Competitive goals should focus on customer rather than product segments. Products have no inherent value; they have value only to customers. Since customer segments *use* products differently, they likely *value* products differently. Since pricing's goal is to capture value, effective pricing strategy must reflect these different values. A one-price policy overprices in some segments while failing to capture increased value in others, and invites competitive entry to save these customers whose needs are unmet.

Competitive Information

Firms cannot properly respond to, and influence, competitive prices without understanding competitor price setting. Marketers must develop and implement formal procedures to monitor and evaluate competitive prices and pricing strategies. Good information permits fast response to competitive moves and limits

customer ability to mislead suppliers. Information sources include published price lists, sales force call reports, competitor public statements and reports, trade reports, and industry analyses.

Price information should also be communicated to the market. Planned price increases should be preannounced and justified, or the firm is competitively disadvantaged while competitors delay in matching the change. Preannouncing in a public forum provides the opportunity to evaluate competitor response before implementing the increase, and decreases the risk of having to reverse it if competitors fail to match.

Finally, firms should communicate their ability and commitment to protect the customer base from competitive threats, *before threats are made*. For example, lower unit *cost* companies should publicize that information since it demonstrates ability to win a price war. If communications are credible, competitors will avoid aggressive pricing that could lead to costly price wars.

Competitive Resources

Company resources are limited; managers must select competitive confrontations carefully. When threatened, too many managers feel they must respond in kind. Managers should select competitive confrontations they can win and avoid those they may lose. Confrontations should not be based on achieving short-term sales goals, unless a long-term win is forecast. The firm is better off walking away from no-win competitive battles and focusing resources on markets with long-term firm value.

Effective competitive management should embrace running fast or changing to favorable battle weapons when threatened. For example, when the Swiss watch firm SMH was threatened by low-price Japanese competition, it did not respond in kind. Rather, it scaled back market share objectives and capacity to cover feasible segments. In those segments, it changed the rules of the game to compete with the stylish Swatch brand, knowing the Japanese had long lead times and could not make rapid styling changes.

AUDITING THE MARKETING FUNCTION

William H. Rodgers, Hamilton Consultants

Gerard A. Osborne, Hamilton Consultants

Philip Kotler, Northwestern University

THE EMERGENCE AND APPLICATION OF MARKETING AUDITS

The marketing audit, an organized review of the strategy, systems, activities, and organization for carrying out the marketing function, dates from the early 1950s. Use of audits grew rapidly in the 1970s and 1980s as business environments became more turbulent and complex, and managements increasingly questioned their marketing approaches.

Our experience tells us that not all firms need a marketing audit. New growth companies run by customer-oriented CEOs (chief executive officers) can often progress for many years without reexamining their marketing principles. In addition, large packaged-good companies, like Procter & Gamble and General Mills, have successful marketing formulae that have worked well over the years.

Between these two groups is a broad set of firms continually adjusting complex marketing strategies to a changing web of customers, competitors, products, media, and distribution channels. Many firms, large and small, in industries ranging from fishing boats and semiconductors, to industrial uniforms and minicomputers, have turned to the marketing audit as a means to reexamine their marketing efforts. Though developed nearly forty years ago, the marketing audit is an accepted tool in management's sustained effort to improve marketing performance.

CHARACTERISTICS OF A MARKETING AUDIT

A marketing audit, sometimes called a marketing opportunity analysis, a marketing performance evaluation, or a marketing checkup, takes many forms, but the common approaches generally cover the marketing mix elements of product, price, distribution, and promotion, as well as marketing objectives, systems, organization, and productivity. A marketing audit may be defined as a *comprehensive, systematic, independent,* and *periodic* examination of a company's—or business unit's—marketing environment, objectives, strategies, and activities with a view to determining problem areas and opportunities and recommending a plan of action to improve the company's marketing performance.

A marketing audit is comprehensive: it cuts across many marketing functions rather than focusing deeply on a single area like pricing or product development. The audit assumes that marketing elements interact and must be examined in concert. In addition, the audit extends beyond the marketing department to all functions having an impact on customer satisfaction. For example, finance (through

Exhibit 2-24. Marketing Roles for Different Areas of a Firm

Marketing Tasks	CEO/General Manager	Sales Department	Marketing Department*	R&D/Engineering	Manufacturing/Customer Service Departments	Finance
Innovation (Finding new ways to meet customer needs)	Imagining new approaches to business	Bringing back new ideas from the field	Researching unmet needs	Developing new products	Developing new manufacturing processes and logistics	Inventing new billing and customer information
Customer Service (Making the customer feel he or she is well taken care of)	Letting customers know the person at the top cares	Responding to customer needs on a timely basis	Providing useful information	Listening to what customers want	Meeting delivery schedule and being responsive on the telephone	Having easy-to-use credit and invoicing systems
Analysis and Research (Research and planning all customer-serving activities)	"Poking" around competitors and customers	Gathering customer and competitor data	Conducting survey research; developing market plans	Researching new technologies and applications	Researching better ways to service the customer	Analyzing product-line profit
Persuasion and Education (Convincing customers to choose the company's product)	Selling the big customers	Selling every day	Having effective, informative advertising and sales promotion	Making products and user instructions "idiot-proof"	Promoting the company on every customer contact	Making terms and conditions clear and fair

* Includes advertising, marketing research, and product management.

Exhibit 2-25. Candidates for Conducting an Audit

	Advantages	Disadvantages
New CEO	Findings will be acted on. Whatever is learned stays in the organization. Customers feel "the boss cares."	Managers may withhold information. CEO may not be a marketer himself or herself.
Academic: a marketing professor	There is good knowledge of marketing concepts.	There is no team to conduct research.
Internal committee	Whatever is learned stays in the organization. Committee members learn from experience.	Managers may withhold information. Committee members may not be fully objective.
Corporate internal consulting group	Consultants know the corporation (but may not know the division).	Managers may withhold information.
Independent consulting team	Knowledge of marketing concepts is high. Team has experience bringing change to organizations.	It is the most expensive alternative. Knowledge may leave with the team.

flexible but sound credit policy), manufacturing (through good delivery and consistent quality), and research and development (through market-focused product development) all play marketing roles. Four dimensions of marketing—analysis and research, innovation, education and persuasion, and customer service—cut across all functional areas of a business (Exhibit 2-24).

The audit is systematic, but not rigid; it thus contrasts with regimented accounting audit procedures. The data are collected and analyzed systematically using probing questions and a vast arsenal of analytic approaches. Typically, an audit takes six to ten weeks, encompassing research with salespeople, distributors, customers, and often competitors.

Independence is critical for an effective marketing audit. Confidential conversations with managers, objective examination of market share and financial performance, and unbiased surveys of distributors and customers can only be accomplished well by persons without a career stake in the business. Independent parties who can conduct an audit are several, each with advantages and disadvantages (Exhibit 2-25).

Periodic examination is also fruitful, in part because market conditions can change considerably in a five- to ten-year period. For example, a gas utility conducted a marketing audit in both 1978 and 1987. In the 1970s, it was reeling from the aftermath of the energy crisis; the 1978 audit helped pinpoint attractive opportunities that even regulators could applaud. By 1987, with environmentalists turning against electric utilities, and with gas prices relatively low, a much more aggressive approach to marketing could be undertaken.

THE AUDIT PROCESS

Auditors must prepare for the marketing audit by holding discussions with the CEO and executive staff, and briefly reviewing some financial and marketing data. Audits

Exhibit 2-26. The Marketing Audit Process

Part I
Review background materials:
  financial results, organization chart,
  business plans.
Interview management and tour
  facilities.
Ride with salespeople and visit
  customers.
Hold interim meetings to discuss
  findings and likely alternatives.

Part II
Gather additional information:
  —additional management and
    salesperson interviews.
  —interview and written surveys
    with customers and trade.
  —internal written survey.
  —outside expert interviews.
  —competitor interviews.
  —product costs and profits, sales
    results, marketing budgets.
Perform analysis and develop
  alternatives.
Hold work sessions to develop
  marketing strategy and next steps
  for implementation.

are often in two parts. The first part begins with a meeting between the auditors and business unit management, and reviews of the unit's financial statements, product literature, and organizational plans (Exhibit 2-26). The auditors explain objectives, procedures, time frame and expected audit output, and required participation from each manager. Participation usually comprises an initial two-hour interview; then others are designated for potential interviews and provision of operating and financial information. The auditors typically tour manufacturing and other operations areas to better understand product features, quality levels, and cost differentials that distinguish the business from competition. The auditors also review customer service, shipping, credit operations, order entry, advertising (if in-house), research and development, and manufacturing engi-

neering. The auditors collect memos, reports, and analyses that help them understand the firm's marketing strategy and business processes.

Managerial interviews are conducted. Managers discuss their responsibility areas in depth; many questions are asked of several managers to elicit different perspectives.

All interview data are confidential. Good auditors project a professionalism in understanding the business and maintaining confidences that allows business unit managers to "open up" on controversial topics. Manager candor is particularly important when two or more powerful executives hold opposing views. Auditors surface these views by using unattributed quotes when reporting findings. Competent auditors continually draw upon their experience to probe the consistency, appropriateness, and sufficiency of the firm's marketing plans and actions.

After initial interviews, auditors usually take two parallel steps. First, they conduct a library search for independent published material on the firm, competition, and industry. Second, they become familiar with the sales force and customer buying behavior by making joint customer calls. Through this process, auditors gather clues in several areas including market needs, firm competitiveness, sales and purchase processes, and where the organization is functioning well and poorly.

Visits with salespeople provide invaluable "soft" data; salespeople are notoriously irreverent regarding "what's really going on" at headquarters, including manager disagreements, rivalries, and favoritisms.

Following these steps, the auditors analyze and organize information and report key issues and observations to the management team in a two- to three-hour working session. Surfaced issues are discussed, and preliminary ideas for eventual audit outcome and alternative action courses are laid out.

The second part of the audit is typically more time consuming than the first part. It comprises customer and trade surveys; further secondary data gathering; analysis of competitive products; evaluation of marketing strengths and weaknesses; interviews with industry experts; detailed analysis of internal financial, sales, and operating information; and second managerial interviews. Management is formally surveyed to compare its views on the firm and competition with customer viewpoints. Finally, all data must be analyzed (see Exhibit 2-27 for examples).

The audit concludes with the presentation of findings and recommendations, first privately to the CEO and one or two executive staff, and then at a day-long meeting with the entire management group. The goal is to gain a common understanding of audit findings so a consensus on future marketing needs, opportunities, and actions is formed.

Exhibit 2-27. Diagnostics and Analyses in a Marketing Audit

Marketing strategy and objectives verification	Individual managers state independently what they believe are the strategy and objectives. Often major differences exist and must be resolved.
Product-line profit	Auditors calculate which product lines produce profit and which do not, using direct costs and activity-based allocations of overheads.
Comparison of company to competition	Customers and internal managers are surveyed on how the company stacks up against competition on several dimensions.
Allocation of additional marketing	Managers are surveyed on how they would spend an additional $1–5 million among ten to fifteen marketing activities. This provides evidence of agreement and disagreement on what areas of marketing are most important.
Customer market share	The company's and competitors' market shares are calculated for key customers or segments to identify company areas of strength and weaknesses.
Sales penetration	Territory penetration versus sales potential of territory by individual salesperson is measured to determine if some territories should be split.
Product development tracking	Case studies are analyzed to determine possible bottlenecks and improper procedures in product development processes.
Price-profit interaction	Demonstration of impact of price increases or decreases on profit.
Product-line additions and deletion	Product-line length is measured over time to see if complexity has escalated beyond manageability.

MARKETING AREAS FOR REVIEW

Data collection, analyses, and reporting are organized around set comprehensive marketing constructs. The authors use a six-part framework.

1. *Marketing environment*—The auditors investigate all key aspects: customers, competitors and suppliers, and social, political, technological, and regulatory trends. This analysis both identifies important trends for the business and gauges firm performance versus competition. Management frequently speaks proudly of historical sales increases, yet analysis can reveal market share losses in growing markets.

2. *Marketing strategy and objectives*—Marketing strategy and objectives should be realistic and understood by all managers; this is not always so. A semiconductor firm's goal was 25-percent growth from new products; analysis revealed less than 10 percent historically; management reassessed goals. An auto parts company sought high performance on service, quality, and price; however, rapid product line expansion caused substandard performance in each area.

3. *Marketing organization*—Auditors must assess if job roles and responsibilities are clear, and if measurement and reward systems motivate performance. A typical issue is that marketing and sales are often viewed as having marketing responsibility for the entire company; of course, each department—manufacturing, R&D, and so forth—must be customer driven. Marketing should plan and help coordinate the marketing effort, and carry out key functions like advertising and product management. It should not try to carry out marketing for the entire business.

4. *Marketing systems*—Auditors assess the efficiency and effectiveness of marketing systems: new product development, marketing research, customer satisfaction measurement, sales forecasting, sales lead generation, customer database design and update, competitor intelligence, and product pruning. Often these processes are languishing or are nonexistent; the audit provides impetus to get back on track.

5. *Marketing productivity*—Marketing productivity raises questions of product line profitability. Do some products merit additional marketing effort? Should others be repriced, cost reduced, or discontinued? A door panels manufacturer also distributed frames and sills with its doors. Product profitability analysis revealed the same dollar contribution from distribution as from manufacturing and prevented an exit from distribution.

How should marketing resources be allocated across the marketing mix (e.g., product improvements, trade incentives, additional sales staff)? Asking managers to allocate an additional $5 million of marketing resources is a very telling exercise when framed against customer and distributor comments regarding necessary improvements.

6. *Marketing mix*—Marketing auditors examine the four P's (i.e., product, price, promotion, and place [distribution]) to determine company performance versus competition and to assess internal consistency. Managers often place too much emphasis on one element (e.g., advertising copy) and shortchange others (e.g., pricing, distribution).

BENEFITS FROM A MARKETING AUDIT

Four major benefits flow from a marketing audit. First, management is provided with an independent, objective review of the firm's marketing performance and opportunities. Audits often reveal inconsistencies in opportunities and marketing efforts. For example, in a photographic products firm, pricing and product policy were at odds. The product was positioned as superior in quality, yet dealer prices were set below competition in an attempt to provide dealers with higher margins. However, using standard markups, many dealers set retail prices below competition; consumers therefore perceived the product as inferior.

Second, marketing audits often lead to strategic marketing change. Careful assessment of the changing environment, customers, channels, and competitors may lead to a reassessment of firm direction, not just fine-tuning of pricing, advertising, or sales force deployment. As a result of an audit, the semiconductor division of a large communications firm refocused efforts on serving other design and manufacturing divisions in the firm, and deemphasized the merchant market where prices and margins were slipping precipitously.

Third, the audit helps set priorities for marketing programs. Ideas for improved marketing frequently exist somewhere in the firm, but controversy and political in-fighting make choices difficult. A seasoned auditor with group process skills, using new data and analyses, can focus managerial effort on important moves, circumventing political struggles that bog down the business.

Fourth, audits educate managers that satisfying customers is a joint responsibility, not simply a task to be delegated to sales and marketing.

MOST COMMON FINDINGS IN AUDITS

Based on over forty marketing audits across a broad range of industries, some common marketing failure patterns emerge:

- *Insufficient knowledge of customers' behavior and attitudes*—Many consumer durables and business-to-business product firms fail to survey customers deeply or frequently enough. When surveys are conducted, data on needs, perceptions, preferences, and behavior are frequently never seen or used by senior management.

By contrast, the story is different in consumer packaged-goods firms; in start-up firms where CEOs are in active contact with customers; and in many Japanese firms where managers are continuously in the field with distributors or customers. More general managers should follow the late Sam Walton's example. While chairman of Wal-Mart, he visited two or three Wal-Marts a day, spent time with employees and customers, and, by his own example, emphasized the importance of customer knowledge and satisfaction.

The audit process should focus on both the firm's direct customers (e.g., wholesalers and dealers) and final customers. Enlightened firms increasingly view channel members as *partners* with whom to work toward satisfying ultimate customers.

- *Failure to segment the market most advantageously*—Many managements believe all customers are driven by the same needs and responses. They may view customers as geographically segmented (viz., geographic sales force deployment), or segmented by size (viz., different distribution for small and large customers). More subtle differentiation in how different segments buy or use the product is overlooked.

For example, a cellular telephone company used industry segmentation based on Standard Industrial Classification (SIC) categories for traditional products; cellular opportunities were also examined by SIC. Analysts determined that types of people driving frequently and needing inbound or outbound communication service were a better segmentation system. Occupation—for example, salespeople, repair and maintenance service people, construction contractors, and service professionals like physicians and consultants—was a far better way to segment than SIC classifications like agriculture, manufacturing, and distribution.

- *Cutting price vs. increasing value*—Management personnel in many firms too frequently listen to sales force complaints that prices are too high. They reduce price more than necessary and have too little profit to reinvest in value-adding activities or product features. Introduction of low-price second and third lines may help hold market, but often management fails to invest in a high-value-added line that can be priced high with good margin.

- *Failure to invest in the future, particularly in human resources*—Too often, managers view marketing expenditures as a today cost rather than an investment in the future. Packaged-goods companies understand that expenditures like advertising build future demand, but less sophisticated marketers view expenditures other than plant and equipment, and R&D, as here-and-now expenses: they are reluctant to spend money if profits are not immediate.

A common shortcoming is failure to view the sales force as an investment. Frequently firms in mature businesses, particularly during or after recession, add sales people reluctantly, if at all. They bet on more sales from existing salespeople and fail to add salespeople in underpenetrated territories. The cause is often an almost unconscious agreement between sales management and salespeople to maintain the status quo. Sales managers dislike adding salespeople and cutting territory sizes. Salespeople agree, as they fear a lower income with smaller territories. The result is both suboptimal sales and profits for the company.

■ *Tendency to delegate new product development to the developers*—All businesses need continually to improve products, or to introduce new products, to keep up with changing customer tastes and expectations, and to stay ahead of competition. A close marriage between technology and customer needs is essential. Too often, senior management delegates product development to technical people who are disinclined to talk to customers in sufficient depth to understand real needs. Also, sales and marketing people report new product ideas from the field, but these are ignored or "handed off" to developers and dealt with on a secondhand or thirdhand basis.

Best product development occurs when senior management is in frequent touch with customers and knows firm technology well. The turnaround at Harley Davidson motorcycle company was driven in large part by improved products based on detailed management knowledge gained from circulating among Harley owners at motorcycle rallies.

■ *Considering marketing as the job of the marketing department*—For over twenty years, the "ideal" organizational move to improve marketing was appointment of a marketing vice-president. Identification of a high-level marketing officer was expected to bring a marketing orientation to the entire firm. Unfortunately, the reverse often happened; marketing was viewed as the marketing department's job; others took no marketing initiatives. Some, like Tom Bonoma, formerly of the Harvard Business School, now believe the marketing director's job really should be to "self-destruct," leaving marketing in the hands of other functions—sales, advertising, customer service, manufacturing, development, and finance.

LEGAL IMPERATIVES FOR MARKETING DECISIONS

Ray O. Werner, Professor of Economics, Emeritus, The Colorado College

THE EXPANSION OF LEGAL RESPONSIBILITY OF MARKETERS

Since the mid-1960s the major development that marketing managers should recognize is the emergence of the concept of caveat venditor—"let the seller beware." In an earlier time the rule of caveat emptor—"let the buyer beware" dominated, although there were important limitations and modifications. Many factors, especially the consumer movement, account for this shift in emphasis. Regardless, marketing managers must be alert to the changed and changing legal environment.

Because of these changes, marketing managers should not attempt to be their own legal counsels. Not only does every enterprise require legal counsel but legal counsel per se is not enough. Marketers need legal counsel specializing in the area of law, sometimes very narrow, in which advice or representation is needed. More important than finding a law firm with impeccable credentials is securing the services of legal specialists with the skill, initiative, and resources to maintain an awareness of changes in their specialization area. Managers must be equally ready and willing to engage new legal counsel at the slightest intimation that currently retrained

counsel has failed to keep abreast of the latest developments. Shifts in the legal fabric, ranging from changes in composition of the U.S. Supreme Court to the propensity for lower courts and administrative agencies to modify existing marketing regulations, significantly mean that marketers would be imprudent if they believed the best informed and current of legal counsel will not err.

However, knowledge of a relevant legal specialty is insufficient for legal counsel to provide competent management advice. Knowledge of commercial and industrial organization is a desirable if not necessary qualification for counsel providing direction in a profit-making enterprise, just as knowledge of educational organizations is indispensable for legal advice in marketing not-for-profit educational institutions.

A FRAMEWORK FOR THE ANALYSIS OF MARKETING REGULATION

Marketing regulation impinges on marketing behavior in one of three ways. Laws, judicial decisions, and administrative orders may determine, alter, or completely destroy the organization of the marketing institution; they may condition and control the operations of the marketing institution; they may impose procedural requirements that determine or restrict the ability of the marketing institution to attain its goals.

These three processes affect organizations regardless of their goals. For business firms pursuing profit maximization, some legal regulations impinge; for nonprofit organizations pursuing philanthropic goals, limitations on how to market their services or causes are encountered. Organizations need a framework to facilitate analysis of what they wish to do and how they wish to do it—to facilitate thinking about marketing regulations that condition and constrain their behavior.

Evidence of the legal environment's ability to influence the organization of the marketing enterprise is almost limitless. Federal Trade Commission (FTC) rules operate to determine if an existing business may effectively extend its marketing area by adopting franchising arrangements. Merger rules, administered in part by the FTC and the Department of Justice, may constrain the corporation from expanding. Laws governing taxation may determine whether a firm organizes as a sole proprietorship, a corporation, or a limited partnership. Court decisions involving medical malpractice may lead medical practitioners to join health maintenance organizations rather than operate unincorporated sole proprietorships.

Illustrations of the impact of marketing regulations on the operations of businesses are more numerous. Regulations governing pricing decisions are common; these range from prohibitions on setting minimum or maximum prices, to restraints on methods by which price changes are communicated to customers or social-cause supporters. Limitations on billboard advertising, slack-filled packaging, or sales of nonpatented items conditioned on the purchase of a patented product constrain marketer practices. As society has grown in complexity, so has the number of restraints on the operations of marketing institutions attempting to attain their goals.

The growth of procedural requirements that function to regulate the ability of marketing institutions to attain their goals is also ex-

tensive. The expansion of class action suits, development of the market share liability concept, or the procedure for substantiating advertising claims may cause a firm not to market a product of potential usefulness to society. Court rulings on who must pay for the mailing of proxy statements opposing a firm's investment in a South African subsidiary may alter the international investment plans of existing businesses.

Illustrations of the impact of statutes, court decisions, and administrative orders on the organization, operations, and procedural actions of marketing institutions are endless and constantly growing. The question that expansion poses for marketers is simple: What statutes, court decisions, guidelines, and rules of administrative agencies exist that may facilitate or impede attainment of my goals?

SOURCES OF MARKETING REGULATIONS

Expansion of marketing regulations has increased the number of agencies with power to influence the organization and operations of marketing institutions. In the legislative branch of government, Congress and state legislatures have the legal authority to create or modify statutes governing the form and size of institutions. Statutes prohibiting mergers may, in most industries, be modified or declared nonapplicable by legislative action. For example, Congress might authorize mergers prohibited as anticompetitive under existing statutes. Thus, in an industry such as newspaper publishing, mergers to save "failing" newspapers may be permitted. Similarly, Congress may enact legislation to allow development of joint ventures so the United States can compete effectively in international markets, even though the joint action might restrict domestic competition, thereby violating prevailing law. Statutory enactments by state legislatures allowing incorporation of practitioners in one profession but disallowing incorporation in another condition the firm's organizational structure. Marketing specialists must be constantly alert to legislative proposals before Congress and state legislatures that might limit, expand, or even destroy their organization forms.

As the economy grew more complex, legislatures created administrative agencies to interpret and implement broad grants of power in acts passed by legislatures (e.g., FTC, FDA, EPA, FERC, FDIC). These agencies, characterized as the "fourth branch of government," have long been accorded the Supreme Court's stamp of legitimacy. Agency scope of action combines power to determine specific meaning of general legislative provisions with authority to investigate possible offenses and corrective orders. If these corrective orders are not voluntarily agreed to by firms, agency lawyers seek judicial enforcement. The breadth of power of even a single administrative agency is very broad. In the famous *FTC v. Sperry & Hutchinson* case (1973), the Supreme Court declared the FTC may determine whether a specific practice is "immoral, unethical, oppressive, or unscrupulous." The Court allowed the administrative agency, in interpreting acts it was enforcing, to consider "public values beyond those enshrined in the letter or encompassed in the spirit of the . . . laws." The Court agreed the agency could enforce the act and apply sanctions against firms using practices it finds in violation of the act.

It is not clear whether, after Congress has created and granted power to an administrative agency, Congress may subsequently act to modify agency decisions. According to prevailing judicial precedent, agencies are created, given authority, and empowered to act by the legislative branch of government. However, after creation they are held by the Supreme Court to be a part of the executive branch of government. As such, Congress may not establish a procedure to enable itself to veto an administrative agency action.

Although Congress wrote provisions to give it power to veto specific actions of agencies it created, the Supreme Court found such veto provisions unconstitutional. In the *Chada* decision (1983) involving Immigration and Naturalization Service actions, extended to the FTC the same year, the Court found such a legislative veto would abridge executive branch power. Since separation of legislative, executive, and judicial branches of government is sacrosanct under the Constitution, the Supreme Court would not allow legislative veto of agency actions. Congress and legislatures retain power to control agencies by modifying appropriations and by passing specific acts governing issues that concern it. Yet in a complex economy with millions of individual transactions taking place daily, marketers can place little hope in an active and effective legislative control of the legislatively created administrative agencies.

As legislatures and administrative agencies regulate the marketing environment, so does the judicial system. Increased numbers of courts, judges, and lawyers attest to the increasing importance of the judicial system in regulating marketing activities. Legal theorists often argue that a specific court decision resolves only the unique issues characterizing that case, but they also acknowledge that judicial precedents arising from specific court cases have tremendous power to determine what actions marketers may or may not undertake. Precedents, especially if approved by the appellate court system, have a life of their own. Wise lawyers caution marketing clients that precedents have the virtual force of law in governing marketing managers' behavior.

Occasionally, as in the *Illinois Brick* price-fixing case (1977), Congress is infuriated by a judicial decision. Individual Congress members introduce bills to overturn the court's action and Congress may even threaten to adopt legislation. However, in the *Illinois Brick* case, despite introduction of bills to "repeal" the *Illinois Brick* holding in every Congress since 1977, no bill has become law. So for marketers, the decision in that case has the force of a legislative act.

Complicating the judicial system's role in determining marketing's contours is the constant retiring and replacement of members of the judiciary. Some fluctuations in judges' and lawyers' views may occur from time to time, but very few contemporary judges refuse to accept openly, or tolerate implicitly, the reality that changing conditions give rise to new and broader regulatory powers of legislatures, administrative agencies, or the judicial system itself. So the judicial system does not operate to modify or limit regulation of the marketing environment. The marketing manager who asks: "Who is going to limit the powers of those who determine what the limits of power are?" might not receive a very satisfactory answer. The full impact of the changing regulatory environment on business and other marketing institutions is quite apparent.

MARKETING REGULATION GUIDELINES

Despite regulatory expansion and flexible interpretation of regulation, some general, relatively well-defined and fixed guidelines exist in some spheres of marketing activity. These guidelines may be very valuable in daily management activity.

Price Fixing

The historic independence of businesses in setting and changing prices has been significantly restricted. A rule governing pricing behavior has evolved. The rule is simple: Do not tamper with the pricing mechanism because it is the central nervous system of the market system. The rule is based on Section 1 of the Sherman Act (1890) providing that, "Every contract, combination in the form of trust or otherwise, or conspiracy in restraint of trade is illegal." In addition, Section 5 of the Federal Trade Commission Act reinforces and supplements the Sherman Act by providing, "Unfair methods of competition in or affecting commerce, and unfair or deceptive acts or practices in or affecting commerce, are . . . illegal."

The definitive interpretation of the rule originating in the Sherman Act arose from and gave rise to a line of court precedents. The most clear statement by the Supreme Court was made in *United States v. Socony-Vacuum* (1940). In its simplest form the rule warns marketers to undertake no joint action with anyone that might be interpreted as "raising, depressing, fixing, pegging, or stabilizing" price. In the *Kiefer-Stewart* case (1951), the Supreme Court was confronted with the question of whether prices might be fixed at a maximum level so that consumers might not be gouged by too-high prices: the Court restated its insistence that price manipulation was illegal. The Court noted that whether a

price, either minimum or maximum, was fixed at a "reasonable" level was an irrelevant consideration. All fixed prices are "banned because of their actual or potential threat to the central nervous system of the economy." Despite this position, the Department of Justice has noted that in many industries various price-fixing methods have become "virtually institutionalized."

Predatory Pricing

The practice of predatory pricing also violates the Sherman Act. Predatory pricing occurs when a firm sets prices at a level designed to destroy competition. Antitrust scholar Robert Bork argues that predatory pricing is an exercise in "commercial folly." He argued that, for sound business reasons, wise marketers should not engage in predatory pricing. Nevertheless, predatory pricing cases occur and marketers must be conscious of the threat. Professor Kirk-Duggan of the University of Texas, a leading scholar of marketing law, has summarized the requirements for proof of illegal predation. The firm charging a competitor with predatory pricing must prove four things: First, the alleged violator intended specifically to control prices or destroy competition in some part of interstate commerce. Second, the alleged violator was attempting to achieve monopoly power by the predatory acts. Third, the conduct must be shown to have a dangerous probability of success. Fourth, proof must be accepted that the alleged violator had injured a plaintiff by actions *specifically* in violation of the antitrust laws.

Just when a specific price meets the first criterion is difficult to determine. The so-called Areeda-Turner rule is the prevailing formula: "Unless at or above average cost, a price below reasonably anticipated (1) short-run marginal costs or (2) average variable costs should be deemed predatory." Economists have long noted the theoretical difficulty of determining marginal costs (particularly when some costs are shared in production of more than a single product); marketers are aware of the practical implications of this difficulty. Notwithstanding difficulties in determining when predatory prices are established, marketers should not set prices that can be proven predatory.

Resale Price Maintenance

Resale price maintenance is an important pricing practice strongly affected by regulatory guidelines and precedents. Marketers attempt to persuade, cajole, convince, or coerce firms selling their products to maintain producer-set prices. The law looks with disfavor on price maintenance contracts but, unlike price fixing arising from conspiracy or combinations, the Supreme Court has not applied a rule of per se illegality to all resale price maintenance agreements. In the *Monsanto v. Spray-Rite Service Corporation* case (1986), the Supreme Court created the standard that applies before resale price maintenance agreements may be declared illegal. "There must be evidence that tends to exclude the possibility of independent action by the manufacturer and the distributor" in applying sanctions against a reseller who has not followed resale prices established by the producer. The issue is difficult to resolve. It requires determination of whether competition among different brands of a product offsets the loss of competition among sellers of the same brand of a product if a seller refuses to continue to deal with a firm that refuses to follow suggested resale prices. The literature on interbrand competition versus intrabrand competition is voluminous. For the marketer, the controversy surrounding the proper regulatory viewpoint is compounded by the uncertain position of the Supreme Court with recently appointed justices.

Price Discrimination

The Robinson-Patman Act governs discrimination in pricing and in the provision of promotional services. Though judicial interpretations have wavered and remain murky, the act still applies to activities of marketing institutions. Yet as recently as 1991, Professor Stern of Northwestern University issued a challenge to government enforcement agencies. Said Stern of the Robinson-Patman Act: "Either enforce it or get rid of it." Congress has not yet repealed the act; the regulatory agencies have not enforced it, except fitfully

and rarely. The act restrains marketers' pricing decisions and hangs, as the sword of Damocles, above unsuspecting marketers.

Penalties for Illegal Pricing Practices

Penalties for illegal tampering with the price mechanism can be severe. They may include imprisonment, although this is rarely applied; fines are more common than prison sentences. Under the November 1990 Antitrust Amendments Act, the maximum fine for price-fixing or other Sherman Antitrust Act violations was raised from $1 million to $10 million for corporations and from $100,000 to $350,000 for individuals. In addition, damage suits may arise from pricing actions the regulatory system finds illegal. Private parties may institute legal action, based on government evidence, to collect damages for losses suffered as a result of price fixing. In a private action, the price fixer is liable for treble damages. In addition, the 1990 act gave the federal government the right to recover treble damages. Congress's intent is clearly to persuade marketers to refrain from actions violating the price-fixing and other provisions of the Sherman Act.

The FTC may also prohibit activities that violate the extensively amended Federal Trade Commission Act and other acts it is empowered to enforce. The commission's enforcement powers frequently overlap the Justice Department's; it uses corrective methods not available to other enforcement agencies. Marketers must be constantly alert to the breadth of enforcement of regulatory power with the attendant penalties.

Specific exceptions occur in the coverage of some laws and administrative regulations. The behavior of regulatory agencies is sometimes vacillating and unclear. Sometimes the judiciary wavers in interpretation of laws and precedents. Marketers, however, can best act with safety by following the guideline suggested earlier: Do not tamper with the unfettered pricing mechanism. The pricing mechanism remains the central nervous system of the economy and, in the long run, rationalizations for interfering with it will fail.

Mergers and Joint Ventures

Marketers, in attempting to broaden markets and achieve scale economies in production or distribution, frequently contemplate mergers with other enterprises. In our legal system, mergers are not accepted with favor, and many laws regulate, and prevent expansion of, marketing units by mergers. The Clayton Act (1914) was the pioneering legislation. In 1950, Congress feared a wave of mergers and adopted the Celler-Kefauver Act as an amendment to Section 7 of the Clayton Act that applied specifically to merger activity. Supreme Court interpretations of merger cases are extensive.

In 1968, in 1982, and again in 1992, the Department of Justice attempted to formulate merger guidelines so that marketers might know if plans to create a new unit by merger would be accepted by the regulatory agencies as legal. The 1982 guidelines incorporated somewhat esoteric market dominance calculations known as the Hirschman-Herfindahl Index. The overall result is that knowing when and where mergers may be carried out, and exceptions to laws and guidelines, is now beyond most managers' legal expertise. Yet mergers do take place and mergers are challenged and prohibited. A lengthy process of premerger notifications and hearings is embodied in present administrative regulations of the Justice Department and the FTC. Marketers contemplating merger activities cannot proceed with freedom and impunity.

Joint ventures, like mergers, are subject to extensive regulation. When two firms wish to pool resources to achieve scale economies, enter new markets, or engage in cooperative research, a joint venture often seems desirable and plausible. The key legal issue is whether Section 7 of the Clayton Act, or the Sherman Act, prevents the joint action. In the *U.S. v. Penn-Olin Chemical Company* (1964), the Supreme Court tried to clarify the guiding criteria. The length, complexity, and ambiguity of the elaboration precludes an explanation of what it seemed to say; the Court's attempt to explain its rationale was more noble than successful. Marketers, wishing to know if a specific joint venture is legitimate, can do no better than to seek legal counsel analysis of the Supreme Court explanation.

Franchising

Franchising has grown in importance since the end of World War II. Its advantages are well known to marketers; the horrors of misuse are legion and chronicled in the popular press. The FTC is the primary regulator, although the judicial system has been extensively involved in interpretation of FTC-adopted rules. The complexity of franchise regulation is derived from implementation of the Magnusson-Moss Federal Trade Commission Improvements Act of 1975, the principal act governing franchising. The FTC Franchising Rule created after thirteen days of public hearings, 22,787 pages of public record, and 1,756 pages of transcript did not become effective until almost four years after the act's passage.

FTC rules define what constitutes a franchise and elaborate in great detail disclosures that franchisors must make to potential franchisees. Penalties for violation of franchising rules are severe. A civil fine of up to $10,000 per violation may be assessed. However, each single day in which the franchise rule is violated may be interpreted as a single violation. The possible multiplication of penalties is frightening in potential scope. Some judicial decisions have given limited protection to franchisors from attack by the FTC or franchisees believing violations of franchising regulations have occurred. Marketers contemplating franchising should acquire, consult, and adhere with rigor to the bundle of requirements that govern the creation and operation of a franchising network.

Tying Contracts and Requirements Contracts

Marketers wishing to distribute products and services may wish to use two distinctive, though questionable, contractual devices. The first, *tying contract*, attempts to condition the acquisition and use of one product over which the producer has significant control or market power upon acceptance of another product over which the producer does not have power. The rules governing tying contracts are elaborate, but if regulatory agencies determine that a tying contract exists that might "tend to" lessen competition "substantially," the contract may be nullified with significant legal penalties. The tying contracts literature is voluminous, especially in the growing realm of contracts involving medical practitioner services and the institutions where they work.

Similarly, *requirements contracts* in which marketers agree to secure all wares or services from a single supplier are extensively regulated. In the *Standard Stations* case (1949), the Supreme Court recognized the possible benefits of requirements contracts for both the seller and the buyer; it established some guidelines, elaborated by the FTC. Because requirements contracts pose the threat of destroying competition by foreclosing markets to competitors, marketers should use them carefully.

Regulation of Product Promotion and Product Characteristics

Marketers try to place products or services before possible users in the most attractive way. Regulation of product and service promotion is almost unbelievably extensive and frequently contradictory.

Most regulations implement Section 5 of the Federal Trade Commission Act declaring illegal "[u]nfair methods of competition in commerce, and unfair or deceptive practices in commerce." The FTC adopts trade regulation rules designed to clarify acceptable practices or those falling outside the act's scope. FTC regulations embrace labeling as well as advertising; most conditions of sale also fall under the act. In addition, specific regulatory statutes governing marketing (e.g., the Comprehensive Smokeless Tobacco Health Education Act, 1986) are implemented by the FTC.

To carry out provisions of the FTC Act and other acts under its jurisdiction, the FTC has established three bureaus: Consumer Protection, Competition, and Economics. These bureaus are the commission's working arms; they are the basis for actions before the FTC's own administrative tribunals before administrative law judges. Enforcement through consent orders, accepted or refused by individual firms, is supplemented by FTC ability to se-

cure readily available and precedent-laden support from the judicial system. The entire system is complex; marketers should secure legal advice if they anticipate any advertising approaching deceptiveness or unfairness narrowly construed.

EMERGING AREAS OF MARKETING REGULATION

Among the areas of increased regulatory scrutiny is "intellectual property." Copyright and patent law has long been present; marketers should be aware of these laws, though they are outside the scope of this chapter. Marketers should also understand that as electronic media—telefax machines and transmission, computer software, optical character readers—proliferate, new problems of just treatment of competitors and new firms alike arise. The law is taking shape in this field; its growing importance suggests that marketers should keep familiar with emerging doctrines and procedures.

KEEPING ABREAST OF THE MARKETING REGULATORY ENVIRONMENT

Two "C's," *caution* and *currency*, should dominate marketers' actions in avoiding pitfalls of the growing legislative, administrative, and judicial regulation of marketing. The best marketing rule is to take no actions, operational or organizational, that carry any suggestion of impropriety. Penalties for indiscretions are too high to do otherwise. Moreover, marketers should avoid actions of dubious legality or morality, and keep current with the changing legal environment.

Good sources for keeping abreast of regulatory issues are by Stern and Eovaldi, *Legal Aspects of Marketing Strategy* (Prentice-Hall, 1984), and by Werner, *Legal and Economic Regulation in Marketing: A Practitioner's Guide* (Quorum Books, 1989). The "Legal Developments in Marketing" section of the *Journal of Marketing* provides an up-to-date review of the most important new developments. Weekly reports of new developments in related areas, and in not-to-be-underestimated state regulatory areas, can be secured by subscription to the Bureau of National Affairs *(Antitrust and Trade Regulation Report)* and the Commerce Clearing House *(Trade Regulation Reports)*. This brief survey does no more than indicate the scope and the direction of marketing regulation. As the inscription above the entrance to the Library of Congress advises: "The Past is Prologue!"

INDUSTRIAL MARKETING

V. Kasturi Rangan, Professor, Harvard Business School, Harvard University

Bruce Isaacson, Doctoral Student, Harvard Business School, Harvard University

Industrial marketing comprises the marketing of goods and services to commercial enterprises, governments, and other nonprofit institutions for use or support in providing the goods and services that they, in turn, produce for resale to other customers. By contrast, consumer goods marketing is the marketing of goods and services to individuals and family units for personal consumption, and to wholesalers and retailers in consumer goods distribution systems. In industrial markets, goods are usually bought for processing and subsequent resale, but in consumer markets goods are bought for their final consumption or use.

Products sold in industrial markets can be grouped into eight general categories: (1) *heavy equipment* (e.g., radiology equipment, diesel engines, air compressors) that is technically complex and usually requires a substantial investment by the buyer; (2) *light equipment* (e.g., portable air compressors, hand tools, personal computers) that involves smaller investments; (3) *systems* (e.g., information systems) of equipment, peripherals, and accessories that provide "solutions" for buyers; (4) *raw materials* (e.g., crude oil, iron ore, cotton fiber); (5) *processed materials* (e.g., rolled steel, fabric, plastic polymers) developed from raw materials that serve as primary input for the next stage of manufacturing; (6) *consumable supplies* (e.g., coolants, abrasives, medical syringes) that are consumed by end users in the course of regular business operations; (7) *components* (e.g., engines and motors) purchased for incorporation in the buyer's end product; (8) *industrial services* (e.g., engineering services, management consulting, and contract maintenance insurance) that may involve comprehensive design, installation, and operation of a major system.

Exhibit 2-28. Key Linkages

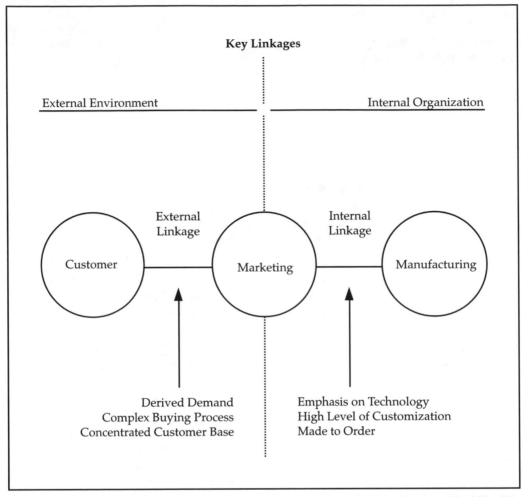

Source: From V. K. Rangan and B. Isaacson, What Is Industrial Marketing? *Harvard Business School Note N9-592-012;* copyright © 1991 by the President and Fellows of Harvard College. Reproduced by permission.

To understand key elements in marketing industrial products, and key differences between industrial (business-to-business) and consumer marketing, it is useful to consider the industrial marketing system as comprising two key linkages: the external interface between the producer's marketing/sales function and the end user; and the internal interface between the producer's marketing/sales function and the production function (Exhibit 2-28). While each of these linkages is quite complex (e.g., R&D's role in the internal interface; the role of distribution channels in

the external interface), the two sets of linkages serve as convenient handles to explore business-to-business marketing.

THE EXTERNAL LINKAGES

Derived Demand

Demand for industrial products is usually driven by the primary demand for consumer goods. For example, an automobile is built from hundreds of components including engines, wheels, the exterior body, and the dashboard. Each of these in turn is the end result of a supply chain comprising many other components and raw materials. The dashboard is usually molded from ABS plastic. ABS plastic is made from three chemicals, including styrene. Styrene is made from ethylene; ethylene is made from petroleum. The demand for each of these intermediate goods is influenced by demand for automobiles. When demand for automobiles slumps, ABS manufacturers are directly affected. Similarly, when downstream demand picks up, ABS producers are automatic beneficiaries. Industrial marketers can improve demand for their products by stimulating demand for customers' or distributors' products. Thus, many manufacturers have "missionary" sales forces that locate and develop potential customers for distributors.

Consumer preferences, economic cycles, and social trends affect industrial markets by influencing final consumer demand. Consumers can adjust their buying habits quickly, while industrial customers are often locked into technology or machinery that cannot be easily adapted to meet the latest market trends. Consequently, industrial customers must purchase in anticipation of economic and market conditions that they are likely to face. Industrial buying, therefore, has a longer-term orientation.

Complex Buying/Selling Process

In consumer markets, the decision-making unit for purchasing a particular item is often the individual, and rarely is larger than the household. In industrial markets, the decision-making unit is usually much more complex and may involve many departments within the organization. The purchase of one piece of industrial equipment may involve a host of departments, such as purchasing, engineering, finance, and manufacturing, and may require approval from top management. Several factors increase the complexity of the buying process: the influence of the formal organization, the strategic importance of the item being purchased, the cost of the item being purchased, and the complexity of the need being serviced.

The complexity of the buying decision increases the time, expense, and experience required of companies selling to industrial customers. Also, industrial customers, unlike consumers, often buy for multiple operations from multiple locations. Each individual unit may use the same basic product, but unique requirements may necessitate service at the buying headquarters as well as at the individual plant locations. The aggregation of selling tasks at two or more levels only makes the selling task much more complex.

Although the selling and buying process is more complex in industrial markets, several aspects of the industrial sale make it easier to establish close vendor relationships in industrial markets. First, industrial purchases tend to be relatively rational and based on specific performance characteristics or benefits sought by customers. Second, with consumer goods, consumers' interactions with sellers are typically short term, intended simply to fulfill immediate needs without implying a long-term dependency; many buyer-seller relationships end with the sale. By contrast, industrial purchases often cause the buyer to become dependent on suppliers for consistent provision of subassemblies, parts, service, support, or product upgrades. Consequently, many industrial customers evaluate suppliers as candidates for long-term relationships.

Concentrated Customer Base

Consumer marketers often reach millions of consumers; an individual consumer is insignificant in such a large customer base. By contrast, industrial marketers generally have a much smaller base of potential customers. In many industrial markets a small number of customers represents a large percentage of the industry's buying potential. Industrial marketers selling high-ticket items such as power-generation equipment can count their customers on their fingers. Also, because of the special infrastructural support required, many industrial product manufacturers are concentrated in geographical areas, such as Silicon Valley in California for high-technology electronics. As a result, industrial marketers are more likely than consumer marketers to use direct sales forces. Moreover, the targeted and concentrated nature of the industrial customer base makes direct marketing and face-to-face selling economically viable. By contrast, many consumer marketers use mass-media communication techniques to reach broad and dispersed consumer bases.

THE INTERNAL LINKAGES

Emphasis on Technology

Technology is a far more visible component in the sale of industrial products than consumer products. Technology and performance superiority can provide industrial products with competitive advantage in the marketplace; there is a heavy emphasis on product improvements in successive generations of industrial products. For example, manufacturers of semiconductors and disk drives are constantly improving the performance-to-price ratio of their components over successive generations of products so end users can make better products for subsequent sale. In industrial markets, performance, functions, and features are of primary importance in the design, manufacturing, and marketing of the product. Many consumer products manufacturers also constantly offer innovations in their markets, but emphasize "solutions" rather than technology.

High Level of Customization

Often, a high level of customization is required for industrial products. The customization of consumer products, on the other hand, is usually in the packaging, labeling, or promotion; the basic product is standardized over a broad range of customers and markets. Unlike consumer products, industrial products are used in the further manufacture or assembly of the next level of product, so it is very important to meet the user's technical requirements. Industrial technical requirements are often very inflexible; consumers may accept a different flavor or color than initially required, but industrial customers will not, for example, accept welded pipe if seamless pipe is out of stock. Many industrial product manufacturers even tailor operations or facilities to meet unique requirements of key customers. Engineers and design teams may often be assigned to learn the needs of key end users, and customize products accordingly.

In many cases, industrial firms may actually sell standard products, but the complexity of the machinery or system may cause the accompanying information and service support to be customized. For example, Digital Equipment Corporation sells a standard line of VAX minicomputers for businesses computing needs, but the system's operating characteristics are adjusted from site to site. Universities and research institutions typically use a VAX computer for analytical modeling involving a variety of nonrepetitive data processing. Consequently, the package of hardware, software, and peripherals needs customization even though each individual component may be from a standard offering.

Made to Order

A large variety of industrial products are made to order. Even if produced to standard specifications, actual manufacturing may commence only after the customer order is received. Thus, much industrial goods manufacturing is essentially job shop oriented; by contrast, production for consumer items (e.g., packaged foods) tends to be based on large-scale batch or continuous flow operations. Raw material and work-in-process inventory levels may vary across types of industrial product and market, but finished good inventory levels are frequently low for many industrial goods manufacturers. As a result, when an industrial customer initiates an order, the order fulfillment chain often triggers a manufacturing operation directly linked to the order somewhere on the factory floor.

Consumer goods manufacturing, on the other hand, is often matched against finished goods inventory because the product specifications are usually standardized. When a consumer initiates an order, the order fulfillment warehouse or customer service department is the trigger point for fulfillment. Finished goods inventory is used by manufacturers of consumer products to insulate manufacturing from day-to-day changes in customer demand; manufacturing of consumer products is usually geared to meeting sales forecast, not individual customer orders.

THE STRATEGY

Given the distinguishing characteristics of both the internal and the external linkages, the formulation and execution of marketing strategy poses different challenges in industrial as compared to consumer markets (see Exhibit 2-29).

Market Selection and Development

Since technology plays such an important role in industrial markets, a key function is customer education and market development. As with consumers, industrial customers might not, a priori, express appreciation or enthusiasm for an untested new product; it is the marketer's responsibility to demonstrate a product's use and value to the customer. Because industrial products are often technically complex and may require a change in buyer operations, adoption usually follows intense application trials and productivity analysis. Many industrial marketers actually create and build a market for their products, rather than merely serving existing needs.

Market Segmentation

Consumer markets can be segmented by psychological or sociological factors such as life-

Exhibit 2-29. Differing Emphasis of Industrial vs. Consumer Marketing

	Industrial Markets	*Consumer Markets*
Market selection and development	The emphasis in the early part of the life cycle is clearly on market development.	Market selection and segmentation are often more important than market development.
Market segmentation	Tends to be along demographic variables, such as size or industry.	Usually along personality or lifestyle variables.
Advertising	Rarely used to create demand. Some manufacturers use it to convey product information.	Extensively used to create demand and brand differentiation.
Pricing	Pricing is usually geared to customer needs and competitive situation.	Pricing is usually standard from which promotional discounts and quantity allowances may be made.
Product policy	Product positioning is usually based on functions/features.	Product positioning is often based on psychological attributes.
Channels of distribution	Fairly extensive use of direct sales force to reach customers.	Wholesalers and retailers are dominant modes of reaching consumers.
Marketing research	Tends to emphasize technical development more than customer research.	Extensive feedback from consumers sought in design of new products as well as repositioning of mature products.

Source: From V. K. Rangan and B. Isaacson, What Is Industrial Marketing? *Harvard Business School Note N9-592-012;* copyright © 1991 by the President and Fellows of Harvard College. Reproduced by permission.

style or attitudes; industrial markets are more likely to be segmented by industry characteristics, purchase quantities, or technical requirements. More recently, industrial marketers have realized the need for benefits-based, or, better still, buying behavior-based market segments. Unfortunately, these segmentation schemes are often very difficult to implement in industrial markets. Industrial customers, unlike consumers, do not self-select into segments and shop accordingly. Rather, they must be approached with the appropriate marketing mix at the outset. Thus, if a consumer needs a dress for a special occasion, she is likely to visit a specialty retailer rather than a discount store. In the industrial situation, the sales force, rather than the customer, makes the visit and offers the appropriate product.

Advertising

Consumer marketers often use advertising to establish brand image; industrial marketers use advertising more often to communicate specific price and performance information. Brand image in industrial markets is achieved by a combination of product quality and service that accompanies the delivery and installation of the product.

Industrial marketers often rely on trade shows to communicate new product information. Trade shows are also used to establish personal contact with buyers, maintain visibility for the firm and its products, recruit distributors, obtain feedback on market needs, evaluate competition, and locate suppliers. Bringing personnel, equipment, and promotional materials to trade shows is expensive, so careful evaluation is necessary to ensure that the trade show attracts the audience sought by the manufacturer.

Pricing

In most consumer markets, retail prices are easily communicated and assumed to be set on a "take it or leave it" basis. By contrast, industrial marketers set prices by three primary methods. In *cost-plus* pricing, often used for large contracts of uncertain length, including military weapons systems or R&D projects, the buyer pays the seller's full cost of providing the product or service, plus an agreed-upon profit margin. In *competitive bidding*, often used for large projects or for those projects where the buyer seeks a product customized to a very specific set of specifications, potential sellers submit bids to the buyer explaining their prices and product offerings. Competitive bidding is a matter of policy even for smaller purchases in many companies and in most government agencies. In *published list pricing*, manufacturers use printed price lists to communicate prices. Published lists are often most appropriate for standard, low-priced items sold to a wide variety of buyers. Often, large customers negotiate discounts off list prices. However, the long-term nature of industrial relationships sometimes means that customers are willing to pay a higher price to ensure delivery, product quality, and service.

Product Policy

As the result of a more technology-oriented buying approach on the part of industrial buyers, industrial products are often sold on the basis of technology, product features, or other functional properties. However, when core product advantages wear out over time (e.g., patent expiration), little supplier differentiation may exist in the market. In mature industrial markets, competitive price pressures are common. The marketing effort to arrest such commoditization is a key aspect of industrial product policy for many suppliers. Product differentiation in industrial markets is secured either through physical product improvements or through the accompanying service. In consumer markets, by contrast, careful product positioning, niche marketing, and brand pull advertising can maintain the franchise value without major improvements in product or service. Industrial products are loosely categorized as either *specialties* or *commodities*. Price is the dominant buying criterion for commodities because all suppliers' products appear essentially the same to the buyer; for specialties, buying criteria often transcend price. Vendor relationship, technical characteristics, or service may provide the necessary differentiation.

Channels of Distribution

Industrial markets usually have narrower customer bases than consumer markets; thus, it is economically viable to reach at least a segment of end users, especially large users, directly. Moreover, given the technical nature of products and the complex buying processes involved, it is often a sales team, rather than a lone salesperson, that closes the sale to industrial customers. Thus, key account (or customer) sales teams comprising technical as well as commercial personnel are frequently employed.

Industrial marketers have many distribution channel options. Selecting the right method of distribution is a difficult task. In general, industrial marketers prefer a direct sales force to distributor channels when there is a manageable (small) number of customers; customers are concentrated geographically; the sales process is long and complex; customers require a lot of information and training in product use. Direct sales forces typically provide manufacturers better feedback about market needs and better control over the marketing mix in the channel than indirect external methods. However, sales force costs are estimated to vary between $150 to $250 per sales call, thus restricting deployment in situations requiring extensive market coverage.

In selecting external channels, a company must decide whether to use *merchants*, who take possession of goods and title, or *agents*, who take neither possession nor title. For example, electrical supply houses buy and inventory electrical items and are thus merchants; manufacturers' representatives receive commissions on orders generated but do not take possession of the product or receive title, and are classified as agents. Merchants relieve manufacturers of the risk associated with inventory and credit in the channel.

Industrial product distributors (merchants and agents) tend to be well trained; the technical nature of the products they carry forces them to be well informed regarding product technology. For example, computer value-added dealers have highly trained teams of technicians to tailor software to solve specific customer problems. Chemical distributors must be well trained regarding safety considerations. In short, industrial distributors often provide channel functions that go beyond the usual assortment, inventory, and convenience that accompany consumer products distribution.

In selecting a channel of distribution, companies must also consider whether *company-owned* distribution (i.e., *captive* distribution) or *independent* distribution is appropriate. Both act as merchants with respect to the channel functions they perform. Company-owned distributors provide the firm with control over channel policies (e.g., pricing), but may complicate management's task by expanding the firm's business from manufacturing to distribution.

Marketing Research

Because of heavy R&D and upfront engineering expenditures involved, new industrial products are often tested sequentially at various critical development stages at selected customer sites. This is feasible because of the separability of the product's functions and features. Consumer products, on the other hand, have to be in their near-finished form before testing because of the difficulty in obtaining consumer response to partial subsets of the product's final attributes and features. This type of intensive testing at customer sites, *beta site testing*, requires very close cooperation between manufacturer and customer. Beta site testing provides the manufacturer with feedback on product design and features generated from actual product use. Customers whose facilities become beta test sites receive a head start on obtaining new technology, but accept the technical risk of potential failure.

Not only does industrial marketing pose key challenges in the formulation and execution of marketing strategy but there are also unique distinctions in organization of the industrial marketing function. Because of the emphasis on technology, higher product customization, and the nature of the order fulfillment cycle, the selling and operations functions of industrial marketing firms usually need much closer integration. This may be achieved by a supporting field technical organization that assists sales representatives in developing customer applications and solving customer engineering problems. As noted earlier, large customers may be served by a joint team of sales as well as technical personnel. Depending on the nature of the industrial product and the complexity of the buying process, such a team approach may also be appropriate for some smaller customers.

The need for closer marketing and operations integration often means that industrial marketers have to make or assist in decisions that cut across functional lines in a "general management" fashion. Product development,

applications engineering, capacity planning, and quality assurance are only a few among the many nonmarketing functions in which an industrial marketing manager has to participate. By contrast, the consumer marketing function tends to be more specialized.

Industrial marketing must be approached quite differently from consumer goods marketing. Key linkages between the firm and the external environment, and between the sales/marketing function and other internal firm functions, take on special characteristics in industrial marketing. As a result, marketing strategy development and implementation must be developed on the basis of assumptions that are peculiar to industrial markets.

ADVERTISING AND MASS COMMUNICATIONS

Bernd H. Schmitt, Associate Professor of Business, Graduate School of Business, Columbia University

The success of many businesses depends on effective advertising and mass communications. As a nonpersonal form of communications, advertising is not always the most effective communications tool. In addition, a firm may decide to use other, more personal communications. For particular communication tasks, however, such as building brand awareness, creating a brand image, or inducing new product trials, advertising is the method of choice.

Advertising planning is a key element in implementing marketing strategy; marketing strategy thus has direct implications for the advertising plan. For example, the segment targeting decision leads to various media decisions. Brand positioning influences advertising objectives and creative strategy. Other decisions determine advertising expenditures. If marketing strategy relies primarily on "push" via retailers, the role of mass communications may be minor. But, in a "pull strategy," where firms target ultimate consumers, advertising plays a major role.

Every advertising plan has five components: advertising budget allocation; advertising objective formulation; message creation; media planning; and measurement and evaluation. Advertising planning decisions are interdependent: budget size influences what objectives can be achieved; messages put constraints on media, and media options limit the use of creative appeals.

Research also plays a major role in advertising planning. Early on, focus groups and survey research are useful methods to understand consumer needs. As part of creative decisions, advertising messages should be pretested before dissemination. When the campaign is finished, its overall impact must be assessed relative to advertising objectives.

Advertising planning typically proceeds in consultation with other organizations, in particular the advertising agency. The agency's role typically includes message creation, media planning, and advertising research.

Successful advertising planning also requires an intricate understanding of communication and persuasion processes. What attracts consumers' attention? What makes an advertisement memorable? What makes an ad persuasive? Research has shown that when consumers are highly involved in processing advertising messages, rational arguments may persuade via central persuasion. When consumers are less able and motivated to process messages, peripheral cues (e.g., background music, celebrities, and scenes) may persuade. Moreover, centrally induced attitudes are stable, resistant to competitors' counterattacks, and predictive of purchase behavior. Peripherally induced attitudes are transient, easy to change, and less predictive of behavior. Depending on the campaign's objectives and the target audience's psychological state, advertisers should therefore put differential weight on central and peripheral cues.

THE ADVERTISING BUDGET

A rational approach to advertising budgeting is marginal analysis: increase the budget as long as incremental expenditures are exceeded by marginal sales revenues. In practice, however, determining the shape of the function behind advertising and sales is difficult. Also, sales are rarely determined solely by advertising expenditures. Other advertising mix components, such as message creativity and media, play equally important roles in a campaign's success or failure.

Despite the availability of sophisticated budgeting models, most firms use simple rules of thumb. The simplest, used by two thirds of major firms, is percentage of sales, based on past-year sales, anticipated next-year sales, or a combination. Though a useful starting point, percentage of sales has one major flaw: its inconsistency with the notion that advertising can stimulate demand. It is a static method and is insufficiently responsive to changing environments.

Another common heuristic is matching major competitors' estimated expenditures. However, competitive parity assumes that competitors spend rationally, and that the firm's situation is comparable to competitors. Both assumptions are often unfounded.

A logical, research-based way to set budgets is objective and task. Is the firm trying to reposition its brands? Are most brands in maturity and being managed for cash? Does the firm need to create awareness for a new product? The objective and task method defines advertising objectives for each brand, then specifies tasks to be accomplished to reach these objectives. Only then does the firm determine costs. As a result, the budget may be substantially different from previous years' or from competitors' budgets. Companies subscribing to this method in principle often use a more cautious approach in practice: adjust the budget by percentage of sales or competitive parity before or after allocating funds according to objective and task.

ADVERTISING OBJECTIVES

Advertising objectives serve three functions. First, they are coordination devices. Objectives coordinate the interactions between account executives, the creative team, and the media and research departments. Second, advertising objectives facilitate decision making. Third, advertising objectives may be used to evaluate results and determine whether the campaign was successful. To serve as coordination, decision-making, and evaluation devices, advertising objectives must be clearly defined, easy to communicate, and operational.

Sales Objectives

Sales objectives are clearly defined and easy to communicate. Yet they are ineffective as operational criteria to guide advertising decisions. Sales is an aggregated measure; it does not specify the communications tasks necessary to motivate and influence consumer behavior. Should the firm convert nonusers to users? Is the goal to motivate brand switching? Does the firm intend to increase customers' usage? In sum, what behavioral changes should be induced to increase sales?

In addition, sales objectives are ineffective in guiding the campaign evaluation. Advertising is a form of mass communication and should be evaluated in terms of its communications impact. Sales, market share, and overt consumer behavior changes are, at best, indirect measures of communications impact. In addition to advertising, a firm may have revised its pricing structure, expanded distribution channels, and made product changes—all of which may have influenced sales. Moreover, sales objectives are often formulated on a short-term basis (e.g., for a fiscal year), whereas mass communication effects on sales often occur after a longer time period. Convincing consumers to break old habits, to try a new technology, and to switch brands takes time. Using sales as an objective may lead to misjudgments about what has actually been achieved.

Communication Objectives

Advertising objectives are best formulated as communication objectives. Awareness, comprehension, image, and affect are all useful in formulating communication objectives.

Brand Awareness. Achievement of brand awareness is a key advertising and mass com-

munications task. Awareness can induce product trials, and for some low-involvement products (e.g., gum, soda, soap), awareness may be sufficient to sustain repeat purchase.

One well-known awareness commercial was Apple Computer's Big Brother introduction for MacIntosh. The visually striking commercial (production cost: $400,000), aired during the 1984 Super Bowl (cost: $500,000), created an elaborate version of Orwell's 1984, with hundreds of drone-like characters listening to a big-screen Big Brother. Facing a major struggle with IBM's PC ($40 million advertising budget), Apple decided to do something dramatic to create new product awareness.

Brand awareness is typically measured as *unaided recall* of the brand name. Alternatively, *aided recall* measures may be used: consumers check all known brands from a list of brands. Aided brand recall is, of course, easier than unaided recall, and recall difficulty further depends on the items on the list. Therefore, different measures produce different results and should be interpreted cautiously. Recall measures rarely indicate absolute awareness, but may measure awareness relative to competitor brands.

Brand Comprehension. A second communication objective is consumer learning of product features and benefits, and correcting misinformation, false beliefs, or other sales obstacles. When consumers must learn and comprehend much product information, print is often chosen as a medium.

Because advertising focusing on brand comprehension includes propositions and claims, consumers often generate their own thoughts in response to advertisements: these may support or disprove the message. For example, a new camera advertisement may lead consumers to infer the camera is superior to others, but more difficult to use than suggested. Therefore, advertisements should be carefully tested for their potential to induce support and counterarguments.

Verbal protocols test for the presence of support and counterarguments. During, or soon after, ad exposure, consumers are asked to write down all thoughts that come to mind. In addition, consumers may be asked to rate the degree to which they agree or disagree with the advertising claims.

Brand Image. Brand image embraces any permanent associations consumers have with a brand. It is most important for hedonistic and relatively intangible products. Fashion designers (e.g., Ralph Lauren, Claude Montana, Georgio Armani) successfully use brand images to associate their clothing with distinct lifestyles. Because brand images are evasive, projective techniques best capture consumers' brand associations. Young and Rubicam asks consumers to relate brands to personality traits ("Is Holiday Inn cheerful?") or to animals ("If each brand was an animal, which animal would it be?").

Brand Affect. Advertisers often try to create positive brand affect or associate brand usage with positive feelings, such as joy, pride, fun, or love. For example, AT&T's late 1980s "Reach out and touch someone" campaign tried to convey the human contact and emotions provided by a phone call from far away. Conversely, public service campaigns try to associate consumption with negative feelings (e.g., fear with drug use). That is, affective advertising tries to transform actual or imagined user experience into something that may result in repeated product use or, for antidrug ads, product avoidance.

General positive or negative feelings are often measured on bipolar attitude scales. For specific feelings, consumers check word lists of emotions for relevance or irrelevance. More subtle, physiological measures include monitoring galvanic skin response, eye movements, brain activity, and facial movements.

Hierarchies-of-Effects Models

Since many advertising campaigns involve several communications objectives at the same time, it is useful to construct a hierarchy-of-effects model that specifies the order in which various communication effects take place. Three hierarchies are commonly distinguished: the learning hierarchy, the low-involvement hierarchy, and the affect transfer hierarchy.

Learning Hierarchy. Before purchasing an unfamiliar, complex product (e.g., a new technology product) a consumer must become aware of the brand, be convinced of its differential benefits, form a positive attitude, and be motivated to purchase. The advertiser may thus need a long-running campaign involving different creative executions and media selections at different stages to guide consumers through this learning hierarchy. To create broad awareness and interest, the campaign may start with flashy TV commercials, such as the MacIntosh introductory commercial, then switch to print media to convince potential consumers of relevant benefits (e.g., superb graphics and networking capabilities). To reinforce a positive attitude, print and TV commercials may stress repeatedly one or two crucial benefits. Finally, co-op advertising with local retailers, which provides price information, may motivate purchase.

Low-Involvement Hierarchy. For low-involvement products, consumers process information in a simplified awareness-to-trial sequence. Advertising's primary task then is to provide top-of-the-mind brand awareness constantly, as for many grocery items. Advertising messages are supported by promotional tactics such as in-store product trials, point-of-purchase displays, and price promotions. The media campaign emphasizes repetition for brand awareness, but should also create positive brand attitude or brand image, since consumers may need justification for repeated purchases.

Affect-Transfer Hierarchy. The key element is associating the brand with positive feelings. The first campaign goal is building brand awareness and brand benefit comprehension. Yet the crucial goal is subsequent association of the brand name and benefits with positive consumption experiences. Positive feelings may be evoked, for example, in various ways: by presenting people or situations that trigger strong emotions (e.g., evoke nostalgia or feelings of joy), or by providing symbolism linked to a target group's sense of identity (e.g., city or country icons). Advertising with the American flag in the background suggests that buying a Chrysler supports America; driving a BMW provides a personal feeling of power; the Infinity experience compares with a Zen-like state of mind. Feelings generated by the ad may be associated with the brand and may be remembered during consumption of the product.

Hierarchy-of-effects models simplify and idealize communication tasks. Moreover, hierarchies depend on the product category, the choice situation, and the target audience. They are, nonetheless, useful in advertising planning because they force the firm and agency to conceptualize the communication task in a detailed manner with a long-term perspective.

ADVERTISING MESSAGES

Creation and production of creative output is the most visible part of advertising. If the creative product is good, the agency looks good; if it is bad, the agency looks bad. Although judging creative output may be relatively easy, the creative process seems to be an enigma, more art than science, mysterious and unexplainable. The essence of creativity seems to be a willingness to alternate between divergent and convergent thinking, between brainstorming and analytical reasoning, between pushing the limits and being reasonable and practical. The process typically begins with fact finding and problem immersion. It moves through a stage of inactivity and frustration when nothing seems to happen. It culminates in an illumination—the Big Idea.

The advertising community continues to debate what seems to be a false dichotomy between creative advertising and advertising that sells. Although many examples of *l'art pour l'art* exist in advertising, there are many more examples of original, creative campaigns that also increase consumer demand. Creative advertising that sells attracts attention, is memorable, gains publicity and, ideally, enriches its creators and recipients. But it also sells because it targets the right segments with the right messages.

The Absolut Vodka Campaign

An excellent example of a highly successful campaign, both creatively and financially, is the ongoing campaign for Absolut Vodka. In the late 1970s, no one would have predicted success for a Swedish vodka with such an unusual brand name and bottle. But in ten years, Absolut sales soared from 5,000 cases (1979) to 2.5 million cases (1989); its market share among imported vodkas rose from 1 percent to 60 percent. Today, Absolut ranks third behind U.S.-made Smirnoff and Popov in the whole vodka category. Its campaign has won prestigious awards for creative advertising and has been imitated by other liquor firms. Its outdoor prints have become collectors' items.

The typical Absolut ad seems simple and straightforward. It displays the distinctively shaped bottle with a two-word headline starting with "Absolut." The attractiveness of the execution lies in the unexpected touches that surround the imagery. "Absolut Perfection" features the crystal-clear Absolut bottle depicted as jewelry topped by a halo. "Absolut Original" features a stone bottle with cracks as if excavated from a prehistoric site. "Absolut L.A." shows an aerial view of a bottle-shaped swimming pool. "Absolut Centerfold," a special ad for *Playboy* (run only once), displays the spotlit bottle as a sexy object accompanied by the "Absolut Data Sheet" listing the bottle's bust, waist, and hips sizes (all $11\frac{1}{4}$), ambitions ("To always be cool, with or without ice"), favorite books (*The Iceman Cometh*), and turn-ons ("Swedish massages"). Artists Andy Warhol and Keith Haring and trendy fashion designers have contributed to the campaign, creating artistic visions of the bottle or designing clothing modeled after it. During Christmas seasons, magazine ads included microchips playing Christmas carols and fake snowflakes in a liquid sealed in plastic. Such original ideas have set the Absolut campaign apart from traditional "bottle-and-glass" liquor advertising and established a distinct product image for the Swedish vodka.

Creative Strategy

The Absolut campaign illustrates the underlying principles of creative advertising that sells. Although seemingly freewheeling and intuitive, behind the campaign is a clever creative strategy: present the right appeal and the right execution. Hundreds of different appeals can be used in advertising—for example, sensory and mental stimulation, affiliation, aspiration, respect, and self-fulfillment. The Absolut campaign presented a particular appeal, one highly attractive to its target group—an appeal to image as such: to be cool and hip and part of it; at the same time, to be different and individual, even in one of the most undifferentiated of choice situations—the choice among vodkas.

The Absolut campaign provides the right appeal, instantiated in a unique execution. It does not use a simple product presentation like a straight sell; nor does it simply use slice of life, a sexual approach, testimonials, demonstrations, or drama. It stands apart from standard message formulas, yet uses all these formulas in a sophisticated fashion. The city ads present slices of life from each city; the *Playboy* ad makes sexual allusions; testimonials are implicit in artists' renderings and designers' clothes; the Christmas campaign has some demonstration and dramatic element. Moreover, the campaign uses humor but avoids excessively funny gags and repetition. Most important, Absolut ads combine appeal and execution in one inseparable, irresistible gestalt.

MEDIA PLANNING

Media planning comprises decisions regarding the best means to deliver advertisements to target customers. A media plan defines media classes (e.g., television or print), media vehicles (e.g., *Late News* or *Tonight*; *Time* or *Newsweek*), media options (full or half page; fifteen seconds or thirty seconds). It also specifies scheduling over time.

Because there are so many feasible media options, media planning is highly quantitative. Computer models are used to search databases from media research suppliers such as Nielsen and SAMI Burke for best media alternatives. Nevertheless, managerial judgment is crucial for most decisions: quantita-

tive comparisons across media are often difficult because some data are either nonexistent or unreliable (e.g., outdoors and transit advertising). Moreover, qualitative differences between media classes may influence campaign success or failure. Finally, since media decisions interact with the creative strategy, cost effectiveness is not the only decision criterion.

Effective media plan selection is based on three broad criteria: (1) number of exposures to the target segment, (2) number of times a potential customer is exposed to the message, and (3) advertising impact in medium/vehicle options.

Ratings, Reach, and Frequency

Agencies and television networks spend more money for rating data than for any other research. A rating is the percent of individuals (or homes) tuned in to a television or radio program. Rating data vary by program, region (television market), season, time of day (daypart), and within program by quarter hour.

Media planners often calculate gross rating points (GRPs)—sum of ratings delivered by a given list of media vehicles. Two other important measures are reach (the number of individuals or homes exposed to the schedule) and frequency (the average number of times individuals or homes are exposed to advertising messages).

Reach and frequency must be traded off: numbers of different people reached versus how often they are reached. Advertising effectiveness research indicates that, for most product categories, two or three exposures per purchase cycle is optimum; beyond three exposures diminishing returns set in.

Print vehicle circulation data (e.g., newspapers, magazines) are also available, but they must be supplemented by estimates of pass-along readership. Also, perhaps in-home readers should be weighted more heavily than out-of-home readers, since they pick up magazines more often and pay more attention to them. Because in-home and out-of-home readership patterns vary by magazine, informed judgment must make readership adjustments.

Qualitative Comparisons

Aside from calculating GRPs, shares, frequencies, and other measures, advertising impact by medium must be evaluated qualitatively. Print and broadcast media differ substantially in the way messages are delivered and perceived by consumers. Involvement levels in print media are generally higher than broadcast media while print media are read at the reader's convenience; messages from broadcast media may be viewed only when broadcast (except if recorded on VCRs). Print media are less intrusive than broadcast media; they interfere with editorial content only to a limited degree but broadcast messages interrupt programs. Print media may be carried to different locations; television and radio are less transportable.

Scheduling

In terms of campaign scheduling, media planners must consider seasonal sales patterns, decide whether competitive advertising should be countered, and assess the relative importance of introductory versus sustaining campaign phases. Spending may be constant over time (continuous), may alternate periods of activity with inactivity (flighting), or may combine the two (pulsing).

ADVERTISING RESEARCH

Prior to running an advertising campaign, marketers should use consumer research as a benchmark for campaign evaluation. For example, a cereal company that intends to reposition its brand should determine the brand's current position vis-à-vis competitors on relevant dimensions (e.g., nutrition, sugar content) before the campaign starts. Copy tests are used to assess how the advertisement may be perceived. Posttesting researches the impact of a campaign.

In day-after recall, consumer panel members, contacted by phone, are asked if they saw a specific product placement in a certain television show. Split runs are like experiments. Different advertisements appear in the same medium—print or broadcast—at the same time. The advertisements are viewed by different matched groups to compare relative

effectiveness. Split-cable testing, coupled with computerized retail scanner systems, allows monitoring both media behavior and actual purchases.

CURRENT TRENDS AND THE FUTURE OF ADVERTISING

The most pervasive advertising trend since the mid-1980s is increased clutter. Satellite and cable television have dramatically increased media and advertising opportunities. U.S. cable penetration is well over 50 percent and strong in all regions. In Western Europe, many private television channels shun rigid advertising regulations existing on state-supported television. Direct mail increases. Since consumers are bombarded with advertising messages, the major advertising challenge is to create clutter-breaking messages.

Critics complain that advertising agencies have not developed more innovative and original advertising. Unusual ideas, such as black-and-white commercials on color television, are quickly copied and lose impact. Original slogans (e.g., "The Art of . . .") become fads when applied broadly to fountain pens, cognac, and dishwashers.

In fact, the advertising industry as a whole has been diminished. Some believe the problem is terminal. Declining creativity, lack of impact, and diminishing importance are commonly cited symptoms. Advertising has lost its glamour as a career. The bad news was broken in the front page of *The New York Times:* "Advertising is dead!" This announcement, however, may be premature. Agencies have changed in the 1980s and trends have emerged that may contribute to advertising's resurrection, albeit in a different form. Mass communications will stay with us, especially in a global environment. Long live advertising!

The Japanese agency Dentsu is a good example of how advertising agencies have changed. In 1986, Dentsu adopted "total communications services" as its new management philosophy; it now offers a large variety of marketing and communication services. Activities include production of exhibitions, international trade shows, sports and cultural events, and satellite broadcasting, in addition to the classic advertising services of media planning, creative consulting, and advertising research. Moreover, Dentsu has established a worldwide network of agencies and subsidiaries, including joint ventures with Young and Rubicam and the French agency Eurocom. Finally, in the Dentsu Institute for Human Studies, researchers pursue in-depth studies of behavioral trends in today's rapidly changing commercial, industrial, and social climate.

Such trends cause traditional boundaries between advertising, promotions, and public relations to become obsolete to the benefit of companies because successful campaigns use these communication devices in a complementary way. Mars's sponsorship of the XI Asian Games (1990) in Beijing is a good example. Although China imposed many legal and bureaucratic hurdles that made fruitful business relations difficult, a sponsorship campaign for M&Ms was an unprecedented success, in large part because marketing communications were effectively embedded in a public relations, advertising, and promotions campaign. Visitors to the Asian Games were greeted at the airport with M&Ms product samples. Flashy M&Ms cars drove through Beijing's bicycle-dominated streets. The M&Ms brand was displayed on T-shirts, balloons, uniforms, umbrellas, and boats in public parks. A Lucky Draw Competition was shown live on Beijing television. M&Ms received more media coverage than any other Asian Games sponsor, including Coke, which spent three times as much as Mars. M&Ms' brand awareness skyrocketed from zero to 70 percent in Beijing— not a bad start for targeting China's 1.3 billion consumers.

This example illustrates another mass communications trend: one country cannot exist independent from the rest of the world. Mass communications and marketing as a technology are now global. Ideally, global communications transcend national boundaries, speak to common human values, and are universally understood.

In the early 1990s, the British agency Saatchi and Saatchi pioneered the ideas of global communications and world brands. Saatchi and Saatchi argued that consumer tastes and preferences were converging around the globe due to common demographic trends (e.g., falling birth rates, aging populations, increased female employment), social changes (e.g., nuclear family decline, higher living standards), and a shared culture offered by television and the entertainment industry. Backer, Spielvogel and Bates Worldwide and other agencies have collected data in fifteen countries on five continents to identify similarities and differences in values and attitudes among consumers as well as global segments to help clients build internationally accepted brands.

Widespread communalities in consumer preferences and behaviors require a universal language for advertisers to speak to consumers. For the global corporate campaign for British Airways ("The World's Favorite Airline"), the Saatchi and Saatchi creative team specified several conditions for global communications: advertising has to be simple and single-minded, instantly understood throughout the world, visual rather than verbal, and likable. Image and affect advertising most likely fall into these categories. Image is best illustrated with pictures, background music, and similar peripheral cues. Many emotions (e.g., joy and anger) are universally understood. Therefore, both image and emotions were featured prominently in the British Airways campaign's initial phases.

Two seemingly opposed trends will determine whether advertising's pivotal role in marketing strategy will diminish, or whether an advertising and mass communications revival will occur. On the one hand, major threats to mass communications result from marketers' needs to target ever smaller consumer segments with increasingly specialized needs and desires. On the other hand, tendencies toward standardization in consumer perceptions and developing global consumer markets present opportunities. Very likely, marketers at the turn of the century, like today, will need both: mass media advertising to create awareness and raise demand for products targeted to substantial segments, and personal messages to communicate specific benefits to consumers with specialized needs.

DIRECT MARKETING

Marjorie Kalter, Executive Vice-President, Wunderman Cato Johnson
Elizabeth Stearns, The Stearns Group

Direct marketing is an interactive system of marketing that uses one or more advertising media to effect a measurable response and/or transaction at any location. In recent years, uses of direct marketing have skyrocketed. Direct mail accounts for one third of national advertising spending. As examples:

> A giant packaged-goods company profitably sells excess inventory produced by an overseas subsidiary to upscale consumers in the United States. It uses direct-mail and direct-response print advertisements to sell only to mail-order subscribers.

> With zero share of voice in television and magazines, a U.S. firm launches a new credit card that quickly becomes a formidable competitor to long-established bankcards; it repeats this success in international markets.

As these examples show, direct marketing is action advertising because it causes the target to act. It can result in an immediate sale; it can turn a customer into a multiple buyer; it can generate a highly qualified lead that can be converted to a sale; and it can command attention when a salesperson cannot.

It is also accountable advertising because its effectiveness can be measured by sales generated. Direct marketers know the cost of acquiring each customer or lead and the relative costs of different media, different creative versions, and different incentives to motivate purchase.

Every aspect of the advertising can be tested and analyzed as a separate variable and adjusted to improve profitability—from the source of each customer (which mailing, which magazine advertisement, which television commercial) to the factors that affect the purchase decision (which price, which incentive).

Increasingly, direct marketing is also described as database marketing. Companies take information they receive from responders and store it in computer files. They can compare and analyze these data to develop prospective customer profiles, to sell other products to existing customers, to obtain information for use in loyalty and relationship programs, and to refine their marketing plans.

In contrast to image advertising, direct marketing is action oriented, is accountable, and can provide marketers with valuable databases. While image advertising builds awareness and shapes attitudes, direct marketing affects behavior by motivating action—purchase—or indication of interest in purchase. Accountability is its greatest advantage over image advertising. Since every sale can be analyzed against other sales, direct marketing program managers have the potential for maximum knowledge about how well or badly profit objectives on a per-customer, per-impact basis are being met, and what is needed to improve profitability.

Direct marketing growth in the United States (30% per annum since 1985) has been driven by both consumer and corporate trends:

- Increased database use by large firms, especially in telecommunications, financial companies, transportation, and manufacturing.
- Acquisition of direct marketing businesses by large firms.
- Increasing sales call costs, requiring more efficient prospecting.
- Less time and more discretionary income among two-income families.
- Increased dissatisfaction with retail shopping.
- Improved quality and variety of mail-order goods and services; reassurance of guaranteed satisfaction, easy ordering, and easy return.
- Higher comfort level for consumers and business persons making purchase decisions without a retail environment or salesperson. Consumers vote on mail order with their pocketbooks; 50 percent of U.S. adults per annum order merchandise via direct marketing.

Direct marketing has a long history in its own right, but increasingly it is included in the marketing mix as a strategic approach to reaching customers. As such, it is a key element in the integrated marketing of goods and services where advertising and direct marketing are developed together, so that brand imagery is consistent in message and tonality.

Direct marketing's key features in integrated marketing programs include action and accountability; the renewed focus on direct marketing stems from an understanding that the most important goal is customer satisfaction. The better a firm is able to understand and communicate directly with individuals, the more it can deliver satisfaction and, therefore, action in the form of sales.

THE NATURE OF DIRECT MARKETING

Direct marketing entails four key elements.

1. *Interactive systems*—Direct marketing is a form of two-way communication: customers respond to, or are in dialogue with, the marketer. The marketer gains firsthand feedback on programs by target segment; customers may seek more information, make a purchase, or set up a meeting. Customers have a measure of control that is atypical of one-way communication like advertising.

2. *Multiple media*—The list of media available to marketers is almost endless:
- direct mail
   brochures
   newsletters
   catalogues
   coop mailings
   statement inserts
   product- or service-specific mailings
- telephone (inbound, outbound)
- fax
- broadcast (radio, television)
- print (magazines and newspapers)
- interactive cable and computers
- on-package messages
   ticket jackets (airline/train/bus)
   matchbooks
   cereal boxes
- package inserts at point of sale and fulfillment
- warranty cards
- surveys (mail, in-person)
- sweepstakes or contest applications
- take-ones

3. *Measurable response*—Databases comprising information about responders and nonresponders allow marketers to refine programs. Because actual buying behavior is tracked, managers can develop models to predict and improve response and profits.

4. *Any location*—Direct marketing provides an additional distribution channel. The channel does not require face-to-face contact; it occurs whenever marketer and customer can be connected through a media vehicle. Marketer reach and customer options are increased.

Other elements make direct marketing effective:

- Targeting can be at a precise level using databases. Also, the marketer's customer database can be enriched with information about lifestyle and demographics from outside lists and information files.
- Communications can be personalized to an individual or target segment.
- Marketing spending can be keyed to the profit potential of customer segments, based on net present value and lifetime value.
- A range of key variables that leverage sales and profit can be tested on small yet statistically significant samples, avoiding costly errors.
- Communications and products can be tested in a "live laboratory." The data surpass quantitative and qualitative research.

DIRECT MARKETING PROGRAMS

Direct marketing programs comprise several interrelated elements: creative strategy; creative execution; and media selection.

Creative Strategy

Creative strategy results from target audience analysis. Strategy is based on insight as to how the product can have a new and positive effect on the target audience. Strategy must be consumer driven—ideally by research.

Developing and describing the strategy precedes efforts of the creative team (e.g., art director, copywriter) to design an ad, and media department to develop a plan (e.g., television, print, mail). The creative strategy is part of a briefing document that outlines relevant product information from the marketing plan. It is used as a creative briefing for the art director and copywriter, a benchmark for researchers, a media briefing for media planners, and a guide for the entire marketing group to monitor all process stages

of executing the marketing plan. Key elements of the strategy document are:

- Description of target audience (e.g., demographics, psychographics, geographics; amplified by prior quantitative or qualitative research); summary of marketplace and relevant competitive activity.
- Profile of target audience's perception of current product, service, or brand.
- List of key product benefits that advertising will feature; reasons why the product delivers.
- Obstacles or marketing problems that advertising must overcome.
- Key message advertising should convey, including the offer, and its tone.
- Action the target audience should take as a result of advertising.

Creative Execution

In direct marketing the creative execution must be compelling and distinctive—like advertising—but it also has to sell, immediately. Thus, direct-response print looks different from image advertising; direct-response television looks and sounds different from image commercials; also, direct mail always comprises special elements.

First, the required response or call to action is highlighted, generally as an offer. It should be clear, prominent, and presented graphically in the most compelling way. Response should be simple; consumers are told how to order, via an easy-to-use reply form or prominently placed telephone number.

Clear offer presentation is essential, but brevity is not; copy is often long and direct mail packages are often complex. The copy has to sell; it should be long enough to answer all possible questions and overcome hestitation.

Typically, qualitative and quantitative research is used to help develop the best executions. Qualitative methodologies (e.g., surveys, mall intercepts, mail, telephone), customized one-time studies, and tracking studies (e.g., attitude and usage and brand/advertising awareness) are fed into the creative process.

Most important, creative execution must work. Success depends on highly objective criteria such as required number of orders or inquiries at an allowable cost per order/inquiry. If not, the chosen method will not be used again.

A creative test against a control should be budgeted in every effort. What worked previously may not work now. Managers should not be overly influenced by history; they should be open to new and even radical concepts that are strategically sound.

Media Selection

The goal of media selection is to reach the most consumers who are most likely to buy. Actual media choice depends on allowable cost per order, ability to target, and potential for expanding the initial buy at rollout.

Target audience assessment is based on classic advertiser sources: syndicated research services (e.g., Simmons and MRI), available category and brand research, and specific market research for the proposed program. These findings determine whether mass media, targeted media, or a combination is most likely to succeed. The key criterion, demonstrated propensity to buy by mail order, governs choice of mailing lists, publications, and television markets.

Direct mail can develop or supplement a house list of customers. Noncompetitive marketer list rentals provide a supply of prospects (onetime use), as well as purchase history, lifestyle, and/or demographics. List brokers provide suggestions, selection criteria (e.g., recency, frequency, size of last purchase, credit card use), and rental cost (per-thousand name basis). Names can be selected by zip code. A merge-purge process adds to the house list and eliminates duplicates.

A major advantage of direct mail is discretion since competition cannot monitor the medium, product, offer, price, or list, and creativity can be tested quietly. Also, the target has time to read, reflect, decide, and order. Disadvantages include rising postal costs, mailbox clutter, and privacy and environmental issues that are leading direct marketers to reconsider mail or to redesign it (e.g., smaller size, fewer pieces, recycled paper).

In contrast, print creates awareness and sells. It has advantages for introducing or testing a new product or service, building a mailing list when the target audience is unclear, reinforcing a television campaign, adding credibility and awareness to a direct mail campaign, and reaching audiences for whom lists are not available.

Media may reach mass markets via large, general audience publications such as *TV Guide,* Sunday newspaper supplements, and newsweeklies or special-interest segments through targeted magazines (e.g., fashion, home, travel, do-it-yourself, finance, sports).

Direct-response print ads must include response devices (e.g., coupon, reply card, postage-paid mailing label, telephone number). Each response device is coded for analysis by publication, issue, format, creative, and offer. The advertisement may be preprinted and inserted into some magazines at the binding stage; the marketer can thus test several versions in the same publication.

Direct-response television is used when high order volume or inquiry is needed from a broad audience. Cable can be used to reach segmented audiences. Television can sell products directly or generate leads to be followed up by mail and telephone. Because viewers must decide and act, direct-response commercials are longer than image/awareness commercials; historically, the most successful length is two minutes, typically on local stations for cost reasons. Shorter spots may succeed for familiar products, or reinforce campaigns including longer spots and other media.

Radio is rarely used to sell direct since the listener must remember how to order. However, it often supports mail, print, and television. Telemarketing, an interactive direct-response medium, is rapidly growing. Well-trained telephone salespeople customize scripts to adapt offers to prospects and close sales. Most products are purchased via *inbound calls* placed by consumers. Some marketers use *outbound telemarketing* to sell, to elicit information from nonresponders and responders, to qualify prospects, to obtain further information for house files, and to reinforce existing relationships.

DATABASES

The database is the core of a market intelligence system that drives strategic marketplace operations via stored information and customer insights. Its key task is to define the customer so that behavior can be measured, analyzed, understood, and managed.

Basic customer performance data accessible from databases are *recency*—the date of the last purchase or inquiry; *frequency*—the number of sales or inquiries within the past six months/one year; *monetary value*—the sum of purchases. Database management encompasses list management (merge/purge), name selection (e.g., segmentation, testing, profiling, modeling), production (e.g., schedules, lettership, file scoring, fulfillment), response analysis, and accountability reporting.

Database management systems facilitate updating, adding, sorting, and manipulating data. Data must be accessible by multiple computer programs and users, contribute to marketers' ability to manage relationships over time, allow for enhancement from external sources, and have a high level of quality, accuracy, and security. Finally, external data (e.g., demographic, geodemographic, psychographic, lifestyle) can be appended to databases to provide marketers with better individual or segment information.

CLUBS AND CONTINUITY PROGRAMS

The profitability key for many successful direct marketing businesses is that selling to an existing customer costs less than to a totally unknown prospect; the house file contains useful information about prior purchase behavior. Even better are sales that initiate a series of orders: club and continuity.

Club and continuity programs can provide a special service dimension: large product selection; established member benefits or discounts; toll-free telephone service; several low payments to acquire substantial collections (e.g., books, recordings, collectibles); opportunities to purchase products unavailable from other sources; mail-order convenience.

For marketers, the advantage is substantial. Each customer represents an ongoing revenue source from a series of orders. Customer acquisition cost can be higher since management can project future sales with zero advertising cost. Thus, music clubs can offer ten cassettes for a penny and book clubs can offer three books for a dollar. (Of course, shipping and handling charges help.) In addition, inventory levels are predictable. Examples include Columbia House and BMG music clubs and Book-of-the-Month Club. Two program types are most successful:

1. *Negative option*—Members are regularly sent next product shipment announcements. A reply card provides three options: featured selection, alternate, or nothing. If the card is not returned on time, the featured selection is automatically sent. Some negative-option programs entail commitments to purchase a minimum amount of product; marketers can thus project long-term sales for each customer. Others offer no commitment, preferring higher initial sales from more customers attracted by the lack of commitment.

2. *Continuity plan*—This plan is a subscription to a series of product shipments. The initial purchase is offered on trial, at reduced price, free, or with a premium. If the customer keeps and pays for the first shipment, subsequent products are sent automatically, usually every four or six weeks, until the series is completed or the subscriber cancels. From historic data, the marketer can predict attrition of front-end buyers who cancel out and revenue flow from back-end sales to remaining customers (e.g., Time-Life Books, Franklin Mint, and Lenox collectibles).

Increasingly sophisticated database management will permit direct marketers to manage club and continuity customer relationships individually. Decreased attrition, increased revenue, greater cross-selling, and improved initial-order volume will follow use of such database-oriented techniques as:

- Segmentation based on attitudes and behavior, to motivate larger or longer-term sales and to predict purchase behavior of prospective customers.

- Targeted offer, creative action, shipment sequence, and frequency of shipments, based on analysis of current customer base, to increase sales among similar groups of prospects.
- Individualized incentive programs.
- Customized product sampling through interactive telephone services and downloading of text/audio/video to personal computers.

RELATIONSHIP MARKETING

Relationship marketing—retention, repeat sales, cross-selling—depends on precise message targeting on a highly segmented basis. One or more of these factors should apply:

- Segmentation is feasible (adequate data to group customers effectively).
- Significant consumer inertia, resistance, or ignorance requires a long-term, costly program.
- Dialogue is perceived by customers as helpful and informative.
- A discreet competitive thrust is needed.
- Building loyalty as well as sales volume is important.
- Marketers can secure, store, and use specific information about customers to improve marketing effectiveness and efficiency.

Targeting is essential. The objective is to reach the right prospect or customer with the right message, at the right time, in order to elicit information to make a dialogue meaningful, to motivate loyalty, and to convey the feeling that even the largest of companies is responsive to individual customer needs. Relationship programs use a series of targeted communications. Frequently, the initial one is a survey for the marketer to gather the information to construct or supplement a database. Subsequent mailings are customized to respond to individual or segmented requests or needs. Each contact should invite some response: the cumulative effect is establishing an ongoing dialogue.

Since consumers are dynamic, and purchase needs change, relationship programs should be monitored, evaluated, and refined to reflect the research findings. In addition, new prospects or customers should be added on a regular basis.

BUSINESS-TO-BUSINESS MARKETING

Marketing directly to business customers is a significant growth area: for lead generation and prospecting; for sales to low-volume customers; for low-margin product sales; and for companies relying on mail order for supplies. It can also help manage existing customer relationships. Direct marketing can help identify and rank all members of a buying group (e.g., purchasers, decision makers, influencers, end users); appropriate messages are sent to each.

Direct marketers can establish a form of dialogue and relationship by telephone, fax, or mail, prior to the sales meeting, to learn about the prospect and analyze the relative value of promotional materials. Each contact and each response/nonresponse provides valuable data for eliminating unproductive leads, revising communications, and refining list information to better identify purchasers and influencers. Therefore, many of the principles of relationship marketing apply here, especially for companies that sell high-end goods and services.

SECTION 3

Sales and Distribution

Noel Capon, Section Editor

Introduction   *Noel Capon*   3-3

The Tasks of Sales Management   *Noel Capon*   3-5

Designing the Sales Organization   *Raymond W. LaForge and
     Thomas N. Ingram*   3-11

Managing the Distribution System   *Jan B. Heide*   3-19

Major Account Management   *John F. Martin and Gary S. Tubridy*   3-26

Designing Sales Force Compensation   *Gary S. Tubridy*   3-35

Sales Promotion   *Scott A. Neslin*   3-41

INTRODUCTION

Noel Capon

In Section 2 we focused on identifying and selecting market opportunities and truly understanding customer needs so that the firm might develop marketing offers that provide it with competitive advantage in the market segments it chooses to address. In this section we assume this job has been done; the focus of interest here is on communicating with, and distributing products to, target customers.

Communication strategies must be designed with the explicit objective of, ultimately, persuading customers to purchase (or recommend to others) the organization's products and services. Broadly speaking, communication with target customers can involve personal or impersonal communication. Personal communication is typically achieved through sales force effort; impersonal communication is achieved by various forms of advertising or public relations.

Whereas advertising messages are frequently focused on individual products/services or product lines to well-defined customer groups, sales forces often sell multiple products/services or product lines to multiple customer groups. Perhaps the key challenge for many organizations in the 1990s is to improve the effectiveness and efficiency of their sales force effort, in the face of increasing competitive challenges, rising sales force costs, and greater customer concentration. In this section, in a manner parallel to Section 2 where we highlighted the core tasks of marketing management, we lay out the key tasks of sales management, those tasks that must be successfully completed for optimal sales force performance. We then focus on selected issues that must concern all sales managers.

First, we discuss the key issues involved in designing the appropriate sales organization for implementing marketing strategy, taking due note of the trade-offs involved in different design options. Increasing concentration of the customer base is a crucial matter for sales managers; here we highlight major account management as a means of successfully dealing with this challenge. Finally, we address the ever critical issue of designing appropriate compensation systems for the sales force and highlight key issues in managing distribution systems.

Turning to impersonal communication, marketing managers must be aware of the benefits, limitations, and application of the various options for spending the promotion budget. We focus both on traditional persuasive methods of advertising and mass com-

munications and on an increasingly important internal competitor for the firm's budget,
sales promotion. Sales promotion expenditures have risen dramatically in recent years
as many firms have switched at least part of
their budgets from advertising.

Cross reference: *Relationship Selling in Service Industries,* J. I. Coppett and W. A. Staples, Section 15.

Noel Capon, *Ph.D., is Professor of Business at Columbia Business School. His teaching and research interests are in the areas of strategy and planning, and sales force management. Recipient of teaching excellence awards, Professor Capon directs several of Columbia's marketing and sales management executive programs. He is coauthor of* Corporate Strategic Planning, *a study of planning practices in major U.S. manufacturing corporations.*

THE TASKS OF SALES MANAGEMENT

Noel Capon, Professor of Business, Graduate School of Business, Columbia University

TASK 1: MEET SALES OBJECTIVES

Typically, sales forces undertake a variety of activities aimed at achieving many different goals. For example, they may be asked to secure information, collect payment for products and services, deliver goods, and entertain senior company management. However, notwithstanding the importance of these different activities, there is only one goal that is ultimately crucial to the success of any sales organization: achieving sales objectives. The firm only survives and prospers to the extent that it receives revenues and makes profits from customers for the goods and services it offers to the market. There is only one function in the organization that is typically charged with making sure that the firm does sell its products and receive revenues; that is the sales force.

There are several implications that follow from this first sales management task. First, for the sales force fully to embrace its sales objectives and work diligently to ensure that they are achieved requires senior sales management to be fully involved in the objective-setting process. In many companies, the starting point for developing sales objectives is the marketing planning process. All too frequently, marketing objectives developed in the marketing planning process are transposed into sales objectives and delivered to the sales force without any meaningful discussion. Under such circumstances it is not at all unusual for these sales objectives to be discarded by sales management as being developed in the "ivory tower" and being out of touch with reality.

In many companies, such a lack of integration between sales and marketing is seen as a critical issue. In these companies every effort is made to involve sales management in the objective-setting process for marketing and consequently in the transposition into sales objectives. In some firms, marketing–sales coordinator positions have been developed to ensure that the appropriate sales and marketing managers are present at the appropriate meetings.

A second implication is that the choice of form of objective is a crucial decision. Not too many years ago, sales forces were typically set gross volume objectives based in terms of unit or dollar volume. In recent years, there has been a growing realization that sales forces should also be set profitability objectives. Frequently such objectives are not bottom-line profit objectives but rather are contribution-type objectives. Contribution-type objectives are based on sales revenues less direct costs, including sales force costs. Typically these costs do not include costs out of sales management control such as head office, research and development burden allocations, and so forth. The intent is to set sales managers' objectives over which they have control.

Another dimension of objective setting is the particular product/market areas that generate sales and profits. For example, sales of new products may be more difficult to achieve than sales of existing products; also, such sales may be more important to the long-run health of the firm. Thus, objectives should be set by product type along the existing versus new product dimension. In addition, if manufacturing capacity is an issue, objectives may also be set by product group. An associated dimension of objective setting is by market segment. As noted elsewhere, marketing strategy is developed for market segments. Since marketing objectives are the basis for sales objectives, the setting of sales objectives by market segment should be seriously considered. To the extent that market segment–based sales objectives are achieved, so too are marketing objectives. Another possible objective-setting dimension is sales to existing versus new customers.

The critical issue for sales managers to focus on in deciding the basis for objective setting is what basis is strategic for the firm. If the firm is unconcerned about whether sales and profits derive from one product group or another then setting objectives by product group is a meaningless exercise. If the firm is unconcerned whether sales and profits derive from one market segment or another, or from existing versus new customers, then setting objectives by market segment or by customer type is a meaningless exercise. However, if the firm does care about one of these dimensions, or indeed any other, if one of these dimensions is strategic for the firm, then this

(these) dimension(s) must figure in the objective-setting process.

Finally, results from sales force execution must be monitored against sales objectives. To the extent that objectives are not being met, clear analyses should be made of the reasons. The results of such analyses may imply redefinition of sales force effort, selection of alternative customer targets, and so forth.

TASK 2: ALLOCATE SALES FORCE EFFORT

Sales objectives are achieved by sales force effort, the work of salespeople in the field. To achieve sales volume and profits, sales management must ensure that efforts of the sales force are targeted against those customers most likely to generate sales and profits. Sales force time is the scarce resource that sales management must allocate to achieve its objectives. In order to achieve appropriate effort allocations, a careful analysis must be conducted of all major customers and customer groups to see where allocated sales force effort will provide the best results. A well-developed marketing plan should provide significant guidance for this task.

When discussing task 1, we made the point that objectives should not just be made on the basis of gross measures. We suggested that sales objectives might be broken out by product (existing versus new), by market segment, or by customer type (existing versus new). Given that sales effort is a key determinant in whether or not sales objectives are achieved, it is crucial that sales management allocate sales force effort in a manner that is isomorphic with sales objectives. In other words, if sales objectives are set separately for existing products and new products, sales force effort should be allocated to existing products and to new products; if sales objectives are set separately for new customers and existing customers, sales force effort should be allocated to new customers and existing customers.

Of course, we should not expect sales effort to mirror sales objectives proportionally. For example, suppose sales objectives are set on the basis of volume for existing and new products, and suppose that 80 percent of sales are supposed to come from existing products and 20 percent from new products. We would not expect the allocation of sales force effort to be in the same 80/20 ratio. Rather, we might expect that proportionately less effort would be necessary to achieve the 80-percent sales of existing products than the 20-percent sales of new products; perhaps a 70/30 or 60/40 ratio might be appropriate.

The set of resource allocation decisions for sales force effort should be made as part of the sales planning process. This process comprises both a top-down element flowing from the marketing planning process and a bottom-up element whereby each member of the sales force performs an analysis of his or her sales territory. As part of the sales planning process, top-down and bottom-up elements are integrated. There are two broad approaches to securing the required effort allocation; these are discussed under task 3.

TASK 3: DESIGN THE SALES ORGANIZATION AND ORGANIZATIONAL PROCESSES

The major function of the sales force organization is to ensure that the appropriate types and levels of effort are applied against the designated customer targets. Decisions regarding the form of line sales organization play an important role regarding type of sales force effort; relative allocation of salespeople within the organization addresses the levels of effort. In both cases, the line sales organization is designed to reflect the strategic realities faced by the sales force.

There are a variety of ways to design the line sales organization, each of which is most appropriate in particular strategic situations. The simplest form of line organization is geographic; salespeople in a geographic organization have the responsibility to sell all products to all market segments within a defined geographic territory. This form of organization is most appropriate when there is comparability across products, customers, and applications. The advantages are minimiza-

tion of sales force confusion via the single company-customer contact, lowest travel and administrative costs, maximization of selling time, and close supervision of salespeople. The disadvantage is that the salesperson is a jack-of-all-trades.

When the product line is large and heterogeneous, when products are at different life cycle stages, or different products are sold into different market segments, a product organization may be appropriate. Salespeople are specialized by product, meaning that more than one salesperson from the firm may call customers in a specific geographic area. Such an organization is less efficient than the geographic organization as regards travel and administrative costs; it is less efficient for customers who now have to receive more than one salesperson; and it can lead to internal competition among the different sales forces if product development blurs the lines of product use and performance. On the other hand, salespeople become product experts and there is much greater sales and operations coordination.

When different products are sold to different market segments but the products sold in each segment are similar, when selling problems differ by market segment, or when specific types of salespeople are appropriate, a market segment organization may be appropriate. Sales forces organized by market segment may be based on industry, application, or end use; key account sales forces also fall into this category—the sales force is organized by account size. The advantages of this form of organization are that salespeople (via selection or training) or teams of salespeople can be matched to market segments. In addition, customers have a single firm contact and can be offered the "best" solution, rather than having to choose from competing offers from salespeople in the same firm. Finally, salespeople learn the customer's business, thus ensuring a greater flow of new product and service ideas. The disadvantages of this form of sales organization are the relative lower efficiency compared to geographic organization, the large breadth of product knowledge required, and the problem of "feast or famine" for individual salespeople if individual market segments fall on hard times.

A form of sales organization designed to focus attention on new products is the division of sales force effort into developmental and maintenance sales forces. New products or new customers are provided to the developmental sales force; when these get off the ground they are handed over to the maintenance sales force. The key advantage of this organizational form is that new products and/or potential new customers get attention and that the firm makes the best use of its developmental salespeople. Disadvantages include lower efficiency, coordination of the developmental and maintenance functions, and handover from the developmental to the maintenance sales force. This form of organization may be appropriate when the firm is in a growth mode.

In addition to the various line organizational forms discussed above, large sales organizations especially may employ combinations of the various forms. For example, the basic organization may reflect a product split, but within the different product organizations salespeople may be specialized by industry (market segment).

Regardless of which sales organization form is selected, sales force effort must be allocated to designated market targets. The product, market segment, and developmental/maintenance forms of organization have the additional advantage that effort allocation can be based on salesperson assignment. For example, if a 200-person sales force is organized by product such that the three product groups' sales forces comprise 40, 60, and 100 salespersons, the allocation of effort across the product groups has already been accomplished.

In the case of a geographic sales organization, or for other dimensions (e.g., market segments, existing/new customers) in the example in the previous paragraph, sales force allocation decisions must be made via the planning process. However, compared to salesperson assignment, sales management cannot be certain that the required effort allocation will be achieved. To ensure that market targets receive the planned allocation, sales management must develop processes to ensure that planned activities are carried out.

Whereas the form of sales organization sets the framework within which the allocation of sales force effort is decided, the extent to which planned effort allocation is implemented and equals actual effort allocated depends on managerial processes. There are a variety of processes available to sales management to ensure that the required effort allocation is achieved; we focus on two. The first process emphasizes the role of the first-line sales supervisor. Sales managers in this role have the responsibility to monitor and control the day-to-day activities of their direct reports. The sales supervisor should play a major role in the bottom-up phase of the sales planning process, working with the salesperson to analyze fully the sales territory, and later to make decisions regarding effort allocation in the territory. Then, through week-by-week monitoring and control, the sales supervisor has the responsibility to ensure that planned levels of effort are implemented.

The second managerial process is the sales compensation scheme. Sales compensation plans are essentially based on three elements: salary (compensation paid regardless of sales performance); commission (variable compensation based on product sold); bonus (compensation based on attaining a level of sales). The compensation scheme is a powerful method for securing the required levels of sales force effort. For example, if effort is required on new products, commission schemes that pay more for such products or bonuses paid for a given level of sales will encourage the appropriate effort. Unfortunately, however, in many sales forces the compensation scheme does not move in sync with sales objectives and the required effort allocation, with the result that achieving the desired effort is very difficult.

TASK 4: DEVELOP SALES APPROACHES

A key output of the marketing planning process is the core strategy or key buying incentive. For each market segment targeted by the firm, the core strategy states the basic reason why customers in the segment should buy the firm's products and services rather than those of competitors. Necessarily, the core strategy is written at a fairly general level for the market segment as a whole. Within the sales force there must be a translation process from the generalized market segment offer to the specific message(s) delivered by the salesperson to individual customers.

During this translation process it may be necessary to develop regional or other focused sales approaches. For example, in one region customer needs may differ from the customer average across the market, and/or major competition may come from a focused regional competitor rather than major national competitors. Such customer need variation and localized competition may have been only slightly taken into account when market segment strategy was being developed. However, for this particular region, positioning by the sales force for these particular customers against local competition may be crucial.

The key issue is that the salesperson should be given the best ammunition with which to approach customers. Sales management has the responsibility to take the core strategy statements for the various market segments that the firm addresses and turn these into actionable sales approaches for the sales force at its specific customers.

The translation process involves three distinct steps. First, salespeople and their managers must analyze the specific customer needs and the specific competitive threats at their accounts. Second, they must take the core strategy statements and translate these into specific benefits for their accounts, dealing both with customer needs and competitive offers. As part of this process, they must be prepared to answer objections and to sell against strong competitive offers.

Finally, customers do not typically comprise a single individual or role position. In many buying situations there is a buying center or group, each member of which may have a different perspective on the purchase. For example, a typical buying center for a manufacturing company might comprise individuals from purchasing, engineering, and manufacturing. Each of these people has a different perspective from which to view the offer. In general, purchasing is concerned with price and delivery; manufacturing is concerned

with the performance of the product in the production process; engineering is concerned with the design ability provided by the product. Sales management must assist the sales force in taking the core product benefits and orchestrating the offer among the various decision makers.

TASK 5: RECRUIT, SELECT, DEVELOP, AND MOTIVATE PEOPLE

Whereas task 3 focused on designing the organization, the line sales organization, and the set of processes to make it function effectively, this task is focused on the firm's human resources. For sales managers, people are the single most important resource. For first-line sales managers, the most important resource is the sales force; at higher managerial levels, sales managers form part of the critical human resource pool.

Regardless of whether we focus on salespeople or sales managers, their ability to function effectively in the sales organization depends on how they are chosen, trained, developed, and managed. To secure an effective salesperson, sales managers must work with the three key variables of recruitment (size and definition of the search pool), selection (the set of criteria used to choose salespeople from the recruitment pool), and training (the degree of knowledge, expertise, and so forth necessary to make the newly hired salesperson effective). Of course, organizations differ regarding their approach to securing effective salespeople. Some search widely, have loose selection criteria, but train extensively; others, preferring to hire only experienced salespeople, search narrowly, have tight selection criteria, and offer little training; most operate between these extremes. Regardless of the organization's hiring strategy, sales managers must ensure it is implemented effectively.

In addition to securing and developing salespeople, senior sales management has a critical role to play in securing and developing sales managers. As they plan this task, sales managers should recognize that the best salespeople do not necessarily make the best sales managers, in large part because the set of skills needed to be an excellent salesperson is different from that required to be an excellent sales manager. Indeed, promoting an excellent salesperson who subsequently fails as a sales manager costs the firm in two ways: loss of sales from promoting the excellent salesperson and loss of sales by poor management of the promoted salesperson's direct reports. Sales management must think long and hard about the criteria that are needed to select sales managers and their subsequent training and development needs.

Finally, sales management must understand that the recruitment, selection, training, developing, and managing nexus is a moving target. As the business environment changes and becomes more competitive, and as the firm's strategy also changes to match new environmental realities, so too must the competencies and skills of the firm's sales force, salespeople, and sales managers also change to be effective. In some cases these new competencies can be achieved through training; in others, sales managers will have to make tough replacement decisions. Regardless, ongoing development of the sales force must be a continuing concern of sales management.

TASK 6: FEEDBACK MARKET INFORMATION

The final task reflects the reality that the sales force is the one element of the organization that is in day-to-day contact with the marketplace. As such, salespeople are in a position to secure significant quantities of information regarding marketplace activity, shifting customer needs, competitive activities, and so forth. Much of this information is provided to salespeople as part of the selling process; for other types of information the sales force is in a position to secure it by asking the appropriate questions. For most firms, this market-based information is critical to the long-run health of the organization. Sales management can play an important role in developing the appropriate systems to ensure this information is collected and used.

In many organizations, the sales force is insufficiently used as a market information source, largely because of poor management of the process. Salespeople are neither recognized nor rewarded for the information, or the information is not used or not seen to be used; the marketing group is often the major culprit in this regard. It is up to sales management to work with marketing to develop information objectives and a managerial process that can effectively tap this most valuable information source.

CONCLUSION

Each of the six tasks of sales management are important and together form an integrated whole that defines, at a broad level, the job of sales management. The underlying imperative is that as the business environment changes, the job of the sales force is becoming tougher. As a result, it is critical that the sales force be managed strategically; accomplishing these six tasks is a way to ensure that this occurs. Finally, it should be noted that the six key tasks of sales management differ from those of marketing. To a very large extent, marketing management plays the role of designer; the sales force must make it happen!

DESIGNING THE SALES ORGANIZATION

Raymond W. LaForge, Brown-Forman Professor of Marketing, University of Louisville

Thomas N. Ingram, Sales and Marketing Executives of Memphis Chair in Sales Excellence, Memphis State University

IMPORTANCE OF SALES ORGANIZATION DESIGN

Sales organization design is increasingly important for success in the marketplace. First, today's dynamic and turbulent business environment forces many firms continually to make major strategic changes. Increased global competition, the changing needs of customers, accelerating technological developments, and industry structure changes alter success requirements in many industries. Firms respond by modifying mission, downsizing operations, diversifying into new products, repositioning, expanding geographic scope, changing target market focus, and other strategic actions.

Successfully implementing these strategic changes typically requires sales organization design changes. For example, many firms traditionally employed sales forces specializing in selling specific product types to all customer types. Market fragmentation and firm restructuring to focus on specific market segments makes product-specialized sales forces less effective. Leading firms have changed sales organization design to specialize by customer type; salespeople sell all product types to defined customer types.

Second, personal selling is increasingly expensive. Cost pressures force firms to search for sales productivity improvements. Sales organization design changes may improve sales productivity for many firms. For example:

- A personal sales call (average cost: over $200) is replaced by a telemarketing sales call (average cost: around $20).
- Sales are maintained/increased with fewer salespeople.
- Average sales calls to close a sale are reduced from eight to six.

Finally, sales organization design "machine" decisions are closely related to sales management "people" decisions (e.g., recruiting, hiring, training, motivating, supervising, compensating, evaluating). For example, shifting sales force specialization from product to customer, or adding a telemarketing sales force likely changes the appropriate salesperson type, training, methods of motivation and compensation, and many other "people" decisions.

Many firms spend insufficient effort on improving sales organization design. Firms frequently focus attention on improving training programs, hiring procedures, motivational plans, and so forth. Of course, these efforts are critical, but the best training programs, hiring procedures, and motivational plans cannot overcome faulty organization design. Successful firms closely integrate "machine" and "people" decisions.

SALES ORGANIZATION DESIGN OBJECTIVES

Sales organization design has three basic objectives. First, effective sales organization design fully supports salespeople and sales managers in performing necessary selling activities. For example, if generating new customers is critical, the sales organization should facilitate identification and qualification of leads and making new prospect sales

calls. Field selling might be integrated with telemarketing and direct mail, the sales force might specialize in developing new customers, and territories might be designed to promote new customer prospecting.

Second, an efficient sales organization allows salespeople and sales managers to perform required selling activities productively, not necessarily at lowest cost. Consider field selling and telemarketing trade-offs. Replacing field sales calls with telemarketing sales calls always reduces cost per call. But some selling activities (e.g., product demonstrations) cannot be performed by telephone. Thus, effectiveness and efficiency objectives must be traded.

A flexible sales force can be readily changed when conditions warrant. The environment forces firms continually to make strategic changes. Thus, designing sales organization is not a onetime task. Management should expect to redesign, or at least reexamine, the sales organization periodically to ensure it is still appropriate.

Although effectiveness, efficiency, and flexibility objectives provide criteria for evaluating sales organization design alternatives,

Exhibit 3-1. Sales Organization Design Decisions

they often conflict: the most efficient design may not be effective; the most effective may be least flexible. Management must achieve the appropriate effectiveness, efficiency, and flexibility balance in designing the sales organization for its particular selling situation.

To achieve its objectives, sales organization design (Exhibit 3-1) requires three interrelated sets of decisions:

1. *Sales channel strategy* specifies customers to be sold, selling method employed, and selling activities to be implemented and stressed.
2. *Sales organization structure* requires decisions concerning sales force specialization, degree of decentralization, number of management levels, and spans of control.
3. *Sales force deployment* encompasses sales force size, territory design, and selling effort allocation.

SALES CHANNEL STRATEGY

The most common sales channel strategy is a company field sales force performing all selling activities to all accounts and prospects. More recently, firms are using multiple sales channel strategies, some combination of team selling, field selling, telemarketing, direct mail, and other sales channels. Multiple sales channels are used for different selling activities for different accounts.

The major sales channel alternatives represent a wide range of cost per customer contact and personal contact per customer. They also demonstrate the effective/efficiency trade-off, since cost per customer contact and personal contact per customer are directly related.

Team Selling

Team selling employs multiple-person sales teams to initiate and develop customer relationships. Major firms such as IBM, Baxter Healthcare, and Digital Equipment use team selling. Team selling is sometimes used solely for a firm's largest and most important customers, often as part of a national, major, or key account program. For example, in the late 1980s General Electric used fifty salespeople from eight different product areas to secure a significant contract with General Motors. Other firms use team selling for all customers: either specific teams for each customer, or ad-hoc teams as needed. For example, an accounting firm might form selling teams comprising tax, audit, and business consulting personnel. Multilevel selling matches individuals from specific functional areas or management levels in the selling firm with counterparts in buying firms (Reynolds Metals, Exxon, and Mobil use this system).

Team selling is expensive, but produces significant personal contact with customers. Although very effective, team selling may only be efficient for specific customers or particular selling activities. Team selling flexibility depends on the program's level of formality. Thus, team selling in national major or key accounts programs is less flexible than using ad-hoc sales teams.

Field Selling

Field selling features individual salespeople performing selling activities to establish and develop customers. Most commonly, company-owned field sales forces are employed, but manufacturers' representatives (reps) and distributors are valuable variations for many firms.

Reps are independent sales organizations selling complementary, but noncompeting, products from different manufacturers. Rep firms typically do not carry inventory or take title. Distributors may or may not sell products from competing manufacturers. They generally both carry inventory and take title. Distributor salespeople provide most field selling effort to final customers; manufacturers usually employ a field sales force to service distributors.

Field selling can be very effective, but increasing cost pressures have led many firms to investigate more efficient sales channels. Use of reps and/or distributors has cost benefits and offers more flexibility than company-owned sales forces. However, firms exert more control over selling activities with their own sales forces.

Telemarketing

Telemarketing, both inbound (customer calls firm) and outbound (company calls customer), is an increasingly important sales channel. Some firms use telemarketing as the major sales channel for certain accounts; others integrate telemarketing with field selling and other sales channels for specific selling activities. Telemarketing is efficient—cost per customer contact is extremely low compared to a field sales call—but has some effectiveness limitations. It is, however, very flexible; telemarketing firms can be hired on a project basis for new product introduction or special sales promotions.

Direct Mail

Although direct mail is not a personal selling channel, it is an important supplementary sales channel for specific selling activities. Direct mail is very efficient and flexible for reaching many customers and communicating a controlled message. It is frequently used for identifying and qualifying prospects or providing after-sales service and warranty information.

Determining Sales Channel Strategy

Different sales channels are used for different customer types and/or different selling activities. The sales channel matrix (Exhibit 3-2) can be used to examine alternative strategies. This matrix can be completed using detailed analytical methods or may be used to stimulate thinking about alternatives.

In the example, customers are classified by dollar sales potential (e.g., small, medium, large); selling activities are categorized as prospecting, sales presentation, or customer service. Other classifications or more detailed categories may be appropriate for specific situations. The matrix is used to consider different sales channels for each selling activity for each customer, using the effectiveness, efficiency, and flexibility criteria.

The example illustrates selection of a sales channel strategy employing direct mail, telemarketing, field sales force, and team selling. Each sales channel is matched to customer type and selling activities for the most favorable blend of effectiveness, efficiency, and flexibility.

SALES ORGANIZATION STRUCTURE

Sales channel strategy is implemented through a sales organization structure that defines which activities must be performed, by whom, in the organization. Sales organization design translates sales channel strategy into selling operations in the market.

Developing sales organization structure is a difficult task. Basic underlying concepts of specialization, decentralization, management levels, and spans of control may combine to yield a final structure including multiple levels and numerous interdependent activities between system elements.

Specialization

In the simplest sales organization structure, each salesperson performs all selling activities for all customers; each sales manager performs all sales management activities for all salespeople under supervision. This approach is typically cost efficient, but may not be very effective.

Exhibit 3-2. Sales Channel Strategy Example

Selling Activities	Type of Customer Based on Dollar Sales Potential		
	Small	Medium	Large
Prospecting	Direct Mail	Telemarketing	Field Sales Force
Sales Presentations	Telemarketing	Field Sales Force	Team Selling
Customer Service	Telemarketing	Field Sales Force	Team Selling

Sales organizations specialize when specific salespeople and sales managers perform a limited set of selling and sales management activities to the exclusion of others. By concentrating on a limited number of activities, salespeople and sales managers can become experts, leading to better performance for the entire organization.

The major forms of specialization are products sold, markets served, or functions performed. Geographic "specialization," involving responsibility for all selling activities to all customers in an assigned area, is really nonspecialization since no specialization by product, market, or function occurs.

In a product-specialized organization, the salespeople sell specific products or product lines to all customers; salespeople should become experts in assigned product categories. A drawback to product specialization is that customers purchasing more than one product category may have to deal with multiple-firm salespeople. Most customers prefer a single salesperson per firm to save buyer-seller transaction time. Also, customers often seek volume discounts for combined purchases from a given vendor. These are often unavailable from product-specialized salespeople; they typically offer volume discounts only on their specific product(s).

In market-specialized organizations, salespeople are assigned specific customer types; they are responsible for selling all of the firm's products. Salespeople should be experts on how customers purchase and use products. Many variations of market specialization exist: consumer versus industrial markets; specific industries; distributor type; account size; or other customer categorization type. Moore Business Forms, for example, specializes by industry type, account size, and geographic location. Unisys (computer firm) specializes by industrial/commercial; financial services; communications/airlines; federal government/defense; and public sector including health-care and education institutions.

In functional specialization, salespeople perform certain selling activities for all customers. For example, some salespeople may specialize in generating new customers, others in servicing existing customers. Integra-

tion of telemarketing with field selling is a type of functional specialization. Telemarketers typically specialize in prospecting and servicing; field sales forces specialize in sales presentations. In the pharmaceutical industry, "detailers" promote prescription drugs to physicians; other salespeople sell to drug wholesalers and pharmacists.

Specific advantages and disadvantages of each type of specialization are indicated in Exhibit 3-3. Less specialized sales organizations normally have efficiency and flexibility advantages; more specialized sales organizations generally rate high on effectiveness. The specific degree and type of specialization depends on the particular selling situation. Firms frequently employ several types of specialization within their sales organizations.

Decentralization

Decentralization refers to taking important decisions at lower sales organization levels, such as first-level sales managers and salespeople. Most sales organizations decentralize some activities and centralize others, but each tends to have a basic decentralized or centralized orientation.

Centralized structures are often used when sales organizations are highly specialized. Centralization is one way to integrate the activities of specialized units. Decentralized structures provide less integration capability, but promote responsive decision making in the field. Decentralized structures are usually preferable when the sales organization is not very specialized. A decentralized orientation typically has effectiveness and flexibility advantages; centralized orientations often have efficiency advantages.

Management Levels and Spans of Control

Management levels define the hierarchical levels of management in the sales organization; spans of control refer to the number of individuals reporting to each sales manager. Typically, management levels and spans of control are inversely related; flat sales organizations have fewer management levels and larger spans of control than taller sales organizations.

Exhibit 3-3. Advantages and Disadvantages to Specialization

Type of Specialization	Advantages	Disadvantages
Geographic	Low cost No geographic duplication No customer duplication Fewer management levels	Limited specialization Lack of management control over product or customer emphasis
Product	Salespeople become experts in product attributes and applications Management control over selling effort allocated to products	High cost Geographic duplication Customer duplication
Market	Salespeople develop better understanding of unique customer needs Management control over selling effort allocated to different markets	Geographic duplication Customer duplication Need for coordination
Functional	Efficiency in performing selling activities	

Management levels and spans of control are also closely related to decentralization. Generally, decentralized orientations lead to fewer management levels and larger spans of control. Spans of control tend to increase at lower sales management levels; at higher levels the number of supervised individuals typically decreases.

Sales organization structure development decisions concern degree and types of specialization, decentralization versus centralization orientation, number of management levels, and spans of control. These decisions are highly interrelated; they depend on the firm's selling situation and sales channel strategy.

SALES FORCE DEPLOYMENT

Sales force deployment decisions address three interrelated questions:

1. How much selling effort is needed for customers and prospects to achieve sales and profit objectives?
2. How many salespeople are required to provide the desired amount of selling effort?
3. How should territories be designed to ensure proper coverage of customers and prospects and to provide each salesperson with reasonable success opportunities?

Decisions in one sales force deployment area affect decisions in other areas. For example, selling effort allocation provides input for determining sales force size, which provides input for territory design.

Many firms could substantially increase sales productivity by improving sales force deployment. Generally, sales forces are too large or too small; some customers receive too much selling effort whereas others do not receive enough, and/or sales territories are improperly designed. Appropriate changes in sales force deployment require detailed examination of current selling effort allocation, sales force size, and territory design.

Allocation of Selling Effort

Determining selling effort needed to provide sales coverage to customers and prospects is the starting point for sales force deployment analysis. These decisions are more complex if multiple sales channels are used. The allocation decision for a firm using both telemarketing and field selling embraces the degree of telemarketing and field selling effort for each customer and in total.

Theoretically, effective and efficient allocation of selling effort is obtained when (1) sales calls are allocated to customers based on potential sales to be generated from each customer; (2) each customer receives sales calls to the point where marginal sales from the last sales call equal the costs associated with that sales call. However, because it is very difficult to determine exact potential sales and costs for individual sales calls to specific customers, management must approximate these analyses.

Three different analytical approaches can assist management in making allocation decisions. Single-factor models classify customers on one factor (e.g., market potential), then assign all customers in each category the same number of sales calls. For example, higher market potential customers receive more sales calls.

In portfolio model approaches, each customer is a member of a customer portfolio; customers differ in attractiveness for selling effort investment. Customer attractiveness depends on the customer opportunity available and the firm's competitive position. Customers are evaluated on opportunity and competitive position, then classified into similar attractiveness categories. Selling effort is allocated to customers in each attractiveness category; more attractive customers receive more sales calls.

Decision models comprise mathematical formulations allowing management to forecast sales to individual customers for different selling effort levels. Management evaluates potential sales to customers for all feasible ways of allocating selling effort. Decision models help management determine selling effort–specific allocations that promise the highest level of sales and profits.

Each approach can help management evaluate alternative ways to allocate customer selling effort. They differ in sophistication and complexity, but each provides a structured procedure for determining productive allocation of selling effort. Final allocation decisions provide direct input for determining sales force size.

Sales Force Size

Sales force size determines the total amount of selling effort available on accounts and prospects. The sales force size decision is most straightforward with one generalized sales force. For multiple sales channels and/or specialized sales forces, management must decide both the total number of salespeople and the size of each specialized sales force. Since both generalized and specialized sales forces are normally organized by geography (e.g., district, zone, region), these allocations are a type of sales force size decision.

Determining appropriate sales force size requires assessment of sales, costs, productivity, and turnover. If decisions on amount of selling effort allocated to each customer and prospect have been decided, summing these selling effort decisions across all customers and prospects establishes the total selling effort needed. Sales force size is calculated by dividing total amount of selling effort needed by selling effort per salesperson.

Alternatively, sales force size is determined in aggregate by comparing forecast sales and costs associated with various sales force sizes. Since both sales and costs rise with addition of salespeople, management should add salespeople until marginal salesperson cost equals marginal profit per last salesperson added. This approach forces management explicitly to consider sales, costs, and productivity associated with alternative sales force sizes.

Regardless of method used, the sales force size decision must reflect expected salesperson turnover. If a firm decides its appropriate sales force size is 200 and 10-percent annual turnover is typical, desired sales force size should be increased by 20. When sales force size is determined, territory design can commence.

Territory Design

A territory is an assignment of customers and prospects to a salesperson. Customers and

Exhibit 3-4. Territory Design Procedures

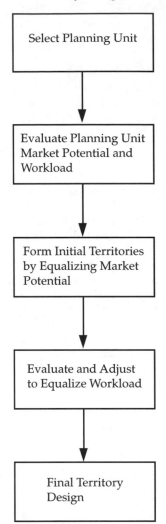

prospects should be assigned to specific sales-persons such that each salesperson provides desired selling effort levels. Territories are the salesperson work unit; salespeople are typically responsible for selling activities and per-formance in a territory. Salesperson compensation and success are normally a function of territory performance.

Although different territory criteria may be desirable for different salespeople (e.g., new versus experienced), more typically territories are equal in opportunity for all salespeople. The goal is to try to equalize market potential and workload for all territories (Exhibit 3-4).

First, planning units are established for analysis. Planning units are some entity smaller than a territory (e.g., individual customers, zip codes, counties) that can be grouped to form territories. Once selected, market potential and workload for each planning unit is estimated. Initial territories are formed by equalizing market potential for each territory. Territory workload is estimated in terms of time taken to provide adequate sales coverage. Workload requires estimates of number of customers, time per average sales call, sales call frequency, and other factors such as travel and administrative task time. Workloads across territories are evaluated and adjustments are made to equalize territory workloads. This iterative procedure balances equal market potentials and workloads. Nowadays, computer software allows many alternative territory designs to be easily evaluated.

CONCLUSION

Management must realize that sales organization design is an ongoing process. Changes are made and fine-tuned, results evaluated, and additional changes made. Continuous redesign of the sales organization is needed to implement sales strategies developed to compete in the increasingly turbulent environments faced by most firms.

MANAGING THE DISTRIBUTION SYSTEM

Jan B. Heide, Assistant Professor of Marketing, University of Wisconsin–Madison

THE NATURE OF DISTRIBUTION CHANNEL DECISIONS

Distribution channels are the means by which manufacturers or suppliers reach designated sets of buyers. Typically, a variety of channel arrangements is theoretically available to a manufacturer. For example:

Sherwin-Williams, the paint manufacturer, distributes through company-owned retail stores.

McDonald's distribution system largely comprises a selected number of independent restaurant owners who have acquired the right to use its trade name within a particular geographical area, subject to a franchising contract.

Mary Kay Cosmetics distributes directly to final buyers, using a "home party" approach.

Alloy-Rods Corporation sells most of its welding electrodes through external distributors; these in turn sell to end users.

In some industries, different firms place their major distribution efforts in fundamentally different channels. Moreover, individual firms frequently use multiple channels for the same product. Thus, one of Alloy-Rods' main competitors relies primarily on an internal sales force, yet also sells products through distributors. Similarly, McDonald's deliberately operates several company-owned fast-food outlets, in addition to the majority that are franchised.

Distribution channel decisions have important interrelationships with other marketing decisions such as product positioning. For example, Paul Mitchell deliberately limits distribution of its hair-care products to selected hair salons to reinforce its exclusivity strategy. Similarly, Honda developed an entirely new distribution system for Acura, as opposed to using its existing Honda network, a deliberate attempt to disassociate Acura from Honda. The firm believed that the market's perception of Honda as economy cars was inconsistent with Acura's intended luxury and performance position.

Distribution channel decisions are important because they are frequently irreversible, at least in the short run. Of all the marketing decisions made by a firm, the establishment of a channel frequently takes the longest. It involves selecting channel members, providing product training, developing communication and control systems, and establishing working relationships with other firms. Such commitment of resources may be idiosyncratic to a particular channel and not easily redeployable.

Channel decisions may provide significant strategic advantages by serving as entry barriers for other firms. Thus, the long-term nature of channel arrangements makes them difficult to duplicate in the short run, and existing channels may be difficult for new firms to penetrate. In addition, strong channel relationships represent launching pads for new products and serve as communication channels for market information.

The foregoing suggests that channel decisions should be made in an explicit and systematic fashion. Unfortunately, evidence suggests that firms frequently make distribution channel choices in a less than deliberate manner, more often based on tradition and past practices than on the existing and predicted situation.

THE ELEMENTS OF CHANNEL STRATEGY

Channels exist to carry out certain functions designed to bridge gaps between producers and consumers. These functions (e.g., physical transportation, promotions, storage, market information, servicing, selling) are generic; they must be performed by someone for transactions between manufacturers and consumers to occur. However, these functions are both shiftable and divisible; they may be performed by the manufacturer, the consumer, a third party like a distributor, or divided among the three. In principle, functions should be performed by the party that can perform them most efficiently. Employing middlepeople or distributors is not desirable per se; it may simply represent the most efficient means of performing a particular function.

Frequently heard claims of eliminating the middleperson should be viewed with much scrutiny. When this occurs, someone else, either manufacturer or consumer, has assumed a particular function. For example, the ability of discount brokers to offer reduced commission rates by eliminating traditional brokers is a systematic effort to target investors who make their own investment decisions; these investors perform functions otherwise undertaken by traditional brokers.

Channel length decisions are concerned with how certain functions are allocated: most

Exhibit 3-5. Distribution Alternatives for Air Compressors

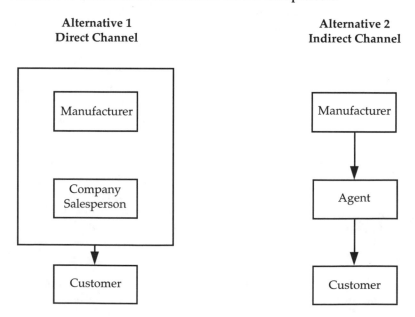

Alternative 1
Direct Channel

Alternative 2
Indirect Channel

Exhibit 3-6. Market Coverage Alternatives

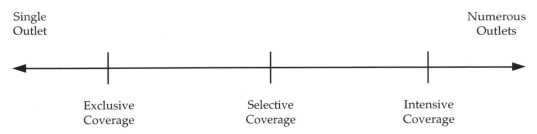

simply, whether a manufacturer or other entity performs them. For example, consider a manufacturer selling air compressors to industrial buyers; two key functions must be performed, namely, personal selling and postsales servicing. One alternative is to establish a direct channel and rely on company salespeople for selling and servicing (Exhibit 3-5). Alternatively, the manufacturer may allocate these functions to a manufacturer's agent who performs them on a contractual basis.

Channel breadth decisions focus on the desired level of market coverage. The manufacturer must decide the number of different outlets at which its products are available. Thus, convenience products manufacturers (e.g., soft drinks) frequently seek intensive coverage, placing their products in as many outlets as possible. By contrast, in exclusive or selective coverage, products are distributed through a limited number of outlets (Exhibit 3-6). For example, Acura employs a selective coverage strategy for its luxury cars, purposely limiting distribution to a few dealers in any given area.

Channel length and channel breadth questions comprise a firm's channel design decision. A complete channel strategy also includes decisions on channel management. Distribution channels often consist of independent firms whose individual goals fail to overlap perfectly with those of other system participants. For example, McDonald's franchisees are independent businesspeople who may have fundamental disagreements with, or even oppose, company policy regarding customer service and product development. A compounding factor is that many individ-

ual channel members (e.g., manufacturer's agents) simultaneously belong to multiple channel systems; the manufacturers they represent compete for the agent's time and resources. Thus, many channels are closer to being loose coalitions than integrated systems, and the interaction patterns among channel members are frequently most accurately described as adversarial collaboration.

Individual firms have incentives to enter into various interfirm alliances and to cooperate with other channel members because of rewards created by their interaction. At the same time, interfirm alliances inevitably involve interdependencies that represent the basis for ongoing conflicts, in particular, how system rewards should be distributed. Management of the ongoing relationships among channel members is thus a key aspect of channel strategy.

THE CHANNEL STRATEGY PROCESS

The starting point for channel strategy decisions is an explicit analysis of the target segment(s) (Exhibit 3-7). The firm should identify the segment's particular preferences with respect to channel output. In a broad sense, channel output comprises the dimensions of product availability and other services. Channel design and management decisions follow from analysis of output requirements.

A distribution channel's ability to produce outputs allows buyers to economize their own efforts. For example, the high degree of product availability for convenience items

Exhibit 3-7. The Channel Strategy Process

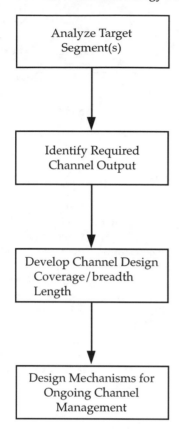

permits buyers to economize on search and transportation costs. Similarly, immediate repair and technical support supplied in the industrial equipment channel eliminates buyers' needs to maintain these services. Of course, channel output requirements reflect segment needs. In the discount brokerage example, one segment of investors made its own investment decisions; another segment required the traditional range of broker services.

THE MARKET COVERAGE DECISION

Three main categories of variables influence a firm's coverage decision, or the choices on the continuum shown in Exhibit 3-6. Each of these variables follows directly or indirectly from the nature of the target market segment. First, coverage depends on the target market's willingness and ability to engage in search activity to secure the firm's products. Search activity, in turn, is determined in part by purchase frequency. Thus, wide availability is a key channel output for convenience items (e.g., toothpaste, soft drinks), and the appropriate coverage strategy is intensive. In contrast, automobile head gaskets can be distributed more selectively because of their infrequency of purchase. A second search determinant is the target segment's degree of brand loyalty. High brand loyalty permits a manufacturer to cover the market selectively or exclusively since buyers have an incentive to search for the brand (e.g., fashion clothing).

Second, coverage depends on the specific functions or support services channel members must undertake. For example, in personal computer purchases, many buyers' service needs are very high, because of inexperience with the product category, its technical complexity, and perceived risk in the buying decision. Buyers tend to rely heavily on retail salespeople for presales services and demonstrations. The manufacturer who requires such services and support from channel members may find an intensive coverage strategy to be infeasible. Conversely, in some buying situations (e.g., soft drinks), buyers have virtually no need for channel services; middlepeople have only to provide shelf space.

Third, coverage strategy depends on the manufacturer's desire to limit competition between resellers of its own brand. Intensive distribution facilitates buyers' ability to comparison shop; this creates a free-riding potential where one channel member can take advantage of services provided by others. Thus, in the personal computer example, buyers may secure extensive presales services (e.g., product demonstrations, technical information) at one dealer, then purchase the product from a low-cost, low-price free riding dealer. Extensive free riding limits the incentive for dealers to maintain the full range of customer services, thus negatively impacting product sales. In such situations, selective or exclusive coverage may be required.

THE CHANNEL LENGTH DECISION

The channel length decision basically involves determining who should perform the relevant functions; channel length is a vertical integration decision. Manufacturers must choose between performing functions with company employees (vertical integration) or contracting them out to an external entity (e.g., an agent). This decision should be based on joint consideration of efficiency (i.e., cost-related) and effectiveness (getting tasks accomplished) criteria.

In the air compressor example (Exhibit 3-5), the manufacturer had two options for the selling function: a company-owned sales force (direct), and manufacturer's agents (indirect). Because agents can economize on selling costs, they may be a desirable option. For instance, manufacturer's agents frequently represent multiple firms with complementary product lines; thus, fixed costs can be spread over many different products. For example, air compressor agents may sell both air compressors and other industrial products. These economies of scale benefit the manufacturer, especially when its own product line comprises a limited number of items.

Notwithstanding such economies of scale, transactions costs in running the system make contracting out a less desirable alternative than integration. Transaction costs include costs associated with collecting information, bargaining, adjusting agreements to new circumstances, and monitoring performance. Vertically integrated organizations generally fulfill these functions more economically as their centralized authority structures facilitate decision making, and comprehensive control systems facilitate performance monitoring.

In the air compressor example, ongoing changes in customer preferences and competitive strategies are likely to require modifications in the relationship between the manufacturer and channel members (e.g., selling strategies, customer service, product development). In an agent system, not only may modification of an original agreement involve significant bargaining costs but the agent may have acquired idiosyncratic expertise in selling the manufacturer's products and may be in a superior bargaining position. By contrast, the existing authority structure greatly facilitates ongoing adaptations with company employees, and allows firms to economize on adaptation costs.

Monitoring is frequently more efficiently carried out when a formal employment relation exists, because of the wider range of control mechanisms available. Thus, employee behavior (e.g., compliance, or following procedures) can be monitored much more easily than verifying the extent of contractual compliance on the part of an agent. Contracts with agents may be limited to measuring output (e.g., sales volume).

To summarize, the two relevant dimensions of efficiency tend to be in opposition. Economies of scale usually favors nonintegration; transaction costs tend to favor vertical integration. However, in many circumstances efficiency must be considered in combination with effectiveness criteria. Thus, to be certain that specific channel outputs are produced, a manufacturer may seek control over certain channel functions via vertical integration and may be less concerned with efficiency considerations.

The efficiency/effectiveness trade-off in channel design should follow from the nature of a firm's overall competitive strategy. Thus, cost leadership strategies are efficiency oriented; firms pursuing these strategies must consider the efficiency implications of all marketing decisions, from product design to channel decisions. By contrast, firms pursuing differentiation strategies are likely to be less efficiency oriented and more focused on achieving control over key functions, for example, by emphasizing customer service. In this case, the relevant channel design criterion is the quality with which the services are provided; vertically integrated distribution channels may be appropriate, leading to disregard of more efficient channel arrangements.

The efficiency dimension of vertical integration decisions is seldom clear-cut, as vertical integration embraces some inherent costs. First, initial investment costs for vertically integrated systems may be substantial. Second, the relevant investments are typically long term and frequently idiosyncratic. Third, investments in channel systems often give rise

Exhibit 3-8. Conceptual Dimensions of Vertical Integration

Nonintegrated
Channel

Vertically Integrated
Channel

←——→

Short-term
  relationship
Ad-hoc bargaining
No formal rules and
  operating procedures
No formal
  control system

Long-term
  relationship
Centralized planning
  and decision making
Extensive use of
  standard operating
  procedures
Comprehensive
  control system

to switching costs, effectively committing a manufacturer to a given distribution arrangement for a long period of time. Thus, while the ability to exercise control over channel functions is enhanced, strategic flexibility may be greatly reduced.

In addition, many benefits of vertical integration can sometimes be achieved without outright ownership of the distribution channel. In fact, vertically integrated and nonintegrated channels are best viewed as end points on a continuum with different forms of "quasi-integration" in between. The end points of key dimensions are illustrated in Exhibit 3-8.

Many vertically integrated end points of these dimensions can be achieved in relationships between independent firms. For example, contracts between manufacturers and distributors are frequently long term in nature, and contain many of the features shown in Exhibit 3-8. Similarly, franchising systems provide franchisors with many integration benefits without the investment requirement of ownership. Centralized planning and control systems allow franchisors to economize on transaction costs, in addition to enjoying close to complete control over key decisions like product quality and promotional efforts. Furthermore, since franchisors are independent businesspeople, they are often able to benefit from high levels of channel member motivation, otherwise found only in nonintegrated channels.

Finally, many manufacturers establish and market through multiple channels, for example, through direct salespeople and external distributors. Frequently, multiple channels correspond to a firms product-market strategy of simultaneously targeting multiple market segments with distinct channel output requirements. Other times, the simultaneous use of multiple channels may have more subtle motivations. For instance, McDonald's decision to maintain both company-owned and franchised restaurants is motivated in part by a desire to continuously stay informed about franchise operations. Company-owned stores provide a strong basis for evaluating franchisee performance, and serve as testing grounds for new products and procedures, thus greatly facilitating implementation in the franchise system.

CHANNEL MANAGEMENT

The performance of a channel system depends critically on the manufacturer's ability to manage ongoing relationships among its members. For example, the competitive viability of McDonald's franchising system is a direct function of its ability to achieve coordinated action among the different parts of the system, and to ensure participation in new product development and promotional programs.

Problems arise due to fundamental goal incompatibilities existing among the firms involved. Thus, McDonald's, as a franchisor, may be concerned with building market share relative to other fast-food chains by introducing new products on a regular basis. By contrast, franchisees' main concerns may be to maximize their own return on investment and may resist new product introductions that require short-term investments. Similarly, in industrial markets, distributors may be reluctant to undertake activities such as new accounts development and servicing that do not have immediate paybacks. These examples illustrate the fundamental channel management problem: manufacturers seeking channel member support for their marketing programs; channel members trying to maximize control over their own product-market strategies, which may be inconsistent with manufacturer goals.

From the manufacturer's perspective, the appropriate starting point for channel management decisions is the general objective of providing certain channel outputs to designated target market segments. The assessment of aggregate channel outputs provides the basis for defining the roles, or expected set of behaviors, of individual channel members. The specific functions comprising a given channel member's role (e.g., customer service, inventory maintenance) may be specified informally, or explicitly included in a contractual agreement.

Frequently, channel members' roles are expressed in terms of specific restrictions on their marketing decisions. For example, manufacturers often impose restraints on intermediaries' product policies, by requiring that certain products be carried ("full-line forcing"), and competing items excluded. Similarly, manufacturers may seek to impose distribution restrictions, in the form of limits on sales territories and customers. Use of such restrictions by manufacturers may have legal implications and should be carefully considered prior to use.

In addition to specifying roles, mechanisms must also be present that allow manufacturers to enforce the relevant roles. Basically, these mechanisms fall into two categories: authority and interfirm dependence. Authority relations provide manufacturers with the ability to secure desired role behaviors from channel members due to the latter's perception that the manufacturer has the right to make certain demands (e.g., a manufacturer's relationship with an employee salesperson; a franchisor's relationship with a franchisee).

Presence of a dependence relation represents a similar ability; channel members have a strong incentive to carry out roles that the manufacturer prescribes. Conceptually, the dependence of a party A on another party B is a function of two conditions, namely, the nature of the rewards that A derives from the relationship with B, and A's difficulty of replacing B. Thus, distributor A may be dependent on manufacturer B due to the income generated by sales of B's products, or from the particular types of distributor support provided by B. In addition, it may be difficult for the distributor to replace the manufacturer, or replacing the manufacturer might result in extensive switching costs. For example, a distributor may have made manufacturer-specific investments in technical knowledge, training, equipment, and record-keeping systems that would have to be reincurred if the manufacturer was replaced. To the extent that the dependence condition is asymmetric, the distributor is more dependent on the manufacturer than vice versa and the manufacturer has a basis for enforcing the distributor's channel role.

Thus far we have assumed goal incompatibility among channel members and implicitly discussed the channel management process in terms of applying some form of power, based on authority and/or dependence. A fundamentally different approach to channel management is to develop strategies designed to eliminate or reduce goal incompatibility in the first place. Specific actions include selectively screening channel members prior to entering an agreement, and/or deliberately socializing members such that they internalize or identify with the manufacturer's goals. For example, much of the initial training conducted by McDonald's and Lexus is designed specifically with the objective of cultivating company-specific values in their channel members.

Strategies designed to eliminate goal divergence tend to be very costly and time consuming. However, they may be efficient in the long term, since they reduce the need for on-going monitoring and control. Nonetheless, in most cases, socialization efforts alone are an insufficient basis for securing reliable role behaviors; other control mechanisms are also needed.

CONCLUSION

Channel strategy decisions, channel design, and channel management should be set with the objective of producing a particular set of outputs for target market segments, subject to certain constraints. These constraints include the firm's overall competitive strategy, which requires that channel arrangements be evaluated in terms of efficiency and effectiveness; company resources constraints that may preclude certain channel design strategies like vertical integration; and legal restrictions that may limit the types of controls that can be imposed on channel members. Finally, the firm's historical or existing channel arrangements may preclude an "ideal" channel strategy due to existing switching costs, or may cloud the firm's perceptions of what constitutes an appropriate channel.

MAJOR ACCOUNT MANAGEMENT

John F. Martin, President, John Martin & Associates, Inc.

Gary S. Tubridy, Senior Vice-President, The Alexander Group, Inc.

Major accounts are generally defined as purchasing a significant volume (absolute dollars and percent of firm sales); buying centrally for geographically dispersed units (e.g., stores, branches, plants); and desiring long-term, cooperative relationships as a means to innovation and financial success. These accounts expect specialized attention and service including information and reports about usage, logistical support, inventory management, favorable discounts, and ideas for line extensions or new applications. Major accounts are frequently national accounts, but since firms are taking an increasingly international view of their largest customers, we embrace all large accounts, regardless of country location.

Major account emphasis is extremely important. First, although major account programs offer significant strategic sales advantage, they are frequently undervalued and underutilized. Second, the increasingly complex markets of the 1990s place a premium on effective major account programs.

Successful major account programs must clearly demonstrate customer value added by defining the major account sales function's mission and communicating it to customers and the firm's field sales force. Effective working with field sales personnel is achieved by clarifying the major account manager's (MAM) sales role, and minimizing barriers between the MAM and other sales positions. Finally, the best people must be recruited for the major account role, not necessarily "top"-volume producers who may fail in the more structured major account environment.

Successful major account programs are embedded in firm sales strategies that optimize effective use of total sales resources. Sales strategies bridge corporate business goals, and the sales coverage and sales processes needed to sell products or services. Building a successful major account program requires a focus on three key topics:

1. What are the "best" company practices?
2. What are the steps to a more effective major account program?
3. How is the account planning process constructed?

BEST COMPANY PRACTICES

Successful major account programs have several common elements. First, there is a clear definition of program mission and relationships (e.g., between the MAM, top sales marketing executives, the CEO, and customers) needed for optimal benefits for both company and customer. Most important is a direct linkage between customer and company, which may involve multiple company executives, depending on the size of the account opportunity. Executives may be assigned specific accounts; they become part of the MAM's team and play an active roll by making calls and participating in key account presentations.

In the best programs, customers play a prominent role in developing the major account mission statement. Customers should know why they are major accounts, and what it means to be a major account. Ask the following questions of your key account program:

- Do your customers know why they are designated as major accounts?
- What does this status mean to your customers?
- What are their top three expectations from this status?
- Give examples of the value a MAM provides to the relationship with a major account.
- Give examples of a MAM's activities that help major account customers reach their goals.

Second, internal and external communication is highly effective. Communication practices in the "best" programs are directed internally to top executives through regular result overviews and future plans for account penetration. They are also aimed at field salespeople through account planning sessions that help define their role in the major account sales process. Externally, communications to customer executives demonstrate benefits received from the firm's products and services, and the firm's actions in addressing expectations.

Third, appropriate measures of critical program elements must be taken. For example:

- Value to the company from this coverage strategy.
- Successful implementation of account plans by MAMs.
- Cost of this sales focus.
- Firm rank versus competitive vendors by major account customers.
- Specific performance measures to evaluate individual MAMs—for example, total customer revenue, sales percent from remote locations, specific profit or product goals?
- Milestone measures for MAMs—for example, gain commitment for pilot installation by end of the second quarter; expand headquarters usage by current customers 50 percent by end of the third quarter.
- Customer service improvement over last year.
- Quality of direct field sales regional assistance, service, and technical support.

Measures should minimize contention for sales credit with the field sales force. Clearly defined objectives for field sales representatives and MAMs, and appropriate credit for sales, can minimize this problem.

Fourth, incentive compensation plans for MAMs must effectively motivate and reward them for cooperation and coordination with field salespeople. Split and duplicate credit are alternative approaches. Split credit awards all participants to a sale with a share of total credit based on a predetermined formula (e.g., MAM sales rep: 75/25 or 50/50 or 25/75) or managerial judgment. Judgment systems include such criteria as contribution, influence in the selling process, account control, and buying decision location (i.e., centralized or decentralized).

Duplicate systems require sales credit for both MAMs and the field sales representatives covering remote locations. Duplicate credit does not necessarily mean double payment for the same sale. Sometimes remote account sales targets are included in field sales representatives' total quota and incentive compensation paid as a percent of total quota achieved.

Fifth, appropriate MAM selection and rotation is critical. Successful MAMs have both sales experience and managerial experience. They must be competent to provide consistent high-quality customer service, internal coordination through effective team relationships, and have proven track records in managing accounts. In the best programs, MAMs are important career development positions; assignments should be for a minimum of three to five years: large accounts do not wish to retrain too frequently.

Sixth, competitive pay levels are necessary to attract and retain the skilled people assigned major account responsibilities. Effective compensation plans are customized to reflect both strategic sales objectives at major accounts and the special nature of major accounts with remote field locations. Typically, MAMs are targeted one or two pay levels above the general territory sales representative at target performance. (Market pricing surveys can aid here.) Typically, salary to total incentive mix ranges from 65/35 to 90/10.

STEPS TO MORE EFFECTIVE MAJOR ACCOUNT PROGRAMS

First, sales strategies should optimize effective use of the firm's total sales resources. Sales managers must meet several objectives: profit and volume targets, specific product or service goals, growth in new industries, competitive win-backs, new business sales, and account penetration in targeted accounts.

Unfortunately, these objectives are often lumped together into one sales target: increase sales results 15 percent over last year; achieve $500,000 in total sales revenue; or produce gross margin on sales of 25 percent. These traditional targets do not differentiate between products, markets, or customers; the national sales manager and the field sales managers must determine what to sell and to whom.

Four selling strategies can guide sales management in allocating field sales resources and directing the sales process: (1) sell in-line products to current customers, (2) sell new products to current customers, (3) sell in-line products to prospects using competitive products, and (4) sell new products to nonuser prospects.

Sales potential from these four groups determines the appropriate sales process. For example, if 80 percent of sales are expected from current customers, in-line products, or new products, the sales process should focus on account retention and growth rather than on competitive win-backs or missionary selling.

With the in-line and new product sales strategies as top priorities, the firm must determine the necessary customer base for the 80 percent of projected sales volume. One way is to categorize customers as large, medium, and small on the basis of potential sales revenue. If the 80/20 rule applies—80 percent of sales from 20 percent of customers—significant emphasis should be focused on large customers—that is, the major accounts.

For successful results at major accounts, it is important to determine (1) the buying process of these accounts, (2) the appropriate sales organization to effectively cover them, and (3) the sales roles to drive desired behavior resulting in optimum account relationships.

Second, major account selling requires sales managers to consider two buying processes: Is the buying process centralized or decentralized and does the customer have one or many locations? There are thus four possible buying processes: (1) enterprise (headquarters) centralized purchases, no buying decision authority at remote establishment location (e.g., regional offices, plant sites); (2) enterprise centralized purchases, no remote locations (i.e., a single large account); (3) establishment buying decision authority after enterprise selection and vendors placed on approved list; (4) establishment buying decision authority at all remote locations, no approval from enterprise headquarters. Buying authority location is the major factor in determining the most effective sales coverage and field sales organization. The most common buying processes in major accounts are options (1) and (3).

Third, sales organizations have become more complex, evolving from a single territory sales force to multidimensional sales organizations (Exhibit 3-9). Criteria for reporting relationships include major account sales contribution to overall sales objectives, and whether the account is a national or regional company. Typical titles include national or major account manager, account executive, "account manager—ABC Company." Proper title selection is important. First, to the customer, the title positions the major account salesperson as having a different sales role from the traditional sales representative. Second, it conveys the importance and role of this sales position to the sales force. Major account managers typically report to a national major account sales manager or directly to the field sales manager in whose geographic territory the account enterprise location resides.

The relationship between MAMs and the rest of the sales organization is critical for optimizing the firm's share of account purchasing volume. For example, in centralized buying situations where account relationship maintenance is key to success, the geographic sales force may have to call on account locations to ensure the firm's products are properly used, or provide postsales installation service. MAMs may sell an annual commitment to buy a certain volume, but program success is predicated on field sales representatives making regularly scheduled calls to remote locations to provide on-site technical assistance and necessary pull-through sales activity.

Fourth, clearly defining the desired sale roles for both field sales representatives and MAMs is paramount to building a strong cooperative selling effort; otherwise, a friction zone can develop. Exhibit 3-10 displays typical sales responsibilities in major account selling. In fact, three types of behavior are common in major account geographic sales organizations: adversarial, separate, and team.

Adversarial behavior occurs when field

Exhibit 3-9. Evolution of Sales Organizations

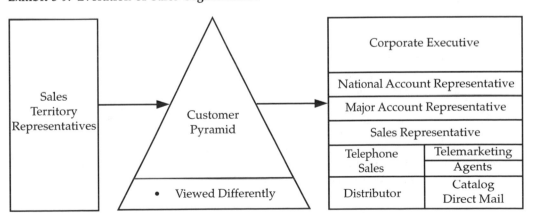

Exhibit 3-10. Sales Responsibilities in Major Account Service

| Establish High-Level Contacts
Maintain Current Contracts
Run Internal "Interference" | Develop Account Plans
Coordinate Company Resources
Negotiate New Contracts | **MAM Role** ← |

Friction Zone

| **Field Sales Role** → | Service National Account Sales
Develop Local National Account
  Contracts
Close Locally Controlled Sales
  Opportunities | Maintain and Grow Sales at Local
  Accounts
Prospect for New Accounts |

sales representatives and MAMs clash over account control and/or credit for sales. Rather than work together, much nonproductive time is spent debating with sales management how the other salesperson negatively impacts sales performance. Disruptive customer situations often arise: local selling efforts bypass customer headquarter's procedures; order entries may be manipulated. The customer is placed in the middle of a sales crediting issue: customer service suffers because neither salesperson agrees to accountability for total customer satisfaction.

Separate behavior occurs when field sales representatives and MAMs work independently. They do not recognize the joint roles that each should play for optimizing account strategy; the field salesperson sees little gain from responding to the MAM's sales direction. For example, a field sales representative has one customer branch location and projected sales of that location are less than one percent of sales quota. The salesperson sees little gain from spending time with this account because his or her sales strategy is tied to medium-size local account opportuni-

ties. If a hundred field salespeople took this attitude, the loss of sales from major accounts would be tremendous!

MAMs are also at fault if they fail to recognize the important role local sales representatives can play in successfully maintaining a strong competitive account presence. MAMs may not fully consider the field rep's role in growing account purchases of new products or services at remote locations where initial demand must be created. When the field rep's role is not recognized, the customer suffers. The vendor's sales force might not provide committed technical support at establishment locations. Responsiveness to customer needs slows because the vendor team works independently; regular communication is informal or nonexistent. Customer remote locations are not presented with new products or services to determine applicability and the account is not serviced satisfactorily.

With team behavior the field sales organization supports and contributes to the MAM's objectives for quality customer satisfaction and optimal account sales growth and penetration. They jointly recognize that functioning as a team is a critical step in achieving account control and competitive leadership among other vendors.

Two barriers can negatively impact team success: first, turf battles, resulting from the desire for account control and when each sales position has different account geographic objectives strategies; second, compensation, when the reward does not recognize the effort of both sales positions.

For example, from the field salesperson: "I closed that sale and hardly got any credit," or "I had nothing to do with that sale, but I sure lost all the sales credit." From the MAM: "I wish I could get more field support. The field rep wants it both ways: 100-percent credit for all sales, with no downside risk." In such cases, no foundation for a team environment is present: Both sales positions appear to be working for different companies—they see no reason to work together.

The desired team environment must be built through effective communication. Field salespeople understand MAM objectives and identify with their roles to ensure a strong competitive account position; MAMs understand the need regularly to communicate what is happening in the account that will ultimately benefit field salespeople through sales to establishment locations.

Selling to major accounts requires more than a "calls plus demonstrations equals sales" approach. Major account selling is generally divided into two sales cycles: short-term (current years sales) and long-term (investment selling). MAMs should thus have two major selling objectives: (1) sales volume objectives for the plan year; (2) specific strategic sales objectives that lead to broader account penetration and increase sales in subsequent years (e.g., gain commitment for a new product pilot installation at one test location in the current year; expand to multiple locations in subsequent years). These objectives and strategies should be grounded in a major account plan.

ACCOUNT PLANNING PROCESS

Effective account plans are more substantial than show-and-tell presentations or data written on file cards. They are working documents serving as road maps for accomplishing strategic objectives such as maximizing account penetration and providing quality service to maintain account relationships.

Three key elements are necessary for successful and effective account planning. The first is market research at the account level. Data are collected on account demographics, past sales history, market presence (e.g., leader, minor player), competitive assessment (e.g., strong position and sole provider versus competing with multiple vendors for similar products), account-specific data (e.g., annual reports, 10-K reports, secondary research from newspapers or other publicly published sources), and trade or industry data.

Account opportunity analysis highlights where the MAM plans to focus primary attention. Opportunity analysis includes examination of product groups (e.g., strategic new versus core products; commodity versus custom products; product maintenance; service offerings), applications or uses of products (e.g., expansion at specific remote plants, branches, or stores; new uses for current products; establishing trial installations for new products), and gaining sales by expanding the account's sales opportunities through use of the firm's products.

The third essential element for account planning is account prioritization when MAMs are assigned more than one account. Accounts can be profiled as maintenance, growth, or endangered. Maintenance accounts require quality service and attention to immediate needs, but immediate changes in buying patterns are not expected. They may be on an annual contract. The sales process requires regular, routine contact to ensure that products sold are properly used and that commitment to fulfill annual contract purchase volumes is being kept. Customer responsiveness and attention to detail (e.g., order entry, shipment scheduling, invoices) are extremely important. The MAM's primary job is to manage the company's position at the account and to sell proactively against competitive inroads.

Growth accounts generally experience rapid change and require a different sales strategy. They may operate in expanding markets and may be faced with "real" time challenges. MAMs must be on the outlook for new opportunities; they must ensure the account is aware of the company's new product developments or new uses of in-line products. MAMs may identify new users and, hence, new decision makers in the account. The account plan must be constantly updated to reflect shifts in account buying patterns.

Since growth accounts look for new ways to increase volumes, the MAM's job is to broaden the partnering base within the account. Internal sponsorship is necessary to uncover new pressure points for growth. An account buying the company's core product line may look elsewhere for new technology equipment to solve growth needs. Accounts become comfortable with their MAMs and routinely bought products. MAMs must beware of the comfortable profile and aggressively seek new opportunities.

Endangered accounts send shock waves to MAMs. They are courted by competitors and there is risk of lost sales or overall account loss. Maintenance is insufficient; the account plan must be directed to specific action plans to fend off competitive activity. The MAM may establish an action team, comprising technical support, plant engineers, contact negotiators, pricing specialists, and so forth. Plant visits, panel meetings, quality improvement team meetings, and product benchmarking are ways to win back customer confidence.

DEVELOPING KEY ACCOUNT PLANS

The MAM's sense of urgency and direction in protecting and growing the account should depend on the account stage. When MAMs have multiple account assignments, account plans must be developed that appropriately reflect, maintain, grow, and deflect competitor activities.

1. *Account classification* — Accounts should be classified as maintenance, growth, or endangered.

2. *Account opportunity identification* — This process should develop required activities for each account and list opportunities for additional revenue in the current year. Opportunities are matched to specific activities and timetables.

3. *Account profiles preparation* — This includes business, account status, and account service profiles. First, the account's business profile should include a mission statement and relevant information about the customer's business including:

- Primary products and services.
- Geographic dispersion of the account's marketplace.
- Types of markets served.
- Sizing statistics (e.g., volume, market share).
- Organizational structure.
- Key decision makers.
- The account's current objectives and strategies.
- The account's three to five critical success factors.
- Financial performance for the last two years.
- Competitive forces affecting the account's industry and business.

A business profile for a major office equipment manufacturer account may include the following items:

- *Mission statement*—to produce high-quality word processing, copiers, and facsimile products. To maintain a leadership role in word processing equipment while improving market position in the two other product areas. Aggressive customer service goals will be established to create a significant competitive advantage over competitive products.
- *Primary products and services*—complete range of word processors, including typewriters. Copier line ranges from desktop to full production models. Plain paper facsimile products are being introduced.

- *Geographic dispersion*—national markets, with stronger positions in the Southeast, Mid-Atlantic, Midwest, and Western states.
- *Types of markets served*—large end-use buyers sold by direct sales force, authorized dealers and distributors, and mail-order catalog purchasers.
- *Sizing*—projected sales volume from core business (word processors) seeing a potential decline of 3 percent over last year; copier sales growth projected at 15 percent; plain paper facsimile products, now receiving investment selling effort, projected to reach $100 million in three years.
- *Organization*—including organizational charts.
- *Key decision makers*—list of all key executives that influence the buying process. MAMs should evaluate friendliness and commitment to the company. Also, those executives that may inhibit increased company presence should be identified and their motivations understood.
- *Objectives and strategies*—increase coverage and market acceptance of each product line; increase maintenance revenue; reduce selling expenses. Key supporting strategies are increasing use of dealers and distributors; introduction of competitive maintenance offering; reduction of the direct field sales force.
- *Critical success factors*—successful growth in alternate channels and ability to manage these channels profitably.
- *Financial data*—for example, published annual report data, 10-K data.
- *Competitive position*—description of the account's competitive position.

Second, the customer status profile provides a description of current customer product and service use. The MAM should gather the following internal information: major account business transactions in the past year; status of current products/service contracts; total customer expenditures for similar services (current or past year); estimated customer expenditures for the next two years;

qualitative assessment of competitive strengths and weaknesses in selling and servicing the account.

Lastly, the account's service profile is a critical assessment in developing account plans. The growing emphasis on building quality performance throughout the firm (viz., Malcolm Baldridge National Quality Award) has led many major accounts to demand their suppliers meet prescribed quality standards to retain relationships. MAMs must prepare an assessment of their firm's performance as a quality vendor and supplier.

Data for a company account service profile may be generated qualitatively by MAMs and their managers, or from a regularly administrated company survey. The survey allows creation of a customer service index with which to measure MAM performance. Key elements would include:

- *Account rating*—a descriptive summary of account executives' attitudes toward firm performance according to their expectations.
- *Product and service appraisal*—a descriptive summary of the account contacts' view(s) of all aspects of the firm's products and services, including assessment of nonsales areas (e.g., shipping, accounting, billing, and technical support).
- *Competitive comparison*—a descriptive summary of the firm's rating versus other vendors competing for the same product sales or sales budgets.

4. *Account potential development*—MAMs should forecast plan year sales by product and service units and revenue, and seasonality (if appropriate). Because major accounts comprise a significant share of total firm sales, MAMs must produce credible forecasts. One approach is to require both unconstrained and constrained forecasts.

Unconstrained forecasts are not required in most major account organizations, but can have significant value for the national sales manager. An unconstrained forecast is based on an "ideal" world—no economic, competitive, or account budgeting restrictions. The

MAM should project dollar or unit forecasts for the enterprise (account headquarters) and for establishment locations. Estimates should be made for current in-line products and services and for new products and services to be announced in the plan year. These forecasts give the national sales manager a look at what could be! Unconstrained forecasts provide sales management with an understanding of potential opportunities before traditional constraints such as local market conditions, account cutbacks, competitive pressures, product weaknesses, and so forth are applied to projections.

Developing both unconstrained and constrained forecasts may highlight areas where potential sales are possible by adding resources, changing pricing strategy, improving products, and so forth. For example, an unconstrained forecast may indicate that current products are only sold at 50 percent of the account's remote locations; lack of on-site technical help to install firm equipment may be the key constraint. The MAM may be able to build a business case justifying on-site installation assistance.

An estimated probability should be applied to the total constrained forecast. A constrained forecast of $1.5 million in sales and 80-percent probability raises the question, What actions would boost the probability to 85 percent or 90 percent? Or, if 80 percent is the best achievable, the national sales manager should plan on generating $1.2 million. Realistic forecasting is critical for the firm's total sales projections. Sales management should assist and train MAMs in the forecasting process so they can do a better job.

5. *Account plan implementation*—The MAM should review the plan with the account and formulate sales initiatives to achieve the desired results. Account activity planning and scheduling provides the road map for plan execution. Gaining internal commitments to ensure the plan is supported may involve technical sales support from manufacturing, marketing, or R&D; a sufficient budget to visit field customer locations; direct access to firm policy executives; information systems to track year-to-date sales volume and a budget to visit field sales offices. Scheduling activities

reduces pressure and provides the MAM with checkpoints against progress made.

Inhibitors, dependencies, and roadblocks must be overcome or alternate strategies established. For example, delivery schedule changes, terms and conditions are modified, or planned pricing actions and product announcement delays might call for alternative strategies. Resolution of these internal roadblocks may require decision escalation. Accounts sufficiently important for major account status must receive top management attention. For top-fifty accounts, senior management should be receptive to direct calls from MAMs including being available to assist MAMs in customer situations beyond their authority level. This principle also applies to regional sales managers being directly involved with MAMs handling major regional accounts.

Implementation activities must be specific and established objectives must lead to desired account plan results. MAMs' account plans should contain specific action items directing their activities. Action items should be planned quarterly. For example, a first-quarter plan may require ten calls to field offices for updates and direction at account remote locations; account briefings to review pilot benchmarking test results; internal briefings with firm R&D management to review product development needs to enhance equipment programming efficiencies. Quarterly calendars allow MAMs to identify pressure points in timing and lead times necessary for internal support.

Collaborative working sessions with account executives offer benefits both to the company and accounts. For the company, these sessions raise the level of influence in decision making at the account, lessen competitive influence, and build a sense of partnership, thereby gaining greater commitment to firm recommendations. For the account, these sessions increase their knowledge of the company's account planning and coverage techniques. This should improve effective delivery of high-quality service to the account's remote locations and provide a common, jointly developed measure of expected results from the company's products and services.

6. *Measure development*—Sales management must measure account plans to determine effectiveness and cost to overall sales. Most programs are measured against objectives that reflect consistent results rather than traditional total sales achieved. Such measures may include a two- or three-year performance attainment. They consider the investment selling associated with long selling cycles, show greater interest in qualitative measures of account plan implementation, and use customer surveys to judge MAM effectiveness in servicing the account.

DESIGNING SALES FORCE COMPENSATION

Gary S. Tubridy, Senior Vice-President, The Alexander Group, Inc.

WHAT TO EXPECT FROM A SALES COMPENSATION PLAN

Whereas salespeople typically judge sales compensation plan effectiveness by a dollars-and-cents yardstick—that is, "Are we making more money this year than last year?"—management uses multiple criteria.

■ *Does it attract the right caliber of salespeople?* Most companies aim to attract top performers by offering a competitive total compensation package that include fixed compensation (i.e., salary and benefits) and performance-based compensation (e.g., commissions, bonuses, contests, recognition programs). Attracting good candidates means designing a compensation plan that draws persons capable of producing results. The salary/incentive mix must match job demands: more risk invites a more entrepreneurial, higher-pressured selling style; less risk implies greater service orientation.

■ *Does it help us retain the best salespeople?* Retaining the best people also requires a competitive compensation package. The focus is delivering competitive pay, given desirable sales results. Top performers should earn significantly more than average performers; if not, morale problems and increased turnover may result.

■ *Does it motivate the sales force to fulfill company goals?* Sales and marketing executives should judge a compensation plan's success according to results achieved in areas such as key market segments, product mix, and gross margin. The sales force must understand the level and type of sales results needed to achieve the business plan. The compensation plan is an important communication tool: Does management want specific product emphasis? Does management want increased profit? If salespersons cannot identify key firm objectives from the sales compensation plan, it is not providing sufficient direction.

■ *Does it motivate salespeople to achieve expected levels of performance?* Sales compensation plans should motivate salespeople to achieve performance that meets firm goals. Thus, when target sales performance is achieved by field salespeople, firm revenue objectives are achieved; target product and price mix is sufficient for contribution margin goals; incentive compensation is sufficient to motivate salespeople to sell at or above established target levels.

Salespeople should always know the level of performance expected of them, extra performance needed to reach that level, and how much money they will earn for reaching or exceeding expected levels. In designing motivational plans, salespeople should be measured in areas on which they have direct impact. It is highly demotivating to be measured on criteria that you cannot affect.

Furthermore, goals should stretch salespeople, motivating them to turn in superior performance. But they should not be unrealistic. It is highly demotivating to have significant incentive dollars contingent on achieving performance goals that are unachievable for even the best salespeople.

There are several telltale signs that the sales compensation plan may be a source of problems. Common indicators are:

■ *Sales goals are missed by a small margin.* If the deficit is huge, the problem is probably not the compensation plan. But if the deficit is small, a well-tuned compensation plan might provide the needed boost.

■ *The sales goal is achieved, but not the profit margin goal.* Salespeople may put too much attention to low-margin versus high-margin products, or they may cut prices too much to close a deal. A compensation plan more sensitive to product mix and pricing can help avoid this situation.

■ *Strategic objectives are missed.* Revenue targets are reached, yet strategic objectives regarding emphasis by product, industry, or new accounts are not achieved. This may spell long-run trouble.

■ *Quotas are adjusted frequently.* Adjustments are sometimes indicative of turbulent business environments; more frequently, they correct poorly allocated goals. Overall incentive plan credibility is diminished and the sales force loses trust in management.

■ *Percent of sales goal achieved differs significantly from percent of sales compensation budget spent.* There should be a symmetry between these measures. If the compensation budget is exceeded yet the sales goal has not been achieved, or vice versa, the sales compensation plan probably needs modification.

■ *Turnover and/or morale problems are increasing.* Are the best salespeople leaving? Are the below-plan performers too comfortable? The sales compensation plan may be subsidizing poor performers at the expense of top performers.

Even the best-designed plans do not meet expectations. Yet the compensation plan may be blamed for problems for which it has little effect. For example:

■ *Poor product quality or availability problems*—Today's customers demand that vendors provide top-quality products on time. If the firm cannot perform, its reputation may be seriously damaged and sales suffer. Encouraging salespeople, through the incentive program, to make promises that cannot be kept only damages customer relations further.

■ *Product recognition problems due to poor marketing*—In crowded markets, buyers have difficulty differentiating between products. Without proper marketing support, salespeople face uphill selling battles. Target performance levels required by the compensation plan cannot be met and, if allowed, sales forces frequently cut price.

■ *Lack of effective sales support*—Presale and postsale support (e.g., administrative, technical, and installation) are necessary both to sell products and to keep them sold. Absence of support affects sales volume, customer relations, and sales force morale.

■ *Poor sales training*—Poorly trained sales forces have problems selling products effectively, especially new products that require different selling strategies. For example, a sales force that has always sold to purchasing departments may not be capable of effectively communicating with end users. No amount of incentive compensation will buy success; training is also needed.

■ *Inappropriate deployment*—There are too many products or accounts (or both) and insufficient time to sell effectively. Through the compensation plan, management directs how salespeople spend their time. Yet even sophisticated plans fail if salespeople are overburdened with too many products or accounts. The results: high turnover in sparse territories, "cherry picking," and underpenetration in lucrative territories.

■ *Poor communication and understanding*—Management must clearly communicate the compensation plan's intricacies and objectives. However, management frequently neglects to communicate to the sales force what it wants, how the compensation plan relates to these objectives, and how salespeople can earn money under this plan. Absent this level of understanding, any compensation plan is suboptimal; the sales force does not understand the plan's message or how the plan works.

PRINCIPLES OF EFFECTIVE SALES COMPENSATION

Successful sales compensation plans depend on several factors. Adherence to five principles derived from direct experience increases the chances that the plan will do the job.

1. *Compensation level*—This guiding principle states: "You get what you pay for." Pay level policy must consider the nature of the sales job—how much knowledge, skill, and effort are required to succeed; and the competitive job market—how much firms with similar positions pay their salespeople and the level of demand to fill these positions.

Typically, positions that require significant knowledge and skill levels command high pay in the job market. Conversely, positions calling for easily acquired skills require only average pay levels to attract and retain desired talent.

The common compensation relationships discussed here should not substitute for internal comparisons or market price investigations. The sales representative is the "base" position; it is assigned a relative total compensation value of 1.0. Product specialists are generally promoted from sales representatives. They are responsible for a broader geographic territory, and typically are not assigned specific accounts. Typically they are members of a sales team and are highly planning oriented. Their pay is often targeted at a 20 percent premium over sales representatives.

Account managers are usually on par with product specialists. They sell all products, but only to selected large accounts. Account managers are highly oriented toward planning and team selling. Product specialists and account managers are generally promoted to sales managers. Sales managers are typically targeted at a 20-percent to 25-percent premium over account managers and product specialists.

Major account managers may report to sales managers or second-line managers, or directly to headquarters. They manage the largest accounts and are oriented toward relationship building and long-term selling. Typically, major account managers earn as much as or more than sales managers. Commonly, total compensation is targeted at 5 percent to 10 percent more than first-line sales managers.

2. *Mix of base salary and incentive*—The guiding principle is: "Tailor the mix to the

Exhibit 3-11. Factors Affecting Mix of Base Salary and Incentives

	Mix between Base Salary and Incentive as a Percent of Total Compensation	
	More Base ←—————————→ More Incentive Salary Compensation	
Direct influence of the sales job on sales results	Low ←—————————→ High	
Length of the sales cycle	Long ←—————————→ Short	
Sales personnel freedom to act independently	Low ←—————————→ High	
Level of dependence on team members to support sales effort	Dependent ←—————————→ Independent	

sales job." Sales managers often believe increasing the incentive portion of compensation, thus increasing risk, helps drive desired sales results. Yet more risk is not always the answer; degree of risk should depend on several factors, as shown in Exhibit 3-11.

Taking these factors into account, we identify common ranges of base salary/incentive mix by sales position that work in many sales organizations. Of course, specific sales positions may fall outside these ranges.

Sales representatives are typically the most highly leveraged 50/50–70/30. Greater emphasis on the incentive component is generally found for salespersons focused on undifferentiated products; the value of a sale is measured only by revenue produced and more calls generally yield more sales. Because product specialists and account managers are typically more planning oriented and more dependent on other positions to close sales, they are generally less leveraged than sales representatives.

Sales managers are almost always less leveraged (70/30–80/20) than line sales persons. Base salary is increased to recognize management quality in such areas as training/monitoring, coaching, counseling, and developing. The major account manager is frequently the least leveraged (70/30–90/10): first, because sales generally require long lead times; second, the relationship-building requirement over time is very high.

3. *Performance measures*—The guiding principle is: "Complex selling environments increase sales job complexity. Sales volume alone may not be an adequate measure of sales performance." Many sales organizations rely primarily on sales volume to measure sales performance; frequently, that yardstick alone is insufficient to reflect the whole sales job.

- *Existing products sold to current customers is maintenance selling*. Performance is typically measured by preservation of the sales base from last year and percent by which the sales base is increased.
- *New products sold to current customers is leverage selling*. Performance is typically measured by the quantity of new products sold into assigned accounts by geography.
- *Existing products sold to prospects is conversion selling*. Performance is typically measured by quantity of sales to prospect accounts, or quantity of new accounts acquired.
- *New products sold to prospects is new market selling*. Performance is typically measured by quantity of new product sales and the sales value to prospects.

When salespeople have to perform several or all of these sales functions, multiple mea-

Exhibit 3-12. Typical Sales Performance Measures

	Total Sales Volume	Product Sales Volume	Gross Margin	Account Objectives	Strategic Objectives
Major Account Manager	F	S	S	F	*
Sales Manager	F	F	S	*	F
Account Manager	F	S	*	F	*
Product Specialist	*	F	S	*	S
Sales Representative	F	S	*	*	*

F = frequently used; S = sometimes used; * = infrequently used.

sures are used and weighted according to the importance level of that particular responsibility. Some more common performance measures are in Exhibit 3-12.

Account objectives are typically expressed as dollar or unit volumes by account. Strategic objectives are typically expressed as specific activities to achieve account or product sales objectives. Individuals are measured on whether planned activities are implemented and on implementation quality.

Careful selection of performance measures is essential for sales compensation plan success. Objectives should be four or fewer, and balanced between volume, profit, product, and account objectives.

Establishing relative weights between measures is also important; this signals how management wants salespeople to use their time. For example, in a sales representative plan, undifferentiated volume may account for 60 percent of target payout, new product sales for 30 percent, new customer sales for 10 percent. The translation is: Make your overall sales volume number; be sure new products have high priority; sell new accounts if possible. *Measures* tell salespeople what is important; incentive *weights* tell how important.

4. *Incentive formula*—The guiding principle is: "Customize it to the type of sales behavior desired." The decision to use *commission* (e.g., percent of sales dollar volume) *versus bonus* (e.g., dollar amount paid on sales quota achieved) in a sales compensation incentive formula depends on firm objectives and the sales job. Generally, commission formulas (with or without base salary) signal volume production is the sales force's primary job.

Fixed-rate commission formulas tell salespeople: "The more the company earns, the more you earn." Commission rates can be varied according to the percent of quota or prior-year sales achieved. Commissions are frequently used with sales forces with limited product lines, commodity-oriented products, or very new products.

Bonus plans always use performance quotas to calculate incentive pay. Payout is expressed as a percent of base salary or as a fixed dollar amount, based on percent quota achieved. Bonus formulae give management better control of compensation budgets and make it easier to relate pay to performance. Bonuses are most common with sales forces selling multiple products and responsible for maintaining sizable sales bases. See Exhibit 3-13 for factors to consider in the bonus/commission decision. Of course, a combination of both may be used.

Accelerators are a plan formulae that increase the rate of incentive payout above a specified performance level. Accelerators can be placed at any performance level yet they usually kick in after salespeople achieve 100 percent of quota. They are used to draw salespeople to increasingly higher levels of performance and proportionately to reward top performers.

Linkage prevents salespeople from "shopping the plan," deciding what they like and focusing on it—often to the detriment of management's objectives. This is a real problem if the plan comprises two or more elements, especially if one element has a significant share of the incentive compensation budget. To prevent shopping the compensation plan,

Exhibit 3-13. Considerations in Selecting Commissions versus Bonus Plans

	Bonus	*Commission*
Number of sales transactions per month	Few ⟵————————→	Many
Importance of account relationship	High ⟵————————→	Low
Sales cycle/lead time	Long ⟵————————→	Short
Accuracy of quotas	Accurate ⟵————————→	Inaccurate

designers can link several incentive formulae. *Hurdles* are the simplest form of linked incentive formulae. A hurdle is a performance level in one measure that salespersons must reach before incentives for another measure are activated. For example, sales volume must be at target level before the new account bonus is paid. A *matrix* incentive formula links two competing measures (e.g., sales volume and operating profit margin). Rather than allowing a trade-off of one measure versus the other, the matrix encourages maximum performance in both categories. Payouts are constructed so that outstanding performance in both measures provides the highest incentive payment (Exhibit 3-14).

Caps stop salespeople from earning beyond a predetermined, maximum earnings level. Generally, setting a cap or maximum discourages overachieving salespeople. Caps are frequently used when management cannot accurately set sales quotas due to business volatility or frequent windfalls, or when the sale of products or services beyond a certain level cannot be supported.

5. *Quotas*—The guiding principle is: "Management should use quotas in sales incentive plans to link individual salespeople to the business plan." Firms establishing quotas (or goals) frequently use them to provide quantitative performance standards; motivate desired performance; improve distribu-

Exhibit 3-14. A Matrix Incentive Formula

Bonus Formula
(Percent of Base Salary)

Sales Volume (Percent to Quota)					
Excellent	16	21	27	35	40
	13	18	25	30	35
Target	8	15	20%	25	27
	5	10	15	18	21
Threshold	0	5	8	13	16

Threshold   Target   Excellent

Operating Profit
(Percent to Quota)

tion of rewards and recognition; and obtain tighter sales and expense controls.

Quotas link salespeople to the business plan inasmuch as the sum of all quotas equals the overall revenue requirements. Linking incentive pay to quota achievement ties the compensation plan to the business plan. For example, pay no incentive until quota is achieved; accelerate the rate of incentive pay once quota is achieved.

Effective quotas should be attainable with normal effort, and their base should be understood by salespeople. Quotas or performance standards should be established for all measures on which incentive compensation is paid, not just sales volume. Because they fulfill many objectives, quotas are not easy to set. Correct assignment requires a thorough analysis of growth potential in each territory. Managers must acquire knowledge of the market, specific accounts, and competitor ac-

tivity. Also, salesperson experience and capability should be taken into account when setting quotas.

Firms often find it difficult to retain salespeople in highly penetrated territories when the quota allocation process is based on insufficient analysis. Quotas are set too high, and sales incentive earnings are minimized. Conversely, typical quota-setting techniques in high-growth, low-penetration territories frequently result in walk-over goals and undermarket penetration.

Quota-setting processes should account for the unique characteristics of each territory both to encourage market penetration and to minimize undesirable sales turnover. Despite difficulties, sales quotas are very important. If quotas are not fully integrated into the incentive plan, management misses an opportunity more effectively to communicate, direct, and motivate the sales force.

SALES PROMOTION

Scott A. Neslin, Professor of Business Administration, The Amos Tuck School, Dartmouth College

Sales promotions are action-oriented marketing events designed to directly influence customer behavior. Sales promotions are events limited in duration and often comprising more than one promotional tool (e.g., retailers couple one-week duration price cuts with feature advertising and special displays; durable goods manufacturers combine rebates and financing incentives). Sales promotions are action oriented: they impel customers to action (e.g., buy, try, use the product; cut out and redeem a coupon; mail in a rebate offer; collect proofs of purchase).

Sales promotions can be grouped into three major types: (1) consumer promotions—from manufacturers to consumers; (2) trade promotions—from manufacturers to retailers; (3) retailer promotions—from retailers to consumers. Trade promotions and retailer promotions are closely related: often the purpose of trade promotions is to induce retailers to promote ("pass-through") to consumers.

Exhibit 3-15 lists specific promotions grouped under each major type. Exhibit 3-16 proposes a simple framework for planning and managing sales promotion.

Exhibit 3-15. Major Forms of Sales Promotion

Consumer Promotions

Coupons — savings certificates that award the consumer a discount equal to the "face value" when presented to the retailer at the same time that a purchase is made.

Contests — games and other participatory events that require skill on the part of the consumer in order to win and receive a prize or other reward.

Sweepstakes — games or other participatory events in which winning is due to chance.

Sampling — a program for getting the consumer to try a product at reduced risk. Risk is usually reduced by making a smaller package or version of the product available for free or at nominal cost.

Premiums — merchandise or services awarded to the consumer for taking a particular action. The premium may be a free gift or the offer to buy additional merchandise at a special price.

Bonus packs — special packages of a product that offer more quantity at the same price.

Continuity programs — promotional programs that require the consumer to make several purchases of the product in order to receive a reward.

Financing incentives — a variety of techniques for making money more easily or more cheaply available to the consumer for the purpose of buying the product.

Rebates — a certificate that entitles the purchaser of a product to receive a financial refund if the certificate is mailed to the manufacturer with an accompanying proof of purchase.

Refunds — similar to rebates, except the term is usually applied to packaged goods, whereas the term *rebates* is usually used for durables.

Trade Promotions

Case allowances — price discounts offered to the retailer on the basis of the number of cases ordered.

Display allowances — money offered to the retailer, possibly on a per-case basis, under the condition that the product be specially displayed.

Advertising allowances — money offered to the retailer, possibly on the per-case basis, under the condition that the retailer specially advertise the product, often in a newspaper circular.

Salesperson incentives — financial rewards paid by the manufacturer to the retailer's salespersons for selling quantities of the product.

Financial incentives — a variety of techniques for making money more easily or more cheaply available to the retailer for the purpose of buying the product.

Contests — games or other participatory events requiring skill in order for the retailer to receive a reward.

Sweepstakes — games or merchandise awarded free or at a reduced price to retailers for taking certain specified actions.

Retailer Promotions

Price discounts — special price discounts from regular price available in the store for a short duration.

Displays — special in-store methods for displaying the product, such as end-of-aisle displays or in-aisle displays that clearly distinguish the product from competition.

Feature advertising — advertising taken by the retailer that emphasizes the available price of the product. The advertised price is often a special price discount.

Sampling — an in-store program for allowing the consumer to try the product at lower risk.

Coupons — distributed by retailers through either newspaper circulars, special mailings, or through in-store methods.

Exhibit 3-16. The Promotion Planning Process

Exhibit 3-17. Objectives of Sales Promotion

Sales Impact

Increase sales
Increase market share
Increase consumption
Attract new triers
Attract brand switchers
Enhance repeat purchasing
Increase usage rate
Gain trial for another product

Competition Related

Preempt a competitive action such as
   the launching of a new product
Defend market share
Signal competition
Deter new product entry
Function profitability in "prisoner's
   dilemma"

Enhancing Other Marketing Mix Elements

Increase distribution
Cushion a regular price increase
Motivate the sales force
Reinforce print or television
   advertising
Help to reposition the product
More directly control retail price

Specific Retailer Objectives

Generate store traffic
Reinforce positioning as discount or
   low-price store
Increase sales of complimentary
   products
Attract consumer to higher-margin
   items
Generate or maintain store loyalty
Increase category profit

SITUATION ANALYSIS

All marketing planning begins with a thorough situation analysis. Topics include recent brand and profit performance; current brand marketing plans; company resources; previous and predicted competitive activity, customer buying patterns; market segments. Special attention is given to reviewing previous types of sales promotion used for the brand, and how successful they were. The situation analysis is the vehicle for reviewing all relevant information from which objectives, strategies, and tactics of the promotion plan follow. Sales promotion does not exist in a vacuum; it is an integrated marketing plan element and it must be consistent with the competitive, consumer, and trade environment.

OBJECTIVES

Although increased profit is the ultimate goal of most promotions, intermediate objectives are ends in themselves. A listing of such objectives is given in Exhibit 3-17.

Promotions often enhance some other marketing mix element. For example, steep trade deals can help manufacturers gain distribution for a new product, or avoid losing distribution for an existing product. Coupons may cushion a regular retail price increase among price-sensitive consumers. (The retail price may increase by 20 cents, but a 25-cent coupon both compensates the consumer and gets him or her used to the new regular price.) Special displays reinforce advertising if the display contains the same slogan or depicts the same well-known spokesperson.

The objectives of sales impact, competition-related and enhancing other marketing mix elements, apply to manufacturers, and often to retailers. In addition, retailers have objectives that especially apply to them. Generating store traffic is perhaps the most important retailer objective. Another important issue is conflict between retailer and manufacturer objectives. Manufacturers want to increase brand sales; however, many retailers have little preference for which brand they sell. Retailers' interest is not to sell more Maxwell House coffee than Folgers, but to generate more profit from coffee overall. If a retailer promotion simply switches a fixed stock of consumers from Folgers to Maxwell House, the retailer is uninterested unless the Maxwell House profit margin is higher than Folgers. For this reason, Maxwell House may offer the retailer discounts (trade promotions) on Maxwell House coffee.

STRATEGY

Sales promotion objectives drive strategy specification. If the objective is to increase sales by 50 percent, the strategy may require a steep consumer price discount. A more sophisticated objective-strategy combination might preempt competitive product launch (objective) by "loading up" consumers with product (strategy); this combination is particularly relevant for infrequently purchased products or services. For example, a computer workstation manufacturer may attempt to thwart a competitor's new workstation introduction by offering special rebates on its own workstations. This promotion may simply accelerate forward customers who, absent the new competitive workstation, would have bought the promoting firm's workstation anyway. Nonetheless, if this acceleration re-

moves customers from the market and insulates them from competition, the strategy may be worthwhile.

Four additional aspects of sales promotion strategy bear close attention. First, strategies must be formulated considering long-term implications. Steep temporary price decreases to consumers will probably achieve sales objectives. However, the steep price decrease may cheapen the brand image; in the long term this hurts sales. In addition, a steep price decrease implemented once may require steeper increases the next time because consumers are not impressed with the same price decrease. However, if promotions are viewed as more than a strictly financial incentive as, for example, if successive coupon programs are coupled with different and creative contests, sweepstakes, or advertising, the novelty is less likely to wear off.

Second, competitive response should be anticipated, particularly in a "prisoner's dilemma." A prisoner's dilemma is a competitive situation wherein each competitor's marketing efforts cancel the other's efforts, resulting in the same share of market for everyone at higher marketing costs. One strategy for functioning effectively in this situation is to design a promotion that the competition cannot copy. For example, a firm might offer premium discounts on its full line of products, assuming its product line is broader than the competition's. Promotion timing can also prevent copying. For example, a holiday theme contest may not be copy-able if it appears close to the holiday. Of course, competition may not just copy: to a regional promotion they may promote in another region: to a 15-percent trade deal they may offer 17 percent. Nonetheless, consideration of competitor actions should result in sounder strategy.

Third, sales promotion's role in the overall push-pull marketing strategy must be considered ("push" through the distribution system; "pull" by causing consumers to demand product from retailers). Traditionally, consumer advertising acts to pull; trade deals operate as push. However, couponing and other consumer promotions can also serve as a pull strategy. These strategies can be coordinated by thinking of consumer promotions as short-term pull and advertising as long-term pull.

Fourth, the sales promotion strategy should be consistent with overall product positioning. For example, a high-quality tennis racket for higher-income players should probably not offer steep rebates, but might offer a can of high-quality tennis balls as a premium. Everyday low-price retailers should not try to outprice discount competitors. Promotional strategy might emphasize less steep price discounts but on more products.

TACTICS

Sales promotion strategy typically suggests a few possible promotion forms; much work is then needed to generate alternatives, select the specific promotion to implement, and fine-tune the details. The net result is a promotion calendar and detailed promotion budget.

Because it is innately difficult to be creative, generating alternatives often turns up promotions used previously by the firm or competitors regardless of whether they worked. Some firms run formal brainstorming sessions to create new promotions, or rely on sales promotion agencies to generate new ideas. Despite difficulties, many firms generate creative promotions. For example, Jello faced a perennial problem that consumers purchased the product but they tended not to use it: promotion objective—increase usage; strategy—consumer promotion tied to the Christmas holiday; tactic—a Jello mold premium in the shape of Santa Claus. The mold was a festive reason to use Jello; the Christmas tie-in ensured usage would occur in a given time period.

Generation and selection often occur hand in hand; the key selection task is to ensure the chosen alternative is on strategy. This is easily checked if the strategy is well specified. Of course, competitive response, marketing plan coordination, and other long-term considerations must be revisited here.

IMPLEMENTATION

Because implementation is considered unglamorous and not intellectually stimulating, it is easy not to pay attention to it. However, the entire promotion's success can ride on successful implementation. The key issues are adhering to the planned time schedule and coordination among managers implementing the promotion. Timing is often important for seasonal or competitive reasons; for example, holiday promotions must be available before the holiday. More delicate timing issues arise, if for example, a trade deal is coordinated with a consumer promotion. Suppose the promotional strategy calls for a "big event" to break through the promotional clutter faced by consumers; the tactics call for trade promotions to stimulate retailer promotions the first two weeks in July, and a coupon in the newspaper the first Sunday in July. Unfortunately, the manufacturer cannot control when (if ever) retailers pass through trade deals to consumers.

Several communication steps must happen: brand managers planning to use the promotional calendar must communicate with sales managers, who communicate with the sales force, who communicate with supermarket buyers, who communicate with store managers. Obviously, this communication can go awry in several places, even if everyone wants to cooperate. In addition, the distribution service might have its circular booked for the first Sunday in July; negotiations, search for alternative distribution, or even a promotion calendar change may be required. Effective implementation requires motivated employees, open communication lines, and a well-conceived promotional calendar.

EVALUATION

Sales promotion can influence sales in three time frames: (1) the immediate term—while the promotion is implemented; (2) the intermediate term—the weeks or months surrounding the promotion period; (3) the long term—within several months or perhaps a year of the promotion period.

Immediate-Term Effects

The principal immediate effects of sales promotion are brand switching and increased consumption. Sales promotions are typically effective brand-switching devices, especially if consumers are indifferent among available brands, because they often include strong financial incentives. Even if consumers have a preference for the nonpromoting brand, the financial incentive can compensate for switching to the second-choice brand. Sales promotion can also reinforce brand switching in markets with high-variety seeking (e.g., restaurants, food products) where consumers naturally want to switch among brands. Brand switching also takes place in durables markets. For example, a rebate may cause a consumer to buy a Chevrolet Lumina rather than the Ford Taurus that would have been bought had the rebate not been available.

Brand switching is a market share battle among competing brands. If increased consumption occurs, all brands might "win," or at least not "lose." For example, in the prisoner's dilemma cola wars, Coke versus Pepsi, the two brands trade market share; however, sales promotion has probably expanded the cola market considerably. First, sales promotion can attract nonbuyers, especially if they are out of the market for financial reasons. Especially important for durable goods (e.g., camcorders, personal computers, expensive clothing), a promotion may attract consumers who otherwise would view these goods beyond their budgets. Second, light buyers may be attracted; for example, some families only buy cookies when an acceptable brand is on sale. Third, it can increase purchase frequency of products consumed soon after purchase. For example, promotions for carbonated soft drinks place products in the family refrigerator where they are consumed rapidly. Fourth, and related, promotions can train consumers to purchase products in shorter interpurchase times. This is especially important for durable goods; for example, automobile promotions may induce a household to trade in their car after five years rather than keep it for seven.

Intermediate-Term Effects

The intermediate effects of promotion concern repeat purchase and purchase acceleration. A positive repeat-purchase effect is very beneficial, especially since the subsequent purchase is likely at full profit margin. However, the repeat-purchase effect may be positive, negative, or zero. Positive effects might occur first, because the consumer learns about the brand's attributes and reacts favorably to them. This is the prime motivation for new product promotions. Second, the promotion serves as a reward; rewarded behavior is more likely to persist. This view is often reflected in the promotion strategy of enhancing repeat purchase among current buyers. Third, the promotion might be habit inducing among relatively uninvolved consumers; for example, among consumers tending to repeat purchase the brand bought last.

Negative repeat-purchase effects involve weaker brand attitudes and lower consumer brand reference prices. Promotions can weaken brand attitudes first, because consumers question why the brand "resorted" to promotion; the brand must be low quality! This is particularly an issue in markets where promotions are rare; for example, Chrysler's early use of rebates, "Buy a car, get a check." Second, the promotion distracts consumers from thinking about brand attributes; promotion availability becomes the reason to buy.

Lower reference prices occur when consumers become accustomed to a discount price, making the regular price seem especially high. For example, a consumer who repeatedly buys Nabisco Chips Ahoy cookies at $2.59 may adopt that price as his or her reference price (subjective standard or benchmark). A promoted $2.29 price looks especially attractive but, after buying at $2.29, the reference price may decrease, possibly to $2.29. A subsequently available price of $2.29 does not seem like such a good deal.

But perhaps promotions have no repeat-purchase effect. First, consumers may be uninvolved with purchasing the product category; promotions may be just a simplifying heuristic for deciding which brand to purchase with no other impact. This may prevail in many packaged-goods categories among today's busy, preoccupied shoppers. Second, high-involvement consumers may carefully consider product attributes. Buying on promotion is part of a carefully derived calculation, but the promotion does not color these consumers' relatively objective scrutiny of product performance, which determines repeat purchase. This situation may occur in durable goods categories, services such as dining or dry cleaning, or industrial products.

Purchase acceleration refers to promotions'

ability to displace the timing of category purchases. The promotion induces the consumer to purchase earlier than he or she otherwise would have, or purchase additional quantities than one normally buys. Both timing and quantity acceleration aspects can occur at the same time—buy sooner, buy larger quantities. Timing acceleration might be more prevalent for infrequently purchased categories; quantity acceleration for frequently purchased categories. For consumers, motivation for acceleration is economic. The benefit is decreased price; the cost is extra storage space. Depending on storage availability, acceleration propensities vary vastly among households.

For manufacturers and retailers, acceleration can be profitable or unprofitable. If acceleration merely displaces sales that would have occurred at full price, it is unprofitable; if it takes consumers out of the market to preempt competitors, it may be profitable; if it helps increase consumption, it may be profitable. The acceleration/increased consumption relationship is especially relevant for durable goods, but it may be difficult to distinguish between them.

Stockpiling by retailers, a common result of trade dealing, is called forward buying; the retailer buys enough product to satisfy current plus future demand. The retailer trade-off is between the price discount on the inventory and the cost of carrying that inventory. Manufacturers usually view forward buying as undesirable because it cannibalizes future sales that would be made at the full wholesale price. Some retailers regard forward buying as an important profit source.

Long-Term Effects

Long-term promotion effects include cumulative intermediate effects as well as additional phenomena. Repeat purchase effects may be relatively small in the one or two purchase occasions after a promotion, but become more significant after a few years. For example, a single purchase of a ketchup brand on promotion is unlikely to erode brand attitudes significantly. However, after years of heavy promotion purchasing, the cumulative effect may be significant. Some managers are fearful that

whereas immediate effects of promotions are clear and enticing and intermediate effects are small, long-term effects are highly significant. However, these long-term effects are difficult to detect because they are so intertwined with other long-term market trends, and difficult to plan for because they are less predictable.

One major long-term effect is consumer response evolution. In the long term, continued promotion may produce a cadre of consumers trained to buy only on promotion, and to wait for a promotion if one is not available. As a result, fewer and fewer people buy off-promotion. The reference price effect can mutate to a situation where steeper and more dramatic discounts are needed to have any effect. There is some conjecture that in the auto industry consumers now consider rebates to be part of the normal marketing environment.

Competitive response is a major long-term effect. The promotion ante to compete may increase gradually, but after several years firms find themselves in a prisoners' dilemma of heavy promotion expenditures. Unilateral withdrawal results in huge market share declines; explicit cooperation is illegal, but would only move firms to their initial position, with a strong temptation to promote. However, in stable environments, firms learn to anticipate countermoves better; they learn which competitors are aggressive and which are relatively passive. Promotions planning and results forecasting become more accurate.

CONCLUSION

Any evaluation of promotion efforts should consider immediate, intermediate, and long-term effects. Usually the immediate effects, which result in a noticeable sales "bump," are easy to quantify. Intermediate-term issues such as repeat purchasing and acceleration are less easy to quantify. Long-term issues are often extremely difficult to quantify. A good approach is to quantify the immediate and perhaps intermediate effects first. If the net result is not profitable, this points to a qualitative judgment as to whether the long-term benefits justified the promotion. In this way, quantification methods and qualitative judgment can work hand in hand.

Human Resources

Michael Z. Sincoff, Section Editor

Introduction   *Michael Z. Sincoff*   4-3

Effective Supervision   *Jack L. Simonetti*   4-6

Human Resources Planning in the 1990s   *John A. Passante*   4-12

Personnel Selection and Psychological Assessment
   Michael Merbaum   4-16

Managing the Diverse Work Force   *Susan L. Pedigo*   4-20

New Dimensions in Work Scheduling   *Caleb S. Atwood*   4-24

Training and Development to Improve Employee Performance
   Ronald R. Sims   4-28

Employee Compensation   *Barry Bingham, Barry Blitstein, Elizabeth J.
   Hawk, and Herschel V. Sellers*   4-35

Employee Benefits: Options and Alternatives   *William R. Maher,
   William S. Comfort, and Robert L. Rosenheim*   4-40

Retirement and Pension Planning   *Thomas C. Farnam*   4-46

Managing Pension Plans   *Clifford A. Rand*   4-51

Compliance with Government Regulations   *John F. Wymer III*   4-55

The Performance Appraisal Process   *Michael Z. Sincoff and
    Kathleen D. Sincoff*   4-60

Evaluating Human Resources Information Systems
    Joseph L. Tufano   4-64

Human Resources Management in International Operations
    Frank L. Acuff   4-66

Dealing with Corporate Restructuring   *Milton F. Droege, Jr.*   4-69

Effective Communication   *Evan E. Rudolph*   4-72

Relations with Organized Labor   *Fred M. Reichman*   4-76

Employee Health Promotion   *Michael Goldberg and Deborah Wiethop*   4-86

Employee Substance Abuse   *Victor Schachter*   4-89

Privacy and Personnel Security Issues   *Dennis J. Morikawa*   4-92

INTRODUCTION

Michael Z. Sincoff

One word captures the human resources function and the people in it in the 1990s and sets the tone for the foundation of the next century: *professional*. As such, those in the function will be required to demonstrate technical mastery and a high standard of ethical conduct and integrity.

Probably the first seriously acknowledged studies focusing on the individual in the workplace were the early twentieth-century pioneering efforts of Henri Fayol and Frederick Taylor, and the advent of scientific management in which work methods were quantified and routinized. Later, Elton Mayo and his team of researchers from Harvard conducted studies at Western Electric's Hawthorne plant. The Hawthorne studies in the late 1920s and early 1930s—particularly the bank-wiring room studies on levels of illumination—spurred further research in group dynamics and, more importantly, the behavior of individuals and small groups in complex organizations. An ancillary Hawthorne finding—actually a listening technique—coupled with techniques developed by clinical psychologist Carl Rogers in nondirective client-centered therapy, provided the genesis for the role of the human resources professional as counselor.

A who's who of researchers, writers, and theorists—Roethlisberger and Dickson, Barnard, McGregor, Herzberg, Blake and Mouton, Argyris, Likert, and many others—all added to the body of behavioral science knowledge that a human resources professional needs today.

Separately, companies practiced improving morale in order to improve employee satisfaction and increase productivity. From the human relations approach of the 1940s and 1950s, to the employee participation and employee involvement approaches of the 1970s and 1980s, to the current view of employee empowerment, individuals and groups in organizations have been a central and deserving focus. Throughout this evolution, the human resources professional played a decisive role in formulating, shaping, and administering the necessary personnel policies and procedures. Today, the human resources professional is required to have the knowledge and skills to understand and apply information in a wide variety of disciplines.

In compensation, Henry Ford led the way with his promise of five dollars a day for a fair day's work. Compensation schemes are no longer that simple yet they still attempt to link pay to performance. Their complexity requires specialized knowledge of compensation theory and philosophy, joined with the ability to develop and implement appropriate programs. Compensation specialists are faced with duties from the relatively simple tasks of preparing and evaluating job descriptions and developing a graded salary structure to grappling with taxation issues of expatriate compensation in a global economy; from automatic wage increases dictated by a collective bargaining agreement to the nuances of executive stock options and performance payouts.

Benefit plans that provide appropriate coverage at acceptable cost require skill and knowledge to create. The issues associated with pretax plans like 401(k) or Section 125; with retirement income plans, the subtleties of ERISA, and retiree health plans; with antidiscrimination testing; or, with simply helping an employee complete a dental reimbursement form require not only close attention but also thorough understanding.

Many other legal considerations in human resources have come to the fore ranging from knowing what questions are permissible to ask during recruitment to what ramifications exist when providing retiree benefits. Take the doctrine of employment-at-will as a salient example. In its purest form, employment-at-will allows a company to terminate an employee at any time for any reason or for no reason at all. An employee may terminate under the same conditions. The doctrine is no longer pure. A collective bargaining agreement may modify the doctrine as may an employment contract between the individual and the company specifying duration or term of employment. Legislative and statutory laws, rules, and regulations, as well as evolving case law with respect to age, race, sex, national origin, Vietnam Era veteran status, and handicap or disability have properly eroded the purity of employment-at-will. As a result, in any personnel transaction—recruitment, selection, training, placement, transfer, promotion, wage and salary adjustments, demotion, discipline, layoff, termination—a trail of clear, thorough, and verifiable documentation must be maintained to assure that an individual receives industrial due process and that the company's actions are defensible as work-related and nondiscriminatory. As total work force diversity becomes more pronounced, understanding the legal labyrinth by the human resources professional, and championing both the letter and spirit of the law, will become even more vital.

Record keeping is no longer placing a piece of paper in a manila folder. Computerized information systems store and process vast amounts of applicant, employee, terminee, and retiree data. Rights of access, privacy, searches, retention, security, and use of such information are issues faced daily by human resources professionals.

Relations with organized labor—grievance handling and settlement, arbitration, contract negotiation—have their specialized rules. Observance of these rules should lead to labor-management harmony; violation of them may result in allegations of unfair labor practices against the company. Management must be aware not only of the rights of the employee to be, or not to be, represented but also of its rights in the labor arena. The human resources professional spearheads this understanding and is typically on the front line.

In many smaller organizations, the human resources function frequently comprises those company functions that in larger organizations are separate departments. These may include but are not limited to (1) safety (safety policy and programs, accident prevention and review, safety audits and compliance); (2) environment (hazardous materials handling, waste disposal, recycling, compliance with regulations promulgated by the Environmental Protection Agency, the Occupational Safety and Health Administration, and related state agencies); (3) facilities (building and grounds maintenance, site selection, office construction, building HVAC [heating, ventilating, and air conditioning], telecommunications systems, and a variety of support services); (4) purchasing (acquisition of supplies, materials, equipment, inventories, vendor selection, and price negotiation); (5) public relations (newsletter preparation, company brochures, investor relations, government relations, press releases, and press relations); (6) training, education, individual development, manpower planning, organizational development, organizational design, total quality processes, resizing, and restructuring. Other areas of expertise include corporate travel services, supervision of the corporate air fleet, risk management, contract review, and just about any function that a company wants to assign.

When reading this section, the reader will appreciate the professionalism and breadth required of those in the human resources function. Jack Simonetti and Susan Pedigo reflect on values and the changing demographics in the work force. John Passante explores work force planning and ways to improve the quality of work life, and Caleb Atwood proposes two innovative and provocative approaches to work scheduling as food for thought. Ronald Sims describes program components needed in training the work force. Milton Droege identifies problems and opportunities in organizational restructuring, and Evan Rudolph suggests ways to make written and oral communication more effective in the workplace.

Michael and Kathleen Sincoff highlight components of the performance appraisal process with emphasis on the performance evaluation review and the need for written documentation, and Barry Bingham, Barry Blitstein, Elizabeth Hawk, and Herschel Sellers recommend approaches for linking pay to performance results. William Maher, William Comfort and Robert Rosenheim describe a variety of employee benefits alternatives that can be used to attract and retain employees. Thomas Farnam and Clifford Rand discuss issues in retirement and pension planning, and Frank Acuff examines selection, compensation, and repatriation issues affecting employees holding international assignments.

John Wymer identifies the primary federal equal employment opportunity laws and discusses compliance with them, and Michael Merbaum offers suggestions on how to use testing to screen for work-related employee characteristics. Fred Reichman describes relations with organized labor within the context of the National Labor Relations Act, and Vic-

tor Schachter presents the issue of employee substance abuse including recommendations for implemention of antisubstance abuse programs. Dennis Morikawa discusses company compliance with employee privacy rights. Michael Goldberg and Deborah Wiethop describe advantages to the company of promoting employee health, and Joseph Tufano identifies the major components in a computerized human resources information system.

The reader will observe that human resources is a function broad in scope that has evolved as a legitimate organizational activity. In many companies it reports to the CEO (chief executive officer), is represented as a full partner in the highest executive councils, and shares equal voice with other key organizational functions. No longer does the function have successful people in it who just bring the watermelon to the company picnic. At once, in addition to being skilled in traditional business disciplines, the human resources professional must be knowledgeable in the psychology and sociology of human interaction, counseling, investigative techniques, employment and labor law, compensation and benefits, administration, the politics of organizations, and broad societal issues. This person must be a clear, insightful thinker capable of expression orally and in writing; a good listener capable of understanding, evaluating, and reacting; one who has the ability and interest in handling many issues concurrently with the integrity to do so; and an innovator—in short, a professional.

Michael Z. Sincoff, *Ph.D., is senior vice-president, Human Resources and Administration, with DIMAC DIRECT, Inc., Bridgeton, Missouri. Previously, he was vice-president, Human Resources, with ADVO, Inc., and held senior-level personnel positions with the Mead and Hoechst-Celanese Corporations, as well as professorships at Ohio University and the University of Minnesota. He currently serves on the Human Resources Council of the American Management Association and the Editorial Advisory Board of the* Journal of Applied Communication Research.

EFFECTIVE SUPERVISION

Jack L. Simonetti, Professor of Management, The University of Toledo

Managing can be one of the most satisfying professions on earth, but it can also be one of the most frustrating. Managing others is different from doing the actual work yourself. It involves a set of basic duties and responsibilities and an understanding and awareness of human behavior. People who move into the job of managing must change what they do and how they do it because the most complex, confusing, and at times, the most rewarding aspect of the manager's job, is the human element. Performance and productivity take the combined efforts of many people and it is the manager's job to coordinate those efforts. Yet trying to get others to do what you want them to do, when you want them to do it, and in the way you want it done is the ever-changing challenge of a manager.

Great insight is required to understand why people behave the way they do. Although all managers have some basic ideas about human behavior as a result of their lifetime of experiences in living with and among other human beings, that storehouse of information is not usually sufficient to enable the manager to direct others at work effectively. Managers need additional concentration and formal study to prepare them for their "people responsibilities," enabling them to cope with the human element in their job.

When most of us finish our formal school-ing, we step into the business world in search of a job. We have acquired a certain knowledge, which we might call "technical" or "professional," and we are anxious to apply this knowledge in an organization. After searching, we are initially offered a job based on our technical skills and we are expected to apply our knowledge and skills in order to accomplish certain technical tasks.

Because we do our individual jobs well over the years, our bosses and/or organizations eventually reward us by promoting us to managerial or supervisory positions, thereby increasing our duties and responsibilities, giving us, we hope, more authority and more responsibility. As managers, we are now required to apply certain knowledge and skills not only to ourselves but also to other individuals who, in turn, are expected to apply their knowledge and skills to job tasks that we, the managers, direct and are responsible for in a collective form (i.e., productivity and profit).

RELATING AND REACTING TO PEOPLE

The transition from doer—a person who accomplishes tasks himself or herself—to manager—a person who accomplishes tasks through and with others, is typically a difficult one. New knowledge, skills, and attitudes are required for the functions of managing and how those functions can best be performed. To make this transition in an era of rapid change is an even more difficult task. If a manager is going to avoid eventual obsolescence, he or she must not only acquire an understanding of key management concepts and strategies but also must keep abreast of the emerging trends of tomorrow and what their impact will be on the management profession. It requires a person who can adapt and modify the knowledge and experiences of the past to fit the needs and demands of the future. It takes time, effort, and determination to become an effective manager. The challenges are great, the opportunities exciting, and the personal satisfactions and rewards unlimited.

Therefore, to be successful in moving from an individual employee to a managerial position requires a person to think like a manager, rather than like an employee, and this requires the following knowledge and skills:

1. *Knowledge of the job*—the technical and operational aspects of the job. Technical skills imply a body of knowledge applied to the specific skills required of a profession resulting in effective performance. A systems analyst, for example, would have a specialized body of knowledge, the ability to analyze related data, and the skill to use specialized equipment, methods, and techniques.

Our capabilities as good technical individual performers are still needed as managers. Actually, a good portion of the day requires the application of these technical and professional skills, particularly at the lower levels of management. However, the percentage of time spent doing things ourselves and having others do things seems to change as we climb the organizational ladder.

At the first level of management, a small percentage of the day is spent in directing the work of others (applying managerial knowledge and skills). The major portion of the day is spent doing the same, or similar, type or work as those being supervised. Consequently, the manager should possess those

technical and professional skills and know-how that relate directly to the work being performed. As a person moves into higher levels of management, more and more of the day is spent managing others. Thus, today's managers must learn how to better relate and react to the human resource, make decisions, and solve problems, because at this level managers rely less on their technical and professional skills and more on their managerial skills and competence.

It soon becomes obvious that the knowledge and skills we applied as individuals, called technical or professional skills, are different from the knowledge and skills we apply as managers. The knowledge and skills required of managers might be called managerial skills and include people and conceptual skills. Therefore, an additional body of knowledge and skills is required in management. In essence, doing the job yourself is different from trying to get others to work with you to get it done. Unfortunately, many managers do not recognize this basic fact. They continue to function in the same way they did as individual employees. When this happens, the organization loses a good individual performer and acquires a poor manager.

Most managers who fail do so not because of a lack of technical skills but due to a lack of people and conceptual skills. Most people are trained to carry out a particular technical skill, whether it be accounting, data processing, nursing, or engineering, and are hired by organizations to apply this skill in an entry-level capacity. A significant majority of these people prove to be individually capable and knowledgeable. The organization then rewards them by promoting them to managerial positions without providing them with proper people and conceptual skill training and development. It would appear that organizations generally assume that if a person can do a good job technically, he or she can also do a good job with people and conceptual skills. *Wrong!*

2. *Knowledge of people*—the ability to recognize why people behave the way they do; the ability to communicate, lead, and motivate people to get things done; and the ability to

develop teamwork and recognize the needs of team members. Indicators of this category of skills would be the ability to tactfully receive and check the accuracy and understanding of assignments; the ability to tactfully work out changes in assignments—such as more time, more workers, more equipment, or different methods if original assignments are unrealistic; the ability to assign tasks fairly and to cause employees to be committed to achieving work assignments; the ability to train employees to perform required tasks; the ability to motivate and lead employees to complete jobs as assigned; the ability to relate and communicate with employees in such a way that they feel satisfaction from the job; and the ability to keep other managers informed as requested. People skills are vital for earning the respect and allegiance necessary to cause employees to *want to work with*, not just for, the manager.

3. *Knowledge of leadership and decision-making practices* — making and assuming responsibility for decisions and the solving of problems—that is, possessing conceptual skills. These skills include the abilities to first identify and then solve problems and make decisions. Conceptual skills are vital because they represent the ability to think out a problem and develop a plan that will result in a decision on how best to solve it.

Leaders are expected to make decisions. If there is one universal mark of a leader, it is decision making. Sound leadership action requires a good grasp of the total situation. Most problems or decisions involve several related factors: workers' attitudes are conditioned by organizational environment, the manager's actions must take into account the superior's expectations, and staff and peer groups may also have an interest in the final decision that is made. When managers have conditioned themselves to be aware of the possible relevance of several or even all of these factors in a given situation, they have developed a broader vision that will lead to better decisions.

4. *Knowledge of self* — judging the effects of words, behavior, and attitudes on team members. Knowing yourself and understanding how and why you behave the way you do is a necessary first step toward improved relations with your employees and improved performance. This self-awareness and assessment is often called *intraview*.

In order for managers to effectively interact with employees in today's work environment it is imperative that they realize today's employees behave and perform differently than employees in past decades because of an ever-changing social and business environment. Managers must be adaptable and flexible enough to interact differently and effectively with these changing individual employee attitudes and behavior.

THE MANAGER AND TODAY'S CHANGING ENVIRONMENT

There is a growing awareness by effective managers that since culture and the external environment have such an important influence on the attitudes, values, and behavior of the individuals in an organization, and since these factors help determine the needs and drives of individuals, it is paramount that managers take them into consideration in carrying out the people skills of their management functions. Today, some trends are already shaping our ideas and strategies of managing people for the years ahead.

There are many changes occurring in our business and social environments, both on a national and an international basis, that will have an impact on both current and future managers and their employees. All around us we hear about the rapidly accelerating rate, complexity, and intensity of change. The time lag between technical discovery and application for commercial use has been reduced sharply in recent years. For example, the silicon chip developed for computers in the 1960s can now be found in many consumer products—from microwave ovens to calculators and personal computers; from toys to cars. More new knowledge in technology has been developed since the 1970s than in any other time period.

An increasing interdependence of government, business, and education has developed. Events in one part of the world now have increasing impact on people in other parts of the world. Rapid, unexpected events are occurring in all phases of our society, creating turbulence and uncertainty. We see this in our companies, our schools, our churches, our governments, and our labor unions. We also frequently hear reference to "revolution"—technological change, civil rights, women's rights, gay rights, moral and ethical obligations, and the social responsibility of organizations.

Another factor influencing today's environment for the manager is the trend toward large-scale, complex multinational companies. Bigness, on a worldwide basis, seems to be part of the future.

More and more time, money, and energy are being directed toward the solution of people problems such as unemployment, discrimination, welfare, crime, drug and alcohol abuse, and mental health disorders. Also, greater attention is being paid to chemical and nuclear waste disposal, pollution, conservation of resources, and locating new sources of energy, resulting in the growth of both business and government operations to deal with these issues.

Also affecting the environment in which organizations and individual managers must function is the reversal of roles between management and labor. In many parts of the business world, management is now viewed as the proponent of change, especially with regard to technology (i.e., robotics), whereas labor is seen as the champion of the status quo, focused on the job security of its union members.

There is a steadily rising level of education in our society and in the work force. Many more college graduates compete for the same positions formerly filled by high school graduates. The trend toward continuing education is the result of rapid technological change, which requires those in the work force to be updated in their fields. Technology is also responsible for diverse new fields of endeavor.

Equal opportunities for minorities are a result of social consciousness and awareness, group pressures, and many other factors.

These changes have resulted in five key values that affect the behavior of many of today's employees:

1. *Changing attitudes regarding work and leisure*—There has been a steady increase in the number of days off negotiated in collective bargaining agreements since the 1970s. For example, today's agreements provide for more paid holidays; two-week vacations are often granted to employees with three years or less seniority; sick days have increased from one or two per year to ten or more in some organizations.

2. *Revolt against conformity*—Organizations that once had a policy against nepotism now have husbands and wives working for them. The increase in both married partners working outside the home has resulted in a call for on-site day-care centers. Another example of the revolt against conformity is that workers are less likely to be "good soldiers"; for example, more and more employees are refusing to transfer to small-town plants and operations from the friendly confines of corporate headquarters.

3. *Desire for more involvement*—The growth of organizational activities, many of which have strong union support and involvement, has skyrocketed; for example, flextime, quality of work life programs, and employee awards.

4. *Commitment to themselves rather than the organization and job*—More complex and intangible is the refusal of today's employees to subordinate their personality and loyalty to the work role. One of the most striking characteristics of the old value system was the tendency for people to identify themselves with their work role by saying, "I am a production foreman," "I am assistant manager of the local bank," and so on. In the new value system, the individual says, in effect, "I am more than my role. I am myself." Today's employees demand that their individuality be recognized.

5. *Higher levels of wants and needs*—An increasing number of people see little or no virtue in holding jobs that they consider menial or unpleasant, and the millions who do hold paid jobs find the present incentive system so

unappealing that they are no longer motivated to work hard. As a consequence, not only do they withdraw emotional involvement from the job but they also insist, as evidenced by recently negotiated collective bargaining agreements, on steady increases in pay, job security, and fringe benefits to compensate for the job's lack of appeal. The less they give to the job, the more they seem to demand—a process that cannot continue for long without breaking down. This deep flaw in the incentive system, signified by the failure of the old incentives to catch up with the new motivations, leads to deterioration in the workplace, threatening the position of the United States as the world's foremost industrial nation. In the future it will only become harder to motivate people. Today, many workers have already sampled material benefits (e.g., cars, televisions) before age thirty-five.

CHANGING EMPLOYEE ATTITUDES, VALUES, AND WORK BEHAVIOR

People do not adopt new attitudes, values, and work behaviors and discard old ones without serious thought. There are many ways of achieving these goals, but the major method is the application of incentives and motivational techniques as stimuli to increase individual and collective output.

An organization's productive capacity is a result of many factors such as machines and materials, but these are inanimate objects. They are translated into productivity only when the human element (an animate object) is introduced. However, the human element interjects a variable into the productive scheme over which management has only limited control. This human quality gives rise to what is probably management's greatest problem—motivation. Individual and group performance behavior depends on the ability, skills, and motivation of the individual or group.

The productivity of employees is an indication of the success or failure of management efforts. Motivating employees is one of the

very important human skills that a manager must develop to be successful. No matter how hard you work, or how organized you are personally, if your employees do not accomplish what they are expected to do, you will not be a successful manager.

Conditions and Consequences

Often attitudes and values can be changed by altering conditions and consequences. Most people have trouble recalling exactly how they developed many of their attitudes and values. For example, if you love music but hate mathematics, can you pinpoint when you began to feel this way? Thus, the conditions that surround a subject and the consequences associated with it are of major importance in forming your attitudes and values.

These findings are not limited to any one field. Conditions and consequences also shape attitudes and values in the business community. Managers, supervisors, and anyone else involved in shaping attitudes and values should keep this simple rule in mind. Whenever an experience is followed by positive consequences, it is more likely to be repeated in the future. If you want people to arrive for work on time, reward this behavior in some way. If operating expenses are too high, look for ways to encourage workers to cut costs and reward those who manage to reduce expenses. As a rule, people will not deliberately do things that bring about negative consequences for themselves. Many opportunities for the manager to apply these basic principles of reinforcement arise every day in the workplace.

Organizations are becoming more aware of the impact of negative consequences on worker attitudes and values. Many organizations are taking steps to reduce boredom, physical discomfort, frustration, and anxiety. The major goal of job enrichment, for example, is to identify ways that the scope of the job can be improved. Job enrichment may involve something as simple as giving the receptionist responsibility for ordering supplies, or it may mean redesigning an assembly line to provide production workers with more challenging and interesting work experiences. Many jobs, though quite specialized, can be redesigned so the worker performs less routine tasks.

Role Modeling

Role modeling provides a second way to change attitudes, values, and work behavior. The term *role* comes from the field of sociology. It is defined as a pattern of behavior expected of a person in activities involving others. Each role calls for a different type of behavior. When you want to learn how to behave in an unfamiliar situation, you usually turn to role models. Think about your first job. How did you determine correct behavior? Very likely you watched to see what others did and then imitated their actions. People tend to learn by imitation.

In the work environment an employee may have several role models. The new machinist in the factory may look at the department supervisor, the union steward, and a highly skilled senior employee for clues about correct and incorrect behavior. In an organizational setting, role models can have considerable influence on employee attitude development.

Of course, management personnel have the greatest impact on employee attitudes and values. The manager's attitudes and values toward safety, cost control, accuracy, dress and grooming, customer relations, and the like become the model for subordinates. Generally, employees will pay more attention to what the boss does and says. If managers want to shape employee attitudes and values, they must set the example and demonstrate the kind of behavior they want others to develop. This is known as the reflective technique of management.

Self-Awareness and the Importance of Feedback

A key stage of personal growth is self-awareness, meaning the individual understands the basic "self" who thinks and feels. Increased self-awareness helps individuals discover the barriers they have in getting along with other people. When they discover that something they do bothers someone else, they have the option of changing their behavior. To see themselves as others see them can set the stage for improving their interpersonal relations.

One key to changing attitudes, values, and work behavior is often feedback. Feedback is information that helps a person develop greater self-awareness. For a manager who must deal with an employee's bad attitude, the most appropriate time for changing that bad attitude and providing feedback and self-awareness is during the performance evaluation.

Performance standards are statements of the results that will exist when the job is satisfactorily performed. They are important because they establish an ideal target considered to be desirable and attainable, and they help the manager and employee understand one another. There are three basic steps for developing an effective standard:

1. List all the essential areas of responsibilities as noted in the job description. Be sure there is agreement.
2. Frame each area of responsibility with a statement of standard with these key words: "Performance will be up to standard when . . ."
3. Complete the above statement. This will lead you to look at the elements and begin asking questions related to proper performance.

Although you will have the final say regarding a standard, it can be very revealing to have employees write their own because it gives you additional insight into the employees' understanding of the job and it helps employees think through their responsibilities from statements on a job description to results.

Remember, for a standard to be effective, it must be realistic. Standards should be written and rewritten until they do the proper job of appraising people's performance. One way to accomplish this is to consider more than one specific standard for each job responsibility. You sometimes hear standards cannot be established for some kinds of jobs because the jobs are too unstructured. While this may be true, you must ask yourself, "If no standard can be developed, is any work being done?"

Work must end in accomplishment, so if there is a job, you should be able to establish a standard and a suitable measure. In every real sense, writing the standard is a test of the validity of the job and organizational structure.

Finally, standards should be worded carefully to avoid misunderstanding. They should stress facts, figures, times, and dates. Quantitative measures are much better than qualitative measures. Avoid words like adequate, approximate, as soon as possible, and reasonable. Be specific! Both the manager and employee should be able to answer the three basic performance questions: (1) Did the subordinate do all the jobs he or she was required to do? (2) Did he or she do them up to standard? (3) Did he or she do them above/below standard?

SUMMARY

Managing cannot be considered in a vacuum or as a function of a few variables. It is too complex a process. For this reason, it is impossible to conclusively say that particular methods and/or techniques should be implemented by managers. What works successfully for managers in one organization or situation could bring disastrous results if applied by managers in another organization or situation. Management methods and techniques must be designed and tailored to fit the individual manager, the organization, the work group, peers, the boss, and the situation. Therefore, most importantly, *the manager must be adaptable and flexible.*

HUMAN RESOURCES PLANNING IN THE 1990S

John A. Passante, Senior Vice-President, Human Resources, Moog Automotive, Inc.

EMPLOYMENT TRENDS

One does not need to be a human resources professional to be aware of the tremendous labor shortage that is occurring in the United States. "Workforce 2000," a study that was published in 1987 by the Hudson Group and sponsored by the U.S. Department of Labor, warned us of the serious consequences for society and the economy of certain critical trends and their implications. Some of those trends are:

1. There will be slow growth in population and the labor force through the year 2000.
2. The pool of young workers entering the labor market will shrink.
3. The proportion of the youth labor force that is minority will increase greatly.
4. The average age of the work force will rise.
5. More women will enter the work force.
6. Immigrants will represent the largest share of increase in population and in the work force since World War I.

7. Jobs will continue to shift from goods-producing industries to the service sector.
8. Many new and existing jobs will require higher levels of analytical skills.
9. Work force diversity will force companies to find new ways to manage their employees by encouraging open and honest communications among work groups.

WHO SELECTS WHOM?

A shortage of qualified candidates requires creative and innovative ways of recruiting and retaining your most important assets—people. The days are over when the world beat a path to your personnel department—it is not even called that anymore. Today's candidate is just as particular about where and for whom he or she works as today's company is about selecting the best candidate. In today's interview, it is the candidate who is asking the questions—questions such as: "Is the company environmentally responsible?" "Are employees on work teams?" "Does the company offer tuition reimbursement for employees?" "How many female managers are on staff?" "Is day care available?" "What is the five-year outlook for this company?" "Does the company recognize the diversity of its work force and encourage open discussion of issues?" "What are the chances for advancement?"

Succession Planning

The human resource planning process should rely heavily on a carefully developed succession planning program. We as professional managers must concentrate not only on the hiring needs of today—although they are important—but also on our future needs. For every key position/person in an organization, another person should be identified as a successor, and plans should be made toward the developmental process of that person.

Because the domino effect may no doubt cause other openings when key individuals move up in the organization, we need to be aware of where entry-level people are and how we can attract them to our organization. Since the pool of young workers entering the job market is shrinking, there will be fewer individuals available with the skills we need to fill our openings. Organizations will continue to become more specialized. Therefore, perhaps the time has come to rethink when the recruiting process should begin. Perhaps we should begin much earlier, such as before college graduation.

By communicating to a young audience the kinds of skills an organization needs, it is much more likely that potential applicants will have those skills at the time of hire. Human resources professionals could save themselves a lot of recruiting headaches if they would enter into partnerships with local high schools and seek out potential candidates at that level for future hiring needs. By developing partnerships with these schools, high school students can be exposed to the business environment through cooperative education programs. These coop experiences could continue through college through internship programs. By graduation, the organization then has an employee who can do a job and is comfortable with the organization's culture.

Classified Advertisements

Recruiting ads are larger and more descriptive, include graphic aids, and are sometimes even colorful. They must compete with a plethora of position descriptions from numerous companies competing for job applicants. Companies may do well to connect with a professional advertising company that can design and develop an advertising campaign that builds on a consistent theme throughout all recruiting materials.

Just as important as how your ads look is knowing your particular market and which publications on a local level will serve you best. While your weekly newspapers are often the best place to include your classified advertisements, other publications such as college/university newsletters, trade journal publications, and professional organizations' magazines are excellent resources.

Interviews

Interviewers should know exactly what kinds of skills are essential for the job. This requires interaction with the hiring manager. The interviewer should know (1) the most important duties and responsibilities; (2) any key involvement with superiors, subordinates, and customers; (3) potential sources of satisfaction; and (4) career opportunities.

Human resources planners should fill jobs considering three categories of factors:

1. *Can do factors*—What specific experiences, skills, equipment knowledge, abilities, prior training or education, and physical requirements are necessary or desired for successful job performance?
2. *Will do factors*—What specific behaviors are required or desired in order to be sure that individuals will apply themselves and behave in ways that are associated with success on the job?
3. *Fit factors*—Will the person fit into the specific environmental circumstances of the job? Include information about the type of industry or business atmosphere of your organization, the circumstances of work at department or area level, and the circumstances of the specific job.

The interview itself can be a source of problems. Common errors are:

1. *Talking too much*—As an interviewer, you should only be talking 10 to 20 percent of the time.
2. *Jumping to conclusions*—Do not allow cursory observations to influence your decision.
3. *Not using an organized approach*—A different approach for each interview makes it impossible to measure one candidate against another.

In the time span of thirty-five minutes or less, interviewers should be able to cover work experience, education, activities and interests, self-assessment, as well as giving information and concluding the interview.

THE CHANGING WORK FORCE

Part-Time Employees

One of the fastest-growing trends of the work force is the permanent, part-time worker who, in many cases, has replaced one employed by an outside agency. Many companies are find-

ing that by creating their own in-house temporary staff, they can use these employees to cover emergency staffing needs at a much reduced cost. The company can devote many hours of training to these individuals to prepare them for the variety of assignments that may occur in a peak period or emergency situation. This investment will serve the company well, since each one is already a part of the organization and is much more prepared than the average agency "temp."

Temporary part-time employees may also be used for a specific period of time—perhaps over the winter holidays or during the summer—when the duration of work assignments is limited. High school and college students are excellent sources of seasonal labor, and the experience they gain from these types of internships is immeasurable.

Retaining Older Workers

Our nation is graying. By the year 2010, half of the work force will be age forty or over. We must do everything we can to retain older workers. Instead of forcing retirement, we must look at offering incentives to keep people working longer. Gradual retirement programs allow older employees to slowly move from full-time work situations to part-time. Rehearsal retirement programs give older workers the opportunity to try out their newfound retirement and the chance to come back to work if they discover that retirement is not for them. When they return, many companies offer a list of available jobs from which these former retirees can choose what they would like to do.

Women in the Work Force

Two out of three jobs are filled by a woman and one in three families is headed by a woman. Yet there is a disparate ratio of female managers to male managers. It is not enough to recruit women in the work force. It is equally important to help them succeed. The formation of women networks and information-sharing meetings is critical in providing them with pertinent business data, such as planning, development, and company performance. The sponsorship of mentoring career development programs that focus on goals, opportunities, expectations, standards, and pressure to fulfill one's potential is also a key to the success of female leadership programs.

NEW EMPLOYEE ORIENTATION AND FOLLOW-UP

Once the candidate has joined the company, he or she should participate in a formal orientation program. This program may be carried out on an individual basis or in a group setting. The purpose of this orientation is to (1) present an overall picture of the company and its products; (2) provide information on specific benefits; (3) introduce the new employee to key management staff as well as other new employees; (4) provide an opportunity to ask questions; and (5) tour the facility.

A typical orientation format is shown in Exhibit 4-1.

Approximately thirty to ninety days after the new employee has joined the company, the human resources department might consider sending each manager of a new employee a feedback form that asks questions, such as:

1. Is the employee aware of organizational and departmental goals?
2. Has the employee been given the mission statement for his or her particular department?
3. Have personal goals been set for the employee?
4. Does the employee understand the company's system for performance appraisal?
5. Has the employee experienced any difficulties so far in the employment period? If yes, please discuss.

This form can then include a number of open-ended questions that encourage a personal interaction between the manager and employee. The form can also provide for remarks by the employee. It is then signed by both parties and forwarded to the human resources department where a manager reviews the form to screen for potential problems before including it in the employee's personnel file.

Exhibit 4-1. Typical Orientation

15 minutes	Network with all new employees and staff members
10 minutes	President/CEO addresses group; discusses mission of the company and corporate philosophy
15 minutes	Human resources executive addresses group; explains major programs including performance appraisal system; discusses organization chart
10 minutes	Human resources manager explains benefit programs; employee handbook
10 minutes	Company history shown on videotape
10 minutes	Sales department overview
10 minutes	Engineering department overview
10 minutes	Financial department overview
10 minutes	Systems overview
10 minutes	Tour of office and manufacturing facility

Performance planning and review is a process that fosters initiative, encourages imagination, and develops a sense of responsibility to achieve results. Through concentrating on observable and measurable elements of on-the-job behavior, the process allows a supervisor and employee to resolve such questions as:

1. How am I doing?
2. What can I do differently or better?
3. Where can I go from here?

Most companies conduct some form of formal annual appraisal that is completed around the same time each year. No matter what type of appraisal you use, it is always a good idea to train all employees in your particular form and explain how it works within your organization. One reason for training all employees in the particular system being used is to ensure the consistent application of the rating system by all participants.

While completing the form usually occurs once a year, it is advisable to include an informal quarterly goal review process so that performance appraisal is ongoing, forces open communication between manager and employee, surfaces problems quickly (within three months) before they become insurmountable, and allows for new goals to replace ones that have been met or that are no longer being pursued for one reason or another.

PERSONNEL SELECTION AND PSYCHOLOGICAL ASSESSMENT

Michael Merbaum, Professor of Psychology, Washington University-St. Louis, and Hazelwood Farms Bakeries, Inc.

In future decades professionally sophisticated personnel selection will play a more conspicuous role in the hiring and development of personnel than is currently the case. Greater attention to rigorous selection procedures is prompted by a number of practical contingencies. In the United States as well as other Western economies the value of the educated, literate worker has escalated sharply and, for companies to be successful in this competitive marketplace, the advantage in attracting these assets is formidable. While this fact represents an economic reality, it is complicated by the pressing social challenges emerging from demographic trends within our increasingly heterogeneous society. Most significant is an increase in the number of women and culturally diverse group members entering the work force along with the large-scale aging of our population.

Concurrently, substantive concerns have recently been expressed about the educational preparation of prospective employees in mastering a high-tech business environment. The probable shortage in the number of well-educated labor to handle new and complex technological innovations is receiving special attention from social planners. From the perspective of forward-thinking companies the success in identifying people with the requisite intellectual aptitudes and social emotional skills is a high-priority assignment. Unquestionably, the substantial costs incurred in time and money during the initial hiring process and the eventual responsibilities for salary, benefits, and ancillary social emotional expenses for both parties require that optimum judgment be exercised at the front end of selection to identify and attract the best talent available. Finding the "right person for the right job" is for all organizations an admirably attractive cliche.

Despite a keen awareness of the value of a well-articulated personnel assessment program, most managers are either uninformed or naive about the available tools, theories, and empirical data that might enhance the accuracy of their assessment decisions. What contemporary personnel selection and psychological assessment have to offer is a sensible balance between subjective, gut-feeling impressions and methodologies that incorporate supplementary objective data into the decision-making equation. Working in close collaboration with managers, psychologists with experience in industry are now able to offer a variety of psychological tools and perspectives that can extend the range of information about an applicant's assets and liabilities in handling various job functions.

For many years, clinical and organizational psychologists have served business groups in a variety of areas. The selection function has been particularly auspicious because of the specialized training in test theory and test development that is a unique feature of the psychologist's formal education. However, familiarity with interviewing, testing, and group theory, and other industry-related skills are not the only attributes needed by the psychologist to make a tangible contribution to the business environment. For the psychologist to be truly useful in an assessment role a number of qualitative factors should be present. Most relevant is an understanding of basic business operations and, through job analysis procedures, an awareness of the range of skills required to fulfill different position requirements. Furthermore, the psychological expert should have an intimate knowledge of the needs of an organization, sensitivity to its eccentricities, and a feeling for the business culture of the organization being serviced. Thus, the skillful psychologist must be part artist, technician, clinician, and scholar who is adept in extracting information, processing it cogently, communicating it clearly, and possessing sufficient credibility to be taken seriously. Without credibility within the organization, the psychologist will have little impact no matter how incisive or clever the contribution may actually be.

Personnel selection and psychological assessment is a decision-making process naturally embedded within our ongoing social experience. Assessment is a euphemism for problem solving and requires the acquisition of relevant information that will directly increase the probability of making a valid choice. Assessment technology like any other enterprise is dependent on the efficiency of its tools. In the main, industry assessment is composed of two basic tool categories. The first set consists of common methods traditionally preferred by business organizations in the evaluation of new hires. These procedures include application forms, resumes, letters of intent, reference letters or reference conversations, and interviews. Occasionally, work samples are also requested. Other tools, defined as psychological tests, and assessment centers are more specialized and require the professional expertise of psychologists who are trained in their use and are familiar with their theoretical and empirical foundations.

LETTERS OF INTEREST AND RESUMES

The initial stage of selection invariably involves a letter of interest in a job or an indication of general availability. This letter may be accompanied by a resume describing background, interests, educational achievement, and other details that might catch the eye of the reader. The company assessor should obviously be consciously aware of these realities and approach the evaluation of this material from two perspectives.

1. *Content of the material*—Are the educational accomplishments and experience factors relevant to the general job specifications?
2. *Judgment*—Has the applicant used the kind of judgment in selecting the introduction format, letter style, and resume style that suggests good self-discipline and relevant problem solving?

In addition, the manager who appraises these materials should be sensitive to his or her prejudices often activated by cues contained in the personal data shared by potential job candidates. Research suggests that selection preferences are consciously or un-consciously influenced by ethnic back-ground, age, gender, socioeconomic status, geographic place of origin, and other legally unsupportable variables that have been shown to have little relevance to effective job performance. A nondefensive attitude about preferences is the first step in countering biases that may in fact sharply reduce assess-ment accuracy.

REFERENCE CHECKING

Reference checking is much like deciphering a coded message. The facility to read between the lines of reference conversations and letters is a uniquely challenging effort. The following considerations apply when weighing the value of reference observations.

Applicants will invariably select references who should predictably furnish positive re-views. This behavior is both functional and sensible. An issue that should be addressed in assessing the actual worth of reference ma-terial is the degree of accuracy that might be legitimately expected. Frequently, the man-ager who receives reference information has insufficient details both about the character of the relationship between the candidate and the reference and the real qualifications of the reference to provide an objective view of the candidate's assets. This issue arises whether the reference content is positive or negative. Thus, the degree of trust in the competency of the reference to make a skilled appraisal must be carefully confronted. To increase va-lidity, more than one reference should be con-tacted. Attention to the consistency of evalua-tion is critical in using reference observations practically. Without consistency, the assessor is in the precarious position of trying to sort out a plethora of conflicting impressions.

Finally, our society is litigiously sensitive. In this light, references may be notoriously restrained in candor because of legal concerns about defamation of character. Thus, figur-ingout the subtle meaning of carefully shared personal descriptions is a challenging assign-ment for the company assessor.

INTERVIEWING

The interview is the most popular and widely used assessment technique. Interviews are our most natural and convenient medium for social communication. Not without good rea-son it is believed that by sharing ideas and feelings we are able to learn important details about our conversational partner and in the process gain personal familiarity. The inter-view is an experience that on the surface facil-itates a sense of emotional intimacy. Within this interaction each member of the dyad can see, hear, and touch the other, thereby receiv-ing direct sensory data about many qualities we intuitively and intellectually value. It is not surprising therefore that the interview is regarded by both the candidate and company assessor as a logically compelling vehicle for information gathering.

Research data evaluating the interview as a viable selection procedure are largely incon-clusive. Unfortunately, there is a noticeable lack of predictive validity in estimating effec-tive performance based exclusively on inter-view data. Why should this be the case? While one of the apparent strengths of the interview is its sense of convenient intimacy, this subjec-tivity is also frequently its undoing. Research emphatically intimates that the interview is an easy arena for stereotyping, bias, and prej-udice. As a consequence, interviewers are often overly responsive to personal character-istics that may be unrelated to the criteria of competence in work settings. Nonetheless, employers continue to base most of their impressions of value on how a person comes across during the initial job interview.

Psychologists consulting in industry have been active in devising more valid strategies so that the interview as an assessment tool has greater predictive efficacy. To counter this effort, most out-placement firms, business schools, and tutorial texts are sophisticated in cleverly teaching applicants how to interview better. The question of course is whether the enhancement of interviewing skills of appli-cants is correlated with future success in the business world. The evidence for this relation-ship is likely to be unconvincing.

PSYCHOLOGICAL TESTING

The introduction of tests in our society to establish credentials, to enter educational institutions, to gain admittance to remedial programs, to evaluate learning performance in schools, and to offer insights about the skill to perform certain jobs in industry is so ingrained that arguments against testing serve more as a conscience against their misuse than as a deterrence to their use. In the main, psychological testing when applied in industry is an attempt to introduce an objective methodology to help clarify a qualitatively subjective decision-making event.

Two major guidelines should apply when psychological testing is used as a component of meaningful decision making:

1. The criteria for making a relevant decision should be as clearly established as possible. For example, a highly skilled accountant should possess effective numerical skills or a competent manager should, among other virtues, display flexible social judgment.

2. The structure and content of the test should meet acceptable psychometric rigors of reliability, validity, and appropriate standardization of administration procedures. The test should have normative data available on groups relevant to those being targeted for assessment. A most important condition is that the test development data should be public and available for careful professional scrutiny.

Psychological tests generally fall into a number of categories:

1. Cognitive ability or aptitude tests focus on capacity to learn or perform a job that has been learned. The popular intelligence tests are found in this group and measure facets of verbal and numerical reasoning and even visual-motor performance skills. Other aptitude tests highlight specific proficiencies in, for example, spatial, musical, and perceptual domains.

2. Psychomotor ability tests measure coordination, strength, dexterity, and a variety of discrete functions such as finger dexterity, manual dexterity, and arm movement speed.

3. Other classes of tests evaluate job knowl-

edge in designated functions such as welding, carpentry, electrical, and other trades. Questions are designed to differentiate between experience levels and are particularly useful in identifying the basic sophistication of the applicant.

4. Vocational interest tests are given when there is a lack of clarity about occupational direction. These tests focus on social preferences, personal interests, and value satisfactions that are statistically correlated with vocational attraction. Usually, the testee's responses are compared to the responses of professionals who have indicated success in their work. Similarity between these sets of responses suggest that the testee might seriously consider the same occupational group for employment.

5. Work sample tests are also frequently used by companies who are looking for "face valid" indicators of performance that are highly job focused. Typing, filing, clerical speed, and precision tests are the most obvious examples.

6. Personality tests are also especially popular because they are touted as a vehicle for the identification of personal traits and social tendencies. It is assumed that for many industry positions certain personality qualities may facilitate or impair job success.

7. Honesty assessment tests claim to offer data bearing on such common industrial concerns as application and resume falsification, drug abuse, criminal activity, and the potential for employee theft. Undeniably the direct and indirect costs incurred from illegal behavior of employees is substantial, and any economical steps to reduce financial and social injury in these areas is welcome indeed. In the past, employers frequently used polygraphs or lie detectors to identify risky employees or ones actually accused of infractions. With federal restrictions on the use of polygraphs the interest has shifted to "honesty" as a valid replacement.

These pencil and paper polygraphs are often based on strict definitions of honesty that are frequently anchored in the admission of prior transgressions. Thus, if a job applicant admits to performing an infraction or expresses a set of values that condone cheating, lying, stealing, or any number of dishonest acts, the risky employee label would be applied. It is assumed by the test that admission of these attitudes is correlated with the future performance of illegal acts. Aside from basic problems in defining the construct of "honesty" and the equally critical fact that these tests usually have only a modest relationship with overall work competence, their usefulness in the workplace is ambiguous at best.

There are literally thousands of psychological tests in the marketplace. Psychological testing is big business and many testing services and publishing houses naturally vie for a substantial piece of the expanding economic market. The industrial consumer of testing is frequently exposed to a bewildering array of extravagant claims that can be confusing and enticing at the same time. The admonition "let the buyer beware" is as appropriate a warning for testing products as any other commercial item.

The appropriate use of testing requires professional expertise. Reliance on a clinical or industrial psychologist is therefore advisable to ensure that the most valid test tools have been selected, to protect the company against legal action in which it is claimed that the rights of job applicants have been violated, and to be in compliance with Equal Employment Opportunity Commission guidelines.

MANAGING THE DIVERSE WORK FORCE

Susan L. Pedigo, Managing Editor, *The Wyatt Communicator*

Through most of the first half of the twentieth century the work force in America was fairly homogeneous—white males held the majority of jobs in management, the general work force, and the trades. Since the 1950s, the composition of the work force has been changing and will change even more dramatically as we move toward the twenty-first century. The work force is becoming more diverse and more heterogeneous.

DEMOGRAPHIC AND ECONOMIC TRENDS

In June 1987, "Workforce 2000" documented the major changes occurring in the American work force. This study highlighted demographic and economic trends that will affect business over the next twenty years and beyond:

1. The work force is growing more slowly and is getting older. Projections indicate that overall population growth in the United States will fall to only 0.7 percent in the year 2000. While labor force growth does not exactly parallel population growth, the decrease in population growth will have a definite impact on the size of the labor force. U.S. Bureau of Labor Statistics figures estimate labor force growth will slow to a low of only 1 percent annually by the year 2000.

The average age of the work force is also rising. In 1987, the average age of the work force was thirty-six. It will rise to thirty-nine by the year 2000 and forty-one in the year 2020. At the same time, the number of young workers (ages sixteen to twenty-four) entering the work force will decline by approximately 8 percent, or two million workers, between 1987 and 2000.

2. Women will continue to enter the work force in increasing numbers. Almost two thirds of all the new entrants to the work force between 1987 and 2000 will be women, which means that 60 percent of all women will be working.

3. The proportion of minority and immigrant workers will increase. According to the Bureau of Labor Statistics, minorities and immigrants will hold 26 percent of all jobs in the year 2000.

4. The new jobs that will be created will require much higher skill levels than the jobs of today. As technology expands into all areas of business, the jobs that will be created will demand literacy, mathematical competence, and the ability to reason through problems. This will affect all jobs—from the production line to the CEO's office.

These demographic and economic realities create challenges for the management of the emerging work force and its environment. Frequently these challenges are thrown to the human resources function for solution. How can the modern human resources professional meet these challenges? There is no single solution but some practical ideas can be useful in developing strategies for meeting the challenges of a diverse work force.

For a very long time, management meant melting the members of a fairly homogeneous work force into a cohesive group. Those members who were different due to race or sex were a small minority and could be convinced to conform to the overall practices and policies of the larger whole.

Today, the different workers are becoming the majority. Asking these different workers to suppress their cultural and sexual differences to a single norm—usually the white male norm—will no longer work. The goal will become not to subordinate individual values and experiences to a single norm but to utilize these individual values and experiences to expand and enhance the whole. This means changing the longstanding theory of the "melting pot" where every worker adapts to fit into a similar mold to a theory of "valuing diversity" where business can understand and utilize the variety of backgrounds, skills, and experiences that workers bring to the workplace.

EXAMINING THE CORPORATE CULTURE

Begin managing a diverse work force by examining your organizational culture. Examine the principles that govern the organization; identify the skills and behaviors that are valued and rewarded within the organization. Each organization is different: Each takes its culture from a combination of business goals and the personalities and philosophies of its leaders.

Whatever the corporate culture, some adjustments will probably be necessary to manage a diverse work force. Cultures that foster individuality will need to expand these efforts. Cultures that establish rigid norms for performance will need to build in more flexibility. Cultures that rest on the values of a few senior executives will need to expand their horizons to encompass different backgrounds and experiences.

EXPANDING RECRUITMENT EFFORTS AND DIVERSITY

Organizations that hire large numbers of workers are already finding increased competition for competent and willing employees. Restricting recruitment efforts to the most traditional labor pools—white high school and college graduates—will bring organizations up short. There are simply not enough of these young people to go around. Increasingly, organizations must look to other sources for employees—minority and immigrant communities, older workers, and the disabled.

Successfully reaching the different pools of potential workers may be as simple as placing an ad in the local newspaper's "Help Wanted" section. Or, it may mean trying new strategies—advertising in neighborhood and ethnic media, establishing recruitment offices in community and recreation centers, working with civic groups and shelters.

Once an organization begins hiring diverse workers, the potential for these workers being productive will depend on the climate within the organization itself. Helping the managers—many of whom will themselves be minorities, immigrants, and women—to both recognize and value diversity will foster productivity. This calls into question the traditional "melting pot" image of fairness: of treating all employees exactly the same. A more modern image of fairness is one that recognizes the differences in workers' backgrounds, experience, education, and cultural heritage and accommodates these differences. Practicing this broader image of fairness requires both training and support for managers.

Training courses can help managers explore differences, both their own and those of their workers, and to begin to understand how to recognize, value, and fairly accommodate the differences individuals bring to the workplace. Managers can share and analyze their own personal experiences managing employees from different cultures or races. For example, a manager might describe her use of different development plans for two new employees. For one, a young white male, she might focus on the technical aspects of the job and let the employee use his past experiences in school and sports to establish relationships. For the other, a young Asian woman, knowing the employee's technical base is strong, she may coach the employee on establishing strong relations and negotiating with her peers.

EVALUATING SYSTEMS

Training managers is just one of the ways an organization fosters an appreciation of diversity. A variety of formal and informal systems exist throughout every organization—performance appraisal, compensation, promotional ladders, mentoring or sponsorship programs —that can support or hinder a productive and diverse work force. If the systems are a roadblock, then modification may be necessary. For example, if your organization says it supports a workplace that builds on diverse backgrounds and knowledge but your performance appraisal system measures all workers' performance based on the same criteria, your system may be a roadblock that sends the wrong message about what is truly valued. Changing the system to recognize and measure different experiences, knowledge, and skills will more effectively support the organization's stated goals and values. Adding a dimension to your performance appraisal system that holds managers accountable for encouraging an understanding of diversity in the work force will send an equally strong message to your employees.

Promotional and compensation systems can also have an impact on successful management of a diverse work force. Such systems that continue to reward a narrow range of behaviors or skills will tell employees that if they want to get ahead or make more money they must conform. They can suppress new ideas and perspectives that could give your organization a competitive edge. Modify these systems by expanding the criteria used to identify individuals for promotion or for granting a salary increase.

Another key system within your organization is benefits. When the work force was composed mainly of married men with wives who did not work outside the home, it made sense to offer a standard package of health and life insurance, retirement, and vacation benefits. One program satisfied the needs of the majority of workers. However, today it is unlikely that one package of benefits will effectively meet the needs of most of your workers. Many organizations are turning to flexible benefits to provide a number of choices for employees in the type and depth of coverage they need for health care.

Allowing for flexible work schedules or work from home is another way of accommodating the needs of workers with very different home situations. Providing this type of option may mean jobs need to be restructured to facilitate part-time workers, job sharing, or a reduction of direct supervision.

TRAINING AND RETRAINING WORKERS

The commitment to training workers must begin at the time of hire. One study estimated that between 50 and 60 percent of new hires leave their jobs within the first seven months. A well-designed orientation program can help ease the transition of the new worker into your organization and increase the chances that the new worker will stay.

As organizations hire an increasingly diverse work force, they will find a greater variation in new worker skills. Providing training opportunities for both basic office skills and English-language and reading skills may become an economic necessity for organizations to retain workers and make them productive.

The workplace changes quickly. New technologies bring new machines, systems, or procedures. Increasing automation brings with it the need for workers to have computer literacy and higher levels of mathematical and problem-solving skills to be effective. Even workers at very high levels of education require ongoing training to remain current in their fields and to master new technologies.

As workers stay with an organization, they move into positions with more responsibility requiring ongoing training in management principles and techniques to remain productive. On-the-job training, sponsoring, and mentoring programs where newly promoted workers are paired with more experienced workers, or a series of management training workshops, are just a few ways to provide this type of training.

MANAGING THE OLDER WORKER

Older workers can be a valuable resource for many organizations. In general, they have a wealth of experiences and skills, tend to be very stable and dependable, and may have more loyalty to the organization than younger workers. Older workers may also be less willing to change or may have physical limitations. How can an organization best utilize the older worker? Most basic principles of good management apply to the older worker, but there are a few additional guidelines that may be helpful.

Match worker capabilities and experience to the job. Place older workers in jobs that they can handle physically. If operating machinery is part of the older worker's job, be sure that instructions are close at hand and easy to read. Consider printing instructions in bold type that can be seen easily even in soft lighting. Some older workers may not have the stamina to perform at high levels for long periods of time. Consider using older workers in part-time positions or floating positions where they can pace themselves for greatest efficiency.

Provide regular information about jobs and performance. Most older workers will be primarily interested in job security. They will usually want more information about their current position, expectations for their position, and readings on performance than their younger counterparts. Managers must be frank and honest about worker performance—recognition of good performance can strengthen loyalty and motivate the worker to bring even more effort to the job and honest evaluation of poor performance and planning for improvement can bring the worker up to standards.

Adapt training to older workers' needs. Training for the older worker utilizes the same principles of adult learning that all employee training does, but a few adaptations can make training more useful for the older worker. Design training for older workers to cover longer time periods, using multiple short sessions over several weeks or months, and incorporating self-paced learning techniques. Make sure that written materials use large or bold typefaces that are easy to read. Use bright colors in illustrations to attract the eye. Build in lots of practical examples for teaching new techniques. Make sure trainers know they must speak clearly and distinctly.

Involve older workers. Involving older workers in teams, task forces, quality circles, and other activities that bring them in contact with younger and less experienced workers can take advantage of their life and work experiences. Involving the older worker demonstrates the value the organization places on the worker, enhancing the worker's feeling of self-esteem and dignity. It also sends the message to younger workers that they can look forward to similar treatment as they grow older.

NEW DIMENSIONS IN WORK SCHEDULING

Caleb S. Atwood, President, E.R.I.Q., Inc.

Advocate paying overtime after thirty-two hours of work rather than forty, or challenge other sacred work scheduling paradigms, and management is likely to respond as enthusiastically as it would to a hostile takeover or tax increase. Consequently, although a growing number of conventional five-day, forty-hour schedules are grandly inefficient, most companies are trudging merrily along scheduling employees "the way we've always done it."

With customers demanding products and services precisely when they need them, workloads are fluctuating as never before. Concurrently, companies are often seeing labor costs skyrocket and work habits deteriorate as employees fluctuate between working extensive overtime and having relatively little to do. Meanwhile, employees who want to rearrange schedules to suit their changing personal needs and interests are seldom allowed to because it is expensive to accommodate them.

All this is both unfortunate and unnecessary. Our businesses will not crash and burn if we pay overtime for *less* than forty hours per week, and dire consequences are not the inevitable result if, in other ways, we abandon conventional scheduling concepts. On the contrary, breaking with many of these sacred cows can enable us to lower labor costs, be more responsive to customer requirements, and profit financially by being more considerate of employees' needs. Following are two schedules I created—Just-in-Time and Win-Win—to show how businesses can break away from conventions yet remain successful. These schedules are explained in the context of manufacturing, but can be used in other businesses as well.

JUST-IN-TIME

Just-in-Time calls for paying time and a half after thirty-two hours rather than forty. Consequently, employees who take a day off lose twelve hours of pay (eight hours at time and a half) that week. When they make the time up in a subsequent week(s), they receive time and a half and break even. Consequently, companies can accommodate their requests for schedule changes without being penalized financially.

Changes can also be made across the board. For example, employees are often extremely busy at month's end and then underutilized until the push begins to make the next month look good. With Just-in-Time, companies can have them work extra hours/shifts at month's end and compensate by shutting down on a following Friday or Monday so employees get three-day weekends.

Free time is so highly prized that many employees should also be anxious to obtain compensatory time off. Such employees can be used to cover absenteeism, vacations, or workload surges, and be compensated with time off when it is mutually convenient.

One way Just-in-Time can be introduced is by reducing employees' wages so that, with built-in overtime, they break even. Employees paid $12 per hour, for example, earn $480 with a conventional forty-hour week. If their wages are reduced to $10.91 per hour, but they receive time and a half after thirty-two hours, they continue to earn $480 per week. Another alternative is to introduce Just-in-Time in lieu of a general wage increase. (Proportional arrangements are also possibilities. In the example, a company could reduce hourly wages to $11.20 instead of $10.91, and provide about a 5-percent increase.)

Providing forty-four hours of pay for forty hours of work appears equivalent to a hefty 10-percent increase. The actual investment, however, is much less because every time employees take a day off when they are not required, companies save all, or the better part of, their pay. When employees make up the time when workloads are heavy, companies avoid overtime. In the process they can save up to twelve hours of pay each time they allow an employee to trade workdays. If employees are rescheduled this way frequently enough, labor costs may actually decline.

Furthermore, absenteeism should decline significantly because this flexibility minimizes employees' motivation/need to miss work, and because those who do, will lose twelve hours of pay rather than eight. Even if absenteeism does not decline, its cost should because others can be scheduled to cover for absent employees and given compensatory time off at convenient later dates. As a result, employees missing work will lose time and a half and be replaced with the equivalent of straight-time employees. Think about that. Every time someone is absent, a company could save four hours of pay!

In sum, with the flexibility this concept can provide, companies can accommodate customers' requirements more effectively, schedule employees more efficiently, and actually save money by being more responsive to employees' needs.

WIN-WIN

Most manufacturing companies are "out of business" most of the time. Typically, day shifts are full, afternoon shifts are about half full, and night shifts, when they exist, are sparse. Consequently, such companies are only operating about 40 percent of the time. Even with overtime, utilization often fails to increase significantly because of such factors as employee fatigue and absenteeism.

Since fixed costs—machinery, equipment, taxes, and so on—usually constitute about 30 percent of total manufacturing costs, and labor costs about 15 percent, doubling utilization can halve unit fixed costs and save an amount roughly equivalent to a company's entire cost of labor. This is far from an earth-shattering revelation. The problem in harnessing the power of productivity is not in understanding the value of increasing utilization but in finding an effective way to induce and schedule employees to work on Saturdays, Sundays, holidays, afternoon and night shifts.

The Win-Win schedule provides a practical solution to this dilemma by offering employees such things as alternating three- and four-day "weekends" and an average of about sixty fewer workdays each year without loss of pay. This sounds prohibitively expensive, but it may actually *reduce* unit labor costs.

Here is how Win-Win works. Employees are assigned to either of two groups—X or O—and are scheduled to work ten-hour shifts. In odd-numbered weeks, employees in

Exhibit 4-2. Win-Win Work Schedule for Groups X and O

Week #	Sun.	Mon.	Tue.	Wed.	Thr.	Fri.	Sat.
1	X	X	X	X	O	O	O
2	X	X	X	O	O	O	O
3	X	X	X	X	O	O	O
4 Etc.	X	X	X	O	O	O	O

group X work Sunday through Wednesday. In even-numbered weeks, they work Sunday through Tuesday. Note that employees work either Saturday or Sunday, but not both (Exhibit 4-2).

Seventy hours of utilization of machinery, equipment, and facilities—almost twice what most companies are getting on all three conventional shifts—can be obtained on the day shift alone. Employing two shifts will double utilization again. Production can be increased even further by scheduling three shifts and reassigning some employees to other duties (assembly, packaging, shipping, etc.) when shifts overlap.

Working forty hours one week, followed by thirty the next, employees will average thirty-five hours per week. Win-Win calls for "cashing in" (i.e., providing pay in lieu of) holidays and vacation time, to help offset the cost of making up the five-hour pay differential.

Employees would object strenuously to reduction in holidays and vacation time with a conventional schedule, but with Win-Win it is a good investment because they will actually gain days off without losing pay. "Trading in" half of the holidays a company recognizes is entirely painless because, on any given holiday, half the employees will not be scheduled and will not suffer a loss of pay.

Trading in vacation time is relatively painless because Win-Win can produce unexpected results. To illustrate, three days of vacation can produce up to ten consecutive days off, as shown in Exhibit 4-3. In sum, with Win-Win, employees work essentially the same number of hours each year, but in a different configuration.

Win-Win provides forty hours of pay for thirty-five hours of work by paying time and a half for Saturday and Sunday work. Exhibit 4-4 shows how this would work for employees in group X. Compensating employees this way, rather than by increasing base rates, is advisable because:

1. It provides added incentive for good attendance on Saturdays and Sundays.
2. It avoids increasing benefit costs, which are related to base rates.
3. Since employees only work two or three shifts each week at straight time, they can be scheduled to work one or two extra shifts each week at straight time and still receive the same pay as with a conventional schedule (i.e., time and a half after forty hours).
4. It makes it practical for companies to use present employees who would like to earn extra income to cover vacations, leaves, and so forth and to avoid having to force anyone to work overtime.
5. It enables companies to be more responsive to employee needs. In addition to letting employees trade shifts during the same week, companies can allow them to trade shifts between weeks (Exhibit 4-5). As with Just-in-Time, employees who work extra shifts can be allowed to take compensatory days off when business is slow. The company may then save up to fifteen hours of pay—ten hours the day employees are off and five hours of overtime pay when they are rescheduled during a busy period.

Exhibit 4-3. Results with Win-Win

Three days of vacation can produce up to ten consecutive days off:

Week #	Sun.	Mon.	Tue.	Wed.	Thr.	Fri.	Sat.	Consecutive Days Off
1	X	X	X	X	OFF	OFF	OFF	3
2	VAC	VAC	VAC	OFF	OFF	OFF	OFF	7
								10

Seven days of vacation can produce up to eighteen consecutive days off:

Week #	Sun.	Mon.	Tue.	Wed.	Thr.	Fri.	Sat.	Consecutive Days Off
2	X	X	X	OFF	OFF	OFF	OFF	4
3	VAC	VAC	VAC	VAC	OFF	OFF	OFF	7
4	VAC	VAC	VAC	OFF	OFF	OFF	OFF	7
								18

Ten days of vacation can produce up to twenty-four consecutive days off:

Week #	Sun.	Mon.	Tue.	Wed.	Thr.	Fri.	Sat.	Consecutive Days Off
1	X	X	X	X	OFF	OFF	OFF	3
2	VAC	VAC	VAC	OFF	OFF	OFF	OFF	7
3	VAC	VAC	VAC	VAC	OFF	OFF	OFF	7
4	VAC	VAC	VAC	OFF	OFF	OFF	OFF	7
								24

Exhibit 4-4. Win-Win Pay Schedule for Group X

Day	Week #1	Week #2	Total Hours of Pay
Sunday	15 (time and one-half)	15	30
Monday	10	10	20
Tuesday	10	10	20
Wednesday	10	0	10
Total for two-week period			80

Exhibit 4-5. Sample Shift Trading between Group X̲ and Group O̲

	Sun.	Mon.	Tue.	Wed.	Thr.	Fri.	Sat.
Week #1	X	X	X	X	X̲	O	O
Week #2	X	X	O̲	O	O	O	O

Employees "win" because they are able to get:

- Alternating three- and four-day, two- and five-day, etc. "weekends."
- Approximately sixty fewer regular workdays annually—120 fewer trips to and from work.
- Thirty-five-hour regular work weeks with forty hours pay.
- Far greater scheduling flexibility.

Companies "win" because they are able to:

- Reduce overtime costs.
- Increase output from machinery, equipment, and facilities.
- Reduce overall manufacturing costs.
- Save substantial amounts of capital otherwise required to expand capacity.
- Improve working conditions and employee morale.

- Provide better service to customers on weekends.
- Utilize most productive machinery and equipment to a greater extent.
- Increase capacity very quickly if customer needs change.
- Reduce the cost of absenteeism.
- Utilize volunteers rather than "conscripts" to work extra shifts.
- Consolidate operations in most productive facilities.
- Increase profits.

Both parties "win" from stronger, more flexible, and more competitive companies that are able to provide greater security, more opportunities, and greater rewards. The alternatives are endless, the potential rewards great, *if* we can rise above principle and free ourselves from the shackles of scheduling paradigms.

TRAINING AND DEVELOPMENT TO IMPROVE EMPLOYEE PERFORMANCE

Ronald R. Sims, Associate Professor, School of Business Administration, The College of William and Mary

For many years, training had connotations of rote or mechanical learning. Now we know it is a systematically planned approach to learning knowledge, skills, abilities, and attitudes, with certain important features. Further, it is a process of changing the behavior and motivation to improve the match between employee characteristics and the demands of a job. The process consists of planned programs designed to improve competence and performance at the individual employee, group, and organizational levels. Improved competence and performance, in turn, imply that there have been measurable changes in knowledge, skills, abilities, attitudes, behavior, and motivation.

The primary impetus for training in organizations is change in employee performance. Managers enhance profits and stockholders' returns by increasing sales or reducing operating costs or both. Managers and private-sector executives at all levels face continuing pressure to provide more effective and efficient services. Organizations must respond to challenges while realizing that advances in technology and knowledge are rendering many traditional employees' skills obsolete. Simultaneously, new skills must be developed. The ultimate success of organizations depends on the ability of their employees to perform their present duties and to adapt to new situations successfully.

Training can play a key role in improving employee performance from the first day an employee is hired. During the first few days on the job, new employees form their initial impressions of the organization, other employees, and its managers. These impressions may range from very favorable to very unfavorable and may influence their job satisfaction and productivity. Therefore, managers must make an effort to train new employees during orientation to the organization, the job, and expected performance levels.

On-the-job training can continue to affect employee performance. Employees who perform unsatisfactorily because of a deficiency in skills are prime candidates for training. This focuses on the removal of performance deficiencies, whether current or anticipated, that are the result of the employee's inability to perform at the desired level. Although training cannot solve all problems of ineffective performance, a sound organizational training program can be instrumental in minimizing those problems.

Training can help overcome a scarcity of financial, human, and other resources. Managers are expected to attain their objectives in spite of personal conflicts, vague policies and standards, absenteeism, turnover problems,

and even labor-management disputes. Such organizational problems are addressed in many ways, including training. Functional training programs may concern personnel, marketing, accounting, finance, information systems, and general management. Employees with the proper functional skills will cause fewer problems in difficult situations.

TRAINING AND PERFORMANCE

Training can serve the organization by updating employees' skills so on-the-job performance can be increased. It is also the proper use of technological advances that will make organizations function more effectively. Especially relevant to the need to incorporate new technologies rapidly, training can assist in making the current work force more flexible and adaptable. Technological change often means that jobs change. By improving skills, organizations keep up with the technological advances and ensure that they are successfully integrated into operations.

Sometimes a new or newly promoted employee will not possess the skills or knowledge needed to be competent on the job. This occurs because:

1. No employee selection device is able to predict success or failure all the time. Training may be necessary to fill the gap between predicted and actual performance.
2. Companies knowingly hire and promote employees who need training to perform at standard levels.
3. The number of applicants may be small. In such a situation, management has little choice but to hire or promote an applicant with limited job-related skills and to remedy deficiencies through training.
4. Management may wish to hire employees who possess the aptitude to learn but not the skills. This is particularly important when organizations seek to hire historically disadvantaged individuals in protected classes. Training can remedy prior educational, social, vocational, or physical shortcomings.

TRAINING AND CAREER DEVELOPMENT

One important way for organizations to attract, retain, and motivate employees is through a systematic program of career development. The benefits of such a program are many, including:

1. Developing an employee's capabilities is consistent with a human resources policy of promotion from within. Training is important in a career-development system.
2. Training enables an employee to acquire the knowledge and skills needed for promotion to higher-level positions. It eases the transition from an employee's present job to one involving greater responsibilities.
3. Training assists in retention. Organizations that fail to provide training often lose their most promising employees. Frustrated by the lack of opportunity, achievement-oriented employees often seek employment with organizations that provide training for career advancement.
4. Training can increase an employee's level of commitment to the organization and improve perceptions that the organization is a good place to work. By developing and promoting trained employees, companies create a competent, motivated, and satisfied work force.

With respect to career development, training can lead to greater employee commitment, less turnover, and reduced absenteeism. Ultimately, training provides benefits to employees and a higher level of well-being in the organization. The implication is that training should be designed and evaluated in terms of its contribution to individual and organizational effectiveness.

TRAINING FOR COMPETENCE

Competence includes not only job-related skills but also well-rounded training that prepares employees to apply integrated knowledge in a practical and job-related manner. Thus, the challenge for the organization is to select appropriate competencies, specify evaluation indicators, and develop a functional training system.

Failure to design training programs that train for competence can result in inadequate design or implementation of a training program. This means the program, even if implemented effectively, will not meet an organization's needs because it will provide no improvement in employee performance. Training based on desired competencies can be evaluated to measure the extent to which the competencies have been achieved. Therefore, training programs should focus on outcomes rather than development of knowledge alone. Some key points to this process are:

1. Competencies should guide the planning and development of training. Each competency should describe a desired behavioral outcome that guides the planning of the program, implementation of training experiences, and the prescription of methods of evaluation.
2. The skills and skill levels required for various positions must be specified in advance. Competencies are perceived as a result of adequate job analyses and emphasize performance outcomes rather than knowledge alone. A competency emphasizes how the training program participants will use the acquired knowledge in real-life settings. The application of knowledge should not end with simple recall. The competencies are always stated to answer the question, "What will the participant be doing with the competency?"
3. Competencies should state the conditions under which a participant performs the actions or behaviors and the standard of performance required. An example might be: A client needs to report a failure of a product to comply with a warranty. A participant in this training program will be able to complete all steps to assist the client in achieving that goal.
4. Competencies should be tied to role models, mentors, and evaluators who can guide and advise the training participant as he or she pursues the mastery of specific skills.

5. Competencies should recognize that individuals vary in their learning styles, abilities, and life circumstances. Training programs should be designed to create an environment for developing and maintaining structures, conditions, and climates for individual learning.

TRAINING PROGRAMS

Design

The realization of training benefits is contingent on the degree of planning and effort expended designing and evaluating training programs. Haphazard training programs result in wasted resources, poorly motivated employees, and few measurable increases in employee performance or organizational productivity. On the other hand, programs that are designed, conducted, and evaluated properly have innumerable benefits to both the employee and the organization.

With budgetary constraints, organizations should consider the following when designing training programs:

1. Training should have the intent of ensuring that trainees are capable of solving problems and attaining training-related goals.
2. Training should provide employees with opportunities for professional growth and development.
3. Training programs should seek to overcome deficiencies that result from stringent hiring policies or other inabilities to hire employees who possess appropriate skill and knowledge levels.
4. Training goals must be expressed in terms of both monetary expenditures and employee time.
5. Training should be designed after a thorough analysis of employee and organizational needs. Such assessments facilitate the design of improved training programs.

Clarifying the Psychological Contract. The psychological contract is an implicit, yet important, agreement between trainees, their supervisors, trainers, and the organization. The psychological contract should specify what each expects to give and receive from each other in the training relationship. The process goes to the heart of motivation, productivity, training program satisfaction, involvement, and the management of the training environment. The design of competency-based training programs should recognize that the functions of training are broader than merely imparting knowledge. Program design must take into consideration the psychological contract.

Training programs should be designed to build an effective learning environment. Such an environment is often dependent on a psychological contract that influences the functioning of both trainers and trainees in training programs. Some considerations are:

1. The development of a psychological contract should occur early in the training process. Once achieved, it should be carefully managed throughout training.
2. A clear understanding of the expectations from the trainer and trainee will help form better contracts. What you do not know can hurt you in wasting training time.
3. The key to contract formulation is achieving a match or a fit between individual and organizational needs. It is not getting more training, the "best" training, or achieving some other goal.
4. Seek out and eliminate mismatches. A program participant, his or her supervisor, and the training staff should have the same or similar goals and expectations. Otherwise, the training can easily become wasted at best and counterproductive at worst.
5. The psychological contract begins with a process of self-directed learning and setting personal directions for learning for individuals.

Identifying Training Needs. Training programs can lead to improved employee performance when trainers, trainees, and supervisors discuss specific training needs, program objectives, and strategies to develop programs. Typical questions that can clarify the psychological contract include:

1. What two or three things are most important to you in this training program?
2. Do you believe that your training needs are being fully addressed in this training program? Previous organization training programs? Why or why not?
3. If you had complete freedom to reconstruct this training program, what changes would you make?
4. How would you describe the positive and negative aspects of this or previous training programs?
5. How well does/has the organization's training program(s) meet/met your personal and professional needs?
6. What do you think this training program expects of you at this point?
7. What have you learned are the objectives of this training program?

While not intended to be all encompassing, these questions help define changing expectations and the current fit between the training program, trainees, and organizational expectations. Essentially, the goal is to ensure that the training program meets personal and professional needs of employees. If the program does not meet needs, modification of the design of the program, improved management of implementation, or a change in training methods may be necessary. If it does meet the needs, the trainer, trainee, supervisor, and manager have congruent goals and the training effort should move forward.

Evaluation

Training evaluation is another area on which organizations can focus attention if they are committed to improving employee performance through their training efforts. Evaluation results should be seen as a vehicle for developing and carrying out training program efforts that facilitate improvement in employee performance and the organization in general.

There is no best way of evaluating training efforts. Because of the diversity of training programs, techniques and methods used, the wide range of training circumstances, and the different purposes of evaluation, various evaluation techniques are needed. The best evaluations occur through a systematic identification of the important factors that produce effective training. Some of the factors are:

1. Does the training program produce the results intended?
2. Is the program visible and important to the program sponsor and potential sponsors of future programs?
3. Is the trainer credible for conveying knowledge or skills on how to do a better job?
4. Is the program cost effective? Are resources well spent?
5. Do the participants show a strong commitment to the training program? Do they seem to understand the experience more fully, make up for deficiencies, and confirm management's beliefs about the value of the program?
6. Are managers better able to assess the program and make effective determinations on whether to send employees to future programs?
7. Does the training produce quantifiable data for improving future training programs?

Resources Affecting Evaluations. Those responsible for designing and implementing training program evaluations in organizations must also pay particular attention to the availability of resources and constraints for such an endeavor. Resources are needed to evaluate training. Constraints can limit evaluation effectiveness. Both are considerations in selecting evaluation method and procedures. Some resource/constraint issues are:

1. *Funding*—This refers to the dollars allotted to cover training evaluation planning and implementation.
2. *Time*—Evaluation can take place immediately or at periodic intervals after trainees return to the job. A sequence of "milestones" can be used, including completion of pretest and posttest data collection, data analysis, and dissemination of results to appropriate audiences.
3. *Human resources*—Trained personnel such as statisticians, computer specialists, research methodologists, and other trainers can be resources in evaluation.

4. *Organizational climate*—Evaluation is facilitated or hampered by the level of trust and openness of managers, supervisors, employees, or trainees. Do people seek, and are they receptive to, evaluative feedback?

5. *Availability of data*—Evaluation is improved by the availability and quality of organizational information. Examples are records of individual, group, department, and organizational performance, reports, and personnel training records. Data can also be obtained from surveys, interviews, and observations of employees.

6. *Details of the training evaluation action plan*—A good evaluation plan contains objectives, a timetable, procedures, participants, locations, and possible use of strategies.

7. *Audiences*—The success of evaluations depends partly on the information needs and interests of the key participants in the training process.

8. *Technical ability*—Evaluation requires the availability of standardized instruments, computerized analyses, stored data, logistics in collecting and disseminating results, and the abilities of persons involved.

9. *Ethical concerns*—Evaluations must recognize issues of privacy, employee and organizational confidentiality, obtrusiveness, and other harmful or illegal aspects of data collection and reporting.

Evaluation Checklist. Improvement in employee performance and overall productivity is the goal of the evaluation of training outcomes. A checklist of such a process might include:

1. Does the evaluation design fit the objectives of the training program?

2. Does the design address important issues such as trainee needs and expectations? These include learning style, trainee culture, expectations about authority, and performance views.

3. Does the evaluation method reflect the standards incorporated by the devel-

opers of the training program and required by the organization?

4. Does the evaluation structure provide a framework in which emergent issues can be addressed? Can the design be modified to address trainees' perceived needs without sacrificing objectives?

5. Can the design be carried out in the time allotted?

6. Does the design provide a mix of activities that appeal to different learning styles such as listening, discussing, and performing?

7. Is the material logically and psychologically sequenced?

8. Is there appropriate redundancy in information presented in training?

9. Does the evaluation design allow for ongoing development of a learning climate?

TRANSFER OF TRAINING

Transfer of training concerns whether behavioral or performance changes taught in training are expressed on the job. That is, transfer refers to the extent to which knowledge or skills learned in training can be applied by the participant on the job. The potential for improving employee performance during training is a result of designing training programs that also give adequate attention to the transfer of training. In other words, the best designed training programs are of little benefit to the organization or the employee if the training cannot or is not transferred to the work situation.

Some key questions can be linked to the success of transferring training:

1. Can trainees now do things they could not before? Can they negotiate a contract? Can they conduct an appraisal interview?

2. Do trainees demonstrate new behaviors on the job after the training is completed?

3. Has job performance been improved after training? With respect to this question, transfer may be positive, negative, or neutral. That is, it may enhance, hamper, or not affect job performance.

Improving Positive Training Transfer

The positive transfer of training is perhaps the most critical goal of any training. Since training represents a step toward improving job performance and organizational effectiveness, a lack of positive transfer to the job indicates a wasted training effort. The potential for improving employee performance through training can be enhanced when the organization pays particular attention to facilitating the transfer from learning to doing. Positive transfer requires the organization to:

1. Encourage the trainee to take the material learned in training and apply it on the job.
2. Encourage the trainee to maintain learned skills over time on the job.
3. Design the training situation to parallel the job situation as closely as possible.
4. Provide practical experience performing new tasks so trainees can learn behavior, not textbook, examples.
5. Provide a variety of examples and applications of teaching concepts or skills.
6. Ensure that the trainer label or identify important features of a task.
7. Ensure that general principles are well understood. Knowing a series of steps can be useless without a foundation. This is particularly true in technical training, such as computer programming.
8. Ensure that the application of newly learned competencies is rewarded on the job.
9. Ensure that the design of the training content is clear so trainees can see its applicability to their jobs. In its simplest context, the skills that are learned today in training should be useful on the job tomorrow.
10. Use questions and interactive formats to guide the learning process.
11. Assign or allow the trainees to generate their own behavioral goals for applying what was learned in training.

Positive transfer is facilitated when certain conditions exist:

1. Trainees should be able to visualize or practice the use of knowledge or skills on the job. As an example, a training program on interviewing skills should include role-playing with "applicants."
2. Higher levels of management should be trained first. This is particularly important when managerial behaviors or leadership styles are being taught. This sequence assures that when each manager returns from training, his or her supervisor is already familiar with the new behaviors and should be willing to encourage their use.
3. Peer support groups can be formed, which means that trained managers meet periodically to reinforce each other and share their experiences in applying the new ideas they have learned.
4. Refresher training can be helpful.

CONCLUSION

The pace of change in our society and its affect on organizations is forcing them to increase their productivity by improving employee performance. Well-designed training programs can serve as important vehicles for achieving optimum improvements in employee performance.

A well-designed training program pays particular attention to clarifying the expectations or psychological contract between employees, training efforts, and the organization. In addition, special program design attention should be given to ensuring that employee training facilitates the positive transfer from learning to doing. If no positive transfer occurs, little value results. Employee performance can be improved when training programs are designed to be evaluated. By continually stressing the role of training, managing the design of training programs, and improving training programs based on evaluative data, organizations will be able to improve employee performance and productivity.

EMPLOYEE COMPENSATION

Barry Bingham, Director of Compensation, Monsanto Company

Barry Blitstein, Vice-President of Human Resources, Monsanto Company

Elizabeth J. Hawk, Senior Consultant of Compensation, Monsanto Company

Herschel V. Sellers, Director of Corporate Benefits, Monsanto Company

Successful organizations make use of a variety of tools to help them be competitive and improve performance. One of those tools is pay. Pay can play an integral role in achieving organizational goals.

Management can expect more from a pay program than attracting, retaining, and rewarding employees—the traditional objectives of compensation. A growing number of organizations are seeking ways to link pay and organization performance at every level in the work force in order to encourage commitment and employee involvement in achieving results. Pay is being used to help set direction and communicate what is important to the organization. Especially in organizations that are changing the nature of work itself through work teams or other new work designs, pay can provide an answer to the inevitable employee question, "What's in it for me?" Increasingly, what is in it for them is a share in the results they help to generate. Organizations that want to use pay as a tool to achieve results will need to consider the elements of total compensation as well as the principles of pay system design.

ELEMENTS OF TOTAL COMPENSATION

Pay systems at every employee level can be more than just pay based on time worked (e.g., hourly wages, annual salaries). In addition to base pay, organizations should consider incentives and reward systems.

Incentives establish and communicate the link between pay and performance up front, so the employee understands what is expected and comprehends the payout potential. Incentives can be paid for individual and/or team performance. They are most often associated with executive compensation, but a number of organizations are extending incentive pay to every employee level. The amount of the incentive is frequently expressed as a percent of base pay or as a flat dollar amount. The incentive opportunity should be large enough to encourage a change in performance. At lower levels, the incentive opportunity could be 5–10 percent of base pay. Chief executives of corporations often have incentive opportunities of 50 percent or more.

Alternatively, *rewards* recognize performance that has already occurred, without the up-front link to goals. For example, an organization might use awards for an outstanding achievement, completion of a special project, or a cost-saving suggestion.

Both incentives and rewards are usually delivered in cash, but other forms of delivery are available. Equity (stock and related vehicles) is ownership in a business. Equity has most commonly been used for executives, but some organizations now use it at lower levels to increase employee identification with the company and its performance for shareholders. There are several different varieties of equity, but three common examples are stock options, performance shares, and restricted stock.

Stock options give employees the right to purchase company stock at a set price. The option becomes valuable if the market price of the stock rises; in this case, the employee is in effect buying the stock at a discount. Stock options are used to link employee and shareholder interests, because when the share price rises, both groups will benefit. Performance shares are company stock earned based on achievement of a preestablished performance criterion. The value of the award is based both on the number of shares earned and their value in the market. Restricted stock is stock granted to an employee that cannot be sold for a period of time. Restrictions on sale may lapse after a period of continued employment or upon achievement of a performance goal.

Noncash awards can include a variety of alternatives; some of the most common are merchandise, travel, plaques, and dinners. Either incentive or reward plans can be structured to provide for noncash awards.

A full look at total compensation also includes benefits. Some of the more commonly used benefit programs include pension plans, medical and dental coverage, savings plans, and vacations. Traditionally, this package of benefits has been standard for all employees, but in more and more cases employees are provided with choices to use in tailoring their benefits program to meet their needs. Often a supplementary benefits package is provided for executives that addresses issues created by tax regulations. Top management may also be eligible for a final element of total compensation—a perquisite. This could include financial planning services, club memberships, and company cars.

PRINCIPLES OF PAY SYSTEM DESIGN

The manager faced with the prospect of using these pay elements to develop a pay system for a new organization—or the manager trying to update an existing "system" that may be simply a collection of past practices—could easily become discouraged by the complexity of the task. It can help to begin with a few principles on which a total pay system can be built. These serve as guidelines both as the process begins and later as proposals are developed. The following discussion outlines nine principles for pay systems.

Pay Should Support the Organization's Strategy

The first, and most important, thing a manager must do is to become fully immersed in the organization's strategy: What does it take to be successful, now and in the future? The strategy will have implications for the way work is organized, the performance required, the types of employees needed, and how those employees should be paid. The manager interested in using pay as a tool should be an active participant as the strategy is being developed, so the consequences for pay system design can be built in from the outset.

Thus, a pay system cannot simply be "pulled off the shelf"; instead, it should be tailored to the organization's unique needs. Consider three examples: a small high-tech start-up, a large service business that must compete by offering the lowest price, and a school system. The start-up might combine relatively low base pay and modest benefits with significant opportunities for ownership in the business, encouraging all employees to make the venture a success. The service organization might pay a premium in base pay for broadly skilled employees who can operate without expensive layers of supervision, then add incentives for cost control. The school system could offer rewards and recognition to teachers who achieve model accomplishments. In short, the system that works in one organization may be unsuccessful in another. Part of the benefit of pay system design is the opportunity it creates to look thoughtfully at what the organization really needs to accomplish. By articulating the business strategy more clearly, management will make it easier to achieve this goal.

The terms *business strategy, management,* and the like are not intended to limit this discussion to the traditional corporate environment. The organization in question might also be a university, a social service agency, a church, or a city government. The business strategy is simply what it takes to make the organization successful.

When we design pay strategy around business strategy, we also help guard against the familiar "program of the month" syndrome. Compensation, like any function, has its fads. Perhaps this year the catchphrase is gain sharing; next year it might be skill based pay or lump-sum merit pay. Another example from a few years ago, now largely discredited, is two-tier base pay. This system created lower pay levels for new hires, and it became a problem as employees found themselves doing the same job for two different rates of pay.

In these examples a design captures attention; soon it seems that "everyone" is putting in such a plan, and a bandwagon effect develops. Unfortunately, unless the fashionable design happens to support the organization's strategy, it may well fail to accomplish anything. Worse, it may create such animosity toward new pay designs that other, more reasoned, attempts become impossible. So it makes sense to focus first on what the organization needs in designing a pay program.

Pay Should Fit the Organization's Culture

The pay system must be part of the total fabric of the organization, not some alien element.

It needs to fit the existing culture, so that it delivers a message that is consistent with other aspects of the way the organization operates. Perhaps more important, if culture is shifting, pay can and should be part of the change.

To illustrate, perhaps an organization is moving to a participative culture. Layers of hierarchy are reduced, self-directed work teams take responsibility for results, and people are provided the tools needed to get the job done themselves. A traditional closed-pay system with narrow job descriptions, limited or no communication about pay, and all decisions made in a black box simply would not fit the emerging culture. Such a system fails to involve employees, fails to share information about pay and what determines it, and fails to recognize the impact employees have on results and share those results with them.

A better pay system for this organization would reflect the direction toward which the culture is heading, reinforcing the new values of shared information and shared commitment. Employees would certainly be involved in examining the old system, then scoping, designing, and implementing a better one. As part of the process, they would be expected to understand the organization's strategy and the elements of pay that can comprise total compensation. Thus, the process of changing a pay system, and the new system itself, can be an integral part of the evolution toward participation.

A Statement of Pay Philosophy Should Be Developed

A statement of pay philosophy is something like a statement of business strategy. Brief and clear, it defines the organization's pay principles in a way that is understandable to employees and shows how business direction and pay at all levels are intended to support one another.

A statement of pay philosophy developed at an organization-wide level can also guide the development of customized pay systems in subunits. It defines limits and provides standards against which to test proposals. And it reassures management that everyone is moving in a proper direction, even though subunit design details may vary.

An organization's pay philosophy will most likely address:

1. Whether pay is to be linked to individual, group, and/or unit results, and at which employee levels.
2. How to define "the competition." Is it those organizations we compete with on products or services? Those we compete with for people? Some of both?
3. How we want to pay versus the competition when our performance is at expected levels. When is our performance outstanding? When is our performance poor?
4. How much of total pay should be guaranteed or fixed (base wages or salary), and how much should vary with results (i.e., incentive pay). The answer may be different at different employee levels.
5. How much customization in subunit pay system design the larger organization is comfortable with, and how important a factor equity among subunits will be.
6. Whether pay programs should be periodically and formally reviewed to keep them current with changing needs.
7. The degree of employee involvement and communication expected.

Pay Should Be Linked to Performance

Pay for performance is a concept familiar to some organizations and some employee groups. Executive incentive plans that pay in cash or other forms for short-term (one year or less) or long-term performance of the organization and the individual are common. Merit pay plans for salaried employees that determine the size of a person's increase based on performance are also widespread. Incentive plans are becoming more common among other employee groups, including production, clerical, and service employees; awards are based on performance against preestablished goals.

Yet most pay, for most employees, is still determined by time worked (dollars per hour or per year) and by how fast pay in the marketplace is increasing. Notice there is no mention of performance of any kind. This can produce inappropriate pay practices. For example, if an organization is performing extremely well in the market, yet pay is simply tracking the average of what others are doing, employees are not sharing in results. The best employees, perhaps the very ones behind the top performance, may be tempted to move to greener pastures, where performance is reflected in pay. Conversely, if an organization is performing poorly but pay keeps rising with the market, it may actually price itself out of business. Everyone, most of all employees, suffers.

Part of the problem may be our traditional definitions of performance and their poor translation to pay. Organizations with management by objectives or other performance management systems for salaried employees often pride themselves on their measurement of individual performance. Yet there are two problems with these systems. First, because they typically focus only on individual performance (and most people do not really work alone), they fail to encourage commitment to team, group, or organization-wide results. Second, once a base pay increase is awarded, it becomes locked in permanently, and there is no continuing performance link or motivational impact.

The other level at which performance has traditionally been measured is organization-wide profitability. Profit-sharing plans that share a portion of profits with employees are rather common in the United States. Awards do, in fact, go up and down with business performance. Yet there is still little or no impact on employee behavior or commitment, because—except in very small organizations—most employees simply do not feel they can affect profitability.

How much better it would be to use our principle of linking pay and performance to design a pay system in which an element of *every* employee's pay varies based on performance he or she can impact. One or more levels of performance measurement would be established up front; these could include individual, team, group, or other measures.

Awards would be delivered separate from base to avoid locking them into fixed base pay. Total pay (base plus award) would be above market when results are good, below market when results are poor. Employees would have a stake in the results they produce. The organization would be more competitive, because total pay costs would go down when performance is poor.

Internal and External Equity Must Be Considered

Internal equity is the degree of equity from group to group within the organization. External equity compares an organization to its marketplace. In either case, the distinction must be made between *actual pay* and *pay opportunity*. If the organization is determined to have absolute equity in actual pay, then the pay for performance discussion above will be of no value, because pay will proceed in lock-step regardless of performance. On the other hand, pay opportunity can be held similar from group to group or with the market, and actual pay (base plus variable incentives or other elements) can be allowed to go up or down with performance. Using the pay opportunity approach, different groups would be paid about the same in total for performance at expected levels, but higher or lower performance could cause the variable elements of their pay to rise or fall.

The organization's business strategy will go far in defining its need for internal equity. A relatively homogeneous organization that needs to move people easily among groups will need to attend to internal equity. A highly decentralized organization will have less of this need.

Of course, any pay program should be developed with knowledge of what the competitive marketplace is paying for similar jobs. Total compensation levels that are too low may contribute to turnover; pay that is too high may make the organization uncompetitive.

Good Communication Is Essential

Communicating about pay used to be easy. In many organizations, it simply was not done at all. At best, an across-the-board base pay increase was delivered to a large group of employees with words about "maintaining our position in the market." Or an individual employee received a salary increase and an admonition not to tell anyone about it.

Keeping people uninformed about their pay programs is easy, at least in the short run. But there are strong arguments in favor of talking openly about pay—not necessarily who gets what amount but rather how the program works. These are:

1. Whether or not one buys into the idea that pay is a motivator, people do pay attention to pay. What the organization pays for is what is seen as important, and what it pays for is what it is likely to get. So an open discussion of how the program works, what determines pay, provides a great opportunity to get everyone moving in the same direction.

2. Open communication of the pay program implies that employees can be trusted with sensitive information. It also implies that the organization can be trusted to shoot straight, because it has told employees what the rules are. This mutual trust can spill over into positive outcomes in many nonpay areas.

3. Simply put, open communication about pay provides an opportunity to better use pay as a motivator and reinforcer.

Employee Input Is Essential to Improve Quality and Plan Success

The quality and success of a pay program will improve with employee involvement in all phases of the process: design, implementation, evaluation, renewal. Of course, most employees are not compensation experts. They may not be familiar with the organization's strategy at the outset. But employees can be coached to do a very effective job. In the process, they learn about business direction and what it takes to be successful. Greater ownership of the plan is achieved because the program is viewed as theirs, not just management's. Thus, while involving employees takes time, it is an investment that gives the pay program a far better shot at success.

No Program Is Forever, So Flexibility Is a Necessity

Early on, we argued that the pay program should fit the organization's strategy and culture. Both, of course, are always evolving. Therefore, the pay program must be dynamic, not static. The organization should not imply to employees (directly or indirectly) that the pay program or any element of it is fixed. The pay philosophy may remain relatively stable over time, but details will and should change to meet changing needs. Plans can be defined as having limited duration, or regular review dates can be preannounced, or the organization may simply tell employees to expect changes to occur. Without this kind of proactive stance, employees will naturally assume that the design of their pay program is permanent, an entitlement.

Governance Issues Should Be Considered

In publicly traded companies, the compensation of certain executives must be the responsibility of members of the board of directors. A committee of nonemployee directors provides oversight to ensure an independent view and protect shareholder interests.

At lower levels in the organization, similar principles need to be developed. These include defining who approves new or revised program elements and individual or group pay decisions. Many successful pay-for-performance organizations have moved authority to recommend pay actions as close to the recipient(s) as possible, often the next level of supervision. This helps ensure that pay recommendations are made by those most familiar with the performance in question. Approval authority is often at a higher level, to provide a larger perspective on performance.

EMPLOYEE BENEFITS: OPTIONS AND ALTERNATIVES

William R. Maher, Maher, Rosenheim & Comfort

William S. Comfort, Maher, Rosenheim & Comfort

Robert L. Rosenheim, Maher, Rosenheim & Comfort

An employee benefits plan, if properly designed, implemented, serviced, and communicated, can help to recruit and retain quality employees. Development of some objectives when reviewing your benefits package can be the beginning of a successful plan. Employee benefits are intended to promote economic security in employees and their families. A human resources director should establish a plan that sets benefit objectives, controls cost, and implements and communicates these benefits to all employees and their families.

There are many types of employee benefits offered in the United States, some of which are required by law (social security, unemployment insurance, workers compensation). Others are voluntary benefits provided by employers.

HEALTH BENEFITS

Group health insurance is the most valued and much needed core benefit an employer can offer employees. There are three basic types of health insurance:

1. *Traditional major medical*—fee-for-service plans.
2. *Preferred provider organizations (PPOs)*— arrangement between an insurance company or an employer and medical providers to receive discounted fees for services.
3. *Health maintenance organizations (HMOs)*—arrangement in which doctors, hospitals, and health-care providers are paid in advance for services rendered.

The majority of employers offer their employees the traditional fee-for-service major medical plans with the PPO option. These plans seem to be most affordable since they offer the employer more premium and benefit choices. The deductibles and coinsurance can be adjusted based on the amount of premiums the employer is willing to pay.

Traditional Major Medical

Major medical plans are the most comprehensive type of coverage since they cover such a wide base of medical services such as hospital charges, surgeons' charges, doctors' office visits, X-ray and laboratory fees, prescription drugs, mental, nervous, alcohol, and drug charges.

The benefit structure typically does not pay 100 percent of all medical expenses incurred. Most major medical plans have a calendar-year deductible that ranges between $100 and $1,000 per year. The deductible is the initial expense that is paid by the employee. Most deductibles are on an annual calendar-year basis and some plans provide a carryover provision that allows an employee to satisfy his or her deductible in the last three months of the calendar year and have that deductible carry forward to the following year.

After an individual satisfies the deductible the insurance company and the individual share in the cost for the next dollar amount. This is called coinsurance. The coinsurance can vary based on the major medical plans or PPO plan that is chosen. Typically, if an employee has no PPO benefits the coinsurance would be an 80/20 split, meaning the insurance company would pay 80 percent of the expenses and the individual would pay the other 20 percent.

Most plans will provide a limit as to the amount shared with the insurance company to prevent an individual from having a major financial burden. To illustrate, after the annual deductible is paid the insurance company would pay 80 percent of the next $5,000 in medical charges with the individual paying 20 percent. Thus, the individual's financial obligation is only $1,000 plus the annual deductible. Most plans will have the insurance company pay 100 percent of the medical expenses after the coinsurance limit is reached.

Preferred Provider Organizations

PPOs are contractual arrangements between health-care providers and insurance companies or employers to provide fee-for-service care at a discount. The PPO encourages the employee to go to a PPO or network provider by creating a financial incentive. Employees are free to choose any doctor or hospital they want, but when they stay in the network they may receive a 90–100-percent reimbursement after the deductible versus going out of the network and getting an 80-percent reimbursement.

Health Maintenance Organizations

HMOs are the alternative to fee-for-service health insurance plans. The hospital, doctors, and other health-care providers provide services and care on a prepaid basis. HMO allows for the employee to eliminate his or her deductible and copayments and receive a wide range of medical services for a nominal cost, usually $2 to $10. In addition, the HMO covers more services than major medical plans to include preventive care, immunization for children, and well-woman exams and encourages wellness.

The employee that chooses the HMO *must* use the doctors and hospitals and other health-care providers who are part of the HMO network. If an employee does not use one of the HMO providers there is no reimbursement at all for his or her medical expenses unless they were due to a life-threatening emergency situation. There would also be limited benefits when the covered person requires medical services outside the HMO area.

PAYING FOR YOUR COMPANY'S HEALTH INSURANCE PLAN

There are two basic ways to pay for health-care benefits: fully insured plans and self-insured plans. Most employers with less than a hundred employees typically have a fully insured plan. The rating of the group premium is based on census information, age, sex, and marital status, but very little credit is given for either good or bad claims experience. For groups over a hundred employees, there are a few more financing methods to consider.

A fully insured experience rated group insurance plan shifts 100 percent of the claims liability to the insurance company. This method allows for a budgeting of the employer's medical premiums since the employer is given a guaranteed rate for a single employee and an employee with family coverage. This premium method is typically the most competitively priced since the insurance company does not have to refund any premiums back to the employer if its claims experience is good. At an increase in premium, a participating contract can be purchased that allows the employer to receive a dividend or refund when it has a good experience.

Many medium-size companies (i.e., one hundred to five hundred employees) consider the minimum premium contract for financing their medical plans. The employer has some very distinct cash flow advantages and very little additional exposure than the fully insured plan just discussed. The minimum premium contract is broken down into three basic components: retention, claims, and reserves.

Retention is the employer's fixed cost in a health insurance contract. These costs are billed each month by the insurance company and typically they would include the stop loss and aggregate premiums, administrative costs, and other incidental expenses such as access fees and managed-care charges. The retention figure is approximately 13–18 percent of the total fully insured rates.

The next component is the claims liability. Under the minimum premium contract the insurance company establishes a maximum claim liability either on a monthly or annual basis for employer budgeting purposes. These two components within the claims section are called specific and aggregate insurance. Specific insurance protects the employer from paying more than a certain dollar amount for any one individual covered under the plan. Aggregate insurance protects the employer from paying more than a certain dollar amount either monthly or annually.

The reserve component to a health insurance contract is established primarily in the first year. These reserves are typically 20–30 percent of the fully insured premium rate and are adjusted each year. These reserves are set aside by the employer to pay for claims that were incurred but not presented for payment prior to the contract being canceled with the insurance company. The reserves represent a future liability that the employee might incur if the employer were ever to cancel the insurance contract or change insurance companies.

Self-insured plans are typically for the employer who has five hundred or more employees. An employer with five hundred to a thousand employees could purchase from a third-party administrator or an insurance company an administrative services contract to take care of its administrative needs. Some employers may want to administer their own plans. The basic fixed cost or retention charges mentioned above can be further reduced because self-insured plans are not subject to state insurance premium taxes. Since self-funded plans are not subject to state laws, the avoidance of state-mandated benefits can lower the potential cost of some large claims, and the employer can determine what medical benefits will be provided or excluded.

CAFETERIA OR FLEXIBLE BENEFIT PLANS

This benefit for employers with larger numbers of employees gives the employees choices about their benefits. An employee can determine how the employer's premium dollars will be allocated among the benefits being offered. In addition, employees may decide to reduce their salary to purchase additional benefits (see "Section 125—Pretax"). Some benefits that may be included are group health insurance with choice of deductibles, dental insurance, group term life, dependent life, accidental death and dismemberment, short-term and long-term disability, and medical reimbursement accounts.

Flexible benefit plans offer the following advantages:

1. Employees are given the opportunity to choose which benefit plans would be best for their own family needs.
2. Employees are more appreciative because they are involved in their benefit decisions.
3. Since all employees are given a core level of benefits and a fixed amount of dollars with which to work, they are more aware of the cost.
4. Employer cost becomes more controllable because a certain dollar amount per employee is being allocated.

Disadvantages of flexible benefit plans include:

1. These plans are expensive and extremely complex to administer. Many insurance companies and third-party administrators (TPAs) do not offer these plans to employers with less than three hundred employees.

2. Having the average employee understand the plan is very important. The commitment to communication is much greater than with the traditional group plan.

Cafeteria or flexible benefit plans are growing in popularity with corporate America. The employer may shift the burden of future increases in cost to the employees.

Group Term Life Insurance

The most commonly used method of providing death benefits for the families of employees is through group term life insurance paid for by the employer. The first $50,000 of all group term plans provided by the employer on a nondiscriminating plan is tax-free to the employee, and the cost is tax deductible as a business expense to the employer. Death benefits are tax-free to the beneficiaries. Group insurance in excess of $50,000 is taxable to the employee based on the uniform premium table under IRC Section 79.

A plan is not discriminatory if the benefits are a multiple of salary or a level amount for all covered employees. In the past, most plans were based on job classifications that today may or may not be considered discriminatory with potential tax problems depending on whether job classification and salary multiple are approximately similar.

Accidental Death and Dismemberment Coverage

One of the least expensive benefits that an employer can provide is indemnification to the family of the deceased, resulting from accidental death to the employee, or dismemberment resulting from an accident. This is particularly valuable for employees whose occupation results in substantial airplane or automobile travel, where the risk is greater than normal. Some accidental death plans will pay a higher benefit for death occurring in a common carrier.

Long-Term Disability Coverage

Monthly benefits after a waiting period of perhaps ninety days at 60 percent of pay to age sixty-five are the most common form of disability income for employees. This can be made available on a group basis or individual basis wherein the employer can pay all the cost or the employer can split the cost with the employee.

To the extent that the employer pays the cost, the expense is tax deductible to the employer, but benefits to the employee are taxable income. To the extent that the employee pays the cost, benefits are received tax-free. Any costs that the employee would pay are paid with after-tax income.

Dental Insurance

Dental plans were developed to help an employee pay for dental costs and to encourage regular dental care, which can prevent serious problems from occurring. Most plans provide four basic levels of service:

1. *Preventive services* — These would include services for an exam, scaling and polishing, X-rays and emergency treatments once every six months. For children under age eighteen, fluoride treatments with each six-month exam are included.
2. *Basic services* — These would include basic restorative services, endodontic services, periodontic services, oral surgery services, anesthesia, and antibiotics.
3. *Major services* — This area covers restorative services such as inlays, onlays, crowns, and major prosthodontics services such as bridges and dentures.
4. *Orthodontia services* — Many plans limit orthodontia services to children under age nineteen.

Most dental plans have features often found in health insurance such as deductibles and coinsurance percentages. These features are designed to require the employee to pay some portion of the overall cost.

Vision Care

Most vision-care services are provided by ophthalmologists, optometrists, and opticians with the vision plan providing reimbursement for the doctors or opticians. Most vision-care plans have deductibles and impose limitations on frequency of services. As an example, an insured may be limited to one eye exam within a twelve-month period, one set of lenses within a twelve-month period, and one set of frames within a twenty-four-month period.

Group Long-Term Nursing Care

People over age sixty-five constitute the fastest growing segment of our population, and by the year 2030, one in every five Americans will be over age sixty-five. Long-term-care protection for the aging is not found with the two public programs, Medicare and Medicaid, due to their specific limitations. Private long-term-care insurance can protect an employee and family for the costs of skilled nursing care, intermediate care, and home care. It will ensure that an employee can pay the cost of the quality of care desired and protect the family from being impoverished in the event that long-term care is needed. It protects assets. The program will be guaranteed continuable and portable, and is available to parents, parents-in-law, and retirees.

SECTION 125—PRETAX

Section 125 is referred to in many ways: pretax plans, premium-only plans (POPs), or cafeteria plans. This provision in the law allows the employee to pay for his or her medical contributions with pretax dollars. Thus, the employee saves on federal and state income taxes and both the employee and employer save on FICA (Federal Insurance Contributions Act) taxes, which means more take-home pay for the employee. The employer must have a written document and must communicate the plan to the employees.

KEY PERSON DISCRETIONARY BENEFITS

Key Employee Life Insurance

Since the loss of a key man or woman could be disastrous, particularly to a small company, many employers purchase "key man" insurance on the key person for which the employer is the owner and beneficiary. Death benefits are tax-free to the employer, and thus there are extra funds to cover the potential loss of the services of the key man or woman, and to train a suitable replacement.

The extra funds can also be used to fund some form of salary continuation to the family of the deceased if this is desirable. The money paid to a deceased employee's family would be taxable to the family as received. It would be tax deductible to the employer.

Split-Dollar Life Insurance

A split-dollar plan is an arrangement between an employer and an employee wherein both parties split the benefits and the costs of a permanent insurance contract. Such an arrangement allows the employee to use the employer's cash flow to purchase personal permanent life insurance at the lowest overall cost to the employer and the employee.

These arrangements can be in the form of a collateral assignment plan whereby the employee owns the policy and assigns to the employer its interest in the cash value and death benefit. It may also be in the form of an endorsement plan wherein the employer owns the contract and the benefit split is provided by endorsement.

Under either arrangement the employee will have taxable income equal to the economic benefit of the death benefit less the employee's contribution to the plan measured by Revenue Ruling 64–328,1964–2CB11 and Revenue Ruling 66–110,1966-lCB12. If the employee is a majority stockholder and wishes to assign his or her insurance to a third party for estate tax savings, special assignments are required.

Key Employee Disability Coverage

Since long-term disability coverage is a desirable benefit for an employer to make available to all employees, it is also attractive to provide special disability benefits to a select group of employees. Under group plans where benefits are frequently paid to age sixty-five, with decreasing duration for those disabled after sixty-five, it is possible to extend the full benefits to age seventy for key employees. Furthermore, key employees can be carved out of the group plan, and individual policies provided

where the contracts may have other bells and whistles that would be desirable but more expensive, such as disability income for life.

Instead of only paying 60–66⅔ percent of salary under the plan, the employer can self-insure the difference and pay the disabled key employee 100 percent of his or her income (including salary and the prior year's bonus, etc.) for some designated period of years. There are two other types of key employee disability coverage:

1. Office overhead provides a payment to cover overhead to run a business if an owner or key person is out on disability. The person's benefit is usually for a short period of time such as twelve to twenty-four months. The benefit is payable to the employer.
2. Buyout disability coverage provides an amount of money to buy out an ownership share of a disabled owner/employee.

Medical Reimbursement

Current tax laws make it difficult to take a personal deduction for medical expenses, and then only to the extent of out-of-pocket medical expenses in excess of 7.5 percent of income. A self-insured medical reimbursement plan, however, must satisfy nondiscriminatory requirements before payment made to key employees can continue to be excluded from their taxable income.

An insured medical reimbursement plan solves the above problem and is a highly visible fringe benefit. It reimburses an employee for his or her family's medical expenses not covered under the employer's group medical plan and permits discrimination by covering a select group of executives.

Death Benefit Only

One of the many methods of providing the family of a deceased key employee with monthly income is to have the employer merely pay monthly benefits to the spouse and/or children. This can be set up on a discriminatory basis. However, there must be a plan in effect prior to the benefits being paid.

The payment is tax deductible to the employer and taxable income to the recipient of the income, unlike group insurance or split-dollar insurance. Should the employer buy "key man" insurance on the valuable employee to fund the benefit and should the employee die, the death benefits payable to the employer are tax-free, so that some leverage is possible.

COBRA OR CONTINUATION OF COVERAGE

The Consolidated Omnibus Budget Reconciliation Act (COBRA) became law in 1985. This act requires employers with health insurance plans to offer the group insurance core benefits to qualified beneficiaries for either eighteen or thirty-six months depending on the qualifying event (such as termination of employment). Benefits can be extended for an additional nine months for an individual if that individual is disabled at the end of the eighteen months. All employers that have had at least twenty employees working for them whether or not covered under the medical plan within the past twelve months are required to provide this option to all employees. The employer can charge up to 102 percent

of premiums or the COBRA equivalent. Employers that violate COBRA must pay penalties of up to $100 a day for the duration of the compliance period.

Note that there are very specific rules to follow in notifying terminated employees or eligible dependents. The plan administrator should understand these rules and keep records to be able to prove they were followed. This COBRA law should be very carefully administered. It should be understood that it is the employer's responsibility to follow this law. Some states have laws dealing with continuation of coverage for companies with less than twenty employees.

BIBLIOGRAPHY

Employee Benefits Surveys. U.S. Chamber of Commerce, 1989.

Fundamentals of Employee Benefit Programs, 4th ed. Employee Benefits Research Institute.

Leimberg, Stephen R., *Tools and Techniques of Employee Benefits and Retirement Planning,* 2nd ed.

Rosenbloom, Jerry, *The Handbook of Employee Benefits,* 2nd ed.

RETIREMENT AND PENSION PLANNING

Thomas C. Farnam, Attorney-at-Law, T. C. Farnam & Associates

Why should employers be concerned about retirement benefits for their employees? The concept is as old as the feudal system, under which a vassal was required to serve "his

lordship" for life. In return, the lord had an implied duty to provide the servant with land, tools, and a place to live. In more modern times, some "company towns" provided homes for retirees, but these have now been largely replaced by retirement plans of various types.

Retirement plans and programs help employers persuade older employees to vacate jobs in order to make room for younger workers. (In fact, the British refer to pension plans as "superannuation schemes.") Of course, retirement income has become much more important as modern medicine continues to extend life spans.

There are a wide variety of methods and techniques available to provide retirement benefits. Some government-mandated programs, such as the social security system, are financed by payroll taxes paid by employees and employers. Social security, however, was never intended to provide complete replacement of preretirement income. It was created as a "New Deal" welfare program and still provides a safety net based on a low level of retirement income, which assumes employees will supplement this from other sources. To assist, many employers provide some additional form of continuing salary or wage compensation for their retired former employees.

SALARY CONTINUATION

The simplest technique available for this purpose is continued payment of the salary by the employer. This may not be attractive to payees, since changes in company ownership often eliminate such payments. Also, as a mere "promise to pay," these payments depend entirely on the long-term financial viability of the employer. Last, but not least, from an accounting standpoint this approach does not match the employer's costs with the time goods or services are produced by the employee's efforts.

To solve the accounting issues, a set-aside can easily match the cost of salary continuation with the income from the employee's services. Unfortunately, any unfunded set-aside still has the other problems of the continued salary payment, especially dependence on continuing financial viability of the employer. Therefore, the next logical step seems to be

funding of this reserve for retirement benefits in order to assure the availability of cash for the retirees.

The instant a U.S. business actually funds retirement benefits there are problems with federal laws including the U.S. income tax system. If employers hold the assets, they get no current tax deduction, since the tax law generally treats compensation as a deductible expense only when it is actually paid out to employees. In addition, there will be income tax payable by any employees who have a nonforfeitable right to benefits, under the "constructive receipt" rules.

A number of other problems are created by a set-aside of employer assets, including book-to-tax differences, which most financial officers consider undesirable, and practical problems with handling such set asides for large numbers of employees. Despite problems, book reserves are useful for small groups of higher-paid employees, if employers are willing to forgo current income tax deductions and employees will accept a mere promise to pay.

QUALIFIED RETIREMENT PLANS

The problems of simple accounting set-asides led to alternative approaches for providing deferred retirement income. The concept that we now refer to as qualified retirement plans resolves many of the problems of book reserves. In order for a retirement plan to be qualified it must meet the standards of the Employee Retirement Income Security Act of 1974 (ERISA) and the Internal Revenue Code. When an employer-sponsored plan is qualified:

1. The employer gets a current income tax deduction for cash deposits to the plan.
2. Employees incur no income tax when the employer makes plan contributions (tax is postponed until the employee actually receives retirement income from the plan).
3. Plan assets are separate from the employer's assets (in a trust fund or insur-

ance contract) and are protected from all claims of the employer's creditors.

4. Plan assets are generally exempt from claims of employee creditors until they actually become payable.

5. Plan assets are exempt from income taxes on interest, dividends, and capital gains, resulting in faster asset growth.

Practical and tax advantages of qualified retirement plans have led to a variety of different plan designs to meet particular types of employment situations. The choice among designs is affected by the corporate culture, financial and human resources considerations, and collective bargaining relationships. Adoption of pension plans was a major element in collective bargaining during the first two thirds of the twentieth century, and most of the collectively bargained plans were the defined benefit type.

Since unionized employers often provided nonbargaining unit employees with comparable benefits, many large companies established defined benefit plans during the decades after World War II. In fact, so many of these plans were established that for many companies the term *pension plan* is substituted for the more accurate *defined benefit pension plan*.

In current usage the four major types of qualified plans are defined benefit, money purchase (or defined contribution pension plans), profit sharing, and cash or deferred arrangements (CODAs, often called 401(k) plans). Proper plan design is critical, since changes may be difficult, and any qualified plan *must* be designed and operated so it does not discriminate in favor of "highly compensated employees" (defined in Code Sec. 414(q)).

An exhaustive review of each plan type's effects, advantages, and disadvantages is the topic of numerous articles and many hours of consultation, which is clearly beyond the scope of this chapter. However, a brief analysis may be useful for managers involved in the process of trying to decide among the different plans.

Defined Benefit Plans

Defined benefit (DB) plan design begins, as the name suggests, by defining the benefit payable at age sixty-five or other "normal retirement age." This benefit may be a fixed dollar amount for all employees, a percentage of the employee's salary, or computed under a formula using dollars or salary percentage and years of service. Under the terms of the DB plan, this amount is then paid to each employee who meets the eligibility requirements of the plan, when they retire. This payment is typically in the form of an annuity for the balance of the employee's life.

Funding of a DB plan is based on an actuarial analysis of the covered employees. If a sixty-five-year-old lives twenty years and is entitled to a benefit of $100 per month, a total of $24,000 will be paid by the plan. However, the gross amount will not be required at sixty-five if the plan's assets are invested during the payout period. In addition, for an employee who is forty-five years old when the plan is created, assets put in the plan at the outset will earn investment income for twenty years before payouts begin.

An actuary calculates the annual deposits required to fund the plan's benefits, taking into account projected benefits and current ages of all employees. Actuaries also select other assumptions pertinent to the plan's accumulation of sufficient funds to ensure availability of assets as each employee reaches retirement age. The assumptions will include investment income—possible funding gains from employees who leave before their benefits are fully earned (or "vested") as a result of death or other cessation of employment.

The cost of a DB plan is also affected by the standard form of benefits paid by the plan. The most basic form is a monthly benefit for the life of the retired employee. Another common benefit form is a joint and 50-percent survivor annuity that pays one half of the participant's monthly benefit to a designated beneficiary still living at the participant's death. Married employees are required by ERISA to take a qualified joint and 50-percent survivor spousal annuity (QJSA) unless their spouse consents to a different payment method. Some plans charge the participant for the QJSA benefit by actuarially reducing the monthly benefit. ERISA also requires DB plans to provide a qualified preretirement survivor annuity (QPSA) as a death benefit.

This annuity is paid to the surviving spouse of a deceased employee, equal to 50 percent of the employee's accrued pension benefit. Plans may either subsidize the QPSA or actuarially reduce the employee's primary benefit to offset the extra cost.

DB payments to employees are not affected by the age at which employees are first covered by the plan. Even when a plan calculates benefits on years of service, past service credit can be provided for employees. Thus, DB plans may provide equal benefits for employees regardless of their age at the time the plan is adopted. Of course, this requires greater employer contributions to fund the older employee's benefits.

A variety of ancillary benefits may be included with a DB plan (or any other type of plan). For example, plans frequently provide some level of death benefits beyond those required by ERISA or the Internal Revenue Code or include disability benefits. Under ERISA and the code, all plan benefits must become vested (nonforfeitable) when employees complete specific periods of continuous service. (Generally, full vesting is required after no more than seven years of service, and in some cases after as little as three years of service).

Money Purchase Plans

Money purchase (MP) pension plans are not based on a predetermined retirement benefit, but instead start with a specific level of contributions. Frequently, MP contributions are based on a percentage of compensation, but they may also be based on a formula using hours, days, or years of employment. Once again, there are many variations of plan formulae, taking into account variables like the participant's social security benefits.

The MP plan's actual benefit at normal retirement age depends heavily on the investment performance of plan assets. As each year's contributions are made, they are allocated to an account for each participant. Investment earnings and losses are periodically allocated to those accounts, based on their relative values. When participants reach normal retirement age, the balance in the account is then paid to them. ERISA's QJSA and QPSA

rules apply to MP plans, but many of these plans allow participants to elect lump-sum payments or installments in lieu of an annuity. Because its benefits rely heavily on the compounding of tax-free investment performance, the MP plan provides relatively small benefits for employees who are covered for only a few years before retirement. Instead, it is usually more effective for employees covered by the plan for several years before normal retirement age. When plan participants terminate their employment, their benefits will be forfeited if they are not fully vested. In an MP plan, forfeited account balances may be reallocated among remaining plan participants, increasing benefits for longer-term employees. (This reallocation, like all qualified plan operations, must be made in a manner that does not discriminate in favor of highly compensated employees.)

Profit-Sharing Plans

A qualified profit-sharing (PS) plan is more accurately referred to as a deferred profit-sharing plan (any plan making payments based on employer profits is a profit-sharing plan). However, in general usage the term *profit-sharing plan* typically means a qualified profit-sharing plan, not a cash bonus program.

PS plans function much like MP plans, with each participant's account receiving an annual allocation to his or her account consisting of employer contributions, investment experience, and (generally) reallocated forfeitures. Again, the account balance at retirement is used to provide the participant's retirement benefit.

There is one major distinction between PS plans and MP plans: PS plan employer contributions may vary each year, whereas MP plan contributions must be fixed (or at least definitely determinable). Each PS contribution may be left to the plan sponsor's discretion, or the PS plan may use a formula for determining annual contributions. For example, a plan could provide that contributions will be made to the extent that profits exceed a specific dollar amount, a specific return on invested capital, or other financial measures. Some profit-sharing plans use elaborate formulae to measure the profitability of the current year compared to prior years and base plan contributions on the resulting ratios.

Annual PS plan contributions may vary, so these plans must include a nondiscriminatory method of allocating employer contributions. Such allocations are often based simply on the ratio of each participant's compensation to the compensation of all participants. However, plans may also follow the IRS permitted disparity rules in order to allocate more to higher-paid employees (compensating for social security's bias toward lower-paid employees). There are also techniques to adjust for age or years of service, and in fact virtually any allocation technique or formula can be used so long as it does not discriminate in favor of highly compensated employees.

Under the Internal Revenue Code, PS plans enjoy some other unique attributes. They can invest up to 100 percent of plan assets in qualifying employer securities or distribute plan assets to participants as soon as two years after contribution to the plan.

Cash or Deferred Arrangement Plans

The 401(k) plans (technically cash or deferred arrangements or CODAs) became common in the late 1970s when the IRS promulgated regulations under Internal Revenue Code section 401(k). These are a subcategory of PS plans, since 401(k) requires that all CODAs be profit-sharing or stock bonus plans. By 1990 they had become the most common single type of qualified retirement plan, having been adopted by over half of all businesses that have retirement plans.

The 401(k) plans work like PS plans for employer contributions, but they also allow employees to make pretax contributions (deferrals) for their retirement benefits. Under the code, deferrals that meet the 401(k) limits are deemed to be employer contributions that the employee never received as income. This "tax fiction" accelerates growth of employee funds, since they have not been reduced by federal (and in most cases state and local) income taxes.

A variety of tests in 401(k) and its regulations ensure the plans do not provide a significantly greater benefit (as a percent of compensation) for highly compensated employees than for lower-paid participants. To help meet the tests, 401(k) plans often provide matching contributions or other incentives to reward lower-paid employees who participate in such plans.

By emphasizing employee participation in funding retirement benefits, 401(k) plans have helped increase employee awareness of retirement benefits. Conversely, they have been panned by some critics as not providing sufficient retirement benefits. As defined contribution plans they inherently favor younger employees (for whom the compounding effect of interest earnings over a number of years is magnified) but disfavor older employees. Among younger employees, many studies indicate these often lower-paid employees have a lower propensity to save, reducing their benefits from such plans.

Other Types of Qualified Plans

In addition to the four broad categories of plans just described, other types of retirement plans have been developed to meet particular situations. The IRS developed plans called simplified employee pensions (SEPs) based on an aggregation of individual retirement accounts (IRAs) for each employee. The major advantage of SEPs is great simplicity in installation, but their disadvantages are 100 percent immediate vesting of all contributions and coverage requirement of virtually all part-time and full-time employees. By comparison, a qualified plan may exclude any employees who do not work 1,000 hours per year and some other groups.

Employee stock ownership plans (ESOPs) are special defined contribution plans designed to invest primarily in qualifying employer securities. Special financing techniques use ESOPs to borrow funds for the purchase of employer stock, with the loan secured by the stock held by the ESOPs, creating a so-called leveraged ESOP (LESOP). There are also stock bonus plans that operate much like a profit-sharing plan but invest primarily in employer securities.

Qualified Plan Distributions

A variety of unique tax rules affect the taxation of distributions from retirement plans.

However, there is a general overriding concept—retirement plan distributions are taxable as ordinary income at the time of distribution. After all, they constitute income that has not been previously taxed! Special income averaging techniques are available for participants who take the entire balance from the plan in the form of a lump-sum distribution. Large excise tax penalties apply to participants who take funds either before age fifty-nine and a half or do not begin taking money out by age seventy and a half. In addition, excise taxes apply to participants whose retirement benefits are too large in relation to the specific standards of Code 4980A (basically over $150,000 per year). (Many of these tax distinctions are being reexamined by Congress and may not continue in the present form.)

Investment Management

The impact of investment management on all of these plans is extremely significant. In the DB plan, if investment performance is lower than projected by the plan's actuary, the employer must make additional contributions to fund plan benefits. If DB plan investment performance is better than anticipated, the company may not be able to make contributions as projected. In MP, PS, and 401(k) plans, risks and rewards of investment performance fall directly on plan participants. Any defined contribution plans' ultimate benefits are determined by the investment performance of plan assets.

CONCLUSION

Retirement benefits have become sufficiently common and so highly regulated that many consultants devote all (or most) of their practice to such plans. These include attorneys, accountants, actuaries, and many financial resources such as securities and insurance firms. The best resource for a particular situation may be from any of these disciplines, but virtually no single source can be expected to provide all the answers. In addition to consultants, there are a variety of self-study courses, books, pamphlets, and other materials available for those seeking further knowledge about retirement benefits.

MANAGING PENSION PLANS

Clifford A. Rand, Partner, Cowen and Company, and Senior Vice-President and Registered Investment Adviser, Cowen Asset Management

Pension plans have become the largest single source of money for our capital markets. As such, they are subject to myriad regulations, public relations concerns, and the dictates of public policy that may conflict with the best interests of an individual plan's sponsor or beneficiaries. Care is needed in defining pension plan goals so a shortfall does not negatively impact employee morale or create a burden for the sponsor.

GOALS OF A PENSION PLAN

Having a plan is an act of either altruism or business necessity. Contributions to qualified plans are tax deductible to the sponsoring company and are therefore no more onerous than other fringe benefits. Most pension plans exist to help attract and retain desirable employees. Vesting and portability regulations have diminished a plan's usefulness in the retention function. Other things being equal, if competitor firms in your labor market offer plans, you probably have to offer one too. Setting up a plan entails the costs of funding, administration, management, asset custody, and compliance with regulations.

Alternatives to pension plans lie in the realm of direct compensation, bonuses, vacation and overtime policies, health benefits, working conditions, education reimbursement, and company-sponsored activities. The so-called cafeteria approach to employee benefits is gaining in popularity, whereby an employee has a pool of dollars to allocate among health, dental, and life insurance, additional current pay, and pension plan contribution, according to personal preference or need.

A whole new industry has developed around the need for expert advice in the employee benefit area. Consultants range from sole practitioners to nationally recognized organizations and large accounting firms and cover everything from cost-benefit analysis to the creation and administration of programs tailored to an individual company's requirements and resources. Such consultants can also provide immense help in pension plan decisions.

SELECTING A PLAN

In determining which kind of plan to have, the sponsor should consider the particulars of its business and the plan's participants. What kind of a funding onus does the sponsor want to place on the organization? Is the business stable, growing, or cyclical? Is it in a highly competitive industry? Is it conservatively financed or highly leveraged? Specific considerations regarding the participants include their ages and financial sophistication. Is the work force likely to expand or contract in relation to the retirees in the years to come?

The pension plan's objective is an overall statement of what the plan is intended to accomplish. Investors invest to preserve capital, obtain income, and seek appreciation from their investments. They do so with short-, intermediate-, or long-term time horizons and low, moderate, or high levels of risk acceptance.

For pension plans, the preservation and growth of capital are the financial objectives. The plan theoretically has a longtime horizon but must maintain liquidity and constrain the volatility of its asset values to accommodate the possibility of unforeseen withdrawals. The obligation of the plan's trustees is solely to the plan's participants. Still, the plan should not be allowed to get into such a posture as to threaten the sponsor's well-being. These considerations place the plans in the low–moderate end of the risk spectrum.

DEFINED BENEFIT PLANS

A defined benefit plan pays specified dollars at retirement based on factors such as years with the firm or salary level. Each employee will receive a stated amount of money upon retirement that may be paid monthly, in a lump sum, or according to some other specified schedule. An actuary must be employed to ensure that funding and reasonable return on investment will be sufficient to meet the plan's benefit obligations. A cost of living adjustment (COLA) may be built into the defined benefit plan.

Defined benefit plans can be the safest and best for the employee-retiree. They are the most burdensome and risky for the plan sponsor, contingent upon investment results and the rate of inflation. Few new defined benefit plans have been formed in recent years. Rather, the trend has been to liquidate existing ones.

DEFINED CONTRIBUTION PLANS

Three types of defined contribution plans comprise the preponderance of pension plan assets. Under each the sponsor is obliged to make or facilitate contributions according to a preset formula but is not responsible for investment results beyond the exercise of due diligence and prudence in the making of investment decisions for the plan. The plans are:

1. *Money purchase plan*—This obliges the sponsor to fund the plan annually. Funding must be fair and equitable to all participants.

2. *Profit-sharing plan*—This is similar to a money purchase plan, except that funding need only occur when the company achieves a specified level of profits.

3. *401(k) plan*—Most 401(k) plans embody a money purchase or profit-sharing element but a principal difference is that 401(k) plans are also a vehicle for employees to shelter a portion of their pretax compensation by placing it in a pension plan. As with other pension plans, the same tax laws apply to withdrawals. Originally limited to $7,000 per employee per year, the maximum contribution allowed has increased annually according to an inflation index set by Washington. The sponsor must offer employees at least three investment options, typically a short-term money market fund, a common stock fund, and a bond or balanced fund. The sponsor is responsible for the choices offered and the employee is responsible for allocating his or her pension dollars among the choices.

ERISA

The Employee Retirement Income Security Act of 1974 (ERISA) required sponsors to abandon unrealistic approaches to the investment process and imposed a set of rules to make sponsors act responsibly in both setting plan objectives and seeking to achieve them. ERISA broadened the definition of fiduciary and attempted to codify the "prudent man" rule as it applies to the investment of pension plan assets. It expanded the list of forbidden transactions and limited the percentage of a plan sponsor's securities that a plan might own. Wall Street and plan sponsors have been chipping away at ERISA's restrictions for many years.

In plain English, ERISA defined the principles of sound, responsible investment management as pertinent to pension plans and required sponsors to adhere to these standards. Investment decisions had to be based on independent analysis. Asset mix decisions had to be based on responsible forecasts of asset class performance. Extreme market-based investment decisions had to be avoided. Investment decisions had to reflect the demographics, nature of the business, and any other characteristics unique to the plan sponsor.

ERISA and its subsequent related legislation, derivative regulations, and judicial holdings have vastly expanded plan documentation and reporting. Since the stock market crash of 1987, laws and regulations have prompted a shift toward 401(k) plans and the use of investment managers. Plan sponsors are legally liable for imprudent investment practices. They are deemed to act prudently if they employ a registered investment adviser, bank trust department, or insurance company to manage plan accounts. These are known generically as investment or money managers, although they are still sometimes referred to as "funding agents."

INVESTMENT POLICY

A pension plan's investment policy statement translates its objectives into quantified guidelines that will enable the investment decision-making process to achieve those objectives. The policy statement cannot specify precise return on investment requirements that simply might not be obtainable. It can create ground rules by which a prudent investor might reasonably expect to achieve reasonable rates of return.

The underlying rationale is that over time asset values will reflect their intrinsic values against each other and the measures of return, growth, and inflation characterizing the economic environment in which they reside. Shorter-term variability can be caused by investor psychology, shortages and excesses of a temporary nature, and "random walk" factors that can continue for extended periods. Investment policy therefore weighs the latter against the former and, based on financial history, defines the ground rules for the percentage to be placed in each class of asset.

Two components of policy not likely to change are diversification and quality standards. History is replete with eggs-in-one-basket stories. As a rule of thumb, no more than 5 percent of assets should be in the securities of any one issuer except the U.S. government and no more than 20 percent of assets should be in a single industry group. The objective of a pension plan is not to maximize results per se but to maximize the chances of good results. Asset mix is the overriding determinant of investment results, responsible for as much as 80 percent of overall results according to some studies.

Investors have essentially seven categories to choose among: stocks, bonds, insurance products, money market instruments, real estate, special items, and various types of futures and options (under specific rules). These latter instruments should not be confused with commodities contracts in the traditional sense.

Investment policy should therefore blend the long-term attractiveness of stocks with their recent high valuations and allow for the possibility that positive economic news could actually be negative financial news if incremental capital flows out of the market and back into the purchase of goods and services. Contingent upon the degree of conservation and caution the sponsor may wish to exercise, the investment policy might therefore limit investment in common stocks to say 50–60 percent of total assets, in bonds to say 30 percent, and allow cash instruments to be up to 50 percent of the plan's portfolio. Conversely, minimum commitments could be at least 10 percent in cash and 20 percent in each of the other categories with the balance at the discretion of the investment managers. These suggestions have no legal standing but are offered to reflect the price vulnerability in the securities markets and the need for diversification.

As an overlay, investment in foreign securities has grown increasingly popular in recent years. While many offer great potential, it should be borne in mind that most foreign markets except the British and Japanese are thin, few have accounting and disclosure standards comparable to those of the United States, and all embody the additional risk of currency fluctuation.

INVESTMENT MANAGEMENT

Having set policy guidelines, presumably with flexibility and a bias toward erring on the side of caution, the sponsor's next task is to find a means of implementing that policy. Increasingly, sponsors are turning to insurance companies, bank trust departments, and registered investment advisers including mutual fund organizations. The problem with the funds, though, is that they do not provide guidance regarding changes in asset mix or strategy and those decisions are left to the sponsor.

More and more sponsors are employing consultants to help them find a manager or managers responsive to their goals. The key tests are, as in any consultant selection, that the consultant have an established reputation for knowledge, skill, and business integrity. An investment consultant should also have a sizable database, thorough understanding of manager responsiveness to individual goals, and fully disclosed relationships with the managers under review. A competent investment manager should be able to invest assets cautiously or aggressively according to the client's needs and to reallocate assets of a given type according to those sectors of an asset class that offer the most potential.

The ultimate problem is that plan sponsors only have so much time to allocate to their responsibilities and are bombarded with articulate, well-reasoned written and verbal presentations to do this or that or to choose this or that manager. It is hard to know what or whom to believe. Decisions as to policy, strategy, manager choice, and the like should therefore boil down to the same rules used in business and life. If it sounds too good to be true, it probably is. Stick to what makes common sense, is credible, and includes some vestige of intellectual honesty and humility. Expect to err, and as a fiduciary, err on the side of caution.

COMPLIANCE WITH GOVERNMENT REGULATIONS

John F. Wymer III, Partner, Jones, Day, Reavis & Pogue

Beginning in the mid-1930s the U.S. Congress enacted laws that regulate and restrict numerous aspects of the employee-employer relationship. Additional regulations, guidelines, and court decisions have been issued that have expanded upon those restrictions. As a result, there presently exists a large body of complex and sometimes inconsistent employment laws. Gaining a basic familiarity with these laws is an important component of every manager's training.

TITLE VII OF THE CIVIL RIGHTS ACT OF 1964

Title VII makes it unlawful for an employer "to fail or refuse to hire or to discharge any individual, or otherwise to discriminate against any individual with respect to his compensation, terms, conditions, or privileges of employment, because of such individual's race, color, religion, sex, or national origin." Title VII not only prohibits sex discrimination in general but also discrimination on the basis of "pregnancy, childbirth, or related medical conditions," as well as sexual harassment. The Americans with Disabilities Act added physical or mental disability as a protected category effective July 26, 1992.

Title VII applies to the federal and state governments as well as to any employer in an industry affecting commerce that has fifteen or more employees. Where an employer exercises control over the work assignments and hours of work of a temporary employee provided by a temporary agency, the employer may be subject to liability under Title VII for an adverse employment decision affecting such an employee. Labor organizations, employment agencies, and joint labor management committees are also covered by Title VII.

Title VII also makes it unlawful for an employer to publish or cause to be published advertisements that "indicate any preference, limitation, specification, or discrimination, based on race, color, religion, sex, or national origin."

Title VII is administered by the Equal Employment Opportunity Commission (EEOC). To exercise their rights, affected individuals must file a charge of discrimination with the EEOC within 180 days of the unlawful occurrence. In states that have a state statute similar to Title VII, individuals have 300 days in which to file a discrimination charge with the EEOC. Although the EEOC has the authority to investigate discrimination charges, and to issue findings of "reasonable cause" or "no reasonable cause," such findings are not binding on the parties. Only federal courts can determine discrimination after both parties have had the opportunity to proffer evidence in support of their positions.

Trials usually take place in federal court before either a federal judge or a jury. Where discrimination is proven, remedies include an injunction, back pay, lost benefits, seniority, and other equitable relief. Where intentional discrimination is alleged and proven, a jury could award punitive and compensatory damages. Where reinstatement is not appropriate, a victim of discrimination may be awarded future damages in lieu of reinstatement, known as "front pay." However, reinstatement is usually the preferred remedy.

There are two theories of discrimination under Title VII:

1. *Disparate treatment discrimination*—occurs when people are treated differently because of some legally prohibited reason, such as sex or race.
2. *Disparate impact discrimination*—occurs when people are treated the same but the effect of such treatment is discriminatory.

Title VII does acknowledge that in limited circumstances, national origin, religion, or sex may be a "bona fide occupational qualification reasonably necessary to the normal operation" of the employer's business. In other words, an employer may discriminate where it can be shown that being of a particular religion, national origin, or sex is essential to the satisfactory performance of the job.

It is important to keep in mind that this law prohibits discrimination based on a legally prohibited reason. Mere unfairness, unaccompanied by unlawful discrimination, is not actionable under Title VII. Employers are also prohibited from retaliating against persons because they seek to invoke the protections of this statute.

THE CIVIL RIGHTS ACT OF 1866

This law provides that all persons in the United States shall have the same rights to make, enforce, and be parties to contracts as "white citizens." This right to make and enforce contracts has been construed to apply to employment discrimination cases against private employers. White people have stand-

ing under the act to litigate claims of "reverse discrimination." The Supreme Court held that Congress "intended to protect from discrimination identifiable classes of persons who are subjected to intentional discrimination solely because of their ancestry or ethnic characteristics."

There is no federal agency entrusted with the enforcement of this law. Anyone can file an action in federal court without resorting to any administrative remedy. The statute of limitations is the most nearly analogous state statute of limitations. Also, a plaintiff can have a jury trial and obtain compensatory and/or punitive damages.

AGE DISCRIMINATION IN EMPLOYMENT ACT

The Age Discrimination in Employment Act (ADEA) covers all private employers "in an industry affecting commerce" who have twenty or more employees for each working day in each of twenty or more calendar weeks during the current or preceding calendar year. Employment agencies and labor unions are also covered.

With respect to private employers, ADEA prohibits age discrimination against individuals who are at least forty years old. ADEA makes it unlawful for an employer to "fail or refuse to hire or to discharge any individual . . . with respect to his compensation, terms, conditions, or privileges of employment, because of such individual's age." Like Title VII, ADEA prohibits retaliation against individuals who oppose practices made unlawful by ADEA or participate in ADEA investigations or litigation. It is further unlawful for an employer to print or publish employment advertisements "indicating any preference, limitation, specification, or discrimination, based on age." This provision has been held to have been violated by employment advertisements that specify such things as "student" or "recent graduate."

ADEA also recognizes the bona fide occupational qualification defense. Employers have been more successful in the ADEA area in prevailing on this defense, particularly in cases involving safety considerations. Thus, a bus company's policy of not hiring bus drivers over a certain age was upheld based on "compelling" medical evidence of the increased safety risk associated with hiring older drivers.

A charge of age discrimination must be filed within 180 days (300 days in a deferral state) of the alleged discriminatory act. Someone suing under ADEA is entitled to a jury trial and may recover back pay and an equal amount in "liquidated damages" if the violation is "willful."

In 1990, Congress passed the Older Worker Benefit Protection Act, requiring nondiscrimination based on age in employee benefits, and imposing substantial limits on an employer's ability to obtain a written waiver of an employee's rights under ADEA.

EQUAL PAY ACT

The Equal Pay Act applies to all employers "engaged in commerce or in the production of goods for commerce." The Equal Pay Act prohibits sex-based discrimination in wage payments or other compensation for jobs that require "equal skill, effort, and responsibility, and that are performed under similar working conditions." Differentials in compensation for equal jobs are permissible when such differentials are based on a seniority system, a merit system, a system measuring earnings by quality or quantity of production, or any factor other than sex.

VETERANS REEMPLOYMENT RIGHTS ACT

The Veterans Reemployment Rights Act requires a preservice private employer to reemploy a veteran in the same position held prior to entering the military service without loss of seniority. The employee must present a certificate evidencing satisfactory completion of military service to the employer. An undesirable discharge or a discharge "under other-than-honorable" conditions does not entitle a veteran to any reemployment rights. The

veteran must make application for reemployment within ninety calendar days of the date on which he or she was unconditionally released from military service, or from hospitalization that continued after discharge for a period of not more than one year.

If these conditions are met, the preservice employer must offer to reinstate the employee to a former position or to a position of like seniority, status, and pay. The offer must remain open for ninety days. Upon reemployment, the veteran cannot be discharged for a period of one year except for "cause."

Reservists who participate in weekend or other limited training are also protected from adverse employment decisions that are motivated by a reservist's need to be away from work for training purposes.

THE REHABILITATION ACT OF 1973

This act requires that any contractor or subcontractor entering into a contract with the federal government in an amount exceeding $2,500 take "affirmative action to employ and advance in employment qualified individuals with handicaps." The term "individual with handicaps" is defined as "any person who (i) has a physical or mental impairment which substantially limits one or more of such person's major life activities, (ii) has a record of such an impairment, or (iii) is regarded as having such an impairment." This act also provides that "otherwise qualified individuals with handicaps" shall not "solely by reason of his handicap, be excluded from the participation in, be denied the benefits of, or be subjected to discrimination under any program or activity receiving Federal financial assistance."

THE AMERICANS WITH DISABILITIES ACT

Title I of the ADA prohibits discrimination in employment based on disability. ADA defines a disabled American as a person who has a mental or physical disability, a history of such a disability, or who is regarded as having such a disability. A "qualified" person with a disability is someone who, with or without reasonable accommodation, can perform the essential elements of the job. Employers are required to reasonably accommodate persons with disabilities, except where such accommodation would constitute an undue hardship. Examples of reasonable accommodation include job restructuring, modified job schedules, reassignment to a vacant position, modification of physical surroundings and structures, providing of readers or interpreters, or other similar accommodations. Undue hardship is defined as any action requiring significant difficulty or expense. Factors to be considered in determining undue hardship include the size and nature of the business, the number of employees, and the financial resources of the employer. Hence, it appears that larger employers with greater financial resources may be required to go farther in reasonably accommodating disabilities than smaller employers with lesser financial resources.

ADA prohibits conducting medical or physical evaluations of job applicants until after an offer of employment has been extended to the applicant. However, preemployment screening for illegal drugs is not considered a medical evaluation, and hence is permissible under the statute.

THE NATIONAL LABOR RELATIONS ACT

The National Labor Relations Act applies to any employer involved in any industry affecting commerce as well as to labor organizations. There are two major types of cases:

1. *Representation cases*—The law guarantees employees the right to form and/or join a labor organization or engage in concerted activity. A question concerning representation exists when 30 percent of employees in the employer's work force indicate an interest in being represented by a labor organization. Only where there is at least a 30-percent showing of interest will the National Labor Relations Board (NLRB) conduct a representation election. The culmination of a representation case is a secret ballot election conducted by the NLRB to ascertain whether a majority of the employees in a "unit appropriate for collective bargaining" wish to be represented by the labor organization.

2. *Unfair labor practice cases*—The law guarantees employees the right to support a labor organization or to refrain from such support. It is an unfair labor practice for an employer or union to interfere with employees' rights. An unfair labor practice case arises when an employer and/or a labor union is accused of interfering with employees' rights to engage in concerted protected activity, or to refrain from such activity. Examples of unfair labor practices include discrimination because of union activity, or refusing to bargain in good faith.

Representation and unfair labor practice cases are conducted and decided by the NLRB. Violations of the law may be remedied by injunctive relief and back pay. Appeals from the decisions of the NLRB may be taken to the appropriate circuit court of appeals.

THE FAIR LABOR STANDARDS ACT

The Fair Labor Standards Act establishes the minimum wage and overtime requirements for employees. It also places restrictions and limitations on the use of child labor.

The law requires that employers pay employees the minimum wage. The act also requires employers to pay one and one-half times the employee's regular hourly rate for every hour worked in excess of forty hours in a workweek. There are certain overtime exemptions for administrative, executive, or professional employees who are paid on a salary basis and who perform duties that require the use of independent judgment and discretion.

THE OCCUPATIONAL SAFETY AND HEALTH ACT

The Occupational Safety and Health Act requires an employer to maintain a working environment free of recognized health hazards. The Occupational Safety and Health Administration has also promulgated numerous regulations and guidelines affecting various industries and the way they do business.

In general, the scope of OSHA's coverage is extremely broad. The vast majority of American employers fall within the provisions of the act. The act applies to any employer who is engaged in a business affecting commerce and who has employees, regardless of the size of business operation.

The provisions of the act apply to virtually all employees regardless of whether they are full- or part-time, permanent or temporary. Thus, for example, an employer would not only be responsible for the safety of his or her regular, full-time employees but would also be responsible for the safety of workers who were borrowed from another job site or for those leased from a temporary personnel referral service.

The primary obligation imposed on an employer is to furnish a place of employment free from "recognized hazards" that are either causing or are likely to cause death or serious physical harm to his or her employees. As defined by the cases that have dealt with the application of this clause, the term "recognized hazards" refers to those hazards that are either detectable by means of the senses, or are so commonly regarded as being hazards in the industry that even if not detectable by means of the senses they are generally known. This clause was not meant to impose absolute liability on the employer since there are some hazards that are unforeseeable and thus unpreventable. However, the general duty clause is meant to cover nonobvious as well as obvious hazards in situations where detection of a nonobvious hazard can be obtained through the use of instrumentation generally accepted by a given industry.

The second basic responsibility of the employer is that he or she must comply with the safety and health standards promulgated under the act. There are literally hundreds of standards currently in effect, and many of these standards are constantly undergoing the process of review and revision. These technical safety standards cover not only such subjects as the proper construction and maintenance of equipment, machine guarding, fire prevention, and permissible levels of air contaminants but they also specify when and what type of personal protective equipment must be worn by employees and define the training requirements necessary to ensure that employees follow safe work practices and procedures.

OSHA has established exposure levels for a number of hazardous substances. Due to the complex and ever-changing nature of these standards, the employer should be careful to consult an expert concerning any questions as to the applicability and/or operation of these standards.

If, after a careful evaluation, employers determine that they are unable to comply with a particular safety standard but that their present practices and procedures, while not in literal compliance with a particular standard, are as safe as those specified by the OSHA standards, they may apply for a variance under the act. These variances may be either temporary or permanent in nature, and are granted at the discretion of OSHA.

WORKER ADJUSTMENT AND RETRAINING NOTIFICATION ACT

This law was enacted in order to provide workers and their families transition time to adjust to the prospective loss of employment, to give workers time to seek and obtain new jobs, and to give workers adequate time and financial resources to enter skill training and retraining programs. This act requires an employer to provide sixty days of advance written notice of a plant closing or mass layoff. A "plant closing" is the permanent or temporary shutdown of a single site of employment if the shutdown results in employment loss of fifty or more employees. A "mass layoff" is a reduction in force that is not the result of a plant closing and results in an employment loss at a single site for at least 33 percent of the active, full-time employees where at least fifty employees are affected.

THE PERFORMANCE APPRAISAL PROCESS

Michael Z. Sincoff, Senior Vice-President, Human Resources and Administration, DIMAC DIRECT Inc.

Kathleen D. Sincoff, Director of Human Resources, Spectrum Emergency Care

The performance appraisal process provides a mechanism for a supervisor to evaluate an employee's performance, rating it against predetermined expectations based on specific job responsibilities. Performance appraisal systems are used by organizations to provide a rationale for, and justification of, personnel transactions—training, placement, transfer, promotion, wage and salary adjustments, demotion, discipline, layoff, termination. (Indeed, many aspects of a performance appraisal system apply to recruiting and hiring decisions as well.) The process also enables an individual to achieve personal growth through appropriate counseling and coaching activity. A successfully managed appraisal system will produce candid, regular supervisor-employee communication and, in most cases, improve the quality and quantity of employee performance results.

Performance appraisal systems are commonplace in most organizations. They range from the elaborate and complex, carried out in a predetermined manner according to specific guidelines, to the informal and much less structured "hallway" coaching conversations. Underlying all of them, however, is the premise that improving employee performance will result in improved productivity and, in turn, improved business results.

PERFORMANCE APPRAISAL SYSTEM OBJECTIVES

The performance appraisal process entails more than a discussion of performance at the end of the appraisal period. Ideally, the process starts when the employee is hired and encompasses the following objectives:

1. To inform the employee about overall organizational goals, to clarify how the employee's position fits into the organization, and to give direction and purpose to the employee's work activity.
2. To define the essential functions, responsibilities, duties, and expected performance levels of the employee.
3. To provide prompt, objective, documented, job-related performance feedback to the employee.
4. To recognize individual achievement and growth.
5. To funnel information from the evaluation interview into decisions affecting

training, development, organizational mobility, compensation, and the like.

6. To avoid charges of discrimination and costly litigation by assuring that all personnel transactions, particularly those that result in disciplinary action, are treated in a uniform, consistent manner and are grounded in work-related, documented data.

For these objectives to be achieved, a performance appraisal system must have at least these elements: (1) planning and establishment of performance expectations at the start of the appraisal period; (2) periodic review, feedback, and coaching during the appraisal period; (3) performance evaluation review at the end of the appraisal period; and (4) thorough and complete written documentation at all stages.

PREPLANNING AND ESTABLISHMENT OF PERFORMANCE EXPECTATIONS

For a performance appraisal system to be effective employees should have a clear understanding of broad organizational goals and direction, operating philosophies, and a sense of why the organization exists. Typically, such information can be found by an employee in an annual report, descriptive brochures, a statement of mission or values, or in a conversation with the supervisor. A job description will provide information about how the position fits into the organization, its overall purpose and function, specific duties, responsibilities and essential functions, and required education and competencies of the incumbent.

The stage is now set for the employee's understanding of specific job performance outcomes and performance expectations. Moreover, an employee should be able to set goals that are the same, similar, or compatible with those of the organization. And when written down and approved by the supervisor, the outcome of the preplanning effort will memorialize what specific results will measure fulfillment of particular responsibilities, and

what competencies and critical performance skills are required for successful performance in this position.

For example, an organization may indicate in a mission statement that it values its people above all else. A human resources manager in that organization may have responsibility for recruitment. Compatible goals, consistent with the mission, would be (1) to fill 80 percent of all exempt openings within sixty days and nonexempt openings within thirty days; (2) to maintain voluntary turnover at no more than 10 percent; (3) to keep recruiting expense within budget.

Competencies would include knowledge about specific jobs, questions legally permissible to be asked, counseling techniques, budgeting, and the like. Skills in employment interviewing and budget control would be required as well.

PERIODIC REVIEW, FEEDBACK, AND COACHING

After having been verified in the planning meeting at the outset of the appraisal period, competencies, standards of behavior, and goals should be reviewed periodically. Competencies represent basic knowledge, skills, and abilities necessary for successful accomplishment of results. Standards represent the performance criteria against which quantity and quality of performance will be measured. Behavior represents the ongoing ways of acting and exhibited traits necessary for successful accomplishment of results. Goals identify performance outcomes to be accomplished in each area of responsibility.

The purpose of the periodic review is to provide the employee with information as to progress being made toward desired results. Feedback given should be positive or negative, as appropriate, supporting accomplishments that exceed expectations and encouraging improvements in those areas where expectations are not being met. Where deficiencies exist, ways to improve them should be identified and agreed upon to eliminate problem areas. During the periodic reviews, intervening factors that may modify performance expectations should be identified and adjustments taken into consideration.

In sum, performance feedback should be provided regularly, frequently, and always when warranted. Under no circumstances should it occur only at the end of the appraisal period.

PERFORMANCE EVALUATION REVIEW*

A formal performance evaluation review should be conducted by the supervisor at the end of the appraisal period (e.g., thirty days, six months, annually). If conducted properly, the performance evaluation is a powerful tool for individual and organizational growth. Positive outcomes will be more likely if feedback is event specific with clear explication of what behaviors should be maintained, which ones should be discontinued, and which should be initiated. Performance evaluations that are vague and subjectively based will fail. A supervisor should be trained to give factual, sound reasons for a performance rating. Specific strengths and weaknesses, and specific examples of events and behaviors should be presented to support the rating given.

Objectives of the performance evaluation review are to:

1. Review and discuss the employee's present job performance in relation to previously agreed-upon job responsibilities, goals, and performance expectations.
2. Allow both the supervisor and the employee to discuss specific strengths and weaknesses in the employee's work performance during the appraisal period.
3. Allow the employee to discuss and obtain assistance in solving day-to-day job problems and to give the employee the

opportunity to suggest methods of improving work performance.
4. Allow the employee to express feelings about personal and work-related variables affecting performance and career direction.
5. Allow the supervisor and the employee to modify the employee's job responsibilities, goals, and performance expectations.
6. Develop jointly between the supervisor and employee plans for improvement, their implementation schedule, and milestones to be noted as the improvement plans are accomplished.
7. Determine the employee's needs for long-term training and development leading to improved performance in the present position, to promotion, or to transfer.
8. Provide a basis for subsequent wage and salary reviews and promotion decisions.
9. Provide documentation for later disciplinary action up to and including termination.

WRITTEN DOCUMENTATION

Not enough emphasis can be placed on the need for written documentation. Written records should be kept of all periodic feedback discussions as well as of the performance evaluation review. While detailed notes, memos to file, letters of warning for poor performance, and completed performance evaluation review forms are preferred, in their absence other contemporaneous records will be better than nothing. Notes in a phone log, appointment schedules on a desk calendar, and return receipts showing delivery of certified mail help document that an employee has been notified of a performance evaluation. Keep in mind that disciplinary actions, which include both oral and written warning notices, are an integral part of the performance appraisal process.

To offset the "sue the company" attitude that is held by so many people, many organizations have adopted so-called "written oral"

---

* Information in this section is based on a more detailed discussion in Sincoff, Michael Z., and Robert S. Goyer. 1984. *Interviewing*. New York: Macmillan, pp. 126–154.

warnings. After an oral warning is given, to document it, the employee is asked to sign a written statement acknowledging receipt of the warning. While this may seem extreme, such written documentation prevents subsequent denial that an oral warning was given and supports later disciplinary action by the company.

In today's litigious society, organizations are frequently exposed to charges by current and former employees of discrimination, favoritism, or wrongful discharge. The first line of defense against such charges is consistency of treatment and the second line of defense is documentation. By following the guidelines in this chapter and by documentation of each step, although charges and suits may not be eliminated, at least the company's position will be defensible:

1. Explain clearly the company's overall goals, how the employee's job fits into them, and what the employee's duties and responsibilities are.
2. Develop and present clear, agreed-upon performance expectations for each area of responsibility. Quantify them to the extent possible.
3. Provide performance feedback frequently, regularly, and as needed.

4. Identify specific instances of performance proficiency and deficiency.
5. Document in writing all discussions with the employee about performance, but especially discussions about poor performance. Be candid and truthful. Under no circumstance should performance be evaluated as "good" when it is not, just so the supervisor can be perceived as nice by the employee or as running a trouble-free department by upper management.
6. Written evaluations should be reviewed by the next higher level of supervision and by the appropriate person in the human resources department to eliminate discriminatory or other inappropriate or unclear comments.
7. In any evaluation discussions, but particularly in those where poor performance is the topic, describe the undesired behavior, detail the history of the offending conduct, if any, indicate the corrective action to be taken and the time frame allowed, and be explicit about the penalty for not improving.
8. Have the employee sign and date any reprimand or performance evaluation review form to acknowledge receipt of it so that proof exists that the evaluation was given and received.

EVALUATING HUMAN RESOURCES INFORMATION SYSTEMS

Joseph L. Tufano, Managing Partner, Management Consulting Services

A human resources information system (HRIS) applies to a series of modular components, both automated and manual, that maintain, track, manipulate, and store data in safeguarding the human assets of an organization. Just as financial systems play a vital role in accounting for and maintaining the financial health and stability of a company, so do HRISs account for the human element.

There are two alternatives in choosing an HRIS: (1) custom develop a system or (2) select a suitable software vendor package solution. To develop a custom system is very time consuming and expensive. There are many effective HR systems on the market today. The decision will depend on the complexity required to support the organizational and human resource management needs.

DEFINING THE ORGANIZATIONAL NEEDS

To define the organization's needs, the company must identify and document all of the business processes currently being performed by all human resources staff. One approach is to prepare diagrams depicting the flow of each process using flowcharts and narratives in combination. This will assist management in sketching out the components of each job performed. With this approach, the HR group can identify the needed requirements and problem areas, including duplication of efforts.

Once all processes have been documented, a thorough review of diagrams and narratives will be necessary to ensure a complete and thorough job. This forces the group to look at the current manner of doing business and plant the seed on how the job can be performed better. An analysis will determine any cost savings that could be realized in eliminating duplicate functions and increasing productivity. One valuable review approach is structured group discussions, bringing together various functional human resources areas to assist groups in building the systems requirements.

For these group discussions to be successful, a skilled leader should control and direct meetings. Once the diagrams and narratives have been reviewed, the next step will be to identify all inputs from the appropriate senders and outputs generated to their various destinations. As this is completed, a group review should be conducted to identify any duplicate and unnecessary paper flow. Throughout this phase there should be approvals of all work performed and conclusions agreed upon by the group. This will strengthen the requirements and assist in cost justifying any proposed processing changes presented to management. At this point, the project team can develop the necessary systems and functional requirements that will be the basis for the selection of the final software vendor solution.

SOFTWARE SELECTION PROCESS

A request for proposal (RFP) will be the document that each software vendor will follow in order to respond with a proposal. The contents of the RFP must include the following information:

1. Company background describing the reasons for the RFP.
2. The hardware desired.
3. A description of the RFP contents including the main contact's name and phone number, a time schedule of the selection process, and a description of how the finalist(s) will be selected.
4. The format for response by vendors.
5. Systems and functional requirements.

There are several ways to identify reliable vendors. They could be discussed with the management information system (MIS) department or contacts within human resources professional organizations could help.

Once the RFP has been sent, a scoring method must be developed to evaluate the responses from the vendors. One approach is to use a weighted scoring method. Assign each requirement a code such as critical, desired, or nice to have. Give each code a numeric weight and develop a performance rating table or matrix. For example:

3 = Fully satisfies the established requirement.

2 = Does not fully satisfy the requirement but the system provides an acceptable work-around to meet it.

1 = Would require a systems modification that could affect the installation of any future software updates.

Apply the mathematical weighing scenario to each vendor. Match the total scoring and select the two or three vendors with the highest scoring for the next round of evaluation.

After narrowing the field of vendors to a short list, set up vendor demonstrations of their products. To be as thorough as possible, you may want to divide the demo into two segments: (1) a complete vendor demonstration in which they will walk you through the system giving you a sense of what the system can do, and (2) a review with the vendor of system and functional requirements that were part of the RFP. After all vendors have gone through this process, rescore the results. Then, check vendor references and make a decision.

SYSTEM DESIGN AND DATA CONVERSION

After a software package has been selected, the real work begins. The first step in the process is to develop a work plan that will cover all the tasks and work steps to be performed. To control the project, include due dates and assign responsibility for the completion of each task and step.

One of the first and most important steps is review of the software package documentation, comparing it to the requirements developed in the first phase. This step is necessary in identifying where your requirements have a good match to the software. In performing the matching, you can determine where the software package must be customized to fit the requirements that were not matched. If there is a need for the system to interface with other systems within the organization or to third-party vendors, interface requirements and plans must be developed.

Another major step is comparing data elements resident in the current system to those of the software. This will help you determine the data needed to be converted and/or added to the new system. This phase will also include the actual designing of report and screen layouts, screen hierarchy, forms, and stationery. If the screens supplied with the new software package do not conform to your functional needs, you should modify them. A good rule of thumb is, "If it is a cosmetic change and not a functional one, then do not make it."

TESTING

The testing phase includes members from both users and technical MIS staff to perform systems testing. Prior to the test, these representatives should have been trained on the systems operations. Once trained, they will develop the test data. The data should be developed from cross-sections of the current system covering all aspects of the human resources and payroll areas currently in use. The testing should include the following examples:

1. Applicant tracking with applicant information having the ability to be transferred from applicant system to the employee database upon hire.

2. Benefits, 401(k) plan, pension/savings plan definition setup.
3. Salary and wage grade table setup.
4. Employee setup and processing of changes that will flow through from hire to termination.

Upon completion of the systems test, all users of the system must be trained on the operation of the system. As part of the planning process, an implementation plan should include (1) the strategy of what modules will be implemented along with the timing and (2) a time plan as to who will go up first on the system.

HUMAN RESOURCES MANAGEMENT IN INTERNATIONAL OPERATIONS

Frank L. Acuff, Director, Human Resources International, and Adjunct Professor, Northwestern University

The complexities of international human resources management have increased along with the growth of multinational organizations. Selection, orientation, compensation, and many other issues require additional attention in the international arena. The guidelines used for effective domestic human resources management are often less applicable internationally. In other cases, international assignments bring unique issues to the forefront of human resources management, such as multicountry relocations, tax protection, and repatriation.

Domestic human resources specialists normally administer programs for a single set of employees with one pay and benefits system and a single currency. Employees are taxed by a single government. International human resources managers, on the other hand, often deal with several nationalities who are on different pay and benefits systems and are paid in more than one currency. Further, the income tax laws of more than one country may be involved. Thus, functions such as wage and salary administration, employee benefits, relocation and orientation, human resources planning, and labor relations become extremely varied.

INTERNATIONAL FUNCTIONS

A typical international human resources department performs a number of functions, including:

1. *Taxation*—This is a major issue since most U.S. expatriates are subject to the tax laws of the host country (where the expatriate is working) and the United States. Tax policies may be designed by human resources personnel. Actual tax calculations are usually performed by either the internal accounting staff or an outside accounting firm.
2. *Orientation*—The expatriate's international experience will be strongly influenced by a successful orientation to the host country. Information can be provided on visa and travel arrangements, relocation of personal effects, assistance in moving into new accommodations, and other factors. Additional planning is needed when family members are involved.
3. *Administrative services*—The human resources function may be involved in arranging housing and travel services for employees assigned overseas. The department may arrange for work permits, visas, and may perform other services.

INVOLVEMENT IN EMPLOYEES' PERSONAL LIVES

The human resources department may become involved with:

1. *Spending habits and lifestyles*—Organizations must establish allowances to help pay for increased costs of living abroad.

The human resources department makes assumptions about the expatriate's typical "bread basket" (eating habits) and living arrangements to establish a home country baseline when computing the size of the living allowances.
2. *Employee health*—The organization must be concerned about health care for the employee and his or her family, particularly if a third world country is involved.
3. *Recreation*—The organization may be concerned about the employee's physical and mental health. This is commonly done by sponsoring recreational and social activities, perhaps with other members of an expatriate community.

SELECTION OF EMPLOYEES FOR INTERNATIONAL ASSIGNMENTS

The selection of the right person for the right job is a challenge under any circumstances. It is especially true in the selection of expatriates. Information may not be complete on the host country job, culture, housing, education, and other areas. The skills that have propelled a manager to success in the home country may not be those that will enhance performance internationally. Some useful characteristics of a potential expatriate are:

- *Reasonable expectations*—Is the employee looking forward to an international experience? Research indicates that those who have both positive and realistic expectations are likely to adjust better to life in a foreign culture than those who do not look forward to an overseas experience.
- *Open mindedness*—How strongly does the individual feel about home country values, ideas, and ways of doing things? Is the individual receptive to new ideas and different patterns of behavior?
- *Tolerance and flexibility*—Tolerance measures the capacity to endure unfamiliar surroundings and circumstances. Flexi-

bility measures the ability to consider new approaches in dealing with a task or problem. Coping in a foreign environment requires both.

- *Patience*—This factor is important in international assignments where a slower pace and delays are typical. A patient person is more likely to adjust successfully.
- *Interpersonal interest*—This characteristic measures the extent to which one enjoys being with other people. A "loner" might find it very hard to establish intercultural relationships.
- *Spouse communication*—Do spouses get along well? The challenges of intercultural adjustment are not usually a good place to build a relationship where there has been a substantial lack of open and constructive communication.
- *Foreign-language interest and ability*—Learning the language of the host country enhances an international assignment. Is the expatriate willing to learn about the foreign culture and language?

KEY FACTORS IN INTERNATIONAL COMPENSATION

The pay packages of U.S.-based employees are quite straightforward compared to those of expatriates. Expatriate pay packages have more components, have relatively compli-

cated tax ramifications, and may differ considerably from country to country, even for the same organization. Special care must be taken to ensure that the expatriate is neither underpaid nor overpaid, and that there is a thorough understanding of the expatriate pay package. Common expatriate compensation issues are:

1. *Foreign service premium*—This is additional money to attract an employee to a foreign assignment. This premium is usually a percentage of base salary.
2. *Hardship premium*—This is a financial allocation to compensate for any special hardships of a given location. Some locations would have no hardship premium. This premium is also usually a percentage of base salary.
3. *Equalization allowance*—This is a financial allocation to "keep the expatriate whole" with respect to food, housing, and other items. In general, it compensates the expatriate for the difference between the host country cost and the home country cost for designated items. These payments are usually paid monthly.
4. *Tax payments*—An expatriate's taxes will be influenced by both the U.S. and host country tax laws. Most companies have policies to compensate employees for extra taxes paid as a result of the international assignment.

Exhibit 4-6 compares a typical domestic and expatriate pay package.

Exhibit 4-6. Typical Domestic and Expatriate Pay Package

	U.S. Pay Package ($)	Expatriate Pay Package ($)
Base Pay	70,000	70,000
Foreign service premium (20%)		14,000
Hardship premium (10%)		7,000
Commodities and services allowance		6,000
Housing and utilities allowance		8,000
Tax coverage		20,000
Total	70,000	125,000*

* This amount excludes any payments for relocation, vacation airfare, schooling, and other potential expenses that could add substantially to the total pay package.

THE REPATRIATION OF EMPLOYEES

Repatriation is a bigger adjustment for many individuals than going abroad. Once the assignment has been completed in the host country, one is caught in an in-between state, not knowing exactly what the future holds or how one will adjust to it. The organization, as the expatriate knew it, has probably changed significantly. The adjustments are not only to new faces and new positions on the job but also to the personal change of pace between the host country and the home country.

The excitement surrounding one's departure to an exotic foreign adventure may be missing from family, friends, and co-workers when returning home. The returning expatriate may be alternately excited, disappointed, and perhaps even depressed. Organizations can take steps to make the experience of returning home as positive as possible, including:

1. Outline the anticipated career implications in advance. Keep the individual apprised of any changes. A well-thought-out effort here goes a long way, even though no one can predict the expatriate's future with certainty. How long do you expect the expatriate assignment to continue? What kind of factors will most affect the timing of the return to the home country? What types of opportunities will typically be available upon repatriation?

2. Establish a mentoring relationship between a senior domestic executive and the expatriate. This will help the expatriate stay in touch with policy and organizational changes. Such knowledge is likely to make reentry far less traumatic.

3. Find a meaningful job for the individual upon return.

4. Encourage the individual to use what was learned in the foreign assignment as the springboard for new perspectives in the organization. This makes the individual feel valued in the home office while helping to broaden the thinking of others in the organization.

DEALING WITH CORPORATE RESTRUCTURING

Milton F. Droege, Jr., President, Droege & Associates

Corporations have structures that designate division of accountability and assignment of authority. Structure, as a rule, is documented in the form of organization charts that reveal the official network of titles of command and specification of functional assignments.

The inner workings of the organization on a day-to-day basis cannot be understood merely from the chart. Legitimate interactions not accounted for on the chart must and do take place constantly. Cooperative ventures that cross chart lines are normal and extensive. The chart, or visible representation of the organizational structure, does not, therefore, attempt to explain how the organization works. It deals only with the formal starting point for accountability and authority.

An organization chart may display duplicate assignments for reason of geographic dispersion. It may reveal greater or lesser centralization. All these and more are merely characteristics felt to be necessary to control the differing management styles, industry requirements, locational variables, and talents and motives of the work force.

CHANGING THE STRUCTURE

Technically, one could claim to have changed the organization merely by exchanging one employee for another. While this would alter the balance of the organization, the structure itself changes only with a shift in the designation of the division of accountability or the formal assignments of authority.

In recent years it has become popular in the press to use the terms *restructure, downsize,* or *right size* to explain organizational cutbacks in times of financial distress. Such cutbacks usually result in a restructuring, but it is not automatic nor is it necessarily the only driving force behind such actions. Such action may occur for any number of reasons, including:

1. Merger with another organization.
2. Divestiture of part or parts of the organization.
3. Geographic relocation of any given part of the organization.
4. Division of accountability by virtue of location or market rather than by function or vice versa.
5. Addition or deletion of a function.
6. Desire for tighter internal control.
7. Desire for greater opportunity of individuals in the organization to have room for initiative.

IMPACT AND OPTIONS FOR RESTRUCTURING

Restructuring disrupts established relationships and work patterns. It creates under-standable doubts and fears and may create a defensive environment. The work force tends to hold back, share little, and take minimal risk. The legitimate questions that relate to the work force's own security will be open to answers from virtually any source. The less information made available through formal channels, the more will be generated in the grapevine. The longer this goes on, the more bizarre and believed will become the inventions.

Simple reassurance from management tends to magnify the problem. Structure is very real. It explains to employees who is accountable to whom, and who administratively is in charge of their fate. To change this is to leave them, at least for some time, on shaky ground. For it to be known that change is in the works and not have information forthcoming invites seriously unproductive reactions. At best, it slows things down. At worst, the talented but concerned employees with other alternatives will jump ship.

A restructuring sequence begins with a driving force and its attendant symptoms. The profits may have been down for some time. The technology of the industry may have left the organization in a less competitive position. The press may reveal interest in the organization by an outsider. A key retirement or resignation may occur.

Suspicions of change begin to enter into normal daily office conversations. There are conversations about change, wanted change, needed change, and possibilities of change. As time passes, rumors become broader and more intense. The amount and quality of work suffers.

COMMUNICATION

If there are legal or competitive reasons to keep things as secretive as possible, such reactions will have to be lived with for a while. If there is going to be a change and it can be shared, it should be. Sending word down through the chain of command is risky. It subjects the information to multiple possibilities for distortion and error. It may also lack the appropriate impact.

When serious announcements must be made to great numbers in a tight time frame, the message should not suggest any course of action that is uncertain. The messages should avoid nurturing reassurances. While neither blunt nor insensitive, they should be matter-of-fact and businesslike. If there are some unknowns, there can be some measured acknowledgments of this. If further announcements are certain, they may be promised.

These announcements or promises of announcements should presume a well-thought-out scenario. An organization is a delicate synergy of both formal and informal concerns. It should be pictured much as a room full of Ping-Pong balls, each suspended from others by elastic bands. When a ball is removed or relocated, the entire arrangement is altered. New sizing, new assignment, new grouping, new titling, new levels or scopes of responsibility are all interrelated. There is no such thing as a simple restructuring. One change begets three or more.

As the needs of the organization unfold and the management team examines the necessary actions, the impact should be considered from every angle. While the financial implications will traditionally come first, they should be accompanied by an analysis of the necessary layoffs, transfers, and reassignments. If the organization has a human resources professional, that person should be involved from the start. Otherwise, some organizational and procedural considerations might be overlooked.

It may also be advisable to bring in an outside professional. No matter how well you may understand your organization and its needs, the odds are that no one person in a key position has gone through many serious restructurings. The ability to anticipate and predict outcomes and prescribe appropriate actions comes with repeated exposure in diverse arenas. Some corporations choose to bring in third parties to handle large numbers of layoffs. This can reduce the emotionality of the event. It can also reduce the possibility of the wrong things being said and causing misunderstandings regarding layoff benefits, outplacement activities, and legal implications.

THE ANNOUNCEMENT

It should be mandatory that the process be confidential until such time as official revelations are forthcoming. If possible, the first announcement should be the last. It should explain the why, the what, and the how to all employees simultaneously. The "one shoe at a time" approach has no redeeming value. "Waiting for the other shoe to fall" will keep everyone tight and defensive. There will be little, if any, discretionary effort and productivity will suffer. Furthermore, if it goes on long enough, it will become part of the work culture and the work force will not ever be fully prepared to refocus entirely on the job.

The first announcement should include as much as possible of the total picture. Decisions that cannot yet be announced should be acknowledged and promised for the future. Dates for future announcements should not be promised unless there is no chance for failure. If layoffs are involved, they should be announced as early in the sequence as possible. Management needs to have arrived at a number in its own mind. Layoffs simply cannot afford to be invented as they go along.

The ideal is to announce all layoffs in the first revelation and to indicate that there will be none further. While ideal, this is dangerous. If there is any chance that there will be further layoffs in the near future, do not make the promise. A broken promise on the subject of layoffs will live with the management team for years. At some point, the sooner the better, there does need to be a formal acknowledgment that the reorganization is complete. It should be pointed out to the work force that there may be the usual turnover or attrition in the future, but that those actions tied directly to the restructuring are past.

RESPONSE TO RESTRUCTURING

During the restructuring period, be prepared to deal with employee speculation. No matter how well organized and forthright the management team may be, a restructuring gets everyone's attention. There will be gallows humor. Do not try to squelch it and do not participate in it. Management is the source of the nervousness and is the wrong source for humor. Be prepared to have many of the normal little glitches in the work process blamed on the restructuring. If it is legitimately a glitch, handle it as such, point out its nonrelationship to the restructuring, and move on. There will be great concern with morale. Those who traditionally see big morale problems will continue to see them and will put them at the feet of the restructuring. Those

who are prone to predicting gloom will not suspend their activity.

It is important for everyone to be busy doing productive work during a restructuring. Downtime is a breeding place for lamentations and negative speculation. Top management should remain as visible as possible. The management posture should not be greatly different than is normal. Forced humor or forced seriousness shows little understanding of the real issues at hand. The overall guide to conduct and momentum should be "business as usual."

EFFECTIVE COMMUNICATION

Evan E. Rudolph, Vice-President
Southern School Media

Communication is the primary function of a manager. Managers spend at least 75 percent of their time communicating with other employees. The complexity of today's business environment makes the achievement of that function difficult. Why? Talking is easy. Communicating effectively is not.

Because we have been doing it since birth, communication becomes commonplace. We become nonchalant about the fact that communication and successful communication are not the same. Successful managers understand that successful communication is the transfer of information with understanding as its goal. The key word here is *understanding*. Whether a manager is communicating verbally or nonverbally, or attempting to inform

or persuade, the objective should be to ensure that the receiver of the message understands the information.

VERBAL COMMUNICATION

Verbal communication is overwhelmingly the method of choice for managers. Effective verbal communication comes only after careful preparation. When communicating verbally, managers will improve their effectiveness by following these suggestions:

1. *Develop understanding.* All communication is designed to produce a response. Sometimes the response we get is not the one we

expected, however. Regardless of where things go wrong, let us start at the source of the message—the sender's mind. Each person communicates according to his or her ability to understand. The sender's language must be in terms the listener or receiver can understand.

2. *Express empathy.* Even successful communication is never 100 percent accurate. The reason is that each person is at the center of his or her own world. If we are to communicate at all, we must share enough thoughts and feelings to develop a common ground. To develop this common ground, empathy is essential. Empathy is defined as understanding how another person thinks or feels.

3. *Read feedback.* Feedback is the response given by others indicating how our message was received. Here are some examples of feedback and what they might mean. If the listener/receiver crosses his or her arms tightly, it might mean anger, hostility, or rejection. If the listener/receiver changes the subject, he or she might not be interested. If the listener/receiver smiles, frowns, or moves around, it might mean agreement, disagreement, or boredom respectively. Feedback is open to interpretation and misinterpretation. Even if you are certain that the feedback you have received is what you wanted, ask a question to make sure.

4. *Smile.* Try it the next time you talk with someone. Give him or her a big, sincere smile and see how the person reacts. Someone once said, "If you see someone without a smile, give him one of yours." That is good advice, particularly for managers.

5. *Be modest.* The temptation to toot our own horn is strong but usually results in negative feelings from receivers. Colleagues and peers know what is going on and will give credit where credit is due.

6. *Take an interest in others.* Interest is flattering. Sincere interest translates into a positive approach to communication. Good communicators and good managers express a sincere interest in the people with whom they communicate.

7. *Avoid arguments.* It has been said that nobody wins an argument. Ben Franklin put it best when he said, "A man convinced against his will is of the same opinion still." Little or nothing can be accomplished through arguing.

8. *Begin on a positive note.* When a conflict is obvious, start by pointing out the things on which you agree. The instant people are told they are wrong, they are forced to defend themselves in order to save face. It does not make sense to back a wild animal into a corner. Backing people into corners will almost certainly result in their being so committed to defense that they stop listening.

9. *Know what you want to say.* It sounds ridiculously simple, but it is critical. Too many people jump into a conversation without first deciding what they want to say . . . then wish they had waited.

10. *Be aware.* An effective communicator is alert and aware of the communication process. AWARE can be an acronym: *A*—assemble your message before you speak; *W*—watch your receiver to see if you are understood; A—adapt your message and delivery to the situation; R—relate your message in the order you assembled it; E—Evaluate your effectiveness by asking questions.

11. *Be yourself.* Communication is not something that exists in a vacuum. All effective communicators are aware of the need to take a natural approach to communication. Forcing an attitude or forcing mannerisms unique to a particular situation does little more than make the receiver wonder what is going on.

LISTENING

When listening skills are needed, managers will improve their effectiveness by following these suggestions:

1. *Watch out for prejudices and biases.* Being aware of personal prejudices and biases will allow you to keep them under control and prevent them from interfering with your listening ability. Try to be open minded, interested in the topic, and enthusiastic.

2. *Ignore distractions.* It takes hard work to

concentrate on the speaker, but the habit of giving in to things like windows, people in the hall, thinking about yard work, or plans for the weekend will seriously detract from your ability to listen effectively.

3. *Take concise notes if necessary.* All too often we assume that we will remember the details needed to make a decision or follow up on a project. Good listeners, good managers, and effective communicators realize the importance of using notes to ensure that things get done correctly and on time.

4. *Give physical feedback to show physical involvement.* Use facial expression and body movement. Sit forward in your chair. Nod when you agree, tilt your head when you have a question, or perhaps raise an eyebrow if you disagree. The speaker and the listener both gain when the listener shows involvement.

5. *Ask questions.* Any time effective communication takes place, you will find that both the speaker(s) and the listener(s) have accepted the responsibility for asking questions if they do not understand.

6. *Agree or disagree.* Do this with the logic or information, but not with the speaker. All too often listeners allow the subject to become confused with the speaker. Good listeners can separate the speaker from the subject and not allow their personal feelings, likes, dislikes, or attitudes to interfere with their ability to listen objectively.

7. *Look for nonverbal cues.* When listening, remember that facial expressions, tone of voice, and gestures should be consistent with the verbal message. If a speaker's words seem to be saying something different than the speaker's actions and the message is unclear, it is time for a question.

8. *Summarize as you listen.* The normal American speaking rate is about 125 words per minute. Your mind thinks several times faster than that. Take advantage of this edge by summarizing as you listen.

NONVERBAL COMMUNICATION

Here are some reasons why nonverbal communication is so important:

1. *Nonverbal and verbal messages sometimes contradict one another.* For example, a manager might say, "It's about time to get to work around here" while smiling. The smile would contradict the seriousness of the verbal message. Some receivers/listeners would believe the smile rather than the words.

2. *Messages may be affected by the overall flow of sound.* Jerky speech patterns convey a message of uncertainty. When long pauses dot a conversation, receivers or listeners become uneasy. If managers do not sound as if they know what they are talking about, many listeners assume they do not.

3. *Lack of facial expression is often interpreted as boredom or apathy.* The lack of facial expression will generally be accepted as a negative rather than a positive.

4. *Eye contact can make or break communication attempts.* When the speaker does not look at the receiver or listener, it can give the listener the opportunity to wonder whether the speaker is simply nervous or has something to hide. Either way, the message is affected negatively.

5. *Movement in itself is a message.* Movement (or the lack of movement) gets the attention of the receiver or listener. Movement is a necessary part of effective communication because it is almost always what we do when we are comfortable. Immobility can make a speaker look stiff and uncomfortable.

WRITTEN COMMUNICATION

Writing is not easy for most managers. It does not come naturally like speaking and listening. On top of the fact that it is not easy, many managers write poor letters and memos because they:

1. *Give in to pressures at work.* They do not plan letters and memos before writing. This often results in the omission of important points, a disorganized letter or memo, and often confusion in the mind of the reader.
2. *Fall into a rut.* If all your letters and memos sound the same (use the same opening, closing, and phrases) there is a good chance they will not get the action you want because they all look the same. The reader sees the same opening and immediately assumes that there is nothing new to follow.
3. *Refuse to write as naturally as they speak.* There is a big difference in writing to write and writing to read. Writing to write results in rigid, formal, stiff prose that lacks the sincerity and warmth to which people respond. Writing to read produces conversational prose that puts the reader in a positive, receptive frame of mind.

For some managers, avoiding these problems simply means resisting the temptation to write pompous, "important"-sounding letters and memos. Successful writers write simply and directly. There are hundreds of books available on business writing. Successful managers do not hesitate to use them.

Some easy to follow suggestions can make letters and memos look and read better:

- Write as you talk, in a natural, conversational tone.
- Be yourself. Do not try to imitate anyone else's style.
- Write to express, not to impress.
- Use your imagination. Find new ways to say the same old things.
- Be sincere. Be friendly. Let people know that being of service is a pleasure, not a chore.
- Use live words. Use active verbs.
- Play up the reader's interests and play down the company's.
- Write in terms of "you" rather than "I" or "we."
- Use "little" words that you know your reader understands. Lincoln's Gettysburg Address is considered one of the greatest works ever written in the English language. Only 265 words long, it contains: 197 one-syllable words (74.3%), 48 two-syllable words (18.1%), 13 three-syllable words (5.0%), 7 four-syllable words (2.6%).

COMMUNICATING WITH EMPLOYEES

Effective communication between management and employees is important. It should go up as well as down. Successful employee relations programs have at least four things in common:

1. A company mission, vision, goal, or objective.
2. Carefully selected means of communicating that mission, vision, goal, or objective to the employees.
3. A means of evaluating the program.
4. An ongoing commitment to effective communication.

An employee communications program may be centered around a company mission such as:

1. Providing superior service, quality, product, and price to customers. This is achieved by knowing the job; doing the job; caring about the job and the customers; delivering service, quality, product, and price; realizing that urgency is essential.
2. Developing and maintaining trust and credibility in the marketplace. This is achieved through the same five activities mentioned in item 1.

A company can communicate its values in many forums, including:

- Monthly budget meetings
- Weekly management meetings
- Department meetings
- Employee meetings
- Bulletin board programs
- Employee orientation programs

- Employee handbooks
- Performance reviews
- Employee newsletters
- Employee suggestion programs

COMMUNICATING THE RIGHT MESSAGE

Effective communication requires a knowledge of the important messages to communicate. Some such messages are:

- The mission/vision is working.
- We are in the game to win, not simply to have the experience of playing and feeling good about it .
- Delegation is the key to our success.
- We are an affirmative action employer.
- We must and will make a profit.
- Senior management does not have all the answers.
- Criticism is welcome. Suggestions are more welcome.
- We are an industry leader.
- How we can better serve our customers?
- We will reward employees for helping reach the mission/vision.
- We have the right people in the right jobs.
- We have high expectations.
- We will succeed.

RELATIONS WITH ORGANIZED LABOR

Fred M. Reichman, Attorney-at-Law, Reichman & Associates

Anyone in the field of labor relations should be familiar with the National Labor Relations Act, union organizational activities, recognition of unions, and the process of collective bargaining.

NATIONAL LABOR RELATIONS ACT

Today, relations between management and organized labor are circumscribed by the provisions of the National Labor Relations Act, which together with its 1947 amendments contained in the Labor-Management Relations Act and the Labor-Management Reporting and Disclosure Act of 1959, constitute the basis of our national labor relations policy. That policy, controlled as it is by federal law, establishes a unified, well-balanced method for management, unions, and employees represented by them to interact with one another. However, prior to 1935, little was done to promote the growth of organized labor and the development of collective bargaining. As a result, an enormous inequality between the power of management and labor existed. In an attempt to establish a balance of bargaining power between the two, the National

Labor Relations Act, or Wagner Act as it was known, was passed in 1935.

Development of Our National Labor Relations Policy Under the Act

The cornerstone of this act was Section 7, which created and gave employees three legally enforceable rights: the right to organize, the right to bargain collectively through representatives of their own choosing, and the right to engage in strikes and picketing. Enforcement of these rights was established by the act through the creation of specific restrictions on management's actions. These restrictions and any subsequent violations of one of these restrictions have come to be known as unfair labor practices. These unfair labor practices continue to play a large role in governing the relationship between management and labor as it exists today.

After passage of the Wagner Act it became evident that instead of creating a balance of bargaining power between management and labor, the act simply transferred the bargaining advantage to labor. After World War II, a groundswell of adverse sentiment led to amendments designed to achieve the desired balance of power.

The first of these amendments was the Labor Management Relations Act, or Taft-Hartley Act, enacted in 1947. The purpose of this act was to curb growing union power by placing restrictions on union activities similar to those placed on management by the Wagner Act. In addition, while the Wagner Act created and gave employees the right to organize, bargain, and strike, the Taft-Hartley Act gave employees the right to refrain from engaging in those same activities.

The second amendment was passed in 1959 and is known as the Landrum-Griffin Act or the Labor-Management Reporting and Disclosure Act. This act was designed to regulate the internal affairs of the unions. Its goal was to prevent certain improper or unethical union practices by requiring unions to report various activities to the Office of Labor Management.

Enforcement of the Act: The Board

In order to enforce the substantive rights created by these statutes, a federal administrative agency was needed. As a result, the National Labor Relations Board was created in 1935. From its inception in 1935 to the Taft-Hartley enactment of the amendments in 1947, the board was responsible for investigating, prosecuting, and adjudicating all cases over which it had jurisdiction. However, this format caused an abundance of public criticism contending that no board could act fairly while serving as prosecutor, judge, and jury. In 1947, in response to the growing criticism, the single National Labor Relations Board divided into two separate and independent units: the five-member board and the general counsel.

The five-member board has become primarily an adjudicatory body. It does not initiate cases and, as a result, must wait until a charge is brought before it by the general counsel. In addition, the five-member board has complete authority over elections.

The general counsel has assumed the investigative and prosecutorial functions formerly performed by the board. The main duty of the general counsel is to investigate and determine whether, when, and upon what basis charges of unfair labor practices should be prosecuted. The decision of the general counsel is final and cannot be appealed to the courts.

Today, the field of labor management is governed by the general counsel, the five-member board, and the federal statutes that are collectively referred to as the National Labor Relations Act. The goal of the statutes is to strike a balance between the rights of employers, unions, and employees. In order to fully understand how the act affects management, it is essential to examine its major provisions.

Employees' Protected Activities: Section 7

Section 7 of the act pertains to protected employees' activities and it gives employees the right to self-organization, the right to form or assist labor organizations, and the right to bargain collectively through representatives of their own choosing. In addition, this section enables employees to engage in concerted activities for the purpose of collective bargaining or other mutual aid or protection. Generally, concerted activity is any action engaged in by employees acting together or an action by one employee on behalf of other employees. This activity must be designed to enforce a collective bargaining agreement or it must be for mutual aid or protection.

Mutual aid or protection has been defined as any activity that is engaged in for a common cause. An example would be employees on a particular shift refusing to work under unsafe conditions. Under such circumstances, the employees would be protected by Section 7 of the act from being disciplined. It is important to understand that the rights included in Section 7 apply to all employees, not just those involved in organized labor, which means that an employer could be found to have violated the National Labor Relations Act by disciplining any of the employees involved in the above conduct even if they were not represented by a union.

Restrictions on Management's Activities: Unfair Labor Practices

To ensure protection of employees' Section 7 rights, the act imposes restrictions on management's activities. These restrictions are referred to as unfair labor practices.

The first unfair labor practice discussed in the act restricts management from interfering with, restraining, or coercing employees in the exercise of the rights guaranteed in Section 7. Accordingly, management cannot impede an employee's desire to join a union; nor can it discipline or discharge an employee for engaging in concerted activity for mutual aid or protection. When determining if management has committed this unfair labor practice, the motive of management will not be considered. All that is examined is the question of whether management engaged in conduct that may reasonably tend to interfere with the free exercise of employees' rights under the act.

The second restriction discussed in the act makes it an unfair labor practice for an employer to dominate or interfere with the formation or administration of any labor organization or contribute financial or other support to it. The purpose of this provision is to make

certain that the union representing the employees is completely independent of the company and of company interference. A wide variety of conduct has been held to constitute illegal domination or support by an employer. Again, the employer may not argue that the assistance was done in good faith without any intention of violating the act. Some activities that are likely to violate this provision of the act include giving preferential treatment to one union over another, or soliciting members for a particular union and extending recognition to a union that does not represent a majority of employees.

The third restriction discussed in the act makes it an unfair labor practice for an employer, by discrimination in regards to hire or tenure of employment, to encourage or discourage membership in any labor union. That is to say, management cannot impose different conditions of employment on an employee, or fire, discipline, or refuse to hire him or her because of that individual's involvement in union activities. This provision of the act would be violated, for example, when an employee who is a known in-house union activist with a spotless record is discharged for one unexcused absence, when no other employee has been so disciplined for similar conduct.

By discharging the employee because of his activities on behalf of the union, the company has clearly violated this provision of the act. However, it is important to understand that being involved in a union does not preclude an employee from discharge or discipline for good cause.

Since management is accused of discrimination more than any other violation of the act, it is important to point out a few rules that management should follow: First, treat all employees in the same manner regardless of whether they are involved in union activities or not. Second, make sure that every decision made by management is substantiated by a legitimate reason. Finally, apply all work rules and policies in a consistent, uniform, and even-handed manner. Following these three short rules can save management from being found to have committed an unfair labor practice for discrimination.

The fourth restriction stated in the act

makes it an unfair labor practice for an employer to discharge or otherwise to discriminate against an employee because he has filed charges or given testimony under the act. Thus, management cannot discipline, discharge, or treat differently an employee who testifies in a board proceeding or files charges with the board. As in the previous section, management can take action against an employee who has given testimony or filed a charge as long as management can show that it would have taken the action for legitimate reasons regardless of the employee's protected conduct. Some activities that are likely to violate this provision of the act include assigning undesirable work or hours to an employee who has testified and discharging an employee who announces the intention to file an unfair labor practice charge.

The fifth and final provision of the act restricting management action makes it an unfair labor practice for an employer to refuse to bargain collectively with representatives of her employees, which means that the company must engage in good faith bargaining with a union that has been recognized or certified as the collective bargaining representative of an appropriate unit of a company's employees. That is to say, a company cannot engage in sham or "surface" bargaining with the intention of not producing an agreement.

UNION ORGANIZATIONAL CAMPAIGNS AND REPRESENTATIVE ELECTIONS

The first step in any union's attempt to become the bargaining representative of a particular group of employees is the organizational campaign. This campaign is an attempt by a union to collect authorization cards signed by 30 percent of the employees in an appropriate bargaining unit. As a general rule an appropriate bargaining unit is made up of employees, other than supervisors or management personnel, who share a similar community of interests. Thus, the unit should consist of employees who have a substantial mutual interest in wages, hours, and other conditions of employment. Once the union

acquires the requisite number of authorization cards it can file a petition with the National Labor Relations Board for an election to gain representative status.

Solicitation and Distribution by Nonemployees

The requirement that a union must obtain authorization cards signed by 30 percent of the employees in a particular bargaining unit presents a major obstacle to the union. The problem from the union's perspective is that it does not have ready access to the employees. Usually, the union does not have a list of the names, addresses, or telephone numbers of the employees. As a result, a union will be forced to look for alternative ways to contact employees.

One of the ways unions attempt to organize employees is through the use of nonemployee union organizers. Typically, they will stand just beyond company property and wait for employees to enter or exit work and talk to them while distributing information fliers with attached authorization cards. The union's goal is to create an active nucleus of pro-union employees whom they hope will spread the union's message to other employees.

The general rule of law is that an employer can prohibit all solicitation and distribution by nonemployees at all times on company property. However, this does not give management the right to prevent solicitation and distribution outside of the company's property or even on such property in circumstances where alternate means of access are not available to such organizers.

In order to implement its rights, management must expressly restrict all solicitation and distribution by any nonemployees on company property. Therefore, management must not only restrict actions by union organizers but also solicitation and distribution by the nonemployee representative from Fred's Diner who wants to inform employees about his restaurant's great orange roughy. By applying this rule uniformly, management deprives the union of the argument that it is being discriminated against.

Solicitation and Distribution by Employees

The second way employees are organized is through disgruntled employees coming to the union seeking representation. If this occurs, the union automatically obtains an employee spokesperson willing to spread the union's message and help organize fellow employees. Under these circumstances, management is faced with employees instead of nonemployees who are attempting to solicit and distribute literature to other employees. As a result, management's rights change.

In discussing management's power to curb solicitation and distribution, it is important to draw a distinction between the two terms. Solicitation is generally defined as oral communication, which includes attempts at convincing employees to sign authorization cards. Distribution, on the other hand, is regarded as the passing out of literature. This activity is doomed to pose special problems because of the possibility it presents for litter as well as safety. It is important that management understands the difference between the two terms as defined, and the difference between the rights management has to limit each particular activity.

In general, management has the ability to restrict union solicitation by employees during working time. Thus, management can prohibit employees from soliciting during those times that they are working, but not necessarily during all working hours. This distinction allows employees to freely communicate during break times, lunch times, and any other period when they are not expected to be working, such as before or after work.

Before management can use its right to restrict solicitation by employees it must draft and post a general no-solicitation rule. In order for this right to be used during union organizing campaigns, the rule must have been drafted and posted prior to the beginning of the campaign. There is no uniform language that must be used in writing this rule, but it should contain a clear statement that solicitation is not allowed during working time. In addition, this rule must be written and enforced in a nondiscriminatory manner.

Thus, all solicitation, not just that which pertains to unions, must be restricted during working time.

Management also has the right to limit the distribution of literature by employees. Generally employers can restrict distribution in working areas, whether work is being performed or not. Thus, an employer can restrict distribution during a lunch hour or break time if the employees choose to remain in the working area. The reason behind this distinction is that if employees were allowed to distribute papers and leaflets in the working area, it could create a problem with littering. In addition, if the papers are left in the work area they are presumed to create a safety hazard. Once again management should inform employees of this rule by posting a well-drafted, clear statement detailing management's position. Finally, it is imperative that management apply this rule uniformly.

How Management Should Act During an Organizational Campaign

The primary goal of management during a union organizational campaign is to prevent the union from obtaining authorization cards signed by 30 percent of the employees in the targeted bargaining unit. If that fails, management must then be prepared to conduct an intensive election campaign. The first defense is the posting of no-solicitation and no-distribution rules described above. At the first indication of an organizing effort, management must initiate a counteroffensive. This may consist of telling the employees, either through letters, posters, or small group meetings, about the detriments of signing union authorization cards and belonging to a union. Management should also state its attitude toward organized labor and unions. Included in this statement should be a summary of management's collective experience with unions. In addition to talking with the employees, it is imperative that management listen to the employees. Often, management appears oblivious to the problems faced by employees. By simply becoming concerned and listening to employees, management would be able to effectively defeat a union-organizing campaign.

While it is important that management become apprised of what it can do during an organizational campaign, it is equally as important that management becomes aware of what it cannot do. To avoid the commission of an unfair labor practice, management should be aware of the following rules.

First, do not threaten any employee. Management may not make statements such as, "Unionization will force the company to reduce benefits and privileges." Management may not, of course, do such things as threaten to fire or punish an employee for engaging in union activity, or to close its facility if the union gains representation.

Second, do not interrogate employees. Management may not ask employees if they prefer a union or if they have engaged in card signing. Management should not inquire about attendance at union meetings. However, some employees may, on their own accord, volunteer such information. It is not an unfair labor practice to listen, but management may not ask questions to obtain additional information concerning employee sentiment about the union.

Third, do not promise additional benefits or wage increases to any employee for not joining or supporting the union, or imply that benefits will be given if the union fails. For example, it is unlawful to tell employees that if they had only come to the company's management before they sought union representation, the company could have resolved their problems. Such a statement implies a promise to provide a benefit.

Fourth, do not engage in surveillance of union activities. Management may not attend any union meetings, park across the street from the union hall to see which employees are present, or otherwise spy on those engaged in union activities.

Overall, the best advice to management during an organizational campaign is to maintain normal day-to-day relations with employees while always being cognizant of these rules.

Representation Election

In the event that the union succeeds in obtaining authorization cards signed by 30 percent of the employees in a particular bargaining unit, the union is then able to file a petition for representative status with the National Labor Relations Board. This petition marks the beginning of the formal process of a board-conducted representation election.

The first step in the election process commences when a board representative phones management and attempts to arrange a hearing. This hearing will generally be preceded by an informal conference for the purpose of the board resolving any outstanding issues. Those issues might involve such things as whether the employer is within the jurisdictional standards; the appropriate bargaining unit determination; supervisory status and the eligibility of certain employees in that bargaining unit; and the date, time, and place of the election. In setting this election date it is important that management realizes that time favors its position. Pursuant to board procedure, elections that both parties stipulate to must be set within fifty days of the filing of a petition. It is suggested that management make full use of the time allowed by the board by setting the election on the latest possible date. This strategy allows the immediacy of the union's initial appeal to wear off and it gives management ample time to conduct its own campaign. The purpose of such a campaign would be to provide the employees with information regarding union practices and to respond to the union's campaign.

How to Run an Election Campaign

Management's campaign should concentrate on three points. First, management needs to show the employees the financial needs of unions and the demands that unions put on their membership to achieve these needs. One way to accomplish this is by obtaining from the Department of Labor the union's latest financial disclosure statement, the LM-2 form, which includes all income of the union and the salaries being paid to all union officials. This can be distributed to the employees.

Second, management should review the union's constitution and bylaws with its employees. This enables management to point out and explain to the employees the amount of control that the union exercises over its membership, and its right to collect fines, fees, dues, and assessments.

Third, management should describe the collective bargaining process and explain to its employees that if the union wins the election management is bound only to bargain in good faith with the union. Employees are generally under the impression that once a union has won representative status they will automatically receive everything the union promised during the campaign. The fact that a breakdown in the negotiations between management and the unions can produce strikes should be thoroughly reviewed together with the impact of such actions.

All three of these points can be presented to the employees through the use of letters, posters, or speeches. These communications must be designed with due regard for the rules that were discussed earlier.

Management Compliance with Board-Mandated Requirements

The company should be aware of certain board-mandated responsibilities that it must perform. First, management has to prepare two copies of an alphabetical list of eligible voters and their addresses, and file them with the regional director of the board. This list, known as an excelsior list, must be filed within seven days of the date on which the regional director approves a stipulation for election or orders the election. Second, management is required to post a notice of election that will be supplied by the board. Although the board may not state a time when the notice must be posted, it is required to be done at least seventy-two hours before the election.

The Election

The last step in this process is the board-conducted election. The board is responsible for supplying all the essential items necessary for running of the election. Eligible employees are provided a written ballot by a board agent that is marked in an enclosed voting booth to ensure secrecy. The ballot is marked "Yes" if the employee wants the union and "No" if the employee wants to reject union representation. The union must receive more than half of the votes to be certified as the collective

bargaining representative of the employees, in which event management is required to recognize and bargain with the union.

RECOGNITION WITHOUT AN ELECTION

The previous section detailed the process through which an election is used to establish management's duty to recognize a union as the employee's representative for the purposes of collective bargaining. Generally, an election is the vehicle a union will use to gain recognition. Yet, there are exceptions. Management may also be required to recognize and bargain with a union that has not won an election if that union has authorization cards signed by more than 50 percent of the employees in an appropriate bargaining unit and management does one of three things: voluntarily recognizes the union; involuntarily or mistakenly recognizes the union; commits an egregious unfair labor practice that makes the holding of a fair election unlikely.

Voluntary Recognition

It is Monday morning and management has just held its weekly meeting. In this meeting a decision has been made to accept the inevitable and recognize the union that is engaged in an organizing campaign of the company's employees. Can this be done? Yes, it certainly can, as long as management remembers one simple requirement. A company can voluntarily recognize a union only upon the union's showing of a majority interest by the employees in the appropriate unit for bargaining. This is normally accomplished by the union's display of authorization cards to the employer, but can also be accomplished by such things as the taking of straw polls. If the union does not demonstrate that it possesses a majority showing of interest through cards or otherwise, management will have committed an unfair labor practice by extending such recognition.

Involuntary Recognition

It is the middle of a workday and two union organizers approach the plant manager saying, "We have authorization cards signed by more than 50 percent of the employees in an appropriate bargaining unit," and hand him a stack of signed authorization cards. After examining each card carefully, the manager says, "Yeah, so what! Some of those guys will change their minds during the election." Then, on Friday the company receives a letter from the union stating that in view of the fact that it has recognized the union, the union would like to schedule a meeting to begin negotiations for a collective bargaining agreement. The manager laughs and says, "Those guys are crazy. There is no way I recognized the union, is there?" The answer to this question is "yes." The examination of the cards was sufficient to confirm majority status of the union and would be held by the NLRB to constitute recognition. In fact, it is very easy for management to recognize a union involuntarily and mistakenly once a demand for recognition has been made. Proper response to these demands should take the following points into consideration.

First, management should be cognizant of the fact that a demand for recognition can be made in various ways. Regardless of the method chosen by the union, its main objective remains the same. That is to secure an acceptance by management of the union's claim that it possesses authorization cards signed by a majority of the employees in a particular bargaining unit. It is very easy for management to involuntarily and mistakenly express its acceptance of the union's claim. In order to avoid this mistake, management should remember one rule, if any doubt exists about how to deal with a situation: It is better to *not* act than it is to act. For example, a union official comes to the plant and says, "I have cards signed by a majority of the employees and if you do not believe me you can check them." Under no circumstances should the cards be accepted or examined.

Second, management should not engage in any extensive discussions with the union. By limiting what is said, management decreases the chances that someone will accidentally extend recognition to the union. An appropriate response to a union's demand for recognition is: "The company is not aware of the circumstances under which any union authorization cards might have been signed and as a result the best test of the desires of the employees regarding representation would be a board-conducted secret ballot election." Management should also make it clear that it is willing to cooperate with the board and with the board's procedures for conducting an election.

Third, management should try to obtain the name of the person making the demand for recognition as well as the union represented, as it is important to identify the principals involved.

Fourth, management should politely ask the union representative to leave the premises. If at all possible, management should avoid using physical force with the individual. Management is reminded to be as courteous as possible.

Commission of Serious Unfair Labor Practices

A union with a majority of authorization cards has petitioned for an NLRB election. During the course of the election campaign the CEO has promised all the employees raises if the union loses and, in addition, he has fired the union's biggest advocate. As he sits down the CEO smiles and proudly states, "The election is ours. This company will never have to recognize a union."

Wrong! The above hypothetical is a perfect example of a situation in which the board could order a company to recognize a union without an election because the company committed an egregious unfair labor practice. In this type of situation the board would examine the facts for conduct that would foreclose the possibility of holding a fair election. If this conduct is present and the union proves that it represents a majority of the employees, the board will order the company to extend recognition to the union and begin bargaining.

As a general rule of thumb, if a company wishes to avoid inadvertent recognition of a union, it should never act precipitously or inconsistently with its past practices. The place to challenge the union is not in your office or on the floor of the plant, but in a well-structured election campaign designed to inform employees of the detriments of union membership and persuade them that it is, indeed, in their own best interests to avoid unionization.

COLLECTIVE BARGAINING

After a union has gained representative status, the company is required under the law to commence collective bargaining in good faith over rates of pay, wages, hours, and other conditions of employment. The result of such bargaining will be a collective bargaining agreement, or labor contract, that will generally be negotiated for a term of up to five years. Thereafter, upon expiration of each successive contract, the parties are required to meet and negotiate. There is a considerable difference in the negotiation of the initial labor contract and subsequent renewal agreements.

Negotiating the Initial Collective Bargaining Agreement

The dynamics of any negotiation are complex and multilayered. Labor negotiations seem even more so. In the process of negotiating the initial contract, more often than not the parties come to the bargaining table by force of law rather than a desire or need to resolve problems and come to an agreement. They have generally just finished what may have been an intense and bitter election campaign in which unkind things were said by both sides; there are issues at stake affecting the direction and viability, if not the very existence, of the company, the livelihood of the employees, and the institutional concerns of the union; there are external forces that must be taken into account such as market conditions, the state of the economy, inflation and the cost of living, competitors' labor costs, and the like; there are the inevitable problems of conflicting personalities and egos with varying degrees of sophistication and experience among the participants in the bargaining; and, underlying it all, there is the ultimate measure of the strength and power of each party.

It is absolutely essential to set aside feelings

of hostility and to resolve or rise above personal conflicts—in short, to adopt a professional attitude toward the negotiation. Continued antagonism will only prove destructive to the interests of both sides, and worse, management's objectives, whatever they may be, will be much more difficult, if not impossible, to achieve.

It is important to understand the nature of a collective bargaining agreement and the issues to which management must be alert. A labor contract should reflect the needs and concerns of the parties. Irrelevant provisions or those that address problems that may only hypothetically arise in the future should be excluded from the contract. For example, in a craft-oriented industry where skill has always been the determinative factor for advancement or retention on layoff, a rigid seniority system is inappropriate. Again, in a new company in existence for only a few years, provision for an enhanced vacation benefit of, say, four weeks for twenty years of service, is inadvisable. It deprives management of future bargaining chips when such a benefit may become relevant and it gains the company no bargaining advantage when conceded earlier than necessary. Management should not accept a proposed provision simply because it appears in some of the union's other contracts, even with the company's direct competitors, if the provision does not make good sense for the company.

Negotiation of a labor contract is segmented into noneconomic or language concerns on the one hand and economic or cost items such as wages, hospitalization insurance, pensions, vacation entitlement, holidays, and the like, on the other. Negotiation of the language provisions will include the structure under which economic benefits are given as well as other purely noneconomic matters. That is, the company will want to negotiate the eligibility qualifications for benefits, such as length of service, and other restrictions such as working the day before and the day after a holiday to be eligible for holiday pay. This can be done prior to any negotiation over the actual benefit.

In negotiating the initial contract, management must insist as forcefully as it can that the noneconomic issues be resolved before the cost items are addressed. The obvious reason for this is that noncost items can have a direct and significant impact on actual cost of production, and should be factored into determining how much actual money management is willing to put on the table. A company that is able to maintain greater flexibility and discretion over the elements of its operations will clearly be more cost effective than a company bound by such things as rigid rules of seniority, voluntary rather than mandatory overtime requirements, and inflexible bidding procedures.

Unions also want to see the language issues resolved before consideration of economics, but may insist on getting into economics before all the language is resolved. Currently, it can constitute bad faith bargaining for a company to insist to the point of impasse on making the resolution of all language issues a precondition to discussion of economics, but short of that, skilled management negotiators will do everything they can to accomplish that end.

The provisions that management should attempt to include in the initial agreement are a strong and detailed management rights clause, a full no-strike provision, and a "waiver of further bargaining" provision, also known as a "zipper clause," since it confines the agreement between the parties to the actual contract language and waives any right to further bargaining during the term of the contract over issues not covered.

The union will be most concerned with obtaining a recognition and jurisdictional clause, asserting its jurisdiction over the employees in the appropriate unit for which it is bargaining, as well as perhaps the work they perform; a union security provision such as a union shop clause requiring membership in the union after thirty days as a condition of employment; a check-off clause requiring the employer to deduct union dues from its employees' paychecks; a grievance-arbitration provision; and a seniority clause. The no-strike and the grievance-arbitration provisions of a labor contract have been held by the courts to constitute a trade-off of equally legitimate interests between the parties. If a union is going to give up its right to strike over the term of the contract, it is entitled to have the grievance-arbitration mechanism available to resolve disputes over the interpretation and application of the terms of the contract.

There are, of course, many other provisions that both parties may wish to include, depending on the industry, the individual practices that have developed within the company, and the union's institutional requirements. The ultimate content of the agreement, including the concessions made by management on the economics, will be determined by the dynamics of the negotiations, the relative strength of the parties, and the skill of the negotiators. One might expect to devote a considerable amount of time and effort to these initial negotiations. It is not uncommon for such negotiations to take many months. All the time and effort devoted to the development of a viable agreement, however, will prove to be worthwhile in the future as it becomes evident that the relationship of the parties has been more or less permanently shaped by that initial agreement.

Negotiating Successive Renewal Agreements

In contrast to the lengthy negotiation of an initial collective bargaining agreement, negotiation of renewal agreements, although intensive, may be accomplished within one or two months. Typically, serious negotiation starts one month before expiration of the agreement. If one of management's strategies might contemplate bargaining to an impasse and implementing its final offer after expiration of the contract, it should provide the union with a written notice of its intent to terminate the contract upon expiration. This must be delivered at least sixty days prior to expiration. The union will typically provide the company with a similar notice as well as a notice of expiration of the agreement to the Federal Mediation and Conciliation Service at least thirty days prior to such expiration.

Although revision of the noneconomic language of a contract is not uncommon, the emphasis is generally on resolving economic issues such as increased wages and benefit costs. Internal surveys of a company's needs and problems that have developed over the term of the prior contract with administration of the agreement, as well as external surveys of similarly situated companies' labor costs and relations with the union, will prove invaluable in developing a bargaining strategy and goals. A good negotiator will need to be realistic in setting the company's goals and flexible enough to adapt to the inevitable changes in position by both parties.

Contract Administration and Maintenance

The execution of a collective bargaining agreement does not end a company's concern with its provisions. A labor agreement is less like a binding commercial contract designed to resolve all problems than it is a blueprint or guideline for the manner in which the parties relate to one another. There are some portions of the contract that are strictly enforceable in accordance with its terms. Other provisions may not be precisely applicable to a fact situation or unforeseen events may have intervened.

When a dispute arises as to the application of contract terms to a particular situation or the interpretation of language, the parties should be prepared to engage in the grievance process pursuant to the grievance procedure in the agreement. If that fails to resolve the problem, they may be forced to submit the dispute to a neutral third party—an arbitrator—for resolution. Management should carefully prepare its case for submission of any matter to arbitration. It should pay particular attention to the selection of an appropriate arbitrator, researching prior cases of each of the panel of arbitrators it receives from FMCS (Federal Mediation and Conciliation Service) or AAA (American Arbitration Association). If a company is uncertain that it will win an arbitration, it would be better off seeking a settlement of the dispute to avoid setting a precedent with an adverse ruling by the arbitrator.

Contrary to the original concept of arbitration as an inexpensive and expedient way to resolve disputes, the process has become time consuming, cumbersome, and costly. It should be seen only as a method of last resort for resolving disputes with a union.

EMPLOYEE HEALTH PROMOTION

Michael Goldberg, Director, Managed Care Development and Education, Blue Cross/Blue Shield of Missouri

Deborah Wiethop, Editor, Communications Projects, Blue Cross/Blue Shield of Missouri

Since the 1970s the employer's cost of health care for workers has increased dramatically. It has been estimated that companies are seeing their health-care premiums increase about 20 percent per year. It has also been estimated that about 50 percent of the dollars spent on health care each year in the United States can be attributed to illnesses that result from poor lifestyle choices, including poor diets, lack of exercise, and smoking.

One method companies have adopted to help reduce these costs, while improving their employees' health habits, is health management, or wellness. These employee health promotion programs stress the prevention and early detection of health problems in order to improve employee health and to reduce later use of expensive health care services.

The premise of wellness is simple: Help develop healthier employees by giving them access to early detection programs, and they will see their medical risk factors for serious illness decrease dramatically. This will translate into future dollar savings for the employer.

MOTIVATING EMPLOYEES TO PARTICIPATE

Companies also are finding that successful wellness programs increase employee productivity, reduce absenteeism, and improve employee morale. Most companies are able to offer the programs either free or at minimal cost to their employees. Some are able to offer programs for spouses and children.

Many programs offer tangible incentives for enrollment and completion of activities. Health-related gift items, such as exercise clothing, are welcome incentives. Others are financially rewarding employees for taking no sick days and filing no medical claims each year. Some programs are taking a negative approach: Those employees who smoke or are 20 percent heavier than their ideal weight are being asked to pay more for their health insurance.

A myriad of wellness activities, often designed through the cooperative efforts of the employer and outside wellness experts, are being offered by companies nationwide: exercise/fitness, cholesterol screening, stress management, smoking control, nutrition education, weight control, blood pressure control, health assessments, alcohol/drug programs, back care, cancer screening, on- and off-the-job accident prevention, and prenatal education.

Companies are primarily concerned with programs that deal with the high rates of cardiovascular disease and lung cancer. To help fight these diseases, the investment in intervention activities, such as lectures, handouts, risk-assessment screening, and personalized treatment programs, is inexpensive while the dividends—employees having fewer major health problems—are high.

DO WELLNESS PROGRAMS WORK?

The jury is still out on the effectiveness of wellness programs. Supporters argue that since the wellness effort is only a decade old, there has not been enough time to assess its cost effectiveness adequately. The majority of corporations offering health promotion programs are establishing them—and do plan to continue them—with little quantifiable proof that the programs actually save money. Some surveys, however, are showing that for every $1 invested in a company wellness program, $3 or more were saved in future health insurance costs.

IMPLEMENTING WELLNESS PROGRAMS

In order to start a fitness program, it is a good idea to get key employees from all levels involved in the planning, start-up, and ongoing process of a wellness program. This will ensure that the program will be attentive to everyone's needs while developing a strong base of support and commitment.

Having the chief executive officer's support is crucial. The employees need to know that the top executive is taking the program seriously. And management employees need to have realistic expectations about the program. Companies are probably looking for employees to stop smoking, add an exercise program to their routine, and have some fun; they are not looking for candidates for the next Olympic tryouts.

In fact, many companies have been disappointed in their wellness programs because the wrong employees are taking advantage of these activities. Aerobics classes, for example, are usually taken by employees who already know that exercise is beneficial, not by those individuals at high risk for heart disease who desperately need some cardiovascular conditioning.

In order to build a healthier work force, companies need to help employees become aware of their individual health risks. Only then will employees start to change attitudes about their health, and then, lifestyle behaviors. Companies should seriously consider administering health risk assessments to evaluate employee needs.

And not every company can afford a new gymnasium. Other programs, much less expensive and probably more important, are those that deal with smoking cessation, alcoholism, obesity, high cholesterol, and hypertension. In helping employees with these health problems, do not treat them like school children. Ask employees what activities they would find valuable, and take their advice. Fun, innovation, and common sense can make a wellness program highly effective.

AVOID THE HARD SELL

Remember, a lot of glitz can turn people off. Full-color brochures and expensive newsletters are perceived as wasteful in these cost-conscious days.

Incentives and rewards go a long way in getting and keeping employees interested. There is no need to invest much money as small prizes work well. Companies also need to communicate the fact that effort and regular participation, not super-athleticism, will be rewarded. Companies should not be focusing on marathon runners or softball stars.

Promotion of your company's wellness program is important. But beware of a hard sell: Let employees know the value and rewards of their participation. And remember that your employees are busy. They may not have time for regular classes, but surveys are showing that activities, such as company-sponsored softball games, are effective in encouraging people to adopt healthier lifestyles. Some companies have found that a well-designed wellness program can become a major factor in creating positive change in the culture of the organization.

CONCLUSION

Companies with successful wellness programs are not making cost containment their first priority. They are finding that if they meet the health-care needs of their employees, cost savings will follow. If employees believe that a company is interested in primarily saving money, rather than in their health and well-being, they probably will not participate.

Companies also are finding that workplace environments can sabotage the best of intentions. Smoking policies, cafeteria and vending machine choices, and safety policies all should be studied to make sure a company's corporate culture is not undermining its wellness efforts.

Most of all, remember that wellness and fitness need not be expensive. And it must be fun. Have a brown bag awards banquet. Or encourage employees to climb the steps every day by hiding coupons for prizes in the stairwells. Creativity can go a long way in developing a program that employees will enjoy.

EMPLOYEE SUBSTANCE ABUSE

Victor Schachter, Partner, Schachter, Kristoff, Orenstein and Berkowitz

SCOPE OF THE PROBLEM

The epidemic of substance abuse in our society is all too well known. It is estimated that 66 million Americans have experimented with illegal drugs, 6 million Americans regularly use cocaine, and 2 million smoke marijuana daily. A Gallup poll reported that drug abuse has become the most important problem facing the nation in the opinion of the American public. Illegal drug use is not the only substance abuse issue. An estimated 9 million Americans are alcoholics.

Since our workplace reflects society, it comes as no surprise that substance abuse pervades corporate America. It is estimated that 23 percent of American workers use drugs on the job, and between 10 percent and 20 percent of all workers have a serious alcohol or drug problem. A telephone survey of callers on the 800-COCAINE hot line indicated that 75 percent of the callers used drugs on the job. Drug and alcohol abuse unquestionably is responsible for many instances of workplace accidents, injuries, deaths, mistakes, productivity lapses, quality control problems, absenteeism, theft, interpersonal difficulties, and morale problems, costing employers an estimated $100 billion per year.

Current investigative techniques to combat workplace substance abuse range from urine and blood testing to random searches and video surveillance. These approaches raise difficult legal issues relating to employee privacy and criminal liability. In addition, with the emergence of wrongful discharge liability, employers must exercise caution in disciplining employees who are suspected of violating company drug/alcohol rules.

Employers must answer three basic questions in addressing substance abuse. First, what investigative techniques will be implemented to identify drug or alcohol abuse, while avoiding the creation of a "police-state" atmosphere? Second, what discipline will be taken against abusers? Third, to what extent will the company support rehabilitation of substance abusers? These questions require a fine balancing of management rights with the rights of individual employees.

INVESTIGATIVE TECHNIQUES AND TESTING

Employers have a broad right to investigate suspected violations of company rules, and employees have a corresponding duty to cooperate in such investigations. Investigative techniques include reasonable searches, undercover agents, and video surveillance. In particular, sobriety and drug screening, such as urinalyses and blood tests, are being used more frequently to detect abuse.

While drug and alcohol testing in the workplace has been the subject of controversial litigation since the 1980s, certain trends have emerged that provide clear guidelines for employers. For example, an employer's right to test employees upon reasonable suspicion that they have used illegal drugs on the job, or that they are impaired by illegal substances, has been universally upheld. Similarly, the right to require tests of those responsible for accidents that cause personal injury or property damage in safety-sensitive industries has also been recognized.

Preemployment testing of job applicants and random testing of employees have been the focus of intense litigation in recent years. Courts have generally upheld preemployment testing, noting that not all privacy intrusions give rise to liability. They balance the competing interests of privacy, safety, and efficiency to determine if the applicant screening is "reasonable." Courts have recognized that employers "unquestionably have a legitimate interest in a drug- and alcohol-free work environment," and an employer "may reasonably determine that the results of a drug test are directly related to job fitness."

Reasonable safeguards should be implemented by the employer to minimize the intrusiveness of the drug tests. In one court case, advance notice was given to applicants of the test requirement, the tests were conducted in a medical environment by independent laboratory personnel, the test results and accompanying medical history information were kept confidential, and the tests were not used to detect pregnancy or other conditions. In addition, applicants were not observed while furnishing the urine samples, positive test results were confirmed by a second testing method, and applicants were given the opportunity to question or challenge test results they believed to be erroneous.

Random testing of employees has received a much "rockier" reception in the courts, particularly in nonsafety-sensitive industries. Such testing involves a systematic method of testing employees using a random selection process where there is no individualized suspicion that the persons being tested have used or abused drugs. In one case, Southern Pacific directed its employees to undertake a random urine test as part of a drug and alcohol detection program. One of its computer programmers refused, claiming that her privacy would be unduly violated as the drug test was

irrelevant to her desk job. She was fired for her refusal. The employee sued for wrongful discharge, among other claims. The railroad argued that such tests were job related, noting that 17 percent of the employees tested positive for marijuana, cocaine, alcohol, or heroin use. The jury decided in the employee's favor to the tune of $485,000. The lesson from such a case is clear: "Suspicion-less" random testing necessitates a more direct justification, such as an actual safety-sensitive job or threat of public harm.

Federal, state, and local governments have enacted various laws regarding workplace substance abuse testing. It is important to identify what enactments might affect your business, and take affirmative steps to comply. However, it is helpful to know that courts generally will find tests lawful if they are implemented in a reasonable, confidential, and nondiscriminatory fashion for legitimate business purposes. Future legislation and court cases will continue to define the parameters of substance abuse tests.

WORKPLACE DISCIPLINE

All companies should have in place a policy clearly setting out the company's rules pertaining to drugs and alcohol. These rules should set forth the types of conduct prohibited, including use and possession on premises, selling or providing drugs to other employees, and reporting to work while impaired by alcohol or drugs. Abuse of prescribed drugs, a very common problem, should also be included within the proscribed activities.

Management should conduct proper investigations of suspected rule violations, and violations should be dealt with consistently in implementing the company's disciplinary guidelines. Employees should be disciplined for performance problems or violation of company rules, not for dependency on drugs or alcohol. Emphasis on dependency, rather than performance or other job-related conduct, could lead to serious handicap discrimination claims. Supervisors should be trained on how to identify and respond to disciplinary problems, and be sensitive to employees' privacy rights.

REHABILITATION

Discipline is not always the appropriate response to a workplace substance abuse problem. In fact, rehabilitation may be preferable, since it is a constructive alternative that allows the abuser, who may be a very skilled employee, to return to a productive and healthy career path. Such a result is desirable not only for humanitarian reasons but also to retain qualified individuals who could be difficult to replace.

Alcoholism and drug addiction are protected "handicaps" under various federal and state employment discrimination laws, including the Americans with Disabilities Act. Therefore, employers covered by such laws may not discharge or refuse to hire an individual because of the employee's alcohol or drug dependency if, after reasonable accommodation is made to his or her condition, the employee is qualified to perform the job in spite of the disability. Of course, none of these laws requires an employer to retain an employee whose current use of alcohol or drugs prevents the employee from performing the duties of his or her job, or whose employment, due to current substance abuse, would threaten property or the safety of others.

While not clearly defined, the duty of reasonable accommodation probably requires employers to give employees (who are willing to acknowledge a chemical dependency) an adequate opportunity to rehabilitate themselves, unless the granting of such an opportunity would impose an undue hardship on the employer. Other possible means of reasonable accommodation may include transfers, reassignments, scheduling changes, or adjustments in employees' duties designed to change conditions that may be contributing to the problem. The duty to reasonably accommodate is an emerging area of law, and employers should carefully monitor legislative and case developments that further define a company's obligations.

RECOMMENDATIONS

The following recommendations provide a useful framework for a corporate response to drugs and alcohol in the workplace:

1. Address the problem of alcohol and drug abuse squarely. The "ostrich approach" is not advisable. Employers, including top management, should be committed to the establishment of a comprehensive approach to the problem, tailored to fit the company's circumstances.

2. Establish clear rules and enforce them consistently. Rules should clearly set forth the types of conduct prohibited and the penalties for violation. The rules must be widely disseminated, so that all employees know what is proscribed and have the opportunity to conform. The rules should be consistently enforced at all employee and managerial levels including the executive level. Toleration of drug or alcohol abuse on an exception basis will probably render the rules unenforceable.

3. Conduct proper investigations of suspected rule violations. Employers should thoroughly investigate suspected violations. Rather than make a hasty judgment on incomplete information, it is better to suspend an employee pending further investigation. If the investigation does not reveal sufficient evidence of an infraction, the employee can be reinstated with pay.

4. Follow appropriate disciplinary guidelines. All employees should be held to the same standards of performance, productivity, and attendance. Principles of progressive discipline should be followed, as with other rule infractions. Employees showing a dependence on alcohol or drugs should ordinarily be given a firm choice between rehabilitation and discipline. It is important that employees be given clear notice of possible discharge if their conduct does not change.

5. Train supervisors. Managers and supervisors, especially first-line supervisors, should be fully trained about the company's substance abuse policies. They should clearly understand their responsibility to implement the company's policy goals.

6. Develop a policy on rehabilitation or employee assistance. All employers should establish a program through which employees may receive appropriate assistance or treatment. While a sophisticated in-house employee assistance program may not be feasible for small companies, a variety of outside referral sources are available in most locales.

7. Be sensitive to employees' privacy rights. Special care must be taken to respect employees' rights of privacy and confidentiality. Participation in an employee assistance program or any other form of rehabilitation should be kept in strictest confidence. Medical records should never be disclosed to third persons without the employee's written authorization. Investigations, reasonable searches, and the administration of chemical tests should be handled in as confidential and dignified a manner as possible, out of the presence of other employees. Confirming tests should be conducted before an employee is disciplined on the basis of a test result. However, if an employee refuses a reasonable request to take a test or submit to a search, and the circumstances indicate that the rules pertaining to drugs or alcohol have been violated, the refusal may justify discharge or other disciplinary action.

8. Take reasonable steps to protect employees and others from harm caused by substance abusers. Employees who are under the influence of alcohol or drugs should not be permitted to work. An employee who appears to be impaired should not be permitted to drive home; other arrangements should be made.

9. Know the applicable statutes and regulations. Each company should determine whether it is subject to state or federal disability discrimination or rehabilitation statutes, and identify what state privacy laws may limit the techniques the company may use to investigate employee substance abuse.

PRIVACY AND PERSONNEL SECURITY ISSUES

Dennis J. Morikawa, Attorney-at-Law,
Morgan, Lewis & Bockius

Privacy, or "the right to be let alone," is a concept that affects numerous aspects of the employment relationship. The sources of law that limit an employer's ability to intrude upon an employee's "privacy interest" are many. The U.S. Constitution provides to public-sector employees protection against infringements on their individual rights. In particular, employees most often invoke their Fourth Amendment protection from unreasonable searches and seizures, their Fifth Amendment right against self-incrimination, and their Fourteenth Amendment right to due process and equal protection. Federal employees also are protected by the Privacy Act of 1974, 5 U.S.C. Section 552a, which restricts federal agencies in their efforts to compile and disclose information and records about individuals.

Private-sector employees generally are not protected by the U.S. Constitution. Nonetheless, private employers are restricted in many ways from infringing on the privacy rights of their employees. Federal, state, and local statutes govern the use of wiretaps, polygraphs, AIDS (acquired immunodeficiency syndrome) testing, and drug and alcohol screening. Other laws restrict the gathering, use, and disclosure of employee records. Other sources of privacy protection are found in collective bargaining agreements, employee handbooks, policy statements, and employee practices, as well as common law restrictions on the invasion of privacy. Finally, a number of state constitutions contain express privacy provisions.

RETENTION OF, ACCESS TO, AND DISCLOSURE OF EMPLOYEE RECORDS

For various reasons, employers often are required to or desire to retain employee records including personnel files, medical histories, credit histories, educational records, criminal arrest and conviction records, workplace hazard information, and medical screening records. The law often regulates retention, access, and disclosure of this information.

A number of federal statutes, including Title VII of the Civil Rights Act of 1964, 42 U.S.C. Section 2000e et seq., and the Age Discrimination in Employment Act, 29 U.S.C. Section 621 et seq., require that employers retain personnel files for certain periods of time. Many states also have adopted similar laws.

Many states require employers to allow employees to inspect their personnel files and some require employers to grant access to employer-maintained medical records under certain conditions and restrictions. For instance, many statutes require that the employee submit a written request, and access may be limited to working hours.

The Fair Credit Reporting Act, 15 U.S.C. Sections 1681–1681t, requires an employer to notify an applicant if an adverse employment decision is, in whole or in part, taken based on a credit report. Employees are entitled to access to certain records under the Occupational Safety and Health Act and its implementing regulations. 29 U.S.C. Section 657; 29 C.F.R. Section 1913.10 et seq.; 29 C.F.R. Section 1910.20.

An employer may not have to, and in some cases must not, provide third parties with information concerning an employee without the consent of the employee, particularly if the information is of a confidential nature. Moreover, the granting of access to confidential employee information to third parties may subject an employer to liability in tort for a claim such as invasion of privacy.

Employers may be required to divulge seemingly confidential information regarding an employee's compensation, including salaries, fees, and personal service contracts, when requested by a union preparing for collective bargaining.

EMPLOYEE TESTING AND SCREENING

Employers use various screening mechanisms in order to reduce theft in their workplaces, to protect the health and safety of their employees and customers, and to evaluate the ability of employees to work together compatibly. These interests, however, can sometimes conflict with an employee's privacy interests.

Drug and Alcohol Testing

Public and private employers are subject to differing legal constraints on the nature of the drug and alcohol testing programs they may impose upon their employees. Private-sector employees generally are not protected from their employers' actions by the U.S. Constitution. The widespread use of drug and alcohol testing by employers, however, has caused state and local authorities to establish their own legal parameters for drug and alcohol testing. Over one half of the states have enacted or have proposed legislation regulating drug or alcohol testing. Some municipalities also have enacted ordinances to address the issue of testing by employers within their respective jurisdictions. Employers are required to negotiate with their unions over the implementation of such policies. Therefore, employers should review their existing collective bargaining agreement or bargaining histories to determine if such bargaining will be necessary.

Public employers and federal contractors should review federal regulations that have been issued requiring and/or governing drug and alcohol testing. Among those affected are employees of aviation companies, commercial motor vehicle operators, railroad employees, urban mass transit workers, employees in pipeline and liquefied natural gas facilities, and certain employees of national defense contractors. Many of these regulations have been challenged on various constitutional grounds, but, for the most part, they have been upheld particularly where there is a safety or national security interest at stake.

Some employers have utilized hair analysis tests and papillary reaction tests to screen for drug and alcohol use. These tests raise concerns about accuracy and some of the same concerns about privacy, albeit they are less intrusive than traditional drug and alcohol screening tests.

AIDS Testing

AIDS testing by public employers is governed by the Fourth Amendment to the U.S. Constitution that proscribes unreasonable searches and seizures. Depending on the position involved, the government interest in these test results may be too low to warrant the intrusion on the individual because the current scientific evidence indicates that the risk of AIDS transmission is extremely slight. The recently enacted Americans with Disabilities Act (ADA), 42 U.S.C. Section 12101 et seq., prohibits private employers from requiring any preemployment examinations, including AIDS testing. Moreover, most states have equal employment opportunity laws or agency policies that protect AIDS victims from employment discrimination, reasoning that AIDS is a physical handicap that interferes with major life activities. At least twelve

states have regulations or legislation prohibiting either the requirement of HIV testing or the discrimination against HIV-infected persons. A number of localities also have adopted ordinances prohibiting AIDS-based discrimination. Furthermore, state common law principles and legislation may limit the disclosure of AIDS-related information in the employment context.

Even if an employer is not legally prohibited from implementing an AIDS policy or testing program, it likely will have a duty to bargain over the matter in collective bargaining, at least with respect to incumbent employees. Also, the discharge of AIDS victims may violate a "just cause" standard in a collective bargaining agreement.

Genetic Testing

Some employers require either a onetime test of individuals to determine the existence of inheritable traits that would predispose an individual to occupational illnesses or periodic examinations of blood or other bodily fluids of groups of workers to determine whether damage has occurred from exposure to workplace agents. Some states regulate such genetic testing directly. Furthermore, prescreening for susceptibility to occupational injuries or diseases now will violate the ADA.

Preemployment Physicals

Depending on the type of toxic chemicals employees will encounter in the workplace, some federal OSHA standards require applicants to undergo preemployment physicals, provide a medical history, and take certain medical tests. On the other hand, the ADA prohibits all preemployment (as opposed to posthire) medical exams, and the regulations under the Federal Rehabilitation Act, 29 U.S.C. Section 701 et seq., governing public-sector employers, federal contractors, and federal aid recipients, prohibits most preemployment medical exams. Employers, however, may make offers contingent upon satisfactory results of posthire medical exams. Under both acts, when an employer requires such an examination, however, it must be required of all entering employees in a particular category. Such results must be kept confidential, and may not be used to discriminate against applicants with disabilities unless the results of the examination show the individual to be unqualified for the job.

Numerous states prohibit employers from discriminating against employees on account of their use of tobacco outside the workplace.

HONESTY TESTING

The Employee Polygraph Protection Act of 1988 (EPPA), 29 U.S.C. Section 2001 et seq., generally prohibits any use of a broad range of lie detector tests in the private-sector employment context. EPPA does not apply to government employers and does not prohibit the federal government from administering lie detector tests in certain situations to experts, consultants, or the employees of federal contractors engaged in national security, intelligence, or counterintelligence functions. All employers covered by the act are required to post and maintain notices prepared by the secretary of labor that summarize the pertinent provisions of the act.

There are exceptions to EPPA. A private employer may request that employees undergo a polygraph examination if:

1. The employee has access to the employer's property and is reasonably suspected of involvement in a workplace incident that results in economic loss or injury to the employer, provided that this specific incident or activity resulting in economic loss or injury is the subject of an ongoing investigation.
2. The individual is a prospective employee of an armored car, security alarm or security guard firm, or an employer that protects certain facilities, materials, or operations that affect health, safety, or national security or currency, negotiable securities, or other like instruments.
3. The individual is a prospective employee of a pharmaceutical or other firm authorized to manufacture, distribute, or dispense controlled substances and has direct access to those controlled substances.

Current employees having access to persons or property that are the subject of an ongoing investigation of criminal activities or other misconduct involving controlled substances may also be tested. Furthermore, more than twenty states and the District of Columbia regulate the use of polygraphs and many of those laws are more restrictive than federal statutes.

Some states, by legislation or regulation, restrict the use of other test forms such as paper and pencil honesty profiles that are not covered under EPPA. Where federal limits on the use of polygraph testing by employers have led to increased use of psychological tests, such as the Minnesota Multiphasic Personality Inventory (MMPI), their validity and reliability, and their impact on employee privacy, are subject to challenge. For example, such tests have been challenged on the ground that the preemployment tests constitute an invasion of privacy and a violation of state statutes that limit the disclosure of confidential medical information.

SEARCHES

Again, private-sector employees are not governed by the U.S. Constitution, although in a few states they are governed by state constitutional provisions. Private employers may, however, be restricted by state or local statutes in their ability to search the persons or property of employees. Moreover, private employers may be subject to tort liability if searches are not justified and are conducted in an unreasonable manner.

Workplace searches and seizures by government employers of private property of employees are subject to Fourth Amendment restraints based on reasonable expectations of privacy, and on similar state constitutional provisions. The reasonableness of a search requires balancing an employee's privacy expectations against the government's need for supervision, control, and efficient operation of the workplace. Of all types of constitutionally restricted searches, body searches are the most intrusive and, therefore, must be supported by a strong need. After the threshold problem of establishing a need for the search, courts consider the methods by which the search was conducted and whether less intrusive means were available.

ELECTRONIC SURVEILLANCE

The federal Omnibus Crime Control and Safe Streets Act, 18 U.S.C. Section 2510 et seq., which applies to both public and private employers, provides criminal and civil penalties for wiretapping of conversations without the consent of at least one party to the conversation. An exception is provided, however, that allows employers to monitor business, but not personal, phone calls. A number of states also have statutes restricting an employer's right to use electronic eavesdropping devices and several states have legislation that restricts an employer's right to conduct video surveillance of employees.

SECTION 5

Accounting

Athar Murtuza, Section Editor

Introduction   *Athar Murtuza*   5-3

General-Purpose Financial Reporting and Financial Statements
  Jeffrey L. Harkins   5-5

Managing Accounts Receivable   *Cecilia L. Wagner*   5-12

Inventory Valuation and Control   *William Brunsen and
  Athar Murtuza*   5-16

Analyzing Operating Results   *Daniel Haskin and William Brunsen*   5-23

Managerial Uses of Accounting   *Athar Murtuza*   5-27

Federal Taxation: Management Responsibilities and
  Opportunities   *Herbert J. Lerner and S. Theodore Reiner*   5-31

Managing State and Local Taxes   *Shelby D. Bennett*   5-37

Internal Auditing   *Bruce L. Whitaker*   5-40

The Independent Audit   *John J. Willingham and Mark J. Allen*   5-43

Investor Relations   *T. Carter Hagaman*   5-49

Accounting in the International Environment   *Gerard Huybregts*   5-52

INTRODUCTION

Athar Murtuza

A major portion of a manager's time is devoted to making decisions that involve the use of organizational resources to help realize organizational goals. These resources include assets listed in the balance sheet as well as intangible assets not directly listed in accounting statements. Steel used to make cars and eggs used to bake cakes are more tangible than efforts expended by the artist/designer to design a new car model. Resources can refer to intellectual and creative elements that must be a part of the organizational resource repertoire.

Using resources effectively means keeping track of them and their use. Given the wide diversity of resources, it is not an easy task. An organization may find it difficult to directly track the efforts being expended to design a car, to better motivate its labor crews, and to win over customers. Not only the deployment of its resources but also the benefits acquired through their deployment are difficult to track and/or measure.

In contrast to tracking the resource use directly, it is much easier to track the money associated with the deployment of varied resources. Doing so can *approximate* the extent to which those resources were expended and the resulting benefits. There are times when the benefits resulting from the deployment of organizational resources may not be easily translated into monetary terms: How does one place a value on what is accomplished by the state's spending on higher education? Despite such difficulties, tracking the monetary resources must be seen as a useful, albeit imperfect, tool for managers, since it can help them make more informed decisions.

Accounting is the discipline charged with the tracking of monetary resources. It does so by means of financial statements that translate in monetary terms what is going on in an organization, where it is headed, and how it is handling its resources. The branch of accounting responsible for record keeping and for preparing financial statements is called financial accounting.

The interests of external investors are served by the statements, but managers ask for more detailed information. Managerial accounting seeks to provide managers with information that tracks the use of resources and can be used by managers to make more informed decisions.

Accounting departments are charged with meeting the needs of external investors and internal managers. Often one hears accountants described as "bean counters" and "number crunchers," but accountants do much more. The various chapters in this section testify to the diversity and complexity of the roles performed by accountants. Through them managers can learn how accounting and its diversity can help them manage better.

Athar Murtuza, *Ph.D., CMA, is an associate professor of accounting at Seton Hall University. His teaching interest is managerial and cost accounting, and his research and consulting interests include effective communication of accounting information, activity-based costing, and process design. Dr. Murtuza has published in a number of professional and academic journals and is a certified management accountant.*

GENERAL-PURPOSE FINANCIAL REPORTING AND FINANCIAL STATEMENTS

Jeffrey L. Harkins, Department of Accounting, University of Idaho

Management's responsibility for reporting on the performance and financial position of a business enterprise is founded in common sense and has deep roots in American economic history. Business ventures of fifteenth-century Europe led to the discovery of the New World. Owners and venture capitalists financed joint ventures to exploit the resources of the newly discovered continent. The absentee owners expected an accounting of the success of these ventures. Records of the Mayflower's pilgrimage, the Plymouth colony, and the Massachusetts Bay Company document the efforts of the colonial managers in providing financial information to their overseas venture capitalist investors.

Today, most business enterprise continues to be financed by investor-owners, who expect a financial return from their investments through dividends, interest, and capital appreciation from share price increases. The owners are not usually involved directly in the day-to-day management of the entity; rather, the owners hire professional managers to direct business affairs and appoint directors to oversee the enterprise policies and plans. The separation of owners and managers creates a fiduciary responsibility for managers to account for their decisions regarding the sources and uses of the entity's capital. As a practical matter, financial reporting serves another purpose: it provides a means for managers to apprise owners of their stewardship or how well they have used their skills to manage owners' business affairs.

In addition to serving the information demands of owners and investors, financial reporting also serves others who have direct and indirect interests in the activities and accomplishments of the business. Creditors, suppliers, employees and employee associations, financial analysts, brokers, underwriters, taxing authorities, financial media, and governments are among the users or potential users of financial information about a business entity. These stakeholders are often not in a position to obtain information about the financial activities and financial position of the entity for themselves, and consequently they look to management to provide such information.

THE ENVIRONMENT OF THE MODERN BUSINESS ENTERPRISE

Contemporary business entities operate in a complex economic environment that impacts the nature and form of financial reporting. Most goods and services are provided through a highly developed system of integrated markets. In addition to highly structured production processes—the means by which raw materials, labor, and capital are converted into finished consumer products—the economy depends on elaborate support systems to efficiently and effectively allocate resources. These support systems include capital formation and investment systems, marketing and distribution systems, government and industrial regulatory systems, and communication and information systems.

To effectively serve the diverse interests of users of financial information, given the complex nature of the economic environment, a finely tuned financial accounting and reporting system is required. The purpose of this chapter is to enhance your understanding of the financial accounting information system and the responsibilities of management in operating that system.

CONCEPTS AND OBJECTIVES OF FINANCIAL ACCOUNTING AND REPORTING

Underlying the financial accounting and reporting system used by business entities and their managers is a complex set of accounting concepts defining the fundamentals upon which financial statements are based. Although a number of individuals and organizations have participated in the development

of the modern financial accounting and reporting system for business enterprises, the primary responsibility for promulgating standards is the Financial Accounting Standards Board (FASB). The FASB, a nonprofit organization, was formed in 1973 by business leaders, accounting organizations, and government "to establish and improve the standards of financial accounting and reporting by defining, issuing, and promoting such standards" (Certificate of Incorporation/By-Laws, Stamford, Conn.: FAF, 1973, p. 1). Since 1973, the FASB has developed a six-part framework of concepts underlying financial accounting and reporting for business enterprise, as well as over a hundred/statements detailing financial accounting and reporting policies and procedures.

The primary role of external financial reporting by business entities is to provide information that is useful for business and economic decision making. In coming to a general objective for financial accounting and reporting, the FASB considered the fact that some financial information users have the authority or opportunity to obtain the information that they require directly from business entities. Consequently, the FASB determined that users not able to acquire information directly should be considered a primary group for which financial accounting and reporting standards are focused. Thus, the FASB narrowed the scope of users and declared that "Investors and creditors and their advisers are the most obvious prominent external groups who use the information provided by financial reporting and who generally lack the authority to prescribe the information they want" (FASB, Statement of Financial Accounting Concepts No. 1, 1978, para. 30).

It would appear that the FASB recognized that it would be difficult and costly to satisfy all the information demands of investors, creditors, and advisers. Consequently, the FASB adopted the concept of general-purpose financial statements (GPFS) to satisfy the general or common interests of selected users of financial accounting information about business entities. The FASB explained that investors, creditors, and advisers "have been studied and described to a much greater extent than those of other external groups, and their decisions significantly affect the allocation of resources in the economy. . . . Information provided to meet investors' and creditors' needs is likely to be generally useful to members of other groups who are interested in essentially the same financial aspects of business enterprises as investors and creditors."

Thus, the FASB narrowed the scope of objectives for financial reporting to meeting the common needs of investors, creditors, and advisors. Specifically, the FASB determined that financial accounting and reporting should provide information:

1. "that is useful to present and potential investors and creditors and other users . . . who have a reasonable understanding of business and economic activities and are willing to study the information with reasonable diligence."
2. "to help present and potential investors and creditors and other users in assessing the amounts, timing, and uncertainty of prospective cash receipts from dividends or interest and the proceeds from the sale, redemption, or maturity of securities or loans."
3. "about the economic resources of an enterprise, the claims to those resources . . . , and the effects of transactions, events, and circumstances that change resources and claims to resources."

These broad objectives provide the framework by which more specific concepts, standards, and principles of financial accounting and reporting are determined. The FASB and others interested in financial accounting and reporting issues (managers and executives) can utilize the broad objectives to better understand the nature of financial reporting and the role of financial reporting in economic decision making. Also, individuals responsible for financial reporting about an entity might better understand how to manage a difficult or unusual financial reporting problem. In the same way that the FASB approaches a financial reporting problem, a manager, armed with a thorough understanding of financial reporting objectives, can critically evaluate a financial reporting problem and develop a means to satisfy the objectives.

GENERAL-PURPOSE FINANCIAL STATEMENTS

An infinite array of financial reports can be prepared for a business entity. The FASB defined the central purpose of financial reporting around the common interests or needs of investors and creditors and determined that the common interests would be best served by a defined set of financial reports called general-purpose financial statements (GPFS). The common information interests are financial position at the end of the period, earnings (net income) for the period, cash flows for the period, and investments by and distributions to owners.

Most managers are familiar with the process by which financial statements are created. Financial statements are compiled by a process that recognizes and measures selected economic events (called transactions analysis). These events are classified, summarized, and aggregated as the building blocks of the financial statements. These building blocks or elements, properly organized, are part of an integrated structure that can be translated into financial statements—financial statements that are specifically articulated to each other.

In the simplest case, financial statements are merely classified and aggregated transactions. Although the accounting process may, at times, appear to be quite confusing, the underlying mathematics of the process is rather straightforward, involving algebra, addition, and subtraction. The basic financial statements are also familiar to most managers, but it may be useful to review each statement.

The Balance Sheet

The balance sheet or statement of financial position is a classified summary of an entity's resources and the claims against (or sources of) those resources (from creditors or owners) at a particular point in time, usually at year-end. The balance sheet is a summary of an entity's investment base (the assets) and the financing of the investments (credit or equity). Although the balance sheet may be used to assist in forming predictions about the value or worth of an entity, a balance sheet does not report the current value or worth of the firm. The FASB recognizes that there may be many different ways to calculate the "value" of an economic event and attempts to use a valuation system that provides relevant and reliable measures about transactions. Under current generally accepted accounting principles (GAAP) several measurement systems can be used, including historical cost, replacement cost, current market value, and net present value. Under GAAP, the asset, liability, and equity accounts are reported using a value system that satisfies specific measurement concepts.

The balance sheet portrays the basic relationship between assets and the claims to those assets in an equation form:

Resources = Claims Against Resources

or, in more conventional form:

Assets (*A*)
        = Liabilities (*L*) + Owners' Equity (*E*)

where:

Assets = Resources

Liabilities + Owners' Equity
        = Total Claims Against Resources

This basic statement of financial position (balance sheet) provides a periodic view (at least annually) of the investment/financing structure of a business enterprise. By comparing balance sheets over time, a user can get an idea of how an entity's investment/financing structure is changing. The balance sheet is a primary source of information about the firm's liquidity and financial flexibility.

The balance sheet is usually presented in a logical format designed to assist users in understanding a firm's resource structure. The common balance sheet is usually classified by liquidity; that is, the assets and liabilities are arrayed in the order of the expected convertibility of the items into cash. Thus, users can expect to see the current assets (assets that are expected to mature to cash in one year or less) followed by long-term assets and

current liabilities followed by longer maturing debt.

Note that the balance sheet itself can lead users to information about the net changes in the various assets and liabilities of an entity. However, most decision makers are interested not only in the net changes in resources and the claims to those resources but also the events that led to the changes. The statements providing an explanation of the changes in financial position are discussed later.

While it may seem trivial, the relationship between assets, liabilities, and owners' equity and the changes that occur in these elements over time define important measures used by many investors and creditors to evaluate the relative periodic performance of entities. Some of the changes in the assets, liabilities, and equities result from the profit-directed activities of the firm. These changes are reported in the income statement. Since the firm also engages in transactions not directly affecting profit for the current period (e.g., investing, financing, and transactions with the owners), additional financial reports are used to provide users with information about those changes.

The Earnings or Income Statement

The income statement is a primary means of reporting on the changes in financial position. The primary purpose of the income statement or earnings statement is to report on the changes in owners' equity that resulted from transactions and events associated with an entity's primary profit-directed business operations. The income statement presents the components of the entity's earnings: revenues, gains, expenses, and losses. The general equation for the income statement is probably familiar:

Revenue
−Expenses
+Gains
−Losses
Net Income or Earnings

The effect of earnings (loss) on financial position is usually described as the increase (decrease) in owners' equity resulting from the profit-making activities of the entity. However, the effects of earnings are also reflected in changes in the assets and liabilities of the firm. This effect is a natural result of using the double-entry recording system (initially developed by Luca Paciolli in the seventeenth century) to enter transactions into the accounts.

The income statement is usually prepared in a single-step format or a multiple-step format. The single-step method presents the income from the normal continuing operations by presenting the revenues (as a group) and subtracting the expenses and the costs (as a group). The multiple-step process presents the income from operations through a series of calculations, such as:

```
 Sales
-Cost of Goods Sold
 Gross Profit on Sales
-Selling and Administrative Expenses
 Operating Profit
±Other Revenues or General Expenses
 Income from Continuing Operations
```

Statement of Cash Flows

The most recent addition (and probably the most controversial) to the basic financial statements is the statement of cash flows. The statement of cash flows replaced the statement of changes in financial position, which was usually prepared as a summary of the changes in working capital (working capital equals current assets less current liabilities). The cash flow statement is intended to present a summary of an entity's cash receipts and cash disbursements organized in a way that describes the entity's cash flow from operating activities, investing transactions, and financing transactions. It is argued that the statement of cash flows is useful in describing information about sources and uses of cash and in explaining the time interval between the recognition of accrued earnings and the conversion of earnings into cash. However, professional analysts and knowledgeable users are able to generate cash flow statements by analyzing the earnings statement, the balance sheets, and the changes in working capital. While the statement of cash flows

may save some time in providing cash flow information, the statement is more likely a convenience rather than an essential financial statement.

The cash flow statement may be prepared using the direct method (which presents the classified sources and uses of cash, including cash sales, collections from customers, payments for merchandise) or the indirect method (which presents a reconciliation of net income to cash flow, by adjusting net income for noncash items such as depreciation and accrued items). The cash flow statement must also include a listing of significant noncash financing and investing activities (e.g., exchange of capital stock for fixed assets). Under GAAP, if an entity uses the direct method, the indirect approach must be provided as supplementary information.

The Statement of Changes in Stockholders' Equity

The statement of changes in stockholders' equity, also called the statement of investments by and distributions to owners, presents a summary of the changes in the owners' capital accounts. The statement is usually prepared in a format that provides an explanation of the changes of the major components of the owners' equity section: paid-in-capital and earned capital (retained earnings). The paid-in-capital section presents the changes resulting from additional capital investments and disinvestments between the firm and its shareholders (the issue and redemption of the firm's capital stock). The earned capital section presents a summary of the changes in the earnings retained in the firm (beginning balance of retained earnings plus earnings for the year less dividends declared for the year equals ending retained earnings).

BASIC ELEMENTS OF FINANCIAL STATEMENTS

The FASB identified ten categories, called elements, as the basic building blocks of financial statements. As an entity engages in economic activity, the economic effects are analyzed and classified according to the element affected. Knowledge of the elements permits one to be able to identify the effects of transactions and summarize the effects in the form of financial statements:

1. *Assets* are probable future economic benefits obtained or controlled by a particular entity as a result of past transactions or events.
2. *Liabilities* are probable future sacrifices of economic benefits arising from present obligations of a particular entity to transfer assets or provide services to other entities in the future as a result of past transactions or events.
3. *Equity* or net assets are the residual interest in the assets of an entity that remains after deducting its liabilities.
4. *Investments by owners* are increases in equity of a particular business enterprise resulting from transfers to it from other entities of something valuable to obtain or increase ownership interests (or equity) in it.
5. *Distributions to owners* are decreases in equity of a particular business enterprise resulting from transferring assets, rendering services, or incurring liabilities by the enterprise to owners. Distributions to owners decrease ownership interest (or equity) in an enterprise.
6. *Revenues* are inflows or other enhancements of assets of an entity or settlements of its liabilities (or a combination of both) in return for delivering or producing goods, rendering services, or other activities that constitute the entity's ongoing major or central operations.
7. *Expenses* are outflows or other using up of assets or incurrences of liabilities (or a combination of both) from delivering or producing goods, rendering services, or carrying out other activities that constitute the entity's ongoing major or central operations.
8. *Gains* are increases in equity (net assets) from peripheral or incidental transactions of an entity and from all other transactions and other events and circumstances affecting the entity except those that result from revenues or investments by owners.
9. *Losses* are decreases in equity (net assets) from peripheral or incidental transactions of an entity and from all other transactions and other events and circumstances affecting the entity except those that result from expenses or distributions to owners.
10. *Comprehensive income* is the change in equity of a business enterprise during a period from transactions and other events and circumstances from non-owner sources. It includes all changes in equity during a period except those resulting from investments by owners and distributions to owners.

RECOGNITION AND MEASUREMENT STANDARDS

In order to complete the financial accounting and reporting process, given a framework of objectives and a set of defined accounting elements, there must be standards or criteria to guide the recognition of economic events in the formal records of the entity. Recognition criteria and measurement standards are necessary to determine what economic events should be included in the financial reports and when those events should be reported. The final pieces of the FASB's conceptual framework project delineated the standards for the measurement and recognition of economic events.

The FASB defines recognition as the "process of formally recording or incorporating an item into the financial statements of an entity as an asset, liability, revenue, expense, or the like" (FASB, *Statement of Financial Accounting Concepts No. 5*, Recognition and Measurement in Financial Statements of Business Enterprises, para. 6). The process by which economic events are recognized in the financial records is a four-stage system comprised of the following criteria:

1. *Definition of an element*—The economic event under consideration must satisfy the definition of an element of a financial statement, for example, asset, liability, equity, and the like.
2. *Measurability of elements*—The elements identified with respect to the economic event must be measurable (quantifiable) by a scale that satisfies standards of reliability.

3. *Relevance of information produced*—The result of the recognition process must provide information that is considered relevant, that is, information that is capable of making a difference to the users of the information. Generally, this has been defined as information that has either feedback value or predictive value (or both) and is available on a timely basis.

4. *Reliability of information produced*—Reliability, like relevance, is a primary quality of information. Reliability refers to the extent to which information represents that which it purports to represent, or how well the information, as a representation of some economic event, communicates the sum and substance of the economic event to the user. The FASB determined that reliability can be assessed by evaluating the faithfulness (the degree to which the measure or description used conforms to the event being recognized) and verifiability (the degree to which the resulting information item would be replicated by another independent measurer) of the information produced.

Recognition is also subject to two pervasive constraints: a benefit-cost criteria and a materiality threshold. The benefit-cost constraint is satisfied if the expected benefits of recognizing an economic event in the records is at least equal to the cost of providing and using the resulting information. Materiality refers to whether or not the quantitative effect of the information will make a difference in the decisions of users. Throughout the accounting function, materiality is an important and complex issue and, like evaluating the benefits and costs of recognizing economic events, requires professional judgment.

The measurement process, the means by which values are assigned the economic events of interest, deserves special attention. There are a number of value systems that could be used in financial accounting and reporting, including historical cost, current cost, replacement value, current selling price, price level or inflation-adjusted price, and net present value. Because there are alternative valuing systems, the measures used for any specific type of transactions can be subject to criticism. Different measurement systems may produce different levels of reliability and relevance, depending on the nature of the economic event being measured and the tools available for measuring. The FASB acknowledges the problems associated with measurement and has determined that, to fulfill the overall objectives of financial reporting, it will be necessary to continue to rely on the use of a variety of measurement systems. Currently, there are five measurement systems used in the financial accounting and reporting process:

1. *Historical cost* is based on the amount of cash or cash equivalent involved at the date of a transaction or event.
2. *Current cost* is based on the amount of cash or cash equivalent that would be required to complete a transaction currently. Current cost is usually associated with the acquisition of assets, particularly inventory.
3. *Current market value* is based on the amount of cash or cash equivalent that could be obtained by negotiating a transaction in the current market. Current market value differs from current cost in that it is usually associated with the disposal of assets in an orderly market, for example, the securities market.
4. *Net realizable value* is based on the non-discounted amount of cash or cash equivalent that would be involved in the completion of a transaction in the due course of business, less any direct costs that will be incurred in completing the transaction, for example, advertising and settlement fees.
5. *Present value of future cash flows* is based on the discounted estimated cash inflows and outflows associated with an economic event. This method requires two estimates: the selection of the appropriate discount rate and the forecast of the future cash inflows and outflows.

Under contemporary accounting standards, transactions are recorded in the financial accounts by satisfying the four criteria for recognition of economic events. Throughout the process, managers and their designated accounting experts are called on to render judgments in determining whether, when, and how financial transactions will be captured by the accounting information system and ultimately reported in the financial statements. Judgment is inherent in the process. But, as long as those making decisions are knowledgeable in the nuances of financial accounting standards and they exercise proper professional conduct, the end product can provide users with a quality information product.

DISCLOSURE STANDARDS

In most financial reports, narrative explanations are required to inform users adequately about the judgments made in recognizing and measuring financial transactions. And, at times, there will be circumstances that preclude the recognition of an economic event into the formal accounting records of an entity. In order to ensure that users are fully informed about the accounting policies and procedures used in preparing the financial report and to provide for information about significant events not as yet accounted for by the accounting records, footnotes and supplemental disclosures are required to be included as a part of the general-purpose financial report. The three required disclosures are:

1. *Summary of significant accounting policies* — a description of the general application of accounting principles employed by the entity, for example, inventory and depreciation methods, asset cost methods.
2. *Notes to the financial statements*—qualitative and descriptive comments necessary to amplify or explain items in the financial statements, including loan covenants, compensating balances, contingent liabilities.
3. *Supplemental information*—used to add information to the financial statements that would normally not be captured by the accounting system (e.g., effects of inflation, industry segment data) and to provide management with the means to discuss the effect or impact of the statements themselves (e.g., management's discussion and analysis).

Notes and disclosures permit managers to fully describe and analyze the performance of the entity and such disclosures are essential in describing the entity's activities to a reader of the financial statements.

MANAGING ACCOUNTS RECEIVABLE

Cecilia L. Wagner, Associate Professor, School of Business, Seton Hall University

Maintaining accounts receivable results in both costs and benefits to a firm. The firm hopes that selling on credit will increase sales and profits. There are, however, costs associated with maintaining receivables, including the cost of financing the investment, administrative and bookkeeping expenses, credit investigation costs, collection costs, and bad debt expenses.

These costs are a function of the level of

sales, the firm's credit philosophy, the terms on which the firm sells, and the methods used by the firm in its collections. Accordingly, the management of credit has three aspects: to whom to extend credit, on what terms, and how to collect.

EXTENDING CREDIT

The decision to extend credit typically involves an effort to standardize the process as much as possible. The level of standardization is often dependent on the firm's competition. If there is high competition, the firm must offer credit or lose sales. If the firm has flexibility in setting its standards, the credit decision is based on the customer meeting certain conditions.

One approach to credit decisions categorizes customers based on their operating stability and financial strength. Called the risk-class approach, the firm identifies categories ranging from strongest to weakest and defines a separate credit policy for each class. When a customer applies for credit, an investigation is initiated. The investigation may incorporate information received from the potential customer, including both trade and bank references, and information received from credit services, such as Dun and Bradstreet. A credit report will contain data on the customer's current payment record, public filings, and credit history. Based on this investigation, the customer is placed in one of the risk classes. This eliminates the need to make a separate decision on extending credit each time the customer places an order. Exhibit 5-1 presents examples of risk classes, a descrip-

tion of the type of firm in each class, and a statement of the applicable credit policy.

TERMS OF EXTENSION

After the firm has decided to grant credit, it must determine the terms of the credit extension. In a competitive industry, firms must meet or exceed the terms offered by their competitors, or lose sales. For these firms the decision is fairly straightforward. Firms with less competition may decide on terms of credit based on some sort of cost-benefit analysis.

One example of such analysis is the cost-volume-profit approach. This approach is representative of the approaches used in this decision-making process. Several steps are required in the cost-volume-profit approach to making credit decisions:

1. *Forecasting sales*—This task is usually undertaken as a joint effort of the marketing and finance departments. For our purposes, we will assume that the marketing department has provided us with the appropriate sales forecasts.

2. *Forecasting discounts taken*—If the firm is evaluating terms of trade that include discounts for payment within a certain time period, these discounts result in reduced revenues, a fact that must be built into the analysis. Historical experience may be helpful in estimating the percentage of customers who will accept the discount. Eventually, a percentage must be estimated in terms of the dollar value of sales.

Exhibit 5-1. Risk-Class Approach to the Extension of Credit

Risk Class	Description of Firm	Credit Policy
1	Well-established firms whose financial position and past record indicate virtually no risk	Open credit up to certain limit without approval required
2	Financially sound firms not supported by a detailed past record	Open credit with approval required for purchases in excess of certain amounts
3	Solid firms with past records that indicate some risk	Limited credit line with frequent checks

The formula for discounts taken is:

$$\begin{array}{ll}
\text{Discounts} \\
\text{Taken}
\end{array} = \begin{array}{c}
\text{Percent} \\
\text{Who Take} \\
\text{Discount}
\end{array} \times \begin{array}{c}
\text{Percent} \\
\text{of} \\
\text{Discount}
\end{array} \times \begin{array}{c}
\text{Dollar} \\
\text{Value} \\
\text{of Sales}
\end{array}$$

If it is estimated that 70 percent of customers will take the discount, a firm with sales of $30 million and terms of 2/10, net 30 (a 2 percent discount can be taken if payment is made in 10 days, otherwise the net amount is due in 30 days), will have discounts taken of $420,000 ($30 million × 70 percent × 2 percent).

3. *Determining cost of goods sold*—Once sales estimates have been made, the firm can forecast the cost of producing goods or providing services. This prediction is usually made by assuming cost of goods sold is a percentage of sales. This is an acceptable assumption because certain fixed costs, such as depreciation, have already been covered and only variable costs are incurred as sales rise. The best technique for determining cost of goods sold is to separate it into fixed costs and variable costs calculated as a percentage of revenues.

4. *Forecasting administrative costs*—The firm's general and administrative costs may also have fixed and variable components tied to the sales level. In addition to the basic general and administrative expenses, two costs vary directly with changes in the terms of trade: collection costs and bad debt losses.

a. *Collection costs*—The costs of collecting delinquent accounts tend to be a fairly constant percentage of the total receivables. For example, a firm may have collection costs of $50,000 when its receivables are $800,000. This ratio is 50/800, or 6.25 percent. If the firm adopts a policy that increases receivables to $1.2 million, the collection costs might rise to $75,000 ($1,200,000 × .0625). It should be noted that the relationship between collection costs and receivables holds even though firms may be making sales to riskier customers when they relax credit standards. This is due to the economies of scale that accrue with the larger collection activities.

b. *Bad-debt losses*—If a firm increases credit sales by a fixed percentage, bad-debt losses often rise by a larger percentage. Relaxing credit terms allows more time for something to go awry for customers. In addition, customers experiencing liquidity problems may increase their purchases or switch suppliers to obtain longer payment periods. More delinquencies would be expected with these customers.

5. *Forecasting the receivables balance*—When forecasting the size of the investment in receivables under different credit terms, several steps are necessary. First, we must determine the average collection period (ACP), or the number of days customers typically take to pay. The ACP is calculated as follows:

$$\begin{array}{l}
\text{Average} \\
\text{Collection} \\
\text{Period}
\end{array} = \begin{array}{c}
\text{Percent} \\
\text{Taking} \\
\text{Discount}
\end{array} \times \begin{array}{c}
\text{Discount} \\
\text{Period} \\
\text{in Days}
\end{array}$$

$$+ \begin{array}{c}
\text{Percent} \\
\text{Not Taking} \\
\text{Discount}
\end{array} \times \begin{array}{c}
\text{Net} \\
\text{Period} \\
\text{in Days}
\end{array}$$

$$+ \begin{array}{c}
\text{Lag} \\
\text{Factor} \\
\text{in Days}
\end{array}$$

where the lag factor is an estimate of the delays in payment as a result of mail and processing floats and customer slowness to pay. As an example, a net-30 policy may result in an average collection period of 45 days. This would be a lag factor of 15 days. Next we calculate the receivables turnover. The receivables turnover formula is 360/ACP. Then, this ratio is used to determine the balance of receivables. The estimated receivables balance is calculated by credit sales/receivables turnover. For example, a firm offers terms of 2/10 net 30. Forty percent of the customers will take the discount, and the lag factor is 12 days. If the average collection period is 34 days (.40 × 10 + .60 × 30 + 12), the accounts receivable turnover will be as follows:

$$ART = 360/34 = 10.6$$

and the average receivables balance will be $943,396 (10,000,000/10.6).

6. *Forecasting financing costs*—If a change in credit policies causes an increase or decrease in receivables, this increased or decreased investment must be recognized. For example, suppose receivables are currently $4 million and the incremental cost of funds is 7 percent. The firm is evaluating two credit policies. The first will increase receivables to $5 million, and the second will decrease receivables to $3.2 million. What is the financing cost or benefit with each policy? The answer is a cost of $70,000 with the increase in receivables ($1,000,000 × .07), and a benefit of $56,000 with the reduction ($800,000 × .07).

7. *Calculating after-tax profit*—Once all the previous items have been calculated, an income statement can be used to calculate the firm's profit.

COLLECTING ACCOUNTS RECEIVABLE

After the firm has made sales on credit, it must collect on the accounts receivable. The goal in collecting on accounts is to collect as quickly as possible in order to optimize the availability of funds. This is achieved through several methods, all of which attempt to shorten the float, which is the time period between when the payor has sent the funds and when they are available to the payee.

There are three basic types of float: (1) Mail float is the time during which the check is in the mail. (2) Internal float is the time it takes the company to process the payment and deposit it in the bank. (3) Clearing float is the time it takes for the check to clear.

Shortening the float is typically accomplished in one of three ways:

1. *Concentration banking*—Firms with numerous sales offices designate certain of these offices as collection centers for their regions. Customers are directed to remit their payments to these centers, which in turn deposit the receipts in local banks. Then, funds from these banks are periodically transferred to a central or concentration bank located in the city in which the firm has its headquarters.

A concentration banking arrangement reduces collection float by shortening the mail and clearing floats. Mail float is reduced because the payor is sending payment to an office in his or her geographical region and the mail is delivered more quickly. The clearing float is decreased because the payee's bank is likely to be in the same region as the payor's bank; it may even be the same bank.

2. *Lockboxes*—In a lockbox arrangement, the payee directs the payor to send the check to a post office box. A bank in the same region as the post office box then empties the box, called a lockbox, one or more times each business day. The bank takes the payments, deposits the check in the firm's account, and sends a copy of the check and payment slip to the payee.

This arrangement is considered superior to concentration banking because it reduces the mail, internal, and clearing floats. The mail float is reduced because the lockbox and the payor are in the same region. The remaining float is decreased because the internal processing and clearing are occurring simultaneously. Additional reductions in mail float may occur since payments do not have to be delivered but are picked up at the post office.

3. *Direct sends*—The final method of decreasing the float and therefore speeding collections is to use a direct send. With this method, firms that receive large checks drawn on distant banks or a large number of checks drawn on banks in a given city may arrange, via express mail or private express services, to present the checks directly, for payment from the banks on which they were drawn. Thus, the firm receives immediate payment. In most cases, the funds will be transferred by wire to the firm's bank. This method decreases only the clearing float, and is thus considered less useful than a concentration or lockbox arrangement.

RECENT DEVELOPMENTS

There have been several recent developments in the field of accounts receivable management. These developments may be divided into four areas:

1. *A focus on credit and collections*—This is a result of concern about cash flows. The trend is toward the centralization of the credit and collection functions into a single area under one manager. The commitment of top management is viewed as crucial to this process.

2. *Computerization of credit and collection processes*—This is gaining momentum since computerization generates both time and financial savings. Some firms are designing their own systems, while others are using packaged software.

3. *Integration of more personnel into credit and collection processes*—This is an additional development. As regards internal personnel, continuing education, training, and certification are recent trends. In addition, involving the sales force in the monitoring of accounts seems to be an effective method of increasing collections.

4. *Electronic payment systems*—These appear to be the tools of the future, both for firms and the government. For example, General Motors converted all of its suppliers to electronic payments, and the federal government is implementing a program called Vendor Express for electronic payments. The objectives are to increase the information available to credit and collection managers and decrease the inefficiencies associated with paper transfers.

INVENTORY VALUATION AND CONTROL

William Brunsen, Eastern New Mexico University
Athar Murtuza, Associate Professor of Accounting, Seton Hall University

It would be no exaggeration to assert that inventory represents a firm's reason for being. Both manufacturers and merchandisers are in business to sell, and without inventories there will be nothing to sell. Furthermore, inventories can represent a major portion of a firm's working capital. Not only do inventories tie up capital but their storage and safekeeping also consumes considerable resources.

Inventory refers to goods held for the purpose of sale. The goods held in inventory by a merchandiser like Sears are sales-ready finished products. But, in the case of a manufacturer of automobiles, like Ford, it will include the raw materials, work in process, finished goods, component parts for factory machines, and supplies. The costs directly related to inventory are briefly defined as follows:

■ *Purchase costs* refer to the value of the inventory itself.

■ *Ordering costs* define the managerial and clerical expenses incurred to prepare the purchase order, or in the case of manufacturing firms, the production order.

■ *Carrying costs* are those incurred for inventory's storage, handling, insurance, pilferage, spoilage, obsolescence, taxes, and the opportunity cost of capital tied up or invested in the inventory.

■ *Stockout costs* are incurred when the needed item is not in stock. It may take the form of lost sales revenue, the cost of delayed production, or penalties incurred for not meeting customers' deadlines.

■ *Setup costs* occur because different products require equipment to be reset to meet specific needs of each batch of product. In addition to equipment setup costs, to make a batch of product different from the one previously made will involve obtaining the raw materials from the warehouse, moving out the previous stock at the workstations, and filing paperwork. In addition, while setups are being changed, workers involved in operating the equipment may be idle, even while they are getting paid. The setup costs are non-value adding to the firm; they can be minimized by redesigning the production process and simplifying the product design.

The value of inventory on hand must be determined periodically along with the value of other assets to enable a company to determine its cost of goods sold and to state the firm's financial position. The basis used for inventory valuation has a significant effect on the costs and earnings reflected in the operating statements and on the asset value shown on the balance sheet.

A variety of methods can be used to value inventory. Income tax computation, accounting principles, ease of application, management reporting, and control considerations all influence the approach used. From a management point of view, the evaluation method that is selected should take advantage of benefits that may affect the operating statement but should also be easily used or converted to effective reporting for management evaluation and decision making.

COST DETERMINATION

The principal methods of cost determination for financial statement preparation begin with standard costs and/or average costs. The development of standard or average unit costs allows the extension of physical units by these costs to determine the ending inventory value, which, when subtracted from the beginning inventory plus materials purchases and conversion expenses for the period, equals the cost of goods sold for the period. Ending inventory values and, correspondingly, costs of goods sold may be further adjusted by the use of FIFO (first in, first out), LIFO (last in, first out), or cost-of-specific-lot methods. For retail and distribution companies, which do not incur conversion costs, the gross margin retail method is the commonly accepted valuation method.

Standard Costs

A simply administered technique for determining inventory cost is provided by standard costs. To facilitate its use, standard costs representing the expected costs of purchase and conversion must be established for materials, labor, and other expenses directly related to each inventoried unit. Those manufacturing expenses (overhead or burden) not directly identified with a product or inventory item are usually assigned to each unit of production on a realistic basis. Thus, supervision might be assigned on the basis of the labor hours required to make a product, whereas depreciation, insurance, and taxes might be allocated on the basis of machine-hours required to make a product.

When actual costs are not equal to the standards, variances result and must be recorded. If these variances are substantial, they are accumulated and reallocated to all the production of the period and the inventory on hand. If the variances are minor, they are generally taken as an expense as they occur. To remain accurate and effective, standard costs must be revised at least annually by correcting for changes in costs and methods; otherwise, the values lose validity either for valuing inventory or for controlling purchasing or operations.

Average Costs

Many companies use an average unit cost to determine inventory value. Two methods are used for this purpose: an average calculated by dividing the total cost of beginning inventory and purchases by the total number of units represented; and a moving average, calculated after each new purchase is made. Where the time lapse between valuations is long or price changes are rapid, the two methods produce somewhat different results. It is important to note that the moving average requires the maintenance of perpetual records, while the weighted average may be computed periodically. In either case, the use of averaging tends to spread the effect of short-range price changes and level their effect on profit determination.

FIFO

The FIFO method assumes that the goods are sold in the order in which they were received or manufactured. With the use of FIFO it is not necessary to identify lots or physically segregate items in the order of purchase. Under this method the final inventory is priced by determining the costs of the most recent purchases or using the most recent standard costs. Generally, this is done by working back from the most recent invoices of units manufactured until the quantity on hand has been covered.

LIFO

The LIFO method assumes that the last goods received or manufactured were sold first. In a period of rising prices, this method reduces profits and postpones tax payments because the highest-cost items are used to compute the cost of sales. This method assumes that all items in inventory, or in a segment of inventory, are homogeneous. This assumption allows the use of price indices to convert the final inventory priced at current prices to the same inventory priced in terms of the base year (the year in which LIFO was adopted).

Generally, any company with the following characteristics should adopt the LIFO method if it desires to postpone the payment of taxes and thus receive an "interest-free" loan from the government: (1) inventories that are significant relative to its total assets (a manufacturer or distributor); (2) inventory costs that are increasing; (3) an effective tax rate that is not expected to increase significantly; and/

or (4) inventory levels that are expected to remain stable or increase. Conversely, if inventory levels or unit costs are expected to decline or the tax rates increase, a company should not use the LIFO method because LIFO could increase rather than decrease the company's future tax liability.

Cost of Specific Lot

For the capital-goods industries and some other industries it is usually desirable to maintain the identity and actual costs of specific lots or items. This is done by recording the actual raw-materials purchase price and conversion costs for each lot or item in inventory. The application of this method is usually limited to inventories containing high-value, low-quantity items or to those situations where such records are practical or mandatory.

Gross-Margin Method

The gross-margin method of pricing inventory has been developed in the distribution and retailing industries to facilitate inventory valuation by having items in inventory priced at an adjusted selling price rather than cost. The basis for computing this ratio is an established average margin, or markup, to the cost to arrive at the selling price. Assuming that the goods in inventory are representative, in terms of their markup, of goods purchased during the recent operating period, their cost is easily determined by using the ratio to recompute the inventory value. Using this method, the ending inventory value is determined by extending the physical units by their selling prices and then reducing the extended amount by the average markup percentage. As with other methods, cost of goods sold is calculated by subtracting the ending inventory value from beginning inventory plus purchases.

Selection of Method

The size, age, and type of inventory must be considered in selecting the method used for valuation. The techniques chosen should provide for the requirements of financial and tax reporting as well as relate to the methods used by management for measuring its performance in inventory management and control. For consistency in financial reporting, it is mandatory that the method of inventory valuation remain constant. If at any time a change in method is made, the effect on the financial results must be clearly stated.

ELEMENTS OF INVENTORY MANAGEMENT

The job of managers responsible for inventory may be said to revolve around some basic questions: What should be ordered? How much should be ordered? When should the merchandise be ordered? Where should it be delivered? Who should the merchandise be ordered from? In addition, the inventory managers also need to keep track of what has been ordered and received.

The inventory to be ordered or manufactured is dependent on sales forecasted. In the case of merchandisers, the quantities of various items to be ordered are unrelated to each other: The number of appliances to keep in stock is not related to the number of shirts on hand. This is described as independent demand. On the other hand, for a manufacturer, the number of tires to be ordered is related to the number of automobiles being manufactured. When goods being ordered are so related, their demand will be called dependent.

While manufacturers are more likely to order goods that have dependent demands, they can also order items that are independent of the decision to manufacture a certain quantity: The amount of supplies and the number of machine parts ordered may not be directly related to the number of cars being made.

In the past the job of purchasing managers was to shop around among a large sample of vendors for the best value. But old ways are changing. A manifestation of the change involves going directly to the wholesalers. This changed thinking means the number of vendors that buyers deal with can be much smaller. This also means longer-term, closer relationships with vendors. Vendors are expected to be more quality conscious and to make deliveries on time; in return, they are assured business.

One consequence of the new thinking has been a reduction in ordering costs. Advances in information technologies combined with fewer, more reliable vendors have allowed changes in accounts payable procedures: Payments are made faster with less paperwork and reduced clerical staff to process purchase orders and receiving reports. Bar codes allow arriving shipments to be identified sooner; such identification of shipments received can allow automatic bank transfers to vendors' accounts.

For manufacturers, the need for reducing inventory on hand has led to having vendors deliver goods directly to work centers on the factory floor as needed. However, not everyone is able to do so since the production facilities may not have been built to accommodate such deliveries. In any case, the manufacturers' concern is to have the goods delivered to the factories, but retailers have more of a problem since their warehouses and stores may be far apart. Instead of storing inventory in their facilities, the mega-retailers can have the vendors deliver it to their stores directly. This trend is increasing in popularity.

The issue of when to order inventory is handled differently, depending on whether the goods are demand independent or dependent. For dependent demand, the issue revolves around a certain point in time when desired goods must be ordered, or in many cases, reordered. That point in time is described as the reorder point. For most firms the reorder point is reached when the quantity on hand of a certain item falls below a certain level. At this level there is still some quantity on hand, termed safety stock, to last until the reordered stock reaches the warehouse. The quantity of safety stock is dependent on the lead time needed for stock ordered to be delivered. When the stock falls to the reorder point, the quantity ordered may be determined through economic order quantity (EOQ), which is discussed next. The reorder points, when drawn graphically, resemble the teeth of a saw; hence, the sawtooth model. There are variants of the basic model that address uncertainty of future demands.

One measure of change in retailing has come about through the point of sales computers that link the sales registers to the vendors, alerting them to items that need to be replaced. Such electronically determined reorder points can be of benefit to both the vendors and the buyers.

While demand-independent methods described above can be particularly useful for retailers, they may not be suited to manufacturers. The needs of such firms are not met by relatively simple sawtooth models; they require material requirement planning (MRP) or manufacturing resource planning (MRP II), discussed below.

In the past the quantities being ordered were related not only to the sales projected but also to a decision to have safety stock on hand. Managers were motivated to provide themselves with safeguards for variation in the deliveries of goods ordered as well as to take advantage of the economies of purchasing in bulk. More recently, the rules of the game dictate that the burden of carrying inventory be shifted from the seller or the manufacturer to the supplier. This has brought on the popularity of just-in-time production, which minimizes work in process inventories. There is also a greater emphasis on matching production to market requirements.

Despite the advent of the new gospel of inventory, the old rules that governed the quantities to order are not quite extinct. Two independent demand models discussed here are economic order quantity (EOQ) and open to buy.

Economic Order Quantity (EOQ)

The economic order quantity method calculates the theoretical minimum annual cost for ordering and stocking an item. The EOQ computation takes into account the cost of placing an order, the annual sales rate, the unit cost, and the cost of carrying the inventory (interest, insurance, obsolescence, and so forth). The formula is illustrated in Exhibit 5-2,

Exhibit 5-2. Economic Order Quantity

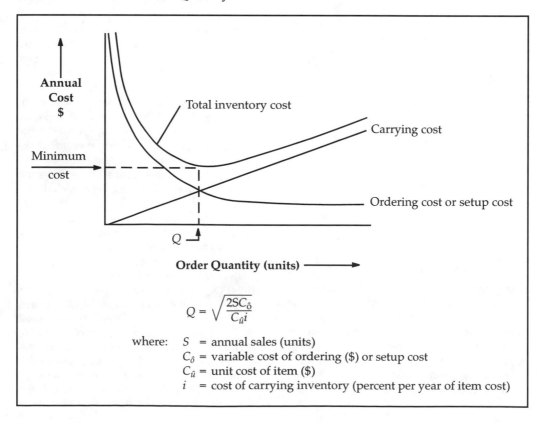

$$Q = \sqrt{\frac{2SC_{\hat{o}}}{C_{\hat{u}}i}}$$

where: S = annual sales (units)
          $C_{\hat{o}}$ = variable cost of ordering ($) or setup cost
          $C_{\hat{u}}$ = unit cost of item ($)
          i = cost of carrying inventory (percent per year of item cost)

which also shows that, as the number of orders placed is reduced, the cost of ordering is reduced but the cost of holding (carrying) increases. The economic order quantity and frequency occurs where the sum of the two costs is minimized. Once determined for an item, the EOQ is not frequently changed except for changes in sales or use requirements.

The Open-to-Buy Method

Retail businesses have used an open-to-buy inventory control system for many years. Simply stated, under this system a department buyer is limited to a specific account of funds that may be committed to the total of inventory on hand and on order. This amount is related to the sales expected in the immediate future, usually a month or season. To calculate the open-to-buy amount, the allowable closing inventory for the month, at retail price, is added to sales planned for the month. The goods on hand (at retail) beginning inventory and open purchase orders (at retail) are subtracted from this total and adjusted for markup percentage to arrive at the funds available for purchases. Adjustments for markups and markdowns are made so that the available amount is not affected by these changes. The allowable closing inventory value is usually related to the average inventory turnover performance expected in the buyer's department and the sales expected in the succeeding month.

Although the open-to-buy method is usually thought of in relation to retailing, it is also being applied in other fields. In one application, for example, a manufacturer may establish a limit for the number of units that may be planned for production on the basis of the sales plan, the units in inventory, and the units already in process or planned for production. The open-to-buy amount for the purchase of parts and materials can be similarly related to the production plan and the dollars of materials on hand already on order.

The two models discussed above pertain to independent demand goods, but in order to determine quantities and delivery time of dependent demand goods, other models such as MRP and MRP II are useful.

MATERIAL REQUIREMENTS PLANNING

Material requirements planning (MRP) is a planning system concerned with the acquisition of dependent demand goods. The focus of MRP is on knowing the quantity and timing of inventory items needed in accordance with the master production schedule. It seeks to ensure that materials, components, and subassemblies needed are available in the right quantity. When used effectively, MRP can reduce the various inventory costs, as well as improve scheduling effectiveness and response to changing market conditions.

The details pertaining to MRP are highly involved, but at its very basic level, MRP is similar to the kind of planning needed to have all the ingredients for a recipe on hand while cooking. Baking one's favorite cake is a discrete item, and the acquisition of the needed ingredients to coincide with cooking is easily done. It is immensely more complex when one is dealing with continuous production of goods that have many models, requiring hundreds and often thousands of parts, components, and subassemblies with differing lead times and vendors. MRP helps to address the immense complexity.

The key factors in an MRP system are a master production schedule (MPS), a bill of materials (BOM), an inventory profile, and lead times of all inventory items. Using these factors, computer algorithms can help schedule the acquisition of inventory and its subsequent release for production. The same algorithms can quickly respond to unexpected changes in the customers' demands for products. Closed-loop MRP includes feedback from both internal production sources and vendor reports. Regenerative MRP systems use batch processing to replan the requirements on a regular basis, such as monthly or even weekly. In contrast, net-change MRP systems are online and can respond continuously to transactions pertaining to production schedule, vendor reports, and inventory status of various items.

The success of MRP is closely tied to making effective use of a firm's production capacity. Capacity requirements planning (CRP) is to personnel and equipment what MRP is to materials. The acquisition of materials per schedule is of no use unless capacity is available to subsequently convert the materials into finished products as planned. Thus, CRP must be effectively integrated with MRP.

In recent years it was realized that requirements planning cannot be limited to material and capacity. A firm does not live by material and capacity alone; other company functions such as purchasing, marketing, management, and accounting must also be involved if the firm is to endure. Material requirements do not effectively describe a planning system that involves all the company functions. To describe the system that involves all the resources of a manufacturing firm in requirements planning, a new term has been coined: manufacturing resource planning (MRP II). It is perceived to be a system that allows all the departments of a firm to work according to the same plan. A number of application software packages are available that allow implementation of MRP II; among them are IBM's MAPICS, Arthur Andersen's MAC-PAC, Hewlett-Packard's FMS, and Martin Marietta's MAS II.

At present MRP is mostly limited to manufacturing environments. However, the potential exists to use MRP in the service sector. Hospitals and academic institutions can use it to schedule equipment, space, and personnel.

Despite the considerable usefulness of MRP, problems have been encountered in its implementation. Problems can occur because of an insufficient management commitment or a failure to realize that MRP is only a computerized scheduling tool; it is only a part of the system, not a replacement for the system. There are instances when MRP is taken to mean no more than meeting the schedule: such a limitation defeats the spirit of MRP. One can argue that MRP's effectiveness is ultimately constrained by the personnel using it and environments in which it is used.

An alternative to MRP is synchronized manufacturing. It seeks to optimize the use of resources such as production time, inventory, and operating expenses by focusing on the actual and potential bottlenecks in the production process.

JUST-IN-TIME INVENTORY MANAGEMENT

The JIT system is characterized by an adherence to goals such as minimizing inventory investment, uncovering quality problems, reacting faster to demand changes, and shortening throughput, that is, the time needed to process a batch through the production process. It insists on the production of the exact number of units to be produced or to be brought in by the vendors as they are needed and where they are needed. Under JIT, the production line is run on a demand-pull basis. As a result, the work at each station is authorized by the demand of the station following it. Production is stopped when problems occur, such as absent parts or defective work.

The underlying philosophy of JIT is constant improvement; it is sought by simplification of the production process and elimination of nonvalue adding activities. The elimination of nonessential activity, the underlying basis of what has come to be known as activity management, can extend to accounting. Under JIT the entire bookkeeping is reduced to two entries: one made at the start of the process and the second made when finished goods exit production and are received by the warehouse.

INVENTORY CONTROL

One of the prime responsibilities of managers at all levels is the optimum use of assets. A balance between customer service, efficient use of production facilities, and minimum inventory investment must be achieved as part of effective profit and asset management.

Inventory losses may affect company profits. Several types of conditions account for most inventory losses. Obsolescence is caused by purchasing or producing products that are displaced by newer or more desirable goods. The difference between the cost of the inventory and its disposal price is the loss caused by obsolescence. In addition, the investment in excessive inventory of these items generally precludes the purchase of other more desirable items, requires space for storage, and increases the effort required for taking physical inventory.

Inventory not used quickly, or stored in inadequate facilities, is exposed to damage or spoilage. A certain amount of such losses may be expected under any condition, but they can be minimized with careful planning, handling, and facilities maintenance. The most effective control is the limitation of purchases and inventory to necessary quantities.

Pilferage or theft is a special loss consideration, especially in certain industries where inventoried items are small or of high value and may be consumed by employees or easily disposed of without identification. In addition to the control of inventory areas, preventive measures include extra care to limit (1) opportunities for access to the inventory, (2) the number of people with access, and (3) the routes for removal of the most susceptible items.

In many states, the value of the inventory has yet another direct influence on profit performance—it is the basis for personal property taxes on corporations. This consideration usually prompts managers to plan substantial reductions in materials and finished goods on hand immediately before the valuation date.

PHYSICAL INVENTORY

Regardless of the accuracy of perpetual inventory records and the care with which they are prepared, the unit stock records must be adjusted periodically (after a physical count) for confirmation of accuracy and balancing to the general ledger. Of course, if no perpetual records are kept, such a count is required to determine the number of units on hand at a specific date. Since no system is flawless, the count also serves to test the effectiveness of the control systems and identify weaknesses requiring improvement.

Many companies have switched to a cycle count system, that is, count one twelfth of the inventory each month or one fifty-second each week. This method will improve accuracy, pinpoint errors in the record-keeping systems quickly, avoid shrink "surprises," and avoid the expense and disruption of an annual physical inventory. Cycle counts can also be administered to concentrate on the high-value or high-movement items, with less frequent count of the low-value, low-movement items.

ANALYZING OPERATING RESULTS

Daniel Haskin, Eastern New Mexico University
William Brunsen, Eastern New Mexico University

The role of management can be described as consisting of planning and control. Management's objectives for the enterprise are stated in financial terms in the form of budgets. A budget is not the only statement of the objectives of the enterprise but is one of the most important forms. Other forms might be narratives related to the company's responsibility to shareholders or its contribution to the well-being of its community or employees.

Once management has stated its objectives in financial terms (planning), its function becomes control. That is, management guides the individuals within the organization to achieve the objectives of the organization.

One of the best methods of evaluating the results of operations is to employ a responsibility accounting system in which individuals at various levels are responsible for controlling costs within their respective areas. A key feature of responsibility accounting is that the individual manager is evaluated on the results of operations under his or her control. For instance, the supervisor of a producing department cannot control the salary of the enterprise's president and therefore is not allocated part of that cost. The concept of controllable and noncontrollable costs is central to the functioning of responsibility accounting. Budgets and budget variances are used to motivate individuals to accomplish their objectives.

A primary responsibility of financial management is to provide appropriate data for external and internal reporting. The collection and reporting of operating results normally are part of the accounting stream of an enterprise's information system. The information system will vary, depending on the size and sophistication of the organization. Accounting data is governed by generally accepted accounting principles, which are highly formalized, and carry significant weight with external users.

For internal reporting, management has the prerogative to define the rules and sacrifice precision to gain time, as in the case of "flash" reports. For example, once actual sales data are available, standard costs and budgeted expenses, as opposed to actual costs, might be used to obtain a quick view of profits.

PRESENTATION METHODS

Operating results can be presented in a variety of reporting formats such as orally, in visual displays, as written reports, or by a combination of these methods, depending on requirements of the presentation. Further, such reports may be for either external or internal purposes. They may be summary reports focusing on the enterprise as a whole or segment reports focusing on one or more areas within the enterprise.

Formats for external reports are usually standardized, since these reports are subject to scrutiny by independent bodies. The format of internal reports depends on the prevailing management philosophy as well as the cost system in use. For our purposes, reports concerning operating results can be categorized as summary reports, control reports, and special-purpose reports.

Summary Reports

Summary reports of operating results can focus either on the entire enterprise or reportable segments and profit centers. These summary reports are usually the income statement, the balance sheet, and the statement of cash flows.

The income statement, also known as the statement of operations or profit and loss statement, was at one time considered the most important operating statement. In recent years, the statement of cash flows and the balance sheet have become equally, if not more, significant. Internal summary reports usually demand more detail than external reports.

Control Reports

A control report provides an even finer focus on the details of the operations of an enterprise. Generally it focuses on a specific area of interest, but it is distinguished by the fact that it is keyed to other control reports that magnify the details. As an example, expenses may be compared with budgets to disclose variances, which in turn call attention to the possible need for corrective action. Or, the profit contribution of a specific product in a particular profit center may be analyzed in detail, showing each cost and revenue component. Still another use of a control report is to identify problem areas by comparing actual results with budgets and prior periods.

Special-Purpose Reports

Reports reflecting operating results may uncover areas that require further analysis. For example, negative variances for a department may be large, indicating the need for more detailed analysis. Such an analysis may then be requested and presented in a special report to the appropriate level of management. Such reporting normally occurs at irregular intervals and is tailored to the specific needs of the situation.

FINANCIAL STATEMENTS

The analysis of financial statements contributes to the evaluation of the firm's operating results. Over the years, guidelines have been developed that allow comparisons with goals, plans, objectives, and standards. Many of the guidelines take the form of financial or operating ratios—ratios that express relationships between items or groups of items extracted from the balance sheet and/or income statement.

To be used effectively, financial ratios must be compared with a standard of some sort. This standard may be a goal established by management, an industry norm or average, the performance of selected competitors, or the performance of another segment of the firm. Several firms including Dun & Bradstreet, Robert Morris and Associates, and others annually publish tables of ratios for most types of businesses. Although operating results can be analyzed and ratios compared to standards, interpretation of ratios is ultimately subjective.

Most analysts who analyze financial statements on a regular basis have a specific group of ratios on which they rely. Although some of the ratios selected may be unique to the industry within which the firm operates, there are ratios that are used for most industries. Such ratios are available from trade groups and other sources such as Robert Morris Associates. It should be noted that ratios from different sources may differ only slightly in definition/content but may be known by various names.

In a profit-oriented enterprise, the primary objective of operating statements is to provide relevant and timely information for making rational economic decisions concerning prof-

itability and solvency of the enterprise and its segments. While analysis can aid in the decision-making process, each individual must interpret the performance data according to his or her criteria and frame of reference.

NONFINANCIAL PERFORMANCE MEASURES

In recent years, nonfinancial measures of performance have been increasingly discussed in the professional literature, reflecting perhaps a greater reliance on them in practice. These measures can pertain to product quality, inventory and material usage, equipment utilization and maintenance, and throughput time. Some representative measures in each category are:

1. *Quality*—includes number of units rejected for defects, customer complaints, and the number of warranty claims.
2. *Inventory and material usage*—includes inventory turnover for raw material, work in process, and finished goods, scrap generation, number of parts used, cycle count accuracy, and level of inventories.
3. *Equipment usage or maintenance*—includes machine utilization, idle time ratios, setup time ratios, and number of repair calls.
4. *Throughput and delivery time*—includes on-time delivery, lead time, amount of production backlog, and setup time.

Both financial and nonfinancial measures have useful roles to play as a means of improving performance and, by implication, profitability.

MEASURING DIVISIONAL PERFORMANCE

Most major firms have several profit or investment centers. The existence of multiple units requires performance measures to evaluate them. Among the most well-known measures are return on investment (ROI) and residual income.

ROI is a product of margin and turnover, where margin may be defined as the percent of income left after paying all the operating expenses. Turnover may be defined as the number of assets sold and then replaced. It may be represented as margin multiplied by turnover, where margin equals net operating income divided by sales, turnover equals sales divided by average operating assets. ROI can be improved by increasing sales, reducing expenses, and/or reducing operating assets.

Notwithstanding its wide uses, ROI has been criticized for promoting short-term performance over long-term growth. An increase in the value of operating assets that can result from new investment may not lead to immediate increases in sales, thus lowering the ROI. Such a decrease in ROI may keep managers from undertaking long-term investments. ROI has also been criticized because it fails to evaluate performance of a manager independent of the operating assets with which he or she works: A manager operating an obsolete plant is handicapped as compared to rivals operating more cost-efficient factories.

Residual income, another performance measure, is the net operating income that an investment can earn above a minimum rate of return. It is described in actual dollars rather than as a percent. The following illustration will help explain its workings:

> Division A is considering an investment that will require $500,000. The minimum return the division is required to earn is 10 percent, in other words $50,000 in net operating income, given its asset base of $500,000. The investment will provide $60,000 in its first year. This equates to $10,000 in residual income.

A large number of firms use measures such as growth in market share, product leadership, product innovation, employee turnover, and increases in productivity instead of, or in combination with, ROI and residual income for measuring divisional performances.

TRANSFER PRICING

A transfer price is defined as the amount charged for products or services when one division of a firm provides them to another division. Whenever segments of a firm are doing business with each other, a problem can arise in pricing intrafirm sales and purchases. The purchasing division would like prices to be lower, whereas the seller would like them to be at least equal to prevailing market prices. Otherwise, the seller's divisional ROI and residual income will decline. Among approaches used to set transfer prices are:

1. Interdivisional negotiations that balance the interest of the divisions and the parent firm.
2. The use of market prices when available.
3. The use of direct variable costs to produce the product.
4. Full costing, that is, direct variable costs plus an allocated portion of fixed costs.

With the spread of multinational corporations and their facilities globally, in setting prices firms have to take into consideration international tax laws, currency fluctuations, and different operating environments in various parts of the globe.

A general rule for setting transfer prices may be expressed as transfer price equals direct variable costs plus lost margin per unit from an outside sale. Such a price-setting approach preserves the profit margins of the selling division. If used as the basis of negotiation among the divisions, it may lead to balancing the interests of all involved. It is equally useful whether the selling division is operating at capacity or below capacity.

MANAGERIAL USES OF ACCOUNTING

Athar Murtuza, Associate Professor of Accounting, Seton Hall University

Financial statements are historical records, like the scores at the ends of games. They summarize what occurred in given fiscal periods, but they do so after the fact. But managers need to keep making decisions that deal with the present and the future. Their interest is not confined to the final scores of completed games.

An income statement gives total revenue, but managers want to know the sales in each store, each department, and by product. The income statement does not help much in performance evaluations, nor does it reveal whether the organizational goals were met. To overcome such inadequacies, managerial accounting tools have been developed. There are a number of differences between managerial and financial accounting. Managerial accounting:

- Focuses on the needs of internal users.
- Places more emphasis on the future.
- Is not bound by generally accepted accounting principles (GAAP).
- Is not mandated by government regulations.
- Emphasizes relevance and flexibility in its reports.
- Uses nonmonetary information.
- Emphasizes the parts rather than the whole organization.

Despite these differences, both managerial and financial accounting rely on the same database.

To better appreciate managerial accounting, one needs to start by learning its vocabulary. *Cost* refers to the expending, sacrificing, or using up of resources. One can track, analyze, and report costs by relating them to the reason for which they are being incurred. *Cost objective* is the reason for which a resource is being used. An example is operating a vehicle or defending a lawsuit. *Cost driver* refers to the activity that causes a cost change. An ice cream maker's cost will increase if he makes more flavors as a result of an increase in the stocks of inventory on hand.

MANUFACTURING COSTS

To make something, be it as simple as a cake or as complex as a space shuttle, one needs three types of resources. In the case of a cake, these are the cake mix, the baker, and the kitchen. In accounting vocabulary, the three resources are called direct material, direct labor, and manufacturing overhead. The work done on the assembly lines of a factory is direct labor. The labor expended in the storeroom or machine maintenance is indirect as it cannot be related to a specific order.

In contrast to labor and material, manufacturing overhead is a composite cost. Overhead includes depreciation on the factory building and equipment, property taxes, utilities, research and development, indirect material, and indirect labor. The support services provided by accounting, purchasing, and human resources are also part of the overhead.

Overhead is more difficult to track and control than labor and materials. Overhead in today's environment is becoming a larger portion of total costs. Direct material and labor may amount to less than 10 percent of the total cost of making a computer. The rest is overhead. Perhaps the major challenge facing managerial accountants today is the task of assigning overhead to various products over their life cycles.

CLASSIFYING COSTS

There are a number of useful ways of classifying costs, including:

1. *Timing of recognition* deals with product versus period costs. Product costs are recognized as expenses when goods are sold. Period costs are recognized as expenses in the period they occur. Manufacturing costs are usually product costs, whereas administrative and selling costs are often period costs.

2. *Traceability* deals with direct and indirect costs. Direct labor, direct material, and sales commissions are usually direct, as they are associated with a single cost objective. In contrast, overhead is indirect because it is shared among different cost objectives.

3. *Authorization* deals with controllable versus noncontrollable costs. When judging performance, it is useful to know who authorized expenses. A major tenet of managerial accounting is that a manager's performance should be judged on how well he or she used resources that he or she actually controlled. Differentiating on the basis of the controllability of costs helps makes this judgment.

4. *Relevance* is helpful to identify costs that change as a result of a decision. Sunk costs are never relevant to a decision.

5. *Variability* deals with fixed and variable costs. Fixed costs do not change with the volume of business. The depreciation on factory machines as well as advertising expenses are

examples of fixed costs. Sales commissions, direct labor, and materials are examples of variable costs, as they do change. A number of expenses behave as mixed costs. An example would be phone bills, which have a fixed portion, irrespective of the number of calls made, and a variable portion stemming from the number of calls.

COST SYSTEMS

The purpose of a cost system is to track costs within an organization. The tracking of costs helps to accomplish objectives such as planning and control, inventory valuation and income determination, and product pricing. Cost tracking in a cost accounting system is mainly accomplished through ledger accounts and journal entries describing various transactions.

Process costing is the cost system used when the product consists of identical units that are produced for long periods continuously. A typical user of this system would be an oil refinery or a maker of chemicals.

A job costing system may be used by firms that make many different products each period. It is used when one is custom building a house or making space shuttles.

Both cost systems track direct material, direct labor and overhead, and seek to determine per unit cost. Given the increased automation in recent years, some have argued that the system should track costs associated with factory machines instead of making them a part of the overhead.

Both process and job costing use similar manufacturing accounts such as those for work in process (WIP), overhead, finished goods, and raw material. The flow of cost through both systems is similar. A major difference between the two is that process costing tracks the work-in-process costs by department whereas costs get tracked by the individual job under job costing.

Some accounting systems combine the attributes of process and job costing. Under such systems, direct material costs are charged directly to each batch being processed as in job costing, while other costs may be charged to the department. Such hybrid systems are well suited to those firms who manufacture related products in batches, including ice cream, books, and automobiles. Each batch can be customized using a different combination of material and processing steps.

An activity-based cost (ABC) system focuses on activities as the basic cost objective. The more parts a product has, the more it is likely to cost, since all those parts have to be ordered and stored. Additionally, more complex products require more production and setup time, thus driving up the costs.

The ABC system functions by first pooling the various costs associated with a given activity, such as procurement of raw material. Then it assigns costs based on the activities that cause the costs.

Among the benefits of ABC systems is the correction of distorted allocation. It is common under the older systems for a high-volume product to be charged a larger share of the indirect costs, while a low-volume product is assigned a lower share. But, in reality, the two products may have equal procurement costs.

A number of costs have multiple reasons for their occurrence. A major problem facing the cost system is how to allocate them. How do we allocate common costs to various products or departments? In recent years machine costs have become a larger share of product costs. Yet most firms bury them alongside other overhead items. If the machines are being used inefficiently, the problem may be buried within a pool containing a wide assortment of diverse costs.

ABC systems have evolved in order to better allocate common costs, using improved causal relationships between cost objectives and their cost drivers. As a result, these systems better track inefficiencies.

Joint costing represents another variation associated with the allocation of common costs. Joint products are produced from a common source. An example is crude oil refined into gasoline, kerosene, jet fuel, and asphalt. Similarly, a cow turns into a variety of joint products: steaks, roasts, ground beef, and hide.

The source product is split into joint products at the split-off point. At this stage in processing, some products may be ready to be sold while others may need additional work. What must be remembered is that one may not obtain only one of the several products. From crude oil we get asphalt as well as gasoline. Similarly, it is not possible to obtain only steak and not the hide once we are past the split-off point. Joint costs are associated with the source product. All costs incurred up to and including the split-up are called joint costs. To allocate joint costs, one may use either the volume or the revenue generated by each of the products.

Why Allocate?

No matter what system is used, allocation of common costs remains a major problem. For the purpose of external reporting, it is immaterial how common costs are apportioned. The net income will not change. Therefore, the question arises: Why bother with cost allocation? Several answers are given:

1. Allocation is a necessary chore mandated by GAAP.
2. It is needed for costing inventories which, in turn, determine tax liabilities.
3. Allocation can show how resources are being used and whether they are being used efficiently. Allocation can motivate managers to better use common resources. If a department is not charged for common costs, it may treat them like a free lunch.
4. Allocation may help in planning by showing the demands being placed on common resources.
5. Allocation can help with product pricing and cost reimbursement.

Budgets, Standard Costs, and Variance Analysis

Budgets, standard costs, and variance analysis help managers plan and control organizational activity. *Budget* is the overall plan. *Standard costs* translate the budget to the operational level. *Variance analysis* helps with performance measurement, to plan subsequent budgetary goals, and directs managers to areas that need attention. Without variance analysis, budgets have the potential of turning into mere intentions.

What Do Variances Reveal?

Variances are the differences between what happened and what was expected. The failure to meet the budgetary goals or expectations can be a result of assorted problems. A variance is a symptom that alerts managers to potential or actual problems. By following up on the symptom, a manager can take corrective steps. Some variances are:

1. *Material price variance*—the impact of price differences that could be due to a price change or the use of material of a different quality than specified in the standard.
2. *Material quantity variance*—occurs as a result of differences between the planned and actual quantity of material used. The variance can result from the use of a lower-grade material, inexperienced workers, or poorly maintained machines.
3. *Labor rate variance*—caused by a difference between the budgeted and the actual wage rate.
4. *Labor efficiency variance*—the variance of workers' efficiency in terms of the time they took to complete a job and the time that was budgeted.

A standard cost system and variances it reports should have the following characteristics:

1. The reporting of variances should allow management to know as early as possible when the costs are getting out of hand. Management can then take steps to address the problem and control it.
2. The variances should be broken down so that individual variances do not cancel or offset each other.
3. The standard must be based on the current work environment and not on past historical figures alone. Workers may

have grown more experienced, material may be more expensive, and/or machines may be more advanced.
4. The standards must be developed as a cooperative effort among many parties, including engineers, purchasing departments, accountants, and production personnel. Accounting's role is to translate the standards into dollars and report the variances.
5. The system should be cost effective. It should not take more resources to operate than what it will save.
6. The system's reports should be relevant and understandable to managers at different levels within the organization.

Benefits of Standard Costing

There are a number of benefits associated with standard costing and variance analyses:

1. Standard costing permits "management by exception." Variances tell managers what problems need attention and what can be left alone. A manager does not have to waste time over minor problems.
2. Standards help with planning. A manager can better estimate what resources will be needed and in what quantity.
3. Standards help with performance measurement. They translate into expectations that can be used in the evaluation of a manager's performance.
4. The presence of standards requires regular reports and feedback from departments. Such reports can improve the chances that managers will be motivated to manage better.
5. The breakdown of variances into various components makes it easier to trace the source of trouble. This, in turn, can permit timely correction of problems.

Disadvantages of Standard Costing

Standard costing is a mixed blessing. Incorrect standards or their inappropriate uses can make variance analysis into something damaging. For one, they concentrate on the problems and are not concerned with what is working well. This can make workers feel that only the troublemakers get attention.

Unrealistic standards can also have a negative impact. Exceptionally easy standards can make the workers slow down, and hard-to-attain standards can make workers give up.

Standards can be seen as a means of "witch-hunts"—attempts by management to "get" the workers or even the managers. Such a perception can lead to game-playing with the budget. An example is introducing slack in the budget so that standards will be easier to attain.

FEDERAL TAXATION: MANAGEMENT RESPONSIBILITIES AND OPPORTUNITIES

Herbert J. Lerner, Ernst & Young
S. Theodore Reiner, Ernst & Young

From an operating perspective, management's responsibility to the shareholders and the corporation is to produce maximum net-after-tax income. To do this, it should view the federal government as having a stake in the taxable income of the business. But, like other expenses of doing business, taxes can be controlled by management. Taxable income and financial reporting income are not always identical. The maximum tax rate on corporations is 34 percent on taxable income, but management can often reduce taxable income below economic income.

In pursuing its goal of maximizing after-tax profit, management must balance business decisions against tax choices. Businesses do not succeed solely by taking advantage of tax benefits. However, successful businesses can and sometimes do pay excessive taxes because tax concerns are not considered. Successful management will seek to develop corporate policies that minimize the administrative burdens of tax compliance and avoid exposure to tax penalties. Management should use internal and external tax advisers as tacticians who implement effective tax strategies.

In some instances, management is limited in its ability to make a decision purely on business consideration. What intercompany price or fee structure may be used without the IRS (Internal Revenue Service) being able to reallocate income or expenses? Is the cost of a repair currently deductible or must it be spread over the useful life of the asset being repaired? And, the IRS always comes first in the priority of payment of bills.

CORPORATE STRUCTURE

Regular "C" Corporation Versus "S" Corporation

For federal tax purposes there are two types of corporations: the regular or "C" corporation and the "S" corporation. A corporation meeting certain requirements—number and type of shareholders, classes of stock, and so forth—can elect to be an "S" corporation and avoid being taxed at the corporate level. A "C" corporation is taxed on its income before distribution to shareholders and then the distribution is again subject to tax in the hands of the shareholders. An "S" corporation's income flows through to its shareholders. It is not subject to tax at the corporate level except in unusual circumstances. Because the corporate level of taxation is eliminated, the "S" corporation election provides more after-tax income.

Capital

In general, management has broad discretion in creating and modifying corporate capital structure. There are caveats, however. Since virtually all forms of interest are deductible and dividends are not, a capital structure that makes use of debentures or other bonds results in lower taxable income. Debt is therefore subject to close IRS scrutiny as to whether the debt instruments are actually disguised equity. This is also relevant in determining whether, on corporate insolvency, stockholder advances to the company will be treated as bad debts (deductible against ordinary income) or as equity (capital loss deductible against capital gain but limited deductibility against ordinary income).

In addition, "S" corporations by statute are limited to one class of stock. And because "S" corporations may have only one class of stock, the IRS may challenge whether a variance in rights between stockholders should be treated as a second class of stock that disqualifies the "S" election. However, if the necessary tests are met, a "C" corporation's capital structure may be reshuffled in various ways pursuant to a tax-free recapitalization.

The corporation may make preferential tax treatment available to purchasers of its securities by careful choice of the language, book treatment, and tax treatment of the certificates issued. For example, debt instruments issued and redeemed (retired) at face are done so on a nontaxable basis. A stock redemption when there are current or accumulated earnings and profits may be treated as a dividend unless the redemption meets one of the special exceptions provided by the Internal Revenue Code. Examples include a redemption to pay death taxes, the complete elimination of a shareholder, and a partial liquidation.

Multicorporate Entities and Consolidated Returns

In some instances, a business may want to operate through several corporations. For example, a retail business may want to have separate corporations for each state in which it transacts business. Or a corporation may wish to separate a high-risk business from low-risk businesses.

Under certain circumstances, all the separate corporations may file a single consolidated federal income tax return. The advantage of this procedure is that both losses and gains of all the companies are consolidated. To file a consolidated return the companies must meet certain ownership requirements. Once management decides to operate in a multicorporate form, it must make sure that the ownership requirements are met and continue to be met. An inadvertent disaffiliation can have negative tax results.

CORPORATE TAXATION

Consolidated return filing is only available to "C" corporations. A "C" corporation is subject to two federal income tax systems: the regular income tax and the corporate alternative minimum income tax. The former is a graduated tax applied to a moderately broad tax base. The latter is a flat tax applied to a substantially broader tax base. The corporation pays the higher of the two taxes.

Regular Tax

"C" corporations are subject to an income tax in a manner similar to that of individuals. Corporate gross income is reduced by deductions to arrive at corporate taxable income, to which the following rates were applied in 1992:

Taxable Income	Tax Rate
Less than $50,000	15%
Over $50,000 but less than $75,000	25%
Over $75,000	34%

When the corporation's taxable income exceeded $100,000, an additional tax of 5 percent on the excess over $100,000 was imposed. When taxable income reached $335,000, this surcharge ended. At this point, corporations with taxable income exceeding $335,000 paid a flat tax of 34 percent on all taxable income. Because of the many deductions to arrive at taxable income, the effective tax rate—the ratio of tax to corporate income—was ordinarily lower than 34 percent.

Alternative Minimum Tax

"C" corporations were also subject to an alternative minimum tax. This was a flat tax of 20 percent applied to alternative minimum taxable income, which was regular taxable income increased by certain preferences and adjustments. Examples were depletion allowances, charitable contributions, and tax-exempt interest on certain municipal bonds. The purpose of the alternative minimum tax was to prevent taxpayers with substantial income from avoiding all tax. It was a separate tax system that came into play in lieu of the regular corporate income tax only if tax under it was higher than the regular tax.

ACCOUNTING CONSIDERATIONS

Timing

The tax law provides that an amount is included in income in the tax year when received unless the method of accounting allows a different year. This provision means

that management can control, to some extent, the timing of income for federal tax purposes by employing such techniques as delaying deliveries of goods or making sales on consignment or approval.

Periods

Taxable income is computed on the basis of a taxpayer's tax year. This is generally the taxpayer's annual accounting period. It can be a calendar or fiscal year. In some instances, an accounting period ends on the same day every year, for example, the last Saturday in January. The accounting period adopted by a taxpayer generally ends on the last day of the month following the end of a business cycle. For example, a retail business that has a substantial holiday business might select January 31 as the close of its accounting period. Generally, management can select its tax year in the first tax return filed for the business. Once selected, the business cannot change the tax year without permission from the IRS.

Methods

The generally accepted tax accounting methods are the cash method and the accrual method. Taxpayers on the cash method report their income when it is received and claim deductions for expenses when they are paid. Taxpayers on the accrual method generally report income when all events entitling them to the income have been fixed and claim deductions for expenses similarly.

Other more esoteric methods can be selected, such as the percentage of completion method. These are applicable only in special situations.

Within limits, a taxpayer can select an accounting method. An example of a limit is that a business using inventories must use the accrual method. In the absence of such a limit, the taxpayer selects its accounting method on its first filed tax return. Like the selection of a taxable year, the method cannot be changed without IRS approval.

Inventories

The taxpayer may choose any inventory method, as long as it conforms to the best accounting practice in the industry and clearly reflects income. Thus, the choice is not confined to the most common methods—cost, market, or lower of cost or market. During an inflationary period—or any time when the replacement costs of inventory exceed original cost—the LIFO (last in, first out) method will reduce taxable income by charging out goods at current prices rather than at the lower costs of the past. But the IRS will permit the use of LIFO only if the taxpayer generally agrees to use this method on all financial statements, reports to stockholders, credit reports, and the like (except for foreign subsidiaries).

Depreciation

New or used assets with determinable useful lives, placed in service after December 31, 1986, would be written off under the modified accelerated cost recovery system (MACRS) or the straight-line method in 1992. Under the MACRS, each item of property is assigned to one of the following property classes: three years, five years, seven years, ten years, fifteen years, twenty years residential rental property, and nonresidential real property. However, depreciation under the alternative minimum tax system may be less than that under the regular tax system. If this is the case, that difference will be an adjustment to taxable income in reaching alternative minimum taxable income.

If property subject to an allowance for depreciation is sold at a gain, the gain was ordinary income to the extent of depreciation previously taken. Gain in excess of that amount was a capital gain. If the facts and circumstances warrant, taxpayers could use a non-time-related depreciation method such as units of production or mileage. To use a non-time-related method, the taxpayer had to keep records to show that its replacement policy provided for the retirement of assets at the end of their use cycle. Depreciation on the tax return was not necessarily the same as depreciation on the books. The former is what the Internal Revenue Code allowed, while the latter is what management believed appropriate for financial reporting purposes.

Write-Offs

Management has considerable discretion in the tax year to be used for write-offs for abnormal obsolescence, abandonment, or other loss. However, the Internal Revenue Service will expect the taxpayer to support its position with substantial evidence.

CURRENTLY DEDUCTIBLE EXPENSES

Compensation

In creating compensation arrangements, management should be concerned with the question of reasonableness. It is a two-edged sword, depending on whether the corporation is a "C" corporation or an "S" corporation. With "C" corporations, the IRS scrutinizes wages paid to shareholder employees to ensure that a high salary is not in part a disguised dividend. This is more frequently a problem for closely held "C" corporations. The corporation can deduct salary payments but not dividend payments.

With the closely held "S" corporation, in which the shareholder-employee's family members are also shareholders, the IRS may well view an unreasonably low salary as an opportunity for abuse. Because the corporate income is attributed to the shareholders, claiming an unreasonably low salary can be a device used to distribute income to other family members. Thus, management should proceed in the development of executive compensation packages with caution.

Charitable Gifts

Corporations are entitled to a deduction for charitable contributions made of up to 10 percent of the corporate taxable income computed without considering the charitable contribution. Any contributions in excess of the 10-percent limitation can be carried over to the next five tax years. If the board of directors authorizes, corporations using accrual accounting can elect to deduct, on the return for the prior tax year, contributions made up to two months and fifteen days after the end of that tax year. The board's authorization and the corporation's election must be made annually. Management should make sure that such an authorization is in effect for each year even if it is ultimately not used.

Another benefit that a "C" corporation can realize is an enhanced deduction for the gift of inventory. Usually, gifts of property that would generate ordinary income if sold will generate a deduction limited to the cost of the property contributed. However, if ordinary income property is given for the care of the ill, needy, or infants, the corporation will be able to claim a deduction for the appreciated value of the inventory of up to twice the cost. Management should be conscious of these opportunities to dispose of surplus inventory at year-end.

Travel and Entertainment Expenses

The Internal Revenue Code restricts deductibility of most travel and entertainment (T&E) expenditures. Taxpayers must meet certain business purposes tests and satisfy strict record-keeping requirements in order to successfully claim the deduction. Only 80 percent of most expenses for meals, entertainment, and entertainment facilities is allowed. This rule alone presents significant record-keeping problems for many taxpayers. Management should review the company's procedures to ensure that the general rules are being followed and the record-keeping requirements are being met.

MERGERS AND ACQUISITIONS AND OTHER REORGANIZATIONS

Mergers

Unless specifically excepted by statute, if a corporation disposes of property, any gain will be taxable. In the area of mergers, acquisitions, and other reorganizations, if the exchange meets rigid requirements, the transaction may be effected on a tax-free basis. This may include:

1. A statutory merger or consolidation.
2. The acquisition by one corporation —solely for voting stock—of stock of another corporation.
3. The acquisition by a corporation —solely for voting stock—of substantially all the properties of another corporation.
4. The transfer of assets to a controlled corporation for stock.
5. A recapitalization.
6. A mere change in form or place of organization.

The dividing of a corporate entity, such as in a spin-off or a split-up, and insolvency reorganizations are among other types of reorganizations that receive tax-free treatment.

Involuntary and Enforced Divestitures

Ordinarily, a corporation may choose the time of a sale or other disposition of property so that it will take place when it is most advantageous to the corporation's tax situation. This is not always possible. In the case of an involuntary conversion such as destruction, theft, seizure, requisition, or condemnation of property, gain is not recognized to the extent that the proceeds from the insurance company or government agency involved are invested in replacement property within two years of the close of the tax year in which the property was converted involuntarily. In addition, gain or loss is generally not recognized if securities are disposed of pursuant to an enforced divestiture mandated by a Securities and Exchange Commission (SEC) or Federal Communications Commission (FCC) order.

Expansion of Business

The growth of the business is a natural process if not a compelling objective. However, it should be recognized that growth can bring tax problems.

Earnings retained to finance expansion or for other purposes can create an accumulated earnings tax problem. The accumulated earnings tax is a penalty tax designed to prevent excess accumulations of cash or cash equivalents in a corporation and thus to compel dividends. The risk will vary depending on the circumstances and the type of corporation involved ("S" corporations are not subject to the accumulated earnings tax). The mere fact that the corporation intends to expand will not necessarily avoid tax. Something must have been done about it and there must be proof that management took this into account when dividends were considered.

Net operating losses and tax credit carryovers of an acquired corporation are subject to special, technical rules that must be met for the acquirer to use these "tax attributes" of the acquired corporation.

A corporation may consider entering a different form of the business in which it is engaged. All the incurred expenses of determining whether to enter the other business are not deductible for tax purposes upon entering the business. They are amortizable over a sixty-month period. Thus, market surveys, feasibility studies, and even salaries and travel expenses may be start-up costs.

FEDERAL TAX LEGISLATION

Management must be aware of potential tax law changes so that the company can meet the challenge either by modifying internal procedures to avoid coming within the scope of a negative change, or affiliating with other companies to lobby against the change. Should the change become effective, management must be prepared to establish dialogue with the Treasury Department in Washington, D.C., to soften the impact of a negative statute once it has been enacted.

Return Preparation and Filing

The tax return is the principal means by which a taxpayer communicates with the IRS. Technically, it represents a self-assessment of the indicated tax liability. Its preparation has become an involved process because of a myriad of penalties that can be imposed for failing to file an accurate return or to provide the IRS with all the needed information. In some instances, management members may be personally subject to penalties for acts of noncompliance of the company.

IRS Examinations

The task of negotiating any and all portions of the company's tax liability with government agents is a clear and present probability. Management can at some time in the corporation's life expect to be involved with the IRS attempting to redetermine the corporation's tax. The large corporation is examined by the IRS virtually every year. Smaller corporations are examined less frequently. An examination may be a lengthy, drawn-out process for which a strategy is essential.

An independent professional is often the best person to handle the examination. Such a person is better able to fend off requests to interview management that can be damaging. It is often in the best interests of management not to have to testify before an IRS agent because nontax management lacks the professional knowledge of tax rules. Nevertheless, it is important at all times during the continuing negotiations that top management be kept advised of the progress and be given reasonable estimates of success for the company's position on the various contested issues as opposed to the government's chances of success.

The process of negotiation continues to settlement of the dispute, which may be attained administratively at the local district director's level or at the appellate level, or through litigation in the federal courts.

Internal Tax Department

The large corporation's internal tax function typically performs its role under the supervision of a director or vice-president of tax who usually reports to a controller or chief financial officer. It can operate successfully as a division of the general counsel's office and frequently is located there, with indirect ties along functional lines to corporate finance, controller, treasurer, accounting, and data processing. In a few instances, the top tax officer reports directly to the CEO.

External Tax Professionals

Most managements retain external tax professionals even if the corporation maintains an internal tax department. Management can benefit from the breadth of experience that an independent tax professional can bring to a particular problem. In addition, the external tax professional will generally have developed an expertise in a tax area that the internal tax department staff person will not have.

For example, external corporate merger and acquisitions specialists have experience with many corporate merger and acquisition transactions, whereas the typical corporate tax staff person will experience only a few during his or her tenure with the corporation.

MANAGING STATE AND LOCAL TAXES

Shelby D. Bennett, The University of North Carolina at Asheville

Knowledge of the provisions of state and local taxes is critical to any business that wishes to minimize its total tax liability. Knowledge of state tax provisions is particularly important for businesses engaged in interstate commerce. There are many factors within the control of the taxpayer that may establish the ability of a state or local taxing jurisdiction to impose a tax. The controlling factor is whether the taxpayer has established a sufficient connection with the taxing jurisdiction to warrant the imposition of the tax in question.

CONNECTION TO A STATE

It is well established that an individual or corporate resident of a state can be taxed by that state. To avoid constitutional barriers, a taxing jurisdiction must satisfy certain criteria in imposing a tax on any business engaged in interstate commerce:

1. An activity must have a substantial connection with the taxing jurisdiction. This connection is called a nexus.
2. It must be fairly apportioned.
3. It must not discriminate against interstate commerce.
4. It must be fairly related to the services provided by the state.

A state can, through careful drafting and administration of its tax provisions, ensure that the last three criteria are met. However, whether or not sufficient nexus has been established is not entirely under the control of the state. The following activities, for example, will almost certainly establish sufficient nexus: maintaining a business location (including an office) in a state; owning real property in a state; owning a stock of goods in a public warehouse or in the hands of another representative if the stock of goods is used to fill orders for the owner's account; making contracts; operating mobile stores in the state (for example, trucks with driver-salespersons).

Taxpayers who wish to avoid taxation in a state should avoid engaging in activities that establish nexus. However, it is not possible to provide a complete list of such activities. Not all states apply the rules with equal vigor. Some states push the boundaries of their taxing authority to the limit while others are less aggressive. An activity may establish nexus in one state but not another.

States may not impose a tax on the income derived within a state through interstate commerce if the taxpayer's only business activities within the state are the solicitation of orders for sales of tangible personal property if the orders are approved outside the state and are filled from a point outside the state. For this purpose, a tax means a tax imposed on, or measured by, net income. Thus, a franchise tax measured by net income is not permitted whereas a franchise tax measured by net worth may be permitted.

Some state courts construe the term *solicitation* narrowly and some construe it broadly. Some state courts have held that normal activities that are incidental to solicitation (e.g., setting up counter displays; giving free samples to customers) do not destroy the immunity against state income taxation. Other state courts construe the statute more narrowly.

UNITARY TAXATION

A unitary business exists when there is a unity of ownership, operation, and management within the group or when there is an interdependence between activities within and without the state, even if the members of the group are separate corporations (e.g., parent and subsidiary).

One of the most controversial areas in state taxation is that of unitary taxation. Frequently, the assertion by a state that a group of affiliated corporations is a unitary business is an attempt to include the income of subsidiaries in the income of the parent for apportionment purposes. If a unitary business is present, sufficient nexus exists to include the income of the out-of-state entity in the income of the in-state entity for purposes of apportionment.

The U.S. Supreme Court has held that it is up to the states to make the factual determination of whether or not a unitary business exists. As a result, one encounters considerable variability with respect to the application of the unitary doctrine. For example, California has aggressively classified businesses as unitary while other states do not consider themselves "unitary states."

Theoretically, a state that in fact finds a business to be unitary can tax an apportioned part of the business's worldwide income. However, in practice, the states currently restrict themselves to a "water's-edge" approach to unitary taxation. That is, they seek to include income only of U.S. entities in the apportionable base.

CORPORATE INCOME TAXES

The typical state pattern for the determination of taxable income of corporations is to start with federal taxable income and make adjustments required by state law to arrive at state taxable income. However, although the correct determination of state taxable income is essential, it is not the major issue in state taxation. The major issue in state taxation is apportionment.

Allocation refers to the assignment of income in its entirety to one jurisdiction. That is, only one state taxes the income. *Apportionment* refers to the division of income among several states. That is, each state taxes a portion of the income.

Ordinarily nonbusiness income is allocated entirely to one state and business income is apportioned among the states in which the taxpayer is taxable. Some states do not follow this guideline. For example, New Jersey requires "allocation" of all corporate taxable income, but allocation is really apportionment. Taxpayers must be careful about state definitions of terms. The same term does not always mean the same thing in every state.

Apportionment is an important issue because of the danger of multiple taxation when income is subject to tax in more than one jurisdiction and the different jurisdictions use different apportionment rules.

The Multistate Tax Commission is active in improving uniformity among the states. Many states have adopted uniform apportionment rules. The big issues in apportionment are (1) whether a taxpayer is entitled to use apportionment and (2) what constitutes apportionable business income. The condition that allows apportionment in a given state is the fact that income is taxable in another state. A taxpayer may seek to establish taxability in a low-tax state in order to obtain apportionment in a higher-tax state.

BUSINESS INCOME

In most states, business income arises from transactions in the regular course of the taxpayer's trade or business. Income from property is classified as business income if the acquisition, management, and disposition of the property are integral parts of the taxpayer's regular trade or business.

Any income that is not classified as business income is nonbusiness income. In some cases, classification as nonbusiness income can be beneficial. For example, a large gain on the sale of property located in a state with no income tax would not be taxed at all if the gain is nonbusiness income. On the other hand, classification as nonbusiness income can be unfavorable to a taxpayer if it results in allocation to a state with a high tax rate.

CAPITAL STOCK TAXES

The typical capital stock tax is imposed on domestic corporations for the privilege of existence and on foreign corporations for the privilege of doing business in a state. It is imposed on some definition of "value of capital stock," usually an approximation of the net worth.

The primary issues in capital stock taxation are (1) determination of capital stock value and (2) allocation and apportionment. The issues of allocation and apportionment, in general, are the same as those discussed previously. Individual state statutes must be consulted to determine taxable value of capital stock.

SALES AND USE TAXES

Sales taxes usually are imposed on sales or leases of tangible personal property. In some states the sales tax is also imposed on specified services. The sales tax may be imposed on the consumer, with the vendor having the responsibility to collect and remit the tax. Or the tax may be imposed directly on the vendor. Most states provide for the exemption of certain items such as food, clothing, or items held for resale.

A use tax may be imposed on the use of taxable items within a state. It is designed to prevent the avoidance of sales taxes as a result of purchasing taxable items in another jurisdiction and bringing them into the state to use. Most states use a destination rule to determine taxability. Thus, if property is delivered to the customer within a state, the transaction is taxable in that state.

Because of pressures on states to increase revenue collections due to budget shortages, the base of the sales tax is constantly being broadened. The result is that sales and use tax provisions have become extraordinarily complex. Taxpayers must review the state provisions with care to ensure adequate compliance with sales and use tax provisions.

One of the most controversial issues in sales and use taxation is that of mail order sales. States have vigorously sought for years to tax sales made to state residents by out-of-state vendors. So far, their efforts have been thwarted by the Supreme Court, which ruled it is unconstitutional for a state to collect use tax when the vendor does no more than communicate with customers by U.S. mail or common carrier. The states continue to pursue aggressively out-of-state sales.

ADMINISTRATION

Most states have commissions or departments that are state counterparts to the Internal Revenue Service and are charged with the collection of taxes and the enforcement of the revenue laws. The administrative procedures ordinarily are quite similar to federal procedures. Like federal law, there are usually provisions for administrative and judicial review of conflicts between taxpayers and the state.

Because each state is different, it is important that taxpayers be familiar with filing due dates, statutes of limitations, appeal procedures and requirements, and other administrative provisions in each state where business is transacted.

INTERNAL AUDITING

Bruce L. Whitaker, Certified Internal Auditor, Eastern New Mexico University

The Institute of Internal Auditors (IIA), formed in 1941, celebrated its fiftieth anniversary as the worldwide professional organization for internal auditors in 1991. During that short period of time, the institute had grown to include a variety of chapters and organizations in Africa, Asia, and the South Pacific and chapters from Canada to South America. Nearly 50,000 internal auditors are members of this organization, and they live and work in more than a hundred countries.

Internal auditors developed and adopted a common body of knowledge in 1972, which led to the certified internal auditor (CIA) program in 1973 and the first CIA examination in 1974. Over 40,000 internal auditors have taken the CIA examination and more than 8,000 have passed all parts. In 1978 the Institute of Internal Auditors adopted the standards for the professional practice of internal auditing. The standards provide essential goals and guidelines for the professional practice of internal auditing and provide guidance for internal auditors and internal auditing organizations.

"PROFESSIONAL INTERNAL AUDITING STANDARDS VOLUME"

The Institute of Internal Auditors makes available their looseleaf binder, titled "Professional Internal Auditing Standards Volume," with updating inserts. The volume is the institute's authoritative reference source and includes three basic documents: (1) the Institute of Internal Auditors code of ethics, (2) standards for the professional practice of internal auditing, and (3) statement of responsibilities of internal auditing. They are referred to here as Code of Ethics, Standards, and Statement, respectively.

The Code of Ethics, a single-page document, is divided into three parts: purpose, applicability, and standards of conduct. The purpose of the Code of Ethics is to provide specific standards of conduct and define to whom the standards of conduct apply. The eleven standards of conduct are applicable to all members of the Institute of Internal Auditors and CIAs. Code of Ethics standard of conduct number seven requires compliance with the standards for the professional practice of internal auditing.

There are five general standards, twenty-five specific standards, and numerous related guidelines within the Standards. The specific standards and guidelines provide guidance to facilitate compliance with the five general standards. The five general standards, reprinted from the Standards,* are:

100 Independence—Internal Auditors should be independent of the activities they audit.

200 Professional Proficiency—Internal audits should be performed with proficiency and due professional care.

300 Scope of Work—The scope of the internal audit should encompass the examination and evaluation of the adequacy and effectiveness of the organization's system of internal control and the quality of performance in carrying out assigned responsibilities.

400 Performance of Audit Work—Audit work should include planning the audit, examining and evaluating information, communicating results, and following up.

500 Management of the Internal Audit Department—The director of internal auditing should properly manage the internal audit department.

The Standards require compliance with the Code of Ethics, and when utilized in unison with the Code of Ethics, provide sufficient detailed guidance for internal auditors, internal audit departments, and those responsible for creating or relying on the internal auditing function. The Statement, on the other hand, provides a basic definition and summary of internal auditing. A single-page document, it is the authoritative summary of the responsibilities of internal auditing and is reprinted below in its entirety.*

---

* Reprinted with permission from "Professional Internal Auditing Standards Volume"; copyright © 1991/1978 by The Institute of Internal Auditors, Inc., 249 Maitland Avenue, Altamonte Springs, Florida 32701 U.S.A.

STATEMENT OF RESPONSIBILITIES OF INTERNAL AUDITING

The purpose of this statement is to provide in summary form a general understanding of the responsibilities of internal auditing. For more specific guidance, readers should refer to the *Standards for the Professional Practice of Internal Auditing.*

Objective and Scope

Internal auditing is an independent appraisal function established within an organization to examine and evaluate its activities as a service to the organization. The objective of internal auditing is to assist members of the organization in the effective discharge of their responsibilities. To this end, internal auditing furnishes them with analyses, appraisals, recommendations, counsel, and information concerning the activities reviewed. The audit objective includes promoting effective control at reasonable cost. The members of the organization assisted by internal auditing include those in management and the board of directors.

The scope of internal auditing should encompass the examination and evaluation of the adequacy and effectiveness of the organization's system of internal control and the quality of performance in carrying out assigned responsibilities. Internal auditors should:

- Review the reliability and integrity of financial and operating information and the means used to identify, measure, classify, and report such information.
- Review the systems established to ensure compliance with those policies, plans, procedures, laws, and regulations that could have a significant impact on operations and reports, and should determine whether the organization is in compliance.
- Review the means of safeguarding assets and, as appropriate, verify the existence of such assets.
- Appraise the economy and efficiency with which resources are employed.
- Review operations or programs to ascertain whether results are consistent

with established objectives and goals and whether the operations or programs are being carried out as planned.

Responsibility and Authority

The internal auditing department is an integral part of the organization and functions under the policies established by senior management and the board. The purpose, authority, and responsibility of the internal auditing department should be defined in a formal written document (charter). The director of internal auditing should seek approval of the charter by senior management as well as acceptance by the board. The charter should make clear the purposes of the internal auditing department, specify the unrestricted scope of its work, and declare that auditors are to have no operational authority or responsibility for the activities they audit.

Throughout the world internal auditing is performed in diverse environments and within organizations that vary in purpose, size, and structure. In addition, the laws and customs within various countries differ from one another. These differences may affect the practice of internal auditing in each environment. The implementation of the *Standards for the Professional Practice of Internal Auditing,* therefore, will be governed by the environment in which the internal auditing department carries out its assigned responsibilities. Compliance with the concepts enunciated by the *Standards for the Professional Practice of Internal Auditing* is essential before the responsibilities of internal auditors can be met. As stated in the Code of Ethics, members of The Institute of Internal Auditors, Inc., and Certified Internal Auditors shall adopt suitable means to comply with the *Standards for the Professional Practice of Internal Auditing.*

Independence

Internal auditors should be independent of the activities they audit. Internal auditors are independent when they can carry out their work freely and ob-

jectively. Independence permits internal auditors to render the impartial and unbiased judgments essential to the proper conduct of audits. It is achieved through organizational status and objectivity.

The organizational status of the internal auditing department should be sufficient to permit the accomplishment of its audit responsibilities. The director of the internal auditing department should be responsible to an individual in the organization with sufficient authority to promote independence and to ensure a broad audit coverage, adequate consideration of audit reports, and appropriate follow-up action on audit recommendations.

Objectivity is an independent mental attitude that internal auditors should maintain in performing audits. Internal auditors are not to subordinate their judgment on audit matters to that of others. Designing, installing, and operating systems are not audit functions. Also, the drafting of procedures for systems is not an audit function. Performing such activities is presumed to impair audit objectivity.

CONCLUSION

The institute is actively encouraging universities, through its College & University Relations Committee, to develop university-level internal audit programs. At least fifteen major universities now have such IIA-approved programs. The CIA examination, now offered in English, Spanish, and French, and the institute's required continuing professional education program promote the professionalism of internal auditors worldwide.

The internal auditing profession has experienced tremendous growth since the creation of the institute in 1941. The profession will continue its worldwide growth as more firms and organizations recognize the need for periodic objective reviews of their internal controls and reviews of the efficiency and effectiveness of their operations and management by professional internal auditors independent of those audited.

THE INDEPENDENT AUDIT

John J. Willingham, Partner, KPMG Peat Marwick
Mark J. Allen, Senior Manager, KPMG Peat Marwick

FINANCIAL STATEMENTS

The annual report by management is the principal communication used to present financial information to the owners of a business. This report enables the owners/investors to assess their investment. For companies with shares traded on a national stock exchange, the financial statements presented in the annual report to shareholders are required to be audited.

Although the annual report is addressed to shareholders, the financial statements are often used by many groups, including credit guarantors, financial analysts, regulatory authorities, taxing agencies, labor unions, credit agencies, and employees. Even though the annual report is prepared primarily for use by investors and lenders, the report is also for general use.

The audited financial statements in the annual report generally consist of a comparative balance sheet as of the last two fiscal year-ends, comparative statements of earnings, retained earnings and cash flows for the last three fiscal years, and notes to the financial statements. The information contained in the notes varies depending on certain regulatory requirements, such as the disclosure rules required by the Securities and Exchange Commission (SEC).

The financial statements are the representations of management. Management is responsible for the financial statements and all the other information contained in the annual report, except for the report by the independent auditor. Although primary responsibility for the financial statements rests with management, the responsibility for approval rests with the board of directors.

Audit committees have become common among larger companies. They share some of the management responsibility of ensuring the credibility of the financial statements. Responsibilities of audit committees vary among companies. Audit committees are generally comprised of three to five outside directors who are not involved in the day-to-day running of the business. Their duties may include recommending to the board of directors the selection of an independent auditor, discussing the scope of the external audit with the independent auditor, monitoring internal controls, and reviewing the independent auditor's report prior to issuance. Audit committees often have free access to the independent auditor without the presence of management.

The audit opinion issued by the independent auditor does not limit management's responsibility for the financial statements and all the additional information contained in the annual report.

Financial information may be prepared and presented in different forms. It is the responsibility of management to ensure that fairness is achieved in presentation. As guidance, a set of generally accepted accounting principles

(GAAP) have been developed to ensure fairness in presentation of the financial statements. It is the auditor's responsibility to opine on the fairness of the financial statements as a whole in conformity with GAAP.

Generally accepted accounting principles consists of rules, guidelines, and conventions concerning the measurement, classification, and disclosure of financial events and transactions. Commonly applied conventions may be broadly based or very specific in application. In the United States, generally accepted accounting principles are established in statements issued by the Financial Accounting Standards Board (FASB). The board is a freestanding body in the private sector supported by the accounting profession and others. The board has approved authoritative pronouncements of predecessor private-sector standard setters, including the former Accounting Principles Board and the Committee on Accounting Procedure of the American Institute of Certified Public Accountants (AICPA).

Although the pronouncements issued by the various accounting bodies are extensive, they do not deal with all areas of accounting due to the vast numbers of different businesses, changing business practices, and consumer needs. Therefore, in addition to authoritative pronouncements, some accounting practices may be found in scholarly writings, textbooks, and previously issued financial statements. For example, a principle may apply to a particular industry but not to other industries. As a result, diverse accounting practices exist among companies, all of which present financial statements in accordance with generally accepted accounting principles.

The SEC is also a source of generally accepted accounting principles for public companies. The SEC views the annual report to shareholders as the primary communication of financial information to the shareholders and the public. The general policy of the SEC is to rely on the FASB standards of financial accounting and reporting, but it reserves the right to reject any standard it finds unacceptable.

Income tax rules often have an effect on GAAP even though in many instances accounting for income tax differs from financial statement reporting. However, conformity between tax and financial statement reporting is common. One example of conformity is the last-in, first-out (LIFO) method of valuing inventories, which must be used in financial statements if used for income tax purposes.

Underlying the rules and guidelines are some concepts that have been accepted in practice. Their use is generally assumed in the preparation of the financial statements unless specifically stated to the contrary. They include:

- *The going-concern concept*—The entity is viewed as one that will continue in the foreseeable future. No closure or liquidation is contemplated in the foreseeable future.
- *The accrual basis of accounting*—Revenues and costs are recognized in the financial statements when they are earned or incurred. Costs incurred are matched to revenues they produced and are included in the income statements in the same time period.
- *The consistency concept*—The accounting principles must be applied consistently in each accounting period to allow for comparable financial information from year to year.

Financial statements consist of factual monetary information, but also include many estimates and judgments by management. Not all measurements are precise. Some require judgments as to the outcome of future events, such as the life of certain machinery and equipment. The amount of disclosure in the financial statements is also a matter of judgment. Underlying all these judgments is the consideration of materiality as a measure of accuracy of the financial statements. There is no precise definition of materiality. However, the effect on the financial statements as a whole and the nature and extent of disclosures must be considered.

The notes to the financial statements are an integral part of the presentation and are considered vital to understanding the financial statements as a whole. Both the SEC and the FASB require many specific disclosures in these notes. Management must present a summary of the underlying significant accounting policies, details of certain financial statement items, and certain future commitment and contingent liability information.

THE INDEPENDENT AUDITOR

The duty of the independent auditor is to express an opinion on the financial statements as a whole. To enable the auditor to express an opinion, the audit must be conducted in accordance with generally accepted auditing standards (GAAS). The auditing standards require the audit to be planned and performed to obtain reasonable assurance that the financial statements are free of material misstatement. The audit includes examining certain evidence to support the amounts and disclosures in the financial statements and also an assessment of accounting policies, significant estimates and judgments made by management, and the overall presentation.

The auditor is expected to adhere to the ethical and professional standards of the profession. The ethical standards are set forth in the rules of professional conduct and ethics set by each state society and/or board of accountancy and by the Code of Professional Ethics of the American Institute of Certified Public Accountants (AICPA).

A certified public accountant (CPA) shall not express an opinion on financial statements of an entity unless he or she is completely independent of that entity. The CPA cannot have a financial interest in the entity being audited, or be a director, officer, employee, or engage in certain restricted transactions. The CPA shall possess integrity and objectivity and shall not defer to the judgment of others.

The CPA must comply with professional standards when associated in any way with financial statements. When financial statements are presented in a manner that is not consistent with GAAP, the CPA is required to describe the departure and its effects in the auditor's report.

The CPA shall not disclose any confidential information obtained in the course of an engagement except with the consent of the client. However, when the CPA is required by a court of law to reveal information, the CPA must do so without reservation.

GENERALLY ACCEPTED AUDITING STANDARDS

Generally accepted auditing standards were adopted by the AICPA in 1948 and 1949 and have been continuously updated since then by the AICPA Auditing Standards Board. Compliance is mandatory by all members of the AICPA. The standards are broken into three major areas: the general standards, the standards of fieldwork, and the standards of reporting.

The general standards are:

- Adequate professional training and proficiency.
- Independence of mental attitude.
- Due professional care in the performance of the examination and preparation of the report.

The standards of fieldwork are:

- Adequate planning of audit work and supervision of assistants.
- Sufficient understanding of the internal control structure in order to determine the nature, timing, and extent of audit procedures to be performed.
- Sufficient evidential matter through inspection, observation, inquiries, and confirmations to afford a reasonable basis for an opinion on the financial statements.

The standards of reporting are:

- The report must state whether the financial statements are presented in accordance with GAAP.
- The report must identify accounting principles that have not been consistently applied.
- Unless stated in the report, disclosures in the financial statements are to be regarded as reasonably adequate.

■ The report must contain either an expression of an opinion on the financial statements as a whole, or an assertion to the effect that an opinion cannot be expressed and the reason why.

To a great extent, these standards are interrelated and interdependent. Two elements underlie the application of all the standards, particularly the standards of fieldwork and reporting. They are materiality and relative risk. Materiality and risk significantly affect the amount of work required by the auditor to render an opinion.

The two standards that require the most attention during an audit are the auditor's understanding of internal controls and sufficient competent evidence. These are the areas where the client has the most contact with the auditor and they are the sources of most client confusion.

Auditor's Understanding of Internal Controls

GAAS requires that the auditor understand a client's internal control structure sufficiently to plan the audit. An additional purpose of understanding the internal control structure of a client is to establish to what extent those controls may be relied on by the auditor. Once this determination has been made, the nature, timing, and extent of audit tests can be determined and applied to the examination of the financial statements. This understanding of internal controls frequently provides a basis for constructive recommendations to the client for improvement of the internal control system, usually in the form of a letter to management.

An internal control structure consists of policies and procedures established by management to provide reasonable assurance that the entity's overall objectives will be obtained. Only certain of these policies and procedures may be relevant to the production of the financial statements. For the purpose of an audit, an entity's internal control structure consists of three elements: the control environment, the accounting system, and control procedures.

The control environment represents various factors establishing, enhancing, and/or mitigating the effect of specific policies and procedures. Such factors include management's philosophy and operating style, organizational structure, assigning authority and responsibility, control methods, personnel policies and practices, as well as external market and regulatory factors.

The accounting system consists of methods to identify, assemble, analyze, classify, record and report transactions, and to maintain accountability of the entity's assets and liabilities. An effective accounting system should identify and record valid transactions, properly classify and value transactions for financial statement purposes, record transactions in the correct accounting period, and properly present transactions in the financial statements on a timely basis.

Control procedures are those policies and procedures in addition to the control environment and accounting system that provide assurance that specific entity objectives will be achieved. Control procedures are applied at various organizational levels and are generally integrated into the control environment and accounting system. They include proper authorization of transactions, segregation of duties, and safeguard controls over access (physical and logical) to assets and records.

In understanding the internal control structure the auditor also must take into account other general considerations. They include the size of the entity, the organizational and ownership characteristics, the nature of the business, the diversity and complexity of the operation, the method of data processing, and legal and regulatory requirements.

Internal control systems are generally dependent on the competency and integrity of personnel, the independence of their assigned functions, and their understanding of the procedures. These factors can sometimes be achieved by segregation of functions and duties so that no one person is in the position to conceal errors or irregularities. This system usually requires separating the authorization duties, the recording functions, and the custodial functions.

Regardless of how comprehensive the internal control structure may be, there are always inherent limitations to its effectiveness.

The possibility of errors arising from misunderstood instructions, mistakes in judgment, distraction, fatigue, and carelessness is always present. Circumvention and collusion may substantially reduce the effectiveness of the best of internal control systems. Also, senior management may override control procedures that would otherwise monitor the occurrence of errors and irregularities.

Increased public awareness of the internal control structure has increased management's awareness. This has led to an expectation that the independent auditor assist management in evaluating its internal control structure. Indeed, certain governmental regulations applicable to audits of governmental entities require specific reporting on internal controls by the independent auditor.

Sufficient Competent Evidential Matter

Most of the independent auditor's work in forming an opinion on the financial statements consists of evaluating assertions made in the financial statements. The amount of evidence necessary, and its influence and validity, lies in the auditor's judgment. The objectivity, timeliness, and existence of corroborating evidence all have a bearing on the auditor's final opinion on the financial statements.

The financial statements embody the assertions/statements made by management. These are classified according to the following broad categories: existence, occurrence, completeness, obligations, rights, valuation, allocation, presentation, and disclosure. In obtaining evidential matter in support of the assertions, the auditor develops specific audit objectives and considers the economic activities and accounting practices unique to the entity's industry. The auditor considers the risk of material misstatement, and the effectiveness of each test that is selected. The nature, timing, and extent of audit procedures is a matter of professional judgment to be determined by the auditor.

Evidential matter consists of the underlying accounting data and all corroborating available information. This evidence may consist of books of original entry, reconciliations, memoranda, contracts, invoices, minutes of meetings, observations of physical inventories and assets, analysis of trends, confirmation by third parties, recalculations, inquiry, and inspection.

To be competent, evidence must be both valid and relevant. The validity of evidence is dependent on its source and its reliability. Independent evidence obtained outside the entity generally provides greater assurance than evidence obtained within the entity. Evidence obtained by the auditor directly provides greater assurance than evidence obtained from outside the entity. When evaluating evidential matter, the auditor considers whether specific audit objectives have been achieved. The auditor must be thorough in his or her search for evidential matter and must be unbiased in the evaluation.

THE AUDITOR'S REPORT

Upon completion of the audit, the auditor issues a report in accordance with GAAS. Ordinarily, any differences between the views of management and the independent auditor are discussed and resolved to their mutual satisfaction so that the auditor can issue an unqualified opinion on the financial statements. The typical unqualified audit report consists of three paragraphs:

1. *Introductory paragraph*—states the entity, the statements covered by the report, and the periods that have been audited. Additionally, it discusses management's and the independent auditor's responsibilities in relation to the financial statements.
2. *Scope paragraph*—states that the audit was conducted in accordance with GAAS, and that GAAS requires the independent auditor to plan and perform the audit to obtain reasonable assurance about whether the financial statements are free of material misstatement. This paragraph also includes a brief description of the general procedures performed in the course of an audit and a statement that the independent auditor believes his or her audit provided a reasonable basis for his or her opinion.

3. *Opinion paragraph*—reads as follows: In our opinion, the financial statements referred to above present fairly, in all material respects, the financial position of the *Company* as of December 31, 19X2 and 19X1, and the results of its operations and its cash flows for each of the years in the three-year period ended December 31, 19X2, in conformity with generally accepted accounting principles.

A standard independent auditor's report is usually expected by the reader of the annual report. However, when the audit report varies from the standard, the auditor's report takes on added significance. The four basic deviations from the standard audit report are:

1. *Addition of explanatory language*—Certain circumstances, although not affecting the auditor's unqualified opinion, may require the addition of explanatory language to the standard report. Examples of circumstances that would require the addition of explanatory language include:
 ▪ Uncertainty about the entity's ability to continue as a going concern or other significant uncertainties (e.g., outstanding litigation).
 ▪ Lack of consistency of application of generally accepted accounting principles.
 ▪ Departure from a promulgated accounting principle which, due to unusual circumstances, is allowable.

2. *A qualified opinion*—The auditor qualifies an opinion due to a material departure from GAAP, a lack of sufficient evidential matter, or a limitation in the scope of the audit. Qualified opinions state that the financial statements are presented fairly "except for" the item or items that led to the qualification. A common reason for qualifying the independent auditor's report is the inability of the auditor to observe the physical inventory and to obtain audited financial statements of investees that are accounted for as long-term investments. In instances in which a qualified opinion is issued, the opinion paragraph is preceded by an explanatory paragraph describing the reason for the qualification.

3. *Disclaimer of an opinion*—This is issued when the auditor is unable to obtain sufficient evidential matter to enable him or her to express an opinion on the financial statements. Examples include management's refusal to make certain significant representations to the auditor, incomplete accounting records, or destruction of all the company's records. In instances in which a disclaimer of opinion is issued, the opinion paragraph is changed to reflect the disclaimer and an explanatory paragraph is added.

4. *Adverse opinion*—If a departure from GAAP is so great that the financial statements do not present fairly the financial position, an adverse opinion will be issued. The opinion paragraph will state that the financial statements are not presented fairly and an explanatory paragraph is added describing the reason for issuing an adverse opinion and the principal effects on the financial statements of the item causing the adverse opinion, if practicable.

The decision to qualify an opinion rather than disclaim or issue an adverse opinion is a matter of professional judgment.

Both the SEC and FASB require certain supplementary information in the annual report in addition to the audited financial statements and notes. Ordinarily, the auditor will not need to expand the report on the additional information.

The auditor's responsibility is to read the information contained in an annual report, and consider whether it is materially inconsistent with the financial statements. If the auditor determines that a material inconsistency exists, he or she should discuss it with management to resolve the inconsistency. If it is not resolved, the auditor should consider other actions such as withholding his report, adding an explanatory paragraph describing the inconsistency, or withdrawing from the engagement.

ADDITIONAL SERVICES OFFERED BY THE INDEPENDENT AUDITOR

Today, accounting firms offer clients more than just the traditional audit. As the auditor has knowledge of the client's business, operations, and systems, coupled with the auditor's technical training and experience, he or she is able to provide additional services.

Independent accounting firms offer three basic areas of expertise: income tax services, management consulting services, and auditing services. These services often are organized independently, but generally complement each other. A firm's ability to audit the client may well be enhanced by the knowledge gained through special assignments.

Although nonaudit services are an integral part of an independent accounting firm's practice, some critics contend that the performance of nonauditing services may impair the auditor's independence or at least the appearance of independence. When accepting nonauditing services auditors must consider whether or not their independence could be jeopardized.

INVESTOR RELATIONS

T. Carter Hagaman, Kean College of New Jersey

Investor relations attempts to reduce any disparities between investors' expectations for the company and subsequent performance through a continuous and credible flow of information. This process has the twin goals of reducing investors' perception of risk and contributing to the maximum sustainable price for a company over time.

Most investor relations programs are focused primarily on investors and security analysts who make recommendations on the purchase of common stock. While the applicable principles bear on a company's dealings with all providers of capital, this chapter is limited to common equities.

BENEFITS TO THE COMPANY

A good investor relations program has several practical benefits to the company:

1. Dramatic swings in the price of the company's stock can be reduced. Investors and analysts tend to avoid companies whose stocks show sharp market fluctuations. Unreasonable expectations about a company's prospects can be reduced by developing and maintaining an informed market.

2. A stable and reasonable stock price allows the company more frequent access to the public market for new issues over time. It is difficult to sell a new issue of a volatile stock. Also, the company is effectively precluded from an attractive financing when the stock is depressed. Further, even when the price is strong, an announced offering could trigger a decline.

3. The risk of proxy fights or takeovers is reduced by developing long-term satisfied stockholders. Stockholder loyalty to management is enhanced through an investor relations program. If management is challenged, stockholders will tend to support a management in which they have confidence in preference to an unknown group. Long-term investors are significantly more loyal than traders or speculators.

4. An effective program builds good relations with security analysts and other investors' representatives, thereby widening the reception for a company's securities. Such a program helps to reduce analysts' concerns about surprises and provides them with a basis for understanding and comparing the company. Analysts value their contacts with management, and a continuing dialogue helps to maintain their interest in the company.

5. The growth of capital markets has increased competition among companies seeking capital. Since capital is a scarce resource, the company that can reduce investor concerns through good communications gains a competitive edge.

6. A program can provide management with useful information about investors' requirements and objectives. This, in turn, can help management set financial policy. Dialogue with analysts and investors is a two-way street, offering insights about why certain investors bought or sold their securities, what factors prevented a recommendation or blocked a sale, how investors feel about their dividend policy, and whether the company's message is getting through.

7. An established reputation for credibility and willingness to communicate can enhance the company's standing with government units such as regulatory bodies and with other third parties.

ESSENTIAL ELEMENTS IN A GOOD PROGRAM

A good investor relations program has several elements:

1. It accurately reflects management's business philosophy, policies, attitudes, and perspectives. In the annual report and in meetings with investors and security analysts, management should describe its goals for the company and how it plans to accomplish them. Understanding of management is always the cornerstone of good security analysis.

2. A good program provides a continuous, regular flow of information to investors irrespective of the state of the company's business, the stock market, or the economy. Analysts who follow companies are committed to their clients or to their employers to provide continuous coverage over time. Sudden or unexpected inability to obtain information places them in an embarrassing position and they resent it. Ordinary investors become apprehensive if there is a break in the flow of information they have come to expect.

3. The company's communications should acquire a reputation for being complete, timely, and accurate, thereby establishing credibility. Management must be willing to apply the same standards of disclosure to both good and bad news. It is better to have no program than one dealing only with favorable developments. On a related note, great care must be taken to avoid unrealistic optimism.

THE MOST COMMON PROBLEMS

In setting up an investor relations program, some difficulties may be encountered:

1. A good program requires a significant commitment in time from senior management. However, its effectiveness is difficult to measure and this can put management's commitment at risk. The commitment to the program must be strong enough to withstand the frustrations of market cycles and other uncontrollable factors that affect stock prices.

2. Loss of credibility can occur if disclosed information is not accurate, timely, and complete or if the company assists analysts with earnings forecasts that turn out wrong. Offering to help analysts with earnings forecasts is a no-win proposition. Analysts expect company projections to be correct and they will blame management if actual earnings differ from the forecast.

3. Publicly disclosed information is subject to review and interpretation by security analysts who may reach incorrect conclusions. This raises the added problem of deciding

what, if any, corrective action is needed. By taking action, management may inadvertently find itself making forecasts.

4. Competitors have easy access to any investor relations disclosures. However, all required disclosure is readily obtained by competitors in any event. As a practical matter, competitors have many sources of information and an incentive to draw on them. Only investors are penalized by withholding information. Admittedly, some voluntary information that is useful to investors may be competitively sensitive, but this concern frequently receives more attention than it deserves.

5. Pressure to promote the price of the stock is a danger in investor relations because changes in the market price are frequently used to measure the benefits of the program. Short-term changes in market price are a poor test. Market prices move for many reasons, many of which have greater impact, such as a general market break or FDA approval of a new wonder drug. A declining stock price is no more an indictment of an investor relations program than a rising price is cause for congratulations. Use of this standard can induce promotion and destroy the program.

6. From time to time, a company may be tempted to use its investor relations program to offset the negative impact of business problems that may arise. Altering the program's balance by emphasizing positive news of minor importance in order to gloss over major adverse developments seldom works for long, but it can seriously damage management's reputation for candor.

DESIGN OF A PROGRAM

The following actions should be taken to design an investor relations program:

1. Develop an accurate and consistent image of the company to be conveyed through the program. This image must be supportable by performance and sustainable over time. For example, only companies with significant market opportunities, aggressive management, and a high rate of return can successfully adopt a "growth company" image.

2. Realistically assess what the company is offering to stockholders—high yield, stability, high return, growth, specific industry focus, international diversification, or whatever. Then, determine the types of stockholders whose investment objectives are compatible with what the company can do for them. For example, investors who place a premium on steady, predictable earnings are not candidates for volatile stocks. Those who want high growth are not in the market for electric utilities. Analysis of the company's current shareholders can help to identify target segments in the marketplace.

3. Define the specific goals to be achieved. These goals should be measurable over time. Examples are a 20-percent increase in individual shareholders, a specific reduction in the percentage held by institutions, greater geographic distribution of shareholders, or following of the company by a certain number of additional analysts. Each measurable goal is selected for its contribution to overall program objectives.

4. Select the level of activity. This can range from a minimal program to meet disclosure requirements to an aggressive program that sets out to broaden or even change the company's investors.

IMPLEMENTATION

The following steps can implement an investor relations program:

1. Define senior management's role in carrying out the program. Focusing overall responsibility for the program is essential; so is providing the investor relations head with continuous direct access to senior management. The company must keep that person fully informed on all matters of consequence. This will permit the investor relations head to speak with authority. It can also reduce, but not eliminate, the time required for top

management to meet with analysts personally.

2. Appoint a person to administer the program and establish a reporting line for the function. Both large companies and others with aggressive programs should make investor relations a full-time professional assignment.

3. Develop job specifications and provide suitable titles to convey credibility, such as vice-president of investor relations. Ideally, the head of investor relations should report to the CEO, since many parts of the company must provide information. However, many companies place the function under the chief financial officer. Some companies place it in public relations, an action that is not recommended.

4. Adopt a disclosure policy for all public communications. Authorized spokespersons should be limited in number and coordinate with the investor relations executive. All public statements or communications with analysts should be arranged through the investor relations function. Timely responses should be given to all legitimate requests from the investment community. The investor relations function should be directly responsible for the nature, content, and frequency of all company disclosures, for supervising all contact with analysts and shareholders, and for maintaining the company's image in the investment community.

5. Prepare a specific operating plan for the program, determining what actions will be taken within specific time intervals. This permits performance assessment.

ACCOUNTING IN THE INTERNATIONAL ENVIRONMENT

Gerard Huybregts, Eastern New Mexico University

Increasingly U.S.-based companies are being encouraged to "go international," to seek growth opportunities and markets overseas. Some companies go international by exporting or importing goods. Others penetrate foreign markets by establishing overseas branches, joint ventures, licensing, or some other form of local presence. A consequence of international involvement is the need to provide financial reports that accurately portray the "real picture" to existing and potential shareholders, creditors, government agencies, and others.

Some of the different situations a firm operating in foreign environments must deal with include:

1. Foreign countries have different accounting standards to which all firms operating in that country must conform.
2. Foreign countries use their own cur-

rency. As a consequence, international firms may have to translate financial reports from one currency to another, and there may be gains or losses associated with currency fluctuations rather than with a business transaction itself.

3. Performance evaluation based solely on financial ratios may be measuring factors other than the performance of the international manager.

4. Other accounting-related factors include the opportunity for multinational transfer pricing, international taxation, and means for minimizing foreign exchange–related losses. Managers must understand the forces behind these situations and develop strategies for successfully coping with them.

ACCOUNTING STANDARDS

Reliable accounting information is required by current and potential shareholders and creditors in order to evaluate the performance of the firm. Government agencies need this information in order to levy appropriate taxes. Management needs it in order to evaluate the performance of the firm and of the various units. Owners of capital need reliable information in order to compare performance and potential against other opportunities. Companies looking for joint-venture partners need it in order to accurately evaluate potential partners.

Within some countries, such as the United States, accounting professionals have formed private boards to establish generally accepted accounting principles (GAAP)—standards or guidelines by which the financial reports of publicly listed U.S. companies must be prepared. In the United States these principles are formulated by the Financial Accounting Standards Board (FASB), circulated to the membership for comments and revisions, and finally officially established. Statement 52, for example, sets standards for foreign currency translation. Enforcement of these standards is by the Securities and Exchange Commission (SEC).

The U.S. standards are the outcome of an environment where the needs of the various groups and the economic and business climate all have a hand in determining the scope of the standards. Other countries establish their standards based on their own environments. This may lead to problems when the standards are different, yet people in country A need to have access to, and an understanding of, the standards in country B.

In the international arena, there is an International Accounting Standards Committee (IASC) attempting to establish worldwide accounting standards. This is also a private organization with representatives from over seventy-five countries. Standards from this organization are advisory only, as no enforcement mechanism exists.

TRANSLATION AND TRANSACTION ISSUES

A major difficulty in international business is the need to deal with different currencies having constantly changing values. Newspapers will quote exchange rates in their financial section on a daily basis. The *Wall Street Journal*, for example, lists the exchange rate for over fifty countries, to four decimal places, under Currency Trading. *Business Week* limits itself to only seven countries, to two decimal places at most, under Foreign Exchange.

To understand translation and transaction issues, let us use an example. *Business Week*, December 9, 1991, quoted the value of the Japanese yen for November 26, 1991, to be 128 yen for each U.S. dollar. The previous week it was 130 yen, and on November 26, 1990, it was 133 yen. These rates are used to examine the impact of changing currency values on the balance sheet and income statement of Big One Company, a hypothetical U.S. company establishing operations in Japan on November 26, 1990.

Assume that Big One invested $1 million on November 26, 1990. The initial balance sheet may look something like this:

	In Yen ('000)	In $('000) ($1 = Y133)
Assets		
Inventory	66,500	500
Fixed Assets	66,500	500
Owners' Equity	133,000	1,000

Exhibit 5-3. Example of Translation and Transaction Reporting

Balance Sheet	"A" Actual Results (Yen)	"B" At Year-End Rate ($)	"C" Autonomous Units ($)	"D" Subsidiary Units ($)
Cash	39,900	311.72	311.72	311.72
Inventory	66,500	519.53	519.53	511.54
Fixed Assets	66,500	519.53	519.,53	500.00
Total Assets	172,900	1,350.78	1,350.78	1,323.26
Accounts Payable	13,300	103.90	103.90	103.90
Owners' Equity	159,600	1,246.88	1,204.61	1,219.36
Translation Adjustment			42.27	
Total Liability & Equity	172,900	1,350.78	1,350.78	1,323.26
Income Statement				
Sales	266,000	2,078.13	2,046.15	2,046.15
Cost of Goods Sold	200,000	1,562.50	1,538.46	1,538.46
Other Expenses	39,400	307.81	303.08	303.08
Translation Adjustment	—	—	—	14.75
Net Income	26,600	207.82	204.61	219.36

After operating for a year, the company reports the following results for Japan in yen in column A of Exhibit 5-3. Columns B, C, and D report results in U.S. dollars based on varying assumptions.

What do the results indicate? Let us examine each column:

Column A: yen results— A Japanese investor in his or her native currency would have a 10-percent profit margin and a 20-percent return on investment. Owners' equity has increased by the profits earned that year.

Column B: dollar results, year-end rate—If the year-end exchange rate is used to translate all of the accounts, some strange results appear. Fixed assets and inventory have increased in value simply because of the currency translation. Owners' equity has increased by more than net income. Net income, which would have been $200,000 at the old exchange rate, has benefitted $7,820 by the increased value of the yen, not by any effort on the part of management. Owners' equity has also benefitted by the increased value in fixed assets

and inventory accounts occasioned by the change in exchange rates.

While management may appreciate the increase in performance implied by the account translations, its attitude would be different if the yen had decreased in value relative to the dollar with a consequent decrease in subsidiary performance. How, then, to appropriately evaluate these results is one problem; that the accounts do not reflect historical costs, the basis of generally accepted accounting procedures, is another problem.

Column C: self-sustaining and autonomous units—For self-sustaining and autonomous subsidiaries, where the functional currency would be the local currency, FASB Statement 52 provides that a modified current rate method be used. Under this method, balance sheet items are translated at historical cost and income statement items are translated at the average exchange rate for the year. Owners' equity has a balancing account that records translation gains or losses.

Column D: subsidiaries of U.S. companies

—For subsidiaries that are an integral part of the company and that have the parent currency as the functional currency, FASB Statement 52 provides that historical (temporal) costs be used. Under this method, account items are translated at the exchange rates in effect when the transaction occurs. Fixed assets, for example, would be carried on the books at $1 equals Y133. Inventory would also be carried at historical exchange rates. On the assumption that transactions occurred evenly throughout the year, revenue and expense items would be translated at the average exchange rates for the year. Assume that the exchange rate for inventory, expenses, and revenues is $1 equals Y130. The results of this method are shown under column D. A trans-

lation gain or loss account in the income statement is established to report any gains or losses resulting from currency translations.

CONCLUSION

Over 170 countries have over 170 different accounting systems. Efforts are being made to standardize reporting results. These efforts work better with multinational companies that currently follow the FASB standards than for companies that do not. Managers must recognize the possible inconsistencies and inaccuracies when dealing with accounting data from other countries.

SECTION 6

Finance

Gordon Cummings, Section Editor

Introduction   *Gordon Cummings*   6-3

Finance's Increased Role in Management   *George Willis*   6-5

The Role of the Chief Financial Officer   *Denis Guerette*   6-7

Planning, Budgeting, and Forecasting   *A. Douglas Hartt*   6-9

Corporate Restructuring   *Ashley James Sinclair*   6-14

Capital Expenditures: Analysis and Decision Making
   V. Bruce Irvine   6-21

Sources of Financing: Traditional and New   *Robert W. Hiller*   6-25

Cash Management   *Cecilia L. Wagner*   6-33

The Effects of Financial Deregulation   *Bruce Lunergan*   6-36

Global Financial Thinking   *John Huguet*   6-40

Managing Foreign Exchange   *John J. Hampton*   6-42

INTRODUCTION

Gordon Cummings

Accounting and finance have gone through an evolution in recent years, as greater demands have been made by both internal users of information and external stakeholders, such as investors, creditors, and regulatory agencies. At one time, financial people perceived their role as following generally accepted accounting principles, dealing with banks, and providing financial advice as asked or needed. Now, changes in financial markets, electronic information processing capabilities, and a global arena for production and marketing have produced new expectations.

Finance has become a tool that can be used by managers at all levels in an organization. It plays specific roles, including:

- *Strategic direction*—At its highest levels, organizations determine their mission and the strategies to achieve various goals. In this part of the planning process, financial analysis helps determine the viability of strategies. Can capital be invested under costs and terms that are likely to yield an appropriate return for the level of risk? Finance helps answer this question.
- *Asset management*—A company has resources that are deployed in pursuit of specific objectives. Does the company have the right level and mixture of assets? Are the assets financed appropriately given the risk in debt and required

return needed by owners? These, too, are financial questions.

- *Profit planning*—Companies prepare budgets and expend monies in pursuit of operational goals. They are expected to show profits in the long-term consistent with the risk they undertake. They are expected to make short-term decisions that lead to long-term results. Finance helps keep score in whether organizations are achieving profit goals.
- *Cash flow*—Firms invest cash and expect to receive cash back on a basis that reflects the time value of money. The tools of finance separate cash from accounting profits and help determine whether adequate cash flows are being achieved or are likely to be achieved.

In this section, financial experts discuss issues that directly affect nonfinancial managers. The authors make sense out of a growing complexity of financial options and alternatives. The process begins in the first chapter where finance is identified as a provider of information in a process of informed decision making. Denis Guerette continues with the management role of the chief financial officer. A. Douglas Hartt examines the role of management accounting in budgeting, planning, and forecasting. These chapters show finance as an activity that must participate fully in strategic and tactical planning and lead the company to a full consideration of the financial impact of changing markets and conditions.

Ashley James Sinclair examines the various kinds of corporate restructuring. V. Bruce Irvine covers the evaluation of capital expenditures. Robert W. Hiller describes both traditional and newer sources of financing, pointing out the need to observe the basic fundamentals of sound investments and to manage the balance between debt and equity. Although these chapters deal with traditional finance functions—raising and investing capital—they reflect modern techniques and methodologies.

The next two articles deal with specific areas that must be understood by managers if the company is to make correct decisions involving money. Their common thread is that the world is rapidly changing. "Cash Management" outlines practices that produce benefits from the timing of inflows and outflows of cash in the firm. Bruce Lunergan examines the deregulation of financial institutions. Under new rules, users of financial services have greater choice but also more confusion.

The reader is then moved into the international arena. "Global Financial Thinking" is somewhat futuristic, covering major financial changes resulting from the globalization of trade and operations. The author provokes social and economic thinking, as well as financial thought. John J. Hampton's chapter is more technical, as it presents techniques for managing foreign exchange.

All of the chapters offer hints and techniques that work for practicing managers. If the tone of some arguments carries a sense of urgency, this is to be expected. Finance keeps score in a world of increased competition and declining resources. To be sure, the viewpoint is always the long run. Managers are encouraged to avoid pursuing short-term profits, but realities of quarterly earnings reports and other immediate measures are all short-term in focus. The viewpoint is always responsible. Corporations must be good citizens, even as they earn a proper return. But the viewpoint is always that companies should earn a fair return for a fair risk in the marketplace. This is the essence of competitive markets and the proper use of finance for the managers of modern organizations.

Gordon Cummings, *MBA, FCMA, is currently the CEO of United Co-operatives of Ontario, an agricultural supply cooperative. Prior to this position he was CEO of National Sea Products, before which he spent fifteen years with Ernst & Young, the last ten as a partner in the consulting practice. He has taught and authored lesson notes on a wide range of management accounting topics.*

FINANCE'S INCREASED ROLE IN MANAGEMENT

George Willis, Controller, Industry, Science and Technology Canada

INCREASED MANAGEMENT EDUCATION AND TRAINING

Throughout the world, there has been a dramatic increase in the level of education and training that people need to qualify for management positions. For example, the MBA is becoming the professional credential of the general manager. American business schools graduate more than seventy thousand MBAs each year. Counterpart programs throughout the English-speaking world and in Europe are burgeoning. This development has two distinct effects. First, the typical manager outside the finance function has been schooled in corporate finance, financial accounting, management accounting, and collateral fields of quantitative methods, economics, and information technology. This makes for knowledgeable and demanding users of financial information. Second, the financial specialist has been exposed to the full body of knowledge of management. This enhances his or her credibility with other managers and enables the financial specialist to play a greater role in the direction of the enterprise.

The result of these changes is that the financial personnel in an organization participate in a wider range of activities as more is expected of the financial people by other members of the management group.

THE EVOLUTION OF STRATEGIC MANAGEMENT

The practice of management has been materially changed by the widespread use of strategic planning as an integral part of the management processes. This factor and the globalization of business have expanded the role of financial personnel.

The senior financial officer is often a key participant in strategic planning for many reasons. He or she is the provider or validator of much information and analysis used in decision making. This role is enhanced by the fact that financial people are often seen as having comparative objectivity in advising on competing priorities among operating managers.

Globalization of business has changed the circumstances governing financial decisions. Financial markets are integrated with financial decisions on the source and disposition of funds. Again, the result is financial personnel playing a significant role in operating activities and transactions.

Corporate restructuring through mergers, acquisitions, and divestiture has become a major result of strategic planning and management implementation of the strategic plan. Almost always, a major financial dimension is involved.

An Emphasis on Accountability

Increased accountability has forged a stronger-than-ever link between executive responsibility for managing external relationships, and the reporting dimension of the finance function. This accountability is both to security regulators, such as the Securities and Exchange Commission SEC, and government agencies for issues such as environmental compliance, employment equity, health, and safety. These accountabilities have expanded the traditional role of external financial reporting.

Increased emphasis on accountability has also arisen from marketplace pressures, from the decentralization of management responsibility to operating units, and from the movement toward downsizing of organizations. These developments require close interaction between line managers and finance specialists in the exercise of the control function.

The Impact of Advances in Information Technology

The proliferation of low-cost, high-powered information technology has impacted every aspect of the finance function. Asset portfolio management is enhanced through the use of computer modeling. Cash management is conducted in real time on a global scale. Control information is provided precisely and instantly on the operational and financial results of ongoing performance. One financial analyst with a personal computer and support software has the same analytical capacity as had twenty of his or her predecessors just a generation ago.

The merging technologies of office automation, data processing, and telecommunications have resulted in high reliability and low cost. Technology allows the linking of physically distant locations and places new demands on data integrity.

All these advances have moved financial people into the arena of managing information. This new knowledge-intensive role replaces a previous activity of being laborious producers of data.

Developments in Finance

Several developments within the function have enhanced finance's role in management. A few of the most important are:

1. In the treasury area, a plethora of new financial instruments such as swaps, note issuances, and tradeable debt claims has provided new opportunities and attendant risks in capital markets.
2. External reporting has evolved from traditional financial statement to forecasting, and accountability reporting on results and anticipated results, in addition to a range of political, economic, and social issues.
3. Reporting on management performance within the organization is now based on financial and nonfinancial measures, rather than being focused exclusively on the "bottom line."
4. Management of costs has moved from the shop floor to all levels, including strategic and policy discussions.
5. The total quality management (TQM) movement necessitates the development of new perspectives on the accumulation and analysis of costs.
6. The control function, particularly in high-technology manufacturing, has become a continuous rather than periodic activity that is fully integrated into ongoing operations.
7. The internal audit function continues to evolve into a broad-based management control instrument.

In terms of corporate human resource management, an intimate knowledge of financial decision making acquired through academic study and practical experience is becoming an essential qualification for assuming general management responsibilities.

THE ROLE OF THE CHIEF FINANCIAL OFFICER

Denis Guerette, Executive Vice-President of Operations, Societe de Services Financiers

The evolution of the financial function in an organization has resulted in the expanding role and complexity of the chief financial officer (CFO). Today, an intelligent and dynamic CFO is an essential prerequisite for survival and growth in the vast majority of organizations. It is important that stakeholders, associated directly or indirectly with company management, become familiar with the CFO's role and that their expectations be clearly defined. The role of the CFO can be divided into three principal areas:

1. Participation on the senior management team in general company management and in the strategic planning process.
2. Planning and financial management.
3. Treasury functions that include establishing and maintaining close relations between the company and relevant external financial markets, taxation, and asset preservation.

GENERAL MANAGEMENT AND STRATEGIC PLANNING

As a member of senior management, the CFO plays an active role in general management as well as in the strategic planning process. Whether the strategies are based on the growth of existing markets, on penetrating new markets, or on decisions to divest or acquire a company, the contributions of the CFO can be invaluable.

In a growth or expansion situation, the CFO must invariably examine financing needs and anticipated profitability. Devising financing that minimizes the cost of capital, within an acceptable level of risk for the company, is a crucial dimension of the CFO role. It is also an area in which expertise is key to the future well-being of the organization.

In the case of acquisitions, or of divestment from certain activities, the CFO is often assigned the task of structuring the agreements that are undertaken between parties. This job is in addition to obtaining competing financing if the case warrants.

Within the senior management group, the CFO is almost always consulted on the financial analysis of past results, and the viability of present and potential operations. This role results in the CFO being the interpreter of key information underlining the strategic planning process of the management group. This role can earn the respect of the remaining members of senior management if the CFO provides and interprets data in an objective manner. Maintaining the reputation of having a balanced, objective perspective results in the CFO having a greater input in the overall planning process.

In short, the CFO must evaluate the financial impact of various strategic options, ensure that other members of senior management have the information to reach balanced decisions, and make sure that the results create value for the stakeholders.

PLANNING AND FINANCIAL MANAGEMENT

Financial planning is an essential dimension and a natural consequence of the strategic planning process. Well-managed companies do not spare any efforts in this regard. A well-prepared financial plan contains a complete pro forma financial statement spanning several years, the capital expenditures required to preserve or improve the competitive position of the company, the financial objectives and benchmarks against which future performance will be evaluated, and how the organization expects to obtain the financing required by the plan.

This process helps to define the interaction between financing activities and investment activities for the benefit of the entire management team, including the consequences of their decisions for the future. It also involves an in-depth analysis of the vulnerability of results with respect to certain factors such as the fluctuations in interest rates and various sales growth scenarios.

The CFO's financial management responsibilities entail, in conjunction with other senior managers, an involvement in setting policies in various areas. These include product pricing, inventory management, credit and collection of receivables. In addition, the CFO has the responsibility to ensure that there is timely, relevant reporting on results so that management can react quickly to changing circumstances. This involves collecting data on results, preparing forecasts, and analyzing and interpreting performance and trends.

TREASURY ROLES

It is incumbent upon the CFO to establish and maintain close relations with financial markets and the financial community as a whole.

These markets expect to be kept abreast of the future plans of the company and their anticipated impacts on results, and the company's likely financial requirements. The wide range of financing options available today place greater pressure on a CFO. Other members of management expect the CFO to be fully conversant with all the financing options. The CFO usually achieves this through ongoing contact with participants in financial institutions, and a fair amount of reading.

The CFO is almost always the ongoing link between the financial marketplace and the organization. A good CFO also ensures that his or her CEO is known to the financial community. As part of this process, the CFO tries to develop a climate of openness and trust with the providers of funds. Extensive communications are essential, for all financiers have one thing in common: They do not want any surprises.

A major treasury role involves taxation. Because earnings retained in the business are the largest single source of financing, it follows that prudent tax management creates added financing for the organization. The evolution of so many organizations doing business in many jurisdictions has compounded the complexity and importance of the CFO's role in taxation management. This is particularly the case for multinational firms.

Most organizations have current and fixed assets that must be controlled so they are properly utilized. The CFO has the responsibility for the custody of assets, which usually involves procedures for acquisition and disposition, insurance and other risk management, and internal auditing to ensure compliance with laws and company policies.

A RAPIDLY CHANGING ROLE

The role of the CFO has evolved over the years. To reflect remarkable changes occurring at an accelerated pace in the business world:

- The growing internationalization of companies adds an important dimension to the CFO, who must now be able to adapt to legal and financial frameworks that are different from the home country.

■ The intelligent use of information technologies has freed the CFO from information gathering. Now, the CFO can focus his or her efforts on the activities where analytical contributions can make a difference.

■ The creation of new, innovative financial instruments offered by financial intermediaries has introduced a wide range of entirely new possibilities. These demand a comprehensive knowledge of their accompanying risks. The role of the CFO in this case consists of finding the right balance between the needs of the company and the products offered to properly manage financial risks. The goal is to create a flexible and competitive financial structure.

PLANNING, BUDGETING, AND FORECASTING

A. Douglas Hartt, Treasurer, Maritime Telegraph and Telephone

Through plans, management communicates the vision, mission, goals, objectives, strategies, and values of the firm. This long-range view is used to formulate sales, expense, and capital budgets to meet the corporate plan. Annually, the budget for the upcoming fiscal year expresses the frontier of the longer-term plan in a one-year, very specific segment. Regularly, these budgets are updated, based on year-to-date results and current outlook, to produce current forecasts of the short-term expectations for the firm, usually to the end of the fiscal year.

Planning is hard work. The process of creating a plan consists of analyzing the situation, creating potential solutions, and judging which solutions are best. The initial analysis of the situation and first solutions usually commence as a variation of the status quo. The real value of planning occurs when the planning group moves beyond the status quo, focuses on change in the firm's environment, and seriously evaluates new solutions. To develop alternate solutions that may improve on current decisions requires the skill of reaching beyond conventional thought and seeking new perspectives.

Management can look to its own skills or to many outside sources including courses, books, conferences, and professional magazines and periodicals. Managers can also consult peers and professional firms and consultants who specialize in the process or those with industry knowledge. No matter what sources are used, the plan must ultimately be created by management. And it is still hard work.

Budgeting flows naturally from the creation of the corporate plan. A budget is the price of the plan for a specific upcoming period, usually the next year. This connection to the corporate plan is critical in translating the value of the corporate plan into the operational realities of the firm. The budget prices the expectations embodied in the corporate plan for that year. As such, the process of creating a budget is almost as much a communication opportunity as it is a financial management process. It embodies the mission, goals, and objectives of the corporate plan for a particular twelve-month period. In essence, the budget is a financial expression of the longer-term plans for the next fiscal year.

Responsibility for creating the budget is broadly shared around an organization. Co-ordination is usually led by the chief financial officer (CFO) and the financial professionals in the firm. Commitment to budgeting rests with all decision makers in the firm authorized to acquire resources and charged with earning revenues. To be meaningful, the budgeting activities of the corporation should be directed to identify the most appropriate individual and component of the organization to give the best information on company financial activities. Each organization is different, but the results of the budgeting process must be a projection of sales, expenses, and resource requirements reflecting the most realistic perspective of the forthcoming period the firm can generate. To model the assignment of these activities, the CFO and his or her team should begin with the corporate financial model.

CORPORATE FINANCIAL MODEL

At this point, business plans and decisions become a numbers game. When all is said and done, the corporation must annually report its successes and failures to its investors as described in an income statement, balance sheet, and cash flow statement. These financial statements are created by the CFO and reflect the company's successes, or otherwise through translation of all activities using a set of consistent accounting rules.

In order to develop budgets that reflect the corporate plan and the company's expectations of the needs of its investors, the company's budgeting process must produce a result that fits the financial reporting model to shareholders. In other words, if all of the company's assumptions built into its planning

and budgeting process were to come to pass precisely as projected, the corporate financial model and the ensuing annual report would be identical. Although this will not occur, any deviation from the plan can be analyzed by reference to the specific results accumulated in the budget.

Since the corporate financial model will be employed in the budgeting process to accept or recycle the twelve-month plan put forward by managers, it is important that the model have "integrity." Integrity in this context means that the input is consistently created under a fixed set of principles and is then processed to develop the financial results in a manner that substantially mirrors the corporation's accounting model used in financial reports. It also means that it is fully repeatable by anybody using the same starting point and assumptions. Ideally, the corporate model will be built in a convenient computer system allowing for multiple iterations and "what if" exercises.

Some corporate models are linked across the entire corporation so that budget preparers, their managers, and the coordination function in finance are able to go back to the source when a change to an assumption is appropriate, when a funding proposal is accepted or rejected, or when a value should be changed. Such a well-linked corporate model would be the envy of many organizations. The dynamics of new information leading to changes in the budget input along with changing assumptions and shifting priorities within the firm is a burden well avoided. Keeping all necessary parties updated is a more manageable task in such an arrangement. A typical corporate model is built under the direction of the CFO of the company. It allows the various organizations within the firm to describe their activities as anticipated in the corporate plan both verbally and numerically in ways most familiar to them. The CFO's team then uses the model to translate these elements into the company's financial projections.

To maximize the skills of all of the parties, the more of the accounting responsibility that can be handled by the CFO's team, and the more of the computations that can be handled by the model, the more that the individual budget preparers will be able to focus on their real contribution to the planning process, that is, inputting what is going on in their part of the business, what are they going to be doing, what resources will they require, and what will they accomplish.

With this in mind, the CFO's team should build a model that contains as much of the pricing assumptions as can be specified. For instance, if the resource requirements include employees whose pay is either standardized or formalized within the company in a way that the program can resolve, then the budget preparers need only identify the full-time equivalent employees that will be needed throughout the year. The model would then extend this staffing requirement into salaries, related benefits, and other salary-related costs and thus complete the price of the human resource requirement for that operation. Similarly, if the operation uses materials, photocopying services, or other resources where standard unit costs are employed in the company, the model can extend these unit costs times the volumes projected by the preparer to provide the financial result.

Obviously, if the costs are the result of the operation of another part of the firm, and if there is a transfer pricing algorithm employed to assign or attribute these costs within the firm, the financial model can again mimic that transfer pricing algorithm to distribute costs in the budget. Some operations in companies result in spending resources, which then must be distributed among expenses on the income statement, or cost of goods sold (still within the income statement), or they will show up on the balance sheet as a deferred charge. The accounting model should solve the accounting resulting from such a transaction. Otherwise, the operating managers in the field will be required to become accountants.

With the model just described, the operating manager provides the kind of information best understood in the operations of the company and in terms that are meaningful to those operations. The work of mathematics and arithmetic extensions are carried out by the model as are the application of the financial and accounting rules as defined by the chief financial officer.

An accounting model built as previously described will more effectively use the knowledge, skills, and abilities of operating managers and the chief financial officer's staff. As a by-product, managers will become more knowledgeable of the financial impact of their operation as the communication has become more appropriate to what they do and what they must manage. They will also gather a clearer understanding of the dynamics of their operation and its impact on the firm while pleasantly avoiding the confusion imposed on them by the application of accounting rules to their use of resources. It allows them to think of three employees on their back shift, a ton of raw material, and of a dollar as a dollar.

One observation in any performance evaluation system is that the employee being managed will try to build in some safety margin so that the results will allow room for a positive performance report. In a process such as the one described, the large volume of budget-preparing units could result in a safety margin that is sizable to the firm. At the same time, the overall budget plan may be rejected as unworkable. A tightly run and administered model will counterbalance that with leaving little, if any, room for unspecified safety margins.

Implicit safety margins are unmanageable. Explicit safety margins in the hands of the right decision makers are good planning. The budget program should isolate authority to provide such margins.

THE BUDGET PROCESS AND REVIEW

To actually build a budget, the starting point is the corporate organization chart, the authorizations practice, the accounting model, and the corporate plan. Using the accounting model, the CFO's budget team can determine the inputs required in order to meet all of the requirements for the budget. Translating this into corporate responsibilities, the team can determine which executive/manager should have responsibility for each element of budget input, and then should be able to follow down the organization chart, assigning increasingly more detailed budgeting responsibilities. Typically line managers or organizational professionals will actually prepare the budget inputs. The budget team will then communicate this list of responsibility assignments across the corporation. This communication is critical to ensure acceptance of the responsibility and determination of any overlaps or gaps in the planning process.

Once all of these structures are planned, the process must be initiated. This is done by either the CFO or the entire executive team issuing a directive to generate a budget setting the overall theme of the budget in terms of the corporate plan and the specific components of the corporate plan for the following year. The guidelines should indicate the overall corporate measures that are expected for the upcoming year as well as significant factors expected to impact on the firm during the budget year. The underlying assumptions should be used by all budget preparers in building their budget proposal for the year. The assumptions and guidelines typically would indicate the corporate view of the economy and how it will impact both sales and costs in the upcoming year, major acquisitions, diversifications or operational changes, plant closures, plant openings, extensions or further investments, expected changes to employment levels, material or labor price changes, especially union and other agreements, and any other matter of an executive or corporate perspective that should be considered by the wider body of management and budget-preparing staff. The letter would close with the indication that the head of the budget management team will be issuing schedules and other details along with providing training sessions on any special items.

The modeling process will demand input in a specific format. Although this will be accomplished on an interactive terminal system within the firm, both input forms and output reports that support the individual budget preparer's stories must be designed. The chief financial officer's team will design these documents and reports and will set standards for their completion and the schedule of events that must be met in order for a successful budget to be completed on time.

As the budget is constructed, it will be found that the first result employing this many inputs from this many diverse re-sources will not satisfy the objectives for the firm. It is thus important to design the system and to create an atmosphere in which the iterative nature of this process is obviously intentional. The process is one of altering assumptions, accepting or denying proposals for resources and for business plans, changing prices, and increasing or reducing discretionary expenditures until the result for the year that maximizes the resources available to the firm and yields an acceptable result is obtained.

Thus it is important that budget preparers and their managers expect this circumstance from the start. In this way, the budget has augmented the corporate plan as a vehicle not only for meeting the expectations of management but of communicating those expectations and priorities to a wide component of the organization. This method must be planned to avoid both overload of budget and "administrivia" on the preparers and with due regard for confidentiality of corporate planning and projected financial results. The entire modeling system should be designed to provide every preparer with only the assistance and feedback required while protecting information on a need-to-know basis.

The budget input document or file on the system should be constructed in a way that the preparer can identify what activity is included in the budget, what resources are being employed, what results and measurements can be anticipated from the budget, what parts of the corporate plan are satisfied within this budget element, and, to what degree, with the funding proposed. The design of the system should give the preparer the opportunity to present the minimal level of funding needed to achieve the minimum of the envelope of results proposed in the corporate plan for that activity.

The preparers should also be provided with the opportunity of proposing additional activities and their associated resource requirements along with the value and the benefits of undertaking these activities. The additional level of funding proposal(s) allows the proposal to represent both the minimum and recommended level of activity for the upcoming year for this component of the business. The budget system should also provide for the communication by the preparer of issues and concerns, explicitly noting whether such issues or concerns are provided for in the plan or represent new risks and opportunities not yet built into the plan.

The budget file should also indicate connections between this activity and other budget areas, especially if those activities are interdependent. Such subjects would indicate that the level of funding required and the results expected of this subject relate directly to other budget areas as indicated. A prime example would be a budget being prepared in the marketing area that relates directly to sales, inventory, cost of goods sold, operations, as well as advertising and promotions budgets. When a change to a particular budget alters other areas of the firm, the preparer should indicate where that influence may be directed. This charge will result in further alterations to the entire plan.

The head of the budget operations team, frequently the comptroller, will set out the schedule for budget preparation and review with senior management. This communication will also include directions on any special reporting that is necessary as part of the process, will identify the final list of budget responsibilities, and will oversee the training of any budget preparer or supervisor to ensure maximum commonality of budget preparation throughout the entire process within the firm.

A special responsibility of the comptroller's department will be a large number of budget items, which are either extensions or computations based on input from the various preparers such as pension expense, personal taxes, other salary-related expenses; corporate expenses such as audit fees; and so on. These items typically either require an accounting expertise in order to create them, or are the result of a corporate commitment whose budget responsibility is best set as close to the end of the process as possible.

As well, specialized input will be required of the tax professionals to compute income tax expense and related cash requirements. Finance professionals in the treasury side would be responsible for financial planning, interest rates, other costs of capital, and their implications below the operating income line.

They would also provide input on capital structure and allowable financial ratios and targets.

Now that everyone has been trained, has their assignments, and has prepared all of their budgets, what do they do with them? The most effective way to ensure that a budget will fit with the corporate objectives and reflect all of the considerations with the corporate plan is through communications and review. Budgets are typically prepared at the operational level within each organization of the firm. The individual charged with preparation of a budget would start with a briefing by the responsible planning team member to get a clear top-down message of the plans and expectations to be assumed in preparing the budget.

Having prepared the document, it should be reviewed through the organization both with superiors and with the other affected parties in related budget areas. This will ensure commonality and comprehension of the budget, completeness, and the elimination of overlaps. It will give the budget the discipline necessary to ensure that perceptions of the best idea for the right reasons are being delivered as part of the budget message. And finally the preparer and other members of that organization will have the opportunity to identify issues, concerns, problems, and opportunities which that part of the firm is expecting or experiencing and will be able to communicate how this budget proposal will deal with those matters.

As the budget is assembled, the CFO's team will create the full model together and provide the executive organization with an overview and a summary of how well the budget meets the corporate requirements for the upcoming year. Other sensitivity tests such as sizable dollar percent changes in revenue generation, expense, and other resource requirements can be isolated mostly with the screening process within the budget model itself. The executives can then focus on those matters, as well as the issues, concerns, problems, and opportunities that have filtered up in the review process within each of their own organizations. The executives can then determine how they are going to deal with those issues and what is next for the budget. Budgeting should be expected to be an interactive process. The preparers and middle management will be expecting communication back as to required changes to their budget proposal. Either the CFO, his or her team, or the respective executive team member can carry the message back so that any alterations to plans and assumptions can be executed by the preparers.

This is a cyclical process allowing the preparers to create a new perspective based on the directions given by the executive. Some or all of the budgets are presented in summary form to the executive to enhance the process of communication and comprehension among the executive team of the underlying assumptions inherent in the budget and to promote a greater understanding of how the resources are acquired and maximized in the firm. Although it may take more than one iteration, generally speaking budget recycling with this model can be very well sized to meet the needs of the corporation.

Once the budget plan as composed meets the needs of the corporation, it is finalized. Communication is addressed back to the preparers that the budgets are approved as they now stand. The next request is for them to take that budget and isolate it by reporting periods, usually months, to be used as a control mechanism in the following year. The final stage in the annual budget is to prepare a budget book containing the final documentation associated with the entire budget. It will include financial statements not only for the years but for the individual months of the following year. It is recommended that the income statements for the months of the year also be subject to review by the CFO's team to ensure that quarterly reporting to shareholders, if the plan is met as now proposed, will satisfy investors. It might be necessary at this time to go back to certain budget preparers to try to encourage earlier or later activities during the year depending on affordability and do-ability.

CORPORATE RESTRUCTURING

Ashley James Sinclair, President, Krell Capital Corporation

An organizational restructuring may be simply the examination of the corporate organization chart to introduce a more effective business structure. This may involve such actions as the sale, purchase, merger, centralization, or decentralization of the organization or its parts. Depending on the success of the

restructuring, it may even be a determinant of the organization's life span.

The corporate restructuring of a holding company involves more of a macro perspective than the change of a single corporation. A holding company is basically an umbrella company that owns other companies, usually operating units. It is possible that the single corporation, in turn, may have one or more divisions that give it greater complexity than a holding company.

Geographic considerations introduce another element of complexity involving corporate restructuring. The laws of different countries may also be a determinant of the corporate structure. Tax considerations on an international level may influence the restructuring of a corporation. This problem is then brought into a smaller focus as federal, state, provincial, municipal, and other governing authorities extend their influence into the corporate lives of an organization.

Corporate restructuring is seldom done in isolation by a few persons acting alone. The cost of restructuring must be reviewed from a cost-benefit perspective and will require the involvement of the finance and accounting departments. Tax issues may require the consultation of the external auditors or accountants. Decisions on staffing, union issues, hiring and terminations, pensions, and other personnel-related matters require the involvement of the human relations department and outside specialists. Changes in product lines, advertising, research and development considerations, patents and licensing, and other business matters will involve sales, marketing, production, and research personnel as well as in-house legal counsel.

Senior financial officers, external auditors, and company accountants perform specific functions for the corporation that is considering restructuring. They provide strategic direction, tax advice, securities advice, and valuations to provide a basic understanding of the proposal.

REASONS FOR RESTRUCTURING

Corporate restructuring encompasses different scenarios that appear to have financial considerations as a common denominator. This is not always the case as there may be nonfinancial considerations that precipitate the restructuring. For example, as the organization expands, it may require restructuring

from a single division unit into a multidivisional organization along product or geographic lines or both. Many events and issues may initiate the process of corporate restructuring, including:

1. *Acquisitions/divestitures*—The acquisition or divestiture of companies, divisions, and assets will likely result in some form of corporate restructuring. In its most simple case, the assets are added or deleted, as the case may be, and the organization continues as before. However, the magnitude of the transaction may be a factor in requiring the change from the existing structure.

2. *Refinancing*—Certain refinancing transactions result in a corporate restructuring. The issuance of shares or debt under a public offering alters the corporate ownership structure and may be accompanied by a new corporate structure to accommodate the intended uses of the proceeds of the offering.

3. *Joint ventures*—This is a business decision to create a new entity that requires substantial financial and decision-making input from the participants. The joint venture may have a limited life span or may result in the creation of a new corporation.

4. *LBO/MBO*—These are reorganizations that involve new owners of a company's capital stock. A leveraged buyout (LBO) involves third parties. A management buyout (MBO) has key members of the existing management team as the purchasers.

In an MBO, the managers participating in the buyout become the new shareholders, and the lines of decision making may be redrawn. Corporate ties that existed with the previous owners may be severed or may continue during an accommodation period depending on the extent of related business between the companies.

The LBO, by its nature, involves the levering of acquired assets to raise additional financing for completion of the transaction. This may involve the disposal of redundant assets to facilitate the transaction. The acquirer is normally another corporation that is actively seeking target companies. Corporate restructuring may occur at two levels: the acquirer and the acquired. The acquiring company may be much larger than it was prior to acquisition. The purchase may be partially financed by the issuance of additional shares of stock.

Both LBOs and MBOs may experience changes from a private to a public corporation as part of the acquisition financing. If venture capital companies become involved to assist with the acquisition, then another dimension is added to the corporate restructuring. Board representation becomes a major issue with these companies as they put procedures in place to protect their investments.

TAX FACTORS IN RESTRUCTURING

Companies with significant tax loss carryforwards may be acquired by companies with stronger financial positions that are seeking some tax sheltering of profits. The extent of the losses available to shelter other income may be viewed as an important motive for an acquisition. The role of the acquiring company is expanded from seeking profitable companies seeking suitable tax loss companies.

Many corporate restructurings are determined by tax considerations or by long-term tax planning incorporated into a strategic plan. Various taxing jurisdictions often amend their tax laws and corporations must respond using tax planning to maximize the returns to their shareholders. The expiration or reduction of particular tax benefits, structures, or deductions may trigger a corporate restructuring to accommodate the window of opportunity that remains. Management accountants must be in communication with their tax advisers to properly plan the corporation's financial affairs. There are preferred regions in which to incorporate subsidiaries, and such factors may have some effect on the final corporate structure. International tax havens have greater significance to companies operating on a global basis.

It is not necessary for senior management to be fully versed in the latest corporate tax laws. It is most important to ask about and recognize that a particular corporate structure

or transaction may be of benefit to the corporation. It is then up to the financial officer to follow up with appropriate professional advice from the relevant disciplines.

MONOPOLY LIMITATIONS

There may be some instances whereby government legislation may require the dismantling of a corporate structure due to monopolization of an industry. Such instances may have occurred in the past. More proactive practices by management have anticipated such concerns and corporate structures have been designed to minimize exposure in this area. As an example, companies often seek advice from a major accounting, investment banking, or law firm prior to making acquisitions or expanding their activities into various markets.

CORPORATE STRUCTURE OPTIMIZATION

Selecting the most appropriate corporate structure is a complex matter. Proper planning and advice is needed to achieve the desired results. It is not just a matter of drawing organization charts but rather considering all the elements affecting a business to determine which is most appropriate. One of management's primary concerns in corporate restructuring is the impact of the resultant organizational structure on the operational decisions that have to be made. If the restructuring involves outside organizations, a decision has to be made with respect to the continuation of these relationships. Corporate restructuring will affect many external parties, including:

1. *Corporate lenders*—One of the more common decisions is the choice of the corporate lenders. Assume that all of the corporation's financial matters are handled by a single bank, including operating facilities, term loans, real estate mortgages, and other financing. Under this scenario, it is likely that the

financial institution also has a blanket debenture or other security registration over corporate assets. Further assume that property owned by the corporation can provide funds for expansion or acquisition. The most likely source of funds would be the sale or increased refinancing of the real estate. The bank would be involved in the decision.

As the size of an organization increases, more than one financial institution will be likely lending to the organization, usually with various security interests. This makes restructuring more complex, but the basic principles set out above remain the same.

2. *Corporate auditors and accountants*—The corporation may have different auditors or accountants, depending on the number of affiliated companies, divisions, geographic locations, and other factors. It may be necessary to change the auditors or accountants within the organizational structure as a result of an amalgamation or merger.

In any corporate restructuring, management must take into account the timing of such changes. In most instances, current or pro forma financial statements may be required as part of any refinancing. The corporate restructuring may have also resulted in an accelerated year-end and financial statements of the new entity would be required. Another concern arises if the year-end remains the same but the corporation is midway through its fiscal period. Lenders have been known to request more recent financial statements if the year-end is too far away. Remember to allow for review and preparation time of the financial statements before a report can be issued.

3. *Insurance*—A new approach to corporate insurance and risk management may be required after the restructuring. For example, the major assets of a corporation may be placed into one company and the operating business may be resident in another company. The reduced creditor risk and other related factors arising from the separation of the corporate assets from its operations may result in an overall reduction of premiums, depending on the type of insurance policies that the corporation may have or require.

4. *Other entities*—Depending on the size of the company and the scope of its operations, other external entities affected by a restructuring should be considered at an early date. A choice may have to be made between advertising agencies that handle the corporate account and the account of the company that was recently acquired. Restructuring may present opportunities to have access to a preferred supplier that was previously restricted from doing business because of competitive reasons. Law firms may present a similar situation where a change can be made to improve legal support.

Since corporate restructuring can occur in any company, industry, country, or some part or combination thereof, other considerations may be endless. Some of them are:

1. *Guarantees*—If refinancing is necessary for the corporate restructuring, corporate and perhaps personal guarantees might be brought up by the lender. Proper planning during a restructuring will enable the company to minimize the requirement for guarantees.

2. *Staffing and cutbacks*—Corporate restructuring accompanied by a major increase or decrease in the scale of operations requires personnel planning. The elimination of similar or redundant functions can result in substantial labor and benefit savings. Again, proper planning during the early stages will avoid confrontations with labor groups, interest groups, and other affected parties.

3. *Salary levels*—A problem in any corporate restructuring is the matter of compensation. If the acquiring or dominant company is the one with the higher salary or wage base, fewer problems will arise than if the roles are reversed. One problem may occur when a senior counterpart of the acquired company is paid less than a junior counterpart of the acquirer. These cases can be dealt with as exceptions and addressed before a problem occurs.

The reverse situation whereby the acquired company has a higher compensation level creates a problem that may not easily disappear. The cost to bring all salary levels to a par may be too great. Selective staff reductions may occur to reduce overall payroll levels to an acceptable level with the required workers.

4. *Unions*—If one of the entities is unionized and the other is not, several points must be considered, including wage levels, benefits, number of unions, and past strike history. In other cases, different unions will represent similar classes of employees. Some lenders have been known to ask when all contracts are up for negotiation and what the prior history of settlements has been. This affects the success of the combined entity to continue with business and fund obligations as they are due. If there is a chance that cash flow may be interrupted, the company should ensure that maturing obligations have appropriate maturity dates.

5. *Corporate cultures*—The organizational cultures of two combining entities may be substantially different. This reduces the likelihood of the transaction succeeding.

6. *Physical relocation*—Corporate restructuring may involve consideration of the cost of premises. The choice of head office location may be a natural decision. On the other hand, a corporate restructuring may result in the senior management team continuing to be located downtown, while the majority of administrative staff may be relocated to lower-cost suburbs. In this manner, the corporation maintains its prestigious downtown address for its corporate offices. Decisions such as these do not have to wait for an acquisition to take place. With the increasing cost of prime office space, it may be prudent to consider such a move as part of the corporate restructuring.

7. *Appraisals and business valuations*—A restructuring may involve financial transactions that require the written support of appraisals of real estate, machinery and equipment, and inventory or valuations of the business itself. The company should be aware of the lead time required to commission and prepare such reports. Consideration should also be given to alternative strategies if an appraisal is substantially lower than expected.

FACTORS AFFECTING CORPORATE RESTRUCTURINGS

Owners and managers must be aware of a variety of factors that influence the structure of a corporation, including the following:

Economies of scale—The theory of economies of scale has been preached to many business students but few are alert to some of the practical applications. For example, a possible acquisition gives obvious savings of management, labor, and premises. There may be additional savings from the combined purchasing power of major suppliers.

Legal agreements—When the corporate structure changes, so also do many existing legal agreements. The company should review these agreements and their implications to ensure that a key business element is not missing in the new corporation. It would not be practical to have an efficient structure in place supported by a patchwork legal program.

Some of these legal agreements include leases, employee contracts, mortgage and loan agreements, supplier contracts, customer contracts, union agreements, royalties, distribution agreements, licenses, and agency agreements.

Balance sheet considerations—One of the functions in a corporate restructuring is to ensure that the balance sheet of the company is strong. This may involve analyzing of certain transactions to determine the most optimum result for the company and devising a strategy accordingly.

Debt restructuring—Many corporate financial transactions involve the restructuring of debt into other debt instruments or quasi-equity. This may involve the conversion of debt with an approaching maturity into debt with a longer amortization period. It may be possible to convert major trade creditors into equity participants if this is the only way that their credit can be recovered. Another possible arrangement is the structuring of additional business from a creditor under the condition that the company will repay the creditor with the profits from future sales.

Redundant Assets — Assets not crucial to the operations of the business should be considered for disposal to allow for their conversion into cash. Surplus equipment normally falls into this category as does a nonessential division or company.

Sale and Leaseback—Certain assets, such as a manufacturing plant or office building, can be better sold to investors and leased back at an established market rate. The cash from the sale can be used to pay down other indebtedness. Sale and leaseback arrangements are also popular for larger pieces of equipment. Depending on the status of the corporate restructuring, some companies try to extract as much cash out of their assets before offering the company for sale.

Hidden Liabilities—A company should be alert to hidden liabilities, particularly with organizations that are being acquired. The best intentions of corporate restructuring can be set aside when a lender realizes that there are hidden prior claims. Examples could involve pension funds, federal sales taxes, provincial or state sales taxes, and other regulatory remittances that have to be collected by the company. Although the balance sheet may not show such hidden liabilities, the amounts can add up easily between reporting periods. Adjustments can be hidden through large accounts such as cost of sales until they are properly identified and corrected.

MANAGEMENT RESPONSIBILITIES

The chief financial officer will be instrumental in providing financial direction to the company during the restructuring process. Some of the responsibilities are:

1. *Obtaining financing*—The company should be able to raise additional financing at all times without severely straining its credit. Proper strategic planning is needed to detect future needs for, and sources of, the financing.

2. *Maintaining control of the company*—Experienced lenders can sense when a company is in severe financial difficulty. They are able to extract larger concessions and share positions by offering otherwise attractive financing and then holding back on some of the funds until some points of clarification are addressed. There may be an initial advance of some of the funds but this only serves to increase the borrower's optimism. The borrower typically commits the company to other expenditures and quickly runs out of funds. The lender then indicates that additional advances can only be made with further concessions by the borrower. The result can be a loss of control of the company. This should be avoided.

3. *Avoiding lending restrictions*—If the company experiences difficulties, the lender may place restrictive covenants and conditions on a loan. Some of these may limit capital expenditures for a period, reduce shareholder draws and salaries, reduce various expense categories, limit expansion, force staff reductions, provide board representation, reduce research and development expenditures, or force a sale and leaseback on certain assets. Careful planning in a restructuring may avoid these restrictions.

4. *Maintaining competitive prices*—If the business is suffering financially, the management team may decide to reduce prices to secure business. Proper financing can avoid the drop in prices that leads to higher borrowing costs and lower profit margins.

5. *Diversifying lenders*—For the reasons advanced throughout this chapter, it is imperative that the company diversify the mix of lenders and avoid blanket security arrangements. In certain instances, the company may have to change lenders to get out of restrictive covenants.

6. *Seeking professional advice*—The company should realize the relevant professional disciplines that are required for the task at hand. There is a danger that the company assumes that all financial tasks can be performed internally. A do-it-yourself attitude

may be flattering to one's ego but may not get the job done effectively.

7. *Stating proper valuations*—The company should ensure that all aspects of the balance sheet and income statement are properly stated, which means that accounts receivable and inventory are properly recorded. Accounts payable should be complete and aged. Sales and accounts receivable should not have any preinvoiced amounts to inflate sales. Inventory should not include consignment goods. The goods on hand should be owned by the company and not augmented for purposes of an inventory count. Proper valuations will provide a better base from which to prepare projected financial statements. And, it is difficult to obtain the required financing if values keep changing based on new information.

8. *Structuring repayment terms*—During the course of corporate restructuring, the matter of repayment terms will require discussion. The company is well advised to negotiate a variety of options rather than limiting itself to conventional payments. As an example, payments can commence after a grace period of several months to allow for the business to gear up. A minor modification of this allows for payments to be skipped for a few months every year, the few months coinciding with the slow period in the business cycle. A further variation calls for seasonal payments throughout the year that vary in amount from little or nothing in slow periods to larger-than-normal payments in peak periods.

FINANCIAL RATIO CONSIDERATIONS

As part of the restructuring, the company must ensure that the financial picture is not worsening. This involves the review of the traditional ratios that are part of every accounting textbook. However, from a practical financing perspective, some of these are more significant than others and can quickly alert lenders to financial problems. The company must review these ratios when preparing forecasts and ensure that historical and projected numbers are in agreement. Some important areas involve:

1. *Working capital*—This is reviewed by lenders to ensure that the company does not have a cash deficiency during the period of forecasted results. If there is a deficiency, the requested loan amount must be sufficient to cover the shortfall.

2. *Debt to equity*—Lenders are always on the alert that a reasonable relationship exists between borrowed and invested funds. Consistency and quality of earnings can overcome higher debt-to-equity ratios. Normal upper limits of debt to equity for most lenders would be 4 to 1.

3. *Interest coverage*—Lenders expect adequate cash to cover interest payments. The consistency and quality of earnings as well as additional security will affect the tolerance that lenders have for low levels of coverage. A lender may seek to adjust a loan amount to provide for adequate interest coverage. Of course, the company has to ensure that it can still operate effectively with a reduced loan.

4. *Gross margins*—The gross margins are reviewed more for consistency between periods than for other purposes. The margins should be sufficient to absorb general overhead expenses.

CAPITAL EXPENDITURES: ANALYSIS AND DECISION MAKING

V. Bruce Irvine, Professor of Accounting, College of Commerce, University of Saskatchewan

Capital expenditures are relatively large investments from which benefits will occur over a period of several years. As such, capital expenditure decisions reflect management's philosophy and strategy in terms of commitments to future products and services.

Two important implications result. First, capital expenditure analysis is project oriented as opposed to having a short-term orientation. Other financial information systems such as operational budgeting, performance evaluation, and income measurement are short term. Attempting to merge these different time frames can create significant problems when making decisions. Second, it is important to recognize that considerable judgment is required when making capital expenditure decisions. While quantitative analysis is an important aspect of such decisions, the time frame for estimating future net benefits from an expenditure can be quite long. Therefore, the subjectivity and risk involved must be recognized.

While capital expenditures are often examined in the context of management accounting techniques, such decisions are heavily integrated with a company's financing capabilities and costs, behavioral factors, and attitudes toward risk. They also must reflect technology, competition, and inflation. The purpose of this article is to broadly examine the capital expenditure process from a decision-making perspective.

Exhibit 6-1 identifies four basic phases and the related actions associated with capital expenditure decisions:

1. *Initiation*—The need for a capital expenditure must be identified by a person or group within a company.
2. *Evaluation*—If the idea seems reasonable, it is likely to be developed into a proposal for discussion and further refinement. If the exposure through review by others is positive, considerable effort may be put in to develop a formal proposal consistent with the administrative structure, policies, and paperwork of the company.
3. *Appropriation*—The selection phase would examine the proposal in order to evaluate its merits relative to other proposals and company strategy, needs, financial capabilities, risk, and any other factors of importance.
4. *Realization phase*—This is important in that actual expenditures incurred to implement a proposal and the net benefits resulting each year should be compared to planned amounts.

While these four phases characterize the capital expenditure process and should al-

Exhibit 6-1. The Capital Expenditure Decision-Making Process

Actions   *Phases*

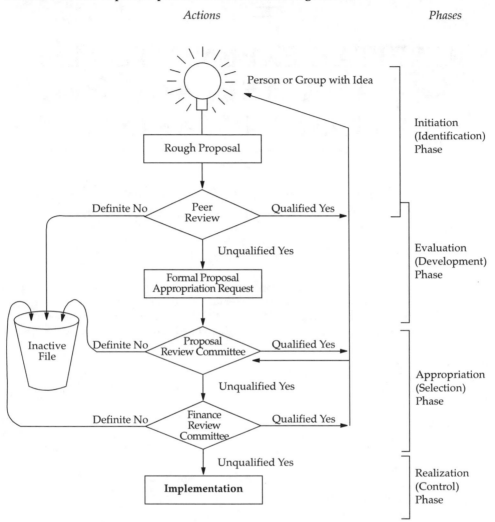

Source: After C. G. Edge and V. B. Irvine, *A Practical Approach to the Appraisal of Capital Expenditures* (Hamilton, Ontario, Canada, The Society of Management Accountants of Canada, 1985), 15; reprinted with permission of the Society of Management Accountants of Canada.

ways be present, it is recognized that the time frame and formality likely varies depending on the nature of a company's management and structure as well as the size and urgency of the expenditure.

Awareness of these four phases provides a useful framework for examining capital expenditure decisions in terms of obtaining a good understanding of specific issues and analytical techniques.

THE INITIATION (IDENTIFICATION) PHASE

The first step in the capital expenditure decision-making process is to come up with an idea for the spending of a large amount of money. Someone in the organization may discover a new potential market for the firm, or changing technology may require more modern assets. Whatever the stimulus, one or more individuals or departments must identify a proposal and bring it to the attention of the company.

THE APPROPRIATION (SELECTION) PHASE

While this is the third phase, considering it first leads to a better understanding of the other phases. To begin, consider yourself a member of a proposal review committee to which several alternative proposals have been presented. Because of various financing and other constraints, all proposals cannot be accepted. Consequently, the question becomes, "What criteria would you consider when comparing the proposals and making an accept/reject decision?" Several criteria are possible:

1. *Maximization of the present value of long-run profits*—The company estimates the investment costs for a capital expenditure and future net cash flows (benefits) from the investment on an annual basis. Then it determines the net present value using an appropriate discount rate for determining how proposals match up to this criterion. Alternatively, the company can determine an internal rate of return for a proposal. This involves finding the discount rate that equates the present value of future net cash flows to the investment cost. The return is compared to a minimum acceptable rate required that also enables ranking alternative proposals.

2. *Risk factors*—Typically, high profitability capital expenditures have a high risk. Consequently, consideration of risk is important when making a decision. Also, the risk of a

particular proposal should be considered within a portfolio of a company's total capital assets. That is, while a particular expenditure may be of high risk, the overall risk to the company may not change substantially because other capital expenditures are of low risk.

When examining risk, it is important to understand what is meant. To some, risk is interpreted as how long it takes to recover the investment cost. This amount of time is called the payback period. More appropriately, risk analysis considers the variability of future net cash flows from a proposal. One way to accomplish this analysis is to estimate a pessimistic, most likely, and optimistic annual net cash flow from an investment and assign a probability to the occurrence of each. Exhibit 6-2 illustrates how this method results in determining an expected value for annual cash flows. By using the expected value of $1,500,000 in a present value analysis or payback calculation, the variability associated with the cash flows would be considered. Using the $2,000,000 most likely amount would ignore this risk and possibly result in incorrectly accepting the project.

3. *Aversion to risk*—Given that information about risk is available, attitudes regarding aversion to risk can influence an accept/reject decision for a proposed capital expenditure. Suppose an investment has an 80-percent probability of generating positive cash inflows each year. A present value analysis could also show high potential profitability. Nevertheless, the proposal may be rejected simply because the decision maker with a high aversion to risk may conclude that the company could not survive if the investment resulted in the $1-million cash loss each year. Alternatively, decision makers with lower

Exhibit 6-2. Risk Assessment

Estimate	Annual Cash Flow	Probability	Cash Flow Times Probability
Pessimistic	−$1,000,000	.2	−$200,000
Most Likely	$2,000,000	.7	$1,400,000
Optimistic	$3,000,000	.1	$300,000
Expected Value of Annual Cash Flow			$1,500,000

aversion to risk would be more inclined to accept the possible loss because of the high probability of increased profitability. While such positions can be exercised only if information on risk is available, what we see here is an attitude of management, rather than the specific quantitative information, being a significant determining factor in reaching a decision.

4. *Impact on reported income*—The net income of a company or operating unit is often considered an important factor in evaluating management's performance. Consequently, decision makers would likely examine the effect of proposals on net income when selecting capital expenditures. When doing this it is important to recognize that net income is an annual accounting measure. It is not the same as annual cash flow, on which determination of long-run profitability is based. It is quite possible that one proposal may result in a future net income pattern that reflects consistent growth while a competing proposal's future net income pattern is very erratic. The latter proposal, however, could have a higher present value of future cash flows.

As with risk aversion, a decision would reflect the decision maker's attitude regarding the results. What we see here is the clash of a period concept (net income) and a project viewpoint (capital expenditure time frame). While it may be argued that the former should be ignored in trying to maximize long-run profitability, this example suggests that it may be difficult for managers to do so.

5. *Company politics*—The previous two criteria suggest reasons why an economically advantageous proposal may not be accepted because of decision makers' attitudes. Other subjective reasons deserve mention in order to have a comprehensive insight to understanding decisions:

- Some companies have an implicit "spread the wealth" philosophy when making capital expenditure decisions, which means there is a belief that each division must have some proposals approved, even if other units have superior proposals in their package. In essence, such a philosophy follows a notion of equity rather than economics.

- Personal biases of decision makers can be an important factor. If a person believes in something and is in a position of power, it is likely to be implemented.
- Decision makers may be influenced by the reputation of those making proposals. If the track record is good, proposals get the benefit of the doubt.
- Some economically profitable proposals may not be proposed by divisions that are already successful. This is because a manager may be evaluated on period-oriented measures (annual income, return on investment). While the company may benefit from an investment proposal, the unit manager's performance may suffer. This phenomenon again indicates the problems that can result by not separating period- and project-oriented decisions.

6. *Environmental factors*—Environmental and social consequences are fairly recent and important aspects to incorporate into capital expenditure decisions. They are growing in significance to the point that some "dirty" assets or projects are almost unsalable. While difficult to quantify, effects of a proposal on the natural environment, community, employees, and other interest groups must be carefully considered. Being socially responsible may not be recognized in terms of profitability, but socially irresponsible decisions are likely to result in significant detrimental consequences.

THE EVALUATION (DEVELOPMENT) PHASE

Different techniques are employed in business to make an accept or reject decision. These are the discounted cash flow methods (net present value or internal rate of return), the payback period calculation, and the accounting rate of return (net income relative to the investment base for each future year). Why do different methods exist? The answer is because different techniques relate to the different criteria for making a decision. The discounted cash flow methods are theoretically superior. They are the only methods that consider cash flows over the entire life of a capital expenditure project and also incorporate the concept of a time value of money. As such, they appropriately provide information to maximize the present value of long-run profitability (criterion 1).

The payback period is viewed as a means of assessing risk (criterion 2). It provides information on how long it takes to recover an investment expenditure. The payback period is somewhat misdirected as a true measure of risk in terms of the variability of cash flows. Nevertheless, payback calculations can be helpful in screening out proposals and in examining proposals of fairly small investment or those investments that are considered automatic, such as the replacement of similar equipment.

The use of the accounting rate of return to evaluate capital expenditure proposals is somewhat of an anomaly. It is based on a non-cash flow measurement of net income. However, to the extent that impact on reported income and performance evaluation (criterion 4 and part of 5) are important in a capital expenditure decision, such a measure does provide a basis for assessing consequences.

What is being suggested here is that there are several criteria against which a capital expenditure proposal can be examined. A company's management should carefully consider the possible criteria and decide which are the important ones in its organizational philosophy, structure, and strategy. While certain quantitative techniques relate to some of the identified criteria, it can be seen that no technique applies to other important criteria. Therefore, decision makers must rely on their judgment abilities when integrating these nonquantifiable factors into their decisions.

THE REALIZATION (CONTROL) PHASE

Accepting a capital expenditure project does not complete the process. The accept decision is based on estimates of the future. Valuable information can be obtained by conducting a postacceptance audit. By comparing estimated to actual investment costs and cash flows, management is able to exercise control. If significant variances occur, it may be necessary to abandon a project. Also, postaudit information can be examined to improve future capital expenditure analysis in the sense of learning from the past.

SOURCES OF FINANCING: TRADITIONAL AND NEW

Robert W. Hiller, Vice-President and Treasurer, General Foods Corporation (Retired)

THE FINANCING FUNCTION

Capital is required to finance both start-up and continuing operations, particularly under the condition of business growth or the need to periodically replace fixed assets. Financing considerations include form, sufficiency, continuing access to sources (availability), and cost. Key sources are the equity and debt markets, both public and private.

The proportions of debt and equity are keyed to the target capital structure of the firm. Traditionally, equity has been viewed as permanent capital. Debt has financed working capital requirements and a portion of fixed assets. While this traditional model retains its validity, developments since the late 1970s have resulted in a significant increase in financing opportunities and flexibility. Facilitated by such factors as globalization and deregulation of capital markets and innovations of "financial engineering," new markets, products, and techniques have been created and continue to evolve.

In addition to financing the firm's requirements for competitively priced capital to support continuing business operations, the chief financial officer (CFO) is also faced with developing and implementing financing plans as part of takeover defenses and corporate restructurings. Clearly, the need to more actively manage the capital structure has taken on added importance. Included in active management are the abilities to rapidly respond to changes in business and financial risk, to change the composition of the capital structure for financial advantage, and to seize market "windows of opportunity" when they occur.

ASSETS TO BE FINANCED

A firm must finance its operating assets, including (1) working capital, principally accounts receivable and inventories; (2) tangible fixed assets, including land, buildings, equipment, and rolling stock; (3) intangible assets, principally intellectual property and goodwill. Given the significant increase in merger and acquisition activity in the past decade, goodwill has been a growing asset category. Goodwill represents the excess of the price paid for a business over the net value of the operating assets acquired. Being intangible in nature, it is usually more difficult to finance on acceptable terms than tangible assets.

The assets financed should be consistent with those required to support the business plan. The financing of excess or underperforming assets should be minimized. How-

ever, there may be strategic reasons, other than financial, for holding such assets temporarily.

Proceeds from the sale of excess and underperforming assets reduce the amount of financing that would otherwise be required. Also, the elimination of such assets can increase the return on investment from the continuing operations. Although this is a disinvestment decision rather than a financing decision, the action has a bearing on the amount and form of financing required.

THE COST OF CAPITAL

Shareholder wealth is created through earning a return on capital in excess of its cost. Operations management is primarily responsible for the returns earned on the capital invested. Financial management is responsible for minimizing the cost of that capital. Both are vital if the "spread" is to be maximized.

Finance theory, subject to simplifying assumptions, holds that the cost of capital of a firm is independent of the proportions of debt and equity in its capital structure. In the "real world" of taxes, imperfect markets and other factors, however prudent the use of debt, may reduce the overall cost of capital. Above a certain level, however, debt financing becomes unavailable, too costly, and risky, thereby having the opposite effect and perhaps endangering the firm.

The cost of debt capital is the effective after-tax interest cost on a yield to maturity basis. It is usually lower than the cost of equity capital because of the deductibility of interest for tax purposes (dividends on share capital are not) and lower risk (debt ranks senior to equity on dissolution).

The cost of equity capital is a required return given the level of the securities markets adjusted for the risk of the common stock. It is somewhat more problematic and difficult to determine with precision. Various methodologies are employed, including, for widely held companies, the sum of:

1. The risk-free yield. Typically the long-term yield on government bonds is used as a proxy.

2. The incremental return from the total equity market. This is called the market risk premium.

3. A premium or deduction to reflect the specific firm's risk characteristics relative to the total equity market. This is determined by the volatility of the firm's stock price compared to the volatility of the market.

The debt and equity percentage rates weighted by their respective proportions in the capital structure provide an estimate of the overall cost of capital of the firm.

THE CAPITAL STRUCTURE DECISION

The appropriate proportion of debt in the capital structure is influenced by various factors. Each should be considered explicitly and objectively. Their respective importance is a matter of management judgment tempered by what the capital markets will support. As such, there is no "right" ratio but rather an "optimal" range tailored to a specific company. Over time the range may change based on shifts in external market or internal business conditions. These factors include:

- *Reducing the cost of capital*—A considered use of debt may reduce the company's cost of capital, thereby enhancing its competitiveness and, prospectively, increasing the return to its shareholders.
- *Nature of the industry*—Capital structures vary significantly by industry segment. Industries that are profitable, predictable, and noncyclical access and support more debt safely than segments with the opposite characteristics.
- *Nature of the assets*—If assets are tangible and readily salable under conditions of business distress, higher levels of debt in the structure can be supported. This provides a second level of security to the lender. The first is a successful business operation to permit servicing and retirement of the debt.

- *Ability to service*—Debt financing must be serviced, both interest and principal, in good times and in bad. Failure to do so results in default. Barring successful renegotiation or replacement of the debt could result in bankruptcy. The cash flow projections, a subset of the business plan, must demonstrate the ability to meet the servicing requirement and should provide a safety factor to allow for the possibility of future adversity.
- *Management and owner attitudes*—The tolerance of the management and owners to risk must also be given recognition in this decision. In addition to the business risk inherent in operations, there is also financial risk in the capital structure. Examples include adverse changes in interest rates and the inability to access markets when financing is required. Compounding high business risk with high financial risk may yield an intolerable result.

TRADITIONAL SOURCES

The debt and equity markets are the principal sources of capital to finance the firm's business operations. These markets are large, well developed, and often volatile. Also, the separation between the two markets is not clean. There are debt instruments with equity characteristics such as convertible bonds and equity instruments with debt characteristics such as preferred stock.

From the standpoint of the firm, financing is frequently categorized by short-, medium-, and long-term debt financing and equity financing.

Short-Term Debt Financing

Working capital is the net investment in short-term assets to support the day-to-day operations of the business, such as trade receivables, inventories, and prepaid items. The principal offsetting liabilities are accounts payable and accruals such as accrued taxes and payroll.

The proportion of working capital to total assets and the degree of volatility vary greatly by industry. For example, working capital management and financing is critical to a manufacturer or distributor of consumer goods. Such a firm has a high investment in receivables and inventories, is subject to varying levels of demand because of seasonality, and sells goods that are price sensitive. For these reasons, a large amount of working capital financing may be needed. Alternatively, in the services sector working capital levels are lower and more stable. Hence, working capital financing is less critical to company fortunes.

Working capital should be actively managed and kept to an efficient minimum to reduce the amount of external financing required. Examples include:

- *Trade receivables*—reviewing and altering the terms of sale to provide a customer incentive for faster payment; more aggressive collection management.
- *Inventories*—clearing out slow-moving items; providing contraseasonal buying incentives; adopting a just-in-time operations policy with suppliers and customers, thereby reducing inventories at all levels.
- *Accounts payable*—not paying before due or discount date; negotiating extended terms with vendors.
- *Other*—minimizing prepayment periods, for example, pay monthly rather than annually in advance for items requiring prepayment; maximizing accrual periods, for example, change from weekly to biweekly payroll periods.

Many of these suggestions merely shift the burden and related cost. The shift may be direct, such as increasing the customer discount for prompt payment, or hidden, such as increased supplier prices to cover higher inventory carrying costs.

The sources of financing for working capital vary with the size, history, and prospects of the firm. Large, established, and particularly multinational companies will have access to more markets and vehicles than smaller firms.

Inventory/Receivable Financing. Typically, the smaller firm and start-up firm will arrange its short-term financing through commercial banks. Loans may be tied to and secured by specific trade receivables and inventories. These loans vary but are commonly limited to 75 percent of receivables and 50 percent of inventories. This provides an adequate security cushion for the lender. The interest rate is usually pegged at a premium above the prime rate. Points or a commitment fee may be additional.

An alternate means of financing receivables is factoring, which involves the sale of the trade receivables to a third party at a discount on either a "recourse" or a "nonrecourse" basis.

Line of Credit. Following start-up, it is common for an operating line of credit to be established with a commercial bank, proportionate to the working capital financing required. Such a line provides greater freedom as specific assets are not pledged as security. Money is available as needed provided the bank has the funds and material negative changes in the borrower's condition or prospects have not occurred. It is not unusual for the lender to request a personal guarantee from the owners as additional security.

An operating line can be replaced or supplemented with a revolving line of credit. A revolver is a binding agreement, reviewed and renewed periodically, providing for an agreed maximum amount of short-term financing to be extended. Costs are negotiable but typically include interest on the portion of the line used on a variable rate basis (prime plus), and a commitment fee on the unused portion. While slightly more costly than an unsecured line of credit, the revolver provides assurance of availability when needed, is often arranged for a longer period (one to three years is common), and may have the right of conversion into a term loan.

Commercial Paper. For large, established companies, it has become common to set up a commercial paper program under which the borrower issues short-term unsecured promissory notes in its own name for varying periods. Such programs, for most borrowers, are used as supplementary to their bank arrangements. Back-up bank lines are usually maintained to provide additional comfort to the lender along with a satisfactory commercial paper rating from one of the recognized rating agencies.

The commercial paper market is large, active, and sophisticated, with a dealer network handling the placement and redemption for all but the largest borrowers. Costs to the borrower are typically below the bank prime rate. For multinational enterprises, it is also possible to access similar facilities in Europe, where base pricing is off of the London Inter Bank Offer Rate (LIBOR).

Acceptances. For firms engaged in importing, banker's acceptances have become an important and growing source of financing. Terms are negotiated between the importer and exporter and a letter of credit is secured from the importer's bank. A time draft is drawn and, once accepted by the importer's bank, provides the financing for the importer for the term of sale period. The draft itself is a negotiable instrument and can be bought and sold.

Medium-Term Debt Financing

Bank term or installment loans are frequently one of the first forms of medium-term financing employed. Such loans are a natural extension of the short-term financing relationship with the banks and are commonly in the one-to seven-year range. Because of the longer period, terms and costs tend to be more onerous than revolvers. Regular payments on principal are necessary and a prepayment privilege, with or without penalty, can be negotiated.

Sources of funds for term loans are banks; thrift institutions, such as savings and loans; and commercial finance companies. Such loans are often asset backed, such as when the financing pays for equipment that is pledged as collateral.

Larger companies can access medium-term funds on an unsecured basis through a variety of sources, both domestic and foreign, such as the EuroCredit market. These are typically referred to as medium-term notes

and are privately placed. Larger issues are syndicated. Interest may be fixed or floating.

Underpinning both short- and medium-term financing requirements is the need for solid commercial bank relationships. Such relationships, earned over time, provide the continuity and reasonable assurance of ongoing support under varying conditions.

Long-Term Debt Financing

Long-term debt financing is generally for periods longer than seven years and is considered part, along with equity, of the permanent capital of the firm. Companies can arrange longer-term financing through capital loans from the banking sector as well as from insurance companies, pension funds, and private investors. Such loans are often secured by the specific assets funded.

For large corporations, most long-term financing is in the form of bonds, either secured by specific assets and called mortgage bonds, or secured by the general credit of the firm and called debentures. Mortgage bonds are particularly appropriate for project financing such as plant complexes and commercial real estate. Debentures, while perhaps issued to fund a particular investment, provide the issuer with greater flexibility to redeploy specific assets at later dates without first having to gain the consent of the security holder. Further, debentures may be senior or subordinated, the latter ranking behind the senior issue on default. Much of the noninvestment grade, including "junk bond," financings, fall into this latter category.

Bond issues usually have requirements to retire a portion of the principal throughout the life. This may be by way of a sinking fund to purchase in the market and retire a given amount of the bonds each year or by way of serial bonds, which have periodic maturities staged over the life of the issue.

Most public issues also have a call feature allowing the issuers to retire, periodically, all or a portion of the outstanding issue. This would be exercised if it gave rise to financial advantage, such as accompanying a decline in market interest rates. If the issuer has excess liquid assets beyond those necessary to take advantage of any call feature, it can engage in open-market purchases to retire additional debt.

Interest rates on these long-term issues are usually fixed, although one variation (not widely used) is the income bond, which only has an interest requirement when earnings of the firm are sufficient. As might be expected, the interest rate on such bonds is higher and often cumulative. Participating bonds, as the name implies, provide a variable sharing in the success of the venture financed as an additional incentive.

In order to more readily access markets and to minimize costs, at least in the early years, various other forms of "sweeteners" have been added to the basic debt instrument. The convertible bond is widely used, giving the holder the right to convert the bond into a fixed number of shares, at certain times, priced at about a 20-percent premium to the stock price on date of issue.

While such a feature provides certain advantages for the borrower (market access, lower interest rate), it can become costly in the long run. For example, it causes an "overhang" in the market for the company's stock, thereby influencing the price and, on exercise, dilutes the current stockholders' proportionate interest.

The public long-term debt markets are large and sophisticated. Investment bankers, which increasingly include the investment banking arms of money center banks, design, price, and distribute issues. Issue ratings are usually secured to enhance marketability. SEC (Securities and Exchange Commission) and similar requirements must be met and followed.

Leasing. Leasing is a large and flexible source of traditional financing. Almost any physical fixed asset can be leased and the term can range from a few years to several decades, limited only by the life of the asset itself.

The traditional operating lease provides that, in return for use of the asset, the lessee (the user) would pay a fixed periodic rent to the lessor (the owner of the asset). At the end of the lease term, the property would revert to the lessor and the lessee would have no remaining obligations.

Numerous modifications have been introduced over the years to "custom tailor" the contract to specific circumstances and to optimize the tax position of the respective parties. These, for example, include variable rents, purchase options and puts, and responsibility for insurance and property taxes.

Lease financing is used extensively for equipment, rolling stock, and building space and is not limited to new assets. The sale and leaseback of an existing asset has become a common source of financing. For large-scale projects, leveraged leasing is often used. This introduces a long-term lender to the equation, in addition to the lessor and lessee. Lessors are varied and include manufacturers who lease their products directly or through a captive finance subsidiary, banks, leasing companies, and partnerships.

Sale of Stock. Equity financing represents the base level of the financing of the firm. It is the owners' equity. Hence, it bears the final risk and rewards. It is the foundation supporting the remainder of the capital structure.

The start-up common equity investment is typically provided by the owner-operator of the firm. It grows with success: earnings less any dividends paid. Success also provides the ability to raise additional equity capital. Eventually, an initial public offering can be made and followed by subsequent offerings to raise additional permanent capital.

Equity is often divided between preferred and common stock with each further divided into several classes. Preferred stock has many of the attributes of subordinated debt. It ranks senior to common equity on dissolution, has a preference over common stock as to dividends, which are usually fixed and cumulative, is restricted as to voting rights, and may be redeemable. Dividends need not be paid unless declared legally by the board of directors and the dividends are not deductible for tax purposes.

Common stock enjoys the unlimited residual rights. It is sometimes divided into several classes. Distinction between classes often centers on voting rights in order to keep control of the company in narrow (often the founder's) hands.

Equity financing shares the ownership and future growth with new investors. As such, a new issue must be considered carefully. The market must be receptive, value the stock fairly, and the issue should be consistent with achieving or maintaining the target capital structure. Existing shareholders' interests may be protected through preemptive rights, allowing them to maintain their proportionate ownership through the right to subscribe, on a privileged basis, in any new issue.

Investment bankers are retained to market the issue, which may be underwritten by the syndicating group or sold on a best efforts basis. Because of market volatility, timing is critical to achieving the best price and distribution. As in any public issue, compliance with securities laws and regulations is essential.

NEW SOURCES

The 1980s saw the rapid expansion of several markets, perhaps most notably the financial futures, the EuroCredit, and the noninvestment grade debt (junk bond) market in the United States. The severe contraction of the latter need not be viewed as failure but rather one, in hindsight, of overly aggressive credit-granting practices, tested and found wanting as the economy weakened. The growth in these markets, however, for much of the period was supported by a generally strong world economy and by progressive deregulation and globalization of capital markets.

These opened up new financing sources for the firm. CFOs were being faced with the challenge of financing accelerated growth on a cost-effective and controlled-risk basis. Custom solutions were designed and, if received well by the markets, quickly disseminated, creating new financing techniques. The investment banking sector acted as a catalyst in the matching of growing pools of capital with business needs through innovative product design.

From the borrowers' perspective, three developments were particularly noteworthy: (1) cost reduction through swaps; (2) the management of risk through hedging; and (3) "designer" products to meet particular needs. The following brief descriptions are illustra-

tive and not exhaustive. Further, many financing strategies and particular products are tax driven and may have accounting implications that must be considered.

Swaps

First developed in 1982 and expanded greatly since then, the interest rate swap is a technique that arbitrages different corporate credits, financial instruments, and capital and money markets. The interest rate swap brings together borrowers, either directly or through an intermediary, who are able to secure lower pricing relative to each other in either the floating or fixed-rate markets.

The basis for a swap is established when one party has access to lower-cost fixed-rate funds but seeks a floating rate obligation and the other has access to lower-cost floating-rate funds but seeks fixed-rate financing. As long as at least one party is able to obtain better pricing than the other on the type of financing it initially raises but does not intend to keep, a swap allows both parties to capitalize on the resultant cost advantage.

Each party remains responsible for its own borrowing. The swap transaction is based on an exchange of payments representing interest on the notational amount. The fixed-rate borrower pays interest on a floating-rate basis and vice versa. The payments may be offset, thereby minimizing credit exposure, or an intermediary, such as a bank, is used. While domestic swaps are arranged, cost savings are often greater on an international basis because of structural differences between the various markets.

The advantages of interest-rate swaps include cost savings, speed, simplicity, minimal disclosure requirements, and low credit risk. Disadvantages are few. A currency swap is a private transaction that allows a company to alter the currency of its outstanding liabilities. It may allow a lower-cost loan in a given currency than is attainable under a direct borrowing. The cash flows, representing principal and interest, are swapped into the other currency by means of forward contracts.

The two forms of swap can be combined. One such product has been called CIRCUS (combined interest rate and currency swap).

The swap market has grown enormously since the mid-1980s and is now considered one of the basic tools to lower costs and enhance flexibility.

Hedging

The ability to manage risk has become an important requirement for the CFO. Market interest rates have become increasingly volatile and, in response, financial futures markets have grown rapidly.

Hedging, using the futures market, is the process of neutralizing or significantly reducing financial risk. The risk is inherent and does not cease to exist. It is merely transferred from the original risk bearer to another risk bearer. While the futures hedge protects against unfavorable changes in price owed, the hedger also forgoes any benefit from a favorable change in the price.

In addition to futures contracts, options are increasingly used to manage risk. An option contract creates an obligation for one party and a right, but no obligation, for the other to sell (a put) or buy (a call) at a fixed price for a given period of time. There is a real cost, the option premium, but also the opportunity for upside gain. The corporate hedger might analogize options to insurance. The payment of a premium is made to avoid possible future real or lost opportunity costs.

There are two fundamental reasons for hedging. The first is to reduce risk. Hedging allows issuers of debt to partially or fully protect themselves from market changes adverse to those anticipated, such as rates rising before debt issuance or falling afterward. Hedging assures the issuer of either an acceptable financial cost or worst case, depending on the hedging technique employed. The second is the ability to separate the timing decision from market opportunities. Pricing and funding can be effectively separated—that is, price today and fund later or fund today and price later.

An example of hedging risk on floating rate debt is through a "cap." The cap refers to the maximum interest rate that must be paid, even if rates move higher. Such a risk-limiting device can be provided through the purchase of put options, or through a private transaction with the lender. As a cost offset, a "floor" (minimum rate paid) could also be provided. The two together are referred to as a "collar."

"Designer" Products. The recent past has seen the creation of new products to meet needs of investors and borrowers alike. While all are constructed from the basic debt and equity building blocks, product customization to meet particular requirements has resulted in a sophisticated balancing of market access, cost, and risk.

A reading of "tombstone" ads and corporate balance sheets no longer provides the whole financing story. Swaps and other hedging activities such as futures, forward rate agreements, and options are frequently used to convert the original disclosed issue to an end result with additional or quite different features.

Further, markets are volatile. They can and do expand and contract quickly. Similarly, product features undergo frequent change in response to market conditions and in the constant pursuit of advantage. The growth of zero-coupon (deep discount) and debt with warrant (puts, calls, conversion) instruments ideally matched investors with borrowers.

An excellent example of the foregoing was the 1990 Berkshire Hathaway $900-million principal amount of fifteen-year zero-coupon-subordinated convertible notes yielding the company $400 million in gross proceeds. This issue allows the investor to convert to common stock at any time but without accrued interest or to put the notes back to the company after five or ten years, but without premium. Also, the company may redeem the notes in three years, thereby obtaining added flexibility. If fully converted, the stock dilution would only be 3.5 percent. The company estimated that this structure saved over 400 basis points versus straight debt. Elegant in design and economic in result!

CASH MANAGEMENT

Cecilia L. Wagner, Associate Professor, School of Business, Seton Hall University

As a result of new technologies and increasing sophistication among corporate treasurers, the area of cash management has changed a great deal over the years. Time is money, particularly when we are talking about the time value of idle funds. Treasurers routinely speed up the flow of funds into investment accounts of the company and take steps to optimize the disbursing of monies. This process requires an understanding of the structure of the banking system and different concepts related to the efficient management of cash.

FLOAT

The term *float* refers to the time periods when cash is not available as a result of lags between the sale of goods or provision of services and the cash on hand in a form that can be disbursed or invested. Four kinds of float can be identified:

1. *Billing float*—time between the sale and the mailing of its invoice.
2. *Mail float*—time period during which the check is being handled by the post office, messenger service, or other means of delivery.
3. *Check processing float*—time required to sort, record, and deposit the check after it has arrived in the company's mailroom.
4. *Bank processing float*—time from the deposit of the check to the crediting of funds in the seller's account.

A major task of cash management is the control of float.

KIND OF BANK

A large corporation should design a cash management system that makes use of cash control features of the banking system. Two distinct categories of banks may be identified.

1. *Depository bank*—This institution specializes in collecting checks, processing them quickly, and making funds available to the firm. Such a bank offers a range of services designed to speed up collections. Generally, depository banks are located in large cities convenient to airlines and other means of transportation.
2. *Disbursing bank*—This institution does not specialize in rapidly receiving and processing checks. Since checks take longer to clear, the float is extended for the individual or firm that writes the check. These banks offer services that ensure that checks will be properly covered by funds in the account when presented for payment. At the same time, it is not necessary to leave large idle balances on hand prior to presentation of the checks.

KIND OF ACCOUNT

A cash management system should distinguish among three categories of bank accounts.

The *operating account* is used to pay bills and conduct the other daily activities of the firm. The balance in this account must be sufficient to satisfy the bank's requirements and provide cash as checks are presented for payment. Usually, the bank does not pay interest on balances in these accounts, and service charges are paid by the company.

The investment account is used to hold funds in excess of operating needs. The institution will pay interest on funds held in this account on a daily basis. Funds may be transferred from this account to other forms of liquid investment, such as the purchase of marketable securities.

The lockbox account is a post office box under the control of a bank. The bank providing the lockbox service collects the mail and deposits the checks directly into the firm's account. The bank then sends a copy of the checks, along with letters or other materials, to the company's accounting department. The lockbox account may be the firm's operating account and may exist at the firm's regular disbursing and depository bank. It may also exist at a bank where the only activity is the receipt of checks into the lockbox account and the transfer of money from that account to another bank.

MOVEMENT AND AVAILABILITY OF FUNDS

An important aspect of cash management is the ability to move funds between accounts and banks. If all collections and disbursements occur in accounts at the same bank, this task is straightforward. The bank moves funds using bookkeeping entries in its computer. When different banks are involved, the task becomes more complicated. Three kinds of movements are commonly used.

1. *Paper transfer with individual checks*—The treasurer can write a check on an account and deposit it in another account. For small dollar amounts, this is a slow but effective way to transfer money.

2. *Paper transfer with depository transfer check*—A depository transfer check (DTC) is a nonnegotiable demand deposit instrument drawn by a bank and payable to a firm or individual. It is used to move money between banks and is generally a faster vehicle for movement than an individual check. The DTC can be written by either the receiving or sending bank; in either case, the movement of funds normally takes only a single day. Thus, a DTC drawn on Tuesday means funds are available in the receiving bank account on Wednesday.

3. *Electronic transfer*—The movement of money in the banking system without the use of paper is referred to as electronic fund transfer (EFT). This is accomplished by wire transfers, electronic depository transfer checks, and direct computer transactions where instructions are typed on a screen and transmitted to banks. Electronic transfers can be accomplished using facilities of the Federal Reserve System or private services offered by large banks. Electronic transfer is the fastest way to move money between banks.

Concentration banking refers to a system of centralizing corporate cash with a goal of controlling the movement of funds and minimizing idle cash balances. A concentration bank is designated to receive funds from lockboxes or other accounts at depository banks. Electronic or depository transfer check movements are made automatically, according to the instructions of the firm. The concentration bank reports available balances daily, so the firm can take maximum advantage of investment opportunities.

To manage the collection of funds properly, the firm should know the bank's policies on converting funds from ledger balances to available funds. Such policies exist within a framework that assists the Federal Reserve in managing the money supply. Three rules apply.

First, the Federal Reserve allows the banking system to provide availability to one party only. Both the drawer and payee on a check cannot have the funds available in a bank account. The check must clear before funds can be available. Although this is a general rule, the Federal Reserve recognizes that delays in clearing can hamper an effective banking system. Hence, an exception exists to this rule.

If clearing cannot take place in two days, the Federal Reserve allows banks to make funds available. Thus, a check deposited on Monday will be available on Wednesday even if the check cannot clear by that day.

Second, funds are made available on each banking day. Thus, if the depository bank allows the funds to be available on Tuesday, the disbursing bank must not allow the funds to be available the same day.

Third, once the first two rules are met, banks are allowed to set their own policies. If a bank is concerned that a check will not clear, it may withhold availability until it verifies that the clearing has taken place.

Bank Policies on Availability

Banks follow a variety of different policies on when funds can be converted from ledger balances to available funds. Common policies are:

- *By individual check*—Large banks with computerized clearing schedules are able to determine when individual checks will clear. These banks can record each check and use an availability schedule to convert ledger balances to available funds.
- *By average availability*—Some banks do not have the capability to determine individual check availability. Consequently, banks use an estimate of the average availability. As an example, since most checks clear in one day, the policy can be one day for all checks received before 2 P.M.
- *By posting date*—Small banks might not have the capability to distinguish between ledger and available balances. The Federal Reserve allows these banks to post checks and give availability when posted. In effect, this is one-day availability since the posting is done overnight.

Clearing for a Depository Bank

A depository bank that specializes in rapid clearing of checks can speed up availability of funds by using different methods of clearing, including:

- *Intrabank*—This clearing occurs when a check is drawn on a bank and deposited in the same bank.
- *Direct send*—This exists when banks clear checks by messenger.
- *Regional check processing center (RCPC)*—Over forty RCPCs have been established in urban areas to allow banks to meet at a given time and location for the purpose of clearing checks. On the availability schedule, times are given for all banks in these cities. This generally indicates that an RCPC, or clearinghouse, exists to assist in clearing checks.
- *Correspondent relationship*—If a check is drawn on a bank that is not a member of a clearinghouse, it may clear through a correspondent bank that is a member. In these situations, the correspondent bank picks up the checks at the clearinghouse and gives them to the drawee bank to post to the depository bank's account.
- *Federal Reserve System*—Many checks are cleared using the facilities of the Federal Reserve district banks. The Federal Reserve charges for these services.

MANAGING DISBURSEMENTS

A disbursement is any expenditure of cash by a firm, whether for the purpose of paying bills, distributing cash dividends, or transferring funds. Efficient disbursing is a key element of total cash management. A disbursement system should have low operating costs, provide accurate management reports, and extend disbursement float where practical and reasonable. Several disbursement techniques are available:

1. *Electronic fund transfer (EFT)*—Cash management systems can make use of the electronic movement of funds. Transactions are recorded on magnetic tape or disk storage and cleared directly using automation. The transactions included range from the payment of salaries to employees to the transfer of millions of dollars to retire loans.

2. *Zero balance account disbursing*—This procedure involves using a regular checking

account in which the firm is permitted to leave no idle funds on hand. Banks offering this service allow the firm to write checks that will clear against operating accounts containing no funds. The checks clear through normal channels and are presented for collection at the bank in the evening. After processing the check, the bank automatically transfers funds from the company's concentration or master account.

3. *Remote disbursing*—This is the practice of using a disbursing bank that is not a member of a clearinghouse and is located outside a major metropolitan area. Checks drawn on such a bank will require more time to clear than checks drawn on money center banks. If a firm writes checks on such a bank, the checks will take more time to clear and the firm will have additional funds to invest.

THE EFFECTS
OF FINANCIAL
DEREGULATION

Bruce Lunergan, Partner, Ash, Craig, and Thornton

TYPES OF DEREGULATION

Deregulation describes a situation in which restrictions are lessened, not eliminated. In the banking world, complete elimination of state controls, such as that experienced in the airlines industry, is not possible. A complete absence of regulation could jeopardize the integrity of a system designed to protect the depositor's funds. For the commercial banker, deregulation represents legislative change that impacts the bank's ability to compete equitably with other financial services suppliers.

Two types of bank deregulation can be identified. *Functional deregulation* allows financial institutions to broaden their current services to customers. For example, banks would be able to offer services previously available at other institutions. Such deregulation is normally opposed by suppliers of securities, real estate, and insurance services. In addition, there is a regulatory and consumer concern that allowing banks to expand their services into risky areas may result in more failures.

In the United States, the principal outcome of *geographic deregulation* would be an increase in interstate banking. Full-scale branching across state lines is generally restricted. Other countries, such as Canada, have no such restrictions. The result is fewer, and relatively larger, banks.

Geographic deregulation has taken place in the United States under an amendment of the Bank Holding Company Act. Commercial banks have been allowed to expand their services across state boundaries through acquisitions of other banks. This amendment allows interstate acquisitions based on mutual agreement by the respective states. The concept of geographic expansion is opposed by community banks who fear the increasing concentration of power within the largest banks.

CHANGES IN U.S. FINANCIAL MARKETS

Banks in the United States continue to be faced with a web of antiquated laws and regulations governing the financial services industry. Until the 1980s, the McFadden Act of 1927 and the Bank Holding Company Acts of 1956 and 1970 made it difficult for banks to consolidate across state lines. The Glass-Steagall Act of 1933 separated commercial and investment banking activities. In combination these acts restrained competition among banks, gave banks advantages over nonbank financial service companies, and forced customers to use banks for the majority of their financial services.

The industrial boom that started in 1940 saw the emergence of large companies whose growth continued into the 1980s. During this time, banks were the main supplier of funds for these organizations. In turn, big depositors and high-quality corporate borrowers supported the growth in the banking industry. Banks were able to maintain stability and high profit levels by imposing high service charges.

In the 1970s, banks began to lose market share as corporations began shifting their financial activities to other financial institutions. Big depositors transferred billions of dollars out of bank accounts into money market mutual funds, which were not subject to interest rate ceilings. Commercial paper became a cheaper source of short-term funds than bank loans. The movement of money away from the banks exploded during the 1980s. Securitization of assets, which is the packaging and sale by investment banks of mortgages, car loans, and credit card receivables, began on a large scale. This process removed assets from the balance sheets of financial institutions.

Banks also lost market share in other lines of business, such as automobile financing. For example, General Motors Acceptance Corporation (GMAC) became the largest U.S. commercial lender. General Electric Capital arranged leases for aircraft and AT&T and Sears issued millions of credit cards. This was in contrast to the situation in Canada, where the banks' share of the residential mortgage market increased during the 1980s.

The International Scene

At the international level, changes also affected financial institutions. The most important factor influencing the growth of international capital markets was significant trade imbalances in the industrialized countries. As a result, international financial systems had to influence domestic financial systems. As an example, in 1987, the Bank for International Settlements in Basil, Switzerland, established minimum standards so banks in one country could not have advantages over those in another country.

U.S. banks have lost market share in international markets. Developments in Japan and the European Community suggest that the current restrictions on the U.S. financial system may further dampen the international competitive position of U.S. financial institutions. In Europe there is a movement toward community-wide banking. In Japan, discussions have begun to reform the separation of commercial and investment banking. Should both of these events occur, European and Japanese financial institutions will benefit from a larger deposit base and be able to offer a greater number of financial services than U.S. financial institutions. The dwindling presence of American banking and financial services in foreign centers is causing concern among bankers and nonfinancial organizations in the United States and abroad.

Regulatory Responses to Changing Conditions

While safety and the protection of funds were the primary goals of early legislation, quality and price of financial services and a lack of competition became the main issues by the 1970s. U.S. legislators passed laws to reform in the financial system including the following:

■ In the early 1970s, Congress passed amendments to the Bank Holding Company Act that expanded permissible activities for bank holding companies.

■ In 1971, the Hunt Commission concluded that previous attempts to regulate the flow of funds had resulted in inefficient markets. The commission recommended that competition be increased by eliminating interest rate ceilings on deposits, allowing depository financial institutions to offer a full range of time deposits, allowing depository institutions to offer checking account services, and broadening the lending powers of institutions.

■ In 1980, the Depository Institutions Deregulation and Monetary Control Act expanded the lending abilities of thrifts and gave them the right to apply to the Federal Reserve for credit.

■ In 1982, the Garn–St. Germain Depository Institutions Act was passed. Its objective was to accelerate the deregulation of deposit pricing by offering a new money market deposit account. It also attempted to revitalize the savings and loans industry by allowing it to participate in commercial real estate lending and development.

■ In 1987, Congress enacted the Competitive Equality Banking Act, which gave "grandfather" protection to so-called nonbanks established before March 5, 1987, to offer commercial banking services. However, it prevented bank holding companies from forming their own nonbank banks. The act also denied bank holding companies and stand-alone banks the power to sell new securities, insurance, and real estate.

■ In 1989, the Glass-Steagall Act was amended to increase the allowable contribution of securities activities to a bank's total earnings from 5 percent to 10 percent.

Although the Hunt Commission and other studies called for more deregulation and greater reliance on market conditions, history has shown that significant financial legislation is more likely to occur during major disruptions in the financial markets. For example, high inflation, interest rate increases, and severe disintermediation as a result of securitization in the late 1970s drove the Monetary Control Act of 1980.

In an effort to improve the competitiveness and stability of financial institutions, the U.S. Treasury Department released a study in 1991. The study contained proposals in five areas: (1) recapitalizing deposit insurance; (2) eliminating barriers against interstate banking; (3) abolishing the separation of commercial and investment banking; (4) permitting the ownership of banks by industrial companies; (5) streamlining industry supervision. To what extent these five components may be approved by the government is uncertain. However, the discussions began and the issues are receiving increased attention.

DEREGULATION'S IMPACT ON FINANCIAL INSTITUTIONS

We may expect a number of impacts on financial institutions if deregulation trends continue, including:

1. *Restructuring of financial institutions*—As more regulatory barriers are relaxed or removed, hybrid institutions will emerge. The result will be a marketplace where a handful of players operate as full-service financial companies. A substantial number of smaller institutions will continue to compete in specialized areas, most often under the ownership, or as an affiliate, of a larger holding company.

The main advantages of merging and restructuring will be cost savings associated with branch closures, staff reduction, the sharing of clearinghouses, joint marketing and advertising efforts, and the integration of electronic networking systems and computer systems.

2. *Increasing technological cost*—Computers linked with satellite communications networks have reduced the financial world to a "a global village." Financial institutions have spent millions of dollars on systems that allow global quotation, trading, recording,

and monitoring of financial transactions. Communication networks can automatically transfer huge amounts of information from one part of the globe to any other. As financial institutions vie for clients worldwide, they must be connected to these global networks and carry the costs of using them.

3. *Increasing emphasis on product availability*—Banks will modify their product and services mix to better meet market demands. A customer's decision to use a certain financial institution will be based more on product availability and less on long-term relationships with that institution. Corporate treasurers will demand access to currencies, maturities, and pricing structures as their awareness of available opportunities increases.

4. *A new breed of financial manager*—As overcapacity and narrower margins plague the industry, financial managers will need to be aggressive, creative, and flexible in order to maintain profit levels. They will have to be more knowledgeable and provide new services quickly given shorter development cycles of domestic and international financial products.

DEREGULATION'S IMPACT ON CORPORATIONS

We may expect a number of impacts on companies using financial services if deregulation trends continue, including:

1. *Use of external advisers*—Corporate financial managers are less likely to be aware of new financial innovations as they occur. As generalists, controllers have to deal with the vast array of new financial innovations. Given the large amount of resources, both in time and personnel, and the degree of specialist knowledge required to make decisions, the corporation's managers will most likely rely on external advisers to identify and use financial services.

2. *Improved management information systems*—As the financial services industry changes worldwide and barriers are reduced, corporations will need information systems integrating a host of financial transactions and information.

3. *Increased cost of financial services*—The cost of searching for tailored financial packages will be paid by the corporation. More time and money will be required to provide made-to-measure packages. Another potential cost rise may occur as excess capacity and the number of competitors in the financial services industry are reduced.

4. *Leveraging with floats*—A float is a sum of money that is in transit—a check that has been issued and not yet cleared. Under geographic deregulation, a corporation's ability to use floats in its scheduling of payments will decrease substantially.

CONCLUSION

The pace of change in financial markets is accelerating. Many of the changes can be traced to external influences, especially the integration of global markets. Although deregulation has taken place worldwide, changes in the U.S. financial system are surfacing at a slower pace than those emerging in other countries. The existing laws do not support the new international climate. Consequently, without the liberalization of existing laws, U.S. banks will find it difficult to compete both domestically and internationally.

Discussions and resolutions of the Treasury proposals will definitely alter the U.S. banking industry. An environment must be created in which U.S. financial strength can match that of other countries and in which the necessary protection of American ownership remains intact.

GLOBAL FINANCIAL THINKING

John Huguet, President, Commonwealth Construction Company

The highest standard of living in the world is found in North America. It is based on Porter's principles of national competitive advantage, which existed long before Porter analyzed them. In free market economies, the United States and Canada have balanced the needs of society, government, and business with a skilled work force that has used applied management to exploit natural resources.

There are challenges ahead. Natural resources are in decline or becoming expensive. Education is not keeping up with the rest of the world. Management practices and technology are being matched in economic systems in different areas of the world. For anyone—not just North Americans—to compete, products and services will have to deliver value in a new context. The finance function must support this effort.

Global financial thinking requires companies to determine priorities for investing their capital and expending funds in operating budgets. Some issues for the allocation of resources are:

- *Quality*—How much should be expended to ensure world-class quality? What percent of profits should be reinvested in projects designed to achieve creative and innovative products?
- *Education and training*—What programs are needed to create and maintain a skilled work force? How can we empower our people?
- *Technology*—What investments are needed to ensure that operating areas make the proper use of new technologies? To ensure the efficiencies and quality available from modern machinery and telecommunications?
- *Markets and competitive advantage*—What should be spent to reach the new markets for our products and services? What capital is needed to use global sourcing as a competitive response to creating our products?

CHANGING FINANCIAL MARKETS

The pressures to compete in a worldwide framework are impacting financial markets in significant ways, including:

- *Worldwide financing viewpoint*—Once upon a time, large companies sought much of their debt and equity financing within the bounds of their national financial markets. This is no longer true, as national markets are losing their independence and becoming integrated with markets all over the world.
- *Transnational investing*—Companies are pursuing higher returns in every corner

of the world, responding quickly to supply and demand factors using computerized models and real-time telecommunications.

- *Transnational financing*—Companies are raising funds using swaps and an unlimited variety of new debt instruments in a continuous effort to lower their cost of funds.

As companies move further afield to fulfill their financial functions, they must recognize new exposures, including:

- *Transfer risks*—Money is moving at rapid rates in a global network. Are all the institutions sufficiently strong? What happens if one institution collapses? Will it even be possible to sort out who pays for what?
- *Reporting risks*—Banks and other institutions use different accounting approaches and standards for capital adequacy. A company must assess whether its foreign partners are financially strong and able to uphold their portion of ventures and operations.
- *Timing risks*—Financial markets are communications driven. Fluctuations in exchange rates and commodity prices occur between the time of offer, acceptance, and final settlement. Companies must determine whether their mechanisms are adequate for the systems they use to move money and conduct their other financial transactions.
- *Currency position risks*—Companies are holding or owing different currencies at different times of the year or in response to the cycle of their markets and sales. The possible disequilibrium from currency exposure can be significant.
- *Political risks*—Governments respond to pressures reflecting local conditions and circumstances. This can pose serious problems with respect to currency movements, taxation of operations, and other actions that can disrupt or destroy investments and operations.

SUCCESSFUL RESPONSES

Companies that are successful in this global marketplace are likely to follow certain financial strategies, including:

- *Telecommunications*—They will invest in modern computers and networks to ensure that they have instantaneous information on the risks and returns that affect their capital investments and operations.

- *Changing investments*—As new markets emerge, companies will explore them and make moves that are consistent with corporate goals. In the 1980s, the emergence of the Pacific Rim created opportunities for companies willing to invest the time and resources necessary to exploit new ventures. Does eastern Europe or the former USSR hold such potential now for an individual company? Only the right financial thinking will result in a course of action to answer the question.

- *Disappearing barriers*—Time, tariffs, and trade restrictions are barriers to market entry in many areas of the world. These are dropping in many markets, either as a result of government policies or because multinational corporations are learning how to use local partners to overcome obstacles to market entry. Successful companies are likely to make investments to take advantage of the strategic alliances that allow the development of new production sources and entry into new markets.

- *Political analysis*—Some countries are taking steps to become the source of operations and likely markets of the future. Companies must invest funds to determine which nations have the government budgets, competitive tax systems, local educational standards, incentives for investment, and other factors that make them good prospects for the conduct of business.

- *Risk management*—Operating in various markets increases the risk of disruption of operations. Exposures must be confronted in a global context. Successful companies are likely to have transnational strategies for managing and financing the expanded risks.

CONCLUSION

The message is clear. A global vision is needed with respect to financial decision making if companies are to survive and prosper in the face of changing business forces. Capital must be invested and operating budgets must reflect the need to obtain new information that allows the selection of solid strategies and business decisions. The finance function will play an important role in successful business activities if it assimilates global financial thinking in its various processes.

MANAGING
FOREIGN EXCHANGE

John J. Hampton, Principal, Princeton Consulting Group

A foreign exchange market is a communications network linking a number of participants, including:

1. *Commercial banks*—Numerous banks throughout the world provide facilities and services for converting currencies or transferring monies across national boundaries.
2. *Brokers and dealers*—A broker refers to a company that brings together buyers and sellers of national currencies. A dealer purchases or sells currencies for his or her own account. The broker is paid a fee; the dealer makes a profit on the spread between what is paid and received for a currency.
3. *Businesses and individuals*—The largest groups of participants in foreign exchange markets are the businesses and individuals requiring the currencies of different nations.

The motivations for exchanging currencies arise from the activities of people who have dealings across national borders. These include:

1. *Exports and imports*—Foreign trade may involve two or more currencies. The exporter may seek to make a payment in its national currency. The importer may desire the receipt of its own domestic currency. The foreign exchange market facilitates the exchange.
2. *Business remittances*—The subsidiaries of multinational firms remit funds in various forms to the parent company or, at the parent's direction, to other subsidiaries. So, foreign exchange is needed for these activities.
3. *Tourist expenditures*—When people travel abroad, they need foreign currencies to purchase goods and pay for services. These transactions are accomplished through the mechanisms of foreign exchange markets.
4. *Securities transactions*—When common stock or bonds are purchased by inves-

tors from other countries, foreign exchange is needed to complete the purchase.

SPOT AND FORWARD MARKETS

Foreign exchange transactions are time sensitive, as follows:

- *Spot market*—A spot transaction involves the immediate purchase of, payment for, and delivery of a fixed amount of a currency. Such transactions are said to occur in the spot market.
- *Forward market*—A forward transaction involves the agreement today to purchase, pay for, and deliver a fixed amount of a currency at a future time. No money is tied up until the delivery date arrives. These transactions occur in the forward market.

Exchange rates between currencies generally differ in spot and forward markets. Two situations are possible. A premium exists when a currency is worth more in the forward market than in the spot market. As an example, suppose the spot exchange rate is $1 to 5.2 pesos and the ninety-day forward market rate is $1/5.3 pesos. The dollar can purchase more of the other currency in the forward market and thus trades at a premium compared to the peso. Conversely, a currency trades at a discount against another currency when it is worth less in the forward market than in the spot market. In the example with dollars and pesos, the peso trades at a discount. Thus, one currency's premium is the other currency's discount.

A premium or discount exists as a result of two factors:

1. *Relative strength of currencies*—Investors prefer to hold strong currencies. Treasurers seek to receive currencies in the future without suffering exposure to exchange rate fluctuations. Forward contracts lock in exchange rates. If a party agrees to deliver a strong currency in exchange for a currency that is declining in value, a price differential will be charged. This is reflected in the premium or discount.

2. *Interest rate differentials*—National capital markets provide various mechanisms for investing the local currency. One market may have a markedly different level of interest rates than other countries. Investors seek higher return but would like to convert back to their own currency at the end of an investing period. Premiums and discounts adjust to reflect differences in interest rates in various markets.

FOREIGN EXCHANGE ARBITRAGE

Arbitrage exists when a guaranteed and riskless profit can be made by simultaneously purchasing and selling a currency in one or more foreign exchange markets. *Space arbitrage* occurs when physical distance separates two transactions. Space arbitrage can exist when a speculator executes simultaneous contracts to buy and sell currencies in two or more money market centers for delivery on the same day. The arbitrage results from different exchange rates. The transaction can occur in the spot or forward market as long as delivery occurs at the same time.

Time arbitrage occurs when an investor makes a risk-free profit by executing a spot and forward contract simultaneously. The arbitrage is created when the purchased currency is invested at a higher interest rate than would have been available for the currency that was sold. The forward contract guarantees a return to the original currency, eliminating any foreign exchange exposure. The higher interest rate provides the arbitrage profit.

HEDGING

Hedging refers to the purchase or sale of foreign currencies for the purpose of avoiding losses resulting from a decline in the value of a currency. The term *cover* is used synonymously with the term *hedge*. When a company hedges a foreign exchange position, it has a covered position.

The most common method of hedging is to execute a forward contract to buy or sell a currency. The agreement fixes the rate of exchange today, even though delivery takes place in the future. Such contracts are routinely available from banks, commodities exchanges, and foreign exchange brokers or dealers.

A second hedging method makes use of foreign exchange facilities but avoids the forward market. A company can make an immediate conversion in the spot market and then hold or owe the foreign currency until the delivery date. As an example, an importer may owe one million lira to be paid in ninety days. The importer can purchase the lira today and hold it until it is needed. Or, the Italian exporter can require payment in dollars but may wish to wind up holding lira. The Italian side of the transaction can borrow dollars today and convert them to lira. In ninety days, the dollar loan can be repaid with the dollars received from the transaction.

FOREIGN EXCHANGE FUTURES

A foreign exchange futures contract is a forward contract executed on an organized exchange, such as the International Monetary Market in Chicago or the London International Financial Futures Exchange in England. The characteristics of foreign exchange futures contracts are:

1. *Contractual agreement*—The purchaser agrees to buy a fixed amount of a currency under terms stipulated in a contract.
2. *Standard contracts*—A futures contract is available only in a standardized amount. The company must purchase a contract to deliver, say, $100,000. This is true even though the actual need may be for $110,000.
3. *Standard delivery date*—The actual exchange of currencies under a futures contract must take place on a fixed future date that is identical for all con-

tracts expiring in that month. Thus, all October contracts for Swiss francs on a single exchange might involve delivery on, say, the first Monday of the month.
4. *Limited range of currencies*—Futures contracts are only available in the major currencies that are used to finance world trade. The U.S. dollar is the common denominator of most contracts. Readily available are forward contracts for deutsche marks, the pound sterling, Japanese yen, and Swiss and French francs.

CURRENCY OPTIONS

A currency option is the right to buy or sell a fixed amount of a currency at a fixed rate in a given period of time. The holder of the agreement has the right to make a purchase or sale but is not required to do so. A put refers to the right to sell a currency. A call is the right to purchase it. The exchange rate identified in the agreement is the exercise price.

Currency options are similar to futures contracts. They are traded on organized exchanges in standard-size contracts with standard termination dates and a limited range of currencies. Currency options are different from futures contracts because:

1. *They cost money.* The purchaser pays a fee that can be as much as 5 percent of the face value of a contract. This reimburses the issuer of the option for the risk of exchange rate fluctuations.
2. *They act like an insurance policy.* An options contract protects against downside exposure from a currency fluctuation. The option is only exercised if a currency moves against the holder. Then, the profit on the option makes up for a loss on holding or owing a currency.
3. *They offer upside profits.* An options contract allows the holder to make speculative profits. They can be purchased simply as a means of speculating on currency fluctuations.

FOREIGN EXCHANGE RESTRICTIONS

Most of the techniques already covered in this chapter deal with currencies that are freely convertible into other currencies. Such a situation exists only with a minority of the world's nations. A corporate treasurer must recognize that operations in developing nations may face currency regulations that are designed to protect the local economy. These rules may restrict movement or exchange of the local currency. Some common restrictions concern the amount of money that a company may remove from the country or the amount of a foreign currency that may be purchased to pay for goods from other countries.

SECTION 7

Research and Technology

Mark D. Dibner, Section Editor

Introduction   *Mark D. Dibner*   7-3

Coping with Technological Change   *Richard N. Foster*   7-5

Management Functions in R&D   *Bela Gold*   7-11

Managing and Prioritizing Projects: Project Assessment
    Pier A. Abetti   7-16

Project Management Methods   *Bert Spilker*   7-21

Setting Up the R&D Team   *Michael Williams and Diana Stork*   7-25

Managing R&D for Strategic Position   *Graham R. Mitchell and*
    William F. Hamilton   7-29

Encouraging Innovation in R&D   *Alden S. Bean*   7-33

Taking Ideas from the Laboratory to the Market   *A. Douglas Bender*   7-36

Licensing, Protecting Intellectual Property Rights, and Other Legal
    Aspects of Technology Management   *Kenneth D. Sibley*   7-39

Technology Management in Consortia and Strategic Alliances
    Raymond W. Smilor   7-42

Using U.S. Federal Government Resources in R&D
    Charles S. Saunders   7-45

Managing Technology in a Global Economy   *D. Bruce Merrifield*   7-47

INTRODUCTION

Mark D. Dibner

The importance of technology to corporate and national attendance is much reported but less frequently understood. Indeed, our ability to compete in a global economy depends on a competitive edge built upon a technological foundation.

In many fields, the United States has been the leader in university-based research. Yet, we have learned that breakthroughs in basic research do not assure a future return on investment. A company must take the new technology and use it to bring products to the marketplace. Once established, the company must keep up with technological advances, manufacture products in a cost-effective manner, and successfully market the products.

These points, while fundamental, are not necessarily intuitive. Many managers have no formal training in the issues related to the management of technology. Few business schools make the management of technology a required course. Many schools do not even offer the course on an elective basis. Once on the job, the basic issues of managing technology do not always come naturally to line managers.

Technology management does not just happen. It needs to be worked into corporate strategies. This can be difficult if the corporation focuses on short-term results, cutting costs, and accounting to produce quarterly profits. Technological achievements do not occur smoothly over time. Many years may be required before profits are realized. The research and development team, which often does not fit the corporate culture anyway, represents a cost that is easy to cut for short-term results.

The management of technology is not easy to learn because there are many issues but fewer answers. Each technology has a different development cycle, numerous competitive approaches, and varying amounts of government control or regulation. The confusion is compounded by the fact that technology fits differently in each corporate culture.

It is possible to present issues that can be used in strategic planning. Understanding how new technologies develop, the limits and discontinuities of technological development, and how to foster innovation in the research and development team can be valuable lessons to help organizations compete.

The following chapters will encourage the reader to begin thinking about a number of issues. These thoughts can be extended to exploring a firm's strengths and weaknesses in technology management. Does your firm have a technology policy? If so, is it shared with all areas of the firm? Does it allow long-term research and development projects? Does the R&D team communicate freely with marketing and manufacturing? Does the R&D team know where its work fits in the corporate mission and plan? Does the firm create an environment that allows innovation? Does the firm have information on technological breakthroughs around the world?

Does the firm take advantage of government research? Does the company use strategic alliances with other companies and university researchers to leverage the R&D dollar? Is the firm poised to compete in a global economy?

Much of the future success of the American system depends on reflective answers to these questions. In this section, the reader will find information to help frame those answers.

Mark D. Dibner, *Ph.D., is currently director of the Institute for Biotechnology Information in Research Triangle Park. He is also adjunct associate professor of technology management and entrepreneurship at Duke University's Fuqua School of Business. Dr. Dibner is an expert in commercial biotechnology and its global development and he writes, consults, and lectures extensively on this subject. He is the author of five books, including* Biotechnology Guide U.S.A.: Companies, Data and Analysis *and* Japanese Biotechnology: A Comprehensive Study.

COPING WITH TECHNOLOGICAL CHANGE

Richard N. Foster, McKinsey and Company

Toward dawn on Friday, December 13, 1907, the age of commercial sailing ships ended when the Thomas W. Lawson ran aground and sank in the English Channel. Able to make 22 knots if the wind was brisk, she had been built to defend against the attack of speedy new steam-powered vessels, which had been winning increasing amounts of cargo business. But to gain swiftness, her designer had been forced to sacrifice maneuverability. The Lawson, with seven masts and a length of 404 feet, was so unwieldy that in a stiff gale her helmsman could not avoid the rocks. Nobody ever attempted to design a faster-sailing ship for carrying cargo. Steamships came to rule the seas. The Fall River Ship and Engine Building Company, constructor of the Lawson, was obliged to seek another line of business.

In 1947, Procter & Gamble introduced Tide, the first synthetic laundry detergent. It contained phosphate "builders" that produced cleaning power greater than that of conventional natural detergents. Tide took off, and Lever Brothers, P&G's major competitor at the time, was left in the dust.

In May 1971, National Cash Register of Dayton, Ohio, announced that it was writing off $140 million worth of newly designed cash registers because they were impossible to sell. Soon afterward it laid off thousands of workers and fired the CEO. The company's stock price fell from $45 to $14 over the next four years. The cause? NCR's electromechanical machines could not defend against new electronic models, which were cheaper to make, easier to use, and more reliable.

In these cases and hundreds of others, companies that were leaders in their fields saw their fortunes suddenly disappear, vaporized by technological change. They failed to anticipate a major shift in technology, estimate its consequences, and take timely action to renew their leadership.

Such failures are rooted in a basic assumption managers make in order to run their businesses: that tomorrow will be more or less like today. Without that belief, controlling day-to-day operations and improving efficiency would be impossible. But it is a fatal assumption to make when developing and implementing strategy. The phenomenon of technological change and its results—commercial innovation and competitive attack—mean that the strategy of nearly every company, whether in ship building, cash registers, or laundry detergent, must assume that tomorrow ultimately will be quite different from today, that it will be discontinuous. And, in most cases, by the time a technological discontinuity begins to have visible impact in the marketplace, the pace of the attack will be swift enough to sweep away all but the best-prepared defenders.

Unlike the legions of victims, companies that have led their industries over the years—IBM, Hewlett-Packard, Corning, Procter & Gamble, Johnson & Johnson, to name a few—believe that discontinuity is inevitable, that it is manageable, and that it is essential to building value for their shareholders. They believe that the attackers, the innovators that exploit technological discontinuities, finally will prevail. Thus, they seek to achieve a precarious balance between attacking themselves and actively defending their existing businesses.

THE S-CURVE

Appreciating the competitive dynamics that crush some companies while enabling others to lead their industries over the long term calls for understanding three basic ideas: the S-curve, discontinuities, and the attacker's advantage. The S-curve is fundamental to the other two ideas. It graphs the relationship between the cumulative effort made to improve a product or process and the performance improvements produced by that investment (see Exhibit 7-1). At first, progress is very slow as researchers grope for understanding. Then, as key knowledge falls into place, the rate of progress accelerates sharply. Eventually the rate slows again, as each increment of performance improvement becomes more and more

Exhibit 7-1. The S-Curve

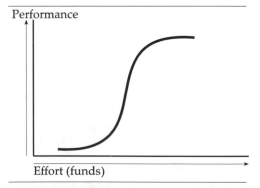

difficult—that is, expensive—to achieve. Regardless of effort, ships do not sail much faster, natural detergents do not get clothes any cleaner, and electromechanical cash registers do not become much cheaper.

The S-curve (also called a logistics or Gompertzcurve) takes its shape because of human learning patterns and physical limits. To master the unknown, humans experiment, just as a child learning to ride a bicycle tries out different combinations of pedal pressure, steering angle, and weight shifts to discover what works. Knowledge grows with each experiment, but the process is woefully inefficient, which is why the lower portion of the S-curve is so flat.

When trial and error reveals basic principles, learning efficiency skyrockets. The child who knows how to balance on a bicycle very quickly learns how to zoom around at high speed, climb steep hills, and jump curbs. Each hour he or she invests in riding returns a large increment of performance improvement, so the S-curve steepens.

Then the bicycle rider collides with physical limits. The mechanical efficiency of the bicycle and the physiology of the body put a cap on performance improvements. Efforts at the margin—using thinner tires, doing more strenuous physical conditioning—can help, but not much. The returns to investments in learning diminish, and the S-curve flattens. The only way the child can perform much better is to circumvent the physical limits of bicycle riding by jumping to the bottom of a new S-curve, by starting to invest in another technology, like that of the automobile.

Learning patterns in organizations, and even in industry-wide technologies that cross organizations, are generally similar to individual patterns. Communities of scientists and engineers experiment with limited success as they overcome obstacle after obstacle, make much swifter progress once they achieve fundamental knowledge, and eventually bump into the limits of nature. Developing an artificial heart that could keep a patient alive for four weeks took more than ten laboratory-years of work by competing teams; another ten laboratory-years produced a device that kept patients alive for about sixteen weeks; and the next ten laboratory-years of work resulted in patient survival of some thirty weeks, eight times the performance that the first ten laboratory-years had achieved. Progress in artificial hearts continues at a brisk pace, for the technologies on which artificial hearts depend have yet to approach physical limits.

It is just the opposite for mechanical watches. Between 1700 and 1850, the thickness of watches shrank from about $1\frac{1}{2}$ inches to about $\frac{1}{4}$ inch. That is roughly the thickness of most modern wrist watches. In effect, watchmakers reached the physical limit of thinness 150 years ago and have concentrated since then on other parameters of performance, such as reliability, ease of use, and cost.

Plotting a technology's S-curve raises important questions about the level and timing of R&D investments. At the beginning of the curve, the lack of big performance improvements may lead to underinvestment or premature abandonment of the new technology. Conversely, there may be overinvestment because of inflated estimates about the likely rate of progress, or because of failure to consider the efforts of other players in the industry, which produce knowledge that can be appropriated. A curve that is getting steeper usually signals an investment race among competitors, since each extra dollar has the potential to produce major performance improvements. A maturing S-curve is especially significant for companies deeply involved with the technology in question. Almost always, they overinvest because of the inertia of R&D programs, which tend to be much harder to stop than to start. If a steep curve is starting to flatten, it is time to scale back and redirect improvement efforts along new parameters, for example, trying to make watches more reliable instead of thinner.

DISCONTINUITIES

But plotting a single S-curve does little to help answer the overriding strategic question: Which technology should be pursued? Sail or steam power? Electromechanical or electronic cash registers? Natural or synthetic deter-

gents? Answering such questions calls for plotting a family of S-curves that will highlight coming discontinuities.

Although a single technology tends to dominate the market, rarely does it meet all customer needs in a superior way. There are almost always competing technologies, each with its own S-curve. Often, several new technologies vie with each other to replace an old technology—for example, the way compact disk players and digital audio tape (DAT) players compete with conventional cassette players and turntables for a share of the home stereo market. It is the crossover points between the S-curves of older and newer technologies that represent discontinuities, the points where one technology replaces another and recasts the competitive order.

A technology can be several things. In some cases it is a specific process—say, a chemical process—that produces a specific product. In that case, technology and product are indistinguishable. Or, it can be a manufacturing process that produces several products, like continuous casting of steel. Here the technology is distinct from the product, as it is also with banking services based on information processing technology. With services or products that rest on thousands of technologies, such as air travel or automobiles, only one or a few technologies are crucial at a particular time. They have the most impact on overall performance, and they are the ones to examine.

The history of tire cords dramatizes the application of S-curves and the importance of understanding discontinuities (see Exhibit 7-2). The performance parameter for tire cord is somewhat complex since it includes factors such as cord strength, heat stability, adhesion, and fatigue. These factors combine to give tires the properties consumers want—a smooth ride, endurance, blowout protection, and low cost. We construct the performance parameter by translating consumer wants (e.g., blowout protection) into relevant technical factors (e.g., heat stability and fatigue resistance) and weighting those technical factors by the values that consumers place on their different wants. In this case, the composite performance parameter is indexed to the

Exhibit 7-2. Innovation

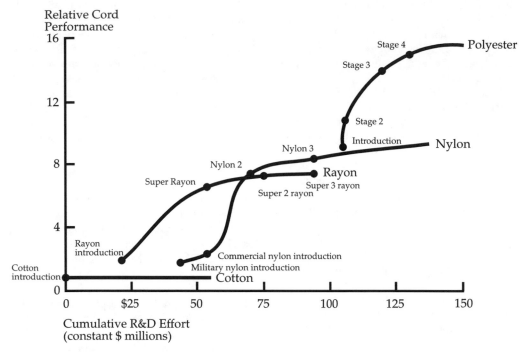

Source: From R. N. Foster, *Innovation: The Attacker's Advantage* (New York: Summit Books, 1986); copyright © 1986 by McKinsey & Company, Inc.

best performance of cotton, since it was the first tire cord material.

As with all S-curves, we measure cumulative R&D effort in terms of dollars invested (or quantities of effort), and not in elapsed time. Effort varies over time as different companies start and stop R&D programs and fund them at different levels. Since most companies do not keep good records of the effort that has gone into a technology, they often try to plot technological progress versus time, only to find the predictions do not come to pass. The problem here is not the difficulty of predicting progress, since we have found the S-curve to be relatively stable, but rather the failure to track and predict investments by all significant participants in the industry. To construct a family of S-curves, it is usually necessary to reconstruct and forecast the efforts of the industry's major players by looking at their R&D spending or at a more direct measure, such as laboratory-years spent to develop a particular technology.

The first synthetic tire cord was rayon, whose leading producers were American Viscose and DuPont. Compared with cotton, it was stronger, allowing the manufacture of thinner tires, and it did not rot, so tires lasted longer. The first $65 million that American Viscose, DuPont, and others spent to develop rayon produced a sevenfold performance improvement over cotton, and rayon came to dominate the market.

Nylon, DuPont's proprietary cord, had performance limits slightly higher than those of rayon, and it became the second dominant synthetic tire cord. The first $30 million that DuPont spent to develop nylon was much more productive than investments in rayon and resulted in performance eight times that of cotton.

But then came polyester and a radical discontinuity. Manufactured to some extent by American Viscose and DuPont, as well as Celanese, polyester had major advantages over nylon from the start and a steeper S-curve.

The first $50 million spent to improve polyester yielded performance twice as good as that of nylon and sixteen times better than that of cotton.

The competitive consequences of these discontinuities in tire cords were stark. American Viscose, prevented by patents from developing nylon, worked at developing both rayon and polyester. But it manufactured rayon almost exclusively. Well after rayon's market share had shrunk to 20 percent, and despite statements by tire producers that polyester was the tire cord of the future, American Viscose executives were asserting that rayon was still the best cord. As Exhibit 7-2 indicates, much of the last $40 million that American Viscose and others spent on improving rayon was essentially wasted—it produced very little performance improvement— and so was much of the capital investment needed to manufacture products such as Super 2 and Super 3 rayon. Plagued by deteriorating financial results, American Viscose was taken over by another firm.

DuPont did not know where nylon was on its S-curve, and that lack of understanding proved costly in terms both of wasted investment and lost opportunity. The last $75 million or so that DuPont spent to develop nylon tire cord could not, in fact did not, make much of a difference. Intent on maximizing returns from its investments in nylon R&D and manufacturing, DuPont underfunded its polyester programs. In five years, in the latter part of the 1960s, sales of the tire cords grew only slightly, but Celanese gobbled up more than 75 percent of the market. DuPont lost a precious opportunity to preempt the competition, an opportunity it could have seized by more accurately predicting the nylon-polyester discontinuity and having the boldness to pursue polyester at nylon's expense.

THE ATTACKER'S ADVANTAGE

The tire cord case underlines the third basic idea needed to understand competitive dynamics: the attacker's advantage. Time after time, in industries as diverse as packaged foods and computers, the leader in one generation of technology loses out to a newer, smaller company that uses the next generation of technology to mount an attack in the marketplace. At first glance, this pattern looks counterintuitive. Leaders seem to have huge advantages over newcomers and also-rans: deeper pockets, greater technical skills, better knowledge of the customer, entrenched market positions. Dislodging leaders, like dislodging skilled defenders on the battlefield, would seem to require a resource advantage of three to one.

At times of discontinuity, though, attackers enjoy three significant advantages of their own. For one thing, they have higher R&D productivity since they are working on the steep part of the curve while the defender is stuck at the point of diminishing returns. When Celanese started spending heavily to improve polyester tire cords, its R&D was about five times more productive than DuPont's R&D on nylon cords.

For another, attackers also enjoy a perceived advantage in R&D yield. While R&D productivity describes technical performance as a function of effort, R&D yield describes profit as a function of technical performance, that is, the economic value of technical improvements. Productivity multiplied by yield equals the return on R&D investments (see Exhibit 7-3), which is a useful summary measure of a technology strategy's worth.

Yield is not a ratio we can forecast straightforwardly, like productivity. It is affected by changing customer preferences, industry economics, and the collective strategies of all the players. Calculating yield is particularly tricky in the case of new technologies, which can have zero yield. This was the case when detergent makers spent heavily to develop powerful optical brighteners. Clothes literally became "whiter than white": brighter as measured by laboratory instruments, but not as measured by the consumer's naked eye. Since brighteners produced no improvement the consumer was willing to pay for, R&D yield was zero (and may even have been negative, since adding brighteners to detergents raised manufacturing cost).

The attacker has a perceived advantage in

Exhibit 7-3. R&D Return

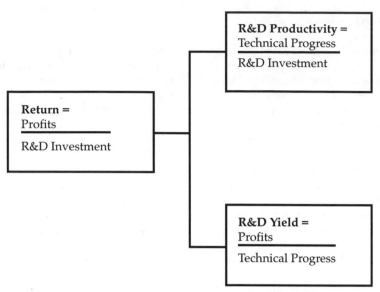

Source: From R. N. Foster, *Innovation: The Attacker's Advantage* (New York: Summit Books, 1986); copyright © 1986 by McKinsey & Company, Inc.

yield because he or she has little or no economic stake in the industry under attack. Leaders are hobbled by their investments in current technology—factories, market franchises, people's skills, and so forth. Like DuPont in tire cords, they conclude that bringing on a new technology will do so much to reduce prices and increase costs associated with current products that the combined yield on current and new technologies will be lower than if they stick to their knitting.

Finally, attackers derive a real advantage from the hubris of leaders who opt to defend today's technology. Defenders typically assume that an evolutionary approach to technology will suffice, even though this approach cannot withstand the enormous and rapid changes brought about by a discontinuity. They assume that economic indicators—market share, margins—will give ample early warning of a threat. But by the time an attack is reflected in such measures, it is usually too late to change course because the technology transition is well under way. After ten years of competing against bias-ply tires in the U.S. market, radial tires had only a 30-percent share, hardly a dominant position. But over

the next three years, they virtually wiped out the bias-ply design.

Another typical assumption that defenders make is that they know what customers want, which competitors to watch out for, and what technologies pose the biggest threats. Those are treacherous assumptions to make during a discontinuity, which typically offers customers benefits they had never thought about before, brings small, niche competitors to the fore, and relies on a technology quite different from the ones familiar to defenders. Hubris turns defenders into sitting ducks.

THE DEFENDER'S CHALLENGE

Ultimately, leaders remain leaders by attacking themselves while going all out to defend their existing businesses. This is an unnatural act. Since the core of major discontinuities is a change in the skill base of the corporation—say, from cutting sails to installing engines—a defender-attacker must figure out a graceful way of making the leap. That may mean hiring outsiders, acquiring other companies, and retraining or retiring today's employees. Negotiating a discontinuity is in many ways a cultural change, and since the strong culture that develops around a defender business is likely to swallow up or reject the fledgling culture of an attacker business, totally separate organizations often are necessary. Even the structures of the two organizations are likely to be different: functional organizations seem to be optimal for stable, established businesses, whereas new ventures appear to do better with project-oriented, cross-functional structures. The differences—and the headaches for leaders under attack—go on and on.

But there is every reason to believe these challenges will confront a growing number of corporations. Discontinuities occur more frequently than most of us realize, and their frequency seems to be increasing. The organizations that ride these waves of technological change instead of running aground will be those that understand the implications of S-curves and the necessity of self-transformation.

MANAGEMENT FUNCTIONS IN R&D

Bela Gold, Claremont Graduate School

STRENGTHENING THE MANAGEMENT OF R&D PLANNING

Prior to the early 1980s, research agendas were primarily determined by research directors and their associates subject only to general periodic review, especially of budgets, by corporate officers. But increased competitive pressures have sharpened awareness of the need for an effectively integrated analysis of a firm's market potentials and vulnerabilities as the basis for determining how R&D as well as other functions can best contribute to improving performance. (See B. Gold, "Emerging Frontiers in Strengthening R&D Programs and Their Integration with Corporate Operations," *Omega: The International Journal of Management Science,* January–February 1991; G. R. Mitchell and W. F. Hamilton, "Managing R&D as a Strategic Option," *Research Technology Management,* May–June 1988.)

Within this broad framework, R&D's potential contributions are also being strengthened by supplementing its traditional focus on emerging research advances reported in technical meetings and literature, or developed by its own staff, through gradually gaining top management support for several additional initiatives. One involves working systematically with other major functions to help strengthen responses to any prospective competitive challenges. Another involves effecting closer working relationships with current and prospective customers to help them cope with emerging product and production problems. And both of these efforts could be further enhanced by the practice, already pioneered by some companies, of offering temporary assignments of R&D personnel to such internal or customer operations in order to help develop more effective solutions to emerging problems.

A third developing sector of R&D activities involves exploring joint approaches with competitors to common industry problems. (See W. M. Evans and P. Olk, "R&D Consortia: A New U.S. Organizational Form," *Sloan Management Review,* Spring 1990; H. I. Fusfeld and C. S. Haklisch, "Co-operative R&D for Competitors," *Harvard Business Review,* November–December 1989.) Familiar issues include threats to the availability of needed materials; governmental and public pressures to reduce health, safety, product liability and pollution problems; and market pressures to develop wider arrays of product standards.

Still another source of common concerns are the foreign advances in a number of leading-edge technologies often based on heavy governmental support despite the unlikelihood of reasonable profitability within practical business time horizons. Such growing threats to the future international competitiveness of wide sectors of U.S. industries urge intensified efforts to strengthen such capabilities, including possible government encouragement for cooperative undertakings by corporations, joint government-industry development efforts, and separate government undertakings.

BASIC OBJECTIVES OF R&D PROGRAMS

To ensure relevance to managerial needs, R&D planning must encompass the wide variety of undertakings necessary to support company objectives. Most analyses of R&D performance concentrate on three forms of contributions (see F. Betz, *Managing Technology,* Englewood Cliffs, NJ: Prentice Hall, 1987, chap. 1):

1. Modest improvements in the capabilities and quality of existing products and processes.

2. Development of new products or processes yielding major commercial advantages over competitors.
3. Advances in knowledge likely to yield future improvements in products or processes.

The first of these tend to dominate the actual activities of most industrial R&D programs, although public statements tend to emphasize the second. Such claims often reflect a rather loose concept of what is meant by "new" products and processes. It may be desirable in some new sectors of industry to emphasize the high proportion of sales attributable to recently introduced products. But such a criterion can hardly be applicable in the industries that supply the dominant sectors of continuing demand for customary products and whose production facilities accordingly represent long-term investments. In such sectors, major advances over comparably competent competitors are unlikely to occur with great frequency. Hence, they cannot prudently dominate a continuing R&D program.

It should be emphasized, however, that R&D programs often generate three additional kinds of important contributions to competitive performance:

1. Reducing, or minimizing increases in, the costs of producing existing products.
2. Reducing lags behind competitors' innovations in products and processes.
3. Adapting designs and processes to shifts in the supply and prices of inputs.

Although the first of these is all too often taken for granted, such individually modest but continuing gains can obviously help to maintain a firm's competitiveness.

But the need to overcome lags behind innovative advances by competitors tends to be an even more pervasive urgency than gaining such advantages over others. To illustrate, even if a firm had only four powerful competitors, it could expect to achieve important creative advances over the others only 20 percent of the time on average and thus to fall behind the current leader 80 percent of the time.

Hence, the ability to catch up quickly is likely to represent an even more consistent need than gaining occasional advantages over all competitors.

Nor can managers ignore the competitive pressures and opportunities resulting from changes in materials and labor markets. The availability of cheaper, or more desirable, or more ample supplies of substitute materials may well present important new challenges to research. So would prospective changes in the supply and price of needed labor skills. And research may also be necessary to learn how to adapt and utilize externally developed advances in process and control technologies for application in the firm's plants.

In short, all six of the preceding objectives would seem to be essential components of an R&D program seeking to improve a firm's competitiveness. It is also worth adding a seventh objective to cover the substantial amounts of R&D in process industries that have had to be devoted to meeting governmental health, safety, noise, and pollution standards. But the relative emphasis to be placed on each of these multiple objectives should be determined by senior management and should be reflected in resulting budgeting allocations and performance evaluations. Hence, if management places primary emphasis only on seeking modest advances over competitors, shortcomings in respect to the other R&D objectives can hardly be surprising and may well exact serious penalties.

Finally, it is important to recognize that advanced research is not a completely programmable activity like production or procurement. Long dominant technologies reflect reasonably widespread acceptance of daunting obstacles to further major advances. But a serious search for occasional major competitive advances may have to include some allocations to pursue recognizably difficult but potentially rewarding targets.

DESIGNING AND IMPLEMENTING R&D PROGRAMS

Prospective R&D programs tend to be evaluated on the basis of expected contributions to sales and to reducing costs as compared with associated development costs and investments, the probabilities of reaching defined goals, and the time required to achieve them. In making such estimates, it is important to recognize that these must encompass not only the requirements for achieving a successful research outcome but also those likely to be needed subsequently to effect any required adaptations in inputs, production processes, and marketing.

In designing R&D programs, managerial choices must determine the allocation of available resources along a continuum of projects including short-term results involving low risks and offering only modest benefits, medium-term results involving medium risks and medium benefits, and long-term results involving high risks and potentially large benefits.

As was noted earlier, most long-established industries have tended to concentrate on short-term results. Common reasons include capital market pressures for attractive short-term profitability; the tendency of senior corporate officers facing retirement within a few years to reinforce such pressures; and the support of research officials responding to managerial pressures for reasonably regular improvements while minimizing associated threats to existing capital facilities and personnel. Hence, the resulting limited foci of research programs are unlikely to be broadened unless managerial pressures and rewards are altered to encourage more risk taking in pursuing more difficult objectives. Indeed, some changes may be required in the composition of research staffs that have long been conditioned to avoid major risks.

But sharp and increasing challenges from foreign producers, with plants in the United States as well as abroad, are necessitating larger R&D allocations for more ambitious, riskier, costly, and longer-term projects, thus conflicting with continuing financial pressures for short-term results. This represents one of the critical issues facing virtually all domestic industries—including such world leaders as aircraft, computers, and biotechnology—as well as older U.S. industries that are major sources of employment and income.

Important changes are also emerging in respect to the organization of research operations. (See B. Gold, "Accelerating Product and Process Development," *Journal of Product Innovation Management,* June 1987; R. W. Schmitt, "Successful Corporate R&D," *Harvard Business Review,* May–June 1985; M. F. Wolfe, "Bridging the R&D Interface with Manufacturing," *Research Management,* January–February 1985; B. Gold, "Integrating Product Innovation and Market Development to Strengthen Long Range Planning," *Journal of Product Innovation Management,* September 1984.) Development projects have commonly progressed through successive separate contributions by R&D, by production, and by marketing, with the results of each being "thrown over the wall" to the next function. But there has been growing awareness of the delayed and limited results of such uncoordinated attacks on largely interconnected problems. As a result, our field studies reveal more frequent efforts to encourage closer cooperation among the relevant functions involved in the development process. The more common forms involve frequent consultations at all stages of progress, but a growing number of firms are establishing interfunctional development teams. Such arrangements seem to be helping not only to shorten the period required for bringing new and improved products to market, but also to ensure the fuller responsiveness of resulting products to the multiple dimensions of practical market demands.

APPRAISING THE R&D PERFORMANCE OF THE FIRM

Because the overall performance of a firm represents the combined contributions and shortcomings of all component activities, favorable results engender competing claims for credit from most functions, whereas shortcomings encourage each to point its finger elsewhere. It is important, however, to recognize some of the special difficulties of assessing the relative contributions of R&D operations to a firm's growth and profitability. (See B. Gold, "Some Key Problems in Evaluating R&D Performance," *Journal of Engineering and Technology*

Management, September 1989.) For example, realization of the potential benefits of R&D-generated advances commonly requires further supportive contributions from all other functions. But efforts to measure the comparative contributions of each objectively do not yet seem promising.

There is also the practical question of when R&D contributions to performance can be evaluated most effectively. Bringing their potential operating and market benefits to fruition often requires extended periods: for gaining the cooperation of other functions in altering their previous operations; for responding to the latter's proposals for modifications of the original recommendations; and for gaining needed additions to capital facilities and to market development efforts. Moreover, resulting effects on sales are likely to become apparent only some considerable period after the preceding adaptive adjustments have been effectuated and commercial levels of production and marketing are well under way.

Given such intertwined contributions over extended periods, it is obviously difficult to measure the distinctive contributions of R&D to subsequent gains in sales, market shares, and profitability. Hence, although a variety of academic studies have reported impressive correlations between R&D expenditures and sales, few experienced executives are likely to regard such findings as offering sound guides for the allocation of resources. Indeed, such relationships often merely reflect the not uncommon practice of allocating a specified percent of sales revenues to R&D.

But any shortcomings in R&D contributions tend to have more readily discernible effects. The lagging development of product and production advances behind competitors, the failure to match them in innovating new products, and long delays in adapting to shifts in input availabilities and costs tend to reflect unfavorably on R&D performance, even when attributable to the inadequacy of their resource allocations. And the frequent practice of reducing R&D allocations when profits decline would seem more likely to further undermine than to increase competitiveness.

A firm's R&D operations may also be appraised, of course, through comparisons with the R&D performance of its competitors. In comparing their respective R&D budgets, however, allowances must be made for the relative diversity of their products and their relative dependence on purchasing technological advances as well as materials and components. Such comparisons should also consider the relative frequency of the firm's leads and lags relative to key competitors and the resulting impacts on their relative market shares and profitability. It should not be surprising, therefore, that persuasive evaluations of the relative effectiveness of the R&D programs of major competitors are still in their infancy.

THE ROLE OF SENIOR MANAGEMENT IN GUIDING R&D PERFORMANCE

The basic responsibility for the quality and effectiveness of R&D performance clearly rests with senior management. It chooses the director of research, reviews program proposals, and allocates the R&D budget. Therefore, resulting performance could be evaluated relative to the managerially approved targets among multiple R&D objectives, as modified by the adequacy of the resources and time provided. But the far more critical criteria concern the effectiveness of the firm's response to the relevant market pressures generated by competitors. And this may well be traceable to the adequacy of management's improvement targets and supporting resource allocations. (See E. B. Roberts, "What We've Learned About Managing Invention and Innovation," *Research Technology Management,* March–April 1988.)

Accordingly, one of the major requirements for catching up with competitors in a wide array of U.S. industries seems to be substantially increased allocations for R&D along with a greater emphasis on seeking larger advances despite the enhanced risks entailed. Although senior executives in industry often deny resistance to such undertakings, any reluctance to support such hazardous projects tends to be reinforced by the fact that even if major research advances do emerge eventually, converting them into sales and profits often requires substantial additional investments over extended periods before expected market rewards are likely to be realized. Hence the continuing pressure in financial markets for maximizing short-term profitability serves to encourage heavy discounting of the potential returns from longer-term R&D.

But continuing inadequacies in the global competitiveness of a wide array of domestic industries may well warrant reexamination of national policies that affect the potential contributions of R&D. Among these may be included changes in tax rules to encourage greater support for R&D as well as investments to utilize resulting technological advances; increasing the availability of credit for technologically innovative enterprises; grants in aid of labor retraining and relocation; increased support for academic and government basic research on industrial processes; and the expansion of government reporting on advances in foreign industrial technologies to help alert domestic producers.

MANAGING AND PRIORITIZING PROJECTS: PROJECT ASSESSMENT

Pier A. Abetti, Rensselaer Polytechnic Institute

Investments in R&D projects are both technical and business decisions. However, the ultimate results of R&D will be measured according to economic criteria, such as the contribution to increased market share, sales, and profits of the company to improved quality of life and international competitiveness of the nation. Therefore, the corporation or independent research entity should decide, as part of its strategic plan, how much money it will invest in R&D, and in what core technologies. (See Pier A. Abetti, *Linking Technology and Business Strategy*, New York, American Management Association, 1989.) This strategic plan, translated into annual R&D budgets, will give direction to the organization responsible for evaluating, prioritizing, selecting, and assessing R&D projects.

The R&D director is faced with the problem of allocating scarce available resources to a broad spectrum of competing projects. In prioritizing projects, a firm should follow four criteria for overall resource allocation: (1) maximize the long-term return on investment; (2) maintain a balanced R&D portfolio; (3) control risk; and (4) maintain a favorable climate for creativity and innovation.

A QUANTITATIVE METHOD FOR PROJECT SELECTION

The R&D literature is replete with project selection methods, both quantitative and qualitative, but very few are used in practice. The most popular quantitative method compares benefit/cost ratios of competing projects according to the following Project Index I.

$$I = \frac{S \times N \times P \times T}{C} = \frac{B}{C}$$

where S is the peak sales volume (dollars/year); N is the net profit on sales (%); P is the probability of success $= pt \times pc \times pf$ (pt is the probability of technical success, pc is the probability of commercial success, pf is the probability of financial success); C is the future cost of R&D; B is the estimated benefit; T is the discount factor to account for the time lag between R&D expenditures and peak sales.

Note that C is defined as future costs of R&D, because sunken costs to date are financially irrelevant. This quantitative method is applicable for projects leading to incremental innovations in products, processes, and services, targeting base technologies and markets of the company. In this case it is not too difficult to estimate, by comparison with the records of similar previous projects, the reliability of estimated benefits and costs and the probability of success.

A QUALITATIVE METHOD FOR PROJECT SELECTION

Qualitative methods are more appropriate for projects leading to radical innovations, targeting technologies and markets familiar to the company. For each proposed project, we evaluate the following three factors (see Thomas H. Lee, John C. Fisher, and Timothy S. Yau, "Is Your R&D on Track?" *Harvard Business Review*, January–February 1986, pp. 34–44):

1. *Strength*—Is the project worth doing?
2. *Timing*—Is the project worth doing now?
3. *Robustness*—Is the project worth doing, in view of foreseeable future changes in the market?

Project Strength

The strength of a project is based on two fundamental factors: technical quality and potential value. These two factors can be displayed on a matrix as shown in Exhibit 7-4. The most desirable projects are clearly those falling in the upper right quadrant. Equally clearly, projects of low technical and low potential value are undesirable. Projects lying in the "questionable" region are ones that should be scrutinized carefully to see whether they should be modified to make them more valu-

Exhibit 7-4. Project Strength Based on Technical Quality and Potential Value

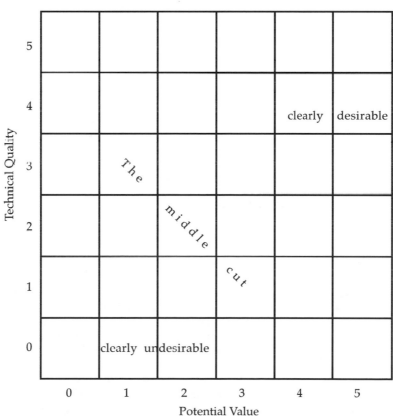

Source: From a 1984 unpublished study by David W. Lillie and Pier A. Abetti.

Exhibit 7-5. Potential Value Based on Expected Financial Value

Rating	Meaning
5	Can achieve leadership in a present large market. Can contribute to creation of a very large market sustainable over a long time.
4	Can achieve significant market share in a present substantial market. Can contribute to creation of a large sustainable market.
3	Can achieve significant market share in a present limited market. Can contribute to creation of a medium market that may or may not be sustainable.
2	Can achieve modest share in a limited existing market. Can help create a small additional or uncertain market.
1	Can have only very limited impact in a present market. May have some impact in future markets.
0	Will have zero or negative impact in present or future markets.

able and thus properly added to the overall program, or eliminated from the program.

Technical quality is a subjective rating that is based on five factors:

1. Clarity of the project goals.
2. The extent of technical obstacles that exist.
3. The extent of institutional or market obstacles that exist.
4. The adequacy of the skills and facilities available for carrying out the work.
5. If the project is successful, how easily can company management find a "home" for the new technology, process, or service?

The potential value rating is based on the expected financial value of the project, if suc-cessful. An example of ratings for a new plastic material is given in Exhibit 7-5. Each organization should define the potential value according to its strategic objectives.

Project Timing

A typical R&D project will follow an orderly progression of technical readiness according to the four well-known stages from idea generation to commercialization. It is equally important that the project follow a similar progression of economic readiness for the marketplace and the environment. In other words, a synchronism is required between states of technical and economic readiness as suggested by the definitions of Exhibit 7-6.

Exhibit 7-6. Technical and Economic Readiness

Stage	Technical Readiness	Economic Readiness
1	Analysis and idea generation	Concept in idea stage, confirming data not yet obtained, applications and markets unclear
2	Laboratory research	Sufficient data available to confirm concept, but many facets poorly understood. Economics not yet established.
3	Development	Phenomena well understood, basic data established. Economic framework established. Surprises still possible.
4	Implementation and commercialization	Phenomena completely understood. Economics established and confirmed. Competition evaluated and manageable. Surprises very unlikely.

Source: From a 1984 unpublished study by David W. Lillie and Pier A. Abetti.

Project Robustness

A project is defined as robust if its potential value is increased, rather than decreased, by the occurrence of foreseeable market and environmental shocks. The corporate strategic plan is based on the most probable future scenario (for instance: no change in oil prices during the next five years). However, alternate scenarios are also described (for instance, doubling of oil prices). Normally, the impact of the alternate scenario could be positive for some energy projects (photo voltaic solar power generation) and negative for others (diesel-electric generators). Thus, the composite robustness of each project can be evaluated based on the probability of the alternate scenarios.

PORTFOLIO BALANCE

The two selection methods previously described, if properly implemented, can be used to allocate resources to the most deserving projects, that is, to those that will yield the highest return on investment. However, there is no guarantee that all the selected projects will represent a balanced portfolio in terms of technologies, markets served, time to positive cash flow, and risk. The relative weighing of these factors will depend on the strategic thrusts and culture of the company. To begin with, we suggest plotting all projects in the matrix of Exhibit 7-7: Markets versus Time to Positive Cash Flow. If too many projects are bunched together, new projects of similar coordinates should be rejected even if their strength is superior to others.

RISK EVALUATION AND BALANCE

Technical, commercial, and financial risk is unavoidable in R&D projects leading to new products, processes, and services. However, this risk can be evaluated and controlled. (See Pier A. Abetti and Robert W. Stuart, "Evaluating New Product Risk," *Research Technology Management*, May–June 1988, pp. 40–43.) The expected value, in statistical terms, of an R&D project is given by the formula:

Expected Value =
    Payoff × Probability of Success

where the payoff is the potential value of the project and the overall probability of success is the product of the technical, financial, and commercial probabilities. All selected projects should have a high expected value. The higher the risk, the higher the payoff required. Therefore, the R&D project portfolio may include products with a broad spectrum of risk, as long as the payoffs are commensurate with risks.

Studies of new technological ventures backed by venture capital give us indications of how risks should be distributed among the various projects. In fact, venture capitalists are interested in making money on the entire portfolio, not on every venture. Exhibit 7-8 gives an indication of the preferred spectrum of product risk. Obviously, there are no new projects with zero risk. There should be plenty of "bread and butter" projects with lower-than-average risk, and moderate payoff. There should also be a few "home-run" projects of high risk, but with high payoff.

Exhibit 7-7. Markets versus Time to Positive Cash Flow Matrix

		Markets					
		Energy	Consumer	Industrial	Government	Services	Other
Time to	1–2 years						
Positive	3–4 years						
Cash Flow	5–6 years						
	7 or more years						

Exhibit 7-8. Program Risk Balance

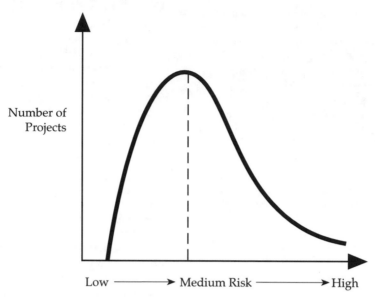

Expected Value = Payoff × Probability of Success
Should be Substantial for All Projects

R&D directors should be neither risk avoiders nor gamblers!

MAINTAINING A FAVORABLE CLIMATE FOR CREATIVITY AND INNOVATION

The R&D director should utilize the project assessment and selection process for maintaining a favorable climate for creativity and innovation in his or her organization. Most researchers and development engineers are aware that resources are limited, and therefore not all meritorious projects can be funded. However, they desire that every person have an equal chance of proposing a project and that the evaluation method be objective and fair.

In practice, in an established laboratory it is difficult to start a new project (particularly if proposed by a young researcher) because all the available resources are already assigned to ongoing projects. On the other hand, it is equally difficult to kill a project that is hopelessly out of control because of inertia, fear of losing face, or alienating senior researchers and sponsors. Thus, the actual project survival rate, as a function of time, is almost a flat curve, as shown in Exhibit 7-9.

Exhibit 7-9. Survival of Projects Over Time

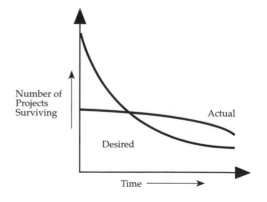

The desired rate, on the contrary, is a steep decreasing curve where many more projects are started, but are eliminated with time, as in an obstacle race. In fact, the R&D director who is selecting a project to be funded may err in two directions:

1. *Accepting an idea doomed to failure*—This is a low-risk error, because the initial R&D cost is quite low and a timely abort is possible, if the project is out of control.

2. *Rejecting an idea with high potential value*—This is a high-risk error, because the frustrated researchers may lose their creativity, or worse, spin off an independent entrepreneurial company, similar to those seen in Route 128 or Silicon Valley.

PROJECT MANAGEMENT METHODS

Bert Spilker, Burroughs Wellcome Company

MATRIX ORGANIZATIONAL STRUCTURE

In the traditional system of management, generally referred to as line-function or vertical management, individuals report through the chain of command to the top of the organization. This type of management is usually described as having a pyramidal structure, because there are progressively fewer managers as one ascends the corporate or institutional ranks. A newer system of management that has become more widespread in recent years has a matrix organizational structure. This is usually described as a horizontal system.

In most instances the matrix system does not replace the more traditional, hierarchical line management system, but is superimposed on it. All individuals continue to report through the line-function organization, but many employees also have a second reporting responsibility. Those individuals report to a member of the project team or group. Likewise, each member of the project team reports to the leader of the project, and all project leaders report to a central coordinator for all projects who then reports up the pyramid to the R&D director.

The reporting relationships in the matrix system may be formal or informal. The optimal system varies depending on the historical traditions of the organization, personalities of the people doing the work, nature of their projects, and styles of management.

Advantages and Disadvantages

A matrix system is often adopted for managing projects because it allows the company to achieve the following benefits:

1. It improves management control. It provides an alternative to line management and is an easier means to monitor progress and current status on multiple projects. It helps resolve conflicts between project requirements and the functional roles of various departments.
2. It improves flexibility of the system used to advance projects.
3. It improves visibility of more individuals to senior management.
4. It improves the visibility of a project's objectives, status, and problems.
5. It provides a simple mechanism to solicit, receive, and use input from all relevant departments, groups, and functions.
6. It applies expertise and resources flexibly and efficiently to multiple projects.
7. It achieves project objective more efficiently than without the matrix, since the entire project team usually operates as a group.
8. It allows skilled professionals to work on multiple projects while working within their area of expertise.
9. It allows the entire project portfolio to be easily viewed as a whole; it may be more readily reviewed, modified, or directed.
10. It provides more leadership positions within an organization.
11. It provides more training of staff for leadership roles.
12. It tends to improve staff morale.
13. It improves cross-functional communication and dissemination of information between different departments and groups working on a project.

The case against the matrix system is that it dilutes authority and creates dual loyalties, especially when a formal reporting system is established on the same administrative level as line managers. This may lead to undesirable competition between line managers and matrix managers. The matrix system requires greater interpersonal skills to operate effectively and is more time consuming. Also, it is often difficult for project managers to accurately assess the contribution of each member of the team, since most work is performed within the team member's line-function responsibilities. The disadvantages are as follows:

- Project members and leaders report to two separate bosses.
- An additional organizational structure must be monitored and controlled.
- Allocation of resources may be more difficult.
- Additional administrators must be hired and trained.
- There is significant potential for disagreements and power conflicts between line and matrix managers, particularly over priorities, competition for resources, and power.
- Policies and standard operating procedures may require excessive amounts of time to create and operate.

Resolving Conflicts in a Matrix Environment

This idealized view of two systems working in complete harmony is difficult to achieve in practice. Most individuals choose the system to resolve a problem that is tied to promotions, salary adjustments, and other administrative matters. If each system's representative has equal input into these administrative matters, then a strong conflict is more likely to result as each attempts to gain a superior position. If, however, one system is defined as having dominance, then there is a better chance of achieving harmonious relationships in operations and facilitating solutions to problems. Within each of these spheres, certain problems and administrative matters will tend to become centered. Making these distinctions as clear as possible to all employees included in both systems is an important goal to pursue.

Conflicts that occur between line and matrix managers are often over clearly defining the types of decisions that lie within each person's purview. One approach toward resolution of complex situations involving many people is to clarify the major roles of the individuals involved in decision making. These roles include those of individuals who (1) have final approval; (2) should be consulted but who are without veto power; (3) may develop alternatives and provide analyses; (4) should be informed about decisions made; (5) have responsibility for implementing a decision once it is made.

Strong Versus Weak Matrices

A perfectly balanced matrix is one in which the power and authority of line managers are on an equal basis with that of matrix managers and project leaders. This situation is, ironically, the most unstable type of matrix because there are forces within both groups that are constantly seeking to tip the balance in their favor. If the matrix managers and project managers win, then a strong matrix results. If line managers win, then a weak matrix results.

The balance of power is usually determined by the most senior manager(s) in a company or other organization. One way to affect the balance is to modify the level in the organization at which matrix managers and project managers report. Bringing project members physically together to work as a group tends to strengthen the matrix, just as keeping them within areas assigned to their functional department tends to weaken it. The amount of decision-making ability line managers have for project activities is the major indicator of matrix strength.

SCHEDULING PROJECT ACTIVITIES

Some of the most popular approaches currently used to schedule project activities are milestones, Gantt, and PERT. Each of these is briefly discussed.

Milestone Schedules

Milestones are the major time points and stages in a project's life. For example, in projects involving therapeutics, these milestones usually include:

1. Project formation.
2. Investigational new drug (IND) filing.

3. Phase I (start, end).
4. Phase II (start, end).
5. Phase III (start).
6. New drug application (NDA) filing.
7. NDA approvable letter.
8. NDA approval letter.
9. Product launch.

Milestone schedules are rarely sufficient on their own to serve as an adequate project schedule. The milestone listings may summarize a great deal of information, avoid complexity, and present the bottom line for individuals to use as a measure to gauge progress. Both start and completion dates for a variety of activities may be listed. Although milestone schedules are easy to prepare and review, they do not indicate interrelationships between activities or any details of the project plan.

Gantt Chart

A Gantt chart is a bar or line chart along an axis of time, usually expressed in weeks, months, and years. This type of chart may be modified in many ways, such as illustrating the time necessary to complete various parts of the overall task represented by one bar, by subdividing it with hatched lines, open spaces, or other markings. One of the drawbacks of this approach is that it is not suitable for most large and complex projects and it does not illustrate interactions between activities. As with the milestone chart, the Gantt chart may be used in conjunction with more complex schedules. In that situation, the Gantt chart may illustrate one or a few aspects of a large project. Activities that lie on the critical path may be identified with specific symbols such as hatch marks.

Program Evaluation and Review Technique (PERT)

PERT is more complex than the preceding two methods and illustrates the interdependence of many activities. PERT (or Gantt) charts are usually accompanied by a listing of all separate activities shown. It is usually desirable to list activities for each individual group or department responsible for those activities. The lists may then be used as a planning tool by those groups.

PERT, as well as the closely related methodologies of critical path method and precedence scheduling, are often referred to as network methods because they illustrate and document how multiple processes of a project may be followed. This approach may document the critical path, whereby rate-limiting activities are indicated. If activities noted as critical are delayed, then the time for project completion will be delayed. Each event on a PERT chart may be viewed as a milestone, albeit a minor one in most instances.

Whereas the critical path method provides a single estimate of time required to complete an activity, PERT requires estimates for the best case, worst case, and most likely case. These three estimates are then used to create a single time estimate. To use the PERT system it is necessary to have:

1. A well-defined set of activities that constitute a project. Usually twenty to several hundred events are listed.
2. Activities that are interrelated with other activities and conducted in a predetermined order.
3. The ability to designate which activities may be initiated and stopped independently of each other.
4. An indication of the time required to complete each activity or the probability that each activity will be successful.

PROJECT MANAGEMENT SUCCESS

Project management represents a rational basis for allocating resources to project activities and provides a means to focus attention on plans to achieve the institution's goal for the future. It identifies rate-limiting steps in current and planned work and improves the efficiency with which work is accomplished. In companies with numerous projects simultaneously under development, the matrix approach is generally viewed as the most efficient approach to manage those projects. A few brief concepts of project management are presented in this final section.

Success is usually defined as the attainment of the project's objectives as soon as possible, which means that the termination of an unsuccessful project is also judged as a success, if it is achieved rapidly and efficiently. The best predictors of project success are the attitude of the project team, the ability of the project leader to act as champion, the quality of the development plan, the commercial value of the project, the support of senior management, and the traditions of the organization.

To calculate the number of people and amount of resources needed for a project it is important to consider both the breadth and depth of each project in the system. Breadth primarily refers to the number of projects in the system; depth refers to the number of activities conducted on each project. Expansion in either breadth or depth must be frequently evaluated by every organization that has some control over the balance between these two. One objective of this evaluation is to ensure that the project team is not expanding beyond its original charge, is not embarking on tangents, and is meeting its objectives. Breadth and depth must also be assessed for the overall project system.

SETTING UP
THE R&D TEAM

Michael Williams, Abbott Laboratories
Diana Stork, University of Hartford

HUMAN FACTORS

In the management of R&D, considerable emphasis has been placed on the team concept. (See M. B. Pinto and J. Pinto, "Project Team Communication and Cross-Functional Cooperation in New Program Development," and H. Thamhain, "Managing Technologically Innovative Team Efforts Toward New Product Success," both in *Journal of Product Innovation Management*, vol. 7, 1990.) Team work, team spirit, and team building are all phrases used in R&D organizations, often well out of proportion to the effort managers make to build effective teams. Too often, the difficult task of setting up an R&D team and implementing the team concept is largely ignored in favor of focusing on the technical aspects of the work. Hiring the brightest and most technically qualified is no guarantee for productive innovation, either by individuals or by teams, particularly in those areas where team skills are necessarily diverse.

The importance of human factors, leadership, and motivation, and the need for clear goals for R&D teams are often overlooked. (See M. Badawy, "Managing Human Resources," *Research Technology Management*, vol. 31–5, 1988.) By not focusing on such team concerns, many organizations prove unable to harness the creative and innovative potential of their R&D staff. Successful research—as assessed by product introductions—does not occur when management thinks wishfully about teams, innovation, and organizational resources.

Such problems, significant in themselves, are magnified in today's R&D environment. A decrease in the number of individuals seeking advanced degrees in various scientific disciplines is anticipated to result in shortages of suitably trained individuals for industry by 1995, a situation already apparent in the pharmaceutical industry, particularly in the field of chemistry. (See R. Pool, "Who Will Do Science in the 1990s?" *Science*, April 1990.) In an environment of increasing uncertainty, the task of managing R&D has become correspondingly difficult due to the greater competition for technical personnel; a more active involvement of government in science policy and implementation; continuing marketplace pressures of competition; mergers and acquisitions; and increasing globalization.

In the past, scientists or engineers who became independently wealthy through the fruits of their labor were a rarity; job security was, however, a given. In today's high-technology industries, with varied employment opportunities and the availability of venture capital, scientists and engineers have many new options. The organization that ignores or overlooks the needs of its scientific and technical people not only stands to lose such individuals but also may become ineffective in attracting new talent.

Goals and resource bases for R&D teams

differ by organization. In a functionally structured R&D organization, teams sometimes draw their human resources from a single department and have goals that relate to departmental expertise. However, it is more common, even in functionally structured organizations, that teams draw resources from several departments, in order to make use of different kinds of talents, skills, and technologies. In R&D organizations structured along market lines (products, therapeutic areas, etc.) teams will include people with different skills, technological expertise, and functional orientations. Thus, typically, the R&D team incorporates different kinds of people, different functional backgrounds, and different kinds of technology.

R&D teams vary in their degree of permanence. Some teams are disbanded when a defined task is completed. Other teams exist as part of the organization's structure and may move to new tasks as old goals are accomplished. The dedicated team has focus, energy, and commitment, but is inflexible with regard to new goals and directions, especially if operating within a large organization. Functionally structured project teams are more permanent and more flexible. They can take on new goals as their efforts lead them in new directions within their functional area.

The effectiveness of R&D teams is influenced by a number of diverse factors: some technical, some organizational and managerial, some cultural, and many related to the individuals who function as team members—their technical expertise, their experience, their needs, and their ability to interact effectively and productively with one another.

ORGANIZATIONAL FACTORS

Before setting up an R&D team, it is important to resolve issues relating to goals, resources, commitment, time frame, and organizational climate in an open and honest manner that engenders trust.

Goals

Before members are recruited, management should have a clear sense of the team's mission and goals. (See Thamhain 1990; J. Pinto and D. Slevin, "Critical Success Factors in Effective Project Implementation," in D. Cleland and W. King, eds., *Project Management Handbook*, 2nd ed. New York: Van Nostrand Reinhold, 1988.) These factors should emerge from a careful analysis of overall organizational strategy, state-of-the-art technology, and commercial opportunities. The goals may be refined and elaborated upon over time, but they are crucial as a foundation for planning in the team forming stage. They can be used to determine the mix of disciplines and the kinds of expertise required within the team. Without them, selecting appropriate team members will be very difficult.

Resources

The most effective way to kill a new project team is with inadequate resources and support. Resources include people, information, equipment, space, funds for travel and collaborative research, access to support groups (research computing, library, legal, human resources, etc.), and so on. Visible support and encouragement from higher levels of management are necessary elements for the nurturing of innovative and successful teams (see Thamhain 1990).

Rarely does an R&D project team operate in an environment where no other project teams exist. Accordingly, there is ongoing competition for finite resources that may cause inappropriate and destructive conflict between teams. Issues relating to resources must therefore be addressed by higher levels of management rather than be delegated (by design or default) to the teams in the spirit of a wrestling match. Resource needs must be addressed before setting up an R&D team. These needs may change over time, but management should have an understanding of the kinds of resources (critical mass) a team might need to accomplish its goals and where these resources will come from. Without resolution of resource issues, the idea of setting up a new project team should be abandoned.

Commitment

In addition to resources, project teams need organizational champions and sponsors, managers within the larger R&D organization who are committed to helping, encouraging, and supporting their efforts. It is the responsibility of higher levels of management to champion, defend, resource, as well as challenge, the project.

Time Frame

In setting up an R&D team, questions of time frame and permanence must also be addressed. A project's time frame should influence resource allocations, the kind of people to be chosen as team members, and reporting relationships within the team and between the team and the larger R&D organization. A failure to deal with such issues allows projects to drag on, draining organizational resources for work that is ill-focused and unrelated to the mission of the larger organization.

Organizational Climate

The climate of the R&D laboratory within which the team functions is an important determinant of creativity, innovation, and effectiveness. A healthy R&D climate is characterized by trust, openness, and a collegial competitive spirit. Secrecy, mistrust, and ambiguous agendas are symptoms of unhealthy R&D organizations, likely to function in an ineffective manner, uncertain of their mandates and of the corporate commitment to their efforts.

TEAM LEADERS

Having resolved some of the organizational issues described above, the next step in setting up an R&D team is the selection of a team leader. The choice of a leader is a critical factor in determining team effectiveness (see Badawy 1988 or Pinto and Slevin 1988). Ideally, the leader should be flexible and should have strengths in technical, administrative, leadership, and interpersonal skills in order to be optimally effective. A sense of humor is also an asset.

Often, a project team leader is chosen from among a group of peers. This may lead to envy and conflicts between the leader and other group members. Typically, the project leader is identified on the basis of technical skills and/or enthusiasm and he or she must be provided with adequate training and support systems in evolving into a leadership role. Few large organizations have programs to support the unique problems of managing teams of technical and scientific staff.

Technical Skills

An effective team leader need not be a specialist in each of the disciplines represented in the team. An appreciation of the different disciplines and how they can contribute to the project are, however, essential, allowing the project leader to see the "big picture," and thus weigh the relative merits and uses of different technologies.

Communication Skills

Effective communication among team members, regardless of discipline, is an essential priority for the project leader and a critical factor for team effectiveness (see Pinto and Pinto 1990). The project leader must help translate between the different disciplines represented in the project. Communicating with scientists and technical people outside their organization is also important to keep the team connected to key external information sources. (See Tushman and Katz, "External Communication and Project Performance: An Investigation into the Role of Gatekeepers," *Management Science*, vol. 26-11, 1980.)

Interpersonal Skills

Effective R&D teams typically draw their expertise from individuals with widely different backgrounds. Conflict and communication problems can arise when members of different ages, experiences, and disciplines work in close proximity.

Effective team leaders are good at managing people and understand how to deal with difficult individuals. They must motivate people to work to their full potential, be good at managing conflicts, and find challenge and reward in helping people grow and develop. Without these appropriate interpersonal interests and abilities, the team will quickly begin to function like a group of individuals rather than as a cohesive unit.

TEAM MEMBERS

Project team members also need certain characteristics. Open communication, motivation, creativity, innovation, flexibility, and cooperation are all assets for the project team and are a function of the individual traits of the team members and their ability to work with one another. The members should also be chosen to achieve synergy and to create a team where all members have a common goal.

Choosing appropriate team members is a difficult task—one that requires attention to individuals' interest, skills, and abilities, their work motivation, their technical backgrounds and experience, and their willingness to work cooperatively in the pursuit of team goals. The team leader should be the primary decision maker in selecting team members, whenever possible.

The sourcing of team members is a critical step in the team-forming stage. Existing personnel within the R&D organization will have certain skills; some will have been hired for these skills; others may have developed them over time, on a "need" basis. If team members can only be selected from within the R&D organization, certain skills may be missing. The organization must then provide the support needed for retraining. Existing personnel know the culture and membership of the organization, making some of the interpersonal issues easier to deal with.

Hiring from outside the organization can avoid the problem of technical skill discrepancy and allows for an infusion of new blood to an R&D organization. On the downside are the inevitable problems relating to the outsider's being an unknown entity and the time required to learn the culture of the organization and become integrated into a team. Regardless of from where team members are drawn, they must be changed into an integrated work group that is focused on the project objectives (see Thamhain 1990).

Communication

Ideally, team members should be comfortable in sharing their ideas (and concerns) and be willing to listen. They need not be eloquent writers or speakers, but should be able to present their ideas in an understandable and convincing manner. Oral communication skills (including listening) are particularly critical during the initiation stage when consensus is needed on difficult issues.

Research indicates that effective R&D teams stay connected to important external sources of information; less effective teams often are cut off from these sources (see Tushman and Katz 1980). This means focusing attention on how new information and novel ideas will flow into the team and how these can be integrated into the work environment. Some team members should maintain and develop contacts within the larger organization and outside to the wider scientific and technical communities.

Motivation and Creativity

Successful teams have members who are motivated by team goals and objectives, as well as by individual ones. The motivation to solve problems and build on opportunities that relate to the project as well as those that relate to their individual disciplines or areas of expertise is essential.

Successful R&D teams typically have some creative members. However, not all team members should have the same creative strengths and abilities. A team composed of "thinkers" without individuals who enjoy "doing" and vice versa can be problematic. R&D teams need highly creative technical talent as well as what some in the pharmaceutical industry call "journeymen." The "thinkers" do not always know how to implement ideas, and may not have the patience to deal with the day-to-day routine of the project effort. A balance between thinkers and journeymen is crucial for R&D team effectiveness.

Cooperation

Perhaps the most important human factor in fostering excellence in R&D teams is cooperation. In evaluating individuals, it is important to identify those who want to be team members and have the maturity and self-confidence to put aside differences and focus on team goals. This means not selecting those scientific and technical "stars" interested in pursuing their own ideas to the exclusion of team and corporate needs.

The graduate training of many scientists often instills a work ethic that favors individual accomplishment, antithetical to the team approach. If hiring straight from school, some time will be required to develop the norms of cooperation and team spirit.

A cooperative team is not the same as a team without conflict. "Intellectual turbulence" requires multiple perspectives and different ideas and implies conflict and disagreement among team members. (See B. Spilker, *Multinational Drug Companies: Issues in Drug Discovery and Development*, New York: Raven Press, 1989.) The resolution of conflict in a well-functioning R&D team means that, after airing different perspectives and reaching consensus, team members can be united in their efforts and can work together cooperatively toward team goals.

MANAGING R&D FOR STRATEGIC POSITION

Graham R. Mitchell, Director of Planning, GTE Laboratories

William F. Hamilton, The Wharton School of Business, University of Pennsylvania

Widespread concern about the competitiveness of American industry and a renewed awareness of the importance of innovation to the U.S. economy have focused management attention on the strategic importance of technology. However, decisions to establish strategic R&D programs and build long-term technical strengths often have to be made before future commercial benefits can be evaluated with precision. Both practical experience and academic research indicate that formal analytic techniques fall far short of resolving the general manager's dilemma: how to balance near-term quantitative analysis of financial returns with reasoned judgment about the long-term strategic benefits of proposed R&D programs. In practice, it has long been recognized that a single financial framework such as return on investment (ROI) is inadequate to guide the funding of the full spectrum of R&D programs:

> In recent years formal business planning has stressed the risk-weighted discounted rate of return on R&D projects. For fast-moving worldwide industries

this has been a disaster. . . . It is inconceivable that today's successful software and computer peripheral producers—or tomorrow's biotechnology companies—started with a careful analysis of ROIs on their research projects. (R. W. Schmitt, "Successful Corporate R&D," *Harvard Business Review*, May–June 1985)

Management has traditionally dealt with the difficulty just described by funding R&D programs under one of two prevailing assumptions: (1) R&D is a necessary cost of business—in effect, an overhead. (2) R&D is an investment, to be funded by the same explicit financial criteria (discounted cash flow, return on investment, etc.) used for making other business/financial decisions.

Of course, there are real limits to the levels of R&D commitments that most executives are comfortable in treating as a necessary cost of business and, effectively, leaving to the discretion of technical managers. The only available alternative is typically to subject the R&D proposal to an ROI or equivalent analysis. Unfortunately, many of the R&D programs that are strategically most important fall between the above two models. That is, they may be too large in funding requirements and too significant in their implications to be treated as a necessary cost of business; and too uncertain in the nature and timing of commercial impact to be treated appropriately as an investment.

STRATEGIC OBJECTIVES

An essential step in ensuring appropriate consideration of R&D programs is to characterize them in a way that is consistent with management's strategic objectives. As technical programs evolve and progress to commercial application, they usually pass through distinct phases where they are targeted to three fundamentally different strategic objectives:

1. *Knowledge building*—This includes exploratory research in industry. Individual projects are generally small and often involve interactions with universities and other external sources of new knowledge. The business impact is often poorly defined but potentially wide-ranging.

2. *Strategic positioning*—To capitalize on any new technical area identified through exploratory efforts, it is often necessary to focus significantly more resources into the area. The objective is one of strategic positioning or building the technical skills and insights needed to exploit potential commercial opportunities.

3. *Business investment*—This is the clear objective of the majority of technical activity within large corporations. The technical programs involved are usually oriented to development and engineering. This is the phase of evolution with which business management is most comfortable. The level of commitment may be one or more orders of magnitude greater than that in the previous phases and generally involves parallel commitments by other functions.

As technical activities evolve from knowledge building through strategic positioning to business investment, the programs become more focused. This progression is usually accompanied by increasing levels of expenditure and reduced uncertainty as illustrated in Exhibit 7-10.

The most reasonable approach to most knowledge-building research is as a cost of business. Business investments in technology are most appropriately justified by the same purely financial criteria that are applied to other business investments for which uncertainty is relatively low. The vexing question facing top management is often what to do with programs directed toward strategic positioning. Here, costs are too high to be justified as overhead and outcomes are too poorly understood to be justified as investment. The answer is that they should be viewed as strategic options.

Exhibit 7-10. Strategic Objectives of R&D

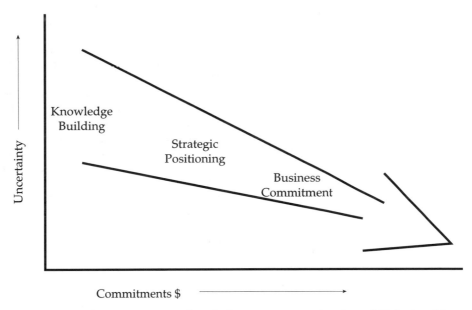

Source: From G. R. Mitchell and W. F. Hamilton, R&D as a strategic option, *Research Technology Management,* May–June 1988, pp. 15–22.

R&D AS A STRATEGIC OPTION

R&D programs directed toward strategic positioning are in many ways parallel to the American call option that permits the owner to purchase stock at a specified price (exercise price) at any time prior to a defined expiration date. The value of the stock option is illustrated as a function of the price of the stock and the exercise price in Exhibit 7-11.

In establishing the parallel between the R&D option and the stock option:

- The price of the call option is analogous to the cost of the R&D program.
- The exercise price is analogous to the cost of the future investment needed by the company to capitalize on the R&D program (PV at some future time T) when the investment is made.
- The value of the stock for the call option is analogous in the R&D case to the returns the company will receive from the investment (PV of expected returns at a time T).

Exhibit 7-11. Value of a Call Option at Expiration

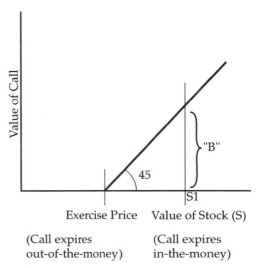

Source: From G. R. Mitchell and W. F. Hamilton, R&D as a strategic option, *Research Technology Management,* May–June 1988, pp. 15–22.

Viewing selected strategic positioning R&D programs in this way can lead to a clearer understanding of the key factors discussed next.

Downside Risk

The downside risk for an investment, whether in the stock market or directly in the business, is that the complete investment may be lost. By contrast, the downside risk for a stock option is that the option will expire "out of the money," and that the option will not be exercised. The loss is thus limited to the price of the option, whatever the value of the stock.

The equivalent situation of an R&D option occurs when the corporation does not make the follow-up investment necessary to capitalize on the R&D program. The equivalent loss is the cost of the R&D program, which in general will be very much smaller than the follow-up investment. In practice, this represents the maximum possible loss, as the results of the R&D program, if not used directly, often provide significant insights into subsequent technical programs and business investments.

Time

In the investment model, the value of returns is discounted as a direct result of the time value of money. For the call option, increasing the time for which the option may be exercised increases the probability that stock price may exceed the exercise price during that period, and thus this increases the value of the option. There is a parallel situation for R&D programs that offer the corporation flexibility in the timing of the subsequent investment or financial commitment, and particularly those providing the opportunity to make a series of investments over a period of time.

Uncertainty

As the uncertainty associated with an investment increases, the value of the investment will be discounted as a result of risk aversion. Often no business investment will be made if the level of uncertainty falls above the range with which management feels comfortable.

Uncertainty has the reverse impact for a call option, as the downside risk is limited to the cost of the option. Increased volatility in the stock price increases the chance that it may exceed the exercise price before expiration, without increasing the downside risk. The R&D option parallels the call option in that high-impact opportunities, with a modest or low probability of success, do not imply higher risk.

In extending the parallel, however, R&D options have one very important advantage over stock options. The purchase of a stock option has no direct effect on the exercise price or the future price of the stock, whereas the major purpose of the R&D option is to influence the future investment favorably, either by lowering costs or by increasing returns.

MANAGEMENT IMPLICATIONS

Faced with these insights, how should the concerned senior executive proceed? There are several important steps to be considered:

1. *Identify strategic objectives.* The most direct and simplest step is to review the company-wide portfolio of technical programs to differentiate the strategic objectives of current and planned R&D activities. It is particularly important to characterize carefully those programs directed to strategic positioning. In many cases, explicit recognition that these programs are designed to produce downstream options can help focus management attention on the strategic, rather than short-term financial, payoffs.

2. *Review impact of strategic options.* The next step involves asking directly, "What is the range of potential benefits to be realized if the strategic option is exercised and the corporation proceeds with downstream investments?" The goal is to estimate future impact recognizing high-impact possibilities. This usually involves speculation on potential future markets and discussion of the multiple ways in which technology might provide future competitive advantages, many of which receive scant consideration at best in most

R&D portfolio reviews. Given the wide range of potential benefits arising from industrial R&D, the assessment process will necessarily be heavily judgmental rather than analytical.

3. *Define strategic positioning targets.* The most fundamental step is to address explicitly the technical areas in which to position R&D strategically. By building expertise in specific areas, management defines the core technical capabilities on which future business success will be based. If these areas are well chosen, significant future benefits will result from applications only dimly perceived when the technical area was originally selected. Viewing the relevant R&D as a strategic option exposes these possibilities and brings the intuition of business and technical managements into closer alignment.

Frequently, the major challenge in strategic positioning is to select rapidly moving areas from among a number of exploratory alternatives. This presents two difficulties: Commitments must be made before all the potential benefits can be determined with confidence. Also, the decision to pursue one area implies that others will not be supported.

In the long run, profitable growth will depend significantly on the balance that is struck between technical programs with different, but complementary, strategic objectives.

ENCOURAGING INNOVATION IN R&D

Alden S. Bean, Lehigh University

Innovation is driven by ideas, and ideas are products of the human mind. Among other things, people involved in R&D are expected to generate novel ideas, or to enhance the novelty of ideas generated elsewhere, using their scientific and technical knowledge.

Two types of ideas are of great importance in R&D: ideas about the application of existing knowledge to new problems; and ideas leading to enhancement of the existing scientific or technical knowledge base. Both can be the basis for innovative products that enhance productivity and create a competitive edge. It is also true that such ideas can create havoc by making obsolete whole bodies of knowledge, techniques, and even industries.

A major challenge in technology management is understanding how R&D managers can stimulate and influence the creation of ideas. It is important to know the conditions under which scientists, engineers, and technicians support the innovative needs of the firm with their best ideas. This chapter focuses on that question.

PROBLEM DEFINITION

Ideas are defined as potential proposals for technical work stimulated by the recognition of a business need or opportunity, and a technical means to respond. A fundamental R&D management concern is whether the number of ideas being generated is adequate to support the firm's needs. If opportunities exceed technical capabilities, the quantity of high-quality ideas is likely to be limited. Investments in innovation will yield modest returns. Conversely, if technical capabilities exceed recognized opportunities, the firm is not likely to properly evaluate the full potential of good ideas. In either case, scarce resources and opportunities are being wasted. Thus, one fundamental problem in R&D management is balancing the supply and demand of good ideas.

A second issue has to do with the emphasis and novelty of the ideas being proposed for funding. Emphasis is concerned with the balance between product innovation and process innovation. Novelty refers to their departure from existing practice. Highly novel ideas are often characterized as radical, whereas ideas for modest improvements in existing practice are termed incremental.

Research has shown that radical departures from existing process technologies have occurred with regularity throughout the history of even such low-tech industries as cement manufacturing and glass-making with devastating impacts on individual firms. However, it is clear that the relentless pursuit of small changes in product features, design, and quality has a lot going for it. The balance of ideas between radical and incremental improvements is clearly an important issue in R&D management. Similarly, it appears that ideas emphasizing product innovation are particularly important in the early stages of the evolution of a product line, whereas process improvements may have greater payoffs as products mature and standardization occurs.

These observations about quantity, emphasis, and novelty problems in idea management suggest the proposition that not all ideas are of equal value for innovation purposes. Therefore, it is important to consider how managers can encourage the generation of potentially valuable and timely ideas for R&D projects.

INFORMATION FLOWS AND IDEA MANAGEMENT

How can idea generation be turned into project proposals? First, people can pay attention to only a limited amount of information at any given time. The ability of management to focus the R&D staff on important needs and opportunities is a major determinant of the ideas that will be generated. Therefore, a critical management function is that of providing R&D personnel with an information environment laced with cues about important organizational needs and opportunities.

To do this effectively, management needs to know what kind of ideas it wants, and it needs to evaluate and act upon ideas that are responsive to the cues, as shown in Exhibit 7-12. Technical personnel will focus their creative energies on needs that have high relevance to the success of the organization. In theory, a carefully articulated strategic technical plan would provide the ideal supporting documentation. Unfortunately, many of these plans lack management's commitment. Research indicates that the R&D staff will learn, over time, to test the credibility of the cues given by management about needs and opportunities, particularly through the network of veterans of previous campaigns for new ideas.

Research suggests that the most credible sources of information about needs and opportunities are the potential users of the research results likely to flow from the ideas. If management is interested in product-line enhancements, R&D should communicate directly with product and brand managers. If process improvements are desired, manufacturing engineers should work closely with R&D. The most difficult need to communicate effectively to the R&D staff may be the desire for radically new products or processes for which there is no obvious internal user or champion. Senior technical and corporate leaders may be the only sources of credible and persuasive information about such needs.

Exhibit 7-12. Behavioral Model of Research Activity

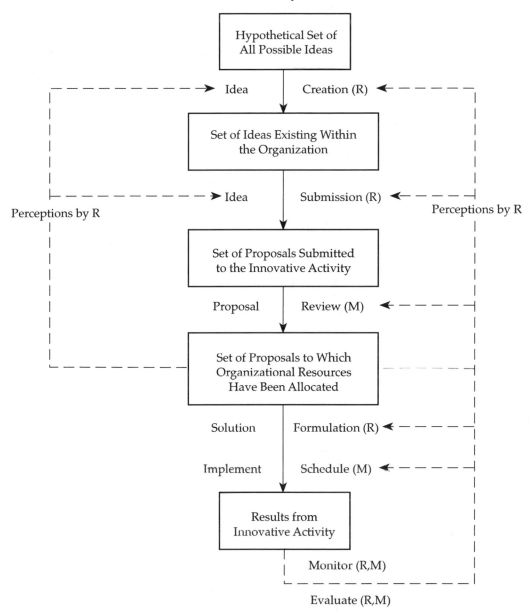

Source: From N. R. Baker and J. R. Freeland, "Structuring Information Flow to Enhance Innovation," *Management Science,* 19(1):105–116, Sept. 1972.

BARRIERS TO IDEA FLOW

A substantial number of high-quality R&D ideas are never submitted for evaluation and review because management values progress on current projects more highly than idea generation for new proposals. This suggests that the project review systems direct undue attention and rewards to the methodical completion of existing work. Moreover, ideas expected to fail the tests of immediate relevance and timeliness are never submitted.

Solutions are straightforward. Idea generation can be explicitly built into the job descriptions and reward structures. Time can be set aside for idea generation. A number of companies have set up databases to record and retain ideas generated out of sync with the formal project review process. Others have created technical advisory boards to meet with the R&D leadership to stimulate thoughtful consideration of the quality and quantity of ideas in the pipeline.

TAKING IDEAS FROM THE LABORATORY TO THE MARKET

A. Douglas Bender, School of Management, Widener University

The new product development process is of growing importance to companies that depend on a flow of new products. Critical issues are the quality, quantity, and timing of potential new products in the pipeline from laboratory to market. Management's interest centers on the question, "How can we get meaningful products to the market faster?" Today it is not enough to be concerned simply with cost, product differentiation, and quality. Speed and flexibility are just as critical.

To achieve speed and flexibility as well as competitive advantage, management must be clear about its strategic focus, be committed to innovation, and create an effective process for bringing new products to the marketplace. Further, management must be balanced in its actions, and not employ a system that is rigid, rule driven, and blind to surprises. Nor should management err at the other extreme and assume that new products just happen;

a shotgun approach will result in time delays, false hopes, and lost opportunities. There needs to be a balance between structure and the tolerance for ambiguity, formal and informal communications, controls and flexibility, specialization and integration, and the "pull" of the market and the "push" of technology.

STRATEGIC FOCUS

There are several important strategic decisions that shape and influence new product development and directly impact the potential productivity of the process. Management must:

1. Identify markets and market segments that best fit the company's strengths and abilities.

2. Decide on how resources will be allocated between creating new products for new markets, developing products for maturing markets, and rejuvenating old products in the product line.

3. Decide if it is more desirable to be the first to market new products or to be second. This is an important distinction; without it, the company may find itself divided with a strategy that does not fit its strength or competency.

4. Create products with a clear "hook." Because of the shortened product life cycle and the introduction of a variety of new products, it is important that this incremental hook be clearly related to anticipated consumer needs. This means being close to the customer. Leapfrogging, not simply catching up, should be the goal. This is particularly critical in markets where low-cost alternatives are available. It will also allow for the natural erosion of optimism and the perceived potential of the product as it proceeds from the initial idea to the reality of the market.

5. Decide on what role licensing will play in the new product development process. Licensing a product can be an important source of future products and technology. Further, out-licensing of technology or a joint venture can represent a viable strategy.

6. Decide on the level of sustainable commitment to new product development and create a contingency fund should the success rate of new product development exceed the plan.

A clear and focused strategy for new product development makes for a more efficient process with fewer delays and mistakes. Resources are spared. Without this focus and direction, costs escalate, productivity declines, and expectations are not met.

CULTURE FOR INNOVATION

Today, the role of top management goes beyond endorsement and support; it must create an environment in which new ideas and new products are an integral part of the culture and style of the organization.

A company that has created such a culture is 3M. The company's goals reflect its commitment to innovation. One goal, for example, states that, "25 percent of sales must come from products that did not exist five years ago." In addition, it has focused on other elements of a supportive culture, including a commitment to excellence, a long-term focus, trusting relationships, and perhaps most importantly, the freedom to fail. Firms that recognize the need for innovation but fail to accept its risks create stress within the organization that will immobilize the process.

There may be times when the new product opportunity does not match the existing organizational culture. The General Motors strategy for creating the Saturn automobile is a case in point. Here the company recognized that a small car that would compete with the foreign imports could not be produced within the structure and culture of General Motors. The decision was to establish a new organization with new rules, a new culture, and a new set of expectations.

STAGES OF DEVELOPMENT

A sound and effective process for bringing new products to the market incorporates critical features involving company stages of development, the R&D team, communicating, and measuring progress.

The steps or phases of the development process are clearly defined. These phases reflect the unique character of the product, the situation, the timing, and the industry. With the completion of each phase a go/no-go decision is based on a set of criteria that reflect the strategic goals and direction of the firm. The quantitative rigor of this process is appropriate to the stage of the project.

To improve effectiveness and efficiency of the new product development process, it has been suggested that the process be divided into a predetermined set of states, each composed of a series of related and often parallel activities. Usually there are four to seven stages each characterized by a set of decision criteria for entry and exit.

The key in the setting of these systems is the ability to establish the relationships among various activities and evaluate the potential to schedule parallel rather than sequential activities. Simultaneous or parallel development is critical in getting new products to the market faster and with fewer mistakes. A predetermined plan can also allow for the identification and assessment of contingent actions. The use of project planning techniques, such as program evaluation and review technique (PERT), are helpful tools in creating these plans.

The R&D Team

The process is managed by a small, multidiscipline product team. A necessary member of this team is a "product champion." Championing was critical to the success of SmithKline's introduction of the antiulcer drug Tagamet. This product arose from a company laboratory in England and in its initial stages faced a doubting U.S. research team. Without the strong commitment of the U.K. team to "their ideas," it is possible that the development of the basic technology inherent in the idea that fostered Tagamet might have been diverted.

Keeping the team together helps it appreciate the complexity of issues and helps develop the communications systems within the team to deal with these issues. Cooperation is strengthened through informal interactions among people working on the project.

Each team member is trained to work as a member of a group. The firm can not just assume that "bright" people know how to work together. Further, the team should understand the changing roles of its members as the project proceeds. In the initial stages, creativity and planning are critical inputs. During the latter stages, the emphasis is on execution of the plan.

Inherent in the team approach is the shift away from a linear and sequential process to a more integrated approach. Simultaneous development or engineering has been an integral part of Japan's success in introducing new products. One key to the success of this concept is to keep workers near each other and to consolidate information.

Some have used the analogy of a relay race versus a rugby team as an example to the more current approach. Under the old system the development process was conducted like a relay race with the passing of the baton from one specialist to another. Under the rugby approach, there is a consistent interaction of team members who work together at the earliest stages in a product development to its final stages. Lastly, the team is held accountable and bureaucratic overload is kept to a minimum.

Communication

Lines of formal and informal communication are open and multidirectional. While formal process focuses on regular team meetings and decision-making sessions, the informal network is encouraged. The physical layout should allow frequent contact between various members of the teams.

Traditional communication barriers are addressed and minimized. Horizontal communication encourages the sharing of information among those engaged in research, manufacturing, and marketing.

Progress

The team monitors not only its progress with the product but also how it is functioning as a team. To do this, responsive intelligence systems are put in place. The processing of a new product through the pipeline will be influenced to a significant degree by new technology, competitive products, new and old, and the changing needs of the customer. Thus, the new product process must define how it will monitor and incorporate change.

Progress on each project is tied to an overall plan that reflects priorities and timing pressures. Management needs to balance the timing of new products so there is a continuous flow of potential new products in the development pipeline.

LICENSING, PROTECTING INTELLECTUAL PROPERTY RIGHTS, AND OTHER LEGAL ASPECTS OF TECHNOLOGY MANAGEMENT

Kenneth D. Sibley, Bell, Seltzer, Park & Gibson

BUILDING THE PATENT PORTFOLIO

Organizations seek patents that will enable them to secure an attractive return on their investment in research. Patents that accomplish this result do not, however, spring gloriously from the research conducted. Instead, a substantial administrative commitment is required: a commitment to implement and carry out a patent strategy that will build an effective patent portfolio over time. Because patents protect new technology, and because the commercial significance of new technology is difficult to assess by the time patent applications must be filed, patent portfolios are pursued to help ensure that the commercially significant patents will be among those secured.

CONFIDENTIALITY AND OWNERSHIP OF TECHNICAL INFORMATION

Rules governing the confidentiality and ownership of technical information within a re-

search organization should be made clear in employment contracts. Typically, employment contracts require that confidential information be kept secret (both during the term of employment and thereafter), that inventions made during the term of employment be assigned to the organization, and that employees cooperate with the patent program of the organization during and after their employment. More stringent provisions that are often found in employment contracts include (1) prohibiting employees from competing with their employer after the term of employment, and (2) requiring employees to assign inventions made by them after the term of their employment. In most states, the scope of these more stringent provisions is strictly limited.

The law governing employment contracts varies from state to state, and varies over time within states as new cases are decided and new legislation is promulgated. While these agreements tend to become settled forms over time, they should be initially established in light of the applicable state law, and monitored to ensure they are current with that law.

As a final note, an organization that accepts

unsolicited invention disclosures from an outsider can find itself in a difficult, yet legally binding, confidential relationship with the submitter. Similar problems can arise when research proposals containing confidential information are submitted to a company—even simple statements like, "I wish to try your drug X to treat condition Y." A program should be established to ensure that (1) research and development personnel are not inadvertently tainted by communicating such information to them, and (2) the information is returned with a request that it be submitted in nonconfidential form.

AVOIDING FORFEITURE OF PATENT RIGHTS

Talks, publications, poster sessions, grant proposals, and offers for sale are some of the acts requiring constant monitoring to ensure that U.S. and/or foreign patent rights are not inadvertently lost.

While the United States provides a one-year grace period to file a patent application, most foreign countries do not. Such countries are said to require "absolute novelty" for patentability. In these absolute novelty countries, a patent application must be filed before the invention is disclosed to the public in any way, or patent rights are forfeited. Several treaties and international agreements govern where a patent application must be filed to preserve patent rights in a particular country, and the steps that must be taken to preserve patent rights vary depending on the countries in which patent protection is ultimately sought.

In the United States, the right to a patent is forfeited if the invention was described in a printed publication anywhere, or in public use or on sale in this country, more than one year before an application for the patent is filed. This one-year "grace period" is strictly enforced by the courts.

AVOIDING PATENT INFRINGEMENT

Anyone who introduces a new product or implements a new process in the United States has an affirmative duty to avoid infringing the valid patent rights of others. Failure to satisfy this duty can result, among other things, in a finding of "willful infringement" and a tripling of the damage award. Even absent a finding of willful infringement, a significant adverse damages award and an injunction prohibiting the sale of an infringing product can bankrupt many corporations. A prudent course is to maintain constant vigilance for potential infringement problems.

The fact that a particular product or process is itself patentable provides no indication whatsoever that it does not infringe the patent rights of others. These are separate issues. Accordingly, one who seeks to satisfy his or her duty to avoid infringement must obtain an infringement search and an infringement opinion for the new product or process.

MONITORING THE PATENT LITERATURE

An effective patent monitoring program is the cornerstone of an effective patent strategy. The patent literature should be monitored continually throughout a research program, and not merely after it is decided that a particular technology should be investigated for patentability. Early monitoring of the patent literature helps prevent costly and duplicative research, can identify technology for licensing, and helps avoid infringement. Since the patent portfolio of a competitor is designed to frustrate a company's efforts to commercialize competing technology, early awareness of new additions to the competitor's patent portfolio is essential to ensure development of competitive, noninfringing technology, without wasting money on research that will ultimately be blocked from commercialization.

It is crucial to place special emphasis on monitoring the foreign patent literature. This is because many foreign countries publish patent applications eighteen months after they are filed. The United States, on the other hand, keeps patent applications secret. Since most commercially significant patents filed in the United States are also filed in at least some foreign countries, one can gain more rapid insight into the patent strategies of one's competitors by monitoring the foreign patent literature.

The patent literature can be accessed easily through a number of online databases. A technical librarian or other information retrieval specialist, if not available in-house, should be consulted in establishing a patent monitoring program: The investment is more than recouped through savings on unwarranted scientific research or legal fees.

THE RECORDING AND DISCLOSURE OF INVENTIONS

Most people with experience in corporate research are familiar with the somewhat tedious ritual of maintaining laboratory notebooks. These records are crucial when a competitor claims to have invented the same technology first, or when certain publications are cited against the invention after an application on the invention is filed in the Patent and Trademark Office.

Laboratory notebooks should record, preferably in ink, all work performed by R&D personnel. The notebook pages should be signed and dated by the person performing the work, and signed and dated by a witness who understands the work reported. The witness cannot be someone who might later be considered an inventor of the work recorded, and should sign a phrase like, "Read and understood by _(name)_ on _(date)_." Notebooks are commercially available that provide appropriate forms at the bottom of each page. Since determining priority of invention involves determining the date the invention was "conceived" (i.e., a mental formulation of the invention was made), notebooks should record and witness proposals for future research in the same manner as actual research.

A standardized invention disclosure form is used in many organizations to initiate the patent process. The structure and content of such forms vary widely. An organization that files patent applications on most disclosures, and seeks an early filing date for its application, would use a form emphasizing complete disclosure of a single "best mode" of the invention. An organization that is more selective in filing might pose questions on the advantages and disadvantages of the invention to aid deliberation on which disclosures should be selected for patent filings. The structure of the form used should be decided on in light of how the organization's patent program is administered.

SELECTING INVENTIONS FOR NATIONAL PATENT PROTECTION

Not all technology is suitable for patent protection. Some can be more effectively protected as a trade secret than through a patent. Other technology is best simply published so that it cannot be patented by others. For example, it is universally agreed that a new pharmaceutical compound should be protected by a patent, but a minor variation on an electromechanical device might simply be published in a technical disclosure bulletin. These decisions should be made with great care, as most purported "rules" on how things should or should not be protected are riddled with exceptions. For example, it is often said that manufacturing processes should be kept as trade secrets, but numerous examples of valuable "process" patents can be found.

For technology that is suitable for patent protection, the difficult question is when a patent application should be filed. Some organizations wait until the commercial value of a given technology is strongly indicated—a strategy that saves on costs, but runs the risk of preemption by others in competitive areas of technology. Other organizations, seeking a more aggressive approach, file a brief and inexpensive "defensive" application early. This establishes a priority date against others who might be working in the same field. Then, if the technology progresses, the defensive application is supplemented in a chain of "continuation-in-part" applications to arrive at the "offensive" application that is ultimately used as the basis for an issued patent.

PURSUING FOREIGN PATENT PROTECTION

Because the cost of developing many new products cannot be recovered by marketing the products in the United States alone, even relatively new corporations routinely file patent applications in foreign countries. For example, there is usually little interest in developing a new pharmaceutical unless patent applications are on file in at least the United States, Japanese, and European patent offices.

Pursuing foreign patents can be extremely expensive, depending on the particular strategy employed. Fortunately, modern procedures provided under the Patent Cooperation Treaty provide a way to control foreign filing costs.

ENFORCING AND LICENSING INTELLECTUAL PROPERTY RIGHTS

The penalties that accompany a finding of patent infringement make it foolish for any company to infringe the patent of another. Yet, numerous patent infringement actions are initiated each year. The high stakes and complexity of legal issues make patent litigation a potentially long, expensive, and acrimonious undertaking. To control these costs, one should consult with litigation counsel at an early time.

You may add to your patent portfolio by licensing the technology of others (license in), or you may add to your income stream by licensing patents from your portfolio (license out). Professional organizations, such as the Licensing Executives Society, are available to help facilitate the licensing of technology.

TECHNOLOGY MANAGEMENT IN CONSORTIA AND STRATEGIC ALLIANCES

Raymond W. Smilor, IC^2 Institute and Graduate School of Business, The University of Texas at Austin

Spurred on by increasing international competition, the rising costs of advanced research, the need to leverage scarce scientific and technical talent, and the desire to share the risk associated with technology generation and commercialization, technology companies are banding together in research and development consortia and innovative strategic alliances. Managers in these new types of organizations face the intriguing paradox of competition and cooperation.

Consortia and strategic alliances are arrangements among organizations to work together to gain access to technology and markets and to accomplish objectives of mutual benefit. They vary in organizational structure, technological emphasis, funding mechanisms, and personnel makeup. They may be formed to enhance positioning in key markets, gain credibility in a new niche, leverage capital and human resources, expand marketing and distribution capabilities, or build stronger and more direct networks to customers. Yet, they all share one abiding task—managing technology in an efficient, timely manner to accelerate the development, transfer, and commercialization of technology and thus speed their access to new and expanding markets.

These arrangements pose unique management challenges. Because the members may come from very different corporate cultures, present different managerial priorities, policies, and procedures, and emphasize different and sometimes conflicting objectives, management faces a variety of organizational, technological, strategic, and cultural barriers to managing technology. To overcome these barriers, managers involved in consortia and strategic alliances should take action in four areas to manage technology. These areas involve communication, distance, equivocality, and motivation.

COMMUNICATION

Communication involves both passive and active links. Passive links have a broad sweep and are usually media based, such as reports, articles, and videotapes. They are best for rapidly communicating the same message at the same time to a widely dispersed audience at a relatively low cost. However, they are impersonal and usually provide little feedback.

Active links are direct, person-to-person interactions. They range from teleconferences to ad hoc teams and on-site demonstrations. They encourage interpersonal communication and provide fast, focused feedback.

The fewer and more passive the communi-

cation links, the less likely the chance that technology will be successfully managed. The higher or more active the communication links, the more likely the chance of effective technology management. Consequently, consortia and alliance partners should increase active communication mechanisms. This involves interacting to understand the politics of each other's involvement, to identify differences and address them early on before they become problems, to select an effective liaison who appreciates and can deal with cultural differences between the organizations, and to plan an exit strategy at the beginning of the association.

DISTANCE

Distance involves both geographical and cultural proximity or separation. Management can lessen the physical distance of those engaged in research activities by promoting more active and direct communication links and by co-locating key players. Cultural distance between organizations poses greater managerial challenges. The lower the distance, the more managers understand the values, attitudes, and ways of doing things in the other organization, and the greater the chance of effective technology management.

To lower geographical/cultural distance, management should utilize champions to bridge the gaps, build support for the consortium/alliance at many levels among all parties, and develop social as well as business bonds among the key players. Actions to enhance geographic and cultural proximity may include expanding the number and type of personnel in activities to build ownership in the success of the venture; incorporating product and marketing personnel in research and development projects; documenting success stories; instituting training and education programs to help instill a service/customer-oriented attitude; conducting workshops on corporate culture issues; and encouraging visits and exchanges among personnel from the member organizations.

EQUIVOCALITY

Equivocality refers to the level of concreteness of the technology. Technology that is low in equivocality is easy to understand, demonstrable, and unambiguous. The lower the level of equivocality, the more likely that the technology will be managed effectively. To lower equivocality, management should clarify the expectations for, and applications of, the technology, protect the technology as intellectual property, create mechanisms to facilitate technology transfer, and implement ways to share and review performance.

Action to enhance the concreteness of the technology may include encouraging collaborative activities; requiring technology transfer objectives in planning efforts; conducting consortia or alliance-wide trade shows; expanding demonstrations of the technology; customizing the transfer process to the specific policies and procedures of each member company; and conducting tutorials.

MOTIVATION

Those involved in technology management among consortia and alliance members can legitimately ask, "What's in it for me?" The greater the degree of variety of incentives, rewards, and recognitions, the higher the motivation for those engaged in the process. Therefore, management should create a system of financial incentives, situational rewards, and personal recognition to increase motivation.

Actions to enhance motivation may include providing expanded teaming and collaborative opportunities; allocating funds for pet projects; ensuring exchanges and on-site visits; implementing a system of bonuses, honorariums, and ownership arrangements for those involved in the successful development and application of technology; recognizing key people in newsletters and videotapes, and with awards; and requiring evidence of technology management in performance appraisals.

USING U.S. FEDERAL GOVERNMENT RESOURCES IN R&D

Charles S. Saunders, Director, Government Relations, ICI Explosives (Division of ICI Americas, Inc.)

Most of us recognize the government as a major sponsor of research at universities and in 700 of its own laboratories throughout the United States. We are also aware that the government sponsors private industry in major technology and demonstration projects associated with the military, space, and energy programs. While we are aware that major prime defense contractors perform a great deal of the sponsored corporate projects, we often overlook the government as a potential sponsor or supporter of our own corporate R&D objectives. This oversight is particularly curious since the government is keenly interested in supporting industrial efforts.

Government funding policy for R&D allows corporations, universities, and research institutes to maintain exclusive commercial rights to inventions developed under sponsored programs. While the government maintains the right to use the technology without paying royalties, it allows the contractor to own and license the developed technology to other parties.

BENEFITS TO INDUSTRY

Government policies offer benefits to industry. The Small Business Innovative Research (SBIR) program not only funds small companies but encourages small-large company interaction and joint-venture relationships, relaxation of antitrust laws, and competing companies to collaborate in R&D.

Legislative actions, such as the Stevenson Wilder Act, the Federal Technology Transfer Act of 1986, and amendments in 1988 and 1990, have opened up federal laboratories to industry. The laboratories can collaborate under the terms of collaborative R&D agreements (CRADAs), and can generally provide a variety of services including intellectual property rights, expertise, and access to equipment. Under such agreements, a company can provide ideas, product, personnel, data, technology, and/or cash for the government services. The only prohibition in such agreements is that monies cannot be provided directly to industry by the government. The assignment of individuals to a laboratory has been shown to be the most cost-effective way to transfer technology and utilize the government assets.

Government laboratories provide ideal collaboration. They will never commercialize their own results. In most cases, they have modern and up-to-date facilities with qualified scientists and engineers who have an end-use orientation, a wide field of view in most cases, and state-of-the-art databases. Government laboratories and personnel have access to a number of reports and assessments from around the world.

OPPORTUNITIES FOR COLLABORATION

The primary responsibility to utilize the available assets resides with the corporate research and commercial development managers. With the vast variety of capabilities at the government laboratories, one must have clear objectives and requirements to be effective in this target-rich environment. Those companies that have received greatest benefit out of collaborations have been those that have quantified their needs and/or problems. Moreover, linkage must be made between the corporate goals and the funding agency's or laboratory's mandates.

While it is apparently simple for a corporation to define its objectives, most may need help in quantifying their technical and marketplace requirements. Government labs and employees can assist in establishing the requirements or in taking audits to support the corporate goals. They can use their massive databases and computational skills to identify and assess the state of the art throughout the world. Such assessments, in combination with the skills of individuals knowledgeable in the field, can save time and expense by rapidly solving technical problems using existing know-how or data. Using the government's physical assets, corporations can arrive at new products and associated performance data at greatly reduced time and capital expenditure.

ACCESS TO THE GOVERNMENT

Linkage with appropriate divisions of the government is made easier by the National Laboratory Consortium, through the Office of Technology Evaluation and Assessment, U.S. Department of Commerce. Other mechanisms include having direct contact with agency personnel via phone and in-person interviews; attending bidders' conferences; reading agency publications, published budgets, press releases and program announcements; predicting future interests by examining the critical technologies lists and general policy statements; tracking programs through the *Commerce Business Daily*, the *Federal Register*, and presentations at conferences; and joining federally managed consortia.

Each federal department and agency has something to offer, and essentially all units, down to the individual laboratories, provide multiple means of access, including detailed written descriptions of their various strategies, programs, and projects. Ports of entry for the uninitiated include the descriptive literature distributed by the SBIR programs that each major department administers and the Small Business Administration oversees. The *Directory of Federal Laboratory and Technology Resources: A Guide to Services, Facilities, and Expertise* is another guiding document, and the AAAS Research and Development study is a concise overview of the government's R&D budgets, programs, and goals.

The telephone may be the most convenient way to access useful information on government programs and activities, so the federal *Yellow Book* may be the key to the castle. Picking the person deemed most relevant to your needs and calling that person may be the most direct and timely route to access key government information.

As one example of this process, a company had a specific environmental interest and called the Environmental Protection Agency. It turned out that the EPA did not have the government's lead in this area, but passed it on to a relevant person in the air force, who in turn referred the caller to the army, who was administering an active funding program. Within twenty-four hours a large package arrived on the company's doorstep providing more information than it had ever expected.

MANAGING TECHNOLOGY IN A GLOBAL ECONOMY

D. Bruce Merrifield, Walter Bladstrom Executive Professor of Management, The Wharton School of Business, University of Pennsylvania

Industrial competitiveness has become the management of change in a competitive global marketplace. Survival and growth require restructuring to manage change, which is driven by powerful forces:

- Advancing technology has collapsed product and process life cycles in many industries to less than five years, obsolescing facilities and equipment long before their useful lives can be realized.
- Companies from foreign nations have targeted U.S. businesses, using low-cost labor and capital, combined with predatory pricing, to capture market share in many existing businesses.
- Moreover, any rice paddy in the world now can be transformed in less than a year to a state-of-the-art facility, operated by low-cost labor, exacerbating a growing world glut of capacity in many commodity businesses.

As a result, wealth no longer will be measured in terms of ownership of rapidly obsolescing fixed physical assets but rather in terms of access to knowledge-intensive, high value-added, largely technology-intensive, proprietary systems. This represents a para-digm shift in management strategy of historically unique proportions.

STRUCTURE TO MANAGE CHANGE

Few organizations hold captive all the skills and resources needed to maintain competitiveness in this period of rapidly accelerating change. Moreover, competitiveness translates not only into a need for continual incremental improvements in existing operations but also into the need for simultaneous development of next-generation systems. Strategic alliances increasingly will be required to accomplish the second of these needs.

Alliances can include licensing of advanced systems, joint ventures, equity participation in new growth businesses, formation of consortia to develop critical technologies, mergers, and acquisitions. Each has an appropriate role, depending on the nature of the opportunity, the cost and risk involved, and the availability of existing skills and resources.

The structure of alliances is important, particularly those involving joint ventures and consortia, since these involve forms of management not well understood. A limited part-

Exhibit 7-13. Limited Partnership Management Model

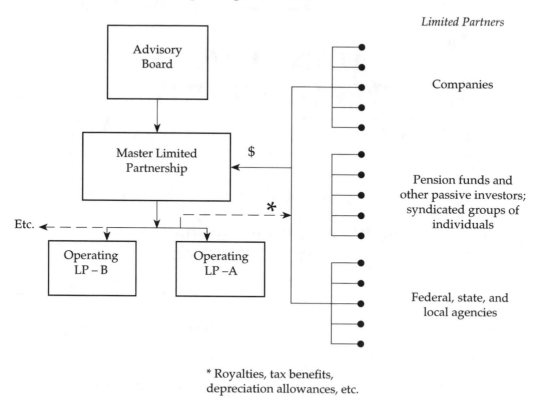

Limited Partners

Companies

Pension funds and
other passive investors;
syndicated groups of
individuals

Federal, state, and
local agencies

* Royalties, tax benefits,
depreciation allowances, etc.

Source: From D. B. Merrifield, A modern Marshall plan for evolving economies, *Journal of Business Venturing* 6(4):235, July 1981.

nership model, as shown in Exhibit 7-13, is one effective form of organization for this purpose.

LIMITED PARTNERSHIP

Properly structured, this model insulates participant-limited partners from both liability and antitrust concerns while preserving responsible management control of the day-to-day operations by the master partnership. It also provides a unique degree of flexibility in accessing diverse sources of funding, as well as needed skills and other resources, on a time-critical basis. The limited partnership avoids double taxation, and provides for all depreciation allowances and tax benefits, as well as profits, to flow back to limited partners in proportion to their investment. Passive-limited partners, by prearrangement, can be bought out at a later day at some agreed-

upon multiple of their investments, thus recapturing 100 percent equity ownership for the active company participants.

Failure modes can involve a lack of commitment by the top managements of participating partners, inadequate up-front specification of each partner's contribution, inflexibility in adjusting to midcourse corrections, based on new information, and lack of open communications. Each of these issues merits careful up-front consideration.

Within the partnership, a form of task force or modified matrix organization, as shown in Exhibit 7-14, is desirable. This structure involves a "champion" for each parallel track of activity. The champion's responsibility is to achieve an assigned mission, accessing and making use of skills and resources, wherever they exist, and whenever they are needed. Managers of the different skill functions (A, B, C, etc.) are responsible for the excellence

Exhibit 7-14. Modified Matrix Organization

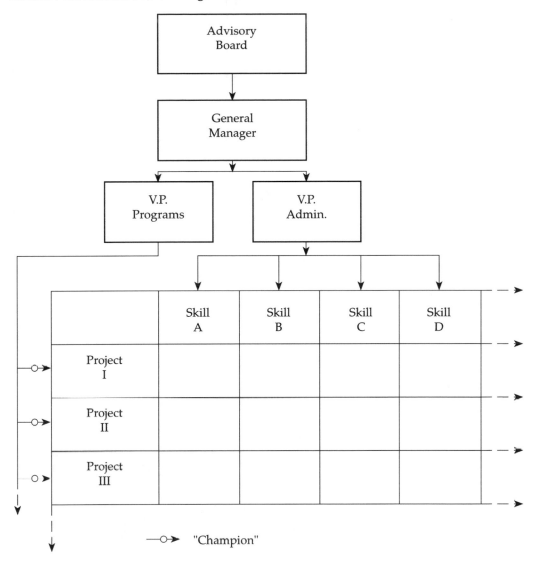

of their function, and for the continuous re-skilling and development of the individuals involved.

Alliances increasingly will be international in scope and an effective model has been developed for forming such joint-venture relationships. This model, International Partnerships for Commercialization of Technology (INPACT), which is shown in Exhibit 7-15, was developed by the U.S. Department of Commerce, and it now operates in Israel, France, Chile, Finland, and India, with re-

markable success. Many other nations are considering its use.

THE INPACT MODEL

Most companies do not have an intimate knowledge of the language, culture, and legal requirements for operating overseas, and do not have the resources to develop such capabilities. Yet many of these companies have leading-edge technology that could be glob-

Exhibit 7-15. The INPACT Model

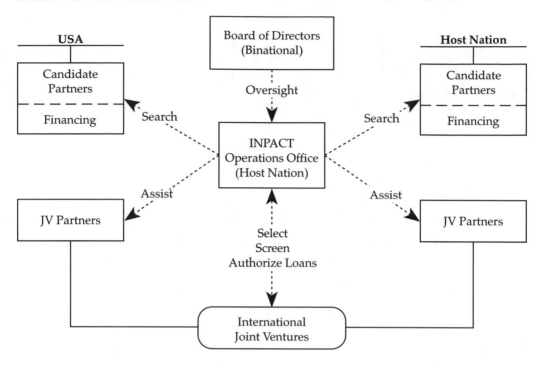

ally marketed. The INPACT program has developed a model that involves creation of a small office of professionally trained individuals who are natives of their country.

The first mission of this office is to search out promising new developments in the native country. A second mission is to find a U.S. partner who can contribute missing skills and resources for both further development and commercialization. The third is to provide seed funding to initiate the cooperative efforts needed. Significant advantages can result from these activities:

- The market potential for a new development is multiplied and access to foreign markets is opened for this and additional successive developments.
- Skills and resources are pooled to reduce cost, risk, and time to commercialization, and trust relationships are developed that tend to persist.
- Access to advanced technology results wherever it emerges. In the Israeli

model, about 70 percent of the technology has come from Israel, and in the India and French models, about 80 percent was initiated in those countries.

SHARED FLEXIBLE MANUFACTURING

Shared flexible computer integrated manufacturing (FCIM) facilities can provide not only the capability for continual incremental improvements in existing products but also the rapid prototyping and start-up production for new products. Such facilities, already in operation, are making multiple products for different companies in different industries, with both the quality and low-cost productivity needed for global competition. As these are "cloned" around the world through strategic alliances, they can be programmed from remote locations for just-in-time production wherever and whenever needed—a revolution in manufacturing, which also will further accelerate industrial globalization.

Manufacturing

Patricia Turnbaugh, Section Editor

Introduction   *Patricia Turnbaugh*   8-3

Developing Strategy in a Manufacturing Business   *Sara L. Beckman*   8-5

Planning Manufacturing Organizations   *Laura A. Lies*   8-18

Human Resources Planning   *John L. Schwab, Jr.*   8-22

Wage Incentives   *John L. Schwab, Jr.*   8-26

Quality Management   *Keki R. Bhote*   8-36

Manufacturing Processes and Materials   *Wendell Leimbach,
   Patricia Turnbaugh, and Michael Perril*   8-51

Managing Technology in Manufacturing   *Tom Inglesby*   8-64

Environmental Management   *L. Hall Healy, Jr.*   8-75

INTRODUCTION

Patricia Turnbaugh

How important is the survival of American manufacturing? A manufacturing expert in a recent roundtable discussion commented:

> I've never seen an example of any country that's maintained any quality standard of living that doesn't have a strong manufacturing base. We've become enamored [in the U.S.] with the service industry concept . . . but it's fundamentally impossible to export services on the scale necessary to maintain a balance of trade. (*Industry Week,* Sept. 7, 1992, p. 14)

The experts from around the world talked about the survival of American manufacturing into the next century. Five factors emerged that are critical to survival: (1) a long-term strategic orientation, rather than a shortsighted "quick solution" attitude; (2) a very strong, healthy competitive attitude; (3) a customer-driven process; (4) a state-of-the-art management of technology; and (5) the motivation to change, "the ability of managers to overcome the anxiety and risk that accompanies positive change" (*Industry Week,* Sept. 7, 1992). All of these survival factors are addressed in the chapters in this section; they support the opinion that manufacturing is a critical component in the country's competitive position and a determinant of our standard of living.

Four management resources are necessary in companies seeking to be world-class com-petitors: (1) technology; (2) a structure that promotes competitive advantage; (3) well-defined and closely integrated information flows that allow continuous improvement; and (4) a commitment to training, educating, and motivating people. To be an effective participant in the global marketplace, manufacturers must *combine* technology with appropriate organizational structures, cultural changes, information flows, and human resource policies. Without the combination, manufacturers will not be able to fully capitalize on technological opportunities and effectively become world-class operations.

The chapters in this section develop the major lessons to help companies compete effectively. The first chapter, "Developing Strategy in a Manufacturing Business," points out the importance of understanding the needs of the customer as a starting point for a solid manufacturing strategy. This viewpoint supports the position of the round-table participants. The "Quality Management" chapter expands the discussion into a "road map" for achieving world-class competition and encourages a recognition of the effectiveness of a strategy that focuses overwhelmingly on accomplishing the highest levels of quality.

Another aspect of competition deals with human resources issues. The chapters by John Schwab deal with human resources planning and wage incentives. Schwab examines the key roles played by effective and economical uses of employee skills and abilities in the production process. Specifically, he examines human resource techniques and systems that can become powerful tools for controlling direct, indirect, clerical, and even managerial costs.

The remaining chapters cover key manufacturing issues that further contribute to effective operations. The "Manufacturing Processes and Materials" chapter examines and deals with strategic issues related to both aspects. The following chapter, "Managing Technology in Manufacturing," expands the discussion into technology issues that affect the competitive posture of a manufacturer. Finally, L. Hall Healy addresses environmental issues facing manufacturers. His chapter points out the pervasive effect of efforts to conserve resources, prevent pollution, dispose of waste, and otherwise deal with producing goods in today's environmentally sensitive world.

Manufacturing has become more complex in the past 10 years, with regard to technology, the environment, and meeting customer needs. The articles in this section offer insights into the new complexities.

Patricia Turnbaugh is a consultant to the Foundation for Manufacturing Excellence and chairperson of the association's Education and Training Committee. Her activities with FME involve identification of manufacturing training needs, development of appropriate courses or programs, and referral of manufacturers to selected providers of training services. She is also the director of continuing studies programs at Dundalk Community College and is responsible for education and technical training for manufacturers.

DEVELOPING STRATEGY IN A MANUFACTURING BUSINESS

**Sara L. Beckman, Haas School of Business,
University of California, Berkeley**

The role that manufacturing plays in a country's competitive position and its effect on the standard of living in that country have been discussed at length over the past decade. The MIT Commission on Productivity summarizes the situation nicely in the introduction to the book *Made in America:*

> To live well, a nation must produce well. In recent years many observers have charged that American industry is not producing as well as it ought to produce, or as well as it used to produce, or as well as the industries of some other nations have learned to produce. If the charges are true and if the trend cannot be reversed, then sooner or later the American standard of living must pay the penalty. (M. L. Dertouzos, R. K. Lester, and R. M. Solow, *Made in America: Regaining the Productive Edge*, Cambridge, MA: MIT Press, 1989)

Stephen Cohen and John Zysman put the issue a bit more succinctly in *Manufacturing Matters: The Myth of the Post-Industrial Economy* (New York: Basic Books, 1987):

> We must reorganize production, not abandon it.... If the United States is to remain a wealthy and powerful economy, American manufacturing must automate, not emigrate. The difference is decisive.

THE COMPETITIVE CHALLENGE

As both sets of authors argue, manufacturing is critical to the well-being of any country's economy and should be considered so by managers in manufacturing businesses. The past decade has seen a significant awakening in U.S. industry, and elsewhere, that manufacturing *does* indeed matter and can make significant contributions to the firm's competitiveness. This new level of awareness has brought with it a new view of the role of manufacturing strategy and its development in an organization.

There are marvelous examples of companies in the United States that have taken on the competitiveness challenge . . . and *won!*

- Motorola set up a highly automated facility in Boynton Beach, Florida, to build Bandit Pagers. The plant has received considerable publicity as a very successful venture, and is credited with allowing Motorola to gain market share from the Japanese, as well as to seek and win the Baldrige Award.* The process is considered a major break with traditional Motorola culture, and one that will be modeled in other parts of the company.

- Copeland Corporation, a manufacturer of compressors for refrigeration, is located in the heartland of the United States. A new president, Matt Diggs, recently put the company on a new path to competitiveness by creating a set of focused factories that caused Copeland to reinvest in its manufacturing function, and to give manufacturing equal status with the marketing and R&D functions. Even the "remanufacturing" business was given a new factory, and has turned around nicely.

- Both Nucor and Chaparral Steel have shown "Big Steel" that an industry seen to be dying can be revived. As mini-mill companies, they have an advantage over "Big Steel" in being less vertically integrated and thus more nimble. Recent innovations in process technology are allowing them to compete directly with "Big Steel" in rolling flat sheet metal for the auto industry, and both companies have been known to sell steel in Japan.

All of these companies have made renewed commitments to manufacturing through investments in people and process technology in the manufacturing function itself, as well as in thinking through major strategic infrastructure decisions, such as vertical integration and facilities focus. In this chapter, the process of developing manufacturing strategies and the critical role that they play in achieving competitiveness are discussed.

In essence, we are saying that a good manufacturing strategy starts with a clear understanding of the customer, and of what the customer wants in the way of cost, quality, availability, and features. Strategic decisions on these dimensions lead to a set of decisions

about capacity, facilities, vertical integration, process technology, information management, organizational design, product generation, and order fulfillment. These decisions are made consistently with the needs of the customer, and are internally consistent with one another. The strategy should be implemented as a pattern of decisions made by the organization, and that pattern of decisions must be fully supported by the accounting and performance measurement systems in place.

PROCESS-ORIENTED MANUFACTURING

Historically, when people referred to manufacturing, they meant the production function itself. More recently, a broader view of manufacturing has emerged. Displayed in Exhibit 8-1, it is labeled "Big M" manufacturing by MIT's Leaders for Manufacturing program.

"Big M" manufacturing suggests that one consider all of the functions in a manufacturing business collectively in decision making and strategizing about the business. It is how these functions work together to provide the customer with the desired results that matters. To make this happen, boundaries between the functional areas—manufacturing, marketing, R&D, finance, and human resources—must be broken down. In some visions of the future manufacturing organization, these functions no longer exist at all. Rather, they are replaced by process-oriented organizations, and exist only as "homes of expertise" to which employees periodically return to be refreshed.

At Hewlett-Packard, we have begun a transition to such a process-oriented organization. Over two years ago, we converted our corporate manufacturing organization to a group we call the product generation team, and we asked that team to focus on the three processes we felt were critical to the future success of the company:

1. *Strategic investment* is the process whereby we make decisions about allocating resources to the various activities

---

* The Baldrige Award is a prize given by the U.S. Commerce Department to companies that achieve particularly high levels of quality in their business efforts.

Exhibit 8-1. The Integrated Manufacturing Enterprise: Overlapping Functions, Disciplines, and Activities

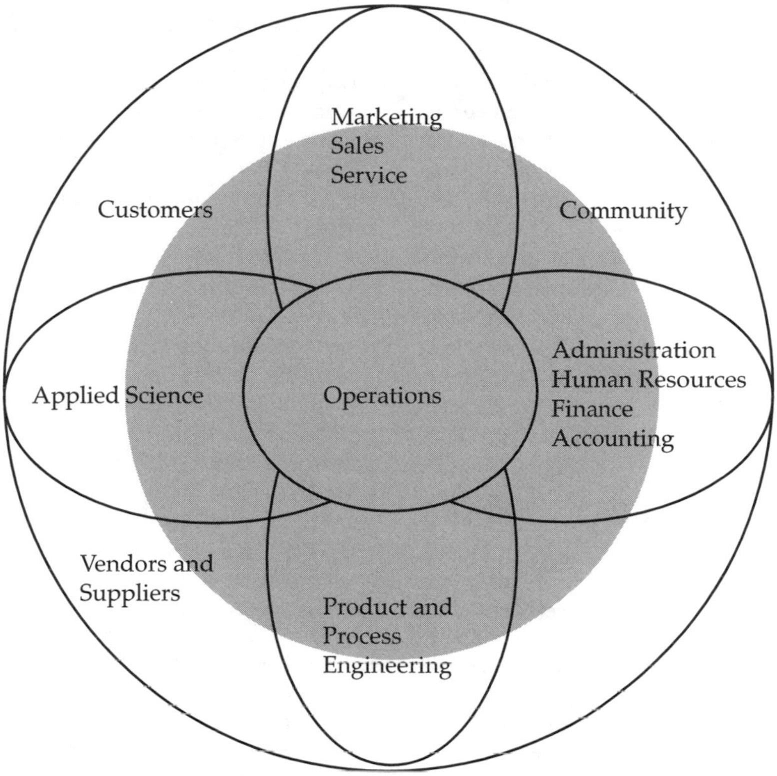

Marketing
Sales
Service

Customers

Community

Applied Science

Operations

Administration
Human Resources
Finance
Accounting

Vendors and
Suppliers

Product and
Process
Engineering

Source: Reproduced with permission from promotional literature for MIT's Leaders for Manufacturing program.

that we undertake as an organization. In a sense, it is the process of strategic planning, but the notion of strategic investment focuses us much more directly on the end result of the strategic planning process: investment in the processes and activities that are critical to the long-term success of the organization.

2. *Product generation* is the process that begins with an initial product concept, continues through product design and development, and ends with ramp-up of production and delivery of the first products to the customer. It is the process around which the time-to-market and break-even time metrics are being placed.

3. *Order fulfillment* is the process that focuses on the ongoing process of taking customer orders and filling those orders. This process clearly overlaps with the back end of the product generation process, which can effectively be considered to be the source of new products to the order fulfillment process.

By focusing our corporate efforts on these three processes (rather than on our traditional corporate manufacturing, corporate engineering, and corporate marketing functions) we began to create a major shift in our thinking as well as in the thinking of the line organizations in the company. We began, for example, to integrate our information systems so that product design information fed directly into manufacturing planning systems. We began to think about new product development teams from a manufacturing perspective and we began to model entire supply chains to minimize inventory throughout, rather than in a specific factory or warehouse.

In most companies, this process perspective is being driven by the need to improve quality beyond previously set limits, as well as by a need to significantly reduce cycle times. Both of these forces create the need to go beyond our traditional functional views and to think about optimization of the process overall. This, in turn, has given rise to a recent fad to "reengineer" processes at a broad level in many of our organizations. It is with this broad process perspective that we approach this chapter on manufacturing strategy. *Only when we view manufacturing as consisting of a full set of process elements will we begin to develop its full competitive capability.*

WHAT IS STRATEGY?

The concepts of strategy development began with the military and provide useful bases for beginning our understanding of business strategy today. In military terms, "Strategy is the art of the employment of battles as a means to gain the object of war. In other words, strategy forms the plan of the war, maps out the proposed course of the different campaigns which comprise the war, and regulates the battles to be fought in each" (General K. Von Clausewitz, *On War,* Princeton, NJ: Princeton University Press, 1984).

Several aspects of this definition are worth noting. First, the definition acknowledges both a *scientific* and an *artistic* aspect to the development of strategy. It is important to understand that strategy development entails a fair amount of data collection and analysis, but it also requires that managers apply some "gut" understanding of the industry and of their own business to the planning process.

Next, the definition emphasizes attaining the "object of the war" through a focus on the enemy. Clearly, in the business case, the objective of the war is to satisfy the customer, and the enemy is the competition. It is critically important to focus on both of these aspects of our businesses. Tom Peters, a well-known management guru and prolific writer, has told us over and over again that the cus-

tomer is critical, yet examples abound of companies that have lost sight of what their customers really want and of how to provide it. Understanding the competition is no less critical. The current craze in the United States to do competitive benchmarking may provide some indication of the extent to which we had lost sight of our competitors and of their core capabilities.

Finally, the definition emphasizes advantageous conditions, which suggests that an organization understand not only its competitors' strengths and weaknesses but also its own. Of particular importance is the need for companies to identify their core competencies as a competitive tool. (This topic is covered in detail in "The Core Competence of the Corporation" by C. K. Prahalad and Gary Hamel in the *Harvard Business Review,* May-June 1990.)

Military strategy definitions have been used as the basis for numerous different definitions of business strategy. Most definitions agree that a business strategy must:

1. Describe the methods of competition (e.g., "We wish to occupy a specific niche of the marketplace that is not currently occupied by other major competitors").
2. Define the contributions of each product and function to the goals of the business (e.g., "Our low-end product offerings will keep low-end competitors from moving into our niche").
3. Allocate resources among products and functions (e.g., "Manufacturing will receive X dollars to develop flexible manufacturing capabilities for building custom products for customers in our niche").

In short, customers are the focus of the business strategy. The strategic statement must describe both the customer-driven goals of the business and the allocation of resources to achieve those goals, and it must be based on facts about the competition.

Defining Customer Need

In simplistic terms, the business strategy must start with the customer. Customers will buy products or services from your organization rather than from your competitors based on their perception of one or more of the following characteristics: low product or service cost, high product or service quality, prompt product or service availability, or distinguishing product or service features.

When a company defines its desired position on each of these characteristics compared to its primary competitors, the company is defining its business strategy. Note that this may vary for different products and different markets, thus requiring proper segmentation of the businesses within the organization. The key question is which combination will allow the company to attract the most customers versus the primary competition.

Notice that these characteristics are no longer considered mutually exclusive, as they once were. We now understand that we can get to low cost through having higher quality. And we understand that flexibility and cost are not necessarily juxtaposed, as we used to think they were. The ability to be competitive on multiple dimensions adds a new challenge to the management of our organizations as we begin to seek multiple objectives simultaneously.

The Strategic Planning Process

The strategic planning process in an iterative one. It has no real beginning and no real end, but rather should operate continuously in an information-gathering and information-processing mode. Many companies still perform their strategic planning processes annually in a major data collection and processing effort that results in a long, written plan that often resides in a desk drawer for the remainder of the year. Recent work by Kathleen Eisenhardt ("Speed and Strategic Choice: How Managers Accelerate Decision Making," *California Management Review,* 1990) suggests that more successful companies perform their strategic planning and development in a more real-time fashion. Specifically, she suggests that speedy strategic decision makers:

- Track real-time information on firm operations and the competitive environment.

- Build multiple, simultaneous alternatives.
- Seek the advice of experienced counselors.
- Use "consensus with qualification" to resolve conflicts.
- Integrate the decision with other decisions and tactics.

According to Eisenhardt, all of these should be done on a real-time basis.

The successful companies constantly scan their environments for information on what their customers want, what their competitors are up to, and what technologies are available to meet both the competitive and customer requirements. They use this information regularly to keep their strategic direction up-to-date and on track with the realities of the environment around them. This real-time perspective of strategy development is new to most of us, but is likely a critical perspective for getting us into the pace of the more rapidly changing environment in which we are attempting to operate. Our definition of strategy and the concept of real-time planning processes provide a framework for thinking about the next important area: the manufacturing operations themselves.

MANUFACTURING CONTRIBUTION TO THE BUSINESS STRATEGY

Traditionally, we have thought of strategy development in terms of the individual functional areas in the organization. In this mode, we developed separate manufacturing, marketing, R&D, finance, and human resources strategies and attempted to integrate these to form the overall strategy for each business in the organization. More recently, we are starting to think about the development of process-focused strategies—product generation and order fulfillment strategies—that cut across traditional functional boundaries, integrating them in fulfillment of the greater requirements of the business strategy.

Manufacturing Strategy Factors

Whether your organization is developing a traditional functional strategy, or a broader cross-functional strategy, several fundamental factors are important:

1. The functional or process strategy must support the business strategy by focusing the functional activity or the process on a small set of objectives dictated by customer need.
2. The strategy should describe allocation of resources within the functional area or across the process in a way that allows achievement of the functional or process objectives.
3. The patterns of actual decisions (e.g., funding, human resource allocation) made over time by the functional areas working on the process should be consistent with the stated strategy. Many times this does not happen; thus, the *stated* strategy is displaced by the *enacted* strategy.

Essentially, these factors encourage the firm to link the manufacturing strategy to the requirements spelled out by the business strategy. Our simple list of the reasons why customers buy products and services—on the basis of cost, quality, availability, and features—is useful here. If the business strategy has spelled out these requirements clearly, then we can determine the ways in which a supporting functional or process strategy will support the business strategy.

Developing the Manufacturing Strategy

If we are concerned about developing a manufacturing strategy, the implications are reasonably clear. Providing an advantage in the cost category implies being able to produce products or services at the lowest possible cost. The attempt in manufacturing will be to minimize materials, labor, and overhead costs associated with manufacturing the product. Advantages in quality must be obtained from conformance to (or betterment of) customer requirements, which requires that the manufacturing organization develop a strong total quality management program. Availability measures the ability to deliver the product or service when and where desired, as well as

the ability to respond to changes in market demand and opportunities. Manufacturing makes a contribution to an availability objective by being flexible and/or responsive. Finally, manufacturing can contribute product or service features whenever its process allows inclusion of unique attributes in the product design or service, which requires that manufacturing be innovative in its development of new process technologies.

The manufacturing strategy, then, can be driven by a clear understanding of the objectives of the business strategy. It must be well integrated with the other functional strategies to create the overall business strategy. The manufacturing strategy itself is composed of a number of critical decisions about various aspects of the manufacturing function.

STRATEGIC DECISION-MAKING CATEGORIES

Once the basis on which the business will compete is well understood, and these objectives have been translated to a set of objectives for the manufacturing function, a set of decisions about the manufacturing activity itself can be made. We typically categorize these decisions into three areas: structural decisions, process decisions, and relationship decisions. Structural decisions, in turn, break down into three areas: vertical integration, capacity, and facilities.

Structural Decisions

Vertical Integration. Each manufacturing business must make decisions as to how backward integrated (toward its suppliers) or forward integrated (toward its customers) it wishes to be. Historically, capital-intensive industries tended to be more backward integrated; labor-intensive industries tended to be forward integrated. Over time, vertical integration strategies may change significantly to meet the changing needs of the industry.

Take the computer industry as an example. Since the mid-1980s, a major shift has occurred in the degree of vertical integration. The older companies (e.g., DEC, HP, IBM) have begun to shed manufacturing processes they once found important, like bending sheet metal, molding plastic parts, and die casting metal frames, in favor of investing in software developers and hardware original equipment manufacturers (OEMs). The younger companies (e.g., Sun, Apple) chose not to backward integrate in the first place, preferring instead the flexibility of choosing, disk drive manufacturers, and the like, based on their current needs.

Interesting questions arise as to which type of company is ultimately in a better position to compete. Is the larger, more vertically integrated company more able to compete on proprietary technology? Or is the smaller, less vertically integrated company more nimble in moving among the most current technologies without the risk of major investments?

Vertical integration decisions may also result in a company moving into a new business entirely. Nucor Steel began as a joist manufacturer catering to the building industry. To assure itself of a low-cost supply of steel, the company backward integrated and began building steel mini-mills. Today, it is giving "Big Steel" a run for the money in the steel market.

Whatever decisions are made about vertical integration, they must be made explicitly. Too often we find that companies make their vertical integration decisions indirectly, through a series of make-buy decisions. Consider an internally focused sheet metal shop that serves multiple divisions in a large company. It is forced by accounting practices to bill out all of its costs at the end of each year. In a low-volume year, large negative variances are charged back to the customers who used the shop the most. The buyers representing these internal customers, in turn, decide that they can likely get a better deal with an outside vendor. And they do. Ultimately, the internal fabricator is put out of business by a series of such events. The company has not made a strategic decision to either keep or get out of the business. In the long run, such decisions will be much more successful if made early and explicitly.

Capacity. Capacity decisions entail deciding how much capacity, and of what type, should be added (or taken away) at what time. These decisions tend to be easier in times of growth, when new increments of capacity can be filled quickly. They are less clear in times of downsizing, when the propensity is to hold onto old and excess capacity too long. A number of dynamics have affected capacity decisions in recent years. The push to improve operations management through total quality management (TQM) and just-in-time (JIT) has significantly increased throughput and decreased resource requirements. This has left a number of organizations with excess capacity. External pressures to develop manufacturing capability in various foreign locations have caused companies to set up new plants, thus adding capacity that in aggregate may not actually be needed.

Capacity decisions are particularly strategic in highly capital-intensive industries, where the decision to add capacity is largely irreversible once carried out. The computer memory business provides an interesting example. In this industry, the product evolves regularly over time (e.g., from 1 megabyte to 4 megabyte DRAM). Memory producers carefully plan to phase out their old process capability and phase in the new so that they maintain little excess capacity of the old, but can quickly fill the new capacity with sufficient volume to have it pay off quickly. Clearly, their ability to make these moves more smoothly than their competitors is critical. Furthermore, they can preempt their competitors by filling their capacity slightly ahead of the competitors and thereby gain market share. Losing in this game can be very expensive.

In less capital-intensive industries, other interesting questions arise. To what extent is the work force a fixed asset? Is the company free to hire and fire at will, thus managing capacity tightly? Many companies use temporary or "flexforce" employees to manage their capacity at lower cost. Recently, companies have begun to manage their labor capacity more closely, particularly in the white-collar work force that was less well managed in the past.

Facilities. Facilities decisions are closely linked to capacity decisions and entail deciding how big facilities will be, where they will be located, and how they will be focused. The sizing of manufacturing facilities has been studied widely over the years. Some argue that a single facility should never be larger than 500 people to maximize interaction among the workers. Notions of economy of scale, however, force many companies to operate with facilities much larger than this. Recent reports on manufacturing trends in Japan (for example, see the *Manufacturing Futures Study* results from Boston University or the *Manufacturing 2001* report from Japan) suggest that the Japanese are moving toward the establishment of small factories located close to their market. They expect, however, that these factories will be highly automated, and will be capable of twenty-four-hour operation. They increasingly view their factories as "design factories" that can rapidly turn around new product introductions or customize products to customer requirements. This model is quite different from the facilities models currently used for U.S.-based manufacturing organizations.

Facilities location decisions are also becoming critically important. As a large number of countries, for example, China, Korea, and India, are trying to grow their industrial base, they are requiring that companies wishing to sell products in the country also build product there. The globalization of our manufacturing base forces more long-term strategic thinking about the location of future manufacturing facilities. It also requires the closure of U.S.-based facilities that may be providing excess capacity.

Finally, an important aspect of creating facilities strategies is focus. As an organization's product line becomes more complex, it is likely that the number of different manufacturing processes it uses will also become large and complex. Organizations develop focus strategies because of a need to reduce complexity. A company with a few homogeneous product lines has simple production processes, and a company with a large number of products with divergent requirements has complex production processes. As shown in Exhibit 8-2, we describe an operation having a small number of process technologies as process focused and an operation manufacturing similar products as product focused.

When the numbers of products and technologies in a facility are both large, it is said to be an all-purpose facility.

Each case in this matrix has different implications. For instance, in an all-purpose facility, several important strategic issues arise. Can the facility be separated into a number of smaller product-focused facilities? Can it be separated into smaller process-focused facilities? Should the facilities be separated physically? Should they be separated organizationally? How would the facilities be governed to meet the overall needs of the company? What, then, are the infrastructure requirements?

The matrix focuses on processes and products as primary dimensions along which an organization might choose to focus its operations. Other dimensions include materials and markets. Paper products companies and food processing companies often choose to focus themselves along the materials dimension. A paper products company would likely choose to locate itself close to its raw materials—the woods. A beet sugar refiner, on the other hand, would likely locate near the beet fields.

A company might choose multiple dimensions of focus. IBM, for example, has product-, process-, and market-focused facilities. It has IC fabrication facilities that are process focused and feed many other product/market-focused plants. IBM has disk drive plants that are duplicated in Europe and the United States, thus allowing both a product focus and a market focus. Larger companies can afford such multiplant strategies. In general, companies that have developed focus strategies outperform those that have not.

In sum, structural decisions entail understanding the vertical integration, capacity, and facilities strategies of the company, all of which are intertwined with one another and with the decisions to which we now turn entailing processes and relationships.

Process Decisions

The second strategic decision category involves process decisions, which focus on a number of dimensions of the manufacturing process itself, on the information systems used, and on the organizational design em-

Exhibit 8-2. Product-Process Flow

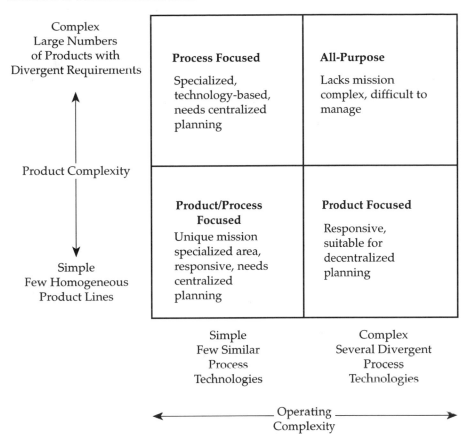

ployed. We might also call them *infrastructure decisions*. Three subcategories are manufacturing process, information technology, and organizational design decisions.

Manufacturing Process. The organization must decide on the type of process it will employ, the degree of automation of that process, what equipment will be used, and how flexible the process will be. A useful tool for thinking about the type of process a manufacturing organization might choose to put in place is the product/process matrix shown in Exhibit 8-3.

The relationship between product life cycle and process life cycle provides a framework for developing alternative manufacturing approaches. The matrix shows a product going through a three-phase life cycle beginning

with product introduction. At that point, the market is small, changes in the product design are frequent, standardization is minimal, and the highest potential for gaining competitive advantage is to offer superior service. As the product matures, it becomes more stable, more standardized, and product quality/performance becomes the primary source of competitive advantage. Finally, the product becomes almost fully standardized, its market volume plateaus at a relatively high level, and competition is primarily based on price. Products that do not necessarily go through this cycle can be classified according to their position in the cycle.

Intuitively, one can define the characteristics of the process technology required at each stage of the product life cycle. A new product requires manufacturing flexibility. A job-shop

Exhibit 8-3. Product Life Cycle and Process Life Cycle

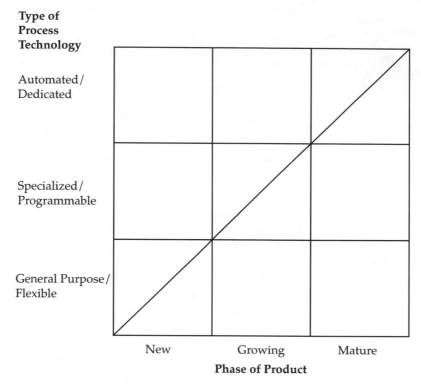

**Type of
Process
Technology**

Automated/
Dedicated

Specialized/
Programmable

General Purpose/
Flexible

New   Growing   Mature

Phase of Product

or general-purpose process best meets this requirement. The middle-age product requires superior quality and room for innovation. A specialized or programmable technology is appropriate. The mature, standardized product must be dependable and must be produced at the lowest cost possible. This is achieved with highly automated and dedicated process technology.

Understanding the position of a company on this matrix provides useful insights. For example, do all products require the same level of technology? If not, should some products be redefined? Or should the process technologies employed be changed? Does the competition define its product in the same way? What competitive niche or position is the competitor attempting to fill? What position should be assumed to meet the competition?

Another view of the product/process matrix is shown in Exhibit 8-4. The framework of this matrix was first popularized by Steven

Wheelwright and Robert Hayes in 1984 in *Restoring Our Competitive Edge: Competing Through Manufacturing*. Here products are described as ranging from one-of-a-kind to commodity-like. Processes range from job-shop oriented to continuous flow. The parallels with the product/process life cycle matrix are obvious.

An evolutionary view of this matrix is interesting to contemplate. Prior to the invention of the assembly line by Henry Ford, the matrix would have consisted of just the oval at the top; everything was made in a job-shop environment. After the advent of the assembly line, the right-hand end of the matrix dropped, creating the diagonal effect described by the second oval. Indeed, for most of this century, we have thought in terms of intersections along the diagonal oval—for example, multiple products with low volume should be handled as a disconnected line flow (batch) process. As flexible manufacturing systems come into vogue, we hypothesize

Exhibit 8-4. Product Structure, Product Life Cycle Stage

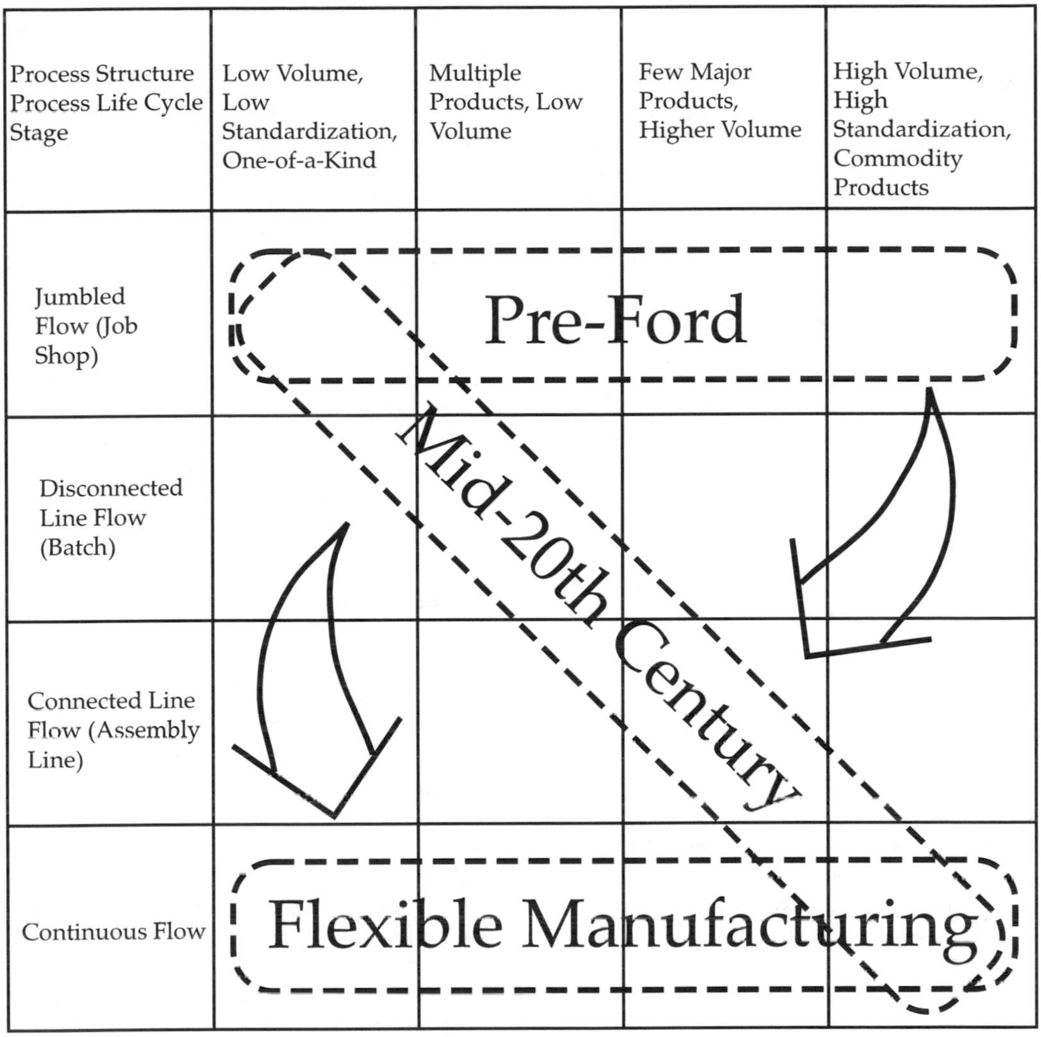

Process Structure Process Life Cycle Stage	Low Volume, Low Standardization, One-of-a-Kind	Multiple Products, Low Volume	Few Major Products, Higher Volume	High Volume, High Standardization, Commodity Products
Jumbled Flow (Job Shop)		Pre-Ford		
Disconnected Line Flow (Batch)				
Connected Line Flow (Assembly Line)				
Continuous Flow	Flexible Manufacturing			

(Diagonal label: Mid-20th Century)

that the other end of the oval could drop, resulting in the oval at the bottom of the matrix. In this environment, one-of-a-kind products may well be built on the same line as commodity products. Imagine, for example, purple, green, and pink pens alternating with black pens in the ballpoint pen factory. Allen-Bradley's motor starter plant in Milwaukee is an example of such a flexible factory.

This has important implications for managing the product generation process, or, more specifically, the prototyping of new products. With a sufficiently flexible system, such as that in place in the Motorola Bandit Pager factory, prototyping can be easily performed on the same line as the regular production. In the Motorola case, prototypes are run on the weekends, and weekly production schedules remain uninterrupted.

Information Technology. Investment in information systems is becoming an increasingly critical dimension of manufacturing strategy. Information systems must be developed to support the process technology chosen as described in the last section. When Tracey O'Rourke, CEO of Allen-Bradley, describes the effort that his company went through to automate the Milwaukee motor starter plant, he emphasizes the difficulty of developing the computer-integrated manufacturing (CIM) software. Scott Shamlin, manager of the Bandit Pager line at Motorola, makes similar comments. Both realize that the information technology is really the source of competitive advantage that their organizations have, not the process technology itself.

Other chapters in this section describe in more detail the evolution of information technology and the role it plays in manufacturing businesses, so we will not belabor the points here. It is sufficient to point out that the amount of integration of the product generation and order fulfillment processes using information technology will radically change the competitive postures of scores of companies trying to win the race against time. Time-to-market and overall process cycle times will shrink radically in companies that choose to invest in information management.

Organizational Design. The last infrastructure that must be made in a manufacturing strategy is to determine what structure, reward and evaluation systems, selection and training procedures, and the like, the organization should use. There is a strong movement in U.S. manufacturing businesses to better understand their organizational designs and to improve them. Many companies talk about empowerment, self-managed teams, and high-performance work systems. Almost all of these approaches entail a thorough examination of the social, technical, and business systems in place in the company and, in many cases, lead to a radical rethinking of these systems. Spans of control are being significantly increased, layers of management removed, and responsibility pushed down in the organization. The result is a very different view of who is in charge, who should interact with the customer, and who should be playing what roles.

It is critical that the organizational design

be integrated with the process and information technologies that are in place. If, for example, employees are rewarded for process innovation, there should be sufficient capital available for them to innovate. Nucor Steel has an innovative incentive system that allows workers to make significant bonuses if they meet established production goals. There has to be sufficient production capacity in the system for them to be able to make their goals. The organizational design is dependent on decisions made in capacity management and process technology.

Thus, we have covered both the structural decisions (vertical integration, capacity, facilities) and infrastructure decisions (process technology, information technology, organizational design) that manufacturing managers must make. Finally, we turn to the relationship decisions.

Relationship Decisions

Earlier in this chapter we talked about the process orientation that many companies adopt for product generation and order fulfillment. Relationship decisions entail understanding these process-oriented views of the organization.

The product generation process is receiving considerable attention as companies rush to reduce their time to market. Manufacturing has a critical role to play with R&D and marketing in the execution of the product generation process. Design for manufacturability and concurrent engineering are reasonably well-understood roles that manufacturing plays. Less often talked about are the roles of procurement and prototyping.

The procurement function is playing an increasingly prominent role in many manufacturing organizations as the percentage of value added by any given organization shrinks. Material costs frequently compose 50 to 70 percent of a product's manufacturing cost, making procurement a key player in keeping product costs in line. A significant shift away from arm's-length management of suppliers to the creation of value-added partnerships and strategic alliances with key technology vendors has also placed procurement in a different role. Increasingly, R&D must rely on the procurement organization to help in the early identification of qualified vendors and qualified parts that will not only function in the ultimate product but that will be easily built, procured, and assembled into the end product.

More and more companies are also learning the critical role prototyping plays and are wresting responsibility away from R&D for the management of the prototyping process. The prototype process for the HP DeskJet was managed by manufacturing. A set schedule of prototype runs was maintained throughout the development cycle. If engineers had submitted their work in time, they could see it in the prototypes produced. If not, they simply missed out, as no prototype run was held up for them. This forced early surfacing of problems with the product design, allowed marketing plenty of opportunity for early test markets, and meant that manufacturing was ready to ramp production quickly once the product was introduced. IBM concurs with the need to do early and frequent prototyping, particularly on large systems. Although the individual parts of a system may work well on their own, problems inevitably surface during a system prototype phase.

Manufacturing strategies must therefore consider the relationships to be maintained throughout the product generation process. In addition, manufacturing must maintain relationships with sales and marketing in the order fulfillment process. How many of us have heard stories about the lack of integration of the sales order-taking system and the manufacturing scheduling system? The recent development of the concept of time-based competition (*Competitiveness through Total Cycle Time: An Overview for CEOs*, Philip R. Thomas, New York: McGraw-Hill, 1990) has emphasized the fact that the manufacturing process itself consumes but a small percentage of the lead time from placement of a customer order to delivery of that order. Much of the time is spent in translating the order as the salesperson received it into instructions that are meaningful to the manufacturing floor. Severe pressures to reduce cycle times are forcing manufacturing to work more closely with sales and marketing on the order fulfillment process.

A number of companies are also starting to worry about inventory management across the entire supply chain from supplier to end customer. By taking this view, they are forcing the functional areas to jointly make trade-off decisions about where inventory is optimally carried. Manufacturing, for example, may be asked to carry inventory of semifinished product to rapidly meet demand for a variety of end products rather than have marketing/distribution carry sufficient inventory of the final product. When each individual function optimizes its inventory by itself, this is not possible.

The need for manufacturing to work more closely with R&D, marketing, and sales will only increase over the next few years. Taking a process perspective—product generation or order fulfillment—will be critical to the transition.

IMPLEMENTATION ISSUES

There are numerous implementation issues associated with the execution of a manufacturing strategy. We focus on two of them here: the accounting system and performance measurement.

Recently, the validity of our accounting systems has been seriously challenged for the first time in nearly a hundred years. Activity-based costing is beginning to replace standard costing systems based on direct labor and direct materials. Leaders of this effort include Robin Cooper and Robert Kaplan of Harvard Business School (see *Relevance Lost: The Rise and Fall of Managerial Accounting,* Cambridge, MA: Harvard University Press, 1989).

Manufacturing is learning, at long last, the actual cost of the activities being performed. Furthermore, managers are able to give good cost information to the R&D organization to use in new product design decisions. This information is critical input to the strategic planning process. It allows for a much clearer understanding of the cost trade-offs being made in, for example, vertical integration decisions.

These costs systems still need to be augmented with information systems that track quality and time throughout the product generation and order fulfillment processes. It is only with a complete set of information that solid strategic decision making can be supported.

The performance measurement system is an integral aspect of most cost accounting systems. Frequently, it is data from the cost accounting systems that are used to judge management performance, and thus provide the basis for their pay. It is critical that the information being collected and used to motivate performance be consistent with the direction being set by the strategy. A food processing company's manufacturing executive once

stated that his critical strategic factor was flexibility. He wanted to be able to respond to marketing's requests for new styles of boxes or packed inserts in cereal boxes. His manufacturing engineers, however, were measured on how well they did at cost reduction on the factory floor. They were clearly not supporting a strategy of flexibility.

It is easy for strategies to fall apart at the point of implementation. Many never become more than the paper on which they are written. Without the support of a well-conceived accounting and performance measurement system, even a well-constructed strategy is likely to fail.

PLANNING MANUFACTURING ORGANIZATIONS

Laura A. Lies, Corning-Asahi Video Products Company

Drastic changes in the global marketplace have forced companies to develop new ways to compete. In the struggle to provide world-class products to increasingly demanding customers, the competitive manufacturing company of today must create a flexible management strategy.

An important part of strategy relates to organizational design or structure, that is, how work is structured within the company. The trend is toward contingency organizational design; different structures are more effective in different situations. The contingency approach requires a transformation of the basic

philosophy that there are preferred ways of organizing that can remain constant over time. As manufacturers are now met with rapid changes, they must be flexible in order to meet the demands of this changing environment.

To assist the practitioner in creating the appropriate structure, in this chapter two basic design types are discussed that highlight the variables of an organization's environment. The effectiveness of each design is considered and processes are suggested for implementing these designs in the organization.

DESIGN TYPES

For simplicity, it is best to consider only two basic organizational design types: formal and informal. The formal design is based on the concepts of division of work, specialization, delegation, linking pins, and span of management or control.

Division of work simply refers to the need to separate tasks into manageable parts. Traditionally, work is divided into levels; the manager has responsibilities and the subordinates perform tasks to serve those responsibilities. This division is referred to as the scalar process, as it offers a scale, or grading, of activities in line with authority and responsibility level. Work is also divided into different kinds of tasks. This process is called functionalization. For example, a subordinate from human resources (HR) who performs applicant tracking and a subordinate from production who performs equipment troubleshooting present two different functional tasks. If each of these subordinates focuses in only HR or production, each becomes a specialist in that function. Specialization is a normal outgrowth of functionalization.

To assure that duties are completed, work is then delegated from the manager to the subordinate. The manager who delegates to subordinates is also to be delegated to by his or her boss. The manager thus acts as the linking pin between the boss and the subordinate. Ideally, the linking pin provides both upward and downward communication between these levels. Finally, the number of subordinates managed by the manager relates to the span of management, or span of control. The larger the span, the more subordinates per manager, the flatter the organization; and the smaller the span, the fewer subordinates, the taller the organization.

In this formal hierarchy, rigidly scheduled roles are clearly defined and communication flows up and down formal lines. From a strategic standpoint, this design is most effective in organizing routine responsibilities. For example, processing payroll is best served through a formal structure: delivery of time card from subordinate to supervisor, approval by supervisor, and data input by the accounting function. Within accounting, specialization of workers to perform data input, processing, and delivery of paychecks is an effective way to ensure consistency and accuracy of the task. Thus, the more frequently a task is performed, the more likely that the formal structure will be both efficient and effective.

By contrast, less frequently encountered issues or out-of-the ordinary events are better performed within an informal design. A popular form of this structure is the team-based design. In this design, autonomous work teams have responsibilities and make decisions as a group. In the team, roles are more loosely defined, communication is multidirectional, and decision making is decentralized. Communication consists of advice and information rather than decisions and instructions.

Less routine tasks that require broad expertise are better managed by the informal work team. For example, consider the payroll procession function of the accounting department discussed earlier. If the same accounting department were asked to find an automated software package to handle payroll processing, a team-based approach would be preferred. Each of the department "specialists" has a different expertise to bring to the team that will enhance the final decision. The manager of the department may or may not make the final decision. What is important is that the team members have input in the decision. The work team approach is more appropriate for events that occur less frequently and require varied functional expertise and multiple patterns of communication.

In adopting the contingency approach to organizational design, we recognize that neither design is inherently better than the other, but that the environments both inside and outside the organization will suggest the optimal design. Within the same organization we can find examples of both design types. For example, the production department may utilize a formal design for its routine batch process of making products, whereas the research and development function requires a more fluid design to manage the growth of fresh and ambiguous ideas among its independent-thinking scientists.

Although the above may appear as two distinct structures, the lines between the formal and informal design are blurring, as the traditional hierarchy has seen much change in recent years. The formal organization of today still includes all of the variables mentioned, but it has adopted some of the concepts of the informal design.

One trend is toward decentralization. The division of work has evolved such that decisions are now made more at a local plant level. The trend is toward pushing decision making down to the level at which the questions and answers surrounding an issue can best be addressed. Another trend is flattening. Span of management has increased; fewer managers at each level along with fewer levels means more employees per manager. The trend here is toward cutting out levels and positions that do not add value and that may in fact impede organizational effectiveness.

The contemporary formal structure is leaner, smaller, and faster as it attempts to meet the demands of an increasingly sophisticated marketplace. Cutting layers is not done merely to cut costs but to get quicker response to the customer. Thus, the formal organizational structure has become more responsive to customer needs in order to meet market demand in less time.

While it has become more responsive, the formal design is still not as flexible as the informal work team. The work team is superior at pulling together expertise quickly to meet customer demands.

APPROPRIATENESS OF THE DESIGN

The trick is to first recognize which design is appropriate and then to know how to implement it. Management can fill this role by constantly looking outside of the organization to anticipate customer demands. Enlightened management can anticipate which design is appropriate by first listening to the customer, then watching the competition, and again listening to the customer.

Listening to the customer means understanding its vision and strategy; knowing where it wants to be in the next five years,

for example, and how it plans to get there. In knowing these, you can anticipate the evolving needs of your customer and can begin investigating the ways that you can best fill those needs. If, for example, you learn that your customer plans to become a just-in-time supplier to its customers by year five, you could investigate what your organization needs to do to help your customer reach that vision. You could form a work team with members from varied functions, such as purchasing, marketing, human resources, production, accounting, and shipping. The team could be assigned the task of exploring how to enable your customer to reach its vision.

The team could meet to brainstorm a list of issues to address, such as:

- Do we also need to become a JIT operation? If so, how do we get our suppliers/vendors to respond to our needs?
- How will the purchasing/receiving process need to be amended? Will billing and payment processing need to be revised? What are the computer requirements?
- Will the manufacturing process need to be revised? Will batches need to be increased or reduced? Can the current equipment handle it? If not, what is the capital investment? Does needed equipment exist or could it be developed?
- Will JIT production require more flexible scheduling schemes of the employees? Will a temporary labor pool better serve fluctuating demands? Is the union willing to consider that? How will the face of the contract change to accommodate?
- Can we sell this idea to our other customers? Or could we still provide traditional delivery (inventories) to some customers while acting as a JIT organization to one?
- Can we ensure JIT delivery with our current trucking company? Do we need a dedicated fleet? Can we afford it?

Such questions must be addressed long before the customer lays a bottom-line demand of JIT delivery on you. This is essential for an organization with just a few customers. It could easily take five years to develop the supplier, transportation, labor, and accounting practices needed to meet such a demand. In today's marketplace, there will be an organization in the industry willing and able to oblige the customer. It is likely to be the company who listens to its customer and anticipates its needs.

To take this example a step further, consider who, within each of the functional groups named above, is most appropriate to participate in the JIT team. As suggested earlier, the trend is toward pushing decision making down to the appropriate level at which questions and answers are most easily addressed. In the team, it may therefore be appropriate to include individuals from all levels of management and employees from both the plant and corporate. Some management types may be more knowledgeable of capital availability, purchasing system flexibility, and vendor reaction. The operators, however, may be more effective at addressing equipment ability, employee willingness, and current warehouse and shipping capabilities. In fact, the line managers and operators are generally in a better position to anticipate cus-

tomer needs, as this group is in more continuous contact with the customer than is higher management.

If we apply this strategy to the formal organizational design, it becomes top management who serves the line employee. Hence, the traditional pyramid is turned upside-down and management provides necessary resources to the employees at the top so that they can serve the customer (see Exhibit 8-5). In this scenario, the job of every line employee and manager is customer service, acting as the linking pin to the customer. The rest of the organization exists only to enable that service by providing financial resources, running interference with auxiliary bodies, and educating the customer servers in communication techniques.

Although it is management's function to plan for customer requests long in advance, it is often the line employee who is in the better position to hear those requests. Thus, the line employee must be empowered with the skills necessary to recognize and to communicate those needs to management. Management must then determine in what structure, formal or informal, that need is best met. If for-

Exhibit 8-5. The Upside-Down Formal Structure

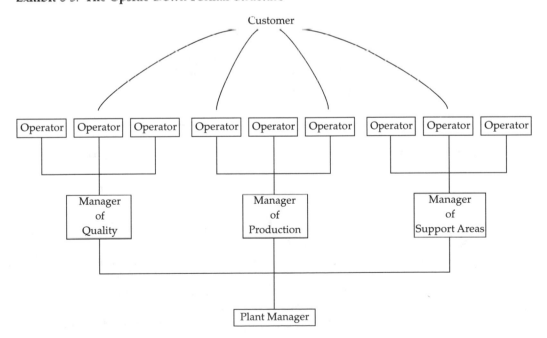

mal, management can just plug it into the current hierarchical system. If informal, management must provide the resources needed to assemble an appropriate team, with all functions represented that may have a stake in the decision-making process.

Watching the competition is the second job of management. By focusing externally, the organization can anticipate how quickly a competitor can deliver something that may be desirable in the industry. Such discoveries should become part of your organization's agenda if you are interested in making the sale before your competitor.

The third job of management is to again *listen to the customer.* Find out how well you are doing in your attempt to both meet and anticipate the customer's demands. Aggressively ask for feedback.

CONCLUSION

There is no one best organizational structure for all organizations or for all activities in the same organization. Formal organizational structure works best in organizing tasks that are routine, occur frequently, and are fairly stable. The "neo-traditional" structure, or upside-down pyramid, is a drastic separation from the normal view of top-down management. It will, however, enable the organization to provide ultimate customer service. To empower this structure, top management must continually look outward, anticipate future customer needs, and provide the resources needed by its internal customers, the employees.

Finally, if management learns of a unique customer request, it may be better addressed through a work team, with membership from various functions and levels of the organization. This team must anticipate and address the requirements associated with the new event well in advance of the competition and the customer's due date. Thus, the work team may develop out of customer needs, frequency of need, and market demand. If the request becomes more common, management should consider fitting it into part of the formal structure or creating a new function to meet the more frequent request.

HUMAN RESOURCES PLANNING

John L. Schwab, Jr., President, John L. Schwab & Associates

The objective of human resources planning is to achieve the most effective and economical use of employee skills, efforts, and abilities in accordance with current and planned operating conditions. Two basic factors in regard to such planning must be known in advance: the human skills *required* and the human skills *available.* Each must be measured in terms of the time available for productive use. In addition, the human resources planner must be concerned with two different types of labor: direct and indirect. Because planning for direct labor is by far the easier of the two tasks, we will begin with that category.

PLANNING DIRECT LABOR

The nature of the manufacturing process itself determines the skills and abilities required. Thus, the planner must have a clear and complete understanding of the available equipment, job methods, quality requirements, and normal working conditions, as well as a calculation of the personnel-hours required to meet varying production schedules established from volume requirements and product delivery dates. Determining the skills and abilities available is a straightforward task, accomplished by evaluating employees in terms of skills, knowledge, physical abilities, and job responsibilities.

In calculating personnel-hours required, the planner has a number of tools at his or her disposal: job process sheets (i.e., descriptions of operation sequences and tools and equipment required), productive job standards (i.e., statements of how much time a task should take), measured nonproductive work, labor variance data, production requirements (per order and per period), information on available equipment, and delivery schedules.

Productive job standards, multiplied by the volume requirements, establish the productive labor time needed. To this calculation, the planner needs to add two additional numbers: (1) a calculation of the predictable, measured, indirect labor hours (such as setup, machine maintenance, and so forth), and (2) the percentage of time required for nonproductive labor variances resulting from waiting for work, training, temporary method allowances, and similar factors. The total represents the expected personnel-hours required at a normal performance level.

The required personnel-hours can be established by operation, cost center, department, or machine. These, in turn, can be easily expressed in terms of required skills and abilities to the same degree of accuracy.

The next step is to deal with the personnel-hours of skills and abilities available. Again, planners have a number of tools at their disposal, such as the job evaluation plan, payroll earnings, and employment records. The job evaluation plan should include job descriptions, define the job requirements, provide an employee performance efficiency list, and state the potential improvement to be expected over and above the schedule developed from the job standards. Employment records will indicate available skills not in active use, which may be saved for emergency or peak periods. To determine the personnel-hours of available skills, the planner multiplies the number of employees who have the required abilities by the working hours available on the particular machine or in the work center, department, or plant.

The planning and administration of a human resources plan and schedule is generally carried out as if the plant were operating a straight-line, paced conveyor system. But it becomes apparent that perfection in balance can never be achieved; it can only be approximated. In scheduling employees, there is always a bottleneck or critical position that limits or restricts every other phase. The major bottlenecks encountered in human resources planning and scheduling may be a critical machine or process, a limited number of specific job skills, limited facilities and space, and uncontrollable production requirements. It is obvious that a human resources scheduling plan designed to improve the complete function must concentrate on minimizing the effect of any bottlenecks indicated by preplanning and analysis.

The most common methods of minimizing the effects of bottlenecks include overtime, extra shift operations, scheduling of longer runs caused by setups, job changeover, provision of relief operators, methods and job improvement, and wage incentives. Management should decide which of these solutions is most effective based on tangible economic considerations, available personnel and, in some instances, labor management agreements.

The additional cost of overtime can be readily calculated and evaluated in terms of its effect on product cost. The addition of an extra shift can be considered in terms of the available personnel who are capable of handling the operation and in terms of the increased operating expenses caused by extra supervision and staff personnel required. The use of longer runs per job order can be evaluated in terms of added inventory costs, additional space requirements for storage, and the increase in invested capital requirements. The use of relief operators to provide greater use of productive machine time necessitates consideration of the available qualified personnel and the added labor cost. Increased job efficiency and performance created by means of job method improvements and an effective wage incentive plan are obvious answers to the improvement of productivity and the operation of human resources planning and scheduling systems. If an effective wage incentive system is in operation, the major portion of the technical details necessary for the development of a sound system is already available.

Many workforce bottlenecks are caused by unique operations or machines requiring long learning times. These are inevitably complex operations. Frequently, such operations can be separated into a series of less difficult operations that are easier to learn and require simple tools and machines. While the ultimate labor cost for the series of operations may be greater than that of the original complex task, the effect on productivity and reduced unit cost may be sufficient to justify the increase in direct labor cost.

In many seasonal industries, the characteristic job skills are required for only a portion of the year. To hire skilled help for seasonal work is difficult under most situations and almost impossible during periods of labor shortage. Furthermore, such practices usually involve major expenses for hiring and training. Careful consideration should be given to evaluating these costs and comparing them with the costs of maintaining a stable, year-round force that may, on occasion, be called upon to perform make-work duties. Properly planned, these make-work occupations can produce results valuable in the overall administration of the business.

PLANNING INDIRECT, CLERICAL, AND WHITE-COLLAR LABOR

For many products, the cost of conversion labor (i.e., direct labor) amounts to less than 10 percent of the sales dollar. Why are conversion labor costs such a small portion? One might suspect that such costs have shrunk as a result of increased productivity generated by new equipment, improved designs, and creative management techniques. Actually, direct labor costs are low because overhead cost factors have gotten so far out of control that the sheer magnitude of these inefficiencies have overwhelmed the entire cost equation.

This is ironic, when one considers that the most significant technological changes to improve productivity since the mid-1960s have been the introduction of the computer and the ready availability of software to increase the effectiveness of white-collar and management personnel. Yet these costs have increased as a percent of total costs instead of showing the dramatic decline that is normally experienced when a technological innovation is introduced on a broad scale. In short, industry has not fully realized the tremendous productivity advantage of the electronic revolution. In terms of controlling indirect, clerical, and managerial costs, we have actually taken a step backward from conditions that existed at the end of the nineteenth century. At least then, manufacturers had piece rate systems in place that enabled them to control unit labor costs, and unit labor costs made up the vast majority of total costs. Today, the vast majority of total costs are managerial and white collar, and the primary control technique is after the fact—that is, "Did we generate enough sales to justify all these people?"

These excessive managerial overhead costs can be reduced, or at least contained, if we realize that they are primarily wage costs (either our own or those of our suppliers). To control them, we must apply the same principles that have been successfully applied to controlling and reducing direct labor costs since the introduction of the scientific management technique. We must plan human resources on the basis of the required skills and abilities, the personnel-hours needed, and the hours that are available. Then, we must motivate individual employees to use their skills and abilities to the fullest extent.

Many companies believe that they already follow this technique. However, if they were to compare current practices used in human resources planning for indirect, clerical, and particularly managerial personnel with those employed in planning for direct labor, they would notice a vast difference in the detail and thoroughness of the techniques. Direct labor planning is based on advance knowledge of the personnel-hours available and the hours required for each skill that is needed. This, in turn, implies that the planners know the process, have standards for the operations, report and measure performance to the standards, and establish variance ratios.

The techniques for measuring indirect, clerical, and managerial costs are much less developed. The costs of indirect and clerical activities are infrequently measured and usually only when they are the direct labor of their industry (as examples, insurance companies and banks where clerks work directly on customer services). Managerial activities are almost never measured and are usually not even reported against except in the most general fashion (i.e., sick time, vacations, personal days, etc).

Resistance for Detailed Planning

The reasons usually advanced for the lack of measurements in these activities are that the activities are too variable to be measured, the costs of measurements are prohibitive, personnel will be upset if they are subjected to measurements, activities are primarily mental and cannot be effectively measured, or work measurements (i.e., standards) do not work and may even cause quality to deteriorate.

These arguments appear to have at least some superficial validity, but they fail to address the provable fact that, in the areas where measurements and reporting are prevalent, costs have decreased as a percentage of the whole. Conversely, in the areas where they are lacking, costs by any measure have skyrocketed.

Closer examination shows that the problems cited for avoiding the measurement activity are far overstated and, in fact, are strikingly similar to arguments that were initially advanced to show the inadvisability of measuring direct labor.

The argument that the function is too variable means that we, as managers, do not really understand the job (i.e., we do not know the method) or we have not established an effective work process (i.e., there are too many variables that should be eliminated or at least minimized). Many managers may not realize it, but they already measure the personnel requirements when they ask for additional people to help perform a particular task. They are really saying, "I don't have enough personnel to complete the task within the period that it needs to be completed. If you allow me to have an additional employee, I will be able to meet the schedule." If managers can accomplish this task by the seat of their pants, either the job is not that variable or staffing is being determined by what is affordable (or salable) to upper management, not what is required to accomplish the tasks. This is an extremely dangerous procedure and, inevitably, leads to the boom-and-bust hiring cycles that are all too prevalent.

The premise that management personnel will be upset at being measured is a matter of opinion, not fact. Managers who achieve high measures usually will be pleased that they are being measured, whereas those who are not achieving will dislike the procedure. This opinion agrees with the findings of direct labor measurement history and also appears to correspond with the experience of schools in using pass/fail programs. What people object to is being measured inaccurately or subjectively (performance rating or leveling). Because we do not know the methods (what must be done, not what is being done) and do not eliminate or at least identify and compensate for variables, this is precisely the form of measurement that is employed throughout industry today.

The contention that work measurements standards have not produced productivity results while they have caused quality to deteriorate does not agree with empirical evidence or any logical premise. Productivity has increased most dramatically in those cost areas where work measurement is extensively utilized. If the "pressure to produce to a production standard" causes quality to fall and costs to rise, then the "pressure to produce to a quality standard" will cause production to fall and costs to rise. Neither statement is accurate. Poor standards of any type are what cause quality and productivity to fall and costs to rise, just as unrealistic goals cause frustration, cutting corners, and lack of effort in everyday activities.

Advantages of Detailed Planning

The rewards for accurately measuring and controlling indirect, clerical, and managerial costs are enormous and the expenditures required to establish the measurements are surprisingly small. When measurement is applied to an unmeasured and highly varied technique, the increase in productivity is historically in the order of 100 percent (i.e., a 50-percent decrease in costs). In today's overhead-encumbered environment, this saving is usually far in excess of anything that can be achieved on the factory floor or, for that matter, through the application of new technology to either the office or the factory.

To achieve these rewards, we must plan office and indirect activities as accurately as we plan human resources in the direct labor sectors. This requires that we accomplish four tasks that are everyday occurrences in manufacturing. First, we must be able to establish a flow for the activities that are required in the performance of the job of managing and providing support to the manufacturing (or any management) function. Second, we must be able to measure or establish how long each of these activities should take. Third, we must determine how often the specific activities must be performed. Finally, we must have in place a procedure for reporting what actually occurred.

When measuring indirect costs, the flow of activities should be more carefully defined than is normally done on management flowcharts. Flowcharts that show a document is handled six times and emerges in an average of ten days are practically useless. The chart must show the times associated with the specific activities that are not subject to direct measurement, such as meetings and nonstructured telephone conversations. Another consideration is that the reporting procedure must be sufficiently detailed so that the reports can be analyzed in a meaningful manner, which means that, as a minimum, the activity accounts must be as defined as the measurement accounts.

These steps are obviously not the final answer to the problem of human resources planning to control overhead wage costs but they are an effective and proven starting point. If used effectively, perhaps in seventy more years writers will be bemoaning the fact that direct labor is over ninety cents of every sales dollar.

WAGE INCENTIVES

John L. Schwab, Jr., President, John L. Schwab & Associates

A wage incentive plan is a wage payment system that offers employees an opportunity to increase earnings by better-than-expected performance. Both labor and management have long recognized the economic value of incentives. The tabulation in Exhibit 8-6 summarizes the production increases a company can expect when it applies an effective wage

Exhibit 8-6. Productivity Improvement from the Introduction of Incentives

	Production Type		
	Unique	Varied	Standard
Average production increase	105%	80%	47%
Average reduction in unit direct labor costs	40%	30%	20%
Average reduction in unit overhead costs	80%	70%	60%

incentive system to work that was previously paid on a nonmeasured, day-work basis. (These numbers apply to labor-controlled operations only.)

It is equally important to consider the losses that will be suffered by improper operation of a wage incentive system. Actual appraisals of more than fifty wage incentive plans currently in use indicate the following losses caused by such improper operation. (These indices also serve to highlight areas for investigation and improvement in existing wage incentive systems.)

1. Seven cents out of every direct labor dollar is lost through improper rate setting.
2. Three cents out of every direct labor dollar is lost because of faulty timekeeping, inaccurate piece counting, and similar errors.
3. Twelve out of every one hundred documents necessary to pay incentives contain arithmetical errors. These cost an average of .2 cents out of every dollar.
4. Unmeasured day work performed by incentive operators costs 25 to 250 percent more than if it were measured and properly placed on incentive.

5. Fifty to eighty percent of labor grievances are due to improper control of incentive plans.

When a moderately effective wage incentive plan has been in use, companies have found that abandoning the system in favor of a nonincentive approach can be extremely costly as shown in Exhibit 8-7. These figures apply only to labor-controlled operations, rather than those controlled by equipment or processes, or where limitations on incentive earnings have been in effect.

INCENTIVE PLANS

Before we examine the various incentive systems currently in use, there is wisdom in looking at such systems from the employee's point of view. The key words in defining and presenting incentives are *opportunity, motivation,* and *acceptance.* An incentive system that is based on real or imagined penalties, rather than opportunities, is usually ineffective. It is rarely accepted or operated with the full cooperation of the employees. In fact, a major problem in gaining the acceptance and use of wage incentive plans is the widespread opin-

Exhibit 8-7. Expected Loss of Production from Abandoning Wage Incentives

Type of Work	With Measurement	Without Measurement
Highly Repetitive	36%	43%
Semirepetitive	44%	58%
Nonrepetitive	47%	59%

ion that incentive systems penalize and restrict, rather than offer additional opportunities.

Motivation

To motivate employees, an incentive plan must meet the following criteria:

- The earnings opportunities must be sufficiently attractive.
- The basis and methods used for determining the rewards must be understandable and acceptable to the employees.
- The rewards must be considered as commensurate with the extra efforts and abilities expended by each employee.
- The employees must be protected against conditions beyond their control.

Opportunity

Inevitably, employees measure the attractiveness of the wage rewards in terms of possible additions to their total pay. Therefore, the earnings opportunity must exist in (1) the performance standards themselves and (2) the percentage of incentive opportunity available during the total pay period.

The average incentive opportunity for a good incentive performance based on measured standards should be at least 25 percent over the day-work earnings level. Thus, employees working 100 percent of the time on measured standards could expect to increase their pay by 25 percent if they provide a good incentive effort over the entire period. It should be emphasized, however, that 25 percent is an average expected opportunity, not a guarantee. Individual skill and effort vary and so will individual earnings potential.

No limits should be placed on incentive earnings; limited opportunity will result in limited performance. Exceptional operational skills exist in many people. Management should encourage these people to use their talents to their fullest capacity, and the pay should reward them for doing so.

Adequate opportunities to achieve incentive earnings must be available. Even though the performance standards themselves offer

a provable 25-percent incentive opportunity, the total earnings potential for a pay period may be insufficient to motivate the employee if too few hours of incentive work are available. If only 20 percent of the hours worked by an employee offer an incentive opportunity, his or her potential payment earnings through the incentive plan will be only 5 percent greater than his or her guarantee.

Employee Acceptance

All employees must fully understand the principles, policies, and practices of the incentive system if they are to accept it, have confidence in it, and be motivated by it. Lack of understanding will result in unavoidable malpractice, earnings inconsistencies, and operational errors that will destroy confidence in the incentive plan and lead to its inevitable destruction.

Employees who work on the incentive plan must thoroughly understand how their incentive standards are established; the methods on which the standard was set; the required quality levels; and the responsibilities and activities covered by the standards. Finally, they must be able to calculate incentive earnings to verify the accuracy of the incentive pay.

Each of these requirements is of vital importance. For example, the incentive standard is usually based on a specified job method that must be followed if the standard is to be valid. If the proper method is not followed, the standard may not be achievable and/or the quality may be improper. In either event, the employee's earnings will suffer.

Job incentive standards seldom—and should not—include allowances for unpredictable, substantial variations. When such variations from normal conditions occur, they must be compensated for over and above the established standard. If they are not, the employee's incentive earnings will be adversely affected. If the employee knows what is (and what is not) included in the incentive standard, these variances can be brought to the supervisor's attention when they occur, and temporary allowances can be made to compensate for the unavoidable condition. Hence, the incentive earnings opportunity will always be available and the motivation provided by the incentive system will continue to exist.

It is equally important that the employee be able to calculate how effectively he is operating and earning. He is then in a position to check and verify his pay and to determine how well he is doing at any particular time during the pay period. This lends further stimulus and motivation to increased performance.

INDIVIDUAL PERFORMANCE INCENTIVES

The incentive opportunities offered by the wage plan must be understood and accepted as being commensurate with extra performance. This relationship can be easily recognized if the incentive system is applied to individual performance. An employee working on an individual incentive fully realizes that her earnings are a direct and personal reward for her own efforts and are not shared with or provided by others. Consequently, the greatest incentive pull exists when the incentive is applied to the individual employee.

The most widely used incentive plans are based on productivity. For such plans, management establishes a productivity standard that can be met by a qualified operator working at a normal or day-work level of effort. Performance standards are usually expressed in terms of money, time, and/or number of units produced. These standards can be exceeded when the operator exerts better-than-normal skill or effort.

If money standards are used, the incentive system is known as *piecework*. Under a piecework system, the standard is expressed as dollars or cents per unit produced. The employee is paid this fixed amount of money for the total amount of units produced in one day's time. Under a piecework plan, the employee's earnings increase in direct proportion to her production. The unit labor cost is constant for normal or better-than-normal performance.

A variation of piecework is the *standard hour system*. The basis of measurement is the standard hours per unit allowed for the oper-

ation. To calculate incentive earnings, the units produced by an employee are multiplied by the standard allowed hours per unit. The result is the standard hours earned by the employee. These hours are then multiplied by the employee's hourly rate of pay to determine incentive earnings. The standard hour system, like the piecework system, provides a fixed unit labor cost for normal or above normal performance. As a result, an employee's earnings increase in direct proportion to his productivity.

There are many variations of the basic standard hour incentive plan. Usually, they have been designed to compensate for measurement and/or incentive control problems or to provide a strong incentive to meet and surpass the normal performance level. The Halsey plan, Rowan plan, and to a large extent, most gain-sharing plans are typical of the first of these variations. They are used primarily where the time standards are estimated and unrefined, or where close control of manufacturing variance cannot be maintained.

The *Halsey plan* shares the time saved between the employee and the company. Excessive earnings resulting from very liberal standards are minimized. Earnings are calculated according to the following formula:

$$[\text{Time Taken} + F(\text{Time Allowed} - \text{Time Taken})] \times \text{Hourly Rate} = \text{Earnings}$$

F, the incentive factor, is usually .5 but other values can be used.

The Rowan plan offers a bonus on the amount of time saved. The theoretical maximum is 100 percent or twice the guaranteed earnings. The formula used is:

$$[\text{Time Taken} + \text{Time Taken} (\text{Time Allowed} - \text{Time Taken}/\text{Time Allowed})] \times \text{Hourly Rate} = \text{Earnings}$$

The various *gain-sharing* plans compensate for ineffective standards by ignoring standards and using past actual output as the basis for establishing normal or expected performance. These plans, in their crudest forms, are direct descendants of the time-honored practice of buying the acceptance of a new standard or methods improvements by sharing the gain (usually by negotiation) with the operator. More sophisticated versions attempt to address the questions of capital investment, improved work flows, and the like. All such attempts, however, suffer from an inherent defect: They incorporate in their base all the inequities that existed prior to the adoption of the plan and they never establish what the cost of the product *should* be.

The Gantt task and bonus plan and the standard time performance-plus plan are typical of the second variation of the basic piecework and standard-hour systems. Both offer a strong additional incentive to meet the established performance levels at which the direct incentive begins.

Under the *Gantt plan,* a low guaranteed rate is offered for substandard performance. Upon achievement of the normal performance level, a higher hourly rate of pay is awarded, and becomes the basis for the calculation of all above normal incentive earnings.

A higher hourly rate of pay is offered under the *standard time performance-plus plan* than under the Gantt plan. The minimum rate is usually the going rate for the proper class of work in the area. A more moderate bonus, up to 10 percent, is offered for achieving and surpassing the standard. Once standard performance is achieved, incentive earnings are calculated at the higher day rate. In both systems, unit labor cost is calculated at the higher rate.

These plans and various modifications of them have been employed where a substantial increase in productivity is required to meet the properly established performance standards. The additional bonus makes such plans appealing to employees because it rewards them for the initial increase in productivity necessary to reach the level at which incentive pay begins.

An infinite number of mathematical formulas can be used. Most of the existing formulas have been tailored to meet a particular set of conditions. However, with the increased accuracy and availability of new and effective wage-control techniques and procedures, the administrative and technical shortcomings of the past (that made necessary these variations to the basic standard-hour incentive system) have been eliminated or at least minimized.

GROUP INCENTIVE SYSTEMS

The various wage incentive plans previously described are most often used for individual wage incentives. However, operating conditions often make the use of individual incentives impractical. Where this is true, a group payment plan may be advisable.

A group incentive system is a system applied to a group of employees working in a common geographical location, on a related type of work, or on an interrelated activity. Its basic purpose is to enable those participating in the group to pool their efforts and performance and then equitably share the incentive earnings of the group.

A common application of a group system is to paced conveyor lines or machine-controlled operations where production is controlled by the equipment. The group system gives employees on such work the opportunity to share the work and share equitably in any incentive earnings. A second application of a group system is to heavy maintenance or construction tasks where a group of craftspeople collectively handle a major assignment. In such instances, it is impractical to specify, measure, and control the individual job assignments. The labor content of the total job is measured and the detailed sharing of the work is handled by the employees on the job. A third application is to a short-run machine group. Here, the majority of the work of each employee is composed of setup time, machine attendance, or troubleshooting. This makes it impossible to establish and control a specific method and a precise standard for each individual job for each individual employee.

The determination of efficiencies and incentive earnings is the same for a group system as it is for an individual incentive plan. The time earned by the group is determined by multiplying the established standards by the units produced. Extra allowed time, such as waiting for work, is added to the group incentive time earned. The total earned hours thus determined are divided by the hours worked by the group members to determine a group efficiency. Each group member's pay is determined by multiplying his or her individual hours worked by his or her individual hourly rate and multiplying the result by the earned group efficiency.

Wherever possible, groups should be limited to fifteen or fewer employees in order to make the individual incentive motivation direct and recognizable. Under proper conditions, a group system will provide a highly practical and effective method for paying labor incentives that are satisfactory to employees and company alike.

There are an infinite variety of overall bonus plans based on productivity, profits, savings, and/or combinations of the three. Examples are the well-known Scanlon and Kaiser plans, which are in effect profit-sharing arrangements. It is imperative, however, that a plan of this type truly reflect the problems and conditions in the plant or company to which it is to be applied.

Despite the proven economic value of well-managed and well-controlled productivity-based wage incentive plans, there has been a tendency over the past fifty years for a decline in their use. The reasons given (rightly or wrongly) vary, but include the following:

- Management cannot control the plans over a long span of time since deterioration is a one-way street.
- The manufacturing cost structure has shifted to one that is dominated by materials, equipment, and overhead and the importance of controlling direct labor cost has greatly diminished.
- The emphasis on output in the productivity systems destroys quality.
- A general deterioration (because of the emphasis on the speed of setting standards) occurs in the accuracy of work measurement techniques that are the bases for these systems.

The need to motivate employees to a better performance level (in all areas) is, however, more widely recognized than ever before. This need, coupled with the inability of many to realize "measurable" improvements from costly programs designed to change work cultures through training, has led to the development of programs specifically designed to promote a desired activity through the payment of a monetary bonus. The variety of these incentives is unlimited. The following quality improvement incentive plan is an example of a situation where a nonproductivity-based incentive has been profitably introduced to the advantage of both the employees and the companies.

One of the more common reasons cited for not adopting, or trying to eliminate, productivity-based incentives is the common belief that the emphasis on output in these plans causes operators to shortcut recommended manufacturing procedures or to "speed up" motions to the detriment of quality and actual unit costs. The validity of this belief is questionable. Productivity incentives do not cause quality problems. Quality problems are the result of improper initial design of the incentive system and/or deterioration over time of management control of the system. The fact remains, however, that practices detrimental to high quality do exist. Furthermore, once these practices are established as acceptable, they are both very costly and extremely difficult to correct because the changes will adversely impact (or are perceived as adversely impacting) employee earnings. These conditions have led to the development of quality-based incentive programs. These programs are either (1) additions to existing productivity-based incentive programs that enable manufacturers to rationalize existing systems without causing labor problems or (2) stand-alone programs to improve quality levels in both incentive and nonincentive environments without diminishing productivity.

The economic impact of quality-based incentives does not as of yet have a substantial quantifiable database comparable to that which exists for productivity-based plans. In specific applications, however, these plans have generated some remarkable achievements that can be measured in dollars and cents. Examples include (1) rework and scrap costs per unit decreased by 68 percent; (2) product designated as seconds reduced from 7 percent to less than 3 percent of output; (3) inspection operations eliminated; and perhaps most importantly, (4) operators asking how they can improve quality.

The quality-based incentives work on exactly the same premise that production-based incentives operate. They motivate employees by affording them the opportunity to increase their earnings by better-than-expected performance. The difference is that the incentive, although linked to productivity, is paid for through the reduction in quality costs per unit.

Effective quality-based incentives must meet the same criteria as the productivity-based systems. The plan must motivate the employee by offering an opportunity, not by threatening a real or imagined penalty. The earnings opportunity must be attractive. The procedures for calculating the earnings must be understood and accepted as being fair by the employees. Finally, the rewards must be considered as being commensurate with the additional care and attention required.

The specifics of the quality incentive plans, however, vary from the productivity-based plans in several significant ways. Some of the most important differences are described below.

■ The earnings opportunities are capped. The maximum incentive occurs when quality costs are zero. These programs approximate a Rowan plan where maximum earnings are limited to 200 percent and occur when time taken equals zero.

■ Additions to production standards mandated by quality are considered to be increases in quality costs for the purpose of calculating the quality bonus. This enables total unit cost to be effectively controlled.

■ All the quality incentive plans are group incentive plans, rather than the individual plans that predominate in productivity incentives. The main reasons for the use of group payment instead of individual payment in the systems are:

1. The primary reason quality suffers in a productivity-based incentive system is that management either cannot or will not enforce quality on an individual operator basis. Group payment enables management to monitor and enforce quality requirements on a department, line, or cell basis. This enables management to pay only for good production while leaving the operating group to

identify and correct the individual who created the poor-quality product.

2. The use of the group system enables the system to be established and maintained with minimum additional paperwork and support personnel. Most of these systems are in fact currently being maintained with the same number of support personnel as existed before the systems were established.

■ The additional earnings potential above the established base rate is not as large as that available under most productivity-based programs. The expected incentive earnings from productivity incentive programs generally range from 25 percent to 33 percent of an established base rate. The quality incentive bonus range is normally from 5 percent to 15 percent of base-rate earnings.

■ The quality plans tend to include a wider range of employees in the bonus payment. Most productivity plans include only direct labor. The quality plans generally include direct labor, indirect labor and, in some cases, support personnel (including first-line supervisors) who directly contribute to improvement in quality levels.

■ The bonus payment is usually by a separate check and is made on a monthly or quarterly basis. The issuing of separate checks is a practice that most users feel enhances the credibility and impact of the system and is not an operational necessity.

Exhibit 8-8 shows the results of a quality-based system.

PROBLEM AREAS

Contrary to popular belief, incentive plans do not police themselves. They must be carefully established and even more carefully maintained by constant audits and checks if they are to remain effective. If these precautions are not taken, the systems will quickly deteriorate and serious labor relations problems and equally serious cost problems will result.

The major problem areas encountered in wage incentive operations are inconsistency of standards, improper control of job vari-

Exhibit 8-8. Results of a Quality-Based System

Item	*Summary of Weekly Quality Costs, Jan–Mar* 1990	1991	1992
Units produced	21,352	22,206	24,750
Total quality costs	$17,358	$5,126	$5,987
Quality cost/unit	$.8142	$.2308	$.2419
Bonus cost/unit	$0	$.2393	$.2291
Total quality cost/unit	$.8142	$.4701	$.4710

Item	*Summary of Monthly Bonus Earned, Jan–Mar* 1990	1991	1992
Number of employees	220	220	230
Total bonus earned	0	$66,627	$73,713
Bonus per employee	0	$303	$320
Monthly bonus/employee	0	$101	$107

Item	*Summary of Annualized Savings* 1990	1991	1992
Gross savings	0	$673,650	$736,550
Bonus payments	0	$291,603	$294,852
Net savings	0	$382,056	$441,698

ances, and inadequate incentive coverage. Each of these problem areas contributes to the others. Unless they are constantly policed, the incentive system will deteriorate. When deterioration occurs, its effects on other important areas of management can be—and usually are—more serious than the obvious labor relations problems created.

If the incentive standards are inconsistent, their use for machine scheduling, departmental manning, production planning, and inventory control will create serious errors. The standard costs of products (if based on inconsistent standards) will be equally inconsistent, resulting in serious effects on pricing, profit determination, and marketing policies. Inconsistent standards will also result in erroneous decisions in purchasing, equipment selection, and plant layout.

A wage incentive system properly established and maintained is one of management's best assurances of the validity of the basic information it uses in most of the management functions and activities. Since employees' earnings are directly in question, a constant check of standards and variance control is maintained throughout the organization. Wage incentives properly used are a most valuable management tool serving other activities as well as employee motivation.

STANDARDS MAINTENANCE

To develop and maintain consistent standards, the following factors must exist: a consistent technique for setting all standards; production standards based on specific, predescribed job methods and quality standards; an established and acceptable procedure for changing standards affected by creeping method changes and employee job improvement suggestions; and a sound wage structure based on an acceptable and consistent job evaluation or job-ranking system.

Predetermined motion times and proven standard data developed from accurate individual time studies are the most effective techniques for establishing production standards. Both procedures require the prior description of the method and quality conditions. The standards developed from them are based on massive data that more truly represent the so-called normal or average performance level.

Regardless of the rate-setting procedure used, the production standards should cover only the predictable conditions and variations of the task. Any attempt to broadly average unpredictable variations into the standards will result in a wide fluctuation of earnings, depending primarily on the existence or nonexistence of these variances.

Proper definition of the method and quality standard on which the production standard is based is mandatory; productivity variations resulting from methods changes and/or shortcutting quality requirements are the single major cause of extremes in performances and variances. When such extremes occur, the employee's concept of a fair standard is inevitably based on the highest figures. If tangible evidence of the basis on which the standard was established is not available, mutually agreed-upon solutions are difficult, if not impossible, to achieve.

The part played by creeping methods changes in the destruction of wage incentive plans is well known. Minor changes may be insufficient to warrant immediate changes in the standard. A series of such minor changes, however, caused by working conditions, minor material changes, or equipment improvement over the years creates loose or inconsistent standards, or both. An ineffective wage incentive is the inevitable result.

The production standards and related incentive administration procedures may be established with accuracy and consistency, but an incentive system will still not function properly unless accurate and consistent controls for variations in manufacturing conditions are in existence. These variances (including temporary material variances, waiting for work, and temporary methods) must be measured and allowed for, over and above the published standards. To control these variances, a factual measurement procedure must be available to set standards for these unusual conditions before or during their occurrence. Variances that are unpredictable (such as waiting time) must be measured and con-

trolled by an accurate timekeeping system that will enable the time variances to be measured and accurately allowed for. A third and final control required is accurate piece counting or production determination. These activities must be established as simple, verifiable procedures accurately reflecting the true amount of work done. If they are not, the wage incentive system will fail.

MAKING THE DECISION

A decision to introduce a wage incentive system, modify an existing wage incentive system, or abandon a wage incentive system must be predicated upon a tangible, factual appraisal of existing productivity, costs, and administrative considerations. The examination (audit) must be an in-depth study that considers the specific operating details rather than a broad overall evaluation of productivity and costs.

Appraising Productivity

The audit should begin by establishing tangible and provable consistent production standards for selected operations. These standards may be developed by any accurate and accepted system of industrial work measurement. Predetermined motion-time standards and provable standard-time data derived from time study are usually the most effective tools for this action.

The operations selected for evaluation should statistically represent the distribution of operations and skills applied in the factory. Using accurate test standards, a direct comparison can be made between existing productivity and actual production studies taken on the floor with a consistent norm. The deviations will indicate the degrees of difference between actual and normal expected production and unit labor costs and in most cases the causes of the variations.

The production and time variances over and above those allowed for in the production standards can be determined by several methods: ratio delay studies or examinations of company records of downtime, lost time, waiting time, losses due to defective material, and the like.

Appraising Administrative Techniques

Equally important are the evaluation and appraisal of the administrative techniques used and the acceptance of the wage incentive plan by supervisors, the bargaining unit, and the employee. An in-depth appraisal of this phase includes:

- The technical aspects of establishing time standards to determine the adequacy and consistency of the base for the most critical controls of management.
- The qualifications of the personnel responsible for the time standards to determine their ability to use the required techniques properly.
- The acceptance of wage incentives by labor and management to determine existing or potential sources of labor relations problems and to evaluate possible solutions.
- Wage incentive controls to determine inconsistencies that might result in disrupting time standards, costs, earnings, or management controls.
- Management control data to determine the quality and quantity of information available to the management team for its assistance in maintaining a sound and effective wage plan, and to determine the effectiveness with which these data and reports are used to control costs, to utilize equipment effectively, and to equitably administer the wage plan.

Each of these areas should be subjected to a thorough investigation through a cooperative study by all who are engaged in the wage incentive system operation. An evaluation or ranking procedure should be developed and applied, so that the appraisal can be conducted as a fact-finding and educational procedure.

The audit, properly developed, will indicate the problem areas, their magnitude, the steps necessary for their correction, the course of action that should be pursued, and the economic justification for the recommended actions.

CONCLUSION

Properly utilized, manpower planning and pay-for-performance systems are management's most powerful tools for controlling and/or reducing direct, indirect, clerical, and managerial wage costs. The effective use of these techniques requires that we understand, and then apply, the following six principles:

1. We must know the activities that must be performed by each employee. This requirement applies to managerial, as well as shop-floor, employees. These are not necessarily (and are probably not) the same activities as those that are presently being performed. This condition also implies that we need to know specifically how the particular activity (the method) should be performed.

2. We must measure these activities as accurately as possible. The extra costs caused by the inaccuracy of macro-work-measurement systems or trying to apply somebody else's packaged data to another person's operations is enormous. If we intend to measure people and to judge their performance by these measures, they must be as accurate as possible. Management is concerned about product quality. This concern should extend to the quality of the standards used to measure and evaluate employees. We should also not forget that these data form the base for the entire management control system.

3. We must learn what activities are being performed by which employees and how much time is presently being spent on each activity. The answers to this step will be extremely revealing, particularly when managerial activities are analyzed.

4. We must compare the differences between what is being done to what needs to be done and develop a plan to improve present practices to mirror what should be done. We also need to put in place a system to capture what is being done on a continuing basis.

5. We must understand that technology,

techniques, and training do not produce advancement. Advancement occurs when people are effectively motivated to utilize these tools. Before we adopt the latest techniques to improve productivity or to reduce costs, we should have the answer to the question asked by employees: "What's in it for me?" Unless we can answer this positively, the potential for successful change is doubtful at best.

6. We must understand that employees at all levels respond positively to monetary rewards that are based on accurate measures and equitable, consistent criteria. Unless we are going to enforce change through fear and punishment, this type of an inducement will be required to obtain and maintain compliance with the recommended changes at every level in the management pyramid. If these rewards meet the basic incentive criteria, they

can be, and have been, designed to foster specific actions in all functions, at every level of the organization.

Only after we have addressed these major points, and the myriad details that accompany them, will we be able to determine whether we have effectively staffed our businesses and if our employees are working as efficiently as possible. Without this firmly established and accepted starting point (the best we can do with what we have), we will not be in a position to evaluate or to fully realize the advantages of new management techniques and technology. Their development and successful utilization in our factories and offices will continue to be ruled by the gods of external public relations and internal salesmanship rather than those of productivity, cost containment, and customer satisfaction.

QUALITY MANAGEMENT

Keki R. Bhote, President, Keki R. Bhote Associates, and Senior Corporate Consultant (retired), Quality and Productivity Improvement, Motorola

The U.S. economy is in the doldrums. Faced with perpetual balance-of-trade deficits, budget deficits, and an alarming attrition in jobs, the Congress and the White House continue to tinker with fiscal and monetary policy—short circuits intended to jump-start the sputtering economy. Yet, the U.S. government can do little by itself to achieve a turnaround. The culprits are U.S. industry in gen-

eral and American management in particular. Our CEOs, drawn largely from the ranks of lawyers, accountants, and MBAs, have almost done us in. Of the many solutions floated to transform our management into a world player, none is as simple, as straightforward, and as effective as an overriding concentration on quality! And, fortunately, it is not too late.

Despite the growing importance of quality, most companies are not fully aware of its far-reaching benefits:

- It can greatly enhance customer satisfaction—the main objective of any business.
- It can increase productivity, market share, profitability, and return on investment in ways that few disciplines can match.
- It can bring job excitement to employees, currently alienated by the drudgery of meaningless tasks.

On a national level, it can increase the U.S. gross national product by 5 to 10 percent, making an appreciable dent in our trade unbalance, our budget deficits, and even our national debt. On a global level, it can mount a war on waste—waste of our dwindling resources, waste of our environment, and waste in the quality of life.

Given these benefits, it would be logical to assume that U.S. managers thrashing around in a sea of mediocrity would reach for quality as a life jacket. Unfortunately, they have been dealing in banal generalities—mission statements, quality policy pronouncements, quality circles, and so forth—without a clear game plan. The purpose of this chapter, therefore, is to provide managers with a practical road map for achieving world-class quality.

Before detailing the road map, it is helpful to trace the progression in the definition of quality and briefly outline its history:

- In the 1960s, quality was defined as "conformance to specifications."
- In the 1970s, quality was defined as "conformance to customer requirements."
- In the 1980s, quality became synonymous with "customer satisfaction."
- In the 1990s, quality is nothing short of "customer excitement."

This ever-escalating concept of quality represents the external view, that is, the customer's view. The internal view of quality can be described as the systematic identification, analysis, reduction, and eventual elimination of variation. In quality, variation is evil, just as in inventory control, inventory is evil. Customers want uniformity and consistency of a product parameter around a target value, not variations all over the lot within specification limits. A second reason for variation reduction is that it is one of the best ways to reduce costs, through the elimination of scrap, repair, analyzing, testing, and inspection—none of which add value.

QUALITY HISTORY AND THE QUALITY GURUS

The history of quality is as old as humankind. The artisan, the craftsperson, dealt with quality long before its recent formalization. The father of modern quality was not Dr. Walter Shewhart, as is commonly supposed, but his mentor, Sir Ronald Fisher, who improved farm quality and productivity, despite its numerous variables, with his revolutionary techniques called the design of experiments. Shewhart's contribution was statistical quality control, using control charts, which distinguish between common causes of variation that should be ignored versus the large, special causes of variation that should be corrected. His junior colleagues at Western Electric, Dr. W. Edwards Deming and Dr. Joseph Juran, went on to coach Japan and make that country the quality juggernaut it is today.

Deming, formerly a prophet without honor in his own country, has not been elevated to a position of preeminence in the United States. This towering curmudgeon tells his audiences that, "America should export everything, except its management!" He regards our business schools as obsolete, our short-term profit outlook as counterproductive, and employee performance appraisal as useless. Instead, he advocates a spirit of continual improvement, invigorated by a sense of joy in work.

Juran's great contribution is the *management* of quality. His 3,000-page *Quality Control Handbook* is the bible of quality practitioners. He stresses that a quality breakthrough can be achieved only by establishing a steering committee that selects chronic quality problems and assigns diagnostic, cross-functional teams to solve them. Dorian Shainin, the least well-known of this country's quality gurus, is undoubtedly the world's foremost quality problem solver. He has initiated and perfected a series of problem-solving tools that are simple and elegant, yet statistically powerful.

STAGES OF QUALITY

The infrastructure of comprehensive processes that a company must construct in order to aspire to world-class quality can best be described in a fourth-stage progression. A company in Stage 1, called the stage of innocence, is in the Dark Ages of quality consciousness. In Stage 2, called the awakening stage, a company recognizes the importance of quality but thrashes around without a firm game plan. In Stage 3, the stage of commitment and implementation, a company has established an infrastructure leading to world-class quality. Finally, a company in Stage 4, called world class, has become a benchmark company.

Exhibit 8-9 is a matrix with the four stages of quality on one leg of the matrix and twelve areas of a typical company—management, organization, systems, measurement, tools, customers, design, suppliers, process/manufacturing, field, support services, and people—on the other leg. Each area is further divided into appropriate subareas. The following pages describe each area, stage by stage, with an emphasis on the practices needed to elevate a company as rapidly as possible to Stages 3 and 4. (It is a sad commentary that there is not a single company—either in the United States or in Japan or elsewhere—that is completely in Stage 4 in all twelve areas.)

Area 1: Management

Deming and Juran have long stressed that 85 percent of quality problems are the responsibility of management; only 15 percent are the responsibility of the worker. Quality starts—and ends—with top management. The issues are twofold:

- *A quality perspective*—In Stage 1, management's perspective is that quality is a necessary evil. In Stage 2, management recognizes the importance of quality, but believes that it costs money (a concept that is still nurtured in business schools). It is convinced that high quality/low cost is an oxymoron.

In Stage 3, managers begin to realize that quality is an economic imperative. This is best illustrated by the famous PIMS (profit impact of market strategy) database, maintained by the Strategic Planning Institute. Studies of the more than 3,000 firms represented in the database indicate that as quality (measured by the customer, not the company) goes from low to high, productivity, market share, profit, and return on investment also go from low to high—by factors of 2:1 and more! In this remarkable correlation, quality is the cause, while the other business parameters are only the effects.

In Stage 4, management elevates quality to a superordinate value. Further, it makes sure that there is a similar "buy-in" of quality values among the company's employees.

- *Quality planning*—In Stages 1 and 2, management does not give much thought to quality in its planning process. In Stage 3, there is a definite linkage to the business plans. Quality has equal weight with financial planning. In Stage 4, top-management quality plans are deployed to all levels of employees, with techniques such as Hoshin planning, where the plans of a higher management level become the goals of the next level and the whole company is "wired together" in terms of quality objectives, goals, strategies, tactics, and plans. Every employee has a set of *personal* goals congruent with management goals.

Area 2: Organization

- *Structure*—In the area of organization, the typical structure in Stages 1 and 2 is bureaucratic, with as many as sixteen levels of management between the CEO and the lowly worker. In Stage 3, the tall pyramid is flattened to no more than five or six levels, thereby reducing the tyranny of bureaucracy and granting each level of management a greater sense of freedom and empowerment. Finally, in Stage 4, the twenty-first-century concept of the upside-down organization—with the customers on top, the customer-contact employees at the next level, the support services below them, the middle managers beneath them, and the CEO at the bottom of the organizational ladder—becomes operational. The CEO is now a servant, in a biblical sense, helping and coaching employees to reach their full potential.

■ *Style*—In Stage 1, management styles are shaped by a vertical structure, and communications tend to flow up and down the hierarchy. In Stage 2, matrix management, with a product or project manager, is the norm. In Stage 3, there is a realization that customer and quality problems are no respecters of vertical management; they tend to move across departments, requiring a horizontal style of management. Ultimately, in Stage 4, the concept of a focused factory, with a narrow line of products, dedicated equipment, and dedicated people from several disciplines, working together as one team under a business manager and serving a narrow customer base, becomes a reality.

■ *Cooperation*—In Stage 1, people work in isolation in "vertical silos" to protect their own turfs. In Stage 2, the team concept—at least within a given function or department—is born. In Stage 3, there is cooperation and problem solving within the organization, through the use of cross-functional problem-solving teams. The team concept blossoms in Stage 4 to self-directed work teams, which take over all aspects of operational management, including establishing goals, contacting suppliers and customers, authorizing expenditures, and even hiring, firing, and evaluating team members. It is the ultimate in organizational development.

■ *Role of the quality professional*—The place of the quality professional in an organization also undergoes a fundamental transformation from stage to stage. In Stage 1, he or she is a cop, blowing the whistle on the rest of the organization's quality shortcomings. In Stage 2, he is given responsibility with little authority. He is the proverbial messenger who gets shot at the first bad tidings. In Stage 3, he is transformed into a coach, consultant, facilitator, and teacher, whose primary role is to *help*

line people in their quality endeavors. In Stage 4, quality becomes so pervasive that all employees reach for quality responsibility cheerfully and enthusiastically.

Area 3: Systems

■ *Type*—Quality systems in Stage 1 are homegrown, boiler-plate quality manuals that get dusted off just before customer's visit. They contain kindergarten directions on quality fundamentals, such as the calibration of equipment and the segregation of nonconforming material. Stage 2 adopts simple quality systems, similar to the old military practices of Mil.Q.9858 or to the much newer ISO.9000 series that is sweeping Europe and is becoming a passport for companies to do business in the European Community. ISO.9000 is procedural, without much emphasis on lifting the sights of a company to world-class quality. Stage 3 can profit from the Malcolm Baldrige National Quality Award guidelines, which have electrified American industry into quality consciousness. The guideline's seven categories and thirty-two examination items can lead to a reasonable quality system. However, it has weaknesses—in terms of its nonprescriptive philosophy, its confusing wording, its lack of powerful tools, and its bias toward the administrative, rather than the technical and statistical, aspects of quality. Stage 4 utilizes the best of several worlds of quality systems—ISO.9000, Malcolm Baldrige Award, the Deming Prize, the NASA Award, the President's Prize (for governmental operations), and other international quality prizes.

■ *Quality audits*—Audits, used to monitor adherence to established quality systems, are unknown in Stage 1. In Stages 2 and 3, quality audits are conducted by quality professionals and by external examiners, respectively. But professionals lack the authority to correct observed weaknesses. In Stage 4, practiced mostly in Japan, top management conducts the audits in order to gain firsthand knowledge of deficiencies, mingle with the people, and force the pace of improvement.

■ *Data collection*—This is haphazard in Stage 1. Vast amounts of quality data are collected in Stage 2, overtaxing the ability of peo-

Exhibit 8-9. A Quality Matrix

Area	Subarea	Stage 1 Innocence	Stage 2 Awakening	Stage 3 Commitment/ Implementation	Stage 4 World Class
Management	Quality perspective	A necessary evil	High cost	An economic imperative	A superordinate value
	Quality planning	Little or none	An afterthought	Linked to business planning	Deployed to all levels
Organization	Structure	Bureaucratic	Tall pyramid	Flat pyramid	Upside-down
	Style	Vertical management	Matrix management	Horizontal management	Focused factory
	Cooperation	Functional silos	Intradepartment teams	Cross-functional teams	Self-directed work teams
	Role of quality professional	Cop	Full responsibility, little authority	Coach	Quality responsibility accepted by all
Systems	Type	Home-grown quality control manual	Simple quality systems	Malcolm Baldrige guidelines	Best-in-class guidelines
	Quality audits	Unknown	Done by quality professionals	Done by external examiners	Done by top management
	Data collection	Haphazard	Data pollution, no action	Data available on timely basis to all employees	Data visible/reviewed for continual improvement
Measurement	Cost of poor quality	No knowledge	Gathered, analyzed	Reduced by 10:1	Reduced to <$1.00 per employee/day
	Defect levels	Not tracked	Posted at each workstation	Measure TDPU across whole line	TDPU less than 0.01
	Cycle time	Unknown	Cycle time reduced	Actual cycle time less than twice theoretical	Actual cycle time no more than theoretical
	C_{PK}	Unknown	Less than 1.0	Greater than 2.0	Greater than 5.0
	In support services	No measurement	MBO	Cycle time the integrator	Internal customer the scorekeeper
Tools	Problem solving	Sorting by brute force	Elementary quality control tools	Design of experiments (DOE) in production	DOE at design stage of product or process to prevent problems

	Statistical process control (SPC)	None	Control charts	Precontrol	Positrol process certification and precontrol
	Customer requirements	Voice of the engineer	Market research	Value research, sensitivity analysis, multiattribute evaluations	Quality function deployment (QFD), conjoint analysis
	Reliability	None	FMFA, FTA	Accelerated life tests, product liability analysis	Multiple environment over stress tests (MEOST)
	Workmanship	Inspection	Video recognition systems	Neighbor inspection	POKA-YOKE (warnings from sensors)
	Equipment maintenance	Fix only when broken	Guidelines to reduce diagnosis and repair time	Operator maintenance	Total productive maintenance (TPM)
	Support services	No tools	Management audits	Benchmarking	Next operation as customer (NOAC)
Customers	Company objective	Profit	Jobs, employee welfare	Focus on all elements of customer satisfaction	Customer enthusiasm, happy, productive employees
	Satisfaction feedback	Intermittent	Market share	Focus groups win/loss analysis	Achieve total customer delight
	Customer contact personnel	Little attention	Customer relations training	Recognition and reward	Empowerment
Design	Structure	Design in isolation	Engineering and manufacturing team	Simultaneous engineering (SE)	SE and early supplier involvement
	Objective	Unclear	Design for manufacturability (DFM)	Design for zero variability	Design for all elements of customer satisfaction
	Strategy	100% redesign	Pushing state of the art	25% redesign	Design in half the time, cost, manpower, and defects
	Design time	Measured in years	10–25% reduction	25–50% reduction	Greater than 50% stream of new products

continued

Exhibit 8-9. *(continued)*

Area	Subarea	Stage 1 Innocence	Stage 2 Awakening	Stage 3 Commitment/ Implementation	Stage 4 World Class
Suppliers	Relations	Adversarial	Suspicion	Goal congruence	Full partnership
	Number	Large, unmanageable	Reduced base	One supplier per part number	Single-digit suppliers for entire commodity
	Top management focus	Direct labor	Automation	Computer-integrated manufacturing	Supply management
	Organization	Purchasing	Materials management	Commodity teams	Supplier an extension of customer
	Modus operandi	Dictatorial, remote	Contractual	Hand-off	Active concrete help
	Quality levels	Supplier defect rates 1–5%	Defect rates less than .5%	Defects <100 parts per million	Inspection obsolete, self-certification
Process/ manufacturing	Process characterization	Muddle through	Equipment manufacturer maintenance and operator inputs	Process capability study	Design of experiments (DOE) (variable search)
	Process optimization	Chasing one's tail	Tweaking	Computer simulation	DOE (scatter plots)
	Metrology	Poor repeatability	Instrument-to-instrument and operator-to-operator variability	Rule of instrument accuracy	Optimization of accuracy, precision, bias
	Latent defect control	None	Burn-in	Thermal cycling	Truncated MEOST, failure analysis

	High scrap, rework, 100% inspection and test yields <75%	Reduced scrap and rework, sample inspection and test, yields >90%	Almost no rework, inspection and test by precontrol yields >99%	Almost no inspection and test yields 100%
Quality characteristics	High scrap, rework, 100% inspection and test yields <75%	Reduced scrap and rework, sample inspection and test, yields >90%	Almost no rework, inspection and test by precontrol yields >99%	Almost no inspection and test yields 100%
Field Warranty period Service	3 months Shoddy	1 year Contracts cover poor reliability	5 years Goals for diagnosis and repair met	Lifetime Built-in diagnostics
Parts	Periodic crises	Excess inventory	Starter kits, exchange units	Redesign for maximum reliability
Support service Internal customer	Unheard of	Concept, no implementation	NOAC implemented	NOAC institutionalized
Structure	Bureaucratic, bloated	Intradepartment teams	Crossfunctional teams	Steering committee, process owner
Improvement techniques	Little or none	Pareto charts, C&E diagrams, control charts	Brainstorming, force field analysis, benchmarking	Value engineering, job redesign, process redesign
People Management view of workers	Pair of hands, Taylorism	Workers capable only of low-grade ideas	Workers respond to Hawthorne effect	Full trust and partnership between managers and workers
Climate	Pervasive fear	Managers not involved	Participatory management	Every worker is a manager
Training	None	Sporadic, no implementation	Focused, with implementation	Cascaded, management to all workers
Management role	Boss-autocrat	Manager-control, manipulation	Coach, teacher, consultant, facilitator	Leader: vision inspiration, help employee growth
Worker	Passive, withdrawn	Team member, problem solving	Small management role, planning, organizing, controlling, improving	Member of self-directed work team having operational management

Source: After K. R. Bhote, *World Class Quality: Using the Design of Experiments to Make It Happen* (New York: AMACOM, 1991).

ple to separate the wheat from the chaff. Computers accelerate this data pollution at the speed of light! In Stage 3, however, the data are gathered in a timely manner, prioritized, and fed back to those who can take action. In Stage 4, the data are made visible at every workstation and are acted upon by improvement teams, with weekly—and sometimes daily—reviews of quality progress.

Area 4: Measurement

■ *Cost of poor quality*—This simple but macroscopic quality metric generally includes warrant and customer returns, scrap and rework, analyzing, inspection, and testing—all nonvalue-added functions. Typically, in U.S. companies, the cost of poor quality runs from 10 to 25 percent of the sales dollar—that is, a cost two to four times the profit on sales. More dramatic, *each employee wastes from $100 to $200 per day* in companies that do not have their quality act together. If every U.S. company could reduce this shocking profit drain to, say, $30 per employee per day, this country could save Uncle Sam $150 billion per year—enough to make a huge dent in our budget deficit, our balance of trade and, simultaneously, increase our gross domestic product (GDP) by 11 percent!

In Stage 1, companies are ignorant of the whole subject (typically, over 75 percent of the companies in the United States are at this stage). In Stage 2, these costs are gathered, sometimes analyzed, but seldom attacked. In Stage 3, the cost of poor quality is reduced by 10:1, to levels below 2 percent of sales. Stage 4 companies reduce these costs to an unbelievable 0.3 percent of sales, or a cost lower than $1 per day! Further, they go after intangible quality costs that accounting systems do not have the intelligence to gather. These include lost sales (especially to hitherto repeat customers); equipment downtime; supplier quality and delivery delinquencies; long manufacturing and design cycle times causing large product and people inventories; white-collar errors/inefficiencies; and the poor quality of management (the worst sin of all!). If these intangible quality costs are included, the average U.S. company could be wasting an astronomical 50 percent of sales.

■ *Defect levels*—In Stage 1, defect levels are not known and not tracked. In Stage 2, they are posted at each workstation, but lack detail and, for the most part, are ignored by the workers. In Stage 3, there is a Pareto analysis of defect causes at each workstation, and the total defects on an entire production line are added up to form a metric called *total defects per unit* (t.d.p.u.). These can run from 0.1 to over 1 t.d.p.u., even in a company with reasonable quality. In Stage 4, the t.d.p.u. is systematically driven down to 0.01 or less, which means that a manufacturing line, starting with material for 100 units, ships 99 without a single rejection anywhere along its numerous workstations.

■ *Cycle time*—This is the actual clock time from the start of a manufacturing or administrative process to its finish. Typically, it includes the actual direct labor time plus waiting, transport, storage, setup, network, and approval times. The last six elements are almost *total* waste and account for ten to one hundred times the actual direct labor time. Cycle time is known as the great integrator. This single metric can simultaneously measure quality, cost, delivery, and effectiveness. Any change in these parameters directly affects cycle time. In Stage 1, cycle time is an unknown quantity. In Stage 2, it begins to be reduced—mainly in manufacturing. In Stage 3, companies approach a cycle time that is just twice the direct labor (or theoretical) time, while in Stage 4, the ultimate in total cycle time, being no more than theoretical cycle time, almost becomes a reality.

■ C_{PK}—*the new language of quality*—If variation is evil in quality practices, it must be measured. Two metrics—C_P and C_{PK}—were developed in the 1980s to measure variation. Although a description of them is beyond the scope of this chapter, they are measurements of the reduction of the cost of poor quality. In Stage 1, no C_{PK} measurements are made. In Stage 2, C_{PK}'s are less than one, indicating defects higher than .27 percent. In Stage 3, C_{PK}'s are less than 2, and in Stage 4, C_{PK}'s are greater than 5, indicating perfect quality.

■ *Metrics in support services*—If quality indices lag in U.S. manufacturing, they are nonexistent in support services, such as finance and accounting, personnel, purchasing, and other white-collar operations. This is especially true of Stage 1 companies. In Stage 2, management by objectives (MBO) is used to link quality goals and plans together, but quantitative measures are a will-o'-the-wisp. In Stage 3, cycle time, as explained earlier, can effectively measure any administrative process. In Stage 4, the concept of next operation as customer (NOAC) is fine-tuned. Every administrative process has an internal supplier and an internal customer. The latter determines its requirements to the supplier, just as an external customer determines specifications. These requirements could include timeliness, completeness, and accuracy (i.e., quality), cost, cooperativeness, and flexibility. These requirements are then agreed upon by the internal customer and internal supplier, along with quantitative measurements to chart progress. The internal customer then feeds back her view of progress made. In the final analysis, it is she who becomes the scorekeeper, the evaluator of performance—not the internal supplier's nominal boss.

Area 5: Tools

One of the sins of American management is that it thrashes around with quality generalities, such as total quality management (TQM), company-wide quality control (CWQC), and quality circles, without giving its good people the tools to achieve a quality breakthrough. Unless these simple but powerful tools are understood and used, no company can ever achieve world-class quality.

- *Problem solving*—In Stage 1, there is no knowledge of problem solving other than brute-force sorting and screening. In Stage 2, elementary quality tools, such as Pareto charts, cause-and-effect diagrams, the plan-do-check-act (PDCA) cycle, and control charts are used, with meager results. Typical is our U.S. automotive industry, which has spent billions of dollars on control charts and has a return on investment (ROI) in the millions—an ROI of 0.1 percent. One could do better in a failed S&L bank! In Stage 3, design of experiments (DOE) (see *World Class Qual-*

ity: Using the Design of Experiments to Make It Happen, Keki R. Bhote, New York: AMACOM, 1991) is used as the best way to solve chronic quality problems in production. In Stage 4, DOE is moved upstream to *prevent* quality problems at the design stage of a product or process.

- *Statistical process control (SPC)*—This is not a problem-solving tool. It is useful as a monitoring technique only *after* chronic quality problems are solved and yields in excess of 99 percent are achieved. Stage 1 companies—a repetitive chant by now—have no inkling of SPC. In Stage 2, tyrannical customers, such as Ford, force their suppliers to use control charts, even though processes are not under control and even though control charts are now an aging technique, with poor discrimination against both good and bad quality. In Stage 3, enlightened companies use precontrol only after products and processes are brought under control, with C_{PK} of 2.0 and more. Precontrol is much simpler and statistically more powerful than control charts. In Stage 4, Positrol is used after a product or process has been characterized and optimized by DOE. It tightly controls important parameters identified in DOE by determining who, how, where, and when such parameters should be measured and kept under control. Stage 4 also uses process certification—a technique to assure that other quality characteristics, such as workmanship, metrology, and environment, are in place and the process is certified before even unit No. 1 is allowed to start in production. Precontrol, then, can continue to monitor excellent quality.

- *Customer requirements*—In Stage 1, "the voice of the engineer" dominates what the customer gets, with little or no input from the customer. In Stage 2, market research is conducted to determine customer needs, but it frequently misses the mark. In Stage 3, a few simple but powerful techniques such as value research, sensitivity analysis, and multiattribute evaluations are the preferred tools. In Stage 4, quality function deployment (QFD) and conjoint analysis are used to capture the "voice of the customer" and the strengths of the competitor and then to translate these into effective product, process, part, and test specifications.

■ *Reliability*—This is distinguished from quality by two parameters—time and environmental stress. In Stage 1, there is scarcely any catering to reliability. In Stage 2, reliability prediction studies, failure mode effects analysis (FMEA), fault tree analysis (FTA), and derating, the tools developed in the 1970s, are the norm. In Stage 3, reliability is demonstrated through accelerated life tests, where environmental stresses are applied to the product one at a time and product liability analysis is conducted to eliminate potential product liability claims and lawsuits. In Stage 4, the ultimate aim is to achieve near-zero field failures through a technique called multiple environment over stress tests (MEOST), where environmental stresses are combined and taken beyond design stress to deliberately smoke out the weak links of design.

■ *Workmanship*—Errors are caught in Stage 1 through external inspection—with an effectiveness under 40 percent. In Stage 2, video recognition systems and computer scans appear to be the technological and mechanistic alternatives to inspection. In Stage 3, neighbor inspection is promoted as a quick and nonthreatening way to feed back defects to the previous operator. Stage 4 recognizes that human beings will make mistakes, no matter how threatened or how well paid. It utilizes a Japanese technique, called Poka-Yoke, where simple, inexpensive sensors warn an operator that a mistake is about to be made.

■ *Equipment maintenance*—"Don't fix it if it ain't broke" is the mindset for equipment maintenance in Stage 1. In Stage 2, maintainability parameters such as mean time to diagnose (MTTD) and mean time to repair (MTTR) are developed to reduce diagnosis and repair time. In Stage 3, maintenance is shifted to prevention and responsibility is shifted largely to operators. In Stage 4, the practice of total productive maintenance (TPM) is institutionalized. Factory overall efficiency (FOE)—measured as a product of yield percent times up-time percent times machine efficiency percent (i.e., theoretical time divided by running time) of 85 percent minimum—is the driving force to move a factory toward maximum equipment utilization.

■ *Support services*—In Stage 1, no tools exist to improve quality and productivity in support services. In Stage 2, management audits of services performed for customers are increasingly used. In Stage 3, benchmarking is a very effective method. It consists of searching for the best-in-class company—either a competitor or noncompetitor—for a particular product, service, technique, or practice; determining the success factors that make it the best; and then mounting a process to close the gap between the benchmarking and benchmarked company. In Stage 4, the full power of the NOAC is used, with powerful tools such as value engineering, job redesign, and process redesign.

To summarize, these are powerful tools that any company can enlist in its march to world-class quality. Yet, there is not a single company—anywhere in the world—that uses all of these tools. For that matter, less than 1 percent of companies use even one tool.

Area 6: Customers

■ *Company objective*—Management gurus, such as Peter F. Drucker, have long argued that the main objective of a business is not profit but customer satisfaction. Yet, Stage 1 companies continue to worship profit, while paying lip services to the customer. In the process, they achieve neither adequate profit nor true customer satisfaction. Stage 2 companies have nobler goals—jobs and employee welfare—but do a poor job in both areas. Stage 3 companies address all elements of customer satisfaction—quality, reliability, maintainability, technical performance, ergonomics, safety, service delivery, and price—all of which, in balance, achieve total customer satisfaction. In Stage 4, customer satisfaction is elevated to customer *enthusiasm,* which can only be achieved by happy, productive employees.

■ *Satisfaction feedback*—This gauge of customer satisfaction is pursued only intermittently by Stage 1 companies. In Stage 2, market share—an unreliable index of customer satisfaction—is used. In Stage 3, numerous survey techniques, focus groups, and panels feel the pulse of the customer, aided by win/loss analysis and such measures as the completeness/speed of complaint resolutions. In Stage 4, the spirit of a famous quote by Konusuke Matsushita (founder of Matsushita empire)—"You must take the customer's skin temperature daily"—is adhered to with techniques such as QFD and benchmarking, on a continuum of time.

- *Customer contact personnel*—These individuals get little attention and even less respect in Stage 1. In Stage 2, these personnel are given customer sensitivity training and taught to smile "with the eyes, but not with the heart." In Stage 3, they are elevated to a position of importance and given recognition and rewards for outstanding performance. Finally, in Stage 4, they are empowered—trusted to act on their own authority in exceptional situations, even to the extent of spending money (within prescribed boundaries) and taking on responsibilities and authority previously reserved for managers.

Area 7: Design

- It is now a truism that a company that designs a product faster than its rivals and gets it to the market sooner will enjoy a distinct competitive advantage. In Stage 1, the engineer designs the product in an organizational cocoon. The half-baked product is then tossed over the wall, with the time bomb ticking, for production to catch and muddle through. In Stage 2, engineering, and manufacturing work together from the start of design to effect a smoother product launch. In Stage 3, simultaneous engineering (a label for an interdisciplinary team consisting of not only engineering and manufacturing but also quality, purchasing, sales/marketing, and finance, under the baton of a program manager) carries the product from concept to production. In Stage 4, partnership suppliers are added to the teams to reduce the design burden through parallel development, offer constructive ideas in design, and help achieve target costs.

- *Objective*—In Stage 1, the design objective has no focus. In Stage 2, it is to design for manufacturability (DFM). This innovative quantitative method rates designs on a scale of 1 to 100, with 80 considered a minimum to assure ease of manufacturing. Many U.S. designs rate from 20 to 50! Stage 3 goes further to assure designs for zero variability, with a minimum C_{PK} of 2.0 of every important design parameter. Stage 4 assures that all elements of customer satisfaction are catered to in the design, especially novel features that can *excite* the customer.

- *Strategy*—In Stage 1, the engineer's natural inclination is to completely redesign a product and put his own unique stamp on the outcome. In Stage 2, he is still obsessed with his own ego, pushing the state of the art in technology, regardless of the consequences of poor quality and reliability. In Stage 3, prudent companies do not allow more than 25 percent of an older product to be redesigned, thereby saving valuable time, improving quality, and enhancing reliability. In Stage 4, the strategy is to design in half the time, with half the cost, with half the manpower, and with half the defects of its predecessor product.

- *Design time*—In Stage 1, the design cycle is measured in years. In Stages 2 and 3, there is a conscious attempt to cut this in half. In Stage 4, the design cycle is measured in months, with a stream of new products arriving at the market in rapid succession to make a competitor's product virtually obsolete before its release.

Area 8: Suppliers

- *Relations*—The relationship between customer and suppliers in Stage 1 is adversarial. In Stage 2, it softens somewhat to suspicion. In Stage 3, there is the beginning of trust and a congruence of each other's goals. In Stage 4, this blossoms into full trust and a sound partnership for mutual benefit.

- *Number of suppliers*—In Stage 1, there is an unmanageably large supplier base. In Stage 2, the base is systematically reduced. In Stage 3, there is no more than one supplier per part number and, in Stage 4, no more than a single-digit number of suppliers for an entire commodity.

- *Top management focus*—In Stages 1 and 2, management is preoccupied with direct labor and with automation, generating the plaintive refrain that our only choices are "to emigrate, automate, or evaporate!" In Stage 3, the obsession is still with production, but now in the form of computer-integrated manufacturing (CIM). It is only in Stage 4 that management realizes that direct labor constitutes less than 5 percent of the sales dollar, while suppliers' materials account for over 50 percent. Supply management—being the partnership, within a narrow base of suppliers, between purchasing, the suppliers' quality assurance, and engineering—becomes a key corporate strategy in Stage 4.

- *Organization*—This is the traditional purchasing department in Stage 1. In Stage 2, this expands into materials management, including inventory control and the physical movement of goods. In Stage 3, the commodity team—consisting of a member from purchasing, quality assurance, engineering, and the partnership supplier—is the solid building block of supply management. And in Stage 4, the supplier becomes an extension of the customer company, with financial ownership the only line of demarcation.

- *Modus operandi*—In Stage 1, the customer's operating style with suppliers is dictatorial remote control. The supplier is a vassal. In Stage 2, it is arms length in nature and contractual. In Stage 3, the customer hands off her requirements to the supplier, with few bridges and little effort to visit the supplier. In Stage 4, however, there is a dramatic change. The customer provides active, concrete *help* to the supplier—in quality, cost, and cycle time improvement—as the best way, *the only way*, to help herself!

- *Quality levels*—In Stage 1, specified acceptable quality levels (AQLs) from suppliers are appalling, with reject rates running 1 to 5 percent; in Stage 2, these are less than 0.5 percent; in Stage 3, less than 100 parts per million (ppm), and in Stage 4, the supplier's quality—following customer help and coaching—is so perfect that incoming inspection at the customer's site is obsolete and the supplier has achieved self-certification.

Area 9: Process/Manufacturing

- *Process characterization*—This is an important discipline to determine which variables in a process are important and need tight control, versus those that are unimportant and whose tolerances can be opened up to reduce costs. Stage 1 companies do not even know the meaning of the term. In Stage 2, important process parameters are selected through equipment manufacturer recommendations, maintenance, and operator inputs, and "the voice of experience." Stage 3 utilizes process capability studies, a modest tool at best. (Ninety-nine percent of U.S. companies have not advanced beyond Stage 3.) In Stage 4, the best way to characterize a process is with DOE, using a Rolls Royce tool developed by Dorian Shainin called variable search.

- *Process optimization*—In Stage 1, the process engineer is a "knob twiddler" who ends up chasing his own tail. In Stage 2, there is considerable tweaking, varying one cause at a time, thereby missing important interaction effects between variables. In Stage 3, sophisticated computer simulation is used. This works if the mathematical relationship between key variables is known. But in many complex products and processes, even an Einstein could not come up with the formula, leaving the much-vaunted computer helpless. In Stage 4, DOE again comes to the rescue, this time with a simple, graphical technique called scatter plots, which can determine *the* very best level of an important variable and its realistic tolerances.

- *Metrology*—In Stage 1, the instrumentation to measure a product parameter is inaccurate, unreliable, and often out of calibration. In Stage 2, there is still considerable variability within each instrument, instrument-to-instrument, and operator-to-operator. In Stage 3, the rule of instrument accuracy—a minimum of five times the accuracy of the specification tolerance of the product being measured—is upheld. In Stage 4, other Shainin DOE techniques, such as multivari and isoplot, are used to determine the correlation between instruments and between operators in order to systematically reduce overall instrument variation. The three elements of metrology—accuracy, precision, and bias—are all optimized.

■ *Latent defect control*—In reliability, one of the objectives is to reduce and eliminate latent defects that can cause infant mortality in products. Stage 1 is a blank. In Stage 2, room temperature or high temperature burn-in is used. Stage 3 employs thermal cycling—a more effective tool to weed out latent defects. Stage 4 uses MEOST in truncated form, along with a quick and thorough failure analysis of repetitive reliability-oriented defects found in the factory.

■ *Quality characteristics*—Stage 1 is characterized by high scrap and rework, 100-percent brute force inspection, and test and yields well below 75 percent. Stage 2 sees reduced scrap and rework, a switch to sample inspection and test, and yields in excess of 90 percent. In Stage 3, scrap and rework are virtually eliminated and precontrol is used for inspection and test. Yields consistently top 99 percent. Finally, in Stage 4, even inspection and test become obsolete and 100-percent yields are the norm.

Area 10: Field

Most companies concentrate on quality up to the shipping dock, but then drop the quality ball when it comes to the field.

■ *Warranty period*—This deficiency in field sensitivity is underlined by the shortchanging of warranties. In Stage 1, the warranty period is no more than three months. Stage 2 is a begrudging one year, hedged with disclaimers and legal jargon. In Stage 3, companies are forced by their competition to extend warranties up to five years. Stage 4 companies, by contrast, are so sure of the product reliability that they extend warranties to the lifetime of the product, albeit limited to single ownership.

■ *Services*—The quality of service continues to be a national disgrace. In Stage 1, field service is an oxymoron! In Stage 2, companies

cover their poor reliability with service contracts that take the customer's money up front. In Stages 3 and 4, quantitative goals for mean time to diagnose (MTTD) a fault and mean time to repair (MTTR) a defective product are established and met. Surveys are also regularly conducted to determine customers' satisfaction with the timeliness and accuracy of service.

■ *Parts*—Customers can forgive an occasional product breakdown. But they cannot tolerate poor service and the nonavailability of spare parts. In Stage 1, a perpetual crisis reigns in parts availability. In Stage 2, there is excess inventory to overcome shortages. In Stage 3, part failure rates are studied to assure availability of high-failure-rate items, along with starter kits of critical parts and exchange units to swap entire products. In Stage 4, the emphasis shifts to reliability to attain virtually zero field failures.

Area 11: Support Services

Manufacturing productivity is 80 percent and rising, while support service (white-collar) productivity is 40 percent and falling. Quality and cycle time improvements are being pursued at an encouraging rate in manufacturing, but in white-collar work, these are foreign terms.

■ *Internal customer*—In Stage 1, NOAC is unheard of. In Stage 2, companies want to embrace NOAC, but it remains a high-sounding concept, with little or no implementation. In Stage 3, NOAC is implemented. Internal customers measure the performance of internal suppliers on a regular basis. In Stage 4, the internal customer's evaluation of the internal supplier is used as the primary performance appraisal tool, not evaluation by the boss. In extreme cases, the internal customer has the power to dispense with the internal supplier's services and even go outside the company to secure those services.

■ *Structure*—In Stage 1, support services are organized in typical bureaucracies. Their common characteristic—large in size, pygmy in effectiveness. In Stage 2, teams are formed in each department to solve administrative problems. In Stage 3, cross-functional teams tackle interdepartmental and even interdivisional problems. In Stage 4, top management provides structure and continual guidance to the effort through the establishment of a senior management steering committee and a process owner who can lead these teams and break down departmental silos.

■ *Improvement techniques*—In Stage 1, improvement of quality, cost, and cycle time in support services is off the screen. In Stage 2, some elementary tools, such as Pareto charts, cause-and-effect diagrams, and control charts, come into play. In Stage 3, more powerful techniques, such as brainstorming, force-field analysis, and benchmarking, strengthen problem solving. In Stage 4, the ideal tools are value engineering, which starts off by challenging every process and explores its elimination; job redesign, which restores meaning and joy to the workplace; and process redesign, which takes the air out of bloated and ineffective support departments and returns most of their functions to line departments at lower overall cost.

Area 12: People

The United States considers itself the world's greatest political democracy, and yet its industries remain autocracies. Top-down, know-it-all management is the order of the day, despite the empty rhetoric that "people are our most important asset."

■ *Management view of workers*—In Stage 1, management looks at the line worker as a pair of hands—as if there were a sign at the guard entrance: "Check your brain here. It will not be needed inside!" This is the direct result of Taylorism. Fredrick Taylor did this country a signal disservice by asserting that, "Managers think and workers do." In Stage 2, managers concede that workers do contribute, but only low-grade ideas, mostly related to working conditions and not to product improvement. In Stage 3, the Hawthorne effect becomes operative. Managers pay attention to their workers and the latter respond in kind. In Stage 4, there is full trust and partnership between managers and workers, with the former undertaking the sacred duty of caring for the workers and orchestrating their growth.

■ *Climate*—In Stage 1, the climate of fear is so pervasive that ideas and suggestions dry up. The employees withdraw into their shells. In Stage 2, management encourages the formation of quality circles or improvement teams in order to promote employee participation. But management itself is nonparticipatory; managers do not mingle with the workers. If communications exist at all, managers are transmitters, not receivers, talking instead of listening. In Stage 3, managers become participatory. They regularly visit their workers, mingle with them, listen to them, support them, and act on their ideas. The workers respond in kind. In Stage 4, there is vertical job enrichment, where every worker becomes a manager in his or her area of operation. There is now job excitement.

■ *Training*—In Stage 1, training is nonexistent. In Stage 2, it is sporadic with no implementation on the job. In Stage 3, training is linked to corporate strategy, focused and followed by coaching on the job. In Stage 4, training is "cascaded." Top management receives the training first. Each member of this group then selects a quality improvement project, implements it, and uses it as part of his or her teaching and coaching. This learning-doing-teaching cycle is cascaded, or repeated, down the ranks so that all workers are taught.

■ *Management role*—In Stage 1, management is bossy. At worst, it is tyrannical; at best, it is parental. In Stage 2, management means control and manipulation. In Stage 3, the manager becomes a coach, a teacher, a consultant, a facilitator. In Stage 4—the ultimate—the manager sheds his or her management skin completely and is transformed into a true *leader*, with vision, inspiring his or her people, helping them, nurturing them, and promoting their growth.

■ *Worker*—In Stage 1, the worker, discouraged by management insensitivity, is passive and withdrawn. In Stage 2, he learns to be a team player and problem solver, with programs such as quality circles and small group improvement activities (SGIA) in place. In Stage 3, the worker breaks through the management glass ceiling and attains the first tier of management responsibilities—planning, organizing, controlling, and improving. The zenith is reached in Stage 4, where a self-directed work team takes on all aspects of oper-ational management, including interfaces with customers, suppliers, and support service personnel; budget and goal determination; even hiring, firing, and evaluating team members.

MANUFACTURING PROCESSES AND MATERIALS

Wendell Leimbach, AME Group, Inc.

Patricia Turnbaugh, Consultant and Committee Chairperson, Foundation for Manufacturing Excellence

Michael Perril, ESI & Associates, Inc.

Company strategy provides the framework for determining what products a company will manufacture. In order to increase competitiveness, manufacturers have learned to bring the focus of the manufacturing strategy in line with the company strategy. Most modern company strategies have a primary focus in one of four areas: quality, flexibility, delivery, or price. The appropriate primary focus is determined by matching the requirements of success in the marketplace with the capabilities of the manufacturing operations. For example, if your company produces high-precision medical instruments for surgery (quality focus) it is unlikely that the company will be successful in producing a children's toy doctor set (price focus).

If there is a strong match between the market requirements and the manufacturing capabilities, the manufacturing strategy will be based on continuous improvement to the products and operations. If there is not a strong match, the company is faced with the prospect of changing its marketing strategy or making major changes to its products and processes.

A manufacturing capabilities audit should be performed to determine the company's strengths and weaknesses in the manufacturing operations. After the audit, the company can determine its appropriate primary focus, and from that, its manufacturing strategy.

Once these decisions have been made, functional manufacturing activities can begin, starting with design work. Management of product cost also begins at this point in time.

This is because a product's design commits the production system to specific processing methods, selection of materials, conversion processes (tools, layout, machinery, etc.), operation sequences, and levels of labor skill.

Since design sets cost, management should exercise constant vigilance in correlating the design with manufacturing process planning. The objective is to ensure that all the elements of the design and the finished product are economically appropriate and support the primary focus of the company.

Since the 1980s, the concept of identifying and satisfying customers through quality improvement has become popular and effective in the United States. American quality gurus such as W. Edwards Deming, Joseph Juran, Philip Crosby, and Armand Feigenbaum have been pushing and/or leading American manufacturing into the quality process. By understanding what the customer (the person who receives or uses whatever the employee personally produces) requires and expects, each employee can be involved in the improvement of the product or service. The concept has a variety of names such as total quality management (TQM), total quality management system (TQMS), total quality control (TQC), and continuous improvement program (CIP). These concepts generally follow the same fundamental principles:

- They meet customer requirements and exceed expectations.
- They continuously improve all products and processes by eliminating errors and waste.
- They empower each employee through extensive training and involvement in the improvement process.
- They measure processes and performance compared to the industry's best in order to know how and where to make improvements.
- They strive to do each activity or process correctly the first time and every time.
- They work closely with suppliers and customers on continuous improvement.

The implementation of these concepts is through active employee involvement on functional quality teams or as members of cross-functional problem-solving teams.

MANUFACTURING PROCESS DESIGN

Three procedures (programs) should be in place to meet customer requirements with minimum waste: design for manufacture (also called simultaneous engineering), value analysis, and group technology. Although the presentation here is essentially sequential, the programs generally operate in parallel.

Design for Manufacture/ Simultaneous Engineering

Design is the primary responsibility of the engineering function. Design activities must be supported and reviewed by (1) management to make sure that the product designs support the company and manufacturing strategies; (2) marketing to make sure the products meet the market requirements; (3) operation to make sure that the product designs fit the capabilities of the operations and support the efforts in continuous improvement; (4) engineering to make sure the product designs will use the appropriate technology to meet the company strategy. The product must be economically exploited for the benefit of the total manufacturing enterprise.

There should be a full written description of the product requirements to guide the designer. These requirements are the foundation of the design effort. In addition, a number of principles can be used to guide development and design review:

- Identify the plannable "core" parts, subassemblies, and materials (i.e., items that reappear across many lines).
- Reduce parts counts.
- Use modules for product functions.
- Use a minimum number of surfaces in parts/modules.
- Design form assemblies from the bottom up and utilize nesting principles.
- Select symmetry and asymmetry to reduce parts and enhance identity.

- Design parts within the capabilities of available or planned processes.
- Utilize group technology classifications.
- Utilize computerized design technology.
- Participate in value analysis.
- Participate in continuous improvement teams.

Obviously, these principles call for cooperation between functional areas. Some companies have pulled product development and manufacturing engineering together under one manager. Others have established design teams, drawing members from various engineering functions as well as from purchasing, finance, and marketing. A number of leading companies, including Xerox, Black and Decker, Cadillac, and Ford, have implemented such programs. The efforts are generally credited with greatly improving time-to-market. The reduction of design to product introduction time greatly reduces the total product cost while improving the ability to satisfy the requirements in the market.

Value Analysis

Value analysis (sometimes called value engineering) basically consists of (1) analyzing and evaluating the fundamental use of a product, (2) systematically attempting to build greater value into the product without reducing its performance or interfering with its functions, and (3) simultaneously reducing its cost. The principles of value analysis should be applied at the drawing board, when a product is initially designed, and continued all the way through each of the operations, to final assembly. In the past, the techniques of value analysis were used primarily on existing products rather than on new ones.

Although specific techniques vary from industry to industry, the goal is the same: to increase the difference between the product worth and product cost, thereby increasing the value to the customer. The goal in organizing a value analysis program is to bring the right people together at the right time on the right product. Because these individuals must temporarily step aside from their regular duties, top management's endorsement of the program is vital. By drawing experts from many different disciplines (including the purchasing, marketing, design engineering, manufacturing, and field service functions) and using their combined creative ideas, management will end up with a superior product, at a lower cost.

Reporting should be to a person high enough in the chain of command so that decisions can be made and then implemented promptly. When value analysis is a centralized function, the overall responsibility often rests with a corporate officer. Quality or problem-solving teams may employ value analysis as a problem-solving tool.

Since materials frequently make up the highest percentage of total cost, value analysis can be particularly valuable in purchasing. Many firms now ask for cooperation from suppliers—that is, partnerships, quality certification, using incentives—to encourage recommendations on quality or cost improvements.

Group Technology

Many products within a company have similar parts and use similar processes. Once recognized, these similarities can be a powerful tool for organizing the production process and reducing costs. European managers named this concept group technology. The Machinability Data Center, a department of the Defense Information Analysis Center, located in Washington, D.C., defines group technology as a manufacturing philosophy based on the recognition of similarities in the design and manufacture of discrete parts. The usual tendency is to consider each manufactured part as unique, since a casual visual examination of a total part population does not usually reveal its commonalities. However, parts can be categorized into groups or families if their fundamental attributes are identified.

Through the systematic classification and grouping of parts into families on the basis of their design or production similarities, a company can achieve significant cost reductions. Parts classification is a necessary activity in group technology systems and can be accomplished using one of a variety of classification and coding schemes. The concept is not new. By 1900, F. W. Taylor had already introduced the use of mnemonic classification, which embodied some of the concepts of what we now call group technology.

The scope of group technology is broad. Its application affects all areas of a manufacturing company, including design, process planning, manufacturing, assembly, and so on. It should also be noted that group technology applies both to mass production where the approach of fixed automation (for example, transfer line machines) is used and to small-lot discrete-parts manufacturing. In the typical manufacturing plant, the excessive setup time caused by the product mix and small lot sizes may be the most significant part of the total production time. Furthermore, plants typically have a functional layout of equipment. Consequently, jobs take nearly unpredictable paths through the plant in order to reach all the necessary processing locations. Production scheduling and production control become very complicated, and actual information on the status of any particular job is nearly impossible to obtain.

Group technology alleviates mass confusion by first grouping parts into families having manufacturing similarities. In this way, different parts requiring similar machines and tooling may be processed in a sequence that increases the quantity per setup, thereby significantly reducing setup times and costs. Machines used in the production of similar part families are grouped together, forming a machine group or cell (hence, the name *cellular manufacturing*). This layout has the effect of reducing the scope of the problems of production scheduling, production control, materials handling, and so on. At the same time, the approach tends to improve the operator's morale. Problems related to tooling, for example, can be simplified through the use of fixtures common to an entire part family. The economic benefits of the application of group technology become significant when the cost reductions in tool design, production control, materials handling, inventory control, and the like are considered.

The concepts of group technology have expanded beyond manufacturing cells into "focus factories" and "plant within a plant."

The drive to organize around families of parts or products is to reduce the production lead time (cycle time). The shorter the distance that material travels in the plant and the faster the setup times, the better the control over the processes and the lower the cost.

Applications

Design for manufacturing should include appropriate applications of value analysis modified by group technology considerations to produce parts and products with the following characteristics:

- Tolerances and specifications optimize the cost/benefit ratio and reduce selective assembly operations.
- Surface-finish requirements are balanced against real need.
- Energy requirements are minimized for changes in configuration.
- Fewer numbers of parts are used to accomplish the product's purpose, to minimize the number of overhead transactions throughout the entire manufacturing process.
- Strategic and scarce materials are conserved.
- Configurations are easy to complete in fewer loadings and handlings, minimizing the setups and the deterioration in geometric relationships and reducing the work-in-process inventory.
- The use of manufacturing cells is promoted and manufacturing lead times are minimized.
- Environment in both manufacturing and use is conserved.
- Manufacturing employees or users are not put in physical jeopardy, minimizing liability.
- Utility is for the broadest worldwide market.
- Minimum replacement activity is required.
- Competitive positions in the industry are enhanced.

As manufacturing processes are increasingly automated, group technology and families of parts can help optimize the use of specific modular parts in the total product line. The whole manufacturing organization should pursue a "search for sameness" that reduces the complexity of parts and processes in the factory. New technology provides a basis for combining machine design, materials handling, and control technology.

MATERIALS MANAGEMENT

Material is the lifeblood of a manufacturing company. After all, if you do not have enough, then what are your customers going to buy? But where do you draw the line? If you have too much, how can you afford to maintain materials without making your product costs too high? Material management is the balancing act we have to perform to optimize our customer service versus the costs of providing the desired products.

Material management is defined by the American Production and Inventory Control Society (*APICS Dictionary*, 7th ed., Falls Church, VA, 1992) as being "the grouping of management functions supporting the *complete cycle* [emphasis added] of material flow." This means from the time we purchase raw material to the time the finished product is shipped to the point of sale. To support the *complete cycle* of material flow, a company must have a coordinated strategy that both defines how various types of inventory are to be used and how the "grouping of the management functions" will be linked into a seamless process. This is the only way an organization can achieve the goals to have the right quantity, of the right end product, at the right time; minimize both the total costs and cash flow requirements; deliver the *required* level of quality; maintain a stable work force.

Materials management can provide either chaos or control in today's factories. Control is the result of a manager's ability to provide a series of balances and alliances related to the planning and scheduling of materials and processes, from acquisition through manufacturing. The end objective is to ensure that the product is available for sale on time.

Materials management's primary concerns are (a) maintaining the *quality* and *quantities* of materials needed to serve the customers,

(2) supporting profitable use of plant equipment and labor, and (3) accomplishing these two tasks with a minimum dollar investment. Materials usually account for approximately four times the labor costs of converting the materials to finished product. Thus, it becomes increasingly important to maintain absolute control over inventory investments—normally one third the capital employed in the enterprise.

To support the profitable use of equipment and labor, the materials manager has a variety of new techniques at his or her disposal, such as manufacturing resource planning and just-in-time (JIT) inventory management. None of these techniques is mutually exclusive in the quest for lowered working capital and elegant planning.

Inventory

Generally speaking, inventories assure the continuous operation of all facets of a manufacturing organization. To smooth out the use of production resources, we maintain *safety stocks* to prevent downtime. To schedule level production, *lot sizes* may be increased for machine efficiencies, or *anticipation stocks* may be built to support seasonal needs. *Decoupling stocks* are useful for separated production processes and *hedge stocks* assure continuous operations even during supplier shutdowns. Finally, *finished goods* help to balance the firm's supply with the market's demand.

Planning for the proper amount of each type of inventory can have a significant effect on a company's bottom line. Inventories are among the largest assets of a company, often representing as much as one third of a firm's invested capital. The issue, then, is to determine how much inventory is worth relative to the benefits expected.

There are two categories of inventory costs: procurement and carrying costs. The cost to order material (including *all* indirect administrative expenses) must be balanced against the costs to maintain the purchased inventories. These material-carrying costs, which may average anywhere from 25 to 35 percent of a firm's annual inventory cost, include cost of money to carry inventory, storage space, and material obsolescence, spoilage, and loss. There are also the hidden overhead costs associated with indirect labor for handling materials (i.e., receiving/inspection, storeroom, dispatching). These indirect labor costs are typically overlooked as part of the inventory-carrying cost. Instead, they are lumped into a general overhead account.

As long as sales were increasing, ever-increasing overhead expenses were not too much of a concern. Unit prices were stable or even decreasing since the overhead could be spread over the larger sales base. Now, however, with sales being flat or even declining, manufacturers must look harder at all overhead expenses. One way to do this would be

to directly charge all labor, as suggested by a cost accounting concept known as activity-based costing (ABC). Then, if inventory levels could be reduced, a corresponding amount of overhead should be reduced.

In general, the more inventory carried, the higher the carrying costs. Of course, by ordering less frequently and in larger volumes, the lower will be the procurement costs. The trade-off between these costs has been represented by a mathematical formula known as the economic order quantity (EOQ). As Exhibit 8-10 illustrates, EOQs are used for more than just defining what quantity of material

Exhibit 8-10. Reduced Setup Equals Reduced Lot Sizes

Conventional Setup

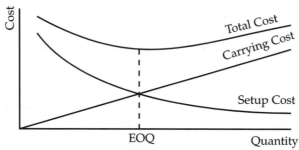

Reduced Setup

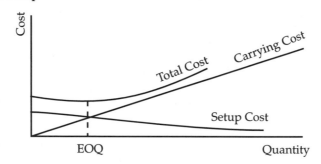

Where:

$$EOQ = \sqrt{\frac{2AS}{CI}}$$

A = annual demand (units)
S = order, or setup, cost
C = item cost
I = carry cost rate expressed as a decimal

Source: From APICS Just-in-Time Certification Course, Viewgraph #87.

should be ordered. EOQ also is used to determine the economic production lot sizes, which directly affect investments in work in process (WIP) inventories. This demonstrates why so much attention has been paid lately to the time to perform a setup. As the setup costs are reduced, so too are the optimal lot sizes, giving manufacturers the means of having greater flexibility in meeting changing demands.

Time-Based Strategy

By cutting the time it takes to produce a product, less inventory is required to meet customer demand. It is no longer the case that customers are willing to pay a premium for quicker turnaround—today that is what it takes just to get the order! Some manufacturers have experienced dramatic successes through reduced cycle times:

- Northern Telecom cut its inventories and operating overhead each by 30 percent, and improved its customer satisfaction level by 25 percent. As part of its strategy, one division alone cut the number of component suppliers from 9,300 in 1984 to 2,500 in 1988. The result has been a 97-percent reduction in the receiving cycle, a 49-percent reduction in the incoming inspection staff, and a 97-percent reduction in shop-floor problems caused by defective material.
- Steve Jobs' NeXT Inc. computer company has streamlined the transition from design to production to enable the company to manufacture a totally new board design in twenty minutes.
- Texas Instruments' antenna department has maintained its competitive position in a downsizing U.S. military market by achieving the following reductions over a two-year period: lead time went from sixty to twenty-five days; work-in-process units decreased from 1,100 to 300; assembly hours and costs per unit decreased 27 percent; rework was reduced by 85 percent; quality (as measured by defects/unit) improved by 90 percent.

What these and many other companies have found out is that by striving to react faster to customer demands, so-called "normal" problems could no longer be accepted. Deliveries of more material than ordered with less than 100-percent quality *do* impact the time to handle, inspect, and put away. The need to rework material due to poor processes *does* take away from the time needed to make acceptable product. Competitive manufacturers can no longer afford to hide behind the excessive inventories that mask the true problems. As the often-cited rocks and stream analogy illustrates in Exhibit 8-11, the less obstructions there are, the lower the level of inventory that is required, and the faster is the flow. Once this can be accomplished, the resources required (i.e., costs) to support the operations can be dramatically reduced.

With increasing customer demands, the ability to quickly provide customized finished goods becomes a distinct competitive advantage. with a faster manufacturing flow, it is possible to reduce the reliance on the sales forecast. The one truism about forecasts is that the longer the time period being forecast, the less accurate it is! Therefore, if you can reduce the time for which a forecast is required, there is likely to be less operating resources and capital invested in finished goods inventories that end up as being unwanted.

Inventory Investment

Given that material accounts for as much as 60 percent or more of a product's cost, control over inventory investments is critical to achieving the goal of minimal cost and cash flow requirements. If viewed as a function of the product's cycle time (see Exhibit 8-12), the longer it takes to complete the production process, the longer scarce capital is tied up.

For example, assume a shop has $80,000 of material in its finished goods per week. If it takes twelve weeks to produce, then 12 × $80,000, or $960,000, of material cost is tied up in work in process (WIP). A reduction of 50 percent in the lead time for the product would reduce the working capital requirements for WIP inventory by a corresponding amount, or $480,000 (6 weeks × $80,000). This also has the effect of doubling the throughput of the facility without any increase in operat-

Exhibit 8-11. Rocks and Streams Analogy

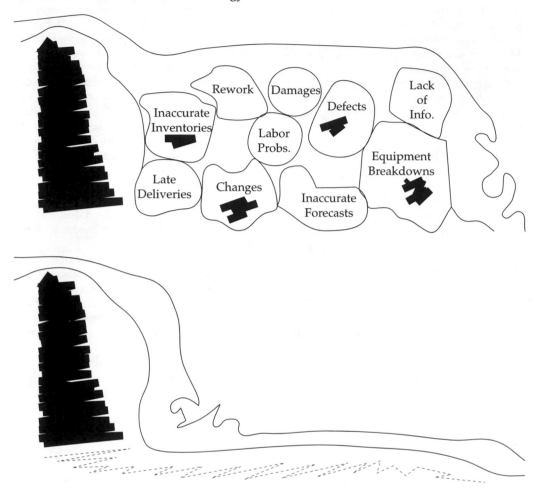

Exhibit 8-12. Investment in Inventory

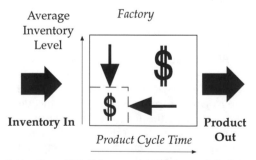

Source: From ESI & Associates Proprietary MRP II Education Program; copyright © 1991 by ESI & Associates.

ing resources! After all, if it takes half the time to produce, then twice as much product can be produced with the same resource base.

Until the production "obstacles" are eliminated, higher inventory levels will also be needed to support the production cycle time—regardless of how long (or short) it is. If less than 100-percent quality is accepted from *either* vendors or internal production, then additional costs have to be incurred. All the JIC (just-in-case) inventory needed to compensate for quality problems does not come for free! By setting ever-increasing standards of excellence, both the level of inventory and the product's cycle time can be reduced.

How Are Reductions in Cycle Time Accomplished?

Key to this time-based strategy is having *all* management functions "supporting the *complete cycle* of material flow." The problem is that more often than not, the organization's departments have objectives that may conflict with one another. Worse yet, their objectives may unknowingly conflict with the true (though unstated) goals of the company.

Although sales and production normally do not agree on much, historically they both agreed on the desirability of larger inventory stocks. For sales, larger inventories support the flexibility and responsiveness required to satisfy customer demands. Production, of course, gets the material it needs to avoid stock-outs, keep lengthier runs on equipment with expensive setups, and have "spare" material to replace scrapped parts. Purchasing does not care as much about on-hand inventory. It does favor placing fewer orders of large quantities to minimize the cost to procure and to get favorable volume discounts. Finance, on the other hand, prefers low on-hand inventories due to the requirement for working capital.

The question that must be answered is whether these are really the objectives each department should have. Is it really sales' objective to meet sales targets regardless of the cost? If not, then what are all of the costs its decisions may impact? Is it really worth the added material expense to keep production running, especially if material is being produced that is not needed yet? Do purchasing's volume discounts offset *all* carrying costs? What about the cost of poor incoming quality? Is purchasing held accountable for this expense? Should financial measurements of return on investment (ROI) for machinery be driving the production department—even at the expense of additional material?

By redefining the objectives (and performance measurements) of all departments, it is more likely their activities will support the company's strategic objectives—those being the balance of cost, product availability (with the desired options), and the required level of quality. Some of the newer measurements of performance that should be considered at the department level include the following:

- *Purchasing*—total material cost (*not* unit price), including the current indirect material costs and the lack of quality (which may require rework or reshipment).
- *Sales/marketing*—finished goods inventory. Since this department forecasts customer demands, it should be held accountable for the forecast's accuracy.
- *Production*—time to produce. By concentrating on the elimination of time detractors, *all* costs (both direct and indirect) may be reduced.

In fact, time to produce should be a key measurement for the entire organization. A good way to measure it is by tracking total output over time based on the total number of employee hours. This way, productivity and lead times are evaluated relative to both indirect and direct labor. As many companies have been finding out, the indirect labor (administrative and material handling) will provide a gold mine of opportunities for increasing company-wide productivity.

Planning and Control Systems. To manage the timing for when material should be made available, it is necessary to plan for its need, as well as to control it effectively. Planning and control systems have been evolving rapidly. In the mid-1960s, material requirements planning (MRP) helped to overcome the deficiencies with the standard order point systems by recognizing component dependencies. In the 1970s, MRP evolved into a closed-loop manufacturing resource planning (MRP II) system to address the master production scheduling and execution or control systems (i.e., purchasing, shop-floor control). In the 1980s, U.S. manufacturers were rudely awakened to just-in-time (JIT) execution concepts. Today, we are in an era where the entire logistics chain must be considered. To support this objective, a new term has been coined: enterprise resource planning (ERP). To date, ERP is merely a concept that recognizes the need to integrate the distribution and manufacturing functions into an organization-wide system. Ultimately, it is likely to integrate the distribution requirements planning (DRP) and manufacturing resource planning (MRP II) systems.

Although this slew of acronyms is enough to give anyone a headache, it really boils down to simply choosing a way to plan and/or control the use of material throughout an organization. If viewed this way, these alternative approaches may not be mutually exclusive. Although much has been written about the use of MRP II versus JIT, there are times when it could be appropriate to use both!

It should be noted that in the following discussion of MRP II, the use of a DRP system may also be warranted. Since it operates in a similar manner for distribution facilities as

MRP II does for manufacturing, they are treated as a single topic.

Instead of viewing the MRP II closed-loop system as it is typically represented by business *function* (Exhibit 8-13), it should be viewed by business *process* (Exhibit 8-14). This perspective indicates that it is possible to consider using MRP II for planning purposes, even though JIT may be more appropriate for the execution systems (or control processes).

The question then becomes, how does one know when to use one approach or the other? To answer this, it is important to understand the concepts of "push" and "pull" systems.

Push Systems. MRP II is known as an order-launching or push system. Driven by a

Exhibit 8-13. MRP II—Manufacturing Resource Planning

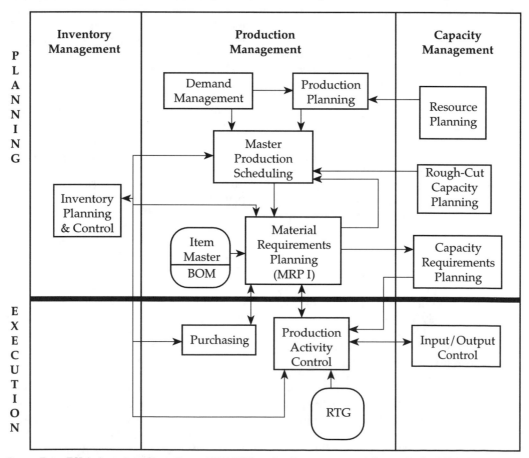

Source: From ESI & Associates Proprietary MRP II Education Program; copyright © 1991 by ESI & Associates.

Exhibit 8-14. Planning and Execution with MRP II

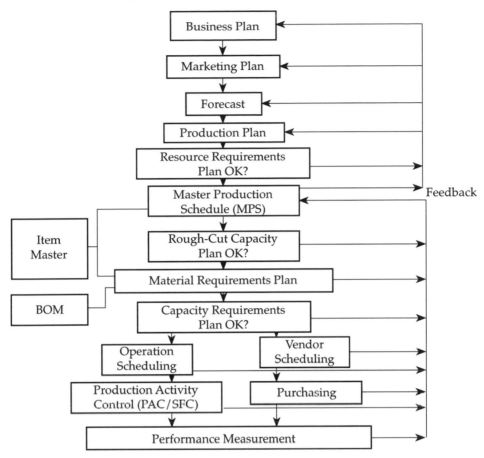

company's business plan, it takes the financial sales and operating targets and translates them into production units. The anticipated build schedule for customer orders and/or forecasted product, known as the master production schedule, is what initiates the calculation of orders for material. Using this highest level of demand for each independent item, the MRP system uses the bill of material for that item and its inventory availability to generate time-phased orders for all components. By backward scheduling with each item's stated lead times, a calculated required date is generated to recommend when orders should be released.

There are several reasons why MRP II has not been the overwhelming success it was originally touted as being. It is dependent on the accuracy of *all* of the data that it uses. Inventory, bills of material, and part lead times' accuracy (for both manufactured and procured material) must be close to 100 percent. If not, more or less parts than are truly needed may be planned, and/or they may be recommended to be available sooner or later than needed. Due to the backward scheduling algorithm, any slip in a component's availability will have a direct impact on all levels above that part. (There is no slack time as in forward scheduling that is typical for project management critical path analyses.)

Even if all of the data were correct, MRP is usually scheduled with the assumption of infinite capacity for all associated resources. There are now many finite scheduling packages available to help address the timing of work in process on the shop floor. Manufacturing execution systems (MES) closely link production processes and order scheduling for more effective use of resources. However, nothing is perfect. There are always going to be random daily events that may affect the fixed lead times upon which these schedules are predicated.

Pull Systems. Recognizing the difficulty in modeling the production environment, just-in-time (JIT) avoids the need to anticipate when work should begin. JIT was pioneered by the Toyota company in the mid-1970s as a production control system known as Kanban (which means card in Japanese). By using two types of cards, one to authorize production and one to signal the movement of parts, each work center (or subassembly line) withdraws parts at the time they are needed.

The process is initiated by the final assembly line. As workers withdraw parts from their feeding work centers, the upstream centers are then authorized to produce replacement parts. In order to do this, these work centers may withdraw parts from those work centers who feed them. In this way, parts are "pulled" only when they are actually required.

In order to be able to rely on such short time intervals for material replacement, it is mandatory that all nonvalue-added activities be eliminated. From this, JIT has evolved into a philosophy of continuous improvement. Its objectives are production to customer demand; process quality improvement; uninterrupted flow; elimination of waste in labor, material, equipment, and space; development of the productive potential of people; continuous quest for improvement; flexibility.

If taken to the extreme, each customer order becomes the initial signal for any production to take place. Since this is not practical, even JIT must rely on a production plan. In light of the second view of MRP II (Exhibit 8-15), it is therefore feasible that the planning process

Exhibit 8-15. Pull Versus Push

	Materials Planning	Control Stage Order Release	Shop Floor
Pull: Continuous Flow	JIT	Rate Based	JIT-Pull
Hybrid Push-Pull: Batch, Repetitive	JIT-MRP	Pull or MRP	Pull
Hybrid Push-Pull: Batch, Dynamic	MRP	MRP	Pull or Order Scheduling
Push: Custom Engineering	MRP	Order Scheduling	Operation Scheduling

Low (top), High (bottom); vertical axis: Lead Time Variability could be that of an MRP II system, while the execution system could be JIT.

Push or Pull? For a pull system to be effective, the operation must have the following characteristics: level flow of material; regular, cyclic final assembly schedule; upper limit on inventory between operations; efficient signaling system for feedback; high-quality, reliable process; quick setup times.

As depicted in Exhibit 8-15, the closer one is to a continuous flow (whether discrete or process), the more likely it is that a pull environment can be employed. The trick for a batch manufacturer is to try and emulate the characteristics of a continuous-flow environment. Cellular manufacturing is probably the best way a non-repetitive manufacturer could look to exploit these concepts. Where a part or a family of parts shares common materials and/or processes, a mini-assembly line may be configured. The means for identifying what parts and processes could share similar production facilities is a process known as group technology.

Even in job shops where irregular demands or highly customized/engineered parts are the norm, there are many JIT principles that could apply. Through setup time reductions and improved quality standards, inventory levels can be decreased significantly. Just as important as the internal improvements, supplier relationships can be developed where smaller and more frequent deliveries can reduce the inventory investments.

CONCLUSION

There are a variety of ways that material management can be performed to achieve the company's goals. What is important is to first make sure that the goals are those that the company wants. A clear, and well-communicated strategy for achieving these goals must then be agreed upon. Performance measurements that encourage activities that support the strategy must be defined and consistently enforced. All of these steps can not be expected from those performing the material management function. This is, however, the domain of executive management. As always, executive management must provide the direction and commitment, in word and deed, to capitalize on the opportunities that are available. Only these managers can empower the entire organization to make the dramatic changes needed to prosper in this increasingly competitive global market.

MANAGING TECHNOLOGY IN MANUFACTURING

Tom Inglesby, President, American Society for Competitiveness; Formerly Editor, *Manufacturing Systems Magazine*

A philosopher, probably a manufacturing manager, once said, "There are only three things that are important: people, time, and money. And since time is money, there are really only two." The current era in manufacturing is becoming more and more in tune with the theory that time is the most valuable thing besides people, that time creates money much as people do. Unfortunately, the reverse is not true: You cannot buy time; you can only buy resources to improve the use of time.

Technology is the major resource available to increase the usable time a company has, and it does it by decreasing the time it takes to bring out new designs, to debug those designs, to bring the products to market, and to improve them to stay competitive. Managing technology requires a knowledge of what the technology is, what it can (and cannot) do, and a belief that, next to people, technology is a company's most important resource.

The modern era in manufacturing turned a fateful corner in the late 1950s with the popularization of the transistor radio ... by the Japanese. Small and nearly disposable, these inexpensive radios demonstrated the capability of the new electronics to reduce size and cost through applied technology. The next stage was the development of the multiple-semiconductor single chip, the microprocessor. Through combining the capabilities of hundreds, then thousands, and now millions of active electronic parts onto a single substratum, the microcircuit age arrived.

Companies such as Motorola, Intel, and Advanced Micro Devices have become closely associated with the microprocessor. IBM, Sun Microsystems, Hewlett-Packard, and others have developed internal chip design and/or manufacturing capabilities to remain competitive while moving the target higher for each generation. And while the chip companies were designing and building faster, more component-laden silicon, developers in all parts of the world were seeking uses for these chips. Some of them ended up in consumer products—everything from toasters to televisions—and some became the controls for modern automobiles, aircraft, and space shuttles. Most important, many became the eyes and ears of manufacturing.

The computer age began before the microcircuit was developed. The difference, some would have you believe, was merely one of scale. Early computers required a room filled with heat-generating vacuum tubes and circuits to process in batch mode a limited variety of software developed by specially trained programmers.

MANUFACTURING COMPUTING

Today's microcircuit-based systems have magnitudes more power, as determined by millions of instructions per second (MIPS) processing speed, require no more space on a desktop than a dictionary, operate in near real time with an operator interface that can be learned in a matter of minutes, and software that can do almost anything the human mind can devise to do. And they cost pennies to buy compared to the first several generations of mainframe systems.

But we cannot dismiss the large-scale computer from this discussion, for the mainframe and its more recent competitor, the minicomputer, are still the backbone of large manufacturing companies. However, this backbone has been splintered into a new, more flexible form of environment known as distributed computing. Even then, that term has several meanings within the structure of manufacturing operations. There are systems that place "dumb" terminals at work locations so employees can access data from a central minicomputer; there are systems that interconnect multiple small microcomputers to create a local area network (LAN); there are systems that combine these approaches by connecting "smart" personal computers with limited storage capacity to a host computer with greater processing power and storage capability. This latter version, known as a client/server architecture, is becoming the most popular as managers move toward the concept of employee empowerment. By having local intelligence in their workstations and access to the data generated in other functional areas, individual workers have the ability to be enterprise employees.

Because so many companies began computerization decades ago, there are significant installed bases of large-scale computers. While these may have lost their edge in speed and capacity to the newer microcircuit-based systems, these companies have too much invested in hardware and software to throw it all away and start over. To protect these companies, and their investments, vendors such as IBM have maintained a migration path for earlier systems owners. By continuing the compatibility of their architectures while utilizing the most modern technologies, these vendors have assured their customers that money spent in the 1960s for computer capability will still be producing information well into the year 2000.

But the American industrial base is composed of more small, relatively new companies than older, well-established ones. These ventures have had the advantage of coming into the computer age when the computer was coming of age. Even then, the dynamism of the market and the speed of development in electronics makes computer systems "obsolete" in a matter of months. But are they really obsolete? Although a newer, faster more powerful chip comes out annually, and in some cases more often, does that negate the value of the existing equipment? The answers are both no.

INSTALLING NEW COMPUTER SYSTEMS

The computer is a tool, like a hammer or drill. The tool rarely becomes obsolete so long as it can do the job it was originally designed to do. If a new-style hammer comes out that can improve a carpenter's productivity, it should be adopted. But if the carpenter is not working at the peak of the hammer's capability to begin with, the new model will not help much. The same is true of computer technology. Too often, companies rush to implement the latest systems without ever coming near the capability limits of the existing equipment. Faster processing speed, as represented by MHz ratings, allows the computer to move information through the system faster. But if the programs being run do not require fast processing, why move to a faster chip? The limitations of today's computer systems lie not in the hardware but the software, the operating system, and most important, the application.

Before any technology is implemented, a detailed plan should be devised to assure that what is being installed will accomplish the tasks at hand. To do this, those tasks must be understood. The first stage of any technology implementation, therefore, is the determination of the problem to be solved by the technology. No problem? Then why bother to add equipment? On the other hand, anticipating problems can be a good exercise in future planning. Doing a classic "what-if" evaluation can point out where problems might develop and where technology can be employed successfully. Because of the time required to implement any new technology, advanced planning such as this can shorten the installation cycle and allow equipment to be up and running in advance of the problem developing. But even this approach has its pitfalls.

Ask any purchasing agent about technology and you will hear the complaint, "Whatever we buy is superseded by a newer version before we can get it in the door." Again, that is true in the fast-moving world of high-tech and especially computers. But it does not mean obsolescence if the equipment ordered will do the job it was ordered for. Do not wait for the next generation of technology before implementing a solution you need now.

INFORMATION TECHNOLOGY

With the introduction of minicomputers and superminicomputers, more activities can be attempted closer to the point where the decisions or activities take place. Typically, the initial response is to automate manual activities. For example, in the engineering department, CAD (computer-aided design/drafting) systems were at first introduced to automate the drawing process. With the passing of time, progress was made and it was possible to go beyond pure automation of manual tasks and offer new possibilities. CAD/CAM (computer-aided manufacturing) systems helped engineers carry out new tasks that were not possible on a drawing board. During this period, it became possible for functions such as engineering to install its own computers rather than rely on a centralized mainframe.

Each department spent months, perhaps years, defining its particular needs and then benchmarking systems from several vendors. However, the analysis rarely took account of interactions with other departments, it looked at the past rather than the future, and it considered local, tactical issues rather than issues of strategic importance to the company. Although it appears that in many systems the software costs twice as much as the hardware, and associated organizational issues cost three times as much, the benchmarks generally were concentrated most on the hardware and least on the organizational issues. The cost justification of such a system often had little value apart from satisfying top management's requirements for paper figures on return on investment (ROI). The financial analysts rarely understood the overall impact of new systems, and the potential users of the system would go to any lengths to get over the hurdle rate set by management.

Up to this point in time, most people in the company had been doing pretty much as they liked when looking for computers. Each department or group bought its own computers and systems to meet its own requirements. Many major corporations found themselves unable to do business without information technology but were saddled with a wide range of computers that did not communicate effectively together. Trying to get information from one program on one computer to a program on another was extremely difficult. What was needed was integration, aimed at connecting the so-called "islands of automation." Whether or not this was necessary from the point of view of the business strategy was rarely considered. CIM (computer-integrated manufacturing) became the buzzword of the 1980s and 1990s.

At about the same time as the integration issue became apparent, the first microcomputers became available. Along with engineering workstations, they offered new possibilities to improve operations. It became possible to automate more manual activities and, for the first time, to provide specific local computer support to individuals.

Before the explosive growth in the use of microcomputers, telecommunications had been a separate area, dominated by engineers adept at splicing cables and interpreting signals on oscilloscopes. As more and more people started to use their own computer, rather than a central computer, the need for communication networks to transfer information between various users became apparent.

The rapid development of communication networks provided the opportunity for another activity: communicating information throughout the company. Corporate mailboxes and electronic mail became familiar buzzwords. Little attention was paid to investigating whether moving information quickly around the company without a massive investment in training and modifying work practices would actually provide an advantage.

Alongside purely technological issues of using computers in manufacturing are associated organizational issues. Two very important and related issues are the procedures governing use of systems and the training of users. It should be obvious that people who are not properly trained will not be as productive as they would be if properly trained. Unless formal procedures are developed showing people how to use systems, people will use them as they see best. There are times when it is sensible to give people free rein to let ambition and imagination lead them to successful, innovative products. However, most of the time, work on engineering systems occurs in a relatively structured environment and the introduction of procedures does not inhibit innovation but prevents anarchy, resulting in a savings of time and money.

Far too many engineering companies spend millions of dollars on technology for product development systems and try to make up for it by saving the few tens of thousands of dollars that would be required to train people properly and implement suitable working procedures. In so doing, they cost the company several more millions of dollars in lost sales, which they see as a sales problem, not an engineering one.

The latest activity to appear is using information technology and communications to gain a competitive advantage. Companies understood they could use technology to create close ties with suppliers and clients. They could use it to help differentiate themselves from the competition through lower costs, higher quality, and faster reaction to market requirements. These are strategic issues and imply that the decision to invest in informa-

tion technology ranked with major investment decisions concerning new product development. As a result, they require significant top management involvement, going far beyond signing off on the management information system (MIS) budget.

Together, the improvements in quality and productivity lead companies to positions as low-cost producers. The improvements in adaptability and flexibility bring products to market faster and increase market share. With reduced costs and increased sales, profitability can rise significantly.

Today, the major issues for manufacturing companies include "information shock." This is the effect of the increasing amount of electronics in products, the possibilities offered by widespread communications networks, and the rapidly decreasing cost of computer power. These factors imply more frequent design and volume changes, smaller volumes, and much more responsive management.

Faced with this environment, manufacturing companies' prime objectives will be to increase their ability to develop new products and services and to find new ways to make and deliver them to the customer faster than the competition. Time, not cost, will become the key parameter. The life cycle of some new electronic products, from conception to obsolescence, is already down to less than two years. As product lifetimes decline further, the effect of being three months late with a product, even if it is cheaper, will be disastrous. Most customers will already have bought the competitor's product. Those who have not will be waiting for the next generation of product. Similarly, producing a product that does not meet customer requirements will be disastrous. There will be no time for trial and error; the product must be right the first time.

Increasing speed typically requires stripping out unnecessary levels of middle management and bureaucratic control, taking a new look at the whole development-to-finished-goods process, and promoting multifunction teams. Instead of engineering doing its job alone, then handing it over to manufacturing, companies will have to bring individuals from marketing, design engineering, manufacturing engineering, and production into a product team with total authority for product functionality, building, and costs.

THE PATHWAY TO CIM

The concept of integration in manufacturing starts with the information flow, continues throughout the operations as information flows from station to station, and ends with information flowing back to the source to confirm the operations were completed and the tasks were accomplished according to plan. In other words, information is the integrator for CIM. Electronic data transfer between operations and locations is the realm of the computer network, and it, in turn, depends on accurate data, in a usable form, and delivered in a timely manner. Throughout the factory, sensors collect information on what is happening, what has happened, and what is expected to happen. If anything, more data are collected every minute than can effectively be utilized. The modern manufacturing operation is in a data overload situation! It is important that the planners determine what data are most immediately needed to provide efficient operation. In many cases, that determination can make or break the implementation of CIM.

The physical world of manufacturing starts with the design. It is here that the idea becomes something tangible, something that members of the product team can discuss, can iterate, can modify, can agree upon. In the computer-driven environment of modern manufacturing, that design begins on a computer screen in the form known as CAD, computer-aided design/drafting. It will later be transformed into other computer programs, such as CAM (computer-aided manufacturing) for metal cutting or CAE (computer-aided engineering) for component placement in electronics assembly. A recent methodology called rapid prototyping may be used to create a first-pass product to compare design with reality. Simulations may be run to test parameters and interferences. Automated test equipment (ATE) may have quality checking programs developed directly from the CAD database as may coordinate measuring ma-

chine (CMM) programs. A bill of materials and shop-floor routing is developed from this same information, often "on the fly" without the designer's active intervention.

These data are compared with existing inventory and orders are placed with vendors through computer links utilizing EDI (electronic data interchange) protocols. The MRP (material requirements planning) system is notified of the new products development stage by stage and constantly updates its database with expected shipment and build dates, inventory requirements, and new component specifications. The MRP II (manufacturing resource planning) system performs computer-aided process planning (CAPP), shop-floor capacity, and machine utilization routines to determine the best way to manufacture the new product when it is ready. Simulations are run to provide engineers with capacity alternatives. Various codes are generated—bar codes, group technology codes, and so on—to make automatic identification of the product, its components, and processes possible.

In the best of all computerized worlds, all of this is done without human intervention. The computer programs, integrated through a common database, interchange information automatically to complete these tasks without paper being produced. The exception would be the only human readable "paper": barcoded labels with code numbers or alphanumeric indications of the product. In most cases, these would be strictly cosmetic, intended to inform the buyer, not the manufacturing operation.

A bane of all manufacturing is the change order. After the product is in production, changes are made to update it, to respond to market forces, to correct a flaw in the design. New variations are implemented to enhance market share; slight or major modifications are made to create new offshoots. All these changes are done through electronic modifications to the common database. Each requirement for operational change in the factory is noted and a continuous file of changes is maintained to track products with each option or variable. In controlled products (those with safety requirements such as automobiles and pharmaceuticals), a database of product numbers and build dates is updated and maintained separate from the ever-changing CAD database. Monitoring this duality is another program that acts as a traffic cop for all operations, assuring that the most current version is in production.

Once the product is in manufacturing, the same database provides information to program the material handling system to bring the raw stock from the receiving dock, where it arrives "just-in-time" from EDI-connected suppliers. The database generates the required CNC/DNC (computer numerical control/distributed numerical control) program to instruct the various machines on how to operate on the material (in metal-cutting operations) or where to route the components for assembly. Robotic machine loaders place the stock in the proper machine and position is checked by machine vision systems comparing the stock to the CAD database for orientation. Inspection of the completed machining is also done with this camera equipment. After machining, the components are moved automatically to the next operation, queues kept to a minimum through capacity planning algorithms. Queued material is considered waste or scrap as no value is being added during the time it sits awaiting the next operation. Like the production line in the classic Charlie Chaplin movie, everything should be moving through value-added operations at all times.

In the assembly area, components identified by bar codes, passive radio frequency ID (identification) tags, or other automatic systems are routed to the appropriate workstations where robotic assembly systems compare the components to the assembly diagrams obtained electronically from the CAD database. Orientation is again determined by machine vision and the use of jigs and fixtures that are flexible enough to accommodate multiple designs. Should human workers be involved at the assembly stage, a monitor shows them the instructions or walks them through the assembly by the application of multimedia (audio/video/alphanumeric) displays. Help is never more than a keystroke away.

As the assembly builds and moves from station to station, inventory records are up-

dated automatically, new components are ordered based on usage, material outages at suppliers are noted, and the line speed is adjusted to maintain a constant flow of production. In those industries where the product is too large to "flow" along a production line—aircraft and locomotives come to mind—the equipment will be moved to the product in sequence and operations will take place at the site rather than along a route.

We use the term *production line* but reality has shown that a line is often the wrong configuration for proper manufacturing. Cells have become more popular as technology supplants human workers. A robot works better if its operations are within an envelope described by the machine's arc or swing. To place material handling systems in a straight line requires multiple robots to accomplish the same work one unit can do if the movement is circular around its periphery. Simulations of robotic and human operations can determine best cell arrangements and avoid conflicts.

As all these operations become computer controlled, humans are moved into more demanding positions. Even though the systems will be self-diagnostic, repairs will continue to be done by humans—for a while, anyway. Preventive maintenance scheduling will be determined by the computer control based on sensor feedback of specification matching and wear factors. If the process starts to slip, alternate routings will be enacted and the out-of-tolerance machine(s) will be repaired or moved out of the loop.

ISLANDS OF AUTOMATION DEFINED

Integration intends to connect the "islands of automation" that have been computerized randomly over many years at so many companies. To connect them one must first recognize them. Depending on the size and complexity of the company, computerization can be done on microcomputers (PCs), mini-, or mainframe computers. The programs range from custom-designed, process-specific to store-bought generic software (Lotus 1-2-3 is probably the most popular) used for a wide variety of functions. The following is a short list of islands of automation most often found in manufacturing. Obviously, different types of manufacturing (process, repetitive, discrete, batch, continuous flow, mixed) will have specific areas computerized and not others. Therefore, the list (from John Stark, *Competitive Manufacturing Through Information Technology: The Executive Challenge*, New York: Van Nostrand Reinhold, 1990) should be considered a starting point rather than an end point. (For convenience, we include the more popular acronyms with their functions. Often, the acronym is more easily recognized than the term it represents.)

Material requirements planning (MRP)
Manufacturing resource planning (MRP II)
Bill of materials processor (BOMP)
Stock control
Purchasing
Manufacturing simulation
Shop-floor routing
Short-term scheduling
Shop-floor data collection
Receiving
Bar-code reading/automatic identification
Machine monitoring
Personnel monitoring
Material handling systems
Numerically controlled (NC) machine tools
Computer numerically controlled (CNC) machines
Direct (or distributed) numerically controlled (DNC) machines
Flexible machining cells (FMC)
Flexible manufacturing systems (FMS)
Automated assembly
Automated inspection
Automated test equipment (ATE)
Robotics
Programmable logic controllers (PLC)
Automated warehousing
Process control
Automated guided vehicles (AGV)
Distribution resource planning (DRP)
Computer-aided plant layout
Work-in-process (WIP) management

Automated storage and retrieval systems (AS/RS)
Coordinated measuring machines (CMM)
Statistical process control (SPC)
Computer-aided quality assurance (CAQA)

THE CAD/CAM CONNECTION

CAD/CAM and CAE (computer-aided engineering) are two of the most important systems in the product development environment.* Although CAD/CAM is most often associated with mechanical engineering and CAE with electronic engineering, conceptually they are very similar. They both refer to the application of computers to the design engineering and manufacturing engineering process of a product and, therefore, refer to the total engineering function of the company. Their aim is to increase the quality, flow, and use of engineering information throughout the activities of defining what the product is to be and the way it is to be produced. This translates more concretely into reduced cycle times, reduced costs, and increased quality. These are the types of competitive advantages that most companies are seeking.

The use of CAD/CAM in mechanical engineering can be taken as an example to illustrate some of the important features of the use of computers. First, there is the very important aim of modeling the part in the computer and of reusing this information at later stages of the engineering process. Geometry modeling is the process of building a model, in the computer, that contains all the necessary information on the part's geometry. The model should be unique, so the part will not be mistaken for another, and it should be complete, containing all the geometry information required in later activities. This information also includes other attributes apart from geometry, such as color and material.

* Much of this section is based on material in *Competitive Manufacturing Through Information Technology: The Executive Challenge*, John Stark (New York: Van Nostrand Reinhold, 1990).

CAD/CAM is a useful computer-based application employing interactive graphics techniques. It can be used for many applications throughout design engineering and manufacturing engineering. However, it is only a tool. It does not automatically provide competitive advantage nor does it automatically design, analyze, or manufacture. These tasks must still be carried out by people, programs, and machines.

CAD/CAM can enable more designs and products to be produced within a given time frame. It can be used in this way to gain competitive advantage. It can be used for a significant amount of design work in projects and can shorten the engineering cycle. CAD/CAM can also lead to an increase in the reuse of existing designs, thus reducing the cost of the design process. Used in conjunction with group technology (the associating of parts and components by their characteristics), it can lead to a reduction in the number of parts needed to produce a wide variety of products. This reduction, in turn, will reduce process planning costs and will lead to a reduction in manufacturing engineering and inventory costs. All these gains can be directed toward attaining competitive advantage. Potential areas for using computers in product development are:

Computer-aided design (CAD)
Numerical control programming (NC/CNC)
Finite element analysis (FEA)
Computer-aided process planning (CAPP)
Simulation computer-aided technical publications
Programmable logic controller (PLC) programming
Robot programming
Automated test equipment (ATE) programming
Machinability data systems
Parts list generation
Computerized piping, nesting, and die selection
Engineering data management
Product modeling
Engineering data exchange

Information models
Integration
Engineering systems procedures
Training

The early view of information technology was very much a set of individual computer systems, each of which would provide a major productivity gain. In practice, in most cases, such systems have not provided the expected gains. Invariably, this has been because the organizational issues have been ignored. Questions such as, "Why are we using this system? How should we use this system?" have been bypassed in the rush to use the system.

A major organizational issue must be the training of the newly empowered workers. Many of them, in the shop, have some limited experience with computers and related technology, but most are inexperienced and, in all too many cases, hesitant to learn. "Computer phobia" is not to be taken lightly as it impedes the required training cycle and can cause a growing distrust among other workers. This is usually a situation found on the shop floor more than in the engineering office, however. Engineers, certainly those coming out of college and university life today, are familiar with computers. As a matter of fact, they might not be able to function without them.

Still, too many companies spend their technology dollars on equipment without adequate funding for training. According to a roundtable discussion (*The Role of CAD/CAM in CIM*, Society of Manufacturing Engineers, 1990), training is the number one issue needing the highest priority and most immediate attention. Four basic types of training were mentioned:

1. *Management training*—the enlightenment of upper management on the capabilities of modern CAD/CAM systems and how they are, or should be, used in the enterprise.
2. *End-user training*—continual user training in the technology available in CAD/CAM systems. Examples would include scanning, photorealistic rendering, file transfer standards, and modeling techniques.

3. *Specific vendor training*—training provided by the system vendor (or third party) on the specific system installed at the user's site. While obviously important to get the most from a system, it was considered to be only part of the answer.

4. *Applications training*—Training mostly required in applying the vendors' capabilities and technology to the job at hand within the enterprise. Many are familiar with certain vendors' claims that the system can be learned in one week or less. That claim may be true when measured by the user's knowledge of the commands but is offset when measured by the ability of the user to apply the system effectively within the enterprise.

NEW TECHNIQUES, NEW TECHNOLOGIES

If there is one constant in modern manufacturing it is that nothing remains the same. Every year, new techniques are guaranteed to increase quality, shorten cycle times, or improve productivity. Many do just what they are claimed to do. Some do not. Either way, it is a fertile area for book writers, consultants, and industry gurus.

Among the conceptual "buzz phrases" mentioned in the past decade are zero defects, world-class manufacturing, just-in-time (JIT) delivery, kanban, continuous flow manufacturing, pull versus push manufacturing, finite capacity scheduling and infinite capacity scheduling, optimized production technology (OPT), and its corollary, the theory of constraints.

Basically, little or no new technology is required to implement these concepts. However, they do require large amounts of one "technology" often in short supply, namely, common sense. They require planning and agreement among the various functional areas impacted by the changes they propound. In the words of Eli Goldratt, author of the "industrial novel" *The Goal*, they require the removal of the syndrome that causes narrow thinking and fails to create mutually beneficial interaction among the functional disciplines in manufacturing.

A "technique" getting significant attention is "employee empowerment." In adopting the idea of giving people at all levels of activity the responsibility—the ownership—of their process and production, we are in effect reverting back to the guild hall concept of the Middle Ages. Ownership of the process in those days was easy: Everyone was a single-person manufacturing operation. Few collections of artisans worked on a project together—building the pyramids being an exception, of course. Manufacturing was an individual occupation. As products became more complex, the requirement for special expertise at various stages of production became necessary. This happened as volume increased, markets opened, and commodity products began to appear. Then individuals grouped together (we would probably call it a merger today) to pool their ideas and talents. Assembly of many identical products was feasible (interchangeable parts, a concept credited to another Eli, Whitney of cotton gin fame, made assembly a repetitive and often tedious job that had once been a craftsperson's venue). Production as we know it today supplanted the inventor-as-builder notion. After all, the Wright brothers could not build all the airplanes the world would want, could they?

In many cases, new techniques spawn new technologies to make the implementation of the techniques easier. It is the "plug and play syndrome" at work—where a manager will call up the purchasing agent and cryptically say, "Order me some CIM, please." Companies seek out technology to make management technique changes more palatable to workers and, not surprisingly, the managers themselves.

The major form of this technology is the computer program. Software is written to make nearly every human endeavor easier or faster. Manufacturing and management are no exceptions. If you want to implement a JIT system, there are several software companies that will provide the required EDI programs to establish constant computer links with your suppliers, to notify them of your order needs and deadlines as inventory decreases during production. The information, a combination of data from the MRP/MRP II systems and shop-floor data collection inputs, will allow the suppliers to schedule your product build times and delivery methods to ship material so it arrives at your loading dock within minutes of the time it is required on the production line or in the work cell. Weather permitting, of course.

Technology is often developed in a vacuum. Someone has an idea for a new approach to making something. It may be a breakthrough concept or the combination of existing components in a new way to accomplish some task. That task, however, may not yet exist. The laser was such a technology, one looking for a use. Light amplification by simulated emission of radiation, lasers were developed in laboratories and slowly found uses outside the ivory towers. Today, the term *laser* is synonymous with two distinctly different areas in manufacturing: data collection and machining/metal working.

In data collection applications, low-energy lasers are used to scan bar codes and optical character recognition symbols for automatic identification purposes. The light beam is automatically scanned across the symbol at high speed, the pattern determined by a rotating mirror system within the reader. The most common systems to the average person are those at the grocery store checkout counter. In industrial applications, the beam may be fixed and the bar-coded item moved through the light pattern on a conveyor or other material handling system. Another major use is in hand-held scanners that allow people to aim the beam at the label and read it from moderate distances. These systems are often used in warehouse and distribution systems for monitoring and checking inventory.

In metal working, two areas employ lasers for two diametrically opposed purposes. A high-energy laser can be used to heat and soften metal at a junction, creating a welding effect. The metal is fused and joined with minimum distortion due to the lack of general heating of the components. Lasers are also used in the fine soldering necessary in some forms of electronic assembly.

At the other extreme, similar laser systems are used at higher temperature levels to cut through metal, composites, and some other materials too hard for economical machining with traditional cutting tools. Ceramics can be cut, as can wood, plastic, and even paper, with a fine beam to eliminate much of the waste generated by more conventional cutting tools with their broader kerf (the width of the cutting tool or blade and its corresponding area in the cut material).

Among the new technologies utilizing lasers are the various rapid prototyping systems that started to appear in the early 1990s. There are several competing technologies that can be used to create a solid from an electronic database. They all use the CAD design information to generate a physical model from raw material in a process that can take as little as a few hours or at most one to two days. The process can create prototypes of products so complex that they cannot be machined or molded in one piece due to internal cavities, recesses, and ports. Yet they can be generated in these prototyping systems in one piece to prove the design, check conflicts, and interferences and other manufacturing parameters before the final, more expensive tooling or molds are made.

The three major technologies involved depend on the application of medium-energy laser beams to raw material. Stereolithography uses an ultraviolet laser to scan a CAD design onto a liquid photopolymer resin, hardening the surface where the beam reacts with the resin. The term stereolithography originated with 3D Systems, Valencia, California. The computer drawing is "sliced" into multiple cross-sections, and as each layer is scanned, the resin hardens a portion at that surface. The hardened material is then incremented so the next layer can be scanned on top of it. This layer-upon-layer building process continues until the item is a completed physical reality of the CAD data. Similar competitive systems differ in using visible light lasers and moving elevators or stationary bases in the resin vat.

Selective laser sintering (SLS) is a technique developed by DTM Corp., Austin, Texas. It can be used with a variety of powdered materials, including wax, polycarbonate, composite metal, metals, and ceramics. A thin layer of heat-fusible powder is heated to just below its melting point and the design is traced on the first cross-section by a carbon dioxide laser. The temperature of the powder impacted by the laser beam is raised to the point of sintering, fusing the particles into a solid. The beam is modulated to sinter only the areas defined by the design geometry. As each new layer of material is deposited on the building object, the process is repeated. The bed of unsintered powder acts as a support for the item as the building process continues and the tray, or elevator, on which the product develops is lowered.

The third rapid prototyping system is based on a high-tech version of lamination. Laminated Object Manufacturing (LOM) is marketed by Helisys, Torrance, California. The materials used are sheets of paper, plastics, composites, or ceramics in various thicknesses. The sheets are precoated with heat-sensitive adhesives and laminated one atop the next to create a multilaminar structure. Once the layer is bonded, a CO_2 laser cuts the outline of the cross-section from the three-dimensional CAD database. The system can operate fully unattended to create the physical prototype. Since the materials are in sheets and the process is noncontact and requires no chemicals, warpage and shrinkage, internal stresses, and deformations are uncommon. Only the edges of the product are scanned so thick-walled components and thin-walled ones are created in the same short time.

In all cases, the developers of the systems have established service bureaus to offer their prototyping to the manufacturing public. Individual machines are being shipped and used by numerous companies involved in the fast-changing world of modern manufacturing.

Because of the pervasive nature of CAD in design and manufacturing, traditional drawing boards are becoming rare. Soon, the computer screen as we know it may go the same way. One of the newest technologies used to modify the designer's work environment is viewing in a three-dimensional and stereoscopic manner.

Because humans view their surroundings in three dimensions, we become accustomed to this viewing technique. When working on a drawing board or computer screen, the image is not "solid" regardless of the claims of three-dimensional CAD made by vendors. But stereo viewing allows this flat image to appear to the brain as a true dimensioned item. To do this, the technology, developed by Stereographics, San Rafael, California, delivers two slightly different images, one to each eye. Software generates the left and right perspectives, displayed sequentially on the monitor in alternating frames. (Computer screens refresh at a rate similar to the normal "refresh" rate of the optical nerves, approximately 60 frames per second.) The Stereographics viewing glasses are synchronized to the right/left images and the result is a depth of viewing not possible with the unaided eye. The technology will allow manufacturing engineers to "walk through" their processes, designers to interpret complex, multilayer designs more readily, and managers to see final products before approving production. In effect, it will allow "rapid prototyping" on the screen.

In a follow-up on technology to stereoscopic viewing, computers are being used to generate an otherworldly world called virtual reality (VR). Again, using glasses—or more correctly, goggles—the viewer is transported into a computer-generated world of sights and sounds that do not really exist outside the database. Connected to the computer by sensors populated in a glove, for example, and wearing the goggles, a user can confuse the brain into thinking the world projected on the glasses is real. As the hand moves, the computer image compensates. You can pick up objects within the database, move them, manipulate them, "hold" them without them existing. So far, tactile feedback is missing, but as the technology finds more uses, this will likely be changed with nerve stimulation through the same glove that now carries the image-enhancement sensors.

Keeping up with the fast-moving world of computerized products for improving manufacturing is a daunting task. Voice systems are available that allow people to discuss complex processes with the computer; handwritten instructions are read by computers;

the feedback environment that connects the human mind to the computer is becoming more and more like HAL in the movie *2001*. The science fiction of ten years ago is commonplace in today's factories. What will the current crop of sci-fi writers develop for us?

In many cases, the technologies are getting ahead of the fiction. Writers turn to the business section of the newspaper to get ideas for the next generation of technology, one that is already being explored to improve manufacturing competitiveness and productivity.

ENVIRONMENTAL MANAGEMENT

L. Hall Healy, Jr., Patrick Engineering Inc.

U.S. industry spent an estimated $129 billion on environmental expenditures in 1991. The growth rate of these costs is three times that of the U.S. gross national product (GNP). Environmental expenses are expected to exceed the Defense Department budget by the year 2005. From October 1990 through September 1991, the U.S. Environmental Protection Agency (EPA) levied $14 million in criminal fines and $1.75 billion in civil penalties, cleanup commitments, and cost recovery. These statistics and others in this chapter are taken from *Hazmat World*, Tower-Borner Publishing, March 1992. They demonstrate the need to understand environmental challenges facing industry and how to cope with them.

The federal government and industry are emphasizing conservation and pollution prevention. At the same time, the government is increasing its enforcement activities significantly. Potential areas of conflict can be identified across a wide range of environmental areas. The topic is a complex one. Environmental matters now touch on almost every aspect of a manufacturing entity, affecting

many things that have been taken for granted for decades. Examples include the value of a firm's real estate, the benefits of packaging, how we dispose of waste, and relations with the public.

Another component is the rate of change. Regulations are becoming more stringent faster. Deadlines are being foreshortened, as in the case of chlorofluorocarbon (CFC) bans. Technologies to deal with some environmental issues are developing rapidly. Constituents, like the public living near a plant, and environmental groups are becoming more activist.

One goal of this chapter is to help synthesize the competing perspectives of government regulators and enforcement with those of the industrialist who wants to minimize the effects of these issues on the bottom line. Exhibit 8-16 shows factory environmental issues graphically. Workers are the focal point of a number of these environmental issues. Exhibit 8-17 provides a listing of the two ways to visualize the difference in points of view. The company is seeking to resolve environ-

Exhibit 8-16. Factory Environmental Activities

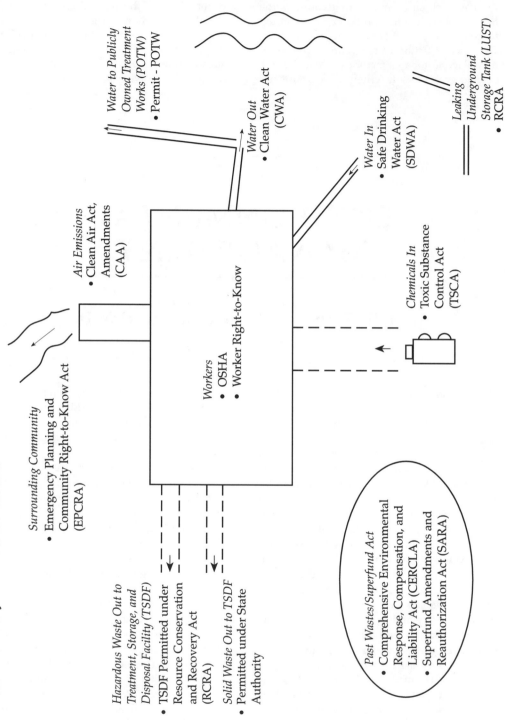

Exhibit 8-17. Industry Versus Government Viewpoints

Industry	Government
Environmental Issue to Resolve	*Federal Legislation to Enforce*
Air emissions	Clean Air Act (CAA), Clean Air Act Amendments
Community right-to-know	Comprehensive Environmental Response, Compensation and Liability Act (CERCLA), and Superfund Amendments and Reauthorization Act (SARA)
Contaminated soil	Resource Conservation and Recovery Act (RCRA)
Emergency spills	CERCLA, SARA
Groundwater contamination	Groundwater Protection Act (GPA)
Hazardous materials	RCRA
Polychlorinated biphenyls (PCBs)	Toxic Substances Act (TSCA)
Stormwater permitting	Clean Water Act (CWA)
Underground storage tanks (USTs)	Hazardous and Solid Waste Amendments (1984), RCRA

mental issues. At the same time, federal, state, and local regulations must be satisfied by government enforcers.

The driving force behind today's environmental cleanup is legislation and regulations—federal, state, and local. Federal legislation set the stage in the late 1960s and early 1970s. Since then, there have and continue to be many modifications. State and local governments now are taking a more active role, both at the behest of the U.S. EPA and due to local political, consumer, and environmentalist pressures. Sometimes local regulations are more restrictive than federal regulations. At times these can be overlapping or unclear. This scenario sometimes creates confusion about how to resolve a particular problem.

Because of the ever-increasing environmental regulations and the cutbacks in government funding and personnel, problem resolution also can become quite extended. Therefore, the best advice might be to hire an experienced environmental attorney and/or environmental consultant. They can assist in determining how regulations and agency actions/citations need to be responded to and in deciding on the most cost-effective solution.

The four categories of environmental issues facing industry today are air, water, land, and "other." Some of the specific issues they encompass include:

AIR
 Air emissions
 Asbestos

WATER
 Groundwater contamination
 Stormwater permitting
 Wastewater treatment
 Wetlands

LAND
 Aboveground storage tanks (ASTs)
 Contaminated soil
 Emergency spills
 Environmental audit/property transfer
 Hazardous materials
 Polychlorinated biphenyls (PCBs)
 Underground storage tanks (USTs)
 Waste handling (reduction, recycling, energy recovery, landfilling)

OTHER
 Community right-to-know
 Energy conservation
 Risk assessment
 Worker right-to-know

These categories are not iron-clad. Pollutants do not necessarily respect boundaries. But the categories do provide a framework that parallels somewhat the governmental and industrial perspectives.

AIR ISSUES

Air-related environmental issues cover a panoply of subjects: global warming, greenhouse effect, the ozone layer, acid rain, and even the indoor air environment. In coming years, air pollution will be a real growth area in terms of regulation formation and enforcement. This is due primarily to passage by Congress of the 1990 Clean Air Act (CAA) amendments. In general, these amendments are more stringent and will result in regulation of more substances at lower emission levels than previous amendments.

The thrust of the initial 1970 Clean Air Act and its subsequent amendments has been to require air quality standard setting by the EPA for ambient air stationary sources and for hazardous air pollutants. Among other things, the 1990 amendments will increase regulation of mobile source pollution (tighter tailpipe emission standards). New programs will require vehicle inspection and maintenance programs, cleaner (reformulated) gasoline, alternate fuels, and carpooling in some areas.

These air quality standards will be the most stringent in so-called "nonattainment zones"—urban areas of the country with the highest levels of six pollutants: ozone, nitrogen, and sulfur dioxide, carbon monoxide, lead, and particulate matter. The states will take a very active role in regulation and enforcement through the State Implementation Plan (SIP) process. The state permitting program and penalties for noncompliance are likely to have a high price tag.

The aspect of the 1990 CAA amendments having the greatest impact on industry will be the regulation of hazardous waste pollutants. At the time of enactment, there were 189 pollutants on the list subject to standard setting. (In the prior twenty years, standards were set for only seven hazardous substances.) The list undoubtedly will grow.

For major "point" sources, the EPA will issue standards requiring the maximum degree of emissions reduction—MACT (maximum achievable control technology)—based on demonstrated technology. The EPA is likely to enact generally available control technologies (GACT) for area sources of these target pollutants.

The 1990 CAA regulations will apply to sources emitting more than 10 tons per year of any listed pollutant (2.5 pounds per hour of a continuously operating source) or 25 tons per year of any combination of listed pollutants. The standards apply to new and existing facilities. Any facility with greater than these levels will be required to prepare and implement a risk management plan. This plan will address detection and prevention, or minimization, of accidental releases of these substances.

For existing sources, the MACT standards will be based on levels achieved by the best performing 12 percent of existing sources in the appropriate category. For new sources, they must be at least as stringent as the best-controlled source in the industry. Of major concern are fugitive emissions occurring at various points in the production process. This will necessitate paying special attention to leak detection and equipment repair.

The Clean Air Act amendments attempt to provide industry with significant flexibility for standards achieved through early compliance and marketplace incentives. Over 700 firms were part of this program in the early 1990s. Many chemical and other companies were reducing pollutants before the amendments were in place. Some were well ahead of the statutory guidelines.

Another incentive allows for emissions trading. This would allow polluters to avoid strict regulation of every emission source by creating a market in "pollution rights." Firms reducing emissions more than necessary would generate credits they could sell to others less able to comply. The number of pollution rights a firm receives at the beginning of the program will diminish each year.

Implications of the CAA amendments are significant for industry. They will entail large investments in plant and equipment to meet MACT standards and to control volatile organic compounds (VOCs). For the chemical industry alone, *Chemical Week* magazine estimated that the cost of complying with this bill will reach $5 billion. To meet a 1995 ban on chlorofluorocarbons (CFCs), firms will need to find technically and economically adequate substitutes for their use as refrigerants, solvents, and plastic blow-molding agents. This deadline is five years earlier than originally dictated by international treaties, due to their documented serious impact on the stratospheric ozone layer.

The CAA also affects such activities as how people get to work. In nonattainment zones carpooling will be required. Some aerosol products will need reformulating. Many businesses (such as some dry cleaners and bakeries, or firms using 5,000 gallons of paint a month or more), previously too small to be affected by the regulations, will be impacted by the new 10- and 25-ton limits.

There will be difficulties with compliance; there are standards that have yet to be enacted; the maximum achievable control technologies are not clearly defined or known. What types of emission monitoring will be required? How will credit trading be done?

It is clear that the trend is toward dramatically fewer emissions of an ever-increasing number of pollutants for an ever greater number of businesses.

> *Hazmat World* (April, 1992, p. 55) suggests remedies for successful compliance, including:
> - A review of existing data.
> - An emissions inventory and source (point and area) operations review. (One input for this information can be previously filed Superfund Amendments and Reauthorization Act (SARA), Title III Section 313 Toxic Release Inventory reports.)
> - Analysis of impact of CAA amendments on the firm's operations.
> - Development of an emissions database.
> - An implementation plan.
> - Employee training.

It also is essential to track deadlines to ensure compliance. Consequences for noncompliance via the CAA amendments include larger felony penalties, field citations, and an expanded citizen award system for information leading to convictions.

Aside from enforcement issues, EPA's clear emphasis is *source reduction*. Publicized examples from IBM, large chemical firms, and others show that dramatic results in cost reduction through lower disposal, legal, raw material, and transportation costs can be achieved.

WATER ISSUES

Water-related environmental issues encompass stormwater, safe drinking water, wastewater treatment, surface impoundments and spill prevention, among other issues. Many of these are governed by the Clean Water Act (CWA) of 1970 and subsequent amendments, the most recent of which were enacted in 1987. These amendments strengthened the standards for pretreatment of water and expanded the number of establishments affected.

Groundwater

Treatment of groundwater is regulated by the Groundwater Protection Act and Resource Conservation and Recovery Act (RCRA). RCRA-licensed hazardous waste treatment, storage, and disposal (TSD) facilities must take water samples and analyze for groundwater contamination when it is first detected. A treatment plan then must be developed and analysis must take place on a yearly basis to ensure no new problems have arisen. There is currently a list of over 400 compounds that must be analyzed to determine groundwater contamination. Challenges do exist in testing for this number of contaminants. Some constituents are analyzed routinely. Technical data for some of those that are not are still lacking. Testing can be expensive and can take significant time. The greatest threat to groundwater supplies appears now to be from leaking underground storage tanks, fuel leaks, and other solvent losses to the ground and the water table (*Environmental Lab*, April/May, 1992, p. 38).

Stormwater

One of the most pervasive of the water issues is that of stormwater, affecting at least 100,000 establishments. Stormwater can pick up pollutants like oil, grease, and heavy metals from many different sources. The Clean Water Act (CWA) prohibits any pollutant discharge from a point source (e.g., storm sewer) into "waters of the U.S." (rivers, lakes, etc.) without a permit. The National Pollutant Discharge Elimination System (NPDES) establishes those permit requirements. At industrial facilities these discharges emanate from any conveyance (e.g., storm sewer) used for collecting and conveying stormwater related to manufacturing, processing, or outside raw material storage areas. Firms with Standard Industrial Classification (SIC) codes of 20 to 39 (lumber, paper mills, chemicals, metal, rubber, leather, stone, etc.) and 10 to 14 (mining) are generally most affected by those permit requirements. Included are outside vehicle maintenance and equipment cleaning and construction activity over 5 acres. Office buildings and associated parking lots are generally excluded.

Water Permits

Due to the high volume of permits NPDES requires, the EPA has established a framework for developing permitting priorities based on reduction of risk to human health and aquatic resources. Essentially this framework calls for group, individual, or general permits. The group permit is appropriate for facilities anywhere in the United States that have similar effluents and operations. These could be different plants within the same corporation or different plants/firms in the same industry. In the latter case, typically an industry trade association will file for the permit. One advantage of the group permit approach is that only 10 percent of the discharges in the group need to submit test data (with a minimum of ten and maximum of one hundred discharges, with one to two from each EPA-designated "precipitation zone" in the country).

Again due to the workload created by NPDES, states are not encouraging individual, site-specific permits. Most states now have general permit programs. For states without them, firms will need to submit at least a notice of interest (NOI) to file an individual permit. The U.S. EPA has enacted a rule allowing most firms to file a general permit. In addition to the basic data required initially (see below), firms having a general permit are required to inspect their facilities annually and submit a report on the condition of their containment and runoff protection measures.

Generally, the permit system calls for information on facility discharge points (outfalls), quantity of water discharged, sampling of water for pollutant content, and the water quality management plan. Sampling must be conducted under a specific set of conditions such as within the first thirty minutes of a storm even with more than 0.1 inch of rain and which also occurs seventy-two or more hours after the last storm event. If an industrial facility's stormwater goes to a municipal treatment system and not into "waters of the U.S.," an NPDES permit may not be necessary. However, the municipality is likely to have its own standards and rules to follow.

The key to whether a permit is required is the potential impact of the effluent on stormwater. Steps that can be taken to minimize the impact and the potential need for a permit include:

- Conducting potential pollution-causing operations inside where effluent is collected and pretreated.
- Process and material substitution.
- Providing secondary containment around stored material.
- Pretreating stormwater.
- Installing sediment basins and vegetative filters.
- Avoiding work in sensitive areas such as floodplains, wetlands, and near waterways.
- Reducing the pollutant source.

Some firms do treat their own wastewater. If so, it may be cost effective to treat stormwater as well. However, storms then can create hydraulic shock loading on the treatment plant. Secondary holding ponds or basins could provide relief. These basins also could serve as holding areas for fire protection water after its use in an emergency, so that it can be tested before releasing.

Spill Prevention, Control, and Countermeasures

Another major water-related issue affecting industry is spill prevention, control, and countermeasures (SPCC). An SPCC plan must be prepared generally by nontransportation-related entities "engaged in drilling, producing, gathering, storing, processing, refining, transferring, distributing, or consuming oil and oil products and which . . . could reasonably be expected to discharge oil in harmful quantities . . . into . . . navigable waters of the U.S." (40 *Code of Federal Regulations* [CFR] Part 112). Exemptions include those facilities with less than 42,000 gallons in underground buried storage or with less than 1,320 gallons stored aboveground (with no single tank more than 660 gallons).

The SPCC plan is to include a description of spills in the last twelve months, spill-prevention structures, a spill contingency plan, site drainage, and other items. There are liability limits on spills at facilities with a 1,000-barrel capacity or less. SPCC plans must be updated every three years or sooner if there are facility changes. The plan must be reviewed and signed by a registered professional engineer. Various additional requirements are placed on water-related environmental issues by other legislation covered in the next section.

LAND ISSUES

While the category of land-based environmental issues is somewhat arbitrary, it can include such issues as PCBs (polychlorinated biphenyls), waste disposal, underground storage tanks, hazardous wastes, and hazardous materials environmental audits. Obviously the pollutants involved can impact air and water as well.

There is a great deal of federal legislation governing land-based environmental activities. Some of these laws also impact air and water issues. Principal among them are the

Resource Conservation and Recovery Act (RCRA) of 1976 and its subsequent amendments; the Comprehensive Environmental Response, Compensation and Liability Act (CERCLA) of 1980; the CERCLA amendments and reauthorization, commonly called SARA (Superfund Amendments and Reauthorization Act) of 1986; and the Toxic substances Control Act (TSCA) of 1976.

RCRA establishes a framework in industry for hazardous waste management, record keeping, permits, proper disposal methods, underground storage tank regulation, and groundwater protection. CERCLA and SARA provide funding to enforce RCRA, emergency spill actions, community right-to-know, taxing, and other measures. Outside expertise generally is advised in helping to determine how these laws impact a firm.

Hazardous Waste (HW)

Wastes are considered hazardous if they are ignitable, corrosive, reactive, or toxic. The TCLP (toxicity characteristic leaching procedure) is used to determine if a waste is toxic. Wastes are also hazardous if they appear on one of four lists contained in the RCRA regulations. It is the firm's responsibility to determine if any of its wastes are hazardous. "Acutely hazardous wastes" are dangerous enough in small quantities that they are regulated in the same way as are large quantities of other hazardous wastes.

It is important to know in what category of HW generator the facility fits. As established by the 1986 RCRA rules, there are three categories:

Quantity/Month Generated	Category
No more than 100 kilograms (Kg) (220 pounds)	Conditionally exempt small-quantity generator
100–1,000 kg (2,200 pounds)	Small-quantity generator (SQG)
More than 1,000 kg	Large-quantity generator

As a conditionally exempt SQG, you must send the HW to an approved waste facility and not accumulate more than 1,000 kilograms of HW on your property or you become subject to regulations of larger generators. Under federal law, it is possible to change generator status, depending on quantities created in a given month. To determine generator status and what requirements to meet, you must determine the quantity of HW generated per month. Wastes include "listed wastes" or wastes otherwise characterized as hazardous that are accumulated on-site, packaged and transported off-site, put in a regulated on-site treatment or disposal unit, or generated as sludge or bottoms from product storage tanks.

Those businesses producing over 100 kilograms of HW per month, as well as HW transporters, storage, and treatment (TSD) facilities need to obtain a U.S. EPA identification number. This is available through the U.S. EPA regional office or the state hazardous waste management agency. A number is assigned to each site. For on-site disposal or treatment of HW, a permit is required in most cases. The process can be costly and time consuming.

While not required by the U.S. EPA, a contingency plan for handling emergencies is a good practice. Steps required include appointing an emergency coordinator, training of employees in emergency procedures and waste handling, and posting of emergency phone numbers and emergency equipment locations. Other steps include establishment of emergency response teams, close coordination with local fire, police, and hospitals, and having emergency communications equipment.

The U.S. Occupational Safety and Health Administration (OSHA) has established a standard to protect workers at EPA-licensed treatment, storage, and disposal facilities. Workers also are covered who respond to hazardous material spills and other emergencies. This standard requires written response procedures and a safety and health program.

Hazardous Materials

The U.S. Department of Transportation (DOT) regulations designate certain materials as hazardous, that is, poisonous, radioactive, flammable, explosive, or corrosive. Other environmental regulations may or may not classify these substances as "hazardous" by DOT's definition. The purpose of the DOT regulations is to promote safe transportation of substances "posing an unreasonable risk to health, safety, and property when being transported." Noncompliance with these regulations can be expensive: $10,000 for civil offenses and $25,000 and/or five years imprisonment for criminal offenses.

Companies involved in transportation of hazardous materials are subject to the regulations, even if they only transport, and do not make, store, use, or otherwise handle these substances. The seven-step compliance process involves proper packaging, marking, vehicle labeling, manifesting, and other actions.

Certain aspects of RCRA are in flux. For example, the EPA wants to label waste as hazardous that is "mixed with or derived from" a substance classified as hazardous. The courts have decided the rules are not valid. Some criticize the EPA for costly delays created by such actions as not settling early in a cleanup process with smaller contributors to toxic Superfund sites. Reauthorization of RCRA is likely to address these and other issues. Emphasis will be placed on streamlining and simplifying the process, waste reduction, and partnering or other less adversarial ways of corrective action.

Underground Storage Tanks (USTs)

USTs have been one of the most ubiquitous of our environmental problems. The U.S. EPA estimated in 1991 that there were some three million in the country, even though many firms already have addressed this issue. USTs have been considered a safe way to store explosive, corrosive, and other hazardous substances, primarily petroleum and petroleum-derived products. For service stations and other facilities with limited space or close to the general population, USTs are the only practical storage method. Many municipalities will allow only USTs.

However, the U.S. EPA has estimated that potentially two thirds of existing USTs leak. Furthermore, almost 50 percent of the drinking water in the United States comes from underground sources. These and other pressures have led to strict regulation of USTs.

Petroleum products and hazardous waste USTs are regulated by RCRA. Congress provided further constraints under RCRA with the Hazardous and Solid Waste Amendments (HSWA) of 1984. HSWA required the EPA to:

- Prevent UST leaks from occurring.
- Locate leaking USTs (LUSTs).
- Require corrective action for UST leaks and spills.
- Ensure owner payment for LUST corrective action.
- Require state programs and regulations for USTs and LUSTs.

To meet these goals for petroleum and petroleum product USTs, EPA established deadlines and required actions, the latest being in 1998.

RCRA regulations dictate procedures for USTs containing hazardous materials governed under CERCLA. RCRA and CERCLA also regulate handling of hazardous wastes. Hazardous material underground tanks installed after January 1, 1989, must have secondary containment and monitoring between tank primary and secondary containment walls (interstitial). Deadlines for installation of monitoring devices on these USTs are similar to those containing petroleum.

There are numerous methods to satisfy the UST leak detection requirements. These include monthly monitoring and inventory control, tank tightness testing, and dedicated leak detection monitoring. Corrosion protection requirements can be met with fiberglass tanks, steel tanks clad with fiberglass, and coated and cathodically protected steel tanks. The options for prevention leaks in USTs depend on state and local regulations, soil type, material(s) stored in the tank, geologic and other conditions.

Piping is a key contributor (two thirds or more) to system failure. Thus, double wall (mandatory only with chemical products USTs) or anode protection of piping is important to the entire UST system. Double wall piping and interstitial monitoring can reduce insurance premiums substantially as well. In addition to piping, other problems that can arise include:

- Incompatibility between the tank and/or liner material and the stored substance.
- Improper installation (RCRA requires certifying that a "qualified installer was used.
- Lack of cathodic protection of tanks.

Should a confirmed leak occur from a petroleum UST, numerous steps must be taken. They include notification of appropriate authorities, containing the leak, cleanup plans, and various reporting procedures.

Many firms now find they do not need USTs. Heating fuel source economics have lessened the use of heating oil as an auxiliary fuel. Off-site car and truck gasoline purchase may be cheaper. If USTs continue to be required, proper tanks, monitoring, and installation are far less costly than subsequent cleanup and potential liability issues.

Aboveground Storage Tanks (ASTs)

ASTs have gained in popularity since federal UST regulations came into effect in 1988. While the U.S. EPA has not established formal AST rules, there is action in the U.S. Senate to adopt an aboveground storage act. It would regulate shop-built, field-erected, and rebuilt ASTs. Under this proposed legislation, ASTs would be subject to similar requirements as USTs. The Clean Water Act (CWA) impacts some ASTs as do the new stormwater regulations.

State AST regulations under development also could affect aboveground tanks. Secondary containment (which could be a double-wall tank in some areas) and interstitial monitoring are advisable. ASTs and AST piping placed right on the ground is still vulnerable to corrosion. Diking and liners for ASTs are frequently mandated; very often dikes must be concrete. Dikes and liners usually are required to have capacity for the contents of the tanks and some amount of stormwater.

Because of the changing nature of AST regulation, legal and technical advice for a firm's particular situation is appropriate. This includes talking to state environmental and local fire marshal officials.

ENVIRONMENTAL AUDITS

Industrial activity frequently involves land transactions. If land becomes contaminated, generally all parties who ever *owned* or *occupied* the premises may be implicated in the cost of cleanup. This can include any tenant, sublessor, and so on, whether or not they are responsible for the pollution. Liability for cleanup is covered under RCRA, CERCLA, SARA, and numerous other environmental and other laws.

To minimize risk of liability, ensure compliance to environmental laws, and to foster environmental cleanup, many states now require owners to make environmental disclosures prior to property transfer. This may mean filling out a form indicating the property is free of contamination. Other measures, such as soil sampling, also may be required. Whether or not an audit is mandated by the state, most lenders (for original purchase and refinancing a loan), attorneys, and major firms will require one.

Typically an audit includes review of the chain of title; review of EPA and other records for environmental incidents; review of laws for applicability to a specific site; aerial surveys; site visits to look for obvious signs such as dead vegetation, discolored soil, asbestos, old transformers with PCBs; evidence of practices that could have caused contamination; underground storage tanks and the like. If there is evidence of contamination in this Phase I investigation, a second phase can be initiated to perform soil borings and more in-depth analysis. Actual cleanup would take place in a third phase.

Environmental cleanup liability and costs can be borne by the buyer or seller, depending on their agreements. These costs can significantly affect the property's price. Environmental issues can even keep a transaction from being consummated. Thus, it is extremely important to know, through a firm's own investigation or its engineering consultants, the extent of contamination. It is wise not to gloss over the need for an adequate and professionally done audit. You do not want to miss such obvious potential problems as vent pipes from USTs or contamination from neighboring property. Prior owners, particularly those with perceived "deep pockets," can be brought in to help pay for cleanup years after a transaction.

OTHER ISSUES

The Emergency Planning and Community Right-to-Know Act (EPCRA, also known as SARA Title III) was enacted in 1986, after the tragic release of toxic chemicals in Bhopal, India, and other incidents. It established requirements for federal, state, and local governments to report on hazardous and toxic chemicals and to plan for such emergencies. The law's provisions will help increase the public's knowledge of hazardous chemicals and releases in their communities. They also will assist communities in setting up ways to improve public safety. Typically, the law applies to manufacturing firms with Standard Industrial Classification (SIC) codes of 20 to 39 and who make, process, or use listed toxic chemicals.

Facilities with certain minimum threshold quantities of over 300 specified hazardous substances must prepare emergency plans. Subject facilities must also be represented on local emergency planning committees (LEPCs). Under the law, plants must notify LEPCs and State Emergency Planning Commissions (SEPCs) of reportable quantity releases of listed (40 *CFR* 355, 40 *CFR* 30.2.4) hazardous substances.

Hazardous substance material safety data sheets (MSDS) or a list of these chemicals also must be submitted to LEPCs and SEPCs. Certain minimum quantities of the substances are needed before these filings are required. Specific forms are available from the SEPC.

There recently has been increasing publicity about toxic chemical releases by manufacturing plants. This information is derived from reports required under Section 313 of the EPCRA. Subject facilities are mandated to file annually with the EPA "Form R," a toxic chemical release inventory (TRI) form. It is meant to inform the public and government about routine releases to the environment. The data are being used in research and to assist in development of regulations, guidelines, and standards.

EPCRA does provide some protection against having to reveal trade secrets via reporting. There is concern over this issue in industry, however. The law underscores the need to establish and to maintain rigorous record keeping. It also reinforces the need for close coordination with state and local public services such as the fire department. Civil and criminal penalties for noncompliance can be stiff. Prison sentences are included. Private citizens also can bring suit against the owner or operator of a facility for failing to meet EPCRA provisions.

RECOMMENDED ACTIONS AND CONCLUSION

There is a major challenge in keeping up with regulatory changes, in comprehending how they relate to your business, and in determining how best to respond. Obviously, the response must be made in the context of maintaining a viable and profitable business.

One of the best ways to satisfy both aims of compliance and profitability is pollution prevention. As underscored by the Pollution Prevention Act of 1990 and by voluntary initiatives, significant costs can be avoided. Compliance, liability, and insurance premium expenses can be reduced, as can processing, waste handling, storage, and transportation costs. These results enhance competitiveness and the public image.

Opportunities are created as well. Marketing of "green" products and use of more environmentally compatible packaging can lead to increased sales. A caution here is that the products have to be proven "green." For example, if claims of biodegradability or recyclability cannot be substantiated, effects on sales could be negative. Recyclable content also must be documented in some areas.

Revenue opportunities do exist to capital-ize on the market for environmental services. Defense contractors are moving into environmental cleanup. With product modifications and additions, old-line chemical and equipment producers are bringing out products to control pollutants.

Some large chemical firms and other companies have made headlines with multi-hundred-million-dollar investments in pollution prevention and waste reduction. For other firms, a smaller, incremental improvement approach can be equally valid.

Small companies can be hit particularly hard by the cost of complying with environmental regulations. They can receive assistance from government and even nonprofit grants, vendors, customers, and trade associations. Municipalities also may help. There is even some precedent for competitors sharing information and doing joint research on environmental issues. Small firms tend to address specific issues as they arise. Larger companies tend to have more comprehensive formal programs. Some corporations are investing in domestic and foreign environmental and conservation efforts. These may enhance public relations. But there are other benefits, too. One pharmaceutical firm is arranging with a Central American country to obtain rain forest plant and animal specimens for new drug research.

In some cases, plant closure may be the best alternative if environmental compliance costs are excessive. However, many actions can be taken in-house to ensure compliance and competitiveness. Here are some examples:

- Establish appropriate controls and incentives to ensure compliance. Conduct periodic, regular environmental audits of internal operations. This is of primary importance.
- Treat the environmental issues as one more *permanent* variable in managing the business, just as health and safety have become. Include them in annual business plans and mission statements. One Fortune 500 firm says that if it has met its revenue and profit but not its environmental goals, it has not met its goals.

- Be proactive. Handle an environmental issue before it becomes a compliance problem. If a problem does occur, handle it with an organized response.
- Consider joining an environmental organization's board of directors or having an environmentalist join your firm's board.
- Ensure training of company personnel in proper handling of environmental issues and hazardous substances. Reinforce that training regularly.
- Ensure good communication and collaboration with the firm's "stakeholders"—vendors, customers, employees, local residents. Have them understand and participate in, to the extent feasible, changes that are made. "Partnering" can create many benefits.
- Look for waste exchanges through which to sell waste products.
- Investigate ways to cooperate with regulators to find cost-effective solutions.
- Assist in creating markets for recycled products by having the firm buy them (recycled paper, etc.). Look at material substitutions that will make your own products or waste more easily recycled.
- Hire attorneys and consultants with proven track records in the specific legal, technical, and geographic areas of concern.
- Become active in trade associations with strong lobbying efforts to uphold the firm's interests. Join other groups that can further the company's goals. One is the Superfund Action Coalition formed in 1992 to eliminate retroactive liability for hazardous waste releases.

Environmental issues will remain and become more a part of the fabric of doing business. We must look proactively for ways to achieve the proper balance between growth and the environment, between production and the resources that make the production possible. Without proper safeguarding of our resources there will be no production.

Information Systems and Technology

Norbert J. Kubilus, Section Editor

Introduction   *Norbert J. Kubilus*   9-3

The MIS Function   *Donald T. Winski*   9-5

Information Strategy Planning   *E. Nancy Markle*   9-10

Hardware and Equipment   *Sara Joannides*   9-16

Software and Applications Development   *Linda J. Ferri*   9-22

Telecommunications   *W. Edward Hodgson*   9-28

Electronic Data Interchange   *Robert Plaut*   9-33

Intelligent Network Management   *Andres Llana*   9-36

Database Management Systems   *Steve Shoaf*   9-42

The Data Processing Center   *Stanley J. Ostaszewski*   9-48

Outsourcing   *Joseph Jackson*   9-52

Disaster Recovery for Information Systems   *Arthur Kurek*   9-56

Training for Users and MIS Staff   *Tony W. Salinger*   9-60

Security and Legal Issues in MIS   *Jack Bologna*   9-64

Managing Transitions in MIS   *Norbert J. Kubilus*   9-68

INTRODUCTION

Norbert J. Kubilus

The information systems challenge for management in the 1990s is how to manage effectively very complex and interrelated computer systems and networks that satisfy ever-increasing customer requirements for information. Who are these customers? What is it they want? What information systems technologies are appropriate for managing and delivering information? How should the information systems function be planned, organized, and managed? These are just some of the questions that management must face in this new Information Age.

The boundaries between the information systems function and the mainline business functions have been eroding for most of the past ten years. Information systems executives and managers are becoming more business oriented, learning to understand the business and how to satisfy information requirements from the customers' perspective. At the same time, the personal computer revolution has made information systems more democratic, turning millions of end users into information managers.

Have the tables been turned? Is there truly a role reversal in information systems? Not really. Customers of information systems and services in the 1990s include end users with desktop computers, as well as vendors, suppliers, and the true customers of an organization's products and services. They want transparent access to information of unquestionable integrity and tools with which to manipulate and otherwise use this information in order to respond to business opportunities. They are usually not interested in the technical detail of the technology being used, relying instead on the information systems function to integrate the components necessary to deliver the required information.

Against this backdrop, there are two objectives in developing this section: (1) to provide managers in general with an understanding of the information systems architecture—computer hardware, software, communications, open systems, and client/server computing—and issues for the 1990s; (2) to provide information systems managers with an insight into the cooperative management of business systems while maintaining focus on availability, reliability, cost of service, and rapid technology changes. Some of the chapters may seem to be directed toward one or the other of these objectives. For the most part, however, the authors keep both in mind.

The integration of information systems with the infrastructure of a business is the subject of the first two chapters. First, Donald Winski looks at the information systems function in terms of the resources it must manage, the benefits that a business may expect to derive from it, and the interaction of information systems management with the rest of an organization. Second, Nancy Markle focuses on the importance of information systems planning to the organization, paying particular attention to the benefits, environmental factors, assumptions, problems, and opportunities involved in this planning process.

The next three chapters address the major technology components of an information systems architecture. Sara Joannides examines the major areas of consideration in selecting computer hardware, including strengths, weaknesses, and features of different types of computers and their components. Linda Ferri discusses the software components of a computer system, the concept of open systems, and trends in application development. Ed Hodgson provides a look at the world of moving information through different telecommunication systems, focusing on the disappearing distinctions between computers and telecommunications.

The communications theme runs through the next two chapters. Robert Plaut discusses the planning and management issues that affect the implementation of electronic data interchange to transfer data in a standardized form from one computer system to another. Network management is an increasing concern of large organizations, and Andres Llana examines the design, control, and performance issues that affect the installation and operation of successful data networks.

Steve Shoaf's chapter addresses what is probably the most central information systems topic: the management of information stored in a company's computers. Organizations can choose from among numerous systems that solve data and information management problems. The author presents the architecture, design considerations, and features of effective database management systems.

Next the focus is on contemporary day-to-day management issues in information systems. Stan Ostaszewski starts by looking at how to maintain a data processing environment that produces information for the business enterprise with reliability, accuracy, timeliness, integrity, and security. Joe Jackson deals with the considerations and issues surrounding the difficult decision of whether to let an outside organization take over one or more MIS functions. Then Arthur Kurek discusses effective disaster recovery techniques used to provide a continuation of information services after major damage to an organization's data processing systems. Finally, Tony Salinger addresses the training needs of information systems professionals and end users, and he reviews different approaches to meeting these needs so they can use information systems effectively.

With the changes in information systems technologies and their business use, information systems managers have to face two issues that are covered in the closing chapters. Jack Bologna examines the changing security and legal environment in which managers have to concern themselves with privacy, piracy, safety, and security. Norbert Kubilus discusses how to manage information systems change, including the elements of planning, resources, human factors, and implementation.

The primary information systems role in the 1990s will continue to be providing integrated systems that satisfy business and customer requirements. Information systems organizations will be smaller and more focused than in the past, with more emphasis on the technical architecture of the business and systems integration of off-the-shelf technology and external services. Business units will be a primary source of innovation and creativity in the use of information systems technologies, and successful information systems managers will be the ones who can bring these technologies to the operation of the business.

Norbert J. Kubilus *is vice-president and chief information officer for BCM Engineers, Inc., in Plymouth Meeting, Pennsylvania. He has also been an information systems executive with Educational Testing Service, National Data Corporation, and Rapidata, Inc., as well as a professor of information systems at New Jersey Institute of Technology. Mr. Kubilus is the author of more than fifty articles, papers, and texts.*

THE MIS FUNCTION

Donald T. Winski, President, DTW Associates

THE INFORMATION TECHNOLOGY RESOURCES

A management information system (MIS) is a collection of elements that rapidly records and manipulates large amounts of raw data. In this chapter, we will examine data processing systems. Such a system must manage eight major information technology (I/T) resources. As shown in Exhibit 9-1, some are fairly obvious; others are more subtle, pervasive, and difficult to control.

Hardware

Hardware refers to the physical computers and peripherals, such as disk drives and printers, that MIS must select, size, and manage. Computers range from personal computers that sit on a desk to mainframes that reside in specially controlled computer rooms. Hardware can also include special-purpose devices such as process control equipment used in manufacturing.

Software

Software refers to the set of instructions that "tells" a computer what actions it is to perform. Applications software contains instructions for performing a business-related application, such as accounts receivable or inventory control. Operating and systems software controls the actions of the computer and its peripherals. Database management software handles the actions related to creating, modifying, and using data stored on a computer. The software used by an organization depends on the implicit and explicit policies and procedures of the organization. A considerable portion of MIS responsibility lies in making sure that the software used by a business reflects the logic of running that business.

Networks

Networks provide the communications medium for transmitting data, voice, image, and video to and among various business units and functions. Increasingly, networks provide an automated transaction interface with customers and suppliers. MIS is responsible for assuring that the networks used by an organization interconnect in a manner that facilitates reliable, accurate, and secure transmissions. This requires managing a variety of local- and wide-area networks, protocols (that is, electronic "handshaking"), communications equipment and media—such as fiber and copper wire, microwave, and satellite—and software that controls and routes electronic traffic over the networks.

People

MIS staff and system users comprise the people resources. The MIS staff is typically organized into systems development, computer operations, and network management groups

Exhibit 9-1. Information Technology (I/T) Resources

	Resources	Examples
Obvious and Controllable	Hardware	Computers and peripheral equipment
	Software	Applications systems; operating systems, policies, and procedures
	Networks	Local- and wide-area communications links
	People	MIS staff, users, vendors
	Data	Numeric, text, image, voice, video
Subtle and Pervasive	Culture	Shared values and traditions
	Time	Timing and harmonics
	Risk	Orientation and avoidance

that consist of employees and contract personnel. System users include the internal users within a company as well as its customers, vendors, and suppliers.

Data

Numeric information, text, images, voice, and video make up the data resource that MIS must manage, often in a custodial role. The ever-increasing challenge is to maintain data security and integrity while providing global access to the data for business purposes. The data resource also includes the relationships between data elements that result in providing useful information to the business.

Culture

Culture is a subtle resource to manage. It is the shared values and traditions that people have acquired. Organizations tend to be multicultural. Some cultures are functional in nature—for example, engineering, accounting, and sales have different functional cultures. Ethnic or national cultures are also present, especially in global organizations where, say, American, Japanese, and English business units are trying to work together as one company. Business units and corporations have their own internal cultures that lead to major management challenges during mergers, acquisitions, and consolidations. MIS must be sensitive to the cultural differences within the organization.

Time

Time is also a real resource that MIS must manage. Managing time means building systems faster, developing new products faster, and eliminating working inventories by employing just-in-time logistics. But there is another aspect of time that has to do with the harmonics of an organization.

Harmonics can be viewed as the pace at which change can ripple through an organization. Depending on the industry and inherited traditions, the cycle-time harmonics for change can vary considerably. For example, the retail grocery business has a natural harmonic of one week based on weekly promotional campaigns. In contrast, the paper industry has a natural harmonic of several years that is directly tied to the growth cycle of trees. When trying to induce rapid change in an organization through the use of information technology, MIS must examine the natural harmonic of that organization carefully to determine the ease or difficulty of implementing rapid change.

Risk

It is important for MIS to understand how risk is viewed within a particular organization and to appreciate the risk orientation or risk avoidance of the business management that will make the systems efforts succeed—or fail. MIS must tune the risk profile of the systems activities to a level acceptable to key business management in order to increase the likelihood of success.

THE INFORMATION TECHNOLOGY PAYOFF

The MIS function within an organization depends on the benefits that it expects from applying its I/T resources to solve business problems. Exhibit 9-2 depicts a spectrum of payoffs as seen from the viewpoints of the chief financial officer (CFO), chief operating officer (COO), and chief executive officer (CEO).

The tendency for the cost-oriented CFO is to view the entire MIS function as a utility that should focus on providing mandatory compliance services at a minimum cost. This may be timely and accurate financial reporting, compliance with government regulations concerning human resources, or reliable and secure voice communications.

The next higher level of benefits relates to those justified by classic return on investment (ROI) analyses that include net present value and hurdle rates. This basically represents a capital investment decision. In many cases, MIS has already implemented systems with favorable ROIs. Head counts may have been reduced, inventory control improved, and cash flows accelerated. As the business changes and technology evolves, however, systems require redesign or new implementations in order to maintain a favorable ROI in the future.

Once organizational control is seen as a benefit of MIS, the application of I/T resources starts to become more strategic and mature. Organizational control here centers on the notion of local empowerment and decentralized decision making while preserving synergies across business units and functions. Through local empowerment, for example, micro-marketing decisions concerning delivery of products and services to customers can be made quickly, thereby reducing costs and improving perceived quality by the customers. At the same time, "back-office" operations such as accounting can perform central functions without impeding decentralized activities.

At the highest end of executive priorities, the MIS focus is on the benefits of enabling management to redesign major business processes. This business process redesign should result in a faster-response organization that has fewer layers of management and at least an order of magnitude improvement in quality. Such a redesign typically depends on an increased dependency on network-based information technology as more functional responsibility is pushed lower into the organization, paperwork and middle management bureaucracy is eliminated, and direct transaction interfaces such as electronic data interchange (EDI) are established with customers and suppliers.

The ultimate I/T payoff is business/technology integration that occurs when management—here the CEO—realizes that I/T can enable new products and services. At this level of I/T payoff, MIS is not viewed as a distinct and separate function in the organization, but instead as an integral part of the busi-

Exhibit 9-2. The Information Technology (I/T) Payoff

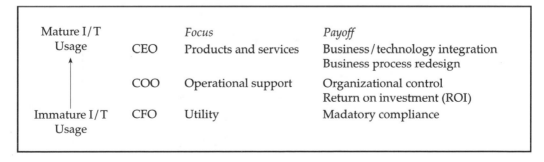

		Focus	*Payoff*
Mature I/T Usage	CEO	Products and services	Business/technology integration Business process redesign
	COO	Operational support	Organizational control Return on investment (ROI)
Immature I/T Usage	CFO	Utility	Madatory compliance

ness. MIS becomes a partner with upper and line management in planning, implementing, and delivering new products and services.

THE MIS RITES OF PASSAGE

The maturation of the MIS function within an organization depends on I/T resource management, the I/T payoffs, and the MIS management role in the organization. Exhibit 9-3 illustrates the MIS rites of passage in an organization. The horizontal axis represents the three roles that MIS management can play in an organization:

1. *Reactive*, in which MIS management is passively responding to ad hoc demands and continual cost-reduction pressures.
2. *Proactive*, in which MIS management initiates and directs projects focused on improving business operations.
3. *Coordinative*, in which MIS management is a consultative business partner focusing on the integration of business requirements and technology.

The vertical axis shows the I/T payoffs in terms of benefits ranging from utility up to

products and services. The diagonal running through the grid in which the I/T resources appear represents the natural maturity cycle of the MIS function.

Resource Focus

If an organization has a reactive (or passive) MIS function, then the focus is on providing an MIS utility consisting of hardware, software, and networks at the lowest possible cost for an acceptable level of service. If the organization, however, wants to benefit from improvements in operational support, then MIS management must take a more proactive role in the organization, placing emphasis on network, data, and people resources. Finally, in order for MIS to help deliver new products and services, it must assume a coordinative role and address issues related to culture, timing and organizational harmonics, and risk. The cultural differences between general management and MIS management, especially their respective comfort levels with the pace of change and risk, can be the greatest barrier to achieving the congruence needed to obtain the ultimate I/T payoffs.

The Flexible MIS Function

This MIS maturity curve recurs as technology evolves and business requirements change.

Exhibit 9-3. The MIS Rites of Passage

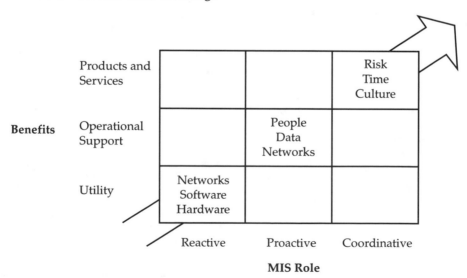

Benefits	Products and Services			Risk Time Culture
	Operational Support		People Data Networks	
	Utility	Networks Software Hardware		
		Reactive	Proactive	Coordinative

MIS Role

Exhibit 9-4. MIS Initiatives in Mode Switching

General Management's Vision (Horizon/Place)	Current MIS Vision (Horizon/Place)	Current Business Health	I/T Imperative Required	MIS Mode-Switching Initiative (From/To)
Long-term/fast	Short-term/slow	Excellent	Critical	Reactive/Coordinative
Long-term/slow	Long-term/fast	Excellent	None	Coordinative/Reactive
Short-term/fast	Long-term/slow	Marginal	Critical	Reactive/Proactive
Long-term/slow	Short-term/fast	Excellent	Absent	Proactive/Reactive
Short-term/fast	Long-term/fast	Marginal	Critical	Coordinative/Proactive
Long-term/fast	Short-term/fast	Excellent	Critical	Proactive/Coordinative

MIS management needs to continuously balance its reactive, proactive, and coordinative roles within the organization. This requires remaining flexible and leveraging MIS resources by establishing partnerships with other functions in the organization and external parties. This leveraging can take the form of cooperative projects with internal users of the I/T resources or joint projects with customers or suppliers such as hardware vendors or systems integrators.

MIS management must self-initiate switching its dominant role among reactive, proactive, and coordinative roles. As shown in Exhibit 9-4, there are six possible mode-switching initiatives involving the three role modes. Experience indicates that four major factors often drive the need for role switching: (1) the strategic vision of general management; (2) the corresponding orientation of current MIS management; (3) the current health of the business; (4) the I/T imperative required by the business.

For example, if general management adopts a strategy of rapid sales growth over a three- to five-year horizon that depends on development of competitive information systems, then the MIS function must shift into a coordinative role in the company. If MIS has been focusing on short-term cost-cutting activities, then the mode shift is from reactive to coordinative. If during this period of sales expansion, one of the business units becomes marginal, management may want to take short-term, quick corrective action in that business unit. MIS management must accordingly shift into its proactive role in order to use I/T resources to assist with the changes being made.

INFORMATION STRATEGY PLANNING

E. Nancy Markle, Information Technology Consultants

Senior information systems executives and their business peers consistently rank information strategy planning (ISP) and aligning the business goals and strategies with the information systems' goals and strategies within their top five issues. In the 1990s, senior management is increasingly recognizing the critical importance of information technology to the competitive growth and survival of the enterprise. Greater emphasis is being placed on the senior information systems executive having a keen awareness and understanding of the needs of the business. Paralleling that trend is a significant rise in the participation of the business executive in the development of the enterprise ISP.

While trends have been toward increased planning and business involvement, there are still several hurdles to overcome. The fact that the two issues—aligning the business and information systems' plans, and information systems planning—are considered separate and distinct suggests that ISP is too narrowly defined and treated. A second factor is that there is an issue of aligning the business and information systems' plans. When the planning process inexorably links the two planning processes, then ISP in its broadest sense is being accomplished. It is only then that the enterprise can most profitably take advantage of the competitive weapons afforded by technology.

Information systems planning in a narrow sense addresses the planning required for a systems development project. From the more global viewpoint, ISP addresses the strategic information needs and the technological architecture required to meet the mission, goals, and strategies of the enterprise. For many, information systems planning has a meaning somewhere on the continuum of these two extremes. To indicate the broader context, information strategy planning (ISP) is used.

Exhibit 9-5 is a planning model depicting the relationships between the business and technology planning when they are in alignment as a function of the planning process. The technology strategy is not necessarily a result of, or reaction to, business plans. The process is ongoing and the business continually feeds and is impacted and changed by the technology.

Exhibit 9-5. Information Strategy Planning Model

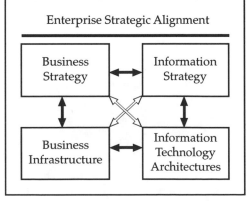

PURPOSE

To build a Stealth aircraft or a Patriot defensive missile without plans would not be feasible. To integrate their technologies, mechanisms, interior and aeronautical design, capacities, launch and repair capabilities requires considerable planning and design. To even consider the capital investment to develop these products requires a great understanding of the offensive and defensive strategies for the country, the current state of weapons products, the critical needs, and the environment and uses for which they would potentially be utilized. Furthermore, deployment of these weapons must be in concert with the overall strategy of the war objective and within the tactical framework of the campaign, the other weapons to be used, and the people and skills comprising the combined forces.

There are numerous pieces and people involved with the development of the tactical weapons to support the technology strategy. The plans for each of these weapons and how they will be used to support the business strategy requires a great deal of continuous planning, integration, and monitoring. Without the master strategy, the efforts are fragmented, though each individually may be superb. Some pieces of the business strategy will be supported; others will not. Some of the systems will be consistent; others will provide conflicting information, based on different assumptions. All will require routines to integrate the systems—a redundant and unnecessary set of routines to implement and maintain.

For large organizations without a strategy process, the cost of technology is unnecessarily large and can impose significant constraints on the work in progress. Even more devastating can be the lost opportunity for improving profits, quality, and service. For smaller companies, while the absolute value of the capital may be lower, the proportional operational overhead may be even more significant. Often because there are less people involved in a smaller organization, the conventional wisdom is that all are communicating and the plans are informal and widely known. This is the most common and costly trap facing the smaller enterprise. It is this "shoot from the hip" type of approach that can lead a smaller business into bankruptcy because of the high cost of information or the lack of timely, critical information.

BENEFITS

In a rapidly changing and complex business and technological environment, it is imperative to develop and maintain an ongoing excellent ISP process. This process will provide:

- *Improved communications*—Communication between senior management, the business entities, and the information systems organization to develop the business and technology strategies provides the necessary forum for ensuring that the technology strategy is complete and that the business has considered the technological opportunities and competitive threats.
- *Strategic business information needs*—Systems will be scaled down, prioritized, and developed to meet strategic business needs, transcending tradition functional barriers.
- *An objective method for resource allocation*—The strategic business information needs and the technical infrastructure required to provide it supply a framework for the allocation of scarce information systems resources.
- *An efficient technical infrastructure*—This develops the architectural framework into which the various systems components must fit precisely so that the components, when designed and developed separately, will function efficiently within the whole.
- *Effective coordination of technologies*—It is necessary to introduce and coordinate the multiplicity of technologies that support the use of information systems such as communications, office systems, end user computing, applications, imaging, document management, mainframes, minicomputers, microcomputers, and networks.

- *Staff productivity*—Effective use of high-productivity tools and the framework for an appropriate training program, supporting staff development for the near term and the future, provide increased productivity, positive reinforcement, and personal growth.
- *Payback*—Opportunities can arise to quickly implement systems, fragments of systems, or decoupled foundation systems with fast payback that meets enterprise needs and solves immediate problems.
- *Control mechanisms*—Progress of the plan and the business strategy are monitored in order to make timely changes and adjustments as the business or external influences require.

IMPLEMENTING THE INFORMATION STRATEGY PLAN

Most major enterprises have some type of formal information systems planning function. Few have an ISP. While the objective of an

ISP is to prioritize systems development and maintenance, the ISP focuses on the strategic direction of the enterprise and:

- Involves the business executives.
- Aims to use information technology as a strategic weapon.
- Focuses on meeting the strategic business information needs.
- Plans for the deployment of new technologies.
- Develops an architecture for the use of technology.
- Identifies skills and training requirements.
- Provides key performance measures and other executive information.
- Is a continuous, monitored process.

There are two evolutionary steps toward instituting an ISP process within the enterprise. The first is the development of the initial plan and process. When it is the first time for an organization, the use of consultant help is valuable to avoid costly mistakes, to bring the practical experience of other enterprises, to provide external, objective questions, and

Exhibit 9-6. Information Strategy Planning Deliverables

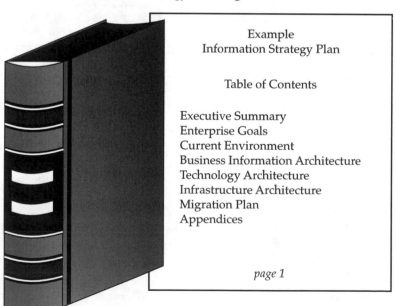

Example
Information Strategy Plan

Table of Contents

Executive Summary
Enterprise Goals
Current Environment
Business Information Architecture
Technology Architecture
Infrastructure Architecture
Migration Plan
Appendices

page 1

Exhibit 9-7. Business Forces Model

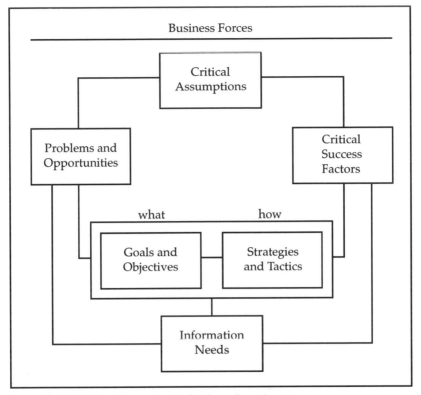

Copyright © 1993 by Information Technology Consultants.

to expedite formulation of the initial plan. The second step is ongoing monitoring, changing, and enhancing the ISP as the business or exogenous factors necessitate. This step is planned and instituted as a part of the initial development process.

There are a number of processes and methodologies being used successfully to develop the initial ISP. It is helpful to use a methodology to develop the ISP; it will facilitate the project, provide direction, and reduce the time frame. Some companies have applied the principles of their existing systems development life cycle methodology to develop the plan. Additionally, tools such as computer-assisted systems engineering (CASE) may be used to accelerate the project.

Regardless of the process selected, there are certain segments that must be analyzed in order to develop a comprehensive ISP. Exhibit 9-6 depicts the deliverables that consti-

tute the ISP. The two models in Exhibits 9-7 and 9-8 illustrate the planning components. The first of these exhibits describes the business forces, which are the instigators of change, and the second exhibit illustrates the building blocks of the enterprise architecture. Each box is a major component to be analyzed in the process and the lines show the interrelationships of the components.

BUSINESS FORCES

The business forces are factors that serve to motivate or drive the business activities. These factors identify what must go right if the business is to succeed. The business forces are used as a mechanism to align the systems strategy with the business strategy and provide a platform for integrating the capabilities

Exhibit 9-8. Enterprise Architectures Model

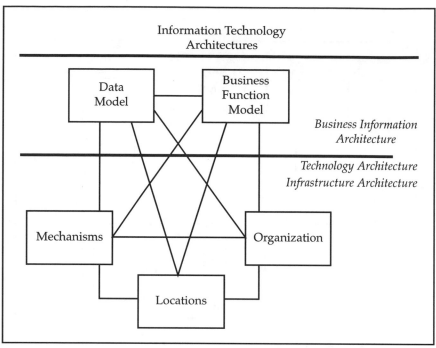

Copyright © 1993 by Information Technology Consultants.

of technology with the development of the business strategy.

Exhibit 9-7 is a model of the business forces that drive the planning process. The model is made up of four primary components that act as sources for change in the enterprise: problems and opportunities, enterprise goals, critical assumptions, and critical success factors.

The problems and opportunities facing the organization are the reasons for change. Problems are the results of unsatisfactory performance or environment. They may be prompted by competitive pressures or internal inadequacies. Opportunities are suitable or convenient circumstances for progress. Rapidly changing technologies and association with suppliers and customers provide a forum for expanding enterprise relationships. They provide opportunities and challenges that should be associated with the business goals and strategies to develop the critical success factors. The growing use of electronic data interchange (EDI) is an example of the use of technology to foster the extended enterprise.

The enterprise mission, goals, objectives, and strategies are the directional statements and targets for the business. The mission defines what the business is and what it should be. The goals are the ideas and plans for successfully achieving the mission. The objectives are the specific achievement targets, shorter in time frame or narrower in scope than the goals. The strategies and tactics indicate how the objectives are to be accomplished; they include the specific tasks to be accomplished, who is accountable, and the time frames for completion. This articulation of the business vision is developed by the business leaders and reflects the needs of the stakeholders and the strategic focus.

The critical assumptions are the beliefs, attitudes, values, and unwritten guidelines that comprise the way things are done. They establish the arena and constraints upon which the business goals and critical success factors are formulated. The critical assumptions are those very important assumptions whose changes will impact goals and critical success factors and therefore they must be identified and carefully monitored.

The critical success factors (CSFs) are key areas where satisfactory performance is essential to achieve the goals of the individual or organization. The CSFs identify a complete set of requirements and their proper priorities. They are specific to the individual or organizational unit and may change with time and perspective. CSFs are easily depicted hierarchically and become more detailed as they are subdivided from those supporting the enterprise to those supporting the organizational unit to those supporting the individual. They provide direct linkages to the enterprise information requirements, functions, and data that are required to develop the information architecture, ensuring completeness and traceability. Most importantly for ISP, the CSF process provides a mechanism for management to focus on its information needs.

INFORMATION NEEDS

The information needs are determined as a result of the analysis required to articulate the sources for change in the business forces model: problems, goals, assumptions, and CSFs. The information needs are the internal and external data requirements that provide the resource for measuring the status of each CSF or goal. The information needs may indicate the necessity for data processing system(s), such as a cost accounting system; or a need for a management support system, such as an executive information system.

Enterprise Architectures

The enterprise architectures model in Exhibit 9-8 is a schematic of the architectures developed during the ISP. The architectures may be divided into two major categories: business systems architecture and technology/infrastructure architecture. To develop the business systems architecture, or list of business systems projects, the architecture for a common data model is created and the fundamental processes of the enterprise are analyzed independently from current systems and pro-

cedures. The technology and infrastructure architectures are developed to forecast the hardware, software, organizational and cultural changes necessary to support the business systems architecture.

The enterprise architectures is a framework for assessing the current environment as well as for determining the attributes of the planned environment. The migration plan is developed by comparing the architectures of where the company wants to be with those of the current environment. The resulting plan is a concise delineation of the major projects (business, technology, and infrastructure), resources, and time frames required, usually in the form of a PERT (program evaluation and review techniques) or Gantt chart.

Business Function Model

The business model represents the activities or functions that are performed by the enterprise. Each function describes an activity, something the enterprise does, independent of the organizational structure. One of the characteristics of the business model is that it documents activities that span the breadth of the enterprise without adhering to organizational ties. The same activity may be performed by several different organizational units but is represented only once in the business model. The activities contained in the business model represent what is done, not how, when, or where.

This emphasis ensures the logical integrity of the business model and provides a vehicle for managing change as it occurs over time within the enterprise. High-level activities (functions) are decomposed into component processes. The processes represent discreet activities that have an identifiable beginning and termination point, and can be executed repeatedly.

Data Model

The data model represents the business view of the information needs, describing the entities of interest to the enterprise and the relationships between the entities. The data model is depicted as a logical map of the entities or data, including the inherent properties of the entities, independent of software, hardware, or performance characteristics.

Organizations and Locations

The organization is the structure that reflects the approach of the enterprise toward accomplishing its mission. The organization is composed of collections of people, their roles and responsibilities, and the relationships between each collection. Because the location of the people has a direct bearing on how, where, and what type of technology is feasible or desirable, location is also an important ingredient in the technical architecture.

Mechanisms

The mechanisms are the methods by which specific processes are carried out. It may be an automated application or it may be manual, and will have characteristics such as description, status, technology, ease of use, response time, and flexibility.

HARDWARE AND EQUIPMENT

Sara Joannides

The computer term *hardware* refers to an electronic device capable of solving problems. Basically, a computer is a machine that accepts instructions and data (input) through a variety of input devices, processes the data in accordance with prescribed rules (programs), and produces an answer (response) that is either displayed on an output device that can be understood by a human being—for example, a printer, a computer screen, a voice-response unit—or is stored on a medium from which it can be retrieved and processed further, such as tape, disk, or diskette.

TYPES OF COMPUTERS

Computers can be categorized by class, generation, and mode of processing.

1. *Class*—A computer is classified as a supercomputer, mainframe, super minicomputer, minicomputer, workstation, or microcomputer depending on its speed, size, and cost. The majority of business settings use mainframes, minicomputers, and microcomputers, the last of which are used either stand-alone or in a network of microcomputers that share printers, modems, and other input and output devices. Workstations, which are powerful desktop machines, also exist in office environments to a degree. The high speeds of supercomputers are useful in solving scientific "what-if" analyses and modeling. Their expense, however, makes it difficult to justify use in a nonscientific or nonacademic environment.

2. *Generation*—The first generation of computers, such as the UNIVAC I in the 1950s, was based on vacuum tube technology. In the

early 1960s, second-generation computers based on transistor technology arrived on the scene. Then in the late 1960s, the use of integrated circuit boards (microchips) marked the beginning of the third generation of computers. These machines, such as IBM's 360 mainframe series, began to make a major impact within business settings, such as banking and insurance companies.

By the mid-1970s, computer manufacturers started to produce hardware based on large-scale integration (LSI) technology, in which anywhere from 100 to 5,000 circuits were placed onto one microchip. These fourth-generation computers are still being used. The fifth generation will see more use of VLSI (very large-scale integration), in which each microchip contains up to 50,000 circuits, closely packed together, thereby increasing processing speed even further.

3. *Mode of processing*—Computers are either digital or analog, with the former being the most commonly used within commercial settings. Digital computers represent values through the use of two states, or voltages; one state—logical ON—represents the value 1; the other state—logical OFF—represents 0. Combinations of these two states are used to represent letters, numbers, and graphics. Analog computers, by contrast, represent values as a continuous variable that can have an infinite number of values.

COMPUTER COMPONENTS

The key components of a computer are the central processing unit (CPU), which performs pre-defined operations on input; internal memory, which maintains whatever data and instructions are needed at the moment; input devices, through which data and instructions are provided to the CPU; and output or external storage devices on which data and instructions not needed immediately can be placed. Together, input and output devices are known as I/O devices.

Central Processing Unit (CPU)

The CPU is the part of a computer that performs arithmetic and logical operations on data based on sets of instructions called programs. It fetches, interprets, and executes instructions and transfers information to and from input and output devices. The early mainframe and minicomputer CPUs contained one or more integrated circuit boards; with the introduction of microtechnology, the entire CPU could be placed onto one chip, thereby leading to the microcomputer revolution.

Memory (Random Access Memory or RAM)

Often, memory and CPU are used together to refer to the part of a computer that processes programs and data. More specifically, RAM represents fast semiconductor storage, directly connected to the CPU, which is used to store and process data and instructions needed for work-in-process. RAM is considered volatile; the data and programs in RAM are not retained permanently and are usually erased when the computer is turned off.

Input Devices

In the early days of commercial computing, data and instructions were typically entered into a computer through a card reader. This device would process a stack of cards, filled with holes representing characters and numbers. Today, there is a variety of means for entering data, and card readers are hardly used at all. The most common current method is through the use of a computer terminal, also referred to as a video display terminal (VDT) or cathode ray tube (CRT). This device consists of a typewriter-like keyboard, on which the user enters data and commands, and a screen that displays information and instructions as well as feeds back what the user keyed in. Early terminals often used paper as a display mechanism, instead of screens, similar to Teletype machines. The common categories of input device are:

- Alphanumeric (or character-based) input devices such as VDTs that have keyboards and a character display.
- Graphics devices, whereby the user points to a menu item or graphical image (icon) on the display screen with

a pointer-type device, rather than keying in text commands. One new example is a graphics tablet on which one can write instructions with a stylus that is interpreted by special character recognition software.

- Readers and scanners such as optical character readers (OCR) that read and interpret printed text, optical mark readers (OMR) that read and interpret pencil or pen marks on a formatted document, bar code readers that read bar codes such as the universal product code found on supermarket items, and image scanners that scan and digitize photographs, documents, graphs, and text so that the information can be stored in digital values understood by computers.
- Voice recognition devices that can interpret human speech, although the ability to recognize and interpret voice commands is still very limited.
- Plastic card readers, such as the slot on an automated teller machine (ATM), that read information from the magnetic strip on a credit card, debit card, or some form of identification card.
- Touch-sensitive screens whereby one simply touches a menu item on the screen to make a selection.

Computers also accept input from information storage media, as well as directly from other computers:

- Magnetic tape and cassettes are similar to the ones used to record speech and music.
- Magnetic disk storage units look like a stack of records. Most are of the nonremovable, "Winchester type," although the removable units are coming into vogue again.
- Floppy diskettes are single-platter magnetic media commonly used for storing data and programs for microcomputers.
- Memory cartridges are plug-in modules for microcomputers consisting of RAM chips. Similar to video game cartridges, the contents of a memory cartridge are not usually erased when power is turned off.

- Optical disks and CDROM (compact disk read-only memory) are nonmagnetic media. An optical scanning mechanism uses a high-intensity light source such as a laser and mirrors to interpret microscopic "holes" etched in a metallic platter as stored information.
- Communications facilities such as telephone circuits, cables, microwave, and satellites provide local or remote transfer of data and programs between computers.

Output Devices

Once a computer has a program in its memory and data to manipulate, the CPU processes the data and puts the results onto a medium that can be recognized by a person, or onto an electronic medium that can be processed by the computer. As with input, output can be stored on magnetic tape, disk, or optical media. It can also be displayed on a CRT, printed, "spoken" via a voice-response unit, or transmitted to a facsimile machine. Common output devices include:

- Line, page, and character printers (impact and nonimpact) for producing hard-copy output on paper and plotters for drawing graphs.
- Other hard-copy devices such as computer-generated microfiche, facsimile, punched cards, and punched tape (the last two are not used very much any longer).
- Displays such as monochrome and color CRTs, flat screen (or liquid crystal display [LCD]) displays, and plasma screens found with notebook-size and portable computers.
- Speech and sound devices such as speech synthesizers used in voice-response units.
- Storage devices such as tape and disk, as well as communications devices, which can also serve as input devices.

Exhibit 9-9 lists the most common input and output devices, categorized by whether the medium is readily understood by a person.

Exhibit 9-9. Common Input and Output Devices

	Human Understandable	*Machine Understandable*
Input devices	Terminal (CRT, VDT) Touch-sensitive screen Mouse Stylus or light pen Voice recognition	Magnetic tape Magnetic disk Optical disk Memory cartridges Readers and scanners Communications devices
Output devices	Printers Plotters Terminal displays Voice response Fax Microfiche	Magnetic tape Magnetic disk Optical disk Communications devices

COMPUTER CLASSES

The distinctions among the different computer classes found in commercial settings are a source of ongoing confusion. Since computers are comprised of microprocessors (integrated circuit boards), the differences between the classes are due primarily to differences in speed, number of microprocessors, external storage capacity, and memory. Exhibit 9-10 lists some of the characteristics of each class.

In earlier days of computing, size and speed generally determined whether a computer was a mainframe or a minicomputer. Today, however, a desktop workstation like a Sun SPARCstation has the compute speed of an IBM mainframe computer—hence the confusion over terminology.

Mainframe Computers

The major manufacturers of mainframe (or host) computers are IBM, Amdahl, UNISYS, and Hitachi, with IBM having the largest market share. Usually, mainframes cost millions of dollars to purchase and have operating and maintenance costs that are many times those of smaller computers. The economics of mainframe computers almost necessitates sharing computing and storage resources by multiple users and applications.

Exhibit 9-10. Comparison of Computer Classes

Attribute	Mainframes	Minicomputers	Microcomputers	Workstations
Cost	High	Medium	Low	Medium
Speed	High	Medium	Medium	High
Memory	High	Medium–High	Medium	Medium–High
External storage	High	Medium–High	Medium	Medium
Security and control	High	Medium–High	Low–Medium	Low–Medium
Environmental needs	High	Low–Medium	Low	Low
Software availability	High	Medium–High	High	Medium
Communications	Medium	Medium–High	Medium	Medium
User friendly	Low	Medium	High	High
Graphics capability	Medium	Medium	High	High
Printer capability	High	Medium	High	Medium

Mainframes need special operating environments, with conditioned water or air cooling. These computers tend to have proprietary operating systems (the software that controls the hardware and the application software) such as IBM's MVS/XA. Mainframes are best where high volumes of data must be stored and where data integrity and software and data security are critical.

Minicomputers

Minicomputers are midsize machines, with power, speed, and memory somewhere between the mainframe and the microcomputer. Often, several are tied together into a network whereby they can share input and output devices, data, software, and can even split the workload in a process known as load balancing.

The cost to purchase a minicomputer is usually within a six-figure range, although some super minicomputers cost well over a million dollars. These machines tend not to need air- or water-cooled environments, and can be located outside of a data center. In fact, the initial attractiveness to users was that they could buy and run their own machines, without the controls and overhead of the mainframe data center environment.

There is a trend within the commercial environment to the use of larger minicomputers and the sharing of machines by multiple users and applications, as with the mainframe environment. Many minicomputers are now kept within data centers so that the end user does not have to worry about capacity planning, hardware and operating system upgrades, backup and recovery, and preventive maintenance. Like mainframes, many minicomputers are controlled by proprietary operating systems software, such as Digital Equipment Corporation's VMS or Hewlett-Packard's MPE.

Microcomputers

These computers on a chip are often called personal computers (PCs), home computers, and micros. Though smaller in size than minicomputers, which in turn are smaller than mainframes, the distinctions are beginning to become more ambiguous. Also, with the in-

creased availability of advanced and less expensive storage technology such as memory cartridges and CDROM, the constraints on microcomputer use are decreasing.

Microcomputers are still largely dedicated to a single user at a time, for applications such as financial spreadsheets, word processing, calendar and time management, and local data maintenance. With the trend toward local-area network (LAN) configurations, whereby multiple PCs are connected for the purpose of sharing input and output devices, data, and software, PCs are starting to process the type of business applications that were previously developed for mainframe or minicomputer setups. A LAN setup allows more than one PC to share a *server*, which is a larger microcomputer, mainframe, or minicomputer, on which data and/or applications are maintained. Microcomputer-based servers are often dedicated to a specific function—for example, data servers, print servers, and communications servers. As capacity becomes exhausted, one can simply add servers and other PCs.

The cost to purchase a PC can run as high as $10,000, depending on the hardware and software options required. Some of the more powerful microcomputer-based servers cost nearly as much as a small minicomputer—upward of $50,000 or more. IBM is the major vendor, but there are many IBM clones made by such companies as Compaq, Dell, Toshiba, and others. Apple has the second largest market share. IBM and IBM-compatible PCs tend to run either Microsoft's MS/DOS operating system (also known as PC/DOS) or IBM's OS/2. The Microsoft Windows operating system is a "layer" above DOS, which provides for a more user-friendly graphical interface instead of DOS-based text commands. Apple has its own proprietary operating system.

Workstations

A workstation is a powerful desktop computer with excellent graphics features. Because of these strengths, workstations were first used within engineering and scientific shops for applications such as computer-aided design and computer-aided engineering. Commercial users began to take an interest, especially in the financial industry, where workstations are now found in trading room operations. The AT&T UNIX operating system and its derivatives are found most commonly on workstations. SUN Microsystems, Hewlett Packard, and Digital Equipment Corporation are the three leading vendors of workstations.

TRENDS

As the price of the microcomputer continues to decrease and its capacity and speed increase, the demise of the "dumb terminal" is at hand. PCs will continue to be used both as "dumb" terminals accessing data and software on mainframes and minicomputers and as intelligent devices able to process their own programs and data. However, users will not need to learn a distinct style for interacting with each type of machine and will not even be aware of the location of the data and software they are using. There will be an increase in local-area networks, with data and software kept on servers instead of on each PC's local storage devices. Minicomputers will increasingly be used as servers within a PC LAN setup.

There will be increasing reliance on "natural" methods of dealing with the computer, through improvements in handwriting and voice-recognition technology and through the use of what is known as GUI (graphical user interface), whereby one chooses from a menu item or picture (icon) on a screen with a pointing device, rather than by keying commands.

External storage for the microcomputer world will become cheaper and will be able to support greater volumes of data, thus eliminating many of the current constraints. Issues around lack of security and the proliferation of software and data will be solved through security and administrative software as well as the growing awareness on the part of users on the need for controls.

The number of vendors will probably be fewer than today. The major ones will offer a gamut of machine sizes, prices, and capacity ranges. There is the likelihood that proprietary operating systems will be less of an impediment as vendors provide open systems as a means to run software on more than one vendor's machines and/or an easy method for communicating across boundaries.

These trends will hopefully reduce some of the current confusion as well as allow the purchaser to make investments that will continue to be compatible with newer technologies entering the marketplace.

SOFTWARE AND APPLICATIONS DEVELOPMENT

Linda J. Ferri, L. J. Ferri & Associates

THE HARDWARE/SOFTWARE RELATIONSHIP

In order to produce desired results, computer hardware must be "told" what to do, when, and with what data. The term *software* generally refers to sets of instructions that people prepare to make computers function in a desired, predictable manner. Exhibit 9-11 illustrates one way to classify the different types of software required to operate a computer, as well as the relationship between the software and the physical hardware environment.

The software used to perform business functions, such as accounts payable, inventory management, and payroll, to provide information to management for making decisions, or to automate office operations belongs to the business application software layer in Exhibit 9-11. Between the business application software and the computer hardware is a software layer that includes:

- *System software*—including the *operating system* that manages the computer hardware resources, maintains data files and controls computer access; the *language translators* that convert various computer languages that people can understand into the binary machine language understood by the computer; and *system utilities* that simplify access and use of the computer.

- *Data management software*—maintains the data stored on the computer—usually on disks—and provides the user with the ability to store, retrieve, and update data without needing to know the hardware-dependent details of how data are accessed and stored.
- *Data communications software*—controls the movement of data between the computer and the user(s) of the computer.

In today's information systems environment, the business application user rarely thinks of this middle layer of software in terms of its components. Rather, the user interacts with the computer hardware through user interface software that is part of the operating system or an adjunct to it. Traditionally, operating systems have provided a character-based user interface (CUI) that accepts alphanumeric data entered on a keyboard and displays information in fixed character positions on a video display terminal (VDT). Business applications that depend on a CUI utilize command languages, menus, and formatted screens for the user to issue instructions to the computer, enter data, and request information. Historically, command interfaces have been used for business applications because commands were simpler to implement and easier to change than menus.

Standard front-end software has emerged as the way to provide a graphical user inter-

Exhibit 9-11. Software/Hardware Relationships

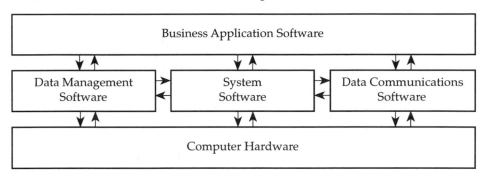

face (GUI) for users that insulates them from the systems, data management, and data communications software that controls their business applications. With a GUI, an application can take advantage of different character fonts, colors, icons, and pictures to communicate with, and present information to, a user. The application can utilize multiple windows to display information as well as to accept data input from the user. User interaction with the application consists of selecting (usually with a mouse) from menus, lists, and buttons displayed on the screen.

GUIs have several advantages from a user's perspective:

- GUIs require little training, thereby allowing users to achieve quickly a level of comfort and understanding with a new application.
- A GUI presents the complete range of choices available to the user at any time during use of the application, which frees the user from memorizing command formats and key sequences.
- Experienced users can be more productive with a GUI because selecting icons

and menu items is often faster than keying commands or menu options.

Three GUIs dominate the market: Microsoft Windows, IBM's Presentation Manager, and Open Software Foundation's Motif. The choice of which one an organization adopts depends on the operating system software being used on its workstations or vice versa—that is, the selection of user interface software first will determine what operating system will be used. Exhibit 9-12 shows the relationships between user interface software and their respective operating systems.

BUSINESS APPLICATION ENVIRONMENT

There are three important characteristics of business applications:

1. Business applications depend on an organization's policies, procedures, management requirements, and data.
2. Changes in information technology, government regulations, business re-

Exhibit 9-12. User Interface Software

Microsoft Windows	Microsoft Windows	IBM Presentation Manager	OSF Motif
MS-DOS	NT	OS/2	UNIX

quirements, and the organization itself necessitate modifications and enhancements to applications.

3. Maintenance costs over the life of an application often exceed the original cost to develop it.

Traditional computerized business applications typically consist of thousands of lines of instructions in one or more program modules. Development can be costly and time consuming, with multiyear projects for major new business applications being not all that uncommon. Indeed, the labor cost for software development and maintenance is one of the top MIS expenditures.

Achieving the business goal of applying information technology to enhance an organization's competitive advantage depends on having a business application environment in which there is a measurable and meaningful return on the investment in business application software; leveraging the use of information technology enhances development staff productivity; managing application change effectively improves the overall performance of the organization. The foundation of such a business application environment is the application architecture of the organization.

Application Architecture

Business applications can be divided into three components: user interface, business (or process) logic, and database. The traditional application architecture, as shown in Exhibit 9-13, has all three of these components resi-

dent on a host computer—typically a mainframe or a minicomputer with a character-based user interface.

In an initial attempt to modernize applications while protecting their investment in "legacy" systems, many organizations move to the back-end/front-end architecture. Here the dumb terminal is replaced by a graphical user interface (GUI) on a workstation. As Exhibit 9-13 illustrates, the application logic and database, however, remain on the host. The workstation handles all of the interaction between the application system and the user, but the host does all of the work.

Sharing processing activities among computers across a network is the predominant trend of the 1990s for business applications. The cooperative processing architecture as shown in Exhibit 9-13 provides the user with a GUI workstation—usually a personal computer—on which all (or a major portion) of the application logic runs while accessing a shared database on a host computer—also known as a server. In its simplest form, cooperative processing involves moving data from a file server to workstations, which do the processing and then send the data back to the file server.

Client Server

In the client server model of cooperative processing, the work is shared between the server and the user (or client) workstations. The

Exhibit 9-13. Three Application Architecture Models

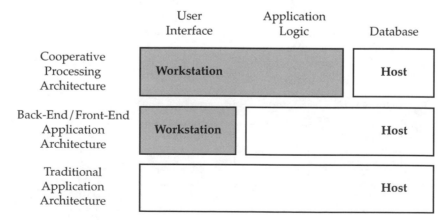

Exhibit 9-14. Client Server Model

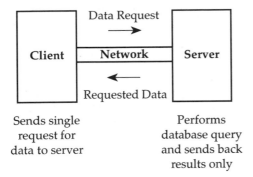

Sends single request for data to server

Performs database query and sends back results only

server in Exhibit 9-14 processes database requests from the client while maintaining data integrity and security. The client takes answers to its database queries from the server and works with them. Only the query and response move back and forth over the network.

The client does what personal computers do better than any other host computer access device—that is, present data in a variety of fashions that facilitate ease of use and understanding by application users. In the simplest form of client server computing, the server provides the computer processing power required to store large volumes of data and retrieve them as quickly as possible in response to data requests from multiple clients. For more complex applications, the application logic may also be shared between the client and server. To the user, the distribution of work between client and server is transparent, and the application appears to be running locally on the workstation.

The goals of the client server model include providing a hardware/software platform that can be scaled to meet business application demands; supporting an integrated, organization-wide approach to data management; and providing a highly productive development environment in which business applications can be implemented quickly. To achieve these goals, the appropriate application software must exist on the client, as well as on the server; an appropriate database management system must reside on the server along with access routines on the client; and the appropriate software must be present on the client,

network, and server to route requests and data. Although the application software itself may be purchased, it is the only piece that today would be developed and maintained in-house by an organization.

Updating the Front End

While moving business applications to client server may be an ideal, the reality is that most MIS organizations have large libraries of business applications code—some of it possibly dating back a decade or more—that was developed to run on mainframe computers and to depend on mainframe databases. A reasonable first step toward moving these applications away from their traditional application architecture is to first address the user interface—the front end in Exhibit 9-13. Software products exist readily that facilitate converting the character-oriented user interface of a VDT to a GUI running on a workstation. But this is only a first step. Taking the next step requires reengineering existing business applications in a cooperative processing environment.

APPLICATION DEVELOPMENT PROCESS

The application development process is a series of activities for creating new business applications and maintaining them during their life cycle. Although technical in nature, the application development process is really a management process that transforms business requirements into computer-based business applications. The application development process consists of five functional steps, as illustrated in Exhibit 9-15.

Planning

Planning is the first step in the application development process. Request for new applications and changes to existing ones come into MIS from management, users, and even suppliers and customers. During the planning step, MIS evaluates these requests, determines the magnitude of effort to meet them, assigns development priorities to them, per-

Exhibit 9-15. Application Development Process Steps

forms a feasibility study for the highest priority requests, and develops a budget and schedule for these applications.

Analysis and Design

The goal of this step in the application development process is to develop a detailed foundation upon which a business application will be implemented. During this step, business and user requirements are translated into a conceptual application approach that will be followed during the implementation step. The evaluation of technical and systems design alternatives occurs during this step, as does the detailed planning for the implementation and testing steps.

The traditional approach to analysis and design has been to break a business process down into a series of subprocesses (or tasks), each of which can be broken down further into work units that can be defined, analyzed, evaluated, and have application logic designed with a reasonable degree of assurance. The application design that results from this approach describes the new system in terms of process and data flow diagrams. Formal methodologies for such structured analysis and design have existed since the early 1970s, such as those developed by DeMarco and Yourdon, Gane and Sarson, and Ward and Mellor.

In the 1990s, the approach to analysis and design is shifting from such functional decomposition of a business problem to one that is object oriented. An object represents a business or technical function, and each object contains the data and procedures (or rules) associated with a specific function. Objects send "messages" to one another requesting information and services. The total set of objects and messages for an organization is its *enterprise model*. The object-oriented approach to analysis and design eventually results in a shorter time for this step. This occurs because existing objects are reusable from a design and coding standpoint. Analysis consists of determining what objects exist, what new objects are needed, how the objects will interact, and how information will be accessed.

Implementation

The implementation step has typically been the largest and most complex part of developing a business application. During this step, the conceptual design for the application is transformed into computer programs that contain the application logic, database interactions, and business rules required by the application. This step also includes preparation of documentation and user training. One of the advantages of the object-oriented approach is that length of the implementation step is greatly reduced with the reuse of existing coded object modules.

Building and Testing

The purpose of this step is to integrate the programs developed and unit tested in the prior step into a business application system, and to perform an efficient, accurate, and complete test of the new business application. Finally, training occurs, data conversion (if necessary) takes place, and the business application goes into production.

Maintenance

By some estimations, over half of MIS development budgets goes to maintaining existing business applications. Ongoing maintenance includes enhancing existing applications to provide new functions, making minor changes, and correcting problems that may be detected during production use of the applications. Maintenance represents an extension of the application development process, resulting often in new requirements that fuel the planning step.

APPLICATION DEVELOPMENT ENVIRONMENT

The traditional application development environment has been manual and labor intensive. It is not unusual in this environment for the application development process to take two years or more for a *single* business application. Planning, analysis, and design can involve numerous hours of interviewing users, studying operations, documenting processes and procedures, and creating volumes of documents including design documents. Implementation depends on individuals developing computer code using one of the programming languages (such as COBOL or FORTRAN), manually debugging the code, and building test suites with which to determine whether or not a business application was ready for production. The final building and testing is no less laborious. And when time is an issue, often implementation begins without proper analysis and design, and documentation is scant or nonexistent.

The emergence of computer-aided software engineering (CASE) has reduced the time needed to develop new business applications, improved application quality, and lowered the cost of maintaining applications. As illustrated in Exhibit 9-16, CASE is a set of applications (or tools) that covers the entire application development process.

Analysis and Design

CASE analysis and design tools concentrate on automating the front end of the applications development process. They allow developers to model applications before implementing them. When used properly, these CASE tools produce higher-quality business application designs that are better aligned with business requirements and user expectations. An equally important result is that applications designed using these CASE tools tend to be better structured and better documented than those resulting from traditional analysis and design.

Application Development

The CASE application development tools tend to be based on what is known as fourth-generation languages (or 4GL). COBOL and FORTRAN are examples of third-generation computer languages, in which hundreds of lines of procedural code are required to perform a function that can be done in a single 4GL instruction. By having to generate less code for a given application, implementation can be accomplished in a shorter time frame and at less cost, and ongoing maintenance is simplified.

Screen Development

Screen development tools simplify design and implementation of user interface screens. By building prototypes, developers can illustrate to users what an application will look like prior to the generation of any application code. Adding GUI front ends to existing applications is usually done with a screen development tool.

Exhibit 9-16. CASE Environment

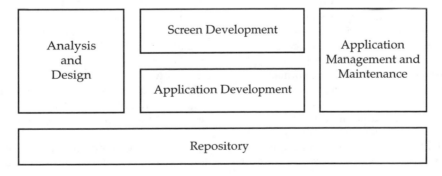

APPLICATION MANAGEMENT AND MAINTENANCE

CASE tools for application management include software to maintain libraries of computer code that include cross-references documenting the data and code used by each application. There is also software to automate building applications from these libraries. Application management also includes tools to facilitate automated application testing, including performance simulation. There are also CASE tools for automated creation of application documentation, including incorporating changes made during application development or maintenance.

The repository provides the foundation for an integrated CASE environment. It is a database used by an organization to hold all of the information needed for developing business applications, starting at the front end with planning, analysis, and design, and right through implementation and maintenance. The analysis and design tools utilize data and business rule definitions that already exist, as well as define new ones that are added to the repository. Application and screen development tools use the definitions in the repository during implementation. The application management and maintenance tools update, maintain, and utilize information in the repository for these activities.

TELECOMMUNICATIONS

W. Edward Hodgson, Manchester Equipment Company, Inc.

The late 1980s and early 1990s have been called the "Dawn of the Information Age"—a time when the use of information has been more important than how it was created, stored, or transmitted electronically. This is a natural progression from the "Computer Age" during which computing power and capabilities rose to unprecedented heights while the cost of computing dropped dramatically. Today, similar dramatic changes are taking place in telecommunications. People can access, share, and transfer information at high data transfer rates and low costs that are unprecedented.

Historically, telecommunications has been based on, and has usually coexisted with, voice telephone services. In the beginning, all telephone service was analog—the human voice is converted from sound to alternating voltages, thereby producing an electronically transmittable form of human sound. First there were switchboard operators with patch cords, then crossbar switches and relays actuated by a telephone's dial pulses. Later, solid-state computers controlled analog switches actuated by either dial pulses or tone. For economic reasons, several analog voice channels would be combined (multiplexed) for transmission between switching centers—locally or even worldwide.

Digital pulses are easier to multiplex and regenerate than are analog ones, and they are less costly to transmit. For these reasons, telephone companies have converted their interexchange and long-distance services to digital technology in which the human voice can be translated into bit patterns for transmission. Since the human voice is analog by nature, it takes a special device to translate it into digital format and re-create it from digital format. This device is a CODEC (COder/DECoder). Depending on the application, a CODEC can be in a local telephone company central office, can be part of a local premises PBX, can be a stand-alone device connected to a telecommunications network, or can be in a telephone desk set itself. The standard that governs this digital encoding—known as pulse code modulation or PCM—is the same for North America and Japan; Europe follows a different standard. The rest of the world uses either the North American or European standard.

With the advent of digital telecommunications, all information transfer is digital, and the technical distinctions between voice, data, facsimile (fax), and video have all but disappeared. Because of digital telecommunications, some industry forecasts see the "distance-sensitive" portion of telecommunications costs all but disappearing in the near future.

SERVICES

If computer hardware and software are the bricks that MIS uses to build systems, then telecommunications is the mortar. A system, like a building, requires a careful selection of components, including the appropriate mortar to hold the structure together.

Analog Services

Transmitting data across an analog telephone circuit requires a device called a MODEM (MOdulator/DEModulator) that converts the digital information from a computer into an analog form. At the low end, there are half-duplex (unidirectional) modems with a transmission rate of 300 bits per second (bps). The most sophisticated modems at the high end provide full duplex (bidirectional) transmission rates exceeding 38,000 bps (38 Kbps). Since the maximum transmission rate for a dial-up modem is 9.6 Kbps, modems achieve 38 Kbps rates through data compression techniques. Many modems today come with error detection and correction logic that provides error-free data transmission over telephone grade lines.

Although the data transmission leaves the building as an analog signal, the telephone company converts the analog output of a modem into a 64-Kbps signal for switching and transmission (see Exhibit 9-17). At the receiving end, the telephone company reconverts the signal back to analog. Though popular in the 1970s and 1980s, leased (dedicated) analog lines are now unavailable in some areas, thereby requiring the use of end-to-end digital services. Even where leased analog lines are still available, the highest transmission rate is 19.2 Kbps.

Digital Services

The basic digital transmission services listed in Exhibit 9-18 are based on the 64 Kbps needed for a single-voice (DS0) channel. The effective rate for a DS0 channel is 56 Kbps because 8 out of every 64 bits are set aside for overhead activities such as synchronization and control signaling. It is possible to obtain a full (clear channel) 64-Kbps DS0—or a multiple thereof such as 384 Kbps—using one of two new framing methods: either ESF (extended super frame) or B8ZS (bipolar 8 zero substitution).

There are current offerings called fractional T1 that are one to twenty-three DS0 channels.

Exhibit 9-17. Analog Data Transmission

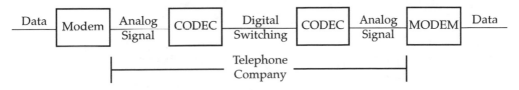

Exhibit 9-18. Digital Transmission Services

Service	Rate	Number of DS0s	Notes
DS0	64 Kbps	1	Voice or data
DS1	1.544 Mbps	24	Also called T1
DS1C	3.152 Mbps	48	$2 \times$ DS1
DS2	6.312 Mbps	96	$4 \times$ DS1
DS3	44.736 Mbps	672	$28 \times$ DS1
DS4	274.176 Mbps	4,032	$6 \times$ DS3

The advantage of fractional T1 is that it is usually less expensive than a full T1 or a comparable digital data service (DDS) channel. Access to the fractional T1 carrier's point-of-presence—that is, the nearest location where a connection can be made with the carrier's network—usually requires a full DS1, which can be used for multiple voice, data, and video circuits provided all of them are handled by the same carrier. For data and video telecommunications, this DS1 may have to be a clear channel.

Leased digital services in the traditional modem data ranges—for example, 9.6 Kbps and 19.2 Kbps—are available in some areas. The costs for these services, however, are usually not less than that for the higher-rate digital services. Finally, carriers also offer switched (that is, dial-up) digital services at 56 Kbps, 64 Kbps, 384 Kbps, DS1 (T1), and DS3.

All digital services require a terminating device called a channel service unit (CSU) that interfaces the customer's equipment to the telephone company's digital services. DS0 services also require a data service unit (DSU) that supplies the standard data interface control signals. As shown in Exhibit 9-19, the DSU often has an integral CSU. Since DS1 and DS3 services often carry multiple lower-rate channels—such as 384 Kbps—a third device known as a multiplexer (channel bank) is needed to combine the lower-rate channels for transmission over the digital service.

ISDN

The latest advance in telecommunications is ISDN, which stands for integrated services digital network. Exhibit 9-20 lists the basic elements of ISDN, where the "D" channel is the data or signaling channel and the "B" channels are the bearer channels that can be used for voice, data, video, Group IV fax, and other information transmission formats. The "B" channels are clear channels that can be used for any application, including uncoded binary or video, and they can be combined for higher data rates.

ISDN BRI is an international standard that supports worldwide end-to-end switched digital transmissions. ISDN BRI uses the same single-pair copper wire facilities used by analog telephones, but it requires a network termination 1 (NT1) unit to convert analog signals into digital ones. The device used to convert these digital signals into usable 64-Kbps data or voice channels are called terminal adapter units (TAUs).

Exhibit 9-19. Digital Data Transmission

Exhibit 9-20. ISDN Services

Service	Rate	"D" Channel	"B" Channel	Notes
BRI	144 Kbps	16 Kbps	2 × 64 Kbps	Basic rate
PRI	1.544 Mbps	64 Kbps	23 × 64 Kbps	Primary rate
or	1.544 Mbps	0	24 × 64 Kbps	2nd PRI
Broad band ISDN	—	—	—	being defined

Why ISDN? Consider two people—one in London and one in New York—who want to view concurrently the same information on screens in front of them with both having the ability to make changes to the information on the screens. With ISDN, one "B" channel carries the data to both screens while the other "B" channel allows both individuals to converse with each other. Other people could be added to the data and audio "conferences" being held on the two "B" channels.

Fiber Optic Services

One of the most significant advances in telecommunications is the conversion of interconnect facilities from coaxial cable and microwave to fiber optic cabling. A single fiber optic strand can support multiple data channels, each at a different wavelength, capable of transferring data at over one billion bits per second (1 Gbps).

Connecting to a fiber-based service usually requires the installation of fiber optic cabling from a building to the carrier's point of presence, which could be as close as the manhole in front of the building or as far as miles away. Whether installing this connection or converting an entire building to fiber optic cable, the costs involved can be two to four times those for a comparable length of copper wiring or coaxial cable.

Satellite Services

Satellite services have been around for over two decades and are the backbone of the television industry. While the installation of fiber optic cabling across the United States has almost eliminated the need for satellite services from a capacity standpoint, satellite still has a place in data communications. Satellite services can provide access to any site, however remote, at data rates of up to 64 Kbps at a reasonable cost. These services use what is called a VSAT (very small aperture terminal) with antenna dishes ranging in size from under one meter to several meters in diameter. Some receive-only units are as small as 18 inches and can be installed inside an office by a window.

Other Services

Other services that may lend themselves to some applications include:

- *Packet networks*—Data are carried very inexpensively by worldwide X.25 packet service providers. Access to these dial-up services is by modem or over leased lines at speeds of up to 56 Kbps. Costs are usually based on usage and the amount of data transmitted rather than on distance.
- *Enhanced service providers*—Value-added services include electronic mail, speed and code conversion, and electronic data interchange (EDI).
- *Digital cellular radio*—Digital cellular radio services provide greater data transmission speeds than possible with analog cellular transmissions.
- *Digital radio*—Private or public radio services can be used for digital data transmission. Private facilities are expensive and require FCC (Federal Communications Commission) licensing. Public services are almost as expensive as cellular radio to use. Probably the largest single use of digital radio is for mobile data terminals (MDTs) in police, fire, and emergency vehicles.

NETWORKS

Telecommunications is rarely just moving information from one place to another on a point-to-point basis. In reality, telecommunications involves networks of computers connected by circuits, channels, or links, whereby:

1. Geographically remote computers can exchange data with other computers.
2. Physically distributed computers can share hardware, software, or data.
3. Computers in a single location can exchange data among themselves as well as share hardware and software resources.

Networks today—especially local-area networks (LANs) found within a single location—tend to be multipoint configurations of one of three types illustrated in Exhibit 9-21: ring, star, or bus. A ring (loop) network has a series of computers or workstations connected to each other in a closed loop. IBM's Token Ring is an example of a ring network. A star network, workstations, or subordinate computers are connected on a point-to-point basis to a central computer that controls the network. The simplest example would be PROFS workstations connected to an IBM host computer.

With a bus network, all of the computers or workstations are attached to a common telecommunications bus. This bus can be a twisted pair of wire, coaxial cable, or fiber optic cable. Bus networks are the most com-

Exhibit 9-21. Common Network Configurations

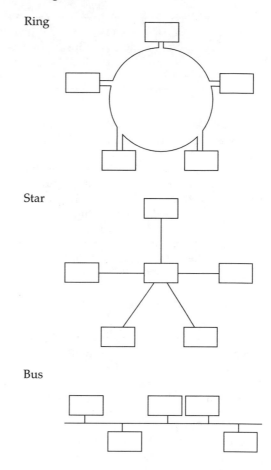

Ring

Star

Bus

mon configuration today for LANs as is evidenced by the popularity of Ethernet. Through the use of equipment known as trans-LAN bridges, bus networks can be connected over digital telephone services to form wide-area networks (WANs).

ELECTRONIC DATA INTERCHANGE

Robert Plaut, Digital Equipment Corporation

An interesting aspect of information systems is the way relatively simple applications and concepts combine and mature into business tools that prove more powerful than the sum of their parts. For example, the combination of word processing, electronic mail, and networking have been combined with conferencing tools, video text, spreadsheets, and other applications to bring about integrated office automation (OA) and work-group systems. The impact of integrated OA on the way business executives can manage information and communicate within their organization has been greater than the prior use of the individual OA components. Electronic data interchange (EDI) promises a similar impact on businesses in the future.

Simply, EDI is the electronic transfer of information from one computer system to another in a standard format. Generally, this is not a new concept to most organizations. For years, related applications within an organization have been exchanging information among themselves in standard formats. What makes EDI different?

- The cooperating applications reside in different organizations or companies.
- The exchanged data adheres to industry-recognized format standards.
- The information transferred electronically bypasses normal human interfaces that rely on traditional, albeit computer-assisted, business procedures and paper documents.

Managers who plan to identify, design, and implement EDI within their organizations can expect to encounter the following:

- *Substantial potential benefits*—Properly planned and implemented EDI applications can provide organizations with significant improvements in the speed, accuracy, and efficiency of intercompany transactions. These benefits result from faster communications between business partners, better control of inventories, shorter order cycles, and reduced processing errors. The total effect is improved competitive advantage and cost reductions to the participants in EDI transactions.
- *Abundance of standards*—In the past ten years, a myriad of proprietary, national, and international EDI standards have been developed, as well as numerous industry-specific guidelines and recommendations for using these standards. While the number of EDI standards and guidelines may be confusing, they represent years of work in this area, and they indicate the interest and willingness of organizations to participate in EDI.
- *Significant challenges*—EDI presents organizations with difficult management, organizational, and personal challenges that must be anticipated and fully satisfied before success can be achieved. The planning requirements and level of sen-

sitivity needed by EDI development teams extend beyond the normal range for in-house development projects.

FOUR CRITICAL DEVELOPMENT ISSUES

The benefits and challenges of EDI are similar to those encountered during the 1980s in integrated OA efforts, and lessons can be learned from those experiences. Both EDI and OA are made up of familiar, usually widely accepted, automation components and concepts. Both have the ability to deliver significant business benefits, and both require individuals to change how they work within an organization. As with OA, EDI implementation efforts require careful attention in the following areas:

1. Detailed and sensitive planning must be conducted to identify and resolve the technical, procedural, administrative, legal, accounting, and human relations issues associated with EDI. Sacred and comfortable business practices such as filing paper copies of orders and inked approval signatures will be eliminated, reduced, or replaced by automated functions in EDI applications. Each of these practices must be addressed for both the company looking to implement EDI and its vendors, suppliers, and customers who will use EDI.

2. There is an exceptional amount of consensus building involved among those who will be affected by EDI. Implementing EDI requires the complete and simultaneous cooperation of many different groups and individuals, and anyone that is neglected can quickly impede the success of an EDI project.

3. Implementing EDI requires orientation and training programs that address the overall business goals that EDI will help the organization meet rather than just covering the operational details of the EDI technology. It is important for people to understand the overall picture up-front so they can bring their unique insights and practical experience to the project based on their day-to-day performance of business functions.

4. The EDI effort must be led by highly motivated decision makers who know how to establish realistic objectives, and how to identify, assess, and manage the risks associated with changing business processes. Success also depends on addressing an appropriate scope of business functions.

The difference between modest and complete success in implementing EDI is not a matter of meeting targeted objectives such as number of users, reports, inquiries, and system availability. Rather, it is a matter of how completely, correctly, and creatively EDI is used. Any EDI implementation effort that seeks to realize the maximum potential benefits—and not just the electronic transfer of documents between companies—must carefully understand the full potential of EDI, plan for how it will change a business, and address these four critical issues.

BUSINESS BENEFITS OF EDI

EDI is a relatively young technology. Although some companies have been developing EDI applications since the 1970s, the major growth in integrated EDI is expected to occur in the mid-1990s. Considering the technical and administrative challenges associated with the proper implementation of EDI applications, the technology must provide significant and easily measured benefits for the business that implements it.

The most important benefits associated with EDI are those related to the increased speed and accuracy of electronically transferring business documents and other information between companies. EDI reduces the time normally taken for document preparation, delivery, and processing from days or weeks to hours. Most EDI systems are designed to work in a batch-oriented, stored and forward manner, which is the most cost-effective means for a wide range of applications. Real-time, interactive EDI can also be implemented for applications where immediate delivery of information is critical.

The EDI benefits related to speed and accuracy vary in importance by industry, by company, and by departments within companies. These benefits are usually related to information timeliness, the ability to manage inventories accurately at the most efficient levels (for example, just-in-time inventory control), reduced clerical and administrative overhead, reduced lead times for materials handling, improved accuracy in forecasting resulting from shortened business cycles, and increased data accuracy due to the elimination of manual data reentry.

THE FUTURE OF EDI

The cost and functional advantages of EDI are viewed today as a means of gaining a competitive advantage. Soon, companies will need these basic elements just to remain competitive. In the automotive and chemical industries, for example, suppliers and vendors have to implement EDI in order to do business with the industry leaders.

EDI applications automate core business functions, and there will be a direct correlation between evolving information systems technologies and the use of EDI. As EDI-related standards, communications protocols, and telecommunications services mature, business managers will be able to use a full range of available technologies to do business electronically across multiple industries and over wide geographic areas.

The inclusion of computer-aided design drawings, graphics, and images in EDI transmissions will help complete the electronic product ordering processing for many industries. In addition, EDI applications will be able to transmit and process spreadsheet data and search central information repositories and computer-based catalogues, thereby enabling the integration of EDI into business decision support systems.

CONCLUSION

Successful implementation of EDI is approximately one quarter technology and three quarters business planning, leadership, and management. EDI requires that business managers take a zero-base approach to planning how automation can be used to facilitate business processes. The traditional development approach of automating individual processes originally designed for manual offices must give way to an enterprise-wide approach that looks at how to take full advantage of available and emerging technologies. This kind of thinking requires an open mind, careful planning, cooperation from top management, and a lot of courage.

INTELLIGENT NETWORK MANAGEMENT

Andres Llana, Jr., Vermont Studies Group, Inc.

NETWORK MANAGEMENT CONCERNS

Faced with a rapid growth in networks due to the expanded application of personal computers (PCs) and local-area networks (LANs), many chief information officers are faced with the management of multivendor networks. The divestiture of AT&T has fostered a greater need for more comprehensive network management support. As networks become more diverse and companies must rely on their networks for the delivery of their products, there is a growing need to manage network resources more closely.

Network management technology has evolved over the last decade through the development of intelligent modems. This technology was further evolved into more comprehensive network management systems and services. These new network management systems support rapid network reconfiguration, automated fault isolation, alarm reporting, as well as proactive trouble ticket management. While these new systems are physical network management systems, they are also capable of supporting an interface to the logical network management process as well.

Centralizing Control

Network management system requirements are heaviest among those industries that de-pend solely on their networks to support their bottom line. These include financial services, transportation services, insurance services, as well as large manufacturing industries. Within these industries, the focus of the network management function is centered in the MIS area. Since these industries were the first to structure network management vehicles, their emphasis has been on older logical and physical network management vehicles. In these situations there is a need to upgrade the older network management vehicles to encompass some of the newer network monitoring and control concepts that will support more centralized control.

The trend now is moving toward carrier-based network management vehicles that cost less to implement and can support the requirements for an integrated voice and data network. These new network management systems are based on proven techniques and software that has been refined by the carriers through years of service. These vehicles allow the carrier's customer to centralize control of his or her network and to reduce the costs associated with a comprehensive network control center.

Performance and Availability

Companies are increasingly faced with the specter of increasing revenues while reducing expenses. One area that is a traditional sinkhole for dollars is the company data center and its accompanying network. Data centers, followed by network costs, represent one of the highest cost items for a company to shoulder. As a result, financial planners often will place pressure on the data center managers to reduce costs by reducing head count and increasing the performance of their networks. The pressure to improve network performance without well-trained communications personnel capable of supporting a comprehensive network structure forces the data center manager to seek outside help. To meet this requirement there are service providers, whose services are based on a partial or complete outsourcing of network support service. This new approach to network management is gaining in popularity with large network users due to the cost savings that are available in terms of improved network reliability and minimized personnel overhead.

The Impact of Downtime

Industries that place great reliance on a network to support their product or services, such as the airlines or financial services providers, face disastrous losses if their networks are down. For some types of services that are highly perishable even the slightest network outage can produce losses in the millions. Hence the need for highly reliable networks backed by alternate or diverse routes is of great importance. Such networks require constant monitoring backed by proactive processes to ensure the survivability of the network under most stringent conditions. Here the emphasis is on the establishment of user-friendly mechanisms that make it possible to proactively maintain reliable networks with personnel possessing minimal network skills. Carrier-based services provide user-friendly management tools designed to support network personnel in diagnosing network problems and reporting network performance in a more comprehensive manner. For some users, this level of support may suffice; for others, it may be just a beginning.

NETWORK MANAGEMENT ALTERNATIVES

Vendor Management

Depending on the company, the techniques for managing telecommunications resources vary. Some companies will stress a multivendor environment playing one vendor off of another with each vendor hoping to gain an ever-increasing share of the customer's business by maintaining an impeccable level of performance. This technique works well where the user has a large enough network and is able to spread his or her network investment over several vendors.

In this situation it is vital that the user maintain a competitive environment among his or her vendors. Further, the vendor contracts must make the vendor responsible for any network service loss that is directly attributable to the vendor. For example, if a PBX vendor cuts over a new PBX that is not properly programmed, forcing the customer to suffer loss through the improper functioning of the user's voice services, the vendor must pay a set fee for the damage incurred. Obviously, in a multivendor network, the task here is to properly organize all of the vendors so that they can be effectively managed.

Since divestiture, some companies have tried to function as their own telephone company, staffing to meet the needs of both their voice and data users. This of course is expensive and demands that network management take on a different dimension than one where the onus is placed on the vendor(s) to maintain an established level of performance. Managing in this situation requires that the user mount a concentrated effort to monitor and diagnose all of his or her own network problems.

Some companies have taken yet another approach to network management by adopting a single vendor policy in support of their network. Such a policy can bear fruit where the stakes are high and the vendor stands the chance of losing a very large account. In this scenario network management is a service that is now being provided by the vendor at modest cost to the user. This provides an option that allows the network manager to migrate to a totally integrated network management strategy.

Outsourcing

Because of the increasing complexity of multivendor networks, a user with a limited in-house staff may not be able to cope with some of the more complicated network management issues. For this reason, one network management alternative is to have a vendor or some other outside company perform the network management functions on a contract basis. This practice is known as outsourcing. Outsourcing can be a viable alternative for the MIS director or data center manager who is faced with managing a large network but is restricted in adding the necessary personnel in order to do the job.

Benefits of Outsourcing. While cost is frequently the driving factor in selecting an outsourcing solution for network management, there are other tangible as well as intangible benefits that bear consideration:

- *Immediate necessity*—Limited budgets prevent a data center manager from performing specific tasks related to the corporate network without additional equipment and staff.
- *Improved corporate focus*—The corporate MIS team is free to concentrate on corporate objectives while contractor personnel can concentrate on the customer's network.
- *Overcommitment of in-house personnel*—Frequently a user with a growing network will overcommit in-house resources due to rapidly changing requirements and priorities. Outsourcing allows for the concentration of in-house resources on more critical projects where retaining and using in-house expertise is an asset.
- *Network availability and responsiveness*—The outside network manager focuses its resources on network availability and responsiveness.

Cost Justification. Justifying the expenditure of funds for outside support starts with properly identifying the cost of not taking action. First there is the cost of downtime. This includes, for example, the cost of lost productivity due to the failure of network components or telecommunications facilities, lost sales where network downtime prevents the

placing of orders in a telemarketing center, as well as the cost to staff an internal telecommunications help desk or call management center. Estimating the cost of downtime should include monthly and annual cost summaries for each type of loss.

There are a number of intangibles that affect the decision to outsource network support. For example, if there is a high rate of personnel turnover coupled with a rapid expansion of the network, there may not be sufficient resources to cope with a dynamic network environment. In addition, network expenses should be reviewed to determine their growth with respect to corporate revenues. Frequently, network costs have a way of outpacing the rate of revenue growth where MIS management does not have the resources to develop a cost-containment strategy for the network.

Other hidden indicators for the need for outside assistance include an inordinately high incidence of network downtime, downtime due to vendor finger pointing, downtime due to many network troubles shown as "no trouble found," or a high percentage of downtime occurring during prime business hours. All of these may be sufficient justification to bring in outside resources to support the corporate network.

Impartial Audit. Bringing in an outside source of support can provide an impartial audit and review of the network. Where necessary, network enhancements can be made that can further ensure the network's availability. During this period MIS management can reorganize available internal resources with the objective of either augmenting or gradually replacing the contractor-supplied help. Further, the outside professional assistance can be used to not only design and reconfigure the corporate network but to develop new network capabilities that may not have been possible before. In this way MIS management can gain the advantage of improving corporate network reliability and responsiveness while also improving the effective utilization of corporate telecommunications expenditures.

COMMON CARRIER NETWORK MANAGEMENT

Common telecommunications carriers such as AT&T, MCI, and U.S. Sprint have had to manage their networks for a long time. They perhaps know more about the process than most others and have been pursuing the issue of network management as a provisioned service for some time. As a result, these carriers have developed comprehensive network management services that can be tailored to most user needs. Of course, these network management services are predicated upon the customer subscribing to a carrier's integrated software defined network, such as AT&T1's SDN, MCI's VNET, or U.S. Sprint's VPN service.

Carrier-based services allow the user to monitor and control both voice and data services that are provisioned by the carrier supplying the network services. There are five basic network management functions provided by the carrier network management services: configuration management, fault management, performance management, accounting management, and network planning.

Configuration Management

Configuration management provides the customer with the ability to control the configuration of the routing of traffic on the corporate network. This enables a user to more efficiently utilize network resources, such as allocating the bandwidth of T1 services on demand. This allows the user to reconfigure and reroute traffic and network calls based on the current needs of the network users. Another example is the ability to control the routing of traffic in connection with bulk calling services associated with incoming 800 call traffic.

Fault Management

This includes the capability to track faults on a T1 link between two locations, as well as the capability to directly access and test dedicated trunks providing access to vendors' network services. It also includes the ability to access circuit and traffic information and to activate call screening and routing controls.

These services are aimed at minimizing network downtime through the delivery of timely alarm and fault status information allowing the customer to take corrective action to minimize (or even avoid) network downtime.

Performance Management

Performance management involves capturing and analyzing information on such things as call traffic, calling patterns, and performance statistics on private line circuits. The carrier-based services allow a customer to schedule traffic reports, which enables the customer to anticipate trends and identify potential problems before they affect network services.

Accounting Management

Both MCI and AT&T provide a range of call detail and billing information that can be structured to support a variety of customer requirements for the management of a large software defined network. Call detail and traffic billing information can be delivered in many forms such as magnetic tape or printed reports. In addition, it is also possible for users to access traffic detail via their own terminals and to structure custom reports suited to their needs. There are also special services that allow the customer to control their own users' access to the network through the assignment of access codes for information that can be retrieved for customer-controlled reporting.

Network Planning

The network carriers also provide planning assistance for network improvement and enhanced design concepts, including line and capacity sizing for access to their network services. AT&T, for example, has special network software design tools called E-INOS that allow the customer to model various network functions as a means of designing and restructuring his or her network to meet changing network traffic requirements.

CUSTOMIZED NETWORK MANAGEMENT SERVICES

Customized network management services are available from a number of equipment manufacturers. There are physical network management services that support the user in the end-to-end management of all physical links within a data network and, in some cases, also support physical monitoring of voice circuits. Originally these services were provided by modem equipment manufacturers to support the off-hours monitoring of data circuits that use their smart modem equipment. These services augment the customer's regular network monitoring so that the customer might have his or her network monitored during third-shift operations and weekends when normal network operations staff are not present.

The major manufacturers of modem and multiplexer equipment have redefined their network management services in recent years to support outsourcing requirements. Major providers of these services include AT&T Paradyne, CODEX, General DataComm, Infotron, and Timeplex. Their services provide for network monitoring, diagnosing network problems, restoring network outages, maintaining network management system files and records and outsourced support.

One of the most critical areas for many network managers has been the ready supply of network operations and control personnel. Many services providers can now offer a pool of well-trained expertise for network backup both at the local and network level. Through the ready availability of trained network professionals, these providers can place experienced personnel on a customer's network to assist in the monitoring and diagnosis of customer network problems. The focus of these services goes beyond the simple identification of faults. Vendor-supplied support specialists are equipped with the tools to accurately diagnose and troubleshoot equipment and line problems. It is through these comprehensive network management tools that the vendor-supplied support personnel are able to dispatch the proper vendor to service the right problem. Armed with an accurate diagnosis, equipment or service vendors are able to deploy resources to resolve problems at a remote location with a minimum of network downtime. This focus on identification of problems with an accurate fix ensures

that the customer's network will be functioning at full design capacity.

Basic Services

In choosing an umbrella network management service from a vendor, the first thing to evaluate is the basic services provided by the vendor, such as:

- *Automatic trouble reporting*—When a failure is detected on the customer's network, an alarm is forwarded to a central network support center, where an assigned specialist who has been trained on the customer's network then dials into the customer's network to diagnose the alarm condition. The alarm condition is then reported and recovery action is taken.
- *Fault isolation*—The specialist who is responsible for a customer's network can diagnose a customer's alarm condition and determine action that should be taken to resolve an alarm condition. The central network support center should maintain an array of diagnostic tools that allow the specialist to conduct a thorough analysis of the user's problems.
- *No-fault support*—The service vendor should absorb any dispatch charges that may be incurred by the user that were the result of a misdiagnosis, causing the dispatch of a field engineer to resolve a customer's network problem.
- *Repair verification*—The vendor should assume responsibility for following up on all repairs that have been made as the result of a service call, verifying that any assigned work is properly completed in a timely manner. As a problem has been cleared, the vendor should call the customer's contact and advise the customer of all completed work.
- *Customer control features*—As part of a network service agreement, the vendor should provide proper network control and escalation procedures to be followed by the assigned support specialists. With this arrangement the customer is able to define the level and degree of

support that will be required to keep the customer's network under control. With such an arrangement the customer can retain the level of control with which he or she feels comfortable.

- *User network database*—The network service vendor should also maintain the customer's network information, at least as an optional service. This can include network profiles, site inventories, service vendor information, as well as service histories. Through this service a network manager is able to maintain an accurate network inventory without having to maintain personnel to support such a service in-house.
- *Management reporting*—There should be reports that summarize network performance data, allowing the customer to track network performance over time.

Additional Service Offerings

The following are added levels of network management support that are available:

- *Network planning and consultation*—This service includes assistance with network configuration and design, network performance evaluation, standards development, development of help desk procedures, and training program development.
- *Project management and implementation support*—Professional assistance with the implementation of any new network design or network enhancement usually consists of the vendor providing a

project manager to assist the customer in scheduling, ordering, coordinating, and implementing any new equipment and network facility arrangements. This service is particularly valuable where there are multiple vendors involved and the customer may not have the skills available internally to provide the needed expertise.

- *On-site service support*—An on-site specialist may serve as the customer's authorized agent and coordinate the activities of several service vendors to include both equipment and carrier facility providers to see that vendor service personnel perform their services in a timely manner.
- *Virtual console support*—Some services offer a form of dedicated support where an assigned network specialist has a network management system console on which the specialist can remotely detect and isolate potential problems before they can affect the customer's network.
- *Contingency equipment services*—Many vendors offer a disaster recovery service for their customers' central site, node locations, and end-user sites. This service provides for the prepositioning of spare data communications equipment stored at a vendor location that can be shipped to a customer's location in the event of a problem. The equipment inventory is usually limited to that which is manufactured, sold, or maintained by the vendor. Equipment shipments are usually made within twenty-four hours of a disaster declaration.

DATABASE MANAGEMENT SYSTEMS

Steve Shoaf, FHP, Inc.

To the businessperson the term *database* is used to describe all of the information stored in a company's computers. This is a typical and correct business view of all the information that is stored and/or managed by a computer system. To a data processing professional the term *database* has an entirely different meaning. To this person, a database is an organization of data managed by a part of a computer's operating system. The part of the computer's operating system that manages databases is called the database management system (DBMS).

Before database management systems existed, and currently, when computers do not use a DBMS, computer systems organized business data into files. Each file contains smaller groups of data called records. The object of the work being performed in the computer for business processing is focused on these records, which may represent customer information, sales information, or data about the products a company sells. Each piece of datum is related to other data within the company—for example, sales records are related to product data, which are related to the parts or component data, and so on. As the business grows, more and more complexities and interdependencies are created. Since data are organized into records for processing by the computer, a complex relationship evolves between the computer files, records, and systems. Born out of this complexity and interde-

pendency is a need for an automated process within the computer to manage the hundreds, even thousands, of different types of records and data/information in the computer system. Database management systems provide a solution to this processing requirement.

COMPUTER SYSTEM ARCHITECTURE

If we view the computer system as if it were a multistory office building, the computer hardware would be on the first floor. The second floor would be where the operating system or main control system is located; this part of the system directs all activities of the system and responds to requests for service from both higher and lower floors (levels) in the building (computer). The third floor would, in many systems, particularly small systems such as personal computers (PCs), be where the business processing is performed. This level may be called the application level; this is where the business programs "run." The application program performs the business work on the data in the computer. When a DBMS is installed on a computer system, it occupies the third floor, or logical level, and business application programs are moved to the fourth floor (level) for data access. In some computer systems smaller than the mainframe but larger than PCs, known as minis, the DBMS may be a part of the main control system (operating system) of the computer. In either case, the database management system provides a greater degree of sophistication in the management of data and information than the typical file manager in most computer systems.

EVOLUTION OF THE DATABASE MANAGEMENT SYSTEM

The first database management systems were very computer oriented; the DBMS was designed to provide services only to application programs performing the tasks of order entry, payroll, accounts payable, manufacturing support, and accounts receivable. These early database systems were designed for speed of processing with little regard given to human needs. Indeed, when two of the most popular database management systems were developed, on-line computer processing through the use of terminals was not in widespread use.

In the years that followed, these large database management systems were being accessed by people within the business departments using terminals to perform on-line and real-time activities of storing and retrieving data. A requirement for greater access to data led to demands for user-friendly tools that the businessperson could use to retrieve, and even change, the data. Unfortunately the data were stored in such a way that people had a difficult time finding and retrieving information, and perhaps more importantly, the database management systems did not provide the means to allow for ad hoc searches of the database. Additionally, even when the early tools were created to allow users to perform these searches, users needed to know how to navigate through the maze of "pointers" that these systems used to store and retrieve information. This eventually led to the development of user-friendly database management systems; these database systems try to bridge the gap between the most efficient way of processing data in the computer and the most efficient and understandable way for people to use the data.

SERVICES PROVIDED BY DATABASE MANAGEMENT SYSTEMS

A DBMS is designed to handle many different types of requests for service. The system must be able to accommodate access to the data and provide for their security, integrity, and recovery in case of system failure. When application systems are designed to be supported by a DBMS, the services provided reduce or eliminate some of the programming effort. Additionally, the DBMS provides data services in a consistent and predictable manner, thus reducing the need for separately developed programs to provide data integrity, security, and business rule enforcement.

When an existing business process is elected to be automated using the computer it becomes clear that the business rules must be enforced in the automated system in the same or to a greater degree as they are using the existing manual procedures. These rules then become processing constraints with which the application system must conform. In non-DBMS applications, each program that performs data maintenance operations (adding customer account records, order entry, and a host of other business processes) must have the business processing rules written into each program. This creates redundant efforts during development and results in higher maintenance costs. The design of the database and the DBMS should enforce the business rules systemwide and independent of application processing method, whether it be batch, on-line, or ad hoc reporting.

Multiple User Support

Many business application systems are used simultaneously by many people in the company (order entry clerks, accountants, manufacturing personnel) who will be performing insert, delete, and change operations to the data. A DBMS ensures the integrity of the data by prohibiting two or more users from changing the same data at the same time. If a database system were not used to control this concurrent access, each program would have to include logic to participate in a design scheme that requires all programs to follow.

This is a significant application development expense and, if control of this type is managed by application programs, the capability for system integrity is reduced.

Data Recovery

One of the more disastrous situations a business could experience is to have its data become inaccessible due to some hardware or system failure. A single storage disk failure could destroy all of a business's critical data, causing severe financial loss and legal liability. Data must be recovered and the recovery process must maintain the integrity of the data, including the content of the data and the relationships between the data. If a non-DBMS-supported application system were used, additional development and maintenance expenses would be incurred to provide these complex functions. Additionally, the time required to recover the data could take much longer and be prone to error when performed using non-DBMS methods. The DBMS system provides controls and programs to perform data recovery operations for all disaster and recovery scenarios.

Information Security

Within every business there are data and information that are considered proprietary or confidential, possibly including trade secret information and other strategic or tactical data such as sales figures or product specifications. The need to protect data from willful or accidental destruction requires that the function of access security be included in system design. If an application does not use a DBMS, this complex function has to be written into each program, increasing development and maintenance expenses and reducing the integrity of the security controls.

Database systems can create "views" of the data that restrict access to an "instance" of information or individual data item. For example, employee salary amounts should be displayed only to authorized company personnel, which would likely be the payroll department staff. The database management system can distinguish one user from all others and allow only a manager to retrieve salary information while other users may only view employee demographic data.

DATABASE ARCHITECTURES

There are essentially three data architectures used by all database management systems. A data architecture is an arrangement of the data into structures that represent how the data are organized and placed in the computer, whether it is a mainframe or a PC. The common thread through each of the designs is that a system of storing and locating the data is built into the database management system. Thus, a DBMS is designed around a specific data structure. The data structure used determines, in a large way, the method of using the DBMS to solve business problems and how an end user accesses data.

A DBMS defines data structures, which are a logical and physical organization of data. These structures are described in terms of relationships. These relationships are one-to-one (1:1), one-to-many (1:M), and many-to-many (M:M). The relationships of 1:1, 1:M, and M:M can occur at the data instance level as well as at the record level.

An important rule toward defining these data relationships is to follow whatever the business rule is for the data during the conduct of business. For example, if a business assigns only one account number to a customer, then this represents a one-to-one relationship between a customer account number and the customer. If a customer is allowed to make any number of orders, then this would be a one-to-many relationship between the customer number and an order (or perhaps an order number). An example of a many-to-many data relationship could be found in a product to part description: A product may have many parts and a part could be in many products. The three data relationship descriptions are handled within all database management systems, but they are implemented in basically three distinctly different ways.

The three basic methods used by database management systems to store and retrieve data in computers are hierarchical, network, and relational. The first two methods use an internal method called pointers to direct the computer to a piece of data in the computer's memory. The relational method was developed to use the data themselves to find the related data/information to the request, or query for data/information. Typically, a relational database management system (RDBMS) is designed to support the end user or the MIS client's needs for information. An RDBMS can also be used for transaction processing systems.

Hierarchical Databases

The term *hierarchical* refers to the organization of the data within a business application or system. Data records in hierarchical databases are described as being either a parent or a child. These notations describe an owner and an owned record. The database management system enforces this rule through internal methods (pointers). This organization of data becomes an operational condition when the system is storing or retrieving data. The overall guiding rule in this type of data organization is that no one record may have more than one parent. Conversely, any one parent may have more than one child. The maximum number of records owned as children by one parent depends on which DBMS is being used. Generally, a mainframe DBMS has higher limits than one found on PCs.

In hierarchical systems the path to the data is always from the top of the hierarchy to the lowest level, meaning that whenever a lower-level record is required the computer must first access all the records in between before retrieving the desired record. This requirement can lead to excessive processing overhead for even small data needs. The navigation overhead is an important consideration when designing computer systems that utilize a hierarchical database management system.

Network Databases

The network database architecture is essentially the same as a hierarchical database design with one very important distinction: In network data structures, any record may have more than one owner. Data record relationships are manifested by describing what are known as set relationships. Thus, the term *network* is used to describe the relationships that are the result of creating linkage, or sets, between many types of records. In a network database the pathways are still predefined, but the access to a specific record is not through just one way—from top to bottom—as is the case in hierarchical systems.

Because each record can have more than one owner, each owner can act as the entry point into the data structure. This allows a greater amount of flexibility in the design of application systems when confronted with performance and business problems. It also greatly complicates the navigational aspect of storing and retrieving data.

Network database systems tend to conform to an industry standard that defines the rules by which database management systems should work. One such standard that network systems employ are insertion and deletion rules. These are rules that govern the operation of the database management system for the data that are defined to it. These rules can be used to enforce the procedures that govern how the business manages its data without regard to a specific program's processing. An example of this capability would be that an invoice cannot be created in the database unless a customer record exists, or an invoice cannot be deleted until payment has been received. This kind of capability of the database management system is an increase of sophistication in computer automation, and provides for a centralized method of control—that is, the DBMS controls when and how records are added or removed from the system and not the application program. This capability is significant in large systems where there are hundreds of programs that use the information stored in the company's database.

Relational Database Systems

The relational database structure has changed the face of database management systems more than any other factor. The implementation of the relational model results in a fundamental change in the way the data are viewed by programs and end users. Essentially, relational systems provide a view of the data in the form of a table. A common analogy is the way the information in a phone book appears to someone searching for a number: The data are organized in columns and rows.

The most significant aspect of a relational database management system is that internal pointers are not used by the database management system to locate related data. Recall that in the network or hierarchical systems the path to the data was created with internal, unseen, and predefined pointers. This led to the requirement that if anyone wanted access to the data, they had to know how to navigate through all the pointers to get to the data. In relational systems a mathematical model is used to tell the computer where to store and retrieve data. The model is a set of algebraic algorithms that define the relations between sets of data. Relational algebra, which is the basis for the relational data structure, is concerned with the identification of a numeric instance in a set of numbers.

When applied to data stored in a computer, the model is the method used to find data that are related to another instance of data. The relationship is predefined only in terms of the data and not through an arbitrary pointer system. The most powerful aspect of this fact is that greater flexibility in data design occurs because there are no artificial constraints on data design imposed by a DBMS pointer system. In relational DBMS systems, when the database designer knows how the business uses data, the data relationships become the design of the database structure. Using this capability, application programming becomes less a computer technical role and more a role that is concerned with how business is conducted.

DATA REPOSITORIES

Perhaps the most significant change that has occurred in data processing has been the emergence of data repositories that contain information about how the business is performing. This information may come from a variety of sources in the business, but primarily it comes from the application systems performing the day-to-day business transaction processing. These systems create a wealth of information about the performance or profitability of the company. Data repositories have been in existence for some time, but their use was not widespread until the introduction of relational database systems. These information databases are accessed directly by the endusers in the business to find answers to business problems.

Enterprise Modeling

The design of a data repository is dependent on a precise definition of business data relationships. When business decisions become dependent on the information in the repository it is very critical to correctly represent business activity that comes from the operational areas of the business. This can be accomplished by performing enterprise modeling—that is, the process of defining in a data dictionary, and subsequently in the data repository, using a DBMS, all of the aspects of the business data or information relationships.

When this enterprise modeling occurs it becomes clear that the business makes extensive use of shared data. These data are found in all the business transaction systems and must conform to a company-wide standard. They can be as simple as product and customer codes, or can be specific business codes that have intrinsic meaning to the business. The implementation of a data repository creates a need for greater consistency in how data elements are defined in the company.

The use of departmental computers—especially personal computers—has increased the complexity of enforcing common data definitions throughout the company. Data repositories can solve this problem by allowing access to the common business data shared across the enterprise, which means the business can control the data definitions and still allow departmental processing and reporting to occur.

End-User Reporting

Businesspeople have long understood that if only they could get their hands on the data they could produce their own reports. It is not uncommon to see managers using the standard reports that come from the transaction processing systems as source material to be entered into PCs where new reports can be generated. This rekeying of data is costly and prone to error, but to many departments in a company it is preferable to waiting for the MIS department to respond to requests for a new report.

The more precisely the company wants to know about the state of its business, the more reporting is required to provide the information. This has led to the backlog that occurs in many MIS departments. Backlogs and the continuing need for business information have given rise to increased direct access to the data and the development of end-user tools to perform end-user reporting. By using an RDBMS and the tools supplied with it, managers in business units use the information in a repository to solve a number of business questions that could not have been answered using a single instance of data.

When users have access to information in a repository that tells them how the business is being conducted, they can run analytic models on their personal computers to make decisions to improve profitability and reduce losses. These systems are sometimes referred to as decision support systems (DSS) because they provide an information base from which business decisions are made.

CONCLUSION

The method used to organize data and information in a computer system is dependent on the intended use. Hierarchical and network database systems are efficient for business systems that perform thousands or millions of transactions per day. These database systems provide predefined pathways to data locations along with definitions of data relationships. The predefined paths eliminate the need for repetitive decisions about the intended use of the data by the computer for a business transaction. Conversely, these systems are not well suited to access by people. When people need access to data, the data are generally used to support a business decision-making process. Information may be needed in a completely different way than was intended in the design of a database supporting a transaction processing system, and processing frequently is performed in ways that cannot be anticipated at all. These requirements are best managed by a relational database management system where entry points are not predefined. The relational database system allows the business professional to define the data relationship within the context of the business need.

The use of database management systems in the business world is becoming more and more widespread. By providing a global view of the data/information needed to run a business, combined with capability to manage the most used and least used data equally, database systems help to make computers more responsive to human needs. The use of relational systems, with their capability of bridging the gap between human needs and a computer's technical requirements, will speed the evolution of greater management of business data within an organization.

THE DATA PROCESSING CENTER

Stanley J. Ostaszewski, Unisys Corporation

Picture a huge factory with all sorts of raw material going in one end and a variety of products coming out the other. In addition, picture a number of roads going to a variety of customers who use the finished products to enhance the quality of their lives. That same picture could hold true for the information processing done in almost any organization. Bits and pieces of data come into the information processing "factory"; useful information is produced from this set of "raw materials" and then distributed throughout the company and beyond to help people make better decisions in their day-to-day activities.

It takes all sorts of people and a number of different disciplines to run a huge factory; the same holds true for the "information factory." We focus on the data processing center, which is the production portion of the factory, the line that produces and distributes the product and makes sure the product is properly produced, is on time, and is delivered to the correct person or group.

There are a variety of ways to describe what happens to information as it goes through the "information factory." The process is simplified into six stages:

- *Stage 1*—idea for a new or different use of information; typically in the form of a report. This can be either in paper or electronic form.
- *Stage 2*—defining and refining what is really required by the final customer (end user) and deciding whether there is a business justification to proceed.
- *Stage 3*—setting up the database and coding the program(s) to produce what is defined in stage 2.
- *Stage 4*—testing and retesting the database and program(s) produced in stage 3.
- *Stage 5*—establishing and maintaining the environment and running the program(s) to produce the desired output and deliver that output to the desired customer(s).
- *Stage 6*—maintaining and enhancing the database and program(s) to meet ongoing business changes and requirements.

The data processing center is the production line where the information product is manufactured day in and day out. The engineers may produce all the specs for the product and the machine to produce the product (analysts and programmers in data processing). When that is done, the creation of an environment that produces the information product to certain standards and on time is the responsibility of the production personnel (the data processing center's personnel). In many instances, the data processing center's personnel are also responsible for the transportation of that output to the customer (end user).

ELEMENTS

Many people characterize a data processing center by its physical characteristics, such as its total floor space or where it is located. These characteristics are secondary to the key elements of a data processing center: its personnel, assets, and customers.

Personnel

Just as in any other area of the enterprise, the most critical component of the data processing center is good people. The personnel can consist of a host of skilled people: data input clerical personnel, computer operators, data communications and database specialists, environmental software specialists, security specialists, disaster recovery specialists, and hot-line personnel. These personnel can work with the mainframe only or support all computers in the organization.

Experienced data processing personnel tend to focus on maintaining an error-free and secure environment. Internal disasters include computer outages, and inadvertent purging of current production files, untested databases, or programs. External disasters include electrical outages, fire, and floods. The more disasters experienced by the department, the more conservative the personnel are likely to be.

Assets

How does the data processing center accomplish its work? Most environments have three major categories of assets:

1. *Hardware*—includes the machines that transform raw data into information.
2. *System software*—controls the hardware operation and allows application programs to run on the hardware.
3. *Network*—provides the transport mechanism by which information is sent to end users.

Customers

When mainframe was king, the data processing center had one set of customers: the end users in the enterprise they serviced with reports, screen outputs, or forms. To a lesser degree, they serviced the "development environment,"—that is, analysts and programmers developing new programs or enhancing others.

In today's dispersed and integrated environment, the data processing center, in addition to serving the needs of the two groups mentioned above, might have to service personnel in the supplier or customer enterprises. With the expansion of dispersed and end-user computing, the data processing center might also have to provide support to a host of departmental or personal systems.

FUNCTIONS

The data processing center's major service is the production of information required for the day-to-day running of the enterprise. Depending on its charter, other services might include capacity planning (making sure there is enough power to run what the company needs in the time that it needs it); security and backup; disaster recovery; the maintenance of the network both internal and external to the enterprise; a hot line for departmental and personal systems; maintenance of standards for data and programming; testing and test bed requirements (ensuring that data and programs work before putting them into production); system development life cycle management (properly managing the maintenance dollar expenditures, getting rid of worn-out programs); repository management (making sure elements and subassemblies of data are called the same, mean the same, and are structured the same).

Daily Production

The day-in, day-out running of production is the mainstay of the data processing center. It truly processes data. Figures vary but the cost of developing solutions compared to that of continuously running them can be in the ratio of 1:7. Over the years, for every dollar a company spends in developing an information solution, it will spend seven in producing that information day in and day out.

In many companies the data processing center does not get a chance to voice its concerns in the design stage of a new application system. There may exist significant benefit in doing so if the cost of ongoing production runs and maintenance can be reduced by allowing the data processing center to fine-tune the product from the design stage onward. As is done in every other part of the enterprise, cost and possible delay of these fine-tuning suggestions must be weighed against anticipated future benefits.

Capacity Planning

For a data processing center to adequately plan for the future it must have an idea of the demands that will be placed on it. In today's on-line, real-time access it is not a trivial exercise to forecast how and when the data processing center's computing power will be utilized. Capacity must be geared to handle peaks. Depending on the accuracy required in capacity planning, the complexity of the processing environment, and the scope of the planning (mainframe, peripherals, network), capacity planning can be a fairly complex and costly exercise.

Another factor in handling capacity accurately is service-level objectives. A service-level objective is how fast a customer needs the data combined with a tolerable level of misses. An example of a service-level objective would be, "All queries will be handled in ten seconds or less 90 percent of the time."

The better the service, the more costly that service will be. A two-second response time will normally require more hardware and more sophisticated data communication equipment than a ten-second response time. A two-second response time 100 percent of the time (not one miss) will normally require more hardware and more sophisticated data communication equipment than a two-second response time 90 percent of the time.

When the customer (end user) and the data processing center come to an agreement on the service-level objectives, they should create a service-level agreement. This allows both sides to have objective criteria against which the data processing center's service to the customer can be measured.

Security and Backup

Most data processing centers adequately handle security and backup. This deals with keeping unauthorized personnel from accessing data and making sure that critical files can be reloaded and restored in the event of a loss of data.

The downsizing trend and distribution of data processing poses a problem in this area. As critical files proliferate throughout the organization, the ability to recover from loss of that data or prevent unauthorized use becomes more difficult to control. Where the data processing center enjoys a solid rapport and good communication with the end-user community, major disasters are normally avoided.

Disaster Recovery

Disaster recovery means being able to recover from a disaster that puts your current information production capacity out of commission. Many data processing centers do not have disaster recovery plans that are tested regularly and take into consideration all aspects of running the core business functions: the amount of terminals required for end users to input critical data; the links required to keep the production lines moving or the trucks being loaded or the orders taken properly.

Information is so pervasive in most companies today that just getting the computer and all its attendant environmental and application software up and running is not enough. The entire aspect of getting the required information into the data processing center and distributing it properly must be considered. A plan to allow the "essentials" of information production to carry on must be developed.

Network and Infrastructure Maintenance

The maintenance of the network is similar to maintaining the infrastructure of a town—that is, the roads, sewer system, electrical system, and so forth. This infrastructure expense is sometimes hard to justify in terms of cost. The data processing center, however, does not do justice to its basic charter if it does not explain the consequences of neglecting this infrastructure. Many CEOs and presidents of smaller companies are really not informed of the exposure they have in using outmoded networks or what the implications of business expansion will have on the current network capacity to deliver critical information.

Help Line Support

Typically the data processing center is the first line of defense for helping the customers get through their difficulties on the departmental or personal computing systems. Systems proliferate in departments with relatively little document support, minimal attention paid to backing up critical files, and inadequate support of the packages that run off the systems. When either programs do not run or a disk drive with significant data cannot be recovered, the data processing center typically gets the first SOS call.

Standards Administration

Setting standards for data and programs may be one of the most advantageous areas for reduced cost that the data processing center can exercise. Since the 1950s, systems have grown up with relatively little standardization: The same elements may have a different meaning in the financial system as opposed to the manufacturing system; two different elements may be named the same across these same systems, or elements that are the same and named the same may be formatted differently.

Costs of maintaining the environment and adding new features can be substantially reduced when the same element is named the same, has the same meaning, and is structured the same throughout the corporate enterprise. There is a significant amount of interest and investment in today's marketplace to provide the data processing center with tools and techniques to achieve standardization.

"LIGHTS-OUT" OPERATION

The whole data processing center operations culture built since the 1950s focuses on the discipline required to minimize mistakes and maximize the ability to return to processing quickly. Yet studies done by the Gartner Group and others indicate that nearly half of all errors in a data processing center are due to human errors. With more and more users connected on-line to the data processing center, even the shortest of downtimes is hard to tolerate. The solution for many data processing centers is to move to a "lights-out" environment. This requires having computer and network management tools such as disk management, security, tape management, and production job scheduling integrated in such a way that all data processing center functions can be performed from one location with little or no physical human interaction with the computers inside the data processing center.

By reducing the number of problems caused by human error, production processing times can be improved, there will be fewer reruns, and the overall quality of service increases. In addition, an automated data processing center generally requires fewer staff to operate it, thereby improving overall data processing center productivity. Whether or not a lights-out operation is warranted depends on evaluating the productivity and efficiency of the current data processing center operation, and then determining whether automation can reduce costs while increasing productivity and efficiency.

PUTTING IT ALL TOGETHER

The data processing center typically falls under the overall information systems (I/S) or information technology (I/T) budget. The entire I/S or I/T department should be dedicated to helping the enterprise achieve both its long-term and short-term objectives. There is much written today about having the I/S or I/T plan follow and support the business plan. The production of information to help the company achieve its mission should be the data processing center's prime objective. Practically, this eventually comes down to a project getting put into the annual plan or having a concerned employee do a little "skunkworks" project, demonstrate its benefits, and then make it part of the production process.

From a data processing point of view, there should be nothing in the long-term or short-term plan that does not have some tie to the objectives of the enterprise. Unjustified technical niceties, in this age of intense competition, are just unwarranted pieces of baggage. There should be a business benefit, whether that be hard or soft, to everything done by the data processing center.

There is a need for the data processing center's personnel to become more sensitive to what the enterprise is all about; to be able to articulate in business terms how the data processing center can help the enterprise achieve its objectives. Information is far too pervasive in the day-to-day running of the business for the data processing center to do anything less.

The data processing center must get close to its customers, work through new procedures and implementations with them, and learn with them. There must be an atmosphere of cooperation that allows both the end user and the data processing center to develop practical solutions for all concerned in the here and now, given current talent, budget, and experience levels of the personnel involved. The data processing center must help make the enterprise more competitive.

OUTSOURCING

Joseph Jackson, Crowley Maritime Corporation

WHAT IS OUTSOURCING?

Outsourcing means having an outside organization (vendor) supply a service. There are numerous examples of outsourcing in everyday life. Cities have hired companies to provide infrastructure services such as transportation, refuse collection, and fire protection. Many companies have turned to third parties to provide security, mail room, and janitorial services. In the context of data processing, outsourcing means that a third party assumes responsibility for the operation and management of one or more key functions, such as the data center or the corporate wide-area network.

Outsourcing involves a long-term investment in a relationship with a third party that should be mutually beneficial to both parties.

It is long term because most outsource vendors want to write a contract for five to ten years. It is mutually beneficial because the outsource vendor stands to make a profit, and the customer should save money, gain access to current technology at a lower cost, or both. One critical success factor in outsourcing is whether the vendor provides technological leadership and innovative information systems solutions that are of mutual benefit to both parties.

The idea of signing such a long-term agreement is a difficult one for many information systems executives to accept, especially when it represents a loss of control over the outsourced functions. Outsourcing is a big step for any company. Once a company gives over control of all or part of its organization to an outside entity, rebuilding—should the need ever arise—it is no simple task. Imagine hiring for difficult positions such as database administrator and network manager five to ten years from now, understanding what has happened to the job market in the last five years. Then think about the future cost of building a data center and relicensing all of the software. Thus, the concept of partnership is obvious and choosing an outsourcing partner is not a trivial task.

WHY CONSIDER OUTSOURCING?

There are six main forces that might drive an organization to consider outsourcing:

1. *Cost reduction/cost predictability*—The outsourcing organization, usually through economies of scale, may provide significant cost reductions, usually in the order of 10–15 percent. Anything less may not be worth the trouble. Outsourcing also provides a means for predicting future data processing costs.
2. *Minimizing business assets*—Many organizations, especially financial ones, take the position that noninterest-bearing assets such as buildings and computer hardware and software should be eliminated.
3. *Business focus*—Elimination of the on-premises data processing function allows the organization to focus on the core business and better utilize all company executives. Of the six reasons, this is usually the most compelling.
4. *Infusion of new technical know-how*—Outsourcing organizations can be a prime source of technological innovation. They have greater exposure to all aspects of data processing and have a wider breadth of experience from which to draw.
5. *Improving application inventory*—Because of different customer needs, outsourcing organizations have a large software inventory. Customers can gain access to software systems at a fraction of the cost usually required.

6. *Obtaining needed skills*—MIS organizations frequently do not hire people with needed skill sets because the need is not full-time, the cost is prohibitive, or the skills are not available. Outsource vendors can afford to overcome these barriers because of economies of scale.

WHAT TRIGGERS OUTSOURCING?

A good place to begin looking for the answer to this question is to answer other questions:

- What pressures are being placed on your company and the industry in which it operates?
- Are there global competitive considerations?
- How will budget constraints affect MIS now and in the future as your company reacts to its environment?
- How do financial markets affect your positioning for the future?

The answers to these questions can come from a management committee in conjunction with the strategic planning function of your company. This allows the company to use a variety of viewpoints in formulating answers.

Unfortunately, many outsourcing studies will be sparked by the wrong motivation. A senior executive will read an article about a firm that saved 30 percent of its data processing costs, or a senior executive will sit next to someone on an airplane who swears outsourcing is the best thing that ever happened to his company. The CEO may be visited by an outsourcing representative. Whatever happens to trigger the issue, the world of the unprepared MIS executive is guaranteed to change overnight.

PREPARATION VERSUS DAMAGE CONTROL

If MIS is not prepared to deal with the question of whether to outsource, then it faces a credibility challenge, and damage control at this point is suboptimal! But how to be prepared? First, understand the advantage from which the outsource operates organizationally. Based on economies of scale, outsource vendors aim for a 15-percent to 20-percent savings—anything less may not be optimal for either party. Then take a good hard look at the MIS budget.

In general, the MIS budget is 40-percent technology—that is, hardware, software, and network—20-percent application development, and 40-percent utility—that is, all the rest of the operations and support functions. Determining the actual breakdown for a company's MIS function is the first step in preparing for the outsourcing debate. Examine the numbers closely. These percentages are just guidelines, and an MIS organization may fall out of line by a considerable amount for very valid reasons.

Look very hard at the technology numbers first. Is the company being well served by the capital invested in its hardware, software, and networks? Are the maintenance contracts reasonable? When was the last time they were reviewed? Is there a lot of underutilized equipment—for example a 3800 printer barely printing one million pages a month?

There is money to be saved on technology in almost every MIS organization, and outsource vendors are very good at figuring out where. Figure out where these weak areas are in your organization and why they exist. The better the weaknesses are known and understood, the more intelligent and informed the debate on outsourcing will be.

Next look at the utility, focusing especially on job descriptions, talent level, and functions performed. This is where the outsource vendor really has the advantage—economies of scale that are almost unbeatable. The opportunities found here will be the most difficult to deal with since they involve people issues and jobs that may not be of strategic importance to the MIS organization. Next try to project MIS staff growth for five, seven, and ten years, complete with estimated personnel count and every direct and indirect dollar that can be imagined. Do not forget raises, bonuses, increased software maintenance costs, and disaster recovery expenditures.

Finally, develop a vision for the future.

Where is the MIS organization going to take the company over the next five, seven, or ten years? The outsource vendor will have a great deal to say about this, and it will be convincing. Most organizations have determined that it is not worth the trouble to outsource applications development, and very little money can be saved here. Accordingly, application development is not part of this outsourcing discussion.

When MIS management completes this budget and future analyses, it has done most of what an outsource vendor would do in preparation for a formal bid. MIS management will also have a different view of its organization and how it functions—and a clearer picture of its mission. But most important of all, it will have identified the areas that will help make the organization leaner and meaner, and hence a more valuable asset to the company. Now, an informed outsourcing decision can be made.

PLANNING FOR OUTSOURCING

If the decision is made in favor of outsourcing, there is a lot of work yet to be done. Outsourcing firms provide shell plans that include the information that they require and the activities that they undertake in starting an outsourcing relationship. MIS management, however, should have its own plan that includes all the steps needed to be done and all the hard questions needed to be answered. Here are a few items to help get started. Answers to some of the questions may uncover some show-stopper and save everyone a lot of work:

- Make a list of the potential providers and keep it private. Do not share this decision with too many people at this stage. Premature disclosure at this stage may result in unwanted staff turnover.
- Prepare projected growth figures in a format easily understood by someone not familiar with your company. The outsource will need all of this information.

- Decide what areas of the process to retain. Most organizations ultimately decide they do not want to give up control over their technical and systems architectures. Remember the data center: Will the space be reclaimed for other use and has this cost been included in the financial analysis? Are there any functions or assets that must be retained?
- Are there any issues that may cause an impasse with an outsource vendor? An example might be retaining control of the network, but making the provider responsible for network response time.
- What are all the resources needed to negotiate a contract? Will outside counsel be needed? Remember issues during negotiations like software licenses, growth factors, future costs, changes in technology, performance, and security of company data.
- How should costs be handled? Outsourcers can handle ramp-up pricing as well as the elimination of up-front costs. There are a lot of opportunities in this arena, and a few consultations with corporate finance will prove helpful.
- Is senior management ready to confront the reality of signing a multiyear contract for what may amount to a huge sum?
- How are the people issues going to be handled? Is MIS, human resources, and corporate management ready for these issues? Will the outsource be allowed to hire the people—understanding that this is not nearly as rosy as it sounds—or will there be layoffs, outplacement, or internal reassignment of people? Who will be retained? Top-quality staff will still be required during the outsourcing relationship.
- Are there activities that may cause costs to be higher than they are today? What about quality of service issues?
- Should an operational readiness study be performed and is it a good idea? The cost may be from $50,000 to $100,000.
- How will the company benefit? If the answer is not clear, there is probably a problem somewhere. The expected returns in cost savings or avoidance need to be specific, not sweeping generalities.
- How much control will the outsource vendor have over operations? Does leading-edge technology need to be addressed in the contract?

Think about current problems and how to articulate these issues to the provider. It is not as easy as it seems. If not done correctly the first time, there will be a lot more work downstream.

Finally, in making the case for outsourcing to corporate management, these points should be emphasized: potential financial savings; increasing complexity of systems and systems management; reallocation of company resources; costs to develop, train, and retrain skilled employees; recruiting costs; exploitation of current and future technologies.

DISASTER RECOVERY FOR INFORMATION SYSTEMS

Arthur Kurek, ALICOMP, Inc.

One way to explain disaster recovery is to examine a company of approximately one hundred employees working in a building in Manhattan. One morning they arrive for work to find police barricades surrounding the building and no one is allowed to enter. The precise cause of the blockade is not known, nor is the duration that they can expect to wait for building access. As company managers arrive at the building, they attempt to corral their personnel, keep them in one place, and attempt to give them as much information as they possibly can regarding what is preventing them from entering their offices.

Hours may go by before a city official, a power company representative, or an Environmental Protection Agency representative appears and advises management that the offices will not be accessible for at least the balance of the day, and that the prognosis for returning is unknown.

At this point, one of two things happens. The company may be ill-prepared to deal with the disruption and may be unable to resume business until it returns to its own facility. In this case, the company would be totally dysfunctional. If the damage to its building or offices is extensive, it will have to find new office space. This may take weeks or even months. The company may be so financially damaged that it will go bankrupt before new offices can be found.

On the other hand, if the company is prepared for this business disruption, then it would move to its contingency space. This space could be its own alternative site, which was prepared in the event of a disaster, a reciprocal partner, or the site of a third-party vendor to whom it subscribes for space, equipment, and/or other business recovery services. If the company has a contingency plan in place, it will probably move effectively off the street and into its contingency space. In this second scenario, the company could resume some critical business functions within hours of the disruption.

This illustration depicts two potential scenarios. The most common disasters are caused by flood, fire, power loss, sabotage, and environmental damage. *Disaster recovery* is the term used to describe the way a company goes from disaster to recovery.

The first companies that planned for and implemented disaster recovery operations were banks—partly due to regulatory pressure imposed by the comptroller of the currency and other regulatory agencies, and partly to be prudent with regard to continuity of services. Some banks began to look for ways to provide themselves with a mirror image data processing environment so they could quickly get critical systems back online. They needed to provide an environment for personnel, some more critical than others, so the computer could be functional. To accomplish this, banks left computers idle as backups to their main computers along with adjacent office space. As real estate costs soared in the 1970s, this option proved to be expensive. Some banks contracted with other banks to provide reciprocal backup arrangements.

At the same time, third-party vendors began to emerge offering duplicate computers, redundant computing capability, and physical space. Their customers are known as subscribers because they pay a subscription fee each month that gives them the right of access when a bona fide disaster declaration is made. It also gives them the right to test their recovery procedures and systems periodically, thus assuring the organization that its contingency plan is workable and comprehensive.

SERVICES DEVELOPED IN THE 1980s

During the 1980s, numerous third-party vendors made disaster recovery services available. Included in those services were hot-site subscriptions, that is, subscriptions to a fully functional computer facility; warm-site subscriptions, which are subscriptions to a computer room equipped with everything except the actual computer hardware; cold-site subscriptions, which provide for an empty computer room for a company to work with its own equipment and stay for a protracted period of time, assuming the worst-case disaster scenario such as a building fire, where the building is nearly or totally destroyed. Companies could buy subscriptions to one or a combination of these services, according to their specific requirements.

During the 1980s, many consulting companies emerged to provide businesses with various options and tools to plan for disaster contingencies. Companies did their disaster recovery plans working with vendors who brought their expertise into the process. Many banks and other institutions brought in dedicated staff members, like disaster recovery coordinators, to take charge of the planning group process and to provide leadership and direct disaster recovery operations.

During the 1980s, federal and state regulatory agencies became more demanding and required banks to test more frequently and to have those tests monitored by their auditing firms so that documented proof could be provided that a test was successfully completed. Reciprocal agreement for hot-site backup became impractical as banks typically do not keep adequate reserve capacity to act as disaster recovery centers.

In the late 1980s, other organizations began to see the value of disaster recovery hot-site subscriptions and planning. The scope of disaster recovery planning expanded into areas such as insurance, financial services, and law firms, as well as large manufacturing firms. Today, virtually every type of organization can be found among the over 3,000 companies who subscribe for hot-site services in the United States.

Other internal pressure, including increased dependence on both mainframe computers and distributed processing, made contingency planning and disaster recovery even more necessary, since theoretically one outage in one of many offices throughout the country could literally have the potential of bringing down an entire company's network. Furthermore, as more and more data were computerized, a company's ability to function without its computers became impossible.

CORPORATEWIDE EMPHASIS IN THE 1990s

In the 1990s, disaster recovery will focus on end-user recovery as well as more comprehensive data processing and telecommunications capability. The pressure on banks comes from the FDIC (Federal Deposit Insurance Corporation), which directed all FDIC institutions to implement contingency planning covering both front- and back-office operations. Other organizations have a heightened consciousness resulting from the disasters such as the earthquake that struck San Francisco, Hurricane Hugo in the southeastern states, and the substation fire that affected thousands of companies in the financial district of lower Manhattan.

Companies have begun to realize that if they were inoperable due to a disaster, their board of directors and officers could be directly sued for malfeasance, meaning that they would be personally liable for the ramifications of not being in a position to provide services to their clients. This has a large impact on law firms, which have the responsibility of being able to provide timely client documentation such as contracts and to litigate lawsuits, as well as impacting banks and security firms, which have the responsibility of investing client money on a timely and efficient basis. For example, it is estimated that some large banks' inability to clear funds at the end of a given day could cost the bank and its customers hundreds of millions of dollars. The corporate directors and/or officers can be held liable for that loss.

The 1990s will find more and more institutions putting together comprehensive and workable disaster recovery planning, buying third-party hot-site subscriptions to cover contingencies that would impair their own computers, and providing a comprehensive working environment for their critical office staff so that operations can be as close to normal as possible. More and more third-party hot-site companies are emerging and providing a vast array of new services to meet these growing demands. They include such items as shadowing, or electronic vaulting, as it is known, which allows companies to keep data current both at their own site and at their recovery facility. This way, at any given moment, should a disruption occur, that company would be able to switch to its backup site having the very latest data available and to continue operating without loss of time.

BUSINESS RECOVERY FACILITIES

A major trend is the availability of business recovery facilities in major cities such as New York, Boston, and Chicago. These facilities provide functional redundant office environment with high-speed connectivity to host or backup computers, thereby allowing large groups of end users, both back- and front-office types, to continue to function on behalf of the organization, in an environment that is conducive to them and is conveniently located. This allows for a more expeditious and successful recovery than having to move large groups of people far away from their normal offices, which especially becomes helpful in a long-term disaster situation.

TELECOMMUNICATIONS AND VOICE RECOVERY

Telecommunications disaster recovery has become more critical than in the past, as well as extremely complicated. Many organizations are tied together through one or more telecommunications networks. If a given satellite office loses its network, that in itself can be considered a disaster. Therefore, companies are beginning to plan network contingency backups, so in the event that a given network is lost, they have ways of redirecting data and voice around those damaged networks in order that the processing of information and voice recovery can resume with minimal interruption.

Voice recovery itself has also become a critical component of disaster recovery. For example, a company using a large quantity of "800" numbers for mail order or customer service must be prepared to use an alternative network should its main "800" numbers fail due to a telephone company disruption, be it long distance or a local company. Again, some companies work directly with their telephone companies and long-distance carriers to provide alternative networks for their voice-recovery purposes. Others, who find it more practical, will use third-party vendors who set up a large voice-recovery offering that allows the company to move its staff to the working voice-recovery facility. Through a series of preplanned switching, those "800" numbers will move over to the alternative site, thereby allowing companies who rely heavily on "800" service to immediately come back on-line and continue their business. One can imagine what type of monetary loss could be incurred by a large telemarketing organization if it were to lose its "800"-number capability for any extended period of time.

DEVELOPING A SUCCESSFUL RECOVERY PLAN

Planning is the key to the most successful recovery, regardless of whether a company uses a reciprocal arrangement, an alternative site, or a third-party hot-site/business recovery-facility. Planning can be complicated. Thus, there are new positions opening up in many institutions for professional disaster recovery coordinators. Some companies and banks employ a dozen or more of these types of people. A coordinator's major responsibility is to manage to put together a contingency plan that is comprehensive and workable. Many coordinators are also responsible for handling a company's disruption and making sure that everything about the recovery process works smoothly.

A recovery plan needs to incorporate many things. Examples include notifying vendors in advance of where the company would relocate should disaster strike; that way, certain checks, stationery, and forms could be made available as quickly as possible. Additionally, phone numbers that would be utilized in the alternative site can be given out in advance to key business contacts.

A business plan must also identify critical applications that would be top priorities in terms of resumption. The disaster recovery coordinators must find out the various levels of priorities for all functions, so all areas are covered by a backup. All departments should be included so a successful plan can be created.

For example, certain people who may not be related to the data processing environment may require PCs or certain types of special technology. Others in an organization might rely heavily on outside data feeds such as Reuters, Quotron, or Telerate. It is possible to redirect those services to an alternative site in the event of a business disruption if planned and tested in advance. Key members of the organization should be identified. Certain people may not be asked to come in to work during disaster mode until a certain point in time. Having all the employees' home phone numbers, therefore, is critical to the planning process. Disaster recovery coordinators rely heavily on managers in determining the requirements of each department. During disaster mode and testing, those managers are responsible for the actions of their employees.

CONCLUSION

Disaster recovery is no longer restricted to banks. Companies involved in disaster recovery include hospitals, utilities, distribution companies, transportation companies, universities, government, and manufacturing. Disaster recovery has proven to be a valuable tool, especially when a good plan is in place and when alternative space is ready. As businesses become more complicated, as networks become larger, as regulatory agencies, boards of directors, and outside auditors become more determined to guarantee business continuity, disaster recovery will continue to grow as a business function.

TRAINING FOR USERS AND MIS STAFF

Tony W. Salinger, Quality Director, AT&T Global Video Phone Systems

One of America's leading business philosophers and consultants speaks of global business as a world turned upside-down. Clearly, among the forces contributing to the dizzying pace of personal and professional life, technology stands out as a major cause. Add to technology global competition, the information explosion, changing business and political boundaries, and a new way of thinking about quality and service and managers have a challenge of unrivaled scope.

The manager as coach in these changing times has to link personal and organization training needs to the business strategy and vision. Analyzing training needs and spelling out what training is supposed to accomplish are key to getting the desired results from training. While there are many ways to deliver training in information systems, what matters most is that managers get what they need to fulfill their part in the firm's strategy.

As world-renowned speaker, author, and marketing consultant Chris Hegerty observes in *Sharing Ideas* (Dec. 1990/Jan. 1991):

> The world is getting even smaller —competition ever more ruthless. Being in business today is like "No Rule" baseball. Once the ball is hit, the opposing team can move the bases anywhere they wish. The future belongs to organizations and individuals committed to increasing competence.

Technology has become a major differentiator. The challenge as well as the risk for managers is that if they do not understand a promising technology, they do not invest in that technology, someone else will. The use of information technology for competitive advantage illustrates this risk. As Robert DeSio, vice-president for development and long-range planning for the National Technological University, writes in the *Training and Development Journal* (Feb. 1990):

> The ability to capitalize on, manage, and adapt technology in the strategic processes as well as the products of an enterprise is a new management need and challenge.

Not surprisingly, several industries are among the champions of newer information technologies. These include banking, insurance, airlines, manufacturing and process industries, common carriers, and mutual funds, to name a few. A survey of the professional literature and the hot topics at leading conferences illustrates the myriad of new technologies and uses: consumer database scoring models; cooperative processing; electronic data interchange (EDI); executive information systems (EIS); integrated voice-data applications; knowledge robots (expert system indexing and topic-searching applications); neural networks; object-oriented programming and databases; optical storage-based image processing.

Like the process of building a system, determining and filling training needs follows a structured process. Born from extensive experience in developing, testing, and implementing training programs, the systematic approach works! Exhibit 9-22 provides a straightforward approach to determining and satisfying training needs. Its major elements are:

- Tying individual and organization training to the firm's strategy—after all, if the work being done and the training required are not tied to the firm's strategy, then why do it?
- Analyzing training needs before reaching for somebody's "canned" training solution.
- Specifying what training should accomplish and what constraints must be observed before selecting a vendor and delivery medium.
- Intelligently select a training vendor to satisfy training objectives and to stay within constraints.
- Evaluating the training experience both on the spot and back on the job to ensure that the training received has met the training objectives.

Much, if not most, of contemporary managers' work is tied to the firm's vision and strategy. Today, the classical competitive forces model has been expanded to include: quality and service-based perception of customers; strategic pricing; information about customer-perceived value and contribution margins; new distribution channels; value-enhancing information provided by over 4,000 public access databases.

According to Dr. Edward Stohr, chairperson of the Information Systems Department at New York University's Stern School, 70–80 percent of the graduate business schools in the United States require a core course in information systems. Following is a list of the typical contents of a core MBA curriculum in information systems based on the MBA programs at the Stern School and Colorado State University:

- The systems approach.
- The strategic role of information systems.
- Micros, minis, and mainframes.
- Computer software.
- Database technology.
- Telecommunications, connectivity, and standards.
- Systems analysis and design.
- Systems development: methodologies, project management, and CASE tools.
- Decision support systems.
- Office automation.
- Expert systems.
- Security and control.
- Information resource management.

Note the parallel between the topics covered in the MBA programs and the contents of this section. Clearly, academics and administrators have voted that business students need grounding in these subjects.

After this broad introduction to information systems in the firm, the MBA in information systems can take major-related courses such as:

- Software development.
- Advanced systems analysis and design.
- Decision support systems.
- Communications-based systems.
- File and database management systems.
- Artificial intelligence: concepts and issues.
- Social consequences of information technology.
- Managing information processing resources.

Again, what works best is a needs-driven approach. Exhibit 9-23 provides a proven procedure for collecting, analyzing, and defining training needs before investing time and money. Before using this approach, pay particular attention to deciding how to gather information and evidence (step 3) and how to analyze, interpret, and "sanity check" the data. The key point is to clarify what skills and competence are needed and how those skills will increase the strategic focus of the people who will be trained.

There is internal instructor training, com-

Exhibit 9-22. How to Select Training

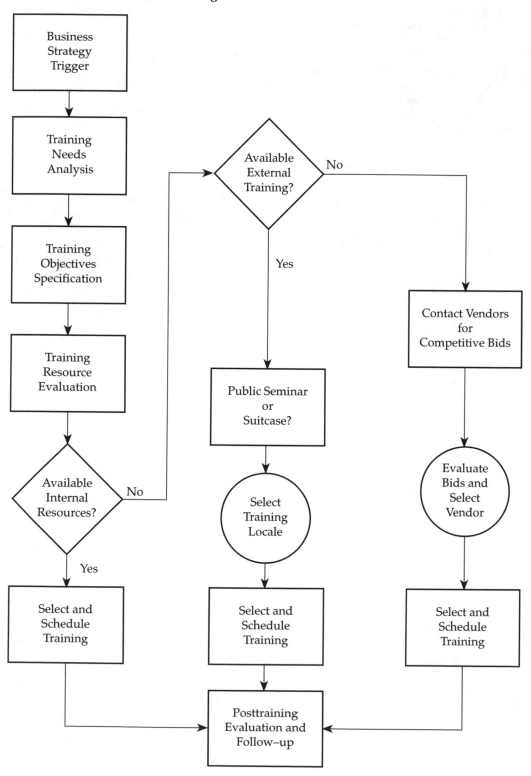

Exhibit 9-23. Basic Steps for Training Needs Analysis

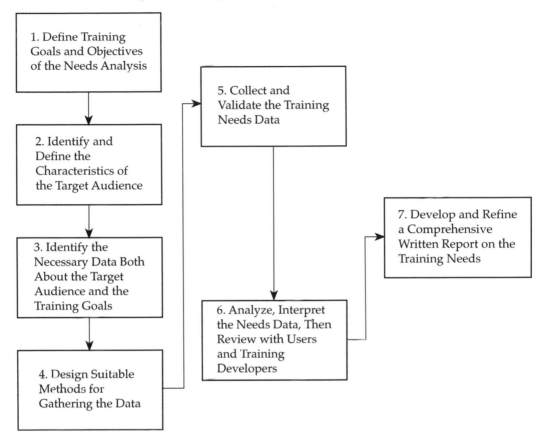

puter-based training, teletraining, thousands of external training vendors, conferences, seminars, and workshops. Each of these varies in cost, medium, approach, and effectiveness (both in general and in meeting specific needs). After having evaluated the availability of internal resources, the manager should follow the process shown in Exhibit 9-22; that is, do some comparison shopping among vendors and training products. The manager should avoid any conclusion that expensive training must be more effective. Consider that Jeff Salzman and Jim Calano built a $63-million-a-year business with CareerTrack® by offering quality training seminars for as low as $48 per person for a one-day program.

In-house training provided by leading ven-dors can range in price from $750 to over $3,000 per class day for an instructor and training materials. Typically these classes are limited to a maximum of around ten students. Classes offered at vendor facilities tend to average in the $200 to $300 range per person per class day, but corporate discounts are usually available that can bring this cost down to $150 per person per day—or even lower.

Local colleges, trade schools, and continuing education programs also are excellent sources of training. Classes may be offered on weekends and in the evenings, as well as during the day. College credit or continuing education units (CEUs) may be granted. Tuition costs can run as low as $25 for a single three-hour session.

SECURITY AND LEGAL ISSUES IN MIS

Jack Bologna, Associate Professor of Management, Siena Heights College

It may come as a surprise to some people that before computers were developed, we had laws: civil, criminal, and constitutional. We also had patent, copyright, trademark, and proprietary information laws. And there were contract and sales laws that governed the way we did business. There were even laws that governed the agency relationship (principal and agent), employer-employee relationship, lawyer-client relationship. Computers did not precede these laws, but early on, computers added a measure of uncertainty and doubt to these laws.

MAJOR LEGAL AND SECURITY ISSUES IN THE INFORMATION ERA

Unclear laws have a way of stimulating litigation and new legislation. For example, the traditional crimes of fraud, theft, and embezzlement had to be updated in the computer era because criminal statutes that are unclear or unspecific are of doubtful validity from a constitutional law standpoint. So we now have computer crime laws in practically every state, as well as several federal computer crime laws. Such laws, in addition to dealing with the crimes of fraud (deceit), theft (larceny), and embezzlement, make criminal

what we euphemistically call "hacking" or unauthorized access of computer and data communications networks, stealing computer time, and planting viruses. Unauthorized duplication of copyrighted software has also been made an illegal act.

Information technology, for all its benefits, has also created some social costs. For example, the sheer volume and easy access to personal information databases pose a threat to our constitutional right of privacy. The technology, as wonderful as it is, is far from foolproof. In sensitive applications like air traffic control, weapons systems, aircraft navigational controls, and nuclear energy plant operations, a system hardware or software failure can have disastrous consequences on human life and the environment. Then there is the problem of VDT (video display terminal)-related injuries like radiation, repetitive action injuries, and miscarriages.

Competition in the information technology industry is keen. On occasion, products are sent to the market before they have been thoroughly tested. Customers are then left to their own devices in installing their systems.

Privacy

Data are collected today by a myriad of private- and public-sector organizations for a wide variety of purposes. The U.S. government alone has gathered and stored four billion records on individuals. The development of database management software for personal computers has extended these capabilities to anyone with a few hundred dollars. While databases have grown explosively (4,000 worldwide; 900 database producers and 300 database distributors in the United States alone, with revenues of $6.2 billion in 1988 [U.S. Industrial Outlook, 1989]), controls over access and disclosure of confidential data have not kept pace. Unauthorized access to databases and disclosure of confidential information contained therein are commonplace. There are legal constraints on the improper collection and dissemination of personal data in the United States, embodied in the Constitution, Supreme Court decisions, tort law, and in federal and state privacy and consumer rights enactments. These laws and rulings are not sufficiently clear to reach consensus.

For example, what degrees of confidentiality should be accorded to such disparate data as medical, psychiatric, credit, employment, school, and criminal records? If medical records are considered the most confidential of the lot, the standard of care accorded such data would be higher; that is, medical records should be gathered, stored, and disseminated with great care and caution.

Piracy

Software piracy is an expression used to signify that the creative work of another has been used or duplicated without permission and/or payment of royalty. The definition assumes that the creator of the software has complied adequately with the legal requirements of the federal copyright law. The software pirate, therefore, commits an act of infringement and may be sued civilly for damages, criminally prosecuted, or both.

Software piracy is probably the most common breach of law in the field of information technology. For each software program sold, developers claim that another two to five copies are "bootlegged."

Safety

Computers and peripheral devices such as terminals and on-line PCs are driven by power sources that may cause humans to be exposed to radiation. High levels of such radiation may cause miscarriages and cancer. The intensive use of terminals and PCs may also bring on muscular-skeletal damage to the neck and shoulders, eye strain, and repetitive action injuries like carpal tunnel syndrome.

Manufacturers should, therefore, see to it that their products are designed and constructed in such a way as to avoid presenting unnecessary risks to users. Users should be made aware of the risks and should be accorded special considerations to ensure against physical harm.

Data Security

The protection of personal information from unauthorized access, disclosure, and duplication obligates a database owner to: formulate and enforce standards for the proper use of the data; communicate, educate, and train users with respect to their responsibility for protecting such information; plan for likely contingencies; establish adequate security controls; monitor control exceptions.

Data Integrity

An incorrectly entered arrest report, credit report, insurance rejection, debt default, or lab test can cause great emotional and financial damage. Yet the error rates of databases with such sensitive information are often higher than the standards set by the designers of these systems. Accuracy, timeliness, completeness, and relevance are what give information its value. Creators of personal history databases have, in particular, a special obligation to compile and process such data accurately and protect the data from the prying eyes of snoops, browsers, and hackers.

Competence

In the race to get new products out of the labs and into the market, compromises in quality, safety, and security are often made. New products, therefore, often contain design flaws, software errors (bugs and glitches), and other impediments to proper functioning. These impediments can be costly to uninformed and unsophisticated users. Accordingly, makers and providers of information technology products, both hardware and software, must take great care and caution in their work, so as to avoid damage or interruption of service to their users.

Honesty

Makers, sellers, dealers, distributors, and installers of information technology products, like all other businesspeople, must be honest in their dealings with one another. Representations must be truthful. Advertising should not be deceptive. Labeling should be accurate. Contract requirements should be fulfilled.

Loyalty

The information technology industry is large, complex, fast-changing, and highly competitive. Indeed, some information products (chips and PCs) have become commodities. So the relationship between buyers and sellers is changing from one in which mutual trust, confidence, and faith give way to arms-length transactions. Sellers attract buyers on the basis of price alone. The service-after-sale element gets forgotten.

These same industry dynamics have also changed the relationship of employers and employees. Loyalty is supposed to be a two-way street. But in today's competitive environment, some high-tech, high-talent employees are loyal only to their paycheck. Obligations, therefore, have become blurred between employers and employees, sellers and buyers, and manufacturers and suppliers.

DISASTER AND RECOVERY PLANNING

Disaster and recovery planning, as an issue in MIS security, deserves expanded treatment. The sequential functions of management are said to be (1) planning, (2) organizing, (3) directing, and (4) controlling. The basic purpose of planning, the first step in the management process, is to anticipate future outcomes on the basis of recurring phenomena and to scan the horizon for threats, risks, and opportuni-

ties by monitoring the trends or changes in needs, wants, demands, and desires of customers. The planning process is intended to guarantee organizational survival in a world of uncertainty. So planning is an effort to control what is controllable. For example, while we cannot control the weather, we can control how we respond to climatic conditions to guarantee survival.

Certainty versus Uncertainty

Yet, while planning is the design of a desired future, our knowledge of the future is not always certain. The degree of certainty we possess about the future then dictates the kind of planning we do. If our knowledge of the future is certain, our planning is done by commitment. If our knowledge is relatively uncertain, we plan by contingency. And if our knowledge of the future is highly uncertain, we do responsiveness planning. Some aspects of the future are virtually certain. For example:

- All things tend to wear out or become obsolete over time. So we set up reserves to replace them in the planning process.
- Every system is subject to random disorder, so we provide for continuous monitoring, self-correction, and validation in our designs.
- All new systems and products have a high initial rate of failure, so we provide backup and tandem support, testing, and debugging procedures.
- All measurements are approximations, so we state our conclusions with an allowance for error.

Some aspects of the future are relatively uncertain. For example, we cannot predict when any discrete event may occur (such as a machine malfunction), but we can determine its probability over time and its cost consequences if we do nothing to prevent it. (Here, preventive maintenance is a form of contingency planning.)

And some aspects of the future are highly uncertain, for example, when a natural disaster will occur and what its cost consequences are likely to be. Here, the effort should be directed to responsiveness planning. (How quickly can we respond to minimize the loss? How long will it take to fully recover? How and where do we operate in the interim?)

Computer operations can be disrupted by both acts of God (natural disasters) and human acts (hardware or software failures, inadvertent errors, and intentional actions such as sabotage and mischief). The objectives of disaster and recovery planning are (1) to ensure against the destruction of human, capital, and information resources (assets); and (2) to minimize the direct and consequential losses attributable to data processing time delays.

Many large organizations depend on data processing capabilities to an extent that even short-term delays in processing time create substantial financial losses and long-term delays can spell organizational ruin. The character of some unfavorable events can be truly catastrophic, such as wipeout of accounts receivable or order processing systems where no duplicate files are maintained and where data cannot be quickly reconstructed on a manual basis.

Strategy for Survival

If organizational survival is, in fact, at stake in a computer disaster, then full standby capability may be required. More and more firms are beginning to adopt that strategy for survival—some because they, in fact, cannot accept anything but very short-term delays in data processing.

Insurance can be purchased as a means for the replacement of capital assets destroyed in a disaster caused by an act of God and even many intentional human acts such as employee sabotage and malicious mischief. Guarding against unintentional human acts,

like incompetence, human error, and negligence, is much more difficult. While insurance is available for such events, the premiums are high and consequential losses are difficult to prove. The physical harm done to employees in the course of a natural- or human-caused disaster can also be insured against through workers' compensation and other forms of medical and liability insurance. But the incidental cost of their replacement (recruitment, selection, and training) is generally an uninsurable loss. And unless your policy includes an "extra expense" clause, you may not be covered for such incidental expenses as the cost of renting other facilities and equipment during the restoration period, or moving expenses, utility hookups, communications equipment, temporary construction, cleaning and maintenance, air conditioning, electrical supply and water for cooling computer equipment; "valuable papers" may also be excluded from loss unless provided for in the insurance contract.

Risk is the product of probability of occurrence of an unfavorable event during a given time period, multiplied by the severity of the impact, if the event does occur:

$$\text{Risk} = \text{Probability of Occurrence} \times \text{Severity of Impact}$$

Thus, the usual problem to be solved in disaster/recovery planning is the calculation of the approximate loss from time delays brought about by the occurrence of the above hazards, threats, and vulnerabilities. One method of solving the problem requires an assessment of the current level of security safeguards, controls, and countermeasures and the costs thereof against a worst-case scenario such as a total loss of computer capabilities.

MANAGING TRANSITIONS IN MIS

Norbert J. Kubilus, Vice-President and Chief Information Officer, BCM Engineers, Inc.

AN ORGANIZATIONAL STATE MODEL

Rapid advances in information technologies over the last decade have been the catalyst for change in business as well as in MIS. Corporate management's view of MIS is no longer that of just a data processing factory and information warehouse. Nearly nine out of every ten top executives see information systems as having a significant impact on the way that their companies will do business in the 1990s, and they believe that MIS holds the key to competitive advantage.

The new reality is that the existing MIS infrastructure must remain operational and productive while management builds a new MIS that is responsive to the business demands for it. Payrolls must be met, vendors must be paid, customers must be invoiced, orders must be filled, and inventories must be replenished. Today and into the next century, business unit and MIS managers have to concern themselves with managing MIS transitions in a planned and controlled manner.

Exhibit 9-24 illustrates the three states of an MIS organization undergoing change. The current MIS environment and the new MIS environment represent relatively stable operations. For example, the current MIS environment in a company may be a central IBM mainframe data center that provides on-line

video display terminal (VDT) access to applications and corporate databases. The new MIS environment may be a client/server architecture that includes distributed IBM PS/2 computers with local transaction databases linked through local-area network connections to a smaller IBM data center.

Moving from the current environment to the new occurs over a period of time during which MIS undergoes a transition state that bridges the current and the new. In the above example, this is the time its takes to distribute processing, applications, and data to the desktop from the central data center. MIS transitions can take anywhere from a few weeks, as in the case of installing a new software package, to a year or more, such as in a consolidation of MIS organizations following a merger or acquisition.

As illustrated in Exhibit 9-24, operating the current MIS environment requires most of its normal resources—such as people and operating budget—while MIS undertakes a transition. The transition itself has additional resources and expenses associated with its three phases—planning, implementation, and audit—with most of the resources being required during implementation. One certain way to doom an MIS transition to questionable results—and even failure—is to commit inadequate resources to the current environment and the transition state in hopes of maxi-

Exhibit 9-24. The Transition Model

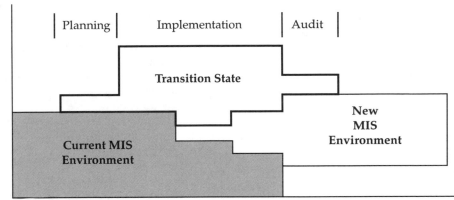

Resources

| Planning | Implementation | Audit |

Transition State

Current MIS Environment

New MIS Environment

Time

mizing the financial return from moving to the new environment.

PLANNING FOR A TRANSITION

Ensuring a successful MIS transition starts with naming a transition project manager who is responsible for planning and eventually managing the transition. A smooth transition requires coordinating and integrating activities related to changing hardware, software, networks, data, operating procedures, and people. These activities often cut across organizational lines. Planning, therefore, requires the transition manager to obtain the active participation and cooperation of staff who will be affected by the transition.

Transition Manager

Every successful MIS transition has a quarterback—the transition manager. The transition manager does not have to come from MIS provided that the person is linked appropriately to MIS—that is, the transition manager should be someone with whom MIS is comfortable, and the transition manager should report to the MIS executive on at least a heavy dotted line basis. A transition manager should be a full-time employee and not a contractor or consultant. Following is a represen-

tative list of responsibilities for a transition manager, according to the phases of a transition:

- Planning, scheduling, and controlling the transition project.
- Defining and creating the transitional organization.
- Creating and training transition teams/working groups.
- Assigning transition activities and tasks.
- Negotiating and coordinating with vendors and users.
- Overseeing testing and cutover activities.
- Monitoring transition progress and reporting to management.

Transition Plans

A transition manager starts the planning process by undertaking a requirements study and then developing a transition strategy. Together, these serve as the basis for the transition plan. A transition plan provides MIS and corporate management with an analysis of the current situation as well as the business rationale for the proposed transition in MIS, sets priorities for transition activities, documents the transition schedule and required resources, provides benchmarks against which progress can be measured and controlled, and establishes critical success factors.

Once management has approved the transition plan, more detailed implementation plans are required for each transition activity. Implementation plans for a data center automation project, for example, specifying the process, deliverables, and acceptance criteria for the hardware, software, and network changes; standards, documentation, and procedures changes; staff retraining, redeployment, and downsizing; application/systems cutover. It is important that the implementation plans be understandable to the members of the transition project team and also to the managers, users, and staffs that will be affected by the transition. An automated project management system is helpful for the scheduling of tasks and the allocating of resources—people, equipment, and supplies.

Transition Resources

The resources needed for a transition involve people and technology—and the funding required for them over the life of the transition. Project staffing can come from existing personnel in the current environment, new hires, temporary help, and consultants. When moving current staff onto a transition project, provision must be made for covering their existing job functions during the transition. Some job functions, especially in data center operations, may be handled with temporary agency staffing. Other positions may require high technical or professional skills that can be supplied by consulting firms.

The technology needed for a transition depends on the nature of the transition. In a project, to automate MIS operations, for example, most of the new technology will be data center automation and network management software with some additional equipment requirements. For a client/server implementation like the one described earlier, there is a significant investment in desktop computers, network servers, and local-area networks. An important but often overlooked adjunct to the technology resources required for a transition is the time and expense for training project, MIS, and user staffs on the new technology.

THE HUMAN FACTOR

MIS managers tend to focus on the technical resources that they understand and can therefore control such as hardware, software, networks, and facilities. The success or failure of an MIS transition, however, depends more on human resources than it does on technical resources. People problems tend to dominate MIS transitions.

Introducing new technology or a new way of operating in MIS will upset the stability or security of the systems, operations, and user staffs. Data center managers, for example, may fear a loss of power following decentralization or downsizing. Computer operators and control clerks who are comfortable with maintaining mainframe production schedules may be afraid of having to learn new jobs or skills due to data center automation.

There is a natural human resistance to change. When uncertainty or ambiguity about the future accompanies change, individuals—and even groups—will take action based on their perception of how the change will affect them. In extreme cases, everything possible will be done to sabotage an MIS transition. Overcoming this resistance to change requires early identification of dissatisfaction among staff members.

Planning how to announce an MIS transition is critical to its acceptance. Following is a checklist of what should be covered in communicating MIS changes to staff. Preparing this announcement and dealing with the staff issues caused by an MIS transition require the cooperation and joint efforts of MIS and human resources management:

- What is changing and the purpose for it.
- When the change will take place.
- Who is in charge of implementing the change.
- What the short-term impact on MIS will be.
- How any planned reductions in force will be handled.
- How information about the change will be disseminated.
- Who will answer questions and concerns for staff members.

IMPLEMENTING A TRANSITION

Managing the implementation depends on having a transition management structure and monitoring progress through maintaining an integrated project calendar, holding regular project review meetings, and issuing periodic project reports to management and key users.

Transition Management Structure

Involvement and communication are keys to any successful MIS transition, and how a transition project is organized is very important. The working group approach is one transition management structure that has met with considerable success. Working groups consist of MIS and user department representatives who are jointly responsible for specific transition activities and tasks. Each working group has a group (or team) leader who reports to the transition manager and is a member of the transition management team. Exhibit 9-25 shows the management structure for an MIS consolidation that followed the merger of two companies. In this case, working group leaders and members came from both premerger organizations.

During the implementation phase, working groups are responsible for completing their assigned tasks on schedule and within budget. Working group staffing will depend on the resources needed for the implementation tasks. Coordination of activities among working groups takes place through the working group leaders.

Maintaining Project Control

Progress against the transition and implementation plans should be tracked on a weekly or biweekly basis using the analysis features of the project management package used for planning the project. Periodic project review meetings provide valuable input from which to maintain the integrated project calendar. These meetings should involve the transition manager, working group leaders and members, and other interested parties as warranted—for example, vendors involved in the implementation, an internal electronic data processing (EDP) auditor, or a human resources representative. The purpose of these meetings is to identify and resolve problems, maintain a current understanding concerning action items and responsibilities, and ensure coordination of activities. Ideally, a problem with the implementation should never go undetected for more than a week, thereby allowing for timely corrective action.

On an agreed-upon schedule, progress reports should be given to management and key users. Reporting progress is not merely sharing copies of the project calendar analysis. Rather, a progress report should be a briefing on the key activities, their status,

Exhibit 9-25. Example of Transition Organization Following a Merger

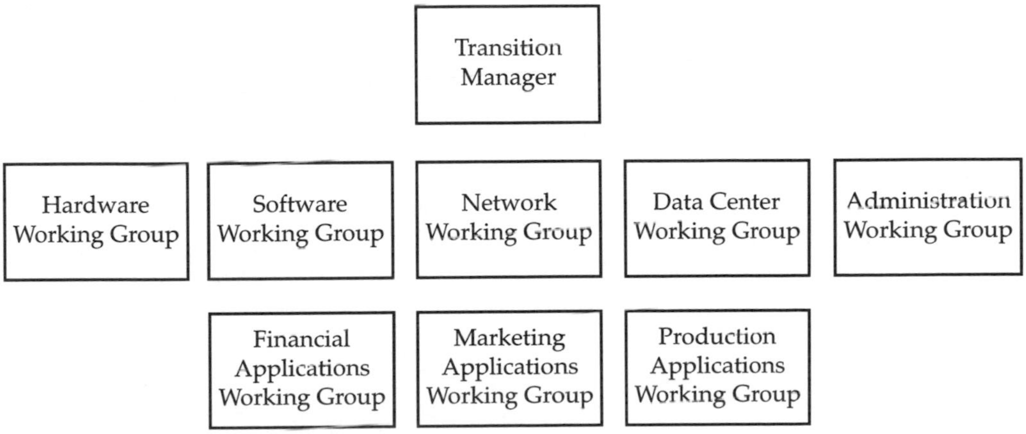

whether or not there are any problems, and what is required to keep the implementation on schedule.

Audit

The purpose of the audit phase is to have an objective assessment of the successes and shortcomings of the transition. Four specific questions should be addressed:

1. Have the goals and critical success factors been met?
2. Are the anticipated benefits of the transition being realized?
3. Was the transition managed in a satisfactory manner?
4. Were costs and schedules met within planned parameters?

Responsibility for this audit (or postimplementation review) should be assigned to a team consisting of MIS and user department representatives who were not involved in the management of the transition. The review team should prepare a report for MIS and corporate management that identifies major variances between actual and planned performance and includes recommendations for improvements.

Four Steps to a Successful Transition

Successful MIS transitions generally follow these four steps:

1. Designate a transition project manager who is dedicated to the project.
2. Develop a transition plan that identifies the transition goals, assumptions, constraints and limitations, project schedule, and resources required.
3. Provide the needed resources in terms of staff, expertise, technology, and funding.
4. Establish a transition management structure that includes the staff and consultants required to make the transition and manage the new MIS environment until a permanent management structure is in place.

Purchasing

Don Bohl and Bobby Zachariah, Section Editors

Introduction   *Don Bohl and Bobby Zachariah*   10-3

Functions of the Purchasing Department   *George R. Quittner*   10-4

Purchasing Techniques and Procedures That Maximize Value
   Warren E. Norquist   10-11

Legal Aspects of Purchasing   *Floyd D. Hedrick*   10-18

Controls in the Purchasing Process   *Donald R. Tieken*   10-22

Physical Distribution and Warehousing   *James M. Guinan*   10-27

Logistics Management   *J. Mike McElhone*   10-31

Leasing   *Randall Vick*   10-33

Capital Purchasing   *Gregory E. Conlon*   10-35

Electronic Data Interchange   *Kathleen Conlon Hinge*   10-38

INTRODUCTION

Don Bohl and Bobby Zachariah

The traditional role of the purchasing department has been to get the right materials to the right people at the right price and on time. Thus, the purchasing approach and the system to implement it affects all steps of the production and marketing processes.

In recent years, major corporations have revised the role of purchasing in business decisions. In effect, purchasing has become a strategic component of the planning process. Purchasing professionals once were quite concerned with the tactical and short-term issues that affect the procurements of goods and services. Now they are increasingly members of the groups that plan corporate direction and implement the policies of the board of directors.

This change is apparent in the chapters in this section. In the previous edition of this handbook, the section was titled "Purchasing, Transportation, and Distribution." Now, the distribution function has been separated and incorporated in a new section entitled "Sales and Distribution." And "Purchasing" has emerged as its own section.

One thing has not changed. The purchasing function deals with practical matters: procedures, techniques, and functions. This section includes procedures that maximize value, legal aspects of purchasing, and leasing as an alternative to purchasing. And it concludes with a discussion on the impact of electronic data interchange.

Purchasing is an important function that will continue to play an important role as organizations compete for scarce resources (and, for that matter, choosy customers who are price and quality conscious). Introduced in the following chapters are the major issues and challenges facing purchasing managers and policymakers who are concerned with the purchasing function.

Don Bohl *is a group editor with the periodicals division of the American Management Association. As editor for the Management Briefing series, he developed monographs for the purchasing, manufacturing, and R&D divisions of the AMA membership. As editor of the AMA Research Reports, he conducted research on the use of electronic data interchange as a purchasing technology. He currently handles* Organizational Dynamics, *a journal in the organizational behavior field, and* Compensation & Benefits Review, *a journal for compensation and benefits professionals.*

Bobby Zachariah *is vice-president of administration and has been with Golden Aluminum/Adolph Coors Company for thirteen years. His areas of responsibility include human resources, management information systems, environmental health and safety services, and corporate purchasing. Formerly, he worked with Babcock & Wilcox and has had various purchasing management assignments. He is a C.P.M. (certified purchasing manager) and a C.P.I.M. (certified in production and inventory management) and is a member of the American Management Association's Council on Purchasing, Transportation, and Physical Distribution.*

FUNCTIONS OF THE PURCHASING DEPARTMENT

George R. Quittner, Coors Brewing Company

PURCHASING RESPONSIBILITIES

Despite the strategic role that this function plays, purchasing must still deal with the basics. It must still deliver goods to the manufacturing, engineering, or construction forces at favorable prices to keep the company competitive in its overall cost of operation. It must still expedite material, manage incoming shipments, check material against specifications, and interface with the receiving function and with accounts payable. But in today's marketplace, purchasing must also add value in a number of other dimensions.

For example, purchasing has a responsibility to ensure that the goods and services it procures are in compliance with federal and state safety and health laws. OSHA (Occupational Safety and Health Administration) and EPA (Environmental Protection Agency) set many of the specifications for materials purchased on a day-to-day basis. Buyers need to be literate in the applicable laws and the impact those laws have on the goods and services they buy.

Sourcing

Sourcing, one of purchasing's age-old responsibilities, has new meaning when one considers minority purchasing programs, "buy local" programs, and "buy American" programs. Moreover, sourcing decisions are influenced by the need to develop strong long-term relationships with key suppliers. These often involve a sharing of market risk between buyer and seller so that both companies can prosper in both good and bad times. Sourcing, therefore, must be performed with an eye toward the overall contribution the supplier can make to the long-term growth of the company, not just by the supplier's ability to deliver goods competitively.

Today's buyers must understand international business laws and customs. They must be cognizant of the impact world events have on their supply of goods, many of which originate overseas in markets driven by forces markedly different from those in the United States. Ten years ago, the United States was *the* marketplace. Today, the marketplace extends to every corner of the world. Buyers need to be able to deal as effectively in the Far East as in Chicago.

Inventory Control

With the cost of money approaching a level equal to the gross profit margins in some companies, effective control of inventories is as important as low material costs. The knowledgeable buyer understands inventory management theory and is able to work with suppliers to reduce inventories without risk of production shutdown or equipment failure. Programs such as systems contracts, just-in-time (JIT) inventory, bin reserve, and electronic data interchange (EDI) provide tools for keeping inventories low, supplier inventory turnover high, and the plant running with a minimum of on-hand supplies.

Buying Decisions

In addition, today's buyers will develop expertise in their respective markets. This expertise implies the knowledge of when to hedge and when to take intelligent risks. Smart buyers understand the forces that affect the marketplace and can therefore forecast material prices as well as product availability. Through close relationships with key suppliers, the buyer is apprised of the market from the seller's point of view and can thus act to assure that his or her operation is at minimal or no risk of running out of key material.

The buyer must possess knowledge of business law and general management theory. Understanding the legal framework that surrounds the deal encourages the wise use of counsel, as appropriate. The buyer manages supplier performance and understands both parties' legal obligations in the transaction, thus ensuring that both parties perform as planned. The buyer is astute enough to recognize problems in their early stages, and can call upon experts both within and outside the organization to move toward win-win resolution of difficult issues.

The modern buyer is also a junk dealer. Every operation has excess and obsolete material that must be disposed of, and the sale of this material keeps idle assets at a minimum and returns dollars to a company's bottom line. The buyer's knowledge of the marketplace creates opportunities with organizations willing to pay top dollar for scrap material. This activity is virtually as important as getting the best price on the original buy.

Cost Savings

Last but not least, the buyer is responsible for saving money on the total acquisition costs for raw materials, services, and supplies. This has always been the key accountability of the purchasing function. It is placed last in this list of responsibilities for two reasons: to allow for an effective enumeration of all the other responsibilities, and to emphasize its importance.

Buyers are able to generate cost avoidances and cost savings when they understand their own operations as well as those of their competitors and suppliers. The old rule, that $10 saved in purchasing is equal to $100 in new sales, is as valid today as ever before. Reducing total cost is still the key to validating the importance of the purchasing function.

Expediting

Expediting is often thought of as punishment for being in the buying profession. Expediting needs to be treated as a purchasing responsibility, performed proactively to ensure the arrival of material in a timely manner.

Expediting should not be relegated to clerks or junior personnel, for several reasons. The expeditor may have to make decisions about substitution of material and logistics in order to ensure arrival as planned. In addition, repetitive expediting of the same supplier may alert buyers to problems within that supplier's organization. The net result may be the need for a new supplier, not more expediting. Such decisions are best made by the person involved with the original transaction, not by junior personnel.

AUTHORITY

The right to commit company funds is usually delegated to the purchasing function by company policy. This is called *express authority*.

When the position of purchasing agent (PA) was the chief authority empowered to spend company money, the PA's obligations and responsibilities were spelled out in agency agreements. These agreements detailed the agent's signature limit, which was conferred to the agent by a supervisor.

Exhibit 10-1. Approval Levels for Purchasing Decisions

Management Levels	Purchase Orders	Contracts/ Blanket Orders	Multiyear Contracts
Buyer I	$ 20,000	$ 20,000	$ 0
Buyer II	50,000	50,000	0
Buyer III	100,000	100,000	0
Senior Buyer	250,000	250,000	0
Purchasing Manager	500,000	500,000	0
Purchasing Director	1,000,000	1,000,000	0
Company Officer	5,000,000	5,000,000	500,000
Board of Directors	>5,000,000	>5,000,000	>500,000

More frequently, the buyer's purchasing authority is now conveyed via department policies and procedures. These can take the form of a matrix, as shown in Exhibit 10-1, or written statements. It is important to remember that the right to commit the company to a financial obligation is not transferrable, that is, not assignable to another department or to an individual outside the purchasing function. Nor should a buyer create the impression of *implied authority* during negotiations. Should the deal go sour, actions undertaken under the guise of implied authority may put the company in jeopardy.

Along with the authority to purchase comes a fiduciary responsibility to spend company money prudently and wisely in support of company goals and objectives. The authority to spend company funds also intends that all transactions are performed at arm's length and for the benefit of the company only.

ETHICS

The purchasing function comes under constant scrutiny, and there should be no room for doubt that every transaction is conducted in the best interest of the company only, and that the buyer has nothing to gain personally from the transaction.

Many companies adopt value statements outlining the ethical environment that the company expects to maintain in its business transactions. The National Association of Purchasing Managers (NAPM) Principles and Standards of Purchasing Practice Exhibit 10-2 includes important guidelines in this regard, as well as the ethics of buying and selling that the NAPM expects its members to uphold.

Buyers need to be aware that *sharp practices,* such as telling a supplier his price is high when in fact it is not, with the intent of lowering that price artificially, is not only unethical but borders on being illegal. Price shopping, that is, sharing supplier A's price with supplier B to induce B to lower the final price, also borders on being illegal under certain circumstances.

Reciprocity—the act of giving preferential treatment to those suppliers who are also your own customers—is a questionable practice and subject to legal debate. Right or wrong, the visible and repeated practice of conveying any favoritism with regard to buying goods and services jeopardizes the ethical standing of a company and may in fact negatively reduce competition, tarnish the company's image, and raise questions as to the sincerity of the company's procurement process.

INTERNAL RELATIONS

The purchasing department is one of the few departments within a company that has direct relationships with almost every other depart-

Exhibit 10-2. Purchasing Principles and Standards

Principles and Standards
of Purchasing Practice

LOYALTY TO YOUR COMPANY
JUSTICE TO THOSE WITH WHOM
YOU DEAL
FAITH IN YOUR PROFESSION

From these principles are derived the NAPM standards of purchasing practice.

1. Avoid the intent and appearance of unethical or compromising practice in relationships, actions, and communications.
2. Demonstrate loyalty to the employer by diligently following the lawful instructions of the employer, using reasonable care and only authority granted.
3. Refrain from any private business or professional activity that would create a conflict between personal interests and the interests of the employer.
4. Refrain from soliciting or accepting money, loans, credits, or prejudicial discounts, and the acceptance of gifts, entertainment, favors, or services from present or potential suppliers which might influence, or appear to influence purchasing decisions.
5. Handle information on a confidential or proprietary nature to employers and/or suppliers with due care and proper consideration of ethical and legal ramifications and governmental regulations.
6. Promote positive supplier relationships through courtesy and impartiality in all phases of the purchasing cycle.
7. Refrain from reciprocal agreements which restrain competition.
8. Know and obey the letter and spirit of laws governing the purchasing function and remain alert to the legal ramifications of purchasing decisions.
9. Encourage that all segments of society have the opportunity to participate by demonstrating support for small, disadvantaged and minority-owned businesses.
10. Discourage purchasing's involvement in employer sponsored programs of personal purchases which are not business related.
11. Enhance the proficiency and stature of the purchasing profession by acquiring and maintaining current technical knowledge and the highest standards of ethical behavior.

Reprinted with permission from the publisher, the National Association of Purchasing Management, Principles and Standards of Purchasing Practice, *NAPM Insights* 1 (9):27, Sept. 1990.

ment in the company. Engineering, production, maintenance, accounting, quality control, law, traffic, planning, and the corporate function all rely on purchasing for information in order to carry out their roles.

Buyers must work closely with these departments to develop specifications, schedules, and procurement plans consistent with the ultimate user's needs. Purchasing must provide commercial analysis, pricing, and cost data to ensure the best value is obtained

in all purchases. The purchasing function must ensure that suppliers maintain the proper level of quality both in their products and in their paperwork to allow other departments to do their jobs efficiently. Improper invoicing is not an accounts payable problem; it is a purchasing problem, in that purchasing is responsible for managing all the deliverables of the purchase, including the invoice.

Purchasing must work with engineering to develop specifications that allow both functionality and reasonable acquisition cost. Those specifications must recognize the needs of the maintenance department for ease of repair and upkeep and, in addition, allow for the ready procurement of spare parts.

As a service organization, purchasing must know how the customer is and keep his or her needs in mind. Buyers should use their own technical expertise in helping solve internal customer problems, thus supporting those departments that have technical responsibility for the company's plant and equipment.

Good internal relationships are as important as good supplier relationships. There is better support of purchasing decisions when all affected departments have participated in the decision and are allowed to perform their respective roles. Purchasing can lead and guide these decisions, but it should not act independently.

PURCHASE OF GOODS AND SERVICES

The buyer may use a number of tools and techniques in acquiring goods and services, the most common being purchase orders, contracts, and leases. There are a number of variations within each category; for the sake of this writing, we will discuss only the general differences among each of these instruments. It is up to the buyer to determine the appropriate instrument for getting the job done.

Purchasing Contracts

Purchase orders generally are used to acquire materials. Delivery of some specified quantity of goods completes the transaction contemplated by a purchase order. Purchase orders may be considered a form of contract, but they are differentiated from other contracts by the standard nature of their terms and conditions.

Since the exchange of tangible property is governed by the Uniform Commercial Code (UCC), buyers need to understand the concepts of *offer* and *acceptance* in order to be aware of the place their terms and conditions play in each transaction. By understanding

what protection the UCC will provide in a given purchase, the buyer is in a position to plan negotiation strategies for any additional protection the company may wish to specify in a particular purchase.

Contracts generally need to be formed when the terms and conditions of a purchase order will not suffice. Contracts can cover purchases of materials, supplies, equipment, labor, and technical or other services. It is important to note that the UCC does not apply to contracts involving labor or service. Therefore, contracts must be complete unto themselves; whatever is omitted cannot be added without written mutual assent.

Contracts should be written clearly and simply, and buyers should avoid using jargon and legalese. The intent of the document should be easily understood by anyone reading it, not just by its writer.

Counsel should review contracts for completeness and conformance with company practices. In lieu of repeated legal review, buyers may have counsel preapprove specific contract language, such as a standard "hold harmless" clause or standard insurance and indemnification language, for use in contract bidding and negotiations. However, the use of "cut and paste" contracts can be dangerous, in that certain clauses taken out of context and used indiscriminately may not have the meaning and intent originally contemplated.

Leases

A lease is a contract or instrument conveying property to another for a specified period of time. Title is not conveyed during the term of the lease, although title transfer may be part of the lease agreement. Leases allow for the use of equipment for substantially lower upfront payments than would be required for an outright purchase.

Most leasing companies have their own forms of leasing agreements, and some states have adopted new UCC provisions covering leases. However, the buyer still needs to make use of his or her company's financial and legal resources to put together leases that provide the best deal for the company.

INVENTORY MANAGEMENT

The inventory management function can be delegated to many departments outside of purchasing. However, true control of inventories can best be accomplished by those purchasing the material in the first place.

As with other purchasing activities, inventory control requires the buyer to coordinate his or her activities with those of other departments. Inventories of production materials, for example, must support manufacturing schedules and efficient production runs. Spare parts inventories must coincide with preventive maintenance and overhaul programs, and inventories of construction materials must support planned work crews and appropriate work sequences.

Buyers of inventory materials must be aware of order multiples and units of purchase. The inventory level of items normally purchased one hundred to a box, or in sets of four, or in pairs must be adjusted when the economic order quantity (EOQ) dictates that the quantity to have on hand is some fraction of the order multiple of purchase.

The inventory minimums and maximums must take into account vendor lead times as well as historical use of the material. Items used every spring or fall in large quantities may average out to a steady yearly on-hand requirement that will leave the user short during the peak demand cycle and long during the rest of the year. Therefore, lead time must be correlated to actual demand to ensure that appropriate levels of material are on hand when needed.

Critical materials and insurance items need to be treated separately from the regular inventory. Items that are needed to prevent a production shutdown, but whose usage cannot be formally planned, cannot be stocked at levels determined by standard EOQ calculations. In addition, the stocking level of spare parts required for overhauls scheduled every eighteen months or two years, for example, cannot be calculated using EOQ formulas. Their inventory level must fit the redundancy requirement level of the plant and also the planned maintenance activity for that particular piece of machinery.

Buyers have a variety of techniques at their disposal to facilitate the management of inventories. These may include just-in-time (JIT) arrangements, with deliveries prescheduled to arrive as needed on the production floor, or consignment purchases, wherein the user pays for parts as they are drawn from the inventory, not when they are delivered to the plant.

Other techniques include the bin reserve system, wherein the supplier actually manages the user's inventories on site by keeping stocks at predetermined levels, and stockless systems/systems contracts, under which suppliers maintain a specified inventory at their facilities and deliver those items with a very short turnaround time.

Most central to all of the above, and key to why inventory management should stay within the control of purchasing, is that the inventory management arrangements are part of the overall negotiations with regard to price and service and should be an integral part of the framework of the entire deal.

INFORMATION MANAGEMENT ROLE

Purchasing passes on to other departments key information regarding expenditures or commitments to spend company funds, delivery dates, specifications, and so forth. This information is normally conveyed via the purchase order. Today, however, the information may be shared with others electronically, through purchasing and materials management systems.

Regardless of the vehicle for sharing data or the number of recipients of that information, the important point is that purchasing information and purchasing systems need to support the act of buying. Often purchasing systems become encumbered with data required by other departments. In some instances, the purchase order (PO) serves only as the system input document and in fact may not contain all the legally required information. In the event that the systems-generated purchase order cannot cover the commercial intent of the document, the true deal must be cut outside of the PO, using a separate document. Each subsequent purchase order acts only as a release against the original signed contract.

Other systems constraints may prevent the true deal from being adequately described on the systems-generated purchase order. The UCC allows for purchase orders and contracts to be silent as to price and delivery terms. Yet, POs often have these as mandatory data fields, when in fact it is fully intended that the price be determined by some future event.

Purchasing systems can interface with a central receiving function, inventory control, and inventory management as well as with accounts payable. Purchasing systems can therefore serve as a repository for much valuable information, including pricing history, supplier history, inventory usage, project master budget, and a specification master file. Recently, purchasing systems have been devised to serve a dual role of providing performance data on both suppliers (on time deliveries) and buyers (number of POs, dollars spent, etc.).

PURCHASING PROGRAMS

The purchasing function has the ability to undertake unique programs that can impact the company's bottom line. Surplus and salvage/investment recovery, minority supplier development, and supplier relationship programs are noteworthy examples of purchasing programs that have such an impact.

Selling Obsolete Items

Every company has excess and obsolete material or equipment that it needs to get rid of on a regular basis. The buyer is best suited to negotiate with the original supplier, or others in the business, to rid the company of these items and maximize the dollars recovered. The buyer's knowledge of the marketplace and established business relationships enhance his or her ability to perform this function. Optimally, the return of excess material can be negotiated up front as part of the original deal, thereby reducing the time spent in returning the excess material.

Minority Programs

Minority supplier development makes good business sense in light of the role that minorities play in the marketplace today, both as consumers and suppliers. However, any supplier-development program needs to go beyond placing purchase orders. These programs need to encompass careful plans for supplier growth and utilization, such that both the buyer and the minority supplier benefit from the relationship.

Minority businesses are often smaller firms that suffer from a shortage of cash and a lack of experience in servicing large corporate customers. Care must be taken not to stretch the limited resources of the small firms in terms of both cash and personnel.

The goal of any minority supplier–development program is to make the minority firm a strong business, competitive in terms of service and price in any market. These efforts may take years, but "growing" a loyal supplier has its rewards in favorable pricing, outstanding quality, and dedication toward improving the profitability of both companies.

Developing Partnerships

Today, long-term supplier relationships and partnerships are in the limelight, overshadowing multiple sourcing and competitive bidding. Buyers have found that rewarding outstanding supplier performance with long-term contracts has more strategic merit than striving for onetime price savings.

Partnership agreements put emphasis on consistently good performance; they are evaluated on the total cost of doing business, not just the unit price of the goods in question. Today, the cost of business includes the cost of correcting errors on packing slips and invoices, the cost of expediting and tracking lost or late shipments, and the cost of ensuring that an adequate supply of material is always available when needed. Working as partners allows both the buyer and the seller to share in the ups and downs of the marketplace and the economy. In addition, partnering focuses on win-win negotiating, not in trying to gain the upper hand against an opponent.

Partnering is a precursor to the formation of

alliances in electronic data interchange (EDI) and stockless purchasing agreements as well as system contracts. These purchasing tools require a great deal of up-front time and effort on behalf of both the buyer and seller. Therefore, partnering requires skillful sourcing, in that a company's ultimate goal is a long-term relationship with a supplier whose goals and objectives parallel its own.

A company's choice of partners must come from its knowledge of the industry, marketplace, and long-term needs and objectives. Picking the wrong partner can allow a competitor to gain a market advantage and can lead to lost opportunities for profit and growth. Buying on the basis of price alone does not allow either party to gain from potential process improvements and subsequent cost improvements; partnering with the right supplier does.

PURCHASING TECHNIQUES AND PROCEDURES THAT MAXIMIZE VALUE

Warren E. Norquist, Vice-President, Purchasing and Materials Division, Polaroid Corporation

A revolution in purchasing is in progress, challenging the traditional search for the lowest price and emphasizing the importance of lowest *all-in-cost*. All-in-cost is the acquisition price plus all in-house costs required to convert a specific material or service into the end product or other use. In-house costs include incoming transportation, incoming inspection and testing, storage, production, warranty, service, returns, and lost sales. All-in-cost also includes any costs resulting from the end product's failure to function in the field due to a defect in the specific purchased material.

TEAMWORK/INTERNAL CUSTOMER CONCEPTS

To achieve all-in-cost, the procurement professional must be concerned with quality, service, technology flow, and purchase of the *right* material or service. Often, this requires

Exhibit 10-3. Categories of Purchase Descriptions

Approach	Advantages	Disadvantages
Brand or trade name	Easily described; readily available; promotional pull of incorporated brand name (e.g., Spandex or Lycra); assurance of quality	Limited competition; higher prices; misses competitors' improvements
Samples	Easy communication of visual requirements; inexpensive	May require detailed specification and testing for nonvisual requirements
Standard spec.	Avoids cost of developing design specification; facilitates communication; wide competition; facilitates standardization program; readily available materials	Specifications may be dated; high test costs; purchaser has responsibility for suitability of purchased item; standardized material may conflict with marketing desires for unique products
Design spec.	Allows unique item; avoids sole source; avoids premium prices; facilitates standardization program; basis for marketing advantage	Expensive to prepare; purchaser responsible for adequacy of specification; higher cost than standard item; more expediting problems; larger inventories; probably requires the most lead time
Performance spec.	Gains latest technology; obtains specified level of performance; increases depth of competition; matches design to supplier's own process, which should result in lower cost	Possible loopholes in specifications; decreases breadth of competition; higher cost than standard item; more expediting problems

work with a procurement team, including representatives from design, manufacturing, quality, traffic, and customer service.

At the same time, purchasing must work with each internal customer to clarify what is really needed from the supplier. Buyers also must be salespeople who convince their "customers" (the requisitioners) to try alternate, lower-cost methods to meet their needs. The buyer often must prove that brand preference and value are not related.

The purchase description is the heart of any procurement. Whether or not a purchase will satisfy the organization's needs is determined at the time the purchase description is written. In no other form of communication is

there a greater need for clarity and precision. The advantages and disadvantages of different approaches are included in Exhibit 10-3.

EARLY INVOLVEMENT

Purchasing is moving to earlier involvement in the new-product development process as a result of the increase in quality and reliability demands; faster product development becoming a major competitive weapon; rapid changes in materials and component technologies. Improving quality and reliability generally requires additional development time.

Thus, the first two trends are in conflict. The most cost-effective way to meet both needs is to involve purchasing early in the design process.

With early purchasing involvement, the procurement team can prequalify suppliers to ensure that they possess the desired technology and the right business/manufacturing capability. The team invites suppliers to suggest how the part or assembly could be more easily manufactured within the process capability of their equipment. Thus, the procurement team and supplier engineer quality and reliability into the item at the design stage. The work done at this stage goes a long way toward determining the final cost of the product, manufacturing scale-up time, customer satisfaction, and market share.

Buyers must demonstrate their ability to assure value by developing and working with one or two suppliers to accept a cost or price model that defines how the final part or assembly will be priced. This advance assurance of value means program managers will be willing to narrow the number of suppliers to one or two at the beginning of a program and not insist on waiting until after the design is completed to get bids from potential suppliers.

VALUE ENGINEERING AND VALUE ANALYSIS

Value engineering (VE) systematically examines every element of cost in a part, material, or service to make certain that it fulfills the required function at the lowest possible cost. VE identifies the functions the user wants from a product or service and establishes a target cost for each function. The product's designers then use knowledge, creativity, and intuition to get the required function at the target cost.

Value analysis (VA) is similar to VE but is performed after the design is completed, or even after it is being manufactured. Value engineering and value analysis are merging as purchasing groups become involved early in new-product development and suppliers' suggestions are incorporated into the design.

PRICE AND COST ANALYSIS

The buyer's objective in performing an analysis is to maximize value. There are two basic types of analysis. The first, price analysis, is the evaluation and review of the total price of an item without regard to the individual elements of cost or profit. Price analysis focuses on the bottom-line price. Cost analysis goes beyond the bottom-line price to consider the necessity and reasonableness of every cost element, including profit.

The professional buyer must conduct price analysis on every purchase. In many cases, however, price analysis alone will not provide an adequate basis for determining price reasonableness or value. Consequently, cost analysis (the element-by-element evaluation) must be performed.

Since price analysis evaluates only the bottom-line price, the analysis involves the following:

- Competitive price quotations.
- Published market prices, catalog prices, or regulated prices whenever they are available.
- Historic prior quotations and contract prices for the same or similar end items.

Competitive price quotations depend on:

- The specifications being clear and adequate so that prospective suppliers may estimate their costs with a high degree of precision.
- There being sufficient time for qualified suppliers to develop realistic and accurate proposals.
- Price being the only variable. If quality, service, schedule, or similar requirements are not firmly established, then negotiation is the better way to set the terms (including price) of the resulting contract.
- The timing, quantity, and specifications being firm. When suppliers anticipate changes, they may bid low, expecting to reap their normal profit plus windfall gains on the resulting changes.

- Special tooling and/or setup costs not being major factors. The allocation of such costs and the ownership of the special tooling are issues best resolved through negotiation.

PERFORMANCE SPECIFICATIONS

The existence of effective price competition may be difficult to determine if one is buying to a performance specification. Under such conditions, all respondents may propose products that meet the performance requirement, but no two of the products may be alike in anything other than claimed performance.

When requirements are defined only by performance specifications, good procurement practice dictates proposal evaluation using technical competition. Then, after selecting the source on technical and quality grounds, price becomes the issue. Cost analysis probably will be required if the procurement is for a significant dollar amount. All-in-cost, which includes both acquisition and in-house costs (or in the case of capital equipment, the total cost of ownership), should be used as the criterion to pick the supplier, not just the acquisition price.

USING CATALOG PRICES

When purchasing a large number of related commodities such as motors, switches, or lighting fixtures distributors' catalog prices should be only the starting point in purchasing's efforts to establish a fair and reasonable price. In such circumstances, the buyer can request distributors of the required commodity group(s) to propose discounts from their catalog prices. After receiving the catalog and proposed discounts, the buyer can compare catalog prices, less the appropriate discount on a usage weighted basis, and award a term contract (i.e., twelve months) for the commodity group(s) to the lowest bidder. This approach allows procurement professionals to gain a large savings on a wide variety of unknown future purchases with a minimum of effort.

USING HISTORIC PRICES

Although inflation distorts historic prices, the professional buyer can use them if he or she calculates the proper adjustment. Price index numbers, calculated by the Bureau of Labor Standards, depict historical price changes with respect to time. They can also be used to analyze, compare, and predict prices for a specific product or service in a future time frame.

Polaroid calculates the price change on the many items bought from a distributor by entering the Bureau of Labor Standards (BLS) index numbers for each category into a personal computer. The change for the item and the weighted change of all items is quickly calculated. This approach avoids reliance on the stack of price increase notices that distributors often bring to negotiation, and which often overstate inflation.

Historic prices might involve onetime engineering, tooling, and other start-up costs. If they need not be duplicated, the buyer should exclude them from the price analysis base.

COST ANALYSIS AND COST MODELS

Cost analysis evaluates the fairness and reasonableness of a price by analyzing the individual elements of cost such as labor, material, indirect costs, and profit. It should be possible to begin cost analysis by comparing the prospective supplier's cost breakdown with that developed by the buyer's engineering department or with a buyer-developed cost model. Ideally, prospective suppliers will supply the data required for such an analysis.

Polaroid's purchasing professionals have found that in many instances they have been successful at starting new suppliers or current suppliers on new programs with an understanding that cost data will be shared. The data are then used to work with the supplier to identify ways to lower cost. Both parties win.

The national trend is to treat suppliers more as partners and extensions of one's own facilities. The extent of this trend depends on building trust. Trust develops through shared data on costs, schedules, market research, future cost reduction, and quality programs.

NEGOTIATION

Negotiation is the process of fair and businesslike bargaining between buyers and sellers, aimed at a sound agreement on price and all other contract terms. Competitive bidding and negotiation are the major methods of arriving at the price paid in private business.

In the private sector, the buyer frequently negotiates with some of the bidders after the bids are received and reviewed. The practice of negotiating after receiving bids should not be misused in an effort to force prices down. Buyers who do this repeatedly do not receive the potential supplier's lowest price offer on the initial proposal. Instead, suppliers play the buyer's game by submitting higher initial bids, hoping to "win" in the subsequent negotiations. Frequently, the result is a higher acquisition price.

On the other hand, professional buyers do undertake discussions with the supplier with the lowest acceptable bid in an effort to reduce the supplier's costs and thereby its price. The practice of discussions after bid opening is especially desirable when bids are difficult to compare. Such discussions frequently result in lower costs and price, because of better understanding of the requirement, elimination of contingency costs, customer revision of requirements, agreement to use alternative materials, and related suggestions by the supplier.

There are three keys to preparing for negotiations before the face-to-face resolution of the issues: (1) collecting and analyzing all available information, (2) establishing realistic objectives, and (3) analyzing the proposal.

Collecting and Analyzing Information

The buyer should know the specifications, the production process involved, and the effect of these on cost and quality. The buyer need not understand all the technical ramifications of the item but should be aware of its use and limitations, as well as its critical components.

The nature of the item affects the price, quality requirements, methods of contract pricing, terms of the resulting purchase order or subcontract, and bargaining position of the two parties.

The buyer should be aware of the procurement history of the item (or similar items) and any of the work that can or must be performed by a party other than the prospective supplier. The buyer should know the language used in the particular industry. He or she should be aware of prospective engineering problems and other areas of uncertainty that the seller is apt to encounter. Several factors affect the buyer's and seller's respective bargaining power:

- *Seller's need for the sale*—The buyer can gain insight into the seller's position through a review of published data, Dun & Bradstreet reports, and the judicious use of preaward surveys.
- *Buyer's bargaining position*—What is the buyer's best alternative to an agreement?
- *Seller's perception of its bargaining position*—If the seller realizes that it is the only or the preferred source, the seller's bargaining position is greatly enhanced.
- *Adequate lead time*—Inadequate procurement lead time weakens the buyer's bargaining position and results in an inability to obtain adequate competition.
- *Availability of cost data*—Adequate cost data and the time and willingness to analyze them greatly assist the buyer in establishing realistic cost objectives. Cost models are useful when supplier-furnished data are unavailable.
- *Knowledge of the supplier and its representatives*—The buyer can never know too much about the people with whom he or she is going to negotiate. The buyer should examine the supplier's past history and study the records of previous transactions with the supplier.

The buyer should have the latest information available on the nature, character, and economics of the industry, and the needs of the firm with whom he or she is about to negotiate. To ensure adequate preparation, Polaroid purchasing offers its buyers the assistance of former buyers who have developed expertise in purchasing research. These individuals specialize in tracking prices, developing economic scenarios, using cost modeling, and searching the best databases for information specific to each negotiation. They help gather detailed data, general economic information, and the special considerations of the specific industries.

The amount of business information being printed is increasing geometrically. But, with the advent of on-line data bases, the buyer has instant access to the most recent information as well as to historical data at a fraction of the time and cost needed for a library search. Dow Jones News Retrieval, CompuServe, The Source, Dialog, and Prodigy are database wholesalers, and each provides access to many individual databases.

With a personal computer and a search program, purchasers can use electronic database searches to locate information including potential suppliers; background information on a supplier, which can include all the information published during the time period being searched; capacity, cost, and price information on raw materials and components; financial data on suppliers and their competitors; the state of current technology and potential technology; labor rates and new processes; forecasts of economic, business, and market conditions.

Being fully informed "manually" is almost an impossible task, even though the buyer knows that in negotiations, business intelligence is power. Now, thanks to the availability of information through electronic means, the buyer can greatly increase the knowledge he or she brings to any negotiation. Polaroid procurement people have used databases like:

- *Magazine Index*™—This is an on-line database that covers 435 general, business, and trade magazines. It has the complete text of more than a hundred magazines since 1983.
- *The Newspaper Abstracts*—This database provides comprehensive indexing and abstracting for nineteen major newspapers published since 1984.

- *TS Newsletter Database*—This database contains the full text of more than a hundred of the specialized industry newsletters.

While databases are unequaled for retrieving historical information (information older than one day), other services now available can provide "current-awareness" information daily to keep buyers updated on developments in the companies or markets they need to be tracking. One current-awareness service used at Polaroid is called *First!* (Individual, Inc., 84 Sherman Street, Cambridge, MA). By taking advantage of new software technology that analyzes the topics and concepts within each article, such services identify those business and economic news items of greatest relevance to a specific buyer. They deliver the information daily to the user's desk via fax or electronic mail. They can make the latest information available to buyers who are in organizations too small to have purchasing researchers available.

Establishing Negotiation Objectives

Several basic objectives are common to most negotiations:

- Agreement on the quality requirements and the procedures for ensuring this quality.
- Agreement on production schedules and the acceptable window around each delivery time.
- Agreement on a fair and reasonable price. (*Note:* If the agreement is to be part of a long-term, collaborative relationship, the price should include a profit objective adequate to allow the supplier to invest in appropriate R&D, process engineering, and equipment to remain price and technologically competitive.)
- Adequate control over the manner in which the purchase order or subcontract is performed (especially in the areas of quality, quantity, and service).
- A commitment for necessary cooperation.
- A continuing relationship with competent suppliers.

If the buyer anticipates employing negotiations to arrive at an agreed-upon price, then the request for bids should require (1) that supporting cost data be furnished with the supplier's bid and (2) that the buyer will have access to such additional cost data as may reasonably be required. The time to establish these rights is when there is competition or the appearance of competition.

Analysis of Negotiation Proposal

The proposal should be broken apart and its elements examined to identify areas that should be explored in detail. The technical details should be compared with whatever requirements were established by the procurement team. Any previous historic costs for similar work can be the basis against which the buyer measures the probable future costs of performance under the proposed contract. Be sure that any historic costs used were based on efficient operations.

When discussions, written or verbal, are required, they should be conducted with all offerors in the competitive range. The competitive range is determined on the basis of price or cost, technical, and other salient factors and should include all proposals that have a reasonable chance of being selected for award. Minor informalities or irregularities and apparent clerical mistakes may be resolved substantially as they would be under competitive bidding, and communications with offerors required to resolve such matters should not be considered additional negotiations.

It is essential that a technically competent buyer review quality requirements before initiating sourcing activities. Requisitions for materials should not be accepted by purchasing until there are clear specifications or a plan to determine the TBD (to be determined) specifications. Progressive buyers increase incoming quality by working with their suppliers to reconcile specifications with the supplier's process capabilities before the design is completed.

Professional buyers prequalify new sources of supply (and may need to requalify known sources) to ensure that the suppliers have the technical, managerial, physical, financial, and attitudinal capability to meet their customer's quality and quantity requirements. This crucial activity frequently requires the involvement of members of the engineering, manufacturing engineering, production, quality, finance, and industrial engineering departments, with the buyer being the team chief. In addition to prequalifying suppliers for current requirements, they should be investigated for technological capabilities that may be required in the future.

The fact that finished product quality standards are met does not guarantee that component specifications are properly stated. A component may be using only part of the latitude allowed. A later shift within allowed specification can cause final product failure.

THE BUYER'S ROLE IN PURCHASING SERVICES

The purchasing department has much to contribute to buying services; unfortunately, this potential contribution is frequently bypassed. Many managers who buy services, especially professional services, do not appreciate the dollars that a purchasing professional could save. Suppliers of specialties and services evaluate their costs as well as customers' costs when establishing prices. If the customer knows little about the product or service and has little price negotiating experience, the price will be significantly higher than need be. As one sales training expert put it, "Raise the price (with extras) until the customer flinches."

Evaluating the price for services on the basis of whether it is within the amount budgeted for the project is not cost effective. However, this frequently is the criterion used by department and division managers. On the other hand, if instead of encountering an "amateur," the potential supplier finds himself dealing with a purchasing professional who is knowledgeable, experienced, and prepared, and if the supplier knows the purchaser has management's support, the final price will represent value.

Buying professional services is very challenging: The value received often is intangible, costs are mainly for labor, domestic competition is frequently limited by customer preferences, and there is hardly ever offshore competition. Without purchasing involvement:

- The amateur buyer settles for vague agreement on output.
- Statements on overall price frequently are only the minimum or starting point.
- Verbal requests and changes, when documented at all, are documented by the contractor.
- The customer usually has let the contractor propose the contract terms.
- The contractor avoids detailing billing changes.

Large savings have been obtained when purchasing has become involved. But, in order to sell the contribution purchasing can make, purchasing should:

- Study the area and learn from others before offering to purchase services in a new area.

- Sell purchasing as a service that can help get what the internal customer wants.
- Sell purchasing as a function that can help by separating the professional relationship from the pricing and billing relationship. This will be well received by many managers, as they really do not feel comfortable discussing price and would prefer to delegate the responsibility.
- Question managers as to how comfortable they are questioning and analyzing price before they buy.
- Show management that one-stop shopping can be costly. For example, the decorator who recommends and then buys furniture may have had a reasonable hourly rate as an adviser. But the effective hourly rate may be staggering when it is determined how much less the furniture would cost without the decorator's markup or commission.
- If the manager is worried by the salesperson's scare tactics, contrast the purchase with other difficult ones where such tactics are regularly surmounted.

LEGAL ASPECTS OF PURCHASING

Floyd D. Hedrick, Chief, Contracts and Logistics, Library of Congress

Certain basic principles of law apply to all common conditions of doing business. A purchasing manager or buyer should be familiar with these principles as a background for a specific understanding of the laws that apply to procurement and contracting. This does not mean that every buyer must be an attor-

ney. It does mean, however, that personnel with procurement responsibility should be aware of the legal obligations to which they commit their companies, and the areas in which they can be held personally liable.

The most fundamental principle is knowing when to consult competent legal counsel.

Certainly, buyers should consult counsel for the phraseology of clauses and conditions on a purchase order or contract before the order is signed. This is particularly true when contracting for a large order or major new facilities, where potential liabilities can affect the operations of an entire plant. Because of the growth in international sourcing, it behooves the professional buyer and purchasing manager to become familiar with business laws applicable to international transactions.

THE UNIFORM COMMERCIAL CODE

The common law, often referred to as the unwritten law, consists of rules and regulations that have developed through custom and that have been accepted and enforced by the courts. Laws adopted by Congress or by the states are known as *statutes* or *statute law*. Laws adopted by a city are usually called *ordinances*. All laws must conform to the Constitution of the United States.

A morass of conflicting state laws would handicap interstate commerce. To prevent such chaos, a group of distinguished scholars, representing the Conference of Commissioners on Uniform State Laws and the American Law Institute, developed what is now known as the Uniform Commercial Code (UCC). The code is reviewed every five years by a group that includes nonlawyer participating observers representing industry, government, and national associations. (The National Association of Purchasing Management, for example, is a participant.)

Because it covers many phases of commercial law in an exhaustive manner, buyers and purchasing managers should thoroughly acquaint themselves with the UCC. At the same time, they must keep in mind that the UCC is not a substitute for definitive contractual language, nor will it override the seller's clear terms. It is vital, from a legal point of view, that every contract be supported by a document from the buyer. In general business practice, the purchase order has evolved as the document that spells out the terms and conditions and thus affords maximum protec-tion. When the seller accepts the purchase order, it becomes a contract. Should a dispute arise, the terms then work to the advantage of the buyer. The UCC states that a definitive and reasonable expression of acceptance or a written acknowledgment that is sent within a reasonable time constitutes an acceptance. The UCC has effectively eliminated a majority of the important differences that existed among commercial laws throughout the United States, and it has also provided new statutory provisions to fill many gaps in prior laws.

FEDERAL LAWS AND ACTS

Buyers and purchasing managers should be familiar with four specific federal laws and acts common to purchasing:

1. *Sherman Antitrust Act (1890)*—This law protects trade and commerce against unlawful restraints and monopolies. Restraint of trade may restrict competition and a monopoly eliminates competition.
2. *Federal Trade Commission Act (1914)* —This law created the Federal Trade Commission and gives it broad authority to litigate against all unfair or deceptive acts or practices.
3. *Clayton Antitrust Act (1914)*—This law supplements general prohibitions of the Sherman Act by outlawing specific distribution practices and structural arrangements.
4. *Robinson-Patman Act (1936)*—This law further expands the Clayton Act. It is an antiprice discrimination law. In general, the act prevents a supplier from offering the same quantity of specific materials to competing buyers at different prices. The act does not, however, prevent a buyer from seeking legitimate reductions in price. But a buyer must be certain that any reductions in price gained are justifiable under the act. A violation of this act could mean a suit for triple damages in addition to attorney fees.

When a doubt exists concerning the legal status of a purchasing transaction, the buyer should seek legal counsel.

RECIPROCITY (TRADE RELATIONS)

Should reciprocity be practiced and, if so, under what circumstances? There are many definitions of reciprocity. One common definition considers reciprocity as the practice of giving preference to those suppliers who are customers of the buying company. There are, however, many gray areas, and it is often difficult to draw a line between legal and illegal. The following guidelines may be helpful:

1. A company with a significant quantity of purchases for one commodity or component should avoid even the appearance of violating the law.
2. Avoid any systematic program of balancing purchases and sales, including compiling statistics on purchase-sales balances between buyer and seller firms.
3. Avoid the practice of providing purchasing figures to the sales department and, conversely, asking sales to provide the procurement function with figures on firms that are buying from you.
4. Avoid maintaining a list of customers on the basis of your purchases from them for the purpose of reciprocity.
5. Avoid having your buyers accompany sales personnel when calling on customers.
6. Avoid making purchases through anyone except authorized sales representatives.

Reciprocity is neither a purchasing problem nor a sales problem. It is a management problem. Management should develop a well-defined, written policy concerning reciprocity to avoid any appearance of illegal activity.

WARRANTIES

A warranty is a guarantee by the seller that the materials or equipment shall be as represented. Warranties can be express or implied.

The Uniform Commercial Code states that a seller's express warranties are created as follows:

1. Any affirmation of fact or promise, made by the seller to the buyer, which relates to the materials or equipment and becomes part of the basis of the sale creates an express warranty that the materials or equipment shall conform to the affirmation or promise.
2. Any description of the materials or equipment which is part of the basis of the sale creates an express warranty that the materials or equipment shall conform to the description.
3. Any sample or model which is made part of the sale creates an express warranty that the whole of the materials or equipment shall conform to the sample or model.

An implied warranty means that the materials or equipment will do the job the manufacturer claims it is designed to do. Unlike express warranties, which are created as a result of negotiations, implied warranties arise from and are created by the sale of the materials or equipment itself. Certainly, a written express warranty should be a part of the original purchase agreement for a large piece of equipment. An implied warranty may serve just as well for small orders in particular if a use specification is involved.

PURCHASE ORDER: A LEGAL CONTRACT

The purchase order is generally regarded as the instrument by which materials and equipment are purchased to fill a requirement. It expresses in specific language the agreement between the buyer and the supplier. Upon acceptance, it has the legal force of a binding contract. In fact, it is a contract. For a purchase order to be considered enforceable, it must fulfill at least five basic elements: (1) competent parties, (2) legal subject matter or purpose, (3) an offer, (4) an acceptance, and (5) consideration.

PATENT INFRINGEMENT

A heavy liability may be incurred through the infringement of a patent. It is desirable to have a clause in purchase orders and contracts denoting that the supplier agrees to assume full responsibility for any loss sustained as a result of an infringement suit. Should a buyer unknowingly purchase an item from a supplier that has infringed the patent holder's rights, the buyer is also guilty of infringement. Particular attention should be paid when purchasing software. Manufacturers have a substantial investment in software and want to protect it.

TITLE TO PURCHASED MATERIALS

A professional buyer must have a clear understanding of when the title of materials passes from the supplier to the buyer. The UCC covers the legal obligations under various shipping terms. In brief, the UCC states that if the purchase order calls for shipment of materials by a common carrier, the risk of loss passes to the buyer when the materials are delivered to the carrier. However, if the purchase order denotes delivery to a particular destination, the risk of loss does not pass to the buyer until the materials are at that destination.

LETTER OF CREDIT

Foreign purchasing has seen a dramatic increase over the past forty years. In 1950, outstanding credits in the United States amounted to $500 million; in 1990 the figure was approximately $200 billion. The letter of credit is the method used to meet the seller's desire to obtain cash promptly upon shipment and, concurrently, to safeguard the buyer's desire that all documents be in order to facilitate entry at customs and carrier delivery upon arrival.

The letter of credit has been used for hundreds of years. Today, letters of credit come in two broad varieties: the commercial letter of credit and the standby letter of credit.

Principally, the commercial letter of credit acts as a payment medium for materials sold. By contrast, the standby letter of credit acts as a backup against customer default on obligations of all kinds, both monetary and nonmonetary. Purchasing managers and buyers who purchase in foreign countries would do well to acquaint themselves with both Article 5 of the UCC, which covers letters of credit, as well as with relevant provisions of the Uniform Customs and Practices (UCP). Until the buyer becomes proficient at using letters of credit, he or she would do well to seek legal counsel for assistance.

FEDERAL GOVERNMENT

Purchasing in the federal government is big business. For the most part, purchasing in this area is governed by the Federal Acquisition Regulation (FAR) and supplemented by individual agency regulations. The Federal Acquisition Regulations system is composed of seven volumes. The federal acquisition regulations in Chapter One are those government-wide acquisition regulations jointly issued by the General Services Administration, the Department of Defense, and the National Aeronautics and Space Administration. Chapters Two through the end are acquisition regulations issued by individual government agencies. The major intended effects of the FAR are to (1) produce a clear, understandable document that maximizes feasible uniformity in the acquisition process, (2) reduce the proliferation of agency acquisition regulations, (3) implement recommendations made by the Commission on Government Procurement and various congressional groups, and (4) facilitate agency, industry, and public participation. Copies of the FAR and Code of Federal Regulations (CFR) may be purchased from the Government Printing Office, Washington, DC 20402.

Purchasing managers and buyers should limit their application of legal principles to the area of preventive law and the recognition of problems and situations that should be referred to legal counsel. Familiarity with basic concepts provides a means of avoiding pitfalls by enabling purchasing personnel to recognize areas in which to seek legal guidance.

CONTROLS IN THE PURCHASING PROCESS

Donald R. Tieken, Riverwood International Corporation

In addition to being a legal and ethical requirement, purchasing controls serve two additional functions. First, they help ensure the purchase of high-quality materials at prices based on market trends. Second, on a more personal level, they are one key to the professional buyer's career advancement. The more skilled a buyer becomes in understanding and working within the parameters of established controls, the more latitude the individual can (and should) be afforded in the performance of his or her duties—and the more valuable his or her contributions to the company.

As the following discussion indicates, purchasing controls take on a variety of forms. They may be externally imposed (legal or government requirements) or internally imposed (a firm's own statements of acceptable practices). Controls in the latter category are inherently more flexible. A company should review these periodically and, if prudent, make alterations that improve overall efficiency.

POLICY, PROCEDURE, AND PRACTICES

The controls in the category of policy, procedure, and practices are necessary to establish parameters within the purchasing department. They should be recognized as constants that give clear guidelines for purchasing direction.

Policies are general guidelines that define the intent, objectives, and commercial aspects of the purchasing function. They include clarifications related to organizational structure, statements on best-value purchasing, guidelines regarding who participates in decisions, and statements on ethical practice.

Procedures assign responsibility, establish documentation control, define practices, and assure adequate training. Practices state how policy is to be carried out. They are considered living documents, subject to change as purchasing personnel explore new methods to implement purchasing policy.

INTERNAL AUDITS

Internal audits are functional reviews done to ascertain purchasing's effectiveness: its relationships with internal clients (other departments), its internal practices, and its relationships with suppliers. In reviewing relationships with other departments, an audit committee generally conducts in-depth interviews with relevant parties. An analysis of these responses forms the basis for recommended improvements.

Audits of the purchasing function itself often include the following: analyses of blanket purchase order (BPO) and straight purchase order (PO) operations; reviews of conformance of the actual expenditures to established dollar limits; BPOs issued without bids; the existence of procurement plans and their quality; practices related to competitive bidding; negotiating efforts; methods for evaluating and rating suppliers; and the like. The review may also cover the quality of the electronic systems for purchasing and communications.

The auditors observe actual practice and compare this with existing procedural guidelines. If discrepancies emerge, management should modify either the practice or the written procedure to achieve conformance.

EXTERNAL AUDITS

Generally, external audits are supplier audits, aimed at improving quality at the supplier's facilities by advocating the application of statistical process control and industrial experimentation techniques. Cross-functional survey teams visit the supplier's facilities and report back to the supplier, providing a rating and recommendations for improvement. Follow-up audits are scheduled as needed. Buyers also receive the audit reports, along with specific recommendations on resultant action items.

Purchasing personnel and personnel from the plant utilizing the raw material reach a consensus on which suppliers are to be audited. The selection criteria include the criticality of the raw material to the consuming plant, physical volume, dollar volume, complexity of specification, experiences with the supplier, and so on.

It is essential that the audit team establish a procedure for recording nonconformances and inform manufacturing and purchasing. The areas to note include specification, condition of the delivery vehicle (including operability as well as appearance), timely delivery, inadmissible short or long weights, and the like. Purchasing communicates instances of nonconformance to the suppliers for remediation.

CONTROLS RELATED TO ORGANIZATIONAL STRUCTURE

Controls related to organizational structure are inherently built into the organization by the way a department or function is structured within a company. Decentralized organizations will, by their very nature, have fewer built-in controls. Generally, purchasing in a decentralized structure reports to nonpurchasing positions such as operations or finance. These positions are usually not trained in the purchasing profession and they are not skilled at monitoring and detecting signs of impropriety. In contrast, central organizations provide for higher levels of career development in the purchasing function within a company. Consequently, it is expected that professionals with better training will be attracted to these organizations. It can be assumed that centralized organizations are easier to control. Obviously, in selecting an organizational structure, many other actors influence the decision.

PERFORMANCE REVIEW AND GOAL SETTING

Purchasing management should establish goals or specific objectives for each employee at the beginning of each year, and each employee should mutually agree to the goals. To keep the employee focused on the goals, management should conduct a progressive review of performance each quarter. At the end of the year, management conducts a formal performance review with each employee. This is summarized in writing. The review should include an assessment of the employee's skills and educational level and a plan for further training and development, taking into account both skills needed to meet current job requirements and future aspirations.

BUDGET AND VARIANCE BENCHMARKS

Regular tracking of purchasing activity helps management monitor performance against established standards. In the area of budgets, management tracks actual departmental operating expenses against planned expenses for each period in order to maintain spending at a reasonable level. Generally, it is important that department heads maintain a level of operating expenses that does not exceed 5 percent of the established budget. Higher variances require approval from the superior.

Effective management practices further specify that benchmarks be established to measure performance in the critical activities of the company. Since most activities that are measured tend to improve over time, benchmarking is an important management technique for improving performance and productivity of vital tasks.

PROCUREMENT PLANS

A company needs a well-planned strategy for meeting its key raw materials and service needs. The procurement plan serves this purpose by summarizing the market conditions for the material or service, identifying the primary suppliers and their capacities, and clearly defining the strategy for acquiring the material or service. The procurement plan becomes a reference document for management as well as a strategic plan. For critical materials, purchasing management should update the plan periodically. Purchasing then monitors actual purchases against the strategic plan. Any deviations must be rationalized and documented.

SYSTEM CONTROL AND SECURITY REPORTS

Effective system controls can best be established through written policies and procedures within the department and proper training of all personnel, both inside and outside the department. Meaningful procedures provide guidelines or boundaries within which employees may carry out their jobs. The procedural statements are meant to provide a framework for systematically accomplishing tasks. But they must depict reality;

thus, they may need to be changed when appropriate.

Security reports provide information on improper attempts to use a system—both deliberate and accidental. If specific and repeated violations occur, management must consider methods for strengthening security, changing existing procedures, or taking other appropriate actions. It should be noted that violations may simply be a matter of insufficient training. Normally, this is the case.

LEGAL CONTROLS

A number of legal and governmental controls apply to performance of the purchasing function. These include:

- *Anti Kickback Act*—eliminates the practice of paying fees or "kickbacks" to obtain or reward favorable treatment in connection with government contracts.
- *Procurement Integrity Act*—designed to prevent contractors who are competing for U.S. government business from knowingly offering, giving, or promising to offer future employment, money, gratuities, or any other thing of value to a government procurement official. It also stipulates that contractors may not knowingly solicit or obtain any proprietary or source selection information regarding the procurement. The act also prohibits government procurement officials from knowingly soliciting, accepting, receiving, or agreeing to receive future employment, money, gratuities, or any other thing of value. Nor may government officials disclose any proprietary or source selection information. In addition, the act also requires that any procurement official immediately report any violation or possible violation of the act.
- *Sherman Act*—declares that every contract combination or conspiracy in restraint of trade or commerce is illegal. In addition, it outlaws monopolization and conspiracies to monopolize.
- *Clayton Act*—makes it unlawful for any

person to lease or sell products on the condition that the lessee or purchaser not use or deal in competing products, if the result will probably substantially lessen competition or create a monopoly.

- *Robinson-Patman Act*—relates to discrimination in price or promotional matters between competing purchasers of commodities of like grade and quality. In some circumstances, the act imposes liability upon buyers as well as sellers.
- *Federal Trade Commission Act*—empowers the Federal Trade Commission to proceed against companies engaging in unfair methods of competition or unfair or deceptive acts in commerce.

The applications of these acts are detailed and, in some cases, complicated. It is advised that all purchasing organizations utilize their legal resources to fully educate their buyers in the content of the provisions and the penalties associated with noncompliance.

DELEGATION OF AUTHORITY

Delegation of purchasing authority sets limits, at all levels of purchasing responsibility, on an individual buyer's power to commit company funds. A purchase commitment can be a contract agreement, purchase order, or other document obligating the company to procure energy, materials, or services. The authorization limits need to be consistent for each job level, in line with that level of responsibility, and appropriate for the skill level of the individual currently holding the position. Authority levels may start low for an inexperienced buyer, then be raised as the buyer demonstrates responsibility and competence.

REQUISITION CONTROL AUTHORIZATION

A requisition can be defined as a control document that allocates funds for the procurement of a requirement identified and specified by a requisitioner who has been budgeted

funds to operate a defined portion of the company. Generally, companies delegate levels of funding authority. Depending on the value of the requested purchase, the individual requesting the material may need to obtain a signature from a higher level of authority. Just as functional groups outside of purchasing have no commitment authority (and as such, cannot obligate their company), purchasing has no authorization-of-funds authority. As a general rule, the individual with budget authority is not the same individual empowered to make purchase obligations binding the company. Thus, to ensure proper controls, a company should establish both funding and commitment authorizations at the appropriately delegated levels.

A requisition must clearly describe the item to be purchased, state the charge codes, and identify any special conditions governing the purchase (specifications, delivery requirements, maintenance, operating clarifications, and the like). The eventual purchase will be written based on the content of the final requisition. Only individuals with a designated budget authority can sign for funds to be spent and charged to a given charge code.

BLANKET RELEASES

To facilitate ease of scheduling or restocking of repetitive purchases, purchasing may authorize designated individuals in an operating environment to release their requirements against an established blanket purchase order. An approved releasor oftentimes is best equipped to determine quantity and timing for obtaining an item, material, or service. Purchasing initially negotiates price, sourcing, and business conditions, and these are spelled out in the blanket order. By reference to controls established by purchasing, an authorized releasor is given authority to contact a supplier to schedule his or her needs in a timely and efficient manner. This activity may be handled by telephone, fax, electronic data interchange, or in writing. While it is possible to handle these activities manually, they are now more often performed using an electronic purchase system.

The blanket order will identify the releaser by name and his or her dollar authority for individual releases. The system will reject any attempt by nonauthorized personnel to release an order, as well as releases that exceed a specified dollar value.

SUPPLIER EVALUATION

For a company to be completely successful in today's competitive environment, it must analyze, coordinate, motivate, and, in part, direct the technical and managerial capabilities of its suppliers. Purchasing's objective should be to develop suppliers who complement their company's own technical, managerial, and marketing capabilities. Purchasing should also seek out and develop promising new suppliers, particularly those whose own long-term supply is secure. Regular surveys and recommendations regarding enhancements to supplier capabilities are another way to continue improving the quality of incoming materials and control the procurement process within a company.

The type of evaluation required to determine supplier capability varies with the nature, complexity, and dollar value of the purchase to be made. In addition to preliminary investigation of a supplier's financial condition, purchasing personnel may also conduct on-site surveys to evaluate a supplier's quality capability. Plant visits also develop a more complete understanding of the details of supplier operations and problems involved in producing materials to given quality levels. Among the factors to be considered are appropriateness of equipment, control of production, quality and cost, competence of technical and managerial staffs, the morale of personnel in general, quantity of back orders, and willingness to handle orders and work cooperatively with customers.

Companies can motivate established suppliers by regularly checking performance and rejecting unsatisfactory work. In addition to representing a sound business practice, inspection of incoming materials provides a quantitative measure of supplier quality performance, which is essential to the development of an effective supplier evaluation program. Such a program must represent a combined appraisal of facts, quantitative computations, and value judgments.

ROTATION OF PERSONNEL

Periodic reassignment of personnel can also serve as a control. Generally, rotational assignments are made to either another procurement area or to sales and marketing. In addition to raising morale and stimulating creative thinking, reassignments prevent a buyer's relationships with vendors from becoming so personal that the relationships influence procurement decisions.

PURIFYING THE PURCHASING FUNCTION

The purchasing activity should remain segregated from the responsibilities of other departments. In other words, purchasing should not be involved in receiving material, approving requisitions, or paying invoices. This separation of duties will maximize efficiency at the same time that it promotes high control standards. If purchasing were to become involved in these other areas, the conditions would be ripe for potential (or actual) abuses. With today's computer systems, a company can create separate security for the various nonpurchasing functions. If a computer system is not in place, the firm can use a manual system, with clearly written policies, procedures, and practices.

PHYSICAL DISTRIBUTION AND WAREHOUSING

James M. Guinan, Retired Senior Executive, Major Retailing Corporations

Modern physical distribution and warehousing, combined with an equally modern transportation system, can provide a company with a substantive advantage over its competition. In addition, the warehouse and distribution systems themselves can become sources of significant additional income.

The key to making distribution and warehousing positive and dynamic (rather than negative and static) has been the full and imaginative use of the computer. With well-managed technology, the processes become faster, more vital, and infinitely more sophisticated and responsive. In companies that have realized the full potential of modern distribution, the function and its executives have earned a place of honor alongside more traditional power positions, such as marketing, production, and finance. Top management recognizes the distribution area as having both the authority and responsibility for a major component of company profitability.

Stripped of its high-tech aura, distribution is a relatively simple set of propositions. First, a company obtains the product needed for its business. The product could vary from primary chemicals and metals to be used in manufacturing processes to finished items for redistribution and sale. In any event, the company wants the items to arrive at its warehouse with as low a freight cost as possible and in those quantities that reasonably guarantee an orderly flow to the business. Second, the company wants to store them for as short a period as professionally reasonable within the context of well-thought-out service needs. Thus, the company hopes to incur the lowest possible inbound and outbound handling costs and money costs while the materials lie fallow. Third, the company wants to move the product to its destination (the factory, the distribution outlet, or whatever) neither faster nor slower than is needed, and at a hauling cost that (in both dollars and percent) is reasonable for a superior distribution player in the company's industry.

Now, if a company's distribution needs are small, little or no high technology need enter the picture. If the firm is buying only a dozen product items from a handful of vendors, and if there are only a few destinations for the material, then the distribution problems are few and the needs simple. These needs can be served by a few good men and women with telephones, clipboards, forklifts, good memories, and—the boon to all warehouse workers—good feet.

From that simple workplace, however, to the most complicated of distribution environments there is a straight continuum of increasing challenge. Consider a warehouse that must handle thousands of suppliers, scores of thousands of diverse products, multiple distribution centers, and hundreds or thousands of final outlets for its products—all interrelating with conflicting timing and service needs. The upward-rising curve of complexity must be matched with a parallel curve of technology and imagination. Only then can the system work profitably, intelligently, and with apparent smoothness.

Next, we look at the major elements of a high-tech distribution environment: (1) inbound procurement and handling, (2) receiving and storing, (3) pulling and distributing, and (4) transporting to final destination. Although our discussion of each element is somewhat general, the basic concepts (reliance on capital-intensive processes, sophisticated selection and individualized service for each demand and outlet, and a just-in-time approach to each step) have application for most large firms in manufacturing, wholesale distribution, and retailing.

IN-BOUND PROCUREMENT AND HANDLING

The process of in-bound procurement and handling typically starts with purchasing. Routine, repetitive purchasing, triggered by electronically reported rates of consumption, provides a first example of how high-tech has streamlined procurement. In other words, the retailer routinely tracks consumption by outlet and transmits this information to each supplier, computer-to-computer. There is only nominal human intervention—mostly monitoring.

Once the order is consummated, the inbound (largely computerized) processes can include such items as (1) specifications for the inbound shipment, (2) designation of the carrier, (3) routing to be followed by the carrier or carriers for minimum freight costs, (4) and a very specific "reservation" so that each truck is assigned a date, a time to the nearest fifteen minutes, and even a specific overhead door to which delivery is to be made.

There are efficiencies to be gained in each of these areas. For example, specifications on how many of each size and/or color per box can be written to provide the ideal minimum shipping assortment per sealed box, so that

cartons need never be broken. Also, specifications can deal with the "look" of the outside carton, including what is printed where on which carton face. For example, the specifications can prescribe where bar codes are to be placed so that these can be easily read by computer scanners.

RECEIVING AND STORING

Again, the process of receiving and storing is highly computerized. When an arriving truck triggers its reservation, the computer produces a special stick-on bar code label for each carton in the shipment. The bar code may include information on carton content and assigned (but random) storage location, usually by pallet load. In addition, the trigger automatically updates other systems, including the inventory-on-hand and the accounts payable systems. Computer-monitored conveyor belts or some variation of AGVS (automatic guided vehicle system) then take the units of product to their storage locations. Neither the conveyor belts nor the AGVS require human intervention until point of put-away.

In the more modern warehouses, storage is in high (45-foot) bays with narrow aisles, making optimum use of cube. Even here the computer guides the high-lift fork truck through the narrow aisles via electronic sensors buried in the cement of each aisle, so that wear and tear and even serious accidents do not happen.

Once the materials are put away, the computer helps keep them from being lost—an event that could easily happen in a narrow-aisle warehouse of this size. Most modern warehousing systems not only provide on-line information by location and SKU (stock keeping unit) but also subinformation on goods that have not been moving, or should have moved based on seasonality or some other factor. Thus, the computer makes management aware of problems that may need addressing.

PULLING AND DISTRIBUTING

If there is a single point at which a computerized distribution environment really shines, it is in pulling and distribution, where the high-level bits and bytes of the computer orchestrate solutions to incredibly complex and competing demands. This can be best described in the context of one day's activities in an imaginary but representative warehouse and distribution center.

Our hypothetical distribution center is 48 feet high with narrow-aisle racks and one million square feet of warehouse space. The center stores some 25,000 different items in quantities of 100 to 10,000 each. It is fully automated with high-speed conveyors from takedown (out of storage) to the outbound doors. The center has thirty overhead doors for shipping, all serviced by the conveyor. In turn, thirty tractor trailers are always available at these doors to service the company's 300 outlets.

The basic software system that drives the automated outbound process is known as batch wave-string loading. A typical day's automated activity begins the night before, when the computer produces the thousands of pull tickets for the thousands of items that are to be taken from the racks and sent to the outlets the next day. Each pull ticket contains information on where in the racks each item can be found and a bar-code stick-on label to guide the carton through the conveyor system to the proper outbound door. In addition, if the outlets are retail stores, folded beneath the bar code will be the retail price tickets for each item in each carton. These will be applied at the store level.

The tickets are issued to the pickers in batches, with batch No. 1 representing all the goods for all the outlets to be serviced by the first wave of trucks outside the thirty outbound doors. Since more than one outlet may be loaded on a given truck, the thirty doors and thirty trucks may, in fact, be servicing fifty or more outlets in this first wave.

To further complicate each batch/wave, picked cartons enter the conveyor system from different points in the warehouse, with some entry points six to eight minutes from the outbound doors and others as much as twenty-five minutes away. The computer system serves as "traffic cop" for each batch wave, using strategically placed laser scanning heads to read the bar codes of each car-

ton as it passes. Thus, the system monitors items individually (to send each to the proper outbound door) at the same time that it orchestrates the entire system. Information so obtained is monitored in several computer rooms throughout the facility, where trained technicians audit the flow of goods on lighted schematics, watching for jams, timing problems, and the like.

String loading is still another software improvement to batch wave. Under this system, the computer "senses" that some trucks in a given batch are fully loaded earlier than others, due to lower quantity, a different mix, and the like. The loaded trailers are pulled away and fresh ones are put in their place. The computer allows the appropriate next-batch goods, just for those doors, to enter the system. Thus, the goods "string along," as it were, on the coattails of the previous batch, thus reducing conveyor downtime to absolute minimums. (Cartons belonging to not-released batches that are put on conveyors in error have their telltale bar codes monitored through the entire conveyor system by laser scanning heads. Ultimately, the system shepherds them down an "abort" line for manual reentry at the correct times.)

Working two shifts, this environment can easily process 140,000 conveyable cartons per day, with error rates so low that conventional material handlers would find them hard to believe—and impossible to achieve.

TRANSPORTATION

Transportation is the final major action in the continuum from purchase of product to servicing an outlet. In its simplest form, an owned or leased tractor trailer rig carries goods or materials from distribution center to outlets and returns to the center. This is very simple, very straightforward, and also—unfortunately—very expensive. Trucking costs, even when well managed, run at approximately $1.00 per mile, which makes managing this step for the least number of truck runs and least miles a significant challenge—and also an imperative.

Again, enter the computer. The most important tool for the hauling fleet manager is one of the very sophisticated routing software packages now available. When fine-tuned to a company's needs and facilities, such a system (1) decides every day which of the outlets will have its product loaded on what trailers, by trailer number, (2) in what batch wave, (3) which trailers will be loaded sequentially for several outlets, and (4) which trailers will be loaded for single destinations. In addition, the system can track all of the trailers, wherever they may be. It can also track and assign tractors and drivers to each of the trailers, thus assuring no downtime except for maintenance.

The system also decides routing for all outbound and inbound rigs. Consequently, it provides access to a major source of hauling revenue: third-party backhauling. Under this concept, your traffic department forms an agreement with major "consolidators" in your hauling universe and with other businesses in the same universe that may not have your trucking capacity. Your agreements with them, stated simply, say that if at any time one of your rigs is returning from any outlet empty (an occurrence that happens dozens of times daily), then the empty rig will swing past the consolidator and load up another party's goods. Since the cost of the empty rig returning is still $1.00 per mile, the traffic department can charge third-party loads at very competitive rates and still maintain a profit center with net income measured in hundreds of thousands of dollars per year. This is a fine offset to the cost of distribution. It is a profit endeavor which, incidentally, can be instituted regardless of whether the truck fleet is owned, leased, or any of combination of leased/owned.

THE HUMAN FACTOR

Because of the high-speed, highly automated nature of the distribution system just described, the company needs to staff the center with workers who are markedly different from those employed in labor-intensive settings. High-speed, high-tech systems do not produce sweat shops. Indeed, the automated nature of the systems requires both less workers and less manual labor per work unit. What is required, however, is (1) people with a good working knowledge of how their function fits into the total picture, and how their performance can enhance or hurt the total effort, and (2) a high sense of urgency, since high speed is very vulnerable to carton jams, frozen rollers, slow truck takeaways, and the like. One choke point left unresolved for twenty minutes can reduce daily production for thousands of cartons. In view of the need for higher caliber, more urgent material handlers, and the relatively low labor intensity of such an operation, one can make a strong case for solving potential labor problems with uncharacteristically high pay, with bonuses tied to both quality and quantity of production.

When a distribution and warehousing center is built, it is usually designed with some overcapacity, since unused capacity is much cheaper than the cost of adding on later. Given the capabilities of the software described above, it becomes obvious that the "stretch" in the system could be used to supply distribution to other businesses, on a contract basis. This could be done at very competitive (and very lucrative) fees, since, as with hauling, the company's costs are largely fixed. The computer does not really care that a given range of SKUs and a given range of outlets, in fact, belong to some other business.

LOOKING AT THE FUTURE

Both the rewards and the technology associated with warehousing and distribution continue to grow. As an example, consider Wal-Mart, now the nation's largest retailer. Twenty years ago, Wal-Mart was a small, essentially unknown discounter from Arkansas. The company's incredible growth was not based on stocking goods that were any different from its competitors. Rather, Wal-Mart shredded its competition by distributing commodity goods with accuracy and timeliness, and at a cost that others could not match. Such is the challenge, future, and potential contribution of modern distribution.

LOGISTICS MANAGEMENT

J. Mike McElhone, Interamerican Transport Systems, Inc.

We often hear the term *logistics management* in today's business discussions. This is partly because the term carries the connotation of high-level decisions and partly because logistics has become a common denominator among businesses. We all participate in some form of goods procurement, regardless of whether we are buying, selling, or making products.

At its most basic level, logistics is simply a system for the procurement of goods, extending from the raw materials stage to the ultimate consumer. Thus, the term can include everything from getting raw materials to feed a production line to shipping finished goods to a retail customer. Some successful companies have learned, however, that logistics management is more than a plan for getting goods from point A to point B. Rather, it is a *strategic* approach requiring reconsideration of practices and procedures that have been around for years.

THE LOGISTICS PROCESS

Perhaps the best way of describing the logistics process is to contrast it with what it is not. Instead of attempting to link the series of freestanding operations that make up a company's distribution process (operations that all function independently of each other), logistics means building a *system* that embraces all aspects of product procurement. Each operation becomes part of a machine whose pur-

pose is to bring goods from origin to final destination.

Several key concepts distinguish logistics management from distribution. In most corporate structures, purchasing, warehousing, production, transportation, and customer service are separate areas. Each is the functional responsibility of a different manager, and each may report to a different executive branch, such as finance, merchandising, or distribution. Each has its own goals related to cost reduction.

A logistics approach recognizes the relationships among the functional areas. The various managers operate as a team, responsible for the total network. This change in structure and accountability forces a change in management decision making.

Consider the premise that all distribution networks are made up of a series of operations with inherently conflicting needs. For example, a company may achieve economies in transportation through consolidation of orders. This is often in direct conflict with the needs of the sales organization, which seeks to deliver goods to the customer in the shortest possible lead time. It also conflicts with the needs of the production area, where raw materials must be on hand to meet production schedules. In a similar manner, centralized inventories reduce warehousing costs, but often impact on transportation expense and lead time. A warehouse manager, traffic manager, and sales manager, when confronted with the same problem, will very often choose different solutions.

The logistics management team, being accountable for all aspects of the problem, would weight the trade-offs involved and select the best total solution.

COST SAVINGS

In most companies, the traditional approach to individual distribution processes has probably yielded most of the cost savings that are achievable. For example, warehouse-operating studies have determined which materials-handling equipment complements the company's warehouse design and operation; purchasing has mechanized order processing to reduce error and improve response times; the transportation department has arranged for volume discounts; manufacturing has automated and streamlined production lines for optimum efficiency and waste reduction; and so on.

Consequently, the big gains needed to improve the bottom line will not be easily found in managing independent operations more efficiently. The future savings will come when management steps back and views the total distribution pipeline, noting the duplication of labor and resources that can be eliminated. The focus must shift from trying to achieve the lowest cost to finding the greatest return on the company's investment. One way to do this is to develop strategic relationships with key customers and suppliers.

LOGISTICS NETWORK

Do not assume that the logistics pipeline begins at your receiving dock. Recognize that the success of your network depends largely on your suppliers. Consider your inventory as extending to their inventory. After all, if the supplier has problems keeping costs down or meeting production schedules, these problems will be your problems very soon. By working together, and by sharing information on strategy and goals with your suppliers, you can find solutions that will solve both your problems. Those solutions will enhance your ability to service your customers and strengthen your market position.

As the cost of technology becomes more affordable, there will be fewer and fewer technical distinctions between products. Customer satisfaction will more and more become the competitive edge that will distinguish successful companies. Strong relationships will be built and maintained with key customers and suppliers by sharing information, especially through electronic data interchange (EDI) partnerships, and by developing joint strategies to address mutual challenges.

Nor should you assume the logistics network ends when goods are turned over to your customer. Just as you must view the pressures on your suppliers as your own, you must also consider the challenges facing your customer as part of the total logistics equation. Trade-off decisions made within your company will always affect your customers. A strategic partnership approach, one that allows your customer to participate in the trade-off decisions, will ensure that he or she buys into the solution and has a clear understanding of what service levels he or she can consistently expect from your company.

STEPS TO SUCCESSFUL IMPLEMENTATION

The best approach is to develop a "logistics map" by listing the activities that make up your company's logistics pipeline. The following steps outline the process:

1. Identify what strategic alliances will be needed, both internally (i.e., with various departments) and externally (with key suppliers and customers).
2. Rank supplies and processes in three categories: (a) critical (other processes cannot move forward without them; substitute materials or processes are not readily available), (b) necessary but flexible, and (c) optional. This ranking will help you set priorities in dealing with trade-off decisions.
3. Rank products in terms of their importance in meeting customer needs. If you do not know, ask. Do not guess.

4. Look for duplication of inventories, labor, resources, and capital investment. In each instance, ask the question: Is this expense being offset by a greater savings somewhere else in the pipeline?

5. Look for areas where EDI can reduce costs or improve efficiency.

6. Examine the current distribution process compared with the map developed from your customer service plan. Identify all areas where trade-offs have been made. Are they the right trade-offs for the total solution?

7. Involve your customers and suppliers in the process. Let them buy into the results you are trying to achieve.

LOGISTICS IN THE 1990s

Technological advances in all aspects of the logistics process will continue throughout the decade. Material requirements planning (MRP) systems will continue to be perfected in the manufacturing sector. Just-in-time (JIT) inventory management, common to the transportation industry for many years, will be applied in other industries. Electronic data interchange will dominate everything from order entry to funds transfer, linking suppliers to customers more closely. Purchasing professionals will be required to consider each technology in terms of new opportunities and impact on trade-off decisions. Through it all, the key to decision making must be based on customer service. It is your competitive edge. Logistics pipelines will continue to grow as international trade becomes a priority, and this will bring about still more opportunities, more challenges, and, of course, more trade-offs.

All of these changes call attention to the need for a basic change in attitude. The most important part of this is a recognition of the supplier and customer as vital links in the distribution chain, not external factors that cannot be controlled and that therefore threaten the process. Sharing information on goals and strategies, not just performance statistics, will be necessary to extend the distribution pipeline beyond your factory. Purchasing professionals will find themselves part of a team effort, with all members accountable for the same goal: total solutions rather than independent ones.

LEASING

Randall Vick, Senior Procurement Specialist, The World Bank

Leasing activity in the United States has become a $120-billion industry, with well over half of the nation's larger companies leasing at least some equipment. Purchasing's role in leasing is almost always carried out in close cooperation with two other functions: the legal department and finance. Even though a requisitioner may contact purchasing first, the financial area generally conducts the lease/buy analysis and approves the decision. The legal staff assists in preparing the initial draft of the contract and reviews the final contract. Within this framework, purchasing is often given the responsibilities of acquiring the property, including selecting the supplier, negotiating the price, and setting the initial terms for the contract. Even though leasing an asset usually costs more than outright ownership, there are clearly circumstances that make leasing an appropriate alternative.

ADVANTAGES AND DISADVANTAGES OF LEASING

Quite often, the existence of particular circumstances, usually financial, will determine if it is more advantageous to lease or own. Historically, the existence of specific tax laws made leasing advantageous for certain firms. As tax laws change, so do the potential advantages in leasing.

There are, however, advantages beyond potential tax savings. For example, leasing allows a company to avoid the risks that may be associated with certain types of developmental or high-technology equipment. In addition, leasing often assures the availability of expert service and technical assistance, thus forming an important complement to the lessee's technical staff. Also, a company often faces short-term requirements that are simply best met with short-term leases. Moreover, a firm often finds that equipment can be on-site and working in a shorter time, compared with typical capital investment procedures.

Finally, leasing involves a lower initial capital outlay. Thus, leasing may be an important tactic during a company's period of expansion, obviating the need to raise capital for all needed equipment. For an infant firm, whose start-up investment requirements exceed its reasonable line of credit, leasing may be the only avenue.

On the negative side, the user has less control of the equipment and, in some cases, a narrower choice of product. But cost is usually considered the greatest disadvantage. Leasing is usually an expensive alternative to borrowing. Generally, the interest cost of funds provided by leases runs as much as 2 percent higher than could be obtained on a loan of equivalent amount and terms. The discrepancy varies according to several factors, including the general credit standing of the lessee, the ease with which the property could be transferred, and the tax obligations of both parties.

In summary, the decision to lease or own should be made on the merits of the alternatives that exist at the time. The total cost of each alternative should be considered in line with current tax laws, present financial needs, the time period during which the equipment will be needed, and other pertinent factors. Financial, legal, and purchasing specialists all need to be involved in the analysis and decision making.

TYPES OF LEASES

Short-term leases, often referred to as rentals, are a special form of lease. Rentals make sense when the company needs to fulfill temporary needs. These present little difficulty for the purchasing professional. Long-term leases, on the other hand, are far more complex, calling for larger commitments and serious financial obligations.

Leases fall into two general categories: operating and financial. A firm uses an operating lease when management is not interested in owning an asset and wishes to avoid the risk and responsibilities associated with ownership. Most operating leases are for a short term and for a fixed period of time, usually much shorter than the economic life of the goods.

Financial leases have two distinct characteristics: (1) a fixed nature of the obligation, which produces a financial burden on the lessee typical to that of debt, and (2) payments that, in total, exceed the price of the assets leased. Usually, though not necessarily, a financial lease is a net lease. That is, the lessee agrees to pay property taxes, maintain the asset, and carry out other obligations as if the lessee were the owner.

Many types of leases are available within these two categories, ranging from a full-service automobile rental to a net lease for real estate. Once a firm decides to lease, it can usually find a vendor willing to tailor the contract to its specific needs.

SELECTING A LEASING COMPANY

Selecting and managing the lessor are the keys to obtaining the desired level of quality, technical support, and service—at the right price. The selection and evaluation processes are quite similar to those for any other vendor, with one exception. A great deal of emphasis should be placed on an evaluation of the potential lessor's financial soundness. In this regard, it is always good practice to enlist your firm's financial specialist to review the potential lessor's financial statements to assure that it has sufficient working capital. Also, dependability is a very important consideration. Look for a vendor with a history of reliable service. Visit the potential lessor's facilities and evaluate as you would for any other supplier. Check the lessor's references carefully.

The advantages of a long-term association with a leasing company are every bit as important, if not more so, than having a long-term source for key goods. Realize that you will be working with this vendor for many years. Thus, careful evaluation is critical.

CAPITAL PURCHASING

Gregory E. Conlon, Champion International Corporation

As an essential preparatory step in any capital project, all parties should understand their roles and responsibilities as well as the roles other members of the project team may play. For instance, there should be a clear understanding that *only* purchasing is authorized to commit or obligate the company to purchase equipment or services. Although making commitments is purchasing's responsibility, in most cases, the actual selection of a vendor is an engineering decision with input from operations, maintenance, purchasing, and sometimes marketing or legal. With that in mind, the purchasing process generally follows these steps:

■ *Project scoping*—This activity establishes the scope of work and an order-of-magnitude cost estimate. Purchasing provides assistance in this phase by obtaining and evaluating supplier data (budgetary parameters, proposals, proposed specifications, shop backlogs, reference lists of users, etc.). All suppliers should know, *early on*, that purchasing is the main hub of information flow. In turn, purchasing has the responsibility to serve as a resource to others, including management, on the project. Purchasing also keeps potential suppliers apprised of the progress of the project.

■ *Establishing purchasing plan, prequalifying vendors*—As soon as is practical, purchasing

Exhibit 10-4. Typical Purchasing Plan and Schedule

Week

ITEM: Crane	1 2 3 4 5 6 7 8 9 10 11 12 13 ... 18 19 20 21 ... 32 33
1. Prepare Specification (4)	
2. Vendor Inquiry (3)	
3. Evaluation and Investigation (2)	
4. Selection (1)	
5. Negotiation and Commitment (2)	
6. Vendor Engineering (6)	
7. Customer Approval (2) of Drawings	
8. Fabrication (12)	
9. Shipment (1)	
Total Time Required:	33 Weeks
Status:	Critical Path Item—Needed to Set Equipment

should work with engineering to establish a list of all anticipated significant purchases for the project, as well as a schedule for each. The schedule should allow time for a variety of factors, including specifications preparation, vendor inquiry, evaluation and investigation, selection, negotiation and commitment, supplier engineering and drawing approvals, fabrication, and shipment to the job site.

Working backward from a "date required" for each item, purchasing prepares a preliminary schedule. This requires establishing a start and finish date for each activity and identifying critical path items as shown in Exhibit 10-4.

Purchasing should then lead the effort to establish a bidder's list for each anticipated

purchase, focusing on the following supplier factors: financial stability, previous experience (reference list), quality assurance capabilities, on-time performance (engineering and equipment), level of interest (commitment to the business or industry).

At this point, it is not necessary that a supplier meet all criteria without reservation. To ensure a competitive environment, an apparently marginal vendor may be allowed to submit a proposal if:

1. The shortcomings are conceivably not insurmountable.
2. The supplier is advised that he or she is marginal and remains interested in preparing a proposal.

3. The supplier is made aware that the buyer reserves the right to reject any and all proposals.

The bidding and evaluation process will often allay or confirm concerns you may have about a particular supplier.

■ *Requests for quotation*—Once the technical specifications and a bidder's list are completed, a request for quotation may be issued. This should include but not be limited to:

1. Technical specification.
2. Plant conditions (i.e., paint type and color, electrical system voltage, any component preferences, the applicable codes, ambient temperature, etc.).
3. Contacts for technical and commercial questions.
4. Commercial terms and conditions.
5. Engineering documentation required.
6. Proposal due date.

■ *Proposal evaluation*—Once proposals are received, the buying company can perform concurrent technical and commercial evaluations. The commercial evaluation, completed by purchasing, may consider the following factors:

1. Price for equipment, services, and spare parts (look for hidden and "life of requirement" costs).
2. Adherence to terms and conditions.
3. Lead time.
4. Response to engineering documentation requirements and schedule.
5. Warranty.
6. Performance guarantee.
7. Erection and start-up and training assistance.
8. FOB (free on board) point and freight terms.
9. Payment terms and cancellation provisions.
10. Union contract expiration dates.

It is important that any significant commercial differences between suppliers are weighted and factored into the overall evaluations. Often suppliers are short listed and meetings are held with suppliers to carefully review the proposals to ensure that you have a good understanding of the supplier's offering and possibly remove any technical or commercial objections that may exist.

■ *Final negotiation, selection, and commitment*—After careful evaluation of the suppliers' proposals, the company makes a tentative selection. This selection then enables purchasing to conduct final negotiations and make an award. Purchasing must understand clearly what is to be purchased (i.e., options selected, specifications to apply, vendor services required, etc.). In addition, it is imperative that engineering's recommendation be kept confidential and discussed on a need-to-know basis only. Premature comments to a supplier about the likely outcome of an evaluation can severely reduce purchasing's chances of negotiating favorable technical or commercial terms in the final agreement.

With large-dollar purchases, customized terms and conditions are usually negotiated between the parties, often with the advice of legal council. These negotiations should be started early (during the evaluation phase) in an attempt to remove any particularly onerous provisions. Often, a letter of intent or conditional purchase order is issued after agreement is reached on all key components (price, delivery, warranty, schedule, etc.) with final contract language to be negotiated and added later. Obviously, suppliers are generally less agreeable to negotiate further conditions once they have received a commitment from a customer.

■ *Documentation*—Purchasing is responsible for maintaining complete files for the company's permanent record (usually five to seven years). These files should include:

1. Quotation request, including specifications.
2. Successful supplier's proposal (original).
3. Other proposals or a summary of their key provisions.
4. Letters of clarifications and vendor assurances.
5. Technical and commercial evaluations.
6. Meeting notes.

7. Purchase requisition.
8. Purchase order, including change orders.
9. Performance test, quality assurance data or reports.
10. Supplier acknowledgment (original).

■ *Expediting / inspection / quality*—Purchasing is responsible for ensuring that the supplier performs all its obligations on time and in concurrence with the terms of the purchase order. Dates should be established, prior to award, for engineering drawings, both approval and certified, instruction manuals, start and completion of fabrication, and delivery. To accomplish this, purchasing should, immediately after the contract is awarded, establish and maintain vigilant contact with the appropriate supplier expediting personnel. Depending on the size and importance of the purchase, company representatives should visit the supplier's plant to verify adherence to schedule. Engineering or technical help may be required to verify the level of vendor compliance.

In addition to the schedule, purchasing is responsible for ensuring that the equipment supplied meets specifications and is of good quality. For major capital equipment, this typically requires visits by quality/technical specialists. The sooner a specification or quality deficiency is discovered, the greater the likelihood it will be remedied to the user's satisfaction and usually at a lower cost to both parties.

■ *Negotiating disputes, performance and warranty issues*—Purchasing should again take the lead in this area and, with proper authorization, negotiate and communicate acceptance or rejection of proposed settlements. Purchasing should be forthright in insisting on complete supplier performance and satisfactory remedies in the case of substandard performance.

ELECTRONIC DATA INTERCHANGE

Kathleen Conlon Hinge

Electronic data interchange may be defined as the intercompany, computer-to-computer exchange of business documents in standard formats. Through EDI, such common business forms as invoices, bills of lading, and purchase orders are transformed to a standard data format and electronically transferred between trading partners. A close look at several key phrases in the definition help reveal the true impact of EDI:

■ "Intercompany"—Data transmission is *between* companies. Therefore, cooperation between companies is required to get the EDI system running properly.
■ "Computer-to-computer" — Information flows directly from the sender's application (say, purchasing) to the receiver's application (say, order entry) without human intervention and without paper.

- "Standard format"—Information must be precisely formatted so that a computer can process the information without human assistance.

DISADVANTAGES OF PAPER-BASED TRANSACTIONS

Because so many companies use computers for their internal data processing functions, including the preparation of business documents, most paper-based business transactions are accompanied by disadvantages. The use of paper in interorganizational document exchange has:

- Slowed the communication.
- Introduced error-prone rekeying of information.
- Added the costs of data entry personnel, postage, data entry errors, and paper.
- Interrupted the flow of information processing.

As a result, paper-based systems limit a company's profitability by directly or indirectly contributing to costs of:

- Administrative lead time
- Overtime premiums
- Premium overnight courier charges
- Late or incorrect shipments from suppliers
- Excess inventories
- Disruptive production schedules
- Poor forecasting
- Incorrect order entry

. . . in addition to a host of other ills.

ROLE AND BENEFITS OF EDI

EDI takes paper out of the loop, by enabling intercorporate computer-to-computer business document exchange. This creates tremendous opportunities for improving inefficiencies. The direct benefits of EDI come from reducing the costs directly associated with handling paper transactions. Indirect—or

long-term—benefits accrue from effective use of data received electronically, as well as from alliances between buyer and seller that may be facilitated through an electronic trading partnership.

Direct benefits of EDI—those that result directly from eliminating paper—are fairly easy to quantify. They include:

- *Savings*—EDI eliminates paper, postage premiums for overnight delivery, and the like. Rooms full of data-entry personnel and equipment become obsolete.
- *Accuracy*—EDI communication is direct, instantaneous, and immediately verifiable. Thus, there is no more lost or misrouted mail. Documents exchanged are 100-percent accurate and complete. Such jobs as reconciliation for payment are made much easier. All this provides additional savings.
- *Speed*—Instantaneous communication is an important EDI benefit to those companies that compete on cycle time. EDI is essential in supporting just-in-time (JIT) delivery schedules.

Indirect benefits of EDI—those that accrue from the more efficient use of information resources and improved business procedures—are more difficult to quantify. They include:

- Decreased required safety stock resulting from shortening the order cycle.
- Decreased labor, freight, and material costs resulting from fewer material returns.
- Improved cash flow resulting from reduced inventory and more timely invoicing and payment.
- Improved sales/purchasing productivity resulting from reduced paperwork requirements.
- Improved business efficiency resulting from the flow of more complete, timely, and accurate information.

The benefits derived from EDI are proportional to both the extent to which EDI is integrated with internal applications and the volume of business transacted electronically. As companies begin in EDI, volumes are low and integration is in the initial stages, if begun at all. Hence, in reality, during the initial stages of EDI implementation, the direct benefits are small and the indirect savings are virtually nonexistent.

However, as the volume of EDI activity increases and the company establishes internal systems to achieve continuous information flow, both the direct and indirect benefits of EDI increase. In the long term, indirect benefits will be substantially greater than direct benefits.

DETERMINING FEASIBILITY

A company's trade association is often the best place to start for unbiased EDI information from a user's perspective. Two organizations focus on serving EDI users across industry boundaries: DISA (Data Interchange Standards Association), which hosts the annual ANSI X12 conference, and EDIA (Electronic Data Interchange Association), which also hosts an EDI conference each year. Both are good starting points for user information. The manager who champions EDI must first evaluate whether it makes sense for the company as a whole. This requires attention to the following areas.

A fertile business environment for EDI is characterized by:

- Large volume of recurring transactions.
- Need for timely transaction processing.
- Product/service described by a code value.
- Transactions associated with large amounts of paperwork.
- Need for careful data tracking and reporting.
- Highly cost-competitive market environment.
- Centralized data processing or distributed data processing with standardized applications.

While difficult to quantify, market factors play a major role in companies' decisions to implement EDI. Even in companies where the short-term costs of EDI outweigh the benefits, the existence of EDI pressure from the market has been enough to justify the investment.

SUPPORTING COMPONENTS

EDI requires a combination of technology and management resources to efficiently communicate business information between the computers of separate companies. Commercially available EDI product and service offerings focus on three main areas:

1. Software

   - For the translation of internal data formats to some EDI format.
   - For interactive completion of a business document and translation to an EDI format (PC software only).
   - For communication of EDI-formatted documents between trading partners.
   - For maintenance of *profiles*—the standards for communication and document format required by each separate trading partner.

2. Third-party EDI network services (also called value-added network services or VANs)

   - For providing instantaneous, twenty-four-hour-a-day delivery of EDI documents.
   - For EDI format translation between trading partners using different EDI formats.
   - For "electronic mailboxing"—the ability to continuously receive and send electronic documents—and other value-added services.
   - For resolution of discrepant computer hardware and protocol issues between trading partners.
   - For support in developing a larger EDI trading partner community.
   - For EDI implementation consulting.

3. Implementation planning and consulting services

- For assistance in strategic, long-term EDI planning; this includes coordinating EDI system development with that of in-house information systems, as well as facilitating adoption of EDI among suppliers.
- For support of implementation and training.
- For information-gathering assistance; resources include periodicals, news services, and market analysis.

ANALYSIS OF SETUP AND OPERATIONAL COSTS

Setup costs refer to one-time, up-front expenditures required to implement EDI, such as:

- Development, purchase, or lease of communications hardware and protocol software.
- Development, purchase, or lease of computer hardware, application link software, and translation software.
- Person-days of effort to reevaluate current business information systems and to design for the EDI data flow.
- Person-days of effort spent in steering group meetings, in implementation meetings, meetings with trading partners, industry group meetings, or at standards organization meetings.
- Education, setup, and training costs.

Setup costs can be substantial, especially if viewed from within only one or two functional business areas. Commitment to EDI from the corporate level will facilitate cooperation among several functional areas, reducing the burden of setup costs for each area. In addition, setup need not be an all-at-once effort. Phased implementation can allow early EDI benefits to mitigate further setup expenses.

Operational costs refer to the ongoing costs of communications and the hardware and software maintenance needed to transmit and receive data electronically. Third-party EDI network charges form the major portion of EDI operational costs.

In evaluating cost/benefit, the company must keep the following in mind:

- Each functional business area has to evaluate cost/benefit separately, since costs and benefits will differ in each area.
- Market factors should be weighted very heavily.
- Setup costs, operational costs, and potential benefits should be amortized over time.
- EDI data volumes, benefits, and operational costs will increase over time.

The foregoing provides the basis for a more formal cost/benefit analysis. In many cases, however, compelling market factors have weighed heavily in the benefit side of the equation. Such factors include:

- Existence of a highly competitive market where EDI can provide much-needed competitive advantage through service distinction, product cost/lead time reduction, high customer responsiveness, supporting a strategic partnerships strategy.
- Pressure from a major customer to accept orders electronically or seek business elsewhere.
- Industry-wide EDI activity, which makes it beneficial to be a front runner in the industry, and reducing the chances of an EDI competitive disadvantage later.

IMPLEMENTATION ISSUES

EDI affects a broad range of disciplines within a company, and each must be represented in system development and installation. Hence, many EDI implementations are managed by a steering committee that reports directly to a high corporate executive and consists of the following members:

- Functional business managers (purchasing, sales, accounting, etc.).
- Systems/communications manager.

- Auditing/legal representative.
- Business managers/technical support from key trading partners.
- EDI consultant.

Functional business managers are responsible for EDI feasibility studies (cost/benefit analyses) within their own departments. Systems and communications personnel assist in the technical system specification and have a large say in choice of EDI software and VAN. Input from key trading partners is essential to cooperative and successful system development. Such choices as the type of information to be exchanged, EDI standard, transaction sets, and implementation schedule require trading partner input and support. The EDI consultant supports the effort by providing experience and a broad perspective.

Definition of a good prototype pilot program is of key importance to successful EDI implementation. The end of a pilot program with one trading partner brings the beginning of a pilot program with another trading partner. The pilot program is of defined duration, consists of defined tasks and milestones, and is conducted with defined trading partners. Proper definition of the pilot program at the outset is essential to evaluating its success at the end. In running the pilot with each trading partner:

- Complete and sign off on all pilot steps.
- Complete and sign off on all pilot milestones.

- Run parallel systems (EDI and paper) for a defined period of time.
- Evaluate results of parallel runs at end of pilot.
- Make changes and define extended pilot period, if necessary.
- Cut over to production.
- Eliminate parallel paper system.

When this process has been completed with one set of trading partners, reinitiate the pilot program with a new set of trading partners. Add trading partners by:

- Contacting new potential trading partners.
- Presenting business specifications for an EDI trading environment.
- Developing time schedule for bringing new partners into a pilot program.
- Cutting over to production as each pilot is completed successfully.

Before long, this cycle of pilot → production → pilot with each new set of trading partners becomes almost automatic. System requirements, decided by the steering committee and tested with early pilot programs, must be conformed to by trading partners added later. Hence, suppliers benefit directly by getting involved in EDI with their customers early on, thereby increasing their say in the EDI system specifications.

SECTION 11

Corporate Relations

John D. Bergen, Section Editor

Introduction   *John D. Bergen*   11-3

Managing the Corporate Relations Staff   *Harold Carr*   11-4

Government Relations   *Margery Kraus*   11-6

Media Relations in the 1990s   *Richard Torrenzano and
     Sharon Gamsin*   11-8

Shareholder and Investor Relations   *Ronald E. Zier*   11-11

Employee Relations and Communications   *William J. Hindman, Jr.*   11-14

Corporate Philanthropy   *George L. Knox III*   11-17

Business-to-Business Communications   *Don Frischmann*   11-20

Trade Relations   *Michael Rourke*   11-23

Risk Management Communications   *Richard C. Hyde and
     Gail H. Marcus*   11-25

Intracorporate International Relations   *David Metz*   11-30

Evaluating Corporate Relations Results   *David N. Richardson and
     James Granger*   11-32

11-1

INTRODUCTION

John D. Bergen

During recent years, corporations have undergone changes that affect their relations with their publics and have confused their corporate identity. It has fallen to those in corporate relations to clarify images, rebuild relations with former publics, communicate with new stakeholders, and restore tarnished reputations.

The mergers, divestitures, and acquisitions of the 1980s altered the organizational structure, corporate portfolios, and even the nationality of U.S. companies. The changes, aggravated by economic pressures, induced employer dislocation and uncertainty that put additional strains on relations with employees and related publics. Finally, social and environmental concern, activism, and regulation thrust business into the public policy arena. Even the media—both print and broadcast—through which corporations speak to their publics were undergoing tremendous changes in their own organizations.

All this took place precisely at the time that globalism became critical to successful competition in most industries. Not only were corporate communicators having to reach out to international audiences but they found themselves helping foreign managers build relations with U.S. publics. It should not be surprising that corporate relations has become a demanding and complex function in the 1990s.

Dealing with new audiences has spawned new ways to perform traditional functions. In these chapters, we address the practice of risk communications. In an era of public scrutiny and liability, every prudent corporation has taken steps to prepare for communicating with its stakeholders during the inevitable future crisis. We also discuss how technology has affected the conduct of the oldest, and still core, practice of corporate relations, working with the media. Satellite press conferences, interactive television, and the twenty-four-hour global financial markets all drive technological change in media relations.

This section also shows how corporate relations staffs have adapted to the new demands and how they have adjusted to the restructuring of all functional staffs during the downsizing era. Even as corporate relations must be more cost effective, so must it achieve the critically important communications goals that grow in significance in difficult times.

John D. Bergen *is president and chief executive officer of GCI Group, a public relations and public affairs agency with offices in twenty-five cities worldwide. Formerly the president and chief operating officer of Hill and Knowlton/USA, he previously served as staff vice-president for corporate affairs at RCA and GE. He also was chief speechwriter to the secretary of defense.*

MANAGING THE CORPORATE RELATIONS STAFF

Harold Carr, Vice-President, Public Relations and Advertising, The Boeing Company

Once upon a time, a large company's communications organization was a centralized function. As was required, communicators were "loaned" to the operating divisions. Over the years, the organizational philosophy has been completely reversed. At present, many companies have most people assigned to public relations and international communications activities in operating groups, and a relatively small corporate staff. At the divisional level, communications staff usually reports primarily to the heads of their operating groups.

Under a decentralized structure, the corporate headquarters staff is responsible for establishing the company's communication objectives and monitoring the efforts of each operating group in meeting those goals. In terms of media and public relations, the corporate staff handles those issues—such as financial, environmental, and human resource topics—that involve the whole company. In the divisions, the focus is on individual products and programs.

It is desirable for the senior executives in charge of corporate communications to report directly to the chief executive officer. The CEO inevitably sets the company's overall direction—and his or her personality and priorities will ultimately determine the strength of the communication function.

An organization in which the senior communicator reports to the chief financial officer, or another senior executive, may also be effective. The communicator must have sufficient access to the CEO to ensure that it is his or her vision that is being accurately communicated to the company's various publics.

It is a mistake for the communication function to report to a group with a short-term horizon, such as sales and marketing. The senior communicator for a company is concerned with promoting and safeguarding the firm's image, credibility, and reputation for the longer term. Good reputations are hard to make and easy to break. The communications function must be, in some sense, the custodian of the company's most cherished values and traditions, and should not be beholden to short-term goals.

If the senior communicator does report to the CEO, he or she will also be faced with the ongoing dilemma of how frequently to consult with the CEO on communication issues. This is one of the toughest day-to-day decisions confronting a communications executive. A lot depends on the management style of the CEO. Some like to manage right down to rewording a press release. Others prefer not to be bothered with the details. The senior communicator should consult with the CEO regularly enough to make sure he or she is informed of broad policy directives but not so often as to waste the CEO's time on routine decisions.

With more and more American companies concerned with productivity, the importance of internal, or employee, communications has taken a dramatic upswing. Many CEOs now view their work force as an asset whose potential has not been fully tapped. The emphasis on continuous quality improvement, breaking down the arbitrary barriers between organizations and functions, and eliminating the traditionally adversarial relations between labor and management all demand an intensive communication effort directed at employees.

The single most important basic skill you should look for in hiring is writing ability. You should also hire those with at least five years of experience in the business, preferably with media experience.

In assigning duties within the department, it is critical to pick the right people for media relations. Not everybody has the ability to respond regularly to media queries without putting his foot in his mouth, and must limit media spokespeople to those who do not risk major embarrassment to the company. Senior management tends to have a very long memory for major media gaffs—even if they resulted from an "inadvertent slip of the tongue."

After you hire the best people, give them access to executives. Restricting access to senior management is not only bad for morale but it is inefficient. If you cannot trust these people to interact with management, you probably should not have hired them in the first place.

Keeping the communications staff informed on pertinent issues is essential and it is one of the toughest day-to-day challenges. You might have a weekly conference call during which key public relations people at locations around the country update everyone on fast-breaking issues in their product area. You can have a daily bulletin for executives to give forewarning on press stories or queries that may surface the following day. Extensive use of fax machines can disseminate information on critical issues. Execution of public relations programs requires fast, coordinated action by communications staff.

A communications plan must clearly support all of the elements of the long-range strategic plan, and it must guide the plans of divisional communication staffs. Most importantly, it unites the staff in accomplishing the organization's goals in a most innovative, disciplined, and strategic way.

GOVERNMENT RELATIONS

Margery Kraus, President and CEO, APCO Associates

The 1990s pose a significant challenge to managers responsible for government relations. In contrast to the deregulation of the Reagan era, most corporations will face a variety of legislative and regulatory challenges compounded by two growing trends:

1. The aggressive movement of state and local governments to outregulate the federal government on popular consumer issues, such as environmental standards for the packaging of products.
2. The growth of citizens' movements, which increasingly results in costly ballot initiatives and referendums or stockholder resolutions.

At the same time that the nature of the issues are changing, so too are the sensitivities of policymakers making decisions on those issues. While much of the Congress changes every few years, recent elections have resulted in turnovers without precedent in modern times. States are examining (and in some cases, have already passed) term limitations for state legislators. Ethics probes have made many legislators ultrasensitive to their relationships with key special interests, even when they fully support the position of these groups. Bans on honoraria and concerns about political action committees also changed the way in which traditional government relations has been conducted.

In light of these changes, how does the progressive corporate relations office handle its government relations function? Here are some observations:

■ *Maximize organizational advantages* — While many companies separate the government relations function from the other corporate relations functions, there is a growing trend to include government relations as an integral part of public affairs or corporate relations. Normally, other functions included in this area are issues management, public relations, corporate social responsibility, and employee communications.

The advantage of this type of approach is that various areas can reinforce each other. For example, if a government relations person knows where key grants are going, he or she can involve government policymakers in the publicity surrounding the awarding of the grant. This accomplishes two things:

1. It provides the company with an opportunity to work with a member of Congress, state legislator, or local official on something of benefit to the community.
2. It provides increased visibility for the company with regard to its contribution.

■ *Conduct affirmative issues management* — Most government relations professionals will tell you they spend most of their time reacting to the crisis of the moment. While crises are inevitable, formalizing an issues management program can improve the effectiveness of the corporate government relations team and allow for proactive action.

Once a year, the company should engage in a formal planning session, identifying primary and secondary issues. You should decide how to handle each issue and what can be done to keep issues from becoming ripe. Can an early communications strategy avoid or delay governmental regulation? Can a small change of corporate policy reduce the chances that the company will become the target of a congressional hearing?

Many issues can be anticipated. Almost every company has to understand a myriad of local, state, and federal sanctions regarding clean air and water standards and packaging considerations as they relate to solid waste. Being prepared, understanding the impact to your company, and knowing what you want is essential to executing an effective government relations program.

■ *Encourage employee action* — While most companies claim they have an employee involvement program, few will say they believe the program is as effective as it should be. Your employees can be a great resource in understanding your concerns about adverse policies and proposed legislation. This is especially true for companies that have multiple facilities or are foreign owned.

Do not wait for a crisis to organize a corporate grassroot program. Inventory the interests and contacts of employees. Inform them about the issues and concerns of your company. Invite members of Congress from plant communities to visit facilities and participate in education sessions. Put a local face on your company so that each politician representing a jurisdiction important to you associates that facility with human concerns and individual people.

Do not stop when employees are organized and informed. Others you conduct business with, from suppliers to customers, are a resource to be developed. Why not conduct an issues audit now so you know which of these matters are most important to you? Perhaps you can take a proactive stand on an issue of lesser importance to your company to create a positive image with policymakers rather than only react in opposition to more onerous policies.

■ *Keep a watchful eye for future developments* — Almost every tactic for a successful government relations program has already been tried somewhere. All of us benefit from knowing what has worked and what has not worked in various situations. The state of the art for government relations responds to the changing nature of our political process.

The growth of state actions, often years ahead of federal action, creates a significant challenge to you and your staff. Some government relations professionals have found it extremely useful to conduct a "best practices" survey or study. This helps managers understand how effective companies manage their government relations activities. What strategies, tools, and tactics do they have at their disposal? What has proven to be cost effective and under what circumstances?

The 1990s will be a challenging time for government relations managers. A creative, proactive approach can help build the linkages between the private and public sectors that benefit both sectors generally and your company specifically.

MEDIA RELATIONS IN THE 1990s

Richard Torrenzano, Director and Senior Vice-President, SmithKline Beecham

Sharon Gamsin, Vice-President, Communications, New York Stock Exchange

Media relations will assume greater importance for corporate success in the 1990s than at any previous time. Business, financial, and economic news affects the daily lives of people around the world, and is now often found on the front page or at the top of TV news.

The 1970s was the period of awakening to this public interest in news of economic issues. In the 1980s, the media's infrastructure expanded to include larger business news staffs, financial news sections, and satellite-based networks for distribution of news. The 1990s will be the decade of more sophisticated use of resources now available to skilled, creative business communicators.

While media resources were expanding and audiences were demanding more sophisticated business coverage, financial institutions, manufacturers, retailers, and service industries evolved into global operations dealing with media worldwide. Smaller companies, divisions of large multinationals, and start-up companies found themselves telling their stories to local audiences. And narrowly focused publications found niche opportunities, with a multiplication of newsletters and business publications for specialized audiences. These developments have set the stage on which media relations will be playing a leading role in the 1990s.

THE MESSAGE

The basic media relations mission can be stated in different ways. The simplest is to assure that coverage focuses on management's vision and delivers its strategic messages.

A communications department, or even one individual, should coordinate these efforts and assure that all contacts with the media reinforce the message. A deliberate strategic policy must be developed and widely disseminated within the company, clarifying an image for the company. All efforts must be directed toward maintaining and supporting that image.

Are you a fast-moving creator of a stream of new products with a welcome mat always out for the media? Are you a reliable long-term supplier taking a low-key, restrained approach? Either can be successful, but not having a defined policy guarantees failure.

The strategic message should be reflected throughout the company's communications programs. Speeches, the annual report, marketing materials, and educational brochures should reflect a similar style in language and look. Consistency of message should be incorporated in internal documents, as these often end up being viewed by the public.

The company's story should be positioned

within the context of the long-term strategic direction, emphasizing continuity. Expansions and contractions, acquisitions and spinoffs, reorganizations and shifts in key personnel should be linked to a strategy rather than presented as isolated incidents.

It is equally important to set policies that assure that public statements by employees are consistent with the message management wants disseminated. The CEO should establish a policy, in writing, that media inquiries received by anyone in the company be immediately referred to one office to be answered by a designated official.

Similarly, the CEO needs to let staff know that every reasonable effort should be made to provide a timely response when the media manager calls other departments for information. If the deadline cannot be met, that individual should be told so unfulfilled promises do not undermine a company's credibility with the media.

Authorized spokespersons, including the CEO, should commit to a consistent policy in responding to the media under all circumstances. The policy should cover routine or exceptional cases, good news or bad, taking the initiative or reacting. If management disappears when the going gets tough, it is likely the media will disappear when management wants to report "good" news.

THE MEDIA DEPARTMENT

To be effective as a counselor to top management as well as a corporate spokesperson, the media department must have the confidence of the CEO. Also, the media needs to understand that the spokesperson has ready access and timely knowledge.

In the high-tech, bottom-line-oriented 1990s, media relations professionals must be business managers able to compete within the company for dollars and show a return on that investment. As images replace or reinforce words, costlier and more effective graphics and visualization may be needed. Media relations professionals should decide whether the company should contract for illustrators and video production or develop in-house capabilities.

For example, the New York Stock Exchange moved quickly to develop broadcast facilities after the October 1987 market crash, an example of a business story being covered as breaking news. Senior management committed to the development of a leading-edge broadcast facility and the creation of the NYSE Radio and Television networks. That facility provided the NYSE (New York Stock Exchange) and the broadcast media enormous flexibility and cost effectiveness in covering market activity and resulted in daily global media access for the Big Board.

The ability to produce video news releases, conduct global videoconferences or broadcast live news conferences, or put a spokesperson, live, on any television broadcast anywhere in the world will provide ongoing benefits to organizations in the 1990s. Depending on the size of a company and the frequency of media coverage, it might consider investing in some type of video editing facilities. However, at the very least, a VCR (videocassette recorder) and television monitor to record, view, and analyze coverage are essential.

MEDIA RELATIONS

Some companies find media attention an asset whereas others find it a burden, if not an outright threat. What makes the difference?

With few exceptions, a company's relationship with the media can make the difference. Developing media policy and sticking to it, knowing and respecting the journalists who cover the company, can help assure that the relationship between the media and corporate management is smooth and works to help the company achieve its goals.

If you are designated to handle the media, you need to have as much information about the company at your fingertips as is humanly and technologically possible. You must know the corporate history and understand the firm's ongoing operations and long-term strategic plan. Being able to answer questions quickly and authoritatively will help you and the media operate efficiently.

If you plan a news conference or press release, try to imagine how you would like the story to appear. Make sure the eye-catching picture, attention-grabbing anecdote, or phrase the reporter needs is part of the package. Do not tamper with the facts. Just make that little extra effort to provide the sound bite, photo, or headline your customers—the reporters and editors—are looking for.

Knowing the media who cover your company is the other major focus of your job. Before you can get to know them personally, you need to know who they are. That sounds simple, but do you have a comprehensive list of the local and national media who might cover your company? When is the last time that contact list was updated? Journalists can change beats fairly regularly, and nothing can derail a successful media campaign as quickly as sending a personal letter to a reporter who has not been on the job for five years.

Take the time to know the deadlines of the various publications and broadcasts who contact you regularly. Read the publications or watch the programs you would like to have mention your company. Your chances of interesting a journalist in a specific story are improved significantly if you tailor your approach to fit the reporter's needs.

As with any other business relationship, personal contact pays off. Successful salespeople visit their customers and establish a face-to-face relationship that creates a better comfort level than just being a voice on the phone. Do not wait until a crisis occurs to introduce yourself and your CEO to the media. Often, a series of informal, off-the-record breakfasts will go a long way toward establishing a relationship of trust that will serve both your company and the journalist well when the going gets tough.

The difference between finding media relations an asset or a burden can hinge on whether the relationship between your company and the media is adversarial or one based on understanding and respect. Keep sight of the fact that journalists have a job to do, they want to do it as well as possible, and their job is circumscribed by certain requirements. In dealing with the media, the tone of the dialogue should be that of one professional to another.

That does not mean you should stand idly by if you think a story contains misleading or inaccurate information about your company. As soon as possible after the story appears, send a letter to the editor and reporter. Clearly point out the errors, outline the actual facts, and, in no uncertain terms, ask for a correction.

INTERNAL RELATIONS

Equally as important, develop solid working relationships within the company with business managers, plant managers, economists, and researchers. If they know and trust you, and know you understand their needs and concerns, they will respect your judgment and make sure you have the information you need to do your job.

Sometimes, it also means you have to be the chief investigative reporter within the company. Find stories that will help the company and make the reporters' jobs easier. If your company has several lines of business, visit those divisions on a regular schedule to learn what is coming up that may be newsworthy.

MAINTAINING CREDIBILITY

Respect and credibility are your two greatest assets in dealing with the media, whether in day-to-day operations or in times of corporate stress. They have to be built and maintained on a daily basis.

Because of legal restrictions or company policy, you may not always be able to tell a reporter everything you know. But attempts to cover up or mislead the media are usually exercises in futility that have a destructive effect on both the company and your credibility.

Attempts to mislead are unsuccessful because journalists have so many other sources of information—your suppliers, competitors, union officials, and industry analysts, to name a few. Their information may be less complete and substantially less accurate than you could provide, but it will be used in the absence of straight talk from your office. Be straightforward and honest. Provide as much information as you can on as timely a basis as possible. If you cannot discuss an issue, say so and provide what assistance you can.

CONCLUSION

The goal is to optimize the benefits the company receives from media coverage. Increasingly, that has come to mean more than getting out an effective message or a satisfactory response to an inquiry. Like the film director,

your overriding concern is building and sustaining interest over an extended period, not the isolated effect of individual frames. Unlike the film director, your raw materials include responses to external forces as well as your own script.

In addition, you have to understand the company's business strategy—domestic and global—and manage increasingly complex communications technology as part of the business. It is a tall order, but one that must be filled by media relations managers in the 1990s.

SHAREHOLDER AND INVESTOR RELATIONS

Ronald E. Zier, Vice-President, Public Affairs, Warner-Lambert Company

GOAL OF INVESTOR RELATIONS

The basic mission of investor relations is to create an understanding about a company so that current and potential investors can make an informed judgment about its potential. To this end, corporations establish communications programs consisting of publications, presentations, personal visits, and telephone conferences to reach shareholders, securities analysts, stock brokers, portfolio managers, and other opinion leaders within the financial community. Three basic concepts guide these programs and help assure their success:

1. *Uncertainty*—It is the greatest obstacle to achieving the goal of corporate understanding. It can result from a simple lack of communication, such as not being in frequent contact with the financial community or not adequately spelling out why the company did or did not do something. A key element in avoiding or rectifying such situations is senior management's full support of a proactive, continuing investor relations program. Management's ability to delineate strategies and project a vision of the corporation's future is invaluable.

2. *Building credibility*—This concept largely revolves around delivering on promises over

the long term. It is founded on candor concerning such factors as earning projections, anticipated management changes, timely product introductions, financial placements, and manufacturing capacity. In elemental terms, it means doing what you say you will do.

3. *No Surprises* — This concept goes to the heart of investor relations. The literature is rife with instances of companies commenting favorably on their operations on a Monday, only to formally announce different results seventy-two hours later.

The only antidote to that kind of event is to become totally proactive. Do not hide. Get on the phone, call an analysts' meeting, and be available. Tell the facts. If you anticipate bad news, make sure you are the messenger. Be out front. This approach will also give you the opportunity to explain why something happened and how its impact can be effectively managed. Experience has shown that the "hit" is often less severe and less prolonged than if you permit the news to simply ooze out over a period of time.

THE INVESTOR RELATIONS ENVIRONMENT

The genesis of investor relations was a series of government regulations promulgated by the Securities and Exchange Commission, established in 1934 to protect the investing public. These rules lay out precisely how corporations are to make adequate and timely disclosure of "material" events. These include earnings and dividend reports, acquisition or divestiture notices, and senior management changes. In short, any event that could influence a prudent investor to buy or sell your shares should be considered "material" and trigger an immediate and appropriate release. This information should be issued to a broad range of media reaching the investing public.

Since the 1970s, corporations have provided a broad menu of investor information and services. The programs have become increasingly sophisticated. For example, the financial analyst community is divided into two segments for targeted communication. Slightly different emphasis and programs are developed for buy-side analysts (pension funds, banks) compared to the sell side (brokerage houses with retail units).

THE INVESTOR RELATIONS PROGRAM

The primary staple of an investor relations program is the informal daily mix of phone conversations and office visits. Wherever possible, these visits include contacts with senior management to provide greater insight into the company. In this computer age, many companies have found it valuable to build their own databases, including comments on an analyst's most recent visit or quotes from any written report they may have issued. They also maintain an up-to-date catalog on the latest information they have released on performance, individual products, and research investment.

The more formal elements of the program consist of comprehensive presentations to analyst groups. A standard program might include an annual presentation in a large financial market, participation in industry-related conferences sponsored by investment houses, and luncheon/dinner sessions with small groups of prospective investors in the top twenty-five worldwide markets.

In recent years, the creation of global markets has demanded an international approach to investor relations. Increasingly, companies are listed on exchanges outside of the United States. A comprehensive investor relations program should include visits to international financial capitals. A standard program could include presentations in such centers as Edinburgh, London, Frankfurt, Zurich, Tokyo, Hong Kong, and Singapore. These visits might be coordinated by the company's investment or commercial banking representative in each country.

INVESTOR RELATIONS DOCUMENTS

Shareholder publications have matured beyond their originally assigned role as disclosure documents. The annual report now frequently serves as a corporate statement about its mission and culture. As such, its utility extends beyond the financial markets to address relations with current and prospective employees, community leaders, government officials, and academicians.

Quarterly reports can be equally informative. As a result of their frequency, they can be used to address timely events and issues. That makes them useful for distribution among media, elected officials, and other interest constituencies.

SHAREHOLDER SUPPORT

Maintaining and servicing established shareholders is plain hard work. Shareholders have already made their investment decision. Now the job is to keep them convinced about the prudence of their investment and to assure that the account is maintained to their satisfaction. The bottom line is that satisfied shareholders are more apt to increase their holdings.

In addition to the myriad details surrounding share ownership, such as registrar and transfer procedures, tax issues, and certificate questions, special services can help enhance a shareholder's appreciation of the company. These include dividend reinvestment programs and bank-sponsored programs that facilitate share purchases without a recourse to a broker.

Many companies have developed share ownership programs that involve one of their most loyal constituencies—their employees. These include ESOPs (employee stock ownership plans) and broadly based stock option programs, which pay productivity dividends by getting employees even more involved in the company's future. During the eighties, companies found that employee share ownership was frequently a useful weapon in dealing with hostile takeover bids.

INVESTOR RELATIONS STAFF

From an organizational perspective, many companies have found value in housing the investor relations function within their public affairs staff. The reasons are straightforward. Whether the company is communicating with the media, government leaders, or investors, the basic information is precisely the same. It is just packaged a bit differently. By maintaining these functions in a single organization, you eliminate the "reinventing the wheel" syndrome in terms of fact gathering and you build teamwork as the staff develops strategies for how and when the information can best be used.

If investor relations can be said to be evolving, so are its practitioners. In the recent past, investor relations was primarily perceived as a function of the treasurer's department. That made particular sense when the financial community was largely preoccupied with scrutinizing balance sheets and P&L (profit and loss) statements. Today, well-informed securities analysts look beyond the numbers. They want detailed information about new product plans, research strategies, and management succession. They want to know how legislative and regulatory events in Washington and Brussels will affect the company. Or about the company's position vis-à-vis social issues, such as South Africa and animal rights.

In that climate, it makes sense to have a well-rounded individual in the post. The ideal candidate should also have experience in sales, management information systems, and strategic planning. The companies should also consider rotating junior staff members from other disciplines into backup positions in investor relations. This provides fast-track managers in accounting, finance, or marketing with a look at the external factors that can frequently influence corporate decision making.

EMPLOYEE RELATIONS AND COMMUNICATIONS

William J. Hindman, Jr., Hindman and Associates

Now you are in the employee communications job. The one you wanted. You are standing at the window in your office looking across the parking lot. And you are thinking: Their bodies are here . . . and their intelligence. But where do I find their minds? With that disquieting question, you have just described your new job.

THE TARGET

The employee mind. Fragile as an eggshell, tough as sheet steel. As cynical as a traffic cop, as loyal as Lassie, as playful as a kitten, as indifferent as a statue. As crowded as a rush-hour freeway, as elusive as a shadow. As essential as your paycheck.

Given the state of the employee mind today, it is little wonder so much time and money are necessary for its care and feeding. It is a mind in which a complex of considerations come together each day, pushing and shoving and vying for attention. And there, scrambling with the rest, are you and your company. If you can acknowledge that company problems contribute to that dicey communications environment—punishing margins, new technology, union demands, layoffs, shifting corporate priorities, cries for reform from groups that did not exist five years ago—then consider what the external world does to the employee mind.

It is a time of breathtaking highs and lows in almost every facet of employee life. Around the dinner table, in front of the television set, in the halls at school, at the shopping center, in church, on the freeway, exhortations in the guise of commercials, instructions, and news crowd in on normal interchange. Relationships between husbands, wives, kids, and friends—already sagging from a lack of time—need relief but often cannot find it.

THE PROBLEM

These emotions come to work each day. The result is that employee communications, the irreplaceable link between the company and its internal audiences, must fight for a place in line with other linkages. It was not always this way. Once upon a time, employee communications managers operated with the certainty that in return for weekly, biweekly, or monthly doses of information the employee mind would grant appropriate behavior.

Today, no matter how flawless your techniques, they must derive from a tight set of strategies that drive each and every message. It is this requirement, the need for sound strategic planning, that makes employee communications one of the major challenges in public relations.

THE ROLE OF PLANNING

All the work you are going to do must be guided by a written plan. And while that may be standard practice for some companies, it is not for many midsize or smaller organizations where employee communications can become, if permitted, almost whimsical.

The plan is not only a statement of objectives and strategies. It provides a tight estimate of what achieving them will cost. Importantly, the plan sets down the assumptions that you must make if you are going to put a time line around the result you expect. Finally, the plan describes the tracking that will be necessary and the intervals at which you will take measurements.

This task, writing the plan, is the toughest work you will ever do. Compared to the solitariness of putting thoughtful objectives in place that stretch both you and the company, then articulating them in prose powerful enough to convey your beliefs, executing the plan—doing things—is duck soup.

Positioning the Company

One aspect of the plan in particular merits attention because it is not always foremost in the mind. It is the positioning requirement. You might observe that the company is already positioned in the employee mind. Of course, that is true. But is that position consistent? Does it place the company realistically in the employee mind? Make no mistake—neither the company nor the employee mind is well served in an atmosphere of contradiction.

Is the company widely believed to be a good place to work? Can the employee mind call up procedures and policies that argue with that reputation? Does the company pride itself on being politically or environmentally sensitive? Does the evidence that drifts into the employee mind reinforce company action or are there clay feet in the closet? Does the company pride itself on quality? Is it demonstrable or ephemeral?

The point is obvious: You need to search for a position that will launch your efforts with a nod, not a shake, of the head. Until you have properly positioned the company, the information you must communicate will fall on skeptical ears. And today, that simply means you are not getting through, that your budget will not last, that the employee mind is not being drawn to you but is pulling back.

Picking Out the Tools

The written plan will outline the themes you need to communicate. For many issue-related topics that call for in-depth treatment, print media remain the basic information distributors. Yet newspapers, magazines, bulletin boards, management and departmental newsletters, even quick delivery vehicles such as posters and table tents, should be appraised as much for the message environment they offer as for the space they provide. Moreover, especially in print, writers need to be reminded that the employee mind, like the external consumer mind, wants information to provide benefits and solve problems.

The electronic media offer both strategists and creative specialists new opportunities. Videotape has a secure place in employee communications. It does a superb job of personalizing messages from the top people in a company. It can also be an effective carrier for motivational information and topics that will benefit from visual emphasis.

Although programs need not be lavish, dollars spent for adequate production values will more than repay themselves in holding viewer interest. Using video does not mean a studio and a staff. You can get bids from a variety of vendors who can build you anything from a video magazine to a report from the CEO. The electronic newsletter that can be accessed through personal computers offers a useful timing advantage. If you have released an important story to the mass media, you can bring employees up to speed before they see it on the early news. Electronic newsletters, together with the increasingly pervasive fax, bring you another advantage in dealing with urgent material. Both can be printed out and posted in high-traffic locations.

An underutilized electronic tool, at least in many companies, sits conveniently on every desk: the telephone. Properly programmed, teleconferencing is quick, personal, and interactive. It is also relatively inexpensive. One caveat—do not load the call with too much information. A single-subject call works best.

A medium that should be mandatory in your company is face-to-face communication. The executive suite needs to move into the trenches on a scheduled basis. Ditto the department heads. And supervisors. If you are implementing a face-to-face program or re-working the one you have, you might consider giving managers some state-of-the-art training. It does not need to be long or expensive. It does need to highlight techniques that work.

The hallmark of effective internal communication is that it seems to seek out and speak personally to each employee. Choosing the proper tool and tuning it for the audience can take your message deeper into the employee mind than you ever imagined.

EMPOWERING THE PEOPLE

Many managers and employees would agree that there is neither a lack of communication nor a shortage of information in today's internal environment. Indeed there may be too much communication, too much information. Like a pail under a spout, the employee mind may be close to running over. There remains one more ingredient critically important in successful employee communications programs. It is called empowerment.

Empowerment is an enabling concept, but one that often requires an attitude adjustment. It is the company's recognition—consistently on display—that each employee is invested with authority and a clear sense of importance. Until you convey the deed of empowerment and provide the communications feedback channels to exercise it, employees may pass through each day disinterested—or worse, believe themselves ineffectual, merely filling up the parking lot at eight and emptying it at five.

The enabling vehicle is, of course, information itself—not shoveled out simply because it is Tuesday and something has to be said. Rather information should be prepared and presented with the conviction that, empowered, the employee mind can better understand the company, its customers, and the need for a quality attitude if jobs are to survive in today's competitive marketplace.

Your challenge is to build an information environment that animates each employee's requirement for self-enhancement and job improvement, that puts inspired dialogue ahead of tiresome preaching, that encourages decision making down the line, that warrants the company's willingness to argue its cases before an audience of employees sitting often as both judge and jury.

When each word you write and each picture you take amplify your commitment to empowerment, you are on your way to the quality and quantity of employee response that both you and your company need to grow and profit.

CORPORATE PHILANTHROPY

George L. Knox III, Vice-President, Public Affairs, Philip Morris Companies, Inc.

THE PHILOSOPHY

Like individuals, corporations are citizens of the world. Unlike individuals, they are endowed by charter with perpetual life and the power to limit the financial liability of their investors. In return, American companies are commonly held responsible to a highly diverse group of constituencies, including not only shareholders but also employees, customers, suppliers, consumers, and communities.

Because these many stakeholders may have different interests, attempting to satisfy all of them can force a company to play multiple roles. An active program of corporate philanthropy is one of the best ways a company can reach beyond its shareholder base to benefit its other constituencies; still, it will not necessarily be able to aid all of them at the same time. Consequently, corporate giving becomes a natural flashpoint for the many paradoxes and conflicts associated with the company's multiple roles. Corporations have little choice in the matter. Their philanthropy is mandated both by business considerations—the expectations of their constituencies—and by a moral recognition of their enduring social responsibilities.

Understanding the company's duty is important because corporate philanthropy is increasingly open to criticism, both from inside and outside the company. Internally, managers may look skeptically at even the most established philanthropic programs, and may want to channel its funds into business projects such as better equipment or more advertising and promotion. Externally, any donation can run into trouble: An outspoken member of the board of a museum receiving funds, for instance, or a provocative artist in the exhibition, can confuse various constituencies about the donor's motives. Developing clear motives, goals, and expectations is crucial to implementing philanthropic programs in the face of so many conflicting pressures.

DANGER: MIXED MOTIVES AHEAD

A typical argument in favor of corporate philanthropy is enlightened self-interest. By this logic, corporate philanthropy is a business investment on behalf of shareholders: Grants to local high schools, for example, might give a company a more educated pool of job applicants; cause-related marketing boosts sales; fund-raising dinners might seem to provide important opportunities to forge relationships with opinion leaders.

This argument appeals to the hard-nosed among us: It makes philanthropy another facet of corporate relations, designed to improve a company's business climate. Rather dangerously, it also suggests that philanthropy will have a quantifiable payoff. But last year, U.S. corporations contributed approximately $5 billion to nonprofit organizations. Few observers could point to an aggregate profit from this $5-billion investment, whether in the form of improved business climate, or of negative events that would have occurred but for the positive impact of the philanthropy.

Planners should resign themselves to the fact that corporate philanthropy is not simply an aspect of the corporation's steward-of-shareholder-wealth role. Instead, philanthropy branches out to include the corporation as major employer in the community; as a significant source of technical skill; as a user of natural resources. Discharging the responsibilities that accompany these roles, companies can properly direct their philanthropy to activities that benefit their shareholders indirectly at best. These may include relief for victims of poverty, disease, or natural disaster; cultural and arts projects that excite their audiences; schools that turn out students better equipped for their future.

Today's sensitive political environment makes it particularly important that companies accept the tensions implicit in their multiple roles. Every day, as the evening news looks for a new story, single-issue groups develop new litmus tests to gauge the social responsibility of a company. These issues include environmental and health impact, animal rights, nuclear power, donations to groups with one or another stance on abortion, employment practices, business in a given African, Asian, or Latin American country. . . . The list will never stop growing, and no company can always please all the list makers. In any case, if the underlying philanthropic motive is to atone for a sense of corporate guilt, the company may not even be permitted to pursue it: At least since Shaw's Major Barbara urged the Salvation Army to refuse large donations of "tainted money," nonprofit organizations have sometimes distrusted prospective funders.

Under these circumstances, the challenge of doing good is extraordinarily complex, and a philanthropic program needs clear and unswerving corporate commitment. Corporate giving will therefore require the same careful strategic planning and consensus building as any other business project.

FOCUS, FOCUS, FOCUS

Giving money away intelligently is not easy. A contributions program will work best if it is a coherent whole that fits the company's corporate culture, reflecting the company's vision of society and the values of its employees or managers. Similarly, the company's long-range planning horizon should also apply to its philanthropic efforts, so that the philanthropy and business do not conflict.

When a company's philanthropy concentrates on defined areas of interest, people inside and outside the company can understand and join in its program. This makes the philanthropy more effective for the program's beneficiaries—hospital patients, arts audiences, or students, for instance. In addition, as funders gain experience and increase their contacts in a chosen field, they will receive more suitable funding applications, and will become better at screening applicants. Funders may also acquire the expertise to develop requests for proposals, guidelines for grant seekers that guarantee a good initial fit between applications and the company's philanthropic interests. Finally, the focusing of a philanthropic program helps to lessen resentment when applications outside the area of concentration are turned down. As with corporate identity, long-term consistency will be crucial to defining and communicating the company's focus.

The areas for focus should be determined not by immediate business advantage, or even by pressure from a constituency, but by a single question of corporate identity: Where can the company, by virtue of what it already is, do the most good? A pharmaceutical company, by its nature, may be well qualified to take a leading role in medical donations, scientific education, or innovation promotion. A consumer products company may want to focus on projects spurring excellence in design, or continuing a tradition implicit in its operations or history. When the company and its selected philanthropic field match, the company can more easily stretch its funding by providing executives' time, employees' expertise, public relations help, used equipment, or unused space.

A proper fit also helps the company shape its programs for impact. An unsolicited contribution to a large national charity might make a store owner feel good, but sponsoring a local junior high school basketball team, or helping a small arts organization, could mean more for the store's immediate community or customers. A company can also use its experience and contacts to leverage its contribution. A corporate lead sponsor has not necessarily donated the majority of the funds; rather, the company may have provided seed money or a challenge grant, and may have helped recruit other funders.

Corporate philanthropy also benefits from a geographic focus, frequently a concentration on communities where the company has operations. This helps funders acquire the information networks that steer them away from potential pitfalls—unreliable administrators or political feuding, for instance—and toward opportunities to do good more effectively.

CONSENSUS BUILDING

Corporate philanthropy needs not only good people and generous resources but also the commitment of the company. Internal briefings to management, forthright explanations to investors, and programs encouraging employee participation are invaluable in building goodwill among constituencies. By their approval, these stakeholder groups can actually contribute to the philanthropy and its beneficiaries; their doubts and fears, especially in the event of controversy, can undermine an entire program.

The more senior the managers involved in the philanthropic program, the more important it is that they understand its philosophy and focus. Properly recruited, senior business managers will help the program meet internal and external challenges, and will understand that running a program by whim can be counterproductive. As sponsors of the program, they will also carry more weight with internal and external audiences than corporate relations executives.

Because corporate philanthropy displays the company's beliefs, values, and multiple roles to a wide public, contributions managers will have to work with powerful constituencies inside as well as outside the company. A large staff of contributions specialists is not always necessary to maintain good relations with these factions; excellent management is.

Ultimately, the amount of good a sponsor does will reflect not only the amount of money it has given but also the boldness, imagination, and discipline behind its commitment.

BUSINESS-TO-BUSINESS COMMUNICATIONS

Don Frischmann, Operations Director, IBM Marketing and Services

GOAL OF BUSINESS COMMUNICATION

Getting the right message to the right people at the right time is the objective of all marketing communications, whether it is advertising, media relations, or direct mail. In today's global, "take no prisoners" environment, companies must continually improve their understanding of industry and consumer requirements and persuade each business buyer that their products or services provide the best solution. And they must do it fast, efficiently, and inexpensively.

With an industry reach that encompasses virtually every product category and a rich depth of detail within each vertical industry, business-to-business communications has been described as the bridge between buyers and sellers, the most effective way to match the trade or product message to the business audience. And with more than 4,000 business press publications and over 8,000 trade and industry associations in the United States today, business-to-business communications has become a science.

Indeed, identifying exactly the right audience and understanding their needs has become the obsession of marketing communications staffs. As a result, there has been an explosion of sophisticated computer tracking programs, audience segmentation studies, focus groups, and feedback surveys.

EXECUTIVE COMMUNICATION

In the blur of all this high-tech media planning, one kind of marketing communications is often overlooked—executive communications. An aggressive, targeted executive communications plan can produce dynamic and memorable messages that not only complement and amplify other media strategies but also directly affect the efforts of the sales force. And because the customers demand to deal with experts in business-to-business communications, the involvement of top executives adds great credibility to the highly rated arena of face-to-face communications.

Developing a strategic executive communications plan to reinforce business communications involves six basic steps that tap into the full spectrum of marketing communications functions and skills.

Develop Key Messages

The first step is to identify the three or four key messages you want to communicate throughout the year in all media. These key messages should serve as the superstructure for all speeches, interviews, byline articles, proactively placed stories, videotapes, and so forth. Encompassing issues such as corporate themes, strategic directions, or short- and long-term plans for products and services, key messages should always be written from the viewpoint of customer benefits.

Identify Opportunities

Once the key messages are in place, begin to match messages and the appropriate executives to the right venues—meetings, industry conferences, roundtables, mass circulation and trade publications, and television. If your company has not traditionally participated in a promising venue, go out and actively solicit it. Do not wait for the phone to ring—it may not. Worse yet, your competition will be filling the slot you want.

When a leading computer manufacturer recently interviewed industry experts and customers, it found that conferences and forums have a strong impact on opinion leaders who ultimately influence customers. It also discovered that the most effective forums for vendors to use are those dedicated to the customer's key issue or industry—again, targeted audiences and tailored messages.

Industry events also provide exceptional trade press media opportunities for extending the reach of executive communications. In response to a survey conducted by the Association of Business Publishers, more than 9,800 subscribers said specialized business publications were their primary source of information on the products and services they purchase. And in a survey of more than 1,000 small business owners in the United States, the trade press was cited as the most credible of all media.

Executive interviews and byline articles that appear in trade publications can build on previously placed stories about the company's offerings, thus providing an integrated, ongoing series of messages that marry products and services to the company's strategy and philosophy. With such an approach, an aggressive vertical industry trade press program can produce significant payback on a minimal investment.

Once opportunities have been booked, it is absolutely critical to spend time with meeting sponsors and editorial staffs to find out what they or their customers want and need. Remember that the audience determines if the speech or the article is a success, so give them value. Once you meet customer requirements, raise the ante. For a speech, offer the addition of a fully staged, live demonstration of a new technology, product, or process in exchange for the keynote spot. For a trade publication, offer to provide original photography or a guided tour of a new facility to elevate the story to cover status.

Use Customer Endorsement

Research has consistently shown that the credibility of all types of communications is strengthened when accompanied by customer, business partner, or industry expert testimony. Consider sharing the stage for a few minutes with a customer or having customers participate in press interviews. Other possibilities include video testimonials as speech support or, in a trade press article, a sidebar about a visit to a customer location.

Make Speeches Theatrical

Unless the speaker has the charisma of Kevin Costner or the cache of Margaret Thatcher, nothing in business-to-business communications carries a greater risk of boredom than a thirty-minute talking head. There are more than enough books and articles available to help make speeches entertaining. What they do not emphasize is the importance of creating an original scenario for a new technology or product demonstration so the audience can easily and quickly apply the demonstration to the needs of their businesses. Some caveats:

1. All speech staging, effects, or humor must tie back into the key messages or the entire presentation will look like a self-serving exercise.
2. Executives—no matter how charismatic—need to rehearse.

Merchandise Speeches

Only half the job has been done if a dynamic, visionary speech—especially one that includes a new product or technology demonstration—ends when the executive exits the stage. At IBM, speechwriters are responsible for coordinating marketing communications staff support from various functions to give the speech a long afterlife. With aggressive merchandising, the secondary reach of a speech can put the audience in the hundreds of thousands. When merchandising is incorporated into the plan at the outset, projected secondary reach numbers can be used as a lever to justify funding for the project. Merchandising possibilities include:

- Speech reprints and/or abstracts of the demonstration distributed to the audience, other customers, the press, and employees. Have copies ready for distribution right after the speech to capitalize on the audience's high interest. If building a mailing list is an objective, gather names and addresses to forward the speech.
- On-the-spot interviews with the executive as soon as the presentation is over. Here again, the media relations staff can use the audience's excitement and interest to capitalize on opportunities with the press. Have the people from your company who actually developed the new product or technology available for interviews and corridor conversations with customers. If the event was held in a second-tier city, front-page coverage in the local press or inclusion in the evening news is a distinct possibility.
- A byline article based on the speech for inclusion in a trade publication, a company-sponsored customer magazine, as well as an employee publication.
- A videotape record of the event. If the budget allows, this can often be the most far-reaching merchandising tactic. Distribute it to the audience. Recent studies have shown that audiences want to share the experience when they get back to their companies. Distribute it to industry experts and consultants who were not at the event so they can start talking about it. Distribute edited highlights to your sales force to use as a dynamic opener to customer calls. Distribute it to employees for their information. If edited immediately following the event, it can be distributed to stations as a video news release. If your company has a customer publication, make the videotape available to your entire customer base. Apple, IBM, and Microsoft have followed this strategy effectively

for major executive presentations. Look at dealer and business partner opportunities for additional uses for the tape.

Get Feedback and Revise Messages

There is nothing like objective, quantifiable data to find out whether or not your message got through. Many associations conduct in-depth evaluations of their conventions. Work with the association's committee to have specific questions about the content of your executive's messages included. If feedback is not built into the program, get permission to distribute a very short questionnaire of your own. One senior corporate executive increased the effectiveness of his speeches from session to session by 54 percent as the result of feedback.

For publications, conduct blind surveys with readers of targeted magazines. A Fortune 50 company found that its image rose 20 percent after the appearance of a proactive article.

CONCLUSION

In business-to-business communications, the inclusion of an executive communications plan into other industry media strategies can have an enormous effect on a company's image. By virtue of their executive credibility and their visionary vantage point, senior officers can often be the architects of the bridge that joins their customers to their sales force. Through the impetus of an integrated, targeted, ongoing industry strategy, customers and industry experts see that a company understands its customers' needs and is producing products and services to meet those needs.

And that brings us back to the opening objective of this chapter—getting the right message to the right people at the right time. When you accomplish that objective and then reinforce it on a regular basis, momentum builds. Industry experts have the information to tout the company in the press. Users have the information to recommend the company's products and services. And your marketing communications staff has a lot more material for next year's customer testimonials.

TRADE RELATIONS

Michael Rourke, Vice-President, Communications/Corporate Affairs, The Great Atlantic & Pacific Tea Co., Inc.

PRINCIPLES OF TRADE RELATIONS

Of the many "publics" impacting the life of a corporation, the one with perhaps the greatest potential for both conflict and cooperation is the "trade." Suppliers, customers, providers of services, and even competitors are the various segments making up an industry. Thus, trade relations encompass the principles and policies that guide a corporation's interactions with those segments, and the implementation of those principles by its personnel.

The philosophy behind good trade relationships is the belief that the overall image of a total industry should be a major concern of all its members. While individual corporate performance is paramount, each trade segment clearly shares some degree of responsibility for the success of the industry as a whole.

This is a delicate balance to maintain, and the best example is the basic buyer/seller relationship. Ideally, it should reflect professionalism, mutual understanding, and integrity—not adversarial to the point that it is either one-sided or unproductive, yet not overly friendly or "chummy" to the extent that employers' interests are compromised.

It is not uncommon to tip this balance either way in the modern corporate environment, where events sometimes dictate the lessening of cooperation and communication. Rapid organizational change and the bottom-line emphasis have, to an extent, eroded both employee-management loyalty and the belief in intercorporate partnership. And such modern-day marvels as computer-to-computer communication, fax machines, and voice mail, while improving speed and efficiency, have decreased face-to-face interaction both within and between organizations.

SHAPING THE TRADE RELATIONS POSTURE

The trade relations posture, while established at the top of the organization, materializes at several levels. As in all key policy areas, it is the chief executive and other senior managers who set the tone by communicating both policy and attitude to subordinates, setting guidelines and parameters, and in general projecting a definitive corporate culture in public appearances and meetings with their counterparts in other companies.

In large organizations, senior marketing and communications executives should play an important role in representing the chief executive in many instances, and might also serve as the initial point of contact leading to relationships across various functional lines. In addition, such personnel are generally responsible for participation in external trade activities and events that bring the various industry segments together.

Finally, there are those "on the line"—the buyers, sellers, and operations personnel who have frequent direct contact, but under the most intense and pressurized circumstances. Their challenge is to maximize results for their own companies while maintaining fairness and integrity in all business dealings. To promote such performance, management must establish and enforce guidelines ensuring propriety, but also allow for a degree of individuality conducive to professional working relationships.

PUT YOUR POLICY IN WRITING

The best starting point is the formulation of a clear, concise document—a corporate code of ethics. Putting such a policy in writing, and making certain it is thoroughly understood by every employee whose job entails outside trade contact, is one of the best ways to establish a reputation for fairness, integrity, and consistency of purpose and attitude. Beyond expressing a general corporate philosophy, such a document must provide very specific policies governing the conduct of anyone in a buyer/seller capacity, covering such subjects as conflict of interest, the use or acceptance of gifts, gratuities, premiums, and other incentives, and other related considerations.

The burden of understanding or interpreting policy must be lifted from those who implement it daily. If it is not, the result is no policy at all, and ultimately no clear image projected to the trade at large. Conversely, clear ground rules observed consistently provide a solid and ethical foundation for individual relationships, enabling them to reflect a larger understanding between organizations as well.

OPPORTUNITIES FOR DIALOGUE

Once such a foundation exists internally, management should then encourage participation in organizations and events that link counterparts from other companies, to promote the objectives of the overall industry. For example, federal, state, and local legislation and regulations often affect all compa-

nies within an industry. Industry interests concerning these issues can best be advanced when various trade sectors join forces on a joint position.

Corporate membership and active participation in industry trade associations at the state and national levels provide such opportunities. Business meetings, educational seminars, sessions with government agencies and consumer groups, and trade conventions promote common interest within industries, in addition to fostering the kind of one-on-one communication and cooperative spirit basic to good relations.

Another catalyst for developing that spirit is the camaraderie that results from the many civic, charitable, and other public-spirited activities that often link industry sectors. For instance, food manufacturers, wholesalers, and retailers donate millions of dollars worth of grocery products annually to food banks and other assistance programs. And the coordinated response of all industry sectors to fund-raisers for a variety of worthy organizations each year has been a source of great mutual satisfaction.

While benefitting those in need, the hours put in on a voluntary basis to coordinate these efforts bring people from every phase of an industry together, and form the basis for ongoing friendships in an informal situation removed from the rigors of daily business.

A NEW ERA OF SOCIAL RESPONSIBILITY

Finally, the business community has long played an active role in helping society in general to overcome some of its larger problems, and that role often involves working closely with trade associates. In the early 1970s, when the first oil embargo plunged the United States into an energy crisis, the manufacturing, distribution, and transportation industries joined forces in rethinking systems, redesigning facilities and equipment, and generally reviewing the way we did business with an eye toward conservation. This marked one of the most significant collaborative efforts by various sectors throughout

American industry, and its benefits are being reaped today by corporations and consumers alike.

Today, corporations can have similar impact as the effort to encourage solutions to pressing environmental problems gains momentum. This may in fact represent the ultimate example of multilateral cooperation, since success will require mutual idea exchange not only among trade elements within industries but among all industries, government at all levels, and consumers.

RISK MANAGEMENT COMMUNICATIONS

Richard C. Hyde, Hill and Knowlton, Inc.
Gail H. Marcus, U.S. Nuclear Regulatory Commission

THE NEED

Increasingly, institutions of all kinds face the need to explain the possible hazards of their products or actions in both routine and abnormal situations. Such communication needs result from increasing sensitivity of the public to the potential risks of the products and processes in a modern industrialized society. The need for effective risk communication is becoming an important element of risk management and corporate public relations. First, two definitions are in order:

1. *Risk management communications* — This is one element of any effective program to manage or control risks. Risk man-

agement communications involves all the efforts an organization may undertake to explain the health and safety or environmental consequences of its products or processes; the efforts it has undertaken to help minimize risks; and where appropriate, the roles of other organizations (such as government agencies).

2. *Crisis communications* — In emergency situations, such as major plant accidents or product tampering, the communication needs are heightened. This special area of risk communication is called crisis communication.

CONSIDERATIONS

Risk communications must take into account:

1. Different audiences including employees, the neighboring community, users

The views expressed in this chapter are those of the authors and do not necessarily reflect the views of the U.S. Nuclear Regulatory Commission or Hill and Knowlton.

and consumers, state and federal agencies, elected officials at all levels, and the general public.

2. The interpretation of complex and highly technical information for a general audience unfamiliar with such specialized concepts as probabilities, uncertainties, or animal research protocols.

3. The recognition that public perception of risks is highly colored by factors unrelated to the absolute level of a risk, including the degree of familiarity, the sense that the risky activity is undertaken voluntarily, the sense of personal control, and the maximum potential consequences.

Effective risk communication requires continual awareness of these audience characteristics. Further, effective communication involves a long-term commitment. It should begin early, should anticipate potential concerns, and should continue for the life of the activity. It should incorporate both routine programmatic elements and plans for emergency situations. While it should use different approaches to meet different needs, it must treat every audience with integrity and respect.

OBJECTIVES

Risk communication can be used to meet different needs:

1. To instruct consumers or employees on the safe use of products or equipment (e.g., appliance instructions, safety posters in the workplace).

2. To meet legal requirements (e.g., warning labels on tobacco and alcohol, information inserts in pharmaceutical products).

3. To gain community acceptance for siting a facility.

4. To address employee and union concerns about the health hazards of occupational exposures.

5. To instruct users or residents on emergency procedures (e.g., announcements and seat pocket cards on aircraft flights, sirens, and radio broadcasts).

6. To provide information to government officials, corporate management, consumers, area residents, and others in the event of a crisis involving an organization's activities or products.

While a good communication program can assure that decisions are made with an understanding of the facts, it cannot guarantee success in allaying public concerns or securing public acceptance. Members of the general public may or may not be persuaded by low probabilities of risk, analogies to other risks, or cost-benefit considerations. Public concern about nuclear power production is a case in point. Nevertheless, a good communication program will assure that the necessary information is available, and will therefore improve an organization's chances of achieving and maintaining acceptance.

For convenience, routine and crisis risk communications are addressed separately. However, in many cases, there will be an overlap in organizational responsibilities and informational materials.

GUIDING PRINCIPLES

While the purposes and audiences of routine and crisis risk communication may vary, the guiding principles remain constant. Risk communication must be:

- *Frank and open*—Misrepresenting risks, hiding or denying facts, or simply failing to supply information is detrimental in the long run.
- *Clear*—Information must be provided at a level, and in language, that the intended audience can understand, but without compromising the factual accuracy or completeness of the information.
- *Available*—Simply responding to requests for information is usually not sufficient. A satisfactory risk communication program requires reaching out to the appropriate audiences.

- *Continuing*—Risk communication is not a one-shot deal. Information that is not periodically refreshed tends to be forgotten or confused. Keeping people current and knowledgeable is particularly critical for emergency procedures, but is important for general risk communications as well.
- *Forthcoming*—Try to be as accurate as possible at all times, but if a mistake is uncovered, or new evidence contradicts earlier statements, admit it promptly and explain what you are doing about it.
- *Timely*—In crisis conditions, the ability to provide information rapidly and to respond quickly to questions is important. The best of information, provided too late, may be useless. Untimely communications can make an organization appear evasive or out of control.

ROUTINE RISK COMMUNICATION

Ordinary low-level releases of effluents from an industrial facility, accidents that can occur from using consumer products improperly, side effects of drugs or medical procedures, and chronic occupational hazards faced by workers are possible normal consequences of industrial activities and products. Depending on the risk involved, communication to consumers, local residents, or employees may be important. The need to communicate such day-to-day risks has frequently been short-changed. However, routine communications needs are often as critical as crisis communication needs.

Any organization that produces products or by-products that may, or are perceived to, impose health or safety risks on consumers, members of the general public, or employees should have a program of risk communications. Simply designating a spokesperson or producing an informational brochure is generally not sufficient. Having a program implies creating an organizational focal point, producing one or more products to convey information, distributing the information, and maintaining the process. In some cases, the program may be simple. In other cases, it may involve many people and components.

In developing an appropriate program, an organization must address the following questions:

- What are the routine communication needs that must be met? Are there any legal requirements? At a minimum, these must be satisfied. Does the organization need to obtain some kind of initial acceptance, for example, to site and build a facility? If so, is there likely to be local concern about the facility? What has the previous experience of the company been? What about other similar organizations? The communication requirements for obtaining local acceptance and necessary legal permits are generally acute where there has been a history of public concern or organized opposition and where misconceptions or misinformation about an activity are significant.

- What information must be supplied? Is a general interpretation of the risk issue required? Are the company's actions to reduce risk the real concern?

- How can the audience best be reached? Mailings, articles, or advertisements in local news media, interviews on local talk shows, and speeches at public schools and community groups are all possibilities. In larger organizations, an internal speakers' bureau may be useful to meet these needs. Speakers should be supplied with adequate information, and may need some training in speaking techniques and in handling difficult questions. In some cases, a visitors' center may be appropriate. However, this should not be undertaken unless the resources are available and the continuing commitment is clear.

- What information already exists? In industries that have long been the subject of public concern, trade groups, professional societies, and even individual companies may already have developed much good information. Taking advantage of this, where possible, is efficient, and helps assure a consistent "voice," and may be viewed as more credible.

However, available information may need to be focused or supplemented. Where such information does not already exist, the potential for initiating some industry-wide response may be considered.

- Are the needs of each segment of the audience addressed? Schoolchildren are a particularly important constituency, and can best be reached with hands-on, interactive displays, information incorporated into games, and information geared to different age groups, with appropriate language and illustrations. Using favorite cartoon characters is popular, but one should be sensitive to any negative connotations. Is there a significant foreign-born community that must be reached? Translation into Spanish or other languages may be necessary. Are there special risks to the fetus that require tailored information or precautions for pregnant women, or for women—and increasingly, even men—of childbearing age? Care must be taken to provide information and opportunities for protection without invading privacy or treating employees inequitably. Are there supervisors who must be able to train others, to assume certain responsibilities in an emergency, or to answer questions? They may require more instruction and more information.

- How often must the information be repeated? The necessary frequency of repetition may vary, but in every case, periodic repetition of information is needed, even to audiences who have heard the message before. The frequency of repetition will depend on how complex the information is, how critical it is for individuals to have correct information (the needs for emergency response are clearly more critical than general information needs), and whether there are any sources of confusing or incorrect information.

- What form should the distribution of information take? Most often, a mix of media and products is necessary. Brochures, warning signs and labels, detailed instructional booklets, posters, audiotapes or videotapes, computerized learning modules, training courses, and formal presentations with slides can all be parts of a good program, depending on the audience and the need for repetition.

DEVELOPMENT OF MATERIALS

The question often arises: Who in an organization should be involved in the development of materials and the dissemination of information? There is no one formula. Some organizations depend heavily on outside consultants with expertise in risk communications. Others have a dedicated public relations staff. Still others, especially smaller organizations, depend heavily on the organization's principals or on technical staff with writing or speaking skills. Much depends on the size of the organization, the risk issues involved, and the skills of individuals.

In all cases, the effectiveness of employees in informal communications within their local communities should not be overlooked. Employees can carry a great deal of credibility within their local communities. An employee living near a plant implicitly makes a statement about his or her perceptions of that plant's safety. Employees who are trusted members of their local community tend to be trusted sources of information. While this cannot be relied upon exclusively, it certainly behooves a firm to assure that employees are kept well informed about relevant risk issues, and also suggests that organizations encourage and, where appropriate, support their employees' efforts to be involved in community activities.

CRISIS COMMUNICATION

Day-to-day risk communication, essential as it is, cannot prevent a mishap or crisis from occurring. *When It Hits the Fan,* using the words of the title of a recent book on crisis management, it is necessary to shift from risk communication to emergency action.

Communicators dealing with day-to-day risks inherent in an organization's products and operations are best equipped to handle a crisis situation. An experienced risk communication team, like a combat-seasoned military force, is far more likely to be a winner and suffer fewer casualties. Proper preparation for crisis communication starts with preemptive planning. The process follows a series of logical steps:

1. *Identify the types of situations most likely to arise.* What crises have struck in the past? Which ones have beset similar organizations?
2. *Identify the audiences that each of the situations would affect.* Precisely who will require notification and further information—individuals within and outside the organization, government officials and agencies, news media, suppliers? A toxic spill, a fatal accident, and a product tampering involve different treatment.
3. *Identify the appropriate spokespersons.* Who will be responsible for communicating with each of these audiences?
4. *Develop a plan.* Ultimately, success or failure in handling a crisis depends decisively on the quality of thought, teamwork, and the abilities of the managers handling the task. But a written crisis communication plan is a must.

Crisis Communication Plan

How detailed should the plan be? Specific organizational needs will determine that, guided by the following recommendations:

- Be sure to develop and keep current a list of all individuals and organizations to notify initially and to keep informed as events unfold. In the heat of an emergency, do not rely on memory to remember everyone who must or should be notified, especially notifications that may be legally required or that will inform those who will be asked questions by the media and others.
- Work out the steps to prevent critical channels of communication like telephone lines and fax machines from becoming clogged. Do employees have to be notified not to call in or report for work? Do key members of the crisis team have to be given direct phone lines

and numbers? Do meeting places, access to files and databases, computer operators, and work processors have to be alerted?

- Anticipate the materials that may be needed, such as fact sheets, photographs, background papers, charts, and graphs. Increasingly, TV is the key channel of communication, so background video footage may be needed. Designate and train spokespersons to be focused, confident, and sensitive to important concerns in communicating with the news media and other groups.
- For the news media, include the names, phone numbers, and fax numbers of individual reporters and editors. Can you reach them at home after working hours and on weekends? For newspapers, include their deadlines for receiving information.

Using the Plan

The best way to test a communication plan and improve a risk management team's performance is to conduct simulated crisis exercises. Valuable lessons, experience, and morale can be gained from simulated crisis scenarios. Videotaped simulations and playbacks are particularly effective aids. These preparations and many others should be thought out in advance, documented, and periodically reviewed. Everyone involved will benefit even if the crisis never happens.

Remember that when any risk situation occurs, newspaper and wire service reporters, along with TV news crews are under deadline pressures. If your side does not provide information, the media will get it elsewhere. The results may be flawed and extremely damaging.

The importance of getting off on the right footing, and fast, is reason enough for careful, thoughtful advance planning of crisis communications. It is a form of insurance that simply cannot be ignored.

INTRACORPORATE INTERNATIONAL RELATIONS

David Metz, Senior Vice-President and Director, Communications and Public Affairs, Eastman Kodak Company

THE PROBLEM

"Think globally. Act locally." This slogan has become a management cliche. Yet when it comes to communications, companies today must do more than "think globally." They must also—simultaneously—think regionally and locally. Also, communicators cannot afford to "act locally" while ignoring regional and global considerations.

The global "image fabric" of any company is made up of hundreds, even thousands, of messages to many different audiences. It is woven from every impression the company makes: from the use of its products and services, from its advertising, from its packaging and promotions, from every message it sends to consumers, dealers, employees, shareholders, and the communities where it does business around the world. Ideally, all of these different messages should be framed and delivered with a single global "voice." But despite satellites, fax machines, computer networks, and sophisticated media strategies, few companies today speak with one voice to all their key constituencies.

Instead, many employ a multinational approach. Major corporate communications campaigns are developed at headquarters and sent out as a "package" to local units. At the same time, local managers and communicators plan their own communications activities independently, country-by-country or even unit-by-unit. Sometimes corporate and local messages reinforce each other. Often they do not. The goal should be one global message, delivered with maximum impact to local audiences.

A SUCCESSFUL APPROACH

A successful international relations program was instituted by a company that sold thousands of products in different national markets. It reviewed its business-to-business advertisements and product literature and discovered "visual wallpaper." Materials were produced individually for each line of business in each local market. It was difficult to recognize the various pieces of literature as coming from the same company.

The company created a global communications effort that played off its organizational heritage and major philosophy and business themes. Materials were tied together by a unified graphic look that could be used around the world.

The results of the umbrella campaign included cost savings in the millions of dollars, the freeing of money for media placement, and gains in generating leads for sales. Of greatest importance, the success resulted in a growing recognition among communications employees themselves of the need to build worldwide usefulness into all their efforts.

A Global Network

One key to worldwide communications is an effective network linking all the people involved. The network must provide good intelligence, both in terms of delivering accurate current data and in anticipating future concerns. Technology, such as electronic and voice mail systems, plays a key role here. Anything you can do to ensure accurate, real-time communications locally, regionally, and globally buys you efficiency and consistency among communicators.

Ultimately, it is people, not technology, who drive your communication program. Your most critical requirement is for seasoned, high-quality people who have worked together long enough to build up a sense of trust. Their ability to work and speak frankly together will determine whether your company speaks with many voices—or in many languages, but with a single voice.

That is especially important in today's changing market environment. As communicators, our budgets are finite. The messages they pay for must go beyond Belgium or Sweden or Thailand to reach the world's increasingly important regional markets.

Regional Communications

Japanese and Korean leadership is sparking development of a bloc of dynamic, export-oriented Asian nations. Initiatives in the Commonwealth of Independent States and Eastern Europe are leading to free trade zones and joint ventures. The prospect of a true common market in Europe is increasingly certain. Even the "three Chinas" (the Peoples Republic, Taiwan, and Hong Kong) may one day coalesce in the economic sense.

For communicators, then, thinking and acting regionally is critical. It is just as important to take account of local differences. In the photographic marketplace, for example, Japanese consumers prefer film with a pinker flesh tone than U.S. or European buyers. Most of the world has shifted to 35mm cameras, but Mexicans continue to hold on to their 110-format cameras. A global communication plan that does not recognize such local differences is unlikely to be persuasive.

A Global Strategy

Realistically, the "globalization" of communications is easier when there is a big event or hot issue around which to focus communications activities. In such cases, it is much easier to get local and regional organizations to buy into global objectives.

However, after these big events, there is a tendency to lapse back into multilocal approaches. That is probably inevitable. The effort to speak with one global voice may always remain, to some extent, an impossible dream. But for most companies, there are many opportunities to bring that dream closer to reality. Here are just a few:

1. Look for those big events where various parts of the communications mix can be coordinated as part of a larger, global tapestry. Look for ways to make that new product launch, for example, not just a headquarters show but a regional and local event as well.
2. Attack the easiest communications events that can be managed on a worldwide basis. New product launches are one example. Sponsorships and point-of-sale materials are others.
3. When you find a big event that lends itself to global coordination, maximize its potential. In the case of sponsorships, for instance, tie in as many products and services as possible. That expands the marketing environment and helps spread costs.
4. Pool global communication resources, such as relationships with vendors, public relations firms, and ad agencies. Frankly, that is often easier said than done. Nevertheless, coordinating your company's worldwide communications activities through one or two agencies can pay real dividends. It can often cut costs and improve effectiveness. Even

more important, it increases the likeli-hood that all your global advertising and public relations activities will speak with the same voice.

5. Measure the impact of your communi-cations across countries and regions. Without some means of evaluating dif-ferences in consumer behavior, we have no way of knowing what makes a com-munication work well in one country or region but not another.

6. As countries group regionally and trad-ing areas emerge, markets for many goods and services will become more similar, with more common customer needs. In turn, that will create more op-portunities to produce regional com-munications with greater impact, at more efficient cost.

7. Make sure your global thinking cuts both ways. Just as there is a natural ten-dency for local communicators to go their own way, it is just as easy for head-quarters staff to think domestically first, and to address international concerns only as a costly afterthought. In today's world marketplace, communicators can no longer afford that luxury.

EVALUATING CORPORATE RELATIONS RESULTS

David N. Richardson, Senior Vice-President, The Wirthlin Group
James Granger, President, The Wirthlin Group

Many public relations professionals do not really believe their work can be evaluated, at least not in the disciplined manner that one normally associates with the word evalua-tion. In a sense, they are right. Public relations will never be as neat, for instance, as advertis-ing. In advertising, despite the impact of indi-vidual creativity, the end product usually has a specific form and is delivered through a spe-cific medium. We can design a range of audi-ence measures that allow calibration of what has been delivered and the impact it has had.

Even though not as neat, PR can also be evalu-ated. Evaluation techniques can help trans-form PR from an amorphous press relations activity into one of a group of program tools for accomplishing communications objec-tives. There are good reasons to build evalua-tion into any public relations program:

1. Public relations almost always involves an expenditure of time or money. Com-petition for these resources often comes from other activities that have seem-

ingly "hard" effectiveness measures. Unless public relations activities can be shown to be worth the investment, it may be difficult to justify them.

2. Evaluation helps an organization gauge the success of its public relations efforts. Regardless of the competition for resources, prudent management should demand that any such activity be able to demonstrate that it serves a useful purpose.

3. Evaluation helps plan for the future. In a complex public relations program, not all components work equally well. Public relations employs an array of tools—press kits, press conferences, special events, media tours, celebrity endorsements, publicity surveys, white papers, and so on. Having a reasonably structured evaluation procedure helps the organization pick out those pieces of its program that work best and worst and plan for future activities.

4. Public relations needs a documented history of successes and failures so it can more effectively communicate in the future.

5. Evaluation forces those responsible for public relations to be clear about their objectives. Our efforts need to be more targeted than "we want people to love us." By identifying target audiences and messages, the public relations manager can judge how well we understand the views of those we want to target.

In the beginning, it was good, or it was bad. The public relations program was a success if the boss saw his or her picture in the paper, if his friends at the club said they had heard his speech, if the press conference was full, or if everybody had a great time at the opening-day party.

Public relations evaluation has evolved from that seat-of-the-pants assessment style. Still, there has been no systematic industry investment in evaluation methods that even begins to approach the structure that exists in the advertising industry. Public relations does not have Nielsen, Arbitron, overnight recall, or pretest methods that are widely used in advertising.

A fundamental reason for this lack of evaluation infrastructure is that public relations is too diverse to fit into the relatively neat formulas used for advertising. There is intuitive understanding that good public relations works, but no systematic cause-and-effect model that says, "Do A, and B will result."

The measurement challenge has to do with the issue of proximity. The closer one gets to the activity itself—the press conference, the news release—the easier it is to measure the impact or effectiveness. At the same time, close proximity gives us little information on the end effects of our efforts, for example, did we influence the way people think about our organization.

EVALUATION PROCEDURE

The most commonly used evaluation procedure splits the difference between cause and effect, measuring the most readily available and most often targeted medium: newspaper clips or broadcast coverage. Clip services provide copies of all the coverage received by an organization in the media, along with the circulation or viewership figures for each source. By counting, an organization can gauge the number or people who might have been exposed to some message about it and the number of times exposed (to use advertising lingo, the reach and frequency). There is a reasonable assumption made that larger numbers of exposures are more likely to be associated with higher awareness and message acceptance.

Some people have manipulated these media circulation numbers to develop an "advertising equivalency" measure, meant to allow direct comparison of public relations and advertising expenditures. This concept is appealing because it seems to provide an answer to the cost-comparison question. But it requires such broad assumptions about the relative value of a printed article versus a printed advertisement or television ad that it might make the comparison almost meaningless.

A more complete use of media clip information is to analyze article contents. Since a key difference between public relations and advertising is that the former exercises less direct control over how the key messages are presented, it is important to evaluate how effectively those messages are delivered. This is a reasonably straightforward content coding task, and a number of commercial services are available that provide this type of media message analysis and reporting.

The main shortcoming of media analysis is that it only measures the medium. More complete systems of public relations evaluation now include surveys of the target population. The added value of using surveys in public relations evaluation is that they provide diagnostic information on the target audience's attitudes, knowledge, and behavior that can be used to help guide subsequent programs.

FRAMEWORK FOR EVALUATION

Given this array of measurement elements, it seems logical to expect a system that ties them together. Such systems do exist, though not on an industry-wide basis. The framework for one such approach to measurement is straightforward:

- Establish objectives and define success.
- Determine what the program will consist of in order to meet those objectives.
- Create measures that mesh with the program components.
- Implement the measurement.

One characteristic of this progression is its similarity to the normal process of designing and implementing a good public relations program itself. The only addition is the development of measures that can capture key program components and the recognition that evaluation measures must be built into the design of a program, not tacked on at its conclusion.

Establishing objectives sounds deceptively easy. Objectives can vary widely depending on whether the task is marketing, crisis resolution, financially or legislatively oriented, and so forth. What counts is to make these

objectives specific. For example, not only should a goal be to raise awareness but it should be to raise awareness levels from 40 percent to 48 percent. Goal setting is often the hardest task if there is little precedent, but without it, conclusions about success are hard to draw.

Each public relations component should contribute to meeting one or more objectives. This should be part of the design of the program. It entails thinking through the outcomes of each program step. For example, if a celebrity is going to visit stores, is the purpose to raise awareness of the stores, to feature a product, to convey a message point for a specific product, or to demonstrate social responsibility? By relating each program component to a specific objective, the manager is able to develop a sense of the relative importance of each component as well as a framework for relating one to another.

MEASURING EVALUATION

What makes a program amenable to evaluation is the measures that are developed to gauge progress. These measures fall into three broad categories:

1. *Execution measures*—These assess the ability of the public relations team to apply creativity, innovation, and state-of-the-art production to each program element. Did the media tour happen? Was it on schedule and on budget? Were the right people there? Was it well orchestrated, creative, targeted? These are all questions that can and should be asked. Sometimes it is possible to quantify: number of attendees, press kits requested, and other information.

2. *Delivery measures*—These cover the intermediate effects of a public relations program. For a public relations program to make an impact, elements must be "sold" through media channels. The primary source for delivery measures is clip reports, coded and analyzed to determine the content and volume of coverage. Other delivery measures might include 800 numbers and mail fulfillment. Examples of delivery measures abound:

- Volume (number and circulation/viewership) of media placements and impressions.
- Quality of media placements (Was the article in the right paper/magazines, or the right section? Was it a detailed article?).
- Quality (or content) of message playback in those impressions (Are key message points covered?).
- Linkage of impressions and messages with the product/company/issue that is the object of the effort.

3. *Impact measures*—These are closest to the attitudes and behavior changes that are the object of the campaign. Examples are awareness, perceptions, attitudes, persuasion, and behavioral intention.

Surveys, with measures before and after the campaign for the target populations, are the best way to get attitudinal, awareness, and behavioral intent information. To interpret these survey data, it is important to overlay both key public relations milestones and other factors that might influence the target audience.

The final ingredient for this evaluation approach is some form of analytical framework that creates a decision structure. It involves a scheme to attach weights to the different measurements. This is a task that will benefit from the attention of someone experienced with analyzing the different measures.

Frequency of Measures

Just as evaluation begins with goal setting, it is better to get results when something can be done about them. With public relations programs that have a degree of regularity, for example, those extending over a one-year cycle, interim measures of performance often can be helpful for midcourse corrections. And for organizations with annual budget cycles, interim results provide input for the next year's plan. For other programs, the frequency of measurement should be guided by the volatility of the situation and the need for tactical fine-tuning.

Measurement Precision and Cost

Not surprisingly, evaluation often is one of the first things to go when budgets get squeezed. Perhaps this is because it is viewed as less crucial than "actual" program activities. Whatever the reason, it is a temptation worth resisting. Program evaluation is an investment in the present and the future. Its immediate value is the discipline it imposes on the public relations team to keep programs focused. Longer term, it provides insight on how to make programs work better.

Full-scale evaluations, covering execution, delivery, and impact components, typically require about 5 percent of a moderate-size program budget. Those costs can be higher if the program is fast-changing or if new surveys need to be designed. Costs are lower if tracking surveys covering key evaluation variables are already in place.

Special Populations

There is no difference conceptually in evaluations where the target audience is the general public or a special group, such as legislators, financial analysts, or physicians. However, there may be a distinct difference in the measures that are appropriate with each group. Media may be a secondary concern and alternative delivery measures may need to be developed. Impact measures of some kind usually exist: votes, recommendations, or prescriptions. And all the groups can be surveyed, albeit not as easily or cost efficiently as the general public. The underlying evaluation philosophy still applies. The public relations manager must understand who he or she wants to influence, what attitudes or behaviors need to be affected, and what outcomes will constitute success.

ISOLATING PUBLIC RELATIONS EFFECTS

There are numerous reasons why it is a challenge to isolate the effect of public relations:

1. Public relations is part of a mix with advertising and promotion that occurs

simultaneously and with similar messages.

2. Responses lag the events driving them.
3. Responses require a cumulative weight of effort.
4. Some effects work indirectly in conjunction with other forces. As examples, does a writer do a story because of the recent press kit he got or because of the cumulative weight of material received? Does a consumer make a buy decision for a big-ticket item solely because of a major public relations event or is she influenced by the full mix of persuading forces operating on her?

This difficulty in isolating public relations effects underlines the value of a measurement system built on an array of measures—some very proximate to the activity (execution), some reflecting intermediate effects (delivery), and some representing end results (impact). At the next level of sophistication, statistical modeling can be used to help determine the relative impact of public relations and other forces. Finally, the best way to isolate public relations effects is to include test cells in any program—areas or populations where, to the extent possible, only public relations or only advertising is used in order to gauge the independent and synergistic effects of each.

CONCLUSION

A number of firms exist that either provide media clips or offer coding service. Many marketing research firms or public relations firms are capable of conducting surveys, though few have the experience to structure a comprehensive evaluation. Nevertheless, assistance can be found. And much of the impetus for effective evaluation must come from the public relations practitioners themselves.

Evaluation is an essential tool to aid goal setting, keep programs on track, identify successes and failures, and plan for the future. There are some clear principles that apply to public relations evaluations. While the discipline falls somewhat short on infrastructure, the approaches and capabilities for executing them exist and are available to any serious public relations practitioner.

SECTION 12

Risk Management and Insurance

Sandra G. Gustavson, Section Editor

Introduction   *Sandra G. Gustavson*   12-3

The Risk Management Function   *Christopher A. Duncan*   12-5

The Risk Management Process   *Jerry D. Todd*   12-8

Property and Income Loss Exposures   *Michael F. Grace*   12-11

Liability Loss Exposures   *Jack P. Gibson*   12-16

Human Resources Loss Exposures   *Michael T. Rousseau*   12-21

Loss Control   *Larry A. Warner*   12-24

Risk Retention   *Elisha Finney*   12-29

Noninsurance Risk Transfer   *Steven P. Kahn*   12-33

Insurance   *Robert B. Edgar*   12-35

Risk Management Department Organization and Policy
   E. J. Leverett, Jr.   12-41

The Role of Insurance Agents and Brokers
    Daniel J. Dean and Karen Epermanis   12-48

Global Insurance and Risk Management   *John J. Hampton*   12-50

INTRODUCTION

Sandra G. Gustavson

The increasingly complex setting in which managers function involves many forms of decision making under conditions of uncertainty. Although many of these situations involve the potential for either gain or loss, there are some conditions that present only the possibility of loss. Obvious examples include the destruction of assets due to fire, injury, or death to employees, and multi-million-dollar adverse liability judgments. These types of occurrences may have a negative impact on profits at the very least; in some cases, they may threaten the survival of the entire organization.

The systematic managing of risks associated with an entity's exposures to loss is known as risk management. The first chapter in this section describes the risk management concept more fully, from both a conceptual perspective and from a practical viewpoint focusing on the risk management function within the corporate environment. The actual process of risk management is described in "The Risk Management Process." The steps of risk identification and evaluation are reviewed, followed by a brief overview of ways to deal with various risks. The point is made that insurance is one form of risk treatment, which should be used within the risk management framework when other alternatives are not appropriate. The days of merely buying insurance to protect against all exposures to loss are long gone for most large and many small organizations.

An expanded discussion of risk identification and evaluation of exposures is provided in the next three chapters. First, "Property and Income Loss Exposures" focuses on exposures to loss arising out of the ownership or use of property. "Liability Loss Exposures" is an overview of the many sources of liability risk, and "Human Resources Loss Exposures" is devoted to the identification of loss exposures associated with a firm's personnel.

Following these discussions of potential loss exposures, the next several chapters in this section focus on ways to treat risks once they have been identified. "Loss Control" describes general approaches for reducing the frequency and/or the severity of losses. "Risk Retention" deals with the financing of losses directly by the organization. Ideally, risk retention should be planned; it should be the result of careful analysis of available alternatives. However, if a source of risk is not identified prior to a loss, by default an organization will be forced to retain the effects of resultant losses.

Another risk treatment method involves the transfer of losses to third parties. An introduction to the topic of loss transfer is provided in the chapter by Steve Kahn. A more detailed description of the best-known loss transfer method—insurance—is the basis of Robert Edgar's chapter.

The final three chapters in this section involve risk management implementation considerations. The organization and policies associated with this function are described by E.J. Leverett, Jr., with a sample risk management policy statement provided therein. In most firms, implementation of some forms of risk treatment may involve insurance agents or brokers. The chapter by Daniel Dean and Karen Epermanis focuses on the role of such people within a risk management context. Finally, some special considerations for firms operating internationally are discussed in the chapter by John J. Hampton.

Sandra G. Gustavson, *Ph.D., is currently department head and professor of risk management and insurance at the University of Georgia. She is a past president of the American Risk and Insurance Association, has published more than thirty articles on risk management and insurance topics, and is the coauthor of* Risk and Insurance *(8th ed., South-Western Publishing, 1992) and* Life Insurance: Theory and Practice *(4th ed., Austin Business Publications, 1987).*

THE RISK MANAGEMENT FUNCTION

Christopher A. Duncan,
Director of Risk Management,
Kentucky Fried Chicken Corporation

Risk management is taking its place as an integral part of sound management as the risks and the associated costs of operating in today's hazardous and litigious environment grow by leaps and bounds. Threats to an organization's critical assets (such as reputation, suppliers/customers, land and equipment, employees, technology, and financial resources) abound. Examples include fire, hurricanes, product tampering, adverse publicity, uncontrolled litigation, punitive damages, worker injuries, thefts, environmental contamination, and loss of consumer confidence, among others. These threats cause tremendous uncertainty in decision making and create potentially unacceptable liabilities for businesses. Increasingly, risk management costs are a critical cost item, as important as payroll and raw materials, and represent a significant portion of sales. The success or failure of this function can mean the difference between profits and bankruptcy. Nelson Bean in the *National Underwriter* reported that 43 percent of all businesses struck by a catastrophic loss never reopen; 28 percent of those that do are out of business within three years.

THE CHANGING ROLE OF RISK MANAGEMENT

In addition to the direct cost considerations of the risk management function, many senior executives are recognizing that sound risk management can help contribute to the resolution of other key management problems such as labor productivity, customer satisfaction, and environmental image. For example, a reduction in the frequency of worker injuries ultimately lowers labor costs and increases productivity by reducing turnover, eliminating additional training costs and wages for replacement workers while increasing job satisfaction, and maintaining the integrity of teamwork within the work force. Responsive and timely handling of customer claims helps reduce customer dissatisfaction following unexpected and unpleasant experiences with a product or service: Given most organizations' desire to retain its existing customer base, a quality claims resolution function can help avoid "turning off" existing and potential customers. How a company handles an incident such as a slip and fall injury by a customer is more important in the return purchase or overall organization perception to that customer, and that customer's friends, family, work associates, and everyone within the customer's sphere of influence, than their perception of all the other wonderful attributes of the firm's product or service!

Gone are the days of simply purchasing inexpensive, broad insurance to cover the risks of doing business. The goal now is the comprehensive management of risks in a proactive manner. The function of risk management has also evolved: Handling of key risks is no longer done by a part-time insurance clerk purchasing insurance (reactive). Instead, sophisticated and well-staffed departments design and manage complex loss prevention and control programs (proactive) and state-of-the-art financing programs to fund losses after they occur.

The objective of risk management has also changed. No longer are risk managers merely expected to find the cheapest insurance available. In fact, insurance is no longer the financial safety net it once was: Insurance companies' financial security may be questionable; critical exposures may be excluded from coverage; recovery or payments under policies is becoming more adversarial; and insurers often limit their financial exposure through high deductibles/retentions and capped limits. Now risk managers are not only expected to negotiate the maze of insurance purchasing but also to prevent losses; educate employees on safety; develop new products and processes to help companies work more safely and efficiently; comply with expanding governmental environmental and safety legislation; guard product/service quality; and avoid unacceptable financial losses and corresponding damage to consumer and stakeholder confidence in the organization and its products and services.

In a perfect world, there would be no need for risk management as a business function, but the truth is that bad things do happen. Preventing unacceptable losses and handling unavoidable ones is the essence of what the risk management function is all about.

CORPORATE CONNECTIONS

Risk management is typically thought of as an overhead function, a specialized area that few in general management understand. While risk management does require specialized knowledge in certain key areas (such as insurance and law), it is one of the few functions within an organization that crosses over into almost every other area of the company—finance, marketing, public relations, operations/production, purchasing, research and development, legal, and others. A working knowledge of all areas of the company and a good working relationship with all these areas is required for risk management to perform its ultimate function of protecting the organization against unacceptable losses.

In some organizations, risk management is a line function, with direct responsibility for safety processes in the production or service efforts. In most organizations, however, risk management is a staff function that advises operations on how to control or prevent losses from occurring. This staff role may have evolved from the infancy of risk management when the purchasing of insurance was its primary responsibility. Today, risk management combines elements of both line and staff responsibilities in an effort to prevent losses or minimize their cost. Whether line or staff, a close working relationship with all other areas of the company is critical to create clear communication of the risks and costs to the company.

One of the risk manager's potential difficulties in relating with other areas is his or her continuing focus on the long term while the business world is often dominated by expedient, short-term decision making. Quarterly earnings probably will not be directly affected by a smart investment in fire safety improvements at a critical manufacturing facility, or by developing a reliable and tested product recall procedure. But the long-term survival and short-term profits of an organization may be at stake without such far-reaching initiatives.

Due to the high cost of the risk management function, most risk managers report to the finance function. There are many exceptions. The Tillinghast/RIMS survey showed that 60 percent of risk management departments reported to a finance or treasury unit, 14 percent to human resources or administration, 10 percent to the chief executive officer, and 16 percent elsewhere.

No matter where risk management reports, a factor critical to its success is frequent contact with senior management so risks are understood and steps can be taken to protect the company. Such understanding by senior management and the board of directors may fulfill a fiduciary responsibility. Since a company's ability to produce income for dividends or stock value appreciation is important to shareholders, it follows that the board has an obligation to ensure that the business's ability to produce income is safeguarded. That means protecting the organization's assets, reputation, customers, suppliers, employees, land and equipment, technology, and financial resources.

APPLICATIONS AND COSTS OF RISK MANAGEMENT

The application of the risk management function varies by industry and by the major risks that face an organization. In a quick-service restaurant like Kentucky Fried Chicken, the primary focus is on preventing injuries to employees and customers arising from the process of preparing and serving food—because that is where the bulk of the risk costs are. For an auto manufacturer, product liability claims from exploding fuel tanks, unpredicta-

ble transmissions, and inability to safely withstand crashes are key concerns. For healthcare companies, malpractice claims from professional services are the primary focus areas. In chemical firms, fire prevention and environmental risks can keep management awake at night. An organization's key, critical risks have the most profound influence on how the specifics of the risk management function are carried out—what loss control programs are in place, how the function is staffed, the particular expertise of its members, what insurance or risk financing is purchased, what retention or deductible levels (the retained financial exposure to the organization) are appropriate, and how the function interacts with other functions of the company.

Just as the application of the function varies by industry and even by company, its costs also vary widely. For example, total risk management costs, including insurance, retained losses, and administration costs, were examined in a Tillinghast/Risk and Insurance Management Society (RIMS) survey. It revealed that the cost of risk could be as high as 2.4 percent in a retail business compared to almost 13 percent in a health-care business. The average cost for all industries was approximately one percent of revenues.

Without good management of risks and its costs, profit margins can easily be destroyed. Conversely, good risk management contributes directly to the bottom line—always an interest to senior management!

THE RISK MANAGEMENT PROCESS

Jerry D. Todd, The Charles E. Cheever Chair in Risk Management, St. Mary's University

To accomplish the objectives of risk management, a systematic process must be established, approved, and communicated to all those responsible for risk management. While the duties can be outlined and described, those responsible must be appropriately motivated and educated to carry out their duties. In this chapter, we examine the risk management process, which has four basic steps:

1. *Investigate and identify possible loss* —property damage, income loss, liability, personnel loss.
2. *Evaluate and measure*—loss frequency and severity, replacement cost, maximum probable loss, maximum possible loss, financial impact of loss.
3. *Control and finance risk*—avoid the activity, prevent or reduce loss, increase loss predictability, insure, retain, transfer to third party.
4. *Implement and systematize*—negotiate insurance, monitor loss reduction programs, monitor changing exposures, create self-funding mechanisms

INVESTIGATION

The first and most important step in the risk management process is to identify all exposures and possible causes of loss in order to prevent overlooking a potential catastrophe and haphazard treatment of a risk. All exposures—buildings, contents, vehicles, equipment, revenues—must be identified to avoid the possibility that the risk of their loss is being inappropriately retained. Next, an analysis should be made of the potential causes and likelihood of loss for each exposure.

The risk manager is the expert in risk investigation. However, he or she simply cannot know at all times about changes in the organization's loss exposures. Consequently, a systematic plan requires an awareness by all employees, particularly department heads, of loss exposures, and a reporting procedure to assure that no exposures will be unknown to the risk manager for long. Help is available from brokers and agents, especially regarding those exposures that are insurable, but it is the responsibility of the risk manager to stay knowledgeable about all of the organization's exposures to loss.

The systematic investigation of risk requires an understanding of the types of losses facing any organization. Exhibit 12-1 shows that all exposures to loss can be divided into two types: property and the loss of use. Property damage involves direct repair costs as well as indirect losses of income and the cost of renting comparable property while repairs are being made. The exhibit also points out

Exhibit 12-1. Loss Exposures

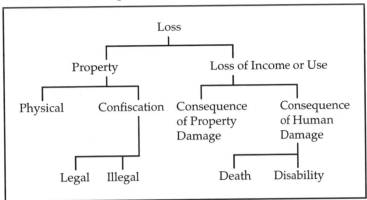

that there are various causes of loss. These range from acts of God such as wind, fire, and water to confiscation by theft or by legal means through liability lawsuits.

Modern investigative techniques should not be insurance based, because so many risks are not insured and some are not even insurable. Four different techniques are useful:

1. *Risk discovery survey*—This is useful because it is thorough. It is essentially a checklist of loss exposures common to most organizations, together with information needed for financial impact and insurance purposes. Completing the checklist involves the use of the other methods: an examination of financial records, physical inspection of properties, and a flowchart of operations.

2. *Analysis of financial records*—This is needed because exposures such as accounts receivable, cash, manuscripts, and revenues will not normally be apparent from physical inspections. Relevant values are also available from such records.

3. *Flowcharts of operations*—These highlight critical points in production processes that could shut down whole plants—for example, the finishing or paint shop. Flowcharts also point out the potential effects on the production line from a loss of a supplier. Flowcharts of funds examine the amounts

and critical areas where funds could be misappropriated.

4. *Physical inspections*—They should be conducted by the risk manager accompanied by the department head. In this way, three purposes can be accomplished: the identification of loss exposures, the identification of weaknesses in the loss prevention program, and an awareness on the part of the department head of the importance of continuous risk investigation.

EVALUATION AND MEASUREMENT

Having identified the various exposures to loss and the potential causes of loss for each, the risk manager is now ready to measure and analyze the risk, evaluating its absolute and relative size for each exposure and cause of loss. This is important for three reasons: to help determine relative importance, to help decide how to treat the risk, and to determine the appropriate values for insurance or self-insurance purposes. In addition to estimating replacement values, the risk manager must analyze the probability distributions of frequency and severity. The importance of an exposure to loss is determined primarily by potential size or severity of loss, not frequency or probability of loss. The maximum probable loss and maximum possible loss arising out of a given event, such as an earthquake, fire, or hurricane, must be estimated. Consider all possible losses: property, income, and liability. Even more important, consider the maximum probable yearly aggregate dollar loss—the maximum total dollar losses that one or a group of exposures is likely to cost in a given year.

The financial impact of a given loss is important, yet often ignored. "Large" loss is a relative term: It depends on the impact a given loss would have on the business. A $100,000 loss might be devastating to a small business, but only a minor inconvenience to a large one. Three useful measures of financial impact are the effects of losses on working capital, the income statement, and the balance sheet. With respect to financial impacts, the avoidance of the potential for catastrophic loss is the first rule of risk management.

CONTROL AND FINANCE

Risk treatment can be categorized into two areas:

1. *Risk and loss reduction or prevention*—Avoiding risky activities or ownership of risky properties, reducing loss frequency or severity, and increasing the predictability of loss so that it can be properly budgeted are examples. This is often called risk control or loss control.

2. *Risk finance*—Insurance, retention, and transfer are examples of financing risk. In other words, this covers the payment for losses that do occur. In practice, these methods may be used in combination. Insurance deductibles, for example, require the insured to retain loss up to the amount of the deductible. Excess loss insurance is an example where the deductible may be hundreds of thousands of dollars. In some cases, the risk may be transferred to a third party other than an insurer. An example is a hold harmless clause in a contract, where one party agrees to assume the legal liability for torts that by common law might fall on both parties.

SYSTEMATIC IMPLEMENTATION

Risk treatment decisions must be implemented through negotiation of insurance coverages, coordination of loss prevention/reduction programs, drafting of legal contracts, and establishing funding methods and claims procedures for self-funded losses. In addition, a system must be established for constant monitoring of changes in loss exposures and for motivating managers and employees to take their share of risk management responsibility.

PROPERTY AND INCOME LOSS EXPOSURES

Michael F. Grace, Insurance Consultant

The exposures normally addressed first during the risk identification step of the risk management process are those related to property and income. They tend to be the most visible, appear to be the easiest to identify and quantify, and may represent the largest accidental loss exposures a business may face.

IDENTIFYING PROPERTY AND INCOME

Three tools that can assist in the identification of the types of property and the level and sources of income a business has that are exposed to accidental loss are checklists, financial statement analysis, and flowcharts.

Checklists

Checklists can be valuable in helping organize a review of a business's exposure to property losses. Unfortunately, many checklists identify only insurable exposures and have left out the types of property exposures that may be considered uninsurable. However, checklists do help in identifying the type of properties that a company may own or control and many of the perils that may threaten the property.

An example of a checklist that goes beyond just insurable exposures was assembled by Gary Robinson in 1986. His categories and examples include:

1. *Real property*—This includes physical structures (complete or under construction) that are on the surface to include manufacturing, offices, warehouses, garages/hangers, dwellings and farms, tanks, towers, and stacks, wharfs and docks, pipes and wires (aboveground), and bridges.

2. *Underground property*—This includes cables and wires, tanks, shelters, caves, tunnels, mines and shafts, wells, groundwater, piping and pipelines, waste lines, and mineral deposits (solid, liquid, gas).

3. *Personal property*—This includes aircraft, animals (farm, domestic), antennae (including towers), crops (gardens, plants, lawns, shrubbery, timber), electronic data processing equipment (computers and peripherals), equipment and machinery (machines, tools, dies, jigs, molds, boilers and pressure vessels, mechanical electrical equipment, engines, meters, turbines, conveyors, lifts, elevators, escalators, cranes, furnaces, electronic machinery), fences and gates, fine art (antiques, paintings, jewelry, libraries, collectibles), furniture and fixtures, improvements and betterments, nuclear and radioactive materials, precious metals, office equipment, promotional displays, recreational facilities (parks, gyms, cafeterias, saunas, exercise equipment), security protection and detection devices, stock supplies (raw materials, goods in process, finished goods), valuable records (blueprints,

formulae, accounts receivable, patents and copyrights, trade secrets, contracts, titles and deeds, securities, tapes, cards, discs, programs, computer chips, cash, plates, mortgages, bond indentures, leases, insurance policies, franchise agreement), vehicles (commercial, private passenger, contractors' equipment, warehouse equipment), watercraft (boats, yachts, barges, ships, submersibles, buoys, drilling rigs), and radio and television equipment.

4. *Intangible external assets*—These normally do not appear in the financial records of the company. This category includes markets, resource availability (finance, suppliers, transportation, employees, public utilities, public protection), communications, natural environment, physical environment, economic environment and stability, social and political environment, and availability of counsel and specialists.

5. *Intangible internal assets*—These include research and development, goodwill and reputation, financial (credit with suppliers, credit lines, insurance, royalties and rents, leasehold interests, company foundations, tax loss carryforwards, tax credits, trust), personnel, and rights (mineral, oil, air, patents and copyrights, franchises/distributorships, trade secrets, royalty agreements, manufacturing).

While these lists compiled by Mr. Robinson are extensive, there may be assets unique to a business that are not listed. The growing use and ownership by private companies of communication satellites is just such a risk. Checklists created by industry associations can be helpful in identifying risks unique to that industry.

Financial Statement Analysis

Financial statement analysis should reveal the overall financial position of the firm and its ability to absorb accidental losses. Financial statements are also valuable in discovering assets and significant liabilities not disclosed through the use of checklists that could affect the survival of a business following a large loss. The income and expense statements indicate the level and the nature of the company's expenses or, in other words, the source and

use of funds. This information is critical in assessing income loss exposures. This analysis will require review of more than just the published financial statements. It will be necessary to see detailed asset and liability ledgers. Particularly useful is the fixed asset ledger.

Flow Charts

Flowcharts are used to diagram or depict the flow from original source through manufacturing or assembling to end user. These charts are particularly useful in identifying critical equipment or locations and unique processes of an operation that could result in significant income loss even though they may appear to be relatively unimportant or of small cost. This approach is helpful in identifying interdependency between or among internal departments, plants, outside suppliers, and customers. A single supplier or a single customer will become very visible once a chart is constructed. A flowchart may also be used to depict the value added by various areas in a firm's operations.

EXPOSURE IDENTIFICATION BY TYPE OF RISK OR PERIL

The process of identifying the types of risks or perils to which business assets might be exposed is critical in order for a business to be able to assess the best means of controlling its loss exposures and develop the most reasonable means of funding the losses that cannot be controlled. There are many checklists that have been developed on this basis. Some tend to be general whereas others are very industry specific.

In volume 1 of two books written for the Chartered Property Casualty Underwriter course CPCU 3 (Insurance Institute of America, Malvern, PA), the authors present a generic peril classification system composed of three groups of perils:

1. *Natural perils*—These include the sun, rain, fog, snow, ice, hail, lightning, static electricity, wind (tornado, hurricane, typhoon, tempest), temperature and humidity ex-

tremes, drought, volcanic eruption, earthquake, mildew, water, flood, tides, tidal wave, perils of the air (icing, clear air turbulence), perils of the sea (icebergs, waves, sandbars, reefs), fire of natural origin, evaporation, rust, mold, corrosion, rot, fungi, vermin, weeds, uncontrolled vegetation, landslide/mudslide, erosion, cave-in, subsidence (sinkhole), meteors, and expansive soil.

2. *Human perils*—These include fire and smoke, pollution (smoke, smog, water, noise), excessive odor, toppling of high-piled objects, building collapse, radioactive contamination, discoloration, contamination, electrical overload, human carelessness (error, mistake, omission, malpractice, incompetence, or incomplete knowledge), changes of temperature, shrinkage, dust, discrimination, sonic boom, water hammer, chemical leakage, vibration, strikes, loss of trained personnel, arson, vandalism and malicious mischief, molten metal, riots, civil commotions, sabotage, war, rebellion, insurrection, theft, forgery, fraud, terrorism, kidnapping, extortion, libel, slander, infringement of personal or property rights.

3. *Economic perils*—These include expropriation or confiscation, inflation, depreciation, obsolescence, currency fluctuations, change in consumer tastes, recession, technological advances, stock market declines.

Perils can be listed differently. In a manual prepared for the U.S. Department of Transportation, a risk exposure checklist lists the peril "crime" and then shows subheadings of burglary, computer manipulation, counterfeiting, depositors' forgery, employee dishonesty, forgery, fraud, misplacement, robbery, and theft.

TYPES OF PROPERTY LOSS EXPOSURES

Property is subject to both direct and indirect losses. A direct loss occurs when property owned by a business or for which it has responsibility is damaged or destroyed by a peril. When a fire in a warehouse owned and used by a business damages the building and

destroys the contents, a direct loss to business assets has occurred. Cleaning up and removing the debris following the fire is also a direct loss. An indirect or consequential loss occurs when the value of other property is lost or diminished because of the direct loss. Direct damage to or destruction of property can set off a chain reaction that affects other property, income, and people. When direct damage to some property results in a lessening of the value of other property, we have an indirect loss. Note that the direct damage does not necessarily have to occur to property of the business suffering the indirect loss.

An example of an indirect loss occurs when a warehouse fire causes a loss of power to refrigerated storage units. The resulting loss due to spoilage of food is an indirect loss. The loss of power could also have been caused by an explosion at the power plant serving the business. Spoilage would be an indirect loss. Another example is when one part of a set or pair of items is lost if the pair or set is worth more than the individual parts. If the jacket to a suit of clothes is damaged, then the lessening of value of the undamaged pants is an indirect loss. Yet another example arises if a building is partially destroyed but sustained sufficient damage that it has to be rebuilt in compliance with revised local building codes. The new code might require that the building be fully sprinklered, whereas the old one was not. The types of property subject to loss are:

1. *Real property*—unimproved land, including all natural resources, improved land, and physical structures both above and below ground.
2. *Personal property*—is chattel, includes all business personal property, inventory, and even improvements and betterments made by a tenant in leased space.
3. *Intangible properties*—rights, agreements, contracts, and so on that a business has an exclusive right to, such as patents and trademarks.

TYPES OF INCOME LOSS EXPOSURES

Many large income losses have arisen following direct losses to business assets. The term most frequently used by the insurance industry to describe this exposure is *business interruption*. Some examples are:

1. *Decreases in revenues*—Following a property loss, revenues decrease when the operation is interrupted and the normal flow of goods or services is lessened or lost; there is a loss of profits when finished goods are damaged in the direct loss. Being unable to occupy or allow others to occupy the space could result in a loss of rents, tuition, admissions, receipts, or other fees charged for the use of the space. If the loss involves accounts receivable records, collections may be reduced or at best slowed down in comparison to normal operating situations.

2. *Increases in expenses*—Many businesses cannot afford to be closed even for short periods of time. Newspapers, banks, and dry cleaners are just a few examples of businesses that would be severely damaged by loss of customers if shut down for short periods of time. Dairies have to keep milking and hospitals need to be able to care for patients. Expenses in excess of normal operating expense associated with keeping the doors open could be prodigious and involve relocation costs, rental expense, security, overtime or the cost of additional labor, and transportation. Recent fire losses have shown the need for large numbers of mobile telephones and other communication equipment. The cost to expedite critical items, such as replacement parts or equipment, or to complete necessary repairs would also add to the amount of the loss. As the business attempts to reassure its customers and keep them informed as to what is transpiring following the loss, they will experience increased advertising expense. Even for businesses where the risk of loss of market share is minimal following a loss, there will still be an extra cost associated with implementing alternative operating procedures.

3. *Rental exposures*—Rent presents an exposure that can result in an increase in expenses to a building owner or to a tenant. If the business owns and uses the damaged premises, or has a lease that does not contain an abatement clause, then the cost to rent replacement space will be an extra expense. A tenant's exposure can arise from a variety of leasehold interests.

4. *Contingent business interruption*—As was noted above, an indirect loss may result from direct damage to someone else's property. This is described as a dependent property exposure. The importance of such exposures depends on the extent to which firms rely on only a few suppliers and/or customers. Additionally, interdependencies within the same company may lead to similar exposures. For example, just-in-time manufacturing techniques may significantly increase a business's exposure to significant loss of income.

MEASURING PROPERTY LOSS EXPOSURES

The easiest of the exposures to measure is the direct loss to owned property. Even this is not simple. Should you consider what it will cost to replace it with a property having equal utility, as in the case of an office building, or does it need to be reproduced or duplicated as closely as possible, as in the case of an antique or unique piece of equipment? Or should you focus on the "book value" based on the financial records of the company, or does the property's current market value really represent its true value?

Up to this point we have avoided referring to insurance. However, insurance does enter the picture for valuation of property since it requires information about insurable value. The terms most commonly used are:

1. *Replacement cost*—This is the cost at the time of the loss to replace the property without deduction for depreciation. Unfortunately, neither replacement cost nor depreciation are clearly defined in the policies. Most insureds expect replacement to actually mean reproduction. In most loss settlements it is not an issue. However, when the structure or item damaged has a unique value, as in the case of a vintage automobile, an antique, or a structure on the National Register, the reproduction cost may be significantly greater than the cost to replace the damaged property with new material.

2. *Actual cash value (ACV)*—This is more difficult to define, but is most frequently described as replacement cost at the time of the loss less depreciation. Depreciation for insurance purposes is different from that used in financial reports. Depreciation is understood by the insurance industry to include the loss in value of a property from all causes: physical deterioration, functional obsolescence, and economic obsolescence. The fair market value is frequently used as the ACV for personal property, such as vehicles or office equipment. Fair market value may also be ACV for real property when a property is completely obsolete. The value a property is carried at on the books of a business is normally irrelevant for insurance loss valuation purposes.

Understanding this terminology is important when a business assesses its exposure to direct and indirect property loss. It is critical to assign the appropriate value to real and personal properties to develop the proper risk control and risk financing response to these exposures. Failing to recognize the additional costs associated with having to reproduce rather than replace with new property could result in a shortfall in resources after a loss occurs. On the other hand, valuing an obsolete building at its replacement cost when it would never be replaced following a significant loss may result in a waste of risk control or financing resources.

MEASURING INCOME LOSS EXPOSURES

Measuring the loss of income associated with potential losses can be difficult and time consuming. Much of the information that will have to be gathered may actually be considered confidential. Virtually every aspect of the business will need to be reviewed. To be successful the effort will require the approval and full commitment of top management.

What has to be measured is the potential loss of profits, plus all continuing expenses, plus any extra expenses that can be projected if a loss were to occur at the worst possible

moment. For a retail store that might occur if the loss happens on Thanksgiving Day. For a school the loss would occur on opening day of the first semester. For a manufacturer it might be the point in time when the finished goods inventory is at its peak. Each business has to identify its most critical time.

The next step is to determine how long it will take to get back to normal or to preloss operating levels and then to normal sales levels. A piece of custom-made equipment may take a year or more to reconstruct. Replacement parts may be difficult to acquire for older, out-of-date equipment. Or there may be readily accessible and acceptable replacement parts or other sources from which the lost or damaged goods might be acquired. It may only take six months to restore an office or apartment building, but it may take years to achieve the preloss occupancy levels.

The development of alternative operating plans or contingency plans as part of an effective risk control program is critical in evaluating the time and expenses required to resume normal operations. A business may never be able to recover the market share it held prior to a loss as customers find acceptable replacement goods or services. Many companies have focused considerable attention on income loss exposure arising from their data processing area. For some it has been a matter of estimating the extra expenses associated with restoring the processing capability and recovering the data that might be lost. Data processing-dependent companies have in place significant contingency plans. Companies need to expand this activity to other areas of their operations.

Flowcharts are one of the best methods for identifying critical equipment, operations, bottlenecks, and interdependent relationships. All must be identified and understood for a company to accurately estimate its potential loss of income arising from direct and indirect losses.

RANKING EXPOSURES

Once values have been established, the next step is to determine the likelihood or probability that a loss will occur. This can be as simple as assigning a numeric factor of, say, 1, 2, or 3, or a factor described as low, medium, or high, as the description of the likelihood that a loss might occur. Thus, it is necessary to have information on losses that might affect property or income of the business.

The first source of information to be reviewed in establishing loss estimates is the loss history of the firm itself. For most firms these data will be insufficient to establish reasonable loss estimates. Second, information about losses from other firms in the same or similar industry can be helpful and may be available through industry associations. Third, insurance agents or brokers have information. Finally, insurance company personnel can also be a valuable source of information, although their information is usually limited to ''insured'' losses.

The final step in identifying and measuring property and income loss exposures is to determine how much a loss may cost. It is important to evaluate and rank loss exposures

so that attention is given to the most critical exposures first. Ranking also helps assure that the most appropriate risk control and risk financing alternatives are used. The following terms can be used to discuss loss levels:

1. *Normal loss expectancy (NLE)*—the level of loss that occurs when established risk control systems and procedures work reasonably well. For example, sprinklers go on as planned, the heads are of sufficient size, and sufficient water exists. NLE may frequently be zero, that is, no losses are expected.
2. *Maximum foreseeable loss (MFL)*—anticipates that some of the control systems are not going to work, but the loss will be contained.
3. *Maximum possible loss (MPL)*—assumes that none of the systems work and that all of the property that can be exposed to a single loss is destroyed. An estimate of an MPL must include a catastrophic loss estimate.

LIABILITY LOSS EXPOSURES

Jack P. Gibson, President, International Risk Management Institute, Inc.

We read about astronomical liability suits every day. People are suing other people, businesses, governments, and even charitable organizations. No one and certainly no organization is immune from potential legal liability. Many commentators compare it to a lottery, and some people win big—while society

pays. The risk management function seeks to identify the specific risks faced by an organization and to handle those risks in the most cost-effective manner possible.

The primary purpose of the law is to protect the legal rights of individuals and entities subject to the law. The three broad classes of legal wrongs are tort, crime, and breach of contract, with each being addressed by different branches of the law. Tort law protects the rights of individuals from civil wrongs. Victims of tort generally have monetary remedies, such as compensatory damages and punitive damages. This obligation of tortfeasors to pay monetary remedies to injured parties constitutes the primary liability exposures with which the risk management process is concerned.

There are so many different types of liability loss exposures, many of which are either quite complex or extremely obscure, that it may be difficult to identify those that a particular organization faces. However, the risk identification process is facilitated when exposures are grouped into related categories. One logical grouping is (1) premises, operations, and related exposures; (2) products and completed operations exposures; (3) automobile, aircraft, and watercraft exposures; (4) professional, errors and omissions, or malpractice exposures.

PREMISES, OPERATIONS, AND RELATED EXPOSURES

People entering the premises of a possessor of property (e.g., the owner or the renter) can be classified under the law as an invitee, a licensee, or a trespasser. An example of an invitee is a customer in a store. A firefighter responding to an emergency at the store is a licensee, and a burglar breaking into the store is a trespasser. In general, under common law, the store owes a high degree of care to avoid injuries to its invitees, a moderate degree of care to avoid injuries to licensees, and a low degree of care to trespassers. Failure to exercise the proper degree of care—such as by failing to either warn of hazardous conditions or to eliminate them—is considered negligence and can lead to legal liability if someone is injured as a result. This is called premises liability.

Many businesses provide services away from their own premises. The so-called operations liability exposure encompasses all types of potential liability arising from activities away from the organization's premises other than liability from its products, completed operations, automobiles, watercraft, or aircraft. For example, the potential liability of a contractor for injuries to people at its job sites is an operations liability exposure. Similarly, the potential liability of an appliance store for injuries to homeowners, or damage to their property, because of the negligence of the store's employees when installing appliances is an operations exposure.

A related exposure is known as the independent contractors liability exposure. In general, a principal is not held liable under common law for the actions of its independent contractors. Over the years, however, the courts have recognized numerous exceptions to this general rule, and it is now dangerous to assume that immunity exists. The exposure is probably most significant with respect to construction activities. However, other industries and activities may also present significant exposures. For example, the deliverers for many newspapers are independent contractors. Independent contractors must be carefully selected, and they should usually be required to furnish liability insurance protecting themselves and the principal.

Another exposure related to the operations exposure is the potential liability for such intentional torts as trespass, invasion of privacy, libel, slander, defamation of character, and false arrest. Intentional torts of this type often occur in conjunction with sales, marketing, and advertising activities; security and law enforcement activities; and personnel relations functions. Note that these torts involve loss of reputation, mental stress, and related injuries but not physical injury. Risk management professionals often call these personal injury perils. However, this moniker contrasts with terminology used by legal professionals, because lawyers use the term to also include physical bodily injury.

Although the basic concept of premises, operations, and related liability exposures is rather straightforward, there are many obscure exposures within this category that can easily go unrecognized.

Contractual Assumptions

Lease, rental, construction, and virtually all other business contracts contain indemnity, hold harmless, and insurance provisions that transfer certain responsibilities and potential liabilities from one contracting party to another. For example, office building leases often require the tenant to be responsible for damage to the building or any liability to people injured on the premises. Such exposures can be handled through insurance or other means if they are identified, but rarely will all of the needed insurance coverages or risk treatment alternatives be in place if the exposures are not known. For this reason, business contracts must be carefully reviewed for their risk management implications.

Liquor Liability

A server of alcoholic beverages can be held liable for injuries to third parties caused by a person who became intoxicated from consuming those beverages. While this exposure is easily recognizable when alcoholic beverages are served or distributed as a primary business activity, there are also less obvious situations wherein it can arise. For example, a business could be held liable for injuries sustained by individuals in an automobile accident caused by an employee who drank too much at a company picnic or sales meeting. The nature of the meeting or activity at which alcohol is served may affect the degree of the loss exposure and the extent to which standard insurance policies will cover any resulting liability, making it important to identify and analyze company activities that may give rise to these exposures.

Environmental Liability

Many businesses face enormous potential pollution liabilities. These potential liabilities arise under common law as well as numerous federal and state statutes. Environmental liability can arise from past and present waste disposal activities, leakage of storage tanks, the inclusion of hazardous materials (e.g., asbestos or formaldehyde) in buildings or other structures, and pollution releases from other activities or operations. The exposure is twofold: (1) liability to third parties for bodily injury or property damage caused by the pollution, and (2) liability to the government or a third party for the cost to remove pollutants.

Generally speaking, an organization that owns property on which hazardous wastes are found may be required to clean up those wastes and may be held liable for injuries arising from them. Similarly, a company may be held liable for the cleanup of a site at which its wastes were deposited, even if its wastes were a small portion of those at the site or if it had no knowledge that its wastes were being deposited at that site. Another major area of potential liability for cleanup costs is underground storage tanks. The steel tanks used in the past eventually rust and leak. When this occurs, they must be removed and disposed of—an operation costing tens of thousands of dollars.

What is most disturbing about environmental exposures is the possibility that conditions with the potential for liability may exist but management may have no knowledge of them. Environmental audits, wherein engineers question operations personnel and inspect company properties and facilities to identify potential environmental problems, are increasingly being used to remedy this situation. Such audits are particularly appropriate when purchasing land, acquiring another organization, or when the company has in the past had operations that generated hazardous by-products.

Property of Others

Another liability exposure faced by many businesses that usually requires special treatment is that of the potential for damage to the property of others, such as customers. The instances wherein this occurs are numerous. For example, garages and many other businesses take possession of customers' automobiles; truckers and other common carriers transport property of others; contractors take custody and control of entire buildings; and jewelers, furriers, cleaners, and repair shops take possession of customers' property.

Many of these types of activities create commercial bailments. In general, a bailee is legally liable to the bailor (for example, the customer) for damage to the bailor's property arising from the bailee's negligence. However, no liability will generally be created when damage is not attributable to the bailee's negligence. For example, damage caused as a result of a fire, hurricane, windstorm, or other act of God would not normally be attributable to the bailee's negligence. This scope of liability may be increased by contract, such as when an agreement or even an advertisement states that the bailee will be responsible for damage to customers' property, regardless of cause. However, attempts to contractually limit or avoid liability, such as by printing a disclaimer on the back of a claim ticket, are generally considered against public policy and are therefore unenforceable.

PRODUCTS AND COMPLETED OPERATIONS LIABILITY

The potential liability to a customer or a third party for bodily injury or property damage caused by the business's product, or if a service company, its completed operation, is known as the products-completed operations exposure. This exposure begins when a product is first put into the stream of commerce (such as when it leaves the manufacturer's premises) or when an operation is completed (such as when a contractor turns a finished home over to the owner). When someone is injured or property is damaged by a product or completed operation, liability may arise under the legal theories of breach of express or implied warranty, negligence, or strict liability.

As an example of the products liability exposure, assume a young boy is injured because of a defective part on his bicycle. All of the businesses involved in manufacturing, distributing, and selling that bicycle face the potential of a products liability claim. Depending on the circumstances, liability could extend to the retailer who sold the bicycle, the wholesaler who distributed it to the retailer, the manufacturer who assembled the bicycle, and the manufacturer of the defective component part.

Dealing with the Statute of Limitations

One unique aspect of this exposure deals with the statute of limitations. The passage of time rarely provides an escape from products liability. Generally speaking, statutes of limitations (which bar lawsuits after a period of time) do not begin to run until an injury occurs (or manifests itself if latent). For example, assume a company manufactured and sold a hammer in 1966. While being used in 1988, the hammer chipped and the piece of metal flew in the worker's eye. Further assume that the particular state with jurisdiction over the case has a five-year statute of limitations. The injured worker could bring a suit against the manufacturer during the five-year period between 1988 and 1993. The fact that the hammer had been manufactured and sold twenty-two years prior to the injury would not normally be a defense.

Inheriting the Exposure

Another unique characteristic of products liability is that one company can inherit another company's exposure. This is called successor liability, and it can occur when one company acquires another company or even just a product line of another company. The main rationale for this legal theory is that an injured party should not be left without compensation simply because the original manufacturer has been absorbed by another organization. Because of the possibility of acquiring a substantial successor liability exposure in an acquisition, merger, or consolidation, it is imperative that an acquiring company look carefully into the products liability exposure of the target company. In doing so, it is necessary to investigate not only the exposure presented by its current products but also any products and product lines of the past that have been discontinued.

Analyzing the Exposure

When analyzing the products-completed operations exposure, the primary consideration is usually the potential liability for bodily injury and, to a lesser extent, damage to other property. However, there are two related exposures that require special treatment: the possibility of liability for property damage to the product or completed operation itself, and the costs of recalling a defective product from the marketplace. The exposure of liability for repairing or replacing the damaged work product is most significant for contractors and certain other organizations in the service sector. Many manufacturers, on the other hand, face a significant products recall exposure. These exposures are typically not insured by standard liability insurance policies, making the use of alternative risk management techniques very important in handling them.

AUTOMOBILE, AIRCRAFT, AND WATERCRAFT LIABILITY

Automobile, aircraft, and watercraft liability may arise under common law, state statutes, federal statutes, or even international treaties. In general, liability may arise from the ownership, operation, maintenance, or use of any of these conveyances.

When an organization owns, leases, or regularly rents automobiles, aircraft, or watercraft, the liability exposure is readily apparent. However, the possibility of being held vicariously liable for injuries or damages caused by the operation of nonowned automobiles, aircraft, or watercraft should not be overlooked. For example, a company may be held liable for accidents involving employee-owned automobiles, aircraft, or watercraft when they are being used on company business. Most risk management programs contemplate and provide for employee use of their automobiles on company business. However, the use of aircraft and, to some degree, watercraft is another story, and the potential liabilities are enormous. Because of the difficulty of identifying these exposures, it is generally advisable to adopt corporate policies prohibiting the use of employee-owned aircraft and watercraft on company business without prior approval.

PROFESSIONAL LIABILITY EXPOSURES

Professional liability is the products liability exposure of individuals or businesses that provide services instead of products. The traditional professions include physicians, law-yers, architects, and engineers. To this list, however, can be added a host of other occupations that, while they have not reached truly professional status in our society, still face a substantial errors and omissions liability exposure. Examples of these businesses and occupations include insurance and real estate agents, corporate directors and officers, financial advisers, financial institution trust departments, insurance companies, the media, pharmacists, auctioneers, consultants, title abstractors, marriage counselors, alcohol and drug rehabilitation centers, and even the clergy.

Professional liability claims may be based on breach of contract or, more commonly, negligence. With respect to proving negligence, a plaintiff must prove that a professional breached a professional standard of care that resulted in the plaintiff's injury or loss.

One of the unique characteristics of these exposures as compared to the other liability exposures discussed in this chapter is that it is often individuals, rather than organizations, who are liable. As such, personal assets rather than corporate assets are endangered by these claims. As an example, consider the directors and officers (D&O) liability exposure. When shareholders believe the directors of a corporation have failed in their duties of diligence, loyalty, and obedience to the corporation, they can bring a claim—or force the corporation to bring a claim—directly against those directors.

People and businesses whose occupations or activities primarily involve rendering professional or semiprofessional services usually have no problem recognizing their loss exposures. However, many organizations face incidental professional liability exposures that are not so easily recognized. A common example is the so-called incidental medical malpractice exposure, which arises when an organization employs a nurse, paramedic, or physician to provide first aid or other medical services to employees or others. Another example is the employment by a contractor of an architect or engineer to assist in preparing shop drawings, designing shoring, or other such construction activities. A fiduciary liability exposure arises when the organization sponsors retirement and other employee benefit plans, particularly when these plans are self-funded.

Whenever a company employs people who hold professional degrees, care should be taken to review their activities to determine if they may present an exposure beyond that

of the premises, operations, and products liability exposures discussed in this chapter. If their activities do present professional liability or errors and omissions exposures either to the individuals themselves or to the organization, special care is necessary to properly manage them.

HUMAN RESOURCES LOSS EXPOSURES

Michael T. Rousseau, Vice-President, Human Resources, Intermedics Pacemaker Division, A Company of Sulzermedica

One of the important functions of human resources is to identify the various loss exposures facing the organization. Once the task has been completed, the exposures should be recorded in a comprehensive policy and procedures manual. Such a manual allows an organized approach to human resources loss exposure. Policies and procedures should be reviewed by competent legal counsel specializing in employment law to provide a defensible position for the company. Policies and procedures regarding discipline need to be specific and followed exactly as outlined in the manual. There should be a procedure regarding exit interviews to cover all "open" items involved with termination. A policies and procedures manual requires a disclaimer stating that the contents are guidelines and do not constitute a contract between the employer and employee.

RECRUITING

Employment is a contractual relationship, that is, an exchange of services for compensation. The initial loss exposure that an employer faces in today's environment is hiring the wrong candidate. Current legislation provides strict guidelines when hiring an employee. The employment application must be nondiscriminatory, with a system to track applications and provide a database to meet EEOC/AAP (Equal Employment Opportunity Commission/Affirmative Action Program) reporting requirements.

Employees conducting interviews require training in what questions are suitable and an understanding of the risks associated with the interview process. Interviewers need to be aware of issues such as age, sex, race, and personal questions not connected to the position. Under the Americans with Disabilities Act, preemployment physical and aptitude testing is not allowable in the hiring process.

Preemployment substance abuse screening is allowed by law on a national basis. However, random drug testing is not permitted in all states. It is wise to investigate state and federal regulations when considering implementing these programs. Substance abuse screening is becoming an employer's weapon in the war against drugs in the workplace. The Drug-Free Workplace Act calls for employers to formulate a policy that must be communicated to every employee; the company should create a drug awareness program to teach employees and their families about the value of a drug-free lifestyle and a drug-free workplace; the company must help, encourage, and support supervisors to identify and refer problem workers; the company must locate reasonable treatment and rehabilitation sources; and the company must begin follow-up procedures considering the disease being treated and its recovery process. Prevention, intervention, and supported recovery are the foundation of any occupational-based program dealing with the problem of substance abuse.

Many companies are implementing employee assistance programs (EAPs) to foster early intervention in the development of life management problems. EAP counselors provide confidential, professional assessment and direction. By making services convenient, available, and nonthreatening, the EAP provides employers with the opportunity to meet most requirements when dealing with employees who are experiencing job performance problems. Legal review of the company's contract with an EAP organization is important and should outline the issues of confidentiality and indemnification.

PERFORMANCE APPRAISAL

Performance appraisal becomes an important legal and possible loss exposure issue whenever the data from appraisals are used for any type of personnel decision. Appraisal systems and the resultant data can be subject to the scrutiny of the courts; for example, appraisals used to promote, discipline, fire, transfer, or provide a basis for merit pay. Performance appraisals play a key role in the human resources function as it addresses the expected performance of an employee. An effective performance appraisal system can also provide a legal defense for the company.

Standards for performance appraisals are based on an analysis of job requirements. Performance standards must be communicated to all employees. Performance dimensions are defined in behavioral terms and supported by objective, observable evidence. Individual raters are assessed for validity in their ratings. Several raters are used, particularly when ratings will be closely tied to important personnel decisions. Documentation of extreme ratings is required and a formal appeal process is established.

REGULATORY REQUIREMENTS

Hiring and Employment Practices

Although there are many regulatory requirements in human resources, the primary areas include EEOC, AAP, FLSA, and ADA. The Fair Labor Standards Act (FLSA) contains five major provisions: minimum wage, overtime pay, equal pay (the Equal Pay Act of 1963 is an amendment to FLSA), record-keeping requirements, and child labor laws. Under the FLSA, employers must collect, store, and report large quantities of information about their compensation system and wage and hour data on nonexempt employees to the Wage and Hour Division of the Department of Labor. Employment law prohibits discrimination based on race, color, sex, religion, age, or national origin in any of the terms, conditions, or privileges of employment by employers, employment agencies, and labor unions.

The Americans with Disabilities Act (ADA) gives civil rights protection to individuals with disabilities similar to those provided to individuals because of race, sex, national origin, age, and religion. It promises equal opportunity in the areas of public accommodations, employment, transportation, state and local government services, and telecommunications to individuals with disabilities.

The Equal Employment Opportunity programs consist of several laws and executive orders. The principal laws are the Civil Rights Act of 1964, Title VII as amended by the Equal Employment Opportunity Act of 1972, the Age Discrimination in Employment Act of 1967 as amended in 1978, the Vocational Rehabilitation Act of 1973, Section 503, the Vietnam Era Veterans Readjustment Assistance Act of 1974, and Executive Orders 11246 of 1965 and 11375 of 1967. While these laws affect all human resources functions, their major influence to date has been on the selection and placement functions. The Civil Rights Act of 1991 allows jury trials and punitive damages for plaintiffs in discrimination suits.

The Rehabilitation Act does not specifically define contagious diseases (such as AIDS) as a handicap. However, the Supreme Court has held that a person with a contagious disease and a "physical impairment" is handicapped. The recent federal law has codified this holding to include a person with a contagious disease under the Rehabilitation Act. Further, the Americans with Disabilities Act prohibits employment decisions based on unfounded fears and prejudices about contagious diseases like AIDS. Eventually, case law will confirm this area; being consistent in hiring practices and maintaining strict adherence to job descriptions and functionality will enable companies to provide a defensible position.

Benefits

The primary regulatory requirements in design and administration of benefits include COBRA, ERISA, and FLSA. Proposed regulations require a group health plan to offer continuation of coverage to people who would otherwise lose protection because of certain events. The regulations will generally affect sponsors of and participants in group health plans, and they provide plan sponsors with guidance necessary to comply with the law. Generally, a group health plan must offer each "qualified beneficiary" who would otherwise lose coverage under the plan because of a "qualifying event" an opportunity

to elect continuation of the coverage. This offer is made immediately before the qualifying event. If a group health plan does not comply with these continuation coverage requirements, the employer will be unable to deduct contributions made to that or any other group health plan and certain highly compensated individuals will be unable to exclude from income any employer-provided coverage under that or any other group health plan.

Congress has extended the eighteen-month COBRA (Consolidated Omnibus Budget Reconciliation Act) benefit period to twenty-nine months for those qualified beneficiaries disabled (under Social Security Act provisions defining disabilities) on the date of the qualifying event. This extension of benefits applies to qualifying events involving a reduction of hours or voluntary/involuntary terminations.

The Employee Retirement Income Security Act (ERISA) of 1974 was passed to regulate the pension programs of employers. Although ERISA does not require employers to offer pension programs, it does require employers who do offer pension programs to follow certain rules if they want favorable tax treatment for both their contributions and their employees' deferral of income. As pension programs continue to evolve, added legislation places more burden on employers, the amount of investment vehicles offered, types of funds offered, and the opportunity to change distribution within those funds. It is critically important that a company remains up-to-date on all changes and requirements and has accurate record keeping for all IRS-qualified plans.

PROPRIETARY INFORMATION

When hiring or terminating employees, a company needs to have an established policy and procedure regarding proprietary information. The primary purpose is to provide protection regarding company trade secrets, patents, and other confidential information. Upon employment, an employee should sign a non-disclosure agreement and then should sign again during the exit interview at time of termination. If the employee is moving to a competitive company, the policy should outline procedures as regards alerting the competitor to the nondisclosure agreement. Some states allow noncompete agreements that place specific limitations on where and when an employee can be hired. However, many states are diluting these contracts and employees are challenging the rights companies hold on the employee's right to employment. Before implementing this strategy, legal review and proper language are critically important.

SECURITY

The company is required to provide protection for employees, curtail disruptions, and provide a secure work environment. Security coordinates those matters that may have an adverse effect on the assets of a company, investigating and reporting on suspected violations of policies and procedures, local, state, or federal laws, or any serious personal misconduct or breach of security that could bring discredit to the company.

WORKERS' COMPENSATION

One of the largest expenses in industry today is workers' compensation. Workers' compensation laws differ throughout the country. Strict adherence to these regulations is critical to prevent severe financial loss to the company. Workers' compensation is an extremely volatile and dynamic area that calls for constant attention and monitoring of changing OSHA (Occupational Safety and Health Administration) state and federal regulations.

Repetitive motion injury (RMI) is a significant loss exposure. Repetitive tasks that place excessive strain on muscles and nerves in the hand or wrist combined with exerted force produce the problem known as cumulative trauma disorders (CTDs). Carpal tunnel syndrome is caused by repeated bending and twisting of the wrist with applied force and is the most well-known of RMIs. Poor workstation designs and constant use of power tools can contribute to this type of injury.

To alleviate RMI, management, safety, and health personnel should learn how to spot existing problems and prevent future problems by introducing periodic rest periods, stretching exercises, and job rotation. Management should introduce programs where design engineers consider ergonomic issues in the design of new products, processes, and tooling.

LOSS CONTROL

Larry A. Warner, Risk Management Analyst, Mars, Inc.

When asked what risk managers do, I frequently respond, "We make sure nothing blows up, burns down, or injures anyone, and if it does, we make sure there is insurance to cover the loss." Notice that insurance is the last resort and all other activities center around the prevention of loss, or loss control.

Specifically, loss control represents the techniques used to reduce a firm's loss frequency and/or severity arising from a loss exposure. Loss control involves a wide range of activities including human safety, asset protection, product safety, crime prevention, and fleet management encompassing both human and property exposures.

The development of an effective loss control program requires the same management techniques as any other company activity. This includes the development of goals, planning, and the commitment of the necessary assets to achieve these goals. Effective loss control for any activity involves a five-step process: (1) risk identification, (2) selection of the appropriate loss control measure, (3) implementation, (4) monitoring the results, and (5) adaptation.

Loss control begins with the analysis of the firm's loss experience in order to identify the perils that have caused losses. Sources for this evaluation process include computer loss runs, OSHA loss logs, and loss investigation reports. Once past perils have been identified, hazards that may cause accidents in the future must be recognized as well. Latent and new hazards can be identified and addressed through safety audits of current equipment/ facilities and through the incorporation of safety features into the design or purchase of new equipment/facilities. It is far more cost effective to address these issues in the design phase than to retrofit in the future.

IMPORTANCE OF INDIRECT COSTS

Although the frequency of losses can be documented and evaluated, the severity of losses is not as easily determined. The direct costs of an accident include medical, rehabilitation, lost time benefits, and the impact on future workers' compensation premiums. The indirect costs are substantially greater, ranging from four to ten times larger than the direct costs. Under most circumstances, indirect costs are not covered by insurance.

Indirect costs impact a company on a broad spectrum. The lost labor and skills associated with the injured party create an indirect financial impact. Although work may be shifted to others or a replacement for the injured employee may be used, a reduction in speed and/or efficiency may result due to a variance in the skill levels of the two parties. The costs associated with spoilage or waste of raw materials or work in process, a disruption in production, cleanup costs, and repair costs of damaged equipment or other property are generally not captured in evaluating the total costs of a loss. Indirect costs also include the labor utilized in the treatment and rehabilitation of an injured employee, the costs of the accident investigation, and the claims administration expenses. The most difficult indirect costs to quantify are the idle time of other employees immediately following the accident and more importantly the impact on the morale of the other employees following a loss. Bad morale can lead to reduced productivity and, in the worst case, additional accidents.

SELECTING LOSS CONTROL TECHNIQUES

Following the determination of the true costs associated with a peril, the selection of the appropriate loss control technique can be made. This includes the establishment of standards or guidelines against which the process can be measured, such as periodic safety audits. Examples of loss control techniques include noise control and hearing protection, eye and face protection, head protection, facility design, machine and equipment guarding, and housekeeping. OSHA regulations address many of these, as well as other loss control methods.

It is important to keep in mind that it is generally more economical to design loss control measures, such as noise reduction and machine guarding, into facilities and equipment during the design and construction period, rather than to retrofit. This should be recognized and included in the overall loss control program.

IMPLEMENTATION

Once the appropriate loss control measure has been selected, the next step is implementation. In addition to the actual execution of the procedure, it is necessary to educate the employees as to the purpose and the use of the system.

Following implementation, success must be monitored and responsible parties must be held accountable for the results. Monitoring tools include safety audits, loss runs, and loss investigation reports—basically the same tools used in initially identifying the hazards. To add further incentive to the loss control program, insurance premiums and claims costs should be directly allocated to the parties responsible. Management must demonstrate its commitment to loss control by holding the line supervisors and their employees directly accountable for the results.

Machine guarding represents an excellent example of the importance of monitoring. Once a firm has made the investment in machine guarding, safety audits may discover situations where employees have defeated the guards. In such cases these employees as well as their supervisors should be reprimanded.

Loss control programs require adaptation and redesign on an ongoing basis. Not all measures will yield the desired results; therefore, changes will need to be made. Furthermore, firms are not static entities. Their loss control programs should be adapted to meet the changes in the business or the technology that the firm utilizes.

ROLE OF MANAGEMENT

No matter how impressive the design of a loss control program, it will not be successful without the commitment of senior management. Not only must management be committed but managers must communicate this commitment and hold their subordinates accountable for the results in order for the program to be a success. They must also play an active role in the loss control process. Management may initially express resistance to loss control. Generally this hesitation involves economic and/or emotional factors. Should this occur, risk management and safety personnel must sell the program benefits to management.

From an economic standpoint, management may be concerned with the initial investment in loss control; however, the ongoing costs to administer and adapt the program may play a role as well. Although the major investment may come initially, the benefits, or savings, accrue on an ongoing basis. In such cases, calculations should be provided to document these savings. Indirect costs should also be included in any analysis.

As an emotional reaction, managers may take the position that loss control is unnecessary under the mistaken belief that catastrophes only happen to others. They may also delay action because action would recognize their imperfect management skills. To prevent or alleviate such a reaction, it is important for the risk manager to present loss control in a positive manner, as a way to improve the operation of the business.

HUMAN SAFETY

Employees are a firm's most valuable resource; it is they who accomplish tasks, not machines. It is of paramount importance for a company to protect their human resources. Loss control makes sense for humanitarian, economic, and legal reasons. The costs associated with industrial accidents and disease have risen dramatically since the 1970s. Furthermore, industrial accident and disease have a far-reaching impact on society. They directly impact the employee, his or her family, and friends, fellow employees, and the employer. From a legal standpoint the Occupational Safety and Health Administration (OSHA) has regulations to which firms have to adhere. Furthermore, firms and their managers may find themselves criminally liable for failing to provide a safe working environment for their employees. Frequently in addressing the hazards that cause accidents, loss control measures will, ironically, have an impact on correcting other problems within a firm, perhaps by making equipment more efficient, as well as safer, as a result of redesign or additional monitoring.

An injury is the final step of a sequence of factors. In chronological order these factors are social environment (character traits acquired through the social environment), fault of person (faults that constitute the proximate cause for the unsafe act or for the existence of the mechanical or physical hazards), the unsafe act and/or mechanical or physical hazard, accident, and injury. (For more detail, see H. W. Heinrich, *Industrial Accident Prevention*, McGraw-Hill Book Company, 1959.) By removing the unsafe act and/or mechanical or physical hazard, the accident will not occur. This is the basis for loss control.

Although research indicates that unsafe acts cause a majority of accidents, defective equipment (design or function) plays a primary role in many injuries either solely or in conjunction with unsafe acts. Thus, any loss control program should address both the human and the equipment elements.

ASSET PROTECTION

The development of an overall property loss control program basically follows that of human safety—risk identification, selection of the appropriate loss control method(s), implementation, monitoring, and adaptation. The major difference is cost. Although the cost of fire extinguishers, fire doors, fire alarms, and smoke detectors may compare favorably with human safety techniques, the cost of sprinkler protection systems can far exceed such levels. Yet sprinkler protection may represent the optimal loss control method.

In evaluating options for asset protection, an understanding of the potential impact from a loss represents the most critical factor. Both direct and indirect costs are associated with asset conservation, just as human safety is. The indirect costs from a fire may be minor or they may be catastrophic and far reaching. In fact, they may extend outside the firm.

Fire Exposure

The majority of asset conservation resources are directed toward the prevention or mitigation of fire. The fire peril generally represents the highest potential for severity of loss. If not prevented or kept in check, fire has the potential to destroy an entire facility.

A fire may not only destroy a facility and cause an interruption in production but it may impact a firm's long-term viability. Although insurance may replace the facility, may provide business interruption coverage for the associated financial impact of the lost production, and may even provide short-term coverage for loss of market share, in the long term the firm may never be able to reestablish its past business position. In the past this has led to the ultimate demise of some firms. Factors such as these should be analyzed when evaluating property loss control methods.

Computer Exposures

Although the major thrust of asset protection is directed toward fire, the exposures presented by computers and their data represent another major area of concern. Businesses now operate in an increasingly information-oriented environment. Protecting a firm's data resources is very important.

Anticipating a loss involving computer hardware can be addressed using one of two methods. In the event of a multiunit business, a firm may have the ability, or be able to develop the resources, to run duplicate systems. If duplicate systems are not feasible, numerous firms provide services to assist in the time of catastrophe. These firms will either bring in replacement equipment or provide access to off-site hardware and software. Here preplanning plays the key role in ensuring ongoing operations following a loss. The outside vendor should have specific details of the firm's computing needs prior to a loss in order to react quickly following a loss.

Insurance policies provide coverage for damage to computer media in the event of a loss caused by a covered peril; however, insurance provides limited, if any, coverage for the cost to reconstruct the data that the media contained. This makes practical sense for both the insurer and the insured. Software worth thousands of dollars may be contained on a computer disk worth less than one dollar. The insurer would never be able to adequately calculate its exposure and the insured can take simple steps to greatly reduce its exposure.

The loss exposures presented by a company's computer software and data can be cheaply and efficiently protected through loss control. All software should have two backups, one on-site and the other off-site. The on-site backup should be updated daily and stored in a class A fire safe. Daily updates ensure that the greatest loss will be one day's work. The on-site backup acts as "insurance" for a broad spectrum of events ranging from a simple "head crash" to a major loss.

The offsite backup provides a company protection in the event of a catastrophic loss from a fire, flood, theft, or any other peril that causes the destruction of all on-site data. The off-site backup should be updated weekly, or more often if convenient. This method should assure that the greatest loss a firm could experience would be one week.

Product Safety

Although frequently overlooked, loss control can play a major role in product safety. The failure of firms to analyze the risks associated with their products, including the inappropriate use of a product by consumers, prior to their production, or to have an appropriate quality control program in place can lead to expensive product recalls, serious product liability claims, and adverse publicity. In fact, there are now federal regulations that require corporations to report products that cause serious harm to consumers. Clearly a loss control program that involves the evaluation of products before they go to market and an ongoing quality control program can yield substantial monetary savings and protect a firm's public goodwill.

Crime Prevention

The crime exposure has two facets: employee dishonesty and street crime, both of which are growing in frequency. Employee dishonesty has the potential for higher loss severity on a per occurrence basis due to the amount of funds or goods to which an employee has access.

Control measures, internal and external, represent the key to employee dishonesty loss control. Internal control measures reduce the opportunity for a crime to occur while external control measures increase the likelihood of discovery in the event that a crime takes place.

Examples of internal control measures include checking references of employees prior to their hiring, separating job tasks, and restricting access to bank accounts and important financial documents. Failure to review references could result in the hiring of a person who is not qualified as stated or has a less than favorable employment history, including past fidelity transgressions. The separation of job functions is critical. Separating such functions as purchasing, receiving, and accounts payable eliminates the possibility of infidelity without collusion. Unless warranted by their job functions, personnel should be denied access to bank accounts and important documents. Failure to limit access increases the potential for a fidelity claim.

External controls, such as periodic audits by CPAs, serve dual purposes: deterrent and discovery. External controls act as a deterrent for employees by increasing the likelihood of discovery, and represent one of management's best external tools for identifying incidents of infidelity.

Employee dishonesty frequently goes undiscovered regardless of the control measures. In fact, many crimes that are discovered are happened upon by chance. Unfortunately, many employers fail to prosecute personnel even with adequate evidence. Although the embezzler may be fired, failure to prosecute sends an inappropriate message to others and partially defeats a loss control program.

Street crime includes such crimes as burglary and robbery. These exposures require different loss control approaches. The burglary exposure is primarily treated by protecting the premises. Loss control measures against burglary include protective fencing; adequate internal and external lighting; the design of windows, doors, and other entry sources; and the use of locks, alarms, security firms, and safes. By addressing these items, an appropriate loss control program can be developed that reduces the likelihood of a burglary.

Training and good business practices reduce the robbery exposure. Employees should receive training on how to handle a robbery. Simple things like not trying to be a hero but being cooperative and attentive to the robber's physical traits may save an employee's life and lead to the capture of the thief. Good business practices like limiting the amount of cash on hand to only that required to conduct business, posting signs stating the limit of the amount of cash on hand, and having two people on hand to open and close operations (one inside and one outside in case of trouble) make a firm less attractive for robbery.

Vehicle Exposure

Automobiles present a unique opportunity for loss control. Unlike the other areas discussed, with the exception of product safety where the consumer may be injured through the use of a product, losses associated with the operation of automobiles usually happen away from the firm's normal place of business operation. This results in less direct supervision that loss control professionals have on this exposure; therefore, hiring practices, training, and automobile selection are the primary loss control measures for this exposure.

The hiring procedures should include a review of the prospective employee's driving history to ensure that a firm does not hire drivers with poor driving records who may put a firm at undue risk. Training classes in defensive driving and the communication of company safe driving standards play a critical role in driver education and performance.

Vehicles have varying degrees of safety features. Optimum handling features, sturdy construction, and the favorable availability of replacement parts directly impact the frequency and severity of accidents. Vehicle handling enables a driver to react more quickly to difficult situations, thereby increasing the likelihood of avoiding an accident. Vehicle construction can offer protection to the driver during an accident, while the availability of spare parts can reduce both the cost and repair time of a car following an accident. Both construction and spare parts availability reduce the severity of loss.

RISK RETENTION

Elisha Finney, Manager, Risk Management and Corporate Credit, Varian Associates, Inc.

Inevitably, losses will occur. Risk financing methods deal with how to pay for these losses. Risk financing can be divided into two major types: risk retention and risk transfer. This chapter explores risk retention. (See the next two chapters for discussions of risk transfer.)

Risk retention is the use of an organization's funds to finance accidental losses. Retention can be planned or unplanned. Planned retention is the result of purposeful, conscious, intentional, and active behavior; unplanned retention is when the firm is not aware that the risk exists and consequently does nothing or when the risk has been recognized but underestimated. Planned retention can be beneficial to the organization in the following areas:

1. *Cost*—Insurance premiums are comprised of estimated losses, administration, and profit. By retaining risks, the administration and profit components can be minimized or eliminated entirely. Retention may also allow an organization to avoid the insurance market cycles.
2. *Coverage*—Insurance may be unavailable entirely or the risk may exceed the available limits. The insurer may require a retention to encourage sound loss control practices or to avoid "swapping dollars" for frequent losses.
3. *Convenience*—It may simply be more convenient to retain frequent, small loss exposures. For example, it is probably not worth the effort to obtain insurance and file proofs of loss for broken plates in the corporate cafeteria.
4. *Control*—Retention affords the greatest flexibility in the areas of loss control and claims management.

The broad risk management objective is to minimize the total cost of accidental losses, which are distinguished by frequency and severity. Efficient management of accidental losses suggests that retention is an appropriate risk management technique where the severity potential is low.

METHODS OF FUNDING RETAINED LOSSES

In determining the best method of retention, many factors such as the firm's size; overall objectives; philosophy; capacity to absorb losses from assets, operating funds, or credit expansion; and ability to predict losses must be considered. While it rarely makes sense to form a business strategy exclusively around tax positions, the issue of tax deductibility should be explicitly considered when choosing among financing alternatives.

Retention can take many forms, including complete assumption of the risk, deductibles, self-insured retentions, and cash flow underwriting plans. Regardless of the name given to various retention methods, the most impor-

tant considerations are how much to retain and how to fund retained losses. Methods of funding retained losses can be categorized in order of their increasing formality or complexity:

1. *Current expensing of losses*—This method relies on working capital to pay relatively small, budgetable losses that occur with such regularity that the frequency and severity of losses can be closely predicted. This is the easiest and least expensive retention method; however, it should be used with caution as the actual cost of losses may differ markedly from budgeted losses. Exposures that are typically retained in this manner include glass breakage, automobile physical damage, and cargo damage. With this alternative, losses are tax deductible as paid.

2. *Borrowing funds*—This method relies on credit, arranged either before or after a loss occurs, to pay for retained losses. The obvious disadvantage with this method is that credit may not be available at the time of loss. Even if a prearranged revolving line of credit is available, the maximum amount may be drawn down at the time of loss or the loss itself may cause a firm to be in breach of the loan covenants. If no prearranged credit is available, the loss itself may prohibit a firm from obtaining the needed funds. For example, if a fire loss destroys a warehouse containing finished goods inventory, a bank may decline to extend credit because it can no longer be secured with inventory. In general, losses are tax deductible when paid and interest is tax deductible when accrued.

3. *Loss reserving (either funded or unfunded)*—This method establishes an accounting reserve in recognition of a loss that has occurred or that is very likely to occur in the future and that should properly be provided for by current charges to operations. Statement of Financial Accounting Standards #5 (SFAS #5) specifies two conditions that must be met before a provision for a loss contingency can be charged to income: (1) It must be probable that a liability was incurred at the date of the financial statement; and (2) the amount of loss must be reasonably estimated. SFAS #5 does not mandate or prevent the dis-

counting of loss reserves; however, most companies report undiscounted loss reserves in financial statements. The major difficulty with this method is preserving the sanctity of reserves. Reserves have traditionally been a popular management device for earnings manipulation and smoothing. While loss reserves reduce current income when posted, tax deductibility is allowed only when losses are actually paid.

4. *Pure captive insurance company*—A pure captive insurance company is a wholly owned insurance subsidiary that is formed to underwrite the risks of the parent company. A captive is the most formalized self-insurance plan in that it is capitalized, and regular premium payments are made to the captive. Over and above the advantages that any retention program offers, a captive can provide a firm with direct access to reinsurers, which are typically more aggressive in underwriting broad policy terms and conditions.

Generally speaking, premiums paid to a wholly owned captive are not tax deductible based on the requirement that a contract of insurance must provide risk shifting and risk distribution to be deductible as a business expense. However, this theory has been challenged recently and there are several litigated cases still pending. In July 1989, the U.S. Court of Appeals for the Sixth Circuit ruled in the *Humana Inc. v. Commissioner* case that in this particular situation of "brother-sister" subsidiaries, premiums paid to the parent company's captive are tax deductible. There are many factors that must be considered in formulating a captive, and it is prudent to obtain a detailed feasibility study before proceeding with this financing alternative.

5. *Association captive insurance company*—Association captives include group captives, industry captives, and "rent-a-captive" insurance facilities that underwrite the risks of several different organizations. Through the pooling of resources these group captives may have the ability to underwrite and retain much larger risks. Some of the benefits of group captives include the potential for both risk distribution and risk transfer, which can have very positive tax implications and in-house expertise in the areas of claims

management, loss prevention, and reinsurance capacity. Group captives, however, can subject individual companies to greater risk due to the poor loss experience of the group. Moreover, they can be inflexible in the coverages and program designs offered.

Arkwright Mutual Insurance Company has found a way to combine the benefits of both the single parent and the group captive without the associated downsides. Through the unique structuring of property and casualty fronting companies, in conjunction with an offshore reinsurance company and excess insurance, the program offers the potential of tax efficiency, flexible coverage, and minimal capitalization.

DETERMINING RETENTION LEVELS

There are various methods of setting retention levels, from "rules of thumb" to sophisticated financial models. Regardless of the methods utilized, retention levels generally reflect the risk management rules: (1) Do not risk a lot for a little. (2) Do not risk more than you can afford to lose. (3) Consider the odds. The "rules of thumb" are as follows:

- *Total assets method*—1 to 5 percent. Retention ability is based on the borrowing power of the firm. If highly leveraged, the retention limit should be at the low end of the range.
- *Working capital method*—1 to 5 percent. Retention ability is based on the financial strength of the firm. If the working capital position is very liquid, the retention limit can be at the high end of the range.
- *Earnings/surplus method*—1 percent of current retained earnings plus 1 percent of average pretax earnings over the preceding five years. Retention ability is based on the earnings and borrowing power of the firm and is a widely used method for determining retention levels. The higher the firm's liquidity, the higher the range that can be used.

- *Percentage of revenues method*—one tenth of 1 percent to 1 percent. Retention ability is based on the firm's financial prosperity. The higher the firm's sales volume and profit margin, the higher the range that can be used. *Note:* This method yields a per occurrence retention level versus an annual aggregate level.
- *Earnings per share method*—3 to 5 percent. A management decision is required regarding the maximum reduction of earnings per share acceptable before serious impairment of stockholder wealth.

Although the rules provide broad retention level guidelines, they should not be depended on solely in structuring a risk management program because of the wide variation in results. Because it is impossible to estimate losses with certainty, most companies take a conservative approach in setting aggregate and per loss retention levels. Also, because most liability risks are "long-tail" in nature, retention levels must be chosen with extreme caution. The retention level should reflect the financial structure of a firm and, just as importantly, legal and psychological factors. Legal restrictions contained in leases and trust agreements may limit the ability of a firm to retain risks. Psychological factors include the reaction of shareholders, and the emotional ability of top management to accept retained losses and resulting earnings fluctuation.

Optimal Retention

The Research and Development Division of Willis Corroon Corporation's Advanced Risk Management Services has proposed a process to determine optimal retention levels. Some components are:

1. *Critical constraint analysis*—The most common way to identify financial constraints is by reviewing restrictive covenants contained within corporate loan agreements. This analysis involves simulating a firm's pro forma financials with increasing levels of insurance and retention levels while measuring preestablished financial standards critical to

the firm's success. Simulations are continued at increasing total cost of risk levels until one or more financial constraints is broken, and the maximum feasible cost level is identified.

2. *Loss probability analysis*—Once the maximum retention capacity has been identified, loss levels are forecasted for each line of coverage at each evaluated retention level at alternative statistical confidence intervals. This analysis is often performed by an actuary.

3. *Present value analysis*—Identify the least-cost retention level by evaluating alternative combinations of retained losses and excess premiums. Present value analysis is the appropriate tool for this measure because of the substantial timing differences between the payout of excess premiums and retained losses. Excess premiums can be conceptually provided by the agent, broker, or underwriter and are typically paid up front or in quarterly installments. Average payout patterns for different types of retained risks can be calculated from a firm's historical experience or from industry averages available from brokers, underwriters, or actuaries. Risk financing expenditures reduce cash available to fund other operating costs, for capital investment, or to reduce debt; therefore, the after-tax borrowing rate, not the weighted average cost of capital, is the appropriate discount rate. The present value costs are then ranked by retention and loss level, and incremental savings are identified.

4. *Discounted payback analysis*—Having identified, by line of coverage, the least-cost retention level on a present value basis, the next step is to evaluate whether the incremental premium savings merit an increase in the retention level. The discounted payback analysis measures the number of years the savings must be invested at short-term, after-tax investment rates to fund a full penetration of the incremental retention level. Retention levels with unacceptable paybacks are rejected, although they may offer reduced costs.

5. *Cross-checking*—Steps 2, 3, and 4 are performed for each line of coverage. Once each line is individually evaluated and optimized, the projected costs for each coverage should be aggregated and compared to the financial

retention capacity identified in step 1. If the results of step 5 reveal an aggregate retention within the financial capacity of the firm, the analysis is complete and optimal. If the result of step 5 yields a program that exceeds the financial retention capacity, adjustments are made by reducing retention levels of individual lines beginning with the longest payback periods.

It is important to note that retention-level guidelines (except the percentage of annual revenue method) indicate aggregate amounts that should be retained in any one year—not any one loss. In a typical risk management program, various retention levels are chosen for different lines of insurance. All retained losses must be considered in total in setting optimal aggregate retention levels. For example, a single occurrence such as an earthquake could result in multiple retentions for workers' compensation, property, and general liability losses.

Other Considerations

In addition to financial, legal, and psychological constraints, underwriting factors must be considered, including:

1. *Premium credits*—Insurance quotes are obtained for various retention levels and the decision is based on a judgmental balancing of premium dollars saved versus losses assumed. For example, the risk management rule, "Do not risk a lot for a little," would lead you to insure an additional $100,000 exposure for a mere $100 premium credit even if you could easily absorb an additional $100,000 loss.
2. *Underwriting leverage*—Retention levels can be used as a bargaining chip when the insurance market hardens because larger premium credits can often be obtained during a hard insurance market cycle. Also, once a retention level is increased, it is psychologically difficult for underwriters to lower the retention at a future date.

NONINSURANCE RISK TRANSFER

Steven P. Kahn, Principal, Advanced Risk Management Techniques, Inc.

An individual or organization can retain the risk of loss or transfer it to others. Risk of loss can be transferred by the purchase of insurance or through noninsurance.

When an individual or organization purchases insurance, it is for the specific purpose of funding accidental losses. The accidental loss for which the insured expects to be reimbursed might be fire damage to owned property, a lawsuit arising from an automobile accident, injury to an employee, or some other unexpected event.

The insurance policy describes the events insured against, events not insured against, and what the insured and the insurer must do to protect their rights. Insurance policies are available to protect against a wide variety of accidental losses.

Noninsurance risk transfer is accomplished through the use of indemnity, insurance, and related clauses in contracts. The risk transfer is incidental to the central purpose of the contract, which may be a space rental, equipment purchase, or construction project. This is different from the outright purchase of an insurance policy where the insurer expects to profit from the risk assumption.

Contracts contain many clauses that must be closely reviewed to determine what risks are being transferred. These include:

1. *Indemnity clauses* — stating that one party (the indemnitor) will compensate another party (the indemnitee) for certain losses.
2. *Return of premises clauses*—stating in what condition premises must be returned to the lessor at the end of the lease.
3. *Rent abatement clauses*—stating the extent to which rent payment is suspended in the event of damage to leased facilities.
4. *Insurance clauses*—specifying the types, amounts, and conditions of insurance that one or more parties to the contract must purchase.

Indemnity clauses, the use of which is the most important technique for transferring risk without using insurance, are included in many contracts. It is important that they be carefully reviewed to ensure that each party understands the extent to which it is assuming or transferring responsibility for certain losses. Points to remember about indemnity clauses are:

1. Their primary purpose is to state who is responsible for injury or damage arising out of work performed under the contract.
2. They do not usually contain a dollar limit. The indemnitor usually agrees to assume responsibility for all losses within the scope of the indemnity agreement, no matter how large.
3. They are usually not limited in the types of injury or damage to which they apply.

Indemnity clauses can be found in many places. They range from simple one-sentence statements to several pages in length. The entire contract must be carefully reviewed to ensure that the scope and effect of the indemnity clause is understood.

Indemnity clauses have been classified many ways. It is helpful to think of three forms:

1. *Limited form*—requires the contractor to be responsible for its own negligence. A simple clause may read: "Contractor agrees to hold harmless and indemnify XYZ Corp. for liability arising out of the sole negligence of contractor and/or its employees.
2. *Intermediate form*—requires the contractor to be responsible for its own activities and liability arising out of the joint negligence of the contractor and another company. A simple clause may read: "Contractor agrees to hold harmless and indemnify XYZ Corp. for all liability arising out of the project, except that arising out of the sole negligence of XYZ Corp."
3. *Broad form*—requires the contractor to be responsible for all liability arising out of the project (including the sole negligence of another company). A simple clause may read: "Contractor agrees to hold harmless and indemnify XYZ Corp. for all liability arising out of the project."

In many states, the broad-form indemnity agreement is unenforceable because it relieves the indemnitee of too much responsibility for its own actions. This leaves a strong possibility that a broad-form indemnity agreement will be declared void.

The intermediate-form indemnity agreement provides good protection to the indemnitee. It protects against claims arising out of the activities of the contractor and against claims that arise out of the joint acts of the indemnitee and the indemnitor. The intermediate-form agreement is widely used in construction and other contracts.

The indemnity agreement places responsibility for certain losses with the indemnitor. Since indemnity agreements usually contain no dollar limit, the indemnitor could be responsible for losses of many millions of dollars. In many cases, the indemnitor will not have sufficient assets to finance the losses for which it is responsible. For example, a medium-size construction company would probably not be able to pay a multi-million-dollar liability claim that could arise out of a construction project. For this reason, the indemnitor is usually required to purchase insurance that is sufficient to pay reasonably foreseeable losses.

The contract should specify the types and amounts of insurance that each party is to purchase. If this is not done, the possibility exists that the indemnitee will not receive the protection it desired when the contract was drafted.

There are several ways to check that the other party has purchased required insurance:

1. Obtain a standard certificate of insurance, which is a document evidencing the fact that an insurance policy has been written. It also includes a statement of the coverage in general terms. It does not guarantee that coverage will be continued throughout the life of the contract.

2. Many organizations draft their own certificates. This is done to better assure that notice will be received if coverage is canceled and that other insurance provisions of the contract have been complied with.

3. Some contracts require that one party's insurance policy be modified in specific ways. It may be possible to obtain adequate evidence of some changes through a certificate of insurance. To increase the certainty that all required changes have been made, insurance policy endorsements can be obtained.

4. The only way to be certain that all policy terms are known is to review a copy of the insurance policy in question. This is time consuming and is reserved for the largest, most complex projects.

Each of these methods is used to obtain evidence of insurance in certain situations. As the necessity of ensuring that the other party has purchased the required coverage increases, a more secure approach to obtaining evidence of insurance should be used.

INSURANCE

Robert B. Edgar, Assistant Vice-President, Chubb and Son, Inc.

Mercifully, most business losses are partial and do not impair results, but this fact has tended to lull management into a false security that the devastating loss "couldn't happen to us." It can! And it does happen to many firms.

Let us assume you acknowledge that all your property could be destroyed in a single loss. Statistics show that, even with insurance, one out of two businesses never reopens following such a loss. The statistics further show that of those that do return, half will file for bankruptcy in the three years following the loss, including those firms with insurance.

What should you know about and expect of property insurance? How must it relate to your risk management (business continuation/disaster) plan?

Let us assume again that you realize your business is vulnerable to a large liability loss that could wipe out its asset base. How would your business survive if your business sustained such a loss? Are there adequate financial resources, including appropriate liability insurance, to defend and resolve the relatively minor and predictable liability claims, much less the large legal claims against your balance sheet? Because of those claims, would your business be exposed to even more complex and serious legal actions by creditors, customers, or stockholders? Can insurance help? How should it be integrated into your risk management plan?

These are valid questions. Alert managers acknowledge their exposures and develop a plan to manage them. The economics of a potential catastrophic property or liability loss requires the plan to include insurance. Many managers feel secure when they have purchased insurance policies that purport to deal with these exposures, but there is much more to insurance than simply buying a policy.

Volumes have been written about commercial insurance. It is a vast and often complex subject, complete with specialized fields of knowledge. This one chapter can only provide broad concepts and prompt the reader with "highlights" of the various insurance coverages that are available. The precise coverage afforded is subject to the terms, conditions, and exclusions of the policies as issued. A more careful analysis and detailed review of insurance is therefore required.

The first step in complementing your plan with insurance is to buy insurance that will enable you to accomplish the goals of your business plan. This means you should work carefully with your professional insurance adviser—agent, broker, or consultant—to understand how the insurance you purchase will perform in the event of a loss. Although underwriters have done much to simplify policy language, remember that insurance policies, much like other types of contracts, are steeped in common and statutory law. If anything is uncertain in your mind, get an explanation regarding the policy coverages.

Your insurance program will not perform as it should unless you can explain to your insurance adviser the types of contingencies that may impact your business. This is where your risk management plan comes in. The plan allows your insurance adviser to match insurance forms to the specific exposures and contingencies of your business.

TYPES OF INSURANCE POLICIES

You can purchase either monoline or package insurance. A monoline insurance policy covers one type of exposure such as fire, general liability, or automobile. A package policy combines multiple coverages into one policy, generally at a discounted price because of the insurer's savings in processing costs. Coverage is usually the same in either the monoline or package policy, but the package typically offers cost and administrative efficiencies to both you and the insurer, not the least of which is unified claims settlement if more than one type of insurance is involved. Large insurance buyers may decide on monoline coverage because their exposures are complex and it makes more sense to use different companies to write the insurance. Perhaps one company has substantial capacity and expert knowledge in property insurance while another is more suited for liability insurance. Your insurance adviser should seek the best policy form when placing your insurance.

THE POLICY ITSELF

The insurance policy, regardless of whether it is monoline or package, is generally comprised of four parts:

1. *Declarations*—It is generally the first page of the policy and includes the insurance company name, the insured's name, an overall description of the coverage provided, limits, locations, deductibles, policy forms that apply, and

any mortgagees. In short, the declarations page customizes the policy for your particular requirements.

2. *Insuring agreements*—This section describes the *coverages* granted in the declarations. These provisions should be carefully examined to ensure that your coverage matches your risk management plan. For example, the property coverage section of a package policy details the exposures insured by the policy unless the coverages are amended by endorsement. The *exclusions* list those perils, conditions, and events that are not covered under the policy.

3. *Conditions and definitions*—This section establishes how the policy provisions will work and the meaning of key words. For example, in the event of a loss, the conditions require the insured to perform specific duties, such as timely reporting of the loss to the insurer.

4. *Amendments*—Also known as endorsements or riders, amendments modify the basic policy coverages that apply specifically to your exposures. The amendments may either broaden or restrict coverages and should be carefully examined.

COVERAGES

There are many types of commercial insurance policies. Specific exposures may require types of insurance not listed in this short chapter. A well-conceived insurance program will, however, typically include the following coverages: property, general liability, auto, workers' compensation/employers' liability, directors and officers/errors and omissions liability, and excess/umbrella liability.

Property Insurance

In general, for a commercial property policy to respond, a loss must be the result of direct physical damage to the property by an immediate or proximate peril or cause (such as fire, wind, flood, theft) that is covered in the policy. Indirect or consequential losses are not covered under most standard policies. To collect under a property policy, you must have an insurable interest (financial loss) in the object of insurance at the time of loss. In addition to your interests, other entities may have insurable interests. A bank, for example, may have an insurable interest if it is the building's mortgagee, or an equipment manufacturer may have an insurable interest if it holds a lien on the machinery. Any of these interests may be listed as a mortgagee or loss payee on the declarations page. Again, you should consult with your insurance adviser about how to best protect other insurable interests under your policy.

Property Coverages.   Just as there are many types of property, there are multiple types of property insurance coverages. Key coverages that should be considered as part of any risk management plan are buildings and personal property, business income, boiler and machinery, crime, and inland/ocean marine.

Building and Personal Property.   You should carefully read the policy's definitions of building and personal property. What you consider to be building and personal property may not be considered as such by the standard policies. For example, the building definition generally excludes foundations and underground pipes. Typically, personal property does not cover personal property of others, so if you have personal property of others (including employees) on your premises, you should purchase insurance specifically for that.

The policy valuation provisions should be carefully reviewed as they establish the basis of a claims settlement. Many policies provide coverage on an actual cash value basis (replacement cost less depreciation) with an option to change to replacement cost if an additional premium is paid. Some insurers automatically provide replacement cost insurance. The differences are critical, and you need to consider carefully what is right for your business. Generally, a replacement cost basis is superior to actual cash value. Many property policies contain a coinsurance clause, which means you must purchase insurance in an amount equal to at least some predetermined percentage of the value of the property at the time of loss. A typical coinsurance percentage requirement is 80 percent. To the extent that the property is underinsured, any loss payment will be correspondingly reduced. Again, coinsurance is an important decision and one you should discuss with your insurance adviser to make sure you are adequately insured.

Most building and property insurance today is purchased on an all-risk coverage form, which does not name specific covered perils but, rather, excludes specific perils from coverage. The list of exclusions will vary by insurance company. When, as part of your risk management plan, you evaluate the types of loss that can impact your property, make sure you have coverage, if it is commercially available, for those potential causes of loss. Typical exclusions found in all-risk policies are (1) wear and tear, (2) rust, (3) dishonesty, (4) war, (5) nuclear damage, and (6) governmental action. Most insurance companies either do not sell, or limit the amount of, flood coverage. Earthquake insurance must be purchased specifically, and the typical policy usually limits the amount. Your policy should include the perils your plan has identified to be covered by commercial insurance.

Business Income/Extra Expense. Business income insurance is necessary to replace income lost by your business because operations have been impaired as a result of an insured loss to your property. Generally, business income insurance should be combined with extra expense insurance to cover (1) net profit that your business would have earned had the property not sustained direct physical loss or damage from a covered cause; (2) those continuing expenses such as overhead, property taxes, and medical costs that you are obligated to pay irrespective of whether or not your business is operating at full capacity; (3) payroll expenses during restoration of property; (4) extraordinary expenses over and above normal operating expenses. Generally these are expenses necessary to establish temporary operations or are those incurred to mitigate the loss.

To determine how much business income

insurance to purchase you must calculate, under a worst-case loss possibility, the income that will be lost during the time your property is being restored to conditions that existed before the loss. You should also estimate the extra expenses that may be necessary to establish substitute or alternate operations. Good worksheets are available to assist in calculating the amount of insurance you should consider purchasing.

Boiler and Machinery. The basic building property forms exclude steam boiler explosions and the mechanical breakdown of your building and process machinery. Some companies will provide this coverage as an amendment to your normal building and personal property insurance; however, most do not. Depending on the amount, type, and essential nature of the equipment, you may need to purchase a boiler and machinery policy. Good boiler and machinery insurers often provide valuable boiler inspection services. You should inquire about those services when purchasing the coverage.

Crime. The principal exposures are employee dishonesty, theft, burglary (forcible entry or exit), check forgery, and protection for money and securities. Many all-risk property policies cover loss by theft, but some are restricted to burglary. If your insurance does not provide coverage for theft, you should purchase a separate crime policy to protect your property.

Even if theft coverage is included in the basic property policy, it will typically not include coverage for stolen money or securities, employee dishonesty, or forgery. These may be severe exposures, so your plan should address them, and appropriate coverages should be purchased either in a monoline or package crime policy.

Marine. Inland marine insurance policies typically are those that provide physical damage insurance protection for property subject to transportation or movement (i.e., goods or merchandise in transit). Some of the more often-required marine coverages are transit (for merchandise in shipment), accounts receivable (reimbursement of uncollected accounts receivable), valuable papers and records (cost to reproduce), and electronic data processing (to cover electronic equipment, software, and media). These marine coverages are traditionally broader all-risk coverage than normally provided under the building and personal property forms. You should note that many of these coverages are included under a well-drafted property package policy. If you ship goods overseas, you may want to explore an ocean or air cargo policy since transit policies do not cover overseas shipment. Again, the advice of a professional is recommended to match your exposures to the appropriate coverages.

General Liability

Property insurance such as that outlined in the preceding paragraphs is first-party insurance because it covers the property of the insured (the first party). Liability insurance is often referred to as third-party coverage. It involves three entities: the insured (the first party), the insurance company (the second party), and a third party who alleges that the insured is legally responsible for damages caused by the insured. The insurance company is responsible, subject to the policy terms, conditions, and exclusions, for the insured's legal defense and the third party's legally established damages. General liability exposures should be insured at limits that best protect the assets of your business. Generally, all businesses should purchase general liability insurance.

Space does not permit a full explanation of general liability coverage. Your risk management plan should identify and economically value your exposures. While the policy is very broad, as with property insurance, there are exclusions and conditions you must understand. The general liability policy generally provides protection in three areas:

1. Those sums the insured becomes legally obligated to pay as damages because of bodily injury or property damage to others. This coverage provides protection for those exposures that arise from business operations, or from the sale of your business products.
2. Those sums you become legally obligated to pay as damages because of personal injury or advertising injury. The policy has an extensive definition of personal injury, but it is important to make sure the policy protects your business from libel/slander, false arrest, or wrongful detention claims.
3. Medical expenses for bodily injury—regardless of fault—when it occurs on premises you own or rent.

All three coverages are subject to the limits of insurance and the exclusions that appear in the policy. The insurer should also pay costs of defending you against these kinds of legal responsibility allegations. The legal defense issues alone make general liability an essential insurance policy for the typical business.

General liability insurance is extremely complex, and your business should not typically operate without it. Only by spending considerable time with your insurance adviser can you be sure you have the proper protection.

Auto Liability and Auto Physical Damage

With few exceptions, general liability policies do not respond to bodily injury or to property damage claims caused by vehicles. Auto liability coverage is required for such exposures. Defense costs for defending against such claims are also covered by auto liability insurance.

Property policies rarely respond to your damaged vehicles. Auto physical damage is required. Since your vehicles belong to you, you may select the coverage that best suits your financial requirements: small or large deductibles, named or specified perils versus comprehensive perils, and collision coverage.

You may also have auto exposures even if your business does not own any vehicles. If you or your employees rent vehicles for business purposes, this presents you with a hired car exposure. If employees use their own cars for your business (even if just delivering a package on the way home from work), you have a nonowned auto exposure.

Many states have mandatory insurance requirements involving minimum insurance requirements, uninsured and underinsured motorists coverage, and medical payments coverage. You will need to carefully review your auto exposures with your insurance adviser. The auto exposures listed here are generally available in a single commercial automobile policy. Some companies may include some or all of these coverages in a single automobile policy.

Workers' Compensation/ Employers' Liability

If employees are injured on the job or contract an occupational disease, there is not any coverage provided under the general liability policy. The workers' compensation statutes of the states determine the benefits afforded employees. To be eligible for benefits, in most situations, employees just need to be injured as a result of their work. This is so regardless of who is at fault—employer or employee.

For this reason, most states require all employers to have some form of workers' compensation insurance purchased from an insurance company or state fund. Some states will permit a self-insured program. Self-insurance workers' compensation programs typically require the employer to post substantial financial guarantees. The programs are carefully scrutinized by regulators to protect workers against an employer's financial irresponsibilities.

Workers' compensation statutes and employers' liability vary by state. All worker injury claims are not covered by the workers' compensation statutes and, thus, are not covered by workers' compensation policies. Accordingly, the typical business should purchase a coverage known as employers' liability. It is usually available as part 2 of the workers' compensation policy. (Part 1 provides statutory workers' compensation protection.) Unlike workers' compensation, which has no policy limit, but is subject only to state statutory limits, employers' liability is subject to the limit of insurance you purchase. A workers' compensation policy is usually a standard state-prescribed form and is written as monoline coverage, not as a part of a package. You must review your exposures with your insurance adviser, especially if you operate in more than one state.

D&O/E&O Liability

Directors' and officers' Liability (D&O) is not subject to any standard form of coverage. This coverage is usually made available only by specialized companies. It protects the corporation, its officers, and directors for damages they become legally obligated to pay because of any claim to which the insurance applies. Such claims must result from a negligent act, error, or omission arising out of the management of the business. This insurance usually includes costs to defend against such claims.

Errors and omissions (E&O) insurance is also not subject to any standard form of coverage and is usually available only through specialized companies. E&O insurance protects you for damages you become legally obligated to pay because of any claim arising out of a negligent act, error, or omission by the insured in providing, or failing to provide, the services your business performs. It usually includes costs to defend you against such claims. These coverages may be important for your business. You will want to explore possible requirements with your insurance adviser.

Excess/Umbrella Liability

The larger your firm, the greater the need for larger limits of liability insurance protection. Excess and umbrella policies provide for limits in excess of the limit provided in your primary or basic general liability coverage, commercial auto policy, and employers' liability coverage. Often several excess policies may be purchased to build a total liability insurance program. A requirement for $15 million of total liability protection would be purchased as follows: primary policy, $1 million; first excess, $5 million excess of $1 million; second excess, $9 million excess of $6 million; and so forth. In the event of loss, the first excess does not respond until the $1 million primary is exhausted, and so on.

An excess policy usually only provides limits in excess of a primary limit that is typically specified in the policy. The coverage is usually the same as provided for in the primary limit. An umbrella policy is similar to an excess policy, but it may provide for certain insurance that may be excluded in the primary policies such as oral or written contractual coverage. You should consult with your insurance adviser to obtain advice about how much liability limit your business might require and the best way to purchase the excess limits of insurance.

These policies are not subject to standard forms. You and your insurance adviser will want to explore the market to determine which insurance company and which policy best suit your requirements.

RISK MANAGEMENT DEPARTMENT ORGANIZATION AND POLICY

E. J. Leverett, Jr., Professor of Risk Management and Insurance, University of Georgia

As a firm grows in size, scope, and complexity, it becomes more difficult for the right hand to know what the left hand is doing. If a firm is to be successful it must overcome this communication problem. The best of facilities and personnel are of little value unless they are properly coordinated and developed. Consistency in the organization is achieved by establishing the proper organizational structure and providing the personnel with a framework from top management. The organizational structure provides the structural parts of the firm with connections of authority and responsibility, which in turn will provide the best results for the firm. The framework, which is frequently called a policy statement, directs the risk manager to act in a consistent manner in the handling of specific situations.

The needs and expectations of the firm will determine the structure of the risk management department organization. If top management views the risk management function as clerical in nature, the organizational chart will reflect that view. In contrast, if top management views the risk management function as one that is broadly based, dynamic in nature, and interacting with a large number of departments within the organization, then the organizational chart will reflect that viewpoint. The desired viewpoint of top management is that the risk management function is dynamic and broadly based.

ORGANIZATIONAL FEATURES

Clarity

A properly functioning organization will have a clear understanding of the nature of the relationships that exist between the people within the organization. This understanding is established by the risk management department organizational chart and the interaction with the overall organization. Authority and responsibility should be clearly expressed in the organizational chart. It is not uncommon in an organization to have overlapping authority. An example of overlapping authority is an individual going beyond his or her expressed area of jurisdiction. The risk management department can easily be involved in overlapping authority because the nature of the activity is so broad. For example, should the risk manager be involved in employee benefits? The author thinks so, but the human resources people might be inclined to disagree. Consequently, the organizational chart should expressly delineate the areas of activity and control to overcome a conflict of this nature.

Flexibility

Modern organizations are dynamic in nature and it is impossible to construct an organizational chart with clearness and completeness that deals with every possible situation. The very nature of the risk management function is dealing with the unexpected; therefore, situations will arise for which specific handling instructions have not been established. As a result, flexibility should be built into the organizational chart.

It is important to consider two features when constructing an organizational chart with flexibility. The first feature is the ability of the structure to change itself to meet the current needs of the organization. The second feature is the inclusion within the master plan of the organization for the perpetuation of the risk management function.

Authority

It is not uncommon for a firm operating with management by objectives to experience difficulties because rigorous standards of performance have been established but restrictions are placed on the performer by limiting authority. A common definition of authority is the right to give orders and the power to exact obedience. Being held accountable for results is known as responsibility. When top managers assign the risk management function to an individual and holds that person responsible for the results, he or she must be given enough authority to match the degree of expected results.

It is proper for top management to hold the risk manager responsible for an economically efficient risk management program, but the risk manager must have the authority to design such a program. Firms within the author's knowledge have indicated to the risk manager that they could do "anything they wanted in the risk management program, except change the broker." This is not to say that all problems originate with the broker or are solved by changing the broker. It is, however, a good example of an all-too-common problem of responsibility without authority.

Communication

No organization can successfully function without good communication. Effective risk managers cannot operate in a vacuum. They must be continually interacting with other people, both internally and externally. The risk manager is an information-dependent person and cannot be effective without the proper channels of communication. The organizational chart of the firm indicates the formal channels of communication, just as the risk management department's organizational chart indicates the communication channels of that department.

In order to do an effective job, the risk manager must establish communication channels with every unit within the organization. At the very least, risk management should have good communication with the following departments: accounting, finance, legal, marketing, operations, personnel, and transportation. These departments are not to be considered the ideal but the minimum communication levels.

Rigid channels of communication will inevitably leave situations unattended because no provision has been made for handling the exception. If the formal organization does not solve the exception problem, it will be solved by the informal communication arm known as the "grapevine." The grapevine is a communication system that operates between friendship, work, and special-interest groups within the organization. The grapevine is normal social interaction among people and should be used, not fought. Managers cannot destroy the grapevine, because they did not create it. In fact, good risk managers do not attempt to destroy, but learn to use this informal communication tool as an information dispenser and provider.

In addition to communicating internally, the risk manager needs communication channels to the industry in general. This external communication can be accomplished by working with various industry organizations such as the Risk and Insurance Management Society (RIMS), the American Management Association (AMA), and industry-specific organizations like the risk management section of the Forest Products Association or the American Bankers Association.

If the agents/brokers are doing the proper job, they can be a great source of information for the risk manager. In addition, consultants and insurance carriers can provide valuable information. State and federal legislators can influence the actions of risk managers, and dialogue with appropriate legislators can be carried out on a regular basis.

ORGANIZATION CHART

Given the choice, the risk manager would choose to report to the CEO. This type of reporting relationship is possible in smaller companies, but as the organization increases in size, the reporting relationship will move further away from the CEO. Nonetheless, positioning the risk management department within the organization's structure and establishing the proper level of reporting is of great importance. A rule of thumb is that the risk manager will report to a position that is

within two levels of the CEO. Generally, the higher the reporting relationship, the more stature and clout the risk manager is likely to have. This posture will enable the risk manager to obtain better and more timely information upon which to base risk decisions.

There is no one in the organization, other than the CEO, that crosses more departmental lines or has greater access to all aspects of the firm's operations than does the risk manager. If the risk management job is done properly, it is more of a risk financing task than any other type of function. Consequently, the proper reporting relationship should be as high up the financial hierarchy as possible.

The organizational chart of a risk management department can vary widely as the complexity, geographical area of operation, and size of the firm increases. Exhibit 12-2 is a sample organizational chart of a fairly typical risk management department. No claim is made that this chart is a picture of all departments, but it is a good place to start.

The head count or staffing may not be available to the risk manager to fill all the slots shown on the sample organizational chart. Nonetheless, the functions must be performed by someone. In the absence of risk management department staffing, the functions must be performed by the broker, the insurance company, or some other person(s) within the firm. The staffing decision is ultimately a cost-benefit analysis of who can best perform the functions.

RISK MANAGEMENT POLICY STATEMENTS

The risk management policy statement provides direction for the risk manager in specific situations. This board of directors–approved statement provides a framework within which lower-level managers can make decisions on repetitive questions and problems. The policy statement should set forth in writing the goals, directions, and attitudes of an organization. A policy statement does not tell how procedures are carried out in an organization; it tells the procedures that are to be carried out. This general guide to action ena-

Exhibit 12-2. Structure of a Risk Management Department

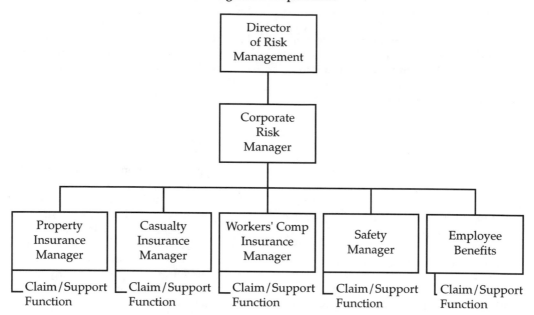

Source: From E. J. Leverett, Jr., Risk management organization, in *Risk Management* (Athens, GA: E. J. Leverett, Jr., 1991), 410.

bles a risk management organization to function smoothly within the corporate structure by anticipating what another unit would do in certain situations.

A policy statement establishes the tone for the risk manager's decisions that are consistent with the remainder of the organization. Some examples of policy statements are as follows: (1) We sell only for cash. (2) We lease rather than buy office space. (3) We insure all property valued at more than $10,000.

Every organization has unique characteristics that play a role in determining the policy statement for each unit within the organization. In establishing the risk management policy, the risk manager needs to recognize the goals of the organization, its environment, and company attributes.

Corporate Goals

If earnings stability is a significant corporate goal, then a firm is likely to have a policy directing the risk management function to concentrate on loss control and risk reduction.

The corporate goal of earnings stability requires the risk manager to do an even more thorough job of risk identification. The goal of earnings stability will likely dictate the purchase of more insurance than if the goal of growth is used. For example, to have earnings stability the risk manager must purchase business income and extra expense insurance to a greater degree than might otherwise be required.

Organizational Environment

An organization's environment will be made up of its clients, competitors, suppliers, and government regulators. Each of these environments can affect the risk management policy statement. For example, a construction company doing cost plus work may be forced into carrying a guaranteed cost workers' compensation policy rather than some type of loss-sensitive program. The loss-sensitive program may be more cost efficient, but the firm is unable to determine the actual cost of workers' compensation on a specific job because of the long tail on compensation claims. It is unlikely that a client would be willing to accept a billing seven years after the completion of a job. The Department of Transportation (DOT), a regulator, will require specific minimum liability limits if a firm is going to operate trucks that involve the DOT. Each of these environments dictates a certain risk management policy position.

Company Attributes

The organizational environment is a major force in determining a firm's development, but history also plays a major role. The influence of a "former" environment reflects the present state of a company's development, but present management cannot be ignored when policy statements are formulated. Present company operations must be analyzed in order to minimize misunderstandings that occur because of failure to differentiate between policies and objectives. A firm's objective is a statement of intention and a policy is more definitive. For example, the objective establishes that the risk manager will strongly endeavor to have "no lost time accidents or no unplanned retentions." The policy is definitive in that it is a directive from top management to perform in a specified manner. Definite limits of authority are prescribed. The policy does not spell out the end result but only indicates a means to achieve the end result. Whereas the objective is a guide, the policy is a specific command.

Policy Statement Format

Managers at all levels of the organization should participate in the establishment of a policy, but the CEO and the board of directors authorize the policy. The risk manager is accountable for the interpretation and application of the risk management policy statement as it is approved by the board. In addition, the risk manager is accountable for developing appropriate regulations to apply to the risk management unit.

A solid format is necessary for a successful risk management policy statement. A good risk management policy statement should contain at least five characteristics if it is to become a solid risk management decision tool:

1. The policy statement should express goals and directions in writing. Even though the document is written, it is not etched in stone.
2. Rules and procedures are not part of the policy statement.
3. A flexible policy statement is essential. The policy should be able to adapt to a dynamic organization.
4. The statement should be consistent with the overall goals of the organization.
5. The statement should reflect the organization's plans and objectives.

Policy Contents

The risk management policy statement should describe where the risk management unit fits in the overall organization and delineate the importance of the risk management function. The policy should outline the scope of risk management and the functions that are to be performed by the unit such as broker selection, insurance purchasing, loss control responsibility, and claims management. The organization's attitude toward staffing for these functions or contracting for their performance should be discussed. The organization's attitude toward risk retention should be spelled out with some minimum and maxi mum levels defined. The establishment of a risk management policy is certainly not limited to the above items, but it should be done in harmony with the overall organization's goals.

Sample Policy

Many firms that do not have a risk management policy statement simply do not know where to start. The task is something that everyone means to do but has difficulty giving it top priority. A sample risk management policy statement is given in Exhibit 12-3. No case is made that sample policy is the ultimate risk management policy statement. It is merely a place to start the process and should be altered to fit the corporate environment to which it applies.

Exhibit 12-3. Sample Risk Management Policy

CORPORATE ENTERPRISES INC.

Corporate Enterprises Inc. is to be protected against significant financial losses, which, in the aggregate during any financial period, would significantly affect personnel, property, the budget, or the ability of *Corporate Enterprises* to continue to fulfill its responsibilities to its customers, shareholders, and the public. Significant means shall be used to prevent or control the probability of loss of life or major personal injury to employees or members of the public.

This policy applies to risks that can cause losses and whose undertaking involves no possible profit. Examples of such losses would be fire, natural disasters, liability suits, theft, workers' compensation, product recall, and other losses both direct and indirect.

Reporting Relationship

The corporate risk manager shall report to the corporate vice-president of finance.

Responsibilities

The risk management department will be responsible for the following areas:

- Identifying and analyzing the company's static or pure risk.
- Quantifying identified risk to determine maximum probable loss.
- Selecting agents and brokers.
- Determining the most economically efficient method of handling the identified risk.
- Where insurance is selected, negotiating the coverage with attention to quality, service, and cost.
- Coordinating information and acting in an advisory capacity with regard to fire protection, safety, security, and employee benefits.
- Carrying out the responsibility for placing or accepting risks at the appropriate levels.
- In the event of a loss, the risk manager will act as the group leader to collect from accounting and the various affected divisions the loss data necessary to collect for the insured loss.
- Working with the legal department in settling liability losses and in analyzing contracts for risk implications.
- Allocations charges of the risk management program to the various divisions of the company.

Risk Handling

The corporate risk manager will recommend various levels of risk retention and administer a retention program when the amount of the potential loss would not seriously affect the corporation's financial position.

The retention guideline for *Corporate Enterprises Inc.* shall be $50.00 in any one loss, and no more than $500.00 in any one year from all retained loss control techniques shall be used in conjunction with all other methods of handling risk.

Loss control recommendations that are received from competent external or internal sources shall be presented to the affected division for implementation. Any charge or credit for the implementation shall be allocated to the affected division.

Exhibit 12-3. *(continued)*

Purchase of Insurance
Insurance shall be purchased when:

1. Required by law or by contractual agreement.
2. Special services (claims handling, engineering, inspection, etc.) that are packaged with the insurance coverage are desired and cannot be purchased more economically as a separate item.
3. Insurance is economically justified because the reduction in the degree of risk is greater than the cost of the insurance.
4. The amount of the potential loss is at least $50.00 or more. Exceptions can occur when the purchase is financially unsound or the exposure is uninsurable.

Insurance shall be placed in insurance companies with a B or better rating in Best's policyholders' ratings. Insurance placed in any other company will require a written report of the particulars. This report is to be filed with the board of directors.

Insurance shall be purchased through licensed agents or brokers who have the technical competence and staff sufficient to service the insurance provided.

Divisional Conditions

Each division manager shall be responsible for conducting operations in accordance with company standards, policies, and statutory requirements. The division manager shall have plans for new projects reviewed by the risk management department for risk implications. The division manager shall report all claims or losses to the risk management department.

Divisions will expense losses to a level acceptable to the division manager, but no less than $1,000 per loss. Insurance charges to the divisions will be determined by the risk management department. They will include a proportionate share of corporate insurance and administrative costs plus a loading to cover losses between the division and corporate loss retention. The premium allocation to the divisions will include a proportionate share of corporate insurance and administrative costs plus a loading to cover losses between the division and the corporate loss retention levels. Loss experience will be part of the premium allocation system and part of the performance system and part of the performance factors at merit review time.

General Conditions

Each plant controller shall be responsible for reporting new property values, disposal of assets, and significant changes in operations to the risk management department.

To keep abreast of conditions in all company operations, the risk manager or a representative shall make visits at least *annually* to all major operating units.

The board of directors shall have the final responsibility of assuring that a prudent risk management program is in effect at all times. A review of the program, including loss exposures, loss control, retention plans, and insurance coverages, shall be undertaken by the board of directors, a committee thereof, or consultant, at least annually. The minutes of the board of directors shall indicate the date of review and the board's approval.

Source: From E. J. Leverett, Jr., Risk management policy statements, in *Risk Management* (Athens, GA: E. J. Leverett, Jr., 1991), 410.

THE ROLE OF INSURANCE AGENTS AND BROKERS

Daniel J. Dean, Vice-President, Frank Crystal & Co., Inc.
Karen Epermanis, Director, Risk Management, Intermedics Inc.

In the insurance industry there is a legal difference between the terms *agent* and *broker*. An agent is empowered to act for another. Therefore, an agent works for one or more insurance carriers and has the power to act on their behalf. A broker is an intermediary that negotiates an agreement between two or more parties. A true broker serves with the interests of both parties in mind.

Although there are legal differences in the terms *agent* and *broker,* in today's insurance environment they are often used interchangeably. This has evolved over time, because in order to maintain a healthy business, the agent or broker must satisfy both the insurance purchasing client and the insurance provider. Thus, the delineation between the role of the agent and broker has evolved to encompass similar services.

One notable exception is an agent of direct writers (for example, State Farm or Farmers Insurance). In this case, the agent has only one insurance company with which to place business. The role of a direct writer agent then becomes more of an extended sales force for the insurance company rather than an intermediary between two parties. For the purpose of this chapter, the discussion relating to the role of the broker generally includes the agent as well.

The broker's service role varies from client to client. This depends on factors such as the client's service requirements, the size of the organization, and the complexity of the insurance program. The role of the broker can vary from negligible participation to performing as an external risk manager. The service functions of a broker can be summarized in the following four categories: (1) insurance administrator/marketer, (2) supplemental staff support, (3) auditor, and (4) innovator/communicator.

INSURANCE ADMINISTRATOR/ MARKETER

The most common function of the broker is to market the client's insurable exposures to the underwriter and to administer the details of the negotiated insurance product. This is perhaps the only function that generally cannot be performed solely by the client. The resources required to adequately maintain a constant view of the marketing process are generally too great for the risk manager/client to handle independently.

The marketing process requires the broker to identify insurance carriers that meet the criteria established by the client. These criteria include size of carrier, financial stability, services provided, product offered, and overall pricing. While many of these factors can be predetermined by the broker, the price and coverage terms and conditions offered within the product are most often resolved by negotiation.

Proficient negotiation skills are essential to being a broker. Some insurable risks are constrained in the market by preset rates (either by the state or the insurance carriers). However, most prices and coverage terms are determined by negotiation. It is during the performance of the marketing phase that a broker can most clearly show the client the added value of his or her role. A broker that is knowledgeable about the client's exposures and is skillful at presenting them in the most positive light can clearly outperform brokers who are not as well prepared.

Once the product and price are negotiated, it is the broker's responsibility to ensure that the product is delivered as agreed and to administer the details inherent in the insurance product. Supplying binders, reviewing policy language, and issuing certificates of insurance when necessary are an integral part of the broker's responsibility.

SUPPLEMENTAL STAFF SUPPORT

The second major function of a broker is to provide the client with an external staff. There are two primary reasons that this is important to the client. First, the broker can more efficiently maintain a staff of specialists to be available for the client's needs. While each client cannot typically justify a full-time staff dedicated to these needs, there are occasions when specialists are needed. Through the use of a broker, the client can effectively expand the expertise of the department without adding unnecessary overhead. Examples of this type of specialist include loss control engineers, claims personnel, and insurance coverage specialists. Coverage specialists are individuals who have job functions that are dedicated to one particular type of insurance policy, such as directors' and officers' liability, fiduciary liability, or international insurance.

A related but secondary function that is filled by this supplemental staff support role is a smoothing of work flow. There are several periods of time that require additional work to be performed in a relatively short time frame. An example would be during the renewal of the insurance program or during the corporate budgeting process. While the client may have the expertise to perform these functions in-house, he or she may not be able to adequately perform the volume of work required within a specific time frame. By shifting much of the administrative details to the broker, the client can meet the short-term work overload while maintaining proper control of normal functions.

AUDITOR

The broker also performs an audit function. Risk management is by its nature a risk-averse environment. Gaps in coverage are highly feared by most risk managers. However, given the complex nature of the function and the large number of transactions that occur, errors are a likely event. Therefore, it is extremely important to have a second pair of eyes watching over the program. This redundancy gives risk managers a good night's sleep.

Where the client is not sufficiently large enough to have its own risk management department, the broker can expand the audit function to a position similar to that of an external risk manager. In that event, the broker is directly responsible for identifying risks of loss and recommending alternatives to handle those risks. These recommendations may include noninsurance risk reduction and/or transfer techniques.

INNOVATOR/COMMUNICATOR

The last major function of a broker is the most subjective and perhaps the most difficult to deliver. The client looks to the broker to provide innovative ideas on how to improve the insurance program and manage risk. Through day-to-day operations, the broker is bombarded with new ideas from the market. By filtering these ideas, building upon them, and communicating the results, the broker is in a position to provide innovative ideas to the client that represent an improvement to the existing program. For large risks, the ability to innovate/communicate is often the difference between obtaining a client and keeping a client over the long term.

FUTURE TRENDS

As the field of risk management develops and the client becomes more educated in the inner workings of the insurance product, the role of the agent or broker continues to change. One trend is the tendency for risk managers to increasingly demand direct access to their insurance underwriters and consequently rely less on the broker for insurance advice. As this occurs, the broker's role shifts more toward that of supplemental staff support and innovator/communicator rather than insurance administrator/marketer.

Another trend is the tendency for smaller clients to go toward direct agency writers. This is increasingly popular for the client who needs insurance but does not want to pay for other services available from multicompany agents or brokers. Therefore, the agent/broker is feeling a squeeze between small clients utilizing direct writer agent services and large clients placing business directly with insurance companies. This loss of market share should continue as free-market forces shake out the inefficiencies of the insurance delivery system. As with any other market, this process will inevitably lead to a smaller, more efficient, and economically healthy industry.

GLOBAL INSURANCE AND RISK MANAGEMENT

John J. Hampton, Professor of Insurance and Risk Management, The College of Insurance

Individuals, multinational corporations, non-profit organizations, government agencies, and others must protect against risk in a worldwide context. The College of Insurance in New York City recognizes two distinct international topical areas. Global insurance refers to national and transnational markets where life, health, property, and casualty insurance policies and programs are provided for individuals and organizations. Global risk management covers the coordination of risk management programs by large organizations.

DOMESTIC INSURANCE MARKETS

Most nations of the world have domestic insurance markets. They range from highly developed to small and insignificant. The most interesting and important markets are:

1. *United States*—This is the world's largest property-casualty market and second largest life insurance market. Thousands of companies offer a vast range of policies and coverages. Insurers offer retirement and other annuity products, either directly to individuals or as group programs. In the property-casualty area, liability exposures are particularly a concern as a result of liberal legal interpretations of tort responsibilities by the nation's courts.

2. *Japan*—This is the world's largest life market and second largest property-casualty market. It is a closed market, dominated by a small number of large insurers. Most coverage is provided by domestic Japanese companies. The market is highly regulated with limited price or other competition. The insurance market provides a capital formation outlet for individuals who are conscientious savers. It also provides property and casualty programs for some of the most expensive assets in the world.

3. *European Community*—This is also a highly developed market with coordinated regulations designed to facilitate the providing of insurance products and services across national borders of member states. This effort began with the 1987 Single European Act and is likely to continue well into the twenty-first century. National markets are, however, quite different in terms of available coverages, distribution systems, and consumer expectations. The markets reflect linguistic, social, and cultural differences as well as varying economic conditions and standards of living.

4. *Four Tigers*—Singapore, Hong Kong, Taiwan, and South Korea have high-intensity economies that cause observers to link them together. With respect to insurance, they are quite different. Singapore is an orderly and well-regulated market that reflects its government's and people's concerns for stable savings and business interactions. Taiwan is a developing domestic market that seeks to expand beyond a relatively limited range of life, retirement, and casualty coverages that were available as the island entered the 1990s.

South Korea is building off a developed life market and seeks to expand into new products and services. And Hong Kong is a nontariff market that reflects its wide-open approach to business. Hong Kong, of course, is building its links with the mainland as it prepares for reunification with China in 1997.

5. *China*—This large market is dominated by a single insurer, the People's Insurance Company of China, that provides the bulk of life and property coverage. Insurance was banned domestically prior to 1979 but grew rapidly in the 1980s. Continued growth is likely, whatever the political climate, as the Chinese government uses the mechanism of insurance to collect capital for investment and provide for the needs of the nation's citizens, including its sick and elderly.

6. *Eastern Europe and former USSR*—This grouping contains many actual and potential national markets with only the most rudimentary mechanisms for providing insurance coverage. These markets are likely to develop at different rates but slowly overall. Unsanitary and unhealthy living conditions pose problems for life and health development. Outmoded and often dangerous physical plants and unsafe work practices require careful selection by insurers of property and casualty exposures.

7. *Other nations*—The rest of the world must be considered nation by nation. In some cases, the domestic insurance markets are highly developed. In other cases, they are devoid of the characteristics that make insurance effective. Generally, domestic insurers dominate the markets. It is common for government-owned companies to have a virtual monopoly in many countries. Customs and practices vary with respect to capital requirements, coverages offered, regulation of the industry, and the social or economic role played by insurance companies.

GLOBAL RISK MANAGEMENT

A multinational corporation and similar nonprofit integrated entities should follow a worldwide plan to manage the various risks and exposures that confront them. Some of the considerations in a program of global risk management are:

1. *Varying standards of coverage*—An organization will have its own philosophy on the mixture of insurance and retention for its property and liability exposures. Some international operations may exist in countries that do not provide the proper coverage. This must be arranged in a worldwide program coordinated by insurers and brokers.

2. *Varying employee relations*—Companies have programs to provide life, health, retirement, and other benefits for their employees. These can be coordinated in a single program that allows for social and economic differences in local operations.

3. *Coordination of coverages*—The laws of different nations may require insurance payments that result in duplicate coverages. It is also possible that the absence of local insurance or loss control services may produce gaps in the organization's overall strategy. A knowledge of conditions and practices in foreign countries is essential to coordinating risk management activities.

4. *Local servicing*—A company may have claims anywhere in the world. The ability to respond to lawsuits, comply with national regulations, and settle injury or other claims by employees, customers, and third parties requires a coordination of the worldwide and local capabilities of a risk management program.

5. *Financial considerations*—The management of risk has a financial side. Some programs may take advantage of tax benefits provided in one or more local jurisdictions. Also, currency restrictions, blockages, or other problems must be included in the evaluation of how to protect against losses and provide local benefits. This can be a particular problem with operations in countries that are highly protectionist with respect to currency exchanges.

6. *Information considerations*—An organization must have centralized knowledge of the workings of its risk management program. Losses can often be more devastating than the local dollars involved. An example might involve safety practices in an organization that manufactures components around the world. A fire may damage a factory that is the sole supplier of an essential subassembly. The business-interruption losses may far exceed the physical damage from the fire itself. Lacking information on local fire hazards, the risk manager may fail to take actions to avoid such disruption.

INTERNATIONAL STRATEGIES

Insurance and reinsurance companies, brokers and other intermediaries, and firms offering risk management services can compete in international markets. Some of the issues that should be confronted are:

1. *Control of the market*—Is market entry controlled by the government or other entities? In some countries, entry is restricted to local nationals. In other countries, entry is strictly regulated.

2. *Culture of the market*—What is the ethnic composition of the purchasers of insurance? As an example, in several of the countries of Southeast Asia business is conducted either by a local ethnic population or by an overseas Chinese community. A different strategy is needed to match the culture of each category of potential customer.

3. *Identity of the customer*—Who is it that actually purchases insurance or related services? In some markets, a broker or agent makes the purchase decision on behalf of the party with risk to be covered. In other cases, a local insurance company may filter all coverages and services on behalf of its client.

4. *The entry strategy*—How should an organization enter a local market? In some cases, it is essential to purchase a local, established provider. In other cases, it may be possible to form a joint venture. In still other cases, it may be possible to open a local branch office staffed with local nationals.

5. *The profit strategy*—Is it likely or even possible to earn a profit in the market? In some cases, the culture precludes a profit. In other cases, currency restrictions make it unlikely that profits could be repatriated if earned.

GLOBAL VERSUS INTERNATIONAL INSURANCE

When operating internationally, large organizations commonly pursue one of two strategies:

1. *Global orientation*—This strategy is to offer services in virtually every country of the world. Through a linkage of brokers, agents, local offices, and other entities, a global company can handle any customer problem no matter where it occurs.

2. *International orientation*—This approach is to offer services in markets where they are likely to produce a profit for the company. Gaps exist, either geographically or by available service, in different countries. The company operates only in markets that make sense at the time and is willing to withdraw from markets if conditions change.

Entrepreneurship and Small Businesses

Donald A. Straits, Section Editor

Introduction   *Donald A. Straits*   13-3

The Role of the Entrepreneur in the Economy   *Alvin Rohrs*   13-5

Preparing a Business Plan   *W. Keith Schilit*   13-6

Sources of Financing for the New Business   *Alan R. Tubbs*   13-12

Human Resources Management in the Small Business
   Donald Grunewald   13-16

Marketing in the Small Business   *Phyllis Elnes*   13-19

Cash Management for Growing Firms   *Jack Rader*   13-22

Customer Service in Small Businesses   *Dick Laird*   13-26

International Opportunities for the Growing Business   *Tom Niland*   13-28

Taxation and Accounting Considerations   *E. Malcolm Greenlees*   13-30

Hiring, Firing, and Avoiding Lawyers   *David S. Machlowitz*   13-34

Family-Owned Businesses   *Dan Bishop*   13-37

The Franchising Route   *Robin D. Anderson and Vance A. Mehrens*   13-39

INTRODUCTION

Donald A. Straits

At some point in time, many of us possess a special dream to start and run our own small business. This dream represents the foundation upon which our country was built. The free enterprise spirit to make things happen on our own has inspired tens of thousands of individuals to begin their own business. Many of these endeavors fall short of their expectations; many succeed beyond the wildest imaginations of their founders.

Entrepreneurship is alive and well. Small businesses combined account for more employment opportunities than all of the major corporations put together. Every year, thousands of new businesses are started by people from all walks of life: young and old, rich and poor, male and female, representing every race and nationality. They all possess the desire, dedication, and determination to make it on their own. They seek to survive and grow through their personal drive to achieve success regardless of the hardships they face.

This section has been designed to share the lessons that lead to success. The authors come from a broad spectrum of experience. They are entrepreneurs, educators, corporate business leaders, and lawyers. They present the knowledge and skills that will enable you to maximize your likelihood of starting a business that will survive and thrive in this highly competitive, global marketplace.

The authors explore a wide range of subjects to help you begin your quest. It is imperative you begin with a sound business plan and so that is one of the first subjects that is examined. Helpful hints on preparing an effective plan are laid out in a step-by-step process.

Another chapter looks at a topic of utmost importance: money. If you already have it, great; if you do not, how do you get it? The author gives you some excellent ideas on the sources of financing and the development of good relationships with banks and other lending institutions.

Other chapters cover the functional areas of small business management from utilization of human resources through marketing, customer service, and cash management. Technical subjects are also examined including tax and accounting considerations and suggestions on dealing with lawyers.

The remaining chapters deal with special issues that confront entrepreneurs or potential business owners. One chapter examines franchising as a viable way of starting your own business. Another looks at the opportunities and obstacles of family-owned businesses. Finally, special attention is paid to the development of sales to foreign markets.

The road to success as an entrepreneur is not easy. The authors show that the opportunity is there, but that the task is not simple. A total commitment by the entrepreneur is a requirement that must be matched with long days of hard, demanding work and creative thought.

But the authors recognize that the entrepreneurial spirit is strong, the rewards are potentially great, the challenges are real, and the problems can be overcome. They have given their best from their wealth of experience. They join me in wishing you the best as you begin your exciting adventure or build on your current endeavor.

Donald A. Straits, M.B.A., *is the founder and president of Leadership Resources. The company provides management motivation, presentation, and leadership skills to corporate managers and executives. Mr. Straits previously served as president of both an industrial machine tool company and a consumer goods marketing company. His academic experience includes sales and marketing professorships at Ohio University, Fairleigh Dickinson University, Seton Hall University, and Linfield College.*

THE ROLE OF THE ENTREPRENEUR IN THE ECONOMY

Alvin Rohrs, President and CEO, Students in Free Enterprise, Inc.

"There is a noble calling. To start a business and to create jobs. We need you, America needs you." These were the words of H. Ross Perot addressing the future entrepreneurs at the Students in Free Enterprise International Exposition in 1990.

Being an entrepreneur is indeed a noble calling because success can only come by serving others. Taking a risk to start a new business and to create new products and services is done out of self-interest with the hope of achieving financial rewards and personal fulfillment. But this cannot be done without serving others. In a market economy, personal growth can only be achieved if the entrepreneur serves the needs and desires of the entire community, and, in particular, the consumer.

To meet the needs of the consumer, the entrepreneur must also provide employment for those people that produce the goods or services. In a market economy the entrepreneur must provide incentives and working conditions that will attract qualified workers.

An old saying is, "Anyone can count the number of acorns in an oak tree but only God knows the number of oak trees in a single acorn." The same is true with the entrepreneur. Anyone can count the number of jobs that exist in the economy but no one can count the number of jobs that motivated entrepreneurs will produce. Who could have predicted that the owner of one Ben Franklin Five and Dime store in Arkansas would create 100,000 jobs. Sam Walton did it by building the Wal-Mart company into the world's largest retailer in less than thirty years. Since the 1980s, small business has created 75 percent of all new jobs, a total of millions of new positions.

Being an entrepreneur is a noble calling because entrepreneurs change the course of history. They take new ideas and turn them into new products and services that raise the standard of living of workers and consumers. Inventions like the steam engine, automobile, airplane, telephone, television, and computer are just a few of the technological breakthroughs that have dramatically changed the world. These inventions would not have been significant if there were not entrepreneurs that took these ideas and turned them into products and services. The cotton gin is one example of the inventor, Eli Whitney, not having the entrepreneurial ability to turn his invention into a viable benefit for others. An entrepreneur took Whitney's idea and made it a practical product that changed the course of history.

Mass production of interchangeable parts, the assembly line, and incorporation to gain capital are but a few of the ways entrepreneurs have taken the ideas of an enlightened age and turned them into higher standards of living for millions of people. Entrepreneurs take calculated risks based on a strong belief in their own ideas and their ability to make those ideas successful. When asked, they do not see their role as being all that risky because of their strong faith in themselves.

The risk of entrepreneurship has often been overstated. The statistic that only 25 percent of the businesses that are started this year will still be in existence in five years is often quoted. Closer examination of this statistic shows that most of the 75 percent did not fail but merely changed their name or form of ownership. Arguably these other businesses were actually more successful due to growth than the 25 percent that stayed in business under the same name and form of ownership.

Business failures do possess an intrinsic value to the economy. In a market economy, failures of products, services, and entire businesses are a result of failing to meet the needs of the consumers. Business failure tells the economy what products and services are not of value and what management strategies do not work. The economy will therefore not allocate limited resources to be used in these inefficient ways.

The entrepreneur also serves a valuable role of turning threats to our quality of life into valuable resources. An example is the problem of pollution where new products and services reduce pollutants or turn them into other valuable products. This is providing jobs for thousands and is improving the quality of life for millions.

PREPARING
A BUSINESS PLAN

W. Keith Schilit, University of South Florida

When the CEO-founder of a computer software firm visited his banker to request a $50,000 line of credit, he kept his business plan tucked neatly under his arm. When the president of a manufacturer of electronic components wanted to establish five-year goals, she, too, resorted to her business plan. And, when a citrus processing company in Florida sought outside investors to finance expansion, it made sure its business plan was

up to par. These entrepreneurs all recognized the value of a business plan.

Only a limited number of investments provide adequate returns. Investors set rigorous standards in evaluating venture proposals. A large majority of proposals are rejected. Thus, as a first step in preparing a business plan, it is crucial to understand how the plan is read and evaluated by the investor.

Many entrepreneurs can prepare a "B" or a "B+" business plan without too much trouble. That would be fine if investors would fund such plans. Investors, however, only fund "A" or "A+" plans. In essence, a "B" business plan is no better than a "C" or "D" plan because it is not likely to get funded. The real skill is to turn a "B" plan into one that warrants an "A+."

What separates a "B" from an "A+"? The key difference is that an "A+" plan is written from the perspective of the investor. The "A+" plan gets the investor to believe in your product or service, your target market, and your management team while it addresses the problems or the key concerns of the business. In addition, the "A+" plan demonstrates that something is unique about this deal— something that distinguishes this investment opportunity from more than a hundred others that are brought before the investor every week.

HOW TO TURN ON INVESTORS

For a plan to receive a favorable review by an investor, it must demonstrate a clear definition of the business, evidence of marketing capabilities, evidence of management capabilities, and an attractive financial arrangement.

Definition of the Business

There are three basic questions that provide a working understanding of the business:

1. What is the product or service?
2. What is the industry?
3. What is the target market?

No small business venture can be all things to all people. In the earliest stages of a business it is critical that the company develop a logical strategy and avoid dramatic changes. Any alteration may result in a riskier strategy for the firm.

Investors are always looking for that something extra that will provide the company with a decided advantage over its competitors. This may include a new product feature, a cost advantage, technical competence, or something else that will benefit the customer. A great way to win the favor of an investor

is to have a unique product that is of a proprietary nature, either by copyright, trademark, patent, or by some other exclusive arrangement. Two classic examples of companies benefiting from their proprietary positions are Polaroid, with instant printing, and Xerox, with xerography.

Although the product or service should be unique, it should also be simple. If you cannot describe it in a sentence or two, it is too complex. Also, keep in mind that investors generally do not have technological backgrounds. If you are dealing with a high-tech product, describe it in such a manner that nontechnical persons will understand it.

The industry should be clearly defined and should have growth potential. Investors prefer to fund businesses in industries that have a high annual growth rate. High growth is more important than high tech, as evidenced by venture capitalists giving greater attention to specialty retailers than to technology companies in recent years.

Many investors are attracted to companies that have the ability to open up whole new industries, as was the case of McDonald's in fast food, Federal Express in overnight delivery, Head in ski equipment, Apple in personal computers, and Digital Equipment in minicomputers. A famous story told by Tom Bata, the owner of one of the largest shoe companies in the world, summarizes the philosophy of opening up new markets: "Two shoe salesmen were sent to a poverty-stricken country. One wired back, 'Returning home immediately. No one wears shoes here.' The other cabled, 'Unlimited possibilities. Millions still without shoes.' "

As a rule, investors prefer innovative companies that are just beginning to grow. They realize their greatest returns as they "ride the growth curve." Investors shy away from revolutionary products in industries that have not yet been developed.

It is critical that you identify a specific target market for your product or service. The difficult issue here is that you want to demonstrate evidence of the market being substantial enough to provide adequate revenues for your business. Yet, capital requirements will make it impossible for you to reach everyone, thereby necessitating you to clearly define or focus your target market.

Marketing Capabilities

There are four features that demonstrate the firm's marketing capabilities: (1) benefit to the user, (2) evidence of marketability, (3) widespread marketability, and (4) selling ability.

Perhaps the best indicator of a firm's marketing capabilities is the ability to demonstrate how the customer will profit, gain, or otherwise benefit from buying the company's product or service. Demonstrating user benefit will strengthen the contention that the company can generate sales and be an attractive investment opportunity. Benefits vary from product to product. However, there are a few guiding questions:

- Will the product save the customer money?
- Will it save time?
- Will it provide status?
- Will it enhance the customer's lifestyle?

When possible, you should quantify the benefits in order to improve the likelihood of investment. For example, a device that reduced energy consumption by 40 percent on average paid for itself within one year. The cost savings to the customer can be measured in terms of lowered reject rate, lowered warranty costs, reduced labor costs, lowered storage costs, lowered inventory costs, reduced downtime, and greater convenience.

Investors generally want to see some indication that customers have used the product or service, even if only on a trial basis, and are happy with it. The best indicator of future customers is past customers. Most investors prefer to fund companies with some operating history, although it is not necessary that the venture be profitable. Stated another way, investors would prefer to have their money used for production and selling, rather than for product development and market research. This reduces the risk and the time needed for profits to be generated.

As a rule, investors shy away from businesses whose basic product or service must be specially designed for each customer. In most of these situations, costs are high due to specialized labor requirements, profits are low due to an inability to achieve advantages from economies of scale, and growth is slow.

You must show how the product will move from the shop floor to the customer's floor. This demonstrates a market-driven, rather than a product-driven, attitude. One essential characteristic of a successful entrepreneur is the ability to sell. You could have the most impressive product imaginable and could be well capitalized; yet, without sales, the business cannot succeed.

Management Capabilities

Most investors fund management rather than products. One prominent venture capitalist goes as far as suggesting, "It's really the people who are important. The plan just gives the investor the opportunity to meet people, see what kind of people they are, learn their visions and their philosophies, and see what kind of intelligence went into the plan."

There are three features that demonstrate the company's attention to the importance of management: (1) the management team, (2) experienced managers, and (3) the board of directors.

Investors would much rather fund an experienced management team than sole entrepreneurs. The management team should have a demonstrated track record and competencies. Furthermore, the board of directors should enhance the team's capabilities. One of the biggest problems faced by less experienced entrepreneurs is that they have "gaps" in their management team. Experienced investors can assist in filling in the gaps by providing introductions to marketing or finance executives.

In some cases, investors will want to take active roles with the company they are funding. For example, Kleiner Perkins Caufield and Byers provided Genentech with the capital to support its early levels of growth. They also provided Genentech with a chief executive officer, thereby enabling Genentech's scientist-executives to return to their research labs to develop new biotechnology products. That decision was largely responsible for Genentech's remarkable success.

In recent years, numerous experienced managers with excellent track records in established companies have been successful in starting their own businesses. Similarly, repeat entrepreneurs such as Nolan Bushnell (Atari & Pizza Time Theater) and Steven Jobs (Apple and Next) have found that securing funding from investors is easy with experience. Investors invariably invest in the experience of the entrepreneur rather than in the growth potential of a given product or service.

Investors are also sensitive to the qualifications of members of the board of directors. An experienced board will partially offset some gaps in the management team. At a minimum, such a board will enhance the capabilities of any management team.

Investors will often make suggestions regarding potential members of the board. In most cases, the investors will want to be represented on the board to remain involved in critical strategic decisions. This is highly advisable as most investors can provide you with experience and important contacts. In essence, you want their advice as much as their money.

The purpose of the board is to aid, challenge, and replace (if necessary) the officers of the company. Thus, a passive unquestioning board can be disastrous. You should consider having two or three "outsiders" serve on the board to assist you in making decisions and monitoring the environment. You will often be able to attract competent directors who would welcome the opportunity to work with a small-growth venture and who will accept a minor token payment of cash and/or equity for their services.

Financial Arrangement

Investors prefer a structured arrangement that describes the capital needs of the venture and proposes a fair equity agreement for the two parties involved. The terms are generally subject to intense negotiation. The business plan should include a specific dollar amount of capital needed for the business. Proposals for any amount of capital may be appropriate. Proposals are generally accepted only above a minimum of $200,000. It is not cost effective to evaluate smaller proposals. The financial arrangement should include an acceptable return for investors, a provision for an "exit," participation by other investors, and a structured deal.

Investors maintain a time horizon of three to seven years in which to realize their returns on their initial investment. During that time period, they expect their investment to increase in value by five- to fifteen-fold net of inflation.

The return on investment is based on the riskiness of the investment. The higher the risk, the greater the expected return. Risk is generally based on the nature of the product or service and the quality of management. New ideas are more risky than established products or services.

Stanley Rich and David Gumpert have developed an evaluation system that identifies four levels to describe the product or service and four levels to describe the management, as shown in Exhibit 13-1. Level 1 is the most risky and would warrant the highest expected return. Level 4 is the least risky. Typical expected returns are given in Exhibit 13-2.

The exhibits are merely guidelines; each venture is evaluated on its own merit. Investors will settle for a lower return if the company has sufficient capital or has a good cash flow, or the owners have invested a sizable portion of their own funds in the business.

Once a proposal has hurdled the risk and return criteria, other factors become important. First, remember that venture capitalists are very conservative. They are interested in making a lot of money and also in not losing the money that they have already invested. It is crucial to demonstrate to them how they cannot lose on their investment. A battle often develops between the entrepreneur and the investor. The entrepreneur argues the upside potential whereas the investor states the downside risk. Eventually an agreement is reached. The important lesson is that the entrepreneur must understand the investor's needs and risk preferences prior to presenting a plan for raising capital.

A second factor to remember is that not all ventures succeed. In a typical venture capitalist's portfolio, there may be one major success, and three or four minor successes, and a num-

Exhibit 13-1. Evaluation System for New Products or Services

Status of Product or Service	Status of Management			
	Level 1 Individual Founder-Entrepreneur.	Level 2 Two Founders. Other Personnel Not Identified.	Level 3 Partial Management Team. Members Identified to Join Company When Funding Is Received.	Level 4 Fully Staffed, Experienced Management Team.
Level 4 Fully developed product/service. Established market. Satisfied users.	4/1	4/2	4/3	4/4
Level 3 Fully developed product/service. Few users as of yet. Market assumed.	3/1	3/2	3/3	3/4
Level 2 Operable pilot or prototype. Not yet developed for production. Market assumed.	2/1	2/2	2/3	2/4
Level 1 Product or service idea. Not yet operable. Market assumed.	1/1	1/2	1/3	1/4

Exhibit 13-2. Expected Returns Compared to Stage of the Business

Stage of Business	Expected Annual Return on Investment	Expected Increase on Initial Investment
Start up business (Idea Stage)	60% +	10–15 × investment
First stage financing (New Business)	40%–60%	6–12 × investment
Second stage financing (Development Stage)	30%–50%	4–8 × investment
Third stage financing (Expansion Stage)	25%–40%	3–6 × investment
Turnaround Situation	50% +	8–15 × investment

ber of projects that lose money or fail completely. Investors need a high return to balance the poor returns. If they secure a 51-percent ownership position in the company, it may reflect the returns necessary to invest in the venture rather than a desire to control the company.

The best way for any investor to realize a gain on an investment is to sell the ownership position. For securities traded on a national stock exchange, there is always a market. For privately held companies, the market is considerably more limited. There are four basic ways in which an investor can "exit" from a deal: (1) a buyback by the founders of the company, (2) finding a new investor, (3) an acquisition by a larger company, or (4) "going public" via an initial public offering (IPO). Going public is often the most attractive because a ready market will then exist for the investors to get their original investment out of the business. It also can be a very profitable arrangement.

An excellent way to attract investors is to demonstrate that other investors, and particularly the existing top management team, have already invested in the business. There is the story of Frederick Smith, who in his quest for $90 million to launch Federal Express, used the tactic of asking all of his potential investors for that "last million," rather than for the "first 89 million."

Investors prefer to see a structured deal. Thus, the answer to the following questions should be stated clearly in the business plan:

- Who is involved in the deal?
- How much money is needed?
- What is the minimum investment per investor?
- How is ownership translated into shares of common or preferred stock, convertible debentures, and other debt?
- What is the price per share of stock?
- What is the projected compounded annual return over the next three to seven years?

HOW TO TURN OFF INVESTORS

In addition to understanding what turns investors on, it is important to know what turns investors off. The sterile standardized business plan packages that many consultants sell to small business owners will often set off a "red flag" to the investor. Such packages use a common skeleton that does not reflect the nature of the company or the industry. Oftentimes, they suffer from "Lotus-itis." Although spreadsheet programs can develop neat, mathematically correct rows and columns of numbers, their end product often fails to meet the needs of the investors. The assumptions surrounding the numbers are more important than the numbers themselves.

One pitfall is to focus on the product rather than on the market for that product. Many inventors fall prey to this problem. True, the product might be innovative and have phenomenal features. The key issue, however, is whether customers will buy the product. Investors tend to shy away from entrepreneurs who are too enamored with the features of the product.

It is difficult to fool investors when it comes to the financial projections for the company. Entrepreneurs have a tendency to overestimate revenues and underestimate costs. Projections of 50-percent growth rates and 60-percent gross profit margins by a company in an industry characterized by 10-percent growth and 25-percent gross margins would be questioned by an investor. Investors like to see a best case, a worst case, and a most likely case set of projections.

It is imperative that the business plan address the critical risks and problems that may be encountered. Investors will generally be aware of some of these risks, so failure to address them will undermine the credibility of the entire plan. In addition, investors would rather fund entrepreneurs who demonstrate that they are "cautiously optimistic" than those who are "recklessly optimistic." Addressing the risks can turn a "B" or "B+" plan into the "A−" range. Turning those negatives into positives can raise it solidly into the "A" range.

SOURCES OF FINANCING FOR THE NEW BUSINESS

Alan R. Tubbs, President, American Bankers Association, and President, Maquoketa State Bank

SELF-FINANCING

Self-financing means using the company's ability to generate capital internally. Stretching trade credit, selling fixed assets and accounts receivable, and cutting expenses will all help generate cash with minimal assistance from outsiders. One of the main benefits of self-financing is its low cost. Self-financing can help firms avoid large interest expenses that can drain limited resources during the early stage of the business.

Creativity is the key to expanding internal capital. Negotiating better credit terms with suppliers can extend payment dates. Tightening up on the collection of funds after a sale can bring money in more quickly. A combination of extended terms from suppliers and faster payments by customers can significantly reduce the need for other forms of financing.

DEBT FINANCING

Debt financing will probably be necessary if your firm is new and not yet generating cash flow. The many different sources of debt financing include both private-sector and government avenues. Commercial banks are the single largest supplier of debt financing for small businesses.

When shopping for start-up capital, business owners should be aware that commercial lenders consider risk an important factor when setting loan charges. Lenders who cater to solid businesses generally have lower loan interest rates than lenders who specialize in newer or less predictable concerns. It is important to remember that some financial institutions target the small business market, and these lenders might be the most receptive to your new business financing request.

Working with Banks

As a new business owner, you will benefit significantly from trying to view your situation from the perspective of the banker. Commercial banks are in business to make money and to increase the value of their bank's shareholder equity. They do this primarily by making loans to new and established businesses. At least 99 cents of every dollar loaned must be repaid if a bank is to maintain a sound capital base. Keeping this in mind, bankers consider the five C's of credit when evaluating loan requests:

1. *Character*—This consists of the borrower's integrity, experience, and proven ability to repay debts. The bank will pay close attention to the business owner's credit history. On a very basic level, good credit starts with proper handling of a checking account. Overdrafts should be nonexistent or kept to an absolute minimum. Many banks offer overdraft protection on checking accounts. If you have

a good credit rating and a steady source of income, a bank will usually grant you a credit line behind your checking account to cover overdrafts. This type of account can help you avoid expensive overdraft charges and allow you to repay your line of credit when your checking account balance turns positive. Some small business owners use this type of account to help them get their businesses off the ground. If you have credit cards, remember to make your scheduled payments on time. By demonstrating to a bank that you are responsible in these areas, you will improve your chances of getting a credit facility for your new business.

2. *Cash flow*—You will need to demonstrate sufficient cash flow to service your loan request, cover operating expenses, and provide for the eventual replacement of the fixed assets of the business. Bankers will often look at cash flow first when making their loan decision. Your banker will also expect you or one of your management team to have past experience in the business field you are entering. Being able to demonstrate past success in your business or a closely related field will be critical to the strength of your loan request.

3. *Capital*—When assessing capital needs, banks generally require that the bulk of the start-up monies for a new business be provided by the business owners. This assures the bank that the business owners are committed to making their new venture successful. You will also be more comfortable if the bank has not invested more in the business than the owners and could be in a position to exercise managerial control if warranted.

4. *Collateral*—With a new business, your banker is almost certain to ask for assets to be pledged as collateral for the loan. The amount of collateral required may differ from one bank to the next but, as a rule of thumb, banks will lend usually 75 to 80 percent of the market value of real estate and 50 percent of the value of eligible accounts receivable, inventory, and equipment. Eligible accounts receivable are those that are current and fully collectible.

5. *Conditions in the economy*—Your banker will look at the economic conditions that may affect your business and the general health of the type of industry/field of which your business is a part.

Your Loan Request

Your loan request should consist of a carefully prepared package including a credit application; financial information, such as tax returns and personal financial statements; and a business plan if you are starting a new business. Your business plan should demonstrate how your business will generate cash flow sufficient to repay the loan, what you will offer as collateral, and how much of your personal funds will be invested in the business. An owner's investment in the business is called equity. Equity investors usually share in the profits of the business and have some say in how the business is managed.

Your business plan should also address the economic environment and why your business will succeed in the marketplace. The business plan describes who you are, what your company is about, what you want to do, how much money you need and why, and how you will be able to repay the money lent to you or invested with you. It reveals the risks the business faces, and it describes in realistic terms what you intend to do to mitigate those risks. A brief outline for a business plan is as follows:

Section One: The Business

   A. Description of Business
   B. Product/Service
   C. The Market
   D. Location of Business
   E. Competition
   F. Management
   G. Personnel
   H. Application and Expected Effect of Investment
   I. Summary

Section Two: Financial Data

   A. Sources and Applications of Funding
   B. Capital Equipment List
   C. Balance Sheet
   D. Break-Even Analysis
   E. Projected Income Statement
   F. Cash Flow Projection

G. Historical Financial Reports

H. Summary

Section Three: The Financing Proposal

Section Four: Supporting Documents

A business plan is a long-range planning tool that will benefit your business regardless of your immediate need for financing. Your business plan will help you:

- Organize your thoughts relating to why you are in business.
- Identify the strengths and weaknesses of your new business.
- Identify your customers and your competitors.
- Set objectives within realistic limits.
- Provide a guide for employees and other managers.
- Demonstrate how the desired loan will further your company's goals and reward the prospective investor.

When preparing your business plan, you may want to hire an accountant or financial consultant to help you organize the financial data section. Your cash flow projections will help you determine when you will be short of cash and what type of financing your business will need. There are three general categories of bank financing:

1. *Short-term financing* is usually paid within one year and covers seasonal inventory loans, short-run production or construction loans, and short-term liquidity problems. The line of credit is a common short-term financing tool that works like a credit card.
2. *Intermediate financing* ranges from one to five years and typically is used for financing equipment or for providing the working capital for businesses undergoing rapid growth.
3. *Long-term debt* provides for long-term needs such as fixed assets that will be used and paid for over the long haul.

Documents to support your business plan might include resumes, letters of intent from prospective customers, recommendation let-

ters from credible supporters, census/demographic data, leases, or buy/sell agreements.

In the final analysis, the potential borrower who has really done his or her homework will stand the best chance of getting a loan request approved. Remember that bankers are not venture capitalists, risk takers, or gamblers. They should not be when they are in the business of investing other people's money. If your banker cannot approve your loan request, he or she may be able to recommend another potential source of financing.

Other Sources of Debt Financing

Other sources of private-sector debt financing include commercial and consumer finance companies, factoring companies, life insurance companies, savings institutions, and leasing companies. A word of caution before you commit your new business to these types of borrowings: Financing from these sources will generally be more expensive than bank financing and high finance costs can tax the limited resources of a new business and hinder its ability to grow.

Finance companies usually charge high interest rates, which reflect the high level of risk in their portfolios. If you borrow from a finance company, be sure to find out the effective annual interest rate you are being charged.

Factoring companies will buy your accounts receivable at a discount, usually at around 50–60 percent of their face value. Once the receivables are collected, the balance is released—minus the factoring firm's share, which can range from 2 percent to 10 percent of the receivables' face value. The overall cost of borrowing from a factor will usually exceed the cost of traditional bank financing.

Borrowing the cash value of a life insurance policy offers the business owner some flexibility in that repayment of the loan can be avoided by canceling the policy. Of course, you then lose your insurance coverage, which could be required in other borrowing situations.

If you qualify, you can apply for a loan that is guaranteed by the Small Business Administration (SBA). These loans, which are handled by banks, are guaranteed by the SBA for up to 90 percent of the principal, to some maximum. The interest rate on an SBA-guaranteed loan floats against the prime rate. In fiscal 1990, the SBA backed 18,301 loans totaling $3.57 billion. The SBA also targets some direct loan programs to the disabled, veterans, and minorities.

Certified development companies (CDCs) provide government-assisted financing under the SBA's 504 program. A mixture of bank financing and debentures makes up 504 loans, which can only be used to finance long-term assets such as real estate or equipment with a useful life of ten years or more.

Small business investment companies (SBICs) make up another source of government-assisted funds. Some 380 SBICs exist throughout the United States, and these privately operated entities have access to federally guaranteed loans for long-term financing of small businesses. An SBIC will usually want to acquire an equity interest in the company it is helping to finance. Minority enterprise small business investment companies (MESBICs) specialize in helping socially or economically disadvantaged entrepreneurs.

Technical assistance is also available through the Service Corps of Retired Executives (SCORE) and a nationwide network of small business development centers (SBDCs). These centers are usually located in colleges and universities and you can contact the SBA to find the SBDC nearest you.

EQUITY FINANCING

Sources of equity financing include common and preferred stock, warrants, convertible debentures, and venture capital. Most firms wait until they are well established to "go public" or sell stock, because the legal assistance and SEC filings required to sell stock can be quite expensive. Also, firms generally have a much better chance of attracting equity investors after they have established a profitable track record. Therefore, this discussion of equity financing for new businesses is limited to the venture capital market.

Both a formal and an informal market for venture capital funds exist. The formal venture capital market provides less than 2 percent of all small business start-up capital. If your deal is large enough and the anticipated payoff is sufficiently high, your firm may qualify for formal venture capital funding. Fundings of over $1 million and anticipated payout rates of greater than 40 percent annually are common in the formal venture capital market.

If your business does not fall into this segment, you may want to consider a more viable source: the informal venture capital market. What we are talking about here is borrowing from rich—or not so rich—relatives and friends. The SBA estimates that the informal venture capital market is putting out $50 billion to $60 billion a year for business start-ups. To maximize your chances of getting financing from a private investor, you should treat that investor just like you would a bank or other financial institution. Prepare a business plan, get an accountant to help you work out the financial section of the plan, and get some professional and legal guidance. An independent third party can help put your potential investors on an equal footing and help avoid surprises, misunderstandings, and hurt feelings down the road.

HUMAN RESOURCES MANAGEMENT IN THE SMALL BUSINESS

Donald Grunewald, Professor of Strategic Management, Iona College

Good leadership, a good team, and a good organization will enable a business to succeed. Human resources management is a key factor in the success of a small business over time. It is just as important as having a good product and adequate financing. Business requires people who can work together effectively under a good leader to achieve good results.

LEADERSHIP

Some entrepreneurs are gifted with qualities for leading and directing others. They just naturally make good managers. Perhaps the foremost qualification lies in being deserving of the respect of employees. When the manager is respected, questions pertaining to the relationship between employer and employee are easily settled. A good manager has mastery over all elements of the enterprise and has the respect of the employees because they know that the entrepreneur knows the business and can intelligently direct them. Add to that personal character above reproach, unquestioned fair dealing, outstanding courtesy, economy and efficiency in business and you have a pretty good manager.

A manager cannot afford a "do as I say and not as I do" attitude. Such an attitude may get results when the employee is being observed by the manager but will not work while the manager is otherwise engaged. An employee who has to be watched all the time is not of much value to most enterprises. For example, if the manager thinks it is all right to use property belonging to the business for his or her own personal use, even down to postage stamps and telephone calls, the employee will feel justified in copying these actions. Similarly, if the manager wastes business time by making personal telephone calls or taking extra time off, the employee will be encouraged to do likewise. Even employee theft of cash or merchandise may be encouraged through the laxity of the manager in establishing proper safeguards and controls over supplies, cash, and merchandise, especially if the manager has sloppy habits.

Employees are generally honest, but it may be asking too much to expect them to protect the property of the enterprise if the manager fails to do so. The manager must lead by example. He or she must create a business atmosphere of systematic, smooth-running competency. The quality and efficiency of employee organization is the reflection of the boss of the enterprise.

Good managers can be friendly with employees provided they do not permit personal friendliness to swerve them from the straight line of good business performance. In today's business world, both the manager and the employees may be well educated and have good experience. The good executive will lead and inspire employees by instilling a spirit of teamwork and cooperation.

TEAMWORK

The need for a team depends on the nature of the business. There are some enterprises that can be successfully run by one person. Most ventures, however, require a number of skilled persons to succeed. Where a team is required, the business will be most successful when the members of the team share a long-term commitment to the business. A strong team will increase the chances for success of the business.

Often the team will have been developed from the inception of the business. Some teams start through the friendship of a group of persons who desire to start and operate a business together. Others start with a single entrepreneur who realizes the need for others to help operate the business and who then begins to build a team. Building a team begins with the founder or founders of the business. What skills and talents does the founder or founders have? What does each of the founders wish to do in the business? What amount of time will each founder contribute to the business?

The next step is to ask what other skills or talents are needed for the business to succeed. In the beginning, the founder or founders often do everything in a business. As the business grows in size, new talents are needed or the founder or founders can specialize in what they do best.

The long-term success of the business requires a team that works well together. If a team is planned before the start-up of the business, the potential partners have the time while planning the business to see how well they work together. If there are conflicts, a partner may drop out at this time more easily than later.

Team members must bring complementary strengths to the team. If one member is good at selling but hates numbers, there must be someone else who can crunch the numbers as needed. Each team member must be assigned responsibilities. These responsibilities may change as the needs of the business change. Team members in a smaller business need to perform a number of tasks. However, duplication should be avoided whenever possible. Whenever possible, each team member should be given the jobs that he or she is most capable of handling. Assignments can also be switched or rotated over time as the needs of the business and the needs of the team members change.

The perceptions of the climate of the workplace are important in the performance of the team. The attitude and conduct of the manager, discussed previously, are important. So are the attitudes and conduct of the other members of the team. Good managers will help create a climate that is conducive to good performance.

A good organizational climate requires high standards. The manager must insist on excellence. Other team members must share this passion for excellence, which is fostered by clarity in the job descriptions and procedures of the company.

Team members must also be committed to the goals of the business if success is to be achieved. They must accept individual responsibility to help achieve these goals and must be given recognition for their efforts in achieving these goals.

Successful teams in sports are the product of teammates helping each other to achieve their goals. This is true in business also. Members of a team in business must be able to seek and give help when needed. They must learn when to seek help and when to give it. There are a number of skills that can be learned in this process. Effective listening and asking questions to illustrate the problem are important. Asking for help and being receptive to receiving help can benefit the business. Ideas and solutions should be considered without bias.

The manager who can become a good team player is more likely to be a good leader. A leader is necessary and managers must evolve into leaders. When there is a difference of opinion among the team, someone must be able to make a decision. The leader who is

looking for status symbols such as a large office or an impressive automobile is less likely
to be successful than the leader who is primarily interested in results for the business.

Each member of the team must be appropriately compensated for his or her performance. In a small business, compensation can
include stock (or other equity), salary, benefits, and titles. Psychological compensation
may be more important to some team members than pecuniary compensation. To attract
and keep a good team requires much care in
both pecuniary and psychological compensation.

Each member of the team will make his or
her contributions to the success of the business. In most cases, the contribution of each
member of the team will be of different value
to the company. Compensation policies
should include these differences. Contributions of team members also may vary over
time.

There are no easy answers to the question
of how team members should be compensated. Such factors as whose ideas are responsible for the development of products or services offered by the business, commitment of
funds and time to the business, skills in marketing, finance, technology, management,
and other areas used in the business, and the
amount of responsibility for success of the
venture should be considered in setting the
compensation. Incentive compensation for
achieving sales or reducing production defects or other areas could also be developed.

ORGANIZATION

Business consists of getting things done
through people. The businessperson must get
things done within the limits of time and cost
permitted by competition. The small business
manager uses organization in a number of
ways:

1. In starting a business, the entrepreneur
   organizes it by bringing together ideas
   with ways and means of putting these
   ideas into operation, in preparation for
   transacting business.

2. If there is to be a team of persons participating in the business, the entrepreneur
   brings together this team as the nucleus
   of the business organization.
3. The business relationship of the members of the team, their duties, responsibilities, and authority, along with the
   detailed work routine that each team
   member is to perform, are established
   by organizing the business operation.
4. The manager also organizes the work
   he or she is to do personally and also
   the time that he or she will make available each day for the purposes of the
   business. The leader of the organization
   may also organize the work of any department, such as sales or production,
   or any other element of the business.
5. The leader may also reorganize from
   time to time elements that require new
   planning or a more efficient system of
   operations.

It is generally recognized that any business
that is well organized as to personnel and
work routine is a business that is efficiently
managed. A business that is efficiently managed has a high probability of being a prosperous business. Some managers of small
businesses are gifted with the ability to organize. They have well-ordered minds with the
facility of readily filling into a smooth working plan the varied details of their businesses.
Many smaller businesses would grow faster
and prosper more with a better understanding and application of organization in business.

In a one-person business the need to organize is limited to the proprietor organizing
his or her own time and work, outlining what
he or she is to do each hour of the working
day in order to attain maximum production
from individual effort. If this time is not well
organized, the minutes and hours will slip
away and be lost. They are then unproductive
and will yield no profit.

In a business with more than one employee,
there is the added need to organize the work
routine of each person. The manager must be
competent to plan and promote efficiency in
the work that others are to do. The owner or

manager of a small business must take the time to properly train all employees.

The smart employer gets this job of instruction, training, and supervision of employees properly organized and reduced to a systematic procedure as early as possible, thus improving the efficiency of the organization. Employees generally appreciate having the opportunity to work where all details of business operation are governed by systematic procedure and routine. It gives promise of job security and advancement and an incentive for their best effort.

Organization in a business permits the owner or manager to run the business. Without organization, the business will run the owner. With business routine well organized and running smoothly, the owner has time to think, to analyze the business position, to study market conditions and trends, and to develop plans for new sales or other expansion of business activities.

The details of a business should be segregated and organized into groups and departments. A qualified person is then selected and given responsibility for each department. The owner or manager can then supervise the activities of each department head.

MARKETING IN THE SMALL BUSINESS

Phyllis Elnes, President, STI International/Sales Training Institute

Being an entrepreneur is like being a composer. Both start with an idea that will not go away. As the idea lingers, themes and embellishments formulate (business plan). Once you decide that the idea must come alive, you write it out to see the structure more clearly and you can share it with others (marketing plan). Finally, someone (sales representative) performs your idea to an audience so they want more, more, more!

The large corporation writes classical music (textbook-perfect marketing plans). Classical music and marketing plans are tightly structured, contain well-disciplined variations on themes, are fully orchestrated, and are presented by accomplished professionals. The result is pure beauty to the audience (consumer), leaving them happy and wanting more. On the other hand, the presentation can be flat and boring if the presentation is not skilled or is presented to the wrong audience (people who have no need or interest).

Small businesses usually write jazz. A great jazz musician has studied classical music, can play it well, and appreciates its beauty. Similarly, the small businessperson must understand market planning. But his or her plan needs more freedom and spontaneity in its execution. Each presentation is different because it relies on the reaction of the audience.

At first, presentations are played solo. Later, they attract other performers who understand the idea and comprehend where it is going. Beyond that, an ability to improvise determines the result. It can bring the audience to its feet, or lose it.

Most entrepreneurs are like the jazz composer. They must understand classic marketing, yet be spontaneous and able to improvise. The bottom line is that marketing for the small business begins, lives, or dies with the founder. You may have the greatest product and fabulous financing, but without clarity in your marketing plan it all goes down the drain quickly.

A wise accountant once told me, "It is easy to get into business, but it is expensive to get out." I agree. There have been many good, hard working people who have lost their life savings in their businesses. While you are still in the planning stage, take the issue of sales and marketing seriously. Without a plan, you can make four mistakes:

1. Find a full partner who can sell alone. It is rare that such partnerships last through tough times. Neither partner can maintain full appreciation for what the other is doing to keep the business healthy.
2. Hire a salesperson. This is like giving a piece of music to musicians who cannot read music. They must hear your song first so they can repeat it. Chances are high that they will miss the point.
3. Go solo. Here, you have so much confidence in your product that you can enthusiastically tell the world how great it is. Your results will be limited. Today's customers are tired of sales pitches.
4. Do no selling. Simply build a good product because you think that a better mousetrap will bring the world to your door. Dreamer!

What is your alternative? The answer is a good marketing plan. The major elements of a good plan are discussed below.

PRODUCT/SERVICE

Careful identification of what you sell, to whom, and what position it will hold in the marketplace is the first step in creating a marketing plan. The more you know, the more you can direct your business and minimize your risks. Some key issues are:

1. *What you sell*—Challenge yourself to state what your business does in one sentence. Then, test it on other people to see if they can accurately explain what you do.
2. *To whom you sell*—Realize that you cannot be all things to all people or you will spread your efforts too thin. Carefully determine who is most likely to need your product or service, has the financial resources to buy it, and is willing to buy it now. This is called your target market. Determine where your target customers live and work, what their preferences are, and the best way to reach them with your message. Make projections of sales for a year, quarter, month, week. Do not follow your gut feelings—do some research. Your local chamber of commerce, state economic development councils, and local library are great places to start.
3. *Positioning in the marketplace*—Customers buy products to fulfill needs. Uniqueness compared to your competitors will make your business thrive. If your product/service is the same as your competitors, the road will be tough.

What are you going to name your company and your product? How will it position or hinder you in the market? The name may describe clearly what you provide. It should not restrict people's perceptions of what you are capable of doing.

The first decision leading to a sale may be influenced by how well the product is packaged. Customers want it to look expensive while retaining a low cost. If you are not a professional graphic designer, get help. A simple design on good packaging does not have to be expensive to be effective.

PRICE AND DISTRIBUTION

Establishing the right price is heavily dependent on the following:

1. *Your experience in the industry*—You know how many units can be sold in a typical time frame as well as their production costs. These data will help you determine profitability in your pricing. Some industries have helpful data regarding this issue in their professional publication.
2. *Your knowledge of the competition's pricing policies*—Shop your competition regularly so you know what it is doing. Listening to customers is another way to get competitive intelligence.
3. *Your goals*—Stay focused on what you are trying to accomplish and the level of profitability required to accomplish it. Cutting prices cuts profitability. Build a margin into your profitability to allow you to reduce a price temporarily. Otherwise, you are cutting into your ability to meet your goals for going into business in the first place.

You must decide the best way to get your product to your target market in the quickest and cheapest manner. Look seriously at how competitors distribute their products. Determine the controls and accountability you must maintain to ensure quality and quantity of deliveries. Ask yourself how this method helps or hinders you in taking advantage of other distribution channels in the future.

ADVERTISING

Stay in touch with what medium is working and how it helps position you apart from your competitors. Customers have become so overwhelmed with advertising that they are developing an immunity to it. Also, buyers want to know how you can meet their specific needs rather than if they fit a mass-produced product/service.

Close monitoring of results is important in assessing advertising efforts. Some advertising is designed to generate leads; other advertising generates name recognition and establishes an image. Carefully consider the following:

1. *Where is the payoff?* How much and how soon will you see a return on your investment? Is that sufficient to warrant the expense in time and money?
2. *Does it reach your target market effectively?* If not, it is a total waste of money.
3. *What is the positioning power?* Does it set you apart from your competition?
4. *Is it professionally done?* Your image is at stake and that affects buyers' perceptions of who you are and what you are capable of doing.

SALES

A great marketing plan can be totally worthless if poor sales efforts exist. Sales and marketing are critically interdependent. Sales gets the product into the hands of the customer and identifies what is and is not working in the marketing plan. Recent research has shown that professional salespeople possess five attributes:

1. *Partnering skills*—They establish a partnership between themselves and their customers. The two work together to find the best solution to a need. They trust each other.
2. *Mission-driven goals*—They love what they are doing, with a driving need to do a better job and serve more people. Money is not the focus, although it is an important motivator. They know that if you fill enough needs the money will follow. Therefore, they do not waste their time on nonprofitable sales calls.
3. *Listening/probing skills*—They are excellent listeners and they know how to ask questions. This allows the customer relax, and it helps the salesperson do a better job of fulfilling customer needs. A skilled salesperson also helps the cus-

tomer clarify his needs in the probing process.

4. *Versatility*—The high-performing salesperson has a wide range of people skills to help the customer feel comfortable.

5. *Higher level of personal growth*—In their drive to improve, high-performing salespeople are compulsive learners. They read a lot and attend training with a passion to find new ideas. Conse-

quently, they grow over time in the skills they apply.

As an entrepreneur, you will need all of the same attributes as outstanding salespeople plus strong skills in managing all aspects of your business. When you are serious enough to put written structure to your idea and go out and sell it yourself, you are ready to go into business.

CASH MANAGEMENT FOR GROWING FIRMS

Jack Rader, Executive Director, Financial Management Association

Once a small entrepreneurial firm is successful in establishing itself as a viable going concern, it will likely enter a stage of substantial growth. During the growth phase, there are a variety of problems or hurdles that must be faced and overcome if the firm is to achieve long-run financial success. One of the most important is the management of the firm's cash flow.

The primary objective of cash management is to maximize the value of the firm. Simply, you want to collect cash as quickly as possible and retain funds as long as you can before disbursing them to others. To achieve this objective, let us determine the cash conversion cycle, the management of collections, and the management of disbursements.

THE FIRM'S CASH CONVERSION CYCLE

The cash conversion cycle is the time interval between the actual cash expenditures a firm makes in order to acquire resources and convert these resources into goods or services and the receipt of cash by the firm. The firm's operating cash flows arise spontaneously from the firm's normal operations. As a result, they are influenced by general economic conditions, industry characteristics, internal operating decisions, and the financial structure of the firm.

Manufacturing, retail, and service businesses all have somewhat different operating cash cycles. For example, a manufacturing firm's cash cycle might include the following steps:

1. The purchase of raw materials on credit (creating an accounts payable).
2. The application of labor to convert the raw materials into a salable product.
3. Cash outflows to employees and vendors.
4. The sale and delivery of a service or good to a customer.
5. The receipt of a cash payment from the customer.

Retail businesses generally purchase finished goods and tend to make a substantial percent of sales on credit. While not subject to the cash demands of a manufacturing process, retail operations can have significant lags between cash payments to vendors and the receipt of cash from customers. Service firms are typically labor intensive and thus incur nontrivial labor costs even when business volume may be down.

Regardless of the specific nature of the firm's cash conversion cycle, the nature of business is that resources must be acquired and paid for before a sale can be made and cash can be collected. Even though a firm may be profitable, without cash it is not a viable economic entity. In short, think of the firm's cash conversion cycle as the lifeblood of the firm. Manage it well and you will prosper in good times and survive the bad times. Let it get out of control and your firm will not survive.

MANAGING COLLECTIONS

Cash

Cash and checks collected at the point of sale should be deposited quickly. Firms that receive large amounts of cash on a daily basis should make arrangements for periodic intraday transfers of the cash to a depository institution. A variety of deposit methods are available, including over-the-counter deposits using a teller at a bank, armored carriers, courier services, and after-hour depositories. The optimal frequency of these transfers will depend on the amount of the cash collected and the cost of making the transfer to the depository institution.

Security and the prevention of theft is particularly important. Where possible, the receipt of cash should be centralized, bank statements and deposit records should be reconciled in a timely manner, discrepancies should be promptly investigated, cash receipt and accounting responsibilities should be separated, and employees who handle cash and checks should be monitored and required to take vacations of sufficient length to allow for the detection of misappropriation of cash. Additionally, a variety of specialized point-of-sale equipment is available for use in discouraging theft and providing a clear audit trail for the detection of such if it does occur. This equipment can also be integrated into the firm's inventory management and financial reporting systems.

Checks received at the point of sale can be handled much as cash received, although the security and theft considerations associated with checks are somewhat different. The theft of checks can be an inconvenience, but since it is difficult for parties other than the payee to cash a check, they are not as attractive as cash. On the other hand, bad checks are a common problem with which firms must deal. Sound customer identification and check acceptance authorization procedures should be established for all check-taking personnel.

Credit

When credit has been extended, certain steps should be routinely taken. For credit provided by the firm, the credit department should be informed of the transaction as quickly as possible. The credit department must then send invoices and statements promptly and ensure that statements and bills are accurate. When credit is provided by a third party (for example, a credit card company), the firm must follow whatever procedures the credit grantor requires so that payment will not be delayed. In addition, the firm should have procedures for notifying the third-party company of a sales transaction as quickly as possible. Finally, the firm must monitor the timeliness of the payment.

Firms that do a large amount of business on credit terms established prior to the point of sale can frequently benefit from using a lock-box system to collect incoming checks. A lock-box system provides an address(es) that is used exclusively to receive customer payments. The lock-box processor separates the checks from the remittance information and introduces the checks into the clearing system to speed up the crediting of funds to the payee's account. At the same time, the remittance information that accompanied the check is processed and/or sent to the firm so that records can be adjusted to recognize the transaction.

Increasingly, businesses are working actively with their customers and clients to convert to electronic fund transfer (EFT) remittance systems. In business-to-business transactions, this is generally accomplished by splitting the float benefits between the two parties and determining in advance what information needs to accompany the transaction so that the accounts of both parties can be reconciled. The overriding advantage of this arrangement is to increase the efficiency by which both firms operate through greatly reducing the processing of paper that would otherwise be necessary. In retail transactions, debit card purchases can be used to speed up the collection of funds. Installment sales and certain forms of credit-based purchases can use automatic funds transfer from the payee's bank to the payor's bank.

MANAGING CASH DISBURSEMENTS

Cash disbursement systems must address and resolve a variety of important issues. These include:

1. The time value of payment float (that is, the earnings the firm generates on funds from the time payment is initiated until the time the payor's account is debited).
2. The opportunity cost of maintaining cash balances in excess of what is needed to settle disbursement transac-

tions (that is, the return foregone because the company is holding cash rather than investing the cash in a more productive asset).
3. The value of maintaining a good credit rating and good relations with vendors, employees, and other stakeholders.
4. The costs of administering the disbursement system.
5. The need for adequate financial controls to reduce the probability of misappropriation of funds.

Paper-based disbursement systems offer the advantage of utilizing float. Examples of float-motivated strategies include remote disbursing (where checks are drawn on a bank located in a remote area) and remote mailing strategies (where checks are mailed from remote locations). While remote disbursing arrangements have been greatly reduced as a result of the Monetary Control and Deregulation Act of 1980, remote mailing systems are still widely used.

Drafts are an alternative to checks, which may, under some circumstances, be useful in a disbursement system. Drafts appear as checks but are actually drawn on the issuing firm rather than the disbursing bank. When a bank receives a draft, the firm is notified, verifies that the payment was authorized, and then approves (or denies) payment. The result is to increase float on the funds by a day or so and to reduce excess cash balances. Bank charges for drafts can be considerably less than for checks. However, drafts are not always liked by payees because they may be difficult to cash in some circumstances.

Internal control for paper-based disbursements is important. Where possible, disbursements should be centralized, financial reports should be prepared in a timely and consistent manner to provide an adequate audit trail, dual signatures should be required, and an independent audit should be conducted.

Electronic disbursement systems (EDS) are growing in importance, particularly in business transactions, payroll, installment sales, and long-term credit payments. EDSs can be quite cost effective but have the disadvantage of reducing the firm's ability to utilize float. This is becoming less important as the U.S. payments system becomes more efficient.

EDSs have unique security concerns but there are a variety of techniques available to reduce the chance of error or fraud. These include restricting the number of persons authorized to order electronic payments, establishing written restrictions on electronic transactions with banks, using controlled access terminals, personal computers, and facsimile devices to verify payment instructions, and using passwords and encryption.

There are three primary alternatives for EDSs. Fed wire transfers (using the Federal Reserve's Fed wire system) are the fastest and the most expensive. CHIPS (the Clearinghouse Interbank Payment System operated by the New York Clearinghouse Association) transfers provide delayed settlement on the same day at a lower cost. Finally, Automated Clearinghouse (ACH) transfers (which are governed by the National Automated Clearinghouse Association) can cost even less when payments are sent in bulk. Since ACH fund transfers are settled at a future date, there is additional credit risk.

Many firms use a technique known as controlled disbursing. In a controlled disbursement system, a firm's bank monitors what is presented for payment and then informs the firm of the aggregate amount so that sufficient funds can be transferred to cover the payments. A commonly used approach to controlled disbursement is the zero balance account (ZBA). In a ZBA, a zero cash balance is maintained, and the bank is given authority to draw funds automatically from another source in an amount equal to the total of the checks that have been presented that day. Frequently, the concentration account, referred to earlier, is the funding source for ZBAs. The fees charged for maintaining a ZBA should, of course, not exceed the economic benefits the firm receives from freeing its cash for other uses.

Cash Flow Matching

Cash flow matching is used by many firms to simplify their cash management program. A cash flow matching strategy forecasts which cash disbursements are likely to occur on a repetitive basis and in relatively stable amounts. The firm then schedules its billing and collection activities so that sufficient funds will be received in advance of scheduled payouts. The most attractive aspects of a matching strategy are its simplicity once it is established and its low cost.

Exact matching strategies are generally not optimal because the company may be foregoing substantial reinvestment proceeds; that is, it is still advantageous to collect funds as early as possible. Sweep accounts can be established so that cash collections in excess of immediate needs can be automatically swept into a short-term investment account.

Credit Decisions

The granting of credit and the use of trade credit are of critical importance to a comprehensive cash management program. From the seller's perspective, the extension of credit should increase the demand for the firm's goods or services because they cost less (the time value of money) and can be purchased more conveniently. From the buyer's perspective, trade credit results in a lower cost of materials or services obtained, is more convenient, and is a potentially low-cost form of borrowing.

In granting credit, the firm must recognize that it incurs an opportunity cost of funds delayed, the cost of investigating credit worthiness, the cost of collection, and the cost of bad debt. For the extension of credit to increase the value of the firm, the economic benefits of increased sales and profitability must exceed the cost of granting credit.

The extension credit affects the firm's cash flows in a variety of ways. Credit shifts the receipt of cash from the point of sale to some future point in time, increases the riskiness of collections, increases cash disbursements needed to pay for credit-related services and, hopefully, increases the total cash payments to the firm. Therefore, when providing credit, firms should:

1. Bill as close to the point of sale as possible.
2. Carefully monitor customer accounts (for instance, comparing aging schedules and receivables turnover ratios to credit terms being extended).
3. Provide incentives for timely payment through use of trade discounts, finance charges, and late payment penalties.

The other side of the credit question is when to use trade credit and how much to use. The objective of using trade credit should be to lower the firm's overall cost of financing by "borrowing" funds from the firm's suppliers. If credit is costless, a strategy of buy now, pay later is economically sound. Discounts for early payment, interest charges, and penalties on late payments make this decision more complex. In determining whether or not to take advantage of trade discounts, companies should use the following guidelines:

- A company with sufficient cash on hand should take a cash discount only if the cost of not taking the discount exceeds the rate of return the company is earning on its short-term, temporary cash investments.
- If the company must borrow in order to take advantage of the discount, the firm should take the cash discount only if the cost of not taking the discount exceeds the rate the firm will be charged to borrow funds.

Firms taking cash discounts should, of course, disburse funds at the end of the discount period, and firms not taking cash discounts should make disbursements toward the end of the invoice due period. Finance charges and penalties, of course, should only be incurred if the cost of paying them is lower than the firm's cost of short-term borrowing and if there are no implicit penalties (such as a lower credit rating).

The practice known as stretching accounts payable (systematically and consistently paying accounts well after the date on which they are due) is an alternative to timely payment of one's own account. If the ethical problems associated with this practice are not sufficiently persuasive to convince one that this is not appropriate, the firm should consider the negative impact such practices will have on the firm's credit rating.

CUSTOMER SERVICE IN SMALL BUSINESSES

Dick Laird, Executive Director, Center for Business and Economic Education, Lubbock Christian University

The most important part of a successful business is the customer. Sam Walton, the founder of Wal-Mart, said "There is only one boss, and whether a person shines shoes for a living or heads the biggest corporation in the world, the boss remains the same." He went on to say, "The customer is the person who pays everyone's salary and who decides whether a business is going to succeed or fail. . . . The minute the business starts treating him badly, he'll start to put it out of business." So the customers can fire everyone in the company from the chairperson on down simply by spending their money with the competition.

If treated well, customers tend to return because they like you. If they like you, they will spend their money with you. Then, because they spend their money with you, you will treat them even better. The more often customers return, they begin to lose their fear of the unknown and may develop a loyalty to your business. This is why you must always make a positive impression when you meet a new customer for the first time. Remember it is the satisfied customer who tells others about your excellent service and who will help you win new customers. This is a never-ending business cycle if carried out properly. The customer must always be "number one."

A onetime customer is of little value. If a customer does not return for repeat business, you will be spending all of your time trying to attract new customers to your place of business. A onetime customer will bring you very little profit. Getting customers once is not a major task, but turning them into repeat customers is where profit is made. The quicker they return, the more profit they contribute to your business and the faster your business will grow.

If we listen to the customers, we will hear what they want. Then it is up to us to provide for those wants. The owner of a local Ford dealership in Texas, while listening to his customers, kept hearing that his service department was always closed after they got off from work. In response to his customers' wishes, the dealer expanded his service department hours to 9 P.M. on weeknights. This one act resulted in a substantial increase in business.

Do not be afraid to ask your customers what they expect from you. Customers will tell you exactly what they want, if given a chance. If customers ask you to perform a service related to your business, always accommodate them. Always allow your customers to buy; do not pressure them. When they buy, they feel good. When you "hard sell," they sometimes develop second thoughts and may grow to resent you. As you serve your expanding customer list, you should always be looking for a better-quality product and/or service to offer them. Anything you can do for a customer makes you look good and will pay dividends.

Know your products and train your employees so that they also know your products well. Customers want salespeople with a working knowledge about the business. Customers like to ask questions about products or services and expect to receive an intelligent answer. Too often in today's marketplace, employees are hired at minimum wage and have no training in the field in which they are employed.

If you are well informed about your product or service, customers sense this and will trust your suggestions. The more customers trust you, the more they will return and become dependent on your expertise. Enthusiasm about your product or service is contagious. A well-known speaker points out: "Enthusiasm is as contagious as the measles and as powerful as dynamite."

Even America's leading retail giants have retreated to minimum-wage employees with little or no expertise in their field. Therefore, the market door is wide open to the business that will provide knowledgeable salespeople.

If your business fails to have in stock an item that your customers desire, call your competition to locate it for them. If you fail to locate the item, special order it for overnight delivery. These customers will return, because you have shown a personal interest in their needs. These customers will tell others about the special treatment you provided, and there is no better advertising than word of mouth.

Always do the job right the first time. If you do not have time to do it right the first time, when will you find time to redo it? If a mistake is made, the person who made the mistake should correct it without pay. Your business cannot afford to charge a customer to correct your mistake. My father used to say, "If you don't make mistakes, you are not doing anything, but when you continue to make the same mistakes over and over, I begin to worry about you." So always learn from your mistakes. Keep your word to your customers. Do not promise something you cannot deliver. Underpromise and overdeliver is the best approach.

Always be prepared for a customer complaint or returned merchandise. View a customer complaint as positive because the customer has pointed out areas that need improving. Sometimes customer complaints allow you a second chance to provide satisfactory service to an unsatisfied client. The way you handle these situations will go a long way in convincing the customer to continue to shop at your business.

INTERNATIONAL OPPORTUNITIES FOR THE GROWING BUSINESS

Tom Niland, Small Business International Trade Program, Portland Community College

Not too many years ago, two thirds of the purchasing power of the world was here in the United States. Current estimates show that we now have only 20–25 percent of the world's purchasing power.

The unfavorable trade balance speaks directly to the problems and challenges that entrepreneurs are facing on a daily basis. The fight to control domestic market shares is a constant lament by small business owners. Some do not understand what is going on or why. Still others are stretched to the limit to maintain domestic market shares, obtain working capital, and husband talented resources. Most require funding for capital expenditures for equipment to keep pace with technological research and meet demands of a consumer-driven market.

The global marketplace can have a profound impact on the health and stability of a small business. Most small and growing businesses focus on domestic markets. Only a small percentage export. Entering the international arena via exporting can improve declining profit margins and overall stability.

Small businesses managed properly have the necessary qualities and skills to successfully penetrate foreign markets. This is made possible by diligent research, developing viable markets, and establishing appropriate target-entry strategies. Usually a small business can adapt quickly to market conditions. It needs to secure only a small segment of the market to be profitable.

Exporting, however, is not for all companies, nor is international trade a panacea or get-rich-quick scheme. On the contrary, international trade requires a commitment in terms of time, energy, resources, and capital. It is imperative that a small business have a successful domestic business before considering exporting. By having a viable, successful domestic business, you will generate the cash flow required for an international operation. Some of the benefits in foreign trade for a small business are:

1. Higher growth rates in some foreign markets than in domestic markets.
2. Orders or markets that may provide inadequate revenues to larger, multinational corporations.
3. A broader marketing base, which can increase growth and profitability.
4. Smoother production runs and utilization of excess production capacity.
5. More effective utilization of managerial and technical talent.
6. Extension of the product life by exporting to those countries where the market requirements differ from those domestically.

A decision to export requires carefully thought-out objectives and the full support of the company's key management people. It is imperative that firms desiring to sell their products or services in world markets develop an appropriate export marketing plan based on their capabilities and the goals set forth by management. Perhaps the single most important element in integrating an international marketing plan is determining the markets of greatest potential.

Before any concerted effort to sell products abroad is made, a firm should conduct an audit of its product and production capabilities to determine whether it can furnish the goods in reasonable quantity on a sustained basis. Small businesses do not have to worry about international trade or penetrating foreign markets by themselves. They do not have to reinvent the wheel. There are many, many resources available to assist them:

- The Small Business Administration.
- Consulates, including the U.S. consulates in other countries and foreign consulates located in the United States.
- The U.S. Department of Commerce.
- Local small business development centers.
- Chambers of commerce.
- World trade centers.

- Export management companies and export trading companies.

Successful small businesses that have entered international trade followed a road map to success. They were disciplined to stay on course, to reach their goals, always reviewing and fine-tuning their objectives. They recognized early that they required the support and service of an international banker and an international freight forwarder. When it came time to enter into an agent or distributor agreement, they utilized the services of an international attorney to make sure the contract was drawn in a manner that was a win-win situation for all parties.

These same companies took the time to learn about the culture of the country that they were trying to enter, the nuances of doing business, and the art of negotiation—when to talk, when to listen. They were willing to take the offensive by thinking beyond their borders.

There are basically two ways a small business can enter the international marketplace. One is the indirect method where you use an export management company or an export trading company. The other is the direct way where you do it yourself by establishing an export department. The strategy for market entry should cover four major points:

1. *Product*—Is the product exportable in its present fashion? If not, what has to be done to it? What modifications or adaptations need to be made?
2. *Price*—How do you price your product? The pricing strategy can take many forms, based on the competition, the distribution channel, and the maturity of your product.
3. *Promotion*—How do you advertise? Where do you advertise? Do you translate your product brochures into the language of the country you are trying to penetrate?
4. *Distribution channel*—The method of distribution will add to the cost of your product and may or may not make your product competitive. Or, it could adversely affect the profit margin on your product.

Today's global economy is subject to the ebb and flow of imports and exports throughout the world. Key points to consider to be successful in international trade over the long term are:

1. To succeed in the international marketplace, you must first have a successful domestic operation and understand fundamental business principles.
2. You must make a firm commitment to international business. This requires allocating resources or time, people, and capital in concert with the domestic business.
3. International trade requires patience. It takes time to develop a business plan, to select the proper products in foreign markets, to make contacts and finalize transactions.
4. International business requires an understanding of specific market conditions, the local economic conditions, competition, and special trade regulations.
5. International trade should be based on trust and the willingness to understand cross-cultural relationships and to develop long-term relationships.

TAXATION AND ACCOUNTING CONSIDERATIONS

E. Malcolm Greenlees, Linfield College

Accounting and taxation are important to a business manager for two reasons: (1) Accounting is the measure of business performance and success. (2) Many reporting and record-keeping requirements must be met if the business is to continue in operation. The key element in a successful accounting and taxation system for a small business is to keep it simple, keep it complete, and keep it current. Managers should also seek the advice of a qualified accountant, attorney, and banker to whom they can communicate easily and seek advice concerning problems. These professionals should have experience with small businesses.

ORGANIZATIONAL FORMS

In deciding on an organizational form, use the old adage, "Form follows substance." The size and complexity of your business will help determine the best form of organization.

Sole Proprietorship

The simplest form of organization for a small business is a sole proprietorship. The business is an extension of the individual. It can be formed with a minimum of difficulty, and has a simple decision-making structure. As an extension of the individual, the sole proprietor has unlimited legal liability for debts of the business.

There is a need to establish and maintain a distinction between the revenues and expenses of the business activity and transactions that are personal in nature. As a sole proprietorship, it is only necessary to obtain the appropriate business licenses to operate and to establish a separate business bank account. Although a husband and wife could work together in a business, for tax purposes the entity could be treated as a sole proprietorship and the income reported on a joint tax return.

For a sole proprietorship, the regulatory requirements are simpler than for other forms of organization. For example, workers' compensation is required only for employees and is either not required or optional for owners of the business. However, social security (FICA [Federal Insurance Contributions Act]) and medicare taxes are higher. No unemployment taxes are due on the owner's earnings and, of course, no benefits are available either. Finally, the income tax situation is simple. An additional schedule (federal schedule C) filed with the individual's tax return reports the net profit of the business.

Partnerships

A partnership represents an extension of several individuals. The main benefits of the partnership are flexibility and the involvement of other individuals in the business decision-making process.

Partnerships have unique problems of liability. Each partner can act for and is liable for the entire partnership, not just his or her share of the business. This joint liability can cause one partner to commit all partners to a course of action. A person must be able to completely trust a business partner. A partnership works well only if all partners share the same goals and objectives.

Partners usually are exempt from workers' compensation coverage requirements. Social security and medicare (FICA) taxes are similar to a sole proprietor. Unemployment taxes are also not due on partners' earnings. However, the income tax situation is more complex. A separate partnership tax return is required. However, no tax payments are due.

Rather, the earnings of the partners are "passed through" to individuals and added to their personal tax returns.

Some form of written partnership agreement is necessary to spell out the methods of compensation and responsibilities of the partners. If no written agreement exists, then the provisions of state law will apply, usually requiring equal divisions of profits and losses. If a business situation calls for any variation, then a written partnership agreement can spell out the allocation of earnings by any desired formula.

Limited Partnerships

This form of business is a variation on the basic partnership form. It offers the benefit of limiting the liability for certain partners. Any limited partnership must have at least one general partner who carries the burden of unlimited liability.

The administrative record keeping of a limited partnership is similar to a small corporation. The taxation structure is similar to partnership with respect to unemployment and social security taxes. A standard partnership tax return is required.

Corporations

Corporations are the most common form of business operation. The corporate form offers the most flexibility for long-term growth from a small business to a large multinational business.

The main advantages of corporations are limited liability, unlimited life and transferability of ownership, access to capital markets through stock and bond issues, and availability of a broader range of fringe benefits to all employees. The advantage of limited liability is lessened by the common business practice of requiring the owners of small corporate businesses to sign personal guarantees for loans. This acts to eliminate the corporate shield of limited liability for debts.

The principal disadvantage of the corporate form lies in the regulatory overhead. There is a large amount of separate record keeping and external reporting required to various regulatory authorities by a corporation. A second major disadvantage is the impact of double taxation, where the earnings of the corporation are taxed when earned by the corporation, and taxed a second time when distributed to individual owners or stockholders as dividends.

The regulatory environment for a corporation is more complex than for a sole proprietorship or partnership. The corporation needs separate business and legal records. Legal expenses are incurred for establishing the corporation as well as for required annual meetings and recording of official actions. The necessity of maintaining this "separate" legal existence of the corporation is the key to maintaining the limited legal liability.

Corporations also face higher social security taxes and unemployment taxes. In a corporation, owners/managers working in the business are considered employees of the business. All employees of the corporation are subject to these taxes. Also, all employees must be covered by workers' compensation and are subject to unemployment taxes.

The corporation must file its own tax return and pay tax on its earnings. The corporate income tax return is subject to special provisions that usually require professional assistance to complete the return.

S Corporations

The S corporation was designed to remedy the disadvantage of double taxation in a regular corporation. An S corporation operates like a regular corporation, but has certain limitations on the total number of shareholders and the characteristics of these shareholders. This type of corporation is taxed like a partnership, with profits and losses being passed through directly to the shareholders, thus avoiding the income tax at the corporate level.

ACCOUNTING RECORDS

Accounting records are needed to meet the requirements of various government regulatory and taxation agencies, and to provide accurate self-evaluation and performance measurement of the business.

A manager must decide how to keep records for the business. The availability of simple and inexpensive computer programs helps speed and ease the process of account-

ing. In spite of this convenience, most small businesses find that the complexity of reporting requirements necessitates finding professional assistance to aid with the preparation of periodic reports.

Record-Keeping Procedures

The following suggestions outline a set of simple business records for a small business:

1. *Chart of accounts*—A simple classification and numbering system keeps track of all revenue or expense items, as well as balance sheet purchases or liabilities incurred.

2. *Income or sales records*—A method of keeping track of all income completely and accurately is necessary. Keep a simple daily log of receipts or income and make bank deposits daily. The bank statement becomes a summary of your receipts and provides an independent third-party record of your receipts. Implement controls over the receipt of cash. Avoid handling cash if possible. If you cannot, then make sure you have good physical custody and records of all cash transactions.

3. *Expense records*—A simple suggestion is to write checks for all possible expenses. This gives you a written record of the expense and avoids the common problem of forgetting about expenses that are proper business deductions. Make sure you mark on each check an explanation of each expenditure. If you pay for items in cash or credit card, make sure that the expenses are reflected in your business records.

4. *Other key business records*—All correspondence to or from regulatory agencies should be retained. It can be important in resolving problems or providing proof of filing or responding to inquiries. Also, business expense records in the areas of entertainment and use of automobiles and computers should be carefully documented.

The majority of small businesses use the cash basis of accounting. Income is recorded when received in cash and expenses are recorded when paid in cash. The use of the cash basis of accounting is often augmented by the use of depreciation for tax purposes and accounts receivable record keeping if credit sales are utilized in the business.

As a business grows larger and more complex, it will use the accrual method of accounting. Here, income is recorded when earned or when the business is entitled to it and expenses are recorded when the obligation to pay is incurred.

Tax Considerations for a Small Business

Taxes can occur in many forms. Income and employment taxes have the greatest impact on a small business. The complexity and rapid change of tax rules for business make it virtually mandatory that the services of a tax adviser be engaged. This person is usually a tax preparer, a tax accountant, or an attorney specializing in taxation matters.

Payroll Tax Planning

Payroll taxes are fairly simple. The tax amount is computed on the amount of earnings of employees. The business records should carefully document the earnings of each employee.

A recent trend is for businesses to hire persons as independent contractors in order to eliminate paying various mandatory employment taxes and to minimize other fringe benefit costs. If a person is an independent contractor, then that person is responsible for paying the employment taxes and providing his or her own fringe benefits. Using independent contractors could significantly reduce payroll taxes. A manager planning to use independent contractors should be aware of the rules and should be prepared to justify the use of the independent contractor status.

Income Tax Planning

The following typical areas of tax planning exist across all types of organizations:

1. *Revenue and timing of revenue*—When the cash method of accounting is used, receipts are taxed only when received. A temporary tax savings can be achieved by delaying the receipt of income into the next tax year. For December receipts, the delay could be only a few days, but the tax impact would be an entire year.

2. *Dividend-received deductions*—The law allows a corporation that receives a dividend from a domestic corporation to deduct up to 70 percent of that dividend. This rule allows small businesses doing business as corporations to avoid multiple levels of taxation on the dividends.

3. *Expenses*—In general, any expense that is "ordinary and necessary" for the conduct of the business is allowed as a deduction against income earned by a business.

4. *Health care*—Self-employed proprietors and partners can deduct a portion of the amounts paid for health insurance for themselves and their families as a business expense. The entire cost of health-care programs for corporations can be deducted.

5. *Qualified pension plans*—Deductions are allowed by proprietors and partners for contributions to various types of pension plans such as IRAs (individual retirement accounts), Keogh plans, or simplified retirement plans. The amounts and qualifications vary and should be discussed with a taxation adviser. Corporate pension plans are allowable provided they meet certain criteria for coverage of all employees.

6. *Other fringe benefits*—Generally, other fringe benefits are deductible on a limited basis to proprietors and partners, and somewhat more liberally to corporations. The key to the deductibility of a fringe benefit is the "ordinary and necessary" test mentioned previously.

7. *Depreciation*—Depreciation is allowed according to specifically mandated rules in the Internal Revenue Code. There are limited deviations from these rates and depreciation methods allowed.

8. *Home office*—A deduction for an office in your home is allowed if it meets certain criteria. It is also the target of considerable attention by IRS (Internal Revenue Service) audits. The home of-

fice must be used regularly and exclusively for business. It should also be used for regular meetings with customers or clients.

9. *Bad debts*—Business bad debts may be deducted as a cost of doing business. It is important that the debt be a genuine business bad debt, and that some effort be made to collect the debt before it can be deducted.

10. *Charity contributions*—Charity contributions made by a corporation are generally limited to 10 percent of its net income. For individual proprietors or partners, it is limited to 50 percent of the adjusted gross income.

11. *Leasing expenses*—Expenses of leasing equipment for business purposes are deductible. However, the lease must be a rental or operating lease, and not merely a form of installment purchase or other financing mechanism.

12. *Research and development expenses*—Certain expenses that are not required to be added to the capital cost of an asset may be currently deductible as expenses or deferred and deducted over some period of time. These expenses may also qualify for a tax credit.

13. *Inventory accounting*—If you have inventories held for production or resale, you may be able to reduce your taxable income by adopting the last in first out (LIFO) inventory accounting method, which tends to reduce your taxable income in periods of rising prices.

14. *Capital loss limitations*—Losses arising from the sale of business assets are subject to complex rules that generally limit their deductibility. In contrast, net gains are taxed as ordinary income in the year of sale.

15. *Tax credits*—A series of special tax credits are available to businesses that offset the tax liability on a dollar-for-dollar basis. For this reason, they are particularly beneficial.

These areas, and others that may be created in future revisions of the tax law, should be systematically included in the process of planning to minimize the level of taxes paid by the business.

HIRING, FIRING, AND AVOIDING LAWYERS

David S. Machlowitz, Counsel, Siemens Medical Corporation

Sooner or later, everyone in business is going to need a lawyer. If you are lucky, it will be when you want to incorporate your business, license one of your products, or lease more office space. If you are not, it will be when the IRS questions your taxes, one of your employees is injured on the job, or you are sued by a customer.

WHERE TO FIND A GOOD LAWYER

Ignore slick television commercials. It may pay to advertise, but it does not pay to pick a lawyer on the basis of self-serving advertisements. First, ask friends, colleagues, or relatives whose judgment you trust. The lawyer who incorporated your sister's business is not necessarily the right lawyer for your commercial litigation, but you might ask for a referral.

If the matter is so sensitive you do not want to discuss it with friends or co-workers, such as an IRS matter, try your local bar association. It will probably make available a list of lawyers with the specialty you seek.

What about your fraternity brother, friend from church, or your cousin, all of whom are lawyers? Yes, it is a familiar face, attentive to your needs, and you may even get a break on the bill. Do you really want your cousin to know the IRS is investigating you? Won't you be uncomfortable telling your friend how much money your business earns? How will you feel if there is a billing dispute or you are unhappy with the results?

WHAT TO ASK THE LAWYER

Feel free to schedule consultations with more than one lawyer. Ask in advance whether you will be charged for the interview. Seek out the following:

1. *Ability*—This can be checked by asking for references. If a lawyer went to a top law school or is associated with a major law firm, the odds are in your favor. Focus on the type of ability you need. To review a licensing agreement, you need a counselor. To litigate a contract dispute, you need a street fighter. To merge with another company, you need a salesperson. If your company's survival is on the line, you need all three.

2. *Availability*—It is the unexpected destroyer of many lawyer-client relationships. The lawyer who fawned over you during the courtship stage may not return your calls promptly or may fob you off on a more junior lawyer. Bear in mind, however, that your law-yer, like you, dislikes constant trivial or nagging interruptions. A good lawyer will be at your service but will not be your servant.

3. *Affordability*—You do not need a Wall Street megafirm to review your lease for 2,000 feet of office space. Sometimes an expensive lawyer can save you money through greater skill or experience. If a matter is adversarial, crucial, complex, or novel, be ready to pay the price. You may be charged a flat fee, an hourly fee, or a contingent fee. Each approach has shortcomings. The flat fee imposes a ceiling and lets you fix a budget. If the matter becomes prolonged, you may receive less attention or a request for additional fees. The danger of hourly fees is that the matter may be dragged out by the lawyer to run up a bill. A contingent fee—a percentage of the recovery or the deal—limits downside risk. It is unacceptable to most lawyers except in liability cases where a big payout is likely.

4. *Affability*—Your lawyer should be patient, courteous, and reassuring, not patronizing, curt, or intimidating. Too many lawyers forget just how nervous many people are when they are making a deal, fighting a lawsuit, or setting up a business.

BUDGETING LAWSUITS

Litigation is also the most likely area to generate larger than expected costs. Often, people enter lawsuits as pigs and exit as sausages. If your opponent thinks it has more money than you, it often will deliberately try to run up your costs.

Instruct the lawyer to provide you with a written budget and fee schedule. Ask to be billed monthly, with a detailed description of all work performed, who performed it, at what hourly rate, and how much has been charged to date. If you have a question about a bill, ask it—and insist you not be charged for the answer. To keep your bill down, prepare carefully for each conversation or meeting. If you are ready with the information and documents your lawyer requests, costly follow-ups can be avoided. In particular, be ready to discuss not only the result you want but the result you are willing to accept. If you are paying by the hour, do not chit chat or call five times a week to learn if there is any news.

DO YOU NEED A SPECIALIST?

The need for specialized expertise is more a matter of specialized law than how much money is involved. Trademark and copyright matters are traditionally handled by lawyers who do nothing else. If a key employee has an immigration problem or the Department of Labor wants to know about your records of overtime pay, you cannot afford for a lawyer to learn the ropes on your tab.

For most matters, you need experience but not specialization. Many areas of law are relatively simple—but only the second time. A lawyer's first venture into drafting a joint venture agreement should not be yours, even if you are not paying by the hour.

DO YOU REALLY NEED A LAWYER?

Sometimes you do not. Maybe you, or one of your employees, can negotiate a resolution of your dispute with your customer or vendor with less ill will or money. Figure out what your total budget is—settlement plus legal fees. Then see if you can settle the case for less.

Consider, too, whether you want to play Perry Mason in small claims court (many people find it fun) or arbitration. Certainly you need a lawyer if serious consequences or com-

plex legal issues are involved. Often, however, lawyers turn a minor dispute into an all-out war or lose sight (if they ever had it) of the underlying business issues.

FIRING A LAWYER

As soon as you begin to have serious problems with your lawyer, you have to consider beginning the firing and the replacing process. Because switching lawyers is often burdensome and expensive, and the likely benefit is never certain, be sure you are reasonable. Identify the sources of your discontent and discuss them with your lawyer. If you want more attention, you can probably get it. If the bills have been too high, there may be cost-saving measures. The most difficult situations involve another party. The deal seems to be moving too slowly. Is your lawyer to blame or is it the other party? Suddenly your lawyer says you may lose the lawsuit. Is your adversary better represented or is your legal or factual position not strong?

Your complaints should be confirmed in writing, since the next step after a lawyer is fired is often a fee dispute. If it comes to that, you do not want to appear to be a deadbeat. Lawyers generally dislike suing former clients, so you may be able to settle any fee issue quickly. This is particularly important, as the lawyer will probably not release your files until all bills are paid.

Line up a new lawyer before firing your old lawyer. You cannot afford a long interval between counsel and there is the chance that talking to the new lawyers will persuade you that you do not want to fire your lawyer after all.

FAMILY-OWNED BUSINESSES

Dan Bishop, Founder/President, National Family Business Association

An interesting aspect of American business is the predominance of family-owned and family-operated enterprises. They include more than 12 million companies, representing 95 percent of all American businesses. They range in size from small to large and have an average life span of twenty-four years.

Operating a family business is complicated by the personal relationships involved. Many family businesses were founded after World War II. Founders were predominantly male and were entrepreneurs willing to take a risk to enjoy independence.

It is the founder's fondest dream to pass the business on to the next generation. Critical concerns need to be addressed by the family in a realistic, unsentimental manner if the family business is to survive. A problem in a family business is the inability of family members to keep family and business matters separated. Emotionally charged family situations influence critical business decisions on a day-to-day basis. The business is governed by the needs of the family, not the market.

NEPOTISM

Webster's defines nepotism as favoritism shown to a relative (as by giving an appointive job) on the basis of relationship. It exists in most family businesses and may be on the rise due to tough competition in the job market making it difficult for young people to find jobs outside the family business. The good news is that the face of nepotism is changing. Founders are recognizing the benefits of having their children complete college and go to work for someone else as the first step in their careers. They gain experience and knowledge before joining the family firm. This alleviates the bitterness felt by nonfamily employees and keeps the children's ego and self-esteem in tact. To reduce the undesirable aspects of nepotism in business, some practical steps can be taken:

- Evaluate each family member's strengths and weaknesses, and assign positions in which his or her particular expertise will be profitable for the company and the individual.
- Have clear-cut job descriptions for family members and other employees so everyone in the company knows the parameters of all positions.
- Treat all employees fairly, and avoid favoritism on the job. Keep relationships businesslike.

RIVALRY

Equality and competition among siblings is an age-old problem that rankles the nerves of parents. It exists naturally in families where there is more than one child and is perpetuated in business when siblings work together.

A wise founder can handle the feelings that exist between siblings in several ways:

- Understand what sibling rivalry is all about and how it manifests itself in the business.
- Consult with experts who can offer objective suggestions and evaluations from an unemotional point of view.
- Carefully consider the capabilities and personalities of each child. Be aware that each individual needs to find his or her own niche.
- Have frank discussions with the children concerning competitiveness and how it could harm the company's day-to-day operations. If everybody understands what is going on, there is a greater chance to keep the rivalry under control.

TRANSITION

There is no mandatory retirement age in the family business. Everyone is aware that the owner will eventually not want to work so hard and will begin to turn over management responsibilities to the children and key employees. This process can be very difficult for the founder who cannot imagine anyone else handling "his baby," not even sons and daughters. This complicated matter should be planned well in advance.

Nonfamily members are an important ingredient in the overall picture of the business. They should be spared the uncomfortable feelings of not knowing where they stand. The need to predetermine roles and responsibilities in a transition process is vital. The following issues should be clarified in writing:

- How will management responsibilities be divided among family members?

- Will key employees be at the mercy of the whims of the children?
- Has the founder planned properly so the business will endure after his or her death?
- Is the founder's retirement plan firmly in place?
- Has it been decided which family member will be the successor? Has that person been adequately groomed for the position?

SUCCESSION

Planning for management transition and succession is not a palatable task for the founder. In doing so, he or she must face mortality. In some cases, it is depressing to be forced to recognize that a lifetime of work can be summed up so quickly and transferred to someone else by the mere act of signing several legal documents.

The structure of the estate plan will depend on priorities set by the family members when they consider protection of the founder's spouse, equitable treatment of children, continuity of the business, and minimizing estate taxes. Begin planning this most important process immediately. The family needs outside counsel that will assess these key issues:

- How is ownership held now?
- What is the business worth?
- Will the business in its entirety be left to the spouse?
- Will the spouse and children inherit equally?
- How will children be compensated if they do not actively work in the business?

When key succession issues are considered in sufficient time to overcome gaps in management and eliminate financial difficulties in the future, the potential for major problems that could threaten the business are reduced.

THE FRANCHISING ROUTE

Robin D. Anderson, Director, Nebraska Center for Entrepreneurship, University of Nebraska, Lincoln

Vance A. Mehrens, Director, International Center for Franchise Studies, University of Nebraska, Lincoln

"More than 540,000 franchise businesses dot the American landscape, generating more than $758 billion in sales" ("The Success Story of the 1980s and 1990s," *Franchise Opportunities Guide,* International Franchise Association, Winter, 1992). This accounts for over 34 percent of all U.S. retail sales. Less than 5 percent of franchise outlets fail, compared to 65–80 percent for independent businesses. With these kinds of numbers, franchising looks like a positive alternative for prospective business owners. However, franchising has some drawbacks. In this chapter, advantages and disadvantages of franchising are examined as they relate to an entrepreneur seeking new ventures.

Franchising is not an industry but a method of distribution of goods and services. It is one of many channels in which goods or services are delivered to the market. Franchising is used in most every industry including accounting, automotive, financial services, construction, food, health, hotels, cleaning, optical, and retail stores.

The primary components of franchising are the product/service, trade name, and payment of a fee. The franchisee is granted the right to sell or distribute goods or services under a system prescribed by the franchisor.

The franchisor in return receives an initial fee and/or ongoing royalty. Although the franchisee may occasionally feel like an employee, franchising is really an agreement between two partners.

Many businesses experience one of three problems that franchising assists in overcoming: (1) The business may lack the necessary capital for expansion. (2) Locating and recruiting good managers and staff has become increasingly difficult. (3) The business may feel a need to expand more rapidly than traditional methods allow.

The franchisee provides both start-up and working capital. Franchisees are generally more motivated because of their direct ownership in the business. Lastly, a business with a timely franchise concept can expand rapidly, dominate the market, and often lock out competition.

The primary advantage to a potential business owner in becoming a franchisee is a reduction of risk. The franchisor has learned from previous mistakes and passes along his or her expertise to the franchisee, as follows:

1. The product or service is established; reputation and consumer awareness have been created. The method of doing

business has been tested and has a solid track record. This advantage will also help the franchisee obtain debt financing.

2. Managerial assistance and training are passed on to the franchisee. This access to information and expertise allows the franchisee to enter the business with little or no previous experience.

3. Because franchisors establish quality control standards, the product/service, operations, performance, and quality are consistent from one franchise to another. Potential customers have confidence in the product/service they will receive.

4. The franchisee benefits from group buying power and established inventory-level requirements.

The extent of these advantages will vary from franchise to franchise.

The primary disadvantages to the franchisee are lack of control and the real risk of becoming overdependent. Entrepreneurially minded prospective franchisees should seriously consider the following:

1. The franchisor may not provide as much assistance as originally indicated.

2. Directly or indirectly, the services and assistance provided by the franchisor are paid for by the franchisee. Thus, a franchisee may be indirectly paying for services that he or she is not receiving or does not require.

3. The franchisee may depend on the assistance of the franchisor too much, neglecting common sense and crisis decisions.

4. Certain restrictions will be placed on the franchisee (i.e., territory, pricing, and advertising). In addition, franchisees may be forced (contractually) to participate in programs that they may not want to be a part of.

5. The franchisee may be at the mercy of the franchisor when the franchise agreement ends. Often, the franchisor determines whether or not to renew the contract.

6. The bad performance or service of other franchisees may have a detrimental effect on your franchise outlet.

After examining the pros and cons of franchising, there are certain areas that you should investigate prior to a final decision:

1. *Self-evaluation*—This process will assist you in determining what industry you are interested in and if you possess the entrepreneurial traits necessary to succeed as a franchisee.

2. *Financial requirements*—The expense of entering a franchise varies widely depending on the business and industry. Evaluating financial requirements is an ongoing consideration for prospective franchisees.

3. *Comparison of several franchises*—The Federal Trade Commission requires franchisors to supply a disclosure document to all prospective franchisees. This document will serve as an initial tool to review and evaluate different franchise ventures.

4. *Talking with franchisees*—Before investing in a particular franchise, you should talk with current franchisees and visit their locations. They are an excellent source of information.

5. *Professional advice*—Prospective franchisees need to have an attorney and accountant review the franchise agreement and disclosure document. The agreement is a contract between you and the franchisor.

The advantages of becoming a franchisee are clear. However, as an entrepreneur, you must decide whether or not you can thrive under the control of the franchisor, and you must weigh the option of whether the reduced risk of failure is worth the additional expense of the franchise relationship.

International Business

Jean Kelly, Section Editor

Introduction   *Jean Kelly*   14-3

Formulating and Implementing a Global Strategy
Françoise L. Simon and Donald E. Sexton   14-7

Looking at the Global Marketplace   *Michele Forzley*   14-26

Overseas Distribution, Licensing, and Technology Transfer
Peter B. Fitzpatrick   14-29

International Sourcing and Strategic Alliances   *Alan Zimmerman*   14-36

Managing Risks in International Joint Ventures   *John J. Hampton*   14-41

Problems and Opportunities in Countertrade   *Leo C. B. Welt*   14-45

Management in Japan   *Christopher E. Held*   14-48

INTRODUCTION

Jean Kelly

International operations services are increasingly being provided in a worldwide context. Events during the 1980s broke down many of the barriers that separated nations. The political occurrences were accompanied by a changing approach to commercial activities that are undertaken by large organizations with operations in different countries and small businesses that participate in international trade. As might be expected, the new realities have affected approaches to operating in national and international markets.

MANAGING INTERNATIONAL RISKS

World trade and capital investments across national borders must be accompanied by efforts to understand and manage the exposures that result from the manufacture and sale of goods and the providing of services. Then, allowances are necessary to reflect the diversity and complexity of activities in different national markets.

Another consideration with international operations reflects the range of exposures facing organizations in various areas of the world. Calcutta or Hong Kong are simply not identical to London or Tokyo or New York. Local conditions must be considered in any effort to understand a market for products or environment for creating goods for export to other areas of the world.

As a result of national differences, a selection process is necessary when evaluating international operations. From the point of view of a specific industry, not all countries are equally interesting or promising. From the point of view of the exporter, importer, or multinational firm, some areas of the world involve greater exposures than others. Decisions on whether to enter markets as a producer or provider of goods or services hinge on local circumstances and opportunities. Decisions on whether to establish a manufacturing or other subsidiary in a country should be made in the light of risks and exposures.

One way to deal with the complexity of global opportunities is to select issues and areas of the world that are most likely to be successful for a company's specific situation. Evaluating selected nations allows a detailed look at exposures that occur when we cross national boundaries.

NATIONAL ECONOMIES

Each country is different. Many countries are isolated by governmental policies and local business practices. Others are relatively open to participation by various manufacturers or service providers from other nations.

A national market can be studied as an individual entity. In this context, we might identify more than 160 countries that are prospects for joint ventures, export agreements, licensing, or other business arrangements. If we began such an effort, we would quickly realize that major differences exist, including:

1. *Size of the economy*—Some countries have large and well-developed economies. An industry with a wide range of products and services tends to be more interesting than a small stagnant market.
2. *Commercial contacts*—Some countries have extensive commercial sectors, with many interactions with the world. A high level of interaction with other nations adds to the likelihood of successful operations.
3. *Regulatory climate*—Some countries have minimal regulation for business operations in specific industries. Others are highly regulated with few opportunities for innovation or growth. Still others exclude foreign participation, either directly or through a variety of nontariff or foreign exchange barriers.
4. *Role of the private sector*—In many countries, certain businesses are the exclusive domain of the government. This may be true for health care, steel manufacturing, and banking. If private participation is not extensive in a company's line of business, the country tends to be of limited interest internationally.

FEASIBILITY STUDY

The opportunities offered by foreign markets can be understood only in economic, political, legal, and cultural contexts. Normally, this requires a feasibility study that covers:

1. *Level of economic activity*—This determines the size of the actual and potential market for selling products or services. From a manufacturing viewpoint, a low level of activity may indicate an underdeveloped infrastructure that will hamper operations.
2. *Structure of the economic system*—Nations have different approaches to managing their economies. Some economies are centrally planned with a large bureaucracy providing the planning for state corporations. Some are true market economies with an active private sector and limited government participation. Some are a mixture. Business opportunities, including the ease of market entry, vary considerably with the degree of government control over an economic system.
3. *Political system*—Some countries are representative democracies. Others are characterized by varying degrees of control exercised by individuals, families, or political alliances. The prospect for profits can be significantly affected by the way business is done in a country. The local political structure, both visible and behind the scenes, must be understood in order to assess the opportunities and obstacles in a market.
4. *Legal system*—Nations have a wide range of approaches to creating and enforcing personal and commercial relations. The differences are reflected in the laws regulating contracts, torts, and business dealings between individuals and organizations. Differences also exist in dispute resolution. The legal system determines the business and financial risks of operating in a country. How may contracts be written? How will they be interpreted? What mechanisms exist to settle disagreements? Reasonable answers to these questions are determined by the existence of reliable and fair laws and dispute resolution systems.
5. *Culture*—The ideas, customs, skills, and arts of a nation are the components of its culture. The national culture determines business practices. Will local ethnic groups deal only with other members of their group? Are contracts between strangers acceptable or must all business be done with old friends? Are business dealings completed in an environment of honesty and trust? Local customs must be recognized in any business venture.

CLASSIFICATION OF WORLD MARKETS

The world's 160 or so countries can be grouped using a variety of approaches. The

World Bank classifies countries by income. This is a useful start to recognizing regions of the world that may be suitable for international operations. The categories are:

1. *Organization for Economic Cooperation and Development (OECD)*—This consists of twenty-five or so high-income countries who are members of the OECD. A few are more accurately classified as middle income. Essentially, these are developed industrial nations with market economies. They work together through the OECD to coordinate their economic policies and activities.

2. *Asia Pacific*—This consists of ten or so middle-income countries grouped regionally along the Pacific Ocean coast of the Asian landmass. A few of the countries are low to middle income. These nations are characterized by market economies that have both an industrial and agricultural component.

3. *Latin America*—This consists of twenty-five or so middle and low- to middle-income countries geographically located on or near the continent of South America. These countries tend to have market economies with mixed industrial and agricultural sectors.

4. *Africa and Middle East*—This consists of twenty-five or so geographically grouped countries. Few similarities exist with respect to their economies or political systems. They include wealthy, oil-producing monarchies and poor democracies and socialist nations. They also vary greatly with respect to customs, religion, and economic structures.

5. *Asian planned economies*—This consists of seven or so low-income countries with directed or planned economies. China dominates the category. These countries offer varying opportunities for the conduct of business and trade or other dealings with other nations.

6. *East Europe and former USSR*—This consists of middle-income countries with changing political systems and generally serious economic problems. In this grouping, the term "middle income" covers a wide range of agricultural and industrial systems. Some of the nations

are moving rapidly toward market economies. Some may take decades to overcome poor centrally planned economic, political, and legal systems.

INDIVIDUAL COMPANY CLASSIFICATIONS

For the purpose of understanding specific prospects for one's own company, a feasibility study might create its own classification. As an example, let us assume that a company seeks to export equipment to other countries. A classification scheme could be:

1. *United States*—This is the world's largest domestic market overall. It could be studied individually.

2. *European community*—This consists of twelve countries plus associated members and a population of over 340 million people. The community has announced a goal of becoming a single European market. Progress has been made toward achieving this goal, even though major obstacles must still be overcome. If a single market is created, it would be larger than the U.S. domestic market.

3. *Emerging former socialist states*—The countries of Eastern Europe and the nations that were formerly part of the USSR represent a large question mark for the sale of equipment. Even though many differences exist among the various peoples of these entities, some equipment will be sold in the near term. Other items will not fit for many years. It may be convenient to consider the geographical region as a single territory.

4. *Japan*—This is a well-developed but somewhat closed economic system. The market is dominated by groupings of companies that work together. Still, Japan represents one of the world's largest markets. Certain items of equipment might sell quite successfully if a company has the patience to learn the Japanese system.

5. *China and the Four Tigers*—China, Taiwan, Singapore, Korea, and Hong Kong

range from the tightly restricted environment of China through the stable and orderly Singapore to the emerging Taiwan and Korea to the wide-open Hong Kong. The year 1997 is a key linkage between China and the rest of the region as a result of the reunification of Hong Kong with the mainland. All sorts of equipment opportunities might exist in this region.

6. *Developing nations*—This encompasses the many countries of the world that are seeking to build their economies. They experience common problems, including unstable markets and limited linkages to hard currency markets. They do, however, purchase equipment that they need but cannot manufacture at home.

7. *Individual exceptions*—This could consist of selected other nations of the world that are not otherwise categorized. They may be too small or otherwise isolated. Examples would be Israel and South Africa as specific markets for lines of equipment.

INDICATORS OF BUSINESS OPPORTUNITY

When preparing a feasibility study, a company can use a number of indicators of potential for business, including:

1. *Population*—Some businesses simply do better if more people exist to produce or purchase products.

2. *Level of consumer or business spending*—Does the country have relatively high levels of disposable personal income that could be diverted to new equipment? Are local businesses suffi-

ciently developed to possess funds to purchase equipment?

3. *Size of existing market*—Does a country already have sales of items that are similar or identical to the company's products? If not, are there indicators of potential demand? Is there currency available to make purchases?

4. *Cost of living*—Is it expensive to establish a local operation? Even if other prospects are positive, start-up costs can be prohibitive in some countries. The cost of living may point to the form of entry in a market. As an example, licensing or a local partnership venture is usually less costly than establishing a branch office. The local partner already has absorbed the costs of operating in a market. For high-cost markets, such arrangements reduce risks. This is less important in countries where start-up costs are lower.

5. *Other considerations*—A company can examine a long list of factors that affect the prospects for a successful operation. These range from existing competition to the structure of taxes to the requirements to provide burdensome employee benefits.

CONCLUSION

Global markets offer opportunities and risks for international operations. The opportunities are best pursued by obtaining knowledge of local conditions. The risks are best managed by carefully assessing the form of entry, nature of the operation, and likelihood for a successful venture. In this section, a carefully selected group of authors assist the reader in dealing with these issues.

Jean Kelly, M.A., M.B.A. *Diplome d'Études Françaises, is presently director of academic programs with the World Trade Institute in New York where she articulates joint-venture programs with selected universities and colleges, and advises on curricula in international business, trade, and languages. For nearly nine years, she also developed and supervised the institute's executive development seminars in international finance, accounting, and law. One of fifteen laypeople who serve in an advisory capacity with the Permanent Observer Mission of the Holy See to the United Nations, she has received numerous commendations for her work on issues dealing with economic development and the protection and advancement of mothers and children in developing nations.*

FORMULATING AND IMPLEMENTING A GLOBAL STRATEGY

Françoise L. Simon, Graduate School of Business, Columbia University

Donald E. Sexton, Graduate School of Business, Columbia University

For companies of almost any size and any industry, a key to keeping a competitive edge in the 1990s will be the existence of a well-defined global strategy based on a series of specific decision steps. For any midsize firms still operating largely domestically, the initial decision will be to develop international operations. The next steps will involve point of entry (country selected) and mode of entry (trade versus investment options).[1]

Given the complexity of options in world markets, these two decision steps must be based on a systematic analysis of company resources, competitive dynamics, and market potential. After entry options have been selected, companies develop an overall positioning strategy, taking into account competitors' positions, the company's own differential advantage, and the main or emerging market segments. Once this strategic framework has been set up, the firm can address marketing mix issues, starting with product line (Which products are global candidates? To what extent, if any, should they be adapted to their new markets?), and in-

cluding pricing, channel, and communication decisions. Finally, companies need to address marketing organization and control issues; these have by no means been resolved even by global giants such as Procter & Gamble or Nestle: In recent years, both have chosen to decentralize some functions and/or recentralize others, and both have dealt with product-based versus country-centered organization modes. Exhibit 14-1 shows the main steps of this strategy development process, and the purpose of this chapter is to describe these stages, with a focus on the global environment, market entry, and marketing mix decisions.

THE CHANGING GLOBAL ENVIRONMENT

The most urgent reasons to globalize tend to be defensive ones, but many firms are now taking a proactive stance in seeking worldwide opportunities. Major defensive drivers of globalization include cost and competitive

Exhibit 14-1. Global Strategy Development

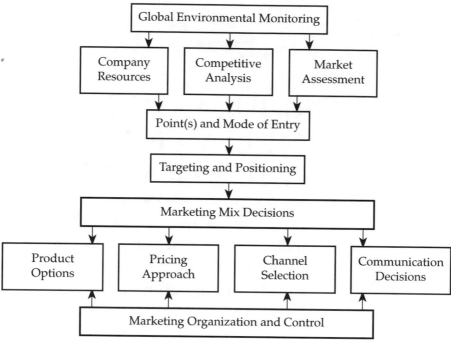

Copyright by Simon Associates.

factors; proactive drivers tend to be market based. Exhibit 14-2 shows the dynamics of this globalization trend.

Defensive Globalization Drivers

Whether we like it or not, we seem to have reached the point of no return in most industries: Competition has globalized and is here to stay. The United States now imports over one third of its computers and semiconductors and over half of its machine tools. Even these numbers are understated, since a growing share of "domestic" production is generated by foreign-owned U.S. plants; this is further reinforced by a "hollowing-out" trend—a personal computer nominally built in California is likely to be full of Asian components and partly assembled in Mexico.

Economies of scale have traditionally driven decisions to internationalize. In some industries, such as pharmaceuticals and biotechnology, the cost of developing a new drug rocketed from $54 million in 1976 to $231 million by 1987.[2] Only a global product designed for a global market can support that level of investment risk. Besides R&D costs, time to market has now become a key source of competitive advantage. The old "cascade" model of international expansion no longer works, as technological lead time and product life continually shorten in high-tech sectors, and as consumer goods require ever faster market response. Accordingly, P&G planned to introduce its latest diaper innovation, Pampers Phases, in ninety countries in fewer than twelve months (vs. twenty-seven months the last time Pampers was modified).[3]

The most traditional—and now least compelling—reason to globalize is the pursuit of lower production costs overseas. This has partly driven the recent rise in foreign investment in Spain, while costs were still below EC (European community) average; by the same token, Japan has shifted some production from the Asian "Four Tigers" (Singapore, Taiwan, Hong Kong, and Korea) to Indonesia and Thailand. However, as the rate of industrialization and the related labor costs accelerate, it is increasingly difficult to recover setup costs before the new site starts to lose its cost advantage.

Exhibit 14-2. Globalization Drivers

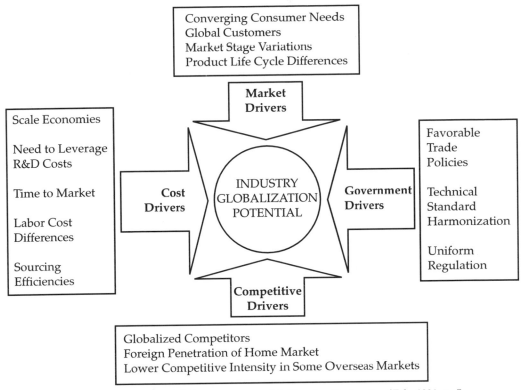

Source: After G. Yip, Diagnosing global strategy potential, *Planning Review*, Jan./Feb. 1991, p. 5.

Proactive Globalization Drivers: Market Factors

Theodore Levitt, former editor of the *Harvard Business Review*, pointed out in 1983 that technology was driving worldwide consumer preferences toward commonality.[4] Six years later, Ken Ohmae still concurred: "Consumers in the Triad increasingly receive the same information, seek the same kinds of lifestyles, and desire the same kinds of products. . . . Everyone, in a sense, wants to live—and shop—in California."[5] While some global segments exist—most notably upmarket, for such premium brands as Mercedes-Benz and Moet & Chandon—entire product categories are still far from global. Pharmaceuticals, for instance, while "born from global molecules," still vary widely to reflect consumer preferences for different formulations (effervescent vitamins in France vs. caplets in the United States) as well as diverse

physician practices (prescription dosages can vary up to 100 percent between Europe and Japan).

For industrial products and services, a firm may need to follow its key accounts as they move overseas. Ernst & Young's postmerger motto, "One Firm Worldwide," therefore reflected the fact that the accounting firm's major clients were multinationals in need of worldwide services. Similarly, Japanese auto parts suppliers followed Honda, Toyota, and Nissan overseas—to the dismay of host governments hoping for a larger "trickle-down" effect on local employment from foreign investment.[6]

The most compelling market driver of globalization may well be the maturity of triad economies and the related fatigue of many major brands. Drugs facing stagnant markets in the triad, such as antibiotics, find a new life in developing countries. Similarly, while

Coke and Pepsi fiercely compete for "share-of-throat" in the mature U.S. soft drink market, they are free to create markets in less-saturated areas overseas.

Barriers to Globalization

While global trade has benefitted since the late 1940s from an easing of tariffs and other restrictions, government policies now appear to run on two tracks that may be on a collision course. Since 1947, the GATT (General Agreement on Tariffs and Trade) system has greatly stimulated trade through many multilateral tariff reductions; under GATT, tariffs on manufactured goods fell from an average 40 percent in 1945 to 5 percent in the 1980s; accordingly, the ratio of U.S. exports to GNP (gross national product) has tripled since the 1950s. However, difficulties in concluding the Uruguay round have stressed GATT's inadequacies, such as the fact that it does not include services (now $700 billion in trade per year vs. $3.1 trillion per year in global merchandise trade),[7] or its very nature as a cumbersome machinery requiring consensus from over a hundred member countries.

As the old East-West political blocs fade into history, the key challenge to the GATT system is the current formation of new economic blocs in Europe, Asia, and the Americas (see Exhibit 14-3). In the past decade, trade

inside these three regions has grown faster than trade between them (interregion trade rose an average 4.2 percent per year in the 1980s vs. 5 percent intraregionally and 6 percent in Asia). There are clear signs that these blocs are now strengthening.[8] The EEA (European Economic Area), which adds to the twelve-country EC its European Free Trade Agreement (EFTA) neighbors, minus Switzerland, may further expand through a web of agreements with Eastern Europe.

The Americas are attempting to follow suit, first with the 1988 U.S./Canada Free Trade Act, then with its extension to Mexico. Within Latin America, links are being forged: Chile signed a free trade agreement with Mexico in 1991, trade between Brazil and Argentina doubled (to $2.1 billion) between 1985 and 1990, and the Andean, Mercosur, and Central American pacts are expected to expand from free trade zones to common markets. While forming a mass of almost 700 million people (over 400 million of whom are in Latin America), this projected American bloc would still be the weakest entity with massive economic imbalances.

The most historic event was the 1993 signing of the North American Free Trade Agreement (NAFTA), signed by the United States, Mexico, and Canada. Although the agree-

Exhibit 14-3. Trade Bloc Evolution (all figures in US$)

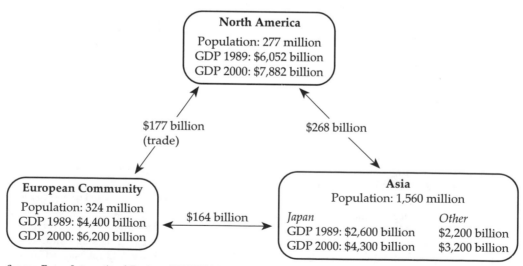

Source: From *International Business/INTERMATRIX*, 11/91.

ment still involves some protections, it has the potential to be a far reaching economic boost for the three countries involved.

While least defined politically, Asia-Pacific dwarfs the other blocs by its population (1.8 billion) and its cohesiveness. It is now a de facto–integrated manufacturing and trading zone led by Japan: Every three days, a new Japanese factory opens in Thailand; Japanese retailers control about half of Hong Kong's department store sales; Japan has massive investments in Indonesian oil and gas, and its exports to the Four Tigers totaled $57 billion in 1990, an amount equivalent to U.S. exports to Germany, France, and Britain.[9] Australia and Malaysia have both proposed to formalize these links with official economic groupings, and the six ASEAN (Association of Southeast Asian Nations) countries (Indonesia, Singapore, Malaysia, Thailand, Brunei, and the Philippines) have recently formed a free trade agreement.

Growing fears that these blocs will close themselves off from external partners have driven a shift from exports to investment; in 1987, the value of goods and services produced by U.S. firms in the EC exceeded $235 billion (four times the value of U.S. exports to the region), and the gap is widening.[10]

Company response to the dilemma of globalization versus regionalization has been largely related to size and resources. Countering the fear of protectionism is the "borderless" company. With $20 billion in revenues, ABB (Asea Brown Boveri, formed in 1987 by the merger of Sweden's Asea and Switzerland's Brown Boveri, and expanded in 1989 by the U.S. acquisition of Combustion Engineering) is nominally headquartered in Zurich but headed by a "Euro-CEO," conducts its business in English, and keeps its books in dollars.[11]

For smaller companies, the path to international success is less clear; if the current trend toward trade bloc formation persists, the traditional globalization strategy no longer applies. This standard stepwise process, aiming to minimize risk and maximize learning time, tended to move from exports to alliances and finally direct investment.

FORMULATING A GLOBAL STRATEGY

Adopting a global strategy does not necessarily entail a presence in every region. It does imply a highly integrated business approach, defining key strengths as they apply across markets, transferring marketing experience and technology from lead markets to others, linking sourcing and marketing activities worldwide, and constantly assessing the balance between standardization and localization of the marketing mix, based on market conditions and consumer needs.

The first step in the globalization process is the selection of entry points, based on a triple assessment of company resources, competitive position, and market attractiveness. In the second stage, the company determines the entry mode, ranging from exports to higher-risk, higher-return options.

Market Selection/Point of Entry

Country selection is a key strategic decision, since adding another market to a company portfolio requires not only initial capital but also significant resources to sustain the venture over time. This business risk can be reduced by a screening process taking into account seven key factors: market potential, company resources and competitive position, the target country's government policy toward trade and investment, its technology level and marketing infrastructure, and its specific consumer needs (see Exhibit 14-4).

How should these factors be prioritized? A stepwise approach groups them into four distinct stages. In the initial stage, a company assesses its resources in order to determine the global candidates, if any, in its product line, their competitive advantage overseas, the management talent necessary to lead foreign operations, and the capital available for the new venture. Stage II starts the external screening process by ranking markets according to their relative attractiveness and balancing this against their competitive intensity. Stage III completes the external screening by actually assessing the potential demand for the company's products or services, and determining the variance between consumer

Exhibit 14-4. Key Drivers of a Market Entry Decision

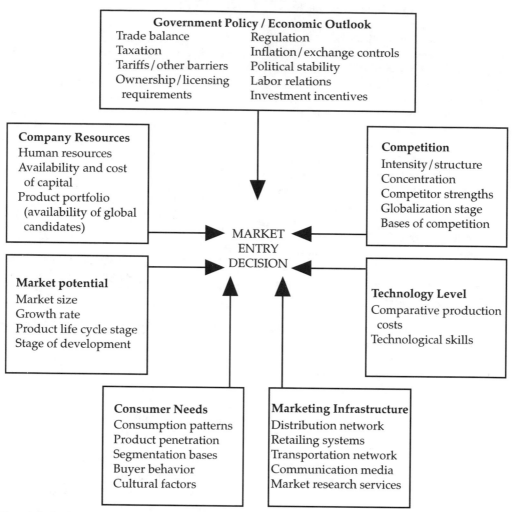

Government Policy / Economic Outlook

Trade balance   Regulation
Taxation   Inflation/exchange controls
Tariffs/other barriers   Political stability
Ownership/licensing   Labor relations
  requirements   Investment incentives

Company Resources
Human resources
Availability and cost
  of capital
Product portfolio
  (availability of global
  candidates)

Competition
Intensity/structure
Concentration
Competitor strengths
Globalization stage
Bases of competition

MARKET
ENTRY
DECISION

Market potential
Market size
Growth rate
Product life cycle stage
Stage of development

Technology Level
Comparative production
  costs
Technological skills

Consumer Needs
Consumption patterns
Product penetration
Segmentation bases
Buyer behavior
Cultural factors

Marketing Infrastructure
Distribution network
Retailing systems
Transportation network
Communication media
Market research services

Copyright by Simon Associates.

needs in the target and home markets. At the end of this process, the markets first identified in Stage II as attractive and competitively favorable should be further reduced to one or two optimal entry points, based on estimated product demand. Finally, Stage IV addresses the question of entry mode, ranging from exporting to joint ventures and direct manufacturing. Exhibit 14-5 summarizes this stepwise screening process.

Market Attractiveness Assessment. Although market size is usually the easiest indicator to define, it is not the most important.

Market growth rate and product life cycle stage are more dynamic indicators of sustainable market potential. For major product categories, the U.S. Department of Commerce, foreign ministries, the United Nations' *Yearbook of International Trade Statistics* and private organizations such as Find/SVP and Predicasts all provide data for main world markets (see Appendix for other sources).

In addition to market size and growth rate, the product life cycle stage is an important selection factor. In the same way as a mature product can be extended domestically by repositioning (as was the case for Johnson's

Exhibit 14-5. Market Selection—Stepwise Screening Process

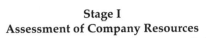

Stage I
Assessment of Company Resources

Are we ready to expand internationally?
With which products / people / capital?
With what competitive advantage?

↓

Stage II
Preliminary Screening: Market Potential Analysis

Which markets offer the highest opportunity?
Which markets show the most favorable competitive conditions?

↓

Stage III
Second Screening: Product Potential Analysis

What is the potential demand for our products / services?
How similar are consumer needs to those in existing markets?

↓

Stage IV
Selection of Entry Mode

How does government policy impact trade and investment?
Does the technology level allow investment options?
How does the marketing infrastructure impact our distribution options?
Do consumer needs require local production?

Copyright by Simon Associates.

baby shampoo, repositioned from baby care to adult use through the "gentle enough to use every day" theme), that same product can grow again in overseas markets where it is at an earlier stage. In pharmaceuticals, for instance, mature categories like antibiotics find new life in developing countries where they are still in a growth stage.

Competitive Analysis. While market attractiveness assessment acts as a positive screen, highlighting the most appealing entry points, competitive analysis may be used as a counterbalancing negative screen, eliminating otherwise attractive markets that show a high level of competitive intensity. A Canadian specialty chemical manufacturer, for instance, when considering an expansion into Europe, found Germany the most attractive market, but eliminated it because of its well-entrenched and technologically advanced local producers.

Consolidation is a current trend that may be a significant entry barrier. Although lagging the United States, the European airline industry, for instance, has started to consolidate: The acquisition of Air Inter and UTA gave Air France a 97-percent coverage of the French market; although a planned British Airways-KLM-Sabena merger was rejected by the European community on antitrust grounds, a number of other airline alliances are now being considered. As a result, new entrants such as Munich-based Wings have rapidly collapsed due to lack of access to airport slots or denial of interline agreements.

Globalization of a given industry is also a factor with mixed impact, since it may open new trade channels but also means the presence, in an attractive market, of strong multinationals as well as local players. Finally, *bases of competition* themselves may vary across markets. In the U.S. context, cost-conscious business travelers may be won through price wars or mileage programs; on intra-European routes, options are more limited, despite the deregulation in progress.

Once entry points have been selected by balancing market opportunity and competitive position, the next stage of the screening process moves from the industry to the product category level, and analyzes the profitability potential of products or services already identified as global candidates.

Potential Demand for Products or Services. While more difficult to evaluate than total market size, actual product potential (either in terms of market share or sales volume) is a key factor not only of market selection but also of entry strategy. While indirect exports can be profitable at relatively low sales volumes, direct production requires high sales levels to offset investment costs.

Product forecasts may be drawn from several sources, such as industry, distributors, and customer estimates, as well as expert opinions and custom surveys. Product penetration data allow a first assessment by showing the relative saturation of a target market.

The frequent noncomparability of product classifications complicates this process: A television set may be classified as an entertainment expenditure in one market versus a furniture outlay in another.

Segmentation bases also impact product potential. While some common trends and segments may exist across regions, such as an aging population, dual-career couples, or single households, one should not assume that these commonalities warrant a standardized product in all cases. A personal-care products firm was able to identify a Pan-European "health and prevention-oriented" segment with common demographics (urban, upscale, educated, etc.). However, the segment was not strategically actionable, since it led to diverse purchase behaviors; toothpaste usage, which was of prime importance to the company, varied from light to heavy within the segment, and other behaviors compensated for it, such as high frequency of professional cleanings. In view of these inconsistencies, the right question to ask may not be "Is our customer global?" but "At what level is our customer globalized?"

A useful way to limit product range while staying responsive to local needs is the lead country model, as practiced by Nissan among others. If Nissan had wanted to design separate cars for each distinct segment identified in the triad, the company would have had to develop four dozen models, which was, of course, beyond its resources. Nissan then looked at the triad region by region and determined each of its core markets' requirements; the successful Pathfinder and 240SX were designed to answer the U.S. needs for a sporty model and a four-wheel drive family vehicle. With a short list of lead country models, Nissan was able to halve its product range and still cover 80 percent of its sales; the remaining 20 percent were covered through minor changes answering local needs.[12] Once possible target markets have been screened and a few candidates have been retained, a company enters the last stage in its decision process, concerning the mode of entry.

Market Entry Decision/Mode of Entry

The range of strategic entry alternatives, which started with four basic options (exports, licensing, joint ventures, and ownership), has now greatly expanded to include innovative alliances covering each stage of the value chain, from R&D to distribution. Given the accelerating rate of change in many industries, flexibility to exit, upgrade, or switch to another entry mode has become a key issue.[13]

Exporting. Exporting is the most traditional entry mode, available to companies of any size, entailing lower risk than equity options but still requiring a significant management commitment. Its benefits include economies of scale from centralized manufacturing and avoidance of risk in uncertain markets. Disadvantages are the possible high cost of tariff or nontariff barriers and the lack of direct presence in a foreign market, which may become subject to protectionist measures.

Direct exporting requires more resources than indirect exporting (which involves brokers or export agents), but provides in return better control over distribution channels. In industries where technical product knowledge and service are critical, a wholly owned sales operation is preferable even to an exclusive distributor. This approach, however, is not a low-investment option: It requires capital for inventory financing, local managers, and facilities, and entails fixed selling and administrative costs.

American producers have been accused of "short-termism," exporting abroad when exchange rates are favorable and exiting markets when conditions worsen. They have looked for export models in Japan, where a pyramid of small companies supplies large exporters in their *keiretsu* (consortia of trading companies, banks, and manufacturers). It now appears that the German *Mittelstand* (midsize sector) provides a far more relevant model.

At $1.4 trillion, Germany's economy is less than a fourth the size of that of the United States, yet in 1990, Germany sold $421 billion worth of exports, well ahead of America's $394 billion and Japan's $286 billion. Most of Germany's 300,000 small and midsize companies, unlike their Japanese counterparts, remain independent but have been highly successful despite the world's highest labor costs and a strong currency. They collectively generate 30 percent of German exports by targeting small but profitable niches abroad and placing quality and training above short-term earnings growth.

While nearly two thirds of these exports are, predictably, technology-intensive, Germany also wins in other sectors: It holds a surprise position as the world's number one textile exporter, selling more than $11 billion worth a year—a third more than Hong Kong. In the United States, a combination of better trade centers and a longer time horizon may play a key role in increasing export competitiveness in the future.[14]

Licensing. Under licensing, one company allows another to use its intellectual property in exchange for a fee or royalty. The property ranges from patents to trademarks, technology, manufacturing processes, or marketing skills.

Licenses are normally signed for limited periods, which depend in part on the foreign licensee's capital investment. The key advantage of this approach is access to a new market without equity investment. In manufacturing, however, licensing is now seen as a high-risk approach. The most obvious threats are the probable transformation of the licensee into a competitor, the lack of direct market participation, and the uncertainty of product quality.

In service industries, licensing presents fewer risks than in manufacturing. Coca-Cola, Avis, Kentucky Fried Chicken, and Holiday Inns have all used franchising (a special form of licensing) as a global expansion tool.

A stellar example of franchising success is the McDonald's empire. In 1990, McDonald's overseas markets contributed, respectively, 51 percent and 24 percent of consolidated company-operated and franchised restaurant dollar margins. A key success factor was extensive training and quality control, but also some independence for licensees allowing for a two-way transfer of experience.

McDonald's accepted short-term losses to achieve long-term growth, waiting on average seven to ten years before making money in a given market. The first restaurants in France were started in the early 1970s with a local licensee, but ran into staffing and quality problems; McDonald's was then relaunched in 1984 and spread to 150 restaurants by 1990, thanks to significant adaptations in architecture (loose cafe-style seating) and marketing (accent on convivial family experience rather than product close-ups, as in the United States).[15]

Joint Ventures. Unlike licensing agreements, joint ventures involve equity participation in the creation of a new entity in which the partners may have a fifty-fifty, minority, or majority position. Joint ventures are common in research-driven sectors like aerospace, computers, and telecommunications, where they allow partners to acquire complementary technologies, achieve economies of scale or scope, or gain access to new markets.

International joint ventures, however, have so far shown a 30 percent to 60 percent failure rate, depending on success factors (survival rate, achievement of profit expectations, etc.). Famous cases include the AT&T-Olivetti venture, hurriedly formed to produce personal computers, and eventually dissolved because of irreconcilable differences in management styles, cultures, and strategic objectives.[16]

A large number of failures have involved U.S.-Japanese joint ventures. The most common "doom formula" involves a U.S. firm driven by avoidance (reducing the risk of entering a new market or developing a new product), paired with a Japanese company motivated by technology acquisition or market learning. This formula paved the way for Japan's capture of the U.S. consumer electronics market, starting with OEM arrangements where Japanese producers gained gradual knowledge of the United States while relinquishing none of their critical R&D skills.

An optimal outcome of U.S.-Japanese joint ventures may be a shift to sole ownership; several firms that, decades ago, cracked the then-impenetrable Japanese distribution system through joint ventures, such as Procter & Gamble, BMW, and Louis Vuitton, are now operating independently. In addition to exit clauses, steps limiting joint-venture risks include reducing the scope of the agreement to cover a single technology rather than a whole range, part of a product line rather than the

whole line, distribution in a limited number of markets or for a specific period of time.[17]

Alliances. A recent response to the mixed track record of conventional joint ventures has been the rise of more flexible strategic alliances, often limited in their scope to one part of the value chain, such as precompetitive basic research, production, or distribution.

Unlike joint ventures, alliances do not require the formation of a new, independent entity, and they may or may not include equity participation. They are now evolving into two concepts with vastly different scopes: limited agreements, which may function as transitional devices to penetration of foreign markets versus long-term networks similar to the Japanese *keiretsu* or the Korean *chaebol*.

While less complex than a *keiretsu*, Ford's network includes owning 25 percent of Japan's Mazda, 10 percent of Kia Motors in Korea, 75 percent of Aston Martin Lagonda in Britain, and 49 percent of Autolatina in Brazil and Argentina for vehicle assembly. Ford has a similar equity network in parts suppliers such as Cummins and Excel Industries, owns 49 percent of Hertz, extends credit through seven wholly owned financing units, and belongs to eight research consortia.[18]

The Ford-Mazda agreement is thriving after thirteen years, thanks to a combination of independence and two-way collaboration. Each keeps certain products off limits to the other, and the partners operate on a project-by-project basis. However, on joint models such as Ford's off-road Explorer and Mazda's Navajo, the two partners fully share in product development, with Ford doing most of the styling and Mazda making key engineering contributions such as steering design.[19]

A 1991 McKinsey study of 150 cross-border alliances in the triad found a number of distinct success factors for alliances versus acquisitions. First, alliances were found to work best in nonconflictual situations, that is, when expanding a core business into new regions, or in penetrating new businesses within the same geographic market. By contrast, acquisitions had the best success rate in building the position of a core business in an existing geographic market. A second factor was equal strength, particularly in product-for-markets swaps—the objective here being to avoid "deskilling" one partner for the other's benefit, thus destabilizing the relationship.

Other success factors included autonomy and flexibility, allowing alliances to evolve according to emerging technologies and changing consumer needs.[20] Exhibit 14-6 reviews the costs and benefits of all these entry options, ranging from exports to alliances.

For companies considering globalization, the most effective entry approach may be a hybrid one. Whereas the traditional path to globalization proceeded in a linear way from exports to joint ventures or ownership, emerging approaches are based on a portfolio of entry strategies, using simultaneously exports, alliances, and direct ownership, depending on market conditions.

Globalizing the Marketing Mix

A central and recurring issue in global marketing is the trade-off between standardization and localization. The more one can standardize the product or service features, packaging, advertising copy, and selling materials across countries, the lower the per-unit costs. Yet the more these elements are standardized, the higher the risks that the product or service will have lower value to the customer in the local country market or, worse, be unacceptable due to local needs, customs, or regulations.

Improvements in operations technology, such as computer-aided design and manufacturing, continue to make these trade-off decisions less prevalent and less urgent. However, most companies still face numerous standardization/localization choices and frequently these surface in the marketing mix: product or service design, distribution, pricing, and communications. Typically, the global marketing strategy sets forth the core positioning of the product or service, but the marketing mix programs are employed to tailor the offer to participants in the local country market. In recent surveys of ninety-two and sixty-eight multinational companies, the product design showed a relatively much higher degree of standardization than programs in the marketing mix such as pricing and advertising.[21]

Country Marketing Strategy. Within the context of a global marketing strategy, often there are several strategic choices left to the country manager. Crucial decisions concern selection of local target segments and positioning for each segment. As noted above, segments attractive in one country may not resemble segments that are attractive in another, due to differences in the number of potential customers, growth rate, needs, buying habits, and so forth. Positioning consists of the key benefits to be provided to the local customers and therefore serves as the foundation for marketing mix decisions within a country. Even though a product is physically the same, its positioning may vary across countries. For example, the Canon AE-1 camera was positioned as a user-friendly camera in the United States and as state of-the-art technology in Europe and Japan.

Country Marketing Research. Local research may be necessary both before and after a marketing mix decision is made. In many countries, the research services available are performed at a high professional level. However, in some countries, conducting marketing research or even utilizing existing data may pose problems. In the early 1970s, many companies were investing in Iran and basing their decisions in part on official census data. These data might have been considered suspect, however, since at the time, if the census takers were unable to obtain data firsthand from local companies, they were encouraged to guess to complete their forms. Subsequent cross-checks of the census revealed huge and unlikely response ranges for several key questions. Basic rules for performing local marketing research include:

1. Get references for the research firm and check them.
2. Examine examples of prior work closely and carefully. Secure the actual interview forms and questionnaires and run cross-checks on key statistics.
3. Use multiple measures for forecasts. For illustration, it may be possible to estimate the automobile population both by registration figures and by production, import, and export figures.

Exhibit 14-6. Global Entry Strategies—Costs and Benefits

Strategy	Benefits	Costs	Key Success Factors
Indirect Exporting	Lowest-risk option	No possible gain of market experience	Selection of agent with strong contacts and good technical and market skills
Direct Exporting	Possible higher return Control over distribution	Financial and human resources investment	Sales subsidiary profitability depends on accurate estimate of significant sales volume
Licensing/ Manufacturing	Access to new market or technology Preemption of competitors	Creating a competitor Dependence on licensee Lack of direct market participation	Protection of core competencies Cross-licensing agreements in noncompeting areas
Licensing/ Services	Fast market entry Low financial investment	Misuse of trademark Quality control problems	Direct product quality control and standardized training Two-way transfer of marketing experience
Joint Ventures	Economies of scale/ scope Value chain synergies Market and technology complementarity	Coordination costs/ problems "Deskilling" one partner	Limiting agreement scope to protect core competencies Limiting markets/ products covered
Alliances	Shared risks and costs Faster time to market	One-way technology transfer Information barriers	Full sharing of product development Best in noncompeting markets/businesses
Acquisitions	Building critical mass Total control	Highest capital outlay Culture integration problems	Best in building core business in existing markets

4. Perform sensitivity analyses on the country strategy by employing both best- and worst-case forecasts. It may be that a high degree of accuracy is not required for some of the parameters being estimated.

Product or Service Options. At the heart of the global marketing strategy is typically the specification of a core product or a core service. The core (or primary) product consists of all those characteristics that will be held in common for all country markets. For a computer, the core product might include most of the internal hardware. Besides the core product, there is a set of characteristics that might be termed the secondary product—the keys and layout of a keyboard for a computer, for example. These characteristics may need to be tailored to a specific country market. There are two major reasons for adapting a product or service to a local market:

1. Adaptation may be necessary just to be acceptable in the market because of the effects of regulations, culture, and buying behavior.
2. Adaptation may add customer value by more closely meeting the needs of local customers.

Many factors can lead to local adaptation of products or services. Broadly, these factors concern the overall country environment or the specific market. Environmental concerns are as follows:

1. *Geography and climate*—The performance of a product or service may depend on natural factors such as terrain, temperature, or weather. Hills require that oil pipes be lighter and easier to handle. Extremely low temperatures require changes in batteries to maintain performance, and water composition affects the efficacy of detergents.
2. *Infrastructure*—Types of road surfaces, parameters of electric current, and nature of wall sockets can affect a product's performance or even whether it can perform.

3. *Regulations*—Contents' form, labeling use, and purchase conditions are just a few of the areas that may be regulated. For example, for some electronic products, required cabinet specifications vary from country to country and must be considered during product design.

Marketing concerns are as follows:

1. *Applications*—Products or services may be used differently throughout the world and therefore must be positioned differently. Bicycles for some markets are essential transportation; for others, recreation.
2. *Culture*—Aesthetics and connotations differ by country culture. The smell of Camay and the flavor of Crest have varied across countries. The number "4" is related to death in Japan and products there should not be packaged in groups of four, as one golf-ball manufacturer discovered due to lagging sales.[22]
3. *Language*—There are numerous international marketing disasters rooted in language. Ford named a truck Fiera, which means "ugly old woman" in Spanish, while American Motors' Matador was interpreted to mean "killer."
4. *Skills*—Ability to use and, therefore, to evaluate products and services may depend on past experience. Cameras that sell well to sophisticated Japanese photographers may do less well in markets earlier in the development phase—unless instructions and personal advice can fill this knowledge gap. Campbell's concentrated soups initially failed in the United Kingdom because the consumers were not accustomed to adding water to canned soups.[23]
5. *Complementary products and services*—Some products and services must be used in concert with others. Country differences in those complementary products may require adaptation of the globally marketed product. Procter & Gamble's liquid detergent—initially called Vizir—succeeded when a

floating dispensing ball was provided so that the detergent could be used more effectively in European top-loading washing machines.

6. *Needs*—For many reasons, customers in one country may seek different benefits than those in another country. A private branch exchange (PBX) in the United States may need the ability to select the lowest-cost long-distance routing for a telephone call. In countries where there is but one rate possible for the call, such a feature would be superfluous.

7. *Attitudes*—Brand names and country of origin may have varying impact on customers. In a Chrysler advertisement, Lee Iacocca asserted, "Two cars come off the same assembly line, in the same American plant. A Japanese nameplate goes on one, an American nameplate goes on the other, and people prefer the Japanese version."[24]

8. *Purchase frequency*—The size and frequency of the typical order may affect package size and inventory policy. In the United States, families with freezers make larger food purchases, whereas in Japan, smaller apartments and storage space help stimulate sales of concentrated laundry detergents.

9. *Distribution channels*—Long distribution channels or slow turnover may require that products have longer shelf life than needed in their home countries.

10. *Competitors*—The relative performance of domestic and global competitors clearly must also be considered when positioning a product or service in a local country market.

Products and services can be adapted by changing the characteristics of the core or primary product or service; changing the characteristics of the secondary product or service; or changing communications, including advertising and personal selling. Changing the core product, by definition, is relatively expensive. That is why global products need to be planned for global markets before production begins. Xerox, for instance, surveys the world to determine the range of dimensions for paper; then it designs its copiers.

Changing the secondary product characteristics is more likely to preserve the economies of the standardized core product while meeting local regulations or creating local value. Pharmaceutical products, among others, can be repackaged to meet local requirements. Communications can be used to spotlight those features and benefits important to the target customers in specific countries, as Canon did with its AE-1 camera. At one point, Volvo focused on performance in Germany, safety in Switzerland, status in France, and economy, durability, and safety in Sweden.

Distribution Channels. Distribution is the key to many markets. In the late 1980s, Eastman Kodak did well in the Japanese market by increasing its marketing, advertising, and research and development efforts there. The most difficult market for Kodak, though, has been the kiosks at railroad stations where typically only one brand of film, Fuji, is stocked.

Channels of distribution around the world often are not well understood. They differ in both length and span. In Japan, for example, half of all wholesalers employ fewer than four people, and the distribution channels are quite long.[25]

Once established, distributors and channels are frequently difficult to change. Many countries have legislation that prohibits companies from altering the products or services sold through them. Since the channel that is optimal for market entry may not be the one that is appropriate later, global marketers must develop global distribution strategies across countries and over time. Within the country, the company must determine:

1. *Current coverage of the target segments*—How do products or services reach the customers now? Are there several routes? Which channels are increasing in importance? Why?

2. *Characteristics of the current distribution channels*—How well defined are their target markets? How quickly can they move products or services to the customers? How effective are their selling

efforts? What skills and expertise are present and at what levels?

3. *Customer needs*—For the resellers or customers at each level of the distribution channel, what information and services are required?

4. *Alternative channels*—Are there other ways to move products or services to the customers? Are they feasible given current buying habits and regulations?

5. *Costs*—What are the expected costs for each channel option? Campbell Soup Company discovered that its distribution costs in the United Kingdom were 30 percent above those in the United States because of the smaller quantities purchased by British food retailers.[26]

The scale and scope of the marketing objectives and how quickly they are to be achieved are a major consideration in selecting distribution channels. However, one must keep in mind that the channel that delivers results most immediately may not be the channel that allows long-run growth. One company awarded exclusive distributorships throughout Central America when it was primarily a one-product firm. Later, when it moved into such diverse areas as medical technology and information systems, those exclusive contracts were a constraint and they had to be renegotiated so that the necessary specialist distributors could be used.

For many companies, the most appropriate distribution channel may well be a system involving several different types of distributors that together allow speed, control, and market coverage. Recruiting distributors must begin with lists of potential resellers developed through discussions with local customers. From these lists, specific distributors are selected that are consistent with the overall distribution strategy. Selection criteria are similar to those used in a domestic market, but they will vary by country and by competitive situation. Possible criteria include: market knowledge and coverage; product or service coverage; service, marketing, and selling ability; inventory, financial ability, and controllability; interest in handling the company's products; local influence, reputation, and trade group affiliations.

Ongoing management of distributors requires motivating, training, and performance evaluation. Contracts must provide for merging operations and for changing or terminating the relationship.

Pricing. Throughout the world, pricing receives substantial regulatory attention. While a company's attorneys likely should review all international marketing mix decisions, they should always be consulted regarding pricing decisions. There are five major considerations for any pricing decision:

1. *Customer value*—What features and benefits do customers in the target segment want? How do they value those offerings? What are they willing to pay? A meal in the Moscow McDonald's costs several hours' wages for a Russian worker, but as one customer declared, "Most . . . have enough rubles. The problem is finding something to buy."[27]

2. *Costs*—What are the variable costs associated with one unit of product or service? In particular, what are the specifically international costs such as transportation, insurance, and duties?

3. *Competitors*—What are their offerings? How do customers value them? What prices are the competitors charging —now and in the future?

4. *Company*—What marketing and financial results do we expect to achieve in this country market? When? What capacity are we allocating to this country market—now and in the future?

5. *Country environment*—What are the laws regarding prices—both on import and on domestic transactions? How are prices typically quoted? What terms are commonly offered?

Answers to these questions would provide the basis for setting a price in a domestic or single-country marketing strategy. However, international pricing is more difficult for a number of reasons.

Gray markets. When prices among country markets for the same product differ, there may be opportunities for arbitrage. If sufficient profit remains after transaction and transportation costs are deducted, products may be shipped outside the regular distribution channels from the low-price country market to the high-price country market. Such product movements are called gray markets or parallel imports. Gray markets often are legal and reflect the globalization of markets with respect to advances in communication and transportation. For a company, they result in decreased short-term profits and breakdown in the morale of distributors as they compete for customers with lower-cost suppliers.

There are many suggested actions to cope with gray markets.[28] Warrantees only valid in specific countries, distinctive packaging, different models, instructions in one language, price adjustments to remove arbitrage opportunities, single price worldwide, distributor contracts prohibiting reshipment, and other legal sanctions are options. These actions vary in their feasibility and likely effectiveness in preventing gray markets. At best, their effects may be short term. The appearance of gray markets signifies that a company may need to reassess its long-run global strategy.

Foreign Exchange Risk. Under floating exchange rates, the deal that looked terrific today may take the company to financial ruin tomorrow. Exchange rates are difficult—many would say impossible—to forecast. In general, most marketing managers will not gamble on exchange rates and will choose to hedge their deals in some fashion. Some currencies are not convertible and buyers may not have sufficient hard currency. For those situations, some form of barter or countertrade arrangement may be appropriate. In countertrade, the seller agrees to receive some product or service or the proceeds from the sale of the product or service in exchange for what is sold. PepsiCo accepts Stolichnaya Vodka from Russian and Premiat wine from Romania in exchange for their soft-drink syrups.

Communication Strategies. The three major decision areas to consider are message, media, and expenditures. Signals that work in one country may have no effect, or even a negative effect, elsewhere. Factors that affect messages include:

1. *Language*—What are the denotations and the connotations of words and phrases? "Come Alive" for one soft-drink company became "Come Alive out of the grave" in Germany, and a U.S. airline's "rendezvous lounges" became "rooms for lovemaking" in Brazil.[29] Are there several languages and dialects in use by members of the target segment? What are the implications of using each language?
2. *Culture*—What meanings are associated with sounds? Colors? White is associated with purity in Europe and in Asia with death. Green is the symbol of the jungle in Malaysia and would not be appropriate for certain health products. Exxon's "Put a Tiger in Your Tank" was successful in many countries but less so in Thailand where the tiger connotes danger, not power.[30]
3. *Regulations*—What restrictions are there regarding claims? In many countries comparative ads are illegal. In France, many superlatives cannot be used on television. What restrictions are there on images? In many U.S. states, Santa Claus cannot appear with distilled spirits. How is promotion governed?
4. *Production resources*—What are the skill levels of local production facilities?

Media factors include:

1. *Coverage*—What media are available? Traditional or nontraditional? What are their audiences? For broadcast media, when are advertisements shown?
2. *Control*—Are the times and space given to our advertisements under our control? In several countries, media companies decide when the advertisement will run.
3. *Regulations*—Are there restrictions on advertising certain products or services? In the European community, pharmaceuticals cannot be advertised to the general public.
4. *Media habits*—Where do customers in the target segment seek information? To what media are they exposed?

Expenditure factors include:

1. *Costs*—What are the rates charged by the various media?
2. *Tax considerations*—Do value added or other taxes affect the nature of the advertising?
3. *Objectives*—Are the company's marketing and financial objectives realistic and cost-effective?

Two key areas of advertising strategy are control and execution. Control relates to the central themes of the campaign, execution to the specific creative and media choices. These areas may be organized in various ways:

Control	*Execution*
Central	Central
Central	Local
Local	Local

The advantages of central control and execution concern cost and the benefits of a uniform global image, whereas the advantages of local execution are found in closer fits with the country markets. There are sufficient differences in communications across most countries that even in the central/central form of organization there ought to be input from the local country representative or local advertising agency. A mixture of central and local organization typifies many companies.

For some companies, the issues of central versus local control and execution are resolved by developing a "pattern" campaign. Such a campaign includes a set of advertisements that local country managers can use, not use, or modify as they wish. There are several global advertising agencies that can provide services in many countries. However, one may wish to select a local agency in a specific country. Selection criteria might include services performed in the areas of creative execution, media, research, promotion, and merchandising. In addition, one may prefer an agency that can relate local communications to a global communications strategy.

In conclusion, the examples we have shown here demonstrate that a successful globalization requires time, management commitment, cultural sensitivity, and a willingness to consider each international opportunity on a case-by-case basis. To win the global battle for market share and brand dominance, companies will have to become increasingly innovative and flexible in formulating their market selection and entry strategies. To implement these strategies at the marketing mix level, managers will need to track worldwide commonalities while being sensitive to persistent local differences. To do both well remains the challenge of global marketing.

APPENDIX: SOURCES OF INTERNATIONAL MARKETING DATA

Selected Organizations Monitoring International Trade

Agency for International Development
Office of Business Relations
Washington, DC 20523

Asian Development Bank
2330 Roxas Boulevard
Pasay City, Philippines

Business International Corp.
One Dag Hammarskjold Plaza
New York, NY 10017

Commission of the European Communities
    to the United States
2100 M Street NW, Suite 707
Washington, DC 20037

Conference Board Inc.
845 Third Avenue
New York, NY 10022

The Economist
25 St. James Street
London, SW1A 1HG, England

European Community Information Service
200 rue de la Loi
1049, Brussels, Belgium

Export-Import Bank of the United States
811 Vermont Avenue NW
Washington, DC 20571

Inter-American Development Bank
1300 New York Avenue NW
Washington, DC 20577

International Bank for Reconstruction &
Development (World Bank)
1818 H Street NW
Washington, DC 20433

International Monetary Fund
700 19th Street NW
Washington, DC 20431

United Nations
Conference on Trade and Development
Palais des Nations
211 Geneva 10, Switzerland

United Nations
Publications/Statistical Yearbook
1 United Nations Plaza
New York, NY 10017

U.S. Department of State
2201 C Street NW
Washington, DC 20520

U.S. Department of Commerce
Herbert C. Hoover Building
14th Street and Constitution Avenue NW
Washington, DC 20230

U.S. Department of Commerce
International Trade Commission
701 E Street NW
Washington, DC 20436

U.S. Small Business Administration
Imperial Building
1441 L Street NW
Washington, DC 20416

World Trade Centers Association
1 World Trade Center, Suite 7701
New York, NY 10048

Selected Sources of International Market Data (Public)

International Labor Office: *Yearbook of Labour Statistics*—data on employment, work hours, wages, labor relations, consumer prices, etc., for 180 countries.

International Monetary Fund: *Balance of Payments Yearbook*—detailed balance of payments data for over 110 countries.

OECD: *OECD Economic Surveys*—cover trends, prospects, and economic indi-

cators for twenty-four countries in the EC, Asia, and North America; other publications include surveys of industry sectors such as textiles, chemicals, and pulp/paper.

United Nations: *Yearbook of International Trade Statistics*—import and export statistics for 166 countries; also statistics by SITC: Standard International Trade Classification. *World Trade Annual*—detailed trade statistics by SITC code and by country. Other useful publications include *Demographic Yearbook* (population data), *Statistical Yearbook for Asia and the Pacific, Statistical Yearbook for Latin America*.

U.S. Bureau of the Census: *World Population*—worldwide demographic data.

U.S. Department of Commerce: *Foreign Trade Highlights*—annual reports on U.S. merchandise trade with major partners and regions. *U.S. Trade Performance and Outlook*—overview of international trade flows.

U.S. Department of Commerce, International Trade Administration: *Overseas Business Reports*—series of reports on one hundred countries, including industry trends, trade outlook, distribution channels, banks and credit, labor, taxation and investment regulation.

Selected Private Sources of International Information

Business International Corp.: Country Assessment Services—corporate service analyzing and measuring country risk, business opportunities, and operating conditions in seventy national markets. Forecasting Studies—series of medium-term (five years) forecasts for major countries, including political, economic, and social trends and key economic indicators.

Economist Intelligence Unit: Series of quarterly reviews covering economic and business conditions and prospects for 160 countries, as well as more specialized, industry-specific publications including *Marketing in Europe* and *Retail Business*.

Major Accounting Firms: Firms such as Ernst & Young, Price Waterhouse, and Coopers & Lybrand publish guides on doing business overseas, focusing on investment factors, trading and taxation practices.

Selected On-line Databases

LEXUS/NEXUS (Mead Data Central, Dayton, OH): Abstracting and full text capabilities for major worldwide business magazines and newspapers.

ABI/INFORM (University Microfilms, Ann Arbor, MI): Bibliographic citations and abstracts covering the most recent five to six years of over 800 U.S. and international business journals.

PTS PROMT (Predicasts Overview of Markets & Technologies): Abstracting index to worldwide articles in over thirty industries.

OECD: Computerized data bank for much of its labor, economic, and industry-specific statistical data.

NOTES

1. For a discussion of the global marketing decision sequence, see Jean-Pierre Jeannet and Hubert Hennessey, *Global Marketing Strategies*, Boston: Houghton-Mifflin, 1992.

2. Pharmaceutical Manufacturers Association, 1990.

3. Zachary Schiller, No more Mr. Nice Guy at P&G. *Business Week*, February 3, 1992, pp. 54–56.

4. Theodore Levitt, The globalization of markets. *Harvard Business Review*, May–June, 1983, pp. 92–102.

5. Kenichi Ohmae, The global logic of strategic alliances. *Harvard Business Review*, March–April 1989, pp. 143–154.

6. For a discussion of globalization drivers, see George Yip, Global strategy in a world

of nations? *Sloan Management Review*, Fall 1989, pp. 29–40, and with G. Coundoriotis, Diagnosing global strategy potential. *Planning Review*, January 1991, pp. 4–14.

7. Tony Riley, The collapse of the GATT Uruguay round: The start of a US-EC trade war? *Journal of European Business*, March 1991, pp. 5–10.

8. Harlan Cleveland, The end of geography? *International Business*, November 1991, pp. 77–83.

9. Angus Foster, Japanese appetite for Hong Kong. *Financial Times*, December 10, 1991.

10. Allen Morrison, David Ricks, and Kendall Roth, Globalization vs. regionalization: Which way for the multinational? *Organization Dynamics*, Winter 1991, pp. 17–29.

11. William Taylor, The logic of global business. *Harvard Business Review*, March–April 1991, pp. 91–105.

12. Kenichi Ohmae, Managing in a borderless world. *Harvard Business Review*, May–June 1989, p. 155.

13. For a more extensive discussion of entry strategies, see Franklin Root, *Entry Strategies for International Markets*. Lexington, MA: DC Heath, 1987.

14. Gail Schares and John Templeton, Think small. The export lessons to be learned from Germany's midsize companies. *Business Week*, Nov. 4, 1991, pp. 58–65.

15. Heather Ogilvie, Welcome to McEurope: An interview with Tom Allin, president of McDonald's Development Company. *Journal of European Business*, July/August 1991, pp. 5–12.

16. David Lei and John W. Slocum, Global strategic alliances: Payoffs and pitfalls. *Organization Dynamics*, Winter 1991, p. 55.

17. Gary Hamel, Yves Doz, and C. K. Prahalad, Collaborate with your competitors and win. *Harvard Business Review*, Jan.–Feb. 1989, pp. 133–139.

18. Kevin Kelly, Learning from Japan. *Business Week*, Jan. 27, 1992, pp. 52–60.

19. James B. Treece, The partners. *Business Week*, Feb. 10, 1992, pp. 102–107.

20. Joel Bleeke and David Ernst, The way to win in cross-border alliances. *Harvard Business Review*, Nov.–Dec. 1991, pp. 127–135.

21. Ishmael P. Akaah, Strategy standardiza-

win in cross-border alliances. *Harvard Business Review*, Nov.–Dec. 1991, pp. 127–135.

21. Ishmael P. Akaah, Strategy standardization in international marketing. *Journal of Global Marketing*, Vol. 4, No. 2, 1991, pp. 39–62. Robert Grosse and Walter Zinn, Standardization in international marketing. *Journal of Global Marketing*, Vol. 4, No. 1, 1990, pp. 53–78. See also John A. Quelch and Edward J. Hobb, Customizing global marketing. *Harvard Business Review*, May–June, 1986, pp. 59–68.

22. Philip R. Cateora, *International Marketing*. Homewood, IL: Irwin, 1983, pp. 565–566.

23. Cateora, op. cit., p. 774.

24. Cleveland Horton, Mitsubishi maps solo success. *Advertising Age*, July 2, 1990, pp. 3, 33.

25. Vern Terpstra, *International Marketing*. New York: CBS College Publishing, 1983.

26. Cateora, op. cit., p. 559.

27. Rosemarie Boyle, McDonald's gives Soviets something worth waiting for. *Advertising Age*, March 19, 1990, p. 61.

28. F. V. Cespedes, E. R. Corey, and V. K. Rangan, Gray markets: Causes and cures. *Harvard Business Review*, July–August, 1988, pp. 75–82.

29. Edward Cundiff and Marye Tharp

LOOKING AT THE GLOBAL MARKETPLACE

Michele Forzley, Managing Director, Forzley and Company

Events of the 1980s and technological advances such as faxes, satellite communications, and high-speed travel broke down many of the barriers that separated nations and their citizens. Political changes were accompanied by trends adopting a free market approach to commercial activities undertaken by both large state organizations and newly established small businesses that began to participate in the global arena. All businesses have been confronted with foreign participants in local markets and a growing awareness that the world is the marketplace. With this awareness, questions begin on how to do international trade.

Almost all trade boils down to a transaction between two parties. When a transaction has one foot in the United States and the other in Paris, that is international trade. It is really only a two-part transaction—just like when you do a business transaction with someone in another state in the United States or with someone across the street. The main difference is that a party to the transaction is a non-U.S. person. Still, a good or service is being bought or sold.

The words *international trade* are misleading. It sounds like international business is a whole lot more complicated than it really is. The fact is that it is really the same old stuff you have been doing domestically. Only now the product or service will leave the U.S. continent or come to the United States. You still have to locate and define a market or source, price, negotiate, deliver, and get paid. Each of the steps is essentially the same for businesses everywhere on the globe.

International trade is conducted in three ways: importing, exporting, and local operation. You could be an importer, meaning you could bring products, raw materials, or partially completed goods to the United States. An importer buys for his or her own consumption or resale. An exporter sells products, raw materials, partially completed goods, or services to someone in another country. You can also set up a business operation in another country. This can be done through an agent, distributor, joint venture, or local operation that could be a branch or representative office, subsidiary, or manufacturing facility. When you think of it, this is how you do business domestically. You buy or you sell finished, partially completed, or raw goods; you set up an office or plant in another city or state, or hire an agent or distributor. I hope to clarify throughout this chapter the differences you must address when doing business internationally The rest you know because it is the same old stuff.

MOTIVES FOR ENTERING INTERNATIONAL MARKETS

You do business in other countries for the same reason you do it here: to make money. The very definition of business requires that the activity be intended to generate a profit. Companies begin to look internationally for several reasons. For exporters, the first reason is to expand the market for their product. You may have satisfied the market in the United States, or have learned there are other markets open to your products in other countries, or perhaps there is less or no competition for your product elsewhere. It may also be that a product has become obsolete or less in vogue here, but that is not the case elsewhere. The first question in analyzing a foreign market is whether someone wants your product.

For the import side, you might be an agent, trader, or distributor for a product that is unavailable here. Or you might buy a product, raw material, or component cheaper from another country, thus increasing your bottom line. Or you may be a manufacturer and you have decided that you cannot produce your product any longer at a sufficiently low price. You can take advantage of opportunity in another country to buy or produce at a lower price. Take a look at the world and investigate how doing business internationally may enhance your own business.

There are other reasons for doing business internationally. The first is that the world market is increasingly interdependent. It used to be that when people were buying a product, they would go within their own country borders to find it. Now, countries and geographic regions are specializing in certain kinds of products and services. Also, one can look at suppliers from several countries to get the best product at the best price. Look at the European community after 1992 as unification progresses. It is very likely we will see that certain products and services come only from certain places. It may be that Milan is the capital of fashion photography. It may be that real estate is only operated out of London or steel out of Korea. The markets are definitely changing. U.S. businesses will change with the world market and find out where to fit in.

The U.S. market used to be sufficient to keep American business busy and profitable. Also, American businesses only had to compete with other domestic companies. Today, enormous markets exist in Europe and to the east; 700 million people live from the border of France to the east coast of Siberia alone. Half of the Earth's population lives in the Pacific Rim. The United States is not the only consuming market. Foreign companies are also rapidly entering the U.S. market as it is seen as large and hungry.

APPROACHING THE INTERNATIONAL MARKET

Your perspective as a business will direct which approach to international trade you take. A product manufacturer looks at whether there is a market in any other country for its products. A manufacturer can also buy parts or materials cheaper elsewhere. A retail-oriented company looks at the U.S. market and others to determine if products can be sourced more cheaply or if they are not available and should be because someone wants them. Service companies do the same, also offering American know-how in great demand. Each company modifies its approach to the making of its product; its marketing, packaging, and pricing must be suitable to the market. McDonald's still sells hamburgers in Moscow and Singapore. Estee Lauder sells lipstick in Paris and Sydney.

The ways of conducting business are the same all over the world. Market entry strategies are:

1. *Direct buying or selling involving your company transacting business from home*—This is done all the time. Your salespeople may occasionally travel to foreign sites to visit customers or suppliers, but most sales are completed via the phone, fax, and mail. Customers or suppliers are identified through various research sources. One can include selling through an export market company or export trading company as direct selling.

2. *Indirect selling through an agent or distributor*—A foreign agent is a local person who acts in the capacity to represent you—a representative who knows the territory, is conversant in the foreign language, and knows the market for your product. You can interview local agents and obtain information about who they are from the local chamber of commerce or similar organizations.

Local governments or your native country's government often have names of people on file who can act as an agent. You have a job to offer. You might talk to other people in your business who have used local agents in the past and get recommendations. Just as you would hire someone in the United States or Canada through these methods, you would do the same in another country. There are employment agencies and executive search firms in foreign countries, especially in the more industrialized countries.

You use a similar method for finding local distributors, although the relationship between you and the local distributor is different than that between you and an agent. An agent is like a salesperson who receives a commission. A distributor buys a product from you and maintains an inventory. A distributor is a separate business. For success the relationship should include after-sales service and some other efforts from the distributor. Using local distributors is an excellent way to do business overseas unless you have unlimited time and an unlimited bank account with which to go on selling missions to other countries.

How do you find out if a potential agent or distributor is honest, reliable, and competent? Many businesses have had experience in analyzing the credit of a customer, and the same technique is used to assess your candidate. Bank references are checked. Are customers and clients satisfied? What does the local government or U.S. Embassy know of this person? No amount of research can protect you from a thief. But take the time to investigate candidates as much as possible.

3. *Local presence*—Another way of doing business internationally is to set up a local presence. All forms of local operations have special legal, tax, and accounting issues to address, since once on the ground, you are clearly subject to local laws. Local manufacturing may make sense if it results in a cost of goods sold that is less than doing business at home. This method needs the same planning and analysis as relocating a domestic operation. The use of a representative office is sometimes necessary to tackle a new market and to service it.

4. *Technology transfer*—Another way of doing business internationally is to license your technology. This method allows another to use your process, method, or technology in another business venture, and you get a fee for it, known as a royalty. Many joint ventures, or combinations of two different businesses, use this concept of technology transfer in order to allow a local company to make a product locally. Coca-Cola is a well-known example of an American product made all over the world by local companies. It is la-

beled and bottled by local companies and sold into the local markets.

5. *Direct investment in a foreign country by setting up a manufacturing facility, office, or some other permanent presence*—This strategy is the most involved and committed level of international business. Such a method of operation subjects the business to many levels of local laws, rules, and regulations, a full discussion of which is beyond the scope of this chapter.

6. *Government business*—Last but not least, you can bid on contracts to do work for foreign governments. All governments hire private enterprises to supply goods and services. You are not restricted from doing business with most foreign governments.

OVERSEAS DISTRIBUTION, LICENSING, AND TECHNOLOGY TRANSFER

Peter B. Fitzpatrick, Executive Vice-President, Center for Innovative Technology

HOW NOT TO DO IT

Joe Jones was the manager of domestic and international civilian sales for Bestcode Software Company located outside of Washington, DC. Bestcode produces an integration software package plus a number of other software tools and two or three pieces of hardware that significantly enhance the capabilities of computer systems that use them.

Bestcode got its start designing systems for the federal government, particularly the Department of Defense, but has since moved on to a civilian market division. At the last strategic planning retreat it was decided that Bestcode should enter the international marketplace and Joe was assigned the duty of developing that market as it seemed to be a natural addition to his domestic operations. His objectives, to be completed in the course of the year, included locating and contracting with a distributor in Europe and the commencement of sales into that market. Due to domestic activity, Joe neglected to develop this marketplace, and forty-five days before his year-end review with the president of the company, he began to address the problem. In a move of desperation he hopped on a plane to catch the last day of a software conference sponsored by a French technology consortium held in

Paris. At the conference Joe met Stan Prescow-itz, an American expatriate who had been living in Paris for the last eight years. After the conference Stan and Joe went to the Crazy Horse Saloon, had some drinks, and Joe asked Stan to distribute his products in Europe. Stan agreed, they shook hands, and Joe returned home knowing he would be able to report that he had located a European distributor and would be sending him the product immediately.

This is, of course, the wrong way to enter any market, but for Americans it is an experience that is all too common. One consultant, Radley Resources, Inc., has identified the twelve most common mistakes in going abroad:

1. Failure to develop a market plan.
2. Insufficient commitment by top management to foreign market development.
3. Insufficient care in selecting distributors.
4. Indiscriminate order chasing worldwide.
5. Neglecting international markets during U.S. boom cycles.
6. Failure to consider all distributors equally.
7. Using the same techniques everywhere.
8. Unwillingness to modify product.
9. Failure to provide local language literature.
10. Failure to consider using an export management company.
11. Failure to consider joint venturing or licensing.
12. Failure to provide service with the product.

FACTORS AFFECTING LICENSING

In deciding to license or otherwise distribute technology abroad, a group of critical questions should be answered to your satisfaction:

1. What are the U.S. laws and regulations that will affect your decision?

2. What are the laws and regulations of the country or regional organization (such as the EC) that will affect your ability to succeed?
3. What are the customs of the marketplace that will affect your ability to distribute or license the technology in question?

Researching the Foreign Market

Any market entry strategy, whether seeking the establishment of a licensing arrangement or a distributorship, should be based on an understanding of the foreign market. Some considerations are:

1. *Cultural research and market research*—No decision should be made as to the appropriate form for entering a foreign market without first preparing a market entry strategy that takes into consideration how best to market your product. For instance, French companies generally prefer having software products tailored to their specific needs, while German companies often will change their procedures to conform to the requirements of a software product. Many sources of information are available in doing this preliminary work.

2. *Research on potential partners*—It is particularly important to determine the reputation of any specific licensee or agent whom you may be considering in the market in question. The image of your product will be dependent to some extent on the quality of the reputation of your licensee or distributor.

3. *Applicable U.S. and foreign laws*—It is important early on to understand if you will have a legal problem with your marketing efforts and whether the local law will be supportive of your ability to protect your intellectual property. For American companies going abroad, the protection of their intellectual property while allowing for the transfer of the technology in question is a critical issue. Often the technology is the heart of what differentiates the quality of the American product from its competitors. If the intellectual property is not appropriately protected, the company can run the risk of losing its marketing edge.

Researching the U.S. Laws

In the case of U.S. laws, it is critical to ensure that you do not run afoul of the following:

1. *Export controls* — In spite of the end of the Cold War, the United States continues to debate the issue of whether it wants to promote national security by protecting critical technologies or national competitiveness by allowing U.S. products containing those technologies to be sold abroad. In all likelihood this issue will continue to be debated in the halls of Washington. Still, it is critical to determine at an early stage whether you will have a problem getting an export license for your technology. An early check with the Department of Commerce on this issue can save heartaches later.

2. *Foreign Corrupt Practices Act* — The FCPA is triggered whenever an improper payment is made to a foreign official to assist an American company in obtaining or retaining business. U.S. companies will be held responsible for illegal payments when they knew or had reason to know of the improper payments.

3. *Antiboycott regulations*—U.S. law prohibits compliance with Arab boycotts of Israel through two sets of laws, one set implemented by the Department of Commerce and the other by the Department of the Treasury under the Internal Revenue Code. These regulations are not straightforward and an unknowing breach of them can occur. If you are dealing in the Middle East, it is worth talking to the Antiboycott Compliance Office of the Department of Commerce to determine the current enforcement intentions and likely pitfalls in this area.

4. *Antitrust laws.* Exclusive dealerships often raise antitrust questions and should be reviewed with these laws in mind. Tying contracts in which a foreign dealer is required to purchase not only the goods he or she wants but additional goods that the supplier wishes to sell may cause problems. In addition, restrictions placed on foreign dealer resales back to the United States may run afoul of antitrust laws. It is worth noting that compliance with U.S. antitrust laws may not be sufficient in foreign markets such as the European community, which has its own antitrust system using a different set of standards.

Role of Agents, Distributors, and Licensees

In the United States the law draws distinctions between agents and distributors as well as licensees. In going abroad, many of these same concepts will hold but the mix of rights and obligations may be different. For example, distributors in the United States are generally independent, being able to buy and sell for their own account and bearing the risk of loss associated with the product. Agents are generally less independent, being paid a salary or commission based on their sales as opposed to a markup of the goods to be sold. In the case of agents, economic risk is generally born by the suppliers and the goods are shipped directly from the suppliers to the customers. Distributors do not have the power to bind their suppliers and usually hold title to the goods being distributed, warehousing them at their own cost. Agents often have apparent or expressed authority to bind the suppliers. Sometimes the foreign dealer concepts do not follow U.S. practices.

Generally, licensees will manufacture the products locally and pay royalties to the suppliers. Often, the suppliers will require the licensees to purchase components from them as well.

Foreign Legislation Affecting Agents and Distributors

Three types of foreign legislation generally affect agent and distributorship agreements: (1) legislation enacted to protect dealers, (2) legislation enacted to restrict dealers, and (3) labor laws of the jurisdiction in which the dealer operates.

It is important to have a feel for how these laws will affect your operations before establishing a relationship in a foreign country. Many jurisdictions, particularly in Latin America, have legislation designed to protect local agents, distributors, and licensees. The effect of this legislation is to limit the ability of foreign corporations to terminate or alter relationships with dealers, often regardless of the terms of any written or oral dealership agreement, unless substantial compensation is paid to the foreign dealer. Often the measure of compensation required is based on lost future profits. The calculation may include such things as the average annual profits of the dealer, goodwill created by the dealer, capital expenditures made by the dealer to develop a market for the supplier's goods, labor and warehousing costs incurred by the dealer, and repurchase costs of goods held in the dealer's inventory. For an example of the scope of this problem, see Chapter 14, Title 10, Puerto Rican Statutes, Section 278, "Dealers' Contracts."

The best protection against the unreasonable enforcement of such statutes is to have a clear definition of the accomplishments to be achieved by the dealer and make these standards just cause for termination. Some jurisdictions seek to restrict the activities of dealers in their country, in particular, the Middle East. Some nations, such as Algeria, prohibit the use of dealers completely. Others, such as Saudi Arabia, prohibit the use of foreign nationals as dealers and require a local national as a dealer. In addition, many jurisdictions require dealer registration.

The labor laws of the dealer's country may substantially affect any severance pay a supplier would have to pay to that dealer. Often the foreign equivalent of social security and disability compensation may be required to be paid at the time of termination. The obligation to make these payments would arise by determining that the relationship between the supplier and the dealer is that of an employer and an employee. For this reason, the independence of the dealer is of significant importance in drafting any dealer agreement.

PROTECTION OF TECHNOLOGY TRANSFERRED AND INTELLECTUAL PROPERTY

Protection of intellectual property is at the heart of retaining a technology-driven market leadership position. In some cases, know-how and trade secrets can also receive certain minimum levels of protection. The issues are:

1. *Patents and trade secrets* — The usual method of protecting know-how and trade secrets abroad is through a confidentiality provision in the contract with your distributor or licensee. Most technology products are patented and it is critical in this context to understand the difference between U.S. patent laws and foreign laws. The U.S. patent system awards patents on a first-to-invent basis. Foreign laws generally award patents to the party who is first to file a patent application. It is important to determine through your lawyer the extent to which your patent rights have been protected both domestically and in the foreign jurisdiction.

2. *Software* — Software is sometimes patented and sometimes copyrighted. In many areas of the world, it is extremely difficult to protect software and a number of organizations have grown up in the United States to try to police software protection rules worldwide. An example is the Business Software Alliance in Washington, DC. In other jurisdictions, a different set of issues must be addressed. For example, the European community is in the process of harmonizing standards for all sorts of products, the effect of which may be to exclude or to hinder the entry of U.S. products into the market. In the case of software, a U.S. company would generally protect itself by copyrighting its source code in accordance with the filing requirements of the U.S. Copyright Office. As the United States has signed the Paris Act (1971) of the Berne Convention for the protection of literary and artistic work, general protection is afforded within the European countries to the same extent as country nationals if registration occurs within twelve months. The United States is also a member of the Universal Copyright Convention (Paris Act of 1971). While filing in the United States will give you the right to protection within the European market, you must register under the national laws of the various countries in which you wish to sell your product to receive protection.

The European community has issued a directive on software protection that raises two troubling questions for software producers concerning the protection of interfaces between computer programs and the encouragement of reverse engineering of software technology. The directive stipulates that the portion of a software product that allows it to communicate with other software and hardware products, and that allows other hardware and software products to communicate with it, would not be protected by copyright. The objective of this ruling is to allow for open access to interfaces to stimulate a stronger European software community. It is intended also that this directive will promote the development of additional peripheral products in the hardware and software marketplace. On the other hand, one effect of this directive is that market leaders, who predominantly tend to be American companies, may lose market share.

Reverse engineering presents a more troublesome issue for American software developers. Reverse engineering is a process in which a software developer is allowed to go into the source code of the software to determine how the software was designed. To the extent that there is unprotected creativity reflected in the source code, the developer may capture that creativity and incorporate it into his or her own products. Software designers naturally do not like to see the capture of this creative element of their software as it could significantly decrease the market life of a product.

3. *Trademarks, trade names, and service marks* — Trademarks, trade names, and service marks have tremendous value in the marketplace. They must be registered on a country by country basis. Registration with the U.S. Trademark Office provides ten years of protection renewable in ten-year increments within the United States. In order to protect trademarks, they must be defended, and therefore it is important that any foreign dealer having a right to use a mark should be required to acknowledge that the supplier has all rights, title, and interest in the trademark. In addition, it is important to restrict the use made by the foreign dealer of the trademark and trade name to uses appropriate to the objective of his distribution or license agreement and to obtain from the foreign dealer a representation that he will report any infringement or illegal use of a mark or name to the supplier and assist in obtaining protection in the dealer's territory.

Obtaining these protections is particularly important as the ownership of a trademark is determined by the control and protection which that owner gives to the mark. If a foreign dealer is allowed to use a trademark randomly and fails to seek to protect it, then the rights of ownership of the supplier in the mark may be weakened.

A related issue is the need to control the use of trademarks and trade names in any advertising or promotional materials used by the licensee or distributor. As pointed out above, copyrights, trademarks, trade names, and patents should all be registered in the country, if possible. The supplier should make sure that this is done in the supplier's name and not in the name of the foreign dealer or some other party, and that upon termination of any dealer or licensing agreement, no right will be held by any foreign party with respect to intellectual property.

OTHER CONSIDERATIONS

A host of other considerations should be taken into account, including:

1. It is wiser to contract with corporations or similar legal entities rather than individuals in order to avoid the application of local labor laws.
2. Once a plan for market entry has been identified, a tax analysis should be made of the components of the plan to determine whether, in fact, the company will make money through this arrangement.
3. If the relationship is that of a distributor or agent rather than a licensee, a short-duration contract (one or two years) is best. It can then be reviewed at the end of this period to determine whether the goals have been achieved. Termination should be for just cause focusing primarily on the commercial viability of the relationship as defined by the business and marketing plans.
4. You must define the territory for your distributor or licensee, although such restrictions will need to comply with

the antitrust laws of both the United States and the European community.

5. Arbitration is often preferable to litigation, particularly in the international arena.

6. To the extent possible, payment should be in hard currencies in jurisdictions where currencies are not blocked. The Foreign Corrupt Practice Act issues should be reviewed in the context of the flow of funds.

7. If inventory-level maintenance, facilities, or specific personnel are necessary, they need to be stipulated in the agreement.

8. The foreign party should agree not to disclose any confidential information to third parties and to return any proprietary information at the end of the relationship.

9. Force majeure provisions generally protect both parties from the claim of failure to perform due to an act of God or other unspecified, uncontrollable force. You must determine whether you will accept labor troubles or strikes as acceptable force majeure under your contract.

INFORMATION SOURCES

Additional information on overseas distribution, licensing, and technology transfer is available from a number of sources, including:

1. Accountants
2. Banks—U.S. and foreign
3. *Business International*
4. Chambers of commerce—Local, U.S., and foreign
5. Consultants
6. Competitors
7. Freight forwarders
8. Interviews
9. State export departments
10. Suppliers
11. Surveys
12. Trade associations
13. Trade publications

14. U.S. government sources, such as the departments of commerce and state, embassies, and commercial attachés.

CHECKLISTS

Some Management Considerations in Going Abroad

1. What are the company's objectives in going abroad?
2. Is top management committed to the effort?
3. What return on investment is management expecting and on what time schedule?
4. Does the company have prior international experience?
5. What products appear to have the best markets?
6. Are domestic clients shipping the company's product abroad?
7. Who are the main product competitors?
8. What in-house international expertise exists?
9. To whom will the international operation report?
10. How much senior management time is allocated to the effort?
11. Who will follow through on the planning?
12. How will the international effort affect production capacity?
13. What changes in production procedures or end product would be necessary?
14. What capital commitments are necessary to enter the markets under consideration?
15. What tax effects will result from this international activity?
16. What additional overhead or production costs will result from the international effort?
17. What are the competing opportunities for the company other than going international?

Some Considerations in Choosing a Foreign Representative

1. What is the representative's reputation in the marketplace?

2. Who are the principals in the organization?
3. What percentage of its total business would you represent?
4. What would be required for the representative to accommodate your market entry needs?
5. How big a sales force does she have and what are her expansion plans?
6. What is her current market area or territory? Are her areas of coverage consistent with your market needs?
7. How many and what products does she currently market? Are they complementary or in competition with your product line?
8. What conflict of interests exist?
9. Will she change her product mix to accommodate your product line?
10. What volume of sales is required for you to be interested and the sales representative to be interested in the relationship?
11. What warehousing facilities, methods of inventorying, and goods protection/insurance does he have?
12. What communication equipment (fax, telephone, telex, computers) does he have and are they compatible with yours?
13. How is his sales staff trained, managed, motivated, and compensated?
14. Who and how large are his key accounts and are they compatible with your marketing needs?
15. Can the representative help you develop your market study?
16. How does the representative promote products and how does he intend to promote yours?
17. Can he provide translation services as required?

Foreign Representative Agreement Checklist

Prenegotiation Preparation
1. Cultural and market research
2. Survey of applicable U.S. and foreign laws
3. Reputation of proposed representative

Contract Provisions
1. Type of relationship
   a. Distributorship/agent/licensee/ other
   b. Offer and acceptance
   c. Corporation versus individual
2. Duration of the agreement
3. Territory
4. Exclusivity
5. Duties of representative
   a. Facilities and personnel
   b. Inventory
   c. Best efforts representations
   d. FCPA representations
   e. Advertising, promotion, and use of trademarks
   f. Sales quotas
   g. Quality control issues
   h. Reporting requirements
6. Terms and conditions of sale
   a. Price
   b. Credit
   c. Passage of title
   d. Currency
   e. Defective goods
   f. Insurance and shipment terms
   g. Taxes
7. Payment and compensation
   a. Currency
   b. Location
   c. Float considerations
8. Termination
   a. Notice
   b. Automatic termination for "just cause"
   c. Curable defaults
9. Arbitration and governing law
   a. Rules: Covered by American Arbitration Association, Inter-State Commerce Commission, or other body
   b. Location and language
   c. Governing law
   d. Fees/currency
10. Confidentiality
11. Intellectual property protection provision
12. Miscellaneous provisions
    a. Force majeure
    b. Severability
    c. Assignment
    d. Waiver
    e. Entire agreement

The management of international partnerships or licensing and technology agreements requires constant vigilance and aggressive steps around the world. The process partly involves taking advantage of legal protections available in different nations and partly the careful legal structuring of agreements with foreign partners and distributors. Attending to the information produced in response to the preceding checklists can help reduce the worst problems or even abuses in such relationships.

INTERNATIONAL SOURCING AND STRATEGIC ALLIANCES

Alan Zimmerman, President, Radley Resources, Inc.

"You can do everything yourself—with enough time, money, and luck. But all three are in short supply. Globalization mandates alliances, makes them absolutely essential to strategy" (Kenichi Ohmae, The global logic of strategic alliances, *Harvard Business Review,* March–April, 1989).

Globalism is a fact of life for most businesses today. If a firm is not competing on a global basis now, it certainly will be in the near future. With freer access to markets around the world, new competitors are arriving in domestic markets while new opportunities are opening in foreign markets. To develop and serve markets throughout the world, companies must examine new strategic approaches.

There is no formula for the correct organization of a business enterprise. Structures both formal and informal are evolving as quickly as technology makes them possible.

Most enlightened firms seek ways to improve their positions through strategic alliances. These alliances include arrangements such as majority and minority joint ventures, franchising, acquisitions, licensing, intellectual property arrangements, contract manufacturing, and marketing agreements. Global sourcing and shared manufacturing are just two examples of the broadest view of strategic alliances.

To take the fullest advantage of these opportunities, the traditional management attitude of all-out competition must be modified. Management must realize that in many instances, cooperation is now preferable to competition.

One example of a firm that has adapted very well to the needs of the global marketplace is Benetton. This firm has chosen strategic alliances of various kinds for tasks where it does not bring significant added value, but has held to itself those areas that are unique to Benetton or in which the company can make a major impact on results. Examples are product design and purchasing. Benetton has been described as "neither integrated nor deintegrated. It looks like Swiss cheese: a large company full of holes. The holes are exactly in those activities of the value chain where external costs . . . are lower than internal costs" (Jarillo and Stevenson, *Long Range Planning*, February 1991).

A strategic alliance can be any arrangement between one firm and one or several others to achieve specific goals. The term *strategic* is critical here. Combinations of this nature between firms are usually difficult to form and require a heavy investment of time and funds by top management. Therefore, these arrangements usually look to a long-term purpose rather than a short-term gain.

EVALUATING STRATEGIC ALLIANCES

As managers look at global operations, they must decide whether they can accomplish all objectives using internal resources. Since more and more firms are facing global competition and opportunities, it is often impossible for one company to finance all the effort required to be successful on a worldwide basis. Yet not moving quickly to take advantage of these opportunities can leave a firm at a severe competitive disadvantage. To solve this dilemma, many firms are rethinking their approaches and entering into some form of strategic alliance. The measure of success for such an arrangement is that it creates efficiencies that the firm cannot achieve on its own. That is, the alliance results in lower costs in logistics, operations, marketing, or service areas.

Management must look at all the aspects of the value chain to decide in which areas it may achieve better results through cooperation. Frequently, a company may find itself too big to perform certain tasks efficiently and too small to perform others while achieving the global cost advantages available. This is often true of large, multinational corporations, especially as they try to operate local retail outlets.

Cooperation has allowed a number of smaller firms to grow rapidly without requiring the massive investment that more traditional approaches might have required. This may mean a lowered cost of acquiring a product because of lower labor or material costs. It may also relate to savings due to purchasing efficiencies or a location closer to a source of supply. Externally to operations, cooperation can lower costs as a result of being closer to the customer, establishing new distribution channels, developing an export base, overcoming tariff or nontariff export barriers, or responding to the preference of local customers for customized products.

Other reasons for entering into strategic alliances may be to access new technology, to diffuse new technology through a market, or just to take advantage of the marketing knowledge of a local partner. Strategic alliances of any form require that management think in terms of cooperation rather than competition. Before moving ahead with any strategic alliance it must be clear that the established cooperation can be sustained over a long time period.

As a company reviews the possibilities of moving into cooperative arrangements, including global sourcing, joint ventures, or any of the others previously mentioned, the firm must look not only at the obvious direct costs that may be saved by moving to these arrangements but also at transaction costs. These include the cost of finding partners, and also establishing, operating, and enforcing agreements with these partners. Also included are the even less tangible costs of establishing a potential competitor or losing critical technology.

For many years, IBM refused to establish any external sourcing just because it was concerned about losing critical technology to its source. Finally, IBM established a joint-venture manufacturing plant in Mexico for personal computers. In this case, IBM may have felt the cost savings outweighed the potential risks or that PC technology is widely disseminated and not as proprietary as mainframe technology.

As the cost of information transfer continues to decline, it will be easier to operate in close cooperation with partners. Those less tangible potential risks are difficult to assess in dollars and cents. Each management must develop its own method for measuring risks and costs versus benefits.

ENTERING A STRATEGIC ALLIANCE

The first and most critical step in developing a strategic alliance of any kind is an internal analysis of the company's strategic needs, advantages, and disadvantages. The firm must fully understand its own business, including where it provides special value added or has proprietary knowledge and where it does not. The uniqueness of this over the long and short term must be examined before the firm begins to look for strategic partners.

Once that analysis is completed, the firm must decide in which area a strategic partnership might be of most use. This is best accomplished by looking at the entire value chain of the company. Once this has been done, the firm can decide on one or two key areas to pursue. A word of caution here: Experience has shown that firms attempting to take on too many different, difficult international projects at the same time end up suboptimizing the results of each. It is important that management concentrate on one or two of the most important projects and attempt to bring these successfully to conclusion.

The second step is to identify potential partners and to analyze these firms thoroughly before approaching them. An analysis should include all public information as well as private information, which may be gathered through the U.S. Department of Commerce and other local sources such as bilateral chambers of commerce, and American law, accounting, or banking firms based in country. The keys to success of any strategic alliance include the following:

- Common objectives, clearly described.
- Clear understanding of management responsibilities.
- Experienced management to run the effort.
- Relative equality in contribution to know-how and/or resources.

- Steady infusion of new ideas, methods, products, leadership.
- Extrication clearly spelled out.
- CEOs involved initially and committed to success of the venture.
- Written agreements.

Once a potential partner is found, and after initial meetings, a memorandum of understanding should be written. After this is reviewed and agreed to within both firms, a joint plan should be developed by a team of individuals from each firm involved in the potential joint operation. This joint plan should not be a wordy document but should detail critical objectives, actions, and responsibilities for each of the partners. Thus, any problems can be ironed out at early stages.

In some cases, the divergence of objectives and even management styles will emerge at this point as insurmountable obstacles. The enterprise can then be stopped before costs get out of hand. It is important to establish a climate of trust over a period of time before the alliance becomes a reality. This establishment of trust and cooperation is far more important to overseas partners than has been the case in dealings between firms in the United States, and requires a shift in U.S. management thinking.

OPERATING A STRATEGIC ALLIANCE

Running a strategic alliance of any kind is more difficult than running one's own business. Management has to be able to live with conflicting objectives, unclear situations, and slower decision making. It is absolutely essential that top management endorse and maintain these strategic alliances. Since the cooperation can be difficult, it must continue to be encouraged.

Often strategic alliances require hands-off management, that is, the ability to allow individuals involved to develop on their own. Many strategic alliances have grown from simple supply or marketing agreements into more formal joint ventures and even acquisitions. This can happen when the partners are given the opportunity to mature.

It is not desirable for top management to assign the day-to-day operation of these alliances to less than qualified or unenthusiastic managers within the firm. These operating managers should also be made to realize that the success of the alliance is important to their careers and not an interference with career growth.

Gaining acceptance for a strategic alliance within the U.S.-based organization is as important as having the support of top management. Implementers in the organization must be fully informed about the proposed alliance before it goes forth and should have input in the decision making and the structure of any agreements. Staff as well as line employees should be involved and should see their involvement as a career-enhancing activity. It is important to match the personal styles of individuals in strategically aligned organizations and it may be more important to sacrifice technical expertise for complimentary personal styles.

There is still some reluctance on the part of U.S.-based companies to engage in either minority or fifty-fifty joint ventures. The need for control represented by majority ownership, while felt strongly by many managements, often yields no tangible benefits. Since local people are generally incountry and are closer to the wants and needs of the market, to suppliers, and to workers, a U.S.-based manager is often well advised to heed the advice of his local partner. This will be true whether the local partner holds a minority, fifty-fifty, or majority interest.

If a U.S.-based company finds itself in a minority or fifty-fifty joint venture, management should be careful to ensure that major decisions cannot be made by a simple majority of a board of directors. This can be assured by requiring "supermajority" votes for major issues such as capital expenditures, shifts in marketing strategy, acquiring or disposing of major assets, and hiring and firing of key executives.

GLOBAL SOURCING

Making products throughout the world is a special feature of the strategic alliance. The basic idea is to secure a product from the best source regardless of location. The difficulty is in determining what makes one source better than another. These sources may be joint ventures, contract or subcontract manufacturers, licensees, or owned subsidiaries.

Originally, multinational firms sourced overseas because they wished to take advantage of lower-cost labor. This reasoning has been expanded to include lower facility costs and tax incentives provided by many underdeveloped countries. In short, the basic reason for sourcing from a particular location could be boiled down to lower cost. Today, managements are looking at many other reasons that include locating closer to an attractive market, moving around trade barriers, locating closer to a source of supply to key raw materials, improving quality, and locating design closer to market to better satisfy market needs. Locating sources close to market can also speed up the design of new products.

While there are many advantages to foreign sourcing for a product, there are caveats. Many firms that rushed to source in the Far East found their product transportation, travel, and communications costs ate up a great deal of the projected cost savings. Distribution charges can easily add 10–15 percent to the cost of a product. The most important indirect cost is the increased cost of "inventory on the water." This is inventory required to make up for the long shipping time and can add as much as 10 percent to production costs. The ability to develop the proper inventory level for a product line sourced from various locations is critical to keeping this buffer cost under control and requires sophisticated analysis. While a plant in the People's Republic of China may be appealing, some firms have had the unpleasant experience of waiting while trucks backed up at key bridges on the mainland as customers fumed.

Other indirect costs include the need to redesign a product because proper equipment is not available in the sourcing location. Another cost is incurred if letters of credit are used, since cash will be required to be on deposit against a letter of credit issued. Sourcing overseas also can create the risks mentioned previously of creating a competitor through shared technology and know-how. Political and currency risks may also be lurking.

Many of the same rules generally apply to choosing a global sourcing partner as to developing strategic alliances. First, overseas sources should be used in parallel with domestic sources until management is satisfied that they will supply quality product in a timely way at the quality and price required.

Successful global sourcing requires that top management show ongoing interest. Partners should be chosen carefully after a thorough background check. An analysis of all costs of moving to a particular source should be completed before potential suppliers are selected. Once selected, these partners should be treated as business partners and nurtured.

The explosion in information handling capability allows for tighter control with fewer trips. While personal visits are critical, they can be limited by the design of a good information transfer system to help maintain deadlines and quality levels. Other risks can be managed through financial planning with a knowledgeable banker to damp out exchange rate fluctuations if a company is doing business in local currency. Political risks can be managed through carefully thought-out contingency plans.

A special case of global sourcing is shared manufacturing. This is especially relevant to smaller firms that wish to try out a new product without building an expensive facility. The idea is that manufacturing centers can be used for short production runs. Firms can lease time on individual machines or networks of machines to experiment with new designs or materials or products. As flexible manufacturing using computers becomes more widespread, the concept of shared manufacturing will become more relevant to more and more firms. One U.S. Department of Commerce executive expects that manufacturing will become a service function with each plant making hundreds of different products for different companies in different industries. Domestic shared manufacturing may be a lower-cost option than moving to an overseas source, especially when reviewing all indirect as well as direct costs.

A firm must be careful that the shared manufacturing approach will not limit its ability to grow quickly should a product become a success. In addition, shared manufacturing may not be acceptable when proprietary technology is being used. A carefully thought-out agreement would be necessary to protect any proprietary materials or techniques, but shared manufacturing offers the opportunity for the smaller firm to use very sophisticated machinery that it otherwise could not afford.

CONCLUSION

Strategic alliances allow firms to serve their customers throughout the world with products and services they might not otherwise be able to offer using their own resources. These alliances can take many forms, but all have several requirements in common.

To succeed, a firm must analyze its business and assess areas in which a strategic alliance will make a valuable contribution. This analysis should be performed before any potential partners are approached. Partners should be carefully checked before a direct approach is made. Once a potential partner is chosen, a joint plan should be developed to test compatibility of goals, organizational climates, and styles. Management should avoid taking on too many strategic alliance projects and should concentrate on a few to complete as thoroughly as possible.

Whatever the strategic alliance, it should be clear to both or all parties what the objectives of the alliance are and what contributions each partner will be making. Most Americans prefer a formal, written agreement, and while overseas partners will generally accept this, the success of the venture generally will depend on developing a climate of trust and cooperation. It is virtually impossible to plan for every contingency in a written document and the goodwill of the partners will be required to successfully resolve inevitable conflicts. A method for settlement of disputes should be built into the agreement as well. The use of an attorney well experienced in international alliances, joint ventures, and the like is strongly recommended once the early stages have been completed.

Global sourcing and shared manufacturing

are specific instances of strategic alliances. These require the same careful, up-front thought that any strategic alliance requires. A thorough analysis of all direct and indirect costs is required before decisions about sourcing can be made. Planning for handling various risks is critical.

As firms face more competition as well as more opportunity, globalism will be a requirement for any management. The ability to look at a business and determine where cooperation or competition will yield the best results will be the hallmark of sound management in the 1990s and beyond.

MANAGING RISKS IN INTERNATIONAL JOINT VENTURES

John J. Hampton, Principal, Princeton Consulting Group, Inc.

The decade of the 1980s was an active period of contractual and equity joint venture negotiations between private corporations and business entities in other countries. Many agreements were concluded and joint ventures were begun and are currently operating all over the world. Managing risks in these ventures is an important aspect of international operations.

Western partners in operating ventures are somewhat reluctant to openly discuss the difficulties they faced in negotiating and implementing their business operations in developing nations. Still, the picture is becoming clear. Many of the hopes and aspirations of the 1970s and 1980s were not realized. In some cases, frustration has turned to bitterness.

Prior to undertaking a joint venture, management should assess the business climate for such ventures. This is appropriate for two

reasons. First, the experience in developing nations has provided an insight into the economic and political exposure confronting joint ventures. The problem is the same—and different—for ventures in Eastern Europe, the former USSR, China, and Latin America. Second, this is a natural time for assessment. We have had decades of experience working with partners in other countries. What did we learn in the 1970s and 1980s?

In the 1990s, the politics of upheaval permeates every discussion on the future of business in many areas of the world. The uncertainties will drain personnel and financial resources from some countries and provide them to others. Western organizations will be reluctant partners in joint ventures in uncertain climates. In this context, a better understanding is needed of risks and potential returns. As a move in this direction, let us examine some major exposures facing joint-venture partners and match them with the lessons we have learned in the past.

OPERATING RISK

An operating risk is the chance that a joint venture will not be able to make money from its major area of business. As an example, can the organization manufacture goods to meet the standards of its markets or others? Can it control expenses so the goods will be sold at a profit? Unfortunately, operating problems plague many new joint ventures. The newspapers and trade magazines are filled with stories of shoddy goods and late deliveries from operations in various areas of the world.

Successful operating ventures take a number of effective steps to reduce delays, minimize faulty goods, and avoid cost overruns in the operation of a manufacturing or services enterprise. Two factors appear to be critical:

1. *Good local management*—Operational control of the venture should be in the hands of skilled and independent managers. The local managers may have to be trained by the Western partner in a home-country factory or elsewhere. When the joint venture begins, a core of skilled personnel should be available on site to train other workers. In most cases, the initial management should consist of local nationals and foreigners working together to solve problems. After a time, the expatriates can be phased out.

2. *Slow learning curve*—The timetable for opening a venture has to allow for delays and failure to meet planning dates. Then more time is needed for detailed training. Then still more delays occur during a testing period when bugs are eliminated and obstacles are overcome. Finally, the venture will be ready for actual operation and will be able to deliver goods or services on a timely basis.

If a future product or service operation is not handled by experienced managers who understand the local system, operating risks will be excessive. If the finances of the venture are not structured to recognize delays, the venture may dig itself into a financial hole. Both of these lessons are widespread from operating joint ventures in the 1980s.

INFRASTRUCTURE RISK

Most developing nations suffer from a lack of roads, vehicles, and railroad rolling stock to deliver their goods to markets. On a related note, communications are likely to be extremely difficult. Utilities, including water and electricity, frequently lack both availability and reliability needed for modern production.

Losses or expenses resulting from unreliable infrastructures endanger joint ventures. To minimize the impact of an inadequate infrastructure, the venture should be physically located in an urban, coastal, or otherwise accessible area where the host country has made progress with roads, communications, and services.

Rural locations may have ample inexpensive labor but possess few advantages sufficient to overcome the problems of poor roads and communications. At the same time, the selection of a site may conflict with the government's goal of developing rural areas or providing jobs in small towns and cities. Tax or other incentives may not be available for the best locations.

FINANCIAL RISK

A financial risk is the chance that a joint venture will not earn the hard currency needed to pay debts and provide a profit for the foreign partner. Prospects for earning a profit are complicated by the view of the time value of money in many developing countries. In negotiations, it may quickly become apparent that the local partner does not have an orientation toward investing money and earning a return on it. This is understandable in countries where high inflation erodes currency value and little cash is held. Such a situation can be a disaster for the Western partner, who is under pressure to earn a return on any invested capital.

The level of financial risk is increased by shortages of hard currency in many nations. Even when the country has favorable trade balances, hard currency can be scarce for joint ventures. For the foreseeable future, it is likely that many countries will continue to have woefully inadequate amounts of convertible currencies to meet their economic needs. The situation is aggravated by recessions in developed countries. And successful ventures are likely to experience difficulties obtaining government approval to repatriating profits to a parent abroad.

Two suggestions are proposed for reducing financial risk in joint ventures:

1. *Limit hard currency investments.* If the Western partner has restricted the amount of convertible currency in the venture, the impacts of delays and other time value of money obstacles are reduced. Stated simply, do not rush in with dollars, yen, or deutschmarks.
2. *Retain a portion of hard currencies in foreign banks.* If the venture does not earn foreign currencies, any discussion of retaining them is moot. However, ventures that earn hard currencies should seek agreements to allow them to deposit a portion of the funds in foreign banks until needed. This will, of course, be resisted by the local government. In spite of this resistance, it may be the price the country has to pay to attract capital. And it is fair to insist on a reasonable return for capital invested.

The likely question at this point is, What happens if the government will not permit either a limitation on hard currency investments or depositing hard currencies in foreign banks? For new ventures, at least, let us answer a question with a question. What happens if the Western partner will not proceed with the venture without some assurance of hard currency profits? Similarly, for existing ventures, what happens if the Western partner gives up on any chance to make profits and withdraws?

In the 1970s and 1980s, many investors were willing to accept likely losses of money in order to do business in certain markets. Now the situation has changed. Competition is strong for scarce resources. Nations can be found where the joint venture is likely to be profitable.

LEGAL RISK

Since the 1970s, many nations have made progress in developing laws and a legal system to deal with the enforcement of contracts and resolution of business disputes. Still, local systems often differ markedly from most developed nations. As a result, joint ventures should recognize a few simple truths:

1. *Local contracts may not be enforceable.* There must be some gentler way to make this statement. In fact, the situation represents more than an opinion of the author or a bias of managers of failed joint ventures. The inability to enforce contracts is deeply rooted in the heritage and culture of many nations. Disputes arise and must be solved by discussions between the parties, perhaps including the government. Disagreements are cultural, not legal, matters.

In spite of this obvious and apparent truth, Western investors often spend a great deal of time examining the local legal system and arbitration clauses in the contract. The documents are reviewed by Western lawyers in the home office or outside law firm. These actions are largely a waste of time in many nations where disputes are seldom resolved in court.

2. *Even if local contracts are enforceable in court, enforcement would end the agreement.* A contract between a Western and local partner is often compared to a Western marriage. Disputes arise but must be settled by the parties themselves. What marriage can continue on a reasonable basis after a serious dispute has been resolved in court? Once again, the Western negotiator must remember that disputes are often cultural, not legal.

3. *The law is part of a grander scheme.* Although some progress was made in the 1980s, the law continues to have little independent

standing in many countries. Hence, it cannot be relied on as a force that is separate from the goals of the local government. This is true in spite of great efforts of some governments to attract foreign capital and protect the rights of Western partners.

We can use China to illustrate the nature of the legal problem. In the 1980s, contracts were governed under Article 9 of the Foreign Economic Contract Law of the People's Republic of China. It stated, "Contracts that violate the law or the public interests of the People's Republic of China are invalid."

The difficulty arises with respect to the timing of the violation. As a result of hard currency shortages following martial law in 1989, a number of contracts were unilaterally declared invalid if they required the use of scarce foreign exchange. The availability of foreign currency was guaranteed at a time when it was in the public interest of China to make such a guarantee. When the public interest changed, so did the validity of the contract.

INSURABLE RISK

An insurable risk is the chance of loss from a source outside a venture's business operations or financial position. Examples are a fire that destroys a factory or a vessel that sinks in a storm. Developing nations have a relatively short history of taking steps to increase the safety practices of their manufacturing operations. A typical factory may have inadequate electrical wiring, cluttered work areas, and numerous fire and other hazards. Accidents are more common than in operations in industrialized nations. Insurable risks pose two important dangers to a joint venture:

1. *Business interruption*—A fire or similar loss can cause a firm to stop production. Even if the direct loss is covered by a policy with a local insurance company, the stoppage of production can be costly. Employees may have to be retained on salary and other expenses continued. Insurance may not be readily available on a cost-effective basis to compensate for business interruptions, particularly when those stoppages affect the hard currencies of the venture.

2. *Physical losses of equipment made outside the local country*—A portion of the machinery in most manufacturing ventures must be purchased using convertible currencies. If destroyed or damaged, they can be replaced using insurance money only if the currency of payment is convertible to other currencies. Depending on the availability of foreign exchange, it may not be possible to replace the equipment destroyed even when it is fully insured.

To reduce the adverse impacts of insurable risks, the joint venture should obtain a portion of its insurance coverage from a Western insurer. This may not be permitted under local laws designed to protect national insurers.

EXCHANGE-OF-PROFITS RISK

The most maddening aspect of any investment in a developing nation is the inability to exchange profits for hard currency to repatriate to the Western investors. How can a Western partner deal with this exposure? Three approaches are possible:

1. *Take it out in product.* If the venture produces goods of sufficient quality to sell in foreign markets, the profits can be incorporated into the pricing of the products. This is called transfer pricing. As an example, a product may cost $15, be sold to a marketing company for $25, and have a final selling price of $30. If it is purchased by an affiliate of the Western partner for $23 instead of $25, a $2 profit is created outside the joint venture. And it will be available in a hard currency.

2. *Negotiate a percentage of foreign exchange earned.* Accounting in developing countries, like accounting everywhere in the world, is subject to whim and manipulation. In a developing nation, it should never be the basis for calculating the profits that accrue to partners. Instead, the agreement should call for a percentage of hard currency earned. The contract might stipulate that the Western

partner may retain, say, 5 percent of gross foreign exchange earned.

3. *Take the profit before it is repatriated to the venture.* Agreements can specify that earned foreign exchange must be deposited in a foreign bank and payment of a percentage of it to the Western partner can be guaranteed by a letter of credit from a foreign bank.

Investors often have unrealistic expectations of opportunities available in developing nations. They overlook political uncertainty and economic difficulties. One way to bring a focus to the situation is to examine the various risks of joint ventures. In the global village, many opportunities exist to make a calculated gamble. Only ventures that deal with local reality are likely to be successful.

PROBLEMS AND OPPORTUNITIES IN COUNTERTRADE

Leo C. B. Welt, President, Welt International

NATURE OF AGREEMENTS

Buyback, compensation and offset, and other countertrade agreements provide for one party to accept a specific obligation to ease the other party's need to locate a hard currency that would otherwise be needed to complete a deal. It is an unconventional form of financing, sometimes called financial engineering, where the seller undertakes the responsibility for developing new or additional exports or services in the client's country, which would in turn generate additional foreign exchange. Such agreements usually span a number of years, and often require the transfer of technology, manufacturing licenses, training, quality control, and many other vital services in exchange for the buyer's commitment to purchase goods, turn-key factories, technology, or services covered by the contract.

On the whole, buyers' and sellers' wishes can be largely compatible in countertrade agreements. Both parties wish the transaction to be a success and expect the package to achieve larger objectives, such as:

- A foreign exchange savings.
- Jobs that will be created.
- Technology and production skills that will be transferred.
- Usually the satisfaction of being able to service and provide some spares for what has been purchased.
- The capital increment of any investment or asset input that can be squeezed from the transaction.

BENEFITS OF COUNTERTRADE

Financial engineering provides a number of benefits to sellers and selling nations, including:

- Make a sale.
- Maintain profit margins.
- Keep old customers or gain new ones.
- Achieve the economies of longer production runs.
- Maintain an ongoing customer-supplier relationship by reserving some servicing functions, and by providing parts, spares, and updating services for the equipment sold.
- Gain foreign exchange from the sale.

When military sales are involved, interested governments want to:

- Cement alliances.
- Rationalize future logistics requirements through standardization.
- Expand and shelter the mobilization base through creation of foreign auxiliary supply sources.

The latter considerations were important enough to gain reluctant U.S. support for such sales in the early post–World War II period, in spite of strong economic arguments against countertrade in some of its various manifestations.

FORMS OF COUNTERTRADE

Each countertrade transaction is unique and the product of extensive negotiations. However, countertrade can be divided into five forms of deals:

1. *Barter*—This is a straight goods-for-goods exchange. Cash is not required: There are no letters of credit, although participants may obtain parallel bank guarantees in the form of standby or performance bonds. These ensure that in the case of default the defaulting party compensates the other in hard currency. In some transactions, the deals run parallel and are linked by letters of understanding, such as exchanging 50,000 tons of black beans for 50,000 tons of soya.

2. *Counterpurchase or buyback*—In this case, the supplier contractually agrees to reciprocal purchases of goods or services from the buyer within a given period of time. The duration of the deal is generally short and the counterpurchase commitment is usually a percentage of the original sale. Counterpurchase or parallel deals really are two separate contracts. Each party pays the other in cash, guaranteed by letter of credit. The two transactions are linked by a protocol or letter of understanding.

3. *Compensation or offset*—Compensation involves the sale of technology, equipment, or a plant with a contractual commitment to purchase a certain quantity of the products produced as full or partial payment. The value of these deals is usually large and the time frame covers many years. The financial commitment to buy back goods is also typically high.

Compensation deals also consist of two separate contracts linked by a protocol agreement. In the contract to transfer technology or plant, special attention must be given to the buyer's right to transfer that technology, use of brand names, and the distribution of the resultant products.

4. *Evidence accounts*—These are commercial agreements, usually between manufacturers and foreign governments, that establish the basis for a bilateral balance of trade. Under this form, the company sells a preset volume of goods and services while buying local products to balance the account. Countertrade products normally can be bought from various suppliers within the country and they may be sold anywhere in the world.

5. *Bilateral clearing agreements*—These are trade agreements between two governments that establish the basis for trade balance. It is agreed that a set volume of goods and services will be exchanged within a given time frame. Accounts are kept in a single currency for effective monitoring. Any degree of imbalance is called the "swing" and brings a halt to two-way trading. At the end of the period

the account is brought back into balance by either a cash payment or "switch trading."

In addition, there are "cross-cutting" countertrade arrangements such as swaps and switch trading. Swaps refer to the exchange of products in different locations to save transportation costs. Switch trading allows any party to a bilateral trade agreement to transfer its imbalance, the "swing," to a third party.

Of course, many variables distinguish one form of countertrade from another. These include the duration of the transaction, the form of the settlement, the relation of the countertraded goods, legal arrangements, the value of deliveries, overall size of the deal, and the nature of the motive for the technology transfer. Individual transactions may fall into one category or another without necessarily embodying all of the characteristics of that particular form. One deal may incorporate features from several forms in the same arrangement.

ROLE OF COUNTERTRADE

The profitability of a countertrade deal depends on the trader's ability to dispose of the goods obtained. Ideally, these goods are used in existing production processes or marketed through already-established networks. This is not always the case.

Countertrade also can be used to upgrade manufacturing capabilities. By entering arrangements under which a Western firm supplies know-how and modern technology in exchange for produced goods, a country gains the management, skills, and industrial plant it might otherwise not have developed.

Finally, countertrade may be used as a way of maintaining the price of exported goods. A country may be able to dispose of goods at a higher price than the market would bear under a cash-for-goods deal. The nominal price is maintained even if the Western company simply inflates the cost of its original sale. OPEC (Organization of Petroleum Exporting Countries) is a prime example. When oil is sold as part of a countertrade deal, it is at the official benchmark price per barrel, which is several dollars higher than the current price on the open (spot) market.

DEVELOPING AN OFFSET CAPABILITY

There are four approaches to developing an offset capability in a countertrade agreement. They need not be mutually exclusive. They are:

1. *Farm it out.* Engage a trading company or clearinghouse to take over offset obligations. In many cases, the fees, commissions, and discounts involved will be so high as to kill the deal.
2. *Hire a consultant.* This should be done early so the consultant can be in on the preparation of the proposal.
3. *Establish an in-house capability.* The selected in-house executive must be assured good lines of communication with purchasing, marketing, and top management. The executive will seek to locate and include in the buyback/offset obligation quality goods at advantageous prices.
4. *Set up an export trading company.* This involves a major commitment that might accompany a decision to engage in multiple countertrade agreements.

The straight farm-out is usually the least desirable alternative. The other alternatives can supplement each other. Sometimes a consultant hired for the maiden buyback/offset deal can also be used to set up the ongoing in-house capability. Subsequently, the in-house unit can hire on a restricted basis specialists to assist with specific marketing problems. If an export trading company is set up, that usually eliminates need for an in-house unit. However, lines of communication must remain excellent, and top management must remain involved.

MANAGEMENT IN JAPAN

Christopher E. Held, Director, Asian Research Center, Concordia College (Japan)

Since the late 1980s, it has become evident that Japanese management techniques are not the panacea that many American managers had come to believe. A major decline in the Nikkei average, a record number of bankruptcies, and scandals in the Japanese financial industry have tarnished the Japanese image of infallibility. However, these events do not change the fact that there is much American managers can learn from their Japanese counterparts.

CULTURAL BASIS OF MANAGEMENT

Management, wherever it is practiced, requires the manager to use human and material resources effectively and efficiently. This process is obviously affected by a nation's cultural characteristics and resource endowment. Just as it is impossible to transplant a nation's resource base from one country to another, it is equally impossible to transplant another country's cultural set.

It would be, however, a mistake to terminate an analysis of Japanese management by attributing its success to cultural advantages that cannot be emulated. Certainly the Japanese were not deterred by the great resource advantage of the United States when they borrowed U.S. material management techniques with great success.

Investigating the cultural attributes that support Japanese management systems is interesting but its practical application is most relevant when engaged in a business relationship with a Japanese company. In this case, the American manager must develop a deeper understanding of the Japanese culture to successfully conduct business.

For others, the objective of studying Japanese management systems is to gain insight into the operations of their own organizations. These benefits are realized by focusing on structures, procedures, and operations in Japanese firms, with less focus on cultural characteristics. For example, an American manager may wish to use a planning strategy similar to that used in a Japanese firm. Although benefits from such a strategy may be similar for both firms, ultimately the American manager must use American cultural attributes and organizational resources for successful implementation.

STRUCTURAL INFLUENCES

Japanese business management practices are the result of a complicated network of interlocking systems. Therefore, it is often difficult to discuss a firm-level activity without introducing broader topics. Since certain aspects of Japanese human resource management have a strong impact on the decision-making process, let us begin with those characteristics. There are three basic components of human resource management that are relevant to this discussion: lifetime employment, job rotation, and the seniority system.

Lifetime Employment

This is often a misunderstood concept among Western managers for a number of reasons:

1. It does not apply to all Japanese employees. In fact, it is estimated that a maximum of 40 percent of Japan's work force is included in the lifetime employment system. To accommodate fluctuations in human resource requirements, subcontractors and temporary employees are used.
2. Lifetime employment is not for life. Generally, between ages of fifty-five and sixty, the employee is required to retire. Since life expectancy is approaching eighty, the growing number of retirees has become a social concern in Japan.
3. Japan's lifetime employment system is not the result of a cultural predisposition to provide worker security. The lifetime employment system was introduced to provide stability in traditionally tight labor markets in a rapidly expanding economy.
4. As Japan enters the slow growth period of postindustrialization, the lifetime employment system has created serious challenges for corporate Japan. During periods of rapid expansion, absorbing the ever-increasing number of middle managers was never a problem. However, in a slow growth environment, the ranks of the middle management have swelled.
5. There are now managers who do little but collect their pay and wait for retirement. In addition, this clog of middle managers prevents the promotion of younger and often technically more skilled employees.

The Japanese lifetime employment system has two operational and behavioral affects on decision making within Japanese firms:

1. Labor is a fixed cost in the Japanese firm. In the United States, it is generally considered a variable or semifixed cost.
2. Maintaining a labor force as a fixed cost alters the cost structure in Japanese firms. As a consequence of higher fixed costs, break-even points are raised and decisions are made with a sensitivity to volume and capacity utilization.

Behavioral aspects affected by the lifetime employment system are varied and more clearly delineated when discussed in conjunction with job rotation and the seniority system. At this point, it should be noted that lifetime employment creates an environment of certainty and stability. Therefore, communication tends to be more open as employees are not inhibited by a need to protect their position.

Job Rotation

From the company's perspective, lifetime employment requires continuous training of employees. Since employees remain with the firm throughout their career, management is not concerned that investments in human resource development will end up in a competitor's office.

This commitment to human resource development leads to the system of job rotation. In a Japanese firm, job rotation is one component of human resource development. Through job rotation, the Japanese manager is developed into a general manager in the truest sense. A new employee may begin his career in the accounting department. He will spend several years in this section learning every function in the accounting section's operation. After several years, the employee may find himself transferred to the personnel section where he will go through the same training process. Then, several years later, the manager may end up in a sales section. Essentially, the early part of a Japanese manager's career is marked by a series of lateral shifts from section to section, learning all tasks within each section.

At this point, the reader should note that in comparison to Western firms, work is organized differently in Japanese companies.

Basically, work is organized around groups called *ka*, or sections. There may be twenty people in each section and it is the section that is responsible for the work: Individual job descriptions do not exist in Japanese organizations.

In contrast, the Western manager is typically a specialist with a well-defined job description. As the Western manager develops expertise through experience, his or her market value increases. Often in quest of advancement, the Western manager will move from one firm to another. This is possible since organizational structures accommodate job specialization and labor mobility. This contrasts with the Japanese firm where careers are tailored to provide the manager with a global view of the company's operation.

The structure of career paths in Japanese companies has a strong influence on the decision-making process, as follows:

1. The most beneficial result of job rotation is improved lateral communications. Since decisions often require information and coordination from several departments, effective lateral communications are essential. In Western firms, the breakdown in effective decision making often occurs because there is no mechanism that establishes lateral communication links. In fact, the specialist in the Western firm tends to be quite parochial in his or her perspective of the operation.

In the Japanese firm, the job rotation creates lateral links that overcome this problem. Through job rotation, the Japanese manager becomes a generalist with a keen awareness of the firm's strengths, weaknesses, personalities, and corporate culture. As a result, the manager will seriously consider a decision's implications for other sections.

2. Over the course of a career, the Japanese manager develops personal contacts throughout the organization as a result of previous job rotations. Through this work experience, a sense of mutual trust develops. These personal contacts facilitate communication and the coordination of activities of sections involved in the decision-making process.

3. Job rotation causes a subtle external control that encourages cooperation and participative decision making. Since the manager has no way of knowing his or her next assignment, he or she is considerate of other sections' opinions. Therefore, the manager will be very reluctant to pass a problem on to another section where he or she might very well be working in another year.

Seniority System

The third component of human resource management is the seniority system of promotion *(Nenko Joretsu)*. The seniority system ensures that a new recruit will move through the organizational hierarchy with an increase in age and experience. Compensation is linked to seniority rank and will fluctuate with the employee's financial needs at various points in his life cycle.

The seniority system has positive impacts on decision making. This orderly method of promotion establishes security for the employee. The Japanese section chief can be certain that he will not be surpassed by an aggressive junior manager. For his part, the junior manager knows that in time he will be promoted. Thus, destructive competition and aggressive behavior are avoided. In this environment, information will flow with greater ease. Since it is not possible to increase the rate at which one moves up the corporate ladder, it is less likely an individual will withhold information in support of a hidden agenda.

There are also disadvantages to the seniority system that have increased in severity with a slow growth economy. Most problematic to the decision-making function is that promotion based on seniority does not reward competency. This has a negative impact on motivation among younger employees and decreases their desire to contribute creatively to the decision-making process.

The system, however, does not ignore competent employees altogether. In the Japanese hierarchy, there is a fast track, of sorts, that recognizes competent employees. This career track is subtle, but indicates to people within the firm, who is on the way up. Essentially, this career track operates by promoting more competent individuals at the minimum age for a given position or promoting individuals to choice positions. As it becomes evident which employees are on the face track, disruptive feelings of inequality are minimized through equal pay, based on seniority.

Of the three components of Japanese human resource management, the seniority system is under the greatest pressure to change and, in fact, is evolving. The most pressing problems resulting from this system are a bloated middle management and the suppression of creativity and innovation among younger employees.

CULTURAL CHARACTERISTICS OF DECISION MAKING

When attempting to understand the Japanese decision-making process, culture and procedure converge. The two cultural characteristics to be discussed are group decision making and consensus formation. Group decision making tends to develop a commitment to the final decision. This increases the ease of implementation. Also, group decision making leads to better decisions because more information is under consideration as a result of an increase in participants. Finally, group decision making compensates for less-competent individuals who might otherwise be left alone to make a decision. This characteristic supports the Japanese seniority system where a section chief obtains his position through seniority, not competency. Through collective decision, poor individual decisions are avoided.

On the negative side, group decision making requires considerable time. Also, group decision making is exposed to risks associated with negative features of group dynamics, such as group-think and suppression of participation by dominant group members.

The second cultural factor is the Japanese affinity for consensus formation. Group tasks tend to operate more effectively in the Japanese setting because agreement is obtained in advance. A consensus is a distinctly unique group decision. As it emerges, it differs from a compromise, which is negotiated. The competitive nature of negotiating a compromise would be disruptive to group operations in a Japanese firm. In contrast, the patient development of a consensus incorporates, or at least considers, the views of all participants in the final decision. The process is highly democratic.

Despite its congenial nature, consensus formation has several problems:

1. *It is time consuming.* The early stages of consensus formation are the most difficult as group members are reluctant to state their opinion in the face of the yet-unknown group opinion. Directly stating one's own opinion would be presumptuous and such that a consensus position develops from inferences and indirect discussion of information before the group.

   As a consensus emerges, group members become more comfortable and support for the decision develops. An outspoken minority view is not acceptable in the face of consensus. Those in dissent will swing in support of the consensus as they are certain their views have been considered in the process.

2. *The behavioral requirements may result in group-think.* Since group members hesitate to offer their opinion, a bad solution may emerge. In the absence of an alternative, the group will support the flawed consensus for the sake of group harmony.

3. *No consensus may emerge.* Since a competitive approach to resolving a deadlock would disrupt group harmony, this is not an acceptable alternative. Consequently, no action is taken in this situation.

DECISION-MAKING PROCESS

The decision-making process in Japanese firms does not always lend itself to a neat delineation of steps. However, the basic process can be defined as proposal initiation, proposal generation, proposal development, and proposal approval.

Proposal Initiation

The Japanese decision-making process is correctly characterized as a bottom-up process.

However, proposals for consideration may originate at any level of the organization. The suggestion is then directed to the section where implementation will occur and the bottom-up process begins.

Proposal Generation

Initially, the proposal takes shape at the section level. Communication within the section is generally more opened and relaxed when compared with interdepartmental meetings that follow. Within the section, people are familiar with one another and, due to job rotation within the section, everyone is familiar with the operation of the entire section. These factors facilitate consensus formation at the initial stage.

If the proposal is considered credible by the section chief, it is presented to the department head for approval. If it is not approved, it is returned to the section for additional consideration. If the proposal is acceptable, it will be passed along to relevant sections for review and consideration.

Proposal Development

At this stage, the proposal leaves the section and a general consensus is sought from all sections involved in the implementation. Members from the relevant sections meet to discuss the details of the implementation. Depending on the complexity of the proposal, there may be a large number of meetings to clarify all the details. The section from where the proposal originated is responsible for supplying required information. Since the participants of these meetings are representatives of their sections, should a difficult or unexpected problem arise, members must return to their sections for consultation with their group.

At this point, the Japanese term *nemawashi* needs to be introduced. Originally, *nemawashi* is a term borrowed from Japanese horticulture to describe a process used when transplanting a tree. In order that the tree will survive, prior to being transplanted, the earth surrounding the trunk is dug up and roots are trimmed so that new roots will grow. In the decision-making process, prior to issuing a proposal for formal approval, spade work

must be completed to ensure the proposal is accepted.

The *nemawashi* practice does not have an exact translation in English. It is vaguely similar to lobbying. However, whereas lobbying involves head counting and pressure tactics, *nemawashi* centers more on establishing or reaffirming personal contacts across the organization in order to gain support for a proposal. The practice of *nemawashi* occurs at all levels of the organization and, depending on what is at stake, the process can be very strategic.

Nemawashi is informal in nature. It may involve dropping by a counterpart's office for a casual visit or having lunch together. In fact, the actual proposal may not be discussed at all, but a personal relationship is developed that will ease future discussions. In other cases, comments alluding to the actual proposal are made, but in either case, both parties understand the actual agenda. Favors and obligations also play a role in this process. Directly reminding a colleague of a debt is unacceptable, although a casual meeting is a sufficient reminder of a favor not yet repaid.

The practice of *nemawashi* is not always successful and a bid to seek support may be rejected. In this regard, *nemawashi* serves as a face-saving mechanism. If the *nemawashi* process is unsuccessful, the proposal will never be issued for formal approval. Thus, the humiliation of rejection or strained personal relations is avoided. If the proposal reaches the approval stage, it is almost certain of acceptance.

Proposal Approval

Upon reaching the approval stage, all details, both formal and informal, have been sorted out. A general consensus has been reached and the proposal is then issued for acceptance. At this point, the proposal is formally issued through a process called the *ringisei*. The *ringi* process is initiated by attaching a standard form called the *ringisho* to the proposal and issuing it to relevant managers for approval. The *ringisho* moves step by step from the bottom of the organization to the top. As the *ringisho* passes from section to section, managers stamp their approval until it reaches the president. The president's approval finalizes the proposal and it becomes policy.

Since all details of the proposal have been worked out during the *nemawashi* process, approval of the *ringisho* is virtually certain. The *ringi* system is an often discussed characteristic of Japanese management. It is in the less structured *nemawashi* process that the fate of a proposal is determined.

LESSONS FOR THE WESTERN MANAGER

Decision making in Japanese firms strongly relies on cultural and structural qualities of Japanese organizations. Emulation in the Western context is difficult. Some insights from the Japanese approach to decision making should be relevant in the Western context, including:

1. *Effectiveness versus efficiency*—The Japanese approach has a bias toward effectiveness over efficiency. There is logic to this thinking. That is, the decision-making process can be more or less efficient, but the solution either works or it does not. Some might argue that solutions can be rated as more or less effective, but the danger in this thinking is that somewhat effective solutions tend to generate problems of their own. Accepting this view, then squeezing the decision-making process for a marginal increase in efficiency, may result in complete failure.

2. *Cost control*—Certainly cost control is crucial. However, it is total cost minimization that is the objective. The costs incurred from planning and organizing, at the preimplementation stage of the decision-making process, are minimal compared to those involved with a botched implementation.

For example, consider a product launch. Suppose all market research indicates the product is a hit. The product is launched and bottlenecks start to pop up. There may be trouble with distribution or production costs are higher than expected. A steady supply of material or components was not secured in advance or production is unable to meet spec-

ifications. Perhaps poor packaging kills an outstanding product.

Now consider the costs involved. The most immediate cost is associated with failure of the product. Even if the product stays afloat, it will be plagued by high costs associated with ad hoc remedies needed to cover problems. The company's reputation will suffer, or worse, a poor reputation will be reaffirmed. Finally, and certainly the most undesirable result, the company has created a great marketing opportunity for a competitor.

3. *Detailed planning*—The key to improving effectiveness and cost control is detailed planning. Unlike the Japanese consensus formation and group decision making, the U.S. company has no mechanism that forces a slow and methodical scrutiny of all information in the early stages of decision making.

Essentially, it is assumptions that dramatically increase a decision's exposure to risk. Assumptions are made because information is not readily available or there is not enough time to nail down a particular number. Therefore, as a matter of policy, management should pursue verification of all details pertaining to costs, time requirements, and coordination of activities and should hold managers accountable for the accuracy of numbers.

4. *Improving lateral communications*—Assumptions often occur because information is not readily available. An open flow of information and coordination between departments provides solid information. Structural components of the Japanese model establish outstanding lateral communications. Job rotations provide insights into various aspects of the firm's operation and develop personal contacts that facilitate lateral communication. In an American firm, there is no such mechanism.

One alternative for overcoming the lateral communication problem is technology. Increasingly sophisticated information systems are establishing lateral links that allow managers to access information from around the organization. Opening systems improves communication. Through information access, the manager can develop a global perspective of the operation.

Besides technical innovations, firms should improve lateral communications through structural mechanisms. Such mechanisms include committees linking individuals from across the organization. In addition, social contacts should be encouraged, creating personal relationships. The bureaucratic tradition of Western management should be reconsidered.

The real message here is that managers must rely on cooperation from colleagues across the organization. There is little formal structure that encourages this cooperation. Therefore, they must develop mutual understanding through developing personal relationships.

5. *Increased time requirements*—Mechanisms that improve lateral communication will slow down the decision making before implementation. Management should plan for this additional time requirement and expect improved implementation as the return on investment.

Slowing down the initial stages of decision making can result in several benefits. First, additional time increases the amount of information that can be factored into the decision-making process. This will tend to improve the quality of decisions developed. Second, additional time encourages a greater amount of participation. Increased participation ensures commitment to the process and commitment results in improved implementation. Therefore, it is the manager's task to direct the process so that time spent is not, or perceived to be, wasted.

SECTION 15

Service Industries

Rachel I. Vecchiotti, Section Editor

Introduction   *Rachel I. Vecchiotti*   15-3

Success in the Service Industries   *Stephen W. Brown and
    Mary Jo Bitner*   15-5

Organizing for Efficient Service   *Charmaine Ponkratz*   15-16

Relationship Selling in the Service Industries   *John I. Coppett and
    William A. Staples*   15-22

The Challenge of New Service Introduction   *Craig A. Terrill and
    Rachel I. Vecchiotti*   15-27

Establishing the Selling Prices for Services   *Kent B. Monroe*   15-33

The Impact of Telecommunications on the Service Industries
    Ann M. Wolf   15-38

The Changing Nature of Professional Services   *Robert A. Smith, Jr.*   15-41

INTRODUCTION

Rachel I. Vecchiotti

To provide a service simply means to assist individuals or companies in performing a necessary task because they do not have the capabilities, expertise, or time to do it themselves. How hard can this be to manage when the buyer is obviously dependent on the provider? Considering the mix of variables, it can be very difficult. Customer perceptions of value, quality, and performance differ from buyer to buyer. The market exchange for a service therefore becomes very hard to pin down.

As we continue to shift from a manufacturing orientation to a service orientation in order to achieve competitive differentiation worldwide, managers will naturally be tempted to apply what they have learned from years of manufacturing products. But services are not the same as products. Managers must realize the essential differences of developing and commercializing a service.

Regardless of the audience—whether it is a consumer of pizza delivery, a business needing package mail service, or a member of an association needing information—the basic principles of service management presented in this section apply. The authors of this section provide a range of timely and varied viewpoints on the service industries. And throughout this section, the intangibility of

measuring the performance of a service is discussed as well as the impact of this intangibility on service management.

Some authors take you along a service idea's path from planning and strategy to building the delivery system to introduction. Others provide effective mechanisms for managers to market and sell services, including pricing strategies. Still others provide practical advice for running a service business, including understanding the increasing role that technology plays in the service industries.

A number of authors discuss aspects of service quality in terms of defining and consistently providing it. They also emphasize the need for education in the marketing and selling of services. Some authors also note the need to focus on direct interface with the customer in terms of training employees on the front line to wear many hats—service provider, customer service representative, sales and marketing representative—with a smile! It is important for managers to motivate these employees because the success of the service falls on their shoulders.

Rapid expansion of services provides a challenging and exciting environment for managers in all industries. This section is a compilation of invaluable viewpoints. It provides managers with a set of vital strategic tools to make the transition less mysterious as we move from products to services. With these tools, managers can enhance their abili- ties to successfully carry service industries into the year 2000 by meeting and exceeding the expectations of their customers.

Rachel I. Vecchiotti *is a consultant with the management consulting firm Kuczmarski & Associates, Inc., of Chicago. Ms. Vecchiotti specializes in conducting new service and new product performance assessments, developing service processes, and creating effective marketing programs. She also helped spearhead research for the firm's nationally recognized business studies, which have advanced today's thinking on new service and new product management.*

SUCCESS IN THE SERVICE INDUSTRIES

Stephen W. Brown, Professor of Marketing and Director, The First Interstate Center for Services Marketing, Arizona State University

Mary Jo Bitner, Associate Professor of Marketing, Arizona State University

Service and service organizations are drawing more and more attention. All the major business magazines run regular features on services; financial analysts track *Fortune*'s Service 500; services consultants and training programs abound.

Services marketing and management has evolved into a distinct field, an area studied extensively since the late 1970s. Leading scholars and executives in Scandinavia, England, and the United States began investigating the differences between goods and services and the implications for marketing them. The exploration soon expanded into the issues of service quality, building long-term relationships with customers, customers' expectations, and so on. Services marketing and management principles have been developed as a result—basics about services, services

This chapter benefitted from the significant contributions of Gretchen Rowe, senior program coordinator of The First Interstate Center for Services Marketing, Arizona State University-Tempe, and Barbara Muller, faculty associate, Arizona State University-West.

marketing, and the implications for managers. Given the trend toward maturing economies becoming service based, the future of services marketing and management looks to be quite an important area for companies of all kinds.

THE IMPORTANCE OF SERVICES

A Services-Based Economy

Services dominate much of the U.S. and world economy. In the United States, approximately 65 percent of the GNP, 70 percent of the labor force, and 50 percent of the family budget are comprised of services. The services sector spawns a majority of newly created jobs and will continue to impact everyone's life and the world's economic growth.

Traditionally, products were considered either goods or services—distinct categories; however, more recently the line has blurred.

Goods and services are often produced and sold as one package. In fact, many services are integral to the manufacturing of goods. Services such as distribution, just-in-time inventory management, and communications are necessary to support the manufacturing function. Thus, it is likely the statistics cited previously actually underestimate the true dominance of services in the economy.

Services as a Competitive Advantage

Furthermore, many companies are using services to distinguish themselves from their rivals and to provide a sustainable competitive advantage. In an age of instantaneous communications and rapid technological change, product innovations provide a company with only a temporary edge. Service advances, on the other hand, are often integral to a company's culture and more difficult for rivals to copy. They thus provide a more lasting advantage over competitors.

Nordstrom, Inc. and Wal-Mart are two firms that have capitalized on service. Most department stores are facing tough times, yet both these firms are succeeding. Though they have different pricing strategies and target markets, both have adopted a strong service orientation that has catapulted them ahead of the competition. Rivals have tried to copy these leaders, but the imitation has been mostly on a surface level—"We Care" slogans, and so on. Competitors have failed in these attempts because customers quickly recognize mere gestures. Customers perceive service to be truly embedded in Nordstrom and Wal-Mart and reward these firms by becoming loyal patrons.

In other words, a good core product alone is often not enough. In many manufacturing industries, where the core product may become more and more a commodity over time (e.g., paper products, computer equipment, etc.), the best way to compete is often through providing superior service. Prompt delivery, error-free billing, customized product bundling, and liberal trade-ins are a few examples of the types of services that often distinguish the top manufacturers in an industry. Leading manufacturers such as Xerox and IBM are increasingly featuring their services to customers as a key competitive differential.

Services as a Necessity of Life

People are finding services essential as a way to improve their quality of life. Lifestyles have changed significantly during the past twenty years. Families are now often single-parent or dual-career households. People are working longer hours with less time for routine chores and leisure. Many families now regularly contract for basic services, such as take-out dining, laundry, and housekeeping, that no longer fit into busy schedules. A dual-career family may also have disposable income to purchase luxury services such as mobile pet grooming, masseurs, personal shoppers, and exotic vacations.

People and companies are outsourcing or farming out jobs they used to do themselves. In fact, many companies are finding that the best strategy is to focus on their core competencies, such as a law firm providing legal services. They contract out those functions, most often services like payroll and office maintenance, that someone else can do better and often at a lower cost.

Services as a Business Imperative

Businesses are increasingly aware of the importance of providing good service—indeed, it may be a requirement for business survival. Tom Peters and other authors and speakers champion companies who have prevailed by focusing on service excellence. Such messages have obviously struck a chord, as books like *In Search of Excellence, Service America,* and *Delivering Service Quality* have shot to the top of best-seller lists. The Malcolm Baldrige National Quality Award was created to recognize U.S. companies that promote the highest quality in business practices. The Baldrige Award has taken the business world by storm, proof of America's refocusing on customer service. Other awards and publications, like Japan's Deming Prize and Jan Carlzon's *Moments of Truth,* illustrate the international business community's obsession with quality and the customer.

GOODS VERSUS SERVICES

Services have unique characteristics that distinguish them from goods. While the marketing of goods and services has many parallels, a number of differences must be pointed out. Insights gained from studying these differences can be used to improve marketing techniques in both the goods and the services arenas.

Intangibility

Services cannot be seen, felt, or touched. A service is done to or for a customer. As such, services effect a change in customers or their possessions, but this change is not always visible. Customers may have difficulty forming a mental image of a service. No place is the intangibility of a service more apparent than in the delivery of professional services. When a consumer hires a lawyer or an accountant, the service being delivered is indiscernible. Any change that takes place is not usually noticed by friends or colleagues, and most consumers do not understand exactly what is being purchased.

For managers, intangibility means that customers often do not understand the service they are buying. Services marketers often use education to help consumers understand the what of the purchase and to instruct consumers about how to consume the service. Several law firms have recently used this approach in advertising. Partners in the firm describe the kinds of cases handled and reasons for hiring a lawyer. Role-playing and testimonials are used to communicate how clients go through the service process and to help consumers know what to expect.

Perishability

Services cannot be saved, stored, or resold. Imagine reselling a medical examination or an oil change. Also, the potential revenues from providing a service are not realized; they are lost. Empty seats on a departing airplane equal unrecoverable income. That revenue potential cannot always be stored and sold at a later, more convenient, time—it is lost. Many American companies are focused on capturing the maximum amount of this revenue potential. Airlines thus offer discounted tickets or travel package deals in an attempt to attract discretionary travelers and fill every seat on their planes.

Perishability leads to supply and demand challenges. Managers need to be constantly alert for ways to better manage supply and demand and for tactics to capture easily lost revenue opportunities. Matinees, midnight movies, and weekend getaways at hotels are among the many methods used to cope with perishability.

Heterogeneity

People such as mechanics, physicians, and bank tellers are involved in service delivery. The human factor means their performance will vary from day to day, causing each service encounter to be unique. A consumer good, for example, a box of soap powder, is subject to much less variability. Because services are often difficult to grasp mentally, this heterogeneity is further amplified by differences in consumers' perceptions. "Good" service is not a universal concept. One person may perceive a brisk, no-nonsense clerk as highly efficient, whereas another consumer may perceive that same clerk as rude. Additional complications arise from consumers' changing needs. What suits a consumer today may be unsatisfactory tomorrow due to mood shifts, perceptual changes, or competitive initiatives. If one mechanic starts offering free loaner cars during repairs, customers may expect all mechanics to do so.

Heterogeneity makes it difficult, if not impossible, to completely standardize a service offering. The ability to standardize goods has allowed for sophisticated systems of quality monitoring, such as statistical process controls. Although these systems may not always be applicable to services, quality control is an issue that management can address. Detailed procedures and "mystery shoppers" are two ways to control and check for quality in services. Services marketers use technology to standardize offerings. Variability is reduced through automation, the banking industry's automatic teller machines being perhaps the most successful example.

Heterogeneity is a two-sided coin. Services

can be far more customized and personalized than most consumer goods. A can of stew is just that; however, a restaurant's entrees can be flavored, grilled, and served to a consumer's liking. For many consumers, this personal attention and flexibility is the joy of purchasing services.

Simultaneous Production and Consumption

The production process for services also has unique characteristics. In many cases, the service process is identical to the service product. The consumer will often be consuming the service while it is being produced. This real-time consumption pattern leaves the manager with very little, if any, time to control and check for errors. The simultaneous producing and consuming of a service means that a small error (or perceived error) is much more apparent to consumers and often has a bigger impact than a similar error in a goods product. Customers experience the performance of a service, not just the service product. For example, an owner who sees an animal's muscle jerk may assume the veterinarian does not know how to give a shot properly when in fact that might be a natural reaction.

Services marketers consider the delivery process an inherent part of the product concept, including it in product planning decisions. For example, heavy equipment manufacturer Caterpillar directly builds in service attributes during the design, engineering, and production process for their products. Services marketers also design service delivery to manage customers through the process. Disney, for instance, snakes its waiting lines, so customers flow smoothly to the ride and do not feel as if they are waiting so long. Disney also uses signs that estimate waiting times to manage customers' expectations.

Also, consumers are often in the "factory" while a service is being produced and become a variable in the production process. The physical setting and the delivery process then become key elements of the service. Services are not generally produced in isolation, away from the consumer. Imagine a haircut. The service is produced right in front of the customer's eyes and that customer can even be

part of the production process, changing the service product at any time. Multiple consumers may be in the factory at the same time, and they can directly or indirectly impact a service performance. Restaurant customers who overhear guests at the next table complaining about the food will be affected. Though the interaction is indirect, their expectations and even their experience of the actual service is impacted. Movie or concert patrons sitting next to a crying baby or to someone who talks during the show will be directly impacted in their ability to consume and enjoy the service product.

Because a service is produced and consumed at the same time, employees often perform marketing activities and actual service operations simultaneously. For example, a teller cashing a customer's check may mention the bank's new check guarantee service. Or a waitress may bring the dessert tray, unsolicited, while serving after-dinner coffee. Management must provide the appropriate cross-training and support to front-line employees to take full advantage of these opportunities. In many instances the employee who provides the actual service is the firm, is the service in the eyes of the customer, and is thus of vital importance to the firm.

The Goods–Services Continuum

The traits of services may give the impression that goods and services are completely distinct categories and that the absence of these characteristics means the product is a good. In reality, products exist on a continuum—a few are pure goods and a few are pure services. Most products, however, are a mix, having traits of both goods and services.

This relationship can be better understood through the goods–services tangible/intangible continuum. This continuum has products dominated by tangible aspects, such as sugar or oil, at one end of the continuum and designated as pure goods. Products dominated by intangible elements, such as education or professional services, are at the other end, and fall into the pure services area of the continuum. Other products are spread along the continuum according to their dominant characteristics. For example, breakfast cereals are considered more tangible, more of a good, while investment management services are considered more intangible, and therefore more of a service. Fast-food outlets fall toward the middle of the continuum since they offer a mixture of goods and services, tangible and intangible products.[1]

Services marketers can use the continuum and other classification schemes not only to classify their products but also to identify other companies (possibly in completely unrelated industries) with whom they may share characteristics. Marketing ideas can be taken from that company, adapted to another organization, and applied to service offerings. For example, Marriott's Honored Guest Program for regular customers was adapted from American Airlines' Frequent Flier program. Through multiple stays at a Marriott hotel and the purchase of other items (e.g., restaurant meals), the guest accumulates points to be used for free nights and other benefits.

EMERGING CONCEPTS AND ISSUES IN MARKETING SERVICES

As a result of the differences in goods versus services discussed above, service marketers face a number of challenges particularly in service design, delivering consistent quality, communicating the nature of their offerings, pricing, and others. Over the years a number of concepts, theories, and strategies have emerged to begin addressing these challenges. The emergence of services marketing is related to other significant developments in business. In some cases these developments have further advanced services marketing. In other situations, services marketing helped catalyze general business trends.

The Services Marketing Mix

The marketing mix refers to a set of variables that can be creatively combined by management to meet the marketing goals of the firm. For example, different media, pricing structures, or distribution methods can be selected for each major product line, or the variables can be mixed and matched between products.

The "four P's" of marketing (product, price, place, and promotion) have been used successfully by goods marketers for years.

Services marketers have found the traditional P's somewhat limited given the special characteristics of services. Based on those differences, an expanded version has been developed for services products. Three elements have been added to the traditional mix to better reflect the challenges and issues facing services marketers:[2]

1. *Participants* are all the people involved in the service delivery setting. Other customers and service providers, in addition to the customer at hand, are included in this category.
2. *Physical evidence* is the total environment in which the service occurs and where the service providers and the customer interact. Also included are any tangible elements that help in the performance of the service or that communicate about the service. For example, business cards, employees' dress, signage, and equipment are in this category.
3. *Process* is the procedures and activities necessary for service delivery. This includes the steps involved in producing the service, mandated specifications, etc.

The expanded marketing mix elements have different impacts in different industries. For example, physical environment will be less important in a telemarketing firm than in a law firm. Also, managers within the same industry may attach different levels of significance to different elements of the expanded marketing mix. An upscale restaurant will spend much more on its decor and furnishings than will a neighborhood cafe. However, the variables will continue to influence customers, whether management chooses to control these factors or not. As with the traditional mix elements, these new P's do not operate in a vacuum; they are interrelated with one another and with the traditional P's. A firm's strategy is reflected in part in its unique combining of the seven elements.

Service Quality

Service quality involves different types of quality. The service itself, the *what* of the service, is one type of quality. Another kind of quality can be thought of as the manner in which the service is delivered, the *how* of the service. For example, a properly performed appendectomy is the *what*; the doctor's sincere concern about the patient is the *how*. True service quality exists when the *what* and the *how* align to meet the customer's expectations.

Along with the difficulty of explaining and describing service quality, the human factor in delivering a service further complicates the situation. Every time a service is purchased, the consumer is uncertain about the level of quality that will be encountered. If a dentist has been overbooked or if the catalog order taker is daydreaming, the level of service quality experienced will be severely impacted. Because of these uncertainties, most consumers feel some risk when purchasing and consuming services. Recognizing the importance of service quality, the service quality model was developed to analyze the gaps that can be used to describe and assess quality:[3]

- *Consumer expectations–management perception gap*—Managers may not always understand customers' expectations and what customers mean by quality. Managers may not recognize consumer needs or the features customers desire. In other words, managers may not be correct in their understanding of consumers' expectations.
- *Management's perception–service quality specification gap*—Even if managers understand consumers' expectations, they may be unable to deliver what customers want. This situation can happen because of resource constraints (not enough people to deliver quality during peak operations periods), market conditions, or a lack of management commitment to quality.
- *Service quality specification–service delivery gap*—Perhaps the specifications and procedures for providing service are up to par; however, employees' "humanness" makes it difficult for the service to be delivered exactly to specifications

every time. Or the delivery system may be poorly designed and may not encourage employees to perform consistently to specifications.
- *Service delivery–external communications gap*—Advertising and other firm communications can influence consumer expectations and perceptions. Overpromising and building up consumer expectations can be a problem. Consumers' expectations may be raised so high that a firm could not possibly live up to them. On the other hand, for some dissatisfied customers, simply hearing about how the firm is attempting to alleviate the problem may help to improve their perceptions of the firm.
- *Expected service–perceived service gap*—Good service comes from meeting or exceeding consumers' expectations. For example, a long wait at the bank to receive attention from a teller may be expected when lines are present, so the customer will not become disgruntled. However, if a customer is not waited on quickly when there are not lines, dissatisfaction may result.

In general, the model highlights potential areas for managers to focus on in identifying service quality gaps and taking actions to narrow those gaps, and the last gap discussed is believed to be a function of any or all of the preceding four gaps. The smaller the difference between the gaps, the more satisfied customers will be with the service.

Service Encounter Evaluation

From the customer's point of view, the most vivid representation of quality happens in the service encounter, also known as the moment of truth. Each time the customer interacts with the firm and its employees, the firm has an opportunity to prove its commitment to quality. And each encounter will in some way influence the customer's overall sense of a firm's service quality. Over time, multiple quality encounters will add up to a sense of excellence. Thus, managing service encounters becomes an integral part of achieving quality.[4] The obvious way to ensure excellent service quality would be to have no service failures, and forward-thinking firms like IBM Canada have instituted a policy of "zero defects" in key service areas. This means having a goal of delivering total customer satisfaction in every moment of truth through ensuring the highest quality in *all* elements of the encounter, from employee attitudes and behaviors to billing accuracy.

However, when inevitable failures occur, carefully designed and monitored recovery strategies can go a long way in turning a service failure into a success. For example, when an airplane flight is delayed, an attendant acknowledging the failure by offering an explanation and compensating passengers in some way for the inconvenience can help alleviate customers' dissatisfaction.

When customers have special needs or requests that are not normally included in the service, the firm's ability to respond can also help tremendously in disposing the customer toward a positive evaluation of the service encounter. Moreover, employees who exhibit seemingly spontaneous attentiveness and concern can delight customers. For example, a hotel van driver might radio ahead that one of the incoming guests is on crutches. The registration desk might then arrange for that guest to be taken directly to the room and register over the phone rather than having the guest stand in line downstairs.

Service Design

Because services are performances or processes, the actual steps involved in delivering and receiving the service take on tremendous marketing importance. Firms are beginning more and more to emphasize the importance of designing in quality from the beginning, both for manufactured goods and for services. For service firms this typically means much greater attention must be given to the service design process when new services are being planned, when the service is being repositioned, or when seeking improvements in customer satisfaction and service quality. When the root cause of a service complaint or failure is finally found, it is frequently the service process that is at fault. Thus, service design tools such as blueprinting and service mapping are becoming more widely used to help ensure that quality is designed into the service delivery process.

Service Guarantees

Service guarantees are one way marketers alleviate consumers' fears and reduce the risk associated with purchases. Though not a panacea, guarantees can help alleviate the risk many customers feel they face when buying services. An effective service guarantee has the following attributes:[5]

- *Unconditional*—A service guarantee needs to eliminate uncertainty and reduce the risk customers perceive they are taking. "Satisfaction or your money back, no questions asked" might be an example of an unconditional guarantee.
- *Meaningful*—This characteristic of an effective service guarantee is twofold. The guarantee must first be meaningful to customers and then must fully cover customer dissatisfaction. An example of a guarantee that falls short in this category may be a photo developing business that guarantees the safety of a customer's film, or it will be replaced with a new roll. This guarantee may not be meaningful because it does not compensate for the damage. With rolls of film, the money spent on the actual roll of film may be quite insignificant compared with the value of what is recorded on the film.
- *Easy to understand and communicate*—An effective service guarantee applies to both customers and employees. The guarantee should be stated succinctly and use as little jargon as possible. What is being promised should be crystal clear. Domino's Pizza has a service guarantee that fulfills these guidelines: A customer's pizza is delivered within thirty minutes or less, or the customer gets $3 off the pizza.
- *Painless to invoke*—The service guarantee should be given proactively. Management should look for all possible opportunities to perform the service guarantee. Customers and employees will then feel comfortable invoking the guarantee, ensuring that customers are satisfied.

A letter-perfect service guarantee is useless and meaningless if it is not used. Management can use a service guarantee to encourage customers in coming forward to complain, so problems can be fixed. Management can reward customers for being communicative about the service. Customers do complain—guarantees get customers to complain to the company rather than to other potential customers. Services marketers use the information to continually build and improve the service.

For example, First Interstate Bank guarantees that its ATMs (automated teller machines) will always work properly, that customers' account statements will be correct, and so on, or the customer gets $5. Through its guarantee, the bank reduces customers' feelings of uncertainty, and it can use the information to find defective equipment, improve the statement-generating system, and so on. Private industry is not alone in adopting service guarantees. Some school districts in the United States are offering "service guarantees" on their diplomas. If a high school graduate is unable to perform on the job because his or her basic skills are lacking, the school district will provide the graduate remedial coursework in reading, writing, and math.

SERVICES EMPLOYEES

The skills, abilities, and performances of employees determine the level of service customers receive and the satisfaction they derive. In most cases, the employee is the personification of the service and of the firm to the customer. Selecting and retaining effective employees is a must for service-oriented firms. Marriott views its employees as its only appreciating asset, referring to them as "associates" and investing heavily in their training and development. This enlightened orientation, in turn, improves employee confidence and satisfaction. The company's leader, Bill Marriott, expresses the philosophy that "Happy employees make for happy customers," because the employees perform better. Many companies now realize that high

employee turnover rates indicate problems and can lead to substandard service.

Services employees lowest on the ladder are generally closest to the customer. They also usually receive the least attention from top management, and the least amount of resources for training, development, and benefits. Yet they are often under the greatest stress due to close daily contact with demanding customers.

Increasing numbers of marketers recognize these factors and are taking steps to help employees feel appreciated and have a renewed service attitude. For example, job rotation and bonuses based on customer evaluations are often used. Recognition, however, may be insufficient. Services employees also need training in the technical and interpersonal skills required on the job. Employees must be trained to listen and communicate well. Most employees could also benefit from a solid understanding of their organization's mission, goals, and service values.

Employee Empowerment

The empowerment of employees has received a great deal of attention. Empowerment means allowing employees to do what has to be done to please the customer without getting management's permission first, and giving them the skills and tools to do so. For example, an empowered hotel employee may be able to express mail a guest's forgotten glasses without supervisor approval. Empowerment can be instrumental in providing timely, attentive customer service in many situations.

However, empowerment is not a panacea and will not work in all situations. An airline mechanic cannot be allowed to violate safety codes to get time-conscious customers in the air. Moreover, not all employees want the responsibility and the accountability empowerment entails. Management must assess the situation, the employees, and the prospective customers before deciding when and where to implement empowerment.

Employee Selection and Retention

Employee selection is critical to a service firm's success. Some marketers use simulation approaches to select employees. Potential employees role-play service situations and are evaluated based on their attitude toward service and whether they have the skills and abilities to learn what is needed to perform the job.

As mentioned earlier, services employees can experience a great deal of stress in performing their duties. Front-line burnout and high turnover can result from being in service-providing positions for long and uninterrupted periods of time. One way to combat burnout is to utilize job rotation whenever possible. For example, one international airline rotates its employees among three different service jobs on a regular basis. They may perform baggage-handling functions one month, ticket counter duties the next month, and customer service phone representative tasks the next. Thoughtful, careful selection of employees, together with an effective training program, helps the firm ensure employees are competent, service-minded workers.

INTERNAL MARKETING

Attracting and retaining service-minded employees and fostering good relationships with and among employees are two objectives of internal marketing. Internal marketing management goals are to hire competent employees, determine their needs, and fulfill those needs in order to satisfy employees and reduce turnover.

Employees will generally give good service when they want to give good service and are able to do so. For good service to happen, employees must be satisfied before they can satisfy external customers. In meeting internal marketing goals, some basic suggestions include the following:

- Sell employees on the service they are providing and educate them about *all* the firm's services.
- Use promotions and advertising to show employees what the company thinks of them. Consider the impact advertising campaigns have on employees as well as on external customers.

- Conduct market research to determine what employees want (i.e., stock options, more vacation, etc.). Use market segmentation to provide different employee segments with benefits that fit their lifestyle. For example, a fast-food restaurant that pays tuition for its part-time workers experiences less turnover and is able to provide a higher level of service for its customers.

Pricing Services

Pricing services presents many challenges and opportunities. Traditionally, the term *price* has not been used in conjunction with most services. Words such as *admission, fee, rate,* and *charge* have been used instead. Additionally, in many services, the exact unit of service is hard to identify distinctly. For example, services can be sold by the hour (legal services) or by the action (haircut). A key pricing issue, then, would be to determine *what* is being sold.

Further compounding the issue is how fixed costs impact the determination of price. High fixed costs mean that volume will significantly impact costs to the firm and the price charged to the customer. The level of customization may also impact the cost per unit and may necessitate several pricing structures to accommodate differing levels of service intensity. The direct costs related to providing a service are often difficult to track, as well.

Services Culture

All the previously mentioned services marketing issues have been addressed by management in various forms. Marketers and managers have initiated programs and instituted activities attempting to develop a service-oriented firm. However, isolated programs cannot work in the long run. Rather, a pervasive service culture has to be fostered. A service culture can be defined, in part, by the existence of the following attributes:[6]

- Top management and the board of directors have a service orientation and want to provide good service, that is, they have a service vision.

- They have an appreciation for and understanding of good service at all levels of the firm, but particularly at the executive level.
- Providing good service to internal and external customers is a way of life, a norm within the company.
- Employees are rewarded and evaluated based on service performance, not based on ROI (return on investment) or cost containment.
- There is a short distance between where decisions are made and where they are executed.
- Service employees have the knowledge and ability to perform their jobs.

Many firms adopting the total quality management (TQM) approach are also fostering the firm's service culture. Most managers accept some or all of these concepts; however, instilling these ideas as a permanent part of the organizational culture is a long-term project. Those companies that have been successful in integrating service quality into their culture have done so, in part, due to the absolute and long-term commitment of top management, the support and recognition provided to employees, and the realization that service excellence is an integral part of quality management.

THE FUTURE OF SERVICES

The services economy is expanding and evolving rapidly, creating an exciting climate for marketers. In considering the future services marketing may take, the following are but a few observations:

- Global competition in the services arena will intensify significantly. When people think of foreign competition, they think mainly of tangibles such as cars and VCRs. However, services are currently being imported and exported, and this will become even more pervasive. Banking, brokerages, advertising agencies, hotels, airlines, and many other service industries will be impacted by global competition.

- Service guarantees will become more pervasive and will be seen as a value-added benefit to consumers. For example, some banks are providing credit card holders with two different protection policies. One covers the item if it is lost, broken, stolen, or otherwise unsatisfactory. A second policy covers the consumer against future sales. If the item goes on sale within thirty days of the original purchase date, the bank will refund the customer the difference between the purchase price and the sale price.

- Reverse marketing will become more widespread. Reverse marketing tries to improve relationships with suppliers and vendors in order to provide the final customer with better service and higher quality. In many cases, the vendors may be forced to comply with stricter service and quality control programs in order to remain a preferred vendor. Motorola, for example, requires its major suppliers to apply for the Baldrige Award.

- Customer contact personnel, the front-line service employee, will assume a stronger role as a salesperson and consultant in services transactions. Firms will rely on these representatives to not only deliver the service but also to cross-sell additional services, conduct market research, solve customers' problems, and ensure customer satisfaction. The term *interactive marketing* will be used increasingly to represent the marketing impact of contact personnel.

- Seamless organizational structure will become more common and workable. Functional teams will work together to better research, design, market, and evaluate a service. Operations and marketing will go hand-in-hand in developing and offering services based on customers' needs. Human resources will provide evaluation and incentive systems that reflect these team efforts.

- Franchising as a method of obtaining widespread service distribution will increase. The marriage between services and franchising is well suited in many ways. Ownership of a franchise helps ensure a high level of service quality. The support, training, and advertising provided can substantially benefit franchise owners. Some services are purchased as a convenience item and, therefore, the wide distribution network provided by a franchise system is advantageous.

■ Services will increasingly involve technology. Firms will use technology to reduce variability and to meet customers' changing needs. However, the high-tech environment will challenge firms to maintain the "human touch" factor. For instance, IBM Canada requires its salespeople to contact within twenty-four hours customers who have left messages on IBM's voice mail system.

■ Firms will increasingly recognize the need to engineer quality into the design of new services, as has been done for manufactured products. Companies will develop and use process design techniques that incorporate the expanded marketing mix, customers' needs, the needs of employees, and so forth, with all elements of the design focused on engineering quality included from the beginning.

■ More and more pressure will be put on firms to customize offerings to customers' different and changing needs. Customers will rarely accept a standard package that does not reflect their unique culture, offerings, employees, and customers.

■ The business-to-business marketing of services will continue to expand. Business-to-business marketers will no longer view the good they sell as their only product; rather, they will market a total product that includes associated services. In addition, business-to-business marketers will rely more heavily on building and maintaining relationships rather than on price alone to compete.

The field of services marketing has grown and evolved quickly. Managers in both services and manufacturing are looking to service quality, internal marketing, empowerment, and so on to help them succeed in an evermore competitive world. People in all functional areas, from operations to human resources, are immersing themselves in services issues. Services marketing will continue to grow and evolve, providing companies with exciting opportunities in the fast-paced, challenging world of business.

NOTES

1. G. Lynn Shostack, Breaking free from product marketing. *Journal of Marketing*, April 1977, pp. 73–80.
2. Bernard H. Booms and Mary Jo Bitner, Marketing strategies and organization structures for service firms. In *Marketing of Services*, James H. Donnelly and William R. George, eds. Chicago: American Marketing Association, 1981, pp. 47–51.
3. Valarie A. Zeithaml, A. Parasuraman, and Leonard L. Berry, *Delivering Quality Service: Balancing Customer Perceptions and Expectations*. New York: The Free Press, 1990, pp. 37–47.
4. Mary Jo Bitner, Bernard H. Booms, and Mary Stanfield Tetreault, The service encounter: Diagnosing favorable and unfavorable incidents. *Journal of Marketing*, January 1990, pp. 71–84.
5. Christopher W. L. Hart, The power of unconditional service guarantees. *Harvard Business Review*, July–August 1988, pp. 54–62.
6. Christian Grönroos, *Service Management and Marketing: Managing the Moments of Truth in Service Competition*. Lexington, MA: Lexington Books, 1990, pp. 114–123.

ORGANIZING FOR EFFICIENT SERVICE

Charmaine Ponkratz, Vice-President, Marketing, Valley Bancorporation

The complexity of many of the services that are being considered for implementation by various corporations results in skyrocketing investments. The temptation is great to stay with what a company is presently doing. At the very least, companies will play a waiting game by letting the competition take the big risks of entering a market first. Realistically in managing the mix of services, a company has only two alternatives:

1. It can pursue its objectives and goals within the framework of a current mix of services. This is a status quo decision.
2. It can modify its present service mix either by adding new services, modifying current services, or eliminating services that no longer fit.

The decision to add, modify, or delete services entails risks. Although certain kinds of risks can be avoided by staying with the status quo, or at least by letting someone else do it first, risks cannot be avoided entirely. The point is that obvious risks are associated with introducing new or modified services, but there are some not-so-obvious risks associated with the status quo.

SERVICE LIFE CYCLE

Organizing for efficient service begins with an understanding of the service life cycle. It can be divided into four stages, as shown in Exhibit 15-1.

Introduction—The Big Gamble

Calling the first stage "the big gamble" aptly describes the risk of introduction. Because the service is new and presumably unique, it is almost always introduced by a single company. Characteristics of the service in this stage can be described as follows:

1. Since there is no competition at the introductory stage of a life cycle, significant variations are not necessary to achieve a competitive advantage.
2. Pricing tends to be influenced by the lack of major competition, and prices generally tend to be higher than they will be when the service matures.
3. Because the new service is introduced by a single company, the market lacks awareness and understanding of the service. This problem puts a special burden on the promotional part of the firm's marketing strategy. To bring about market awareness, the promotional effort must be disproportionately heavy.
4. Finally, the new service probably will lose money.

Exhibit 15-1. The Service Life Cycle

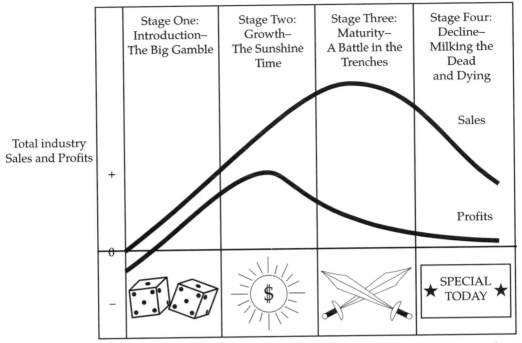

Growth—The Sunshine Time

Why take a gamble? The answer is simple:
to put the organization in the best possible
position for taking advantage of the growth
stage, appropriately called "the sunshine
time." The characteristics in this stage are as
follows:

1. Significant growth occurs as others
   begin to introduce the service, general
   market awareness and acceptance has
   reached some critical mass, and sales
   become substantial.
2. New competitors at this point do not
   present a serious problem. Instead, new
   entrants tend to expand the market at
   an even greater rate because of the increase in the general market awareness
   of the new service.
3. Despite the competition, market sales
   will be increasing. The major problems
   might be production and supply to
   keep up with the demand. Price compe-

tition will be virtually nonexistent during this stage.
4. Service diversity will begin to increase
   as competitors try to position themselves favorably within certain portions
   of the market.
5. The promotion effort will change. During introduction, promotion carried an
   educational burden. In this stage, it will
   emphasize brand or company recognition and preference.
6. Perhaps the most important aspect of
   the life-cycle growth stage is that it is
   going to be the time of maximum profitability for the industry involved in delivering this service.

Maturity—The Battle in the Trenches

By the time a service reaches maturity, total
industry sales have begun to level off. They
may be increasing slightly if the population
is also increasing. In this stage the battle will

be fought in the trenches. The characteristics are as follows:

1. Heavy competitive pressures will exist for the business, making the scramble for market share and profitability very difficult.
2. Costs associated with diversifying the service will increase.
3. Price competition will arise.
4. Promotional efforts will become less effective.

Decline—Milking the Dead and Dying

Eventually the services will enter the decline stage, where:

1. Sales will actually begin to decrease, probably as a result of the introduction of a new service or an elimination of the consumer need that justified the old service. Often this decline stage will be irreversible.
2. Cutthroat competition will develop as companies desperately attempt to survive or to minimize their losses.
3. The organizations that actually profit in this stage are those that are skilled in milking the dead and dying to the end.

Interpreting the Life Cycle

The life-cycle discussion is being presented from an overall industry perspective. Division of sales and profits among competing firms within a particular industry is rarely equal. The organizations that make an investment during the introduction stage are usually in the best position to take advantage of opportunities at the growth stage and usually dominate market share and profitability throughout the life cycle. As a general rule, the later an organization enters a life cycle of a generic service, the more difficulty it has achieving market share and profitability.

Second, the industry profits for a generic service not only peak during the growth stage but actually begin to decline toward the end of the stage, even though industry sales are still increasing. This is because the sunshine time attracts increasing numbers of competi-

tors to the market, causing market saturation and the beginning of price competition. This brings home a key point: Sales are not profits, and increasing sales is not necessarily increasing profits.

EVALUATING PRESENT SERVICE MIX

The first step in services planning is to determine the status of existing services in terms of the service life cycle. It is not necessary to get involved in a complicated mathematical or market research project to determine the position. Take each service separately, analyze its characteristics, and then determine whether that characteristic would indicate it is in the introduction stage, the growth stage, the maturity stage, or the decline stage. Seven service characteristics should be used, as shown in Exhibit 15-2. A grid is formed with the characteristics in the left-hand column and the stages across the rows. The number of checks in each column indicates the stage of the existing service.

After each service has been reviewed, the analyst can determine whether current services have a bright future, a modest future, or a dead-end future. At least three benefits can be derived by completing this exercise:

1. It forces you to consider the most significant market factors and trends within your industry.
2. Based on where the service falls in the life cycle, it can help you anticipate the competitive environment.
3. Knowing what that environment is going to be like, you can make informed decisions with regard to modifications, cost cutting, and the like.

ESTABLISHING OBJECTIVES AND GOALS

A great deal of time could be spent on the subject of corporate goals and objectives, both long range and short range, as they affect marketing and specific services. Corporate

Exhibit 15-2. Analysis of the Life Cycle of a Service

	Phases of Generic Service Life Cycle			
Service Characteristics	*Introduction*	*Growth*	*Maturity*	*Decline*
1. Industry sales				
2. Competition				
3. Segmentation				
4. Service diversity				
5. Pricing				
6. Promotion				
7. Industry profits				

Source: From *Developing Bank Services* (Washington, DC: American Bankers Association, 1982); copyright © 1982 by the American Bankers Association. Reprinted with permission. All rights reserved.

goals and objectives need to be stated in a way that ties them directly to the marketing mix issues of product, price, place, and promotion. Market-driven companies will define their goals in terms of high-priority markets. It is the marketer's job to apply the marketing principles and develop appropriate objectives and strategies.

THE MARKETING STRATEGIES

Determining the marketing strategies to be followed to achieve company goals is a key step in the planning process. Four basic strategies can direct the company's future: (1) market penetration, (2) market development, (3) service development, and (4) service diversification, as shown in Exhibit 15-3.

Exhibit 15-3. Marketing Strategies

Services

		Present Services	New Services
Markets	Present Markets	Market Penetration	Service Development
	New Markets	Market Development	Diversification

Source: From *Developing Bank Services* (Washington, DC: American Bankers Association, 1982); copyright © 1982 by the American Bankers Association. Reprinted with permission. All rights reserved.

The strategy selection will determine the markets to be targeted—either present or new markets. For those companies planning for growth, service innovation is universally recognized as a strategy for building market share in both mature and expanding markets.

Once the marketing strategy has been selected, a company can use three tactical approaches for dealing with the market. These are (1) add a new service, (2) drop a service, or (3) modify a service. Tactically, modifying a service entails specific changes of:

1. *Function*—a change that enhances the usefulness or value of that service to the customer. Adding a capability or enhancement to a service is exemplified by financial institutions' shift from offering traditional second mortgages to offering contemporary equity lines of credit.
2. *Style*—recognizes that customers buy products or services for other than functional reasons. An example might be the success of a costly gold Mastercard compared to a regular Mastercard that offers most of the same services.
3. *Quality*—involves altering the way a customer perceives the value of the service. An example might be to assign a senior account executive to work with a client, thus increasing the perceived importance of the relationship to the service provider.

With respect to tactics, keep in mind the distinction between strategies and the related actions. Strategies are the what, the general path to be followed within a reasonable time frame. Actions indicate the how, with whom, and when the strategy will be followed.

DEVELOPING NEW SERVICES

Generating Ideas

Management often has a general idea about what kind of service addition or modification might be effective. No system for planning new services, however carefully designed and implemented, can produce winning services out of losing ideas. A company's ability to develop successful new services depends on its ability to generate good ideas for new services. Although these ideas occasionally appear out of nowhere, ultimately the success of a company's service planning system depends on developing a formal and rigorous procedure for generating ideas.

Screening Ideas

Single out each one of the services submitted for consideration, measure it against criteria, and rate it as high, medium, or low. This will serve as a way of determining whether or not the service is worth pursuing. Any idea that fails to measure up to a significant number of these criteria should be eliminated immediately. Some of the criteria that can be used include:

1. *Customer transferability*—Will current customers utilize the new service?
2. *Distribution system leverage*—Can current distribution systems be used to deliver this service? Will new facilities or new technologies be required?
3. *Image*—Will this service be consistent with the kind of image that your company is trying to project?
4. *Service synergy*—Will this service complement your company's current menu? Or will it only confuse both the salespeople and the customers?
5. *Skill similarity*—Does current staff have the skills required to deliver this service? Will training be a significant factor?
6. *Personnel policy similarities*—Are compensation and benefit packages for the new employees hired to deliver this service similar to those of the current staff? Commission versus noncommission salary structures can create conflict and dissension within company units.
7. *Risk to company*—What kind of capital investment is required? What kind of human resources investment is required? What is the risk level if the service fails?
8. *Motivation for entry*—Is there a high motivation for entry? Are substantial profits and growths likely?

Business Analysis

After the initial screening, estimates must be made of the expected costs, sales, and profits over some future time period. This will not always be easy, because the service prototype has yet to be developed and costs may be difficult to estimate. Given the inability to determine the expenses of marketing, service production, and the uncertainty of market acceptance, it will be hard to estimate sales and profits.

Despite the uncertainties, the company should make the best estimates possible because the next step—actually developing the service—is likely to be expensive. Only financially promising proposals should make it to that step.

The Pricing Strategy

Several pricing strategies are commonly used:

1. *Cost plus*—The basic strategy here is to determine service cost and price above that cost to provide an acceptable profit margin. The advantages to this method are that it is simple, easy to understand, and its execution is objective and analytical. The disadvantages of cost-plus pricing are that it ignores customer needs, the marketplace, and competition.

2. *Competitive pricing*—Here it is important to determine what competitors are charging. This may not be an easy task. Quantity discounts and prices resulting from bidding situations can be elusive. The advantages to competitive pricing are that it is simple and easy to understand, and it is easier to execute than the cost-plus method. It focuses only on competition, however, and ignores costs and customer demand.

3. *Value pricing*—This pricing is based on what the market will bear and focuses almost exclusively on customer demands and other external factors. Value pricing can be very effective if the perceived value of services is properly identified. It focuses on customer needs and can result in ideal prices as defined by the customer. Because cost factors are ignored with this strategy, it is conceivable that despite an optimal market price, a product might not be profitable. This strategy requires

significant data collection and research time, making it more expensive to develop services.

Once the business analysis of a new service is completed and the decision is favorable, it is time to shift from a research mode to an execution and implementation mode.

Organizing for Delivering the Service

Each service will have its unique set of service management tasks to be completed:

1. *Information-gathering transfer system*—This involves creating the flowchart of information processing. It may be a paper process or an electronic entry. The process must track where and how information is gathered, how it is transferred, and how it gets reported back so management can track the service. This set of tasks must be completed before introduction, because if demand is high, you will avoid many problems in this key area.

2. *Employee training system*—An employee training system must be established for this new service. Employees need the answers to some questions. Where did this idea originate? What is the rationale behind introducing the service? What are the features of the service. What are the benefits from the customer's point of view? Who are the priority target markets? What clues might indicate a sales opportunity?

3. *A cross-selling strategy*—The company should develop a list of services complementary to the one being introduced. Where does this service stand relative to the competition? How does this service fit into the current mix of services? What kind of service tracking information needs to be gathered from employees? What agreements, documents, and contracts are needed for implementation? What are the service or account-opening procedures?

4. *Promotion*—In the introduction stage of a service, the promotion and service strategies must be integrated. This allows advertising, publicity, and personal selling to be used with maximum effectiveness. During this stage, education is critical if the market is to become aware of the product.

5. *Service quality*—A company that is committed to quality will be organized to support the service as a journey, not an event. Service

must become everyone's job, with leadership and communication provided by top management. It is a design issue that implies establishing a corporate environment that can keep the service promise.

Test Marketing

Basically, there are three approaches to testing a service:

1. A separate market may be selected, perhaps a branch office location.
2. A separate segment may be tested. An example might be to provide the service for senior citizens.
3. Focus groups or other research mechanisms can be used instead of an actual market test.

Although consumer input has been an integral component of the development process to this point, the service has not yet been offered in a real-time environment. This is a desirable goal in the testing phase. Still, test mar-

keting exposes the new service to the competitors. Care needs to be taken so that competition is not created prematurely. This is done by discreet testing and avoiding publicizing the results of the test marketing.

COMMERCIALIZATION

The last step of the planning cycle is commercialization. At this point the service development task force steps into the coach's role to provide support and encourage the company to achieve success.

After the service goes to market, the challenge is to manage and monitor its performance relative to the business analysis that was completed. The company also deals with any service problems and pursues opportunities that arise. This requires the skills and leadership of the service manager. At this point the management information system must provide relevant and meaningful data so that service improvements and enhancements can be acted upon quickly to prevent the premature demise of a service.

RELATIONSHIP SELLING IN THE SERVICE INDUSTRIES

John I. Coppett, University of Houston at Clear Lake
William A. Staples, University of Houston at Clear Lake

Buyers in both consumer and industrial markets are too sophisticated for salespeople who are still using the traditional "tell-'em and sell-'em" methods. This chapter examines the

fundamentals of relationship selling within the context of a services marketing environment.

What is relationship selling and how does

it differ from the way most personal selling has been conducted in the past? A formal definition contained in our book, *Professional Selling: A Relationship Management Approach* (South-Western Publ. Co.), states that "relationship selling is planned, goal-oriented interaction between a buyer and a salesperson yielding benefits to both the buyer and the seller, thereby fostering additional purchasing opportunities with the buyer in the future." Brief reflection on this definition will reveal that the salesperson's perspective is crucial. To truly practice relationship selling a salesperson must think about future relations with the customer even as the salesperson interacts with that customer today. For instance, two of the questions an insurance salesperson should reflect on are, If I sell this type of policy to this client today, will the benefits of the purchase be sufficiently apparent to the client in the future? and, Can this sale I am proposing become part of a total investment program for this client? Such questions reflect the salesperson's concern over the establishment of a series of client or customer purchases in the future.

Contrast this future concern to the situation in which a salesperson concentrates only on successfully closing a sale without any regard for how the immediate purchase will affect the future dealings with the client. This short-run approach to selling is referred to as trans-action-oriented selling. Such selling has given rise to several negative consequences. The most obvious effect is the absence of any trust between the buyer and the seller. The sale or transaction, once completed, leaves the buyer to fend for himself or herself. If the purchase is ultimately judged by the purchaser to be satisfactory, so much the better, but if not, the sales representative will just move on to another prospective buyer.

From an economic viewpoint, transaction selling leaves much to be desired. If the salesperson makes an initial sale to a client, but for whatever reason cannot establish a lasting relationship with the client, there is a strong possibility that the onetime sale has resulted in little or no profit to the representative's company. Exhibit 15-4 provides an illustration of this situation. If one compares the costs and revenues associated with "Sale #1," it is easy to see that there is an actual monetary loss to the seller associated with the first sale. How could this be? If all the costs incurred by the salesperson are known (i.e., travel, presale preparation, and so forth), it may be that the salesperson only makes his or her company any profit by holding on to the client and making subsequent sales to the client. In Exhibit 15-4 the break-even sale point occurs when the third sale is made to the same buyer. For this to occur, obviously a satisfactory relationship must be established. This is not just

Exhibit 15-4. Cost-Revenue Comparisons Resulting from Repeat Sales to a Customer

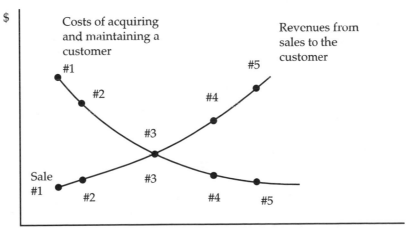

a theoretical straw man established to support a point. Research studies have revealed that it costs approximately five times more to find a new customer compared to the cost of maintaining an existing customer. Relationship selling pays dividends!

What kinds of relationships can salespeople form with their customers and clients? Three basic types of relationships can be established: counselor, supplier, and systems designer.

COUNSELOR RELATIONSHIP

The counselor relationship involves the providing of expertise and extensive personalized attention. It occurs in the sale of financial services, when consumers require assistance making choices in real estate investments, choosing insurance, or purchasing stocks or other liquid assets. It occurs in commercial sales of health plans or managing the retirement funds of employees.

In a counselor relationship, the customer knows that a goal needs to be achieved but does not know the solution to the problem. Thus, he or she places a high value on access to a knowledgeable salesperson. The seller must take the time to understand the customer's needs and goals and respond to them.

This relationship is characterized by patience and trust. The salesperson is listening much of the time rather than closing the sale. The salesperson must engender the trust and confidence of the customer or client. One strategy is to match the age, education, and experience of the salesperson and purchaser. The logic is that buyers are best able to relate to individuals who are most like themselves.

In most service industries, access to accurate and up-to-date information is essential to the relationship. Customized investment programs, real estate pricing and availability, health care options, and other information help build the customer's trust and confidence.

SUPPLIER RELATIONSHIP

A supplier relationship exists when a customer knows the type of service desired and needs assistance in procuring it. The role of the seller is to supply the service and solve any problems in providing it. Building a relationship under these circumstances requires personal attention after the sale. This includes ensuring the delivery of the services as described. It also requires resolving billing or other problems.

An important aspect of the relationship involves keeping the buyer informed on new services that might be available. The customer probably knows other vendors and frequently reevaluates all vendor relationships. Providing new information can be an important part of retaining the supplier relationship.

SYSTEMS DESIGNER RELATIONSHIP

A systems designer relationship is needed when a seller must design a service to meet a specific customer need. Examples are the design of a program of health-care benefits or a computerized network to link various offices of a company.

This relationship is based on the premise that purchasers may need solutions to problems that require several products and services working together. Frequently, the customer is unaware of ways to perform an activity in a more efficient way. Once a solution has been designed, the customer expects a total systems approach to its implementation.

The role of the salesperson is to conceptualize the system and implement it in the customer's environment, which may require the help of technical support personnel. Since the availability of expertise may be the determining factor in obtaining the sale, the company must back up the sales force with extensive technical support resources.

A salesperson needs specific skills to succeed in a systems design relationship. In addition to conceptualizing the solution, it must be explained in advance to the customer. A modest technical knowledge must be combined with strong communications skills. The challenge is increased when several people must understand and approve the purchase.

Because of the complexity of many systems and the speed of technological improvements, the customer expects the sales representative to monitor the service after it has been provided. This is a great opportunity to further cement the relationship. Upgrading and modifying the system to improve its efficiency also results in additional revenues.

When postsale system design and maintenance are part of the sale, great opportunities exist to apply the success in one department or family to other groups associated with the original user. A favorable climate in the first sale can allow sales penetration of an organization, a neighborhood, or other area where word-of-mouth promotion can be passed on by satisfied parties to other potential buyers.

BASIC SALES ACTIVITIES

Within the context of relationship management, salespersons must perform certain activities to successfully sell services. These include:

1. *Prospecting*—This is the task of determining target customers, narrowing the field to the most likely prospects, and identifying the specific person to visit to make the sale. The process begins with a large pool of potential customers. The field is narrowed to leads or prospects— that is, individuals who meet specific criteria. Finally, the salesperson hopes to convert a prospect to a buyer using one of the relationships already described.

2. *Sales lead qualification*—This is the task of converting possible customers to qualified leads or prospects. It involves determining whether a person or organization has (1) a need for the service, (2) a desire for the service, and (3) the economic means to pay for it.

3. *Previsit preparation*—This involves obtaining the information needed for a sales call. It is a critical step in services marketing since an unprepared sales visit may destroy any chance for success. Sources of information that can improve the previsit preparation include:

- *Customer files*—Has the firm ever sold anything previously to the potential customer?
- *Trade papers, journals, or newspapers*—Can a library search turn up information about the customer, similar needs, or competitive circumstances?
- *Credit reports*—Can the customer pay?
- *Annual reports or 10-K forms*—These can reveal information about the business conditions of commercial buyers.
- *Other sales representatives*—Sometimes one's peers in other departments have sold or tried to sell to the prospect. They may have helpful suggestions.

4. *Approaching the prospective buyer*—The first face-to-face contact is a crucial time in the formation of a relationship. The salesperson should have a goal for the visit. An obvious objective is to make a sale. This may not occur as a result of one sales call. Depending on the nature of the service and other factors, the sale may require five or six visits. Some realistic goal is needed. Aside from the goal, the salesperson should project a professional appearance, have several customer-oriented questions to ask, and be prepared to listen.

5. *Sales presentation*—At or after the first visit, a sales presentation may be appropriate, or it may not. The time is mostly passed when formal sales presentations are more effective than questioning the customer, analyzing his or her needs, and working together toward a solution.

6. *Dealing with objections*—Customers can voice objections to the service, the seller's company, or the salesperson. Some of the major objections involve:

- *Price*—The salesperson can justify the price by showing the economic benefits of the service, breaking down the total cost over a reasonable period of time, or asking the customer to explain his or her basis for forming the objection. It is always dangerous to lower the price as the lowering may cast doubts on the quality of the service.
- *Lack of need*—This objection can signal several problems. It may indicate a poor prospecting system. Or it may mean that

the salesperson has not identified the prospective buyer's need and explained how the service can satisfy it. Or it may reveal a hidden objection, such as the customer cannot afford the service.

- *Buyer indecision*—In some cases, the buyer may not yet be ready to make the purchase. A successful salesperson may probe the reasons for the indecision as part of the process of building a relationship.

7. *Closing a sale*—This is not the culmination of the marketing effort. Rather, it is a beginning of a relationship. If the sale is made to an established customer, it is a continuation, not a conclusion. A perceptive sales representative will detect the appropriate time to close. "Taking the temperature of the sale" conveys the notion that judgment is needed on when the buyer is ready to commit to a purchase.

8. *Postsale customer contacts*—The relationship has now begun. The salesperson should follow up to ensure that customer expectations are being fulfilled. The skilled and confident salesperson views follow-up visits as opportunities to make future sales.

CONCLUSION

Because the selling of services requires the salesperson to deal with intangibles, it is usually conceded that services selling requires a higher order of sales skills. Although such selling is inherently difficult, it is even more challenging to establish and maintain a long-term relationship with a customer or client. This is, however, what precisely successful sales professionals are required to do today. The maintenance of a durable relationship with a profitable customer is becoming a measure of a salesperson's productivity.

Sales managers, therefore, are advised to look beyond the superficial surface of sales volume statistics and evaluate where the sales are being made. Are they coming from repeat purchasers who are expressing their satisfaction and confidence in the salesperson, the service being offered, and the salesperson's company? By seizing opportunities for creating relationships with customers rather than conducting short-term transactions, salespeople cannot only work smarter but more profitably as well.

THE CHALLENGE OF NEW SERVICE INTRODUCTION

Craig A. Terrill, Principal, Kuczmarski & Associates
Rachel I. Vecchiotti, Principal and Research Associate, Kuczmarski & Associates

Why are so many companies reinventing the wheel with every new service introduction? What can be learned from successful new service development companies? How do some companies introduce innovative new service ideas while most launch only derivatives of existing offerings? What can be learned from years of new product development to answer these questions? We should recognize that a new service is often viewed as a new product. Like a new product, a new service also responds to an existing problem or created need among a set of customers. But then moving forward to develop a new service should involve an understanding of the uniqueness of services.

Although there are indeed many lessons from new product development experiences that can be transferred, new services managers often try to "force fit" product techniques and approaches to new services. This chapter highlights ten challenges new service managers commonly face and describes how some of these challenges are unique to the development of new services versus new products. Understanding, addressing, and overcoming these challenges is critical if a company wishes to increase the likelihood of successful creation and introduction of new services.

NEW SERVICE DEVELOPMENT CHALLENGES

1. *Securing top management commitment*—If top management truly does not believe in the power of new-to-the-world and new-to-the-company services, then the organization will not launch successful new services consistently. It is that simple. Top management must recognize the potential for new services to increase revenues and profit, and blend the strategic roles and expected results of new services into its long-term business strategies.

2. *Developing truly innovative new services*—Conventional wisdom continues to show that a new service with a high degree of creativity, while riskier, is typically the most successful and well worth the risk. Managers must fight the temptation to develop ideas that only mimic competitive services and minor concept extensions that only respond to short-term-oriented customer complaints.

3. *Reducing the time-to-market*—New service managers are constantly challenged to reduce the cycle time from idea generation to introduction, while increasing the success rate of new services launched. A company needs to focus on time-to-market for all new services. For new services derived from existing offerings, reducing time-to-market should

be the primary focus. It is unreasonable, however, to expect new-to-the-world and new-to-the-company services to meet the same cycle time expectations. They require a different speed-to-market expectation due to the need for additional research, mock-ups/trial runs, and employee readiness.

4. *Killing off failures*—Sometimes a new service cannot be created or the market disappears during development. At the same time, however, a certain momentum has been established, leaving organizations reluctant to stop the process. Companies should set up a system that will aid in disciplining them to kill failing efforts and reallocate resources to more promising projects.

5. *Achieving high quality at introduction time*—Image and identity are critical for any new service offering. If the quality of the service delivered is poor at the time of introduction, then those first-time buyers will be hard-pressed to repeat buy unless convinced the service has improved. Unlike a product in which the customer can physically see and "feel" the improved benefits, new services must build trust immediately in order to convince a repeat buyer. The delivery team, system operations, customer service, and management involvement are all key factors to achieving high quality at the point of introduction.

The preceding challenges result from the lessons learned from both new service and new product managers. However, successful new service organizations, including traditional product companies wanting to increase their services business, do not overlook the following unique challenges of new services.

6. *Securing enough people, capital, and technology resources*—The worst possible scenario for a new service project is to be caught in a budget dilemma where a company allocates too little resources to properly develop a brand new concept. Unfortunately, these same companies, however, usually approve enough funding for a project to keep it bumping along. New service managers should focus on selling the value of the expected benefits up front, along with the investment required to realize those benefits, in order to gain resource commitment from senior management.

For new services, securing critical resources involves freeing up enough time from several key people. This kind of commitment usually requires that at least half of their overall time be dedicated to a given project. In addition, capital is a critical resource needed for a new product development effort. But for services, capital and information technology requirements take on a different emphasis and often are secondary to people resource needs.

The need for people as a resource in new services is slightly different than for new products. First, there is a greater need for help from a broader group of employees, not just a few key development types. A broader group helps bring in a variety of perspectives and completely exhaust definition alternatives for the service. A larger group also helps ready the entire organization. Second, people from different functions in the organization are needed, including customer service, sales, operations, information systems group, and maintenance. Third, people resources must be managed differently, given the intangibility of services during their creation and testing. There should also be a greater emphasis on recognizing people for their individual contributions, because people are the service. A service, unlike a product, cannot sell itself!

Capital requirements for both services and products escalate exponentially from development to introduction. However, unlike new products, which often require investment in fixed assets during ramp-up, new services primarily need investment in new systems, processes, communications, and training.

Successful new service developers often utilize proprietary and applied information technology in the delivery of their services to establish competitive advantage. To establish this competitive advantage, the operations component of the new service (similar to production capabilities for new products) should be developed fairly early in the development process and should include operational capabilities and constraints, cost estimates, and design change parameters. This often means early "negotiations" with the information technology group to free up conceptual thinking talent from a generally backlogged flow of work. Beyond specific people resources, gaining time on the information system to test operational readiness prior to launch can cause major delays if not properly secured far enough in advance. Often new service champions try to circumvent the technology group at this juncture if delays arise in order to "get the thing out." But this strategy can backfire as it destroys buy-in to the new service or results in major problems shortly after introduction.

7. *Involving all employees as part of a broad delivery team*—Services, by nature, have a greater reliance on human interaction than products. Buyers of a new service are not really looking for an explanation of a service's features. Rather, they need reassurance from those individuals involved in the delivery that a new service will in fact create the results expected. Four main factors influencing a buyer's perception are the level of confidence, enthusiasm, knowledge, and personal experience that the service delivery team has with the new service. For example, we are more motivated to buy when we discover that the new insurance policy we are considering is one our agent has taken out personally. Or remember the feeling you had when someone you knew at a bank or an investment firm showed genuine excitement for a new offering.

New service development requires that tremendous attention be given to team dynamics, training, and "dress rehearsals." This attention ensures the delivery of a high level of service quality. Readying the delivery team requires a company to recognize that those delivering the service are at the same time reselling the service. The focus must be on "pumping up" the entire delivery team. Confidence in the value of the service offerings and a thorough understanding of its inner workings will lead to an enthusiastic delivery team as it offers the new service to customers. Delivery team enthusiasm is the insurance policy for a successful new service launch and operation.

8. *Developing a unique partnership relationship with future customers during the development stages*—Conventional wisdom has indi-

cated a high correlation between successful new services and the degree of customer involvement during development. The basic premise is that, more often than services, a new product has its functionality "locked in" and is targeted for a large group of buyers. But new services require greater customization to more specific market segments and customer needs. Thus, the development team can only define a new service concept to the level of surfaced needs for a customer base. It is with the help of customers that specific problems are defined and solution parameters for the problems are established. Customer-shaped concepts lead to a firmer definition of the new service before significant investments are made. Customer input helps guide the final shaping of the service during the later stages of market testing.

If new service developers want powerful new services in the market, they must include customers during the development process, enhance the customer relationship with the new service delivery team, and leverage these customers during the introduction. Most customers will gladly be involved as a way to gain strategic time advantage over their own competition by implementing a new service first.

Customer partnering can also give a new service a tremendous advantage at the time of introduction. Whereas a product can be examined, a service must be experienced. This distinction requires a high degree of referential selling to encourage first-time trials by customers. In addition, customer partners begin using the service immediately, which helps operations reach early volume levels, spread costs, and fine-tune capabilities.

9. *Establishing the right environment to unleash development champions*—Successful new service companies cultivate, encourage, and support development champions. Development champions are essential to provide the needed push within a company to move a new idea along to reach introduction. Moreover, getting a new service out the door takes staying power and endurance just to cut through the bureaucratic clutter that frequently stifles innovation.

However, a development champion cannot

go it alone. Companies will often turn to a multidisciplinary team, drawing upon the different disciplines needed for developing a new service. Increased communication between, and greater commitment and ownership by, key functional managers is more likely to occur when their input is aggressively encouraged from the beginning.

In the best of companies, top management creates and supports a positive environment for new service development by assigning the best managers and supporting entrepreneurial behavior. Top management in successful companies will also compensate managers consistent with long-term goals and treat the process as an investment rather than an expense. A positive climate fosters superior dedication and enthusiasm for success.

10. *Implementing a development process that responds effectively to customization*—In many ways, new product developers are ahead of new service developers. New product developers know how to implement new product development processes that combine formality and flexibility in order to provide efficiency. However, new service developers recognize, unlike many new product developers, that today's introductions often involve more market segmentation and less mass market appeal. Therefore, new service introductions nowadays require heavier and earlier market input, customer partnering, and high-impact delivery in order to respond to the demand for increased customization. Development is further complicated for new service developers because they cannot utilize prototypes to gain important market feedback for customization. Yet new service developers must generate creative answers to provide tangible representatives that are as close to the new service offering as possible. In addition, new service development is complicated by the need to balance an explosion of new service ideas in the beginning with rapid and stringent screening of those ideas throughout the process.

DEVELOPMENT PROCESS

The new service development process displayed in Exhibit 15-5 provides the necessary

Exhibit 15-5. New Service Development Process

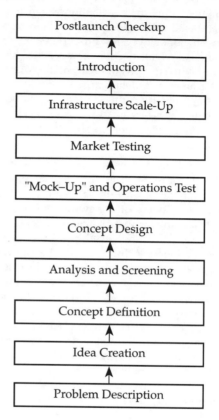

combination of formality, flexibility, and tools for customization that will increase a company's new service success rate.

■ *Problem description*—Typically, companies are not at a loss for new service ideas. The difficulty arises in choosing the right ideas for further development. A successful approach to focus idea generation begins with identifying a customer problem or need that exists in the market. It is important to fully understand and describe the problem in order to generate new service ideas that can address it. This step relies on problem-based exploratory market research.

■ *Idea creation*—With a clear description of a customer problem, a group of people in a room can probably brainstorm hundreds of ideas. But a company must explore beyond internal sessions and look for ideas from sources such as salespeople, current and potential customers, industry "bulletin boards," competitors, and delivery partners. A new services team is forced to look at the market up front when following a customer-oriented creative and analytic approach to idea generation. This will dramatically increase the probability of a new concept addressing a customer need that in fact exists.

- *Concept definition*—To define a concept means to "put meat on the bones" of a new service idea. The idea must take on a more recognizable form so the organization can fully evaluate the end service offering. And to do this, a company needs customer input. It is necessary to flesh out all benefits in the definition. This stage can be very difficult because of the intangible aspects of a new service, but at the very least a company needs to write down a substantive definition of the concept and describe "what it is."

- *Analysis and screening*—Before any additional dollars and time are invested in the service concepts, they need to be analyzed and screened to determine the highest potential concepts. Analysis evaluates the potential revenue and profit streams, market size, competitive environment, cost to develop and introduce, and match to the company's capabilities. Following the completion of this type of analysis, a company should screen all concepts to make sure they can meet company financial and strategic objectives.

- *Concept design*—By this point, internal and external input from the analysis and screening stage may have resulted in changes to the concept definition. Therefore, it is important to again fully document the concept. Design entails developing a detailed description of the service attributes and benefits, customer purchase criteria, and market, cost, and competitive analysis. In addition, all important support systems and processes need to be designed at this point. By developing a working design of the service offering, a development team can present a tangible new service concept to other employees and potential customers for feedback.

- *"Mock-up" and operations test*—Beyond a detailed written description, development teams need to design a simulation of how the service will be delivered and performed. For example, a prominent hotel chain set up a futuristic room with new in-room services for its mock-up. And a major tire manufacturer and repair company used a mock-up to decide on a new system that would best operationalize a new aspect of their customer service program. This stage applies the nuts and bolts to the delivery of the new service offering and prepares the company for market testing. It also provides feedback on the magnitude, potential advantages, major barriers, and cost estimates regarding the operations of the new service.

- *Market testing*—Once a concept gains understanding in the marketplace, service developers often are tempted to immediately move to introduction. But a "hurry-up" new service introduction may jeopardize its success. Therefore, incorporating patterned responses heard from potential customers into the service offering is critical prior to introduction. For service companies, it is also an opportunity to test the system developed for delivery. Does the new service match our internal operational capacity? Does it position our strengths in the marketplace? Are we maximizing our productivity? Does it maximize our position? Did the tested new service meet our financial objectives? Is there customer acceptance? Prior to introduction, new service developers should answer these questions.

- *Infrastructure scale-up*—If the market test is successful, then a company can proceed building the necessary infrastructure. For industrial products, heavy investment is often required to get a facility ready to manufacture a product to quality standards. While creating a services infrastructure focuses more on structure, systems, processes, and people, it nonetheless requires significant investment. Think of what it costs American Express to scale up its global network to offer cash machines around the world. Or what it costs the airlines industry to offer reservations services from home computers. The investment in training and education at this point will pay large dividends in the future.

- *Introduction*—The quality of the new service at the time of introduction can make or break the new offering. To ensure a high level of quality, a company should utilize small company-specific delivery teams, targeted customer segments, well-timed promotional releases, direct communication with initial customers, and immediate feedback to operations.

- *Postlaunch checkup*—Companies that monitor their new services' performances can determine what additional changes are necessary to keep the services competitive and successful. A postlaunch six- to twelve-month review of a new service's performance also determines if the new service is meeting its financial and strategic objectives.

CONCLUSION

To ensure ongoing success, new service managers should take into consideration the following guiding principles to implement a formal service development process:

- Tie new service objectives to business objectives.
- Develop multifunctional teams early on and keep intact after introduction.

- Identify and use communication vehicles, such as a descriptive name, for new ideas to make them tangible.
- Be discerning in the use of market research heavily in up-front stages and also near introduction. Employ market research techniques that provide the closest representation of the new service offering as possible.
- Vary the emphasis of each development stage depending on the strategic type of new service.
- Determine and communicate individual and team accountabilities.
- Build the new services pipeline with a portfolio of new services types.
- Secure commitment both with top management and delivery teams.

The biggest obstacle to new service success today is management's emphasis on short-term profitability. Succumbing to the pressures of current business, managers constrain innovation by channeling dollars away from new services. Although such an attitude may bring profit for existing services, it can be paralyzing to an innovative new service program.

ESTABLISHING THE SELLING PRICES FOR SERVICES

Kent B. Monroe, University of Illinois, Champaign-Urbana

Pricing a product or service is one of the most important decisions made by management. Pricing is the only marketing strategy variable that directly generates income. All other variables in the marketing mix—advertising, product service development, sales promotion, distribution—involve expenditures. In recent years, economic and competitive pressures have led to new strategies in the area of pricing.

Pricing practices remain largely intuitive and routine. Companies often determine prices by marking up cost figures. Thus, pricing has not been a major factor in marketing strategies for services. This is not a good situation. Service companies should be active rather than passive in an increasingly competitive environment.

Organizations that have been successful in making profitable pricing decisions have taken what may be called a proactive pricing approach. They have been able to raise prices successfully or reduce prices without competitive retaliation and have become aggressive pricing strategists and tacticians.

There are two essential prerequisites for becoming a successful proactive pricer. First, it is necessary to understand how pricing works. Because of the complexities of pricing in terms of its impact on suppliers, salespeople, distributors, competitors, and customers, the simple prescriptions of traditional microeconomic theory are not appropriate for a modern market system. Indeed, companies that focus primarily on their internal costs often make serious pricing errors.

Second, it is essential for any pricer to understand how customers perceive prices and price changes. Price plays two roles. It is used as an indicator of how much money the buyer must pay. It is also used as an indicator of service quality. The difference between the prices of alternative choices affects buyers' perceptions. Thus, it is imperative that the price setter knows how buyers perceive price information. Moreover, prices must be consistent with buyers' value perceptions. Failure to follow this basic prescription leads to some major pricing errors.

CONCEPTUAL ORIENTATION TO PRICING

Six essential factors must be considered when setting price:

1. *Demand*—The level of demand for the service provides a ceiling or maximum price that may be charged. The determination of this maximum price depends on the customers' perceptions of value in the seller's service offering.
2. *Costs*—These provide a floor or minimum possible price. For existing services, the relevant costs are the direct

costs associated with the creation, mar-keting, and distribution. For a new service, the relevant costs are the future direct costs over the life of that service. The difference between what buyers are willing to pay and the minimum cost-based price represents an initial pricing discretion.

3. *Competitive factors*—This may narrow the range of pricing discretion, primarily by lowering the price ceiling.

4. *Corporate profits*—The desired profit level must be considered. Normally, this reflects the level of risk in the business and serves to raise the minimum cost-based price.

5. *Market objectives*—Can the price be used to expand sales in desired markets?

6. *Regulatory and legal constraints*—Are there any legal issues that affect pricing? Does the danger of future lawsuits mean the price must be higher?

Depending on the type of service and characteristics of demand and competition, the actual pricing discretion could still be relatively large, or it could be nonexistent. Nevertheless, several very important factors should be considered when setting prices. To focus only on costs obviously ignores many other important factors.

ECONOMICS OF PRICING

One of the most important cornerstones of price determination is demand. In particular, the volume of a service that buyers are willing to buy at a specific price is that service's demand. The discipline of economics provides the basic theory of how prices should be set, as well as some important analytical concepts for practical pricing decisions. Some key concepts are:

1. *Theory of buyer behavior*—Price influences buyer choice because price serves as an indicator of service cost to the buyer. The buyer attempts to maximize satisfaction within a given budget constraint. One piece of information available to the buyer is price. Other pieces of information are not always known. Unknown information introduces uncertainty about the buyer's ability to predict correctly the need satisfaction available through purchasing the service. Hence, buyers may use price both as an indicator of service cost as well as an indicator of service quality.

2. *Price elasticity*—Price elasticity of demand measures the relationship between pricing and changing demand for a service. When quantity demanded falls as price increases, price elasticity is negative.

3. *Income elasticity*—Income elasticity of demand measures the relationship between personal income and changing demand for a service. If demand rises when income goes up, elasticity is positive.

4. *Cross-price elasticity*—Cross-price elasticity of demand measures the responsiveness of demand for a service relative to a change in price of another service. If this relation is negative, the two services are complementary. If the relation is positive, the two services are substitutes. Cross-price elasticity is also often used as a measure of the effects of price changes by competitors.

CONSUMERS' SURPLUS

Pricing decisions are affected by the fact that there are usually some consumers willing to pay more than a posted price in order to acquire the service. Essentially, this means that the price charged may be lower than some buyers' perceived value for the service. The difference between the maximum amount consumers are willing to pay for a service and the amount they actually pay is called consumers' surplus.

In essence, consumers' surplus is what the consumer gains from the trade of money for the service. Value-in-use (what is gained) minus value-in-exchange (the price) is positive. Value-in-use always exceeds value-in-exchange simply because the most that anyone would pay must be greater than what they actually pay. Otherwise, they would not enter into the trade.

The important point is that the price at which exchange takes place is not the equivalent of value as is so often assumed. Total willingness to pay is comprised of value-in-exchange and consumers' surplus. It is that latter concept that becomes an important consideration in the determination of prices. Rather than concentrating on the cost considerations when setting price, the pricing problem becomes one of determining potential customers' perceived value-in-use.

THE BUYER'S PERCEPTION

A successful proactive pricer sets price to be consistent with customers' perceived value. Perception plays a key role in marketing services. Perception basically involves the process of categorization. We tend to place new experiences into existing classifications of familiar experiences. When buyers are confronted by a price different from what they believe they have previously paid, they must decide whether the difference is significant. If not, they may classify the two prices as similar and act as they have in the past. Conversely, if the price differences are perceived as significant, buyers may classify the services as different, and make their choices on the basis of price.

Consumers' perceptions of a price derive from price differences and from their interpretations of the cues in the offer. Consumers make their purchase decisions in a two-step process. First, they judge the value of an offer. Then, they decide whether to make the purchase. It is also possible that they will postpone the purchase decision until they have more information.

Buyers' choices depend on how they evaluate the quality or benefits relative to the price. Purchasing represents a trade-off between the quality perceived and the sacrifice required to pay the price.

Spurred, in part, by business concern with service quality, there has been a renewed interest in the price-perceived quality relationship. Indeed, major business publications indicate that product and service quality can represent potent competitive advantages. If buyers know that there is a positive price-quality relationship in the service market, they are likely to use price as a quality indicator. If they know there is a weak price-quality relationship, they will use other cues to assess quality.

PRICING ERRORS

We know that a buyer has a lower and upper price threshold, implying that he or she has a range of acceptable prices for a purchase. Furthermore, the existence of a lower price threshold implies that there are positive prices greater than zero dollars that are unacceptable because they are considered to be too low. This may be a result of a suspicion that the quality of the service is low.

A pricing error fails to recognize this range. To illustrate this issue, consider the plight of two local accountants who opened a local tax accounting service. They quickly gained a reputation of providing excellent service and enjoyed a competitive advantage over the nationally franchised tax consulting services. However, the competition offered additional service hours and charged a price premium over the local accountants. Instead of raising their price and offering the new service, they maintained a lower price. The result was that they lost customers. The local tax consulting service failed to recognize this relationship between price and perceived value, and that there is an important link between perceptions of quality and perceptions of value.

A second pricing error occurs when a company does not distinguish between absolute price and relative price. Usually a buyer has alternative choices available for a contemplated purchase and normally selects from among these choices. The prices of these alternative choices may provide cues that facilitate this decision process. Even if the numerical prices are different, however, it cannot be assumed that the prices are perceived to be different.

The error occurs when a company initiates

a small price increase. The perception of a price change may be more important than the magnitude of the change. It has also been shown that people are more sensitive to price increases than to decreases. Pricing decisions should reflect the relative nature of price perception.

DEVELOPING PRICING STRATEGIES

There are many kinds of pricing decisions that a company must make. Among these is the decision on what specific price to charge for each service marketed. But the specific price to charge depends on the type of customer to whom the service is sold. If different customers purchase in varying quantities, should the seller offer volume discounts? The company must also decide whether to offer discounts for early payment, and if so, when a customer is eligible for a cash discount and how much to allow for early payment. Normally, the company sells multiple services, and these questions must be answered for each service. Additionally, the need to determine the number of price offerings per type of service and the price relationships among the services offered makes the pricing problem more complex.

One of the most interesting and challenging decision problems is that of determining the price of a new service. Such pricing decisions are usually made with very little information on demand, costs, competition, and other variables that may affect the chances of success. Many new services fail because they do not possess the features desired by buyers, or because they are not available at the right time and place. Others fail because they have been incorrectly priced, and the error can as easily be in pricing too low as in pricing too high. The difficulty of pricing new services is enhanced by the dynamic deterioration of the competitive status of most services as they mature.

The core of new product pricing takes into account the price sensitivity of demand and the incremental promotional and production costs of the seller. What the product is worth to the buyer, not what it costs the seller, is the controlling consideration. What is important when developing a new service's price is the relationship between the buyers' perceived benefits in the new service relative to the total acquisition cost, and relative to alternative offerings available to buyers.

Skimming Pricing

Two alternative strategies can be chosen once the company has dealt with the issue of customer perception. Some services represent drastic improvements upon accepted ways of filling a demand. For these services, a strategy of high prices with large promotional expenditure during market development may be appropriate when:

1. Sales of the service are likely to be less sensitive to price in the early stages than when it is "full-grown" and competitive imitations have appeared.
2. Launching a new service with a high price is an efficient device for breaking up the market into segments that differ in price elasticity of demand. The initial high price serves to skim the cream of the market that is relatively insensitive to price.
3. A skimming policy is safer, in that facing unknown elasticity of demand, a high initial price serves as a refusal price during the stage of exploration.
4. High prices may produce greater dollar sales volume during market development than are produced by low initial prices. If so, skimming pricing will provide funds to finance expansion into the larger-volume sectors of a market.
5. A capacity constraint exists.
6. There is a high consumers' surplus for the service.

Penetration Pricing

This is a second strategy for a new service. Despite its many advantages, a skimming-price policy is not appropriate for all new services. Using low prices as a wedge to get into mass markets early may be appropriate when:

1. Sales volume of the service is very sensitive to price, even in the early stages of introduction.
2. It is possible to achieve substantial economies in unit costs by operating at large volumes.
3. A service faces threats of strong potential competition soon after introduction. Thus, a strong market position becomes an early goal of the introduction.
4. There is no class of buyers willing to pay a higher price to obtain the service.

While a penetration pricing policy can be adopted at any stage in the service's life cycle, this pricing strategy should always be examined before a new service is marketed. Penetration pricing should be explored again as soon as the service has established an elite market. Sometimes a service can be rescued from premature death by adoption of a penetration price after the cream of the market has been skimmed.

MANAGEMENT OF PRICING

Value-oriented pricing can help prevent the error of setting a price that is too high relative to perceived or delivered value. It can also avoid setting a price that is too low relative to the value perceived by customers. Pricing only from the viewpoint of satisfying internal profit needs often ruins attempts to gain a competitive edge and the ability to set prices above average market prices. A number of pricing practices and policies are consistent with the contemporary decision environment, including:

1. *Determine consistent objectives*—Not all pricing objectives may be consistent. For example, increasing volume, improving cash flow, or improving margins may actually lead to very different pricing decisions. In spite of the contradictions, companies often indicate that they are attempting to accomplish each of these objectives simultaneously. Thus, it is important that pricing objectives be clearly stated, mutually consistent, and prioritized. Moreover, everyone concerned with the pricing decision, at any level in the organization, must understand the relevant objectives.

2. *Establish a pricing research program*—In terms of applied marketing research, the relative effect of price changes and price differences is the least understood and the least researched. The lack of data in this area has led to many inappropriate pricing strategies. At a minimum, a pricing research program should develop the relevant cost classifications and determine how customers relate price to quality and value perceptions. Such an effort is necessary to understand the cost and volume effects of price changes and relative price differences.

3. *Maintain feedback and control*—It is important that companies establish procedures to ensure that pricing decisions fit into their overall marketing strategies. Often, pricing decisions are made within the financial management function of the organization, and the potential for ignoring or minimizing the effect of buyers' perceptions is increased. Moreover, such a pricing approach tends to emphasize the cost aspects of the pricing decision. Buyers are typically not interested in what it costs the seller to provide the services. Rather, they are interested in the price-value relationship. Feedback gives information on the perception of this relationship.

4. *Use rigorous thinking*—Service companies also need to avoid me-too pricing strategies and tactics. A careful analysis of the organization's objectives, costs of providing specific services, competitors' offerings and costs, and the value perceptions of prospective and served customers must be completed before establishing specific strategies. Each service must be priced as an individual offering while understanding its inherent relationship to the other offerings in the service line.

THE IMPACT OF TELECOMMUNICATIONS ON THE SERVICE INDUSTRIES

Ann M. Wolf, Vice-President, Robert E. La Blanc Associates, Inc.

Universal switched telephone service is the essential factor of the many different telecommunication services available in the United States today. Yet it has just been over 125 years since the invention of the telephone and the availability of limited telephone service in this country. A few years after the initiation of telephone service, telecommunication regulation was established in 1885. By 1893, AT&T dominated long-distance service, interconnecting with 6,000 telephone companies providing local service throughout the country.

Universal telephone service was an objective established by regulation in 1910 when AT&T became a regulated monopoly charged with providing universal, interdependent service to subscribers of all telephone exchanges. This situation existed until 1984 when AT&T was separated from the Regional Bell Operating Companies (RBOCs) by an antitrust consent decree. This milestone was a major impetus in the deregulation of telecommunication services and has accelerated competition and change in the telecommunication industry.

Over the years, telecommunication technology has changed considerably, enabling telephone companies to continue to develop and offer new services while maintaining affordable prices to their customers. For example, modern switches, digital transmission, fiber optics, as well as other technological advancements have all drastically reduced the telephone companies' need for personnel and equipment, thus lowering the cost of providing telecommunication service.

Digitization of the telecommunication network is taking place today, allowing for new services that were unavailable on an analog network. Digitized services are generally clearer and have less noise than their analog counterparts. Packetized data are another technology that is proving advantageous to businesses. Data that are transmitted via packets are more apt to arrive intact and are less error prone.

Wireless communication is growing at a much faster rate than was originally anticipated. The convenience, ease of use, and widespread geographical availability have encouraged telecommunication users to embrace this technology.

Another technological improvement is the availability of increased bandwidth or telecommunication transmissions. Businesses benefit as they are able to send and receive more information at faster speeds than in the past. Compression technology further improves the amount of information that can be carried over a transmission path, further lowering telecommunication costs.

STANDARDS

Ubiquitous service depends, in part, on the acceptance of standards among the equipment manufacturers and providers of service. The critical issue of standards can be demonstrated with the evolution of fax service. Fax equipment has been available for over twenty-five years, but it was not until the mid-1980s when a fax standard was accepted that this service began to grow. Today, because of the standard that was adopted by both equipment manufacturers and service providers, fax service is ubiquitous.

Other telecommunication services have been similarly slow to develop because the lack of standards allows products and services to be incompatible, for example, the Integrated Services Digital Network (ISDN). The lack of ISDN standards produced a reluctance to develop applications that would promote usage of ISDN service. Recently, a North American standard was established for ISDN that will be deployed in the early 1990s. New ISDN products and services have been available to the business community since this standard has been deployed. When assessing the future availability of new telecommunication services, businesses need to consider the status of uniform standards that could speed up or slow down the deployment of their services.

TELECOMMUNICATION CHANGES

The new technology, increased competition, development of new services, changing regulation, and other changes in the industry are impacting the services industry in many ways. The following issues are examples:

1. *Telecommunication costs*—The cost of making a telephone call has decreased dramatically during the second half of the twentieth century. Today, telecommunication services can be economically employed for eighty services, such as telemarketing, audio and video teleconferencing, that were not even anticipated twenty years ago. It is expected that, as the telephone companies continue to make cost-saving improvements and equipment suppliers develop new technology, the absolute cost of telecommunication will decrease and the relative cost-per-unit of telecommunication will drop even more.

2. *New telecommunication service*—The availability of telecommunication services continues to increase, providing businesses with opportunities to improve efficiency and productivity and enter new markets. Since the 1980's, new telecommunication tools, such as electronic mail, have been developed and have changed the way business is transacted. Using electronic mail, managers are able to effectively communicate with their co-workers on a regular basis, keeping the entire team up-to-date.

Wanting maximum efficiency, businesses need to consider their telecommunication requirements in the structuring of the workplace. Sufficient telecommunication tools, that is, fax, conferencing services, messaging, voice and/or electronic mail, can significantly improve the productivity of the work force. As telecommunication services increase, the requirements for office space, secretarial and other support, and logistical services can decrease. This will reduce the cost of providing services and open the door for new services to be designed and sold.

3. *Networking via telecommunication services*—With the improved voice data telecommunication services available today, people no longer need to work in close proximity to one another in order to work together or exchange information. Business locations can be chosen strictly according to economics and linked to other locations via telecommunications. For example, a telemarketing firm might choose to locate in an area with an adequate labor force rather than in its primary calling area, trading more efficient labor for higher telecommunication costs.

Field workers, whether they provide sales, maintenance, delivery, or other services, can maintain constant contact with their firms, relaying and receiving information through wireless communication as needed. This online sharing of information can save time, improve customer service, and cut down on cost.

4. *Information availability*—Today, telecommunications can dramatically increase the availability of information to businesses. Online databases exist for a wide variety of subjects and are available to users on a dial-up basis. Managers can access needed corporate information directly and no longer have to depend on others to gather information for them.

5. *Customer service expectations*—The availability of improved telecommunication services has raised expectations of customers for a higher level of service. For example, services can be ordered by telephone twenty-four hours a day, information is faxed at the time of request, and problems are solved with a telephone call. This access to rapid service and problem solution has made consumers less willing to tolerate delay. It can be expected that availability of new and improved telecommunication services will continue to raise customer expectations. The business with the best telecommunication network will have an advantage over its competitor.

ISSUES OF CONCERN

Some of the changes taking place in telecommunication services have created concern both to the industry and its customers:

1. *Privacy*—An intelligent network offers many advantages to the user, but by its very nature it must store an enormous amount of data including information about its customers. There is concern that this information could be misused or be available to unauthorized persons.

A privacy issue currently causing a great deal of debate concerns the caller identification service available in some areas. This service provides the caller with the telephone number of the person placing the call. Some regulatory commissions are now debating whether this service should be considered an invasion of privacy and are restricting the availability of the service.

2. *Complexity*—Complexity is a by-product of telecommunication networks offering an extensive array of service. In order to effectively utilize the services available to them, users must understand how they operate and how the service will assist them to do their job. As the number of services escalates, the task of understanding and utilizing them increases.

3. *Obsolescence*—Rapidly changing technology always carries with it the problem of obsolescence. Business decisions must be made as to when is the appropriate time for upgrading a telecommunication system to obtain additional features. As with all economic decisions, the cost of new telecommunication equipment must be evaluated against the expected benefits of the new services for the firm.

THE FUTURE

Some telecommunication changes will be so revolutionary as to be unpredictable in their impact. To illustrate this point, consider a telecommunication network that is no longer based on telephone numbers but instead directs calls to the user, regardless of his or her location. The network will be capable of determining the user's location—that is, home, office, car—and will address the call to the appropriate telephone. The advantages to business customers using such a system are staggering.

Major changes can also be expected internationally as the world's facilities improve and become part of a sophisticated telecommunications structure. The initiative is being driven by multinational businesses that increasingly are taking a global approach to sources of supply, the identification of markets and customers, and the use of partnerships and alliances to restructure their operations and activities. Individuals and smaller businesses will also benefit as worldwide communications capabilities improve and costs continue to decrease.

THE CHANGING NATURE OF PROFESSIONAL SERVICES

Robert A. Smith, Jr., Managing Partner, Smith and Hiatt

THE MEANING OF SERVICE

A profession is a business conducted with a body of knowledge, theory as well as practice, standards for admission, continuing certification, and ethical standards. All of these areas are receiving continued and even increased attention in the 1990s.

What is changing is the meaning of service. A lawyer can assess a set of facts, explain options to a client, and, if needed, file or respond to a lawsuit. Accountants, financial advisers, and other professionals perform similar functions where expertise and skill are sought and provided. Performing the requested duties is no longer an adequate meaning of service.

A lawyer and, by extension, other professionals must be able to provide the timely and often specific behavior, paperwork, or information needed in a complex business society. Service now means:

- *Customization*—A standard court filing is not standard at all. The law firm must use word processing and other technology to customize documents to meet the exact needs of clients.
- *Volume*—Changing conditions mean a feast one week and a famine the next, as clients shop for services and cut off professional providers on short notice. The law firm must be prepared to handle a large volume of a specific business

one quarter and an equally large volume of an entirely different business the next.
- *Range of services*—A law firm can no longer specialize so easily in a single practice, such as real estate or litigation. A simple closing of a sale on commercial property can raise issues of third-party liability, performance under contracts, financing the purchase, and pollution considerations. Bad advice, even in an unfamiliar area, can produce client dissatisfaction or even the specter of malpractice.
- *Fulfilling expectations*—Even when the service is perfectly fine, expectations can be violated. Did the firm send a typewritten reply when a customer expected to see computer graphics executed on a laser printer? Did the client want the paper file, a faxed response, or an electronic document that can be manipulated without the aid of the professional services firm?
- *Compatibility*—Services must increasingly be provided in compatible formats and systems with a client's own system. A billing report may have to meet specific formats as to the activities performed and the accrued charges. Documents may have to be formatted to be electronically read. Financial reports may need to be created with specific software and network features.

It is no longer enough to do a service function using the systems and capabilities of the professional provider. Clients now demand a definition of service that considers their own needs.

CLIENT RELATIONSHIPS

As a result of new services expectations, a senior partner can no longer rely on a personal relationship to solidify the linkage with a client. The power breakfast and golf outing still exist but the "old-boy" network is going in the direction of the manual typewriter. Discussions with clients increasingly cover topics such as accuracy of documents, timeliness of work, necessity of costs, and what can be done in the future to do a better job.

The task of maintaining a client relationship is complicated by the transient nature of many professionals and client contact personnel. Lawyers change firms in response to real or perceived opportunities and clients may stay, go, or divide their business. The client contact person may be rotating through a three- to five-year assignment and depart with almost no notice. The replacement contact person may be transferred from a distant city and have no expectation of staying more than a few years. Or worse, the new contact person may be located in a distant city a long way off from the services being provided.

The changing client relationship is accompanied by new rules of competition. If once it was unprofessional to steal clients, no such barrier exists today. Clients are fair game for any predators in the jungle. But who is feeding on whom? In many cases, clients pit lawyers, accountants, brokers, and others against each other to gain monetary or other benefits. The loyalty of long-term relationships has eroded in the face of boards of directors, managements, consumer groups, and others who are seeking new ways to conduct professional services business.

MANAGEMENT IMPLICATIONS

The changing service requirements have a number of impacts on firms that provide professional services, including:

- *Cost of the equipment*—The firm must budget for the acquisition of new equipment and the maintenance of sometimes elaborate hardware systems. Of equal importance is widespread training of staff members who must respond to business requests using the various pieces of equipment. In a law firm, even the attorneys must be conversant with the systems as the practice of law moves from paper to a mixture of mediums.

- *Dealing with obsolescence*—Essentially, this is an issue of when to change equipment or systems. In the days of typewriters, a change was needed when a machine got old and would not work anymore. A typewriter might hang on for longer than the life of the typist. This does not work anymore. A 1,600-baud modem still sends documents and might last for ten more years. It makes no difference. The client does not want documents sent slowly. A firm that is perceived as being outdated will lose business to the firm with a 9,600-baud modem. Obsolescence decisions have become a new ball game.

- *The person or the machine?*—The new equipment and systems entering professional services organizations are fundamentally changing the way we work. The typing pool is gone. Proofreading of documents is a mixed task of people and machines. Some labor-intensive tasks have disappeared completely as a machine interacts directly with a lawyer, skipping the steps that were previously performed by secretaries, paralegals, or typists. People must be trained to perform new tasks. In many cases, positions disappear forever.

- *Increased role of management*—Overall, these impacts require considerably more attention to the management of the professional services business.

LIABILITY

Up to now, we have examined important and real changes in the delivery of professional services. We have not dealt with a particularly ugly specter that has raised its head, the prospect of malpractice.

Lawsuits are filed against professionals who commit negligence. This is not so unreasonable. They are also filed against professionals who do not commit negligence. This is nothing more than a hunt for money to remedy real or imagined grievances.

Whether real or not, third-party liability has become the great management concern of successful service firms. Some management considerations are:

- *Acceptance of work*—The firm should not accept assignments that it cannot complete properly. If the firm is understaffed, lacks the necessary skills, or has a potential conflict of interest, it may be wise to decline the work.
- *Training programs*—The firm should institute internal and external programs to sharpen employee skills. A current knowledge of the profession, firm policies and procedures, and the importance of specific job behaviors all help avoid mistakes.
- *Work assignments*—Care is needed in assigning work. Highly sensitive and potentially explosive tasks must be identified and completed by people who understand the exposure and need for perfect work.
- *Policies and systems*—In areas where errors are possible or likely, the firm needs procedures to minimize the chance of failure. A docket with more than one person checking on dates can avoid a missed deadline. A conflict-of-interest system can catch possible conflicts before work is begun.

One's best efforts are no longer enough to avoid a charge of negligence. All personnel, from the managing partner to the receptionist, must know the client and the client's business well enough to fulfill expectations when clients call, seek information, or receive service.

Public-Sector and Nonprofit Management

Herrington J. Bryce, Section Editor

Introduction   *Herrington J. Bryce*   16-3

Competencies of Effective Public-Sector Management
   Richard E. Boyatzis   16-5

The Leadership Function in the Public Sector   *Marc Bassin*   16-9

The Power of Government Agencies   *Charles H. Koch, Jr.*   16-14

Evaluating Public Programs   *Joseph S. Wholey*   16-18

Decision Making in the Public Sector   *William John Hanna*   16-22

Ten Principles to Guide the Nonprofit   *Herrington J. Bryce*   16-25

The Management of Nonprofit Organizations   *Dennis R. Young*   16-27

Information Technology and the Nonprofit Manager   *Ahmed Zaki*   16-31

Public and Nonprofit Marketing   *Christopher H. Lovelock and*
   Charles B. Weinberg   16-36

Auditing Nonprofits   *Anne Farley*   16-42

INTRODUCTION

Herrington J. Bryce

The public sector contains a large number of government and quasi-governmental organizations that interact with the private and nonprofit areas of the economy. The interaction can be productive or it can be filled with tension. The nonprofit sector can involve large sums of money, challenges of fund-raising, and the need for both administrative and political skills. The manager can get results or can get fired by a volunteer board.

Managing in both sectors is a great challenge. On the one hand, the manager has control of enormous resources that can be used to fulfill lofty humanitarian and social goals. On the other hand, the constraints of the system are formidable. Operating in a virtual fishbowl, the manager must satisfy a wide range of constituents with conflicting goals and interests. This can produce waste, gridlock, suboptimization, and the frustration of national and local policies and priorities.

In this section, we have asked a number of expert observers to comment on key issues that affect management in the public and nonprofit sectors. The authors have identified issues that reach the core of the problem of managing in the absence of a profit motive. The chapters provide a mixture of technical information to improve management ability and suggestions for ways to solve complex problems under trying circumstances. In fact, this is the reality of managing government agencies, hospitals, school systems, charities, and similar organizations at the end of the twentieth century.

Richard Boyatzis examines the factors associated with competence in public-sector managers. Marc Bassin builds directly on this foundation as he discusses leadership in the public sector. Charles Koch develops the foundation for government regulation of the private sector. In a society of many lawyers, government has been profoundly affected by the rules and regulations that may later be interpreted in a court of law. To answer whether government agencies are getting results, Joseph Wholey discusses the evaluation of program performance. William Hanna encourages quality decision making at all levels of government.

Herrington Bryce offers some principles for effective management for nonprofits. Dennis Young builds an economic foundation for managing in nonprofit organizations. Without the profit motive, agencies and departments must seek other goals and agendas. The focus shifts as Ahmed Zaki introduces the role of management information systems and technology that affects the public sector. If we can measure performance, we should also pursue high levels of achievement. Then, information on performance measurement is contained in the reports of auditors. Next, Christopher Lovelock and Charles Weinberg discuss an increasingly important topic for nonprofit organizations; that is, the need to understand how the functional area of marketing must be adjusted to be a valuable tool to help the nonprofit organization achieve its goals. Finally, Anne Farley shows how to gain useful information from the independent audit of a nonprofit organization.

The public and nonprofit sectors have become complex and pervasive. They affect managers in all areas of the economy. Also, they frequently participate in a sharing of management skills as private-sector managers accept appointments in government agencies or large nonprofit entities and politicians, government bureaucrats, and nonprofit managers accept positions in private corporations. This section encourages thinking about the unique nature of management in the public sector and nonprofit organizations.

Herrington J. Bryce, *Ph.D., CLU, Ch.F.C., is currently Life of Virginia Professor of business administration at The College of William and Mary. He specializes in corporate as well as nonprofit finance and management. He is the author of* Financial and Strategic Management for Nonprofit Organizations *(Prentice-Hall, 1992).*

COMPETENCIES OF EFFECTIVE PUBLIC-SECTOR MANAGEMENT

Richard E. Boyatzis, Professor, Weatherhead School of Management, Case Western Reserve University

COMPETENCIES AS A COMPONENT OF JOB PERFORMANCE

Public-sector organizations need competent managers to reach their objectives efficiently and effectively. People enter the public sector work force "to serve" a mission. Management in the public sector is more complex than management in the private sector because of conflicting demands of this mission and efficiency: to develop and maintain values, policies, practices, and traditions of the governmental institutions serving the society yet juggle limited resources to work toward unlimited objectives.

All of this juggling occurs in the context of an organization. The organization has policies and procedures reflected in the internal structure and systems. It also has a direction in the form of a mission, purpose, or strategy. The organization has physical, financial, and technical resources. It has a tradition and a culture. The organization exists in the context of a larger economic, social, and political community. All of these factors contribute to the internal organizational environment.

Although the goals and environment are different in the public sector, effective performance is as important as it is in the private sector. This means the manager must attain specific results (i.e., outcomes) required by the job through specific actions while maintaining or being consistent with policies, procedures, and conditions of the organizational environment. Certain characteristics or abilities of the person enable him or her to demonstrate the appropriate specific actions. These characteristics or abilities can be called competencies. People use their competencies to respond to the demands of a job.

Effective performance occurs when three critical components are consistent, or "fit." The components are shown in Exhibit 16-1. Although it is possible that effective performance may result when only two of the components are congruent, or fit, the likelihood is less.

IDENTIFYING COMPETENCIES

A job competency is an underlying characteristic of a person in that it may be a motive,

Exhibit 16-1. A Model of Effective Job Performance

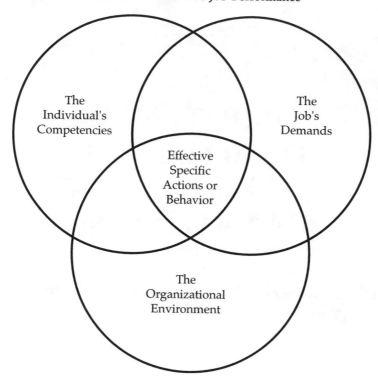

trait, skill, aspect of one's self-image or social role, or a body of knowledge that he or she uses. The existence and possession of these characteristics may or may not be known to the person; they may be an unconscious aspect of the person. Because job competencies are underlying characteristics, they may be apparent in a variety of actions. Therefore, to define a competency, we must determine what the actions were and the intent or meaning of the actions.

It is also important to distinguish competencies from tasks, or functions, which are required in the job. A function such as organizing resources requires a person to use multiple competencies, such as analytic and planning skills, to perform it effectively. In communicating a particular organization of resources to others, additional interpersonal skills would be needed, such as influencing others. Therefore, selecting staff, decision making, delegating responsibility, and repairing a machine are tasks or functions and are not skills.

A study by the author sought to explain differences in general qualitative distinctions of performance (i.e., poor, average, and superior) of managers in a variety of jobs and organizations.

In the research effort, managers in twenty-one management jobs in four federal departments or agencies within the U.S. government were studied. The study involved four steps: (1) determining an appropriate measure of job performance; (2) identifying the elements that distinguished between superior from average performance; (3) conducting interviews to determine critical incidents on the job and to document the behavior of individuals during those incidents, and then systematically coding the events for various competencies; and (4) identifying and administering tests.

One result of the research was the identification of various qualities as indicators of competencies. (For a complete description of the data and analysis, the reader is referred to *The Competent Manager: Effective Performance* [John Wiley & Sons, 1982].)

The Goal and Action Management Cluster

One finding was a group of characteristics clustered under the term of goals and actions. The characteristics were:

- *Efficiency orientation:* a concern with doing something better. Average performers demonstrated more of it than did poor performers.
- *Proactivity:* a disposition toward taking action to accomplish something. Superior performers demonstrated more of it than did average and poor performers.
- *Diagnostic use of concepts:* a way of thinking in which the person applies a concept to a situation and interprets events through that concept. Superior and average performers demonstrated more of it than did poor performers.
- *Concern with impact:* a concern with symbols of power to have impact on others. The superior performers demonstrated more of it than did poor performers.

An implication of these findings is that managerial performance could be improved if the environmental demands placed on the organizations and managers were altered. The changes would have to allow for measurement of performance, establishment of goals and plans, diagnosis of performance problems and potential for improvement with the appropriate concepts, managerial initiative to implement changes, and the power to put them into effect. This is not merely a contention that managers in the public sector would be more effective if their environment were similar to the environment of private-sector organizations. Remember, effective managers within public sector organizations demonstrated more of these competencies than their less effective peers.

This type of change in environmental demands would be complex and require careful thought. Otherwise, the implementation of such changes would wallow in additional procedural regulation. At the core of this implication would be a massive effort to redesign public sector management jobs in terms of responsibilities, tasks, functions, span of control, performance measures, and commensurate rewards. Recent reforms in the civil service system (i.e., a merit-based bonus system for senior federal executives and new performance appraisal procedures) suggest the possibility that some of these changes have been recognized as desirable. The question remains whether current efforts can be enough to have the desired impact. There is also a question whether such programs have taken into account differences in time horizon, institutional response time, policy-directed objectives, and other factors that make public sector management different than private-sector management.

The Leadership Cluster

Another group of characteristics is a leadership cluster and includes:

- *Self-confidence:* often called decisiveness or presence. Superior performers demonstrated more of it than did average and poor performers, and average performers demonstrated more of it than did poor performers.
- *Effective use of oral presentations:* a competency with which people make effective verbal presentations, whether these presentations be in one-on-one meetings or an address to an audience of several hundred people. Superior performers demonstrated more of it than did average and poor performers.

The combination of showing self-confidence and use of oral presentations is critical to public sector managers. They are often under pressure during presentations to reflect "administration" policies and perspectives. The press and the public scrutinize such presentations. Groups within the government (i.e., legislative committees and regulatory agencies) and those outside the government (i.e., special interest lobbies and the press) have access to and examine presentations.

Human Resource Management and Directing Subordinates

The study also covered interactions between managers and their subordinates. Some of the characteristics that became evident were:

- *Use of socialized power:* a competency in which the person uses forms of influence to build alliances, networks, coalitions, or teams. Superior and average performers demonstrated more of it than did poor performers.
- *Managing group process:* a competency in which people can stimulate others to work together effectively in group settings. Superior performers demonstrated more of it than did poor performers.
- *Developing others:* a competency with which managers specifically help someone do his or her job. Average performers demonstrated significantly more of it than did superior and poor managers.
- *Use of unilateral power:* a competency with which people use forms of influence to obtain compliance; that is, managers act to stimulate subordinates, or others, to go along with their directions, wishes, commands, policies, or procedures. Average performers demonstrated significantly more of it than did poor performers.
- *Spontaneity:* a competency with which people can express themselves freely or easily. Superior and average performers demonstrated significantly more of it than did poor performers.

Effective managers build networks and are able to establish identity, spirit, and cooperation within work groups. They appear to do it in a way that does not threaten to violate these other concerns about interagency or interdepartmental functioning. Managers who consistently coach, counsel, and seek to develop others or who "swing a mighty stick" appear less effective. They are possibly too involved or too naive about their human resources.

CONCLUSION

It should be obvious, then, that there *are* competencies that enable a manager to be effective, and beyond, to be superior. The human resource management systems, including selection, promotion, training, career pathing, performance appraisal, and compensation must be focused on getting and keeping people with these abilities. Many managers in the public sector began their career as professionals committed to public service. For them, the organization should develop and nurture these competencies early in their careers as managers.

It should also be clear that effective public-sector management cannot be achieved by simply importing managers from the private sector. The environments, mission, resources, and challenges are vastly different. The competencies needed and the mix of them, vital to superior performance, are not the same in the public and private sector.

THE LEADERSHIP FUNCTION IN THE PUBLIC SECTOR

Marc Bassin, Vice-President, Human Resources Development, Montefiore Medical Center

Leadership is an intricate and delicate art, not a science, developed like all arts through desire, dedication, continuous assessment and correction, and perseverance. Its function is to initiate, instill, and maintain the quest for peak performance as the fundamental and primary operating premise of the organization.

Leadership centers around two basic and interdependent themes: direction and energy. Without direction, energy leads nowhere. Without energy, direction is meaningless. Most major public-sector organizations labor under difficult and adverse conditions surrounding issues such as education, health care, crime, drugs, government, and the environment. Energy and direction are precisely the two areas most lacking. Thus, while the nature of leadership does not differ between the private and the public sector, both the need and difficulty are significantly greater in the public sector. This is overcome to some degree by the noble and emotionally engaging nature of most public-sector organizations. Their capacity to excel and desire to reach higher performance levels may be greater than the same attributes of many private-sector counterparts.

While the challenges encountered in the public sector are generally enormous, the resources available are often quite limited. This applies to money, supplies, capital, technology, and people. With lower salary levels, less flexibility in hiring (licensing and civil service regulations), and an undeserved but often negative image, the public sector may have greater difficulty attracting and retaining desirable staff. In the public sector, it is also more difficult to fire weak performers.

Public-sector organizations are often "behind the times" in the sophisticated use of management tools and human resource systems. They tend to plan and implement poorly, rarely pay enough attention to quality control, and are often chaotic or hectic environments. Morale in such places may be poor. The politics may be intense, often driven by various groups fighting for scarce resources and attention.

As a result of these problems, management is often characterized by a "we do the best we can" mentality. Such a mentality reinforces the reactive nature of many organizations, reaffirms limited standards and expectations, and enhances cynicism. It may leave the organization muddled and troubled.

In the public sector, outstanding service tends to be occasional and isolated. Leadership is often the exception rather than the rule. Instead of leadership, we may find acquiescence. This is not enough. The "rougher conditions" of the public sector make leadership all the more essential.

Despite all of its shortcomings, people generally choose to work in the public sector because they feel deeply about making a contribution to others, or to a cause. It is precisely around these values that they can be empowered and motivated to reach high performance and satisfaction. This underlying passion around purpose, if unleashed by effective leadership, is a powerful tool. It can be a more powerful motivator than the tangible resources and incentives available in the private sector. The ignition of energy in an empowered and focused organization guided by vision is the essence of leadership in the public sector.

CHANGE AND RENEWAL

To appreciate the function of leadership, it is important to understand the "open systems" nature of organizations. They are systems of interdependent parts (subsystems) open to physical, social, economic, and psychological forces. Organizations, like individuals, must adapt and adjust to environmental changes if they are to survive and prosper. This process is called renewal. It is not a simple process. Change is always accompanied by forces of resistance from individuals or groups in the organization who perceive themselves to be losing something. Change is also associated with stress. This is true even when change is perceived to be positive.

Without leadership, the organization becomes disassociated and disjointed from its environment. It thereby becomes less relevant and less effective. Eventually it will die. However, the need for renewal also has positive benefits. It can provide the opportunity and impetus for initiating the leadership process, developing a vision, and combining future needs and conditions with desired outcomes.

LEADERSHIP VISION

Vision is an ideal, dreamlike picture of what an individual or group would like an organization to be in the future. It answers the questions: Where should it be going? What should it look like? How should it operate? Vision also asks: What are the primary values around which the organization will be built?

Vision is a simple concept, easy to say and understand, yet hard to develop and use. When present, it captures the hearts, minds, and spirit of the people. In this role, it serves as the ultimate motivator. When absent, it leaves the organization and its people mired in the present.

Vision provides both a sense of purpose as well as a sense of direction for the enterprise. It must be an extremely compelling purpose so that it can generate an empowering sense of hope. It forms the foundation for leadership.

Visions rarely come from one person. They are usually formed by groups of people sharing their values and dreams for the future. It is the leader's function not to single-handedly develop a vision but rather to facilitate its development for the organization. Developing a vision is tricky. A vision must have just the right amount of intensity and ambition. If it is too grandiose, it can overwhelm rather than motivate. This drains energy. If it is not sufficiently ambitious, it can leave people cold with a "why bother" attitude. A powerful vision can be the ultimate motivator and driving force for an organization. To achieve this goal, the vision must be well formulated, jointly developed and owned, and communicated throughout the organization. Also, the vision must be linked to the deeply seated values and beliefs of the organization's employees.

While vision can be the most powerful of all motivators, there are two areas of serious vulnerability for leaders in the public sector. The first concerns the basic choice around vision. Once a vision is developed, communicated, and owned, it creates a large gap between itself and current reality. This gap in turn causes tension in the organization that can either be incredibly stimulating and challenging or turn into deadly cynicism. The gap between vision and reality can only be resolved in one of two ways. If the people in the organization see some significant progress in moving reality closer and closer to the vision, they will feel more and more empowered and capable. This is precisely the essence and function of leadership. The leader creates a gap between vision and reality and then works to close the gap by slowly but deliberately changing reality. The other resolution is to compromise the vision due to reality; that is, close the gap by expecting less. This is acquiescence, the opposite of leadership—an approach too often used.

The second vulnerability around a vision is very personal. Powerful visions are always deeply connected to values. Once the vision is stated, people expect leaders to serve as role models for the values inherent in it. If the organization perceives basic contradictions between the behavior of the leader and inherent values, the vision fades and the leader loses credibility. One merely needs to look at many of today's politicians to see how common and deadly this dynamic can be. Personally representing the vision clearly falls directly upon the leader. As a matter of fact, many leaders are almost fanatical about the values inherent in the visions they create.

EMPOWERING OTHERS

Empowering others is the leadership component that releases the energy needed to pursue the vision. It centers around two basic and interdependent principles: high expectations and trust. These, in turn, are coupled with involvement and ownership.

The idea behind empowerment is to unleash as much energy as possible within an organization in a targeted and aligned manner. Every person who feels empowered adds to this energy base, which grows in a synergistic fashion. However, this can only occur when leaders behave in such a way as to expand power by actively extending it to others. The function of leadership is to create ownership and mutually held high expectations around goals. The leader then stays out of how to achieve goals, leaving that to those

accountable. The leader does remain supportive, adding value in a coaching capacity.

Empowering individuals can be quite threatening to the status quo of the organization, because individuals often feel bound by senseless layers of authority, professional or functional roles, and other traditional organizational boundaries. Some boundaries are tangible, as the one often existing between union and nonunion workers. Others are more subtle, such as those surrounding diversity and bias.

Misalignments between the organization's vision and its actual functioning must be acknowledged and removed by leadership if true empowerment is to occur. This is even more crucial in the public sector where the intrinsic sense of motivation that accompanies empowerment is often the primary incentive mechanism. The importance of empowering others cannot be overemphasized. Without it, there may be compliance or obedience but no leadership or inspired performance.

ONGOING ASSESSMENT AND CORRECTION

Vision and empowerment are enough to start the leadership process but not enough to sustain it. This requires ongoing assessment and correction. Change and adjustment are inevitable and must be built into the leadership process. A critical function of leadership is to periodically stop the action, check progress, make adjustments, inject new data, set new targets, and proceed in a planned, proactive, and disciplined manner.

Public-sector organizations tend to be particularly poor in this regard. Few incorporate a planned, disciplined process into their modes of operation. Rather, they submit to everyday pressures and thereby contribute to what is often perceived as the chaos around them. It is similar to time management. Those who need it the most are often the least able to find the time to do it.

The leadership function requires two levels of focus and discipline. The first revolves around the assessment and correction component. If done seriously on a regular basis, assessment provides the organization with the focus and discipline to systematically accomplish the objectives related to its vision.

The second requires leaders to remain centered around the components of the leadership function. With so many constituencies vying for their time, attention, and energy, public-sector leaders often get diverted from strategic functions. They become consumed in daily operational issues. Indeed, the reputation that public-sector leadership has for being absorbed in crisis management is often well deserved. This is not a question of how hard leaders work but rather of where they are focusing their energy.

THE ROLE OF TEAMS

Leaders are under continuous and mounting pressure to increase productivity. With limited vehicles for incentives, demographic trends resulting in a smaller and less qualified work force, and workers demanding greater job satisfaction, public-sector leaders can easily be driven into a reactive, chaotic, and crisis mode of leadership. There is, however, one major powerful counter to these pressures, which remains largely untapped in most organizations. That resource is the team.

Most public-sector organizations are structured as professional, bureaucratic hierarchies. Such a structure becomes more and more strained under adverse conditions. The leader can restructure the organization into a series of semiautonomous, interconnected, interdisciplinary family or work teams. Each team can focus on key critical success factors and objectives from the vision.

Restructuring into a team model generally requires major changes. The leader must significantly flatten the organization, shedding unneeded layers of supervision and extending individuals' roles beyond their traditional functional boundaries. There are compelling reasons to realign public-sector bureaucracies into a team structure:

1. Well-functioning teams outperform individuals or bureaucratic entities. They do so by providing more access to needed information, stimulating and enhancing creativity, synergistically generating more energy and support among its members, and promoting higher levels of ownership, commitment, and loyalty.
2. Teams tend to be more flexible, more adaptable, more informal, and quicker moving than individuals working in traditional hierarchies.
3. Teams provide higher levels of job satisfaction for their members.
4. Teams are ideal vehicles for generating empowerment and its accompanying productivity.

Teams do not generally emerge naturally. They must be carefully structured, actively developed, constantly nurtured, trusted, and empowered if they are to maximize their potential. The leadership of a team centers around exactly the same four components as presented above. Each team is a mini-organization that must develop a vision, align itself with the organization, empower its members, use a process for assessment, correction, and development, and stay focused and disciplined if it is to succeed.

LEADERSHIP VERSUS MANAGEMENT IN THE PUBLIC SECTOR

A great deal has been made over the distinction between leadership and management. Leadership is about change, renewal, direction, and the future. Management focuses more on the present, on task coordination and completion. Leadership is about empowerment and energy. Management is about control and compliance. Certainly the boundaries between them are sometimes gray. We might note that management is an essential component of leadership. Leadership, however, is not an essential component of management. This is demonstrated by the fact that so many managers do not lead.

In the public sector, the distinction between leadership and management is particularly important. Organizations tend to suffer from an abundance of management and a corresponding lack of leadership. So many institutions have neglected leadership. The individuals in management positions have been socialized to a nonleadership mentality that they perpetuate themselves. Breaking out of bad habits calls for radical change, including removing many of those individuals in key middle management roles that have been too socialized to make the fundamental changes required to truly lead.

THE PERSONAL SIDE OF LEADERSHIP

The responsibilities of leadership can be stressful. This is particularly so in the public sector. The stakes of the enterprise are invariably high. "Screwing up" has visible negative consequences. Leaders face the need to continually inject energy and a sense of possibility into their organizations. In many cases, leaders must deal with malaise and cynicism. In other cases, they are overwhelmed by the tasks they face. Overall, the need to be a constant giver of energy puts a tremendous emotional and physical burden on public-sector leaders.

One useful way of characterizing individuals is to think of them as having three interdependent and interconnected spheres: a work sphere, a family and relationship sphere, and a self sphere, as shown in Exhibit 16-2. Each of these spheres is interconnected and open to each other. Activities in one sphere affect the others. Also, stress in one sphere moves into the others.

Many public-sector leaders have an uneven and unbalanced profile. The work sphere is large. The relationship sphere is smaller. The self sphere may not be developed at all. A measure of the size of each sphere is the number of hours spent per week in each.

An unbalanced profile does not provide a strong foundation for leadership. It is similar to a stool whose three legs are of unequal length. When unbalanced, the stress from

Exhibit 16-2. Three-Sphere Profile of an Individual

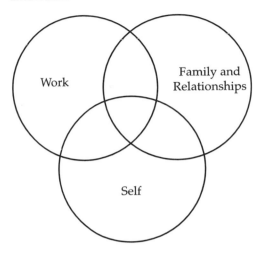

work may dominate the rest of an individual's life. Gradually, a person will suffer energy loss, illness, burnout, and stress-related syndromes.

Just like stress moves from one sphere to the other, energy also transfers. Here lies an antidote to stress. Instead of structuring their lives so they are dominated by the work sphere, leaders must put time and energy in the relationship and self spheres. In this way, they gain the strength of the three-legged stool. They can seek refuge from the strain of work.

Even more important, leaders can use energy generated in the other two spheres and bring it back with them to their work. They can experience rejuvenated attitudes and energy levels. Leaders need a nonwork passion—a hobby or some interest that gives a sense of physical, emotional, or spiritual energy.

Energy is a critical part of the ability to lead. Without a source of energy, a leader cannot provide energy. And so a requisite for effective leadership in the stressful world of the public sector is a balanced lifestyle that provides a source of energy into which a leader can tap in response to the demands of the workplace.

THE POWER
OF GOVERNMENT
AGENCIES

Charles H. Koch, Jr., Woodbridge Professor of Law, School of Law, The College of William and Mary

THE EMPOWERING PROCESSES

Administrative agencies are not specifically recognized in the Constitution. The Constitution establishes three branches of government: legislative, executive, and judicial. Many agencies are in the executive branch but some are independent, that is, they are not technically in any of the constitutional branches. Moreover even those agencies located in the executive branch have a life of their own, with only limited presidential supervision.

The relationship between the bureaucracy and the three constitutional branches is primarily defined by the constitutional principle of separation of powers. Many agencies, although part of the executive branch, may adjudicate cases and hence perform a function confined by Article III of the Constitution to the judicial branch. Only in the most egregious situations is a violation of the doctrine of separation of powers likely.

A fundamental administrative law question is how much authority the legislature may delegate to the agencies. The nondelegation doctrine holds that the legislature may not delegate legislative authority. The crux of the question is the definition of legislative power. In general, a delegation must establish some standard if it is to be upheld. The standards may be as broad as "feasible" or "in the public interest."

By this test, the delegations to the Securities and Exchange Commission are reasonably specific. For example, the language of section 10b-5 empowering the SEC to prohibit "any manipulative or deceptive device or contrivance" is clearly within the prescriptions of the nondelegation doctrine.

The public-sector manager will do well to understand whether his or her agency's mission is legislative, judicial, or executive in intent.

INTERNAL DECISION-MAKING PROCESSES

Administrative agencies perform an almost infinite variety of functions and they must have procedures tailored to these functions. The procedures should constrain the administrative process in the interest of fairness and justice and yet permit the flexibility necessary for government to be effective.

The search for this balance is one of the continuous challenges to administrative law and public management. Because public managers regulate the decision-making processes concerning a variety of substantive issues, they must manage the administrative law upon which they must rely. Substantive issues should be grouped according to shared characteristics.

Areas to Be Administered

The public manager might be involved in processes in three areas:

1. *Economic regulation*—This was once the major business of the administrative process. Generally it involves fixing rates and allocating business through licensing. It is intended to correct perceived market failures. Justification for the SEC, for example, was based on market failures in the securities industry demonstrated by the crash.
2. *Public-interest regulation*—This has attained more recent dominance. It involves command and control regulation to protect health, safety, and the environment.
3. *Social programs administration*—These include income support and educational enhancement programs.

Issues of Law

Administrative law deals with several categories of issues. The first consists of issues of law, which occur when the agency engages in statutory interpretation and applying traditional law as evolved by the courts. This is called common law. Two basic types of internal decision-making processes are used for such issues:

1. *Adjudication* determines individual rights or duties. An example is whether a broker has violated a securities law. Adjudication allows an agency to evolve policy, as courts do, on a case-by-case basis. Policies are created in the course of deciding individual rights or duties through adjudication.
2. *Rule making* involves the making of generalized decisions that affect the future. An example would be the required disclosures by corporate officers. Rule making is a process specifically designed to make policy.

Formality

Formality is defined as employing the methods of trial. A formal procedure is more trial-like than an informal procedure. Both adjudication and rule making may employ various elements of a trial and hence may vary as to their formal nature. Agencies may engage in formal adjudication, informal adjudication, formal rule making, and informal rule making. Usually formal, or trial-like, procedures are considered more appropriate for adjudicating individual rights or duties than for rule making. Rule making is characterized as quasi-legislative and the methods of legislation are considered more appropriate. Agencies have considerable freedom to choose among the degree of formality.

DUE PROCESS CLAUSES AND STATUTES

Due process clauses of the Constitution are an important source for the law, establishing procedural requirements by public agencies. The Fifth Amendment applies to federal agencies. The Fourteenth Amendment applies to state agencies.

The due process clause provides that no person shall "be deprived of life, liberty, or property, without due process of law." The language does not prohibit the government from depriving an individual of life, liberty, or property but only that it must do so through proper procedures.

In a seminal 1970 decision, *Goldberg v. Kelly*, the Supreme Court broadened the definitions of the interests protected by the clause. That case recognized a "new property," bringing within the definition of property "entitlements," such as welfare benefits and the like. Subsequent cases have recognized a "new liberty" interest as well, bringing values other than protection from actual restraints into the definition of liberty.

Applying these expanded definitions in specific cases has been complicated. In general, however, the Court has found protection where the agency or official must make a judgment before denying a benefit. For example, if a school principal may suspend a student for "disrupting" the educational environment, the student has an "entitlement" to remain in school until the official has conducted "some kind of hearing" to determine whether the student committed a disruption.

Due process law has developed an extremely flexible approach to the kind of hearing required. The required hearing may be as informal as a conference with the principal and teacher or as formal as a trial-like proceeding. As a guide to making this decision, the Supreme Court in *Mathews v. Eldride* recognized three dominant factors:

1. The private interest that will be affected by the official action.
2. The risk of an erroneous deprivation of such interest through the procedures used and the probable value, if any, of additional or substitute procedural safeguards.
3. The government's interest, including the function involved and the fiscal and administrative burdens that the additional or substitute procedural requirement would entail.

In addition to the constitutional minimum, two types of statutes regulate administrative procedures:

1. *Administrative procedure acts* set procedures for a broad range of agencies. They are the most important acts for regulating due process. All federal agencies and most state agencies are governed by these acts.
2. *Enabling acts* set procedures for specific agencies.

ADJUDICATION OF ISSUES

An adjudication may be initiated in several ways, including:

1. An enforcement agency may issue a complaint that immediately leads to a hearing.
2. An agency may issue a citation, much like a traffic ticket, in which case the private party must ask for a hearing to contest the citation.
3. The private party may request some action or benefit— a license, rate increase, Social Security benefit— that initiates a hearing to decide on that request.

The general principle is that the agency must give adequate notice upon the initiation of an adjudication to allow the private party to represent its position. When the agency adjudications are formal, it usually employs many of the discovery devices seen in a judicial proceeding. It may issue subpoenas or summons compelling documents or testimony. Then, the agency may have a prehearing conference. The government and the parties may agree on disclosure of documents, trim the issues, or negotiate a settlement.

There is almost always some type of presiding officer. In more formal hearings, the presiding officer is independent of the agency and performs like a judge. In less formal adjudications, the presiding officer may be a member of the agency's staff. The presiding officer controls the hearing.

In a formal hearing, there may be witnesses, cross-examination, and evidence introduced into the record. The rules of evidence and the examination of witnesses are usually relaxed compared to a courtroom, but are still followed in principle. Relevant evidence may be admitted for what it is worth. Hearsay, for example, is usually admitted. The function of a lawyer then is to assure that the evidence is introduced in a manner calculated to afford it the greatest weight.

Several concepts protect the integrity of the hearing process. Communication outside the hearing between the agency's enforcement staff and outside interested persons is generally prohibited. Bias and prejudgment, particularly arising from personal interest in the case, are not permitted.

The presiding officer may issue a recommended decision to a higher agency authority or merely certify the record to that authority. In more formal proceedings, the officer issues an initial decision that is final unless appealed. In those processes, the higher authority acts much like an appellate court. The final decision may ultimately be appealed to a court.

RULE MAKING

A rule or regulation sets a standard for a group or regulates a practice. It has general applicability and future effect. Rule making is considered a quasi-legislative function and hence the process often follows that of a legislative hearing. Although some enabling acts require trial-like procedures, the dominant process is "notice and comment" rule making. The basic requirements are notice, some opportunity to comment, and a statement of reasons accompanying the final rule.

Rule making usually has broad impact. Therefore all interested persons should be able to participate. This demands broad distribution of the notice of rule making and of the final rule. Administrative procedure acts require publication of the notice in the *Federal Register* along with information about how to participate. The final rule will not take effect until it is published in the *Federal Register*.

The effect of a rule is complicated. Legislative rules are given binding effect, even on courts. They are made pursuant to delegated authority to make rules and hence in a sense take the place of legislation. Nonlegislative rules are not binding on courts. They are generally exempted from the requirements of public procedures. They may have a variety of labels including "interpretative rules," "statements of policy," or "guidelines."

MONITORING ADMINISTRATIVE DECISIONS

Several processes exist to monitor and control bureaucratic decisions, including:

1. *Judicial review*—The decisions can be appealed in court.
2. *Executive review*—The president and governors have developed various means for monitoring agency action. In the federal system, the Office of Management and Budget (OMB) exercises much of this control through its authority to approve the agency budgets and legislative comments. It also exercises some direct control over rules. In the

states, in addition to other controls, the governors may have authority to veto rules.
3. *Legislative review*—Congress and the state legislatures have several methods for controlling agency action. Before the fact, they describe the agency's authority in the enabling act. After the fact, they use the appropriation process to communicate their desires to the agency. They also conduct oversight hearings and other oversight functions. The staff of the relevant committee has tremendous power over the agency. Hence, informal power exists to force agencies to submit rules for their approval.

PROCESSES FOR ASSURING OPEN GOVERNMENT

Open government is a necessary condition of democracy. The electorate must have the information to evaluate government performance. Several methods have evolved over the last few decades for assuring open government. These are generally classified under the phrase "freedom of information." The federal Freedom of Information Act (FOIA) releases most of the documents in the possession of the federal government. It requires federal agencies to grant access "upon request" to "any person." The import of these words is that anybody, whether or not directly affected by an agency proceeding, must be given access.

An agency may only protect documents that fall within one of nine limited exemptions. Thus, the strategy of the act is to grant access to everything and take back, through the exemptions, a few categories of documents. The exemptions then have become the focus of much of the law because they are the only impediment to disclosure. The exemptions that provide the major protection for government information are:

1. *State secrets*—There is limited protection for sensitive military and foreign affairs information.

2. *Deliberative process*—Internal documents involving the agency's deliberative process can be protected to the extent that they contain opinions and do not constitute "secret law."
3. *Law enforcement records*—Some law enforcement records may also be protected.
4. *Privileged or confidential business information*—This is protected if disclosure would interfere with the agency's ability to obtain information or would harm the business.
5. *Private information*—This is protected if disclosure would constitute a clearly unwarranted invasion of personal privacy; however, a surprisingly limited protection for personal privacy is provided.

While the FOIA benefits the public by fostering open government, it may create problems for individuals and businesses who deal with the government. Managers should always consider the potential of disclosure in submitting information to the government. Most states also have a freedom of information act. These acts vary but are similar to the federal act.

Privacy Act

Some additional protection is afforded by the Privacy Act, which provides two types of protection:

1. It regulates the government's ability to collect and distribute personal information.
2. It allows individuals for whom the government maintains a file to view that file and challenge any information contained in it.

Sunshine Act

"Sunshine" or open meetings provisions are often extremely important to state and local agencies and those who deal with such agencies. Basically they require agencies, including elected authorities, to conduct their business in public view. These acts permit closed meetings on certain sensitive issues. Efforts to avoid the impact of these acts by state and local officials, however, have been unsuccessful. These open meetings statutes have been strictly enforced. There is also a federal sunshine act, requiring open meetings for all federal authorities governed by collegial body.

EVALUATING PUBLIC PROGRAMS

Joseph S. Wholey, School of Public Administration, University of Southern California

A program is a set of resources and activities directed toward one or more goals. Any public agency, organizational unit, or local project can therefore be thought of as a program. A group of related activities can be thought of as a single program.

In the public sector, effective program performance includes success in gaining needed resources, delivering high-quality services, and attaining intended outcomes, as well as success in satisfying internal and external constituencies such as legislators, agency and program staff, grantees, professional groups, clients, and taxpayers. Program evaluation includes measurement of program costs, services provided, service quality, and outcomes achieved, comparisons based on those measurements, and use of the resulting information in policy and management decisions. Although not usually calling it "evaluation," public-sector managers have long been familiar with three forms of program evaluation:

1. Their own monitoring of program costs, activities, outputs, and outcomes (results).
2. Outside audits of program performance.
3. Qualitative studies of program operations. In total quality management (TQM), for example, evaluation of customer satisfaction is a key element in stimulating continuous improvements in program quality and productivity.

Over the past ten to twenty years, managers have become more familiar with additional forms of program evaluation:

4. Use of randomized experiments, time series analysis, and evaluation synthesis to estimate the extent to which program activities cause observed outcomes.
5. Use of benefit-cost analysis to compare the value of program outcomes with the value of the resources consumed by the program.

THE IMPORTANCE OF EVALUATION

Managers can use performance monitoring and other forms of evaluation to improve the productivity, quality, and credibility of the programs for which they are responsible. Using appropriate evaluation systems, managers can project the image and the reality of cost-effective, results-oriented management, stimulate improved program performance, communicate what their programs are accomplishing, and gain the resources needed to maintain and enhance program operations.

Since "red tape" and other constraints often inhibit effective program performance, managers may be able to enhance program performance by getting agreements with policymakers substituting outcome accountability for process accountability. This is the direction being taken, for example, in the educational reform movement.

Using periodic reports and other incentives, managers can stimulate higher program performance. Policymakers and managers can reward high performance, improved performance, or performance above expected levels. Higher-performing units can be rewarded through honor awards, removal of constraints, and delegation of authority. Policymakers and managers can provide financial incentives for higher performance through performance contracts or budget allocations.

Through periodic reports on program performance, program managers can enhance the credibility of their programs. The director of the Harlem Valley Psychiatric Center, for example, dramatically improved center performance and staved off threats to close the center by establishing clear, outcome-oriented objectives (rapid reduction of the inpatient census, appropriate placements in the community, and high-quality care for all patients in the hospital and in the community), getting periodic reports on the performance of units within the center, reallocating resources and responsibilities to the managers and staff of high-performing units, and publicizing unit performance within and outside the center.

The U.S. Public Health Service used a performance-based resource allocation system to stimulate improvements in community health center performance and to demonstrate to Congress that the community health center program was well managed, effective, and worthy of legislative and budget support. The U.S. Employment Service developed a performance-based resource allocation system to stimulate state agencies to improve services and to demonstrate to Congress and others that efforts were being made to improve U.S. Employment Service performance.

THE MANAGER'S ROLE IN PROGRAM EVALUATION

Managers can and should play central roles in evaluation of the programs for which they are responsible, as follows:

1. They can negotiate agreements on the criteria that will be used in assessing program performance. The key step in program evaluation is agreement on the types of evidence to be used to assess resources expended, services delivered, service quality, and program results.
2. They are well placed to identify sources of data on the costs, quality, outcomes, and value of the programs for which they are responsible and to encourage the production of evaluation data that will be useful in improving program performance.
3. They are ideally placed to use evaluation findings and to ensure that findings are communicated to other important constituencies.

PERFORMANCE MONITORING

A performance monitoring system periodically measures resources expended, services delivered, service quality, and program outcomes. It typically focuses on short-term and medium-term program outcomes rather than attempting to estimate the ultimate impacts of program activities. A performance monitoring system may compare different units or compare program performance with prior performance or standards of expected performance.

Some monitoring systems measure results achieved in different geographic areas or in different population subgroups. The most advanced performance monitoring systems compare units operating under comparable conditions or use statistical analyses that attempt to correct for differences in client char-

acteristics, community characteristics, or other factors.

State and local governments have developed outcome-oriented performance monitoring systems in such areas as economic development, elementary and secondary education, higher education, hospital care, mass transportation, police and fire services, public assistance, public health, road maintenance, and solid waste collection. Many states, for example, have developed systems for monitoring the performance of local school districts or individual schools in terms of such performance indicators as student achievement test scores, teacher and student attendance rates, dropout rates, and graduation rates.

Unadjusted program outcome measures may not provide valid indicators of program impacts. Thus, performance monitoring systems could reduce program impacts by encouraging services to clients for whom favorable outcomes would have been likely even in the absence of program services. Performance standards can be adjusted to avoid such errors. Though it appears that unadjusted performance standards did encourage such "creaming" in the early years of the Job Training Partnership Act (JTPA) program, the Department of Labor has since improved its adjustment models and encouraged services to more disadvantaged clients. Most states now use the Labor Department's models or similar procedures to adjust local JTPA performance standards to reflect the influence of participant and community characteristics.

Qualitative Evaluation

Qualitative evaluation is also important for management purposes. Qualitative evaluation uses observations, detailed descriptions, open-ended interviews, extracts from documents, photographs, videotapes, and expert judgments to assess "hard-to-measure" phenomena. Case studies and other qualitative evaluations can help policymakers and managers to understand program operations and results from the perspectives of clients and direct service providers, communicate the meaning of quantitative findings, and help explain variations in program performance.

Other Important Evaluation Options

To provide stronger justification for their programs when changes are being considered in budgets or authorizing legislation, managers may also find it helpful to commission or encourage evaluations of program impacts. Through randomized experiments, for example, evaluators can estimate the extent to which programs cause observed outcomes. Through time series analyses, evaluators can use differences in outcome trends before and after program implementation to estimate the extent to which program activities cause observed outcomes. Through evaluation syntheses, evaluators can use the results of many studies to produce more conclusive findings than those that could be produced by any single study. Through evaluations that include benefit-cost analyses, evaluators can compare program costs with estimates of the economic value of program impacts such as productivity improvements and cost savings in other programs.

IMPLEMENTING USEFUL EVALUATION SYSTEMS AT A REASONABLE COST

The measurement of program quality and program outcomes is likely to require new data collection, for example, through ratings by trained observers or telephone surveys of clients. The costs of data collection and data analysis can be minimized by using existing data to the extent feasible and by using random samples rather than data from the entire universe of interest. When there is a sufficient research base, it may be possible to reduce data collection costs by using output measures or short-term outcome measures as proxy measures of longer-term outcomes.

Cost-effective evaluation efforts can be facilitated through the use of advisory committees that represent major constituencies such as policymakers, appropriate management and staff levels, and relevant interest groups. Such advisory committees can be helpful in decisions on what data should be collected, what comparisons should be made, and how the resulting information should be disseminated and used.

Since it will seldom be possible to be definitive in predicting either the costs of data collection and data analysis or the usefulness of evaluation information, managers and evaluators will often find it helpful to pilot-test evaluation systems by collecting and analyzing small samples of data on program performance and reviewing the resulting information with intended users. In some cases, such pilot studies will provide sufficient information for policy or management decisions; in other cases, the pilot studies will lead to implementation of useful full-scale evaluations.

DECISION MAKING IN THE PUBLIC SECTOR

William John Hanna, The University of Maryland, College Park

A few years ago, the National Academy of Science's Committee on Science, Engineering, and Public Policy prepared a report identifying the nation's most vital subjects for additional research and study. One of these was decision making:

> The work of managers, of scientists, of engineers, of lawyers—the work that steers the course of society and its economic and governmental organizations—is largely work of making decisions and solving problems.... Nothing is more important for the well-being of society than that this be performed effectively, that we address successfully the many problems requiring attention at the national level. . . and at the level of our individual lives. (*Research Briefings 1986, National Academy Press, Washington, DC; copyright © 1986 by the National Academy of Sciences*)

Decision making is a challenging and complex process. Yet many public-sector managers think that decision making involves choosing among a small set of action alternatives. For instance, should we locate that new homeless shelter in neighborhood A or B? Should we hire a specialist to implement the new disability law? Alas, such choices constitute only one step in a complex and dynamic process. The components of a quality decision making effort are of two types:

1. *A series of sequential steps*—These include activation, diagnosis, the generation and choice of alternatives, implementation, and evaluation.
2. *A set of pervasive factors*—These include who decides, information, interpersonal dynamics, timing, and communication. Each component may be linked with one or all of the others.

ACTIVATION AND DIAGNOSIS

A manager usually gets involved in a decision-making effort as a consequence of becoming aware of a nonroutine problem or opportunity, caring about it, and believing that something should be done about it. This is activation. Unfortunately, activation does not always happen. Many important problems persist or opportunities remain unexploited by default. Sometimes, the manager is unaware, does not recognize the importance of the situation, or underestimates the possibilities of change. Or the manager may simply choose to duck a problem. Not actively making a decision is actually a decision to continue the status quo.

Failure to act may have good or bad consequences. Problems or opportunities do not remain at a constant level. Avoided problems may get worse or they may fade away. Opportunities not seized may expand or disappear. Sometimes, problems or opportunities are not "ripe" for a decision. They may be too "fuzzy" to address and strategic delay may be the best course of action.

At this step, the problem or its symptom must be diagnosed. In other words, we must try to identify the actual problem and its likely cause. To make the decision-making effort manageable, we may well have to simplify by focusing on the major problem and its likely cause. Medical doctors regularly face this challenge. The patient who complains about a headache must be diagnosed to determine whether she has a brain tumor, a chemical imbalance, or something else.

The range of diagnoses is limited by the values and beliefs of the diagnostician. Medical research has shown that national culture and professional specialty are among the determinants of a diagnosis. A manager's diagnosis is also influenced by his or her perspectives. Those having business management backgrounds, for instance, may well differ in their diagnoses from those trained in psychology. The story is told about the clinic where clients complained about waiting time. One staffer, trained in business management, diagnosed the problem as staff inefficiency and began a time-and-motion study to speed up intake and clinical procedures. But a staffer with a background in psychology saw the problem in terms of client restlessness and therefore proposed waiting room redecoration, piped music, and better magazines to read.

ALTERNATIVES

Having made a diagnosis, the manager must generate possible courses of action and then select one. Alternatives should be related to the organization's mission and goals. This still leaves the manager with choices in the specification of objectives and even the time horizon for results. Quality decision makers consider a broad range of alternatives. At a later point,

they narrow them down. In this process, it is useful to brainstorm, consult, and think imaginatively. If reasonable, the status quo should be included as an alternative.

To select among alternatives, decision makers should outline a set of objectives and time horizon. Each alternative must either be judged by a set of accept-reject criteria or by a broader selection method. A wide range of tools has been developed to select among a limited set of alternatives. The simplest is a coin flip, a technique that is appropriate for trivial choices. A more complex tool is the checklist of pros and cons. Its main defect is the failure to weight and rate. More powerful tools are usually needed. Two challenges arise in choosing among alternatives:

1. *Trade-off*—This arises when some alternatives are preferable on one factor but others are preferable on another. A useful tool for analyzing trade-offs is the decision matrix, a modification of the checklist that attaches weights to each factor and comparative assessments of each alternative on each factor.
2. *Risk*—A risk or uncertainty means that we do not know for sure what result will occur if we select a particular alternative. All we can do is estimate probabilities. This situation is usefully analyzed with a "decision tree," a tool that weights each outcome in terms of its desirability and the probability of occurrence.

With more powerful tools, trade-offs and risks can be analyzed together.

IMPLEMENTATION

Public-sector managers know the great gulf between selecting an alternative and implementing it. Implementation is the next step in decision making. The quality decision maker makes several implementation subdecisions:

1. Should we recheck the decision-making effort before implementation? The more important the decision, the more rechecking may be needed.

2. What specific actions must be taken to implement the decision?
3. How will we monitor implementation?

Managers recognize a hard truth. Many chosen alternatives are difficult to implement. If the decision must be implemented in steps over a period of time, the odds are often against success. Implementation is difficult, in part, because there are so many possibilities of failure. They range from rainfall when an outdoor event is planned to the illness of a data-entry staffer with a report deadline hours away. Some hurdles regularly get in the way of implementation. Examples are communication failures, poor timing, active opposition, passive noncooperation, and competing demands for resources.

EVALUATION AND INFORMATION

Quality decision makers evaluate—that is, they learn from experience and adjust their decision-making efforts in accordance with new information and understandings. This requires a great deal of self-confidence. The decision maker should know when to assess rather than advocate. It is also important to think about a chosen alternative as an experiment to be tried rather than a commitment to be permanently defended.

The key evaluation goal is to assess the impact of the implementation on the target population. Such an assessment is hazardous because it is difficult to disentangle change caused by an implementation from other causes of change. Another matter of concern should be the spillover effects. These result from changes in the target clients or situations that were not taken into consideration in the decision-making effort. Sometimes, for instance, one may help a client but unexpectedly disrupt her family.

Next, the pervasive factors that influence the entire decision-making process should be examined. The first is the person who makes the decision. Each member of an organization has a different set of job skills as well as organizational and personal perspectives. These perspectives are the product of personal abilities and experiences as well as organizational positions and subcultures. Perspectives shape how the decision is made. The choice of who is making a particular decision may well determine what the choice will be.

Managers should think about decision-making personnel, both who and how many. The manager should consider whether to make a command decision, delegate responsibility, or create some form of shared decision-making process. The breadth of participation depends on the issue, the situation, and especially the decision stage involved. Important considerations include expertise, cooperative abilities, personal preferences, and time available.

A second factor that affects decisions is the information needed to make the right decision. Information is needed at every stage of the decision-making process. Information is of varying usefulness and cost. There are many threats to information quality. The classic warning is garbage in, garbage out. Information is constrained by limitations of time and other resources for collecting, processing, and analyzing data.

A serious threat is reliance on easily obtainable or vivid information. Often, the decision maker avoids digging for quality information. Another threat is to assume that quantity is equivalent to quality. A great quantity of information may submerge the critical thinking required by quality decision making. Management information systems may significantly increase the information available but sometimes they serve to mislead the decision maker by providing an abundance of information that may not be of high quality.

Quality decision making often requires innovative, open, and critical thinking rather than conformity, and cooperation rather than conflict. Unfortunately, the presence of colleagues may have a negative impact on the manager's thinking or that of his subordinates. A group-think phenomenon can cause inadequate thinking.

Sometimes group pressures are political. The term "syco-think" has been coined to refer to active or passive agreement with a leader for political purposes such as popularity and tangible favors.

The quality manager must take steps to minimize dominating behavior and encourage dissent during the process of decision making. Hearing praise and achieving a consensus may at times be desirable near the end. It can be quite harmful at a number of stages during the decision-making process. Peter Drucker wrote that there is no argument for a decision if there is not argument against it.

TIMING AND COMMUNICATION

Time is critical in decision making, and a key element of time is timing. Decisions must be made at the right moment. Perhaps anyone who has asked, "Will you marry me?" has thought about this matter.

Some moments are likely to be better than others for proposing marriage, opening a homeless shelter, or closing a street for repair. There are, in other words, windows of opportunity. Indeed, at every stage of the decision-making process there are issues of timing. It may well make a difference when a needs assessment is conducted, information is collected, or a choice among alternatives is made.

Timing matters because the situation facing a decision maker at one point of time is invariably different than the one at another point in time. An obvious example would be timing a needs assessment pertaining to people who are homeless. The season, the weather, and economic fluctuations are factors that change seasonally or over time.

The communication of information is central to the decision-making process. Evaluation efforts provide an example. One of the major concerns of evaluation specialists is utilization, and that involves failures in communicating results from the evaluators to the managers and subordinates in a way that is not threatening.

An effective communication must be sensitive both to the interests of an organization's members and to the hazards that message sending and receiving create. The quality decision maker gives special attention to communication because he or she wants to receive useful and accurate information from others as well as have it received by them. Crafting the message and selecting the medium are two important responsibilities. Even redundancy should be considered. For years we have known that redundancy is an effective means of error suppression.

TEN PRINCIPLES TO GUIDE THE NONPROFIT

Herrington J. Bryce, School of Business, The College of William and Mary

Serving Society—The first consideration of every nonprofit manager is how well the society or community is being served. Each state and the federal government define what is to be construed as public welfare. The three most common activities are education, health, and religion. The laws also stipulate that there may be no distribution of dividends or assets to individuals. Thus, the whole motive and orientation of management is to satisfy a larger society.

Fufilling the Mission—The second factor motivating managerial decisions is the mission of the organization. Nonprofits acquire their tax and legal statuses based on their mission and annual reports. These documents may be amended but amendments must be reported to local, state, and federal government agencies who assess whether the organization is following a public mission. Unlike the private sector, missions are more like contracts than plans. They cannot be changed at whim or ignored.

Pursuing Efficiency—The third principle is the need for efficiencies. A manager should not get carried away with the charitable nature of the organization and tolerate inefficiency. The end result would be a constant state of financial crisis as the nonprofit wastes scarce resources that are needed elsewhere.

Respecting the Marketplace—Nonprofits are not government agencies. They must compete for donations and clients, unlike government that is financed by a compulsion called taxation. Furthermore, governments rarely go bankrupt and disappear. Nonprofits do. Governments can pass laws to perpetuate themselves in spite of the marketplace. Nonprofits cannot. Observe and follow the market. It gives useful clues.

Following Strategic Plans—Because nonprofit managers are constantly pressured to produce, they often find it difficult to accept the need to follow a plan. The manager who does not stop to pull the troops together in pursuit of a plan will soon be in trouble. Even natural disasters require preplanning so emergency teams can respond quickly and effectively. Planning determines the efficacy of responses and the success of many missions.

Working with Others—Nonprofit organizations compete for funds, are challenged by outsiders, and are sought to perform specific and possibly conflicting missions. Yet many managers operate as though they were on a deserted island. The ability to carry out a mission and stretch resources is enhanced by involving others who might be natural partners to achieve certain goals.

Paying Attention to Resources—The government and public play a small role in the collecting and spending of money by private organizations. This is not the case for nonprofits. Many activities are not permitted or would be unwise. Lobbying is restricted. Political expenditures are generally prohibited.

On the other side of the ledger, revenues are also scrutinized. To keep a tax exemption, some nonprofits must prove that they are publicly supported. The proof relies on a demonstration that a large percentage of their revenues comes from contributions and membership fees. Receipts and expenditures will be used by the government and public to determine whether the organization is abiding by its mission. The manager must pay attention to the pattern of receipts and disbursements.

Understanding Laws and Regulations—Nonprofit managers must understand the laws and regulations that govern them. The organization can be held liable for violations and some of the penalties are quite severe.

Recognizing the Key Role of Trustees—Nonprofit trustees represent the public. It follows that management has to be accountable to them, inform them, and obtain their approval and guidance. Many actions require specific affirmative decisions by the board. In this process, the trustees are held to a high standard under the law. Violation of the public trust involves penalties.

Watching the Bottom Line—Nonprofit managers often believe they are not permitted to make a profit. The law has long said otherwise. Profits are acceptable but not as a main goal. Although the continuous accumulation of profits year after year is dangerous, accruing profits to provide stability and endowments is a wise strategy. It encourages the manager to watch the bottom line.

THE MANAGEMENT OF NONPROFIT ORGANIZATIONS

Dennis R. Young, Mandel Center for Nonprofit Organizations, Case Western Reserve University

THINKING AT THE MARGIN

One of the most powerful ideas of microeconomics is that decisions are best made on an incremental basis. That is, we ask the question, "What happens if I buy or sell or produce one more unit of a good or service?" In this framework, one seeks the cost of the next unit produced (the marginal cost) rather than the average cost of all units produced so far. Similarly, the decision maker seeks the marginal revenue from the sale of the next unit of product.

To appreciate the concept of marginal analysis, one must recognize fixed and variable costs. Fixed costs are resources that must be expended to start an operation. Within broad bounds, they do not vary with the level of operation. To run a child-care agency or museum, you must have a facility, administrative staff, and some equipment before you can take in your first child or visitor. These involve fixed costs.

Once you open your doors, there will be additional costs that increase with the number of customers. In the case of the child-care agency, food, instructional and recreational supplies, and staff hours would be variable costs. In the case of museums, the variable costs might consist of extra maintenance associated with visitor traffic.

How do we go from fixed and variable costs to marginal versus average costs? Average cost is the total cost divided by the units of service. For a child-care center having $100,000 of fixed costs, $50,000 of variable costs, and 50 children, the average cost would be $3,000 per child:

$$(100,000 + 50,000)/50 = 3,000$$

The marginal cost is simply the additional cost of providing one more unit of service. In this example, if serving 51 children increased the variable cost to $51,000, the marginal cost would be $1,000, which is much lower than the average cost.

APPLICATIONS OF MARGINAL ANALYSIS

Of what use is the distinction between marginal and average cost? One application concerns the pricing of services. Presumably, the nonprofit organization is in business to serve the public, not to make a profit. If one prices to break even, one must charge the average cost so that fixed costs are covered. This price might not be best from a social point of view. An economist would argue that pricing according to marginal cost is more efficient. If you charge more than this, you will exclude someone who is willing to pay more than the additional amount it costs to serve him or her. And a social benefit will be lost.

Of course, this argument may not allow a museum to pay its mortgage! But part of the fixed costs can be covered through grants or public subsidy rather than through pricing that excludes customers.

Another application lies in the area of fund-raising. What level of funds should a non-profit try to raise? Presumably, more money is better. This is not necessarily so. Raising funds costs money. It is clearly inefficient to spend more money than you bring in. But what is the correct rule of thumb? Under marginal analysis, you expand your fund-raising operation until the next dollar spent brings in just over a dollar. If we use average cost, we might make a mistake.

As an example, a charity can raise $300,000 by spending $125,000, or $400,000 by spending $250,000. The average costs are 41 cents (125,000/300,000) and 62 cents (250,000/ 400,000). Either level seems to make sense since, on average, it costs less than a dollar to raise a dollar. However, only the first level really makes sense. On an incremental basis, it costs an additional $125,000 to raise an additional $100,000 above the $300,000 level. On an incremental basis, this is not sensible. Thinking at the margin avoids this trap.

Let us extend this concept further. A frequently applied standard to judge the efficiency of a charity is the percentage of raised funds used for administrative costs. This standard reflects the average cost of fund-raising. Charities with low percentages of administrative costs are judged to be efficient. The standard fails, however, in some cases. A new, small charity might be efficient for its size but may have high average costs as it covers its fixed costs. Should an individual donate to such a charity? At the margin, the charity might allocate a high percentage of the next dollar to direct service. This would be efficient from the donors' point of view and would make the charity a worthy object of giving. This truth emerges only when we think at the margin.

Other counterproductive actions are set up by "average" thinking. If fund-raising organi-zations know they will be judged by average costs, they may maintain lean operations. That is obviously all to the good. However, they may also be reluctant to undertake costly but worthwhile initiatives. One example is the United Way, which has historically raised money at low cost via payroll deduction. It has used low fund-raising costs as a marketing concept, explaining that a large proportion of funds goes directly to charitable causes. This approach has created a disincentive to raise funds from smaller employers where the cost of fund-raising is substantially higher than in large organizations. Thinking at the margin would lead to more efficient decisions to undertake such fund-raising so long as the marginal revenue exceeded the marginal cost.

OPPORTUNITY COST

An important concept from economics involves opportunity cost, defined as the value foregone when a scarce resource is used. To an economist, all real costs are opportunity costs. Conversely, expenditures of resources without an alternative use are costless. For example, if markets are functioning well, the price I pay for supplies or equipment represents their value in the next best alternative use. If I do not buy the fax machine at the stipulated price, it will be sold to someone else whose business or personal satisfaction just exceeds the price.

The situation is different when no alternative use exists. If I have a room in my agency that goes unused during the evening hours, the cost of letting someone else use it at that time is low, equal to the additional maintenance, cleaning, and security that might be required. I should be willing to charge a low rent to gain some additional revenue rather than holding out for my average cost of floor space.

The concept of opportunity cost is powerful when applied to more subtle issues of resource use, program initiatives, and timing of revenue and cost flows. Let us revisit fund-raising for a moment. One question is, "Who should be involved in fund-raising?" How much time should university faculty or doctors in hospitals spend on it? This question can be answered by comparing opportunity costs with the benefits of employing resources in this manner. The wages of such individuals would reflect the opportunity costs of their time if they would be working rather than fund-raising. Thus, one should ask, how much value is received from fund-raising versus what these individuals would be doing otherwise?

Participation in fund-raising or other administrative tasks is often cast in terms of obligations and duties of the individuals involved. This can be a wasteful practice. Nonprofit organizations would do well to evaluate the activities of their star faculty members, symphony players, or surgeons, in terms of opportunity costs.

TIME VALUE OF MONEY

Economics is also helpful in terms of the timing and size of gifts and donations. The concept is simple. The sooner money is received, the more valuable it is for two reasons:

1. *Inflation*—In an inflationary environment, a dollar received next year is worth less because it has less purchasing power. That is why economists talk in terms of constant dollars corrected for inflation. If we want to compare what we are spending this year to what was spent five years ago, it makes no sense to compare actual dollar numbers. We need to compensate for inflation in order to compare actual purchasing power or resource value.
2. *Opportunity costs*—Even if we deal in constant dollars, however, it is still true that dollars now are more valuable than dollars later. If we receive a dollar now we can use it now to produce benefits, or invest it to produce more than a dollar a year from now. If we have to wait a year to receive that dollar, we have lost that opportunity.

The time value of money affects fund-raising strategy. As an example, suppose a pro-spective donor is willing to give a $500,000 endowment now or a $1,000,000 endowment when she dies? The choice would depend on the lost opportunity cost associated with the time value of money, which in turn would depend on such factors as the donor's age and the rate of return on investments.

RESOURCE CONSTRAINTS

Economics helps us because social decisions involve the allocation of scarce resources. Organizations in the nonprofit sector often think in terms of addressing social needs in some absolute sense without considering the alternative use of resources. Yet nonprofit organizations always have limited budgets that require pragmatic choices. Should a hospital, for example, open up a kidney dialysis unit? The need for such a unit, in terms of patients waiting for this expensive treatment, may be clear. But the same limited resource might expand a program of prenatal care for poor, pregnant teenagers.

Making life and death choices is always difficult and involves other considerations as well as available resources. But a failure to recognize constraints is tantamount to making the decision in ignorance.

Nonprofit organizations must recognize the impact of limited resources. Donors often attach stipulations to their gifts and certain kinds of expenditures are more popular than others. Bricks and mortar, and treatments rather than preventive programs, are more tangible and hence sometimes more likely to be the objects of largesse. But development officers can be more effective in shaping donors' stipulations if they can explain the results in terms of resource implications. Additional money spent on operations can be more effective than on a new facility that will be undermaintained. Money spent on treatment may forego greater benefits from prevention. Donors can understand that. If managers and development officers understand it, they can try to find ways to provide recognition to donors that will induce them to donate funds to their best alternative uses, even if those uses are less tangible.

ECONOMIC INCENTIVES

A final concept from economics is the notion of economic incentives. It is widely held that the nonprofit sector runs on altruism. This is only partly true despite the fact that the nonprofit sector derives a good fraction of its support from voluntary donations and the volunteering of time. Economists argue that selfish behavior can be exploited to promote unselfish, charitable ends. All we need to assume is that individuals giving or working for charities have mixed motives, some selfish and some altruistic. Let me suggest two applications of this idea:

1. Charities raise money for what economists call "public goods." These are services or causes such as protection of wildlife or a cure for cancer. The incentive for the selfish individual is to "free ride." Others pay for the good while the individual enjoys the benefits without paying. Yet the selfish person may have some degree of altruism and public responsibility. The solution for the nonprofit organization is to give donors or volunteers a "private good" or "selective incentive" that encourages contributing to the public good.

To make this transaction worthwhile for the charity, the cost of this private good must be less than the solicited contribution. Museum tee shirts or public TV tote bags are examples. The value of the incentive as a purely private good may be less than store-bought similar products. But the cost of the donation provides a combined satisfaction from altruism and self-benefit that is worthwhile. Nonprofits are learning this lesson well, as demonstrated by the explosion of souvenirs, magazines, art reproductions, sponsored trips, and other products and services that raise money.

Other economic incentives can appeal to selfish donors. The tax code gives incentives by allowing the deducting of charitable contributions. People do not give just to obtain the tax deduction but that deduction does provide an inducement.

2. The second example is somewhat controversial. Should development officers and other fund-raisers be paid partly on a commission basis? We might not want to attract to the fund-raising profession individuals who are simply out for the money. Such people might employ unsavory tactics that undermine the organization's integrity. But neither does it seem sensible to ignore the possibilities that additional funds may be raised by providing more direct incentives to fund-raisers. Finally, however, one must also ask whether donors would be inclined to give less money if they knew that a share of each dollar they give will go into the fund-raiser's pocket.

INFORMATION TECHNOLOGY AND THE NONPROFIT MANAGER

Ahmed Zaki, School of Business Administration, The College of William and Mary

The terms *data* and *information* are often used synonymously. This is not an accurate use. Data represent facts, such as the number of units sold, the percentage of suppliers, or census data. Information, on the other hand, is data that has been organized or processed in a meaningful and usable format. It can be communicated to a user to assist in choosing an appropriate course of action. Information is used to describe past performance, shows trends and characteristics, monitors the present, and provides warning signals for the future.

Decision makers in modern organizations are essentially information processors and organizations called information processing systems. The apparatus for collecting, processing, and distributing information at the right time and in the correct format is called a management information system (MIS). A functional definition of a management information system is that it (1) is an integrated person-machine system; (2) provides information in the form of data, voice, image, or video; and (3) supports managers at the operational, tactical, and strategic levels of the organizational hierarchy.

To perform the above functions, a management information system consists of (1) one or more computer systems, (2) one or more telecommunications systems, (3) one or more databases, and (4) management support software such as executive information systems, decision support systems, and expert systems. An MIS should support all levels of management. However, few of the current MISs in organizations achieve this goal. Also, few organizations have executive information systems, decision support systems, or expert systems. Those organizations that have such systems do usually fare much better in terms of the quality and timing of their decisions.

COMPONENTS OF A MANAGEMENT INFORMATION SYSTEM

This section presents the functional definitions of a management information system's main software items.

Databases

During the 1960s and early 1970s, file systems were used to store the organization's data. Each application such as payroll, personnel data inventory, and so forth had its own separate file. Each application programmer had his or her own file and program format and design, thus making the acquisition of information/data from two or more files very difficult, if not impossible. Thus, if an application required data from both the payroll file and the personnel file, the application programmer usually found it easier to create a new file containing data from both the payroll and personnel files. This resulted in the creation of a substantial number of files in the organization containing a large amount of redundant data.

To alleviate these problems, the concept of a database emerged. A database is best described as a repository of the organization's interrelated data stored together according to a certain format and standards to serve more than one programmer and/or application and to control redundancy. An organization may have more than one database to serve different management levels with different data needs or a database for each location in the case of widely dispersed organizations. An organization with only one central database is said to have a centralized database. When more than one database exists at different locations or managerial levels, the organization is said to have a distributed database.

Executive Information System (EIS)

Executive information systems are usually targeted for top management. They provide managers at the strategic level with user-friendly on-line access to relevant, and appropriately and conveniently organized internal information about the organization. They also provide important external information concerning the organization's environment, such as government regulations and taxes. In addition, most EISs provide projected trends and data analysis capabilities. The information is often displayed in a graphical format. For convenience and speed of access to information, EISs sometimes have their own dedicated databases. Several software manufacturers now sell EIS packages that the organization can buy to build its customized EIS.

Decision Support System (DSS)

DSS refers to a class of software whose purpose is to support the decision-making process at any level of the organization hierarchy. The main characteristics of a DSS are:

1. The system consists of decision models such as spreadsheet models, scheduling models, and so on. These models have the capability of retrieving data from the organization database or a DSS-dedicated database.
2. The DSS must fully support the decision maker but not replace his or her judgment. Thus, a DSS should neither provide the answer to the problem nor impose a predefined sequence of analysis on the decision maker.
3. The DSS must be able to support the solution of complex problems that cannot be totally programmed, such as some semistructured problems, or any structured problems that can be solved at a much slower time.
4. The DSS must provide the ability to interactively test different courses of actions or strategies. It also must provide the decision maker with the capability of "what-if" analysis to test the decision under different scenarios or conditions.

Expert System (ES)

Artificial intelligence (AI) evolved during and after World War II. The ultimate goal of AI scientists is to produce computer programs that can in some sense "think," that is, solve problems in a way that would be considered intelligent if done by a human. Advances in that field have been very slow. Expert systems are a subclass of AI that emerged in the 1960s and are now being widely used. The sale of ES in the 1990s is estimated to reach $4 billion.

The idea behind expert systems is simple. Human experts' knowledge is translated into "rules" using special programming languages and stored in a computer's memory. Decision makers interact with the computer using a user-friendly interface system and input the questions they need to be answered. The computer then uses the human expertise stored in its memory in the shape of rules to infer an answer/decision. Thus, in essence, the computer performs as a human expert and advises the nonexpert user. Most expert systems also provide an explanation of the logic they used to reach the decision, which is very useful and educational for the user. The main advantages of expert systems are:

1. They can contain the expertise of more than one expert.
2. They can be used in more than one place simultaneously. Human experts cannot be in more than one place at the same time.
3. The expertise is always there even if the experts leave the organization.
4. There is consistency in the sense that the ES will always make the same decision under the same circumstances.

ES use was limited to highly technical organizations because of the high degree of technicality required to build an ES. However, there are currently several software manufacturers that produce ES "shells," whereby the user only provides the rules (expertise) in a relatively simple English-like programming language and the ES is ready to be used. Some software manufacturers even sell ready-to-use (that is, the decision rules are already installed) ES for specific applications in financial organizations, manufacturing plants, and other areas.

Networks

Historically, computers and the data processing operations were centralized in one department known as the data processing department (DPD). Then, personal computers (PCs) with their user-friendly software came into the picture and managers at all levels discovered their effectiveness and usefulness in helping them perform their managerial functions.

To be able to share databases, software, and hardware, and to be a member of an electronic mail system, managers realized that it would be expedient if they were to connect their PCs with other equipment. To achieve this objective, local-area networks (LANs) evolved. As the name implies, LANs connect several personal computers distributed in a small geographic location such as a building or a campus. The PCs are physically connected to each other by cable (hard-wired). The cables used for hard wiring are either a twisted pair such as the old telephone lines, coaxial cables such as the TV cables, or fiber optics, which is a relatively new transmission media designed to handle efficient and very fast rates of data transmission. Personal computers that are attached to a LAN are usually referred to as workstations instead of PCs.

In large geographically distributed organizations, networks are also used to connect large computers and PCs via telephone lines, microwave, or satellites. Such networks are called wide-area networks (WANs).

Electronic Mail

Electronic mail systems allow the users to send long or short messages to one or more users on the network simultaneously without the necessity of producing a hard copy. The message is usually stored in the intended receiver's electronic mailbox until he or she retrieves it, reads it, and either disposes of it, saves it as is, or sends it to other destinations as is or after modifying it. Electronic mail systems may be set up within a building or campus on a LAN. They may also be installed on WANs to service several sites across the country or the globe.

PLANNING FOR INFORMATION SYSTEMS

Information is a valuable resource. The effective use of information systems or information technology has enabled organizations such as American Airlines, United Airlines, and American Hospital Supply to gain and sustain a competitive advantage. In most of the cases where organizations gained competitive advantages, information systems did not just facilitate line management functions by increasing efficiency but were an integral part of the product or service offering.

The 1980s were the years when information systems were hailed as the sources of competitive advantage. However, by the end of the decade, many top-level managers were dissatisfied with their information systems. In the May 1990 issue of *Datamation*, Jeff Moad gave two reasons why IS is not accepted at the executive suite:

1. Top management blamed its information system managers because the latter did not deliver on competitive advantage promises. This results from an overestimation of the role of information systems. An organization consists of an integrated number of activities that are performed to plan, produce, market, deliver, and support its product. Information systems enable the organization to efficiently perform each of these activities. In addition, IS serves to provide the necessary internal linkage between all these activities and the external linkage with the suppliers, buyers, and channels of distribution. Thus, information systems by themselves will not provide a competitive advantage. However, information systems, like any other activity such as finance or production, will help reshape the activities and processes that will enable the organization to achieve competitive advantage.

2. Top management also complained that IS strategic planning is inadequate.

Information Systems Strategic Planning

Strategic planning is the process of (1) identifying where the organization is relative to its competitors, (2) analyzing the environment and anticipating opportunities and possible threats, (3) assessing the organization's resources and constraints, (4) setting the goals and objectives that need to be pursued, and (5) planning the appropriate strategies to achieve the stated goals. Once the plan is articulated, it is then implemented and feedback is collected to help design future plans.

Historically, strategic planning and IS planning have not gone hand in hand. In many organizations, especially in the public sector, information system managers are not adequately involved or, sometimes, even informed about the organization's strategy;

hence the inadequacy of the IS strategic plan. The prominent reasons cited are (1) there is no corporate strategic plan of sufficient quality that IS managers can use to develop their IS strategic plan, and (2) the IS managers have been shut out of the boardroom.

An interesting study in the *Journal of Information Technology Management* in 1990 by Kenneth Calhoun and Albert Lederer investigated what they called "the missing link between corporate planning and information systems planning." The researchers surveyed both business and IS planners in eighteen organizations in the United States and Canada and asked them whether the quality of the strategic business plan and/or the quality of the communication of the strategic business plan influence (1) the extent of the strategic information systems planning effort and (2) the level of understanding of the strategic business plan possessed by the information systems executive. The responses indicated that the missing link is not the existence of a good business plan but the quality of communicating the strategic business plan to the IS executives.

The quality of communication between business executives and IS executives, by itself, is necessary but not sufficient to ensure that information technology–extensive capabilities will be sufficiently utilized. In many cases where IS management was informed about corporate strategy, its own plans played a subordinate role. The capabilities of information technology should be recognized by both business and IS planners. Such an understanding can be achieved by educating line managers on the capabilities, breakthroughs, and management of information technology. This goal could be accomplished by (1) formal programs such as executive education seminars or a series of short sessions, (2) informal programs such as technology demonstrations of actual equipment or by showing videotapes in a brown-bag meeting. In addition, every organization should consider establishing a steering committee.

Using a Steering Committee

A steering committee consists of the heads of the organization's agencies and is usually chaired by the organization's top executive. The IS executive should be a full-fledged member, participating fully in the decisions of the committee and acting as an adviser to the other members on information technology opportunities, capabilities, and constraints. In *Managing Information as a Corporate Resource* (1987), Tom Paul states that the function of the committee might include:

1. Determining appropriate levels of expenditure and capability for the IS department based on the organization's strategic and tactical plans.
2. Approving specific proposals for the acquisition of major hardware and software.
3. Approving long- and short-term information systems plans.
4. Determining whether specific projects are to be undertaken on the basis of criteria such as expected return on investment, business value to the organization, effect on competitive position, effect on internal organization, and conformity with corporate plans.
5. Determining project priorities.
6. Reviewing and approving cost allocation methods.
7. Reviewing project progress.
8. At specific decision points, determining whether projects should be continued or abandoned.

9. Resolving territorial and political conflicts arising from new systems.

The advantages of having a steering committee include:

1. IS executives will be adequately informed about the organization's strategic goals, objectives, and thrusts.
2. The IS manager will be able to advise the strategic planners about opportunities where information technology can lead to competitive advantage and/or streamline their operations.
3. Information systems will gain top management support, which is critical to their success.
4. There is user involvement in specifying the systems that meet the committee's needs and in prioritizing, planning, implementing, reviewing, and evaluating these systems.
5. There is a sound flexible IS plan that dovetails with the corporate strategic plan.

If properly structured, the steering committee provides the kind of direction that makes strategic planning an effective tool in designing an organization's management information system. It also provides an opportunity to involve various constituencies in a process that allocates resources to solve information problems, in accordance with organizational priorities.

PUBLIC
AND NONPROFIT
MARKETING

Christopher H. Lovelock, Lovelock Associates
Charles B. Weinberg, Professor of Marketing, University of British Columbia

ORIENTING THE ORGANIZATION TO THE MARKETPLACE

In many public and nonprofit organizations (PNPs), especially those offering services, management attention focuses on operational issues. Often, the culture leads to the development of operating programs with little regard for meeting customer needs. Marketing, if present at all, is often an "add-on" activity, centered on advertising and promotion campaigns to increase revenues by pushing existing offerings. Yet the real problem may be a need radically to rethink those offerings and their delivery.

Instituting a formal marketing function is a relatively recent event in most nonbusiness organizations; many still lack such a function. Of course, non-marketing-oriented organizations often quickly fail, but even large and seemingly well-established organizations may not possess the sensitivity to users and the general public required for long-term survival. Several clues provide warning signs that management thinking is product rather than market oriented:

- Managers (and board members) are so taken with organization programs and services that they believe these must be what the public needs.
- Marketing activities center on stimulating awareness through advertising and publicity; low usage is blamed on ignorance or inertia, rather than on organizational shortcomings—products, pricing, or distribution.
- User focus is on consummating discrete transactions, rather than creating and maintaining long-term relationships.
- Marketing research is little used; when done, findings conflicting with management beliefs are ignored.
- Market segment distinctions are ignored or played down in preference for "one best strategy" for all.
- Competition is little recognized; at most, only competition from similar organizations is recognized. "Generic" competitors offering alternative solutions to similar consumer needs are ignored.

Why do these attitudes and behaviors occur? Basically, current employees and volunteers are so convinced they are dealing with socially important issues and services that they assume the public views these topics with equal concern. This commitment to a cause is often what keeps public and nonprofit managers going. They forget that thousands of issues and services compete for public attention, and that most citizens may not consider any given activity relevant to their situations— if, indeed, they are even aware of it.

Often each program has its own advocate who may enjoy professional qualification status or board member "protection." Unfortunately, all too often the organization's collective offerings fail to represent a coherent whole with clear links to a well-defined institutional mission. Additional problems from a product-centered mindset are the assumption that potential customers will go to great lengths to obtain information about the organization's activities and use its services. But service availability does not guarantee use. Neither does a minimal announcement of availability attract interest from a public continually bombarded with messages sent through all possible communication media.

There is also a real risk that customers may be seen as tolerant and forgiving. After all, if the service (or cause) is so important, won't the customers or audience forgive a few shortcomings in delivery, delayed schedules, missing materials, substitute personnel, canceled exhibits, or changes of location? Unfortunately, the answer is often "no." Many users demand quality service from PNPs just as from private firms.

Marketing's fundamental contribution is to help organizations become more externally focused. In doing so, PNPs must keep in mind their organizations' distinctive aspects. These differences make marketing implementation very challenging, but also very rewarding.

DISTINCTIVE CHARACTERISTICS OF NONPROFIT MARKETING

PNPs typically provide services or seek attitude or behavior change rather than manufacture and sell physical goods. Despite increased attention to services marketing, it is less well developed than physical goods marketing.

Dominance of Nonfinancial Objectives

By definition, PNPs do not seek profits to distribute to owners or shareholders. Because they rarely seek financial surplus and do not expect operating revenues to cover costs, nonfinancial objectives invariably have priority.

This focus on nonfinancial goals can be a strength. Peter Drucker argues that the best nonprofits avoid sweeping mission statements full of good intentions and instead focus on objectives that have clear-cut implications for the work that staff and volunteers perform. As examples, he cites the Salvation Army's goal of turning society's rejects—alcoholics, criminals, derelicts—into citizens and the Girl Scouts' goal of helping youngsters to become confident, capable young women who respect themselves and other people.

The lack of even a theoretical profit maximization goal makes measures of success or failure in strictly financial terms difficult. Is one university or nonprofit hospital more successful than another? Is a children's museum in one city better than one in another city? More difficult still: How can the performance of a university be compared to a hospital, or a museum? Nonfinancial measures (e.g., wilderness areas preserved, attitudes changed by a conservation society) must be used to document performance.

Need for Resource Attraction

All organizations need resources to function. Nonprofit organizations (NPs) sometimes secure resources free (e.g., volunteered labor, services in kind, donated facilities, property tax exemptions), or at a reduced rate (e.g., discount postal rates, tax concessions). In addition, most NPs cannot cover costs from sales revenues; they devote major efforts to seeking new donations and grants, and/or preserving revenue flow from existing sources. So NP marketers must deal with two interrelated marketing tasks: programs to *attract* needed resources and programs to *allocate* resources in pursuit of organizational mission.

Multiple Constituencies

Pursuing both resource attraction and resource allocation, NPs must deal with two sets of "customers." Balancing the needs and expectations of both groups can be difficult. For example, some donors may demand that money serve a population group or supply a product different from management's decision. Often, results are unsatisfactory. Some arts groups, for example, feel compelled by terms of government grants to attract populist audiences for whom their performances are not designed.

Other constituencies include third-party payers (e.g., health insurance firms, parents paying children's college tuition), politicians, regulatory agencies, former consumers (e.g., college alumni) with a continuing interest in their institution's performance, and the mass media. Few business managers have to juggle the interests of as many constituencies as their nonprofit counterparts.

Tension Between Mission and Customer Satisfaction

The basic marketing tenet holds that organizations do best if attentive to customer needs and wants. Not all firms adhere rigorously to a "customer is always right" philosophy but most seek to satisfy consumer needs. For NPs, consumer sovereignty is sometimes alien to fulfilling their institutional missions.

For example, many nonprofit missions require a long-term view rather than pandering to popular tastes. Medical treatments must consider long-term patient needs, not how he or she would like to feel or act tomorrow. Religious organizations have spiritual missions often involving self-sacrifice. Universities transmit skill, knowledge, and ways of thinking that have extended student value—not simply to amuse and inspire for the course duration. This tension is not always adjusted smoothly. Many NPs are in constant conflict over mission interpretation by their constituencies; these tensions are exacerbated when resources are scarce.

Ability to Obtain Free or Inexpensive Support

NP managers often draw on donated labor and services. For example, United Way and member agencies receive millions of dollars of free advertising during televised profes-

sional football games. Volunteers play key roles in helping universities raise money from alumni, providing nonmedical services to hospital patients, operating retail stores in museums, and serving as guides at historic properties.

These benefits compensate for some of the disadvantages facing PNP managers. Wisely sought and carefully used, they provide a powerful way to stretch resources. But free or discounted resources need strong (yet sensitive) management, perhaps more than those purchased at market prices. For example, a museum shop will be unsuccessful if volunteer sales clerks have high absenteeism rates and do not acquire needed selling skills and product knowledge.

Management in Duplicate or Triplicate

Finally, in NP marketing programs, many "managers" are involved. Often trustees or directors assume management responsibilities, and volunteers have management roles. Since individuals seldom have direct reporting relationships with the administrative staff, they can be a help, a hindrance, and sometimes both.

Duplicate management problems are compounded when the service is planned and delivered by professionals who outrank managers responsible for operations. In the arts, higher education, and health care, disputes often arise between management personnel and professionals such as curators, faculty members, and doctors. Professionals (e.g., college faculty) typically produce the product and usually possess considerable expertise in their chosen fields. Frequently, they resent a strong user orientation that suggests an outsider may know more about a service than they do. Professionals asked to act in more customer-oriented ways may find this threatening and inconvenient.

MARKETING MIX CONSIDERATIONS

Collectively, public and nonprofit organizations create an immense variety of "products." Most PNPs produce services, ranging from health care to higher education, and from performing arts to postal service. Others market causes or social behavior patterns: Their goals range from saving sea mammals to saving souls, from banning handguns to banning abortion. A few organizations, such as sheltered workshops, use productive work as therapy for their clients, producing in the process useful physical goods that are sold as a profit-making sideline.

Many PNPs view their products from a different perspective than potential customers. This is especially true of advocacy organizations. For example, highway safety organizations view wearing seat belts as vital; much of the population is indifferent or even hostile to this behavior. Managers must avoid thinking that what they do or market is viewed universally as indispensable or morally compelling.

Most PNP products can be grouped into one of three categories. First are *core products* tied directly to the institutional mission. *Supplementary products* facilitate or enhance customers' use of the core products (e.g., film or lecture programs at a museum, paid parking at a hospital), and *resource attraction products* secure the financing needed to run the organization (e.g., bingo games in church halls).

PNPs offering multiple products must think in terms of a product portfolio. They must choose which products to emphasize. Each product offered by a PNP must be evaluated against two criteria: net financial contribution and ability to advance institutional mission (Exhibit 16-3). Core products (and some supplementary ones) advance the mission. But many supplementary products are sometimes deliberately priced to operate at breakeven so as not to discourage users of the core product. Many core products (not least those of advocacy groups) lose money, even after accounting for earmarked grants and donations; hence resource attraction products such as sale of gift items, rental of facilities, and so forth may be needed to cover the deficits.

Political or financial restrictions may constrain a PNP's ability to engage in expensive communication efforts. In both instances, the organization may be condemned to operating far below its potential. Well-planned communication efforts should realistically be viewed as an investment that will yield greater success in achieving institutional goals and perhaps higher revenues, too. The role of communication is not just to persuade but also to inform and remind. Absent effective communications, an otherwise well-planned marketing strategy, designed to deliver, say, counseling or family planning at a reasonable price, and at times and locations tailored to customer needs, may fail if people are unaware of the service or when and where to obtain it, or are not convinced that the program offers them meaningful benefits.

For some PNPs, seeking out sources of "free" communication such as public service advertising, donated public relations activities, and volunteer salespeople works well. For others it may represent a false economy. In any event, decision makers should note that relying on donated services may lead to loss of control over message content, format, and scheduling.

COMPETITIVE POSTURE AND POSITIONING STRATEGY

Competition has traditionally been associated with the private sector. NPs were typically formed to provide services that high-minded citizens believed were desirable for society but where profit was either inappropriate to mission or unattainable. Consequently, few long-established NPs were conceived with competition in mind. Most met an established demand that was insufficient, at prevailing prices, to attract profit-seeking competitors. Yet, over time, a competitive posture has become necessary for survival.

In some cases (e.g., higher education), demand has shrunk relative to supply; institutions that once peacefully coexisted now fight for a larger share of a shrinking pie. In other instances (e.g., hospitals), the private sector has focused on certain segments with a subset of profitable services. Changes in technology and consumer needs have resulted in an upsurge in generic competition, such as telecommunications competing against postal services.

Exhibit 16-3. Product Portfolio Analysis

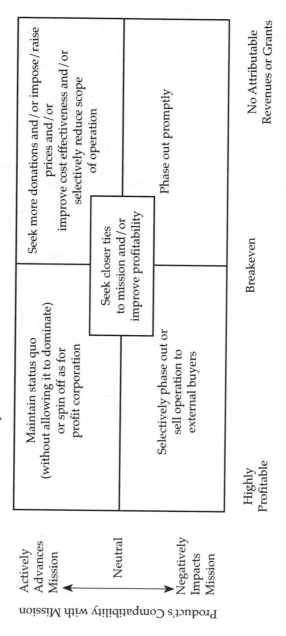

Source: From C. H. Lovelock and C. B. Weinberg, *Public and Nonprofit Marketing*, 2d ed. (San Francisco: The Scientific Press, 1989), 213.

16-40

Finally, to make better use of existing resources and skills, and to provide financial contribution to operating overhead, many NPs have added profitable new goods and services; some compete directly with the private sector. Examples include retail shops, printed materials (e.g., calendars from Sierra Club), educational programs and vacation activities (e.g., historical tours hosted by university professors). To this litany of new competitive factors, we should also add increased competition for government funding, philanthropic donations, and volunteers' time.

Some organizations find the market perceives minimal distinctions between offerings. For example, a community center offering preschool day-care programs thought it was differentiated because of religious affiliation and content. However, a parent survey showed this affiliation made little difference. Parents saw five or six local day-care centers as roughly equivalent on all important service dimensions; they chose on price and location.

Some organizations are perceived as relatively distinctive. In the day-care example, parents believed one preschool had a particularly effective educational program. It attracted children from a wider geography and at higher fees than the other schools. By developing a unique competitive position, this center prospered while others were barely surviving.

A positioning strategy involves selecting target market segments on which to concentrate, identifying positions held by competitive offerings, and choosing a position that is (currently or potentially) important to the segments. Positioning brings together market analysis, competitive analysis, and internal analysis of organizational resources and constraints. Once chosen, positioning strategy forms the framework on which to build the marketing mix. Product, price, and distribution create the chosen position; communication conveys this position to the relevant target market.

In short, positioning establishes and maintains a distinctive place in the market for an entire organization and/or its product offerings. A position is held with respect to performance on specific characteristics. In a competitive market, position is usually related to competing products or organizations. Thus, a hospital stressing emergency services for patients may seek the image of a well-equipped, quick-response health-care center—a different position from one sought by a hospital specializing in the latest techniques of heart surgery and appealing to an international market of patients referred by physicians practicing on several continents. Of course, the position should be consistent with the organization's basic mission and purposes.

Positioning analysis is a diagnostic tool to help organizations understand the relationship between products and markets. The analysis suggests where new opportunities lie: developing new products or repositioning existing ones. An organization should choose its position; if it avoids positioning, the market or competition may force it into an unappealing stance.

AUDITING
NONPROFITS

Anne Farley, CPA, Former Partner, KPMG Peat Marwick

Experienced executives know that their independent auditors are an important management resource. An independent auditor not only enables management and the board to carry out their fiduciary responsibilities but also serves as a source of objective advice and counsel about a wide range of business needs. To reap all of the benefits of an independent audit, executives should be familiar with the basics of an audit and then make their needs and level of service expectations known.

The primary output of an independent audit of financial statements is the rendering of an opinion by the auditor as to whether an organization's financial statements are presented fairly, in all material respects, and conform with generally accepted accounting principles.

The auditor renders his or her opinion on financial statements in writing. The financial statements, which are the subject of the audit, are the responsibility of the organization and should be prepared by management. In its purest form, an audit consists of various tests of data supporting management's financial statements and the notes thereto. Depending on the capabilities resident in an organization, the auditor may assist by drafting all or a portion of the financial statements for management.

Professional standards of performance and conduct guide the auditor in his or her work. These standards specify expected levels of competence, requirements for supervision of personnel, independence, and requirements

for the content of the auditor's opinion. Professional standards also recommend audit procedures to be used in specific circumstances.

SELECTING AN INDEPENDENT AUDITOR

Because nonprofit organizations have special needs, they are best served by auditors who have extensive experience with their kind of activity. For example, nonprofit organizations use their financial statements to communicate messages to prospective donors and others interested in the organization about the organization's activities and its financial health. Experienced auditors can advise management and the board about ways to most effectively "tell the organization's story" through the financial statements. Further, recent activities by the Financial Accounting Standards Board to set standards in the nonprofit area and activities by government agencies to mandate audits for recipients of federal grants and contracts are creating issues for not-for-profit organizations that require planning and special expertise.

Most organizations seek continuity of auditors. There are many hidden costs in changing from one auditor to another, the most significant of which is internal personnel time required to familiarize the new auditor with the organization's operations. Consequently, if the level of service and fees are satisfactory, many organizations retain their auditors indefinitely.

If a decision has been made to select a new auditor, the organization usually will solicit proposals. Executives should specify in advance the information that should be included in the auditor's proposal. Typical questions include:

> Who are the members of the audit team, and what are their qualifications and experience with similar not-for-profit organizations?
>
> What is your firm's expertise in serving colleges and universities, arts, religious, human service organizations, etc.? In specialized audit areas (pledges, joint costs, indirect cost recoveries, federal grant programs)?
>
> What major clients do you serve in your geographical area?
>
> What is your firm's policy for rotating personnel?
>
> What are your firm's independence policies? How does your firm determine adherence to its independence policies?
>
> What would be the current year's audit fee? How will future fees be determined?
>
> How will you coordinate your audit with the internal auditor?
>
> What management consulting and tax services does your firm provide specifically for not-for-profit organizations?
>
> How do you consult with management during the year on accounting and reporting matters?
>
> What firm resources are available for resolving technical accounting issues?

Most auditors will visit the organization, review the accounting records, and estimate the amount of effort required to perform the audit. After the written proposals have been received, management usually narrows the selection to two or three finalists, who then make oral presentations to a committee of the governing board. Because the auditor is primarily responsible to the board of directors or trustees, it is essential that the board, or a committee of the board, participate in the selection process.

PLANNING THE AUDIT

The best way to ensure a productive audit is to plan. Typically, at least one planning meeting between management and the auditor should be held before any audit work begins. Things usually discussed include: (1) major changes within the organization during the year; (2) problems and concerns that should be addressed during the audit; (3) timing of the audit and important deadlines for reports and board meetings; (4) fees; (5) internal audit participation in the external audit.

By identifying these factors in advance, the management group and auditor are, in effect, focusing the audit. This focusing increases the likelihood that the process, once begun, will move smoothly to an effective conclusion. The focus of the audit can be increased even further if the organization has an audit committee. If a group of individuals reviews the plan of management and the auditor, additional input is received that can produce modifications to the plan so as to better meet the needs of the governing board of the organization.

NEGOTIATING FEES

Audit fees are composed of service costs and expenses. Fees may be quoted on a cost plus expenses basis or on an all-inclusive basis. At the time a proposal is obtained, and for each ensuing year, the auditor will provide an estimate of his or her fees. This estimate is based on the number of hours anticipated to perform the work and the standard rates per hour. Some CPAs will adjust their standard rates up or down depending on their perception of the risk associated with a particular audit. Work on business acquisitions or debt offerings is frequently done at a premium, whereas work for charitable organizations or work done at an off-peak time may be done at a discount.

It is important to keep in mind that the auditor's fee estimate is based on a certain level of assistance from management in preparing the financial statements and account analyses, and in retrieving documents needed for the audit. Because professional rates are generally higher than internal personnel costs, it is essential that any and all work that can be done internally be done internally.

UNDERGOING THE AUDIT

After the audit has been planned and fees have been agreed upon, the audit will begin. Generally, an engagement team led by a partner and supported by a manager and several staff is responsible for conducting the audit and overseeing services provided to the organization. The manner in which an audit is conducted depends greatly on the individuals who have been assigned to the work. Consequently, "personal chemistry" is an important factor in auditor/client organization relationships.

Audit test work may be performed to determine whether an organization's internal control structure is functioning properly. In addition, auditors perform test procedures to verify the amounts and account balances reported in the financial statements. The test procedures to be performed are selected based on auditor judgment, and the exact nature and extent of procedures to be performed is generally not shared with organization management.

The auditor will also obtain a letter from the organization's attorney that describes pending litigation, read all minutes of meetings of the board of directors or trustees, and request copies of contracts, including leases entered into by the organization. At the completion of the audit, the auditor will request a representation letter, usually signed by the chief executive and chief financial officers, which asserts that all information has been provided to the auditor. The letter is further tailored to include other representations that are appropriate in the circumstances.

Interpreting the Auditor's Opinion

At the conclusion of the audit, the auditor will prepare his or her written opinion on the or-

ganization's financial statements. The language of the standard opinion is recommended by the AICPA, and the typical unqualified or "clean" opinion is presented in three paragraphs:

1. *Paragraph 1* lists the financial statements subject to audit and indicates that they are management's responsibility.
2. *Paragraph 2* indicates that the auditor followed professional auditing standards, describes the nature of audit procedures, and states that audit work was performed on a test basis.
3. *Paragraph 3* states the auditor's opinion on the financial statements.

Sometimes a paragraph may be added if the organization presents supplementary schedules or to highlight other matters.

Under special circumstances, the auditor's opinion language will differ. For example, if the auditor believes that accounting principles have not been appropriately applied, or if the auditor was prevented from making a full examination of the organization's accounts, then a fourth paragraph may be inserted describing the situation.

The opinion may be further modified under certain circumstances to indicate that the financial statements do not present fairly the financial condition or results of operations of the organization or the auditor may decline to express an opinion on the financial statements. Naturally, management would want to cooperate with the auditor in every way possible to avoid language of this type.

Using the Management Letter

In addition to receiving the auditor's opinion on the financial statements, the organization will receive a management letter at the conclusion of the audit. This letter includes the auditor's recommendations with respect to operations, internal controls, and other financial management matters. By its nature, a management letter is intended to be constructive and therefore addresses only matters that require attention. Each year, the auditor will address the status of recommendations made in the previous year and make new recommendations.

Because the initial input for comments may come from the junior staff performing the audit, observations generally need to be discussed thoroughly between management and the auditor in order to yield practical, valuable recommendations. This process is undertaken in the letter-drafting stage so that all parties are in agreement as to the facts in the letter long before it is submitted to the governing board. Management will usually respond in writing to the governing board with its plans to implement or not implement the recommendations, either in a separate letter or in the body of the management letter.

ESTABLISHING AN AUDIT COMMITTEE

Although there is no regulatory requirement for a nonprofit organization to establish an audit committee of the governing board, there has been an increasing level of interest in audit committees in the nonprofit sector in recent years. To a large extent, the interest is attributable to a growing awareness of the fiduciary responsibilities of governing boards and a better understanding of how audit committees assist in fulfilling those responsibilities.

The primary objective of an audit committee is to provide additional assurances about the integrity of financial information used by the governing board, disseminated to constituencies, and provided to regulatory agencies such as state attorneys general. Of equal importance is the audit committee's responsibility for ensuring that the organization has the necessary controls in place to safeguard assets.

Many audit committees have charters defined in the organization's bylaws or otherwise have their role specified in writing. Although the size of the audit committee should be determined by an organization's needs, several studies show that three to five members is a typical size. Because of the long-term nature of the committee's activities, membership continuity is important. Reappointments and membership terms that end in different years contribute to achieving this objective

because they prevent all experienced members from being replaced at one time. The most common audit committee responsibilities are to (1) oversee the organization's internal control structure; (2) review the internal audit department; (3) select the external auditor; (4) review the external auditor's annual audit plan; (5) review the annual report, management letter, and the results of the external audit.

Audit committees generally meet at least twice each year with the external auditor. The first meeting, scheduled before the audit begins, serves as a planning meeting. The second, held on completion of the audit, serves as the audit review meeting at which the management letter and financial statements are discussed.

OBTAINING OTHER BENEFITS

Many executives find the resources of their independent auditing firm helpful for a broad range of business needs. Opportunities to leverage limited internal capabilities are frequently available through extensive management consulting and tax capabilities resident in CPA firms.

Among the areas where the management consulting arm of a CPA firm can assist are (1) management systems design and implementation; (2) strategic planning and marketing; (3) organization, governance, and operations reviews; (4) cash management; (5) financial planning and analysis; (6) human resources management assistance.

Typical tax services include (1) review of activities to identify potential unrelated business income; (2) planning for tax minimization and estimated payment calculations; (3) penalty exposure reviews; (4) personal financial planning advice; (5) private inurement reviews; (6) review of compensation schemes and retirement plans.

Executives can also benefit from the training resources of CPA firms. For example, many audit firms offer courses available to the public on various management and accounting topics. Also, some firms have training facilities that can be borrowed or rented by clients at a minimal cost. And auditors can be helpful in training board members and nonfinancial managers in understanding complex fund accounting financial statements. Some, but not all, of these opportunities for training will have fees associated with them.

GETTING THE BEST RESULTS

Auditors, by the very nature of their profession, are motivated to providing competent, quality service. While licensing requirements help to ensure basic competence, the auditor's need to generate and maintain business while avoiding losses arising from legal liability motivates him or her to provide top-quality service. The kinds of things that disappoint executives can frequently be prevented or eliminated if service expectations are clearly known. Problems will be avoided if care is taken to:

1. Select an auditor with relevant experience, industry expertise, and good references.
2. Obtain advice about issues (accounting and operational) during the year before decisions are made.
3. Keep organizational commitments to prepare information requested for the audit.
4. Instruct organization personnel to cooperate with the auditor and keep communication lines open.
5. Provide honest feedback about the performance of on-site staff.
6. Establish clear, reasonable deadlines for review of draft financial statements and management letters.
7. Understand the basis for fees, billing practices, and expectations about payment.

The best audit execution results from careful planning and open communication to avoid surprises on both sides.

INDEX

[Proper names in *italics* refer to contributors.]

AAA. *See* American Arbitration Association
ABC. *See* activity-based cost system
Abetti, Pier A., **7**/16–21
ABI/INFORM, **14**/25
aboveground storage tanks (ASTs), **8**/83–84
Absolut Vodka campaign, **2**/112
accelerators, **3**/39
acceptable quality levels (AQLs), **8**/48
acceptances, **6**/29
accidental death/dismemberment coverage, **4**/43
account
  investment, **6**/34
  lockbox, **6**/34
  operating, **6**/34
  opportunity identification, **3**/32
  plan implementation, **3**/34
  potential development, **3**/33–34
  profiles preparation, **3**/32
  rating, **3**/33
accountability, **2**/71, **6**/6
account classification, **3**/32
accounting, **2**/10–11
  international environment, **5**/52–55
  management, **9**/39
  managerial uses, **5**/27–31
  rate of return, **6**/24
  small business, **13**/30–34
Accounting Principles Board and the Committee
  on Accounting Procedure of the American
  Institute of Certified Public Accountants
  (AICPA), **5**/44–45
accounts payable, **6**/28
accounts receivable
  collecting, **5**/15
  managing, **5**/12–16
  recent developments, **5**/15–16
accrual basis of accounting, **5**/44
accrual method, **5**/33
ACH. *See* Automated Clearinghouse transfers

acquired immunodeficiency syndrome (AIDS), **4**/93
acquisitions/divestitures, **6**/15
activity-based cost system (ABC), **5**/29, **8**/56
actual cash value (ACV), **12**/15
Acuff, Frank L., **4**/66–69
ACV. *See* actual cash value
ADA. *See* Americans with Disabilities Act
ADEA. *See* Age Discrimination in Employment
  Act
Administration Industrielle et Generale, **1**/13
administrative agencies. *See* government agencies
administrative costs, **5**/14
administrative law, **16**/15
administrative procedure acts, **16**/16
administrative techniques, appraising, incentive
  plans, **8**/35
advertising, **2**/106
  allowances, **3**/42
  budget, **2**/109
  creative strategy, **2**/112–113
  current trends, **2**/114–115
  future of, **2**/114–115
  mass communication, **2**/108–115
  messages, **2**/112–113
  objectives, **2**/109–112
  qualitative comparisons, **2**/114
  ratings, **2**/113
  reach and frequency, **2**/113
  research, **2**/114
Africa, **14**/5
after-tax profit, **5**/15
Age Discrimination in Employment Act (ADEA),
  4/56–57, **12**/23
Agency for International Development, **14**/23
agent
  foreign, **14**/28
  international business, **14**/31–32

AGVS. *See* automatic guided vehicle system
AI. *See* artificial intelligence
AICPA. *See* Accounting Principles Board and the Committee on Accounting Procedure of the American Institute of Certified Public Accountants
aided recall, 2/110
AIDS. *See* acquired immunodeficiency syndrome
AIDS testing, 4/94
air issues, environmental management, 8/78–79
Allen, Mark J., 5/43–49
alliances, international business, 14/16–17
allocation, state income taxes, 5/38
allowances
   advertising, 3/42
   case, 3/42
   display, 3/42
alphanumeric input devices, 9/17
alternative minimum tax, 5/33
amendments, insurance, 12/37
American Arbitration Association (AAA), 4/86
American Production and Inventory Control Society, 8/55
Americans with Disabilities Act (ADA), 4/55, 57–58, 94, 12/22
analog services, 9/29
analysis, political, 6/41
Anderson, Robin D., 13/39–40
annual percentage rate (APR), 2/57
Antiboycott Compliance Office of the Department of Commerce, 14/31
antiboycott regulations, international business, 14/31
antibureaucracy behaviors, 1/59–60
Anti Kickback Act, 10/24
Antitrust Amendments Act, 2/98
Antitrust laws, international business, 14/31
Antitrust and Trade Regulation Report, 2/101
applications, manufacturing processes, 8/54–55
apportionment, state income taxes, 5/38
appraisals/business valuations, 6/18
appropriation, capital expenditure, 6/21, 23–24
APR. *See* annual percentage rate
AQLs. *See* acceptable quality levels
arbitrage, 6/43
Areeda-Turner rule, 2/97
artificial intelligence (AI), 16/32
ASEAN. *See* Association of Southeast Asian Nations
Asian Development Bank, 14/23
Asian planned economies, 14/5
Asia Pacific, 14/5
assessing strengths and weaknesses, 2/29
asset management, finance, 6/3
assets, 5/10
   financed, 6/26
   nature of, 6/27

association captive insurance company, 12/31
Association of Southeast Asian Nations (ASEAN), 14/11
ASTs. *See* aboveground storage tanks
ATE. *See* automated test equipment
ATM. *See* automated teller machine
AT&T, 6/37
Atwood, Caleb S., 4/24–28
audit
   independent, 5/43–49
   networks, 9/38
auditing
   internal, 5/40–42
   marketing function, 2/86–93
   standards, generally accepted (GAAS), 5/45–47
auditor
   independent, 5/45
   insurance broker as, 12/49
auditors/accountants, corporate, 6/17
auditor's opinion, nonprofit organizations, 16/44
auditor's report, 5/47–48
audit phase, MIS transition, 9/72
audit process, 2/88–90
audits
   environmental, 8/84
   most common findings, 2/92–93
   nonprofit organizations, 16/42–46
   quality, 8/39
authority, 1/13
authorization, 5/28
auto liability/auto physical damage, 12/39–40
Automated Clearinghouse transfers (ACH), 13/25
automated teller machine (ATM), 9/18
automated test equipment (ATE), 8/68
automatic guided vehicle system (AGVS), 10/28
automation, islands of, 8/69–70
average costs, 5/17–18
aversion to risk, capital expenditure, 6/23

background assessment, 2/43
bad-debt losses, 5/14
Balance of Payments Yearbook, 14/24
balance sheet, 5/7–8
   considerations, 6/18
bank
   depositary, 6/33
   disbursing, 6/33
Bank Holding Company Act, 6/37
Barnard, Chester, 1/5
barriers, disappearing, 6/41
barter, 14/46
base salary and incentive mix, 3/37–38
Bassin, Marc, 16/9–13
Bean, Alden S., 7/33–36
Bean, Nelson, 12/5
Beckman, Sara L., 8/5–18
behavioral model, 1/48

behavioral theory, 1/15–16
behaviors, antibureaucracy, 1/59–60
Belasco, James A., 1/5–10
Bender, A. Douglas, 7/36–38
benefits, 2/15
Bennett, Shelby D., 5/37–40
Bergen, John D., 11/3
Berra, Yogi, 1/10
beta site testing, 2/107
Bhote, Keki R., 8/36–51
bilateral clearing agreements, 14/46–47
bill of materials (BOM), 5/21
Bingham, Barry, 4/35–40
Bishop, Dan, 13/37–38
Bitner, Mary Jo, 15/5–15
bits per second (BPS), 9/29
blanket purchase order (BPO), 10/22
Blitstein, Barry, 4/35–40
board-mandated requirements, management
    compliance, 4/82
Bohl, Don, 10/3
boiler and machinery coverages, 12/38
Bologna, Jack, 9/64–67
BOM. *See* bill of materials
bonds, 6/29
Bonoma, Tom, 2/93
bonus packs, 3/42
Boyatzis, Richard E., 16/5–8
BPO. *See* blanket purchase order
BPS. *See* bits per second
brand, 2/18
brand affect, 2/111
brand awareness, 2/110
brand comprehension, 2/110–111
brand image, 2/111
Brown, Stephen W., 15/5–15
Brunsen, William, 5/16–26
Bryce, Herrington J., 16/3–4, 25–26
budget, 5/29
    operations team, 6/13
    planning cycles, 2/30
    process and review, 6/11–14
budgeting, 6/9–14
bureaucracies
    decline, 1/59
    knowledge power structure, 1/61
    problem solving, 1/61
bureaucratic model, 1/47–48
bureaucratic theories, 1/13
Bureau of National Affairs, 2/101
Bushnell, Nolan, 13/9
business application architecture (software), 9/24
business communication goal, 11/20
business enterprise, modern environment, 5/6
business function model, 9/15
business income, and state taxes, 5/39
business income/extra expense coverages, 12/38

Business International, 14/23, 34
business plans, mall business, 13/6–11
business remittances, 6/42
Business Software Alliance, 14/32
business-to-business
    communications, 11/20–22
    marketing, 2/121
buyback, 14/46
buyer(s), 2/60
    early majority, 2/22
    late majority, 2/22
    product, 2/21–23
buying decisions, purchasing department, 10/5
buying/selling process, 2/103

C_P, C_{PK}, 8/44
CAA. *See* Clean Air Act
CAD. *See* computer-aided design
CAD/CAM, 8/70–72
CAE. *See* computer-aided engineering
cafeteria/flexible benefit plan, 4/43–44
Calano, Jim, 9/63
Caldwell, Alethea O., 1/43–47
Calhoun, Kenneth, 16/34
call option, 7/31
CAM. *See* computer-aided manufacturing
capacity, manufacturing, 8/11
capacity requirements planning (CRP), 5/21
cap and hedging, 6/32
capital, 1/61, 5/32
    cost of, 6/26–27
capital expenditures, analysis/decision making,
    6/21–25
capital loans, 6/29
capital purchasing, 10/35–38
capital stock taxes, 5/39
capital structure, 6/27
Capon, Noel, 2/3–4, 12–25, 3/3–10
CAPP. *See* computer-aided process planning
caps, 3/40
Carlzon, Jan, 15/6
Carpenter, Gregory S., 2/77–80
Carr, Harold, 11/4–5
carrying costs, 5/17
CASE. *See* computer-assisted systems engineering
case allowances, 3/42
cash conversion cycle, 13/22–23
cash cow, 2/38
cash or deferred arrangements (CODAs), 4/48
cash flow
    finance, 6/3
    matching, 13/25
    statement, 5/9
cash management, 6/33–36, 13/22–26
cash method, 5/33
catalog prices, purchasing, 10/14
cathode ray tube (CRT), 9/17

cause-and-effect diagrams, **8**/45
C corporation, **5**/32
CDCs. *See* certified development companies
CDROM. *See* compact disk read-only memory
Celler-Kefauver Act, **2**/99
centralization, **3**/15
central processing unit (CPU), **9**/17
CEO. *See* chief executive officer
CERCLA. *See* Comprehensive Environmental
        Response, Compensation and Liability Act
Certificate of Incorporation/By-Laws, **5**/6
certified development companies (CDCs), **13**/15
certified internal auditor program (CIA), **5**/40
certified public accountant (CPA), **5**/45
CEUs. *See* continuing education units
CFC. *See* chlorofluorocarbon
CFO. *See* chief financial officer
CFR. *See* Code of Federal Regulations
Chada decision, **2**/96
chaebol, **14**/16
chain of command, **1**/13
challenger, **2**/79
change
    nature of power, **1**/60–61
    obstacles, **1**/8–9
    trends, **1**/58–59
changing corporate climate and culture, **1**/32
changing demographics, **1**/17
changing expectations, **1**/17
changing rate of skill obsolescence, **1**/17
changing workplace, **1**/16–17
channel length decision, **3**/23–24
channel management, **3**/24–26
channel service unit (CSU), **9**/30
channel strategy
    elements, **3**/20–21
    process, **3**/21–22
charitable gift, **5**/34–35
chart of accounts, **13**/32
Chartered Property Casualty Underwriter course
        (CPCU), **12**/12
chief executive officer (CEO), **1**/33–34, **9**/7
chief financial officer (CFO), **6**/7–9, **9**/7
chief operating officer (COO), **9**/7
China, international business, **14**/5–6
CHIPS. *See* Clearinghouse Interbank Payment
        System
chlorofluorocarbon (CFC), **8**/75
choosing among options, **2**/79–80
CIA. *See* certified internal auditor program
CIM. *See* computer-integrated manufacturing
        software
CIP. *See* continuous improvement program
CIRCUS. *See* combined interest rate and currency
        swap
Civil Rights Act of 1866, **4**/56
Civil Rights Act of 1964, **12**/23

classical theory, **1**/20–21
classic directive theory, **1**/18
Clayton Antitrust Act, **2**/99, **10**/19, 24
Clean Air Act (CAA), **8**/78
Clean Water Act (CWA), **8**/79, 83
clearing, **6**/35
clearing float, **5**/15
Clearinghouse Interbank Payment System
        (CHIPS), **13**/25
client server, **9**/24–25
club programs, direct marketing, **2**/120–121
CMM. *See* coordinate measuring machine
        programs
CNC/DNC. *See* computer numerical control/
        distributed numerical control
coaching, performance appraisal, **4**/61–62
COBRA. *See* Consolidated Omnibus Budget
        Reconciliation Act
CODAs. *See* cash or deferred arrangements
CODEC, **9**/29
Code of Federal Regulations (CFR), **10**/21
Cohen, Stephen, **8**/5
COLA. *See* cost of living adjustment
Coll, Joan H., **1**/47–51
collaborative R&D agreements (CRADAs), **7**/45
collar and hedging, **6**/32
collection costs, **5**/14
collective bargaining, **4**/84–86
combined interest rate and currency swap
        (CIRCUS), **6**/31
Comfort, William S., **4**/40–46
Commerce Business Daily, **7**/46
Commerce Clearing House, **2**/101
commercialization, service industry, **15**/22
commercial paper, **6**/28
Commission of the European Communities to the
        United States, **14**/23
common carrier, network management, **9**/39
common stock, **6**/30
communication, **2**/16
    business-to-business, **11**/20–22
    crisis, **11**/25, 28–29
    effective, **4**/72–76
    employee, **4**/75–76
    employee relations, **11**/14–16
    executive, **11**/20–22
    international business strategies, **14**/22–23
    nonverbal, **4**/74
    objectives, **2**/110–112
    right message, **4**/76
    risk management, **11**/25–29
    verbal, **4**/72–73
    written, **4**/74–75
compact disk read-only memory (CDROM), **9**/18
company politics, capital expenditures, **6**/24
company-wide quality control (CWQC), **8**/45

compensation
 deductible expense, 5/34
 employee, 4/35–40
 total, 4/35–36
compensation level, 3/37
compensation/offset, 14/46
competition, 2/43–44
competitive advantage, 2/40–42
competitive analysis, 2/35–36
competitive comparison, 3/33
Competitive Equality Banking Act, 6/38
competitive goals, 2/85
competitive information, 2/85
competitive position, 2/39, 3/33
competitive pricing strategy, 6/19, 15/21
competitive process, 2/84–85
competitive resources, 2/85
competitive response, 3/47
competitor analysis, 2/44–45
competitors' capabilities, objectives, and
  strategies, 2/45
components, 2/101
Comprehensive Environmental Response,
  Compensation and Liability Act (CERCLA),
  8/81
comprehensive income, 5/10
comptroller, 6/13
CompuServe, 10/16
computer
 architecture, 9/42–43
 classes, 9/19–21
 components, 9/17–19
 input devices, 9/17–18
 mainframe, 9/19–20
 memory, 9/17
 new systems, 8/65–66
 output devices, 9/18–19
 processing power, 1/17
 trends, 9/21
 types, 9/16–17
 workstations, 9/20–21
computer-aided design (CAD), 8/66
computer-aided engineering (CAE), 8/68
computer-aided manufacturing (CAM), 8/66
computer-aided process planning (CAPP), 8/68
computer-assisted systems engineering (CASE),
  9/13, 9/27
computer-integrated manufacturing software
  (CIM), 8/16, 48, 66, 68–69
computer numerical control/distributed
  numerical control (CNC/DNC), 8/69
computing, manufacturing, 8/65
concentration banking, 5/15
Conference Board, Inc., 14/23
confidentiality/ownership, 7/39–40
configuration management, 9/39
Conlon, Gregory E., 10/35–38

consistency concept, 5/44
Consolidated Omnibus Budget Reconciliation Act
  (COBRA), 4/46, 12/23
consortia, 7/42–44
consumable supplies, 2/101
consumer promotions, 3/42
consumer response evolution, 3/47
contests, 3/42
contingency plans, 2/48
continual learning, 1/9–10
continuing education units (CEUs), 9/63
continuity plan, 2/120
continuity programs, direct marketing, 2/120–121
continuous improvement program (CIP), 8/52
contracts, 2/99–100
contractual assumptions, 12/17–18
contribution, focusing on, 1/8–9
control, 2/47–48
 of company, maintaining, 6/19
 function, 6/6
 level, 1/53
 reports, 5/24
 spans, 3/15–16
controls
 characteristics and conditions of, 1/44–46
 establishing, 1/43–47
 ongoing, 1/45
 outcome measurement and, 1/45
 plan, 2/48
 traditional vs. dynamic, 1/43–44
conversion labor. See direct labor
convertible bonds, 6/30
COO. See chief operating officer
Cooper, Robin, 8/17
coordinate measuring machine (CMM) programs,
  8/68
Coppett, John I., 15/22–26
copy tests, 2/114
core products, 16/39
core tasks, marketing management, 2/12–18
corporate auditors/accountants, 6/17
corporate climate, 1/30–32
corporate codes of conduct, 1/34–35
corporate culture, 1/31–32, 4/21, 6/18
corporate ethics committee, 1/34
corporate financial model, 6/10–11
corporate income taxes, 5/38–39
corporate lenders, 6/16–17
corporate marketing, 2/61–64
corporate philanthropy, 11/17–19
corporate relations
 evaluating results, 11/32–36
 staff, managing, 11/4–5
corporate restructuring, 6/14–20
 announcement, 4/71
 changing structure, 4/70
 communication, 4/70–71

corporate restructuring (*continued*)
  dealing with, 4/69–72
  factors affecting, 6/18–19
  impact and options, 4/70
  management responsibilities, 6/19–20
  monopoly limitations, 6/16
  and other entities, 6/17
  reasons, 6/15–16
  response to, 4/71–72
  tax factors, 6/16
corporate structure, 5/32, 6/16–18
corporate taxation, 5/32–33, 38–39
corporations
  impact of deregulation, 6/39
  small business, 13/31–32
cost
  allocating, 5/29
  capital, 6/26–27
  classifying, 5/28
  debt capital, 6/26
  determination, 5/14, 17–19
  driver, 5/27
  equity capital, 6/26
  leadership, 2/40
  manufacturing, 5/27–28
  savings, 10/5, 32
  specific lot, 5/18
  structure, 2/82
  systems, 5/28–31
cost analysis/cost models, purchasing, 10/14–15
cost of living adjustment (COLA), 4/52
cost plus, pricing strategy, 15/21
counselor relationship, 15/24
counter, purchase, 14/46
countertrade, 14/45–47
country marketing strategy and research, 14/17–19
coupons, 3/42
CPA. *See* certified public accountant
CPCU. *See* Chartered Property Casualty Underwriter course
CPU. *See* central processing unit
CRADAs. *See* collaborative R&D agreements
creative execution, direct marketing programs, 2/118–119
creative strategy, direct marketing programs, 2/118
credit
  extending, 5/13
  line, 6/28
  terms of extension, 5/13–15
credit decisions, small business, 13/25–26
crime
  coverages, 12/38
  prevention, 12/28–29
crisis communications, 11/25, 28–29
critical success factors (CSFs), 9/15

Crosby, Philip, 8/52
cross-price elasticity, 15/34
CRP. *See* capacity requirements planning
CRT. *See* cathode ray tube
CSFs. *See* critical success factors
CSU. *See* channel service unit
CTDs. *See* cumulative trauma disorders
CUI, 9/22
Cummings, Gordon, 6/3–4
cumulative trauma disorders (CTDs), 12/24
currencies, relative strength, 6/43
currency options, 6/44
current cost, 5/11
current market value, 5/11
customer analysis, 2/45–46
customer base, 2/103–104
customer behavior, tracking, 2/55–56
customer decision making, 2/55–60
customer need, 8/8–9
customer orientation, 2/9
customer price sensitivity, 2/83–84
customer service, 2/7, 13/26–28
customer's relationship to firm, 2/15
customization, high level, 2/104
CWA. *See* Clean Water Act
CWQC. *See* company-wide quality control
cycle time, 8/44

DAT. *See* digital audio tape
database architectures, 9/44–46
database management systems (DBMS), 9/42–47
  evolution, 9/43
  information security, 9/44
  services, 9/43–44
databases
  direct marketing, 2/120
  hierarchical, 9/45
  network, 9/45
  nonprofit manager, 16/31–32
  relational systems, 9/45–46
data collection, quality, 8/39
data communications software, 9/22
Data Interchange Standards Association (DISA), 10/40
data management software, 9/22
data model, 9/15–16
data processing center, 9/48–52
  elements, 9/48–49
  functions, 9/49–51
  human error, 9/51
data repositories, 9/46–47
data service unit (DSU), 9/30
Day, George S., 2/25–34
DB. *See* defined benefit plan
DBMS. *See* database management systems
DDS. *See* digital data service channel
Dean, Daniel J., 12/48–50

death benefit, **4**/45–46
debentures, **6**/29
debt
   restructuring, **6**/18
   with warrant, **6**/32
debt financing, **6**/27–31
   other sources, **13**/14–15
   small business, **13**/12–15
debt to equity, **6**/20
decentralization, **3**/15
decentralizing, sharing, **1**/46
decider, **2**/60
decision making, **2**/26
   negotiating objectives and resources, **2**/31–34
   public sector, **16**/22–25
   types, **2**/59–60
decision-making process, stages, **2**/56–59
decision-making roles, **1**/16
decision-making unit (DMU), **2**/60
decision support system (DSS), **16**/32
declarations, **12**/36–37
deductible expenses, **5**/34–35
deduction, **6**/27
defensive globalization drivers, **14**/8
defined benefit plan (DB), **4**/48–49, 52
defined contribution plans, **4**/53
Delivering Service Quality, **15**/6
delivery measures, **11**/34–35
Deming, Dr. W. Edwards, **8**/37, 52
Deming Prize, **15**/6
Demographic Yearbook, **14**/24
dental insurance, **4**/44
department planning, **1**/38–40
deployment, sales force, **3**/16–18
depository bank, **6**/33, 35
Depository Institutions Deregulation and
   Monetary Control Act, **6**/38
depository transfer check (DTC), **6**/34
depreciation, **5**/34
deregulation
   financial, **6**/36–39
   functional, **6**/36
   geographic, **6**/36–37
derived demand, **2**/102–103
designer products, **6**/32
design of experiments (DOE), **8**/45
design for manufacturing (DFM), **8**/47
DeSio, Robert, **9**/60
deskilling, **14**/17
detailed planning
   advantages, **8**/26
   resistance, **8**/25
developing nations, international business, **14**/6
developmental steps, **1**/28
DFM. *See* design for manufacturing
Dialog, **10**/16
Dibner, Mark D., **7**/3–4

differentiation, **2**/40, 79
digital audio tape (DAT), **7**/7
digital cellular radio, **9**/31
digital data service channel (DDS), **9**/30
digital radio, **9**/31
digital services, **9**/29–30
direct buying, international business, **14**/28
direct investment, international business, **14**/29
directional policy matrix, **2**/38–40
direction-setting approach, planning, **2**/71–74
direct labor, **8**/23–24
direct mail, **3**/14
direct marketing, **2**/116–121
   nature, **2**/117–118
   programs, **2**/118–119
directors and officers' liability (D&O), **12**/20, 40
*Directory of Federal Laboratory and Technology
   Resources: A Guide to Services, Facilities, and
   Expertise*, **7**/46
direct sends, **5**/15
DISA. *See* Data Interchange Standards
   Association
disability coverage
   key employee, **4**/45
   long-term, **4**/43
disaster recovery
   business recovery facilities, **9**/58
   corporate wide emphasis in the 1990s, **9**/57–58
   developing successful plan, **9**/59
   for information systems, **9**/56–59
   services developed in the 1980s, **9**/57
   telecommunications and voice recovery, **9**/58
disaster and recovery planning, MIS, **9**/66–67
disbursements, managing, **6**/35–36
disbursing
   bank, **6**/33
   remote, **6**/36
   zero balance account, **6**/35–36
discer, **1**/10
discipline, defined, **1**/10
discipulus, **1**/10
disclaimer of opinion, **5**/48
disclosure, financial statements, **5**/12
discontinuity, **7**/5, 7–9
discounted cash flow methods, **6**/24
discrimination, **4**/56
   price, **2**/98
display allowances, **3**/42
displays, **3**/42
distribution, **2**/107
   to owners, **5**/10
distribution channel decisions, nature, **3**/19–20
distribution channels, international business, **14**/20–21
distribution requirements planning (DRP), **8**/59
distribution system, managing, **3**/19–26

distributors, 4/50–51
  international business, 14/31–32
diversity, expanding, 4/21
divestitures, 6/15
  involuntary/enforced, and taxation, 5/35
divisional performance, measuring, 5/25–26
divisional structure, 1/49–50
DMU. *See* decision-making unit
D&O. *See* directors and officers' liability
DOE. *See* design of experiments
dog, 2/38
domestic insurance markets, 12/50–51
dominant brand advantage, 2/77–78
doom formula, 14/16
DOT. *See* U.S. Department of Transportation
Dow Jones News Retrieval, 10/16
downtime, 9/37
Droege, Milton F., Jr., 4/69–72
DRP. *See* distribution requirements planning
Drucker, Peter F., 1/16, 2/5, 8/46
drug/alcohol testing, employee, 4/93–94
DSO. *See* single-voice channel
DSS. *See* decision support system
DSU. *See* data service unit
DTC. *See* depositary transfer check
due process clauses, government agencies, 16/
  15–16
Duncan, Christopher A., 12/5–7

EAPs. *See* employee assistance programs
Early, John F., 1/23–27
early adopters, 2/22
early majority buyers, 2/22
earnings/income statement, 5/8–9
East Europe, 14/5
economic approach, 2/66
economic factors, 2/44
economic order quantity (EOQ), 5/19–21, 8/56,
  10/9
economic perils, 12/13
economics of scale, 6/18
economic value analysis (EVA), 2/83
Economist, The, 14/23
Edgar, Robert B., 12/35–41
EDI. *See* electronic data interchange
EDIA. *See* Electronic Data Interchange
  Association
EDP. *See* electronic data processing
EDS. *See* electronic disbursement systems
EEA. *See* European Economic Area
EEOC. *See* Equal Employment Opportunity
  Commission
EEOC/AAP. *See* Equal Employment Opportunity
  Commission/Affirmative Action Program
efficiency orientation, 16/7
EFT. *See* electronic fund transfer
EFTA. *See* European Free Trade Agreement

EIS. *See* executive information system
Eisenhardt, Kathleen, 8/9
elasticity, 15/34
election, board-conducted, 4/82
election campaign, how to run, 4/81–82
electronic data interchange (EDI), 8/68, 9/7,
  33–35, 60, 10/5, 38–42
  analysis of setup/operational costs, 10/41
  business benefits, 9/34–35
  determining feasibility, 10/40
  development issues, 9/34
  disadvantages of paper-based transactions, 10/
    39
  future, 9/35
  implementation issues, 10/41–42
  role and benefits, 10/39–40
  supporting components, 10/40–41
Electronic Data Interchange Association (EDIA),
  10/40
electronic data processing (EDP), 9/71
electronic disbursement systems (EDS), 13/24
electronic fund transfer (EFT), 6/34, 35, 13/24
electronic mail, 16/33
electronic payment systems, 5/16
Elnes, Phyllis, 13/19–22
Emergency Planning and Community Right-to-
  Know Act (EPCRA), 8/84
employee
  attitudes/values/work behavior, 4/10–12
  benefits, 4/40–46
  compensation, 4/35–40
  disability coverage, 4/45
  health programs, 4/86–88
  international assignments, 4/67–68
  life insurance, 4/45
  personal life involvement, 4/67
  protected activities, 4/77–78
  relations and communications, 11/14–16
  repatriation, 4/69
  retention/access/disclosure records, 4/93
  screening, 4/93–95
  selection/retention, 15/12–13
  services, 15/12–13
  solicitation/distribution by, 4/80
  substance abuse, 4/89–92
  testing, 4/93–95
  training/development, 4/28–34
employee assistance programs (EAPs), 12/22
Employee Polygraph Protection Act (EPPA), 4/95
Employee Retirement Income Security Act of
  1974 (ERISA), 4/4, 47, 53, 12/23
employee stock ownership plans (ESOPs), 4/50,
  11/13
employment trends, 4/12
empowerment, 11/16
  services employees, 15/12
enabling act, 16/16

energy, and leadership, **16**/13
enhanced service providers, **9**/31
enterprise architectures, **9**/15
enterprise resource planning (ERP), **8**/59
entertainment expenses, **5**/35
entrepreneur, small business, **13**/5–6
entrepreneurial orientation, **1**/16
environmental assessment, focus, **2**/28–29
environmental audits, **8**/84
environmental concerns, **1**/17
environmental dimensions, **2**/26–28
environmental factors, capital expenditures, **6**/24
environmental liability, **12**/18
environmental management, **8**/75–86
    air issues, **8**/78–79
    land issues, **8**/81–84
    recommended actions, **8**/85–86
    water issues, **8**/79–81
Environmental Protection Agency (EPA), **4**/4, **7**/
    46, **8**/75
E&O. *See* errors and omissions
EOQ. *See* economic order quantity
EPA. *See* Environmental Protection Agency
EPCRA. *See* Emergency Planning and
    Community Right-to-Know Act
Epermanis, Karen, **12**/48–50
EPPA. *See* Employee Polygraph Protection Act
Equal Employment Opportunity Act, **12**/23
Equal Employment Opportunity Commission
    (EEOC), **4**/55
Equal Employment Opportunity Commission/
    Affirmative Action Program (EEOC/AAP),
    12/21
equalization allowance, **4**/68
Equal Pay Act, **4**/57
equipment maintenance, **8**/46
equity, **5**/10
    external, internal, **4**/39
equity financing, small business, **13**/5
ERISA. *See* Employment Retirement Income
    Security Act
ERP. *See* enterprise resource planning
errors and omissions (E&O), **12**/40
ES. *See* expert system
ESF. *See* extended super frame
ESOPs. *See* employee stock ownership plans
estimating, **1**/55–56
ethics
    importance of enforcing, **1**/34
    purchasing function, **10**/6
    training, **1**/33
European Community, international business,
    14/5
European Community Information Service, **14**/23
European Economic Area (EEA), **14**/10
European Free Trade Agreement (EFTA), **14**/10
EVA. *See* economic value analysis

evaluation
    capital expenditure, **6**/21
    sales promotion, **3**/45–47
evaluation phase, capital expenditure, **6**/24–25
evidence accounts, **14**/46
excess/umbrella liability, **12**/40–41
exchange-of-profits risk, **14**/44
execution measures, **11**/34
executive information system (EIS), and nonprofit
    manager, **16**/32
Executive Order #11246, **12**/23
Executive Order #11375, **12**/23
executive review, government agencies, **16**/17
executive summary, **2**/43
expansion of business, and taxation, **5**/35–36
expediting, purchasing department, **10**/5
expenses, **5**/10
experience curve, **2**/40–42
expert system (ES), and nonprofit manager, **16**/
    32–33
Export-Import Bank of the United States, **14**/23
exporting, international business, **14**/15
exports, **6**/42
exposures
    analyzing products and completed operations
        liability, **12**/19–20
    automobile, aircraft/watercraft liability, **12**/20
    computer, **12**/27–28
    environmental liability, **12**/18
    fire, **12**/27
    human resources loss, **12**/21–24
    identification by type of risk/peril, **12**/12–13
    identifying property and income, **12**/11–12
    inheriting products, **12**/19
    liability loss, **12**/16–21
    liquor liability, **12**/18
    measuring income loss, **12**/15
    measuring property loss, **12**/14–15
    premises, operations, and related, **12**/17–19
    products and completed operations liability,
        12/19
    professional liability, **12**/20–21
    property of others, **12**/18
    ranking, **12**/15–16
    Statute of Limitations, **12**/19
    types of income loss, **12**/13–14
    types of property loss, **12**/13
    vehicle, **12**/29
express authority, **10**/5
extended super frame (ESF), **9**/29
extensive penetration, **2**/78
external advisers, **6**/39
external audits, **10**/23
external equity, **4**/39
external linkages, **2**/102–104
external reporting, **6**/6
external tax professionals, **5**/36–37

facilities, manufacturing, **8**/11–12
facility discharge points, **8**/80
failure mode effects analysis (FMEA), **8**/46
Fair Labor Standards Act (FLSA), **4**/58, **12**/22
family-owned businesses, **13**/37–38
FAR. *See* Federal Acquisition Regulation
Farley, Anne, **16**/42–46
Farnam, Thomas C., **4**/46–51
FASB. *See* Financial Accounting Standards Board
fault management, **9**/39
fault tree analysis (FTA), **8**/46
Fayol, Henri, **1**/5, 13
FCC. *See* Federal Communications Commission
FCIM. *See* shared flexible computer integrated
    manufacturing
FCPA. *See* Foreign Corrupt Practices Act
FDIC. *See* Federal Deposit Insurance Corporation
feasibility study, international business, **14**/4
feature advertising, **3**/42
Federal Acquisition Regulation (FAR), **10**/21
Federal Communications Commission (FCC), **5**/
    35, **9**/31
Federal Deposit Insurance Corporation (FDIC),
    9/57
federal government, purchasing, **10**/21
Federal Insurance Contributions Act (FICA), **4**/46
federal laws/acts, purchasing, **10**/19–20
Federal Mediation and Conciliation Service, **4**/85
Federal Register, **7**/46
Federal Rehabilitation Act, **4**/94
Federal Revenue System, clearing, **6**/35
federal taxation
    accounting considerations, **5**/33–34
    management responsibilities/opportunities, **5**/
    31–37
federal tax legislation, **5**/36–37
Federal Technology Transfer Act, **7**/45
Federal Trade Commission Act (FTC), **2**/95, 98,
    10/19, 25
Fed wire transfers, **13**/25
feedback, performance appraisal, **4**/61–62
feedback loop, **1**/25–26
feedback market information, **3**/10
Feigenbaum, Armand, **8**/52
Ferri, Linda J., **9**/22–28
fiber optic services, **9**/31
FICA. *See* Federal Insurance Contributions Act;
    social security and Medicare taxes
field selling, **3**/13
FIFO. *See* first in, first out
Fifth Amendment (U.S. Constitution), **4**/92, **16**/
    15
finance
    and accounting, **2**/10–11
    role in management, **6**/5–6
    theory, **6**/26

financial accounting/reporting, concepts and
    objectives, **5**/6–7
Financial Accounting Standards Board (FASB), **5**/
    6, 44, 53, **16**/42
financial deregulation, **6**/36–39
financial document, **2**/47–48
financial institutions, **6**/38–39
financial management, **6**/8
financial markets, changing, **6**/40–41
financial officer, **6**/7–9
financial planning, role of chief financial officer,
    6/8
financial ratio considerations, **6**/20
financial reporting/statements, **5**/5–12
financial risk, **14**/42
financial services, increased cost, **6**/39
financial statements, **5**/25
    analysis, **12**/12
    basic elements, **5**/9–10
    disclosure standards, **5**/12
    evidence to support, **5**/47
    independent audit, **5**/43–45
    recognition/measurement standards, **5**/10–12
financial thinking, global, **6**/40–42
financing
    forecasting costs, **5**/14–15
    function, **6**/25–26
    incentives, **3**/42
    inventory/receivable, **6**/28
    long-term debt, **6**/29–31
    medium-term debt, **6**/29
    new sources, **6**/31–32
    obtaining, **6**/19
    short-term debt, **6**/27–28
    sources, **6**/25–32
    traditional sources, **6**/27–31
    transnational, **6**/41
Finney, Elisha, **12**/29–33
First!, **10**/16
first in, first out (FIFO), **5**/17–18
Fisher, Sir Ronald, **8**/37
Fitzpatrick, Peter B., **14**/29–36
FitzRoy, Peter T., **2**/34–42
float
    bank processing, **6**/33
    billing, **6**/33
    check processing, **6**/33
    clearing, **5**/15
    internal, **5**/15
    leveraging, **6**/39
    mail, **5**/15, **6**/33
    shortening, **5**/15
floor and hedging, **6**/32
flow charts, and exposures, **12**/12
FLSA. *See* Fair Labor Standards Act
FMCS. *See* Federal Mediation and Conciliation
    Service

FMEA. *See* failure mode effects analysis
focus, facilities strategies, **8**/12
focus factories, **8**/54
FOIA. *See* Freedom of Information Act
follow-the-leader companies, **2**/24
Ford, Henry, **1**/5, **4**/3
forecasting, **6**/9–14
   discounts taken, **5**/13–14
   financing costs, **5**/14–15
   receivables balance, **5**/14
   sales, **5**/13
Forecasting Studies, **14**/24
foreign agent, **14**/28
Foreign Corrupt Practices Act (FCPA), **14**/31
foreign exchange, **6**/42–45
foreign service premium, **4**/68
Foreign Trade Highlights, **14**/24
formality, government agencies, **16**/15
Form R, **8**/85
forward buying, **3**/47
forward markets, **6**/43
Forzley, Michele, **14**/26–29
Foster, Richard N., **7**/5–11
four-cell matrix, **2**/37–38
Fourteenth Amendment (U.S. Constitution), **4**/92, **16**/15
Fourth Amendment (U.S. Constitution), **4**/92
Four Tigers, **14**/5–6
franchising, **2**/99
   international business, **14**/15–16
   service industry, **15**/14
   small business, **13**/39–40
Freedom of Information Act (FOIA), **16**/17
frequency, direct marketing, **2**/120
frequency of measures, **11**/35
fringe, **2**/79
Frishmann, Donald E., **11**/20–22
FTA. *See* fault tree analysis
FTC. *See* Federal Trade Commission
FTC v. Sperry & Hutchinson, **2**/96
functional deregulation, **6**/36
functional management, **1**/13–14
functional structure, **1**/49
functions
   integration, **1**/52–54
   staff vs. line, **1**/52–53
Functions of the Executive, **1**/5
funds, movement/availability, **6**/34–35
funds availability, **6**/35
future cash flows, **5**/11
futures, foreign exchange, **6**/44

GAAP. *See* generally accepted accounting principles
GAAS. *See* generally accepted auditing standards
GACT. *See* generally available control technologies

gains, **5**/10
gain-sharing plans, **8**/29
Gamsin, Sharon, **11**/8–11
Gantt, Henry, **1**/12
Gantt chart, **7**/23, **9**/15
Gantt plan, **8**/30
gap analysis, **2**/33–34
Garn-St. Germain Depository Institution Act, **6**/38
GATT. *See* General Agreement on Tariffs and Trade
GDP. *See* gross domestic product
General Agreement on Tariffs and Trade (GATT), **14**/10
General Electric Capital, **6**/37
generally accepted accounting principles (GAAP), **5**/8, 43, 45, 53
generally accepted auditing standards (GAAS), **5**/45–47
generally available control technologies (GACT), **8**/78
general management, chief financial officer, **6**/7–8
General Motors Acceptance Corporation (GMAC), **6**/37
general-purpose financial statements (GPFS), **5**/5–12
genetic testing, **4**/94
geographic deregulation, **6**/36
geographic dispersion, **3**/33
Gibson, Jack P., **12**/16–21
Gilbreth, Frank, **1**/12
Gilbreth, Lillian, **1**/12
Gimpel, Ronald M., **1**/54–57
Glass-Steagall Act, **6**/37–38
global financial thinking, **6**/40–42
global insurance, risk management, **12**/50–53
globalization
   barriers, **14**/10–11
   defensive drivers, **14**/8
   proactive drivers, **14**/9–10
global network, intracorporate international relations, **11**/31
global orientation, **1**/17
global risk management, **12**/51–52
global sourcing, **14**/39–40
global strategy
   formulating and implementing in international business, **14**/7–26
   intracorporate international relations, **11**/31–32
GMAC. *See* General Motors Acceptance Corporation
GNP. *See* gross national product
Goal, The, **8**/72
goal and action management cluster, **16**/7
goal and objectives, **1**/29–30
going-concern concept, **5**/44

Gold, Bela, **7**/11–15
Goldberg, Michael, **4**/86–88
Goldberg v. Kelly, **16**/15
Goldratt, Eli, **8**/72
Gompertz curve, **7**/6
goods vs. services, **15**/7–9
Gore, W. L., **1**/49
government agencies, **16**/14–18
government business, international business, **14**/29
government regulations, employee relations, **4**/55–59
government relations, **11**/6–7
GPFS. *See* general-purpose financial statements
Grace, Michael F., **12**/11–16
Granger, James, **11**/32–36
graphical user interface (GUI), **9**/21, 23
graphics devices, **9**/17
Gray, Barbara L., **1**/54–57
Greenlees, E. Malcolm, **13**/30–34
gross domestic product (GDP), **8**/44
gross-margin method, **5**/18
gross margins, **6**/20
gross national product (GNP), **8**/75, **14**/10
gross rating points (GRP), **2**/113
groundwater, **8**/79
Groundwater Protection Act and Resource Conservation and Recovery Act (RCRA), **8**/79
group incentive systems, **8**/30–32
group technology, manufacturing processes, **8**/53–54
group theory, **1**/22–23
growth-share matrix, **2**/36–38
GRP. *See* gross rating points
Grunewald, Donald, **13**/16–19
guarantees, **6**/17, **15**/11–12
Guerette, Denis, **6**/7–9
GUI. *See* graphical user interface
Guinan, James M., **10**/27–30
Gumpert, David, **13**/9
Gustavson, Sandra G., **12**/3–4

Hagaman, T. Carter, **5**/49–52
Halsey plan, **8**/29
Hamilton, William F., **7**/29–33
Hampton, John J., **1**/58–62, **6**/42–45, **12**/50–53, **14**/41–45
Hanna, William John, **16**/22–25
hardship premium, **4**/68
hardware, computer, **9**/5, 16–21
Harkins, Jeffrey L., **5**/5–12
Hartt, A. Douglas, **6**/9–14
Harvard Business Review, **14**/9
Haskin, Daniel, **5**/23–26
Hawk, Elizabeth J., **4**/35–40
Hawthorne effect, **8**/50

Hawthorn Works of Western Electric, **1**/14
Hayes, Robert, **8**/14
hazardous materials, **8**/82
Hazardous and Solid Waste Amendments (HSWA) of 1984, **8**/83
hazardous substance material safety data sheets (MSDS), **8**/84
hazardous waste (HW), **8**/81–82
  treatment, storage, and disposal (TSD), **8**/79
Hazmat World, **8**/75, 79
health benefits, **4**/41–42
health insurance plan, paying for, **4**/42–43
health maintenance organizations (HMOs), **4**/41–42
Healy, L. Hall, Jr., **8**/75–86
heating, ventilating, and air conditioning (HVAC), **4**/4
heavy equipment, **2**/101
hedging, **6**/32, 43–44
Hedrick, Floyd D., **10**/18–21
Hegerty, Chris, **9**/60
Heide, Jan B., **3**/19–26
Held, Christopher E., **14**/48–54
Herzberg, Frederick, **1**/15
hidden liabilities, **6**/19
hierarchical databases, **9**/45
hierarchy, **2**/111–112
hierarchy-of-effects model, **2**/111
Hiller, Robert W., **6**/25–32
Hindman, William J., Jr., **11**/14–16
Hinge, Kathleen Conlon, **10**/38–42
Hirshman-Herfindahl Index, **2**/99
historical appraisal, **2**/43
historical cost, **5**/11
historic prices, purchasing, **10**/14
HIV testing, **4**/94
HMOs. *See* health maintenance organizations
Hodgson, W. Edward, **9**/28–32
Hoffman, Donna L., **2**/65–68
Holden, Reed K., **2**/80–85
holding company, **6**/14
honesty testing, **4**/95
Hong Kong, international business, **14**/5
Hosh, in planning, **8**/38
HRIS. *See* human resources information systems
HSWA. *See* Hazardous and Solid Waste Amendments of 1984
Huguet, John, **6**/40–42
Hulbert, James M., **2**/5–11
Humana Inc. v. Commissioner, **12**/31
human behavior schools, **1**/14
humanistic theory, **1**/21
human perils, **12**/13
human relations schools, **1**/14–15
human resources, **2**/9, **4**/12–16
  planning, **8**/22–26

human resources information systems (HRIS), 4/64–66
human resources management
    in international operations, 4/66–69
    public sector, 16/7–8
    small business, 13/16–19
Hunt Commission, 6/38
hurdles, 3/40
Huybregts, Gerard, 5/52–55
HVAC. *See* heating, ventilating, and air conditioning
HW. *See* hazardous waste
hybrid structure, 1/50
Hyde, Richard C., 11/25–29

IBM, 1/9
IIA. *See* Institute of Internal Auditors
illegal pricing practices, penalties, 2/98
Illinois Brick price-fixing case, 2/96
impact measures, 11/35
implementation, 2/26
    sales promotion, 3/45
imports, 6/42
IMS (research firm), 2/49
inbound calls, 2/119
in-bound procurement, and handling, 10/28
incentive, group systems, 8/30–32
incentive formula, 3/39–40
incentive plans, 8/27–29
    appraising administrative techniques, 8/35
    appraising productivity, 8/34–35
    employee acceptance, 8/28–29
    making decision, 8/34–35
    motivation, 8/28
    opportunity, 8/28
    problem areas, 8/32–33
    standards maintenance, 8/33–34
incentives, individual performance, 8/29–30
income, comprehensive, 5/10
income elasticity, 15/34
income statement, 5/8–9
income tax planning, small business, 13/33–34
incremental return, 6/27
IND. *See* investigational new drug
indemnity clauses, 12/34
independent audit, 5/43–49
independent auditor, 5/45, 48–49
indirect labor, 8/24–26
indirect selling, international business, 14/28
individual retirement accounts (IRAs), 4/50, 13/33
industrial consumers, 2/22–23
industrial marketing, 2/101–108
industrial services, 2/101
industry attractiveness analysis, 2/44
industry capacity, 2/44
influencer, 2/60

informational roles, 1/16
information management role, purchasing department, 10/9–10
information security, database management systems, 9/44
information services, 2/8
information strategy planning (ISP), 9/10–16
    benefits, 9/11–12
    business forces, 9/13–15
    implementing plan, 9/12–13
    information needs, 9/15–16
    mechanisms, 9/16
    organizations/locations, 9/16
    purpose, 9/11
information systems (I/S), 2/8–9, 9/51
    disaster recovery for, 9/56–59
    planning for, and nonprofit manager, 16/33–35
    strategic planning, 16/34
    and technology, 9/71–72
    training for users and MIS staff, 9/60–63
information technology (I/T), 8/15–16, 66–68
    budget, 9/51
    impact of advances, 6/6
    and nonprofit manager, 16/31–35
    payoff, 9/7–8
    resources, 9/5–7
infrastructure risk, 14/42
infrastructure scale-up, new service, 15/31
Inglesby, Tom, 8/64–75
Ingram, Thomas N., 3/11–18
initial public offering (IPO), 13/11
initiation, capital expenditure, 6/21–23
initiator, 2/60
innovator/communicator, insurance broker, 12/49–50
innovators, 2/22
INPACT. *See* International Partnerships for Commercialization of Technology
INPACT model, 7/49–50
In Search of Excellence, 1/9, 15/6
Institute of Internal Auditors (IIA), 5/40
insurable risk, 14/44
insurance, 6/17, 12/35–41
    administrator/marketer, 12/48–49
    agents and brokers, 12/48–50
    auto liability/auto physical damage, 12/39–40
    clauses, 12/34
    conditions/definitions, 12/37
    coverages, 12/37–41
    global vs. international, 12/53
    monoline, 12/36
    package, 12/36
    parts of policy, 12/36–37
    property, 12/37–39
    types of policies, 12/36
insuring agreements, 12/37
intangible assets, 6/26

intangible properties, **12**/13
integrated office automation (OA), **9**/33
integrated services digital network (ISDN), **9**/30, **15**/39
integration, of functions, **1**/52–54
intellectual property rights, enforcing/licensing, **7**/42
intelligence, **1**/16
Inter-American Development Bank, **14**/23
interest coverage, **6**/20
interest rate differentials, **6**/43
intermediary levels, **2**/15
intermediate, **2**/17
intermediate-term effects, sales promotion, **3**/46–47
internal audit function, **6**/6
internal auditing, **5**/40–42, **10**/22–23
internal control structure, and audits, **5**/46–47
internal equity, **4**/39
internal float, **5**/15
internal linkages, **2**/104
internal marketing, services industry, **15**/13–14
internal relations, purchasing department, **10**/6–8
internal tax department, **5**/36
International Bank for Reconstruction & Development (World Bank), **14**/24
international business
    alliances, **14**/16–17, 37–39
    antiboycott regulations, **14**/31
    antitrust laws, **14**/31
    changing global environment, **14**/7–11
    choosing foreign representative, **14**/34–35
    classification of world markets, **14**/4–5
    communication strategies, **14**/22–23
    countertrade, **14**/45–47
    distribution channels, **14**/20–21
    exporting, **14**/15
    feasibility study, **14**/4
    foreign legislation affecting agents/distributors, **14**/31–32
    formulating global strategy, **14**/11–23
    globalization barriers, **14**/10–11
    globalization drivers, **14**/8–10
    globalizing marketing mix, **14**/17–23
    global sourcing, **14**/39–40
    individual company classifications, **14**/5–6
    joint ventures, **14**/16
    licensing, **14**/15–16
    management considerations, **14**/34
    managing risks, **14**/3
    market entry decision, **14**/14–17
    market selection, **14**/11–14
    national economies, **14**/3–4
    opportunity indicators, **14**/6
    overseas distribution, licensing and technology, **14**/29–36
    patents/trade secrets, **14**/32
    pricing, **14**/21–22
    protection of intellectual property, **14**/32–33
    role of agents/distributors/licensees, **14**/31
    software, **14**/32–33
    sources of marketing data, **14**/23–25
    trademarks/trade names/service marks, **14**/33
    ways of doing business, **14**/28–29
international compensation, key factors, **4**/68
international environment
    accounting standards, **5**/53
    translation/transaction issues, **5**/53–55
international functions, **4**/67
international joint ventures, risks, **14**/41–45
international marketing data, **14**/23–25
international markets, **14**/27–29
International Monetary Fund, **14**/24
international opportunities, small business, **13**/28–30
International Partnerships for Commercialization of Technology (INPACT), **7**/49
international relations, intracorporate, **11**/30–32
international risks, managing, **14**/3
international strategies, global insurance and risk management, **12**/52–53
international trade, conducting, **14**/26–27
interpersonal roles, skills, **1**/16
interviewing, **4**/18
intracorporate international relations, **11**/30–32
introductory paragraph, auditor's report, **5**/47
inventions, patent protection, **7**/41
inventories, **6**/28
inventory
    control, **5**/22–23, **10**/4–5
    management, **5**/19–21, **10**/9
    materials management, **8**/55–57
    methods, **5**/33–34
    physical, **5**/23
    valuation/control, **5**/16–23
    valuation method selection, **5**/18–19
inventory investment, materials management, **8**/57–58
inventory/receivable financing, **6**/28
investigational new drug (IND), **7**/23
investing, transnational, **6**/40–41
investment management, **4**/51
    pension plans, **4**/54
investment policy, pension plans, **4**/53–54
investments
    changing, **6**/41
    by owners, **5**/10
investor relations, **5**/49–52, **11**/11–13
investor relations programs, **5**/49–52
investor relations staff, **11**/13
involuntary/enforced divestitures, and taxation, **5**/35
IPO. *See* initial public offering
IRAs. *See* individual retirement accounts

IRI (research firm), **2**/49
IRS audits, **13**/33
IRS examinations, **5**/36
Irvine, V. Bruce, **6**/21–25
I/S. *See* information systems
Isaacson, Bruce, **2**/101–108
ISDN BRI, **9**/30
ISDN. *See* integrated services digital network
isoplot, **8**/48
ISP. *See* information strategy planning
issues, identifying, **2**/30
I/T. *See* information technology

Jackson, Joseph, **9**/52–55
Japan
    cultural basis of management, **14**/48
    decision making, **14**/51–53
    international business, **14**/5
    job rotation, **14**/49–50
    lessons for western manager, **14**/53–54
    lifetime employment, **14**/49
    management, **14**/48–54
    seniority system, **14**/50–51
    structural influences on management, **14**/48–51
JIC. *See* just-in-case
JIT. *See* just-in-time
Joannides, Sara, **9**/16–21
job costing system, **5**/28
job rotation, in Japan, **14**/49–50
Jobs, Steven, **8**/57, **13**/9
Job Training Partnership Act (JTPA), **16**/20
Johnsonville Foods, **1**/8
joint ventures, **6**/15
    international, **14**/41–45
    international business, **14**/16
    and mergers, **2**/99
Journal of the Academy of Management, **1**/12
Journal of Information Technology Management, **16**/34
JTPA. *See* Job Training Partnership Act
judicial review, government agencies, **16**/17
Juran, Dr. Joseph, **8**/37, 52
just-in-case (JIC), **8**/58
just-in-time (JIT), **4**/24–25, **5**/22, **8**/11, 20, 55, 59, 62, 72, **10**/5, 9

Kahn, Steven P., **12**/33–35
Kalter, Marjorie, **2**/116–121
Kaplan, Jeffrey, **1**/35
Kaplan, Robert, **8**/17
keiretsu, **14**/15–16
Keith, Robert, **2**/5
Kellerman, Mary, **1**/28
Kelly, Jean, **14**/3–6
key person discretionary benefits, **4**/44–46
Kiefer-Stewart case, **2**/97
Kirk-Duggan, Professor, **2**/97

Kissinger, Henry, **1**/7
knowledge, **1**/61–62
Knox, George L., III, **11**/17–19
Koch, Charles H., Jr., **16**/14–18
Koontz, Harold, **1**/12
Kotler, Philip, **2**/86–93
Kraus, Margery, **11**/6–7
Kubilus, Norbert J., **9**/3–4, 68–72
Kuczmarski, Thomas D., **2**/69–77
Kurek, Arthur, **9**/56–59

labor
    planning direct, **8**/23–24
    planning indirect, **8**/24–26
Labor-Management Reporting and Disclosure Act, **4**/76
LaForge, Raymond W., **3**/11–18
laggards, **2**/22
Laird, Dick, **13**/26–28
laminated object manufacturing (LOM), **8**/74
LAN. *See* local area network
land issues, environmental management, **8**/81–84
Landrum-Griffin Act, **4**/77
large-scale integration (LSI), **9**/17
l'art pour l'art, **2**/112
last in, first out (LIFO), **5**/18, 34, 44, **13**/34
late majority buyers, **2**/22
latent defect control, **8**/49
Latin America, **14**/5
Lawson, Thomas W., **7**/5
lawsuits, budgeting small business, **13**/35–36
lawyers, and small business, **13**/34–36
LBO. *See* leveraged buyout
leader, **1**/15–16
leadership
    energy, **16**/13
    personal side, **16**/13
    strategic, **1**/7
    theories, **1**/15–16
    vs. management, **16**/12–13
leadership cluster, **16**/7
leadership function, public sector management, **16**/9–13
learning, continual, **1**/9–10
learning hierarchy, **2**/111
leases, **10**/8
leasing, **6**/30, **10**/33–35
Lederer, Albert, **16**/34
legal agreements, **6**/18
Legal Aspects of Marketing Strategy, **2**/100
legal considerations, and ethics programs, **1**/35
Legal Developments in Marketing (section of *Journal of Marketing*), **2**/100
Legal and Economic Regulation in Marketing: A Practitioner's Guide, **2**/100
legal responsibility of marketers, expansion, **2**/94
legal risk, **14**/43

legal/security issues, in MIS, 9/64–67
legislative review, government agencies, 16/17
Lehmann, Donald R., 2/48–54
Leimbach, Wendell, 8/51–63
lenders, diversifying, 6/19
lending restrictions, avoiding, 6/19
LEPCs. *See* local emergency planning committees
Lerner, Herbert J., 5/31–37
LESOP. *See* leveraged ESOP
letter of credit, 10/21
letters of interest/resumes, 4/17–18
leveraged buyout (LBO), 6/15
leveraged ESOP (LESOP), 4/50
Leverett, E. J., Jr., 12/41–47
Levitt, Theodore, 14/9
Lewin, Kurt, 1/15
LEXUS/NEXUS, 14/25
liabilities, 5/10
liability, professional services, 15/42–43
liability loss exposures, 12/16–21
LIBOR. *See* London InterBank Offer Rate
licensees, international business, 14/31–32
licensing, international business, 14/15–16
Lies, Laura A., 8/18–22
life insurance
   group term, 4/43
   key employee, 4/44–45
   split dollar, 4/45
lifetime employment, in Japan, 14/49
LIFO. *See* last in, first out
light equipment, 2/101
limited partnership, 7/48–49
   small business, 13/31
line of credit, 6/28
line function, 1/52–53
linkage, 3/39
liquor liability, 12/18
listening, 4/73–77
Llana, Andres, Jr., 9/36–41
local area network (LAN), 8/65, 9/20, 32
local emergency planning committees (LEPCs),
   8/84
local presence, international business, 14/28
local taxes, managing, 5/37–40
locate leaking underground storage tanks
   (LUSTs), 8/83
lockbox account, 6/34
lockboxes, 5/15
logistics curve, 7/6
logistics management, 10/31–33
logistics network, 10/32
logistics process, 10/31–32
LOM. *See* laminated object manufacturing
Lombardi, Vince, 1/9
London InterBank Offer Rate (LIBOR), 6/29
long-run profits, maximization, 6/23
long-term disability coverage, 4/45

long-term effects, sales promotion, 3/47
loss control, 12/24–29
   asset protection, 12/27–29
   human safety, 12/26–27
   implementation, 12/25–26
   indirect costs, 12/25
   role of management, 12/26
   selecting techniques, 12/25
losses, 5/10
loss reserving, 12/30
Lovelock, Christopher H., 16/36–41
lower reference price, 3/46
LSI. *See* large-scale integration
Lunergan, Bruce, 6/36–39
LUSTs. *See* locate leaking underground storage
   tanks

McClelland, David, 1/16
McElhone, J. Mike, 10/31–33
McFadden Act, 6/37
McGregor, Douglas, 1/15, 21
Machinability Data Center, 8/53
Machlowitz, David S., 13/34–36
MACRS. *See* modified accelerated cost recovery
   system
MACT. *See* maximum achievable control
   technology
Made in America, 8/5
made to order, 2/104
Magazine Index, 10/16
Maher, William R., 4/40–46
mail float, 5/15
mainframe computers, 9/19–20
maintenance, equipment, 8/46
major account manager (MAM), 3/27
major account programs
   account planning process, 3/31–32
   "best" company practices, 3/27–28
   key account plans, 3/32–35
   steps, 3/28–31
major medical, 4/41
Malcolm Baldrige National Quality Award, 8/6,
   15/6
MAM. *See* major account manager
Management: Tasks, Responsibilities, and Practices,
   1/16
management
   capabilities, small business, 13/8–9
   cash, 6/33–36
   channel, 3/24–26
   competencies, 1/16
   defined, 1/3
   education and training, 6/5
   environmental, 8/75–86
   evolution of strategic, 6/5–6
   finance, 6/5–6
   functions, 1/6, 7/11–15

human resources, in international operations, 4/66–69
in Japan, 14/48–54
levels, 3/15–16
logistics, 10/31–33
major account, 3/26–35
materials, 8/55–63
network, 9/36–41
nonprofit, guiding principles, 16/25–26
principles, 1/6, 16
public sector competencies, 16/5–8
quality, 8/36–51
quality processes, 1/23–27
risk, 6/41
roles, 1/16
scientific, 1/12
theory and application, 1/18–23
management buyout (MBO), 6/15
management information system (MIS), 8/67, 9/5, 16/31
competence, 9/65–66
components, 16/31–33
disaster and recovery planning, 9/66–67
function, 9/5–9
managing transitions, 9/68–72
organizational state model, 9/68
piracy, 9/65
planning for transition, 9/69–70
privacy, 9/64–65
security and legal issues, 9/64–67
transitions, human factor, 9/70
transitions, implementing, 9/71–72
management letter, nonprofit organizations, 16/44–45
management process school, 1/12–13
management theories
nature and use, 1/18–19
schools, 1/12
today, 1/16–17
Management Theory Jungle, The, 1/12
manager, today's changing environment, 4/8–10
managing
accounts receivable, 5/12–16
corporate relations staff, 11/4–5
disbursements, 6/35–36
diverse work force, 4/20–24
foreign exchange, 6/42–45
international risks, 14/3
older worker, 4/23–24
pension plans, 4/51–54
R&D for strategic position, 7/29–33
risks in international joint ventures, 14/41–45
managing cash disbursements, small business, 13/24–26
managing collections, small business, 13/23–24
managing ethics, 1/32–35

Managing Information as a Corporate Resource, 16/35
manufacturing
and/or operations, 2/10
business strategy, 8/5–18
competitive challenge, 8/5–6
computing, 8/65
costs, 5/27–28
implementation issues, 8/17–18
managing technology, 8/64–75
new technologies/techniques, 8/72–75
order fulfillment, 8/7
organizational design, 8/16
process decisions, 8/12–16
process-oriented, 8/6–8
product generation, 8/7
relationship decisions, 8/16–17
strategic investment, 8/6–7
strategy, 8/8–9
manufacturing execution systems (MES), 8/62
Manufacturing Matters: The Myth of the Post-Industrial Economy, 8/5
manufacturing organizations, 8/18–22
manufacturing process(es), 8/13–15, 51–55
applications, 8/54–55
design, 8/52–55
group technology, 8/53–54
manufacturing resource planning (MRP II), 5/20, 8/60, 68
manufacturing strategy factors, 8/9–10
Marcus, Gail H., 11/25–29
marine coverages, 12/38
marked differences, new product development, 2/7–8
market attractiveness, 2/39
assessment, international business, 14/12–13
market coverage decision, 3/22
market entry decision, international business, 14/14–17
market growth, 2/44
marketing
areas, 2/91
auditing function, 2/86–93
business-to-business, 2/121
concept, 2/5–7
decisions, 2/7–9
environment, 2/91
expenditures, 2/8
future, 2/11
globalizing, 14/17–23
legal imperatives, 2/94–101
management tasks, 2/12–18
mix, 2/91
objectives, 2/47
offer, 2/15–16
organization, 2/91
orientation, 2/62–63

marketing (*continued*)
  plan, **2**/42–48
  productivity, **2**/91
  programs, **2**/47
  public and nonprofit, **16**/36–41
  quality, **2**/65–68
  regulatory environment, **2**/100–101
  relationship, **2**/121
  research, **2**/48–54, 107–108
  researcher, **2**/49–50
  small business, **13**/8, 19–22
  staffing, **2**/63–64
  strategies, **2**/47, 91, 105–108, **15**/19–20
  systems, **2**/91
Marketing in Europe, **14**/25
marketing regulation
  emerging areas, **2**/100
  framework for analysis, **2**/94–95
  guidelines, **2**/97–100
  sources, **2**/95–97
market segmentation process, **2**/13–14, 105–106
market selection
  and development, **2**/105
  international business, **14**/11–14
market size, **2**/44
market testing, new service, **15**/31
Markle, E. Nancy, **9**/10–16
Marsh, Don E., **1**/3–4, **1**/11–17
Martin, John F., **3**/26–35
Maslow, Abraham, **1**/14, 21
mass communications, and advertising, **2**/ 108–115
master production schedule (MPS), **5**/21
material requirement planning (MRP), **5**/20–22, **8**/59, 68
materials management, **8**/55–63
  inventory investment, **8**/57–58
  reductions in cycle time, **8**/59–63
  time-based strategy, **8**/57
matrix
  directional policy, **2**/38–40
  four-cell, **2**/37–38
  growth-share, **2**/36–38
  incentive, **3**/40
  product-process, **8**/13
  structure, **1**/50
Matsushita, Konusuke, **8**/47
maximum achievable control technology (MACT), **8**/78
maximum forseeable loss (MFL), **12**/16
maximum possible loss (MPL), **12**/16
Mayo, Elton, **1**/14
MBO. *See* management buyout
MDS. *See* multidimensional scaling
MDTs. *See* mobile data terminals
mean time to diagnose (MTTD), **8**/49
mean time to repair (MTTR), **8**/49

measure development, **3**/35
measurement precision and cost, **11**/35
mechanisms, information strategy planning, **9**/16
media
  classes, **2**/113
  options, **2**/113
  planning, **2**/113–114
  relations, **11**/8–11
  selection, direct marketing programs, **2**/119
  vehicles, **2**/113
medical, major, **4**/43
medical reimbursement, **4**/45
Mehrens, Vance A., **13**/39–40
MEOST. *See* multiple environment over stress tests
Merbaum, Michael, **4**/16–20
mergers
  and joint ventures, **2**/99
  and taxation, **5**/35
Merrifield, D. Bruce, **7**/47–50
MES. *See* manufacturing execution systems
MESBICs. *See* minority small business investment companies
metaphysical approach, **2**/65
me-too, **2**/79
me-too companies, **2**/24
metrology, **8**/48–49
Metz, David, **11**/30–32
MFL. *See* maximum forseeable loss
microcomputers, **9**/20
Middle East, **14**/5
middle management, decline, **1**/59
milestone schedules, **7**/23
Miller, W. Sanford, Jr., **2**/61–64
millions of instructions per second (MIPS), **8**/65
Miniard, Paul W., **2**/55–60
minicomputers, **9**/20
Minnesota Multiphasic Personality Inventory (MMPI), **4**/95
minority programs, purchasing department, **10**/ 10
minority small business investment companies (MESBICs), **13**/15
Mintzberg, Henry, **1**/16
MIPS. *See* millions of instructions per second
MIS. *See* management information system
mission statement, **3**/32
  at work, **1**/28
  and policies, **1**/27–30
Mitchell, Graham R., **7**/29–33
Mittelstand, **14**/15
MMPI. *See* Minnesota Multiphasic Personality Inventory
mobile data terminals (MDTs), **9**/31
model, **2**/18
  hierarchy-of-effects, **2**/111
model change, effecting, **1**/51

models, organizational, 1/47–49
MODEM, 9/29
modified accelerated cost recovery system
    (MACRS), 5/34
modus operandi, 8/48
Moments of Truth, 15/6
Monetary Control and Deregulation Act, 13/24
monetary value, direct marketing, 2/120
money purchase (MP) pension plans, 4/49
monitoring, execution and performance, 2/17–18
monitors, plan, 2/48
Monroe, Kent B., 15/33–37
Monsanto v. Spray-Rite Service Corporation case, 2/
    98
Moore, Jeffrey A., 1/36–43
Morikawa, Dennis J., 4/92–96
mortgage bonds, 6/29
motivation and rewards, 2/71
MP. *See* money purchase pension plans
MPL. *See* maximum possible loss
MPS. *See* master production schedule
MRP. *See* material requirement planning
MRP II. *See* manufacturing resource planning
MSDS. *See* hazardous substance material safety
    data sheets
MTTD. *See* mean time to diagnose
MTTR. *See* mean time to repair
multicorporate entities, and consolidated returns,
    5/32
multidimensional scaling (MDS), 2/53
multiple environment over stress tests (MEOST),
    8/46, 49
Multistate Tax Commission, 5/39
multivari, 8/48
Murtuza, Athar, 5/3–4, 16–23, 27–31

NAFTA. *See* North American Free Trade
    Agreement
Nagle, Thomas T., 2/80–85
Nakamoto, Kent, 2/77–80
NAPM. *See* National Association of Purchasing
    Managers
National Association of Purchasing Managers
    (NAPM), 10/6
national economies, 14/3–4
National Laboratory Consortium, 7/46
National Labor Relations Act, 4/58, 76–79
    restrictions on management's activities, 4/
    78–79
National Labor Relations Board (NLRB), 4/58, 77
National Pollutant Discharge Elimination System
    (NPDES), 8/80
National Underwriter, 12/5
natural perils, 12/12
Nature of Managerial Work, The, 1/16
NDA. *See* new drug application
nebula model, 1/49

need recognition, 2/56
negative option, 2/120
negotiation
    process, 2/32–33
    proposal, analysis of, 10/17
    purchasing, 10/15–17
nemawashi, 14/52
nepotism, small business, 13/37
Neslin, Scott A., 3/41–47
net realizable value, 5/11
network databases, 9/45
network management, 9/36–41
    alternatives, 9/37–38
    common carrier, 9/39
    concerns, 9/36–37
    customized management services, 9/39–41
network planning, 9/39
networks, 9/5
    impartial audit, 9/38
    local-area, 9/32
    and nonprofit manager, 16/33
    packet, 9/31
    wide-area, 9/32
network structure, 1/50–51
network termination 1 (NT1), 9/30
new drug application (NDA), 7/23
new employee orientation, 4/14–16
new product blueprint, 2/71
new product development, 2/69–77
    culture for innovation, 7/37
    marked differences, 2/7–8
    process, 2/74–76
    stages of development, 7/37–38
    strategic focus, 7/36–37
    successful, 2/71, 72, 76–77
new product strategy, 2/71
    competitive, 2/77–80
    options, 2/78–79
Newspaper Abstracts, The, 10/16
New York Stock Exchange (NYSE), 11/9
Nielsen, A. C., 2/49
NIH. *See* not-invented-here
Niland, Tom, 13/28–30
NLE. *See* normal loss expectancy
NLRB. *See* National Labor Relations Board
NOI. *See* notice of interest
Nolan, Jim, 1/18
nonemployees, solicitation/distribution by, 4/79
nonfinancial performance measures, 5/25
noninsurance risk transfer, 12/33–35
nonprofit management
    applications of marginal analysis, 16/27–28
    economic incentives, 16/30
    opportunity cost, 16/28–29
    principles, 16/25–26
    resource constraints, 16/29
    thinking at margin, 16/27
    time value of money, 16/29

nonprofit manager
  decision support system, **16**/32
  electronic mail, **16**/33
  executive information system, **16**/32
  expert system, **16**/32
  information technology, **16**/31–35
  networks, **16**/33
  planning for information systems, **16**/33–35
nonprofit organizations (NPs), **16**/37
  auditing, **16**/42–46
  establishing audit committee, **16**/45
  getting best audit results, **16**/46
  negotiating audit fees, **16**/43–44
  obtaining other benefits from auditing firm,
    16/45–46
  planning audit, **16**/43
  selecting independent auditor, **16**/42–43
  undergoing audit, **16**/44–45
nontraditional work patterns, **1**/17
normal loss expectancy (NLE), **12**/16
Norquist, Warren E., **10**/11–18
North American Free Trade Agreement
  (NAFTA), **14**/10
note issuances, **6**/6
notice of interest (NOI), **8**/80
not-invented-here (NIH), **2**/22
NPDES. *See* National Pollutant Discharge
  Elimination System
NPs. *See* nonprofit organizations
·NT1. *See* network termination 1
nursing care, long-term, **4**/44
NYSE. *See* New York Stock Exchange

OA. *See* integrated office automation
objectives
  sales promotion, **3**/43–44
  strategic, **2**/23
obstacles, to change, **1**/8–9
Occupational Safety and Health Act (OSHA), **4**/
  58–59, 94, **8**/82, **10**/4, **12**/24
Occupational Safety and Health Administration,
  4/4
OCR. *See* optical character readers
OECD. *See* Organization for Economic
  Cooperation and Development
OEM. *See* original equipment manufacturers
Office of Labor Management, **4**/77
Office of Technology Evaluation and Assessment,
  7/46
office and time realities, **1**/17
offset, **14**/46
Older Worker Benefit Protection Act, **4**/57
older workers
  managing, **4**/23–24
  retaining, **4**/14
ombudsman, **1**/34

Omnibus Crime Control and Safe Streets Act, **4**/
  96
OMR. *See* optical mark readers
open-to-buy method, **5**/21
operating results
  analyzing, **5**/23–26
  presentation methods, **5**/24–25
operating risk, **14**/42
operations, **2**/10
opinion paragraph, auditor's report, **5**/47
opportunities, **2**/13, 28
OPT. *See* optimized production technology
optical character readers (OCR), **9**/18
optical mark readers (OMR), **9**/18
optimal retention, **12**/32–33
optimized production technology (OPT), **8**/72
order fulfillment, **8**/7
ordering costs, **5**/16
organic model, **1**/48–49
organization of future, **1**/58–62
organizational goals, **1**/13
organizational manufacturing design, **8**/16
organizational models, **1**/47–49
organizational needs, defining, **4**/64–65
organizational resources, **1**/58–59
organizational roles, **2**/15
organizational structures, **1**/49–51
Organization for Economic Cooperation and
  Development (OECD), **14**/5, 25
organized labor relations, **4**/76–86
original equipment manufacturers (OEM), **8**/11
O'Rourke, Tracey, **8**/16
Osborne, Gerard A., **2**/86–93
OSHA. *See* Occupational Safety and Health Act
Ostaszewski, Stanley J., **9**/48–52
Ouchi, William, **1**/15
outbound telemarketing, **2**/119
outfalls, **8**/80
output devices, computer, **9**/18–19
outsourcing, **9**/37–38, 52–55
  defined, **9**/52
  planning for, **9**/54–55
  preparation vs. damage control, **9**/53–54
overseas distribution sources, **14**/34
overseas distribution/licensing
  factors affecting licensing, **14**/30–32
  how not to do it, **14**/29–30
  researching U.S. laws, **14**/31
Overseas Business Reports, **14**/24

PA. *See* purchasing agent
packet networks, **9**/31
Pareto charts, **8**/45
Paris Act, **14**/32
participants, services industry, **15**/9
partnerships
  and purchasing, **10**/10–11
  small business, **13**/31

parts, availability of spare, **8**/49
part-time employees, **4**/14
Passante, John A., **4**/12–16
patents
    foreign protection, **7**/42
    infringement, **7**/40, **10**/21
    international business, **14**/32
    literature, monitoring, **7**/40–41
    portfolio building, **7**/39
    rights, avoiding forfeiture, **7**/40
Patent and Trademark Office, **7**/41
Paul, Tom, **16**/35
pay
    communicating about, **4**/39
    performance, **4**/38–39
    philosophy, **4**/37
    system design principles, **4**/36–40
payback period calculation, **6**/24
payroll tax planning, small business, **13**/33
PCs. *See* personal computers
PCBs. *See* polychlorinated biphenyls
PCM. *See* pulse code modulation
PDCA. *See* plan-do-check-act cycle
Pedigo, Susan L., **4**/20–24
penetration pricing, **15**/36–37
pension plans
    goals, **4**/52
    managing, **4**/51–54
    selecting, **4**/52
perceived quality, **2**/66
    approach, **2**/66–67
perceptual distinctiveness, **2**/78
performance, nonfinancial, **5**/25
performance appraisal, **12**/22
    periodic review/feedback/coaching, **4**/61–62
    process, **4**/60–63
    system objectives, **4**/60–61
    written documentation, **4**/62–63
performance evaluation, review, **4**/62
performance expectations, **4**/61
performance goals, **2**/17
performance management, **9**/39
performance measures, **3**/38–39
performance specifications, purchasing, **10**/14
Perot, H. Ross, **13**/5
Perril, Michael, **8**/51–63
personal computers (PCs), **9**/20
personal property, **12**/13
personnel
    psychological assessment, **4**/16–20
    security issues, **4**/92–96
    selection, **4**/16–20
PERT. *See* program evaluation and review
    technique
PEST. *See* political, economic, social, and
    technological

Peters, Tom, **1**/9
physical evidence, services industry, **15**/9
physical inventory, **5**/23
physical relocation, **6**/18
physicals, preemployment, **4**/94–95
piecework, **8**/29
PIMS. *See* profit impact of market strategy
pioneers, **2**/23–24
P&L. *See* profit and loss statements
plan-do-check-act cycle (PDCA), **8**/45
planning
    assumptions, **2**/46–47
    department, **1**/38–40
    financial, **6**/9–14
    human resources, **8**/22–26
    manufacturing organizations, **8**/18–22
    media, **2**/113–114
    process, completing, **2**/34
    project, **1**/40–42
    sales, **1**/42–43
    strategic, **1**/36–38
    systems, **2**/8
planning cycles vs. budget cycles, **2**/30
plastic card readers, **9**/18
Plaut, Robert, **9**/33–35
PNPs. *See* public and nonprofit organizations
policies, **1**/29
political, economic, social, and technological
    (PEST), **2**/26
political analysis, **6**/41
political factors, **2**/44
Pollution Prevention Act, **8**/85
polychlorinated biphenyls (PCBs), **8**/81
Ponkratz, Charmaine, **15**/16–22
PO. *See* purchase order
POPs. *See* premium-only plans
postlaunch checkup, new service, **15**/31
postpurchase evaluation, **2**/59
power shift, **1**/60–61
PPOs. *See* preferred provider organizations
Predicasts Overview of Markets & Technologies
    (PTS PROMT), **14**/25
preemployment physicals, **4**/94–95
preferred provider organizations (PPOs), **4**/41
preferred stock, **6**/30
premium credits, **12**/33
premium/deduction, **6**/27
premium-only plans (POPs), **4**/44
premiums, **3**/42
prepurchase evaluation, **2**/58
present value, future cash flows, **5**/11
price, **2**/15
    discount, **3**/42
    discrimination, **2**/98
    elasticity, **15**/34
    fixing, **2**/97
    insensitivity, **2**/78
    maintenance, **2**/98

price/cost analysis, purchasing, **10**/13–14
pricing, **2**/7, 106
  competition-driven, **2**/82
  cost-driven, **2**/80–81
  customer-driven, **2**/81
  guidelines for strategic, **2**/82–84
  international business, **14**/21–22
  penetration, **15**/36–37
  predatory, **2**/97–98
  procedure pitfalls, **2**/80–82
  services, **15**/13
  service industries, **15**/33–37
  skimming, **15**/36
  strategy, **15**/21
primacy of organization, **1**/13
Principles of Administration, **1**/5
principles of management, **1**/13
printers, computer, **9**/18
privacy
  employee, **4**/92–96
  telecommunications, **15**/40
Privacy Act of 1974, **4**/92, **16**/18
private/privileged/confidential information, **16**/18
proactive globalization drivers, **14**/9–10
proactivity, **16**/7
problem child, **2**/38
problem solving, in bureaucracies, **1**/61
process
  characterization, **8**/48
  costing, **5**/28
  manufacturing decisions, **8**/12–16
  optimization, **8**/48
  services industry, **15**/9
processed materials, **2**/101
procurement, in-bound, **10**/28
Procurement Integrity Act, **10**/24
Prodigy, **10**/16
product
  buyers, **2**/21–23
  class, **2**/18
  form, **2**/18
  generation, **8**/7
  liability, **2**/8
  life cycle, **2**/18–25, 44
  policy, **2**/106
  promotion regulation, **2**/100
  quality, **2**/67–68
  quality and liability, **2**/8
  regulation, **2**/100
  safety, **12**/28
  service appraisal, **3**/33
production management approach, **2**/65–66
productivity
  appraising, incentive plans, **8**/34–35
  and total quality management, **1**/24–27
product-process flow, **8**/13

product-process matrix, **8**/13
professional advice, seeking, **6**/20
Professional Internal Auditing Standards Volume, **5**/40
Professional Selling: A Relationship Management Approach, **15**/23
professional services
  changing nature, **15**/41–43
  client relationships, **15**/42
  liability, **15**/42–43
  management implications, **15**/42
  meaning of service, **15**/41–42
profitable pricing, **2**/80–85
profit impact of market strategy (PIMS), **8**/38
profit and loss statements (P&L), **11**/13
profit oriented, **2**/17
profit planning, finance, **6**/3
profits, **2**/44
profit-sharing plans (PS), **4**/49–50
program evaluation and review technique (PERT), **7**/23–24, **9**/15
progress reporting, **1**/56
project management, techniques, **1**/54–57
project planning, **1**/40–42
  and estimating, **1**/55–57
project proposal standard, **1**/55
project scoping, **10**/35
promotions, **3**/42
property insurance, **12**/37–39
proposed strategic actions, **2**/13
proprietary information, hiring/terminating employees, **12**/23–24
protection of intellectual property, **14**/32–33
PS. *See* profit-sharing plans
psychological assessment, personnel, **4**/16–20
psychological testing, **4**/18–20
PTS PROMT. *See* Predicasts Overview of Markets & Technologies
publications, **2**/8
public and nonprofit marketing, **16**/36–41
  competitive posture and positioning strategy, **16**/39–41
  distinctive characteristics, **16**/37–38
  marketing mix considerations, **16**/38–39
  orienting organization to marketplace, **16**/36–37
public and nonprofit organizations (PNPs), **16**/36
public programs
  evaluating, **16**/18–21
  TQM, **16**/19
public sector decision making, **16**/22–25
  activation and diagnosis, **16**/22–23
  alternatives, **16**/23
  evaluation and information, **16**/24–25
  implementation, **16**/23–24
  timing and communication, **16**/25

public sector management
  competencies, **16**/5–8
  goal and action, **16**/7
  human resource management, **16**/7–8
  leadership cluster, **16**/7
  leadership function, **16**/9–13
published statement, necessity, **1**/27–28
pulling and distributing, **10**/28
pull systems, **8**/62–63
pulse code modulation (PCM), **9**/29
punishment, **1**/60–61
purchase acceleration, **3**/46
purchase costs, **5**/16
purchase order (PO), **10**/9, 20
purchasing
  contracts, **10**/8
  legal aspects, **10**/18–21
  physical distribution and warehousing, **10**/27–30
  techniques and procedures, **10**/11–18
purchasing agent (PA), **10**/5
purchasing department
  authority, **10**/5–6
  functions, **10**/4–11
  purchase of goods/services, **10**/8
  responsibilities, **10**/4–5
purchasing process
  blanket releases, **10**/25–26
  budget/variance benchmarks, **10**/23–24
  controls, **10**/22–26
  controls related to organizational structure, **10**/23
  delegation of authority, **10**/25
  external audits, **10**/23
  internal audits, **10**/22–23
  legal controls, **10**/24–25
  performance review/goal setting, **10**/23
  policy/procedure/practices, **10**/22
  procurement plans, **10**/24
  purifying purchasing function, **10**/26
  requisition control authorization, **10**/25
  rotation of personnel, **10**/26
  supplier evaluation, **10**/26
  system control and security reports, **10**/24
purchasing programs, **10**/10–11
purchasing services, buyer's role, **10**/17–18
pure captive insurance company, **12**/31
push systems, **8**/60–62
push vs. pull systems, **8**/63

QFD. *See* quality function deployment; quality function development
QJSA. *See* qualified joint survivor spousal annuity
QPSA. *See* qualified preretirement survivor annuity
qualified joint survivor spousal annuity (QJSA), **4**/48

qualified opinion, **5**/48
qualified plans, **4**/50
qualified preretirement survivor annuity (QPSA), **4**/48
qualified retirement plans, **4**/47–51
qualitative evaluation, public programs, **16**/20
quality
  attributes, **2**/66
  audits, **8**/39
  characteristics, **8**/49
  consumer perceptions, **2**/66–67
  customers, **8**/46–47
  defect levels, **8**/44
  design stage, **8**/47
  dimensions, **1**/24
  economic approach, **2**/66
  as features, **1**/24
  field stage, **8**/49
  as freedom from deficiencies, **1**/24
  history and quality gurus, **8**/37–38
  improvement, **1**/25–27
  latent defect control, **8**/49
  management, **8**/36–51
  management approach, **2**/65–66
  measurement, **8**/44–45
  metaphysical approach, **2**/65
  metrics, **8**/44
  organization, **8**/38–39
  people, **8**/50–51
  perceived quality approach, **2**/66–67
  perceived risk, **2**/67
  planning, **1**/24–25
  process/manufacturing, **8**/48–49
  professional role, **8**/39
  ques, **2**/66
  services, **8**/49
  stages, **8**/38–51
  as strategy, **1**/23–24
  suppliers, **8**/47–48
  support services, **8**/49–50
  systems, **8**/39–44
  tools, **8**/45–46
  workmanship, **8**/46
quality control, **1**/25–26
Quality Control Handbook, **8**/37
quality function deployment (QFD), **8**/45, 47
quality function development (QFD), **2**/10
Quittner, George R., **10**/4–11
quotas, **3**/40–41

Rader, Jack, **13**/22–26
RAM. *See* random access memory
Rand, Clifford A., **4**/51–54
random access memory (RAM), **9**/17
Rangan, V. Kasturi, **2**/101–108
raw materials, **2**/101
RCPC. *See* regional check processing center

RCRA. *See* Groundwater Protection Act and Resource Conservation and Recovery Act; Resource Conservation and Recovery Act

R&D. *See* research and development

readers, computer input device, 9/18

realization phase, capital expenditure, 6/21, 25

real property, 12/13

rebates, 3/42

recall, 2/110

receivables balance, forecasting, 5/14

receiving and storing, 10/28

recency, direct marketing, 2/120

reciprocity, 10/20

recruiting, 1/60, 12/21–22

recruitment efforts, expanding, 4/21

redundant assets, 6/19

reference checking, 4/18

refinancing, 6/15

refunds, 3/42

regional check processing center (RCPC), clearing, 6/35

regular tax, 5/33

regulation, product promotion/characteristics, 2/100

regulatory factors, 2/44

regulatory requirements, employment practices, 12/22–23

rehabilitation, employee substance abuse, 4/91

Rehabilitation Act of 1973, 4/57

Reichman, Fred M., 4/76–86

Reiner, S. Theodore, 5/31–37

relating/reacting to people, 4/6–8

relational database systems, 9/45–46

relationships
  counselor, 15/24
  marketing, 2/121
  selling, 15/22–26
  supplier, 15/24
  systems designer, 15/24–25

relevance, 5/28

remote disbursing, 6/36

rent abatement clauses, 12/34

repatriation of employees, 4/69

repayment terms, structuring, 6/20

repeat-purchase effect, 3/46

repetitive motion injury (RMI), 12/24

replacement cost, 12/14

reported income, and capital expenditures, 6/24

reports
  control, 5/24
  special-purpose, 5/24–25
  summary, 5/24

representation cases, 4/58

representation election, 4/81

request for proposal (RFP), 4/65

requirements contracts, 2/100

research and development (R&D), 2/10, 23
  federal government resources, 7/45–46
  global economy, 7/47–50
  innovation, 7/33–36
  laboratory to market, 7/36–38
  maintaining climate for creativity/innovation, 7/20–21
  management functions, 7/11–15
  management strategies, 7/30, 32–33
  matrix organizational structure, 7/21–23
  performance, 7/14–15
  portfolio balance, 7/19
  programs, 7/12–14
  project assessment, 7/16–21
  project management methods, 7/21–24
  project robustness, 7/19
  project selection, 7/16–19
  project strength, 7/17–18
  project timing, 7/18
  risk evaluation/balance, 7/19–20
  scheduling project activities, 7/23–24
  strategic option, 7/29–33
  strengthening management, 7/11–12
  U.S. funding, 7/45–46

research and development (R&D) team, 7/25–29

research project
  analysis, 2/52–53
  communication, 2/54
  interpretation, 2/53–54
  problem definition, 2/50–51
  sampling, 2/52
  selection of approach/design, 2/51–52
  stages, 2/50–54

residual income, 5/26

resource attraction products, 16/39

Resource Conservation and Recovery Act (RCRA), 8/81

Restoring Our Competitive Edge: Competing Through Manufacturing, 8/14

resumés, 4/17–18

Retail Business, 14/25

retailer promotions, 3/42

retaining high-quality workers, 1/60

retention levels
  earnings per share method, 12/32
  earnings/surplus method, 12/31
  percentages of revenues method, 12/32
  total assets method, 12/31
  working capital method, 12/31

retirement and pension planning, 4/46–51

return on investment (ROI), 5/26, 8/45, 66

return of premises clauses, 12/34

revenues, 5/10

reverse marketing, service industry, 15/14

RFP. *See* request for proposal

Rich, Stanley, 13/9

Richardson, David N., 11/32–36

RIMS. *See* Risk and Insurance Management
    Society
ringi process, **14**/52
ringisei, **14**/52
ringisho, **14**/52
risk(s)
    currency position, **6**/41
    exchange-of-profits, **14**/44
    factors, capital expenditure, **6**/23
    financial, **14**/42
    infrastructure, **14**/42
    insurable, **14**/44
    legal, **14**/43
    management communications, **11**/25–29
    operating, **14**/42
risk-class approach, **5**/13
risk-free yield, **6**/26
Risk and Insurance Management Society (RIMS),
    12/7, 43
risk management, **6**/41
    applications and costs, **12**/7
    changing role, **12**/5–6
    corporate connections, **12**/6–7
    function, **12**/5–7
    and global insurance, **12**/50–53
    international, **14**/3, 41–45
    process, **12**/8–10
risk management communications
    considerations, **11**/25–26
    crisis communication, **11**/28–29
    development of materials, **11**/28
    guiding principles, **11**/26–27
    the need, **11**/25
    objectives, **11**/26
    routine risk communication, **11**/27–28
risk management department
    organizational features, **12**/42–43
    organization chart, **12**/43
    organization and policy, **12**/41–47
    policy statements, **12**/43–47
risk retention, **12**/29–33
    funding retained losses, **12**/30–31
    optimal retention, **12**/32
    retention levels, **12**/31–33
RMI. *See* repetitive motion injury
Robinson, Gary, **12**/11
Robinson-Patman Act, **2**/98, **10**/19, 25
Rodgers, William H., **2**/86–93
Rogers, Carl, **4**/3
Rohrs, Alvin, **13**/5–6
ROI. *See* return on investment
role modeling, **4**/11
roles, **1**/16
Rosenheim, Robert L., **4**/40–46
Rourke, Michael, **11**/23–25
Rousseau, Michael T., **12**/21–24
Rowan plan, **8**/29

Royal Dutch Shell, **1**/9
Rudolph, Evan E., **4**/72–76

salary continuation, **4**/47
salary levels, **6**/17
sale and leaseback, **6**/19
sales
    analysis, **2**/43
    approaches, developing, **3**/8–9
    channel strategy, **3**/13–14
    compensation plan, **3**/35–41
    cyclicity, **2**/44
    forecasting, **5**/13
    function, **2**/9–10
    management, tasks, **3**/5–10
    objectives, **2**/110, **3**/5–6
    organization design, **3**/7–8, 11–18
    organization structure, **3**/14–16
    people, **3**/9–10
    planning, **1**/42–43
    promotion, **3**/41–47
    taxes, **5**/39
    trajectories, factors affecting, **2**/19
sales force
    allocate, **3**/6–7
    compensation, **3**/35–41
    deployment, **3**/16–18
    size, **3**/17
salesperson incentives, **3**/42
sale of stock, **6**/30
Salinger, Tony W., **9**/60–63
Salzman, Jeff, **9**/63
sampling, **3**/42
SARA. *See* Superfund Amendments and
    Reauthorization Act
satellite services, **9**/31
satisfaction feedback, **8**/46
Saunders, Charles S., **7**/45–46
SBA. *See* Small Business Administration
SBDCs. *See* small business development centers
SBIR. *See* Small Business Innovative Research
SBUs. *See* strategic business units
scanners, **9**/18
Schachter, Victor, **4**/89–92
Schilit, W. Keith, **13**/6–11
Schmitt, Bernd H., **2**/108–115
Schneider, Benjamin, **1**/30–32
Schwab, John L., Jr., **8**/22–36
Scientific Management, **1**/12
scope paragraph, **5**/47
scoping, project, **10**/35
SCORE. *See* Service Corps of Retired Executives
S corporation, **5**/32, **13**/32
S-curve, **7**/6
searches, employee, **4**/95–96
Sears, **6**/37
seasonality, **2**/44

SEC. *See* Securities and Exchange Commission
Securities and Exchange Commission (SEC), 4/
    46, 5/35, 43, 6/6
securities transactions, 6/42–43
security
    for employees, 12/24
    legal issues, in MIS, 9/64–67
    personnel issues, 4/92–96
segmenters, 2/24
selective laser sintering (SLS), 8/73
self-awareness, feedback, 4/11–12
self-financing, small business, 13/12
Sellers, Herschel V., 4/35–40
selling field, 3/13
selling team, 3/13
selling obsolete items, 10/10
seniority system, in Japan, 14/50–51
SEPs. *See* simplified employee pensions
SEPCs. *See* State Emergency Planning
    Commissions
server, 9/20
Service America, 15/6
Service Corps of Retired Executives (SCORE), 13/
    15
service guarantee, 15/11
service industries
    business imperative, 15/6
    commercialization, 15/22
    developing new services, 15/20–22
    establishing objectives/goals, 15/18–19
    establishing prices, 15/33–37
    evaluating present service mix, 15/18
    franchising, 15/14
    impact of telecommunications, 15/38–40
    importance of services, 15/5–6
    internal marketing, 15/13–14
    marketing strategies, 15/19–20
    as necessity of life, 15/6
    new service introduction, 15/27–32
    organizing for delivering service, 15/21–22
    organizing for efficient service, 15/16–22
    pricing strategy, 15/21
    relationship selling, 15/22–26
    service as competitive advantage, 15/6
    success, 15/5–15
    telecommunications, 15/39–40
    test marketing, 15/22
    TQM, 15/14
service life cycle, 15/16–18
services
    culture, 15/13–14
    design, 15/11
    employees, 15/12–13
    future, 15/14–15
    goods-services continuum, 15/8–9
    guarantees, 15/11–12
    heterogeneity, 15/7–8

intangibility, 15/7
marketing issues, 15/9–12
marketing mix, 15/9
perishability, 15/7
pricing, 15/13
professional, 15/41–43
reverse marketing, 15/14
service encounter evaluation, 15/10–11
service quality, 15/10
simultaneous production and consumption,
    15/8
vs. goods, 15/7–9
setup costs, 5/17
Sexton, Donald E., 14/7–26
SFAS #5. *See* Statement of Financial Accounting
    Standards
SGIA. *See* small group improvement activities
Shainin, Dorian, 8/48
Shamlin, Scott, 8/16
shared flexible computer integrated
    manufacturing (FCIM), 7/50
shareholder/investor relations, 11/11–13
Sharing Ideas, 9/60
sharp practices, 10/6
Sherman Antitrust Act, 2/97, 10/19, 24
Shewhart, Dr. Walter, 8/37
Shoaf, Steve, 9/42–47
Sibley, Kenneth D., 7/39–42
sibling rivalry, small business, 13/37–38
SIC. *See* Standard Industrial Classification codes
Simon, Francoise L., 14/7–26
Simonetti, Jack L., 4/6–12
simplified employee pensions (SEPs), 4/50
Sims, Ronald R., 4/28–34
Sinclair, Ashley James, 6/14–20
Sincoff, Kathleen D., 4/60–63
Sincoff, Michael Z., 4/3–5, 60–63
Singapore, international business, 14/5
Singer, Andrew W., 1/32–35
single-voice (DSO) channel, 9/29
SIP. *See* State Implementation Plan
SITC. *See* Standard International Trade
    Classification
situation analysis, 2/43–44, 3/43
situation assessment, 2/26–29
situation structure, 1/19
sizing, 3/33
skimming pricing, 15/36
Skinner, B. F., 1/15
Skooglund, Carl, 1/34
SKU. *See* stock keeping unit
SLS. *See* selective laser sintering
small business
    accounting records, 13/32–34
    budgeting lawsuits, 13/35–36
    cash flow matching, 13/25
    cash management, 13/22–26

corporations, **13**/31–32
credit decisions, **13**/25–26
customer service, **13**/26–28
debt financing, **13**/12–15
entrepreneur, **13**/5–6
equity financing, **13**/15
family-owned businesses, **13**/37–38
financing sources, **13**/12–15
franchising, **13**/39–40
hiring/firing/avoiding lawyers, **13**/34–36
human resources management, **13**/16–19
income tax planning, **13**/33–34
international opportunities, **13**/28–30
management capabilities, **13**/8
managing cash disbursement, **13**/24–26
managing collections, **13**/23–24
marketing, **13**/19–22
marketing capabilities, **13**/8
nepotism, **13**/37
payroll tax planning, **13**/33
preparing business plan, **13**/6–11
self-financing, **13**/12
sibling rivalry, **13**/37–38
taxation/accounting considerations, **13**/30–34
turning off investors, **13**/11
turning on investors, **13**/7–11
Small Business Administration (SBA), **13**/14
small business development centers (SBDCs), **13**/15
Small Business Innovative Research (SBIR), **7**/45
small group improvement activities (SGIA), **8**/50
small quantity generator (SQG), **8**/81
Smilor, Raymond W., **7**/42–44
Smith, Robert A., Jr., **15**/41–43
social factors, **2**/44
socialist states, emerging former, and international business, **14**/5
social security and medicare (FICA) taxes, **13**/31
software, **9**/5
  application development environment, **9**/27
  application development process, **9**/25–26
  application management and maintenance, **9**/28
  business application environment, **9**/23–25
  data communications, **9**/22
  data management, **9**/22
  international business, **14**/32–33
  selection process, **4**/65
  system, **9**/22
sole proprietorship, **13**/30–31
sourcing, **10**/4
sourcing, global, **14**/39–40
South Korea, international business, **14**/5
spans of control, **3**/15–16
SPC. *See* statistical process control

SPCC. *See* spill prevention, control, and countermeasures
specialization, **3**/14–15
special populations, **11**/35
special-purpose reports, **5**/24–25
Spilker, Bert, **7**/21–24
spill prevention, control, and countermeasures (SPCC), **8**/81
split-cable testing, **2**/114
split-dollar life insurance, **4**/46
split runs, **2**/114
spot markets, **6**/43
SQG. *See* small-quantity generator
staff function, **1**/52–53
staffing/cutbacks, **6**/17
stakeholders, **1**/17
standard costing, **5**/30–31
standard costs, **5**/17, 29
standard hour system, **8**/29
Standard Industrial Classification (SIC) codes, **2**/46, **8**/80, 84
Standard International Trade Classification (SITC), **14**/24
Standards for the Professional Practice of Internal Auditing, **5**/41
Standard Stations case, **2**/100
standard time performance-plus plan, **8**/30
Staples, William A., **15**/22–26
star, **2**/38
State Emergency Planning Commissions (SEPCs), **8**/84
State Implementation Plan (SIP), **8**/78
state and local taxes, managing, **5**/37–40
Statement of Financial Accounting Concepts (FASB), **5**/6, 10
Statement of Financial Accounting Standards #5 (SFAS #5), **12**/30
statements
  cash flow, **5**/9
  income, **5**/8–9
state secrets, government agencies, **16**/17
state taxation, administration, **5**/39–40
statistical process control (SPC), **8**/45
Statistical Yearbook for Asia and the Pacific, **14**/24
Statistical Yearbook for Latin America, **14**/24
Statute of Limitations, exposures, **12**/19
statutes
  and government agencies, **16**/15–16
  statute law, **10**/19
Stayer, Ralph E., **1**/5–10
Stearns, Elizabeth, **2**/116–121
Steenkamp, Jan-Benedict E. M., **2**/65–68
steering committee, nonprofit manager, **16**/34–35
stereolithography, **8**/73
Stern, Professor, **2**/98
Stevenson Wilder Act, **7**/45
Stitzel, Paul J., **1**/27–30

stock, **6**/30
  out costs, **5**/17
stock keeping unit (SKU), **2**/43, **10**/28
stockpiling, **3**/47
Stohr, Dr. Edward, **9**/61
Stork, Diana, **7**/25–29
stormwater, **8**/80
straight-line recovery system, **5**/34
Straits, Donald, **13**/3–4
strategic activities, focus, **1**/7–8
strategic alliances
  entering, **14**/38
  evaluating, **14**/37–38
  operating, **14**/38–39
  structure, **7**/47–48
  technology management, **7**/42–44
strategic business units (SBUs), **2**/36, **2**/62
strategic climate, **1**/31–32
strategic decision-making categories, **8**/10–17
strategic direction, finance, **6**/3
strategic investment, **8**/6–7
strategic leadership, **1**/7
strategic marketing approach, **2**/35
strategic marketing planning tools, **2**/34–42
strategic planning, **1**/36–38, **6**/7–8, **8**/9
Strategic Planning Institute, **8**/38
strategic thinking, **2**/26, 29–31
strategy
  developing, **2**/25–26
  early, **2**/23–24
  formulation, **2**/47
  generating and evaluating, **2**/30–31
  manufacturing contribution to development of,
    8/9–10
  planning, **9**/10–16
  quality, **1**/23–24
  sales promotion, **3**/44–45
strong dominant brand, **2**/79
structural decisions, **8**/10–12
structure change, effecting, **1**/51
structure project testing, **1**/56–57
structures, organizational, **1**/49–51
substance abuse, employee, **4**/89–92
summary reports, **5**/24
Sunshine Act, **16**/18
Superfund Action Coalition, **8**/86
Superfund Amendments and Reauthorization Act
  (SARA), **8**/81
supervision, effective, **4**/6–12
supplemental staff support, **12**/49
supplementary products, **16**/39
supplier relationship, **15**/24
support, securing, **2**/16–17
support services, **8**/46
surveillance, employee, **4**/96
Swanson, David H., **1**/52–54
swap, currency, **6**/31

swap, interest-rate, **6**/31
swaps, **6**/6, 31–32
sweepstakes, **3**/42
syco-think, **16**/24
system design and data conversion, **4**/65
systems, **2**/101
  evaluating personnel, **4**/22
systems designer relationship, **15**/24–25
system software, **9**/22

tactics, sales promotion, **3**/45
Taft-Hartley Act, **4**/77
Taiwan, international business, **14**/5
tangible fixed assets, **6**/26
TAUs. *See* terminal adapter units
tax accounting methods, **5**/33
taxation
  corporate, **5**/32–33
  federal, management responsibilities, **5**/31–37
  small business, **13**/30–34
  unitary, **5**/38
tax considerations, small business, **13**/30–34
taxes, state and local, **15**/37–40
tax payments, **4**/68
tax return preparation/filing, **5**/36
Taylor, Frederick Winslow, **1**/5, 12, **8**/50, 54
Taylorism, **8**/50
TBD. *See* to be determined
TDPU. *See* total defects per unit
team selling, **3**/13
teamwork and communication, **2**/71
technical information, confidentiality/ownership,
  7/39–40
technological change
  attacker's advantage, **7**/9–10
  coping with, **7**/5–11
  defender's challenge, **7**/10–11
technological factors, **2**/44
technologies, new manufacturing, **8**/72–75
technology, **1**/17
  emphasis, **2**/104
  information, **8**/15–16, 66–68
  information systems, **9**/1–72
  managing in global economy, **7**/47–50
  managing in manufacturing, **8**/64–75
technology management, licensing/protecting
  intellectual property rights/legal aspects, **7**/
  39–42
technology transfer, international business, **14**/
  28–29
telecommunications services
  analog, **9**/29
  digital, **9**/29–30
  fiber optic, **9**/31
  global marketplace, **6**/41
  history, **9**/28–29
  impact, **1**/17, **15**/38–40

ISDN, **9**/30–31
networks, **9**/32
obsolescence, **15**/40
privacy, **15**/40
satellite, **9**/31
services, **9**/29–31
telemarketing, **3**/14
tenure and experience, **2**/71
terminal adapter units (TAUs), **9**/30
Terrill, Craig A., **15**/27–32
territory design, **3**/17–18
testing, **4**/65
  AIDS, **4**/94
  employee, **4**/93–95
  genetic, **4**/94
  HIV, **4**/94
  honesty, **4**/95
test marketing, services industry, **15**/22
theories, leadership, **1**/15–16
theories of motivation, **1**/14
theory x, **1**/21
theory y, **1**/21
The Source, **10**/16
thinking strategically, **1**/6–8
third-party administrators (TPAs), **4**/41
threat, new entrants, **2**/44
threats, **2**/28
Tieken, Donald R., **10**/22–26
time-based strategy, materials management, **8**/57
timing of recognition, **5**/28
title, purchased materials, **10**/21
Title VII of Civil Rights Act of 1964, **4**/55–56
to be determined (TBD), **10**/17
Todd, Jerry D., **12**/8–10
tombstone ads, **6**/32
top quality management (TQM), **2**/10
Torrenzano, Richard, **11**/8–11
total defects per unit (TDPU), **8**/44
total quality control (TQC), **8**/52
total quality management system (TQMS), **8**/52
total quality management (TQM)
  capacity decisions, **8**/11
  costs, **6**/6
  manufacturing, **8**/52
  productivity, **1**/24–27
  public programs, **16**/19
  services industry, **15**/14
  tools, **8**/45
touch-sensitive screens, **9**/18
tourist expenditures, **6**/42
toxic chemical release inventory (TRI) form, **8**/85
Toxic Substances Control Act (TSCA), **8**/81
TPAs. *See* third-party administrators
TQC. *See* total quality control
TQM. *See* top quality management; total quality
  management

TQMS. *See* total quality management system
traceability, **5**/28
tracking system, **2**/71
tradeable debt claims, **6**/6
trademarks/trade names/service marks,
  international business, **14**/33
trade promotions, **3**/42
trade receivables, **6**/28
Trade Regulation Reports, **2**/101
trade relations, **10**/20, **11**/23–25
trade secrets, international business, **14**/32
training
  career development, **4**/30
  competence, **4**/30–31
  development, employee performance, **4**/28–34
  and performance, **4**/29
  programs, **4**/31–33
  retraining workers, **4**/23
  transfer, **4**/33–34
Training and Development Journal, **9**/60
trait theory, **1**/15
transactions analysis, **5**/7
transfer pricing, **5**/26
transition manager, **9**/69
transition plans, **9**/69–70
transition resources, **9**/70
transnational financing, **6**/41
transnational investing, **6**/40–41
transportation, **10**/29–30
travel expenses, **5**/35
treasury roles, chief financial officer, **6**/8
TRI. *See* toxic chemical release inventory form
TSCA. *See* Toxic Substances Control Act
TSD. *See* hazardous waste, treatment, storage,
  and disposal
TS Newsletter Database, **10**/16
Tubbs, Alan R., **13**/12–15
Tubridy, Gary S., **3**/26–41
Tufano, Joseph L., **4**/64–66
Turnbaugh, Patricia, **8**/3–4, 51–63
tying contracts, **2**/99–100
Tylenol crisis, **1**/28

UCC. *See* Uniform Commercial Code
UCP. *See* Uniform Customs and Practices
umbrella liability, **12**/40–41
unaided recall, **2**/110
uncertainty, **1**/19–20
underground storage tanks (USTs), **8**/82–83
underwriting leverage, **12**/33
unfair labor practices, **4**/58, 78–79, 83–84
Uniform Commercial Code (UCC), **10**/8, 19
Uniform Customs and Practices (UCP), **10**/21
union elections, **4**/79
union organizational campaigns, **4**/79
  how management should act, **4**/80–81

union recognition
    involuntary recognition, **4**/82–83
    unfair labor practices as, **4**/83–84
    voluntary recognition, **4**/82
    without election, **4**/82
unions, **6**/18
unitary taxation, **5**/38
United Nations Conference of Trade and
    Development, **14**/24
United Nations Publications/Statistical Yearbook,
    14/24
United States, international business, **14**/5
United States v. Penn-Olin Chemical Company, **2**/99
United States v. Socony-Vacuum, **2**/97
U.S./Canada Free Trade Act, **14**/10
U.S. Copyright Office, **14**/32
U.S. Department of Commerce, **14**/24
U.S. Department of State, **14**/24
U.S. Department of Transportation (DOT), **8**/82,
    12/45
user, **2**/60
use taxes, **5**/39
U.S. Small Business Administration, **14**/24
USSR, former, **14**/5
USTs. *See* underground storage tanks
U.S. Trademark Office, **14**/33
U.S. Trade Performance and Outlook, **14**/24
Universal Copyright Convention, **14**/32

valuations, stating proper, **6**/20
value-added network services (VANs), **10**/40
value analysis, manufacturing processes, **8**/53
value engineering, **8**/53
    value analysis, **10**/13
value-in-exchange, **15**/34
value-in-use, **15**/34
value pricing, strategy, **15**/21
VANs. *See* value-added network services
variability, **5**/28
    and process capability, **1**/26
variable search, **8**/48
variance, **5**/30
variance analysis, **5**/29
VCR. *See* videocassette recorder
VDT. *See* video display terminal
Vecchiotti, Rachel I., **15**/3–4, 27–32
vehicle exposure, **12**/29
Vendor Express, **5**/16
vendor management, networks, **9**/37
versatility, **1**/16
vertical channel systems, **2**/15
vertical integration, **8**/10–11
very large-scale integration (VLSI), **9**/17
very small aperture terminal (VSAT), **9**/31
Veterans Reemployment Rights Act, **4**/57
Vick, Randall, **10**/33–35
videocassette recorder (VCR), **11**/9

video display terminal (VDT), **9**/17, 22
Vietnam Era Veterans Readjustment Assistance
    Act, **12**/23
Vincent, Julie A., **1**/36–43
virtual reality (VR), **8**/74
vision, magic of, **1**/7
vision care, **4**/44
VLSI. *See* very large-scale integration
Vocational Rehabilitation Act, **12**/23
VOCs. *See* volatile organic compounds
voice recognition devices, **9**/18
volatile organic compounds (VOCs), **8**/78
volume oriented, **2**/17
volume-profit approach, **5**/13
VR. *See* virtual reality
VSAT. *See* very small aperture terminal

wage incentives, **8**/26–35
Wagner, Cecilia L., **5**/12–16, **6**/33–36
Wagner Act, **4**/77
Walton, Sam, **13**/5, 26
WANs. *See* wide-area networks
Warner, Larry A., **12**/24–29
warranties, **10**/20
warranty period, **8**/49
water issues, environmental management, **8**/
    79–81
water permits, **8**/80–81
weaker dominant brand, **2**/80
Weber, Max, **1**/13
Weinberg, Charles B., **16**/36–41
Welch, Jack, **2**/9
wellness programs, **4**/87
Welt, Leo C. B., **14**/45–47
Werner, Ray O., **2**/94–101
Wharton School, **1**/11
Wheelwright, Steven, **8**/14
Whitaker, Bruce L., **5**/40–42
Whitney, Eli, **8**/72, **13**/5
Wholey, Joseph S., **16**/18–21
wide-area networks (WANs), **9**/32
Wiethop, Deborah, **4**/86–88
Williams, Michael, **7**/25–29
Willingham, John J., **5**/43–49
Willis, George, **6**/5–6
Winer, Russell S., **2**/42–48
Winski, Donald T., **9**/5–9
Win-Win, **4**/25–28
WIP. *See* work in process
Wolf, Ann M., **15**/38–40
women, in work force, **4**/14
work breakdown structure, **1**/56
Worker Adjustment and Retraining Notification
    Act, **4**/59
workers, training/retraining, **4**/23
workers' compensation, **12**/24
    employers' liability, **12**/40

work force, changing, **4**/14
   demographic/economic trends, **4**/20–21
   managing diverse, **4**/20–24
working capital, **6**/20, 26
workmanship, quality, **8**/46
work in process (WIP), **5**/28, **8**/57
work scheduling, new dimensions, **4**/24–28
workstations, computer, **9**/20–21
World Population, **14**/24
World Trade Annual, **14**/24
World Trade Centers Association, **14**/24
worldwide financing viewpoint, **6**/40
write-offs, **5**/34
written documentation, performance appraisal,
   4/62–63

Wymer, John F., III, **4**/55–59

Yearbook of International Trade Statistics, **14**/12, 24
Yearbook of Labor Statistics, **14**/24
Yellow Book, **7**/46
Young, Dennis R., **16**/27–30

Zaki, Ahmed, **16**/31–35
Zand, Dale E., **1**/18–23
ZBA. *See* zero balance account
zero balance account (ZBA), **6**/35–36, **13**/25
zero-coupon, **6**/32
Zier, Ronald E., **11**/11–13
Zimmerman, Alan, **14**/36–41
Zysman, John, **8**/5

ABOUT THE EDITOR

John J. Hampton is a management consultant and professor with more than twenty-five years of practical and academic experience. Formerly he was Provost of The College of Insurance in New York City and Dean of the School of Business at Seton Hall University. He has consulted with AT&T, Celanese Chemical, Manufacturers Hanover Bank, the Princeton Consulting Group, and other financial and industrial organizations. He is the author of eleven books on finance, management, insurance, and international business. He holds master's and doctor's degrees in business administration from The George Washington University.

ABOUT
AMERICAN MANAGEMENT
ASSOCIATION

Founded: 1923
Headquarters: 135 West 50th Street
  New York, N.Y. 10020
Telephone: 212-586-8100
Fax: 212-903-8168

Mission Statement: American Management Association provides educational forums worldwide where members and their colleagues learn superior, practical business skills and explore best practices of world-class organizations through interaction with each other and expert faculty practitioners. AMA's publishing program provides tools for individuals to use to extend learning beyond the classroom in a process of lifelong professional growth and development through education.

Organization: AMA operates management centers and offices in the United States in New York, Atlanta, Boston, Chicago, Hamilton (New York), Kansas City (Kansas), San Francisco, Saranac Lake (New York), and Washington, D.C. Through AMA International it operates centers in Brussels and Tokyo and, in addition, has affiliated centers in Buenos Aires, Toronto, and Mexico City. AMA centers offer conferences, seminars, and membership briefings where there is an interchange of information, ideas, and experience on a wide variety of management topics.

AMACOM, the book division of AMA, publishes approximately seventy books annually. Its objective is threefold: to help individuals increase their skills and knowledge, to improve organizational performance, and to illuminate vital business issues. AMA also publishes ten periodicals, including *Management Review, Compensation and Benefits Review, Organizational Dynamics, HR Focus, Supervisory Management,* and *Trainer's Workshop;* numerous research surveys and management briefings; videos; and self-study courses.

Other AMA services include Operation Enterprise, a program for young adults; AMA On-Site, which delivers seminars at the site of the company's choice; AMA by Satellite, which offers videoconferences; the Information Resource Center, a management information and library service for AMA members; and five AMA bookstores.